3497 3666

D1062800

AMERICAN CRITICAL ARCHIVES 10
Langston Hughes: The Contemporary Reviews

The American Critical Archives is a series of reference books that provide representative selections of contemporary reviews of the main works of major American authors. Specifically, each volume contains both full reviews and excerpts from reviews that appeared in newspapers and weekly and monthly periodicals, generally within a few months of the publication of the work concerned. There is an introductory historical overview by the volume editor, as well as checklists of additional reviews located but not quoted.

This book is the first comprehensive collection of contemporary reviews of the writing of Langston Hughes from 1926 until his death in 1967. Most of the reviews have never before been listed in a Hughes bibliography, and many of the reviews are reprinted from hard-to-find newspapers and periodicals. Their collection here, by replacing myths with the actual historical record, will make possible a reassessment of Hughes's initial critical reception.

The American Critical Archives

GENERAL EDITOR: M. Thomas Inge, Randolph-Macon College

Langston Hughes

The Contemporary Reviews

Edited by
Tish Dace
University of Massachusetts Dartmouth

 CAMBRIDGE
UNIVERSITY PRESS

PUBLISHED BY THE PRESS SYNDICATE OF THE UNIVERSITY OF CAMBRIDGE
The Pitt Building, Trumpington Street, Cambridge CB2 1RP, United Kingdom

CAMBRIDGE UNIVERSITY PRESS
The Edinburgh Building, Cambridge CB2 2RU, United Kingdom
40 West 20th Street, New York, NY 10011-4211, USA
10 Stamford Road, Oakleigh, Melbourne 3166, Australia

© Cambridge University Press 1997

First published 1997

Printed in the United States of America

Typeset in Sabon

A catalog record for this book is available from the British Library.

Library of Congress Cataloging-in-Publication Data
Langston Hughes : the contemporary reviews / edited by Tish Dace.
p.   cm. — (American critical archives; 10)
Includes index.
ISBN 0-521-38148-7 (hard)
1. Hughes, Langston, 1902–1967—Criticism and interpretation.
2. Afro-Americans in literature.   3. Books—Reviews.   I. Dace,
Letitia.   II. Series.
PS3515.U274Z6732   1997
818'.5209—dc20   96-24197
CIP

ISBN 0-521-38148-7 hardback

This book is dedicated to the memories of
Glenn Carrington
and
George Houston Bass

Contents

Appendix: Additional Reprints and Checklists

Series Editor's Preface

The American Critical Archives series documents a part of a writer's career that is usually difficult to examine, that is, the immediate response to each work as it was made public by reviewers in contemporary newspapers and journals. Although it would not be feasible to reprint every review, each volume in the series reprints a selection of reviews designed to provide the reader with a proportionate sense of the critical response, whether it was positive, negative, or mixed. Checklists of other known reviews are also included to complete the documentary record and allow access for those who wish to do further reading and research.

The editor of each volume has provided an introduction that surveys the career of the author in the context of the contemporary critical response. Ideally, the introduction will inform the reader in brief of what is to be learned by a reading of the full volume. The reader then can go as deeply as necessary in terms of the kind of information desired—be it about a single work, a period in the author's life, or the author's entire career. The intent is to provide quick and easy access to the material for students, scholars, librarians, and general readers.

When completed, the American Critical Archives should constitute a comprehensive history of critical practice in America, and in some cases Great Britain, as the writers' careers were in progress. The volumes open a window on the patterns and forces that have shaped the history of American writing and the reputations of the writers. These are primary documents in the literary and cultural life of the nation.

M. Thomas Inge

Preface: Using This Book

The reviews reprinted and cited in this book were found primarily among those preserved by Hughes himself and now located at Yale University's Beinecke Library, in the New York Public Library's Schomburg Collection, and at Lincoln University (Hughes's alma mater) in Pennsylvania. Of course, other likely libraries (such as those of the University of Kansas and Howard University) also have been searched, roughly forty serial and review indexes have been consulted, and in some cases whole runs of periodicals likely to have reviewed Hughes also have been searched. I have omitted mere announcements of publication unaccompanied by an evaluative review. Otherwise, I would appreciate being notified of any omissions. Readers should also note that the Beinecke continues to add to its review collections; recent acquisitions will not be found here.

These sources of scrapbooks and clippings collections do not always provide dates or periodical titles for the reviews, and when they do these now and then err. Thus, the review of *An African Treasury* that the Beinecke file leads us to believe appeared in *American Import and Export Bulletin* (no date) did not appear in any issues published between 1959 and 1967, despite four searches carried out in the copies at Columbia University, the New York Public Library, and the Library of Congress. Although I considered that these three libraries might contain a variant page from other copies because the March 1961 issue (vol. 54, no. 3) should, according to the index, contain reviews on p. 249 but does not, I also checked out the possibility that the review instead appeared in another magazine from the same publisher. Voilà! The elusive review shows up in the December 1960 issue of *Air Transportation*. Perhaps two hundred dates on clippings at the Beinecke likewise proved incorrect. For instance, Olive C. Robinson's "Reviews of Recently Published Books: Negro Humor" turned up in the *Lewiston Daily Sun* of 26 March, not 10 April, and E.D.I.'s "Younger Readers" appears in the 31 January 1953, not 1 December 1952, *Kansas City Star.* Moreover, hundreds of clippings lack authorship credit.

Locating the reviews in newspapers, magazines, and journals, verifying dates, and supplying page numbers and other missing information has taken me not just to research and public libraries but also to libraries for business, education, and divinity schools, and for children's books. This work has occupied me since 1977. Even where errors did not slow the search, merely ascertaining that no copy of that publication for that date had survived or figuring out the periodical's origin and location often took months. For example, one of the Beinecke scrapbooks contains a review of *Fine Clothes to the Jew* by P. H. from the 15 April 1927 issue of *The Library*. A printed page cannot qualify as a bibliographical ghost. This review certainly appeared; the question was, Where? The journal title sounded simple enough—some kind of library journal. But not, as research proved, *Library* (Newark), the Bibliographical Society's *The Library, Library Association Record, Library Journal, Library Literature, Library Occurrent, Library Quarterly, Library Review, Library Service* (Detroit Public Library), *Library World, Libraries,* or the *Texas Library Association's News Notes.* The 1926 Ayer's does not list this title, and I could not locate a librarian who had heard of it, not even at the library-school libraries of Yale and Columbia. Returning to the Beinecke to recheck the review as it appears in the scrapbooks, I was temporarily stalled by the disappearance of the scrapbooks (though not the clippings boxes). Since they had still not been catalogued (as of the summer of 1989), the available librarians told me I had hallucinated the scrapbooks, which must, they maintained, never have existed. In mid-September, a letter assuring me they had been located ("They had been removed to a special area for cataloguing and the person who knew that was away on vacation") brought me back to New Haven. Although the review yielded no clue, I finally culled from a nonreview clipping from *The Library* pasted to another page the scrawled pencil notation "New Mexico." Letters to every library in the state that had existed in 1927 elicited a few responses providing the publication's provenance: New Mexico Military Institute. And Kathy Flanary, the librarian at the Paul Horgan Library at NMMI, explained—you guessed it—that Paul Horgan had edited the periodical and written the laudatory review.

Where an entry mentions multiple appearances of a review for which the first reference has been verified, in a few instances I have skipped a search for complete information on the other entries in order to ensure that this volume will appear before the century's end. These few entries simply omit data. In nearly all other instances the entries provide complete, verified information. Where the data may err or the source could not be located, a question mark appears within brackets. Should a reader locate and verify any of these queried entries, please contact me through the publisher. Such assistance will be acknowledged in any subsequent edition.

Failure to locate the source of a review has occurred for one of two reasons. Either no copy of that periodical for that date exists (despite occasional entries in research libraries' card catalogs that originally suggested the periodical had survived) or, in that periodical for that date, the review itself does not appear, and searching elsewhere likewise did not locate the review in its original context.

Users of the scrapbooks and clippings boxes at the Beinecke (and of notations drawn from them in Arnold Rampersad's invaluable two-volume *Life of Langston Hughes*) should exercise caution in accepting the dates and periodical titles attached to these clippings, in view of the many errors contained in Hughes's collection. In most instances the mistakes can be attributed to his clippings service. (A dyslexic friend has confided that he once worked for such a service; enough said.) This book should prove useful to anyone using that and the other collections in either verifying or correcting those attributions.

The reviews reprinted or cited here include only those published in the United States, with two notable exceptions, both from English-language periodicals published in Mexico. Because they seem likely to give the reader difficulty in obtaining copies, I provide these reviews—Alain Locke's of *The Weary Blues* in *Palms* and Lois de Banzie's of *Tambourines to Glory* in *News*—for readers' convenience. I cite no other foreign reviews, no articles (whether published in books or periodicals), and no mere passing references.

Space limitations have prevented reprinting every word of every review. Those reviews omitted entirely tend to be nonjudgmental, repetitive of other reviews, or easy to find in many libraries. Sections omitted in reprinted reviews deal with other books not by Hughes, or repetitively quote from the book under review, or simply do not add substantively to what already has been quoted. No review has been edited so as to alter or censor its critical judgment of Hughes's work. Bibliographical information about the book's publisher and price, as well as section headings in reviews, generally have been silently excised, and typographical errors have been silently corrected.

Hughes included negative reviews along with the raves. No matter how scathing, even in the earliest scrapbook he pasted in the invectives. We can therefore conclude that these reviews do provide a representative and fairly complete representation of the responses in the U.S. print media to those books by Hughes prepared for publication by the time of his death. This book does not consider reviews of those volumes compiled or completed by others after his death on 22 May 1967. These include *Black Misery, Don't You Turn Back, Anch'io sono America, Good Morning Revolution, Langston Hughes in the Hispanic World and Haiti,* and *Arna Bontemps–Langston Hughes Letters: 1925–1967.*

The twenty-eight major books appear here in chronological order, as do the reviews within each section and the checklists of additional reviews. The appendix provides checklists (as well as a few reprints) of five of the six poetry volumes that appeared as limited editions or pamphlets, of the children's tale *Popo and Fifina,* of the five "First" books, the three "Famous" books, the nine books Hughes edited, and three of the four books he translated, as well as selected reviews of fourteen selected scripts by Hughes in production. (Another volume should be devoted to the complete reviews of all the scripts.) In short, my search covered seventy titles; for only two of these (*Dear Lovely Death* and the translation of Federico García Lorca's *Romancero Gitano: Gypsy Ballads*) did this search prove fruitless.

Acknowledgments

My sixteen years' research for this book depended mightily on the kindness of strangers. The institutions and individuals who helped me locate material or, in a few instances when I could not travel to a library, verified dates or located page numbers for me constitute an amazingly large group. So great is my indebtedness, however, that I hope I do not omit anyone in thanking:

The following public libraries: Albuquerque (John Vittal); Anniston and Calhoun County (Ala.; Sunny Addison); Atlanta; Boston; British Library; Brooklyn (Carmen Leon); California State (John Gonzales); Charleston County (S.C.; Steve Roeberg); Chicago; Cleveland (Joan L. Sorger); Colorado State; Columbus and Franklin County (Michael Robbins); Dallas (Gerald Schroeder); Davenport; Dayton and Montgomery County (Clinton Lowell); Detroit (Noel Van Gorden); El Paso; Evansville-Vanderburgh County (Ind.; Nancy A. Higgs); Houston; Indianapolis-Marion County (James Simon); Kansas City (Mo.; John Mort); Kern County (Calif.; John Walden); Lewiston (Maine; Lizette Leveille); Library of Congress (Travis Westly, Susan Manakul); Massachusetts State; Miami (Florabell Webster, Carol Stone); National Library of Scotland; New Jersey State; New Mexico State (Peggy Medina Giltrow); New York (Betty K. Gubert, Charles Morrow, Betty Odabashian, Ernest Kaiser); New York State (Billie Aul, Morris Stilson, Barbara Nicholls Randall); Newark (N.J.; James Osborne); Oklahoma Department of Libraries; Pasadena (Carolyn L. Garner); Philadelphia (James Cooney); Pittsburgh; Pittsfield (Ill.; Helen H. Wright); Portland (Maine); Richmond (Fenton L. Shugrue); Roanoke; St. Louis; San Francisco; San Jose; Springfield (Mass.; Guy McLean, Marcia Lewis, Karen Pirog, Maggie Humberston); Stowe (Vt.; Phoebe Sakash); Taos (N. Mex.; Harwood Library; Nita Murphy); Toledo; Waco-McLennan County (Tex.; S. Kethley); Washington D.C.; Washington State (Ellen Levesque); Youngstown and Mahoning County (Ohio).

The following college and university libraries: Bridgewater State (Kevin Manning); California at Berkeley; California at San Diego (Larry Cruse, Priscilla Krasner); Central State (Ohio; Janet English); Chicago; Santa Fe (Arthur Panaro); Columbia University (Olha Della Cava, Jeff Rosedale); Harris-Stowe State (Mo.; Joe Rogers, Julia Broad); Harvard (Maryellen McCarthy); Hawaii (Nancy Morris); Howard (Barbara Ford Foster); Illinois (Constance A. Fairchild); Indiana (David K. Frasier); John Jay College of Criminal Justice (N.Y.);

xv

Kansas; Lincoln (Penn.; Sophy H. Cornwell); Los Angeles Harbor (Sally Gogin); Massachusetts Amherst (J. Merriam); Massachusetts Dartmouth (Charles McNeil, Linda Zieper, Jane Booth, Lucille Fernandes, and especially Ross T. LaBaugh); Michigan (Tom Burnett); New Mexico (David Null); New Mexico State (Marie Garcia, Karen Stabler); New York University (Angela Chin); Northwestern (Dan Britz); Ohio State (Saragail Lynch); Pittsburgh; Pratt (Josephine McSweeney); Princeton (Emily Belcher, John Logan, Denise M. Shorey); Rutgers; St. Meinrad (Ind.; Doris Hanebutt); San Jose State (Rosemary Thorne); South Carolina (Eleanor M. Richardson); Southern Methodist (John Goolsby); Stanford (James M. Knox); Sul Ross State (Tex.; Eleanor Wilson); Syracuse (Marcella Stark); Tennessee at Chattanooga (E. Ray Hall); Texas at El Paso (Andy Schramm); Toledo (Kathleen J. Voigt); Tulsa; Virginia State; Wilberforce (Ohio; Jacqueline Brown); Yale (Beinecke: Donald Gallup, Patricia C. Willis, George Patterson, Karen Marinuzzi, Anne Badger).

The following historical societies: Chicago; Cincinnati; Colorado (Catherine T. Engel); Illinois State (Laura J. Berk); New Jersey; New York; Ohio (Steve Gutgesell, William G. Myers); South Suburban Genealogical and Historical Society (South Holland, Ill.; Edith L. Degenhart); Western Reserve (John Grabowski); Wisconsin (Carol Crossan, Jim Danky).

The following other organizations: Boston Athenaeum; Community Church of New York; Harvard Law School (Carol Smith, David Kennedy); New Mexico Military Institute (Kathy Flanary); *Omaha World-Herald* (Stephen Allard); *Town and Village* (Millicent Brower, Frank Gribbon); United Teachers of Dade; Urban League of Pittsburgh; Vermont Agency of Administration Public Records Division (Linda Gomo).

Others who provided assistance include: the late George Bass, executor of the Hughes estate, whose enthusiasm and gratitude for my labors provided marvelous compensation for them; my sons, Hal and Ted, who grew up while assisting me; Barbara Jacobskind, Karen Sunde, Leah Frank, Marc Rosenblum, Dennis Myers, and Elaine Fisher, all of whom accompanied me to a library or libraries; Robert D. Harlan, University of California at Berkeley; Jonathan Hicks (*New York Times*), past editor of the *Kappa Alpha Psi Journal*; Giulio Massano, Everett Hoagland, and Richard Hogan, UMD; Judith Rollins, Wellesley; Richard Kornberg, New York Shakespeare Festival; Smoky Moak, who helped me assemble and pack the manuscript; Cambridge University Press editors Julie Greenblatt, T. Susan Chang, and Martin Dinitz; M. Thomas Inge, the series general editor who approached me about doing a book on this subject so many years ago (and who also, by not hiring me to teach Shakespeare when he had the chance in 1971, encouraged me to specialize in modern literature); and the late Glenn Carrington, mentor to innumerable members of the Harlem community, who interested me in Hughes shortly after his friend's death in 1967.

I was fortunate to be granted release time from one course, one semester, by the Southeastern Massachusetts University (now University of Massachusetts Dartmouth) Research Committee and Foundation, which also supported a part of the cost of reprints with a Healey Award. I am especially grateful to the National Endowment for the Humanities for granting me a summer research stipend in 1987. Thanks also to Louise Habicht and Robert Waxler, former chairpersons of the SMU/UMD English department, and Ed Thompson, current chairperson, for assigning me during some semesters a two-day-a-week teaching schedule so as to facilitate the research travel this book required.

I thank all my predecessors who have published scholarship and criticism about Hughes. Special acknowledgment must be made to Arnold Rampersad, whose monumental *Life of Langston Hughes* paved the way for whatever books and articles on Hughes follow it.

I am indebted to Carl Van Vechten for his foresight in persuading Langston Hughes to keep every scrap of paper about himself and regularly send all these items to Yale University.

Finally, I owe an enormous debt to Langston Hughes himself, who had the talent to deserve a book like this one and the wisdom to see to it Yale acquired the sort of collection that facilitated its compilation.

Acknowledgment of Permissions to Reprint: For Elliot M. Rudwick's review in *Annals of the American Academy of Political Science,* copyright © 1963, reprinted by permission of Sage Publications, Inc. For "Three Worlds" by Erling W. Eng copyright © 1951 by the Antioch Review, Inc.; first appeared in the *Antioch Review,* Vol. 11 No. 3 (Fall 1951), reprinted by permission of the editors. For various reviews, *Chicago Sun Times,* reprinted with permission, © 1942, 1949, 1956, 1958, 1959, 1961. For three reviews, *Chicago Tribune,* © Copyrighted Chicago Tribune Company, all rights reserved, used with permission. For "Sunny Preachment," reprinted, with permission, from the *Columbus Dispatch.* For "Negro Poet Contributes Second Book," reprinted with permission of the *Dallas Morning News.* For reviews from the *Journal of Negro History,* ©, reprinted with permission from the Association for the Study of Afro-American Life and History. For "The Negro in America," reprinted with permission of the *Lexington Herald-Leader.* For "It'll Be Me: The Voice of Langston Hughes," reprinted from *The Massachusetts Review,* © 1963, The Massachusetts Review, Inc. For ten reviews, reprinted with permission from *The Nation* magazine, © The Nation Company, L. P. *Newsweek* for reviews from 26 August 1940 and 9 March 1942, © 1940 and 1942, Newsweek, Inc. All rights reserved. Reprinted by permission. For various reviews from the *New York Herald Tribune,* 1 August 1926, 25 July 1930, 27 July 1930, 1 July 1934, 27 July 1934, 25 August 1940, 3 May 1942, 31 August 1947, 9 January 1949, 11 March 1951, 26 March 1952, 30 March 1952, 14 June 1953, 13 December 1955, 18 December 1955, 20 February 1957, 21 September 1957, 7 December 1958, 26 November 1961, 23 September 1962, 26 December 1965; © 1926,

Introduction

Langston Hughes published his first book in 1926, when he was just turning twenty-four. His most recent volumes have appeared posthumously, and others may follow. Most of his more than sixty books have been reviewed, some by fifty or more publications, yet Donald Dickinson, for instance, lists only a brief selection of these in his *Bio-bibliography of Langston Hughes,* second edition, revised (Hamden, Conn.: Archon Books, 1972), and Richard K. Barksdale, attempting in *Langston Hughes: The Poet and His Critics* (Chicago: American Library Association, 1977) to comment on the reception of Hughes's books of poetry, has been forced to generalize on the basis of a small proportion of each work's reviews. In his introduction to the thirty-five reviews he reprints in his *Critical Essays on Langston Hughes* (Boston: G. K. Hall, 1986), Edward J. Mullen likewise reaches inaccurate conclusions based on insufficient examples, maintaining, for example (p. 13), that only Alfred Kreymborg gave *Shakespeare in Harlem* a favorable notice, whereas, in fact, the majority of the reviews praised this work. Mullen especially misses the mark in his assessment of the generally glowing reviews of *Not Without Laughter* as representing a "mixed but generally lukewarm critical response" (p. 16). In the interest of saving space and time, even Arnold Rampersad in *The Life of Langston Hughes* (2 vols.; New York: Oxford University Press, 1986, 1988) generalizes from small samples of reviews. The present volume will make readily available for the first time the primary documents necessary to assess fully reviewers' receptions of Hughes's books.

The absence of knowledge of, and access to, Hughes's reviews in the past led to some hyperbolic and inaccurate generalizations. For instance, Lindsay Patterson in "Langston Hughes: The Most Abused Poet in America?" *New York Times,* 29 June 1969, p. 30-D (a record review of *The Poetry of Langston Hughes* by Ossie Davis and Ruby Dee—Caedmon-TC-1272), falsely states in his first paragraph: "Critically, the most abused poet in America was the late Langston Hughes. Serious white critics ignored him, less serious ones compared his poetry to Cassius Clay doggerel, and most black critics only grudgingly admired him." "The Check List," *American Mercury,* 52 (October 1940), 245, errs likewise by insisting: "The Negro literati have consistently attacked him and his work. He has found patronage and appreciation almost exclusively among the whites."

1

The response to Hughes's books was considerably more favorable than we have believed. His free verse forms, his prose and dramatic dialect pieces, and his "lowdown" subject matter did earn him particularly partisan vituperation, but also won him more champions than detractors. The very qualities in his work that caused some offense early in his career ultimately assured his position as the preeminent African-American writer, one who excelled at poetry, fiction, drama, and the essay, and who communicated effectively to readers of varied races and classes. Never were the majority of Hughes's reviews negative.

Hughes's scrapbooks attest to the comparative lack of attention he gave to his reviews. Although he did employ a clippings service, he must not have scrutinized the reviews carefully. Into the section on *Fields of Wonder* he has stuck one on the book *Alcoholic,* by another Langston Hughes.

To evaluate these reviews, we must know something of Hughes's relations, personal and professional, with the people who wrote them. Rampersad's biography, in particular, provides motives in such "friends" of Hughes's as Alain Locke and James Baldwin for reviews whose negativity may not reflect objective assessments. This collection could make possible examination of the dynamic between personal contact and critical detachment.

Of course, labeling the reviews as favorable, unfavorable, or mixed proves tricky, and each reader doubtless will regard them differently. As a reviewer myself for more than twenty years, I believe few notices emerge as 100 percent raves, yet the critic intends largely positive reviews as praise. I have, therefore, categorized 75 percent or so admiration as the laudatory response I feel the writer intended, a review that is thoroughly ambivalent as mixed, and a wholeheartedly condemning piece as negative. To increase the difficulty of grouping reviews in this manner, some of the most patronizing or, to modern tastes, seemingly obtuse remarks occur in the largely favorable reviews, and some of the critics who appear to understand what Hughes was doing are most deprecatory. In addition, the critical viewpoint sometimes contradicts our expectations formed in response to the nature of the periodical publishing the review—diverse indeed, considering they encompass everything from *Seventeen* and the *Junior League Bulletin* to the *Daily Worker.*

In his first book, *The Weary Blues,* and its successor, *Fine Clothes to the Jew,* Hughes presents poems to two fundamentally different audiences. He wrote both types fluently and must have taken pride in both, but few readers were likely to appreciate these often radically different styles. Therefore a few reviews are mixed, praising the one type but damning the other. Among the more uniform reviews, he is admired by those reviewers who accept the unconventional free verse forms and free-spirited flouting of behavioral norms. And he is castigated by those critics—sometimes middle-class blacks—for whom his earthy and hip poetry proves embarrassing; they would prefer him to stick to the traditional conventions of Western poetry. Yet his notices do not reflect a clear racial dichotomy. He is both lauded and lambasted by members of both races. These reviews tell us a lot about their writers and the times and climes that spawned them.

Hughes replies to unfavorable aspects of Countee Cullen's mixed review of *The Weary Blues,* to other criticism from the "talented 10th," and most immediately to George Schuyler's essay for the *Nation* entitled "The Negro-Art Hokum" in his "The Negro Artist and the Racial Mountain," *Nation,* 122 (23 June 1926), 692–4, where he recognizes "this is the mountain standing in the way of any true Negro art in America—this urge within the race toward whiteness, the desire to pour racial individuality into the mold of American standardization, and to be as little Negro and as much American as possible" (692) and concludes triumphantly, "We younger Negro artists who create now intend to express our individual dark-skinned selves without fear or shame" (694).

In the argument about whether the Negro writer should develop his own style and content (which Hughes advocates) or excel in modes and on matter set by white writers (which Cullen, Schuyler, and others contend), Carl Sandburg weighs in on Hughes's side in "The New Negro Writer," *Chicago Daily News,* 29 September 1926, p. 15. Although he says the truth lies somewhere between, his analogy to singing spirituals, where he contrasts Roland Hayes to the "blacker" Paul Robeson, works all to Hughes's advantage.

Yet, despite such controversy, most of the reviews of Hughes's first book are favorable. The only two that altogether repudiate *The Weary Blues*—as insufficiently true to Occidental poetic conventions—appear to be Donald Davidson's in the *Nashville Tennessean* and Jake Falstaff's in the *Akron Beacon Journal,* the former contrasting it to Countee Cullen's *Color* and concluding Hughes "has rushed into publication before he was mature as a poet," the latter judging Claude McKay a superior poet and dismissing Hughes's volume as offering "hardly enough real poesy to make five good poems."

Five other critics provide mixed assessments. Howard Mumford Jones writes in the *Chicago Daily News* that Hughes in imitating tired literary modes creates insincere "Verlaine and water," but admires "the genuine and authentic blues." Thus Jones recognizes the superiority of Hughes writing in an original African-American mode to Hughes tritely echoing Western conventions. Not surprisingly—given the difference between Cullen's embrace of Western modes and Hughes's frequent departure from them, not to mention the fact the title poem had beaten Cullen's own entry in the *Opportunity* contest—Countee Cullen weighs in with those who prefer the poems resembling his own. His *Opportunity* review praises Hughes's distinctive individuality but regrets that the blues and jazz poems "will be most admired," because he objects to their "dissociation from the traditionally poetic" and regards them "as interlopers," not really poems, even though they prove as affecting as the "frenzy and electric heat of a Methodist or Baptist revival meeting." Cullen does not deny Hughes's skill, but imposes his own definition of a poem as a "quiet way of communing . . . more spiritual for the God-seeking heart." Because Hughes's essay in the *Na-*

tion obviously responds in particular to the negative parts of Cullen's judgments and because some writers have quoted Cullen's repudiation of "The Cat and the Saxophone"—"I can't say *This will never do,* but I feel that it ought never to have been done"—as though he speaks of the entire book, we might be tempted to conclude Cullen panned *The Weary Blues;* clearly that view does not fit the facts, nor would it characterize the reviews in the *Independent Weekly Review,* the *Seattle Post-Intelligencer,* or *New Masses,* none of which agree with Cullen's preference for the tamer poems or damn the book outright.

The large majority of *The Weary Blues*'s reviews praise it either unreservedly or with few demurrers. Thus the *Toledo Times* refers to Hughes as "destined to be one of the great poets of his race," whereas the *Cleveland Herald* calls him "a young poet of amazing promise" and exults in the book's "exquisite unusualness." The *Cleveland Plain Dealer,* after expressing a few reservations, commends it as a "contribution not merely to American Negro poetry but to poetry in general."

Frequently reviewers love the originality of Hughes's jazz rhythms, as when Corinne Meaux in the *New York Amsterdam News* proclaims, "These verses mark a new stride in the poetical field" and the *Double Dealer* commends the "fluidly sensuous rhythm, rich and colorful." Du Bose Heyward in *New York Herald Tribune Books,* however, recognizes that Hughes's rhythms have precedents in the work of Carl Sandburg and Amy Lowell, but praises him for catching the "very essence" of the blues. Heyward regrets that in "one or two places . . . the artist is obscured by the propagandist," but continues, "Far more often in the volume the artist is victor."

The *Chicago Defender* and the *Sioux City Journal* prefer the quiet, descriptive poems. Likewise the *New York Times* acknowledges a distaste for jazz poetry (while conceding Hughes writes this better than other poets do) and expresses high regard instead for "Cross," "The Jester," and "Poème d'Automne." The *New Orleans Times-Picayune,* despite recognizing flaws and conceding some Southerners will be offended, lauds the book as "good" and "unquestionably one of the most interesting of the year." The *Daily Oklahoman* prints another commentary colored by a "southern" perception, expressing astonishment at *The Weary Blues,* "astonishing because of its poetic qualities and because Langston Hughes is a Negro." Somewhat condescendingly, the reviewer nevertheless pays homage to the poetry, particularly to everything subsequent to the opening jazz section. A second *Opportunity* review, by Robert T. Kerlin, although it never refers to Cullen's reservations, praises the Harlem lyrics as "akin to the deathless ones in all languages—Sappho's, Horace's, Herrick's, but most of all the Hebrew Song of Songs."

The *Pittsburgh Courier* appreciates the poet's reflection of his thoughts in his forms, whereas *Crisis* observes, "Never is he preoccupied with form," praises instead his spontaneity, and asserts, "While I do not think of him as a protagonist of color—he is too much the citizen of the world for that—I doubt if anyone will ever write more tenderly, more understandingly, more humorously of the life of Harlem." Theophilus Lewis in the *Messenger* notes, "Six lines of his are painted on a six-foot sign in the lobby of the Harlem YMCA," which he terms evidence "this pagan poet is fast becoming a religious force. . . . [I]n giving concrete and definite expression to the incoherent feelings and impulses of his people he is functioning as a unifying spiritual agent. This is the chief work of the artist—this and to crystallize the beauty of his people." Lewis equally and specifically extols Hughes's craft and his originality. Ethel Arnold Tilden in *Voices* understands how Hughes proves characteristic of his race, universal, and distinctively himself—all in one volume. Llewellyn Jones in *American Life Magazine* praises Hughes's protest against injustices in "The South," yet asserts the poems "are not works of propaganda but of art." Another thoughtful reviewer, Alain Locke in *Palms*, proclaims, "The Negro masses have found a voice," identifies in the race poems the products of "a poet who has gone to the cabaret for some of his rhythms and to the Bible for others," and praises a "mystic identification with the race experience . . . instinctively deeper and broader than any of our poets has yet achieved."

Not until Knopf on 4 February 1927 issued his second, more controversial volume of verse did some reviewers truly trash Hughes's poetry.

Most reviews of *Fine Clothes to the Jew* praised it, yet the negatives approach the vitriol leveled by the press at Ibsen's *Ghosts*. Although the greatest outrage was reserved for his matter, many complaints greeted the manner as well. These pans disqualified his verse as poetry. All reviews, favorable and unfavorable alike, tend to agree as to its attributes—its accurate evocation of low-life African-American spirit—but disagree as to the value of such poetry.

Several critics prefer *Fine Clothes to the Jew* to *The Weary Blues*. V. F. Calverton in the *New Leader* proclaims the second book "well-nigh equal . . . to the Coleridge and Longfellow imitations of the old ballads." Hunter Stagg's *Richmond News-Leader* acclaims *Fine Clothes* as "better art." Howard Mumford Jones in the *Chicago Daily News* regards it as superior because "he has contributed a really new verse form to the English language. . . . Hughes is dangerously near becoming a major American poet." Dewey R. Jones in the *Chicago Defender* regards the second as "more subtle," appreciating the gap Hughes fills: "We have needed someone to interpret the emotions—the inner feelings—the dreams, even, of the great masses of us who are so far down in the scale of things." The *Washington Post* greets Hughes as "in a fair way to assume the laurels of Paul Laurence Dunbar as the poet laureate of his race."

Du Bose Heyward in *New York Herald Tribune Books*, on the other hand, prefers the "high spots" of *The Weary Blues* to the more uniform quality of *Fine Clothes*, although he also affirms the new book "does appreciably increase the number of first-rate poems to the credit of Langston Hughes, and it renews his high promise for the future." Theophilus Lewis in the *Messenger* likewise expresses a mild preference for the former volume, nevertheless remarking similarities between Hughes's later blues and the "ascetic delicacy one finds in the lyrics of Thomas Hardy and A. E. Housman."

Some other periodicals that approve *Fine Clothes* include the *New York World*, *New York Sun*, *Brooklyn Citizen*, *Detroit Free Press*, *Independent*, *Bookman*, *Poetry*, *New Republic*, *Baltimore Afro-American*, *New York Age*, *Boston Chronicle*, *Lincoln News*, *Crisis*, *Kappa Alpha Psi Journal*, and *Opportunity* (all three reviews, including, mirabile dictu, Countee Cullen's). Margaret Larkin's *Opportunity* review compares Hughes to Burns and dubs him "Proletarian Poet." Sigmund Spaeth in the *Philadelphia Inquirer* commends Hughes as—"when he speaks in his natural idiom"—"a great poet." T. Bernard Pace in the *Asheville Times* endorses Hughes's realism and emotional force and exults, "One does not read his poems. One sings them, laughs them, prays them." Alice Dunbar-Nelson in the *Washington Eagle* reminds "some of our folks [who] don't like it" that Aristotle "said that poetry is an imitation of life." R. E. Cureton in *Oracle* affirms the poems' realism and the right of Hughes's subjects' lives to be celebrated in verse. "This latest volume of Brother Hughes'," Cureton continues, "deserves to be read; his reputation has been sustained." Alain Locke more than concurs; he raves about the book, about its tragic vision (comparable to that of the Greeks), and also approves it as "notable as an achievement in poetic realism in addition to its particular value as a folk study in verse of Negro life." Frank Luther in the *Des Moines Register* strikes the same note: "The tragic lot of the black-skinned in a white-skinned civilization is apparent again and again, but there is no explicit propaganda; there is no appeal for help or pity."

Subsequent double Pulitzer-prize winner Paul Horgan in *Library* applauds, "The poet's heart yields beauty here"; and Lewis Alexander in *Carolina Magazine* dismisses those who object to Hughes's originality by arguing: "Those who understand anything about the matter at all will concede that the essence of real poetry certainly does not lie in conventionality." Katherine Garrison Chapin in the *Junior League Bulletin* adulates Hughes: "Here is a young man who . . . has stepped out of the ranks where any social or racial discriminations might hold him, and walks easily among the best writers of his day." But William Russell Clark spoils his favorable review in the *Dallas Times-Herald* by his racist stereotyping of Hughes and other African-American writers: "Many Negroes are poets without half-way trying to be or knowing that they are. A superstitious race, their imaginations run riot."

Fine Clothes received five mixed reviews. The *New York Evening Post Literary Review* pronounces, "It is quite limited, but there is a purity of quality about most of it that cannot be equaled by the studied simplicity of the sophisticated." George S. Schuyler in the *Pittsburgh Courier* finds the verse "both too free and too blank" but credits Hughes with "knowing the Negro proletarian." The *Boston Transcript* condemns the cynicism but praises the blues and spirituals. The *Princeton Literary Observer*, after complaining the collection "does not maintain the same plane of excellence which was attained in his earlier work," adds, "There is much to praise in the volume." Herbert S. Gorman in the *New York Times Book Review* judges the book "uneven and flawed but it displays flashes of authentic inspiration and when it is at its best, as in some of the 'blues' experiments, it gives a vivid sensation of the Negro spirit."

Those who dislike *Fine Clothes*, however, excoriate Hughes. O.C.E. in the *Philadelphia Tribune* avers, "The book leaves, a very bad taste in the mouth," and on the same page Eustace Gay laments, "It's been a long day since I have read anything 'uglier,'" concluding "let us have some books . . . dealing with something else besides the cabaret hounds and 'primitive types of American Negro.'" Both writers object to the free verse. As Gay puts it, "There is no meter, unless it is a gas meter." In the same newspaper's third review, Orrin C. Evans—presumably the same reviewer who launched the first diatribe against *Fine Clothes*—laments both form ("decidedly free verse") and content ("his apparent obsession for the more degenerate element"). William M. Kelley in the *New York Amsterdam News* fulminates, "It reeks of the gutter and sewer." J. A. Rogers's *Pittsburgh Courier* review blasts the book as "trash," accounts for its failure by surmising it "is designed for white readers," and calls upon readers of his African-American newspaper to "discourage this marketing of such books, books that help but to tighten the chains of social degradation."

The *Chicago Whip* castigates both Hughes as the "poet 'low-rate' of Harlem" and Carl Van Vechten—to whom Hughes dedicated the volume—as "a literary gutter-rat." The poems this critic dismisses as "unsanitary, insipid and repulsing." This anonymous purveyor of invective takes offense at Hughes's subject matter, "lecherous, lust-reeking characters." Taking another approach, Roger Didier in *Light and Heebie Jeebies* seems less shocked at Hughes than convinced he displays a trivial talent: "He is an artificer forcing words into odd combinations that sometimes incite a pleasing imagery which means very little." Thereafter, O.C.E. returns to the fray once more, faulting *Fine Clothes* for the third time in the *Philadelphia Tribune*, thereby contributing fully one-third of the book's total venomous reviews and inflating a later generation's erroneous impression that Hughes's second book fared poorly with critics. The reader will notice that most of the negative assessments come from the black press, although by no means all the reviews from this sector prove negative. The sole reviewer to damn the book in the nonblack press, Harry Alan Potamkin writing in the *Nation*, objects, not to the subject matter but to what he regards as lack of superior poetic talent.

In the *Cleveland Plain Dealer* for 27 February 1927, under "Praised and Damned," Hughes writes, "They miss the fact that every 'ugly' poem I write is a protest against the ugliness it pictures." He likewise responds to his critics in two articles in the *Pittsburgh Courier*, for 9 and 16 April 1927, entitled "These Bad New Negroes: A Critique on Critics," as well as in a letter in the September 1928 *Crisis*.

Only three reviews of Hughes's first novel, *Not Without Laughter,* should be characterized as negative—two in the African-American press, the other in a large-circulation Chicago paper. Writing in the *Boston Guardian,* Lillian Lewis Feurtado maintains the novel "leaves a bitter taste" because its "immoral, vulgar, low-down 3rd rate Colored people" may "make the white reader feel that segregation is justifiable." She errs factually in her objection that Hughes has failed to provide "young men with high aspirations," for clearly the protagonist, Sandy, embraces those and, indeed, represents Hughes himself. The reviewer acknowledges the novelist's talent and calls upon him to "write another novel and put in as principals some girls and boys worthy of admiration" so as to "make the whole race proud of him."

This continuation of the sort of objections about subject matter that Cullen had first raised and a few reviewers of *Fine Clothes* had elaborated finds no echo, however, in the other two faultfinders. The *New Freeman* takes Hughes to task for the "shapeless and sprawling" construction and "flat" characters, "types rather than . . . human beings." The *Chicago Evening Post* dismisses the novel as a "readable, rather trite tale" that "has nothing to add to our conception of Negroes as individuals, as a group, or in their relations to their pale antagonists." One other mixed review, in the *New York Sun,* condescends to contrast Hughes to "white writers in a similar field," deciding "his brush is surely not dipped in the magic of *Black April* and *Porgy.*"

Meanwhile, other periodicals greet *Not Without Laughter* enthusiastically, and it is one of only two novels included in the American Library Association's 1931 list of forty outstanding American books of the year. It also outsold Hughes's two Knopf poetry volumes (Dickinson, p. 56, n. 80).

The *Cleveland Press* pronounces it "the soundest Negro book by anyone, black or white, since Cleveland's Charles W. Chestnutt did *The Conjure Woman* 31 years ago." The *New Yorker* praises its humor, whereas the *Philadelphia Public Ledger* opines, "It leaves his reader not without tears" and predicts it "will rank among the most outstanding volumes of the season." The *Pasadena Star-News* praises a poignancy that reflects "an aspect of American life that is in its essence pathetic and heroic." The *Pike County Republican* pays the tribute "Every word is interesting." Martha Gruening in *Hound and Horn,* impressed with the work's affirmation of Hughes's people, terms it "not only uniquely moving and lovely among Negro novels but among books written about America." She devotes a paragraph to comparing the novel with Willa Cather's *My Antonia.* The *Pittsburgh Courier*'s George S. Schuyler enthuses, "I haven't read all of the novels written but I haven't read a better one." Mary Ross in *New York Herald Tribune Books* commends it "to the attention of those who love life and its mirroring in fiction." Sterling A. Brown in *Opportunity* expresses his approbation: "Its simplicity is the simplicity of great art." Some reviewers adopt the phraseology "not without" to express their—usually favorable—responses.

Both African-American and white reviewers rave; both races love Sandy and enjoy the tale of his coming of age, which they find so authentic many suspect—correctly—an autobiographical basis in the character study. The *Oracle* embraces the boy as "an inspiration to the Negro youth of today." The *Philadelphia Record* calls Sandy "the finest fictional type of a Negro boy that literary America has yet produced." One woman, however, Isabel Paterson in the *New York Herald Tribune,* instead discusses Aunt Hager as the "heroine," and Wallace Thurman in the *New York Evening Post* rebukes Hughes for killing off this "indelible" character with more than fifty pages of his tale yet to go. The *Nation* relishes all the characters as "the people who make it live with that quick and intimate reality which is seldom seen in American fiction." The *New York Times Book Review* judges Sandy the "least-successful creation of them all," but praises all the rest: "These are the people who live in this novel as few characters have ever lived in a book." The *Milwaukee Journal* concurs. Herschel Brickell in the *Saturday Review* approves the novelist's "ability to make the reader feel very deeply the problems of his characters." Theophilus Lewis in the *New York Amsterdam News* enjoys Hughes's pioneering effort in portraying "normal Negro life" and argues, concerning his "ability to present character faithfully and vividly, Hughes rates far above any other novelist who has ventured into the field of 'Negro' fiction except Du Bose Heyward, and he is easily Heyward's peer."

Other publications—among them the *Tulsa Tribune* and the *Tuskegee Messenger*—particularly praise the book's prose style. Several appreciate the setting—not Harlem but Kansas. Some commend the author's objectivity; in the words of the *Detroit News,* "Mr. Hughes does nothing to shield his race from just criticism. He depicts Negroes at their best and at their worst and very fairly shows that the black man's best and his worst closely parallel the white man's."

Although many mention the absence of a tightly developed plot, most do not find this a fatal flaw, or necessarily a flaw at all, but appreciate the book's nature, its purposeful focus on Sandy's rites of passage. Alain Locke in *Opportunity,* for instance, suggests, "Despite immaturity of narrative technique, this novel is one of the high-water marks of the Negro's self depiction in prose." The *New York Amsterdam News*'s Aubrey Bowser even insists, "It is just as well for a novel not to have too marked a plot: it tempts the author to make his characters behave unnaturally." *New Masses,* reading the same novel as Lillian Lewis Feurtado, comes to a contrasting conclusion, that this one avoids vulgarity and instead excels in its depiction of class conflict. Several reviewers suggest Hughes should write a sequel.

Hughes followed his successful novel not with another full-length work of fiction but with the first of a series of limited editions and pamphlets containing poetry and drama. These little volumes, appearing during the 1930s and early 1940s, attracted few—but generally laudatory—reviews. Aubrey Bowser, in the *New York Amsterdam News*, for example, after echoing Hughes's racial mountain essay for the *Nation* by calling for "Negro literature . . . written of the Negro, by the Negro, and, most important of all, for the Negro," greets *The Negro Mother* (1931) as "a constructive move" towards achieving that goal. The *Boston Evening Transcript* terms *Scottsboro Limited* (1932) a play "which epitomizes in verse and tragedy the industrial plight of the Negro" and compares "Christ in Alabama" to Cullen's "Black Christ."

The *Daily Worker* lauds *A New Song* (1938), "The ballads and lyrics have the simplicity, straightforwardness, and plain, rhythmical speech of all folk songs," and *Fight* raves, "It is a great intellectual, emotional, common sense treat to read . . . the songs of everyday living and suffering and tears and laughter and hope in Chicago, in Spain, in Alabama." The mainstream daily the *Winston-Salem Journal-Sentinel* finds in this volume "yet another evidence that the best Negro literature is a folk literature, close to the joys and sorrows of the people."

The *Chicago Defender,* upon the publication of Hughes's two wartime pamphlets in 1943, compares the title poem in *Freedom's Plow* to Sandburg and finds *Jim Crow's Last Stand* shows "there are few poets today who can match Hughes for colorful, lilting, pointed quality." Carter G. Woodson in the *Journal of Negro History* interprets each poem in the latter volume, then sets them in the context of African-American history, and *Span's* review of the former pamphlet terms Hughes "one of the great poets of our country" and his poems "gleaming stones in the citadel of a better tomorrow." Finally, William Rose Benét in the *Saturday Review* describes *Freedom's Plow* as "more good rhetoric, rhetoric in a good cause," offering "stirring rhythm. It must be deeply moving, to all who really care about this country."

Back in 1932, Hughes had published his collaboration with Arna Bontemps, the children's tale *Popo and Fifina*. Although Alain Locke dismisses this as a "quite flimsy sketch," four other reviewers greet it more respectfully. The *New York Times Book Review* calls it "a model of its kind," compares it to the popular *The Dutch Twins*, praises "the beauty of the style," and concludes the book "tempts us to wish that all our travel books for children might be written by poets."

Not many more critics reviewed Knopf's 1932 collection for children entitled *The Dream Keeper and Other Poems,* not only because of the age of its intended audience but also because many poems first had appeared in the earlier two books. Yet those who write do so enthusiastically. The *San Diego Union* approves the poems as especially likely to accomplish their purpose of arousing "an interest in genuine poetry in some young ear." The *Boston Evening Transcript* commends the selections as "simple, human, vivid, singing with sincerity." Horace Gregory in the *New York Evening Post* refers to the poetry's "air of outdoor health and vitality" and dubs Hughes the "Carl Sandburg of Negro poetry." The *Boston American,* whose reviewer Charles Hanson Towne has tested the poems' merits by reading them aloud "to my colored servant, James," judges them deserving of high praise and suggests they be set to music by Gershwin or Deems Taylor. More reserved in his endorsement, William Rose Benét in the *Saturday Review* concludes Hughes "is not a first-rate poet, even among those of his own race, but he is distinctly an appealing one, a melodist who touches with sensitiveness the stops of his black flute." The *New York Amsterdam News* does not mince words but adjures us, "This book should be placed in the hands of as many children, black and white, as possible. To the former it is bound to be a great inspiration and to the latter afford a better view of what Negroes can do in the field of literature."

Critics widely and favorably reviewed *The Ways of White Folks*. Only a few voices dissented from the praise; several critics awarded the book such encomiums they could only be described as raves. Yet William Soskin of the *San Francisco Examiner* lambastes the book as "neo-Marxist"; in fact, he goes on in that vein at length, beginning with "Perhaps the Commissars and the Soviet Union of Artists and Writers will approve the latest work of the American Negro writer, Langston Hughes, and perhaps that's all the approval he wants." Although Soskin does not quarrel with the viewpoint he discerns, he believes it has damaged the author's artistry, for it has caused him to produce "little allegories, little arguments." That reviewer also objects to the stories glorifying the black characters. Similarly, George Schuyler in the *Pittsburgh Courier* feels impelled to act as an apologist for—or champion of—whites, instead of devoting much space to reviewing the fiction, which he judges better "race propaganda" than literature. (Sherwood Anderson in the *Nation* also writes an essay on race relations, but nevertheless likes the book.) Schuyler's remarks prompt Dewey R. Jones in the *Chicago Defender* to the rejoinder "I have little faith in Negro critics who feel themselves called upon to take up cudgels for the white race."

Although nobody else pans *The Ways of White Folks,* a few critics turn in mixed notices. The *Philadelphia Evening Public Ledger* discerns "writing of high talent" but objects to the tone—"a little too somber, a little too bitter." The *New York Sun* finds, "at their worst, his stories are dull," but elsewhere admires his "eminently sensible writing, deserving respect." We can observe reservations also in Martha Gruening's *New Republic* remarks and Alain Locke's assessment for *Survey Graphic*. She deplores his creating his white characters, as though by a formula, as "either sordid and cruel, or silly and sentimental," yet terms the collection "distinguished." Locke concludes, "This is an important book for the present time; greater artistry, deeper sympathy and less resentment would have made it a book for all times," and he likewise tempers his praise in *Opportunity*.

In more than fifty other reviews, however, critics express jubilation concerning this first anthology of Hughes's short stories. Repeatedly writers speak of the human tragedy that runs through these tales. *Spokesman* compares the volume's "somber despair" to that in *All Quiet on the Western Front, The Well of Loneliness,* and *Strange Interlude.* Theophilus Lewis in the *New York Amsterdam News* cites Hardy's *Wessex Tales* as he explicates Hughes's irony. The *Hastings News* notes a resemblance to Upton Sinclair. The *Durham Herald Sun* reports, "Hughes has combined the poetic instinct and feeling to the best technique of Erskine Caldwell, Anton Chekhov and Katherine Mansfield." Several critics simply cite the "Russians" as his forebears. Turning to another art form, the *Saturday Review* lauds the "sophisticated jazziness": "Reading the fourteen stories one after another is like listening with eyes closed to a Paul Whiteman concert of fourteen numbers."

Nearly every story is singled out by one reviewer or another as the book's best, although "Home" may be most frequently mentioned among the tragic tales; the *New York Times Book Review* prefers it, and the *Pasadena Star-News* calls it a "masterpiece." (Passages of *The Ways of White Folks* review attributed to E.E.H. in the *Albany Times Union,* incidentally, bear a striking resemblance to this 1 July 1934 *New York Times* review of the book by Leane Zugsmith.) Harry Hansen and others prefer "Cora Unashamed"; Hansen terms the book "an admirable contribution to American writing that counts." The first of two reviews in the *New York Amsterdam News* singles out "Father and Son," calling it "more emotionally satisfying than any other this reviewer has read on the conflict of black and white," whereas the *Chicago Defender* opts for "Christmas Eve," its reviewer terming it "one of the most poignantly touching stories I have encountered in many years of reading." Several, including Mary White Ovington in the *Omaha Guide,* admire "Little Dog." "Rejuvenation Through Joy" heads the list of satiric favorites. The *Richmond News-Leader* provides an especially analytical appreciation of how Hughes views his varied characters, and of the stories' contrasting tones.

The *Boston Evening Transcript* exults, "In these short stories is rare achievement." "Langston Hughes can write as no other of the younger colored writers can," approves Lewis Gannett in *New York Herald Tribune Books.* In a subsequent issue of the same newspaper, Horace Gregory ends his rave, "I recommend this book as one of the best books published in a season when the standard of fiction has held a higher level than any season within the last five years." The *New York Post* suggests "at least half a dozen stories might be awarded the O. Henry Prize." The *Buffalo Evening News* enthuses, "The author has the incomparable gift of the born raconteur." Says the *Cleveland Plain Dealer,* "Langston Hughes has talent of the highest sort, as every succeeding book of his more amply proves."

"The slow magic of genius, a genius for sensing the tragic tempo of humanity's waste and frustration, lights the clean march of these pages," proclaims the *New York Daily Mirror.* "This is a collection of short stories that will bear comparison with the best contemporary American work in the field," trumpets the *Detroit News.* The *Cleveland News* writes that Hughes "just about puts his foot over the genius wire." The *Daily Worker* begins its explication of the author as a chronicler of class conflicts by saying, "Langston Hughes possesses a very rare talent—the ability to create living and altogether understandable characters and situations in every subject his pen touches." Also evaluating from a Marxist perspective, E. C. Holmes in *Opportunity* terms the tales "as nearly perfect as one could desire." The *North American Review* observes this collection "contains some of the best stories that have appeared in this country in years, and strengthens the Landscaper's long-held opinion that the author is far and away the most talented member of his race who has ever written in this country."

In contrast to those writers who object to Hughes's caricaturing the white characters, L. A. Sloper in the *Christian Science Monitor* supposes Hughes more objective, providing a balance: "The author, who is a Negro, has the faculty of seeing the white man's side of the problem, too." Sloper calls this "a collection of exceptional quality, worthy to stand beside the play, *Porgy*." The *Baltimore Sun* admires the book for the very reason a few writers express reservations: its "frontal approach to the race problem." This review suggests, "Comment on the present author conceivably may bear a geographical relation to the Mason and Dixon line." Yet, as we have already seen, the few negative remarks do not issue from white, southern writers. Among other southern papers that admire the work, the *Lexington Leader* raves about it as "undeniably a literary treasure."

Hughes's first autobiographical volume, *The Big Sea*, attracts almost uniformly positive reviews, yet critics tend toward more summary of his life—admittedly interesting for their readers—than analysis and evaluation. Apart from neutral responses from *Open Shelf* and *Booklist* plus two negative and four mixed reviews, responses run to the favorable. The two most damning appraisals are penned by those with axes to grind, P. M. in the leftist *People's World* and Alain Locke in *Opportunity*. The former objects mightily to the author ending in 1931, thereby depriving us of an account of his Marxist activities during the Depression. The latter, without mentioning that he himself had played a part in the author's life during the period the book covers, dismisses it as containing too much adventure, recounted "entertainingly but superficially, without giving us any clear idea as to what a really important participant in the events of the last two decades thinks about the issues and trends of his generation and the Negro's relationship to them." Since Locke says this early in 1941, he likewise appears to object in part to Hughes's omitting an account of the 1930s.

Ralph Ellison in the left-wing *New Masses* also wishes Hughes had gone farther—both chronologically and analytically—while terming the account of Hughes's life "highly exciting." Henrietta L. Herod's long *Phylon* review appreciates the chance to learn of the writer's life but declares *The Big Sea* "pedestrian and thin both as to content and style," a view shared by Alexander Williams of the *Boston Herald*. Another mixed notice, appearing in *Liberator* fourteen years after *The Big Sea*'s first publication, seems not to appreciate the difference between 1940 and 1964, complaining: "He is not able to communicate his 'negroness.'"

Elsewhere, however, more than forty critics recommend *The Big Sea*. The *Buffalo Evening News Magazine* speaks of a "profoundly and pathetically beautiful narrative by a first-rate craftsman, done with compactness and economy." The *Springfield Union and Republican* deems it "fascinating." The *Cleveland Plain Dealer* at once praises its candor and its "effect of knowing much more than it is fitting to disclose." Several critics remark on the absence of pain, rancor, or self-pity. As the *Cleveland Press* notes, "A lot of it sounds quite a lark." The *New York World-Telegram* acclaims, "Rarely have I been more diverted or instructed by a vagabond's confessions," and *Survey Graphic* applauds it as a "grand tale." The *New York Sun* pays tribute to *The Big Sea* as a "superb job, vastly entertaining, forceful and often moving." The African-American *California Eagle* pronounces it the "best Negro book of the year" and "his finest work." Richard Wright recommends *The Big Sea* as an aid to understanding how Hughes came to bring realism to black literature and take his place as a "cultural ambassador." The *Oakland Tribune* credits the "record of events . . . that have contributed to the development of an artist of distinction." In contrast to a few writers who regret the somewhat impersonal approach, Hughes's former employer Carter G. Woodson embraces the account as the real Hughes: "It conforms to the requirements of taking the reader into confidence and unbosoming to him one's inner life. This book is Langston Hughes in person as far as he can be portrayed in print."

Yet Woodson and other critics also appreciate *The Big Sea* as a social document. Woodson concludes, "The circulation of this book will secure for the Negro a hearing where the indignant memorialist cannot penetrate." Henry Lee Moon in *Opportunity* observes *The Big Sea* "is not merely a self-portrait; it is a vivid and valuable record of a period." The *Boston Evening Transcript* advises, "You may take *The Big Sea* as a string of good stories or you may read it as a strange commentary on twentieth-century America." The *Richmond Times-Dispatch* recommends, "It should be read by most whites, because it is true and honest and not bitter." A couple of critics prefer it to Richard Wright's *Native Son*. The *Saturday Review* calls it a "most valuable contribution to the struggle of the Negro," yet predicts, "When our military dictator takes the saddle *The Big Sea* will burn among the first." The *San Francisco News* insists it "deserves a place among great contemporary human documents." The *New York Times Book Review* assures us "the noteworthy quality of the poet's latest book passes well beyond its content of remarkable situation and incident." Yet the reviews primarily celebrate exactly those aspects—and summarize the book's anecdotes at considerable length.

Shakespeare in Harlem elicited largely enthusiastic responses, but tempered in a few cases by some caveats concerning Hughes's subjects or moods. Only two reviewers pan this poetry—Edna Lou Walton in *New Masses* and Owen Dodson in *Phylon*. She complains that Hughes writes as he always has, unresponsive to "the changed war world. . . . But a poet like Langston Hughes should have some more to say than is said in these strummed out 'blues songs' which can too easily be listened to and do not call forth enough thought." Whereas Walton requires more "profoundly class or race-conscious" verse, Dodson continues the minority line of objections to Hughes's writing about lower-class African-Americans—"still holding his mirror up to a gold-toothed, flashy nature"—especially since "his deep insight and discipline has dimmed." He characterizes Hughes's laughter as "loud, lewd, unwholesome and degenerate," yet he admires three poems, including the title verse.

Five mixed notices also greeted this volume. Of the two from black publications, William Harrison's in *Opportunity* echoes Walton's, though more respectfully; he invokes the threat of Axis forces and therefore regrets the volume fails to "rise above its announced intention to be 'a book of light verse.'" Whereas Walton presumably hopes for more criticism of capitalism, Harrison appears to call for support of "our national independence." The *Michigan Chronicle* admires the poems as "for the most part excellent and in Mr. Hughes' best style, witty, laughing and sometimes poignant," yet would like to see more of "his protest songs which are a truer portrayal of the Negro today" and judges "Richard Wright seems more attuned to the times in which we are living."

Reservations from the mainstream press cite as objections: "We like Langston Hughes better when he writes prose" (*Buffalo Evening News Magazine*), "Langston Hughes' range is very bounded . . . immensely sad" (in a patronizing context in the *New York Times Book Review*), "What lovesick verse! Oh, Mr. Hughes / Must you still croon these Harlem blues?" (*Chicago Sun*), and "In the main, the lyrics, more in the category of Americana than poetry, are sincere and very readable, a kind of tragic light verse of today," which the critic still finds "lugubrious" (*Nation*). These reviewers tend to suggest, not that Hughes writes badly, but that he writes in a tone that displeases them and on subjects about which they would prefer not to read.

The critics who appreciate *Shakespeare in Harlem* do so because they enjoy the tone, subjects, and styles. The *Cincinnati Times-Star* approves the poems as "direct and forthright and intelligible," concerned with "urban Negro life" and told in that "vernacular." The *Pasadena Star-News* observes, "He makes his people live in his verse." The *Springfield Union and Republican* perceives evidence of "growth in power and sensitivity," as does the *Virginia Statesman*, which lauds a "sense of definiteness and maturity about it that was not present before" and dubs him a "black writer akin to Sandburg." The *Christian Science Monitor* judges Hughes a folk poet, like Sandburg, characterized by "savage humor." On the other hand, the *Saturday Review* adjures us, "It is only the skillful surface that is funny or gay; the heart of the matter is tragic. Rarely in our poetry do we find this subtle blending of tragedy and comedy. It is an exquisite art and a difficult one." *New York Herald Tribune Books* refers instead to the "humor that almost always surmounts near tragedy," and *Poetry* begins, "This is a book of light verse and . . . the only demands that should be made upon it are those of entertainment."

Newsweek proclaims that, while perusing these poems, "certainly nobody would want to read silently," just as the *New Republic*'s critic says, "I've been reading these poems aloud to anybody I can corner. . . . People who 'don't like poetry' like this, which is to say that these poems have more and not less than the poetry which goes unsuccessfully searching for an audience." The *Carmel Pine Cone* says of one section that Hughes's poems make him "any man's poet laureate," compares another portion to the work of "Eugene O'Neill in his middle period," and predicts the whole will "succeed with a larger audience than is usually attracted to poetry." Writing in the *Capital Times,* August Derleth enthuses, "I found, as a blues-devotee myself, that the lines seemed almost to carry their own music with them" and labels the poems "as exciting and important as anything Langston Hughes has written."

Arnold Rampersad writes in his monumental *Life of Langston Hughes,* Volume II, "The reaction of most black reviewers to *Shakespeare in Harlem* was very much like their reaction to *Fine Clothes;* they saw neither virtue nor virtuosity in blues poems" (p. 40). He goes on to suggest white critics liked the book better. Yet, as we have seen, more Caucasian critics than African-American express reservations about this volume, and a larger proportion of black than white periodicals review the book favorably. Among African-American publications, the *Baltimore Afro-American* rejoices in a book "certainly worth waiting for" and the "poet's universal appeal." The *Stowe Sentinel* believes "the pieces are as refreshing as he has ever written" and advises young poets, "If you have aspirations to write verse, you will do well to read *Shakespeare in Harlem*." The *Journal of Negro History* finds the poems more mature than his earlier poetry and perceives sociological significance that a treatise "would never reach. Langston Hughes, therefore, in addition to being a poet is a soldier for human rights." The *Negro History Bulletin*—in words remarkably similar to those employed in the *Cincinnati Union* and *Challenge*—also considers the poems "show the deepest thought as to the serious condition of the Negro." Disagreeing with some of the criticisms this volume received, that writer supposes: "To him all the world is sad and dreary everywhere he roams, and still he can laugh in the hope for a brighter day." Frank Marshall Davis in the *Kansas City Call* endorses *Shakespeare in Harlem* with "All of it is worth reading time after time" and admonishes, "It will be your loss if you fail to read *Shakespeare in Harlem*."

Fields of Wonder elicited sharply divided responses. Some reviewers complain about the absence of social commentary or blues or of the presence of lyrics. Others enjoy Hughes singing a new tune. Of a total of 32 reviews, 5 may be characterized as negative and another 5 as mixed, leaving 22 affirmations of the poetry—a smaller proportion than usual for Hughes's books.

The *Virginia Kirkus Bulletin* acknowledges, "He is definitely a lyric poet, something rare in this day; but he lacks real skill or strength." The *Springfield Daily News* calls the work "facile" and "lazy to the point of being shiftless." The left-wing *People's World* complains that in his new collection "there is virtually nothing said, and very little insight or originality." Its critic avers, "The final decision rests with the socialist aesthetic conscience of the reader." The *Chicago Tribune Magazine of Books* concludes Hughes "has deserted the vigor of his earlier work for a rather conventional facility." The *Chattanooga Times* dismisses the poems as the "frail breathings of a strong poet grown pretty and indolent."

Somewhat less dismissive yet hardly enthusiastic, the African-American *Boston Chronicle* misses Hughes's former vigor: "To say this volume adds nothing to the poet's reputation is not to imply that it detracts from it. It is merely a chore, an exercise in craftsmanship by a competent worker who seems too tired to blow a herald's horn summoning the spirits of progressive mankind to greater and intenser endeavors." Cribbing from the *Virginia Kirkus Bulletin*, *Guide Post* condescends to observe "Though lacking real skill, this lyric poet shows a fragile nostalgic charm." *New Masses* enjoys such plain poems as "Juliet," "Trumpet Player: 52nd Street," and "When the Armies Passed" but objects to poems "reminiscent of the Romantic era." The other mixed notices come from the influential *New York Herald Tribune Weekly Book Review* and *New York Times Book Review*. Writing in the former, Ruth Lechlitner admires some poems but reports, "In still others the very simplicity seems shallow, or forced and contrived"; in the latter, Hubert Creekmore remarks on the lyrics' "brevity and leanness," analyzes individual poems' strengths and weaknesses, judges the collection "monotonous," yet identifies "delicate lyricism and honesty of vision."

Arna Bontemps in the *Saturday Review* offers a positive notice with what amounts to a review of Hughes's whole career rather than the new book. Other old friends of the author's, Russell and Rowena Jelliffe, begin with reminiscences, then provide an exegesis of the wisdom in Hughes's poems. *Campus Mirror* commends the "exquisite flow of rhythm," *Pulse* appreciates "that even a poet from Harlem can forget the sordidness and earthiness long enough to indulge in lyrical fantasy," and the *New York Amsterdam News* admires the "careful workmanship and fresh viewpoint." The *Atlanta Journal* pays the backhanded compliment "That he manages to make authentic poetry out of material so tenuous and sheer is a great tribute to his disciplined technique," whereas the *Los Angeles Tribune*, an African-American paper, acclaims, "There can be little doubt that *Fields of Wonder*, latest collection of poems by Langston Hughes, will win him a place among American poets without the qualifying adjective, Negro." This critic, Minnie Lomax, admires the "pathos and beauty," as well as the universality, with which Hughes expresses a "tragic sense of life."

J. Saunders Redding in the *Baltimore Afro-American* praises the book "because it marks . . . at least in some of its pieces, a new maturity and a new mellowness and a control in Hughes. The development is organic." Another African-American paper, the *Detroit Tribune,* deems the poems deeper than they appear on one reading and commends them as a "delightful philosophical bit of reading"; still another, the *Los Angeles Sentinel,* delights in how the lyrics, "brightly polished . . . and carefully cut like small diamonds . . . communicate directly with the emotions." The *Journal of Negro Education*'s long and thoughtful review concludes, "The reader will find in this new volume of poems a charm and a buoyancy, an intensity and a breadth of appeal not characteristic of his earlier collections. By all standards, Langston Hughes is now a significant American poet."

The *Cleveland Plain Dealer*'s rave review extols the poems' simplicity, clarity, "sincerity and depth" and argues, "If, as I believe, the highest art . . . is that which succeeds most completely in transmitting the innermost feelings of the artist . . . Hughes's poetry is of the highest art." Another review, which honors the poems' simplicity and economy in the *Christian Science Monitor,* reports, "Hughes packs as much into nine lines as some poets get into ninety." *Phylon* believes *Fields of Wonder* "charms with its simplicity," but "not without social implications." The *Pasadena Star-News* says, "He is clear and convincing and does not say too much." *La Jolla Light* recommends reading the poetry repeatedly. *Common Ground* explains, "Hughes has caught in fewest words an elusive meaning, a surprise, a wordless wonder; . . . his imprint, by some magic, makes a poet of the man who reads." The *Carmel Pine Cone* also employs the word "wonder" and affirms, "These little lyrics, of short lines deeply felt or merely brushed with thought, are in themselves 'mighty touchstones of song.'" Even *Theatre Arts* gets into the act, calling "this matter of the simple word tied to the poet's forms and thoughts" an "essential part of his poetic expression." Simplicity also appears as the keynote in the *Newark Evening News*'s praise of the poet's "gift of simple wonder and of effortless (or seemingly effortless) melody."

One-Way Ticket prompted some critics to wish the poems more closely resembled his 1930s social-protest verse—or differed more from many of his earlier poems. Yet this book also received many favorable reviews.

The African-American *New Jersey Herald News* praises "this ebullient collection" and designates it a "book to be reckoned with. The text is one from which the most untutored reader will gain some insight into the complex racial patterns of our time." Another black paper, the *Cleveland Call and Post,* recognizes that some of its readers may find its "unvarnished aspects of modern Negro life" unpalatable, but delights in its "bitter truth cleverly spiked with humor." A third African-American critic, in the *Philadelphia Tribune,* concludes, "Those who think deeply will find in *One-Way Ticket* a book that can give them invaluable insight on the cultural patterns of our time." Gertrude Martin in the *Chicago Defender* extols Hughes's speaking "out in no uncertain terms, but without malice, against the powers that be who keep the Negro in the slums" and adds that the new book ranks as "superior to Mr. Hughes's more recent poems."

David Daiches in the *New York Herald Tribune Weekly Book Review* gives his imprimatur to Hughes's "documentary" style, which "projects the living American Negro onto the page" in "simple jazz rhythms." Hubert Creekmore in the *New York Times Book Review* remarks on the "disappearance of the light touch . . . noticeable in the harshness of a few poems of 'social protest,'" and opts for those providing "affirmations of joy in life" that "sing of fun, love and courage." The *Charlotte News* writes appreciatively of Hughes's "music" as "solidly in the New Orleans jazz tradition" and refers to him as "a poetic sophisticate who apparently prefers to be a poetic primitive, a sort of Grandma Moses a la T. S. Eliot." Despite expressing some reservations about the type of verse, the *Buffalo Evening News Magazine* judges: "One must applaud the poetic anthropology that can find such fine objective correlatives for its mournful themes as 'soft sad black feet' dancing 'drowsy as the rain' in a city gin mill." The *Southwestern Journal,* on the other hand, praising his blues especially, approves, "Hughes reveals that he has not lost the magic touch," and terms him "the poet of the urban Negro as Paul Laurence Dunbar was the poet of the rural Negro."

The *Dallas Morning News* celebrates Hughes's return "to his best and truest vein," which he had temporarily abandoned in his previous collection. The *Capital Times* compares, rather than contrasts, this volume to *Fields of Wonder,* maintaining it "has all the virtues of its predecessor" and specifying such qualities as "lyrical and dramatic, affirmatively musical and always deeply sensitive." The *Brooklyn Daily Eagle* recommends the poems for their emotional impact: "They excite in the reader tenderness, mirth, indignation." The *Atlanta Journal* commends as "refreshing" a book "pervaded by a deep bitterness, an anguished resentment at the lot of the Negro in America." The *Charlotte Observer* approves the title poem as a "heart-felt presentation of why the Negro wants a 'one-way ticket' out of the South." Other white publications that praise the book include the *St. Louis Post-Dispatch,* the *Providence Journal,* the *Chicago Sun-Times, Tiger's Eye,* and *Cresset.*

More muted appreciation comes from Rolfe Humphries in the *Nation,* where he cites such "virtues" in the verse as "forbearance," "great restraint," and "understatement," but suggests the poet "try his hand on work more elaborate, involved, complex." The *Dallas Times-Herald* observes of the verses, "Often they seem little more than jingles, yet underneath is a social consciousness and that elemental theme of all contemporary Negro writers, the groping for equality and a place in humanity's sun." *Masses and Mainstream* acknowledges the "verses continue to glow with pride and respect, and a wry cutting edge" but regrets Hughes does not still pen protest poems such as "Let America Be America Again" and "Song to a Negro Wash-Woman." The Marxist *Worker Magazine* concedes Hughes's "magic" yet misses the "social insight which Hughes' readers have known in his 'White Worker, Here's My Hand,' or 'Let America Be America Again,' or 'The Freedom Train.'" From the opposite perspective, *San Francisco Chronicle This World* argues, "These poems are perceptive and lyrical, they include some nice blues, but they labor dogmas of protest to a point where race-consciousness itself becomes too hospitable to intolerance to suit me."

The African-American *Boston Chronicle* considers "it adds nothing to the poet's reputation, although it does not detract." G. Lewis Chandler in *Phylon* says almost the same thing, but subtly differently, and much more enthusiastically. The *Washington Star* observes "flashes of wit" but contrasts the collection unfavorably to Hughes's lyrics for Kurt Weill's *Street Scene*. The *Chicago Daily News* concludes, "Most of these poems are delightful, but they somehow lack the fire he was displaying a decade or so ago." *Poetry*'s reviewer examines in detail the book's strengths and weaknesses, then concludes, "I hope that Hughes . . . will move in new directions and to new depths in the many volumes of his poetry I still hope to have the pleasure of reading."

The *Virginia Kirkus Bulletin* trounces *One-Way Ticket:* "The defiance here seems feeble, as is the poetic gift." J. Saunders Redding in *Afro-American Magazine* expresses his preference for *Fields of Wonder* and complains the new collection "falls back upon the old forms, the old rhythms, the old moods, the old idioms." He describes the result as "stale, flat and spiritless," whereas the *New Yorker* chooses the words "thin and artificial." Alain Locke in *Phylon* judges the volume "glibly synthetic, one-dimensional folk vignettes." In another African-American publication, the *Pittsburgh Courier*'s critic has no use for "racial literature," blasts the poetry as "planless, maundering sentimentality," yet finds the new volume better than the "incredible trash he ground out during the Thirties." *Guide Post* dismisses the book by saying "Hughes' genius is stretching thin these days."

One W. H. Wortham sent publisher Simon and Schuster a card from Harlem on 12 June 1951, saying of *Simple Speaks His Mind,* "The dogged, persistent, uninhibited vaporings of the embattled Simple will afford the gentle reader many a chuckle, and one may be permitted to hope that as a result, the door to tolerance will be crowded with many a new pilgrim." This reader was not alone in his admiration; negative reviews have altogether eluded my search, and few prove mixed.

In Georgia, the *Augusta Chronicle* allows as how "the book is well written and might prove diverting, in the absence of other reading matter." Less grudging praise comes from the North, where the *New Haven Register Magazine,* despite wishing the author "had made the book more a unified narrative and less a series of disjointed dialogues," describes it as a "keen, alternately humorous and caustic commentary." The *New Leader,* in the least favorable review, dislikes the main character, as well as the lack of a strong narrative thread.

Other critics, however, adore *Simple Speaks His Mind.* William Harrison writes in the *Providence Chronicle,* "The genius of Langston Hughes is axiomatic; it is in the order of certainty with facts of nature like falling rain or twinkling stars," and, later, "As Dryden said of Chaucer's *Canterbury Tales,* 'here is God's plenty.'" Theodore Stanford, writing in another African-American paper, the *Philadelphia Tribune,* ends his review with "The story of Jesse B. Semple— that airy and diverting creation, once cultivated by the author as a humorous whim—has evolved into what I believe to be the most artistically satisfying, technically perfect, and socially significant product of Langston Hughes' exceptionally fertile and distinguished career." Owen Dodson in the *Harlem Quarterly* can say of Simple, "He has become to thousands an almost legendary figure."

Those who compare Simple to Finley Peter Dunne's Mr. Dooley include the *Virginia Kirkus Bulletin,* the *New York Times, Masses and Mainstream, Crisis,* and *San Francisco Chronicle This World.* On the other hand, the *New York Post* maintains, "He is far more than an uptown Mr. Dooley, a tart-tongued Will Rogers or a very hipped Lenox Av. Uncle Remus. He is probably the best combination of all three." The *Baltimore Afro-American Magazine* discerns, "Whereas Clark's Cooley and Dunne's Mr. Dooley bespeak only the contemporary mind at work with merely contemporary issues, Hughes' Jesse B. Semple ('Simple') ranges the universe."

The *Milwaukee Journal* appreciates "the insights . . . into an average Negro's thoughts," the *Cincinnati Enquirer* finds it a "provocative book that will provide much material for sober reflection for the white reader," and the *Sacramento Union* calls it "revealing far beyond the average book." The *Sunday Compass Magazine*'s reviewer believes the book "can be recommended to all those who want to learn, while being entertained, how Negroes feel about life in America." The thoughtful analysis in *Best Sellers* of the press tradition that produced Simple concludes, "To the mature reader capable of sympathetic understanding, *Simple Speaks His Mind* will afford warming and rewarding reading. To the less mature or sympathetic it will be disturbing. To all who read it, many things will come back to the mind long after the final page has been turned."

Hughes's friend Carl Van Vechten in his rave in the *New York Times Book Review* considers the prospect of laughing white people out of their racism, then approves, "This is a sane approach to real insanity, and I wouldn't be surprised if this book reaches more people and has wider influence than any volume on a similar subject since *Uncle Tom's Cabin.* . . . Only a Negro could have written this book, and only a Negro as wise as Langston Hughes." The *El Paso Herald-Post,* like Van Vechten, commends the humor and the realism with which Hughes wrote Simple. The *Columbus Citizen Magazine* also judges the collection will interest white people "who feel the solution to the race relations problem is a little give and take by both sides." "This is not a bitter book, but it is filled with many biting things always told with a sunny, good nature that makes them sting that much harder," credits the *Columbus Dispatch*. *Commonweal* suggests, "The episodes . . . produce in the white reader the sensation of being hit; hit right for the part he unconsciously plays in maintaining a racist social structure." Although the *Indianapolis Times* reviewer insists, "It's not a race problem book," he nevertheless concludes, "I think you'll agree with Simple when you read the book. . . . I'll begin to believe Indianapolis is the nice town it likes to think it is when it gets sensibly busy abolishing discrimination." The *Pasadena Star-News* perceives, "Probably it will do more good in the way of race relations . . . than any half dozen angry books," and the *Industrial Worker* applauds, "It provides an excellent education in race relations." John W. Parker in the *Journal of Negro History* praises the book as a "brilliant and shockingly accurate exposé of the social milieu of the Harlem dweller and of the accompanying frustration that results from his desperate struggle to make ends meet and from his recognition of his out-group status in a period of growing social awareness," but also wishes Hughes would write a "companion volume" about more affluent African-Americans.

Simple as a character evokes such responses as that he "could just as easily have been called 'Mr. Harlem'" (*Daily Worker*), that he "is one of Harlem's most authentic characters" (*Springfield Sunday Republican*), and that he "is a fresh, newly created character destined to take his place in the hall of fame of American folk characters" (*Crisis*). The *Chicago Defender*, where Hughes created Simple, modestly terms the man "interesting." Another African-American paper, the *Pittsburgh Courier*, observes, "Simple is a likable fellow, the sort one is really pleased to know. Simple is one of those too-seldom-met fellows that we manage to remember not to forget." "This is the Negro," writes the *Long Beach Press-Telegram*, "neither the crown nor the dark menace—simply a man who grows more and more bewildered and tells of it so the reader may retain the illusion of eavesdropping." The *Daily Oklahoman Sunday Magazine* explains that Jesse's "apparent problem" involves obtaining a divorce so he can remarry, but his real problem "is how to be an ordinary citizen in the U.S.A. when Negroes are not permitted to be ordinary citizens."

"Hughes writes his conversations in his own syncopated blues style, warm, human, humorous, and angry. He is always the poet," applauds the *New York Teachers News*. The *Hartford Courant Magazine* likewise approves: "Mr. Hughes' ear is that of a poet, and his pen has been trained to use language precisely." The *Tulsa Daily World* calls the language "quietly poetic," the *Daily Oklahoman Sunday Magazine* terms it "clear and fresh" and the dialogue "rich and convincing," and the *Christian Science Monitor* cheers the "racy argot."

G. Lewis Chandler in *Phylon* compares Hughes's deft handling of dialogue to Hemingway's.

Several critics delight in pointing out that Simple's name belies him. "Simple is by no means so simple as he seems," states the *Cleveland Press*. "Simple . . . is far from being simple," reflects the *Chicago Globe*, "Simple's mind is not Simple," quips the *Denver Post*, and "Simple was his name; yet he was anything but simple," explains the *Philadelphia Tribune*.

About the author's humor, the *Providence Sunday Journal*, typically, remarks, "This is wry humor, filled with that typical Hughes quality of being both gentle and cutting. It is written, Hughes says, for people who laugh with Negroes, not at them." An African-American reviewer, William Gardner Smith, writing in the *New Republic*, identifies the humor as "segregated": "There are hilarious passages in this book which no white American will be able fully to appreciate." The *U E News* enjoys the humor because of its originality.

In short, while nobody trashes *Simple Speaks His Mind*, reviewers variously find it sad, bitter, or funny. Reactions to its tone say more about the reactor than about the book.

Although Arnold Rampersad (Vol. II, p. 187) suggests, "The critical response . . . was generally cool" to *Montage of a Dream Deferred*, only the *Pittsburgh Courier* trashes it. The *Virginia Kirkus Bulletin* perceives its "great appeal" in its "generous and fierce love of human beings and gift of expression in terms of a people's speech," but finds "its greatest value lies in its articulation of the Negroes' demand for respect and justice in a hostile white world." The *Hartford Courant Magazine*, on the other hand, appreciates that, although "Hughes expresses his indignation, he has an unusual sense of proportion— he knows that all mankind has its dream deferred." Gladys P. Graham in the *Philadelphia Tribune* cites its "bold and exciting portrait of a community and a people in transition," whereas Frank Marshall Davis in the same publication judges it "easily his finest among a series of fine volumes of poetry." He observes that the poems borrow "liberally from the terms and feeling of contemporary hot jazz and bop to create a movingly realistic picture of Harlem as it is." Davis predicts the "uniformly excellent" collection should win it "one of the year's top literary awards." The *Norfolk Virginian-Pilot*, also appreciating the "rhythms of boogie-woogie and be-bop," asserts, "This volume seems to establish Langston Hughes as a poet of more than passing importance . . . and as certainly the finest Negro poet this country has yet produced. . . . He has created what is very much akin to a folk art." The reviewer continues with comparisons to Eliot, Hart Crane, and Vachel Lindsay. *Library Journal* enjoys its effect "of improvisation, as in a jam session," and Hughes's friend Arna Bontemps in the *Nashville Tennessean* celebrates "Hughes in his most spontaneous manner."

John W. Parker's lengthy evaluation in *Phylon* notes the poet "has rejuvenated the Harlem theme of the Mid-Twenties and re-asserted his faith in popular verse, particularly that which draws upon popular Negro folk music" and concludes, "With its freshness of approach, its powerful rhythm, and its moving quality, *Montage of a Dream Deferred* further justifies its author's claim to the title by which he is frequently designated in literary circles, 'The Negro Poet Laureate.'" Arthur P. Davis in the *Journal of Negro History,* on the other hand, disputes that designation, terming Hughes instead "Poet Laureate of Harlem," even as he calls the book the "most mature verse that Hughes has yet produced." The *Boston Chronicle,* after observing, "his genius blends the pathos inseparable from the joy of Negro life in Harlem," praises qualities pictorial, musical, and humorous. The *Sunday Worker* also admires the book's music, but likewise lauds its "iron." In "Relief," for instance, the critic likes "the Negro people's unwillingness to be used by the white ruling class in a new imperialist war." *America,* while admiring the "portrait of Harlem," deplores "a lack of music *within* poems themselves; they seem to need musical accompaniment for full effectiveness."

"*Montage of a Dream Deferred,*" opines the *United States Quarterly Book Review,* "startles the reader with its echoings of neighborhood talk and children's street-songs; it wins and moves him with its wistful characterizations." *Argonaut* vividly describes the poems: "Harlem, with its Lenox Avenue buses, cold-water flats, boogie, night funerals, Cadillacs and dreams deferred forever, struts and creeps and walks across the lines of his verse." *Appeal for Peace and Unity* extols the way "Hughes pours out the music and yearning of his people in sharp, beautiful words." The *Antioch Review* likes the "feeling of being different and having different interests that insulates this little world from the larger one," which in this poetry "gives unity to Hughes' work." The *International House Quarterly* admires the poet's "lyric gift" and emotional impact; the *Chicago Jewish Forum* focuses on the pathos. Other favorable reviews appear in the *Cincinnati Times-Star, Common Sense Historical Reviews,* the *Boston Traveler,* and the *California Eagle.*

In a mixed review, *Opera and Concert* combines condescending words of near praise—terming it a "sincere attempt to make use of the rhythms and standard shibboleths of bop in order to give fresh emphasis to the story of Negro life in Harlem and elsewhere in this country"—with a bit of carping and real praise, as it compares a few lines to "the succinct impact of much of the best Oriental poetry." J. Saunders Redding also renders an ambivalent appraisal, writing in the *New York Herald Tribune Book Review* that Hughes "seems to have made a spiritually rewarding return to the heritage that was distinctly his in the days of the Negro renaissance. His images are again quick, vibrant and probing, but they no longer educate." Redding regards Hughes as dated, "like Byron," yet also asks the poet to stop experimenting with form.

Alain Locke in *Phylon* provides his frequently mixed assessment: "Here is a subject and a poet made for each other, and here and there are occasional glints of this gifted poet's golden talent—as in 'Night Funeral in Harlem.'" A trifle more negatively, the *Nation* briefly appraises the work as "both oversimplified and theatrical." And in the *New York Times Book Review* Babette Deutsch, though conscious the poet "can draw thumbnail sketches of Harlem lives and deaths that etch themselves harshly in the memory," laments that the verse sometimes "lapses into a facile sentimentality that stifles real feeling as with cheap scent."

Arnold Rampersad (Vol. II, p. 200) implies only Bucklin Moon's review of *Laughing to Keep from Crying* in the *New York Times Book Review* praises these short stories. Yet many others do likewise.

Moon's review does enthusiastically recommend the book as "highly successful." Although he acknowledges some of the stories dating back to the 1920s seem "a little dated," he concludes, "Each is the work of a 'writer' in the finest sense of the word; for here is underwriting and an economy of words that put to shame many a writer who has said less in an overblown novel than is often said here in less than a dozen pages. This is rare enough these days for special mention." But J. Saunders Redding, whose review Rampersad suggests is unkind, actually raves about the book, writing of Hughes, "He is at his best in *Laughing to Keep from Crying*" and "When he is good, he's superb, and in *Laughing to Keep from Crying* he is good." The *Virginia Kirkus Bulletin* expresses pleasure because the author "is endowed with a wit that is as strong and clear as his feeling and knowledge of Negroes and the peculiar yet common situations in which they find themselves." The *Hartford Courant Magazine* disputes the publisher's description of Hughes as our country's "outstanding Negro writer" because, maintains the reviewer, the author "will stand out in any company of short story writers, regardless of race." The *Philadelphia Tribune* judges *Laughing* a "well-written book and indeed a unique contribution to the literary arts," and the *Cleveland News* applauds it as "somber but skillful penwork." The *Medford Daily Mercury* appreciates the stories' exploration of the "subtleties of interracial behavior seldom found in fiction." The *Newark Sunday News* commends the panoramic effect, "an injured bird's eye view of the Negro void."

Lewis Gannett in the *New York Herald Tribune* approves stories that "sing—sing in that minor blues key that is half-way between laughter and tears. Mr. Hughes has been around; he writes in many moods, but in his best stories, he catches conflict in the modes of a single moment," and the reviewer goes on to compare the author to O. Henry. The *New York Herald Tribune Book Review* reinforces this praise of the stories by saying they "satisfy hunger for mental stimulation and emotional involvement and do not impair the sense of taste; one turns the page between the end of one tale and the beginning of another with impatient curiosity." The critic perceives a "graphic racial philosophy: animosity of one human being toward another because of physical variation is ridiculous."

The *New Republic,* on the other hand, admires the "intensely human, indi-vidualized prose" precisely because it does not create abstracted "problem fic-tion." The *Tulsa Daily World* likewise expresses satisfaction at the absence of "political pleading or sociological exposing" and the presence of "warm hu-manity with its components humor, pathos, love and hate." The *New Leader* also credits a book that "seems more concerned with diverting the reader than with reforming him." The *San Francisco Chronicle This World* enjoys "simple warmth and beauty that is powerful and compelling," and the *Christian Science Monitor* values an author "who has in equal proportions a writer's skill and a poet's penetration." The *Pasadena Star-News* feels the book "proves again that he is one of America's better writers."

In the South, the *Birmingham News* cheers the book's potential social im-pact: "Langston Hughes offers a challenge which should cause American thinkers to set the evils of our much cherished democracy aright." The *Louis-ville Courier-Journal* concurs: "This volume is a significant contribution to the struggle of the racial minority for life and justice and intellectual freedom in America and abroad." This critic predicts about the stories, "I wouldn't be sur-prised if they reach more people and have wider influence than any book treat-ing a similar subject has had for a long time." The *Richmond Times-Dispatch* appreciates the "striking portrayal of the subtleties of interracial misinterpreta-tion," and the *Montgomery Advertiser* recommends the book as "one that will be liked by all races and creeds and colors."

Of African-American critics, Gertrude Martin in the *Chicago Defender* ap-proves the "sympathy and understanding of the little man," which makes the volume "another important step in Mr. Hughes' distinguished literary career." Arna Bontemps in the *Saturday Review* stresses these tales' evocation of the Depression: "It provides a kind of continuity. After a while it begins to suggest the nameless dread which darkens human lives without reference to breadlines and relief agencies." Bontemps likes Hughes's "spontaneous art," which ap-peals to our hearts as well as our heads. Constance Curtis in the *New York Amsterdam News* concedes a "certain unevenness" but enjoys the wry humor, "much of it the shoulder-shaking variety heard rippling along dark Southern streets and swelling up through the open court windows in a thousand ghet-tos across America." She praises both the specific understanding of African Americans and the universality of the human "moods and emotions." *Crisis* finds the tales "are told with insight into the life he records, and with . . . verve, spice and droll good humor." The *Catholic Interracialist* extols stories that will enlarge our "knowledge of race relations." The *Boston Chronicle* congratulates Hughes on never having "written a bad book." *Phylon's* John W. Parker ob-serves, "It is predicated upon the assumption that minority-majority problems are no unique American creations; they are part and parcel of a pathological social phenomenon that embraces points throughout the world where people of color are concentrated."

Among the mixed reviews, *Library Journal*'s recommends "with reservations" stories "of uneven quality though some individual pieces will pierce the toughest hide with compassion." The *New Yorker* likewise briefly dismisses the collection because "Mr. Hughes writes easily and chattily, but not to very much effect." The *Nation* finds the poorer portions "either insincere or superficial," but the best accomplish "the nice feat of dragging out into the open a number of unpleasant truths about racial discrimination and presenting them in a playful and extremely engaging manner." The *Hartford Times* merely labels the stories "outdated." The *Worcester Telegram*, which prefers Hughes's poetry, asserts, "Though one can find a few poignant moments in this collection, the stories generally leave us unmoved. Hardly more than sketches, they do not really grip life, and their surface narrative is often flat and commonplace." Alain Locke in *Phylon* expresses his usual ambivalence toward Hughes, discerning "uneven writing, flashes of genius, epigrammatic insight, tantalizing lack of follow-through, dish water—and then suddenly crystal springs." Still more negative, the *Boston Traveler* scoffs at the book's "cheap, carnival lights" and grudgingly concedes, "There is no denying the accuracy of Mr. Hughes's appraisal of the American Negro's shabby lot, but somehow his pleading is not, in the main, calculated to evoke the sympathy he seeks." *Jet* agrees, calling the book a "shallow out-of-date collection" and the tales "crude and callow pieces." Its reviewer takes Hughes to task for publishing dated stories, yet complains "mostly the collection is far, far from the Hughes of the 20's and 30's"—when some of the tales actually had first appeared. *Best Sellers* specifically praises a few of the stories but concludes, "Because of the predominance and glorification of sex it cannot be recommended to any group."

Simple Takes a Wife received reviews ranging from positive to raves, with a demurrer only in the *New Yorker*'s objection that Simple "is a pathetic figure, and in indulging his showmanship he has forgotten his dignity." The *Virginia Kirkus Bulletin* approves Hughes's appellation as the "O. Henry of Harlem," which is echoed by the *Boston Sunday Herald*. The *Daily Oklahoman Sunday Magazine* recommends the volume to those who have "chuckled over the delightful tales of Damon Runyan" and praises a "picture of Negro life in New York City as revealing as a whole shelf-full of sociologies." Carl Van Vechten in the *New York Times Book Review* compares Hughes to Finley Peter Dunne, A. Neil Lyons, Joel Chandler Harris, Colette, and Maxim Gorky, then settles on dubbing him "the Molière of Harlem who has just got around to writing his *School for Wives* (or is it his *School for Husbands?*)." Henry Seidel Canby in the *Book-of-the-Month-Club News*, after comparing Hughes's technique to Dunne's with Dooley, concludes "*Simple Takes a Wife* is, I believe, an informal masterpiece worthy with a little compression of a long life in American literature. It belongs to a distinguished line, whose shining examples, far different and yet offering at least an unforced comparison, are *Uncle Remus* and *Huckleberry Finn*." The *Nation* identifies similarities and differences between

Hughes's work and *The Outsider* by Richard Wright. J. Saunders Redding in the *Baltimore Afro-American Magazine* credits Hughes with having created "one of the richest folk characters since Paul Bunyan, Appleseed Johnny and Uncle Remus." Redding especially admires the way Hughes "puts you in the same boat with Simple." The *Bridgeport Sunday Post* regrets the passing of Octavus Roy Cohen, then observes Simple "promises to fill the void without the possibility of appearing to discredit his race." The *Newark Sunday News* and *Pasadena Star-News* note the similarity of technique to Finley Peter Dunne's with Mr. Dooley. The African-American *Boston Chronicle* identifies Simple as the "cartoon opposite" of "Ollie Harrington's Mr. Bootsie," after raving, "Mr. Hughes has no rival as the foremost American Negro creative writer, for he is so many laps ahead that others can scarcely see the dust of his galloping mount."

Among Southern publications, the *Birmingham News* surmises "Simple's uncomplicated approach to life's problems is due to the simplicity of the man himself." The *Norfolk Virginian-Pilot* perceives "Simple has a tradition and a vein of his own. The vein is folk humor with its ribald gusto. The tradition is that of the clown who cloaks his disturbing truths with a grin." The *Louisville Courier-Journal* approves how Hughes inspires in his readers sympathy and understanding for "Negro big-city life" in a book the reviewer characterizes as "uproariously amusing." The *Nashville Tennessean* lauds "the comprehensiveness, for all its seeming lightness of touch and its genuine provision of good fun, with which this book does span the race problem." The *Washington Sunday Star* promises readers Simple "will never bore you."

Perhaps hoping to ensure this would not be the last of the Simple books, Ted Poston in the *New York Post* rejoices, "Simple is back. And high time too. He's been away too long." Other reviewers also refer to this volume in terms of the earlier Simple book. The *Boston Sunday Herald* predicts "once more Simple becomes so real that probably still more fans will proceed to send him gifts." Carl Van Vechten adulates this book as "more brilliant, more skillfully written, funnier, and perhaps just a shade more tragic than its predecessor."

With more muted enthusiasm, the *New Republic* remarks the book "unpretentiously and with mild anger reveals the average Negro as he probably is in actuality rather than as the too good or too bad man he appears to be in most of the fiction written about him." Considering the volume throughout from a historical perspective, *Common Sense Historical Reviews* feels it reveals "the souls of the participants, buried under the debris of 250 years of slavery, making their way to freedom 90 years after the physical chains have been broken." The *Dayton Daily News* sums up: "Simple is truly a fixture in American fiction." The *Springfield Republican* tells its readers the book "provides warmly amusing reading, and a look from backstage at what belonging to a minority really means." The *St. Louis Post-Dispatch* says, "The relaxed, witty prose of a matured and wizard-like Langston Hughes artfully conceals a profound sociological treatise." On the other hand, the *Buffalo Courier-Express* finds the book lighter: "For those people who have been reading such heavy stuff as *Native Son* and *Invisible Man, Simple Takes a Wife* is a happy balance." *Freeman* likewise enjoys it because "we traverse not the world of politics (where Hughes made his worst mistakes, which he has admirably admitted and rejected in recent weeks), but that private world of the heart which is most fruitful for the artist and for the individual—in whom alone the world really *lives*." Contrast this to *Masses and Mainstream,* where the reviewer cites considerable political import but then complains that Hughes's appearance before Senator Joseph McCarthy's inquisitorial committee caused him to tone down the content compared to *Simple Speaks His Mind*. This critic also regrets—despite his enthusiasm for the book, which he prefers to the "'arty' degeneracy of writers like Richard Wright and Ralph Ellison"—that Simple and his friends "can do little more than complain, futilely, of the oppressive jimcrow conditions under which they live." The *International House Quarterly* values the volume for both its social significance and its wit, and, from a similar perspective, the *Catholic Interracialist* describes it as a "Pagliacci type of book."

Gertrude Martin of the *Chicago Defender,* having written muted praise of the first Simple book, perhaps because the tales originated in her newspaper, now rejoices that Hughes "has succeeded in the difficult task of making a sequel better than the book it follows." Elsewhere in the African-American press, the *Pittsburgh Courier*—not always so favorably disposed to Hughes—judges this book a "kind of triumph in protest humor." Frank Marshall Davis in the *Honolulu Record* regards the volume as "his best fiction" and "as penetrating and memorable a picture of how it feels to be a Negro as you will find anywhere, including the lengthy and scholarly studies from the pens of social scientists." *Phylon* notes the book's lack of plot and Simple's lack of moral fiber, but nevertheless approves Simple—for "he invites comparison with such rich folk characters as Appleseed Johnny and Uncle Remus"—as well as Hughes, who "has remained true to his ideal of a social poet." Arna Bontemps in the *New York Herald Tribune Book Review* terms the book "even better reading" than *Simple Speaks His Mind*.

The *Denver Post* calls Simple "one of the most engaging fictional characters around currently." The *Providence Sunday Journal,* assuming Hughes will continue to write about Simple, urges him not to let his creation "become respectable or cowed." The *Rocky Mountain News* announces, "The pleasure in meeting Jesse B. Semple—it was all mine! I hope it will be all yours."

Reviewers generally like *The Sweet Flypaper of Life*. Only the critic for *Professional Photographer,* who disputes the worth of Roy DeCarava's illustrations, faults the work on the grounds "much modern photography leaves us cold." The *Nation* offers a mixed assessment of Hughes's contribution as "perceptive and tender—but also a little cute and patronizing." Otherwise critics intrigued by the unusual marriage of verbal and visual images and by a glimpse into African-American daily lives proffer nothing but praise.

The *Los Angeles Tribune*'s critic, who has never liked Hughes's works, enjoys this one: "Here is all of the realism and the redemption of a family album." Another African-American paper, the *New York Age Defender,* observes, "It isn't often that words and pictures are wed together so warmly, and with such passion and inspiration." The *New York Amsterdam News* rejoices that the work "relates some of the happier phases of life in our community" instead of "fights and numbers-playing and loud-talking and dirty ash cans." The *Baltimore Afro-American* lauds it as "typically Langston Hughes, which is about the highest praise I can give." J. Saunders Redding in the same publication celebrates Hughes's folk discourse: "He is a son returned in time to the folk soul, that is passing; and this it is that gives his work its special value. This it is that contributes to its very special enchantment." The *Afro Arts and Theatre Spotlight* comments, "Not since the early illustrated copy of the complete works of Paul Laurence Dunbar has there appeared an adult volume so understanding of the true spirit and nature of a people." *Crisis* considers several aspects of this volume, remarking, for example, "The Negro woman who has taken a sound lashing in many of Hughes' books can thank Heaven for *The Sweet Flypaper of Life,* for by implication it suggests that by and large she is a clean, loyal person who has a husband and a job and who gets the children off to school every morning." The *Philadelphia Tribune* honors the book as an "artistic triumph that encourages us to find and create beauty out of the raw realities we are all involved in."

Gilbert Millstein in the *New York Times Book Review* pays tribute to the book as a "delicate and lovely fiction-document of life in Harlem, told, with astonishing verisimilitude. . . . Its tone is by turns quiet and lively, its rhythms are soft and emphatic, its insights are constant." Although equally enthusiastic, *Variety* appreciates the muting of verisimilitude: "It is done in a warm, human, understanding style, with no more accent on the sordid environs than necessary." The *Kansas City Star* sees a combination of the true and the imaginary: "The text is fictional, the names of characters false, but the scenes are real." Rose Feld in the *New York Herald Tribune Book Review* commends the collaboration "on a little gem of a book that captures the warm human essence of Negro life in upper Manhattan." The *Village Voice* approves the book as "small enough to fit into your pocket and big enough to fill your heart . . . a yea-saying about all of human life." *Community News* admires its "rare and unearthly beauty, the beauty of the caring, searching, yearning, hoping human soul." The *Oregon Journal Northwest Living Magazine* calls it "unique" and a "fine little story." Nat Hentoff in *Down Beat* recommends it "unreservedly" to "anyone who digs music and being alive."

Best Sellers implicitly links it with the force of other Hughes books by term-

ing it a "disarmingly charming plea for mutual understanding in race relations." In a similar vein, the *Charleston Gazette's State Magazine* says of the
people who "look out at you from every page of this remarkable little book,"
"Their eyes are hard to ignore," and the *Hartford Times* applauds the fact that
"it makes one forget his troubles reading about people who have worse ones
and still can be glad to be stuck up in the sweet flypaper of living." Among
other publications, *Picture Week* congratulates Hughes on "a new note: hope,
a feeling of a future." The *Charleston News and Courier* reviewer reflects, "I
hope these two Harlem authors won't be too dumbfounded to read that a South
Carolina book editor thinks their work quite, quite, fine."

Image recommends, "The only way to feel the import of this book is to read
the text and the photographs together—otherwise it's like looking at TV with
the sound turned off." Expressing this view with more formality, the *New York
Herald Tribune* suggests text and photos "achieve a harmony which is more
than poetry or photography alone, but its own kind of art." Orville Prescott in
the *New York Times* enthuses, "I cannot recall any other book in which the
two elements of pictures and words were so artfully mixed." The *Omaha
World-Herald Magazine* acclaims the "superlative mating of talent" in which
"text and pictures here grow out of each other." *U.S. Camera* commends the
"perfect blending of words and pictures." The *Providence Journal* notes ironic
contrasts of text and photos when "Mr. Hughes writes with his tongue in his
cheek." A review in the *Air Force Times Magazine*—a periodical where one
might not expect to find one—greets the volume as "a work of art, a minor
masterpiece." Writing thirteen years later, after Hughes's death, on the occasion
of a new edition, a reviewer for *CLAJ* judges, "Sister Bradley is a distinctive
addition to the folk characters portrayed in Hughes' works."

I Wonder as I Wander receives generally favorable reviews, with one clearly
negative and a few mixed. The *Virginian Pilot and Portsmouth Star*'s pan objects, "This is an autobiographical journey—not an autobiography" and "The
book is easy reading, with many wanderings, but with little depth in the wondering." The *Washington Post and Times Herald* offers praise—"As in an abundant smorgasbord, there is something for absolutely every taste"—but then
wants "more direction" and "emphasis." The *Library Journal* wishes he had
not waited so long to recount his travels, but concedes the volume gives "something of the quality of the man." The *San Francisco Examiner* complains,
"Hughes really seems to do precious little wondering in his wandering" and
terms the book a "peppery, if slight, amusement," which sometimes displays
Hughes's "eye and feeling for the essence of experience." The *Hartford Courant
Magazine* reveals its critic's biases through objections to the lack of "humility"
with which Hughes chose "to buck the color barrier" and a lack of "good
taste" in his mention of a few "love affairs." Yet the reviewer praises his "wonderful tales" and "keen deft strokes and . . . sense of immediacy." The *Providence Sunday Journal* reviewer, who enjoyed the book, especially its humor,

complains only of occasional stylistic flaws: "It is as though a kind of good-natured indolence overtook him from time to time" when he "falls back on folksy usages." Finally, Nick Aaron Ford writes in *Phylon* an extensive appreciation, which he then qualifies with objections to Hughes's having waited eighteen years to write it, related "intimate details of his own sex life," referred to "praise of his work by others," and included "gossip and hearsay."

Other reviews of *I Wonder as I Wander,* however, can be characterized only as favorable. The *Virginia Kirkus Bulletin* terms it an "amusing and often deeply serious account of the interchange between himself and people and countries." W. G. Rogers in the *Hartford Times* and many other publications praises the tales of famous people, but even more "the unnewsworthy people and events." The *Boston Herald* deems the work "poetic, frank and humorous." The *Dayton Daily News* reviewer enjoys how Hughes has "caught so clearly and with such consistent good humor the heart-warming quality of common people everywhere." Although H. A. Sieber in the *Winston-Salem Journal and Sentinel* seems barely to suppress some racial bias or other grounds for patronizing Hughes, even this reviewer does not disapprove of the book. More enthusiastically, the *St. Louis Post-Dispatch* critic writes, "The value of all this? Good autobiography answers that question with the powerful pulsebeat of living men and women, with panoramas of living history. And this is good autobiography." The *New Yorker* pronounces it an "immensely interesting book, written with bounce and zest." Similarly, *San Francisco Chronicle This World* enjoys the fact that "the blue note lurks in his life but, for the most part, the basic beat sounds real joyous." A *St. Louis Post-Dispatch* retrospective review of a 1987 reprint praises both Hughes's prose style and his travels.

I Wonder as I Wander interests left-wing writers especially because of Hughes's account of his stay in the Soviet Union. The *Daily Worker* approvingly quotes him at length on the "Russian experiment," then endorses the book as a "reminder both of what America has gained from great talents like his own and lost in others crushed beneath the weight of racism." *Mainstream* lauds Hughes for remembering "that he was the son of the oppressed. And no matter what city or country he visited there is no mistaking what side he was on." The *Harvard Crimson*'s long review, on the other hand, takes as its premise "Hughes never cared much for ideology" and instead approves the author's senses of both wonder and humor. The *Newark Sunday News* offers still another take on Hughes's politics: "His sympathy for the 'under dog,' whether represented by his own race or the proletariat in general, does not inhibit a tender and charming rendering of the other side."

Whereas the white press generally responds to Hughes's tales of adventure and interpersonal encounters, African-American writers perceive more political import. In a personal account of what Hughes's work has meant to him, Fletcher Martin tells *Chicago Sun-Times* readers the book comprises not only a "delightful recollection of his autobiographical journey through life" but also the "profound and compounded story of Negro life." Ted Poston in the *New York Post* brings a still more personal perspective to the volume, since he shared the trip to the Soviet Union with Hughes and the other black Americans: "If the Moscow which he describes is hardly the one this reviewer recalls, it is at least a little larger than life and more interesting for all that. And that is the charm of this book." Roi Ottley's remarks in the *Saturday Review* conclude, "It proves excellent fare as he recalls dramatic and intimate moments in a life well and vigorously spent." The *Pittsburgh Courier* decides, "There is important sociological significance in Mr. Hughes' book, but he has also woven a yarn of bright, glittering texture." The *Chicago Defender,* after likewise responding to the volume largely on a sociological level, concludes, "Certainly of best-seller caliber, *I Wonder as I Wander* rates well with the other books and poems that Hughes has written." J. Saunders Redding in the *Baltimore Afro-American Magazine,* on the other hand, sees the book as more personal than political, but judges it "fascinating" and its author "especially delightful." Frank Marshall Davis in the *Honolulu Record* approves it as "one of the most refreshing literary experiences of the decade." *Crisis* finds, not insight into race relations, but interesting personal anecdotes. Yet a high school sophomore writing for the *Winston-Salem Journal and Sentinel* judges its topic as "race." The *Los Angeles Tribune*'s critic writes, "The greatest compliment I can pay it is to say that I read it twice and plan to reread its 405 pages."

A Pictorial History of the Negro in America receives generally favorable notices, north and south, from black and white presses—and far more attention than most of the volumes of verse. The demurrers usually note omissions—as does the *American-Statesman*'s paragraph on famous African Americans who should have been considered—or object to the proportions of space allocated to various periods, yet some raves express admiration for the volume's emphases. Racism may creep into certain objections, as when the *El Paso Herald-Post* complains, "The authors are, of course, prejudiced and their emphasis is on the long catalog of wrongs the Negro has suffered." The critic for the *Chattanooga News-Free Press* counters Hughes's charges of cruelty on the part of slaveholders with a claim that plantations were run by humane masters whose kindness prompted their contented slaves to display passionate loyalty. Two others, J. A. Rogers in a two-part review in the *Pittsburgh Courier* and Herbert Aptheker in *Mainstream,* evidently denounce the book because it rivals their own research in the same field; Aptheker also objects to "the volume's underplaying of the Left, and particularly the impact of socialist and communist thinking and organizations upon the history of the Negro people." The *American Examiner,* citing an illustration, charges the book "is trying to curry the white man's favor" and demands the African American "stand up erect and demand what is his by right." Although the *Journal of Negro History* respects the volume as a "significant contribution" to history, the *Virginia Magazine of History and Biography* dismisses it as mere "historiography."

More commonly, however, critics praise the volume in such terms as "We really feel that this book should grace the book shelves of everyone's library" (*Black Dispatch*), "Its publication in itself is an event in Negro history" (P.L.P. in the *Pittsburgh Courier Magazine*), "The authors have presented a surprisingly varied, stirring, informative—and often touching document" (*San Francisco Chronicle*), "Many little known but highly important events and personalities are brought into sharp focus by the painstaking research" (*Jet*), "It is free from bias and distortion" (*Oregon Journal*), "The text is knowledgeable and eloquent" (*Youngstown Vindicator*), "There is a minimum of sentimentality and a maximum of historic fact in Hughes' text" (*Kansas City Star*), and "There is a nice combination of scholarly scrupulousness, objectivity, and attractive presentation" (*Saturday Review*).

J. Saunders Redding in *Afro-American Magazine* responds to his concern about "academic historians who will not like this effort by a skilled story teller" by observing, "Few people learn from history written by scholars. Drama is a better teacher." Similarly, in one of the *Pittsburgh Courier's* several reviews, Benjamin E. Mays commends the work as "simply but movingly and profoundly told." The *Lexington Herald Leader* pronounces it a "worthy addition to the history, not only of the Negro, but of the United States," the *Atlanta World* terms it "amazingly interesting throughout," and *Community* calls it "a well-rounded, valuable book." The *Library Journal* recommends it "for even the tiniest public library." The *New York Amsterdam News* reviewer believes, "To place this volume in every library, every school, and, in fact, every home in America would add greatly to the moral courage and physical stamina of the entire country."

Simple Stakes a Claim appears to have elicited only favorable responses and generally the same kinds of comments as the two earlier Simple volumes. The *Book-of-the-Month-Club News*, for instance, appreciates that Hughes "is, in fact, one of the few authors working today who can write about race relations with humor," the *Library Journal* discerns "that Simple is not really so simple after all," the *Washington Post and Times-Herald* calls Simple "one of the freshest and most fascinating Negro characters in American fiction," and the *New York Times* suggests he "is well on his way to becoming one of those fictional characters who cease being fictional and become historical." The *Philadelphia Independent* explains the title's assertion that Simple stakes a claim "in his country and in his rights." The *Philadelphia Tribune* accurately assesses, "Everyone likes Simple."

Whereas the *Worcester Sunday Telegram* and *San Francisco Chronicle* relish Simple's humor and the *New York Herald Tribune* maintains he "is as serious as a man can be," *Phylon* hedges that he "is mainly a humorous-serious character." The *Los Angeles Tribune* rhapsodizes, "Langston Hughes deserves a medal! . . . by Simple alone . . . Hughes has every right to be considered one of America's leading satirists." The *Chattanooga Times* decides, "One can read them for fun, but should never overlook the deeper implications." J. Saunders Redding describes in the *Baltimore Afro-American Magazine* the tension between moods thus: "He reveals us to ourselves and even while the sharp pain of self-recognition stabs to the brain, he makes our hearts ready for healing laughter." *Mainstream* sees Simple as a peculiarly political prank: "a Negro in Harlem, the eternal butt of the official American joke that all here enjoy democracy."

Inevitably, some critics complain about the particular selections contained in *The Langston Hughes Reader*. And Elizabeth Staples publishes an article (not a review) launching an ultra–right-wing attack on Hughes as a Communist ("Langston Hughes: Malevolent Force," *American Mercury*, 88, 420 [January 1959], 46–50), partly prompted by the appearance of this book. Each review, however, comes down either entirely or primarily (with the noted exception) on Hughes's side. Yet almost every one chooses a slightly different focus for praise.

The *Philadelphia Tribune* finds the collection "has defined the place of the Negro in all of the diverse forms of American literary expression." The *New York Post* salutes the "scope of his prodigious output." The *Virginian-Pilot and Portsmouth Star* dubs the volume "one of the most refreshing collections to come out in a long time." Another Southern paper, the *Charlotte News*, reassures readers, "Anyone who is interested in facing problems and solving them will not feel it offensive." Associated Press reviewer W. G. Rogers judges the book a "fine rich dish of Hughes," and the *Village Voice* terms it a "delight." J. Saunders Redding in *Afro-American Magazine* hopes the collection does not mean Hughes won't be writing a great deal more. The *New Yorker* compares reading a thirty-year cumulation of Hughes to "attending an unusually subtle tolerance lecture," because "his American Negroes are remarkably unexotic and unalien, and, in fact, more like everybody else than most Americans realize." The *Greensboro Daily News* values the revelation "of the inner life of a major American minority in transition," and *Crisis* discerns "the man from Joplin is the chief advocate and preserver of a folk tradition."

The conservative *Stray Notes from the Shrine of the Little Flower* approvingly perceives a "gradual mellowing in Mr. Hughes' racial attitude." The *Tulsa Sunday World Magazine* cheers, "This is a volume to restore one's faith in a little bit of everything." The *Dallas Times-Herald* offers the surprising observation that Hughes "has never achieved enough objectivity to see that the colored problem starts out with the white problem—that persecution starts not with the persecuted but with the neurotic needs of the persecutor—. Be that as it may, Hughes has struck many a blow for freedom and has given heart to many by his wit and grace." The *NAACP Voice* raves the anthology "can only be described in superlative terms." The *Raleigh News and Observer*, while regarding Richard Wright as "America's most important living Negro author," terms Hughes the "most versatile." The *Richmond News Leader* likewise provides a long-term assessment: "Some of the poets and novelists popular thirty-odd years ago have now disappeared because they offered little except novelty and a sense of race. A few have survived because their values ran deeper. Of this second group, Langston Hughes has proved the most durable of all."

Only one reviewer blasts *Tambourines to Glory*. Less than a decade later, after championing black nationalism and changing his name to Amiri Baraka, LeRoi Jones may well have regretted writing contemptuously of Hughes in the *Jazz Review* as a "folklorist" because he fails to write universal art for art's sake, turning out instead mere "Negro literature." "A writer," Jones insists, "must be concerned with more than just the color of his skin." Jones repudiates the new novel as unworthy of publication and faults the "Harlem slang" as outdated.

Nobody else comes close to Jones's indignation, but a few mixed reviews do take Hughes to task as well as praise him. The *Virginia Kirkus Bulletin* argues, "That it ends on a note of melodrama bordering on tragedy somehow fails to touch the heartstrings. But the telling in the vernacular has its poetic overtones and its sense of authenticity." The *New York Times Book Review* describes the work as "skillful and engaging," yet laments the author has "elected to avoid the serious implications of his thesis." In the same vein, J. Saunders Redding in *Afro-American Magazine* praises the tale, but adds, "The book gives the impression of playing around with materials worthy of serious treatment." The *National Guardian* complains some of the language belongs to locales other than Harlem, dubs the novel "one of Hughes' lesser efforts," concedes "Hughes is an able craftsman," and advises, "Taken for what it is—a literary divertissement—some readers may use it for a half-evening of light, after-dinner reading." The *Library Journal,* on the other hand, prefers the language to the stereotyped characters and "labored plot." Finally, among the demurrers, the *Los Angeles Times* remarks, "His dialogue and characters are vivid but one wishes he had put his talents and understanding of his people to work in a stronger book. As it stands, it reads more like the libretto of an opera than a novel and undoubtedly could be effectively adapted." Which, of course, Hughes already had done with the then unproduced play of the same title.

The perspectives from which critics praise the novel vary as much as those from which others damn it. The *San Francisco Call-Bulletin* prefers Hughes's novel to Richard Wright's *Long Dream* because "it is funny, it is touching, it is sad." "There is humor in this little book and there is tragedy," proclaims the *Baltimore Evening Sun;* "It is well done and will be memorable." The *Saturday Review* begins, "Sometimes . . . I think Langston Hughes is one of the greatest folk poets our country has produced" and continues, of this book, "It is full of vitality, earthiness, joy, unashamed religious feeling, and humorous perspective." The *Fort Wayne News-Sentinel* applauds the "colorful, earthy and endlessly inventive Negro speech." The *Chicago Sun-Times* approves, "Langston Hughes has written with knowledge and compassion about a memorable woman and her longing for fulfillment." Because Hughes "knows well the mores and folkways of the urban Negro," *Jet* dubs him the "Boswell of Harlem."

The *Philadelphia Tribune* credits the author with hitting "pretty close to home in his exposé of the way in which religion is misused." The *Worcester Sunday Telegram* commends, "We have had many a hearty laugh in this satire on a sham revivalist movement and we have been shown more clearly than by many a serious book the corruption, the unfair practices, the despair of Harlem." The *San Francisco Chronicle* greets a "slight, Rabelaisian exposé of a certain type of evangelistic chicanery."

The *New York World-Telegram and Sun* reveals insensitivity when it remarks, "The pleasantest thing about this very ingratiating little novel is the way a distinguished Negro author revives the wonderful Amos and Andy humor that has been out of fashion ever since it supposedly became bad taste to find comedy in the manners of ethnic groups." The *Hartford Courant Magazine* asserts, "There's much here to make you smile or burst out laughing every few pages. As always, Hughes makes you feel you are listening to real people talk." Arna Bontemps ends his *New York Herald Tribune Books* critique: "*Tambourines to Glory* is funny as all get out, but it's no joke."

The *Columbus Citizen Magazine* rejoices, "His prose has the liquid rhythm of poetry and his story line is as clean and sharp as an arrow." Another admirer of the style, the critic for the *San Francisco Examiner,* appreciates a "rare sense of life through the speech of its Negro characters." *Crisis* also judges, "Much of the humor and the pathos of the book comes from Mr. Hughes' mastery of the Harlem idiom." The *Kansas City Star* finds the novel "is characterized by its simple but singing prose, its humor, its tolerance of human weakness. But underneath it all is an awareness of the tragic plight of his own people." In a somewhat patronizing review generalizing about African-Americans as "people who love color and music and rhythm," Lois de Banzie in *News* describes the novel as "written with humor, and in a suitably colorful style."

The *Lincoln University Bulletin* focuses on Hughes's message, a "fictional exposé of certain ways in which religion is misused . . . by . . . 'gospel racketeers.'" Similarly, *Community News* derives a thesis: "This book should be a challenge to all churches to do their jobs better and reach the deepest needs of their people." *Phylon* observes that the novel "underscores a wide knowledge of the New York ghetto," and the *Kansas City Call* likewise approves the authenticity: "Hughes' familiarity with Negro religious folk sermons and his interpretations of the uninhibited speech and antics of the typical folk preacher are unsurpassed genre pictures of a typical Negro church life." Yet the *New York Post* finds the novel a fine "fantasy," as well as touching and funny.

While preferring Hughes's poetry to his fiction, *Press Facts* enjoys "this excellent bit of story telling." Though finding its author inferior to "Chaucer, Cervantes, Rabelais," the *Greensboro Daily News* judges this "one of the season's better folk tales" and its two women "among those longest remembered" of Hughes's characters. *CLAJ* deems the "fable" a "sepia Horatio Alger saga" in which "the achievement is slight, but the craftsmanship assured. The result is charming." The *Negro Educational Review* writes of a tale "impellingly told ... compact and lucid." *Marriage* tells its churchgoing subscribers, "This is adult reading, partly satire, partly just good fun." Mimi Clar in the *Jazz Review* offers an alternative reading to that of LeRoi Jones in which she observes that the characters represent "realistically a small segment of the community" and praises the language as a "vivid folk idiom" that "swings with jive talk." The *Durham Herald* recommends the work as "wonderfully readable, a strikingly contemporary book."

Approximately a third of the reviews of *Selected Poems* seem mixed. Harry M. Meacham in the *Richmond News-Leader,* after acknowledging, "Hughes is at his best when he is echoing the simple songs of his people," laments, "Hughes' slender talents cannot support the bitter racialism which pervades too many of the poems. . . . [I]f the poet had continued to use the subject matter Paul Laurence Dunbar found so rewarding, his work might have some enduring qualities." Clearly no improvement in skill would satisfy someone intent on changing the poet's fundamental character. Another Southern review not altogether favorable to Hughes, that in the *Miami News,* begins as an essay on black class structure vis-à-vis poetry, then, without having considered the poetry, dismisses the poet as not "of real stature," although "he is good enough to prove that there is no field of endeavor in which the Negro is not the equal of the White." Similarly, without offering any specific evidence, the *Virginia Kirkus Bulletin* maintains, "If he is not a great poet, he hardly seems to claim to be one. Yet he has flashes now and then of real insight, and he communicates a tenderness that has a wide audience appeal." The *Hartford Courant Magazine* presents a particularly ambivalent judgment:

> The early poems remain the most convincing ones. . . . [A]t their best, the poems ring with stirring conviction. On the other hand, honesty and passion are not always enough. . . . The jazz rhythms, the authentic use of idiom, the genuine insights are all here but all too frequently they fail to fuse together. It is a tribute to Hughes that his poems of social protest are more durable than those of many of his contemporaries; and it is a greater tribute of him as a poet that his best poems need no apology for their social content.

The *Providence Sunday Journal* attributes the reviewer's own mixed feelings to Hughes's race: "He is a poet condemned to be black; and he both triumphs and falters because of this fact. . . . Yet quite a few of these pieces quietly emerge from their sources into poetry—from gospel-shout, say, into literary art—and we are then conscious of the color of the art, so to speak, and not of the color of the artist." This reviewer praises "Spiritual," "Shadow of the Blues," "Wake," "Song for a Dark Girl," and "some of the 'Madame' poems."

Yet he generalizes about others, "That which tries too hard to be deceptively simple can sometimes become simply deceiving." *Mainstream,* surprisingly, writes of the section "Words Like Freedom,"

> Welcome as they may be in a political way, these poems on freedom and equality fail their subject because they never depart from the abstract principles involved. Poetry cannot exist apart from the concrete and Hughes, not being a rhetorical poet, does not render the length of his utterance in a solid fashion. His essential qualities are, in its best sense, flute-like. He is almost always sweet, dear and delicate—great virtues in a man and needed ones in an art as ill with violence and intellectual strutting as poetry today.

Most damagingly, however, James Baldwin laments in the *New York Times Book Review,* "Every time I read Langston Hughes I am amazed all over again by his genuine gifts—and depressed that he has done so little with them. . . . [T]his book contains a great deal which a more disciplined poet would have thrown into the waste-basket." Baldwin complains especially of "fake simplicity," admires "brief, sardonic asides" and "lyrics," but concludes, "He is not the first American Negro to find the war between his social and artistic responsibilities all but irreconcilable." When James Baldwin suggests a lack of discipline, perhaps he really reacts to nontraditional elements. Yet Arnold Rampersad quotes him as saying, "I hadn't really read the book, to tell the truth" (Vol. II, p. 299).

Nevertheless, the bulk of the reviews praise the collection. The *St. Louis Post-Dispatch,* for instance, pays tribute to "a voice of pain and isolation, of a deeply felt contemporary anguish. . . . [T]he voice of this suffering spirit is true, timeless and universal." The *Virginian-Pilot and Portsmouth Star* commends, "Hughes at his best, and it is a very good best, captures the spirit of the northern big-city Negro and the transplanted southern Negro with feeling and truth." *Phylon* asserts, "Even a casual perusal of this newly-published collection of poems reasserts a feeling that enjoyed vogue when *The Weary Blues* came out—namely, that there had appeared on the literary scene a fresh voice and a clear tone and something of a new literary genre capable of penetrating the emotional heights and depths of the Negro people in Harlem and in other ghettos around the world." *San Francisco Chronicle This World* approves, "One is not here conscious so much of omissions as of the consistent fineness of what has been chosen for the book. . . . [W]e have some of the saddest, most humorous and beautiful insights ever given into the heart of a race." After commending Hughes's universality, the *Charlotte Observer* continues, "His poetry is full of passion, as great poetry must be. His verses yearn and plead for the fulfillment of the wordless wishes of his people."

The *Trenton Sunday Times and Advertiser* approves "the power he possesses to put a thought, a meaning, a feeling into a few lines, something like that difficult form of the Japanese. Some of his poems are only three lines long, but that does not mean they are fragments." In the *Baltimore Afro-American Magazine,* J. Saunders Redding praises Hughes generally as a prolific and versatile "18th-Century man of letters," expresses his disappointment—at length—at the absence of "The Cat and the Saxophone," then concedes, "Nearly all the best poems are here." The *Chicago Sunday Sun-Times* approves in Hughes "the brief, quick thrust . . . the simplicity that hides a complex of art and of humanity. Typical of this artlessness that is at the core of art is the poem 'Harlem.'" John Henrik Clarke in the *Chicago Defender* castigates "James Baldwin's inept review," then rejoices, "Unlike the small, though increasing group of alienated Negro writers, who spend so much of their time running from other Negroes and cursing God for making them black, Langston Hughes has never left home. . . . Being our most versatile writer, he has the largest Negro reading audience. . . . His most enduring poems can be found in this volume." The *Dallas Times-Herald,* which celebrates Hughes's blues, echoes that refrain: "There is plenty of Hughes at his best in this volume." *Crisis* also applauds the blues, as well as those poems in which "he is humble enough to live within the experience of his people," where "one finds more authenticity . . . than in imposing cultural histories."

Reviewers of *The Best of Simple* compare Hughes to Thurber and O. Henry. All the reviews praise the book, but many publications appear not to have reviewed it, probably because as the fourth Simple book—and one that excerpts the previous three—it would only prompt the same remarks already published about the character who by now had taken his place as a classic. The *Chicago Sun-Times,* typically, remarks, "Simple is no simpleton. He, and Hughes, know the score: They're way ahead of the rest of us." *CLAJ* commends "spontaneity, sensitiveness and charm" as Hughes's "hallmarks" and asserts of Simple, "As a sort of Everyman for the Negro people, he is perhaps the best-known fictional character in contemporary literature, not only in America, but in Europe, Asia, Africa, and in the West Indies." *Freedomways* tells us Simple "is a latter-day Aesop," and *Community* terms him "one of the warmest human beings in modern literature." *Stray Notes from the Shrine of the Little Flower* expresses its enthusiasm most succinctly: "Oh, we do like him."

Ask Your Mama's jazz rhythms prompt *Berkshire Eagle* critic Milton R. Bass to rave, "His latest work, *Ask Your Mama,* increases the admiration twelvefold." Bass describes Hughes as "a gentle poet whose words are fierce enough to shake your conscience . . . who gets his inspiration from people, from their blood, from their sweat and from their tears. But even more important, he also gets it from their laughter." Bass's review scats much in the book's manner, but others also wax favorable. The *Los Angeles Times Calendar* tells us, "Hughes remains the one poet who has been able to capture the rhythms, melodies and spirit of jazz. This is a *swinging* performance with moments of high comedy, anger, irony, sorrow and puzzlement." Dudley Fitts in the *New York Times Book Review* starts to compare the poems to Vachel Lindsay's, then qualifies this by adding, "The fury of indignation and the wild comedy, however, are very far from Lindsay. The voice is comparable to that of Nicolás Guillén."

New York Herald Tribune Book Week interprets: "'Go ask your Mama' is the retort—half-derisive, half-angry—to the smug, the stupid, the bigoted, the selfish, the cruel, and the blind among us, all those to whom these truths that America was built upon are, even today, not yet self-evident. With this great theme, a talented poet finds a universal voice." J. Saunders Redding in the *Afro-American Magazine* compares the work to *The Weary Blues*: "There is the same passion and the same power." Redding suggests the music "is not always jazz. It is hymns and marches and way-out swing." But he actually finds it superior to Hughes's first book: "It is more sophisticated now and—oddly—less confined: the power, I mean—and the passion, transmuted to the present temper and expressed in the strange, daring rhythms of the current time, is more varied." The *Michigan Chronicle*'s critic hears and feels the rhythms and laughs, but adds, "Although *Ask Your Mama* will delight you, it has a serious theme too."

Another publication weighing in on Hughes's side, the *Washington Post*, notes the "importance" of poems written for performance, but adds that these poems "make good reading too." After explaining the "dozens," *Freedomways*'s reviewer continues, "The presence of humor accentuates the social protest, making it more effective and less offensive." *People's World*, following a still more extensive discussion of the dozens, ends its review "SWING!" The *National Guardian* concludes, "It is a book well worth having—the first substantial body of verse directly made for jazz." *CLAJ* asserts, "Anyone who is still unconvinced that Langston Hughes occupies a major position in the stream of American literary humorists and experimental poets should find convincing proofs in *Ask Your Mama*."

Less enthusiastic comments include: "It should be felicitous when recited at night clubs and will undoubtedly gather partisans, but lovers of real poetry won't be among them" (*Virginia Kirkus Bulletin*), "Hughes is now the man being harmed by his intellectually impotent adversary" (*Dallas Times-Herald*), "written . . . for reading to music. They must be wholly alive and diverting that way. On the page, they are less so" (*Chicago Tribune Magazine of Books*), "thin and topical as much of the beat material it resembles" (*Library Journal*), "It is not good propaganda and is not an indictment. It is merely curiously interesting and enjoyable because of its novelty of presentation" (*Greensboro News*). In addition, *Phylon* remarks ambivalently, "Those who like blues poetry will no doubt find pleasure in another exhibition of the Hughes specialty. But those who have not yet accepted this kind of writing as legitimate poetry will sigh for the return of such moods as those represented by 'The Negro Speaks of Rivers,' 'Let America Be America Again,' and even 'Brass Spittoons.'"

Because here Hughes becomes more than a literary figure, the reviews of

Fight for Freedom move beyond the bounds of literary criticism. Most reviews seem favorable, a few mixed, and two negative.

The *Washington Star* sets the tone of the ambivalent responses by acknowledging that Hughes tells the NAACP's story "with his usual grace, power, and even humor," but also noting he omits the controversies surrounding the organization, including the fact that the "leadership today is under increasing attack from Negroes." The specific, knowledgeable, and enthusiastic account in the *Roanoke Times* terms Hughes "perfectly correct in attributing" most of the country's racial progress "to the leadership of the NAACP," but then criticizes Hughes's failure to give appropriate credit to Presidents Truman and Roosevelt. For similar reasons, the *Louisville Courier-Journal* characterizes the work as a "straightforward, but undefinitive, history." Still more detailed in its categories of omissions, the *National Guardian* nevertheless also argues, "Langston Hughes, the commissioned author, is one of the most skillful writers of this generation. He has done the NAACP a service." And *Annals of the American Academy of Political and Social Science* predictably complains the author "is no academic historian or sociologist and makes no pretense of scholarship," and he sells the organization's accomplishments and thus "ignores the past and current criticism leveled by friends of the organization." Nevertheless, this publication recommends the book "as an introduction for a general reader who knows little about the subject." The *Progressive* finds it "useful" and "skillfully written" but a "superficially researched publicist's tract for the NAACP rather than a critical history."

In addition, one review has nothing good to say about the volume. The *Charleston Evening Post* casts its entire attack on Hughes's work in terms of the firing and reinstating of a Savannah letter carrier named W. W. Law, president of the Georgia NAACP, an event Hughes barely mentions but which the reviewer appears to believe damns the organization as a pressure group protecting incompetent African-American employees.

The laudatory reviews—often supplying extensive summaries of historical accounts Hughes provides—include those in *Publishers Weekly,* the *Book-of-the-Month-Club News,* the *New York Times Book Review,* the *Indianapolis Times,* the *Kansas City Times,* the *Chicago Tribune, New York Herald Tribune Books,* the *Fort Wayne News-Sentinel,* the *Berkshire Eagle, Booklist,* the *St. Louis Post-Dispatch, America, Stray Notes from the Shrine of the Little Flower,* the *Negro Educational Review, Jet, Crisis,* the *Library Journal,* the *Chattanooga Times,* and *Community.* Typically, the *San Francisco News-Call Bulletin* assesses, "There is nothing more powerful, in writing history, than to be accurate, objective and interesting. Author Hughes is all three." The *Springfield Sunday Republican* concurs: "This excellent book, which reflects new credit on its distinguished author, deserves to be widely read, and should be appreciated by all Americans who believe in democracy and fair play." Irving

Dilliard exclaims in the *Saturday Review* concerning "this stirring book," "Somebody ought to put it in every library in the country!" J. Saunders Redding in the *Baltimore Afro-American Magazine* approves Hughes's approach: "A straight and unadorned historical or sociological treatise, written from documents, of which there are thousands, would have been as dry as dust . . . . [T]hen it follows that the history of an institution must be written in terms of biography and biographical narrative. That is what Langston Hughes has accomplished. He has done it simply and directly, with passion and dramatic power and truth." Says the *New Jersey Herald News,* "This brilliant story of accomplishment with facts gathered and written by such an authority in spirit and letters as Langston Hughes is a must for your book collection."

Something in Common and Other Stories elicits few reviews, and still fewer favorable comments. Critics disdain the volume because only a fourth of its stories have not appeared in Hughes's previous collections. The *Library Journal* nevertheless approves, admiring the author's "versatility in style and approach," the varied tones, and the fact that "Hughes almost consistently avoids propagandizing, because he makes his characters real." The *Charlotte Observer* critic likewise endorses the tales as "wonderful" and confides, "I put the book down reluctantly." *Community* concludes, "Hughes treats a broad range of human experiences with the greatest of ease, and his delightful style and humor are worth the reading."

A less sanguine appraisal from the *Quincy Patriot-Ledger* characterizes the collection as a "disappointing grab-bag . . . a combination of questionable sociology and worse fiction." Its reviewer accuses Hughes of sharing the views of race relations harbored by "Southern racists." Though less severe, *CLAJ* judges, "Those stories written in the urban Negro idiom of which Hughes is the undisputed master are by far the best. . . . Some of the less successful stories rely too heavily on the surprise ending and others show a strange ineptness in dialogue and characterization."

Even fewer reviews greet *Five Plays by Langston Hughes*—a not surprising fact considering that plays usually receive critical response only when performed. (See the Appendix for a selective list of some Hughes plays in performance.) Critics react quite favorably to the short collection. The *Library Journal* asserts the scripts "have a definite social and historical significance" and recommends the volume for "all collections specializing in Negro literature or the theater and in at least one agency of all large public libraries." J. Saunders Redding's *Afro-American Magazine* assessment maintains, "Hughes has the rare good fortune of not going stale—of fresh vision and high spirits, of vitality and directness, of projection." *Booklist* perceives, "The same qualities that make them interesting as drama make them enjoyable reading: an earthiness, a basic respect for human beings, and an indigenous American idiom both precise and revealing." According to *CLAJ,* the plays prove "readable as well as stageable" and "Webster Smalley and the Indiana University Press have done American literature of the theatre an invaluable service with the publication" of this collection.

Most significantly, and at greatest length, Doris E. Abramson in a review article for the *Massachusetts Review* individually appraises each play. Concerning *Mulatto*'s power she muses, "It may not be produced in the United States as often as it is abroad, but now we can read it and ponder why." She terms *Soul Gone Home* "one of the strangest little plays ever published anywhere" and shares the valuable information that the playwright has told her "it should be played for broad comedy in order to heighten the tragedy." She regards *Little Ham* as not one of Hughes's stronger plays, although it "moves lightly through a Harlem of the 'roaring twenties'" with dialogue that "ripples along with what we take for authenticity." But *Simply Heavenly* Abramson describes as "a remarkable play about Harlem life, a comedy filled with characters who interest, instruct, transport—and please us. Only Saroyan has created a barroom to match Mr. Hughes' Paddy's Bar." And of *Tambourines to Glory* she opines, "It is far more effective than Mr. Hughes' novel of the same name." In short, says Abramson, "Langston Hughes, like Bertolt Brecht, writes for the theatre as a knowledgeable man of the theatre."

Simple's Uncle Sam, the fifth Simple book, prompts the usual positive reviews. The *Virginia Kirkus Service* calls the protagonist "as simple as a Jesuit," whereas *Publishers Weekly* terms him a "Will Rogers of his time and place." The *Baltimore Evening Sun*'s reviewer, who admits he has been a fan "for a good twenty years," loves the character's "trenchant, witty observations on the indignity, inconvenience and downright peril of being colored in America," as well as the hero's poetic "cadence and internal rhyme." The *Pittsburgh Press* identifies as "Hughes' particular genius that he can make a point as well by suggestion as by detail." The *Nashville Tennessean* pronounces Simple "the truly folk hero, who comments wisely, wittily, not linguistically soundly but morally well of American life as seen through the eyes of a Harlem sage of the tenements." The *Dekalb New Era and North Dekalb Record* praises Hughes's "compassion, a delightfully dry wit, and a writing technique subtle enough to appear artless." *People's World* sums up: "The book supplies the reader with about as fine an insight into the lives, the hearts and the thoughts of Harlem's citizens as one is likely to find."

New York Herald Tribune Book Week analyzes the joking: "I was struck by the similarities between Simple's irony, the wry wit we label 'Jewish humor,' and the kind of joking I heard once among wartime amputees at an Army hospital. Like the 'sick' joke, this humor is self-mocking, but it is also self-respecting." Among other favorable responses, the *Quincy Patriot-Ledger* dubs Simple the "personified laughter of an oppressed people," *Community* praises the way Hughes "distills the essence of the matter and redesigns it in a funny, enjoyable, pleasant manner," yet the *Negro Digest* warns, "When you think they are all froth and humor, there's the keen cutting steel." In the book's most analytic review, W. Edward Farrison considers comparisons to Paul Bunyan and Davy Crockett ("inappropriate" because "he is a product, not of mere fancy, but of his creator's experience") and to Mr. Dooley (who differs because of his "mutilated English" compared to Simple's "more natural and indeed more convincing" dialect).

The last two books included in this study—*The Panther and the Lash* and *Black Magic: A Pictorial History of the Negro in Entertainment*—appeared following Hughes's death in 1967 (although copies of the former had already been printed by then). For the latter, a collaboration with Milton Meltzer, Hughes had just completed his own part in the volume; he did not survive to see it through the press. The poetry collection proves prophetic of the 1967 riots. Both books appeared shortly after journalists had already summed up their responses to the author in their obituaries.

The *Kirkus Service* commends the poetry: "He still writes in an admirably lean, brief, matter-of-fact form which avoids the obvious pitfalls of anger, sentimentality or melodrama inherent in his subject matter." The *Library Journal* judges, "The present selection presents him at his best," and continues that he "deserves more attention than he receives." The *Providence Journal* tells its readers, "Hughes' verse is cold sober, and the violence in it is warned about rather than preached." The *Atlanta Journal and Constitution* evaluates the volume with muted enthusiasm: "As works of art, his poems may not stand; but as human documents, they are written in blood." Keneth Kinnamon in the *Nation* quotes Hughes's manifesto that had appeared in that publication more than forty years earlier, but observes, "Much of his enormous body of writing is admittedly hack work." Nevertheless, he pays tribute to the poet as a "pioneer" and notes, "*The Panther and the Lash* reminds us how accurate a poetic barometer of the Negro mood Hughes has been since his first volume." Two reviews in *CLAJ* provide by far the most extensive and perceptive analysis of the poems and their merits. After commenting in depth on each of the volume's sections, W. Edward Farrison ends his consideration by saying, "From the beginning of his career as an author, Hughes was articulate in the Negro's struggle for first-class citizenship. It is indeed fitting that this volume with which his career ended is a vital contribution to that struggle as well as to American poetry." Theodore R. Hudson, on the other hand, begins his comments by saying, "The late Langston Hughes was never primarily a 'protest' poet. . . . Dipping his pen in ink, not acid, his method was to expose rather than excoriate, to reveal rather than revile. Indeed, in the rare instances when he approached irreconcilable bitterness, his art suffered." Therefore, Hudson prefers the collection's older poems to those brand new. Nevertheless, he assesses the volume as "satisfying." Laurence Liberman in *Poetry* often (but not always) prefers the new Hughes to the old and labels the recent work "many of the best poems of his career."

Among other enthusiastic reviews elicited by *Black Magic,* H. W. Fuller in *Negro Digest* lauds it, "There has not been anything even remotely like it since Edith J. R. Isaacs' *The Negro in the American Theater,* first published in 1947." W. Edward Farrison's *CLAJ* review enumerates some differences the critic has with the authors' emphases but, nevertheless, endorses the volume's value. Gilbert Chase in *Notes: The Quarterly Journal of the Music Library Association* writes, "The text is adequate but makes no pretense of any scholarly apparatus," but further on alters his tone to "It is an impressive and comprehensive chronicle, a pictorial treasury that should be in every library."

By this time, however, Hughes no longer survived to collect his reviews for posterity, so we must now turn to the text of the reviews themselves.

THE WEARY BLUES

J[ohn] T. H[ackett]
Springfield Union, n.d.,
[p. ?]

An uncommonly, if moderately, successful little book is Langston Hughes' *The Weary Blues.* He has a deft and canny touch, this facile twenty-three year old Negro builder of Harlem canzoni, and with the publication of his modest sheaf steps forward to take his place with Charles Gilpin, Roland Hayes, Paul Robeson, Countee Cullen, James Weldon Johnson et al. Only to discourage faddists who have recently hurrahed indiscriminately for every Negro able to hum a tune, mimic a canary or write his name does one specify that Mr. Hughes is not the awaited Negro Milton, for his are unassuming canticles. The jazzed pieces, for example, that one opening, "Me an' ma baby's Got two mo' ways, Two mo' ways to do de buck," are, I think, the more distinguished verses in *The Weary Blues.* Occasionally Mr. Hughes' Waterman does splutter, as when he wrote "Caribbean Sunset"—"God having a hemorrhage, blood coughed across the sky, Staining the dark sea red, That is sunset in the Caribbean"—a somewhat terrible poem, unless I err. *The Weary Blues* is fortunate in its dapper introduction by Carl Van Vechten.

Howard Mumford Jones
"The Poetic Blues"
Chicago Daily News, n.d.,
[p. ?]

The breath of life sweeps through Langston Hughes' *The Weary Blues* at intervals, particularly in the opening section, in the section called "Water-Front Streets" and the one called "Our Land." At other times Mr. Hughes falls back into the literary mode which Miss Garvin and Miss Tilden never escape from—poems with too many "dreams" in them, poems about vague desires to be different, poems about Pierrots, white or black, and all the pale, precious themes over which a thousand minor poets have wept and sighed in books composed of a rivulet of text meandering through a meadow of margin. When Mr. Hughes is genuine he is superb, and when he is not genuine the fact that he is a Negro makes his poetry no better, despite Carl Van Vechten's admiring introduction. By this last cryptic statement I mean merely that the present vogue of Negro art is falsifying a good many values, which, upon cooler inspection after the craze has died, will be found to be fools' gold.

But the title poem of Hughes' book is about as successful an evocation of the blues in terms of an enduring art of poetry as one would wish, and only less successful are such pieces as "Blues Fantasy" and "Song for a Banjo Dance." It is a queer thing that a man who can write as nakedly and directly as Hughes can should also write such poor stuff as "After Many Springs" or "Afraid." A man who writes bitterly and sincerely about the south, for example, ought not to give the impression of writing insincerely a "poeme d'automne," which is Verlaine and water, or such worn stuff as this:

Does a jazz band ever sob?
They say a jazz band's gay.
Yet as the vulgar dancers whirled
And the wan night wore away,
One said she heard the jazz band sob
When the little dawn was gray.

"Wan night wore away" is Owen Meredith redivivus; "one said she heard the jazz band sob" grows worse every time you say it over. "The little dawn was gray" is that false pathos which ruins all the minor poets, and throughout the whole poem you do not know what point of view is intended, who is speaking or about whom the meditation is being meditated.

I have been thus specific about Mr. Hughes' work because he is clearly a poet with something to say. Mr. Hughes' trouble is that he is afraid he will not be literary. I assure him on my honor as a reader of some thousands of verses that literature has ruined more poets than it has ever saved. When Mr. Hughes keeps his eye on the ball he writes keenly and directly and movingly, and this he must do more and more if he is to develop, but half the time he swings around, looks uneasily at his audience and seems to say, "After all, I am a poet, you know, and not a bright colored boy," and then we have a spell of Gottschalk (who was only a cheap Chopin) on the piano. I prefer the genuine and authentic blues when they are played with such consummate skill and I think Mr. Hughes' readers will, too.

It is needless to remark that the other two volumes are quite negligible exhibitions of literature. . . .

. . . the three volumes here listed (barring parts of Mr. Hughes' book) are like a hundred other precious little babies left to die of inanition on the slopes of Parnassus.
[. . .]

Ruth Peiter[?] "Book Review and Latest Book Comment[?]: New Negro Poet Looms" *Toledo Times*, Sunday Magazine[?], n.d., p. 12[?]

With an introduction by Carl Van Vechten comes a first volume of poems, *The Weary Blues* by Langston Hughes, the young colored poet who with Countee Cullen has been much in the public eye recently. Mr. Van Vechten speaks with enthusiasm and one or two poems will convince you that he does so with reason. If one may judge by a slender volume, here is a young man destined to be one of the great poets of his race.

The verses are in many moods, reflecting something of the vividness and enchantment of the wandering, adventurous life which their writer has led. There are tragic poems, and delicate lines, and sea poems and fantasies. And there are poems which are like a cry from the heart of his race.
[. . .]

Ormond A. Forte "*The Weary Blues*" *Cleveland Herald*, January[?] 1926, [p. ?]

Langston Hughes' first book of poems, named after the prize-winning poem in *Opportunity's* first literary contest, "The Weary Blues," has just reached my desk. Hughes is a young poet of amazing promise whom Cleveland delights to call her own, because of the knowledge that during the rambles of his twenty-three summers he sojourned here, attending Central High School, of which he is a graduate.

The first impression of the book is its exquisite unusualness. From the paper jacket—a vigorous study of a jazz hound at the piano with parted lips, tremulous with daring "Doing a lazy sway by the dull pallor of an old gas light"—to the quaintness of its paper binding, the book is expertly singular.

In the preface by Carl Van Vechten vivid snatches of the young poet's nomadic life are given—doubtless to prepare the reader of the poems that follow for the incredible maturity of the youth's sensitive reaction to the vagaries of life. "Rich in experience as a fruit-cake is full of raisins" sums up Mr. Van Vechten in his characterization of Hughes—and this in the short span of twenty-three years!

There were days in Mexico—and in Spain, where the swish of the fandango and the click of castanets must have quickened the warm roving blood of young Hughes—and slow journeys along the African West Coast—in Dakaar—and days in "Gay Paree"—and of beachcombing!

Most arresting of all the poems in the book are the shorter ones with their strangely quickening interest—poems that seemed to have been written with a sudden fury of eagerness that leaped boldly from one subject to another.

SEA CALM

How still
How strangely still
The water is today.
It is not good
For water
To be still that way.

And then there is audaciousness and utter frankness in the poems too:

CARIBBEAN SUNSET

God having a hemorrhage,
Blood coughed across the sky
Staining the dark sea red.
That is sunset in the Caribbean.

And note how Mr. Hughes throws conventionality to the winds and sings of this forbidden thing:

CROSS

My old man's a white old man,
And my old mother's black.
If ever I cursed my white old man
I take my curses back.

If ever I cursed my black old mother
and wished she were in hell,
I'm sorry for that evil wish,
And now I wish her well.

My old man died in a fine big house
My ma died in a shack,
I wonder where I'm gonna die
Being neither white nor black.

Then varying his moods like the kaleidoscopic scenes of his far-blown wanderings, Mr. Hughes shows the catholicity of his art in this poem of indefinable exaltation:

We have tomorrow
Bright before us
Like a flame.
And dawn today—
Broad arch above the road we came!

The book, published by Alfred Knopf, New York, should interest all lovers of poetry at least for the primitive audaciousness of Mr. Hughes' poetic license.

Corinne Meaux
"The Weary Blues"
New York Amsterdam News, 27 January 1926, [p. 9]

I could not help but feel that the *Weary Blues* was like a canvas and each poem a brilliant splotch among the riot of colors that blend themselves into Negro life in America. These verses mark a new stride in the poetical field, something unattempted before, jazzy poetry throbbing with syncopated rhythm. They mirror Harlem's night life in true spirit, lilting with its gaiety.

"Negro Dancers," "To Midnight Nan at Leroy's" and "Blues Fantasy" sing themselves fascinatingly. Refined, sensitive natures may feel that this special group are slightly offensive, too raggy and lacking in artistic value, but they are typical. One would hardly expect an artist to give us meadows and glowing sunset as a portrayal of Harlem. Even though of merit, there is no doubt that the poems in this section are not as fine and as expressive of the writer's own feelings as those found elsewhere.

However, we are not confined to Harlem and its roof jaunts, nor Lenox avenue with its cabarets. Neither does he give poems only of Negro life—for art knows no color line. The stirring emotion must have an outlet and beauty that thrills will find expression. "Dream Variations" is like a piece of music starting quickly and joyfully only to die softly, slowly and sweetly. The loss of a friend he expresses simply, yet exquisitely.

Then with the glad free abandon of the adventurer he charms with tales of the sea, the beauty of the Caribbean sunset and the wild joy of a sailor's life. These are the songs in simple lyric verse which he sings in "Water Front Streets."

He chants of the loveliness of Mexican women, of a beggar lad who plays a wild free tune, "As if Fate had not bled him with her knife."

The more serious poems "Cross," "The South," "The Jester," "As I Grow Older," while they stir with bitterness are not cruel. Like a ripple in a stream they seem to hide a strong undercurrent of deep sorrow and mournful longing that tugs at the heart strings.

It is the voice of suppressed feeling, the love of the open road, which sings in "Our Land."

"Mother to Son" also stirs deeply—but to enumerate these places would lessen the appreciation of the book.

Carl Van Vechten's introduction is a gem sparkling with iridescent fires. Combined with the fine expression of Langston Hughes you will find the book a veritable treasure.

Dewey R. Jones
"The Bookshelf: The Weary Blues"
Chicago Defender, part 2, 30 January 1926, [p. 1]

The much-heralded *Weary Blues* has at last come tonight, and such an arrival it is! Not since the war removed so many budding young poets and stunted the rhyme market has a book been published that gives greater promise of a literary career than *The Weary Blues*. Not in recent days has so much been crowded in a space of 110 pages; nowhere can you be carried along on a maze of words, swept to the depth of despair and then transported to the heights as you can in *The Weary Blues*.

There is a variety of subjects, handled variously. There are flashes of real brilliancy, and again there are spots of mediocrity; but the latter are few. When you get into the second part of the book, where you are allowed to stray from Harlem cabarets and night life in big cities, you are also allowed to forget that Langston Hughes is a Race man, whose works interest white people chiefly because he is not white.

Strange thing about white people; they ignore you, humiliate you, scorn and spurn you until, out of sheer desperation, you develop something better than they could do with the same material, and immediately you become their pet. They take you up and make you a fad, and then you have arrived. Langston Hughes, at 23, has already learned this; consequently he devotes the first part of his book to what his critics will call typically "Negro" songs without music. He tells you in an easy, rhythmic flow of weird scenes in Harlem's famous or infamous night clubs.

Strut and wiggle,
Shameless gal.
Wouldn't no fellow
Be your pal.

Hear dat music
Jungle night.
Hear dat music
And the moon was white.

Sing your blues song,
Pretty baby.
You want lovin',
And you don't mean maybe.

And so he runs on in his monologue to "Midnight Nan at Leroy's."

He follows that up with "To a Black Dancer in the Little Savoy":

Wine-maiden
Of a jazz-tuned night,
Lips
Sweet as purple dew,
Breasts
Like the pillows of all sweet dreams,
Who crushed
The grapes of joy
And dripped their juice
on you?

There are many of these, striking the same note that cubist and circular paintings strike. They are gaudy, though picturesque. They don't carry conviction that the writer was as happy when he wrote them as he pretended to be. He does, however, touch a real depth of the pathetic, tragic note in his "Lenox Avenue: Midnight":

The rhythm of life
Is a jazz rhythm,
Honey.
The gods are laughing at us.

The broken heart of love,
The weary, weary heart of pain—
Overtones,
Undertones,
To the rumble of street cars,
To the swish of rain.

Lenox Avenue,
Honey.
Midnight,
And the gods are laughing at us.

There is something strangely sad in the meditations on the race problem in America. Mr. Hughes, without apparent effort, with perfect rhyme and rhythm, discusses the cross which cannot bear him down because he has the heart of an artist and can fly away from it all, but which he knows does weigh upon the rest of us like the albatross upon the neck of the mariner:

> My old man's a white old man,
> And my old mother's black.
> If I ever cursed my white old man
> I take my curses back.

> If ever I cursed my black old mother
> And wished she were in hell,
> I'm sorry for that evil wish
> And now I wish her well.

> My old man died in a fine big house.
> My ma died in a shack.
> I wonder where I'm gonna die,
> Being neither white nor black?

These are words that make us pause and wonder upon the thoughts that must have passed through Mr. Hughes' mind before he could relieve himself by singing.

But to me his best works are not of his color, nor of Harlem cabarets, but of the color of the sunset in the Mediterranean. He feels that in his travels, where he was given an opportunity to forget his color and race hatreds, he could see the beauties of God and nature through unclouded eyes. What, for instance, is more beautiful than—

> The spring is not so beautiful there,
> but dream ships sail away
> To where the spring is wondrous rare
> And life is gay.

> The spring is not so beautiful there,
> But lads put out to sea
> Who carry beauties in their hearts
> And dreams, like me.

The Weary Blues is introduced by Carl Van Vechten, who tells us something of the colorful history of the young poet. Altogether, no library is complete without the book—it is a gem!

Irvin Shapiro "Langston Hughes a Young Poet of Great Promise: Wardman Park Bellhop Author of Volume of Verse Sponsored by Carl Van Vechten" *Washington Herald,* 31 January 1926, p. 6D

When we think of the magnificent Dunbar High School erected in this city in honor of Paul Laurence Dunbar, the poet, we cannot conceive of the honors the colored race will pay to Langston Hughes.

Hughes is but 23 years old. Six months ago he was a nobody. Two months ago he was a bellhop in the Wardman Park Hotel. Today he is a poet of such promise that Alfred A. Knopf has brought out a volume of his verse. The introduction to this work is written by Carl Van Vechten and the cover design was drawn by Covarrubias.

We first heard of the work of this young colored poet when Vachel Lindsay in his recital at the Wardman Park read several manuscripts that Hughes (then a bellhop) had handed him.

The poems were rich, powerful and spontaneous. The musical effects were striking. There was authentic Negro rhythm running through his verse. With all his moods Hughes attempted to bring in a jungle-reminiscence.

The volume is *The Weary Blues* and receives its name from the Hughes poem, which won a recent contest.

Hughes can forget his race-injustice and be a great poet. It is for this quality that we most admire him. Here is a genuine piece of poetry that is far above the color-line:

SUICIDE'S NOTE

The calm,
Cool face of the river
Asked me for a kiss.

Here is the work of an artist:

PROEM

I am a Negro:
    Black as the night is black,
    Black like the depths of my Africa.

I've been a slave:
    Caesar told me to keep his door-
      steps clean.
    I brushed the boots of Washington.

I've been a worker:
    Under my hand the pyramids arose,
    I made the mortar for the
      Woolworth Building.

I've been a singer:
    All the way from Africa to Georgia
    I've carried my sorrow songs.
    I made ragtime.

I've been a victim:
    The Belgians cut off my hands in
      the Congo.
    They lynch me now in Texas.

I am a Negro:
    Black as the night is black.
    Black like the depths of my Africa.

The first verse of "Negro Dancers" shows Hughes' talent for verse syncopation.

Me an' ma baby's
Got two mo' ways,
    Two mo' ways to do de buck!
Da, da,
Da, da, da!
    Two mo' ways to do de buck!

When Lindsay gave his readings, there was one poem that appeared to be more authentic than all the rest. It was Hughes'

portrait of an African boy after the manner of Gauguin.

All the tom-toms of the jungles beat in
    my blood,
And all the wild hot moons of the
    jungles shine in my soul,
I am afraid of this civilization—
    So hard,
      So strong,
        So cold.
[. . .]

Countee Cullen
"Our Book Shelf: Poet on Poet"
Opportunity, 4 (February 1926), 73–4

Here is a poet with whom to reckon, to experience, and here and there, with that apologetic feeling of presumption that should companion all criticism, to quarrel.

What has always struck me most forcibly in reading Mr. Hughes' poems has been their utter spontaneity and expression of a unique personality. This feeling is intensified with the appearance of his work in concert between the covers of a book. It must be acknowledged at the outset that these poems are peculiarly Mr. Hughes' and no one's else. I cannot imagine his work as that of any other poet, not even of any poet of that particular group of which Mr. Hughes is a member. Of course, a microscopic assiduity might reveal derivation and influences, but these are weak undercurrents in the flow of Mr. Hughes' own talent. This poet represents a transcendently emancipated spirit among a class of young writers whose particular battle-cry is freedom. With the enthusiasm of a zealot, he pursues his ways, scornful, in subject matter, in photography, and rhythmical treatment, of whatever obstructions time and tradition have placed before him. To him it is essential that he be himself. Essential and commendable surely; yet the thought persists that some of these poems would have been better had Mr. Hughes held himself a bit in check. In his admirable introduction to the book, Carl Van Vechten says the poems have a *highly deceptive air of spontaneous improvisation*. I do not feel that the air is deceptive.

If I have the least powers of prediction, the first section of the book, "The Weary Blues," will be most admired, even if less from intrinsic poetical worth than because of its dissociation from the traditionally poetic. Never having been one to think all subjects and forms proper for poetic consideration, I regard these jazz poems as interlopers in the company of the truly beautiful poems in other sections of the book. They move along with the frenzy and electric heat of a Methodist or Baptist revival meeting, and affect me in much the same manner. The revival meeting excites me, cooling and flushing me with alternate chills and fevers of emotion; so do these poems. But when the storm is over, I wonder if the quiet way of communing is not more spiritual for the God-seeking heart; and in the light of reflection I wonder if jazz poems really belong to that dignified company, that select and austere circle of high literary expression which we call poetry. Surely, when in "Negro Dancers" Mr. Hughes says

Me an' ma baby's
Got two mo' ways,
Two mo' ways to do de buck!

he voices, in lyrical, thumb-at-nose fashion the happy careless attitude, akin to poetry, that is found in certain types. And certainly he achieves one of his loveliest lyrics in "Young Singer." Thus I find myself straddling a fence. It needs only "The Cat and the Saxophone," however, to knock me over completely on the side of bewilderment, and incredulity. This creation is a *tour de force* of its kind, but is it a poem:

EVERYBODY
Half-pint,—
Gin?
No, make it
LOVES MY BABY
corn. You like
don't you, honey?
BUT MY BABY. . . .

In the face of accomplished fact, I can't say *This will never do,* but I feel that it ought never to have been done.

But Mr. Hughes can be as fine and as polished as you like, etching his work in calm, quiet lyrics that linger and repeat themselves. Witness "Sea Calm":

How still
How strangely still
The water is today.
It is not good
For water
To be so still that way.

Or take "Suicide's Note":

The calm,
Cool face of the river
Asked me for a kiss.

Then crown your admiration with "Fantasy in Purple," this imperial swansong that sounds like the requiem of a dying people:

Beat the drums of tragedy for me,
Beat the drums of tragedy and death.
And let the choir sing a stormy song
To drown the rattle of my dying
breath.

56

Beat the drums of tragedy for me,
And let the white violins whir thin
and slow,
But blow one blaring trumpet note of
sun
To go with me to the darkness where I
go.

Mr. Hughes is a remarkable poet of the colorful; through all his verses the rainbow riots and dazzles, yet never wearies the eye, although at times it intrigues the brain into astonishment and exaggerated admiration when reading, say something like "Caribbean Sunset":

God having a hemorrhage,
Blood coughed across the sky,
Staining the dark sea red:
That is sunset in the Caribbean.

Taken as a group the selections in this book seem one-sided to me. They tend to hurl this poet into the gaping pit that lies before all Negro writers, in the confines of which they become racial artists instead of artists pure and simple. There is too much emphasis here on strictly Negro themes; and this is probably an added reason for my coldness toward the jazz poems—they seem to set a too definite limit upon an already limited field.

Dull books cause no schisms, raise no dissensions, create no parties. Much will be said of *The Weary Blues* because it is a definite achievement, and because Mr. Hughes, in his own way, with a first book that cannot be dismissed as merely promising, has arrived.

Donald Davidson
"The Spyglass"
Nashville Tennessean,
7 February 1926, p.7[?]

Langston Hughes is a Negro poet, whose volume, *The Weary Blues,* comes forth with a puffy introduction by Carl Van Vechten. Mr. Van Vechten is highly excited over Langston Hughes' nomadic life; the inference seems to be that a young Negro poet who has traveled all over the world from the Azore Islands to Topeka, Kansas, ought to be a regular bear-cat of a writer. The result, however, doesn't come out convincingly in this volume. Langston Hughes' poems are short, sharp exclamations, done with spirit and precision, but having hardly a feather's weight even when he is most passionate or angry. His poems are like fragments, and have an air of improvisation. And there is something incongruous in a Negro poet who runs the gamut from jazzy versions of Negro "blues" to pallid free verse and imagistic miniatures. He is merely sentimentally absurd when he says: "I am a black Pierrot." Nor do we like him any better when, to quote Van Vechten, "he writes caressingly of little black prostitutes in Harlem." His pagan vigor may eventually serve him well, but *The Weary Blues* seems to indicate that he has rushed into publication before he was mature as a poet. His work, in this humble opinion, is far inferior to the work of another Negro poet, Countee Cullen, whose volume, *Color,* is a very fine piece of writing.

Georgia Douglas Johnson
"Book Review"
Pittsburgh Courier, 13
February 1926, p. 16

Langston Hughes, the author of *The Weary Blues,* published by Knopf, comes forward with his own rhythmic and strikingly individual note, to swell the poetic concerto now being rendered by the younger writers of a marvelously rich and intricate race.

With his air of "gay valor" transcendently "More winning than grim philosophy," he tunes in with the ever augmenting orchestra whose music gently modulates from hope's bright major strains to sobbing minors on and on through rhapsodies, elegies, lullabies and brilliant arias.

Langston Hughes has a thought and then models for himself a form to house it, always subjecting the form to the thought.

"My soul grows deep like the rivers," a quiet meditative line disclosing deep forests, dark waters. Coleridge Taylor's "Deep River" sounds alongside this unforgettable line. One is reminded of the author of "Hiawatha" upon seeing Langston Hughes. There is something of the calm, something of the serenity that both possess to a very similar degree.

[. . .]

With a brave smile Langston Hughes faces the world. With a heart full of sympathy he views life around him, in the following lines to "A Little Lover-Lass Dead," his tender regard is well evidenced:

> She
> Who searched for lovers
> In the night
> Has gone the quiet way
> Into the still

> Dark land of death
> Beyond the rim of day.
> Now like a little lonely waif
> She walks
> An endless street
> And gives her kiss to nothingness,
> Pray God his lips were sweet.

Note this transition to the stately elegy:

> Beat the drum of tragedy for me
> Beat the drums of tragedy and death,
> And let the choir sing a stormy song
> To drown the rattle of my dying
>   breath.

> Beat the drums of tragedy for me
> And let the white violins whir thin
>   and slow,
> But blow one blearing trumpet note of
>   sun
> To go with me to the darkness where I
>   go!

The entire book is the song of a soul pulsing with colorful rhythm.

Mary White Ovington
"Book Chat"
New York Amsterdam News, 17 February 1926, [p. 16]; also *Washington Sentinel,* 13 February 1926

Langston Hughes, city bred, told a group of us the other evening that he had never cared for the poetry that as a child he read in his schoolbooks. It dealt with things of which he had no understanding. Why should he, for instance, be interested in Tennyson's

I come from haunts of coot and hern
And make a sudden sally—

when he had never seen a coot or a hern? But one day he read a poem in a Kansas newspaper that the editor was holding up to ridicule. It described the city's narrow street, the shabby house, even the garbage-can. Here he found was poetry that appealed to him, and he began himself trying to write in such a vein.

This, I think, is typical of Mr. Hughes' method. Thousands and thousands of children read Tennyson's book—

I chatter, chatter as I flow—

and enjoy the sound of the words without ever thinking whether they have seen a brook or not. But Langston Hughes never was intrigued merely by the melody of tripping syllables. Even as a little boy he must draw as clearly as he could, the picture of what he really saw.

The Weary Blues is a book full of pictures, word pictures of some of the multitude of things that have swept across a young man's vision. Sometimes they are out-of-doors:

How thin and sharp is the moon
    tonight!
How thin and sharp and ghostly white
Is the slim curved crook of the moon
    tonight!

or this:

Sea charm—
The sea's own children
Do not understand.
They know but that the sea is strong
Like God's hand;
They know
But that sea wind is sweet,
Like God's breath,
And that the sea holds
A wide deep death.

Sometimes they are of people:

When Susanna Jones wears red
Her face is like an ancient cameo
Turned brown by the ages.

But always they are pictures, not reflections upon life, but vivid bits of life itself. All of which tells us that Langston Hughes is very much a modern.

"The Weary Blues," the poem from which the book takes its name, won the first prize at the *Opportunity* contest in 1925. There are other "Blues" verses in which one sees an effort to strike the rhythm of these folk songs. These are cabaret songs, and Harlem stands out among them with her comedy and her tragedy somberly stalking through her mirth.

In the introduction, Carl Van Vechten tells us of the interesting life this vagabond poet has led—a true poet, who preferred to knock about on ship and in strange ports rather than stay in college! I, for one, feel a little piqued at this volume. It says so little out of all it might say. Such wonderful lands as Langston Hughes has seen and such picturesque people as he has rubbed elbows with. He only gives us titbits of all that must be rushing through his mind. We have sat down to the hors d'oeuvre and they have whetted our appetite for more. May the next course come soon!

"City's Negro Poet Offers New Volume" *Washington Post*, 21 February 1926, Amusements Section, p. 6

That the Negro race in America, which has given such undoubted poets to the world as Paul Laurence Dunbar, James Weldon Johnson, Claude McKay, and Countee

Cullen, has produced another poet in Langston Hughes, of Washington, former bus boy at the Wardman Park Hotel, is the contention of critics who have reviewed his new volume *Weary Blues*.

Langston Hughes is a poet of many moods and his imagination of a high order. He has had an adventurous and romantic career, for his 23 years since his birth in Joplin, Mo. The wanderlust has gripped his soul since boyhood, but he managed to stay in Cleveland long enough to be graduated from its high school as class poet and editor of the Year Book. He has been a sailor before the mast and sailed many strange seas and visited many lands, all of which experiences have found their way into his verse.

This young poet has the gift of vivid description and an instinctive grasp of color, warmth and beauty in his work. As interpreter of the soul of the Negro race he has portrayed a deep understanding of the Negro heart and its aspirations toward better things. In his cabaret songs are caught the rollicking refrains of true jazz motifs, while there is a stark realism and a melancholy lyricism in his sea pieces, and now and then he touches poignantly on what he considers the oppressions of his people.

In a few brief stanzas called simply "Proem" he has written effectively the story of the Negro race. It reads:

I am a Negro:
Black as the night is black
Black like the depths of my Africa.

I've been a slave:
Caesar told me to keep his door steps
  clean.
I brushed the boots of Washington.

I've been a worker:
Under my hand the pyramids arose.
I made mortar for the Woolworth
  building.

I've been a singer:
All the way from Africa to Georgia
I carried my sorrow songs.
I made ragtime.

I've been a victim:
The Belgians cut off my hands in the
  Congo.
They lynch me now in Texas.

I am a Negro:
Black as the night is black,
Black like the depths of my Africa.

There is thought in this little fragment:

CABARET

Does a jazz band ever sob?
They say a jazz band's gay.
Yet as the vulgar dancers whirled
And the wan night wore away,
One said she heard the jazz band sob
When the little dawn was grey.

That Hughes has an abiding faith in his own people is told in the simple beauty of these few lines.

The night is beautiful
So are the eyes of my people.

Beautiful, also, is the sun.
Beautiful, also, are the souls of my
  people.

Any poet would be proud of this poem:

We have tomorrow
Bright before us
Like a flame.

Yesterday
A night-gone thing,
A sun-down name.

And dawn—today
Broad arch above the road we came.

Jessie Fauset
"Our Book Shelf"
Crisis, 31 (March 1926), 239

Very perfect is the memory of my first literary acquaintance with Langston Hughes. In the unforgettable days when we were publishing *The Brownies' Book* we had already appreciated a charming fragile conceit which read:

> Out of the dust of dreams,
> Fairies weave their garments;
> Out of the purple and rose of old
>   memories,
> They make purple wings.
>
> No wonder we find them such
>   marvelous things.

Then one day came "The Negro Speaks of Rivers." I took the beautiful dignified creation to Dr. Du Bois and said: "What colored person is there, do you suppose, in the United States who writes like that and yet is unknown to us?" And I wrote and found him to be a Cleveland high school graduate who had just gone to live in Mexico. Already he had begun to assume that remote, so elusive quality which permeates most of his work. Before long we had the pleasure of seeing the work of the boy, whom we had sponsored, copied and re-copied in journals far and wide. "The Negro Speaks of Rivers" even appeared in translation in a paper printed in Germany.

Not very long after, Hughes came to New York, and not long after that he began to travel and to set down the impressions, the pictures, which his sensitive mind had registered of new forms of life and living in Holland, in France, in Spain, in Italy and in Africa.

His poems are warm, exotic and shot through with color. Never is he preoccupied with form. But this fault, if it is one, has its corresponding virtue, for it gives his verse, which almost always is imbued with the essence of poetry, the perfection of spontaneity. And one characteristic which makes for this bubbling-like charm is the remarkable objectivity which he occasionally achieves, remarkable for one so young, and a first step toward philosophy. Hughes has seen a great deal of the world, and this has taught him that nothing matters much but life. Its forms and aspects may vary, but living is the essential thing. Therefore make no bones about it—"make the most of what you too may spend."

Some consciousness of this must have been in him even before he began to wander, for he sent us as far back as 1921:

> Shake your brown feet, honey,
> Shake your brown feet, chile,
> Shake your brown feet, honey,
> Shake 'em swift and wil'— . . .
> Sun's going down this evening—
> Might never rise no mo'.
> The sun's going down this very
>   night—
> Might never rise no mo'—
> So dance with swift feet, honey,
> (The banjo's sobbing low) . . .
> The sun's going down this very
>   night—
> Might never rise no mo.'

Now this is very significant, combining as it does the doctrine of the old Biblical exhortation, "eat, drink and be merry for tomorrow ye die," Horace's "Carpe diem," the German "Freut euch des Lebens" and Herrick's "Gather ye rosebuds while ye may." This is indeed a universal subject served Negro-style, and though I am no great lover of any dialect I hope heartily that Mr. Hughes will give us many more such combinations.

Mr. Hughes is not always the calm philosopher; he has feeling a-plenty and is not ashamed to show it. He "loved his friend" who left him and so taken up is he with the sorrow of it all that he has no room for anger or resentment. While I do not think of him as a protagonist of color—he is too much the citizen of the world for that—I doubt if any one will ever write more tenderly, more understandingly, more humorously of the life of Harlem shot through as it is with mirth, abandon and pain. Hughes comprehends this life, has studied it and loved it. In one poem he has epitomized its essence:

Does a jazz-band ever sob?
They say a jazz-band's gay.
Yet as the vulgar dancers whirled
And the wan night wore away,
One said she heard the jazz-band sob
When the little dawn was grey.

Harlem is undoubtedly one of his great loves; the sea is another. Indeed all life is his love and his work a brilliant, sensitive interpretation of its numerous facets.

Theophilus Lewis
"Book Review: Euterpe Learns the Charleston" *Messenger*, 8 (March 1926), 92

Lyric poetry—and I am almost persuaded to Edgar Allan Poe's opinion that there is no other kind of poetry—springs from the core of the mind where the emotional kinship of races is close enough to make the imagery of each intelligible to all. It sprouts from the youth of humanity, the race or the poet and, as youth is parent to maturity, it reveals the mold or patterns from which the more spiritual and intellectual arts will later develop. While the bard whose songs flow unalloyed from the universal human emotions usually wins quicker recognition, he will, unless he is a master of musical speech, inevitably be surpassed by the vigor and arresting originality of the poet bearing the unmistakable mark of his race. If anybody asserts this is simply an expression of my well-known chauvinism, I reply "Bushwah!" Differentiation is always a step forward in the process of evolution.

The "Blues" poems which make up the first part of the book, *The Weary Blues,* reveal Langston Hughes as a poet of the latter type. On second thought I see no valid reason why the "Blues" should be distinguished from the earlier poems. They are merely an emphatic expression of the mood discernible in his work from the beginning. To people who think a poet is a man who repeats in verse what he reads in books or newspapers, these poems, all of them, will appear either gauche monstrosities or clever innovations, happily or lamentably, according to whether one likes them or not, destined to live no longer than the current cabaret vogue. Which view marks the failure, or perhaps the inability, to understand the function of an artist.

Langston Hughes has gone direct to life for his themes and he has embodied its ironies and . . . harmonies in his verse. He has not consulted life of 1890 as observed and recorded by Theodore Dreiser and Rudyard Kipling; he has caught life in its current incandescence as it roars and blazes in the bosoms of the new race of American blacks. Six lines of his are painted on a six-foot sign in the lobby of the Harlem YMCA, and this is no mere coincidence. It is one of the indications that this pagan poet is fast becoming a religious force. By this expression I do not mean he has invented a novel way to chant hallelujahs to a Jewish Jehovah, a standardized Christ and a Central Islip Holy Ghost. I mean that in giving concrete and definite expression to the incoherent feelings and impulses of his people he is functioning as a unifying spiritual agent. This is the chief work of the artist—this and to crystallize the beauty of his people in stone or verse or enduring drama and so leave behind an impressive tombstone when the civilization of which he is a part has trod the road to dusty death.

As no man can read vivid and thoughtful literature without showing the effects of it, there are places, here and there, where his verse faintly smells like the Public Library, as—

He did a lazy sway . . .
He did a lazy sway . . .

which suggests the rhythm of the Chinese Nightingale, or "To the Black Beloved," with its subdued elegance which somehow carried the mind back to the Song of Solomon. But these reminders of book lore, faint as they are, are few and far between. What we usually hear is the shuffle of happy feet, as in:—

Me an' ma baby's
Got two mo' ways,
Two mo' ways to do de buck!

Or Bessie Smith's robust contralto moaning a seductive ululation like:—

My man's done left me,
Chile, he's gone away.
My good man's left me,
Babe, he's gone away.
Now the cryin' blues
Haunts me night and day.

In "Cross" he takes his theme from the bio-sociological riot of the Aframerican's background, and the first line, which establishes its rhythm, comes straight from the guts of 133rd Street, which cries out against the restraints of the Ten Commandments and the factory system in the Rabelaisian couplet beginning "My old man is a man like this."

It almost tempts one to write him a personal letter demanding something inspired by that other jewel of levity, the quatrain which opens:

"I wish I had ten thousand bricks."

And Hughes, the craftsman, is quite as deft as Hughes the artist is original. His poems which at first sound as simple as the theme of Beethoven's Sixth Symphony on closer examination reveal a good deal of the complexity of that master's music. As an example, I point to "Midnight Nan at Leroy's." You will travel a long day's journey before you find another contemporary poem in which the fundamental poignancy and superficial gayety of life are so effectively blended. Note how skillfully he employs paired iambics to make the Charleston rhythm dance blithely down the surface of the poem while an excess of short feet and weak vowels form an undertow which establishes a final melancholy mood. I can think of no poet since Poe capable of weaving such an intricate tapestry of antithetical feelings.

Hughes is not a solitary figure, of course; there are at least two other poets producing work quite as authentic. But I know of no other poet who keeps in such close contact with life in its molten state or who is as capable of getting expression out of gaseous feelings without waiting for them to cool off. If he doesn't stop to mark time now he will certainly grow into a spiritual force of major significance.

63

"Five Silhouettes on the Slope of Mount Parnassus"
New York Times, 21 March 1926, pp. 6, 16

[. . .]

But the most startlingly human of all in this advance guard from Parnassus is Langston Hughes. Hughes is a natural troubadour; and if there have not been more Francois Villons among the Negro race it is chiefly because the Negro poet has not been able to make himself heard. We can but think it a mistake, however, that Hughes's publisher should have placed the poet's inferior work, his jazz poems, in the forefront of the book and have permitted the book a title (*Weary Blues*) so exclusively connotative of this type of verse.

Yet when we use the adjective inferior, however, we do not mean that as jazz poetry Mr. Hughes's verses are inferior; on the contrary, We believe that they are superior to the jazz poetry that is peddled on Broadway and among its environs. And they are not inferior to Vachel Lindsay's jazz poems. but they are inferior to other poems in the book. They are inferior to "Cross." . . .

If this is poignant with its peculiar sorrow, more poignant is "The Jester." But Mr. Hughes does not dwell upon the burden of his race; he is too light-hearted long to be cast down. In this "Poeme d'Automne" we have a modern Villon, the troubadour in very truth.

[. . .]

We sincerely hope that Langston Hughes will receive the wide reading he deserves. He is scarcely more than a youth, we understand, although he has roved half the world. If he can go on as he has begun, America bids fair to have a poet worthy of far more than passing mention.

Jake Falstaff
"Pippins and Cheese"
Akron Beacon Journal, 30 March 1926, p. 4

The unfortunate feature of this recent awakening in interest toward the serious and lively arts of the American Negro is that things which would ordinarily be found too weak for general attention achieve the spotlight and a temporary enthusiasm merely because they are of Negro production. I would class as one of these things Langston Hughes' *Weary Blues,* in which, to my way of thinking, there is hardly enough real poesy to make five good poems. The principal Negro poet is still Claude McKay, with Countee Cullen a far second.

"Books on Negro-White Relations"
World Tomorrow, 9 (April 1926), 131

Among our younger poets, none, it is safe to say, has lived so adventurous a life as Langston Hughes. Last year, at the age of twenty-three, he put together the sixty-eight of his poems which make up his newly published volume, *The Weary Blues,* to which Carl Van Vechten supplies an introduction and Covarrubias a jazzy jacket on the theme of the title poem. The verses are as varied as might be expected from such a youthful nomad; he sings of the sea, of far tropical lands, of Harlem cabarets, of the freedom and justice he covets for his race. Since the day when, as a bus boy in a restaurant, he dropped some of his verses at Vachel Lindsay's elbow, to have them enthusiastically received, he has trod a hard road valiantly. Some time, however, if not already, he may thank his years of hardship; for to them he owes much of the emotional sensitivity which distinguishes his verse.

"New Books in Brief Review" *Independent Weekly Review,* 116 (3 April 1926), 404

[. . .]

This young Negro poet expresses the strange medley of emotions, memories, hopes and fears of his race in modern America. The heavy heritage of slavery, dim racial memories of Africa, the sharp, self-conscious revolt against the scheme of things today—the delirious "escape" from life provided by Harlem, by music, by syncopation and blues, by dancing, by raw drink and wild love—all these elements are woven through his poems. He is very young, but he has lived feverishly. He has the fine qualities of force, passion, directness, and sensitive perception. Time may give more depth and beauty to his work, which is crude in texture and lacking in distinction.

[. . .]

Eric Johnston *"The Weary Blues" San Jose Herald,* 4 April 1926, p. 8

The Negro's having a great vogue. He's followed, or rather the fashion has been enhanced, by the Charleston, that dance demanding lateral genuflection and joints of water. No longer is his race inarticulate. No longer does it need some white-skinned spokesman, feverish with zeal for his emancipation; he's speaking for himself nowadays, and speaking well.

He has his colleges, he writes his novels, he receives wild plaudits from the concert platform. He reigns supreme in Harlem, and exacts much gold for his performance in a jazz band in many a New York night club. He's depicted in the smart magazines; smart writers like Carl Van Vechten make quite a show of interpreting him. In fact he seems to be a fetish of Van Vechten's.

Anyhow, the self-willed author of *Firecrackers* and *The Tattooed Countess* has written the introduction to *The Weary Blues.* And although after reading it, one approaches the actual work slightly prejudiced against it, Hughes' verses are often extremely lyrical, extremely evocative.

The black boy of 23 has had a fast and furious life. He's shipped around the world. He's seen black, brown and high-yellow prostitutes in its four corners. He's seen the moon hung over the jungles, and jazzed and loved with the rest of his folk in Harlem, the black man's northern metropolis.

Hughes is highly sensitized. Life impinges on him and bears fruit in verses. He smells romance wherever he goes. The rousing female odor is perfume in his nostrils. Hughes isn't preoccupied with sex; any artist with acute senses (as artists must be) knows its vastness in human affairs.

Much inspiration he draws from the piercing, poignant life of the Harlem night clubs where blacks, whites and browns dance, drink and love to the smashing, moaning, wrenching strains of a nigger band.

[. . .]

In "Soledad, a Cuban Portrait," we have him deeply aware of the undertones and overtones of life in the south: . . . .

Sometimes he's in the aching grip of nostalgia and cries, as in "Africa": . . . .

And again in "Poem," for portrait of an African boy after the manner of Gauguin: . . .

Langston Hughes is not the savior of his race; not the greatest singer. But *The Weary Blues* is the first song of one likely to some day sing marvelously well.

John McClure
"Negro Poet of Promise"
New Orleans Times-Picayune Sunday magazine, 4 April 1926, p. 4

The American Negro who has made American music and American folk poetry (if we include all the black-and-tan blues) almost in their entirety is beginning to enrich belles lettres. Five years ago we knew Claude McKay, William Stanley Braithwaite and a half-dozen older poets of more or less solid accomplishment. In 1922 Jean Toomer appeared in the magazines, a couple of years later Countee Cullen and a squad of other youngsters almost as good,

and now comes Langston Hughes. Of these three Jean Toomer is by far the most sensitive artist. He is in fact one of the most promising geniuses in lyrical prose in the United States, and if he had not fallen under the influence of Waldo Frank would have done great things before now. Countee Cullen is the emotional lyricist of the conventional school. He handles certain lilting rhythms most deftly and has a rather immature skill in diction. His danger is glibness. Langston Hughes, whose *The Weary Blues* has just been published by Knopf, falls somewhere between Countee Cullen and Jean Toomer. He is less conventional in his reaction to life than Cullen, and not so glib. Yet his reactions are far less sensitive than Toomer's, and his style is far less subtle, and less finished than either Toomer's or Cullen's.

The Weary Blues is a good book. Langston Hughes is a promising poet. Southern readers will be upset by some of the lyrics and there are a few that they will resent. One on the South will not help the sale of *The Weary Blues* down here. But these questions have nothing whatever to do with the merit of the verse. An introduction by Carl Van Vechten, which largely sidesteps the art of poetry, dwelling almost altogether on the career and personality of the poet, tells how Hughes was born in Joplin, Mo., February 1, 1902. . . .

It is said that Vachel Lindsay "discovered" Langston Hughes when Hughes was a bus boy in a Washington hotel dining room.

Hughes' poetry at the moment is more a promise than an accomplished fact. There are excellent things in the volume, but there are seeds of corruption in his work which he must eliminate if he wishes to build a lasting monument or a thoroughly satisfying art. Most of his poems are difficult in rhythmical vitality—strange, for a man with the Negro pulse, most musical in the world. And his diction is too often vague. He has a tendency, like most of the young intellectuals, to be satisfied with self-expression. Countee Cullen is too glib in his rhythms. Langston Hughes is not liquid enough. And yet *The Weary Blues* is a book of poems that reflects credit on the poet's sincerity and integrity. The personality revealed is both sensitive and intelligent, and the book is unquestionably one of the most interesting of the year. Here is a poem on a dead girl:

> She
> Who searched for lovers
> In the night
> Has gone the quiet way
> Into the still,
> Dark land of death
> Beyond the rim of day.
>
> Now like a little lonely waif
> She walks
> An endless street
> And gives her kiss to nothingness.
> Would God his lips were sweet!

He uses the blues to advantage:

> My man's done left me,
> Chile, he's gone away.
> My good man's left me,
> Babe, he's gone away.
> Now the cryin' blues
> Haunts me night and day.

[. . .]

J.B.C.
"The Reading Lamp"
South Bend Tribune, 11 April 1926, p. 7

Moving poetry is included in *The Weary Blues,* by Langston Hughes, a young Negro songster, whose volume, with an introduction by Carl Van Vechten, is published by Knopf.

[. . .]

Hughes' poems which are strongest in racial consciousness are not necessarily the best in the book. He is an authentic poet and his little volume is rich in transcriptions of universal emotions in forms of beauty.

Robert T. Kerlin
"Singers of New Songs"
Opportunity, 4 (May 1926), 162–4

[. . .]

The story of Dunbar's printing and peddling his first book is well known. Something like that has been the story of all Negro books of verse hitherto. I have a shelf of such books—the cost of printing borne by the author, the burden of selling borne by the author. Is it not a notable event in the history of the American Negro, and of America, that in the first months of the year 1926 two young Negro poets had their books put forth, on their merits and trade value, just as white poets' books, by two publishing firms of first repute for orthodox business? Negro poets are in the market, no longer lost wanderers on Parnassus.

Mr. Langston Hughes has now for three or four years—he is but in his twenty-fifth year—been transposing into verse some of the rhythms of Negro life. He is the interpreter of jazz and of the life from which it springs. Harlem is his, its theatres and dance halls, its streets and tenements, its gaieties and "blues." The

poignant note is not long absent. This is
typical:

She
Who searched for lovers
In the night
Has gone the quiet way
Into the still,
Dark land of death
Beyond the rim of day.

Now like a little lonely waif
She walks
An endless
Street
And gives her kiss to nothingness
would God his lips were sweet!

It's a common story. Why weep?

The rhythm of life
Is a jazz rhythm,
Honey.
The gods are laughing at us.

The broken heart of love,
The weary, weary heart of pain—
Overtones,
Undertones,
To the rumble of street cars,
To the swish of rain.

Lenox Avenue,
Honey.
Midnight,
And the gods are laughing at us.

All this life of Harlem calls for a poet.
No reporter can give it to the world. His
most honest story of any event in Harlem
would be a lie. Mr. Langston Hughes
comes on the scene and we begin to see a
new world—one that night only reveals.
Here are lyrics that are akin to the deathless ones in all languages—Sappho's, Horace's, Herrick's, but most of all the Hebrew
Song of Songs. This is an example:

Would
That I were a jewel,
A shattered jewel,

That all my shining brilliants
Might fall at thy feet,
Thou dark one.

Would
That I were a garment,
A shimmering, silken garment,
That all my folds
Might wrap about thy body,
Absorb thy body,
Hold and hide thy body,
Thou dark one.

Would
That I were a flame,
But one sharp, leaping flame
To annihilate thy body,
Thou dark one.

I would liken you
To a night without stars
Were it not for your eyes.
I would liken you
To a sleep without dreams
Were it not for your songs.

Truly those who see only with their eyes
see not at all. Dancers, and jazz bands, and
chansons vulgaires, and Charlestons, and
Weary Blues hardly tell the whole story,
and tell their own not at all. Hence Langston Hughes.

[. . .]

A little more than a century ago Leigh
Hunt announced, in a paper of which he
was the editor, three new poets. Two of
them were Shelley and Keats. It sometimes
happens—once, in a century, perhaps, two
or three poets of indisputable genius appear linked in some sort of union. It's
in the lap of the gods whether Toomer,
Hughes, and Cullen will be poets of unfulfilled renown or the creators of an epoch
when it will no more seem a marvel "To
make a poet black, and bid him sing."

Joseph Hilton Smyth
"The Weary Blues"
Double Dealer, 8 (May 1926), 358

Much of the stream of poetry that flows endlessly from the publishing fount these days possesses the originality and refreshing qualities of flat dish-water. The parturition of the older poets is somewhat forced, while the younger ones are apparently slightly crippled by adolescent debauches.

It was not so many years ago that poetry became a wonderful and a fearsome thing to behold. At any rate, it was interesting. Fifty-seven varieties of schools were formed, including Futurists, Impressionists, Neo-Impressionists, Dadaists, Vorticists, Expressionists, and God Knows what not! The sweet untempted virgins of Back Bay suffered tobacco heart and parental displeasure by smoking cigars—and incidentally writing verse—in a feeble imitation of Amy Lowell; callow collegiates caught head colds and got blisters on their feet from going hatless and tramping delicately on life in the manner of Harry Kemp. Some followed Ezra Pound to Europe, a chosen few published their brain children in the *Dial*, a great many were lost in the shuffle. Occasional critics asked plaintively where the younger poets were headed. The answer, in the light of the verse now published, is obvious. They weren't headed anywhere.

There are few exceptions, including *The Weary Blues*. The poetry in this volume is far better than the introductory encomium by Carl Van Vechten, which tends to befog the product with the personality of the author, would lead one to expect. George Moore might object to Hughes'

work on the ground that it i[s] tive, too personal. True, the[?] dertone of sentimentality thro[?] does not, however, detract from[?] ——— passages as:

> To fling my arms wide
> In the face of the sun,
> Dance! whirl! whirl!
> Till the quick day is done.
> Rest at pale evening. . . .
> A tall, slim tree. . . .
> Night comes tenderly,
> Black like me.

It is in his jazz variations that Hughes is undeniably at his best. The title poem together with "To Midnight Nan at Leroy's" possess a fluidly sensuous rhythm, rich and colorful. There is, in contrast, a lyric simplicity in some of his other moods—as in "Suicide's Note":

> The calm,
> Cool face of the river
> Asked me for a kiss.

With this volume Langston Hughes takes his place with other poets of his race: Countee Cullen, Jean Toomer, Dunbar and Claude McKay.

Ethel Arnold Tilden
"Contrasts"
Voices, 5 (May 1926), 267–9

Against the background of its author's life, *The Weary Blues*, of Langston Hughes, stands out a picturesque and poignant thing. I think there is no one for whom its gorgeousness, its gallantry and its "lyric cry" would not have an appeal. Mr. Hughes is a young Negro. He is a wanderer. His wanderings have carried him to lands of romance the world over. From these lands, and the lands of his own spirit, he creates those "realms of gold" he shares, realms of warmth and color and beauty. He sings beauty and his own joy and hurt in beauty with an unafraidness which arrests attention and wins for him more than a slight consideration. There is in Mr. Hughes' singing the music of his race—and the melancholy—but there is in it, also, a bitterness and a fatalism and a courage which are, I think, quite his own. His "Proem" spells courage. "Our Land," with its homesickness for the "land of the gorgeous sun," reveals the dream of a poet as much as it mirrors beginnings. "Dream Variations," although significant of the race life of its author, sings his own passion for joy as well. I find it very lovely.

To fling my arms wide
In the face of the sun,
Dance! Whirl! Whirl!
Till the quick day is done.
Rest at pale evening. . . .
A tall, slim tree. . . .
Night coming tenderly
Black like me.

The lyric quality of these poems and their inherent music are characteristically Negro, but above and beyond this underlying foundation of racial reality, they are the expression of an individual soul, sensitive and highly poetic. I, myself, am likely to care for them out of proportion because they are so lovely and so brave—Nothing could be more gallant than the "Fantasy in Purple":

Beat the drums of tragedy for me.
Beat the drums of tragedy and death.
And let the choir sing a stormy song
To drown the rattle of my dying
     breath.
Beat the drums of tragedy for me,
And let the white violins whir thin
     and slow,

But blow one blaring note of sun
To go with me to the darkness where I
go.

Lancaster Pollard
"Books in Review: *The Weary Blues*"
Seattle Post-Intelligencer, 2 May 1926, p. 6D

The sales popularity of *The Weary Blues*, by Langston Hughes, is due as much to efficient publicity and to curiosity regarding its Negro author as to the poetry itself. For, while there is much durable poetry in the book, there are also many trifling and insignificant pieces, and a considerable number that are obvious and undistinguished—common statements of commonplace experiences. Not all these poems contain warmth and charm; they do not deserve the indiscriminate praise they have been awarded.

When the author is writing of jazz he is good, and when he cries out with the woes and joys of the Negro, he is very good. A soul disinherited, in trying to win peace within himself and of himself, he creates authentic poetry, poems full of sorrow and beauty. His imagery is a mixture of that characterizing barbaric and erotic emotionalism. Mostly songs of abandon, there is little that is thoughtful or delicate or exquisite in the body of the work. Of those lyrics simple with the ultimate simplicity of art, his "Fantasy in Purple" is typical: . . .

70

F.B.B.
"*The Weary Blues:* Some Distinctive Verse by a Young Colored Poet" *Boston Transcript,* Book Section, 15 May 1926, p. 2

Only an orchestra of Negro players can cause the weariest jazz devotee to tingle with a desire to dance to their rhythm. So, too, only a Negro poet can write on mundane subjects and fill his readers with a sense of racial rhythm and melody.

The title poem in this collection was awarded first prize in a 1925 contest for Negro writers. It contains all of the singing characteristics so well within the power of the Negro. It also has a dominant note that is a mark of the thinking black man, i.e., a touch of tragedy blended with cynicism and a heart tearing melancholy. What though the poem is concerned only with Sweet Blues? They proceed from a black man's soul. Much of the poetry within the volume is crude. There are grammatical errors here and there. But who wants to haggle over a minor "those sort," when Pierrots, Brides and Souls are being spoken of? We agree with Carl Van Vechten, who writes the introduction to the volume, that Mr. Hughes's life story ought to prove interesting. We add that it ought to be as provocative to read such prose as this youth would write, as it is to read his varying poems.

Langston Hughes is only twenty-three. The education gained from schools has been of a migratory sort for him, but he has learned much from cruising as a sailor to the Azores and Africa. His education was carried on after he left the naval life, for he has been second cook, doorman, waiter in Paris, as well as a beach comber in Genoa. We hope he can be prevailed upon to publish some of the details of such an existence. There are poems within the pages to fit almost any mood. Always do the verses reveal an innate sense of lyricism and always are they personal. From many appealing verses and from many which strike at the writer's endeavor to express his color and racial traits in a touching way, we might select the concluding poem which strikes a warning note more than do any of the others. It warns what may happen when the great black tide of American Negroes becomes an insistent mass and surges out into present-day higher civilization.

I, too, sing America.
I am the darker brother.
They send me to eat in the kitchen
When company comes,
But I laugh,
And eat well
And grow strong.
Tomorrow
I'll sit at the table
When company comes.
Nobody'll dare
Say to me,
"Eat in the kitchen,"
Then.
They'll see how beautiful I am
And be ashamed.
I, too, am America.

It seems safe to say that some of the work of Langston Hughes ranks with that of Paul Laurence Dunbar.

Charlotte Hubbard Prescott
"The Readers' Round Table: Promising Negro Poet Is Langston Hughes"
Sioux City Journal, 16 May 1926, p. 14

Langston Hughes has written some jazz poetry, as the somewhat unfortunate title of his book of verse, *The Weary Blues,* would indicate. But the jazz poetry is not his best. Did you ever read, for instance, a more haunting, poignant thing than . . . "Cross." . . .

Or if that seems a bit jingly, listen to this "Poeme d'Automne": . . .

His publisher, Knopf, says that this young colored poet is determined to put his poetry across to the people who want it. During his recent reading tour of the middle west, he met with an automobile accident which jarred him badly, cutting and bruising his face. But rather than disappoint his large Indianapolis audience he gave his reading according to schedule, a doctor on the side lines, and plenty of ice on the table.

Langston Hughes will go far, or we miss our guess.

Llewellyn Jones
"Poetry of Countee Cullen and Langston Hughes"
American Life Magazine: A Magazine of Timely Features and Good Fiction, 1 (July 1926), [p. ?]

[. . .]

Two of the best known of the younger Negro poets of today are Countee Cullen, winner of many prizes and author of *Color* (Harper & Brothers), and Langston Hughes, another prize winning poet who has recently published *The Weary Blues.* Countee Cullen has, in addition to the endowment of his race, the culture of the European tradition and the background of an American university. Langston Hughes did not stay put when he went to a university, but found his spiritual satisfactions in wide traveling, both as a sailor on equatorial voyages, and as a sojourner in Paris and in Italy.

These two sorts of spiritual disciplines are reflected in the two poets' work. Both men are conscious, of course, of their racial inheritances and racial feelings. Of the two, Mr. Cullen has explored these the more deeply, being by education and predilection an "intellectual," a wit, and a poet in the metaphysical tradition (indeed, some of his love poetry reminds one of Donne's). . . .

[. . .]

Langston Hughes' racial consciousness is social—and Countee Cullen has the social race consciousness too—but not so psychological as Mr. Cullen's. Probably Mr. Hughes has made his "catharsis" through his adventurous life, and so it does not appear so patently in his poetry. Like Mr. Cullen, he celebrates in more than one lyric the night life of the Negro in Harlem: that release of the impulses of living through the dance, the singing of the "Blues" and brilliant light and gaiety of the cabaret and dance-floor—a joyous phase of Negro life which thousands of white people in New York are pathetically eager to join in, that they too may know what it feels like merely to be alive and free from the bondage of machine and desk. And he can see the tragedy that is often implied in this sort of release. Here is a short poem, "Cabaret":

[. . .]

And indeed the disillusion which seeks solace in jazz is well portrayed in Mr. Hughes' pages:

[. . .]

Like Mr. Cullen, Mr. Hughes is acutely conscious of the horrible injustices of which the country at large, and particularly the South, has been guilty. In "The South," he states the gist of the whole situation briefly and eloquently. And it is a good thing that this note of defiance is being sounded. For in the end the Negro will be taken at his own valuation—not his valuation in words only, but at the valuation which he is able to enforce. And when he places it high and proceeds to enforce it he is doing a service not only to his own race, but to the white race, for no man of that race is a good citizen or even a good man who would want to live with inferiors—self-confessed or otherwise. To wish to dominate over others is a sign of barbarism.

Not that I wish to end this article as if the chief value of these poems were in their racial assertiveness. They might have a sociological interest and a practical value in racial assertion and yet not be good poetry as poetry. But they are not works of propaganda but of art. And as works of art they are above all questions of race; they catch and transmit beauty, a beauty new to many of us. They, and other like manifestations in poetry, in music and in painting, all born of this Negro renaissance, are a valuable contribution to our common life.

C. C. Glenn
"Volume of Poems by Negro Author Is Worth While, Says Reviewer" *Daily Oklahoman*, 25 July 1926, p. C-12

In the number of volumes of poetry recently published the most astonishing is that of Langston Hughes; astonishing because of its poetic qualities and because Langston Hughes is a Negro. The Negro literature now being printed in the United States, meager in quantity and sometimes doubtful in quality, consists of perhaps a dozen newspapers, of which only two or three can be considered worth the paper they consume, and a handful of writers who have succeeded in finding publishers of some standing to market their stuff. Among these writers of African descent, whose efforts warrant the attention of both publisher and public, is the poet Hughes in his book, *The Weary Blues,* here under scrutiny.

The name ascribed to the volume does not do it justice, for, to the casual shopper, the title, *The Weary Blues,* printed on a book jacket with a silhouette of a Negro jazz player rampant, suggests anything but beautiful poetry, which, in truth, is to be found throughout the whole volume. I think, too, that the book would have been less inimical to itself, if the first section of

73

the collection had not been given to jazz, for the other sections have much more poetically to recommend them than this first one of typically Negroid syncopation. But once through this section there is writing that transcends the thing expected of the Negro minstrel. There are verses which enrich the present aggregate of American poetic literature, however much the Anglo-American purists may deprecate the fact. It is there, and the objectors can do nothing about it, now that it has once reached appreciative ears.

Hughes' collection contains none of formalism; there are no attempts in the grand manner, but poetry there is in every line of it. Classic flourishes of grandiloquence are passed by for freshness and vivility [*sic*] in both style and feeling. He comes near to the modern style; writing in one place with rhyme and rhythm, in another with rhythm and no rhyme, and again with neither. But Hughes is not concerned with arbitrary standards; bound by no traditions and pursuing no false gods. Rather, he writes out of his experience, with a palpable subjectiveness and personality all through it, at least, when the whole work is considered. In short poems, here and there, he may momentarily escape consciousness that his is the persecuted race, but it is only momentarily at most. The plaintive note is struck in the "Proem." It is inevitable to the end. Personal suffering for his people (and, now and then, a quiver for himself) exudes from the lines when he looks back in his "Black Africa." Exultant joy seizes him when he paints "Our Land," and there is infinite tenderness in his tormented soul when he writes "To F.S.," his lost friend. His sea pieces are simple lyricism. In all it is good poetry; better poetry than most of it now put on the book shelves.

The book has been on the market some weeks now, and I have seen no mention of it in the reviewing magazines; neither have I seen it acknowledged in the various supplements. Only the publisher has mentioned it in paid advertising. I do not understand this. The work is worth space in any of them. It should be brought to the attention of the Anglo-purists-snobs so they may be informed that intelligence and artistic sensitiveness is not amenable to race. It may be difficult to imagine the sons of slaves producing literature, but here is poetry from one of them.

Du Bose Heyward
"The Jazz Band's Sob"
New York Herald Tribune Books, 1 August 1926, p. 4

A little over a year ago the brilliant Negro journal *Opportunity* awarded a prize for a poem, "The Weary Blues," by Langston Hughes. Shortly thereafter *The Forum* reprinted the poem. Previous to the appearance of this poem very few were aware of the existence of the author, although he had been writing for seven years; an apprenticeship the results of which are evident in the pages of this volume, to which his prize poem gives its name.

The Weary Blues challenges more serious consideration than that generally accorded a "first book." Langston Hughes, although only twenty-four years old, is already conspicuous in the group of Negro intellectuals who are dignifying Harlem with a genuine art life. And, too, his use of syncopation in his prize poem suggested the possibility of a conflict in the rhythms of poetry paralleling that which is taking place between the spiritual and jazz exponents of Negro music.

Let it be said at once then that this author has done nothing particularly revolutionary in the field of rhythm. He is endowed with too subtle a musical sense to employ the banjo music of Vachel Lindsay, but he is close kin to Carl Sandburg in his use of freer, subtler syncopation. In fact, he has wisely refused to be fettered by a theory and has allowed his mood to select its own music. Several of the short free verse poems might have been written by Amy Lowell.

But if he derives little that is new in rhythm from his "Blues" he has managed to capture the mood of that type of Negro song, and thereby has caught its very essence. When he is able to create a minor, devil-may-care music, and through it to release a throb of pain, he is doing what the Negroes have done for generations, whether in the "Blues" of the Mississippi region or a song like "I Can't Help from Cryin' Sometimes," as sung by the black folk of the Carolina low country.

As he says in his "Cabaret":

Does a jazz band ever sob?
They say a jazz band's gay.
Yet as the vulgar dancers whirled
And the wan night wore away,
One said she heard the jazz band sob
When the little dawn was gray.

That Langston Hughes has not altogether escaped an inevitable pitfall of the Negro intellectual is to be regretted. In one or two places in the book the artist is obscured by the propagandist. Pegasus has been made a pack-horse. It is natural that the Negro writer should feel keenly the lack of sympathy in the South. That the South is a great loser thereby brings him small comfort. In the soul of a poet, a revolt so born may be transmuted through the alchemy of art into poetry that, while it stings the eyes with tears, causes the reader to wonder.

But far more often in the volume the artist is victor:

We have to-morrow
Bright before us
Like a flame.

Yesterday
A night-gone thing,
a sun-down name.

And dawn to-day
Broad arch above the road we came.

And in "Dream Variation" youth triumphs:

To fling my arms wide
In some place of the sun,
To whirl and to dance
Till the white day is done.
Then rest at cool evening
Beneath a tall tree
while the night comes on gently,
Dark like me—
That is my dream!

It is, however, as an individual poet, not as a member of a new and interesting literary group, or as spokesman for a race, that Langston Hughes must stand or fall, and in the numerous poems in *The Weary Blues* that give poignant moods and vivid glimpses of seas and lands caught by the young poet in his wanderings I find an exceptional endowment. Always intensely subjective, passionate, keenly sensitive to beauty and possessed of an unfaltering musical sense, Langston Hughes has given us a "first book" that marks the opening of a career well worth watching.

"Negro Poet's Blues Lyrics: Youth Sings with Sadness and Gayety" *Cleveland Plain Dealer,* All Feature Section, 1 August 1926, p. 3

The essence of lyric poetry consists of a synthetic rendering of life's color and substance. The author of *The Weary Blues,* a young Negro—formerly of Cleveland—possesses this quality of a lyric poet.

The title aptly defines the book's character. It is a combination of racial sadness and gayety. Hughes' nostalgia for warmth, his description of Harlem's women, his cabaret songs, the jazz-like rhythm of some of his poems, the mellow perspective of his feelings and a certain stubborn buoyancy of his youth—all these indicate poetic depths. His heart reacts to life like that of a poet, and the Negro adjective is applicable only in that it explains certain typical racial moods.

The shortcomings of his poetry consist of a certain cabaret song lightness where a more substantial form would be more appropriate. Evidently the inner rhythm which created the form of these poems was consistent with the youth of their author rather than with the feelings that inspired them. But his book is a contribution not merely to American Negro poetry but to poetry in general.

R.L. "Brief Reviews" *Midland,* 12 (October 1926), 303–4

The work of these two young Negro poets [Countee Cullen and Hughes], while betraying in a few places youthful imperfections of technique and a hasty disregard for the finesse of composition, has nevertheless much strength and beauty and vision.

[. . .]

For a young person, Langston Hughes has an exceedingly adventuresome background of color and romance. It is not surprising, therefore, to find a great diversity of subject and mood in this first book of poems. He follows the moan of a jazz band in a Harlem night club, sings to the little brown harlots in the cabarets, indulges in dreams under the eternal moons of youth, slips into strange seaports, and voices the tragedy at the heart of his race. He traverses with illusive grace the scale from lyric joy to lyric melancholy. While he might write more intensely, introspectively, and maturely than he does, there is really no need for his doing so. And while some of these brief lyrics may live, there is really no need for that either. Even the art of the moment may fulfill its function of beauty.

Alain Locke
"The Weary Blues"
Palms, 4 (October 1926), 25–8

I believe there are lyrics in this volume which are such contributions to pure poetry that it makes little difference what substance of life and experience they were made of, and yet I know no other volume of verse that I should put forward as more representatively the work of a race poet than *The Weary Blues.* Nor would I style Langston Hughes a race poet merely because he writes in many instances of Negro life and consciously as a Negro; but because all his poetry seems to be saturated with the rhythms and moods of Negro folk life. A true "people's poet" has their balladry in his veins; and to me many of these poems seem based on rhythms as seasoned as folk-songs and on moods as deep-seated as folk-ballads. Dunbar is supposed to have expressed the peasant heart of his people. But Dunbar was the showman of the Negro masses; here is their spokesman. The acid test is the entire absence of sentimentalism; the clean simplicity of speech, the deep terseness of mood. Taking these poems too much merely as the expressions of a personality, Carl Van Vechten in his debonair introduction wonders at what he calls "their deceptive air of spontaneous improvisation." The technique of folk song and dance are instinctively there, giving to the individual talent the bardic touch and power. Especially if Hughes should turn more and more to the colloquial experiences of common folk whom he so intimately knows and so deeply loves, we may say that the Negro masses have found a voice, and promise to add to their natural domain of music and dance the conquest of the province of poetry. Remember—I am not speaking of Negro poets, but of Negro poetry.

Poetry of a vitally characteristic racial flow and feeling then is the next step in our cultural development. Is it to be a jazz-product? The title poems and first section of *The Weary Blues* seem superficially to suggest it. But let us see:

> And far into the night he crooned that tune.
> The stars went out and so did the moon.

Or this:

> Sing your Blues song,
> Pretty baby.
> You want lovin'
> And you don't mean maybe.
>
> Jungle lover. . . .
> Night-black boy. . . .
> Two against the moon
> And the moon was joy.

Here, I suspect yet uncombined, are the two ingredients of the Negro poetry that will be truly and beautifully representative: the rhythm of the secular ballad but the imagery and diction of the Spiritual. Stranger opposites than these have fused to the fashioning of new beauty. Nor is this so doctrinaire a question as it seems, when considering a poet who has gone to the cabaret for some of his rhythms and to the Bible for others.

In the poems that are avowedly racial, Hughes has a distinctive note. Not only are these poems full of that passionate declaration and acceptance of race which is a general characteristic of present day Negro poets, but there is a mystic identification with the race experience which is, I think, instinctively deeper and broader than any of our poets has yet achieved.

"The Negro Speaks of Rivers" catches this note for us most unmistakably:

I've known rivers;
I've known rivers ancient as this world
   and older than the flow of human
   blood in human veins.

My soul has grown deep like the
   rivers.

I bathed in the Euphrates when dawns
   were young.
I built my hut near the Congo and it
   lulled me to sleep.
I looked upon the Nile and raised the
   pyramids above it.
I heard the singing of the Mississippi
   when Abe Lincoln went down to
   New Orleans, and I've seen its
   muddy bosom turn all golden in the
   sunset.

I've known rivers;
Ancient, dusky rivers.

My soul has grown deep like the
   rivers.

Remembering this as the basic substra-
tum of this poetry, we may discriminat-
ingly know to what to attribute the epic
surge underneath its lyric swing, the primitive fatalism back of its nonchalance, the
ancient force in its pert colloquialisms, the
tropic abandon and irresistableness of its
sorrow and laughter.

No matter how whimsical or gay the
poet may carry his overtones after this, or
how much of a bohemian or happy troubadour he may assume to be, we will always hear a deep, tragic undertone pulsing
in his verse. For the Negro experience
rightly sensed even in the moods of the
common folk is complex and paradoxical
like the blues which Hughes has pointed
out to be so characteristic, with their non-
chalant humor against a background of
tragedy; there is always a double mood,
mercurial to the artist's touch like an easily
improved tune. As our poet himself puts it:

   In one hand
   I hold tragedy

And in the other
Comedy,—
Masks for the soul.

Laugh with me.
You would laugh!
Weep with me,
Would you weep!

Tears are my laughter.
Laughter is my pain.
Cry at my grinning mouth,
If you will.
Laugh at my sorrow's reign.

James Rorty
"Off with the Black-Face!"
New Masses, I (October 1926), 26

Creatively, New York is not much better
than an ache and an appetite. It is the mon-
strous overgrown belly-plexus of a mon-
strous, overgrown competitive civilization.
It doesn't make anything except money,
and its greed is enormous. It must live, it
says, although of course it would be much
better to have an earthquake up-end the
whole idiot's carnival and let the healed
earth go quietly back to sumach and
timothy.

But New York must live, and its wants
are multitude. It wants girls—not the
worn and jaded local product, but fresh
and shapely beauties from the provinces;
Mr. Florenz Ziegfeld caters astutely to
this need. It wants rustics, eccentrics, lum-
berjacks, cowboys,—James Stevens, Will
Rogers. It wants art—and the writers and
painters and sculptors of a continent pour
their hoarded gains of life and desire,
thought and feeling, into the dry veins

of the metropolis. It wants pottery from Czecho-Slovakia, hooked rugs from New England, idols from Africa, cults from India. New York will pay, liberally, and in cash, the only currency it recognizes.

New York is liberal, sophisticated, enlightened. New York draws no color line. It *wants* the Negro. It wants his dark uncorrupted flesh. It wants his jazz, his songs. It wants his laughter—New York's lips are split with its own wise-cracks. Despite the subways, the elevated trains, the rushing traffic, there is a terrible silence in New York, a white, death-house silence that aches to be filled.

Well, for five or six years now, New York has had the Negro. The black tides have poured north into Harlem. The black jazzers and singers are stars on Broadway. The sharp Jews and Nordics who run the cabarets have found a new decoy—painted black—and how it does pay! The black poets are published by the best publishers. The Negro renaissance. Carl Van Vechten has told us all about it, and New York is amused.

But how about the Negro in all this? I, for one, am sick of black-face comedians, whether high-brow or low-brow. I am sick of the manumitted slave psychology and I should think the Negroes themselves would be twice as sick. I, for one, am waiting and hoping for a new titillation. I want the Negroes to stop entertaining the whites and begin to speak for themselves. I am waiting for a Negro poet to stand up and say "I—I am *not* amused."

Langston Hughes doesn't say anything like this. Nothing as bitter, nothing as masterful, nothing as savage. Why not? Why do the Negroes express so little beyond this black-white relation? Why don't they speak forthrightly as free, untamed *human beings*? Are Negroes really savages? One hopes so, but one doubts. So many of them look, talk and write like sophisticated, tamed, adapted, behavioristic white men,

and if that is what they want to be, it is nothing in the way of an aspiration.

Nevertheless, Hughes is a poet, with a curiously firm and supple style, half naive and half sophisticated, which is on the whole more convincing than anything which has yet appeared in Negro poetry. Here and there in the volume there are pieces startling in their effectiveness.

"WHEN SUE WEARS RED":

When Susanna Jones wears red
Her face is like an ancient cameo
Turned brown by the ages.
Come with a blast of trumpets, Jesus!
When Susanna Jones wears red
A queen from some time-dead
    Egyptian night
Walks once again.
Blow Trumpets, Jesus!
And the beauty of Susanna Jones in
    red
Burns in my heart a love-fire sharp
    like pain.
Sweet silver trumpets, Jesus!

There are others the effect of which is much less pleasing. For example:

All the tom-toms of the jungle beat in
    my blood.
And all the wild hot moons of the
    jungle shine in my soul.
I am afraid of this civilization—
    So hard,
So strong,
    So cold.

I hope and trust Hughes doesn't mean this. If he does, I'd rather have Garvey, who may not be intelligent, but who at least seems more angry than afraid.

Ruth Peiter
"Book Review and Latest Book Comment: Recent Poetry"
Toledo Times Sunday Magazine, 14 November 1926, p. 12

In Mr. Hughes we have a young poet, passionate, keenly sensitive to beauty and possessed of unfaltering musical sense. He belongs to that new group of Negro intellectuals growing up in the Harlem district of New York City, and his poetry expresses the strange medley of emotions, memories, hopes and fears of his race in modern America.

R. E. Cureton
"The Weary Blues"
Oracle, 5 (December[?] 1926), [?]

About a year ago Alfred A. Knopf published *The Weary Blues,* a book of poems by Langston Hughes, and the fame and popularity of this young and versatile poet was firmly established. Prior to this publication of his first book of poems, Hughes had become well known in the literary world, many of his poems having appeared in the leading magazines, both white and colored.

The Weary Blues is a book of poems expressing the manifold moods of a wanderer, a strange soul that touches here and there the veil of life and makes futile efforts to break through. The volume is divided into seven parts, each division has a title-poem, and those that follow have much of the same line of thought. In the first part the poet lifts the veil of Harlem, and shows us snatches of cabaret life, rhythmic dancers, jazz and blues. "Dream Variations"—the title of the second part—are poems of strange muses on life, longings; sensitive reactions to an environment that is cold, yet sometimes colorful and passionate. But in the "Negro Speaks of Rivers," the reader finds the poet's reactions to the grim realities of life, especially as it pertains to the Negro race. The "Jester" and "As I Grow Older" are excellent examples. Then in the "Black Pierrot" little black girls are sung about in the most delicate and musical verse—verses you will read over and over again. "The Waterfront Streets"—the title of the fifth part—contains poems of the sea and sailors. And this reminds me that one of the poems among this group, The "Young Sailor," was reprinted in a prominent Southern daily. In the "Shadows of the Sun," the poet has written in delicate lines about women in foreign lands; sad, decayed women, women of the world. And here, too, the poet speaks of death in the "Suicide's Note." Again, poems of a crying race greet us at the close of the volume.

H. L. Danson
"Black Blues"
Brooklyn Eagle, Book Section, 1 May 1927, p. 18

Langston Hughes has been a truck farmer, a flower boy, a sailor, a cook, a waiter and a bus boy. It is probable that he has been other things, too. But were he this or were he that, Langston Hughes is a poet, and a genuine one. *The Weary Blues* is first hand proof, and *The Weary Blues* is Langston Hughes' first volume of verse.

I have read the title poem a number of times—when it beat Countee Cullen's entry for the first prize offered by *Opportunity,* when it was reprinted in various publications, and last in volume form. It has never failed to thrill. His jazz poems are imbued with the true and earnest spirit of actual syncopation. He gets the tones and effects accurately, and it is no easy matter to get them well.

But Langston Hughes is not only at home in jazz. Other of his poems ("Suicide's Note," "Young Sailor," "Pierrot," "Cross," etc.) reveal the poignance and the tenderness of their author. Hughes has always something strong to say or sing. He is terse, keen, interpretive and stark. Invariably he is plaintive; a melancholy note is ever present in his work. Occasionally his poetry is slightly feeble. It is somewhat strange to remark that his love poems are inferior to the rather objective verses.

Checklist of Additional Reviews

"*The Weary Blues,*" *Afro-American,* 23 January 1926, p. 3.
"Youth Speaks," *Open Shelf,* April 1926, pp. 45–6.
Elizabeth Shepley Sergeant, "The New Negro," *New Republic,* 46 (12 May 1926), 371–2.
"Literature," *Booklist,* 22 (July 1926), 410.

FINE CLOTHES TO THE JEW

V. F. Calverton
"Critical Cruisings: Negro Poetry"
New Leader, 29 January 1927, p. 10

. . . In Hughes' latest volume, *Fine Clothes to the Jew,* it is the Blues motif that prevails. The first eight and the last nine poems in the book are patterned precisely after the manner and form of the original folksong Blues. The poetic pattern of the Blues is interesting because of its distant resemblance to the form of some of the old English ballads. The diction is simple, almost primitive; the metaphors, though few, are unpedantic and uninvolved; incremental repetition, one long line repeating itself in each stanza, is also an arresting element in the technique. The habit of having the third line rhyme with the first also adds charm to the form. As to their spirit, Hughes' own comment is instructive: while "the mood of the Blues is almost always despondency, when they are sung people laugh."

The Weary Blues, Hughes' first book of poems, had attracted interest by its oddness rather than simplicity. *The Weary Blues* was a much more ambitious and pretentious volume than is *Fine Clothes to the Jew.* With its far-flung and often fantastic metaphors, the former collection failed to attain the striking simplicity of the latter. In *Fine Clothes to the Jew,* Hughes, in places, has almost approximated the directness and intimacy of sentiment, the unpracticed phrase and rhythm, of such Blues as "The Awful Moanin' Blues," "The Chicago-Bound Blues," or "The Mason-Dixie Blues." This is a distinct achievement. Although not equal in beauty, it is well-nigh equal in degree of approximation to the Coleridge and Longfellow imitations of the old ballads.

Hughes is still an unfinished poet. He is still young, still fumbling for forms that will give stability and vigor to his verse. In the "Blues" he has found an interesting medium. The scope is small, unfortunately, and what he will do when he starts off on a new tangent still remains problematical. In *Fine Clothes to the Jew,* however, he has undoubtedly made an advance— and in a genre in which he is competent.

These fragments from his poem "Mulatto" are illustrative not of the Blues, but of a spirit that at times gives his poetry something of the verve and defiance that may ultimately be transmitted into that exquisite challenge of revolutionary art. . . .

O.C.E.
"Light Stuff"
Philadelphia Tribune, 5 February 1927, p. 16

We have been asked to review Langston Hughes' "new book of poems," *Fine Clothes to the Jew.* We have read the book from cover to cover and, aside from an odd, but attractive jacket, we were unable to find anything of merit. Our impression is that Hughes lacks a certain necessary sense of refinement. Of course, we may be wrong, as we very seldom are, but the book leaves a very bad taste in the mouth. We don't like to believe that Mr. Hughes had had a bad night, or several of them, before writing some of the decidedly free verse he dignifies with the title of poems.

Eustace Gay
"Facts and Fancies"
Philadelphia Tribune,
5 February 1927, p. 16

[. . .]

The exploitation of the Negro still continues. Everybody knows that he is exploited in the southern section of this land of the free and home of the brave. Up North, however, within the past three or four years there has been set in motion a method of exploitation that is not so apparent on the surface. This exploitation has its center in New York City.

It is the exploitation of the Negro in literature. A few white authors, using the Negro as their subject are reaping a golden harvest by writing such books as *Tom-Toms, Porgy, God's Stepchildren,* and *Nigger Heaven.* Every once in a while, as evidence of this Negro Literary Renaissance, one of a selected group of Negro writers publishes a book of poems (ought to be poorems), which is supposed to be representative of Negro progress in the literary art.

The idea that the popularity of the Negro as a literary theme furnishes a sly way for a favored few to cash in on a much neglected stratum of American society, meanwhile having an occasional book by a Negro author "come off the press," flashed across my mind when I read Langston Hughes' new book of poems *Fine Clothes to the Jew.*

These poems are supposed for the most part to interpret the more primitive types of American Negro, the bell boys, the cabaret girls, the migratory workers, the singers of blues and Spirituals, and the makers of folk-songs. They are intended to express "the joy and pathos, the beauty and ugliness, of their lives."

The author has succeeded in expressing the "ugliness" of Negro life. No doubt about that. It's been a long day since I have read anything "uglier."

They may be true to life. Some of them are. Let us take for granted that they all are. What I am anxious to know is this: "Is this the best this young author can do?"

The Weary Blues made me tired, and *Fine Clothes to the Jew* disgusts me.

It may be, however, that my ignorance of "literary standards" and of what constitutes poetry is responsible for this mental reaction on my part.

The book, significantly enough, is dedicated to one of the "band of brothers," Carl Van Vechten.

Most of the verses are "free." All of them are blank. There is no meter, unless it is a gas meter.

And it does not matter to me whether every poem in the book is true to life. Why should it be paraded before the American public by a Negro author as being typical or representative of the Negro? Bad enough to have white authors holding up our imperfections to public gaze. Our aim ought to be to present to the general public, already misinformed both by well-meaning and malicious writers, our higher aims and aspirations, and our better selves.

I have no objection to the truth, in art or literature, but let us have some books during this so-called Renaissance dealing with something else besides the cabaret hounds and "primitive types of American Negro."

Dewey R. Jones
"Songs of the Lowly"
Chicago Defender, part 2,
5 February 1927, [p. 1]

When hard luck overtakes you
   Nothin' for you to do.
When hard luck overtakes you
   Nothin' for you to do.
Gather up you' fine clothes
An' sell 'em to the Jew.

And thus the second book of poems by this young singer and student makes its bow. Not unlike *The Weary Blues* in many of its passages, *Fine Clothes* is more subtle, if possible, therefore more intriguing than his first book, printed early last year and now said to be in its third edition.

Fine Clothes to the Jew is a combination of typical chain-gang chants, blues songs heard all over the South today and in the large cities of the North since the war, "down home" Baptist church services, and plaints of the person lowest down everywhere. There are also scattered among these reproductions the author's own plaintive note against conditions as he finds them.

When *The Weary Blues* made its curtsy to America, I expressed the belief that it heralded the approach of the real poet of the Race. *Fine Clothes to the Jew* only accentuates that belief. We have needed someone to interpret the emotions—the inner feelings—the dreams, even, of the great masses of us who are so far down in the scale of things. Dunbar treated of the same subjects as they applied in his day. And with his passing there was no one to take up the songs an ignorant "black gal"

sings down on Rampart St., for instance. There was no one who dared go beneath the surface of things and express in poetry the little witticisms of the convict—the gambler—the idler, or the "pimp." White men tried it and failed, and young poets of our Race studiously eschewed the subject. The reason, presumably the fear of antagonizing the white man who must print, and who must read the book, if it is to pay for itself.

Langston Hughes, with master strokes and fearlessness, rips into the problem and lays it bare for all the world to see. The section of *Fine Clothes* devoted to the blues I passed over with almost cursory attention. I know the blues fairly well, having heard them in their various ramifications practically all my life. My experience is that of the average person of my Race. To white readers of the book, however, I venture to say that this section and that devoted to "hallelujahs" will bring real revelations and even thrills. For their sakes I am glad Langston Hughes included them.

But for me and for others of my Race there is real enjoyment—a sort of person pride in those songs from Georgia Roads, the Railroad Avenue group and the Beale Street love. Perhaps no work in the entire book gives a clearer impression of the depth of feeling Mr. Hughes has on his subject than the sketch of "Ruby Brown." Here he gives vent to a feeling of long-suppressed (it seems), deep-burning, but calm resentment at conditions faced by young women of our Race in every small southern community today.

She was young and beautiful,
And golden like the sunshine,
That warmed her body,
And because she was Colored
Mayville had no place to offer her,
Nor fuel for the clean flame of joy
That tried to burn within her soul.

Well, Miss Ruby sits down one day and thinks out her problem, the results of which land her in a bordello where she is the toast of white men who

> Pay more money to her now
> Than they ever did before,
> When she worked in their kitchens.

Ruby's case is typical. But for that matter, so are most of the other cases mentioned by Langston Hughes in *Fine Clothes*. He has the faculty of transporting you into the midst of those about whom he is discoursing—you see them in their rollicking "Saturday Night" at a "drag," and you dance along with the rest—or you stand on the bank of the Mississippi river with the "Ruined Gal" and sympathize with her even when she says:

> Damn ma black old mammy's soul!
> For ever havin' a daughter.

What is more true to our lives than Mr. Hughes' "Feet of Jesus"? Who hasn't sat in one of our primitive churches where worshipers give full play to their emotions, and has not heard:

> At de feet o' Jesus,
> Sorrow like a sea.
> Lordy, let yo' mercy
> Come driftin' down on me.
>
> At de feet o' Jesus,
> At yo' feet I stand.
> O, ma little Jesus,
> Please reach out yo' hand.

Or this "prayer":

> I ask you this:
> Which way to go?
> I ask you this:
> Which sin to bear?
> Which crown to put
> Upon my hair?
> I do not know,
> Lord God,
> I do not know.

Then comes what I consider the boldest yet the most effective bit in the entire collection. "Mulatto."

> I am your son, white man!
> Georgia dusk
> And the turpentine woods.
> One of the pillars of the temple fell.
>
> You are my son!
> Like hell!

I wish I could quote the entire poem, but of course I can't. Mr. Hughes caught the very heart of the situation in that plaintive note of the "little yellow bastard boy" crying out in desperation, pointing an accusing finger at the slinking, shrinking, yet domineering thing that gave him being. I am your son, white man.

Commenting on his book in a letter to me, Mr. Hughes says: "It's harder and more cynical than my first, and it's limited to an interpretation of the so-called 'lower classes,' the ones to whom life is least kind. I try to catch the hurt of their lives, the monotony of their 'jobs,' and the veiled weariness of their songs. They are the people I know best."

And they are the people we all know best, however much we seek to get away from them and submerge them under a blanket of aloofness. I am glad for *Fine Clothes* (in spite of its title) because I know it will be read by many, many white persons who can't help feel the real seriousness of Mr. Hughes' purpose, and who, consequently, will be led to wonder if, after all, these people, whom they are wont to despise, do think, dream, fight and love as the rest of them do. They may be led to look a little more tolerantly upon those who prepare their foods for them—even those who clean their "spittoons" and shine their shoes.

"Negro Poet Sings of Life in Big Cities"
Washington Post, 6 February 1927, p. 5F

In *Fine Clothes to the Jew* by Langston Hughes, there is ample evidence that this young Negro, who formerly worked as a "busboy" is in a fair way to assume the laurels of Paul Laurence Dunbar as the poet laureate of his race.

The poetic ability of Langston Hughes has strengthened and increased since the publication of his first book, which received favorable notice from the critics. For his present volume young Hughes has gone for material to the more primitive types of American Negro, the bellboys, the cabaret girls, the migratory workers, the singers of blues and spirituals and the makers of folk songs. The plantation Negro of yesterday is no more, and in his place has come the city worker, the struggler in the industrial maelstrom of modern life and inhabitant of the Harlems of American cities.

In the poems of Hughes are painted, with swift, deft touches the joy, the pathos, the beauty and the ugliness in the lives of present members of his race. That he understands his own people is apparent from the first word to the last in this book. With the insight of the real poet the secrets of human nature are as an open book to him. The emotional stress of some of the poems is marked; and behind others are the convictions of a thinker, of one who has pondered over the problems of his fellows and come to definite conclusions about them.

Fame touched Hughes early in his career. He is only 25 years old now and a native of Joplin Mo., but he has been a soldier of fortune in many countries and many cities in his short life. His chance in the world of poesy came in 1925, when he won first prize in the contest conducted by the *Opportunity* magazine for the best Negro poem of the year. His first book, *The Weary Blues,* was published in January, 1926, and he has subsequently been enrolled as a student at Lincoln University.

Here is a vivid picture in a few lines of a Crap Game:

Lemme roll 'em, boy.
I got ma tail curled!
If a seven don't come
'Leven ain't far away.
An if I craps,
Dark baby,
Trouble don't last all the time.
Hit 'em, bones.

The religious fervor of his race adorns the little group of modern spirituals appearing under the title of "Glory Hallelujah!" Simplicity of faith is there and rare tenderness, too. For instance, take the two stanzas entitled "Feet o' Jesus!"
[. . .]
His race as he sees it is poetically set forth in "Laughers."

Dream singers,
Story tellers,
Dancers.
Loud laughers in the hands of fate—
My people.

[. . .]

The sex element is portrayed in the raw in several of the poems, but withal it is a vision of a people struggling up to the light, told in simple but powerful verse by one of their own and therefore with more truth and understanding.

Walter F. White
"The Growth of a Poet"
New York World, 6 February 1927, p. 9M; also in *New York Herald Tribune* and *New York Post*

It is probable that most of the sophisticated and near-sophisticated have by now heard Bessie or Clara Smith sing either in the flesh or on phonograph records one or more of the infinite number of songs known as "blues." If the prospective reader of Langston Hughes' *Fine Clothes to the Jew* or his earlier *The Weary Blues* has not heard at least one of these songs as sung by a Negro singer, I urgently recommend that he do so before tackling the poems. For the blues are strictly limited both as to poetic pattern and meaning. As the name implies, blues are sung as plaintive expressions of utter despondency. Almost always there is expressed some idea of suicide through drowning or "laying ma head on de railroad track." Inevitably the repetition of a single emotion in time grows monotonous and often triteness cannot be avoided because there are few changes to be rung on the blue theme. The human voice of a Bessie Smith is needed to transmute and vary the subtle overtones and in that manner give the needed variety.

So, too, is the form rigidly fixed, one line repeated and a third line to rhyme with the first two. In a paragraph Mr. Hughes explains that "sometimes the second line in repetition is slightly changed and sometimes, but very seldom, it is omitted. The mood of the blues is almost always despondency, but when they are sung people

laugh." Frequently a beautiful bit of imagery darts through one of these songs or a poignant catching up of a profound emotion in a single line. Take, for example, two stanzas of Mr. Hughes' "Homesick Blues," in which both of these gifts are seen:

De railroad bridge's
A sad song in de air.
De railroad bridge's
A sad song in de air.
Ever time de trains pass
I wants to go somewhere.

Homesick blues, Lawd,
'S a terrible thing to have,
Homesickness blues is
A terrible thing to have.
To keep from cryin'
I opens ma mouth and laughs.

It may be questioned, however, how much further blues can be utilized as poetry because of its rigid limitations. Out of the blues form it is possible and probable that a more inclusive poetic form may develop, but that form would not be blues as the term is now interpreted. It will be interesting to watch these changes as they are developed by Mr. Hughes and others who may follow him in the growth of either a more universal medium of expression or a broadening of the scope of the moods themselves. Mr. Hughes' friends and admirers may perhaps have some apprehension, but too diligent working of this vein may cramp him or lessen the fine, flowing, ecstatic sense of rhythm which he so undoubtedly possesses.

For he has seen the immense store of material for poetry which is in the life of the Negro. When he leaves the more confining form of the blues Mr. Hughes evokes magnificently stirring emotions from the life of Negro porters and prostitutes and others of humble estate. For example, take the last ten lines of this poem, "Brass Spittoons":

Hey, boy!
A bright bowl of brass is beautiful to
   the Lord.
Bright polished brass like the cymbals
Of King David's dancers,
Like the wine cups of Solomon.
Hey, boy!
A clean spittoon on the altar of the
   Lord,
A clean, bright spittoon all newly
   polished—
At least I can offer that.
Com' mere, boy!

I would like to quote several other poems
and give in Mr. Hughes' own words the
fine flavor of his new book—poems like
"Ruby Brown," "Porter," "Prayer Meeting," "Magnolia Flowers," "Song for a
Dark Girl," "Laughers," or two or three
others equally fine. But that would be fair
neither to Mr. Hughes nor his publisher,
for then there would be some who would
not buy the book. It is a book that should
be bought and one that will grow upon
its readers in its evocation of beauty and
rhythm and color and warmth. And if the
reader has heard Clara or Mamie Smith
croon and moan the blues, the first eight
and the last nine poems in *Fine Clothes to
the Jew* won't seem as monotonous as they
perhaps might otherwise be judged.

"Poetry and Near-Poetry, Sophisticated and Otherwise"
New York Sun, 7 February 1927, p. 20

As Spengler began telling us last year, cultures have their youth of lyricism and their
culmination in disillusioned intellectuality.

And as if to illustrate the idea Mr. Knopf
offers two books of poems by two Southern men, one of whom versifies the sheer
emotionality of Negro culture and the
other the memoried sophisticated culture
of the white. They represent two inheritances—that of the prodigal who lives ri-
otously, but lives nevertheless, and that of
the elder brother who lives also, but in a
more selective, cold-blooded fashion.

John Crowe Ransom in his volume *Two
Gentlemen in Bonds* has let learning and
self-distrust drive his poetry to subtleties,
violences, grotesqueness and even precios-
ity. . . . Langston Hughes, on the other
hand, in *Fine Clothes for the Jew* comes
free, unencumbered by literary inheritances, but charged with the distillations
from a dark and unmeasured, unexpressed sea of feeling.

Here are some of Mr. Ransom's over-
civilized lines: . . .

The contrasts between the excellences
of Mr. Hughes's poetry and of Mr. Ransom's are to their mutual advantage. . . .

W[illiam] M. K[elley]
"Langston Hughes: The Sewer Dweller"
New York Amsterdam News, 9 February 1927, [p. 22]

About 100 pages of trash, that is about all
we can say of *Fine Clothes to the Jew*, by
Langston Hughes. It is not even the kind
of trash made by an accumulation of excel-
sior or straw or waste paper. Instead, it
reeks of the gutter and sewer.

After reading it one feels that he has
just passed through one of those Parisian

sewers so well described by Victor Hugo in *Les Miserables*. True, on the way one passes openings where a little light and fresh air are permitted to penetrate the underground passage, such as when one reads the nine poems grouped under the chapter heading Glory Hallelujah, and "Dressed Up" in the group, Beale Street Love, which shows that Mr. Hughes has both imagination and talent.

> I had ma clothes cleaned
> Just like new.
> I put 'em on but
> I still feels blue.
>
> I bought a new hat,
> Sho is fine,
> But I wish I had back that
> Old gal o' mine.
>
> I got new shoes.—
> They don't hurt ma feet,
> But I ain't got nobody
> for to call me sweet.

It is true that even the sewer is necessary, but we do not understand why so promising a poet as Hughes prefers to linger there and write the kind of dribble that characterizes his *Weary Blues* and the present volume.

We do not maintain that all poetry should be uplifting, or that it should deal exclusively with subjects foreign to everyday existence, but we do not believe that it should debase merely for the sake of debasing—to satisfy the morbid tendencies of a jazz-crazed world—as is done in "Red Silk Stockings."

> Put on yu' red silk stockings,
> Black gal.
> Go out an' let de white boys
> Look at yo' legs.
>
> Ain't nothin' to do for you, no-how,
> Round this town,—
> You's too pretty.
> Put on yo' red silk stockings, gal.

> An' tomorrow's chile'll
> Be a high yaller.
>
> Go out an' let de white boys
> Look at yo' legs.

If poetry of this type is the only kind white publishers will accept, it may be that the world—both the black and the white world—would be just as well off without it.

Orrin C. Evans "Modern Muse Presents New Book of Poems" *Philadelphia Tribune*, 12 February 1927, p. 9

Champions of Langston Hughes as a poet with possibilities will doubtless be disappointed in his new book of poems, *Fine Clothes to the Jew*, published by Alfred A. Knopf. While Mr. Hughes obviously has the "fine qualities of force, passion, directness and sensitive perception," as *The Independent* stated in its review of his preceding book of poems, *The Weary Blues*, he undoubtedly lacks the finer quality of delicacy.

The present volume of poems is somewhat choked with decidedly free verse that has no particular merit nor appeal. Poetic form seems to be irrevocably lost in an attempt to cram as much suggestiveness into the eighty-nine page book as possible.

Aside from his apparent obsession for the more degenerate element as suitable material, his stylistic enigmas contribute much to the lack of appeal. For instance:

> Starter!
> Her face is pale
> In the doorway light.
> Her lips blood red

and her skin blue white.
Taxi!
I'm tired.
O, God, please!
The river and the moon hold
     memories.
Cornets play.
Dancers whirl.
Death, be kind
What was the cover charge, kid?
To a little drowned girl.

It is highly likely, however, that Mr. Hughes is merely following the line of least resistance in the exploitation of the Negro, as are Van Vechten, DuBose Heyward and Vandercook. Art seems to be subsidized in an attempt to snatch the Negro, unblushingly set forth certain of the least desirable characteristics of the race and market it as literature and art.

As a matter of fact, certain sections of the book make interesting light reading. There are two or three of the poems that seem to have had possibilities in them, but there is evidence of haste with the resultant lack of any poetic form. One can go through the book from cover to cover at one sitting—slightly over one hour.

There is in "Mammy" something that attracts the reader's attention. It too lacks meter, but there is a subtle note of despondency that awakens a sympathetic chord. Then too, "Prayer" has a degree of merit. . . .

The poems are, in brief, a study in the perversions of the Negro, and he seems to cast the onus upon the entire race, rather than upon circumstances and environment. The opposite race is bound to gain an entirely mistaken and satisfactory (to them) conception of the Negro.

The jacket is artistically attractive—of the impressionistic sort—by Aaron Douglass. The cover, in harmoniously blending pastel shades, seems incongruous when thought of in connection with the poems.

The book is dedicated to Carl Van Vechten and contains a note on blues which is interesting and enlightening.

It's all in the point of view, however. There will probably be many who will acclaim this new book of poems as of a lasting nature, but we feel that in the course of a few years *Fine Clothes to the Jew* will have been forgotten.

"Langs. Hughes' Newest Book of Blues"
Baltimore Afro-American, 12 February 1927, p. 12

If you're a stranger to jazz and an enemy of realism as it applies to sex, you'll not like Langston Hughes' new book of poems.

The author of the *Weary Blues*, comes back to book lovers this month with *Fine Clothes to the Jew*, dedicated to Carl Van Vechten, author of *Nigger Heaven*, and published by Alfred A Knopf.

The volume contains a number of new poems in addition to those published in current magazines of 1926, including *Poetry, Vanity Fair, The Crisis, The Messenger, New Republic, Fire,* and the *New York Herald Tribune*.

The blues, jazz and spirituals tumble over each other in Mr. Hughes' new book. Here's a spiritual:

Fire
Fire, Soul!
Fire gonna burn ma soul
I ain't been good,
I ain't been clean
I been stinkin' low down, mean.
Fire,
Fire, Lord!
Fire gonna burn ma soul
I been stealin'

Been tellin' lies,
Had more women
Than Pharaoh had wives.
Fire,
Fire, Lord!
Fire gonna burn ma soul
I means Fire, Lord,
Fire gonna burn ma soul.

"Hard Luck" is the title of the poem which gives the volume its name—"Fine Clothes to the Jew." Note the "poetic pattern" of the following stanza which, as Mr. Hughes remarks, contains a long line repeated and a third line to rhyme with the first two:

When hard luck overtakes you
Nothin' for you to do
When hard luck overtakes you
Gather up yo' fine clothes
An' sell 'em to de Jew.

Then there's the "Ballad of Gin Mary."

Old Judge says you's a drunkard
Fact is you worries me
Gwine give you eighteen months
So licker'll let you be.

Here's a bit of introspection dedicated to the porter, polite always with "yes sir," on his tongue continually, to whom life is just one big mountain of "yes sirs."

I must say
Yes, sir,
To you all the time
Yes, sir!
Yes, sir
All my days
Climbing up a great big mountain
Of yes, sirs.

Here's one to the black working girl who dresses her man, but can't keep him and imagines he prefers girls of lighter hue.

I dressed up Albert Johnson
I bought him suits of clothes

As soon as he got out de barrel
Then out ma door he goes.

Another dark girl whose lover was lynched by hanging to the cross-roads tree is made to say:

Way down south in Dixie
Bruised body high in air,
I asked the Lord Jesus
What was the use of prayer.

Love is real to Langston Hughes. It's something that's always accompanied by jazz or blues or liquor and as real and objective as anything in life. Here's the "Young Gal's Blues":

When love is gone what
Can a young gal do?
When love is gone, O
What can a young gal do?
Keep on alovin' one daddy
Cause I don't want to be blue.

[. . .]

Joseph Moncure March "Verse" *New York Evening Post Literary Review*, 12 February 1927, p. 4

There is, as every one knows and most persons admit, an American vogue for The Negro in Art. The "sophisticated" but not always discriminating enthusiasm accompanying this vogue is already beginning to cloud those intrinsic values of Negro work—its naivete and its total lack of self-consciousness. Once the Negro artists are made thoroughly aware of values in their work, some of which do, some which do not, exist, the type of work they produce will become dry. It may resolve into a different product, but there will be a loss: they are at present practically the only unspoiled artists among us.

Anxiety lest the work of Langston Hughes be shortly affected by such self-consciousness makes me advise reading his verse now. It is quite limited, but there is a purity of quality about most of it that cannot be equaled by the studied simplicity of the sophisticated. It is vigorous, spontaneous and so unaffected that the simplest adornment of emotion and thought stands out vividly.

[. . .]

As a preface note says, the "Blues" have a strict poetic pattern; they are made of one long line repeated and a third line to rhyme with the first two. Halving the lines properly, as done above, gives a slight emphasis to the syncopation. Mr. Hughes's gift of rhythm and his easy but accurate syncopation may well make many poets envious.

But occasionally in the book come things like this:

SPORT

Life
For him
Must be
The shivering of
A great drum
Beaten with swift sticks
Then at the closing hour
The lights go out
And there is no music at all
And death becomes
An empty cabaret
And eternity an unblown saxophone
And yesterday
A glass of gin
Drunk long
Ago.

Here Mr. Hughes's distinction is suddenly lost. There is no rhythmic pattern,

half the figures of speech are strained and unconvincing, and the word usage is not in any way peculiarly personal. Mr. Hughes has attempted to speak in an idiom not his own, and the result is flat failure.

Contrast it with the start of the poem on the opposite page:

SATURDAY NIGHT

A glass o' whisky
    An' a glass o' gin:
Strut, Mr. Charlie,
    Till de dawn comes in.

Pawn yo' gold watch
    An' diamond ring
Git a quart o' licker
    Let's shake dat thing!

Skee-de-dad! De-dad!
    Doo-doo-doo!
Won't be nothin' left
    When de worms git through
An' you's a long time
    Dead
When you is
    Dead, too.

Alongside this vigorous mixture of rhythm, gayety and simple philosophy, "Sport" seems like a badly made wax lily. It will be too bad if Mr. Hughes takes to writing more things like "Sport" and fewer like "Saturday Night."

"A New Book of Poems by Langston Hughes"
New York Age, 12 February 1927, p. 4

Fine Clothes to the Jew is the title of a new book of poems by Langston Hughes, the author of *The Weary Blues*. The volume of some ninety pages is dedicated to Carl Van

Vechten, and the poems reflect the author's life of wide rambling and sympathetic observation. Born in Joplin, Missouri, in 1902, Mr. Hughes has lived in many American cities and in Mexico. He studied at Columbia University, which he left for a series of jobs, ranging from truck farming to working on an old ship on the Hudson River. His travels on his own, working his way, have carried him through Europe and to parts of West Africa. Later he lived in Washington, and he is now a student at Lincoln University. His first book, *The Weary Blues,* was published by Alfred A. Knopf in 1926, he having won the first prize for poetry in the *Opportunity Magazine* contest the year previous. Some of his poems have been accepted by the *Crisis, Poetry, Vanity Fair,* the *New Republic* and other magazines.

The poem which gives its name to the present volume is one of a group written after the manner of the Negro folk songs known as the "Blues." A note tells us that the Blues, unlike the Spirituals, have a strict poetic pattern: one long line repeated and a third line to rhyme with the first two. Sometimes the second line in repetition is slightly changed and sometimes, but very seldom omitted. The mood of the Blues is despondency. We give the first verse of *Fine Clothes to the Jew* as an example:

When hard luck overtakes you
Nothin' for you to do
When hard luck overtakes you
Nothin' for you to do
Gather up yo' fine clothes
An' sell 'em to de Jew.

In the group beginning with "Railroad Avenue" we have vivid pictures of lowly life including "The New Cabaret Girl" and "Elevator Boy." Under "Glory, Hallelujah" are given shouting hymns which typify the fervor of a religious revival.

One of the most touching of these, entitled "Feet o' Jesus," runs as follows. . . .

"Beale Street Love" introduces a strain of tragic woe, the incident to the untoward working of the tender passion, while "From the Georgia Roads" presents striking visions of Southern life, the most poignant of which is "Mulatto." The joy and pathos, the beauty and the ugliness of the more primitive types of the American Negro find true poetic expression in these poems.

Mary White Ovington "Book Chat" *Boston Chronicle,* 12 February 1927, [p. ?]

[. . .]

Langston Hughes has chosen a striking title for his second book of poems. It is an achievement to have a publisher bring out, unaided, a volume of verse, and to have him bring out a second is phenomenal. Those who buy verse in America could all be lodged in one of New York's towering hotels and leave plenty of space for the poets who came for shelter of a stormy night. To reach this small group and to have them ask for more is something to be commented upon.

Fine Clothes to the Jew gives a haunting picture of Negro life. No work of fiction that we have shows so naturally and with such sympathy the unsophisticated colored folk as they move through their city streets, into their homes and cabarets, or take to the open road. The girl whose man has left her, the boy trudging up from Mississippi town, these touch our hearts. And yet we are supposed to laugh at them. What is a Blues for but laughter, the laughter that is deeper than tears?

[. . .]

Mr. Hughes' touch has seemed surest when he has written in the "Blues" form, but in this volume his religious group, "Glory, Hallelujah" he calls them, are equally good. They recall the spirituals, but they have their own distinct form. . . .

There are the songs of the city, "Railroad Avenue," "Beale Street," and a group "From the Georgia Roads." They all have a strain of sorrow. How is it that the gay, unconcerned side of Negro life never slips into the verse of our young colored poets? What Dunbar saw still exists. It would be a comfort if fine clothes did not always go to the Jew, or if when safe on their owner, and worn with a flair, the right girl were around to see them. But no, as Bert Williams used to sing: "There's always something wrong."

Well, it is easier to sing of sorrow than of joy. And perhaps in this verse, we should see the joy beneath the sorrow. We can say, with the joy the sorrow. We can say with the boy in the Crap Game:

An' if I craps,
Dark baby,
Trouble
Don't last all de time.
Hit 'em, bones!

J. A. Rogers
"Langston Hughes' Book of Poems 'Trash': Noted Race Critic Attacks Pandering to White Man's Twisted Notion of What Race Authors Would Write"
Pittsburgh Courier, section 2, 12 February 1927, p. 4

The fittest compliment I can pay this latest work by Langston Hughes is to say that it is, on the whole, about as fine a collection of piffling trash as is to be found under the covers of any book. If *The Weary Blues* made readers of a loftier turn of mind weary, this will make them positively sick.

For instance, this so-called poem, the first in the book:

"HEY"

Sun's a settin'
This is what I'm gonna sing:
Sun's a settin'
This is what I'm gonna sing:
I feels de blues a comin',
Wonder what de blues'll bring.

If this is poetry, then verily Shakespeare, Keats, Poe, Dunbar, McKay, were Ainus or Australian Bushmen. But, of course, this book, like *The Weary Blues,* is designed for white readers, with their preconceived notions about Negroes.

[. . .]

And the pity of it is that Mr. Hughes is capable of producing other than such degenerate stuff as this. He is capable of finer, loftier expression. The fact that he writes of Negroes in the humbler walks of life has nothing to do with it. With Mr. Hughes, it is indeed a case of "Fine Clothes to the Jew"; of selling his best clothes to the ragman.

Nor must the blame for this prostitution of talent be laid wholly on Mr. Hughes. The Negro group is even more to blame in that it has made absolutely no provision for its writers, expecting the Nordic to do it. Poets, like ladies, must live, and if they are to get along they must put their feet under the white man's kitchen table or starve. And when one sits to another's table, he can't very well dictate the dishes.

What is aimed at in America is the social degradation of the Negro to a stage where his labor can be had in the cheapest market. The rage over books like this and the vogue of the spirituals among white people is but a red herring drawn across the trail. When it comes to books or articles that vitally affect the question, then these same folk will be found, generally, to be the rankest kind of conservatives. Recently George S. Schuyler sent some of his Southern snapshots to the *New Masses,* a Communist paper, and after the editor had finished trimming it, it looked as if the Imperial Wizard, bitterest foe of the Communists, had been through it, instead.

This book, while it has some modicum of truth and beauty, is plainly an attempt to exploit the jazzy, degenerate, infantile and silly vogue inspired by the success of such plays as *Lulu Belle.* It has 89 pages, and it is safe to say that the matter in the whole could be held in sixteen pages.

Fine Clothes to the Jew is unworthy both of Mr. Hughes and Messrs. Knopf, the publishers. I would very much rather have said a good word for both, especially as Knopf is publisher of *The Fire in the Flint.* But a reviewer owes a duty both to himself and his readers, for, in proportion as one praises the bad, he detracts from the good. We have had enough of Mr. Hughes

in this vein—too much in fact—and the Negro public, if it will not help Mr. Hughes to publish his worthy poems, can do at least this: It can discourage this marketing of such books, books that help but to tighten the chains of social degradation.

George S. Schuyler "Views and Reviews" *Pittsburgh Courier,* section 2, 12 February 1927, p. 8

Langston Hughes' latest book, *Fine Clothes to the Jew,* will doubtless be received by Negro reviewers with as great a shower of bricks as Van Vechten's *Nigger Heaven.* From the technical viewpoint, I think such a reception would be justified. Labeled as "A New Book of Poems," the reader will find a large number that it is difficult to place under that head. Much of the verse is both too free and too blank to suit yours truly.

But Hughes must be given credit for knowing the Negro proletarian. It is precisely because he knows this type of Negro and portrays him that the Negro bourgeoisie, reviewers and readers, will fall on him like a ton of brick. I notice the tendency among Negroes (and whites, too) to become very indignant over such portrayals. The truer these pictures are, the louder the good folks yelp. In his latest book of poems, Mr. Hughes is revealing the soul of the Negro slum proletariat and the lowly Negro worker. I think he knows them very well, but I feel quite sure that what he has said could on the whole be said much more beautifully.

Du Bose Heyward
"Sing a Soothin' Song"
New York Herald Tribune Books, 20 February 1927, p. 5

When Langston Hughes published his first volume less than a year ago under the title of *The Weary Blues,* he sounded a new note in contemporary American poetry. Like practically all first books of lyric poetry, the quality was uneven. At its worst it was interesting, because it was spontaneous and unaffected. At its best the poems contained flashes of passionate lyrical beauty that will probably stand among the finest examples of the author's work. This irregularity of quality is to be expected in a volume that is in a way a spiritual biography of the poet. Writing has been an escape; it has registered the depths, and it has caught the fire of the emotional crises through which its author has passed. Because Langston Hughes had suffered with intensity and rejoiced with abandon and managed to capture his moods in his book, he sounded an authentic note.

Unfortunately, writing poetry as an escape and being a poet as a career are two different things, and the latter is fraught with dangers. In *Fine Clothes to the Jew* we are given a volume more even in quality, but because it lacks the "high spots" of *The Weary Blues* by no means as unforgettable as the first book. The outstanding contribution of the collection now under review is the portraiture of the author's own people. Langston Hughes knows his underworld. He divines the aspirations and the tragic frustrations of his own race, and the volume is a processional of his people given in brief, revealing glimpses. Here is a boy cleaning spittoons, who sings of his work: "A bright bowl of brass is beautiful to the Lord." And here is the psychology of the Negro bad man in a single stanza:

I'm a bad, bad man
'Cause everybody tells me so.
I'm a bad, bad man,
Everybody tells me so.
I takes ma meanness and ma licker
Everywhere I go.

In "The Death of Do Dirty," "The New Cabaret Girl," "Prize Fighter," "Ballad of Gin Mary" "Porter," "Elevator Boy" and the several poems bearing the sadness of the Negro prostitute, we are given sharply etched impressions that linger in the memory.

The "Glory Hallelujah" section of the book contains a number of devotional songs which have the folk quality of the spiritual. A lovely example is the "Feet o' Jesus": . . .

From the section "From the Georgia Roads" tragedy emerges in the poignant "Song for a Dark Girl."

Way down South in Dixie,
(Break the heart of me),
They hung my black young lover
To a cross-roads tree.

Way down South in Dixie,
(Bruised body high in air),
I asked the white Lord Jesus
What was the use of prayer.

Way down South in Dixie,
(Break the heart of me),
Love is a naked shadow
On a gnarled and naked tree.

Fine Clothes to the Jew contains much of beauty, and in most of the poems there is the same instinctive music and rhythm that distinguished the poet's best earlier work. Against this must be set what appears to me to be an occasional conscious striving for originality, as in the title, and the employment in one or two of the poems of a free verse that invades the territory of prose. But if this second book does not lift the art of the author to a new high level it does appreciably increase the number of first-rate poems to the credit of Langston Hughes, and it renews his high promise for the future.

"Under the Lash of the Whip: A Column of Constructive Criticism of Men and Measures in the Hope of Correcting Errors and Evils"
Chicago Whip, 26 February 1927, [p. ?]

Mr. Langston Hughes, poet "low-rate" of Harlem, has just released his latest collection in a volume and dedicated it to Carl Van Vechten, a literary gutter-rat. It is well and wise that such a volume be dedicated to Van Vechten because he at least will revel in the lecherous, lust-reeking characters that Hughes finds time to poetize about. Hughes captions his book *Fine Clothes to the Jew* and shows how poverty-stricken blacks sell their raiment to pawnbrokers, not an unfrequent thing among the literary craftsmen of his group. These poems are unsanitary, insipid and repulsing. Again the harlot is brought to light, the crapshooter and the gin-biber are made to talk in the lingo of their land. Hughes submits these feeble creations as a work of art. If the younger artists have no finer source of inspiration than "sinister shuttered houses" then they would do well

to encase their pens and find a job. This work is a sad commentary on the psychology of the "new Negro."

Gwendolyn Bennett
"The Ebony Flute"
Opportunity, 5 (March 1927), 90–1

Fine Clothes to the Jew, Langston Hughes' new book of poems, is off the press. The greater portions of the book are given over to his studies in blues rhythms. He has been unafraid in his coining new things from old rhythms and ageless things from new rhythms. However, there are those who will not like his blues poems; for them there are poignant slices from life with which he has concerned himself. To those who do not see poetry in blues and spirituals, I recommend "The Sport," which I would say was one of the finest poems I had ever read anywhere. If this book by Mr. Hughes is as warmly received by the reading public as was his first, *The Weary Blues,* which is now in its fourth edition, his name as one of the accepted modernists in the field of poetry will be unquestioned. . . .

Countee Cullen
"The Dark Tower"
Opportunity, 5 (March 1927), 86–7

[. . .]
   Fine Clothes to the Jew, Langston Hughes' new collection of verses, is an

array of poetical vestments in which any poet can find more than one garment he would be willing and anxious to wear. With admiration and some pardonable envy we fingered the fine-wrought texture of "Brass Spittoons," "Mulatto," and "Prayer"; and though we cannot clothe ourselves in Hughes' "Song for a Dark Girl," we can quote it, thus catering to a small extent to our particular brand of vanity which covets this vivid robe more than any other:

> Way down South in Dixie,
> (Break the heart of me)
> They hung my black young lover
> To a crossroads tree.

[. . .]

Margaret Larkin
"A Poet for the People"
Opportunity, 5 (March 1927), 84–5

In casting about for a precise category in which to identify the work of Langston Hughes, I find that he might be acclaimed a new prophet in several fields, and very likely he does not think of himself as belonging to any of them.

There is still a great deal of talk about "native American rhythms" in poetic circles, and the desirability of freeing poetry from the stiff conventions which Anglo Saxon prosody inflicted upon it. In turning to the rhythm pattern of the folk "blues," Langston Hughes has contributed something of great value to other poets, particularly since he uses the form with variety and grace.

> De po' house is lonely,
> An' de grave is cold.

> O, de po' house is lonely,
> De graveyard grave is cold.
> But I'd rather be dead than
> To be ugly an' old.

This apparently simple stuff is full of delicate rhythmic variety through which the long ripple of the form flows boldly. The "blues" are charming folk ballads and in the hands of this real poet present great possibilities for beauty.

Ever since I first heard Langston Hughes read his verse, I am continually wanting to liken his poems to those of Bobby Burns. Burns caught three things in his poems: dialect, speech cadence, and character of the people, so that he seems more Scotch than all of bonnie Scotland. It is a poet's true business to distil this pure essence of life, more potent by far than life ever turns out to be, even for poets. I think that Hughes is doing for the Negro race what Burns did for the Scotch—squeezing out the beauty and rich warmth of a noble people into enduring poetry.

In hearing a group of young poets reading their new poems to each other recently, I was struck with their common tendency to intricacy, mysticism, and preoccupation with brilliant technique. Their poems are competent and beautiful, and the antithesis of simple. To any but other poets, skilled in the craft, they are probably as completely mysterious as though in a foreign tongue. The machine age and the consequent decline of the arts has driven many poets and artists into the philosophy that art is the precious possession of the few initiate. Poets now write for the appreciation of other poets, painters are scornful of all but painters, even music, most popular of all the arts, is losing the common touch. Perhaps this is an inevitable development. Yet the people perish. Beauty is not an outworn ideal, for they still search for it on Fourteenth street. While the poets and artists hoard up beauty for themselves and each other, philosophizing upon the "aristocracy of art," some few prophets are calling for art to come out of rich men's closets and become the "proletarian art" of all the people.

Perhaps Langston Hughes does not relish the title of Proletarian Poet, but he deserves it just the same. "Railroad Avenue," "Brass Spittoons," "Prize Fighter," "Elevator Boy," "Porter," "Saturday Night," and the songs from the Georgia Roads, all have their roots deep in the lives of workers. They give voice to the philosophy of men of the people, more rugged, more beautiful, better food for poetry, than the philosophy of the "middle classes."

This is a valuable example for all poets of what can be done with simple technique and "every day" subjects, but it is particularly valuable, I believe, for other Negro poets. Booker T. Washington's adjuration to "educate yourself" has sunk too deep in the Race philosophy. As in all American life, there is a strong urge to escape life's problems by reaching another station. "The life of a professional man must surely be happier than that of a factory worker," America reasons. "A teacher must surely find greater satisfaction than a farmer." Poets, influenced by this group sentiment, want to write about "nicer" emotions than those of the prize fighter who reasons

> Only dumb guys fight.
> If I wasn't dumb
> I wouldn't be fightin'
> I could make six dollars a day
> On the docks,
> And I'd save more than I do now.
> Only dumb guys fight.

or the pondering on circumstance of the boy who cleans spittoons

> Babies and gin and church
> and women and Sunday
> all mixed up with dimes and

> dollars and clean spittoons
> and house rent to pay.
> Hey, boy!
> A bright bowl of brass is beautiful to
>   the Lord.
> Bright polished brass like the cymbals
> Of King David's dancers,
> Like the wine cups of Solomon.
> Hey, boy!

Yet this, much more than the neurotic fantasies of more sophisticated poets, is the stuff of life.

There is evidence in this book that Langston Hughes is seeking new mediums, and this is a healthy sign. If he were to remain the poet of the ubiquitous "blues" he would be much less interesting. He will find new forms for himself, and I do not believe that he will lose his hold on the simple poignancy that he put into the "blues" as he adds to his poetic stature. The strong, craftsmanlike handling of "Mulatto," one of the best poems in the book, the delicate treatment of "Prayer," the effective rhythm shifts of "Saturday Night" are promises of growing power.

Not all of the poems of *Fine Clothes to the Jew* are of equal merit. Many of them are the product of too great facility. To be able to write easily is a curse that hangs over many a poet, tempting him to produce good verse from which the fine bead of true poetry is lacking. But even the most demanding critic cannot expect poets to publish perfect volumes. It ought to be enough to find one exquisite lyric like the "New Cabaret Girl" surcharged with an emotion kept in beautiful restraint,

> My God, I says,
> You can't live that way!
> Babe, you can't
> Live that way!

and here are many such.

Theophilus Lewis
"Books: Refined Blues"
Messenger, 9 (March 1927), 95

Langston Hughes' second book, *Fine Clothes to the Jew,* disappoints me. Perhaps a poet's private life has nothing to do with the quality of his art or at least it should not color an appraisal of his work. Perhaps too a reviewer's private thoughts had best be kept to himself. But a reviewer must be honest with himself as well as honest with the public, and if he cannot make his attitude toward a book clear without exposing his personal prejudices he must simply grit his teeth and do his duty.

I do not believe there is a reviewer in Christendom who would not prefer reviewing a bad book instead of a good one. Every place where the book displeases him gives him a talking point and the result is he can write a much longer and more eloquent article. When I heard Langston Hughes' next book was going to be another volume of "blues" I expected it to be a let down from his first collection of poems and prepared myself to deliver a long sermon on the folly of a young poet gallivanting around cabarets too much and giving too much heed to the advice of his foreign friends. I find I will have to reserve that sermon for some other book.

Inevitably one compares *Fine Clothes to the Jew* with *The Weary Blues.* While I can truthfully say I like the first volume better I would hesitate a long time before admitting that my preference was caused by the intrinsic superiority of its poems. What I like about the earlier poems is their freshness, vivacity and reckless abandon to life, but, obviously, those are not the only

moods which insure fine verse. In *Fine Clothes to the Jew,* Hughes catches life from another angle; gayety is subdued and wistfulness is thrown out in high relief. Instead of the passion, sensuousness and wild music which throbbed from his first poems the later blues exhale the ascetic delicacy one finds in the lyrics of Thomas Hardy and A. E. Housman.

The later poems are more original, too. In *The Weary Blues* I could often trace his work back to sources, but in the present volume method as well as matter is the poet's very own. This is one of the striking evidences of Hughes' superiority to his contemporaries, his constant tendency to explore and experiment. He is not content to sing about bleeding love the way the troubadours sang about it; he sings in the living speech and rhythms of the present. That is why his compatriots so frequently regard his work as shoddy or freakish. As a true artist he sees deeper into life and is able to discern movements they are unaware of. This is what makes his work appear strange and startling when it is compared with art already crystallized by convention and familiarity. It is also the quality that makes his poetry distinctive and marks it for endurance.

R. E. Turner
"Fine Clothes to the Jew"
Lincoln News, 2 (March 1927), 7

[. . .]

In discussing the latest book of poems written by Langston Hughes, one should have two important questions in mind. He should first ask himself if in *Fine Clothes to the Jew,* which is the title of the book referred to, Mr. Hughes has portrayed the truth. Having satisfactorily replied to this query, one should ask if the truth or falsehood were better expressed now than later, or if it could be better left unexpressed forever.

When one reads this book and is shocked by it, he has merely been struck with the force of truth.

When hard luck overtakes you
Nothin' for you to do,
When hard luck overtakes you
Nothin' for you to do.
Gather up yo' fine clothes,
An' sell 'em to de Jew.

It could be suggested that "yer" or "ye" would more often be used than "you" by the type of individual which this verse intends to depict. Such a person might use "fer" for "for." But it must be admitted that frequently pawn shops, or combination shops owned and operated by Jews, contain many silks, satins, and jewels, etc., which have been sold to them by Negroes in distress.

Let us now consider a poem entitled "Feet O' Jesus," which almost perfectly portrays the humble type of prayer made by the artless:

[. . .]

The first stanza is nearly beyond improvement. The second is likewise, save for the use of "little" in reference to "Jesus." The unlettered conception of "Jesus" is usually that of someone great and powerful and one with a mighty beaming countenance.

It would be no difficult task to name poem after poem in which Mr. Hughes has submitted a true characterization of different types. Though he seems to overlook the fact that the unlearned Negroes have a tendency to sound "or" and "ow" as if they were "er" and "ew," he seldom mistakes their attitude in a given situation. It

seems fair to conclude, in reply to our first query, that, on the whole, the book contains true portrayals of some Negro types.

The question then arises, is Mr. Hughes justified in depicting the truth, or this particular truth at this particular time? Evidently this inquiry involves more ethics and more morality than most of us are willing to admit.

It may be that an egoist would reply without hesitation to this effect: "He is telling the truth and will be well-paid for it, so let him write." Probably an utilitarian would say, "This book reveals many facts to the upper white world and to other refined folk which they would otherwise not know. And since it reveals countless truths pertaining to lower Negro life, Mr. Hughes is justified." Probably a great friend of the Negro would say, "At such a time as this; when the whole world is looking askance at the Negro; watching attentively his every step; noting his merits and demerits; magnifying the latter instead of the former and judging the Negro by his deficiencies instead of his efficiencies; at a time when he is being pushed out of home, school, industry, government, and society; at such a time let no black bard sing of the weakness of his race."

But so much for the probable reactions of others. I now wish to speak for myself. We, the Negro race, are being most rapidly exploited by members of other races. Hundreds of dollars are being made by white men who poorly portray some form of Negro life. The assertion has been made that the Negro's past and present are inexpressively interesting. The threat has gone forth that unless the Negro relates his own past and describes his own present, someone else will do it for him. And even while this threat was being made it was simultaneously being fulfilled. If anyone doubts this fact, let him examine the stories published in the *Saturday Evening Post*. Let him read Van Vechten's *Nigger Heaven*.

For in the *Saturday Evening Post* and in *Nigger Heaven* is the truth made plain that if the Negro does not reveal himself, others will paint him to his sore displeasure, and that picture will be displayed with little regard for truth or for compunction. Thus, it is clear that it is both the right and duty of the Negro to portray his past and present with truth, to "paint the thing as he sees it, for the God of things as they are."

"What to Read"
Crisis, 34 (March 1927), 20, 32

The outstanding book of the month is Langston Hughes' second book of poems, *Fine Clothes to the Jew.* It is a beautifully printed little volume of eighty-nine pages issued by Knopf and has, like *The Weary Blues,* "the fine qualities of force, passion, directness and sensitive perception." There are extraordinarily beautiful bits here and there, and while the poems distinctly confine themselves to lowly types, it is the human feeling and longing there that he emphasizes. Despair at sunset:

A good woman's cryin'
For a no-good man?

The spittoon cleaner, who puts his lowly offering on the altar of the Lord; the porter

Climbing up a great big mountain
Of yes, sirs!

The cry of the religious mourners:

O, ma little Jesus,
Please reach out yo' hand.

Of individual poems one must read the rhythm and abandon of "Saturday Night"; the little "Sun Song"; and the tragic

"Song for a Dark Girl." And then there are phrases here and there: "A passing girl with purple powdered skin"; "I'm midnight mad"; "I'm waiting for ma mammy—She is Death."

And one line which is a sort of key to the book:

Loud-mouthed laughers in the hands
Of Fate.

The book is $2 and has a jacket by Aaron Douglas. You should buy it.

[. . .]

"Fine Clothes to the Jew"
Boston Transcript,
2 March 1927, p. 4

How far is this new Negro movement going to spread? Some people think that those people interested in Negro poetry, art and dancing could turn their attention to the repealing of the Jim Crow laws to a better advantage. In other words, interest in the gifted of a race should be widened to include interest in the general mob.

This Langston Hughes—what of him? Sponsored as is Countee Cullen, by Carl Van Vechten, he does not prove to be as great a poet as Cullen although his life story ought to be more fascinating. *Weary Blues,* his first volume, was full of racial rhythm and melody with a strong undercurrent of cynicism. This second book has much of the rhythm, but it is as though the cynicism had broken over a dam which had previously held it in leash. Now it runs rampant through the poems. Coupled with the cynicism is a something which cannot exactly be called superficiality, but which might be described by saying that the author is using the same things which brought him first into notice, but that he is doing it consciously rather than from his heart. Some of the poems might even be called tawdry. It is often as though the words were there, but discord is clashing and clanging through them.

This statement in no way applies to the sections of the book which contain the blues and the spirituals. The blues, unlike the spirituals, have a second line which is a repetition of the first. They possess rhythm and appeal, and are often as haunting and as pathetically tragic as are the spirituals.

[. . .]

"Magnolia Flowers" and "Mulatto" show more clearly than any other two poems the way in which the genius of Mr. Hughes can vary.

Sigmund Spaeth
"Collections of Afro-American Verse and Music"
Philadelphia Inquirer,
5 March 1927, p. 19

[. . .]

To this actual music of the Negro must be added the language of a young black poet. Langston Hughes has already won definite recognition with his *Weary Blues,* published last year. A wandering Missourian, seeking the truth, educated at Columbia and Lincoln Universities, and in the cities of America, Mexico, and Europe, he is filled with the happy-go-lucky melancholy of the Negro race.

His "Blues" cry out for music, and it will be a pity if some such composer as George Gershwin does not soon heed their call. In an introductory note to his newest book, the author says "The mold of the 'Blues' is almost always despondency, but when they are sung, people laugh." He explains the strict "pattern" of their technique. "One long line, repeated; and a third line to rhyme with the first two." (In the printed form he breaks these long lines in two, thus creating a series of six-line stanzas.)

Mr. Hughes derives the title of his book, *Fine Clothes to the Jew,* from its second poem, "Hard Luck":

When hard luck overtakes you,
    nothin' for you to do
When hard luck overtakes you,
    nothin' for you to do.
Gather up yo' fine clothes an' sell 'em
    to de Jew.

Jew takes yo' fine clothes, gives you a
    dollar an' a half.
Jew takes yo' fine clothes, gives you a
    dollar an' a half.
Go to de bootleg's, get some gin to
    make you laugh.

If I was a mule I'd git me a wagon to
    haul.
If I was a mule I'd git a wagon to
    haul.
I'm so low-down I ain't even got a
    stall.

It is in this mood that the poet is most successful. His rough-hewn verses bristle with forthright expressions of human misery. "Can't you understand a good woman's cryin' for a no-good man?" "I beats ma wife an' beats ma side gal too. Don't know why I do it but it keeps me from feelin' blue." "I'm gonna buy me a rose bud an' plant it at ma back door. So when I'm dead they won't need flowers from de store."

When Langston Hughes takes to verse [sic] libre and correct English, he is less convincing. And it is a pity, in the polyglot "Jazz Band in a Parisian Cabaret," that a careless proofreader should have permit-

106

ted him to mis-spell one of his two words of German.

Fortunately, however, the major part of this little book, with its parti-colored cover, like fancy icing on a cookie, is an honest expression of the American Negro as he is. When he speaks in his natural idiom, Langston Hughes is by every test of truth and beauty a great poet. The dedication to Carl Van Vechten is almost inevitable.

Alice Dunbar-Nelson "As in a Looking Glass" *Washington Eagle,* 11 March 1927, [p. ?]

One must reckon with a poet whose first book of poems, published, not printed, is followed in a little over a year's time by a second book—also published, not printed. And that reckoning must be a sharp one if the poet be a Negro, and the publishers of his verse a white firm, who are not actuated by altruism alone. Therefore, one cannot dismiss Langston Hughes lightly, either with faint praise or with bitter vituperation. He has made a niche for himself; and the poetry of America, whether you agree with Langston Hughes or not, must acknowledge his verse as an integral part of its warp and woof.

Critics accepted Mr. Hughes' first book, *The Weary Blues,* because of its novelty, as well as because of its haunting melody and wistful passion. Here was a new form in poetry. An absolutely new form. The blues song was common enough, but even at that no one thought of it as having a law, a form, a technique. But here arose a writer who embodied the technique of the despised "jazz" song into

literature, and talked about its law and reason. The poem "The Weary Blues" had won a prize in a contest. The book therefore was talked about, and was a nine days' wonder.

And now Mr. Hughes has done it again. *Fine Clothes to the Jew* comes from the press of Alfred A. Knopf. And some of our folks don't like it, and are quite frank in saying so.

Some hundred years ago a storm arose in England over the poetry of the so-called "Lake School" of which Wordsworth and Coleridge were the immediate exemplars. That Wordsworth, in particular, should insult the British intelligence with his poems about idiot boys, gawky girls, simple maidens, and dull clods of workmen sent the *Edinburgh Review* and such other eminent critics into frothing rages of bitter defenses of the noble art of poetry. To which the youthful poets replied by quoting Aristotle. "Poetry is an imitation of life."

An imitation of life. You cannot get away from that. Every rhetoric that has been written for the past thousand years or more in any language, has been but Aristotle, translated, boiled down, emended, amended, amplified, expounded, rewritten. But Aristotle, for all that.

And Aristotle said that poetry is an imitation of life.

Mr. Hughes has chosen to imitate the life of the Negro in diverse places. In the cities, in the slums, in cabarets, in the dust of the Georgia roads. Some of it is poignantly beautiful, and some of it is irritating, and some of it you wish had not been included in the volume. Here and there it is rather as if prose had been cut into lines of indifferent length. But by and large, the hauntingly beautiful overbalances that which is not so excellent. Not even excepting the poem which gives the volume its name, "Fine Clothes to the Jew."

The worst thing that can happen to any young writer is for a storm of adulation

107

untempered by careful criticism to over-whelm him. He needs the pricks and stings of unfavorable comment here and there to goad him to severe self-searching and pruning of his work. If he has the right stuff in him, it will do him incalculable good. It is only the weaklings who sink be-neath the bitter winds of blame.

The heart-breaking philosophy of the Negro is found in the poem, "Homesick Blues." The whole history of the race is epitomized in the two lines,

To keep from cryin'
I opens ma mouth an' laughs.

Which is what the race has been doing since it came from Africa. And the white man thinks it a child-like merry race, be-cause it can laugh with a breaking heart. "Yes, Laughers. Loud-mouthed laughers in the hands of fate."

Some of the same thought is found in "Brass Spittoons," which is a Negroid ver-sion of the "Jongleur of Notre Dame." And you read "Railroad Avenue" over and over, searching for the jewel at its heart, until it thrusts its sharp points up at you, and you recoil from its bitter facets.

Mr. Hughes writes of the low people, the "Dish-washers, elevator boys, ladies' maids, crap-shooters, cooks, waiters, jazz-ers, nurses of babies, loaders of ships, rounders, number-writers, comedians in vaudeville, and band men in circuses—dream-singers all. My people," as he enu-merates them.

And why not? They are. They live and laugh and love and sing, and there are more of them than there are of the profes-sional high-brows, who draw their robes aside and sneer at real life, at red-blooded Negro life, while they shiver in an emas-culated, half-Nordic existence. There are millions and millions of "My People," and they clamor for self-expression. Not for the white man's words or thoughts, but for their own.

And so Mr. Hughes has made articulate "My People" of the cities and slums and the cabarets and the crap dens. There they are, and he sings them as a part of his own life. And sometimes, as in "Shout" and "Baby" and "Dressed Up" and "Crap Game," and "Elevator Boy," it seems like nothing, and sometimes as in "Sport" and "Feet o' Jesus" it grips you with a sharp realization that this is a life like that "Lost River" in the mountains, a deep, dark dan-gerous underground current.

Naturally, I like the group "From the Georgia Roads" best of all. Perhaps it is more familiar soil, and there is not the un-easy feeling that I am treading on danger-ous ground. But in this Georgia group, "Mulatto," "Red Silk Stockings," "Song for a Dark Girl," and "Laughers" have poignant unforgettable lines, as vivid as bare trees etched against moonlit fog. Raped black women, despoiled girlhood, lynched youths, wrecked homes—all sung there, completed. Nothing more to say, but to let the instrument fall with jangling strings.

Tested by the acid test of intense subjec-tivity, Mr. Hughes is a rare poet; testing his verse by the plumb line of imitation of life, it is poetry. And now we shall await his third volume with interest.

Roger Didier
"Langston Hughes Patches Us Up"
Light and Heebie Jeebies [Chicago], 3 (12 March 1927), 10

Langston Hughes' *Fine Clothes to the Jew,* published by Alfred A. Knopf, New York, although it is jacketed as "A New Book of Poems," might just as aptly and correctly be designated "A New Book of Patches." These poems are a Peck's-Bad-Boy description of a less favored element in the Negro race.

We are aware of the criticism which has been directed toward Mr. Hughes as a result of this latest volume and, in some respects, we share it. Hughes has taken exception to the criticism, claiming that he had hoped critics would seize the opportunity to tell him how well or how poorly he had written, rather than to criticize the poems because of their special character.

We have all along been fearful that admirers of Mr. Hughes would delude him into believing that he had shown great talent as a poet. We were particularly apprehensive when his *Weary Blues* was considered as a sort of twin to Countee Cullen's *Color*. Here and there one discovers in Mr. Hughes' vivid patches of words some approach toward the essence of poetic thoughtfulness, but those occasions are rare. For the most part, he is an artificer forcing words into odd combinations that sometimes incite a pleasing imagery which means very little.

Nor do we think that his peculiar forms are commendable. We are rather sure that we have not had many persons using Mr. Hughes' mechanics because they did not in themselves feel that the use of such forms without ideas of any consequence would make poets of them. We know fellows around the streets who can beat Mr. Hughes thinking the stuff he does, who have never realized that they were poets.

Nevertheless, we are hopeful that he will continue to entertain us, for many of his "poems" are entertaining. But we don't want him to fool himself, nor to think that he is fooling Negroes who read him. We don't care about which class of Negroes he writes, but we would enjoy having him write with more point. For purposes of comparison we reproduce, first one of Mr. Hughes' "blue" poems, and second, a stanza caught from an extemporaneous composer who played a piano in small cabarets. Mr. Hughes:

HEY

Sun's a settin',
This is what I'm gonna sing.
Sun's a settin',
This is what I'm gonna sing:
I feels de blues a comin',
Wonder what de blues'll bring?

And this one from the cabaret improvisator:

Somethin' 'bout a woman,
I can't understan'.
Something' 'bout a woman,
I can't understan':
She'll cook cornbread for her
    husband,
Hot biscuits for her man!

Which, if either, is poetry? Why doesn't somebody tell this cabaret singer he ought to put his songs in a book?

Sidney Friedlander
"The Negro Speaks of Rivers"
Brooklyn Citizen,
20 March 1927, p. 7

By the sad waters of Burutu, the mud city, is hidden the heart of Africa. Some who have been in Victoria Nyanza, some who have found the wild head waters of the Congo, some who have eaten the fine dust of Timbuctoo, some who have ridden over the green plain of Kano, have thought they held the heart of Africa fast in their palms. But it is not so. They were but nerve ends, parts of the body structures of a complex anatomy. In Victoria Nature exults madly, the Congo, too, is a secret orgy, and Timbuctoo and Kano are Arabian festivals. But Burutu, the hidden, the lagoon city, is the African essence. It is the softness of the warm muddy waters of the Niger, the greenness of the African bush, the continuous song of the marshes. Burutu is the key city of the Niger, a city of thatch and dried clay. It is an island city, surrounded by the lagoons, wide mysterious, unending lagoons.

In Burutu the poet heart of the world was born, the poet heart that sang because singing was good and a medicine for the jungle soul. Ju-Ju, the jungle magic was born here in high cadences and long rhythms. From Ju-Ju the Blues were born, the wide mouthed Blues. The spiritual is a daughter of the Blues.

And so it was that the poet of the Blues came back to Burutu and found his soul there. The poet of the blues, born on the banks of that other great mud river, the Mississippi, came back to his home through the devious ways of his fate and took from it his native song.

That is the story of the poetry of Langston Hughes. It is told beautifully by Van Vechten in his introduction to *Weary Blues*. It is told more beautifully by the poet himself in a few short poignant stanzas. The soul that he found is warmly revealed in "The Negro Speaks of Rivers." The pain and the joy of it are "The Weary Blues."

There was a sneering, argumentative book written recently which said that the colored races are doomed, that their weaknesses in the face of the dominant white man's strength would cause them to disappear from the earth. The book was written, of course, by a white man and it is from beginning to end a lie. The black man cannot disappear. The tropics and the south belong to him. The Empire-seeking white man cannot even mark the face let alone touch the soul of the tropics. Let him burn away the bush that borders the rivers of Africa and the river revenges itself by carrying away the desolated land, and planting it again in a richer, untouched jungle spot. Let him destroy the thatch villages and plant his great white structures, and the sun and the jungle penetrate his foreign structures till they fall from their own rottenness.

Africa is black and the property of the black man, and the white man who challenges its owners will either become a part of the colored soul himself or surrender to the strength of the jungles. Langston Hughes does not make this challenge. He tells only of the black man's soul and the soul of the jungle countries, and they are the same.

This poetry is primitive. The best of it is more than primitive. It is primal. The cadence and the rhythm are things born of the ideas they sing of, of rivers, of moons, of jungle moons, and tropic seas. In them is none of the fierceness of white verse. These poems are part of the calm, deep surrender of nature to itself. Simple songs, poignant with unwept tears.

I loved my friend,
He went away from me.
There's nothing more to say.
The poem ends,
Soft as it began—
I loved my friend.

Dark night songs, songs of black souls drowned in seas of white men, songs of love, of flesh and of passion, of light hearts but more often of light tongues hiding pain and tragedy.

This is the essence of these two books, *Weary Blues* and *Fine Clothes to the Jew*. But there are also a few poems of the lost life of the Negro amid the crushing lives of the white. They are touched occasionally with revolt, hot and despairing with futile struggle. For Mr. Hughes has been in almost every place where his people may be found, whether in America, North and South, in Europe or in Africa. He has been with them where their fortune and their lives are great and where they are simple and primitive. He knows them all, laborers, singers, and searchers, and his is the voice of all of them. Through him may that voice become a loud cry to drown out the voices of hate and intolerance everywhere.

Hunter Stagg
"Galley Sheets in the Wind"
Richmond News-Leader,
21 March 1927, p. 4

Maxwell Bodenheim has named his new book of poetry *Returning to Emotion*. . . .

Somehow the frigid abstractions of Bodenheim incline us even more strongly than before to the clear cut verities of life which the poetry of Langston Hughes presents with a tropic warmth and a Harlem swing. It has already been stated more than once that when this young Negro published last year the volume called *The Weary Blues,* he sounded a new note in modern poetry. Some people objected to this note on the ground that it was too like the elongated writhe of a saxophone cry, which was the very reason some other people like it. Who would pay any attention, anyway, to the verdicts of such as do not like the saxophone! And recognize it as the authentic artistic expression of something in human nature, we are not quite prepared to say what, only that we are sure it is something very real.

Meanwhile, Langston Hughes, as is probably well enough known by now, has produced his second volume of verse, calling it *Fine Clothes to the Jew,* which sounds peculiar and unnecessarily obscure until you read the poem of that name which is in the book. Reading this new volume, we conclude that if it is to be called a little less fiery than its predecessor, it is at the same time a good deal more considered, more thoughtful—in short, it is better art. The fire, we suspect, has not burned low, it has simply burned deep, which means that it will spring up again in a new place all the hotter for what it has found and consumed beneath the surface of life. This book represents, as it were, the finding and the consuming, and certainly it cannot be denied that much of Langston Hughes' best work is found in such smouldering poems as "The Ballad of Gin-Mary," "The Death of Do-Dirty" and "Song for a Dark Girl."

The tragedies and frustrations of his race Langston Hughes has observed— more, he has undoubtedly experienced— and he has brought out of them lyrics which sing with characteristic barbaric rhythms and native passion. He has not yet reached the profundity of the older Negro poet, Countee Cullen, but he is nearer it than he was before. Meanwhile the chief concern is with portraiture. Harlem types, Georgia types appear in his pages to moan their sorrow-laden blues, then disappear to make way for others. In portraiture, certainly, this young artist excels.

[. . .]

"Partly Undigested Particles of Poetry"
Princeton Literary Observer, 2 (22 March 1927), [1], 6

Mr. Carl Van Vechten has managed to become very much excited because indifference to the literary work of Negroes has stultified expression in that race. But the instant Langston Hughes published his first volume, *The Weary Blues,* in the beginning of last year, it was received with the greatest acclaim. And now there is a second book bearing the name of the talented young colored man; unfortunately it does not maintain the same plane of excellence which was attained in his earlier work. Apparently then, here is a case where too much enthusiasm has hindered perfect expression by tempting it to hastiness.

Although this review begins upon a lugubrious note for Mr. Hughes, there is much to praise in the volume. It is not a very big book, but in it are the subtle suggestions of the rage, despair, and hopelessness; passion, joy and humor; mysticism, worship and love of pageantry of the Negro people. And the poetry itself carries the genuine tone of spontaneity and natural music which has always been associated with the Negro. He sings with a husky crooning plaint. But it is not the traditional poetry of a race in bondage of slavery; it is the expression of a people possessing a growing self-consciousness—a questioning and eager people.

Herbert S. Gorman "Tradition and Experiment in Modern Poetry"
New York Times Book Review, 27 March 1927, p. 2

The idea of comparing four contemporary American poets picked haphazardly from the mountainous pile of new publications with four contemporary English poets, seized upon with an equal indiscrimination, is of no value whatsoever and yet certain points of interest may be deduced. Messers. John Crowe Ransom, Hart Crane, Langston Hughes and James Rorty may be said to exemplify a number of distinct modernistic trends in American verse, while Messers. Humbert Wolfe, Richard Aldington, John Drinkwater and Ford Madox Ford are surely British through and through. Therefore, so far as nationalistic characteristics are concerned there is some ground—exceedingly precarious, to be sure—for comparison. Considering these poets as individuals, however, makes any comparison sheer arrant presumption and arbitrariness on the commentator's part, as none of these men are proper foils for one another. Among the Americans Langston Hughes belongs to the colored race and it is therefore impossible to estimate him beside, say, Humbert Wolfe or Richard Aldington. Surveying these two quartets of poets as groups, however, does suggest certain aspects of the contemporary poetic urges in the two countries.

All of the Americans are modernistic in inclination. Experimentation and uniqueness in both thought and metrical forms are to be found in their work. . . .

... Both Mr. Ransom and Mr. Crane belong to that modernistic category of poets that is dubbed intellectual. The emotions they handle have been translated in passing through the brain.

This is not true either of Langston Hughes in *Fine Clothes to the Jew* or James Rorty in *Children of the Sun*. Here we have visible evidence of two well-defined trends in contemporary American life and letters. Mr. Hughes, of course, is exemplative of the great Negro renascence that has produced half a dozen excellent colored poets in the last few years. His book is uneven and flawed but it displays flashes of authentic inspiration, and when it is at its best, as in some of the "blues" experiments, it gives a vivid sensation of the Negro spirit.

... These four American poets (of whom Mr. Rorty is the last) have one attribute in common—they are all concerned with contemporaneity. Taken as a representation of our poetry, they display such encouraging factors as an excessive curiosity about verse-forms, a bland regardlessness of tradition, a highly sensitized intellectual immersion and a receptivity to new urges of all sorts.

[. . .]

R. E. Cureton
"Our Book Rack"
Oracle, 6 (April 1927), [?]

Fine Clothes to the Jew, Langston Hughes' new book of poems has just come, at this writing, from the press. I have looked with interest at the coming of a new book of poems by the author of the *Weary Blues*, for the critics have said his first book was the opening of a career well worth watching, and if he could go on as he had started, America bids fair to have a poet worthy of far more than passing mention. Thus, it was in a mood of glorious anticipation that I started to read *Fine Clothes to the Jew*. I found the volume of, perhaps, ninety poems to run the gamut of moods, longings and observant wanderings. And yet unlike the *Weary Blues,* they are fashioned on a smaller pattern, depicting things almost purely American. There, too, is more of the racial yearning. The melancholy gal sings her blues in the slough of despondency; the black man, down and out, moans over the loss of his good woman—gone away. And here I might say Hughes is a specialist when writing about, or expressing himself in the mood of the blues, and he sticks to the poetic pattern—seldom, if ever, changing.

Following the group of poems under the title of "Blues" is a group that interpret the life of the porter, the street women, the wine bibblers and bad men in alleys, cabarets, etc. And then comes a group of spirituals, prayers and religious exclamations, written in delicate lines, and woven into weird and strange verses. "Beale Street Love" heads another group of poems that reveal the sordid life of the dregs in the human cup of existence. Here I recall the recent discussion among many leading critics as to how the Negro shall be portrayed in art. Certainly, Hughes will be severely criticised for writing many of the poems in this book that reveal the more primitive and sordid types of the American Negro. But they are true to life, and we all know it; we have seen it with our own eyes. The kind of people Mr. Hughes writes about live all around us; their voices roll in on my ear this moment; we'll rub elbows on the street in an hour or so. They sing and love, yearn and have longings for the life that they know just as the more sophisticated element of our race does. Why shouldn't the joy and pathos, the beauty and ugliness of their lives be expressed in verse—in verse they can't write, but which Langston Hughes can?

This latest volume of Brother Hughes' deserves to be read; his reputation has been sustained.

Babette Deutsch
"Four Poets"
Bookman, 65 (April 1927), 220–1

[...]

The three books mentioned above are linked together, by the sophistication of their authors, if by nothing else. Messrs. Pound, Ransom, and Van Doren are all three learned and, for the most part, urbane gentlemen, whose poetry is fed in almost equal streams by literature and life. The verses of Langston Hughes are completely unliterary, often willfully illiterate, and as naively vital as any old ballad or folk song. The dialect pieces fairly sing themselves when read aloud, and the others show craftsmanship of a high order. Poems like "Railroad Avenue" and "Magnolia Flower" echo in the memory. Typical of the poet's feeling for symmetry is the manner in which the last lyric in the book balances the first.

Loren R. Miller
Kappa Alpha Psi Journal, 13 (April 1927), [?]

I was hard put to it to lay my hands on a copy of *Fine Clothes to the Jew* by Langston Hughes. The book well repaid me for the exertions. You have read his *Weary Blues* of course. Here is the same Hughes grown a bit more cynical, a trifle more disillusioned. He puts aside the abandon of his first book and shows you the half tragedy which makes Negroes sing the blues. Langston Hughes sets himself to catch the spirit of the blues and he does it well. You have not heard his words before, but you have heard their music all your life. And so with the spirituals he has included. Here is the poetry of Negro life, as we live it, set down by a poet. You look on the surface of the Negro's life with Hughes: elevator boys, young gals, shouting saints, prize fighters, and cabaret girls. You know that underneath that surface are troubled waters.

O.C.E.
"Light Stuff"
Philadelphia Tribune, 2 April 1927, p. 16

Of course, while you may not have liked it, H.L.P., we stand by what we have said. While Mr. Hughes may not be, and probably is not, depraved, his *Fine Clothes to the Jew* reminds us more of some of the obscene literature we used to run across while we were passing through the adolescent stage than anything published in book form we have ever had the opportunity to read. Its appeal to you must be due to the similarity of type of one or more of the characters in the book and yourself.

T. Bernard Pace
"Singing Laughter"
Asheville Times, 3 April 1927, p. 11

I am a lover of titles of the book kind. I am a lover of original names. That is one reason why this volume appeals to me so. This *Fine Clothes to the Jew* is a queer title, yet it is an appropriate one. Throughout the book the poems have such names as "Brass Spittoons," "Railroad Avenue," "Gin Mary," "Do Dirty," "Red Silk Stockings." But this reason soon loses its significance. The substance, the plainness of the poems is what really holds one.

Langston Hughes can capture the feelings of his own people. Before working as a bus-boy at the Wardman-Park in Washington (where he was when he gained fame with the publication of *The Weary Blues*), he traveled extensively, and he knows every type of Negro. He has since studied at Columbia as well as at Lincoln University, the Harvard of the Negro colleges.

Though not being as poetical (judging by poetical standards) as that of his contemporaries, his poetry is, nevertheless, more emotional, comes more directly from the heart. It does not have the conventional quietness of the poetry of Countee Cullen and Paul McKay. One does not read his poems. One sings them, laughs them, prays them. You cannot read "Prayer" in this volume without giving it the intonation of a prayer.

> I ask you this:
> Which way to go?
> I ask you this:
> Which sin to bear?
> Which crown to put
> Upon my hair?

> I do not know,
> Lord God,
> I do not know.

There are thumb-nail sketches of every kind: the realistic Hatrack tale of Ruby Brown; a rounder's story in the "Death of Do Dirty"; the cause and effect of the Southern mulatto, elevator boys, ruined gals. But through it all there is laughter. The Negroes seem to say: "We haven't a chance to rise. Make the most of life. Forget irony, forget pity, forget sadness." An outlook quite as optimistic as the Christian Scientists, and quite as effective. After all, they really have nothing except their Spirituals and religion in life. And, is there a more sincerely religious people than the black race?

Alain Locke
"Common Clay and Poetry"
Saturday Review, 3 (9 April 1927), 712

Fine clothes may not make either the poet or the gentleman, but they certainly help; and it is a rare genius that can strip life to the buff and still poetize it. This, however, Langston Hughes has done, in a volume that is even more starkly realistic and colloquial than his first, *The Weary Blues*. It is a current ambition in American poetry to take the common clay of life and fashion it to living beauty, but very few have succeeded, even Masters and Sandburg not invariably. They get their effects, but often at the expense of poetry. Here, on the contrary, there is scarcely a prosaic note or a spiritual sag in spite of the fact that never has cruder colloquialism or more sordid

115

life been put into the substance of poetry. The book is, therefore, notable as an achievement in poetic realism in addition to its particular value as a folk study in verse of Negro life.

The success of these poems owes much to the clever and apt device of taking folk-song forms and idioms as the mold into which the life of the plain people is descriptively poured. This gives not only an authentic background and the impression that it is the people themselves speaking, but the sordidness of common life is caught up in the lilt of its own poetry and without any sentimental propping attains something of the necessary elevation of art. Many of the poems are modelled in the exact metrical form of the Negro "Blues," now so suddenly popular, and in thought and style of expression are so close as scarcely to be distinguishable from the popular variety. But these poems are not transcriptions; every now and then one catches sight of the deft poetic touch that unostentatiously transforms them into folk portraits. In the rambling improvised stanzas of folk-song, there is invariably much that is inconsistent with the dominant mood; and seldom any dramatic coherence. Here we have these necessary art ingredients ingeniously added to material of real folk flavor and origin. "Gal's Cry for a Dying Lover" is an excellent example:

Heard de owl a hootin',
Knowed somebody's 'bout to die.
Heard de owl a hootin',
Knowed somebody's 'bout to die.
Put ma head un'neath de kiver,
Started in to moan and cry.

Hound dawg's barkin'
Means he's gonna leave dis world.
Hound dawg's barkin'
Means he's gonna leave dis world.
O, Lawd have mercy
On a po' black girl.

Black an' ugly
But he sho do treat me kind.
I'm black an' ugly
But he sho do treat me kind.
High-in-heaben Jesus,
Please don't take this man o' mine.

After so much dead anatomy of a people's superstition and so much sentimental balladizing on dialect chromatics, such vivid, pulsing, creative portraits of Negro folk foibles and moods are most welcome. The author apparently loves the plain people in every aspect of their lives, their gin-drinking carousals, their street brawls, their tenement publicity, and their slum matings and partings, and reveals this segment of Negro life as it has never been shown before. Its open frankness will be a shock and a snare for the critic and moralist who cannot distinguish clay from mire. The poet has himself said elsewhere, "The 'low-down' Negroes furnish a wealth of colorful, distinctive material for any artist, because they hold their individuality in the face of American standardizations. And perhaps these common people will give to the world its truly great Negro artist, the one who is not afraid to be himself." And as one watches Langston Hughes's own career, one wonders.

The dominant mood of this volume is the characteristic "Blue's emotion," the crying laugh that "eases its misery" in song and self pity. However, there are poems of other than the folk character in the book—none more notable than "Mulatto"—too long to quote, even though it is a lyric condensation of the deepest tragedy of the race problem. One that is just as pregnant with social as well as individual tragedy can serve as a brief sample of this side of younger Negro genius for tragic vision and utterance:

SONG FOR A DARK GIRL

Way Down South in Dixie
(Break the heart of me)
They hung my black young lover
To a cross roads tree.

Way Down South in Dixie
(Bruised body high in air)
I asked the white Lord Jesus
What was the use of prayer.

Way Down South in Dixie
(Break the heart of me)
Love is a naked shadow
On a gnarled and naked tree.

After this there is nothing to be said about the finest tragedy having always to be Greek.

"Poetry and Plays"
Independent, 118 (9 April 1927), 396–7

The author of *The Weary Blues,* has written and published in this volume a series of authentic songs of the modern American Negro. Blues, spirituals (new style), songs of Beale Street love, and white-Negro, sophisticated songs, all are here, sung from the heart with amazing simplicity and equally amazing effectiveness. Of all, perhaps, Mr. Hughes is best in his "Blues." Take the song from which the volume derives its name. . . .

This is indubitably the real thing. It might be done by any Pullman porter or any suit presser. It could not be done by anyone who was not—to a certain extent—both a poet and a singer. It is hard to praise too highly one who expresses a race's emotion—and a moment in its life. Mr. Hughes has done both—and the result is, in its best sense, literature.

Frank Luther
"More Blues, Hughes Brand"
Des Moines Register,
10 April 1927, p. E9

This latest Harlem contribution to the literature of the New Negro is interesting technically and moving emotionally. Mr. Hughes is known chiefly as author of *The Weary Blues,* published two years ago, and this slim and charmingly made book begins and ends with blues poems. In this author's hands the blues follow a fairly strict pattern; as he explains it in a brief note, each stanza consists of one long line, then a repetition of it usually with a slight change, and finally a long line to rhyme with the first two. In printing—and in reading, I believe—each of these lines is divided; so that the stanza has six lines:

Weary, weary,
Weary early in de morn.
Weary, weary,
Early, early in de morn.
I's so weary
I wish I'd never been born.

There are character pieces, a group of religious songs, and Harlem cabaret and love songs. Many are amusing, but the prevailing mood is of sorrow. Like all the really honest Negro poetry, these verses have a remarkable emotional suffusion.

But the most remarkable thing here is the objectiveness of this picture of Negro life. The tragic lot of the black-skinned in a white-skinned civilization is apparent again and again, but there is no explicit propaganda; there is no appeal for help or pity. Squalor, immorality, ignorance, superstition, fervor, joy, dancing, music, abandon, passion, despair, religion; here they all are in little songs in a slender book between delicately tinted boards.

All these things and hope too:

> "Glory! Hallelujah!
> De dawn's a-comin'!
> Glory! Hallelujah!
> De dawn's a-comin'!"
> A black old woman croons
> In the amen-corner of the
> Ebecanezer Baptist church.
> A black old woman croons,—
> "De dawn's a-comin'."

Harry Alan Potamkin
"Old Clothes"
Nation, 124 (13 April 1927), 403–4

Mr. Hughes is right when he reprimands Mr. Schuyler in *The Nation* for denying the necessity for a Negro expression. Such expression is not only unavoidable, but it is also most desirable for both America and the Negro. The original American from Europe has done nothing with his heritage and is certainly now too distant from it to convert it to contemporary uses. Whatever hope there is for an American art lies with the minor races. To urge a cultural assimilation of the Negro is to urge the Negro to lose his singular identity and to enter into something only nominal. For him to become an American is for him to toss away a unified character for something unestablished and as yet unattractive. For what shall he exchange his native systemic heritage; for contradictions unfused?

The Negro is conscious of his singular identity. But as yet there are few among his artists equipped to meet this consciousness of identity with a consciousness of its material. The Negro artists divide themselves into those who have capitalized the fact of color without paying for it by the study of its essence and peculiarity, those who recognize the need for a separate expression of a racial material but whose aesthetic apprehension or control is not adequate, and those who attack the essential material for what it can yield under aesthetic suasion. It is evident that an artist is great in proportion as he approaches the third category. Of the Negro poets only Jean Toomer has entered it with both feet. Langston Hughes is as yet on the threshold of the second category, and there is no visible progress in his present book beyond *The Weary Blues* to reveal that he has become sensible of his poetic problem, which is *to convert the material.*

Whatever value as poetry the Negro spirituals or blues may have, duplicate spirituals or blues have only duplicate values. In the conformation of the inherent qualities of these indigenous songs to an original personal intelligence or intuition lies the poetic performance. And Mr. Hughes has not made the material so conform. One critic has attributed to his work "force, passion, directness, and sensitive perception." The "force" is the material's, not the poet's. It remains literal, unconverted. The "passion" is not great enough to convert the *attitudes* of his verse (attitudes simply rewritten from the material) into integrated experiences or even effective quasi-experiences. "Directness" in itself is of no importance; it can intensify or sharpen initial power or give precision to inventiveness. His "perception" is not sensitive, for what he sees it takes only eyes to see. He reads what is written, no great feat; he hears well, that is, his receptive pitch is accurate. But what of the final instrument of poetry that recreates the sensations in terms of a personal idiom? He is apparently unaware of even its existence.

Mr. Hughes has been called an interpreter of certain of his race. Perhaps. I see nothing in his verses to convince me of their experiential authenticity. But interpretations are only reutterances at best. Not even a translation creates the new utterance which is a poem. I find in the work of Langston Hughes the recording of certain Negro songs. I have no doubt it is as good a record as we own, for he has here and there done a little rewriting. But beyond that he has made no individual contribution.

P[aul] H[organ]
"A Poetic Artist"
Library (New Mexico Military Institute), 6 (15 April 1927), 3

Langston Hughes, in this, his second book, confirms the enthusiasm which was awakened in the reviewer by certain poems in *The Weary Blues*. It is now clear beyond doubt that here is a poetic artist of definite, high talents.

Mr. Hughes is concerned, in this new book, with the people of his own race in their most elemental moods—the Negro of the revival is here, and the servant, and the dweller in excitement of a world of Saturday nights, and the vaguely troubled Negro with that wistfulness and that simplicity which, of all his traits, are the most attractive and disarming. All of the present poems are intimately concerned with the poetry of such characters and lives, and an absence of the usual trappings of poetry— an "attitude," a "technique," the often-conscious "sounding of a fine note," a

"high eloquence"—allows them to come the nearer to poetry itself.

If his ingredients are simple, Mr. Hughes must none the less have toiled lengthily with them to produce such beautifully contrived lines as

De railroad bridge's
A sad song in de air.
De railroad bridge's
A sad song in de air.
Ever time de trains pass
I wants to go somewhere.

How simply, strangely effective is the slight variation in the repetitions of "Young Gal's Blues":

De po' house is lonely
An' de grave is cold.
O, de po' house is lonely,
De graveyard grave is cold . . .

Music and feeling are warmly blended in this poetry with an almost relaxed simplicity. The poet's heart yields beauty here.

There is little of the virtuoso about Mr. Hughes. The form most happily moulded for his use is the blues. Many of his verses are innocent of any formal arrangement, a sometimes deplorable fact, since a course of stern discipline with more rigid poetic styles might be reflected in a less profuse, less deployed version of the "Mulatto" poem here, a poem containing, as it is, much that is good.

Certain of the inclusions in this collection might be regretted—"Sport," "Porter," "Closing Time," "Laughers," "Jazz Band in a Parisian Cabaret." But our regret at their presence is not nearly so keen and vigorous as our delight in such poems as "Po' Boy Blues," "Homesick Blues," "Ballad of Gin Mary," "Death of Do Dirty," "Saturday Night," "Feet O' Jesus," "Angels Wings," "Song for a Dark Girl," "Lament Over Love" and "Young Gal's Blues." In these poems, the author has felt his subjects warmly and closely. The store of his experience may presently yield poems on more "standard" poetic topics than those of the contents of *Fine Clothes to the Jew.* I hope it may not be too soon, for to come upon poetry of a stirring order in these racial songs of Langston Hughes is to be reluctant in the face of any change, no matter how richly it might yield.

It is, after all, not without significance that such as Vachel Lindsay and Carl Van Vechten should proclaim Mr. Hughes' talents loudly, and that he should be published by the most distinguished American publisher. Further works from this highly gifted young poet will be eagerly awaited.

Lewis Alexander
"Book Review"
Carolina Magazine, 57
(May 1927), 41–4

Fine Clothes to the Jew reveals the fact that Mr. Hughes understands completely the lives of the more primitive types of Negro. No one who knows intimately the Negro crap shooters, gamblers, typical gin Mary's, bootblacks, bell boys, cabaret girls, piano plunkers, makers of folk songs, street walkers, and old rounders can deny this. This poet enters into the spirit of the lives of these people and paints them with a sympathy and understanding not matched in contemporary literature. It is true that there is much sordidness and ugliness in the lives of the more primitive types of the Negro, but yet the same is true of the more primitive types of any racial group. The sordidness and ugliness present in the lives of these folks do not constitute a reason why they are not fit subjects for literary treatment. In real life we find ugliness along side of beauty; hence in literature which is true to life we must expect to find the same conditions existing, and without a shadow of doubt, Mr. Hughes has not failed to portray the life of which he treats with all its terrible reality.

Nowhere does he attempt to cover up; therefore his work has that fine sincerity which is the essence of all true poetry. We may select from his work at random but at all times we feel that the author knows whereof he speaks. He has actually lived with and knows well the people and conditions of which he writes. No vain pretensions or fanciful imagination here—only reality.

In addition to his sincerity, Mr. Hughes possesses an originality in his writing which is quite refreshing. He goes directly to the source for his material and reports his findings as he sees them. The result is quite delightful.

Mr. Hughes also shows that he understands something of the economic revolution which is taking place in the mind of the Negro. Let us read his poem entitled "The Porter."

I must say
Yes, sir,
To you all the time.
Yes, sir!
Yes, sir!
All my days
Climbing up a great big mountain
Of yes, sirs!
Rich old white man
Owns the world.
Gimme yo' shoes
To shine.

Yes, sir!

In this poem the porter realizes the servility of his position. There was a time in Negro history when the porter and other domestic servants of the white folks felt themselves superior to the Negro farm hand or the Negro laborer, or even the Negro mechanic. This condition existed in the minds of the former type of Negro, probably because he wore clean clothes, a tie and collar while the latter wore soiled clothes and greasy overalls. Of course, this is the same fallacy which makes the small white American clerk think himself superior to any and all other workers simply because he has a "white collar" job. There are many poems in this book which might come in for specific mention but as space is limited I cannot consider all of them; but I daresay there is the poem "Mulatto" which is the masterpiece of the book.

[. . .]

Nowhere do we find a more powerful picture of a delicate Negro-white situation. Mr. Hughes has said in the space of one short poem all that can be said about the matter. One could write a volume on what he implies in this one short poem. And the poem is excellently done too— vivid, graphic, poignant. Who has written a more piercing lyric on the terrible crime, lynching, than his "Song For A Dark Girl"?

[. . .]

Mr. Hughes will continue in his good work. He is a real poet and at the rate he is going will develop into a genuine folk poet worthy of being called the spokesman of the black masses of America. He is a real poet despite the fact that he does not adhere strictly to the conventional subject matter and conventional poetic patterns, but those who understand anything about the matter at all will concede that the essence of real poetry certainly does not lie in conventionality.

Howard Weeks
"Three Poets: Another Book of Negro 'Blues,' and Two Reprints That Have Value"
Detroit Free Press, Feature Section, 8 May 1927, p. 8

In the discovery of a literary United States, Sherwood Anderson found dark laughter among the Negroes and Carl Van Vechten found nigger heaven. Waldo Frank wrote a novel about Negroes, but it is more satisfying to let them speak for themselves of their own people, as Mr. Hughes does in this book, which follows his other poetical venture, *The Weary Blues*.

Blues songs, written before the white jazz composers tricked out the tunes and words, and the race records that one may hear today set forth the lyric despondency, the religious fervor, the humor, delicacy of feeling and desire and appreciation of brilliant ostentation that mark the expression of the Negro. And these verses do that. The emotions are honest and appealing and intensely pictorial.

In a piece called "Black Gal," Mr. Hughes says:

> I's always been a workin' girl,
> I treated Albert fine.
> Ain't cut him wid no razor,
> Ain't never been unkind.
>
> Yet it seems like always
> Men takes all they can from me
> Then they goes and finds a yaller gal
> An' let's me be.
>
> I dressed up Albert Johnson,
> I bought him suits o' clothes,
> An' soon as he got out de barrel
> Then out ma door he goes.

121

Yet I ain't never been no bad one.
  Can't help it cause I'm black.
I hates them rinney yaller gals
  An' I wants ma Albert back.
Ma little, short, sweet, brownskin
  boy—
  Oh, God, I wants him back!

And in a longer verse he writes:

Hey boy!
A bright bowl of brass is beautiful to
  the Lord.
Bright polished brass like the cymbals
Of King David's dancers,
Like the wine cups of Solomon.
  Hey boy!
A clean spittoon on the altar of the
  Lord,
A clean bright spittoon all newly
  polished—
At least I can offer that.
  Com' mere, boy!

However, in certain verses, one feels
that Mr. Hughes sacrifices the honesty and
sincerity of his emotion for rhymes. In a
piece called "Workin' Man," he writes:

I works all day
With a pick and shovel,
Comes home at night—
It ain't nothin' but a hovel.

The word "hovel" seems particularly
out of character there and is apparently so
placed for the rhyme which gives the verse
an air of unreality which it otherwise
would not have. But on the whole, Mr.
Hughes's verses are intensely real and moving and reflect the feelings of the American
Negro with vitality and vividness.
  [. . .]

Katherine Garrison Chapin
"Fine Clothes to the Jew"
Junior League Bulletin,
13 (June 1927), 53

This book, and its companion *The Weary
Blues* published a year ago, are two volumes of poems of which we, as Americans,
may be proud. Perhaps when Europe has
again set its seal of approval on something
native to us we will "discover it," but by
the time we are ready to give full honor to
a Negro poet the need for giving that
honor may be passed.

Because here is a young man who at the
age of twenty-five has stepped out of the
ranks where any social or racial discriminations might hold him, and walks easily
among the best writers of his day. He is a
poet, not merely a Negro poet.

Yet his poems, in spite of the title,
which is only a line from one, are distinctly
racial, racial in their feeling, in their sensitiveness to beauty, proudly racial in their
consciousness, and deeply racial in that
most subtle characteristic, their unfailing
rhythm. It is a rhythm which we associate
only with Jazz, but which harks back to
the broken pulse of some primitive drum
beat. Langston Hughes writes in racial
forms, Blues, Spirituals, etc., but even his
free verse has the same rhythmic quality.
"Mammy" is an interesting example of
this.

I'm waiting for ma mammy,—
She is death.

Say it very softly
Say it very slowly if you choose.

I'm waiting for ma mammy,—
Death.

This rhythm walks through the book, sometimes stressed loudly, blaringly as in "Saturday Night," sometimes softly as in "Feet o' Jesus," or with dramatic intensity, or haunting in lines like these:

Night coming tenderly
  Black, like me

Langston Hughes was born in Missouri, and has lived an adventurous life which has taken him to strange corners of the earth. But for the moment he identifies himself with the American Negro. The Negro, humble, unpretentious, not idealized. The boy who cleans the brass spittoons or behind him the dark people of Africa who feel "caged in the circus of civilization." Honest, passionate, crude at times, tender, never sentimental, with a fine ironic economy of words, he sings of them, for them. From a race with whom we associate a mellow loquaciousness one would not expect the splendid compact brevity of this "Song for a Dark Girl."

[. . .]

Perhaps we should take back what we said at the beginning. Langston Hughes is a Negro poet. It is a term of distinction.

Abbe Niles
"Real and Artificial Folk-Song"
New Republic, 51 (8 June 1927), 76–7

[. . .]

To this reviewer, the most interesting portion of Mr. Langston Hughes' book is his dialect verse, and especially the seventeen poems in the manner of the Negro folk-blues, of which he offers far the best concise description in print:

The *Blues,* unlike the *Spirituals,* have a strict poetic pattern: one long line repeated and a third line to rhyme with the other two. Sometimes the second line in repetition is slightly changed and sometimes, but very seldom, it is omitted. The mood of the *Blues* is almost always despondency, but when they are sung people laugh.

The last sentence is remarkable for what it leaves unsaid, for commentators on the blues, including the reviewer, have expressed overdefinite conclusions on the state of mind they represent. Their psychology, or their philosophy, if any, is in fact too complex to fit into any single pigeon-hole such as that of bravery, humility, optimism, "making the best of things," or, since they presuppose no audience, exhibitionism or appeal to sympathy. Although the gusto in their best phrases is unmistakable, even the comfort of having well stated one's grievance will not invariably explain them. For one thing, the singer has quite frequently disguised a real trouble and built his blues on one which is quite fictitious. For another, there has been a curious phenomenon of sympathetic cooperation, which is implied in Mr. Hughes' "Misery": a honky-tonk pianist has been approached by a woman with the request: "My man's lef' me—gimme a blues," and straightway her obscure need has been supplied on such material as she has furnished:

Oh, Sis Kate's lost her rider, so she got
  de blues . . .

The long and short of the matter is that the spirit of the blues, which, unlike their "pattern," is not peculiar to them in American Negro folk-song, can be defined only in terms of their creators themselves: unlettered people who know an inner necessity to sing of their contacts with life, and whose stream of thought takes characteristic jumps and turns, sometimes diverting to others and sometimes, pleasantly, to themselves.

Mr. Hughes' thought need not follow the channel which in those instinctive singers produces such jumps and turns, but at his pleasure it is able to do so. It is still his thought, not theirs, so that he expresses the feelings of the porters, elevator boys, Harlem prostitutes and Memphis bad men into whose shoes he momentarily steps, with an explicitness and coherence which would be beyond most of them; and the resulting absence, in his work, of the streakiness which has been mentioned above, at once takes it out of the category of mere pastiche. It is apparently out of the same ability, and consequent desire, to be explicit, that he resorts to the anomaly of a blues *sequence* forming a single poem. Yet the reviewer finds in this volume but a single line which—since he has never, in his experience, encountered in folk-song a similar assertion that "A *is* B," instead of "A is like B"—he ventures to believe incongruous:

> De railroad bridge's a sad song in de air.

These experiments derive both from spirituals and from secular song, but from only a limited class of the latter. There is none corresponding to the pure fancy of the folk-dance:

> Popped ma whip—*Sangaree!*
> Popped it loud—*Sangaree!*
> Whip got tangled—*Sangaree!*
> Behind a cloud—*Sangaree!*
>
> Popped ma whip—*Sangaree!*
> Popped it strong—*Sangaree!*
> Whip got tangled—*Sangaree!*
> In de wagon-tongue—*Sangaree!*

and there is little to suggest the faint ambiguous melancholy of the folk-blues:

> Oh, de big boat blowed fo' Memphis, but she tuhned aroun' . . .
> She struck high water, an' she went on down

but one does find Hughes' vein in another anonymous verse:

> You don't love me, honey—you don' need to lie . . .
> But de day you leaves me, dat's de day you die

His people are immediately conscious of specific and personal wants, inconveniences and designs, and it is from the depths that they raise their various voices:

> . . . I hates dem rinney yaller gals An' I wants my Albert back. . . .
>
> Gonna buy me a rose-bed An' plant it at ma back door . . .
> So when I'm dead they Won't need no flowers from de store.
>
> I ain't gonna mistreat ma Good gal any more.
> I'm just gonna kill her Next time she makes me sore. . . .
>
> I brought her from de south An' she's goin' on back
> Else I'll use her head for a Carpet tack.
>
> Gonna buy me a knife with a blade ten inches long . . .
> Shall I carve ma self or That man that done me wrong?

Verse of this character should be made complete and its rhythms brought out by music such as the author must have had in mind as he wrote, and it is pleasant to record that there is actually a "Golden Brown Blues" by Hughes and Handy, containing the verse, reminiscent of Van Vechten's Harlem novel:

> If I hits the numbers, I'm tellin' you the fac's . . .

Gonna get a Golden Brown with my
income tax.

Mr. Hughes' range is broader than the scope of this review has indicated; quotations could by multiplied so as to bring out, among other things, his quick sensitiveness to any manifestation of beauty or ugliness, or the exceeding bitterness of some of his reflections. But he has much left to say, he is consistently saying it to better effect, and the variety of his considerable qualities is unlikely to want for critics to number them.

Howard Mumford Jones
"Two Negro Artists"
Chicago Daily News,
29 June 1927, p. 14

The movement of Negro art in this country has been injured by its friends. Maudlin sentimentality of the old sort has been supplanted by a new and complicated sentimentality which purports to see mystic "art" values in crude songs, crude jazz and crude dances, and the devotees of the new sentimentality look with scorn on any who doubt the permanence of these values. A good deal of the work of the "Negro renaissance" is going to be sunk without trace a few years hence, and particularly is this true of the work of many white authors.

But the two books at the head of this review seem to this reader genuine and authentic. James Weldon Johnson has struck bottom in *God's Trombones—Seven Negro Sermons in Verse.* The austere and sustained art of this book is far and away superior to his book of poems. He has been astute enough to abandon Negro dia-

lect—the pitfall of most of the "Negro" literature. . . .

Langston Hughes' earlier book, *The Weary Blues,* was reviewed in these columns some months ago. *Fine Clothes to the Jew* is as much an advance over *The Weary Blues* as *The Weary Blues* is an advance over, let us say, Johnson's *Fifty Years and Other Poems.* Hughes employs dialect, it is true, but he employs it austerely. As Johnson has raised the Negro sermon into art, so Hughes in the poetic form which he calls "Blues" has raised the blues into art, by stripping the crudities off the verse, keeping the repetend, and paring down to the bone. In a sense he has contributed a really new verse form to the English language. In consequence the whole book is on a higher pitch than his earlier volume. It is true that he does not always distinguish propaganda from poetry. "Brass Spittoons," which James Weldon Johnson admires, I do not admire at all. I do not think it is half the poem that "Red Silk Stockings" is. And Hughes has occasionally made the Wordsworthian mistake of confusing with vapidity simplicity. But the book is authentic, it lacks the uneasy air of being a "stunt" book which hung around his earlier production, and one is not conscious that the author is a Negro poet, as he was with *The Weary Blues.* One is conscious only of the material. If he continues to develop, Hughes is dangerously near becoming a major American poet.

Kenneth Fearing
"Limiting Devices"
New Masses, 3 (September 1927), 29

The poems in this volume have a certain amount of power, and a great deal of ease. Hughes is colorful, unsentimental, sharp, and at times strange. He uses Negro dialect and jazz rhythm, in this particular volume, with as much success as anyone has achieved using those limiting devices. But with the American language, to which Hughes will have to turn, he is not yet familiar. An indication of what he may do when he learns a way to use "American" may be seen in the following:

"SPORTS"

Life
For him
Must be
The shivering of
A great drum
Beaten with swift sticks
Then at the closing hour
The lights go out
And there is no music at all
And death becomes
An empty cabaret
And eternity an unblown saxophone
And yesterday
A glass of gin
Drunk long
Ago.

In the main, however, Hughes sticks to dialect poetry; he handles this well, is nearly always successful with it, is precise, imaginative, simple.

De railroad bridge's
A sad song in de air.
De railroad bridge's
A sad song in de air.
Ever time de train pass
I wants to go somewhere.

The trouble with these successes is that they are all small; the poems are little better than poignant playthings. Dialect of any kind, it seems, automatically reduces a poem from the adult to a miniature plane, to a state of unreality. Paradoxically, though the language may be straight from life, a work in dialect is always slightly stagey, a tour de force.

But Hughes has done more with his conventional "Negro stuff"—has used its style to better advantage—than, in my opinion, any other dialect writer.

Julia Peterkin
"Negro Blue and Gold"
Poetry, 31 (October 1927), 44–7

Langston Hughes, in this book of poems, interprets the emotions of primitive types of American Negroes. He has taken the joys and woes of dish-washers and bell-hops, crap-shooters and cabaret girls, broken women and wandering men, and, without losing their strong racial flavor, he has molded them into swift patterns of musical verse.

He has done this without pretension or regard for conventional forms. Stark, fierce, tragic bits of life fall into simple words which keep up an insistent rhythmic beating, beating. No matter what the mood is, each one of these poems has that definite swing, or cadence, which is the sign of an unfailing musical sense.

Cocky black bucks boast defiantly of

their badness, then moan despondently over their bitter loneliness. Deserted side gals cry for faithless yellow papas. Willing wenches beat out frenzied dance-steps that jar the cabaret lights. Brazen gin-flavored laughter chimes high above wailing saxophones that blare out tunes for blues. But the beat of the tom-toms runs through them all, sometimes marking the throbbing of a heavy heart, sometimes drumming measure for eagle-rocking heelthuds. Body-swaying spirituals call on the Creator. Prayers to little Jesus rise from troubled hearts. Apprehensive mothers shriek out warnings to venturesome black babies.

Comedy, tragedy, gayety, despair, sing and moan through the pages. Tragic cries and questions, prayers and hallelujahs, are turned into poetry with an art and skill that makes them available for the enjoyment and experience of all human beings, regardless of color or race.

Certain of the poems, especially, cling to my mind as curious examples of the Negro rhythms to which I am accustomed on our plantation. "Misery," for example, sings as it moans:

Play de blues for me.
Play de blues for me.
No other music
'Ll ease ma misery.

Sing a soothin' song.
Said a soothin' song.
Cause de man I love's done
Done me wrong.

Can't you understand,
Oh, understand
A good woman's cryin'
For a no-good man?

Black gal like me,
Black gal like me
'S got to hear a blues
For her misery.

A more irregular one is "Brass Spittoons," the lament of a boy who has to clean them, which ends consolingly. . . .

"Ma Man" haunts my ear also, and this one, "Gypsy Man," lingers in memory like a whimsical sad tune:

Ma man's a gypsy
Cause he never does come home.

Ma man's a gypsy—
He never does come home.
I'm gonna be a gypsy woman
Fer I can't stay here alone

Once I was in Memphis,
I mean Tennessee.
Once I was in Memphis,
Said Tennessee.
But I had to leave cause
Nobody there was good to me.

I met a yellow papa,
He took ma last thin dime.
Met a yellow papa,
He took ma last thin dime.
I give it to him cause I loved him
But I'll have mo' sense next time.

Love—oh, love is
Such a strange disease.
Love—oh, love is
Such a strange disease.
When it hurts yo' heart you
Sho can't find no ease.

William Russell Clark
"Negro Poet Contributes Second Book"
Dallas Times-Herald, section 5, 4 March 1928, p. 10

The name of Langston Hughes is only beginning to definitely assert itself in the field of poetry. This young Negro first attracted attention when, in 1925, some of his poems were published in *The Crisis*. The same year he won first prize in a contest conducted by *Opportunity Magazine* for the best Negro poem of the year. Subsequent to that time, his poetry found placement in many of the better American magazines, and in 1926 his first book was published, *The Weary Blues*.

To the average Southern intellect, a Negro poet is an inconceivable possibility. With the possible exception of Paul Laurence Dunbar, no black man has ever written a poem recognizable as such among the intelligentsia of the South and Southwest. The place of the Negro has been fixed so definitely that any aspirations he may have entertained have been scoffed at and laughed down.

In truth, however, many Negroes are poets without half-way trying to be or knowing that they are. A superstitious race, their imaginations run riot. Their lives are filled with forebodings, overshadowings, a fine admixture of the spiritual and unreal coloring their talk and enhancing their chants and spirituals. The words of their songs are as potently arresting as are their wails and lamentations and are, for the most part exquisite, if unique, poetry.

In *Fine Clothes to the Jew*, Langston Hughes has made a real contribution to American poetry. The poems in this collection mirror the reactions of the race he represents. He has not encroached upon the white man's privileges and prerogatives, but rather he has depicted and laid bare his people and their hearts. His language is direct and simple, dialectic, if you please, but wholesomely so. He has recorded, in short lyrics, the life of his people as it is lived, day in and day out, with its vulgarity, its barrenness, its delusions, but he has also put into his poems that fine quality of self-sufficiency that only comes naturally from a race of singers.

In practically all of Hughes' poems the quality of music is apparent, not so much in the theme itself, but in the handling of it. He sings as knowingly of a "yellow gal" as he does of Cora, who broke her heart because her lover failed to supply the impetus to keep it beating according to bodily schedule. His "blues" poems are not of the tin-pan-vaudevillian-black-mamma-type, but rather the untutored philosophy of the black man whose woman "done him wrong." In other words, Hughes depicts the life of the Negro as it is and not as paid artists would have us believe.

Never does Hughes forget that he is a Negro and that his poems have to do with those of his race. He is suffering from no form of psychosis, and if he has a complex, it is entirely black. He seems proud of the opportunity accorded him to present his people as they really are. Whether or not the collection with which we are concerned has within it great and indigenous poetry is a mooted question, pending upon the attitude the reader takes in regard to the book. Certainly, the poems are not great as some of the poems of Shelley and Keats are great, but there are within them much of the substance that is akin to greatness.

This young Negro poet should achieve

much. There is substance to his poems; there is music and beauty in them. His field of endeavor is wide and deep and long. He can run the gamut of human emotions in it and never lose himself or his identity. "Prayer," one of the poet's shorter lyrics which originally appeared in *The Buccaneer*, is quoted below:

I ask you this:
Which way to go?
I ask you this:
Which sin to bear?
Which crown to put
Upon my hair?
I do not know,
Lord God.
I do not know.

Checklist of Additional Reviews

Herschel Brickell, "Books on Our Table," *New York Post*, 5 February 1927, p. 8.
"The Literary Almanac," *New York World*, 27 February 1927, p. 10M.
"Negro Poets," *Open Shelf*, April 1927, pp. 51–2.

NOT WITHOUT LAUGHTER

Carlyle Tucker
"Our Book Rack"
Oracle, 9 ([?] 1930),
[p. 27?]

The novel *Not Without Laughter* represents Langston Hughes' first serious work in prose. Mr. Hughes, well known for his poetry, has in his first novel shown himself to be a capable writer of prose, and it is our fond hope that many more novels of outstanding worth will pour from his gifted pen.

The story in itself is a simple one, involving a simple folk, simple customs and manners, but interwoven and intermixed in the general plot is the ever-present strand of propaganda so peculiar and so necessary to a novel dealing primarily with the Negro, his complexities, his struggles and tribulations in a present day world.

The story is laid in the little Kansas town of Stanton. The family involved is that of Hager Williams. Aunt Hager may be typified in a number of old colored families. She is the painstaking, conscientious God-fearing creature, whose chief mottoes are: "God Will Provide," and "Love Your Enemies." Eternally opposed to her is her young incorrigible daughter, Harriett, whose chief aims in life are to have a good time, and to "hate the white folks." It is in the character Harriett that the author has ingeniously interwoven the rebellion of Negro youth against hide-bound, accepted traditions and customs, against religion but only as a thing which prevents individual initiative and freedom of thought and action, and lastly against racial prejudice.

The most interesting character, however, and one who is most outstanding for his philosophical musings, is the boy, Sandy. Here the author has given himself over to a period of profound meditation. Through the eyes of the youth Sandy, he endeavors to puzzle out this complex, paradoxical existence, this world of prejudices and inconsistencies, and is on the verge of surrendering his soul to the inevitable whirlpool of fate, but stretching forth with a supreme effort, snatches himself from the awful abyss of despondency. It is in the portrayal of the boy Sandy that the author is an inspiration to the Negro youth of today.

The novel is primarily one of pathos, interspersed liberally with humorous scenes, but throughout, whether the scene be humorous, pathetic or of dramatic incidence, Mr. Hughes is always the master. His choice of language is most excellent, and his use of the descriptive adjective borders on to genius. The reader's imagination soars to the greatest heights in mentally conceiving the scenes so admirably painted by the author.

The story recommends itself to every thinking Negro for the youthful philosophy of life it contains, and for a thankfulness in the realization that there is a compensating element, that, "no matter how hard life may be, it is not without laughter."

Marion Pinkham
"*Not Without Laughter* Good as Predecessors by Author*"
Tulsa Tribune, 20 July 1930, p. 4C

[. . .]

The talented young poet whose *Weary Blues* and *Fine Clothes to the Jew* have taken their places among the finest of Negro poetry, has here written a novel, bearing the title of the same happy fitness as his books of verse.

Not all the stories of the dark race have to do with hot breathlessness of Harlem or the sentimentality of "coons" and watermelons, cotton fields and banjoes of the old-fashioned southern novels. Hughes presents a cross-section of a group of Negroes in a Kansas town, with the conflict between black and white, older generation and younger, old-time religion and "modern" trend in morals. It is written without bitterness, in a quiet spirit of sympathy and understanding. Here is no educated Negro who wants his people to become poor imitators of the white race, no sullen young reformer trying to lead his fellowmen to a black paradise.

The author tells a touching and convincing story with a skillful blending of pathos and humor. His characters are real creatures, living in the sun, feeling the warmth of summer and the chill of winter; nasturtiums are blood-red and mange, the air hums with great green flies, yellow-black butterflies suckle at the rambling roses; a little boy hurts his heel and limps whimpering through the dust, a storm comes up, and the air is very still and yellow.

There is nothing "literary" about this book. The occasional bits of typically Negro phrasing lend it color. It is somehow fitting that the author should sometimes write "holler" and "licker" or drop into the second person—"You could hear the two women talking"—giving a quality of naturalness and spontaneity that no rule-of-thumb correctness could give.

An interesting distinction of color is made in his description of the different types of Negroes. There are "golden" Negroes, "orange-brown," "autumn-leaf," "ebony," "mahogany," "dark purple," "seal-skin brown" and "chocolate-to-the-bone."

This is the story of Aunt Hager, whose life is lived between her steaming washtubs and the revival meetings where she hopes her children will see the light; of lazy, good-looking, liquid-voiced Jimboy; of patient Annjee and their little son Sandy, of slim Harriett who rebels against the religion of her mother and chooses the carnival tent instead of the revival tent; of Tempy, trying so hard to become white and leave behind her the stigma of a dark skin. Of "plot" in the conventional sense of the word there is none, but the reader's interest never flags.

The poetry of *Weary Blues* and *Fine Clothes to the Jew* is evident again in the magnificent passages describing the dance hall where Benbow's hand makes its insistent melody for the fox-trotters. "Cruel, desolate and unadorned," the wild and savage music is interpreted in prose that surpasses any to be found in modern novels of this type. ". . . the banjo cried in stop-time, and the piano sobbed alive with a rhythmical secret passion. But the drums kept up their hard steady laughter—like somebody who don't care."

The very lack of "pure English," the rude naturalness of these dozen pages devoted to the dance-hall scene make it alive and vivid. This is a Negro writing of his own people, and not a white man looking on from the side lines. This is as they see themselves. In this simple fact lies the whole magic of its strength and power.

The young Sandy wonders if Negroes are poor because they are dancers, jazzers, clowns. "The other way 'round would be better: dancers because of their poverty; singers because they suffered; laughing all the time because they must forget. . . . It's more like that, thought Sandy." For no matter how hard life might be to them, it was not without laughter.

[. . .]

134

Aubrey Bowser
"Invincible Laughter"
New York Amsterdam News, 23 July 1930, [p. 20]

Once in a while we see a book of Negro fiction. There is a sharp difference between Negro fiction and fiction that is written about the Negro. Most of the books written about the Negro are not Negro fiction at all, even when they are written by Negroes; they are Caucasian literature. In the same way, *Othello* is not Moorish drama, for it was written for Englishmen; it is English literature. *Carmen* is not a Spanish opera; it was composed for Frenchmen. And when you write a book about Negroes, every page of which is trimmed to suit a white audience, you are writing "white" literature.

Negro writers address themselves to this white audience because they don't see any other audience. The number of Negroes who can afford to pay $2.50 for a three-hour book of fiction is very small; the number who not only can but will pay it is far smaller. A book about Negroes that does not please a white audience will butter few parsnips, if any.

Thus Negro fiction roughly falls into two categories; it is either pleading or desperate. In the pleading literature the author seeks to convince his audience that Negroes are not so bad as they are painted, that they are really nice people who speak good English and often French, that they wear good clothes and morals. In the desperate fiction the author says: "All you want about us is dirt—damn you, here it is!"

What Negro literature needs is a Marcus Garvey. This man to Negro intellectuals is like a red rag to a bull; but they must admit that he grouped millions of Negroes under a black banner. The man who builds up a group of fifteen or twenty thousand book-buying Negroes will do the greatest thing in the world for the Negro author. With such an audience it is safe to say that our Fishers, McKays and Larsens would write things twice as good as anything they have done, books with no more self-consciousness than Negro spirituals.

Not Without Laughter is that kind of book. Langston Hughes has always been known as a poet, in the opinion of many the greatest living Negro poet. But he has always had a gift for moving prose, and some have wondered why he didn't exercise it. This story is his first long prose work. It is neither argument nor plea, nor is it born of despair; it is simply a story told without self-consciousness.

In fact, the emphasis here is not on the story, but upon the characters, who make the plot by developing naturally. It is just as well for a novel not to have too marked a plot: it tempts the author to make his characters behave unnaturally. In some books you see well-drawn characters doing things that such characters would not do, unless twisted to fit the plot.

The scene of this book is the Middle West, in Kansas. The characters are all members of the average poor colored family trying to wrestle a living and some little happiness out of their unsympathetic environment. The central figure is a little boy called Sandy, who at the end of the story is still adolescent. He lives with his grandmother, an old washerwoman called Aunt Hager. His mother comes home every night after working all day in a white family's kitchen; his father is a rover, who has never outlived the nickname of Jimboy. His mother has two sisters. One is named Harriett; she is in revolt against religion, convention and everything staid. The other,

Tempy, is the "hinkty" member of the family, married to a man some degrees above the social scale of the family and very voluble about it.

With these six characters the author has made a touching story. Their struggles, reverses, disasters, defeats and victories epitomize Negro life in the North and West. There is Aunt Hager, the most appealing character in the book. She washes clothes from the beginning to the end of her life, praying at every plunge into the suds that her children may see the light and carry it on to other and better generations. She never whines at her fate, never flinches, never dodges responsibility; she just works and works for others. In the end her heart is broken because her children do not justify her sacrifices.

Sandy's father, Jimboy, and his young Aunt Harriett are lovable but light in character. Jimboy loves his guitar more than his wife and Harriett likes singing, dancing and fast company. The game is too much for Harriett; her morale is soon gone. The boy's mother, Annjee, is too much in love with her worthless husband to think about anything else.

Her sister Tempy is the kind of woman of whom authors find it hard to write sympathetically; yet she, more than any of the others, represents racial progress. She works hard to be respectable, to have property, to attain culture, to forget the past and go ever forward. All that is very good; but the human side of her is stunted. She is cold and hard, she won't go near her poor old mother if she can help it, for she wants to forget such people. She is obsessed by the ambition to prove to white people that she is just as nice as they, and she is thin-skinned about it. She won't even eat watermelon—it figures too often in cartoons.

Thus at every page of this book the reader has a thrill of recognition. Every person in it, with all his or her faults and virtues, stands out, a definite character truly drawn. Their lives are repeated by the thousands everywhere the Negro lives in America. Jimboy is always losing a job because of white laborers' prejudice; Harriett quits school because she finds she can't get anything to do after she is through; Aunt Hager pounds the tub and prays. When you consider all that Negroes have to contend with, you wonder that any of them should succeed.

Yet, as the author says, their lives are not without laughter. It is to be hoped that Langston Hughes may make this book the first of a trilogy; every reader will wish to know what became of the boy Sandy.

Isabel Paterson "Books and Other Things" *New York Herald Tribune*, 25 July 1930, p. 11

[. . .]

A novel of Negro life, by a Negro, which never comes within sight of Harlem, is a pleasing variation. Langston Hughes has gone back to the scenes he knew in boyhood for *Not Without Laughter*. The heroine, and she deserves the title, is an old Negro washerwoman in a small Kansas town. Aunt Hager Williams could remember growing to girlhood in slavery. She held no bitterness; she had been a house slave, and was well treated and fond of her young mistress. She was worried that her own children and grandchildren were so resentful of the handicap of their color. They hated the white people, when it was brought home to them. Aunt Hager said people were people; some were kindly and some were mean, and hating hurt yourself more than anyone else.

She wanted the youngsters to grow up decent and honest; she wanted them to have an education and do something for their own people. Just the same unselfish ambition that so many mothers, white and black, have cherished for their children. For herself she asked nothing but to be able to go on working and support herself to the end. So much was granted her. One of her girls "went wrong." Aunt Hager whipped her; but when Harriett ran away, and back home again, her mother received her with affection. After all, Harriett "needed to be happy." Her oldest daughter prospered respectably, so well that she was rather ashamed of the poor old washer-woman, and did nothing to help her. Aunt Hager never asked for help.

The clear merit of Mr. Hughes's novel is that his people are just people. He has a sense of character and of proportion. The "color problem" never obscures the human interest. They are simply poor folks with a living to get and a longing for happiness; the story is woven of the texture of life itself.

[. . .]

"Education, Black and White"
Cleveland Press, 26 July 1930, p. 5

Langston Hughes has done pretty nearly everything you can find in a book of adventure since he was graduated from Cleveland's Central High School as class poet and yearbook editor.

Now he has written the soundest Negro novel that has been produced by any of the swarm of Negro novelists that have been active since the war.

That makes it the soundest Negro book by anyone, black or white, since Cleveland's Charles W. Chestnutt did *The Conjure Woman* 31 years ago. Hughes' novel is *Not Without Laughter*.

It is superior to any other Negro's Negro book (except Chestnutt's) because it has perspective; it is not special pleading; it might, so far as either apology or raw passion goes, have been written by anyone of whatever race.

It is superior to any non-Negro's Negro book because it is built from information that no non-Negro could possibly have.

So much for foundation. On that, it is superior to most Negro books because it is not melodramatic; it does not strain for fantastic color; it is a straightforward novel built honestly out of its own material.

That is the life of a whole Negro family, told in relation to a hero who is 5 when the book opens and 16 when it closes, in a Negro community in a white middle western town. The town is called Stanton, Kansas. I recognize in it a good deal of Topeka, where Hughes once lived as a boy.

That is incidental. What is important is that it is in such towns—not in the South, which is traditional, nor in Harlem, which is special—that the Negro social problem reaches the average of its new ferment.

When the boy is 16, as the book ends, he has moved to Chicago. That is more useful than having him go to Harlem, too.

The book is not long, but compressed in it is the whole panorama of the new Negro social history. The boy's grandmother, born in slavery, is the old-style hard working black mammy. Her eldest daughter is of the first flight of the newer Negro—imitation white. The second daughter, Sandy's mother, is in service and satisfied; her husband, an ambulatory guitar-playing, blues-singing yellow buck out of the South. The youngest daughter after rebellion reaches eminence thru the cultivation of her special racial gifts. Sandy might be Langston Hughes himself.

They move thru good times and bad, in relation to the white community and the black, old, changing and new.

H.J.
"Some Midseason Novels to Cool Away Hot Days"
Philadelphia Public Ledger, 26 July 1930, p. 7

Old Hager Williams has raised three daughters. Tempy, rich and aristocratic, by virtue of her marriage to a mail clerk, is ashamed of her old mother, who has spent forty years at the laundry tub; Annjee, wedded to good-for-nothing guitar-strumming Jimboy, cooks for the white folks to buy silk shirts for Jimboy and to send young Sandy to school; Harriett, pretty, life-loving little sprite of joy, who rebels at life's unfairness to her race, runs off to sing and dance at carnivals. Old Hager's only consolations are her religion and her grandson, whom she destines as a leader of the Negro folk. Such lends the atmosphere of Langston Hughes' remarkable first novel.

Not only does the author show decided skill in choice of incident but also in his vividness of word-choosing and, above all, in his employment of restraint. The pathos, the crude brutality, the blind and tireless struggle of his people are told with close fidelity. Sandy's young rebellion against old Hager's doctrine of renunciation and his acceptance of his parents' inability to win a place in life are autobio-

graphic in detail, though there is nothing in Mr. Hughes' history to indicate an autobiographic basis for his work. He calls his volume *Not Without Laughter,* but it leaves his reader not without tears. Mr. Hughes has proved his skill at character portrayal and at prose as completely as he has already proved his skill at verse. *Not Without Laughter* will rank among the most outstanding volumes of the season.

Wilson Jefferson
"Life Comes 'Not Without Laughter' to Kansas Negroes"
Philadelphia Record, 26 July 1930, p. 10C

In *Not Without Laughter,* Langston Hughes, the young Negro poet, has written a novel of Negro life in an entirely new manner. His black characters are real people. Some of them are real sinners. But saints or sinners, one feels that they always do or say the inevitable thing, and not the merely silly nor the fatuously inept thing.

The scene is laid in a small Kansas town. Aunt Hager, a widowed mother, wants her three daughters to grow into honest, sedate and God-fearing womanhood.

Two of them openly rebel. When Harriett reaches the ripe age of 16, she leaves home to live with a jazz-loving girl friend. Tempy finds her mother and her mother's friends beneath her after she marries a post office clerk and joins her husband's progressive church.

Annjee, the one daughter that sticks to her mother, marries a roving, fun-loving husband appropriately named Jimboy, who twangs a wicked guitar and prefers blues songs to Baptist hymns. It is only Sandy, Annjee's son, who remains to the end of Aunt Hager's troubled, harried career, her one comfort and inspiration. She wants her grandson to be a great man some day and a leader of his people.

But Aunt Hager dies and the inevitable family breakup follows. Annjee joins the roving Jimboy in Chicago. The war comes on, he enlists and leaves for the front. Harriett continues to drift, learns to sing and dance, and finally gets on as a member of a traveling theatrical troupe.

The story ends with the meeting of Harriett and Annjee and Sandy in a Negro theatre in Chicago after Harriett has done her stuff as part of the evening's entertainment. Jimboy is still somewhere in France. But Harriett, some of her dreams realized, gives Sandy a small sum of money and promises that she will send him funds regularly to help him complete his schooling and be that great Negro leader his Grandmother Hager visioned for him. Genuine feeling and color are woven in and about the black folk in this simple story. Jimboy is a real, fun-loving, guitar-playing black man who never grew up. Aunt Hager is a sacrificing Negro mother, honest, hardworking, fearful of new ideas and notions, but always ready to go to the limit of her strength and resources to help others. Whites and blacks alike find solace in her wisdom and counsel.

Sandy is perhaps the finest fictional type of a Negro boy that literary America has yet produced. He sees and experiences things that would warp a nature less resolute, or embitter a nature less poised. He feels the touch of poverty from his tenderest years, is thrown around barber shops and second-rate hotels in his efforts to earn a few dollars and help his grandmother—and yet, unlike his Aunt Harriett, keeps clean and wholesome.

I wondered, as I contemplated Sandy's career, just how much of Langston Hughes' own life went into this lovable picture. Certainly he, too, once dreamed dreams under what most of us would call crushing and inhospitable conditions. And he, too, worked at humble tasks without losing faith either in himself or in mankind. How just and well placed that faith was this really fine novel reveals to us.

George S. Schuyler "Views and Reviews" *Pittsburgh Courier,* 26 July 1930, [p. 10]

Bring out the laurel wreath and drape the brow of Langston Hughes for giving us *Not Without Laughter*. It is the novel of Negro life. It is great literature. I haven't read all of the novels written but I haven't read a better one. More than a novel, it is a social document, an epic on the sable lowly that white America and bourgeois black America look down upon. Here we have the suffering, the pleasures, the loves and hates, the hopes, aspirations and frustrations of Negro proletarians. To the ordinary Negro reader it arouses memories of youth, of yesterday and today. I know the people in this novel, every one of them. They are in a hundred little ghettoes from Augusta, Me., to Seattle, Wash. His people are real and their language is real.

"I been known' white folks all ma life an' they's good as far as they can see—but when it comes to po' niggers, they just can't see far, that's all."

"White folks made me leave ma home."

"Evening's the only time we niggers have to ourselves! Thank God for night . . . 'cause all day you gives to white folks."

You get pretty hot under the collar when once more and so effectively you are reminded of the White Terror that smothers and frustrates Negroes. Here is pictured Negro servants, leg- and back-weary, feeding their families on white folks' leavings, girls graduating from school to be faced with the alternative of drudgery or prostitution, poor little Negro children with sick mothers and absent fathers, wanting Christmas presents like the white children—and being disappointed. Hughes bears all the spiritual scars of every American Negro. Despite his title, there is little or no laughter here; he knows too much, feels too much. And yet the tale is not without humor.

These are your folks Hughes has written about in this tale of a Negro family in a small Kansas town; good old earthy, cynical, shrewd, struggling, sometimes bitter, Negroes who eat ham and cabbage, black-eyed peas and salt pork; who twang guitars, sing blues when happy or thoughtful and spirituals when worried and tried. The novel will doubtless have a sequel. At least it ought to.

Mary Ross
"A Little Colored Boy Grows Up"
New York Herald Tribune Books, 27 July 1930, p. 5

To the white man, by and large, Negroes have been people who could cook or launder or sing and play jazz; who were lazy or faithful or religious; or sometimes, in a manner especially surprising because they were of another color, showed talent or even genius in one of the arts, which seemed important initially because it was Negro, and only secondarily because the products were beautiful in themselves. Negroes, even to those whose intellectual protestations were liberal, have not often been accepted as just people, aside from the qualities or defects which are sweepingly attributed to their race as a whole. That racial potpourri which goes by the name of American occasionally comes up against a similar indiscrimination in Europe, for example, when some one announces dogmatically that Americans are merely money-grabbers or that their chief ideal in life is sanitary plumbing.

And on the other side of the color line, that wavering but very real barrier between the two races, there has been in these past years of growing economic and educational attainment by Negroes a wholly understandable tendency to "cash in" on the gifts for which the domineering caste expressed admiration. If they are willing to pay royally for being amused in night clubs by the songs and dancing that they could see without a penny on the sideless streets of Charleston or Harlem, let them pay. All they can pay and more would do little enough to wipe out the debt of agony that produced the spirituals, and then, in a more secular generation, the blues. Personal integrity must have been hard to maintain before this fluctuation from contempt to almost maudlin admiration, which throughout so often has been entirely impersonal—treating the performer, whether in the arts or the professions or merely the economic maelstrom, as though he were no more than a racial puppet. Little wonder that there has grown up one counter-pride, which attempted to deny everything allegedly "Negro" and to imitate the life of the more fortunate whites; another pride, which denied the whites any virtue, and took out in bitterness and in the racial magnification to which subject peoples always are driven the indignities to which their loyalties made them prey. The pendulum has swung fitfully from martyrdom to sterile isolation or boastful mastery.

In this first novel Langston Hughes, already distinguished for his volumes of poetry, achieves the difficult equilibrium of showing Negroes who are essentially human beings. Like the other creatures who aspire to this title, they are molded by limitations from within and without; and for them, that which overpowers all else in power, is the fact of their being colored, and the attitudes which circumstance engenders. But *Not Without Laughter* should not, I think, be called "The Negro novel." It has no need to trade on the color of its characters or the race of its author. Because it is a story of a little boy growing up in a Negro family, with an outlook which no white reader could experience in full for himself, but more especially because it is written with understanding, tolerance and beauty, it lays special claim to the attention of those who love life and its mirroring in fiction.

Langston Hughes, not yet thirty, comes of a generation which was spared some of the need for bitterness by which cultured members of his race, like the early feminists, had to cut through the bigotry of an earlier day. He was born in Missouri, his father a lawyer, his mother a school teacher; and his twenty-odd years have seen life in Mexico City, Topeka, Colorado Springs, Kansas City, Buffalo, Cleveland, New York and Washington, as well as capitals of Europe and voyages to the Canary Islands, the Azores, and the West Coast of Africa. As a beachcomber in Genoa, a doorman in a Paris cabaret, a busboy in a Washington hotel, a friend of poets and writers and singers, he has had a chance to see his own people—and the whites—from angles that a lifetime often fails to compass. And it is this richness of observation, this joy in experience, that he brings to a simple story of a little colored boy living with his grandmother—who was a laundress—in a Kansas town.

This story of Aunt Hager Williams, who had known slavery, and her three daughters and one little grandson gives play for some of the attitudes, white and Negro, which I tried to sketch above. One daughter, Tempy, marries modest riches, becomes genteel in her tastes, deserts the Baptists for the Episcopalians, and draws her skirts aside from all that has been known as "Negro." The second, Annjee, hangs her whole life on her love for her wandering man, Jimboy, and worn out by her unremitting toil to support him and their child, fails to keep before her, as did the old grandmother, the ideal that Sandy must get the education for which he thirsts. The third, gay little Harriett, refusing to accept her mother's faith that she must wait till the next world for the joys denied her in this, goes her dancing and blues-singing way, hating the whites, taking from them what she can get, but generous and loyal to her own people. And wise old Aunt Hager herself saw beyond her children to the possibilities for her grandchild. "For mighty nigh seventy years I been knowin' both of 'em, an' I ain't never had no room in ma heart to hate neither white nor colored. When you starts hatin' people you gets uglier than they is—an' I ain't never had no time for ugliness, b'cause that's where de devil comes in—in ugliness."

Occasionally, as perhaps in the speech just quoted, a bit of philosophizing seems to take one a little outside the story itself, to make its people more mouthpieces or examples than individuals. But to an extent unusual in any novel which deals with issues so cutting and tangled, this is a story of the poignant joys and griefs of a little boy, and the group of women and men who were his life. In places it is cruelly touching—when the colored children in school were placed at the back of the room; when they got to the amusement part with their newspaper coupons for a party for "all the children of Stanton," agog for a ride on the roller coaster, only to be told it was a party for white children only; when Santa Claus didn't bring the Golden Flyer sled. But this is no mawkish pathos, nor is there, even in Harriett's story, the disfiguring touch of rancor—but only regret. Rather it is the simple pleasures, the gayety and good humor of these people, that triumph, and make the whites seem, by contrast, as anemic in spirit as in color. Looking at old Uncle Dan Givens, the town's champion boaster, Sandy thought: "No matter how belligerent or lewd their talk was, or how sordid the tales they told—of dangerous pleasures and strange perversities—these black men laughed. That must be the reason why poverty-stricken old Negroes like Uncle Dan Givens lived so long—because to them, no matter how hard life might be, it was not without laughter."

Wallace Thurman
"Books in Review"
New York Evening Post,
28 July 1930, p. 7

Langston Hughes's novel *Not Without Laughter* will confound many soothsayers and prematurely pessimistic critics. For the poet has proven that he can write prose adequate for the story he has to tell, and he has not concerned himself either with Harlem's Midnight Nans or the southland's cottonfield sweet men. He has depicted, rather, as the blurb on the jacket so conveniently states, a "deeply human picture of a simple people, living in a typical Kansas town, meeting, as best they can, the problems of their destructive, complex environment." He has done this, that is, for 249 pages of his 308-page novel. Remem-

ber this reservation for future reference.

Aunt Hager Williams is an aged Negro woman, a pious, homespun, ample-bosomed individual, beloved by all with whom she comes into frequent contact. She lives her simple life, immersed in the steam and suds of her washtubs, dedicated to the welfare of her children, to the grace of God, and to the service of her neighbor should he be in need of her assistance. And, as a reward for this exemplary conduct, makes such an impression upon the community in which she lives that notice of her death merits, "in small type on its back page," the following paragraph from the *Daily Leader:*

> Hager Williams, aged colored laundress, of 419 Cypress Street, passed away at her home last night. She was known and respected by many white families in the community. Three daughters and a grandson survive.

One of these surviving daughters, Tempy, is a victim of that lamentable American disease for which there seems to be no antitoxin: Keeping up with the Joneses, the Joneses in Tempy's case being bourgeois whites. With a smattering of what she believes to be culture, a few parcels of income property, and a husband who works for the government, Tempy spends her time trying to convince herself and the world at large that she is neither part nor parcel of the peasant environment in which she happened to be born. While Tempy sounds as if she might be interesting, she is actually the most poorly delineated character in the novel. The reason is obvious. Being constantly surrounded by a legion of Tempy's prototypes, Mr. Hughes has not been as objective in this portrayal as he might have been had Tempy, like most of his other characters, been more indigenous to the novel's milieu.

The youngest daughter, Harriett, is a native hedonist, early and easily seduced by flashy clothes, torrid dancing, spontaneous song fests, stimulating beverages and amorous dalliance. Frustrating all efforts to keep her in school or make her amenable to menial labor, she gleefully, if not always successfully, defies the wrath of Aunt Hager's God and Charlestons down a gaudy, primrose path.

The other daughter, Annjee, is the mother of Hager's one grandchild, Sandy. Annjee is distressingly normal. She works hard, complains but seldom, has no desire to be either a Tempy or a Harriett, and loves her husband, the irresponsible Jimboy, intensely, constantly, albeit he is subject to the "travelin' blues," and walks off from Annjee and her child whenever the spirit so moves him.

It is with Sandy, the son of this haphazard union, whom *Not Without Laughter* primarily concerns itself. Around him most of the action is woven, through his eyes much of the story is reflected, and it is the problem of Sandy's adjustment to his environment, a problem more or less peculiar to the maturing Negro child, which occupies many pages of the novel.

It is not Sandy, however, but Aunt Hager, Harriett, Jimboy and Annjee who remain alive in the reader's mind once the novel is completed. And of these Aunt Hager is by far the most indelible, a fact which explains the reference made to page 249 some paragraphs ago. For when Aunt Hager dies and crosses over Jordan, the reader is hard put to retain his former high pitch of interest. Simultaneously with her death, Harriett, Jimboy and Annjee also fade into the background. It is too great a bereavement. Either the novel should have managed to end itself at this point or Aunt Hager's demise should have been postponed. Certainly her heavenly home could have done without her for a few more years. Her presence is vitally necessary to the more mundane *Not Without Laughter*.

Following the death of his grandmother, Sandy is forced to sojourn with the dicty Tempy, his mother having decided to trail the truant Jimboy. Tempy keeps him in school, urges him to abjure bad company, and, being a myopic disciple of Dr. W. E. B. Du Bois, attempts to invest him with ideals diametrically opposed to those disseminated and held dearly by his dead grandmother, a loyal, if vague, disciple of Booker T. Washington. Sandy seems destined to pursue a middle course, and we leave him optimistically facing the future, appropriately misunderstood by Annjee, obligingly relieved by Tempy, and, surprisingly enough, encouraged and aided by Harriett, whose aversion to the straight and narrow path has brought her a measure of fame and fortune on the stage.

Not Without Laughter is an enviable first performance. Belonging to a more decorous school, it lacks the dramatic intensity, the lush color and tropical gusto of Claude McKay's *Home to Harlem*. It also lacks the pallid insipidity and technical gaucheries of certain other contemporary novels by Negroes which are best left unnamed and forgotten. But it does present a vivid, sincerely faithful and commendable picture of peasant Negro life in a small American town, a town which vacillates uncertainly, spiritually and physically, from one side of the Mason Dixon line to the other.

In a moment of post-college exuberance, while considering Mr. Hughes's first book of poems, *The Weary Blues*, the present reviewer stridently declaimed that its author was possessed of "an unpredictable and immeasurable potential." After five years, the language might be more simple and more choice, but the spirit of the phrase would remain unchanged. For, as in his poetry Mr. Hughes carried a beacon light for Negro poets, he now, with this volume, advances to the vanguard of those who have recourse to the novel in an earnest endeavor to depict the many-faceted ramifications of Negro life in America.

Constance M. Green
"A Negro Boy's Childhood"
New York Sun, 2 August 1930, p. 14

In his first novel Langston Hughes has made a vivid, sincere and natural study of a Negro boy's childhood and adolescence. The humorous suggestiveness of the title is hardly justified in so serious a portrayal of life, but not without laughter are the efforts of the little darkey's aunt, Tempy, to dignify her place among the colored Four Hundred of the Middle-Western town.

No big pots of black-eyed peas and pigtails scented the house of the newly prosperous Mrs. Siles. She never bought a watermelon, having advanced to the sophistication of grapefruit and tangerines in imitation of her former mistress. The subtle inference is that Mr. Hughes himself feels that the genius of his race can never find its fullest expression in a servile following of the ways of white people, socially or in the world of art.

While not wishing to judge this young man's work from a racial point of view, it must inevitably meet in comparison that of white writers in a similar field. It may be that the very fact of his inheritance brings the author too close to his canvas, but his brush is surely not dipped in the magic of *Black April* and *Porgy,* novels of strictly Negro life by writers also young. This is accounted for in part by the Middle-Western setting, which though more unusual in a novel of Negro life, lacks its accustomed picturesqueness.

There is an interesting contrast of personalities in Aunt Hager's three daughters—one of whom is the small hero's mother—and the reward of virtue in the wayward Harriett's triumphal career is convincingly lifelike. The best touch in the book is, happily, the closing scene, where in an obscure little Southern church in a Chicago side street, a group of old black worshippers were still holding their nightly meeting as Annjee and her son pass.

[. . .]

A.W.S.
"Recent Books"
New Yorker, 6 (2 August 1930), 58

There is a sadder side of the picture [than in Eslanda Goode Robeson's *Paul Robeson, Negro*] in *Not Without Laughter* by Langston Hughes. This is the story of the ordinary black family living out in Kansas, where, as Mr. Hughes says, "Being black is like being born in the basement of a house . . . with the white folks living upstairs." Mr. Hughes, whose poems you may know, is a first-rate novelist; his book stands the great test of racial literature—it would be just as good, just as sound, if it were written about a group of poor whites. He writes simply, honestly, and sincerely; he would rather touch your heart than shock you. He has the courage to show that a certain class of Negroes are just as greedy, snobbish, and heartless as the shoddy whites. Unlike many modern Negro writers, he dares to be just a little sentimental about the good old people—the hard working old mammies. I also like his humor, which is detached and spontaneous.

[. . .]

Elizabeth Lay Green
"The Literary Lantern"
Virginian-Pilot and Norfolk Landmark, 3 August 1930, p. 6

In a batch of midsummer fiction which ranges from mediocrity downwards, it is a privilege to be able to select two novels of distinction—two which we venture to predict will last a long time in the top rows of their respective classifications. One is a Negro novel and the other deals with white Tennessee Mountain characters.

Langston Hughes, a native of Missouri, one of the best and the most individual of the young Negro poets, has been promising his first novel for a long time, and his poetical gifts would lead us to expect a brilliant performance, though we must admit that his preoccupation with jazz had led to the expectation that his prose style would be mannered and stylized, and his chief interest the surface description and colorful elements of Negro life. We almost feared another Harlem sex piece. What Mr. Hughes has given us in *Not Without Laughter* is a simple chronicle of a Negro boy in a Kansas small town, his childish hopes and disappointments, his growing awareness of the music and discord in the life of his race, his struggle for balance and an upward lift where even those who loved him best are pulling him backward. The author's chief emphasis is on characterization, and his style is a simple straightforward prose which lapses only a few times

into a sort of breathless impressionism. His people, particularly the old grandmother, Hager, and the blues-playing loafer of a father, are full of life and reality. The background of small-town life is sincerely and well described. Mr. Hughes is only a little bitter over race discrimination. His detached attitude is most effective in descriptions such as those of "Children's Day" when the little blacks are excluded from a promised party. Here is perfect understanding and sympathy with a child's petty and enormous woes. It is largely because of Mr. Hughes' depiction of the colored child's psychology that we feel this book could only have been written by a colored man—and it is the only Negro novel we know of about which we do have this feeling.

If we have any quarrel to pick with *Not Without Laughter* it is with the form. There have been too many novels of late which are merely episodic. The character may develop through the succeeding events, as he does here, but his career is picked up and ended anywhere—there is no rounded plot, no great complication, no inevitable end.

[. . .]

"Negro Family Life in Novel"
Detroit News, part 10, 3 August 1930, p. 6

In his first novel Langston Hughes reveals exceptional powers of observation, a fine understanding of his subject and the literary ability that has given him a name as a poet.

He tells the story of a Negro family living in a small Kansas town, and the portrait of each member of the family is remarkably clear. There is old Aunt Hager, an ex-slave and a true "Mammy" type (somewhat different, it might be noted, from the cinema-musical comedy type). There is her daughter Annjee who, with her husband and son, lives with her mother in her heavily mortgaged little home.

Both Annjee and old Hager work for white people, while Jimboy, Annjee's husband, works when he can find a job, but is devoted to the guitar and has the heart of a gypsy. He absents himself for long periods and writes to his adoring wife infrequently.

Sandy, the son of Annjee and Jimboy, is really the central figure of the story. He is a well-mannered boy, eager to gain an education. He has the affection and support of every other member of the family, as well as the regard of many friends and neighbors who like to believe he can become another Booker T. Washington. Even the lad's irresponsible father and his Aunt Harriett, whose early escapades finally lead her to residence in the notorious "bottoms," strongly champion the boy's career.

The story is simple. It moves along easily, telling of Sandy's development as a boy and youth. It offers flawless pictures of a Negro district with all the familiar types of characters. It records the gradual disintegration of the family and the death of the aged grandmother. It reveals the struggling mental development of the Negro and the unselfish determination on the part of some less fortunate ones to aid the rise of one of their fellows who can help to right the wrongs they feel are imposed on them by white men.

Mr. Hughes does nothing to shield his race from just criticism. He depicts Negroes at their best and at their worst and very fairly shows that the black man's best and his worst closely parallel the white man's.

Reading this novel the impression grows that it may be autobiographical. This impression is strengthened by the reflection that the young hero, Sandy, is carried well along the road to the sort of success that has been achieved by Mr. Hughes. Throughout the book the author's understanding of literary values and his poetic ability to express himself stand out as strong evidence of his subtle suggestion that the Negro can ascend to great heights.

"Not Without Laughter and Other Recent Fiction" New York Times Book Review, 3 August 1930, p. 6; as "Brief Reviews of Modern Fiction," Times (Calumet City, Ill., Hammond, Ind., etc.), 30 August 1930, p. 11

Langston Hughes has succeeded in giving us in Not Without Laughter an intimate picture of that type of Negro life which has been so popular with white writers in the recent decade. In the last five years, for example, two Pulitzer prize works, Paul Green's In Abraham's Bosom and Julia Peterkin's Scarlet Sister Mary, have dealt with the same aspects of Negro life that are to be found in this novel. Hughes, in fact, is the first of contemporary Negro writers to treat successfully with the life of the lower class Negro in town as well as city. Claude McKay in Home to Harlem dealt with bottom-rung Negro life in its urban forms, as also did Rudolph Fisher in The Walls of Jericho. Hughes, however, in turning to the country for his setting, has exploited material that is even more picturesque. More than that, he has come to closer grips with this material than have his white contemporaries. In other words, he has made it live as of itself, without resort to artifice or literary stratagem.

Not Without Laughter really has no story at all. It has only characters. The hero, Sandy, who grows up in the novel from a very young boy to a rapidly maturing young man, is the least-successful creation of them all. The other characters, however, are beautifully clear and real. Jimboy, the father of Sandy, a guitar-playing, irresponsible gadabout; Annjee, his wife, who loves him on account of rather than despite his vices; Aunt Hager, the mother of Annjee, the plantation mammy who would rather be a slave than a free woman and whose whole life is spent in service to others; Tempy, the sister of Annjee, who marries Mr. Siles for his wealth and becomes an exponent of middle-class virtues; and Harriett, who despises Tempy and flings herself into the circus-whirl of the stage, winning prominence as a blues singer—these are the people who live in this novel as few characters have ever lived in a book.

One of the most interesting aspects of the novel is the excellent contrast in character that it affords. Tempy and Mr. Siles versus Harriett and Jimboy, the conflict between the Negro type which, preferring wealthiness of money to wealthiness of soul, apes white ideas and ideals, and the type which, despising wealth even when it has it, sneers at white ideas and ideals as the ridiculous conventions of a people who have never learned to live—here we have a striking cross-section of that conflict which has already set in between upper and lower class Negro life. Tempy and Mr. Siles hate the blues and spirituals because "they are too Negro," and condemn those who sing them for "acting like niggers." Harriett and Jim Boy not only love the

blues and spirituals, their very lives are made up of their music. They love them because they are so Negro.

Not Without Laughter is very slow, even tedious, reading in its early chapters, but once it gains its momentum it moves as swiftly as a jazz rhythm. Its characters, emerging ever more clearly and challengingly as the novel proceeds, give it this rhythm. Every character in the novel, it can be said, with the exception of Tempy and Mr. Siles, is a living challenge to our civilization, a challenge that is all the more effective because it springs naturally out of its materials and is not superimposed upon them.

V. F. Calverton "This Negro"

Nation, 131 (6 August 1930), 157–8

Here is the Negro in his most picturesque form—the blues-loving Negro, the spiritual-singing Negro, the exuberant, the impassioned, the irresponsible Negro, the Negro of ancient folk-lore and romantic legend. "Good-natured, guitar-playing Jim Boy"; Annjee Rodgers loving Jimboy no matter where he goes or whom he lives with; Aunt Hager, the old mammy of a dead generation, "whirling around in front of the altar at revival meetings ... her face shining with light, arms outstretched as though all the cares of the world had been cast away"; Harriett, "beautiful as a jungle princess," singing and jazzing her life away, sneering at sin as a white man's bogy, and burying beneath peals of laughter "a white man's war for democracy"; and Sandy, seeing his people as a "band of black dancers captured in a white world," and resolving to free them from themselves as well as from their white dictators—these are the Negroes of this novel, these the people who make it live with that quick and intimate reality which is seldom seen in American fiction.

Not Without Laughter continues the healthy note begun in Negro fiction by Claude McKay and Rudolph Fisher. Instead of picturing the Negro of the upper classes, the Negro who in too many instances has been converted to white norms, who even apes white manners and white morality and condemns the Negroes found in this novel as "niggers," McKay, Fisher, and Hughes have depicted the Negro in his more natural and more fascinating form. There can be no doubt that the Negro who has made great contributions to American culture is this type of Negro, the Negro who has brought us his blues, his labor songs, his spirituals, his folklore—and his jazz. And yet this very type of Negro is the one that has been the least exploited by contemporary Negro novelists and short-story writers. It has been white writers such as DuBose Heyward, Julia Peterkin, Howard W. Odum, and Paul Green who have turned to this Negro for the rich material of their novels, dramas, and stories. These writers, however, have known this Negro only as an exterior reality, as something they could see, listen to, sympathize with, even love; they could never know him as an inner reality, as something they could live with as with themselves, their brothers, their sweethearts—something as real as flesh, as tense as pain. Langston Hughes does. As a Negro he has grown up with these realities as part of himself, as part of the very air he has breathed. Few blurs are there in these pages, and no fumbling projections, and no anxious searching for what is not. Here is this Negro, or at least one vital aspect of him, as he really is, without ornament, without pretense.

All this praise, however, must not be misconstrued. *Not Without Laughter* is not without defects of style and weaknesses of structure. The first third of the novel, in fact, arrives at its points of interest with a pedestrian slowness; after that it picks up tempo and plunges ahead. Unfortunately, there are no great situations in the novel, no high points of intensity to grip and overpower the reader. Nor is there vigor of style—that kind of vigor which could have made of Sandy's ambition to emancipate his race, for example, a more stirring motif. But *Not Without Laughter* is significant despite these weaknesses. It is significant because even where it fails, it fails beautifully, and where it succeeds—namely, in its intimate characterizations and in its local color and charm—it succeeds where almost all others have failed.

Theophilus Lewis "The Harlem Sketch Book" *New York Amsterdam News,* 6 August 1930, p. 9

Not Without Laughter, by Langston Hughes, is more than an intrinsically good book. It marches into a virgin field and establishes a new frontier for the branch of American letters known as Negro literature. In this novel Hughes turns his back on the debaucheries of barrel house niggers and makes a wide detour around the lusts of plantation blacks who are almost as degraded as the authors who record their lecheries with such gusto, advancing into a hitherto unexplored region of normal Negro life. The reward of his pioneering is a story that demonstrates that the short and simple annals of sane, thrifty Negroes can be as intensely interesting as the pornographies of Beale Street or the liaisons of sepia wenches and white overseers in Mississippi cotton fields.

The literary movement which for some obscure reason is called the Negro renaissance divides itself into two schools. The dominant school follows the pattern of Carl Van Vechten's *Nigger Heaven* and includes such novels as *Porgy, Black April, The Walls of Jericho, Home to Harlem, Banjo, Scarlet Sister Mary* and *Sweet Man*. In the dramatic field it includes plays like *Black Boy, Going Home, In Abraham's Bosom, Porgy* and *The Green Pastures*, as well as the entire roster of Paul Green's one-act plays.

In all these books, and all the plays except *The Green Pastures*, the Negro is pictured as a primitive gypsy whose shellac of civilization goes no deeper than his B.V.D.'s. He is a picturesque and picaresque "pagan," as improvident as a Bushman and as sexually avid as a satyr. He is incapable of either sustaining thought or sustained effort, and if a dash of white blood makes it possible for him to have an aim in life, as in *Abraham's Bosom*, it will eventually drive him mad.

Votes of protest have been registered from the left. The authors of *The Fire in the Flint, There Is Confusion, Dark Princess, Passing* and *The Blacker the Berry* have made gallant efforts to portray the Negro as he actually is—as a striver and thinker capable of more self-restraint than any white man ever had to exercise. In *Mamba's Daughters*, DuBose Heyward turns his back on the "pagan" panhandlers of *Porgy* and endows his heroine with a singleness of purpose equal to that of the *Mayor of Casterbridge*. Each of these books is a contradiction of the prevailing theory that the Negro is a thoughtless drifter. *Not Without Laughter* is more than a contradiction. It is a challenge.

Perhaps I give the impression that *Not Without Laughter* is a propaganda novel. If so, I pause to state it is nothing of the sort. Hughes indulges in no maudlin weeping over the injustices perpetrated on the Negro; makes no effort to sugar-coat the obvious shortcomings of his swarthy compatriots. He presents the day to day life of the average black in its natural colors and contours, omitting nothing essential, exaggerating nothing important.

The story describes the fortunes of a colored family of Kansas whose means and standards of living are so similar to those of the bulk of Negro families of Baltimore, Detroit, or even Harlem that a sociologist might readily accept it as the typical Negro family of America. The family consists of a widowed grand dame, Hager Williams, her three daughters, and her grandson, Sandy Rodgers. When the story opens Harriett, the youngest girl, is approaching the borderline between adolescence and womanhood. Annjee, the second daughter, has already been married several years, but as her husband spends more of his life following the call of the wanderlust, she and her boy, Sandy, live with Hager. The eldest daughter, Tempy, has married well and gone dicty, seldom visiting her mother and sisters.

Hager supports the home with the earnings of her wash tub, assisted by Annjee, who cooks for a white family crosstown. The atmosphere of the home is thoroughly commonplace and practically everything that happens in it can be described by the same term. Dominated by the stalwart Hager, the little family strives valiantly to keep its place on the upper side of the line that divides poverty from degradation. While Hager and her daughters seldom agree on the tactics to be employed or the goal to be sought, none of them ever suggests surrender. No one ever thinks of waving the white flag.

The central interest of the story is the

development of Sandy from early childhood to the threshold of manhood. They are years of struggle. Heartaches are many, frustrations are frequent and triumphs are few and far between. But never does the family give in to discouragement or admit the probability of defeat, and in their resistance to the pressure of poverty and prejudice there is more profound passion and genuine humor than you will find in all the books of the barrel house school of literature put together.

There is no straining for bizarre effects in this book; no forced humor or alcoholic eroticism. Yet while Hughes portrays life accurately, the story is not a piling up of photographic detail. It is not a duplication of life; it is life smelted and refined, with its non-essential slag drained off and its poignancy and beauty retained—and that's what art is.

The final test of an artist is his ability to create character. Plot, style, technique, do not make great literature. First-rate fiction is always a convincing portrayal of character in development or decline. In the ability to present character faithfully and vividly Hughes rates far above any other novelist who has ventured into the field of "Negro" fiction except DuBose Heyward, and he is easily Heyward's peer. This is strikingly shown in his depiction of Harriett and Jimboy, Annjee's vagabond husband. Jimboy loafs a lot, tramps a lot and seldom works, and is happiest when sitting on the doorsill strumming his guitar while droning a blues or singing a song of the road. Harriett is no less fond of song and gayety and has her own notions of the value of the religion and morals of white folks. But Jimboy's indolence is more than half intellectual revolt. His presence on a job usually causes friction with white workers, or else the boss wants to pay him less than a white man would be paid for the same toil. Jimboy, who has a mite of Cyrano in his soul, is too much of a romantic to pur-

chase respectability when the price is perpetual insult to his manhood. For a similar reason Harriett chooses the primrose path; not because she lacks the stamina to make the up-grade, but because she sees that for her, as for thousands of other white and black women, the scarlet way is the high road to a freer and better life. Harriett and Jimboy do not depart from the ways of respectability because they are wanting in moral sense; they deliberately follow what is for them the most profitable way of living. This is sensible motivation and plausible human behavior.

Equally well done are the figures of Annjee and Sandy and the profile of Tempy. While Annjee is the yielding, loyal girl who remains by her mother's side and helps maintain the home, it is Tempy who inherits Hager's ruggedness of character. She is hard, cold and aloof, but it is upon her kind that the progress of the race depends, and Hughes has drawn her with sympathy and understanding. In drawing Sandy the author was confronted with the difficult task of presenting the changing mental angle of a growing boy. Hughes negotiates the task with the skill of a veteran, and the reader closes the book with the feeling that he has lived with Sandy all the while the boy was developing from rompers to long pants.

Skilfully as the other characters are limned, it is the fine portrait of Hager that dominates the book. There is a touch of your mother in Hager, and mine, too, and all the other humble but resourceful women who reared the best of this generation of Negroes. Sometimes Hughes permits the reader to look directly at her, sometimes she is seen through the observing eyes of Sandy. Always she is the dauntless and determined character builder, instilling neatness, thrift and industry in her grandson while planning for his future. "You gwine out yonder 'mongst all them white chillens, I wants you to at least look clean." "I wants you to stay nice an' make something out o' yourself." "If Hager lives she ain't gonna to see you go down. She's gonna make a fine man out o' you fo' de glory of God an' de black race. You gwine to 'mount to something in the world. You hear me?" She admonishes him from day to day while her seventy-year-old back bends over the wash tub.

Even after her death her solicitude for his future lingers on and we hear her urging him, "Stand up straight and look like somebody!" Here the voice is the voice of Tempy, but the message comes straight from Hager. And again she speaks, this time through the lips of Harriett, "This boy's got to get ahead. . . . He's gotta be what his grandma Hager wanted him to be—able to help the black race, Annjee! You hear me? Help the whole race!" And so Hager's noble soul goes marching on.

Not Without Laughter may not be a great book. But I am here to tell the world it's a fine one. Furthermore, I am ready to peel off my coat and fight Aubrey Bowser or anybody else who says it is merely a good book.

Lillian Lewis Feurtado "Feurtado's Column" *Boston Guardian,* 9 August 1930, [p. ?]

The novel of Langston Hughes, *Not without Laughter,* leaves a bitter taste. At least, it must do so to every Colored reader. I hope it does not make the white reader feel that segregation is justifiable after the chapter after chapter of contact with immoral, vulgar, low-down 3rd rate Colored people. The story may be very true of a class of uncultured, foul-minded Colored people and also of another class of them— the "white-folks-nigger" class—two that should be hidden from the white world, and those hidden in the book should be put in the limelight. Because there are vulgar suggestions and some plain talk that makes for nasty thought, the book will be sought after and generally read, because the public likes that sort of reading now-a-days, and they will like it all the more because it is the Colored girl who is the fallen one and the Colored boys who provoke their disgust. This story will be generally accepted as typical of the young Colored man and woman coming up today. It is too bad, for we do have some girls of lovely character and fine instincts who think of something besides sex and jazz and some young men with high aspirations, but the readers of that novel would never believe it, for Mr. Hughes is an artist. His word pictures are painted vividly and convincingly and it seems that you stand among these people and that they are in flesh and blood at your side, as you continue reading. He knows how to portray human beings and human nature and has the words to fit his portrayal, and if he would write another novel and put in as principals some girls and boys worthy of admiration, he would give to his people a gift that would make the whole race proud of him.

The old time before-the-war stuff and old time darkeyism is something the Colored people of this generation are trying to get away from, but Mr. Hughes' novel would make the reader believe that we are eternally fastened to it and shows little promise or hope of getting away from it. These people are no doubt real creatures that Mr. Hughes has observed, in his varied travels and experiences, and he has told the story of their poverty, their struggle to get a living by washing and ironing and other menial work, their shiftlessness by running round to dances and jazz parties and living loose lives and has told it with realism. He has made, at the end of his story, the one intelligent character with a desire to live above this sickening atmosphere stand out sharply and save the youth from being swirled in the current of that wretched life. But she is a "white folks nigger" and the reader would not sympathize with her for she is painted a first class snob. The best person in the tale is Aunt Hager. But we don't have Aunt Hagers now-a-days, and what's the use of shoving them under the eyes of the public, to make them laugh at us. *Not without Laughter* is the title. I don't believe anyone but a white person would find much to laugh at in this book. It seems to have been written for their enlightenment. It is depressing and unsatisfactory to a Colored person who cares how we are exploited before the white race.

I do not like the manner of calling almost everybody in the novel a "nigger." The book teems with the word "nigger." The characters call themselves niggers, and as you read, you form a mental picture of nothing but "niggers." This book goes out to the great white public, and after they read it, no matter how light nor how dark your skin they will instinctively think of you in the author's term as "niggers." This is too bad.

The little allusions to Booker Washington, Fred Douglass and Dr. DuBois, are like little pieces of court plaster put on to cover up an unsightly place in the skin.

[*Cleveland*?] *Call,* 14 August 1930, [p. ?]

The writing and publishing of *Not Without Laughter,* by Langston Hughes, marks a new era in the history of the so-called Negro novel. For the first time since the coming of the over-publicized Harlem re-naissance a Negro novelist has had the hardihood to write a novel both about and for Negroes. It is in the nature of an experiment, for the country has been so flooded with the efforts of colored novelists to out-nigger *Nigger Heaven* that there is some doubt that an honest attempt to picture the life of the Negro peasant will be well received.

The scene is laid in the Midwest and the story is homely in its simplicity. An aged grandmother clinging to the memories of slavery and with a touching faith in Jesus has the task of rearing her grandson thrust on her. Perhaps it is wrong to say that the task is thrust on the grandmother, for all her children have a part in it; the mother herself wavering between love for the boy and love for a wandering husband, another daughter who has married a postman and joined that nebulous thing referred to by colored journals as "colored society," the youngest daughter whose hate of working at the country club leads to her singing in night clubs, and even the boy's father, when he can forget the lure of "going somewhere."

The task of rearing a colored child is no simple one in an America that bestows a theoretical equality on all of its citizens the while it bends its energies to dwarfing their souls and hindering their development. This novel portrays that double-edged attitude of mind with a force that is not weakened by propaganda. There is room for bitterness and hate when one contemplates the tragedy of the Negro child in America. Nobody knows quite what to teach him to believe or hope for or expect, and as a consequence he is taught as a white child only to face a more than bitter reality when he comes of age. Langston Hughes indicates the problem and treats it adequately, but nowhere is there any raging or frontal assault on prejudice or race hates. It is a tribute to him as an artist that he performs the task so well.

Those who know Hughes as a poet and a short story writer will not be surprised to learn that his character delineations are excellent and his style a pleasing one. If any criticism is to be urged against the book it is that the plot is not as well developed as it might have been and the story as it now stands a bit incomplete. The central figure stands on the threshold of adolescence as the story ends, and one could wish that the story extended beyond that critical age.

Hughes' first novel is more or less a collection of short stories written around a central figure, but for all that it is far and away the best thing that has issued out of Harlem. Most of the others have suffered from that same defect with the added disadvantage, as was remarked in the beginning, of being written for their exotic effects. Although such a warning has no place in a book review, it ought to be brought to the attention of the colored reading public that the type of the Negro novel of the future depends to a large extent on the willingness of the colored public to lend its buying support. If this book meets with apathy from Negroes they can look forward to a fresh supply of dirt for art's sake. In that eventuality one hopes Hughes will return to his poetry.

Herschel Brickell
"A Poet's Debut as Novelist"
Saturday Review, 7
(23 August 1930), 69

The quality in this first novel by one of the most interesting of the young Negro poets in America that distinguishes it from most of the fiction about Negroes by Negroes is

its tender understanding. It does not burn with the kind of indignation whose heat so easily converts fiction into propaganda; neither does it present its characters as whitewashed whites, with speech and action obviously and pathetically synthetic. It is a subtly simple book, at times bordering on the biblical in the directness of its narrative, and giving one the pleasant impression of listening rather than following with the eyes. Its strength lies in this simplicity, in its author's unflinching honesty, and in his ability to make the reader feel very deeply the problems of his characters.

The life of a Negro boy, son of a ne'er-do-well father who is twin brother to Howard Odum's *Black Ulysses*, although he is a mulatto, and of an honest hard-working mother who cooks for a family of white people, is the chain upon which the story is strung. Sandy, so nicknamed because his hair is sand-colored, has a grandmother, Aunt Hager, who is typical of an older generation; once she was a slave, but her memories of slavery are not bitter. She loved her mistress and was beloved. She is an angel of mercy for white and black, fervently religious, and devoted to her children and to her one grandchild.

There are two other daughters besides Sandy's mother, one of whom marries a man of property and becomes an Episcopalian, the type of the rising Negro who is anxious to forget his racial backgrounds, who speaks with exaggerated correctness, and worships at the shrine of respectability. The youngest of the three is a joy-loving, hot-blooded colored flapper, who goes to the devil in her own way, despite Aunt Hager's earnest pleas and even the use of the cane. Aunt Hager supports herself by taking in washing; her heart is in Sandy's proper upbringing, and in her desire to give him every opportunity she talks to him many times about the problems of their race. She is troubled by the atmosphere of sharp hostility that is about her, for most of her associates, and certainly her youngest daughter, hate white people and express their feelings with complete frankness.

Jimboy, Sandy's wandering father, drops in and out of the picture; when he arrives his "box" comes with him, and he and Aunt Hager's youngest, Harriett, have gay times singing and dancing. He is worthless, and Aunt Hager quarrels with him, but with a certain sympathetic understanding, just as she quarrels bitterly with Harriett, but continues to love her, realizing the child's need for pleasure. This quality, as has been said, distinguishes the book; the life of the Negroes is lived not only not without laughter, but not without understanding of one another's difficulties.

Of this simple chronicle of the life of a Negro family, Mr. Hughes has made a truly poignant novel. Of the minor tragedies of racial discrimination, such as the turning away from the gates of an amusement park of all the Negro children, or the seating of all the Negro children in the back rows of the school room, he has written touchingly, and with no trace of pleading, no underlining, just the simple statement, which is here, as always, the most effective means of stressing a point. Of such scenes as a wild dance, or of Jimboy's singing blues, Mr. Hughes has written vividly and colorfully, imparting the rich flavor of these matters without exaggeration.

In time, to return to the outline of the story, Jimboy's wife leaves Aunt Hager to look after Sandy and follows her wandering man. Aunt Hager dies and Sandy goes to live with his very proper Aunt Tempy, until his mother sends for him to come to her in Chicago, where he is soon installed as an elevator man. Then the "bad girl" Harriett reappears, this time as a singer and dancer, and highly successful. She arranges to help Sandy complete his education, and here again Mr. Hughes makes us see the desire of all these people to help one another no matter what Fate has done to them.

All this occurs in Kansas, so that much of the extreme bitterness that might have crept in had the scene been laid in the South is easily left out. But one feels that it would not have been a bitter book in any event; there is too much understanding in it for bitterness. Mr. Hughes has made a real contribution to Negro literature in Not Without Laughter, and wholly aside from its value as observation, it is a good novel, an unusually appealing story handled for the most part with fine skill. The author's name must be added to the long list of contemporary poets who have turned with genuine success to the prose medium.

Thomas L. Masson
"Books"
Life, 96 (29 August 1930), [1]

In spite of the fact that we are all more or less being fed up with Negro fiction, this story can hardly be passed by. Middle west colored folk. As good as Heyward's Porgy. Written from the heart, with understanding.

Neal F. Herriford
"The Saga of Sandy Rodgers"
Tuskegee Messenger,
30 August 1930, p. 6

With admirable skill and genuine feeling, Langston Hughes has given to us his first novel, *Not Without Laughter.* Turning his back on that over-ripe literary plum, Harlem, he has written a story with a midwestern setting, a novel of the Negroes of Stanton, Kansas; and the young writer's explanation for this is that of the artist— "I am interested primarily in life, not local color." Any second-rate schoolboy can give us local color by the reams; it is the artist, and only the artist, who can give us a portrayal of life that is at once genuine and sincere, and, therefore, convincing. This Hughes has done.

In this book we read of the doings of three generations of the Williams family, each generation having its own arresting philosophy of life. In old Aunt Hager Williams we catch the stifling optimism of the old-time Negro, who believed as firmly in the "good white folks" as in his religion, which would somehow straighten matters out for the black folks. But Aunt Hager is not without her dreams and ambitions for her daughters, Tempy, Annjee, and Harriett, exponents of the second generation with widely differing tenets of living.

Tempy, the oldest daughter, becomes quite high-tone, marries a railway mail clerk, lives in a fine house with electric lights, joins the Episcopal Church where the intellectual tone nullifies the emotional, and thereby damns herself in the eyes of the members of her family, whom she comes to look down on.

Annjee loves her shiftless, handsome husband, Jimboy, more than anything else in this muddling world, thus winning as her share the constant disapproval of her mother, who sees Jimboy as the perfection of nothing in a man. But this means nothing in Annjee's life.

Quite different from her sisters is the youngest, Harriett, the black sheep of the family. Life means more to her than slaving for the white folks, going to revival meetings, and waiting hopefully and blissfully for glory in the Promised Land. Harriett wants Life, and she gets it; that is why we see her finally as a headliner on vaudeville circuits, billed as "Princess of the Blues."

Sandy, Annjee and Jimboy's only child, is of the third generation. He it is whom Aunt Hager wants to be a great man— great like Booker T. Washington. It is really Sandy who occupies for us the center of the stage during the Williams drama; for life in the family centers very definitely around the welfare of this sensitive and intelligent boy, who is determined to satisfy his old grandmother's ambition for him. Aunt Hager struggles hard to give this lad a decent niche in the world. In the midst of her trials she is interrupted by death, and her place in the boy's life is taken for a time by the cold and aspiring Tempy. Existence with this aunt proves irksome to the growing Sandy; so he is overjoyed when opportunity presents him with a trip to Chicago, where his mother has gone in her efforts to be near her nomadic Jimboy. The Great War calls the boy's father away; thus for a while it looks as if he must forego his long cherished hope to further his education and help support his somewhat selfish mother, who has become apprenticed of the hair-straightening industry. It is when Sandy's hopes seem faintest that Harriett, "Princess of the Blues," arrives on the scene and generously offers to subsidize his education. With the genuine feeling and loyalty of the errant member of the family, Harriett refuses to see the ambition old Aunt Hager had for this boy side-tracked by the selfish demands of his mother. It is in the final chapter of the story that Harriett's philanthropy is announced; thus the reader is left to conclude that Sandy received a satisfactory start on his ambition to equal Booker T. Washington.

Quite dexterously has the poet-novelist drawn for us the picture of this family with its conflicting ideals, its conflicting beliefs. Aunt Hager's slave-time love for the white folks elicits a harsh note of protest from her youngest, Harriett, who hates them venomously. Tempy sees them with the eyes of one who hungers for social equality, with the eyes of one who feels Nordic superiority to be no myth; thus life has for her the usual frustration such purblind people experience. Poor Annjee's reaction to them is sublimated into a love for her Jimboy, for whom she steals choice dishes of food from her white employers. To her the white folks are a very definite means to a definitely lovely end—her Jimboy.

All these reactions somewhat mystify the young Sandy; he seems quite inarticulate before the conflicting beliefs of his elders. As a result we have a sensitive youth trying again and again to make something of this riddle of life.

There is no propaganda in this book. Hughes clings closely to his objective and writes truly of life. There is none of us who can truthfully deny the existence of any of the conditions he paints for us. He writes in a charming, naive, arresting manner, and tells his story as only a poet could. Hidden here and there are exquisite passages filled with striking imagery. Doubtlessly the most artistic and delightful chapters are those which tell of Jimboy's presence in the Williams household and the one in which Aunt Hager makes her exposition of the meaning of life— "nothin' but love." Hughes has shown us that he is novelist as well as poet.

"Middle Western Negroes Pictured in New Novel" *Milwaukee Journal,* 30 August 1930, p. 4

Negro life in a small middle western town is the theme and substance of *Not Without Laughter,* the first novel of Langston Hughes, itinerant Negro poet. Stanton, Kans., is its immediate locale; "Sandy" Rodgers, who grows from small boyhood to rapid maturity in the progress of the book, is its protagonist. Of plot, so-called, there is nothing in the novel; the characters alone are important in *Not Without Laughter,* and there are many of them, affording an all-embracing picture of Negro life which aspires to explain something of its philosophy and psychology. Drawn with native, inherent honesty, the picture is one of living, pulsating truth, at times drab and at times lurid with bold, natural colors.

"Sandy," unfortunately, succeeds in being little more than a vehicle to an end in the book. Too infrequently does he become a figure of flesh and blood. He is, in a manner of speaking, a mirror to reflect the thought and action of the other and minor characters. It is they who give the book its glowing vitality. Aunt Hager Williams, young Sandy's grandmother, is a character fully realized. Perhaps because she was "born in slavery," she is more tolerant of "de white folks" in what seems to the younger generation their persecution of the Negroes. She is a washwoman, and by dint of a native capacity to give service she has carved out a bit of a niche for herself in the little town of Stanton. She is respected by both the blacks and the whites; she has a knack for nursing and is always called upon to take charge in sick rooms;

she is honest, kindly, deeply religious, superstitious.

But Aunt Hager has her worries, and they are concerned primarily with little Sandy, to whose future opportunities she dedicates the last years of her life, and with two of her daughters. The third, Tempy, has married well; has left the Baptist church of her mother's training and switched to more elegant Episcopalian services; dislikes the blues and spirituals because "they are too Negro" and condemns those who sing them for "acting like niggers"; apes white folk and ideals and swears by the virtues of middle class respectability. Annjee, the second daughter, is Sandy's mother, is married to Jimboy, a banjo playing, jazz singing, lazy, irresponsible "good-fur-nothing," according to Aunt Hager.

In Harriett, the youngest daughter, Jimboy has his feminine counterpart; except that Harriett has ambitions of a sort, to go on the stage, to be free of the yoke which "white folks" put upon Negroes. Harriett tires of her mother's "preachin'," is lured away by the jazz and dancing and dim lights of "the Bottoms," the one section in Stanton where the blacks and whites mingle. At the end of the book she turns up, not as a horrible example of virtues gone astray, but as a brave, loyal, perhaps a bit hardened, girl who has found success on the stage and who proved Sandy's key to the education Aunt Hager hoped would be his.

There are many other characters in this novel which is significantly called *Not Without Laughter,* and all of them are well and quickly established individuals. Langston Hughes has written his many sided, kaleidoscopic novel of Negro life with no undue display of sentiment and without resorting to any of the cheap tricks of many novelists in their trade.

[Mary White Ovington] "Praises Hughes as an Unusual Colored Writer" *New York News and Harlem Home Journal,* 30 August 1930, p. 8

It is, I think, a fair generalization that a white novelist, writing on the Negro question today, sincerely tries to get new and correct material and is not afraid of it; while a colored novelist, with enormous data on hand that he knows to be true, shies from his stuff. He copies old patterns and skates around dangerous places. He rakes much, gaily clad like Claude McKay, but he fears his emotions and he is timorous about showing us reality. This is a rough generalization with its exceptions, and one of the exceptions is this first novel of Langston Hughes, named *Not Without Laughter.*

Not but what Mr. Hughes' material is old enough. Here is the kind of mammy who loves everyone, the little boy who sits on her lap to hear her wisdom, the no-count husband, playing the banjo and worshipped by his wife, the pretty daughter turning prostitute, all familiar figures and yet fresh and living as they stand in the drab setting of a little Kansas town.

Langston Hughes does not fear his material. He drew, perhaps with some venom, the well-to-do daughter, Tempy, who has made a successful marriage, and who looks down on her mother at the ironing board and her sister going out to work in a little white home. His colored "climber" is as distasteful a sample of the species as one could find among any group in America. Tempy is never there to help out when help is needed. She only comes when coming means patronizing ostentation. She is a tiresome snob.

The book opens with a cyclone, genuine Kansas variety, carrying off the porch of the house where Hager, the grandmother, lives. When the excitement is over, and Hager knows that her children and grandchildren are safe, she looks at the grotesque, porchless house and laughs: "Might ha' been blowed away maself, 'stead o' just my porch, if Jesus hadn't been with us." The laugh and the childlike faith run through the book. The hero is Hager's grandchild, a little boy when the story opens, and like most books built on this pattern, more interesting than when he begins to grow old enough to wear long trousers and to go to high school. He has his experiences with the white race, his humiliations at school. He works at the barber's shop and in the hotel and sees the seamy side of white and colored life, but keeps decent through it all. He likes study and in the end it is his pretty but disreputable aunt who fosters his ambition, telling him, "You got to get your education, Sandy, and amount to something." Turning to the boy's mother who wants the money he could make at work, she says: "Sandy gotta be what his grandma Hager wanted him to be—able to help the black race, Annjee. You hear me? Help the whole race."

Not Without Laughter! Why did Langston Hughes choose that title? At the circus Sandy heard a Negro play the banjo and sing a blues with innumerable verses all ending:

An' I can't be satisfied,
'Cause all I love has
Done laid down and died.

To Sandy it seemed the saddest music in the world, but the white people around him laughed.

Sterling A. Brown
"Our Book Shelf"
Opportunity, 8
(September 1930), 279–80

We have in this book, laconically, tenderly told, the story of a young boy's growing up. Let no one be deceived by the effortless ease of the telling, by the unpretentious simplicity of *Not Without Laughter*. Its simplicity is the simplicity of great art; a wide observation, a long brooding over humanity, and a feeling for beauty in unexpected, out of the way places, must have gone into its makeup. It is generously what one would expect of the author of *The Weary Blues* and *Fine Clothes to the Jew*.

Not Without Laughter tells of a poor family living in a small town in Kansas. We are shown intimately the work and play, the many sided aspects of Aunt Hager and her brood. Aunt Hager has three daughters: Tempy, Annjee and Harriett. Tempy is doing well; having joined the Episcopalian Church she has put away "niggerish" things; Annjee is married to a likeable scapegrace, Jimboy, guitar plunker and rambling man; Harriett, young, full of life and daring, is her heart's worry. She has a grandchild, Sandy, son of Annjee and Jimboy. And about him the story centers.

Sandy with his wide eyes picking up knowledge of life about the house; Sandy listening to his father's blues and ballads in the purple evenings, watching his Aunt Harriett at her dancing; Sandy at school; Sandy dreaming over his geography book; Sandy at his job in the barbershop and hotel; Sandy at his grandmother's funeral; Sandy learning respectability at Aunt Tempy's—and learning at the same time something of the ways of women from Pansetta; Sandy in Chicago; Sandy with his books and dreams of education—so run the many neatly etched scenes.

But the story is not Sandy's alone. We see Harriett, first as a firm fleshed beautiful black girl, quick at her lessons; we see her finally a blues singer on State Street. The road she has gone has been rocky enough. She has been maid at a country club where the tired business men made advances; she has been with a carnival troupe, she has been arrested for street walking. We follow Annjee in her trials, and Jimboy, and Tempy. And we get to know the wise, tolerant Aunt Hager, beloved by whites and blacks; even by Harriett who just about breaks her heart. Lesser characters are as clearly individualized and developed. We have Willie Mae, and Jimmy Lane, and Joe Willis, "white folks nigger," and Uncle Dan, and Mingo, and Buster, who could have passed for white. The white side of town, the relationships of employers with laundresses and cooks, all these are adequately done. The book, for all of its apparent slightness, is fullbodied.

One has to respect the author's almost casual filling in of background. The details are perfectly chosen; and they make the reader *see*. How representative are his pictures of the carnival, and the dance at which "Benbow's Famous Kansas City Band" plays, and the gossip over back fences! How recognizable is Sister Johnson's "All these womens dey mammy named Jane an' May an' Cora, soon's dey gets a little somethin', dey changes dey names to Janette or Mariana or Corina or somethin' mo' flowery than what dey had."

As the title would suggest the book is not without laughter. Jimboy's guitar-playing, Harriett's escapades, the barber shop tall tales, the philosophizing of the old sheep "who know de road," all furnish something of this. Sandy's ingenuousness occasionally is not without laughter. But the dominant note of the book is a quiet pity. It is not sentimental; it is candid, clear

eyed instead—but it is still pity. Even the abandon, the fervor of the chapter called "Dance," closely and accurately rendered (as one would expect of Langston Hughes) does not strike the note of unclouded joy. We see these things as they are: as the pitiful refugees of poor folk against the worries of hard days. It is more the laughter of the blues line—*laughin' just to keep from cryin'*.

The difference between comedy and tragedy of course lies often in the point of view from which the story is told. Mr. Hughes' sympathetic identification with these folk is so complete that even when sly comic bits creep in (such as Madame de Carter and the Dance of the Nations) the laughter is quiet—more of a smile than a Cohen-like guffaw. But even these sly bits are few and far between. More than Sandy's throwing his boot-black box at the drunken cracker, certainly a welcome case of poetic justice, one remembers the disappointments of this lad's life. Sandy went on Children's Day to the Park. "Sorry," the man said. "This party's for white kids." In a classroom where the students are seated alphabetically, Sandy and the other three colored children sit behind Albert Zwick. Sandy, in the white folks' kitchen, hears his hardworking mother reprimanded by her sharp tempered employer. And while his mother wraps several little bundles of food to carry to Jimboy, Sandy cries. These scenes are excellently done, with restraint, with irony, and with compassion.

Sandy knows the meaning of a broken family, of poverty, of seeing those he loves go down without being able to help. Most touching, and strikingly universal, is the incident of the Xmas sled. Sandy, wishful for a Golden Flyer sled with flexible rudders! is surprised on Christmas Day by the gift of his mother and grandmother. It is a sled. They had labored and schemed and sacrificed for it in a hard winter. On the cold Christmas morning they dragged it home. It was a home-made contraption—roughly carpentered, with strips of rusty tin along the wooden runners. "It's fine," Sandy lied, as he tried to lift it.

Of a piece with this are the troubles that Annjee knows—Annjee whose husband is here today and gone tomorrow; Annjee, who grows tired of the buffeting and loses ground slowly; and the troubles of Aunt Hager, who lives long enough to see her hopes fade out, and not long enough to test her final hope, Sandy. Tempy, prosperous, has coldshouldered her mother; Annjee is married to a man who frets Hager; Harriett has gone with Maudel to the sinister houses of the bottoms. "One by one they leaves you," Hager said slowly. "One by one yo' chillen goes."

Unforgettable is the little drama of Harriett's rebellion. It is the universal conflict of youth and age. Mr. Hughes records it, without comment. It is the way life goes. Harriett, embittered by life, wanting her share of joy, is forbidden to leave the house. The grandmother is belligerent, authoritative, the girl rebellious. And then the grandmother breaks. "Harriett, honey, I wants you to be good." But the pitiful words do not avail; Harriett, pitiless as only proud youth can be, flings out of doors—with a cry, "You old Christian Fool!" A group of giggling sheiks welcomes her.

Of all of his characters, Mr. Hughes obviously has least sympathy with Tempy. She is the *arriviste*, the worshipper of white folks' ways, the striver. "They don't 'sociate no mo' with none but de high toned colored folks." The type deserves contempt looked at in one way, certainly; looked at in another it might deserve pity. But the point of the reviewer is this: that Mr. Hughes does not make Tempy quite convincing. It is hard to believe that Tempy would be as blatantly crass as she is to her mother on Christmas Day, when she says of her church "Father Hill is so digni-fied, and the services are absolutely refined! There's never anything niggerish about them—so you know, mother, they suit me."

But, excepting Tempy, who to the reviewer seems slightly caricatured, all of the characters are completely convincing. There is a universality about them. They have, of course, peculiar problems as Negroes. Harriett, for instance, hates all whites, with reason. But they have even more the problems that are universally human. Our author does not exploit either local color, or race. He has selected an interesting family and has told us candidly, unembitteredly, poetically of their joy lightened and sorrow laden life.

Langston Hughes presents all of this without apology. Tolerant, humane, and wise in the ways of mortals, he has revealed beauty where too many of us, dazzled by false lights, are unable to see it. He has shown us again, in this third book of his—what he has insisted all along, with quiet courage:

Beautiful, also, is the sun.
Beautiful, also, are the souls of my
  people. . . .

"The Browsing Reader" *Crisis*, 37 (September 1930), 313, 321

Langston Hughes' first novel, *Not Without Laughter*, is a story of black peasantry of the Middle West: they who work, and laugh, and are finally drowned in the great city. It is a story that is realistic and close to human beings, but being a study of character rather than plot, it is not very strongly knit together and may not hold the sustained interest of most readers. It touches dirt, but it is not dirty, and it ends with the upward note. It is well written.

Betsy Greenebaum
"Some Recent Fiction"
Chicago Evening Post,
5 September 1930, p. 4

The great novel of and by the Negro is still to be written, and with each publication by a Negro author, one hopes. So far as Langston Hughes' first novel is concerned, the hope is vain. It is a competent story of a poor Negro family in the middle west, with the regulation background full of jazz, blues and race consciousness. But it has nothing to add to our conception of Negroes as individuals, as a group, or in their relations to their pale antagonists. One does not for a moment imply that a novel about Negroes should be a thesis novel, or that it should be evaluated on any special basis. On the contrary, it is by becoming so obviously novels of purpose that books like *Not Without Laughter* fail to become novels of significance. Because their material is comparatively unexploited, they treat it journalistically rather than fictionally: that is, they accept it is an asset in itself and play it up to the detriment of the characters, which tend to lose individuality and become lay figures.

The characters in this story are the types we have learned to accept as part of that myth known as The Negro-in-America. There are patient, godly Aunt Hager, bent over her tub, cruelly easygoing Jimboy with his golden flow of music, Harriett who follows the way of black heroines from night light to white lights, Annjee, long suffering and devoted, and Sandy, the sensitive soul from whose point of view the story is for the most part told. All these folk form a sort of decoration, harmonizing with the "colorful" background. They remain remote, as actors seen by alien eyes, or worse still, by native eyes which have submitted to artificially tinted spectacles.

But from the standpoint of enduring art, this formula of easy seeing and easy writing is fatal. Only when the sensitive Negro is seen both as an individual and a member of a race, and portrayed against a background viewed with independence and at the same time subordinated to individual human interest, shall we have the great novel which is inherent in the subject. One supposes that it will be a Negro who finally produces the masterpiece. But he must be one who is less Negro than artist, who regards his material as something to be interpreted rather than exploited, and who is genius enough to slough off the "wishful thinking" which has distorted the concepts of both races. Meanwhile *Not Without Laughter* is a readable, rather trite tale, with a single flash of true lyricism—very much what one would expect from the poetry for which its author is already known.

"Among the New Books: Fiction"
New Yorker, 6 (13 September 1930), 95

[. . .]
Exceptionally fine novel of Negro life.
[. . .]

Mae A. Conklin
"Books and Things"
New Haven Register,
section 4, 14 September
1930, p. 9

Mr. Hughes is one of the most talented of the younger Negro writers in America and in *Not Without Laughter* he turns to the lowly people of his own race for inspiration. We have had all sorts of sensational and emotional stories of Negro life within the past five years—some of them excellent and many of them very poor. But few have told so simple and so unaffected a story as this one. In fact, there is very little story to it. It depends for its strength upon the admirably clear-drawn characters in it. Mr. Hughes has selected a little house in a small country town, and when his novel is finished we have shared in the little springing hopes, the crushing disappointments, the spiritual problems, the gay moments, the hunger and the dreams of those within.

There is, first of all, Aunt Hager, a typical old plantation mammy, her life spent in service to others, loving her little hut and her dear dark children, worrying over them, praying for their welfare, fumbling for understanding when they grow up and out of the reach of her mother arms. There is Harriett, her oldest daughter, married to a wealthy man and given to aping the ways of white society; and Annjee, the loyal, hard-working wife of the jazz-playing, irresponsible Jimboy. There is, lastly, Tempy the laughter-loving daughter who breaks her mother's heart by becoming a blues singer, and Sandy, the little grandchild who goes to the store for cornmeal and returns absent-mindedly a long time afterwards with washing soda.

These half dozen people emerge with remarkable clearness from the book and their universal problems take on an individual emphasis and meaning as our interest in them deepens. It is an interesting cross section of Negro life that the author gives us here. The struggle of the old type generation to retain its simple joys and faith against the inroads of white ways and jazz civilization has never been more effectively told. It is the story of a race that, however sorely tried, always manage to live out their lives "not without laughter."

J. E. Robinson
"Of Making Many
Books"
St. Louis Post-Dispatch,
17 September 1930, p. 3C

This first novel by the well known Negro poet tells the poignant story of a poor family of his race in a small town in Kansas. The widowed Hager Williams, up from slavery, toils a lifetime over the washtub to rear according to her ideas of righteousness her three daughters and her worse than orphaned grandson. Aunt Hager is one of a type fast disappearing, whose concept of duty made a fetish of work and whose hope was placed in some indefinite after life of reward for miseries and hardships uncomplainingly endured.

To her children life seems not so simply ordained, and in tracing the development of their characters Mr. Hughes ingeniously surveys most of the problems confronting the Negro in the present complex social order.

Tempy, the eldest, becomes the maid of a prominent suffragette who trains the girl to ways of efficiency and by encouraging reading arouses in her dreams of overcoming racial handicaps. At her patron's death she inherits a small property, and with this advantage marries an ambitious Negro in the postal service. They acquire several houses and Tempy, casting aside the influences of youth, takes a leading place in the colored aristocracy.

Annjee, the second daughter, a worker like her mother, is seduced by happy-go-lucky, pleasure-loving Jimboy, a shiftless Southern darky, on one of his casual visits to the town. Belatedly he atones by marriage, but leaves to his patient wife and her mother the task of providing for his small son. Jimboy is typical of the irresponsible Negro, cursed with wanderlust, lazy, indifferent, sentimental and unreliable.

Harriett, youngest of the tribe, a brown-skinned beauty at 16, decides life must yield her pleasure at whatever cost. Not for her the supine resignation of her mother or Annjee or the small satisfactions of the snobbish Tempy. Harriett chooses the primrose path. Despising white people, her personal charms readily win favor. A singer and dancer, whose antics horrify her staid old mother, after many frustrations she attains the well paid independence of a vaudeville head-line blues singer.

Sandy the grandson, around whose upbringing from the age of nine to 17 the story is woven, is a handsome intelligent boy who finds unaccountable the difficulties a pigmented skin place in the way of his advancement. We take leave of him half way through a high school training, gravely considering the conflicting counsel of the leaders of his people; weighing the resignation of Booker Washington against the concept of racial equality propounded by Dr. Burghardt du Bois.

Walt Carmon
"Away from Harlem"
New Masses, 6 (October 1930), 17–18

Not Without Laughter, first novel by Langston Hughes, is a definite contribution to both Negro and proletarian literature in America.

Coming at this moment, however, it takes on added importance: it is the first definite break with the vicious Harlem tradition of Negro literature sponsored by Van Vechten and illustrated by Covarrubias.

This literary tradition has vulgarized and burlesqued the Negro as have the stage and the movies. It has seduced talented young Negro writers with easy money and quick recognition to be found in a synthetic cabaret bawdiness which is but a libel on 12 million American Negroes, most of them wage slaves.

Even Taylor Gordon, artist and genial human, makes his autobiography *Born To Be* a series of off-color episodes moralized into: "Don't sit on the green grass nude if you don't know your botany." He can thank Van Vechten.

And our own Claude McKay in *Home to Harlem* and *Banjo*, despite all their virtues, makes them definite products of this travesty on Negro life.

It is not surprising that genuine talent should have sacrificed artistic honesty, race pride and even class consciousness. Like the Negro worker, the Negro writer has been Jim-Crowed unmercifully. Honest novels of Negro life with their tragedy and bitterness were as unwelcome as the novels of the white worker. For years, this perverted literature has been practically the only opening in the literary field for the

Negro writer. He has been allowed only to porter and clown at the literary bawdyhouse.

That Langston Hughes in his first book has had the courage to break with this tradition is evidence of his artistic honesty and a proletarian experience that has served him well. Hughes has been a seaman, porter, busboy and student.

As far back as 1924, I recall how enthusiastically we discussed his first poems then appearing in the *Workers Monthly*. They appeared later in the fine little collection *Poems for Workers* edited by Manuel Gomez, who was also editor of the *Workers Monthly* at the time. The poems were spirited, bitter poems of a proletarian and the work of a sensitive, competent literary craftsman.

In later poems in the *New Masses* and the following two books of verse, *The Weary Blues* and *Old* [sic] *Clothes to the Jew,* the same note was dominant. But here it was already heavily laden with the scent of the vicious Van Vechten patronage which Hughes still acknowledges.

In *Not Without Laughter,* the break with the Harlem tradition is not complete. But the novel is far beyond *Home to Harlem,* for instance. While McKay consciously daubs his canvas for the well paying market, Langston Hughes, closer to proletarian reality, gives us a vivid picture of a Negro working class family in midwest America.

One is struck immediately with the remarkable similarity to Agnes Smedley's *Daughter of Earth*, published last year. The kinship is a proletarian class kinship; the life is one that both black and white workers share in common.

The Indian father in Agnes Smedley's novel is not unlike the Negro, Jimboy, of *Not Without Laughter:* a transient worker, restless, always moving: "Jimboy was always goin ... what was there in Stanton anyhow for a young colored fellow except to dig sewer-ditches for a few cents an hour or maybe porter around a store for seven dollars a week?"

But where the Indian drowns his unrest in drink, the Negro Jimboy plays a guitar and sings blues, shouts and jingles: the songs he learned as a wharf hand, railroad worker and porter in Natchez, Shreveport and Dallas. Some of these are folk-songs he learned in the pine woods of Arkansas from the lumber camp workers, earthy songs "desperate and dirty like the weary roads where they were sung."

Daughter of Earth took its bias from the bitterness of a woman. *Not Without Laughter* is steeled in the hatred of an oppressed race. Both are marred as class novels in this way. Yet both are proletarian as well. Agnes Smedley's story was a bitter, gray story. *Not Without Laughter* also gray, has brilliant gay tones of laughter, dance and music. Some of its passages are unmistakably the work of a poet.

The Negro worker feels the heel of race oppression. He is "Nigger" to his white playmates in childhood. He is discriminated against in grade and high school. Later in life he is restricted to miserly paid menial labor. The white boss exploits him and his white misguided fellow-worker often discriminates against him on the job and in the trade union. Langston Hughes lets us see how bitterly the Negro worker feels this. It is not strange that class issues are beclouded by race feeling.

Harriett, hardheaded funloving girl who turns prostitute and later becomes a successful blues singer is told by her mother that her sister must guard her health. "What for," she asks, "to spend her life in Mrs. Rice's kitchen?"

And Harriett voices all the bitterness against a white religion which helps to oppress such a great part of her race: "Your old Jesus is white," she says, "He's white and stiff and don't like niggers!"

Discrimination, lynching, exploitation,

the proletarian Negro feels as a class. But his oppressor is almost always white, and the bitterness and hatred is misdirected at the white race as a whole.

Not Without Laughter is primarily a race novel. It concludes in a misty pointless fashion. There is no clear class consciousness nor revolutionary spirit which distinguished some of Hughes' early poems. But under its black skin, there is red proletarian blood running through it. With all its faults, *Not Without Laughter* goes far beyond Harlem. It is *our* novel.

E.M.C.
"Sincerity in a Negro's Novel about Negroes" *Kansas City Star,* 4 October 1930, p. 4

Not Without Laughter, not without tears and not without a lasting impression does Langston Hughes's first novel enchain itself to our senses and thoughts. Coming as it does from a Negro about Negroes, it has an essential sincerity and a variance of viewpoint distinguishing it from the ordinary contemporary novel.

After reading this novel, the setting of which is supposed to be Topeka, Kas., one finds himself searching the faces of Negroes seen on the streets and saying with mingled emotion, "There is a hard working Annjee; there is a blessed Aunt Hager." The small brown lad who sits at the newsstand on Twelfth Street becomes a Sandy come alive—so truly has Hughes made his characters parcel of one's memory.

Hughes brings a new phase of the Negro's life to our attention. Too often do we regard Negroes as a race apart, a frolicking race, whose dark laughter, breath-taking

blues and Amos 'n' Andy clowning amuses us because it gives us that feeling of superiority which is the heart of humor. We are apt to forget that this dusky race bears a conscience, that its members have felt the sublime promptings to do the painful right, that they have their unspoken sorrows and their sacred joys, that their hearts have gone out to their first-born and they have mourned over their irreclaimable dead. Long have we known the comedy of their existence. *Not Without Laughter* bids us look to their tragedy.

Perhaps it is true, as in the reasoning of the awakening Sandy: "Are Negroes poor because they are dancers, jazzers, clowns? ... the other way round would be better: dancers because they suffered; laughing all the time because they must forget ... a band of dancers ... black dancers—captured in a white world ... dancers of the spirit, too, a captured dancer of the spirit."

This is distinctly a novel of character, not of story. It could as well have ended at the fifth chapter; the only interest that holds one is the kindly competence of Aunt Hager, the wavering youth of Harriett, the petulant devotion of Annjee, the lovable irresponsibility of Jimboy. What slender webs of story there are in the novel are lost in the loom of characterization.

Instead of the blatant Harlem dance hall rhythm so many stories of Negroes have been written by, the author turns, without hesitating, to tell us of simple family life and of the thoughts of a small brown boy as he eats his supper under the drooping lines of white folks' garments. Only one chapter, "The Dance," resorts to the steady tom-tom of the drums as an accompaniment to Negro life. This chapter, however, is exceedingly well done, almost poetic in its clean-cut imagery.

Hughes finds opportunity in the three daughters of Aunt Hager Williams to contrast as many reactions to "white folks": Tempy, the oldest, who has married a bit of money, is contemptuous of anything "Negro," and is eager and ambitious to make herself as near like white people as possible. Annjee, the wife of Jimboy and the mother of Sandy, takes a quieter view of the situation—white folks are to work for. "They are like spoilt chillens what's got too much of ever'thing—an' they needs us niggers what ain't got nothin'." But Harriett, the youngest and most vehement, cries out in rebellion, "Oh, I hate them! I hate white folks! I hate 'em all!"

It so happens that Harriett makes a signal success of blues singing, and can help Annjee put her son, Sandy, through school and out into the world to "make somethin' of himself," as the book ends.

Mary White Ovington "The Bookshelf: Hughes: Novelist"
Chicago Defender, 4 October 1930, p. 11 (reprints 30 August review but adds an extra paragraph at end)

[. . .]

To many readers the music of this book, for it is written with the poet's sense of beauty, will seem, as the blues did to Sandy, the saddest music in the world. But occasionally there is laughter, not white folks laughing at "niggers," but strong, healthy laughter of a race that can face adversity and yet keep a sense of proportion. A race that after a day at someone else's stove can say, chuckling: "Don't know what white folks'll do in heaven 'cause I'm gonna sit down there myself."

[. . .]

Eugene Armfield "Half Tones"
New Freeman, 2 (29 October 1930), 165–6

Mr. Langston Hughes occupies a conspicuous, practically unique position among the Negro writers who have appeared in the last few years, a position well above mediocrity. Besides possessing a genuine talent irrespective of race or color, he uses, more than any other Negro poet, the elements of race in an appropriate and successful manner. In his best work race is not the occasion for bombast or the purely external exploitation of events or characteristics, but an immediate, pervasive factor which imparts a profound, if indirect, meaning to a whole poem. "Brass Spittoons" represents, in its complete effectiveness, fully assimilated impulses arising from the poet's racial experience. Mr. Hughes's verse fails to reach the high excellence it deserves because he has, as yet, not achieved a form adequate to his imagination or his material.

Any form derived from the "blues" lyric imposes upon itself at the outset limits that are insurmountable by their very nature, since the "blues" song proper depends so much upon the music and instrumentation. The lyric by itself, or any verse modelled upon it, remains cramped and inadequate, bare, without the sustaining rhythm provided by the instruments and melody. Mr. Hughes does not practise this type of verse exclusively, but even when he uses other kinds the form is rarely distinguished.

The same fault and the same qualities are evident in *Not Without Laughter*. Here, too, Mr. Hughes has a firm grasp on the rich materials of race, and handles them with insight and sensitiveness. In addition, he has a sense of humor. His people are treated with a decent pride in their qualities and achievements; for their foibles he has an amused tolerance. But in form the novel is shapeless and sprawling, without force of action or development of character to give it body and direction. It appears too much a series of anecdotes and sketches hung loosely on the framework of a single family. The events comprise various things that happen to the family. The framework fails to support the novel because the characters, with a single exception, are too flat. The principal personages appear as types rather than as human beings. Thus Aunt Hager, the family's head, is too much the old mammy type. As such, she is well and affectionately drawn; but she differs from the other old people in the book only by reason of being more constantly present. The other members of the family are too easily tabulated as a "blues" singer, a social climber, a guitar-playing roustabout, a superior boy. None of these characters develops in any way; they simply pass on from one event to another.

The most interesting person in the family is neglected, with great loss to the novel. Annjee, Hager's second daughter, might have been a deeply moving character, precisely because she represents the normal, the average of Negro men and women. As it is, she is far more interesting than her flamboyant sister or her no-'count husband. By neglecting the possibilities inherent in such a character, Mr. Hughes loses much of the advantage he gained by setting his story in a poor home in Kansas.

Mr. Hughes writes, at times, exceedingly well. The storm with which the book opens is excellently done; excellent, too, is the episode in which Sandy and his friends are kept away from a fair because the merry-go-rounds and pink lemonade were for white children only. But no matter how

skilfully told or how interesting in themselves, such episodes contribute little or nothing to the characters or to any central action. What results is a sensitive, understanding picture of Negro life; but as a novel, the book is neither dramatic nor moving.

J. R. Adams
"News and Reviews of Season's Books"
San Diego Union, World-Wide Features section, 2 November 1930, p. 8

When Langston Hughes published, a few years ago, his first book of verse, *The Weary Blues*, he was immediately recognized as a spokesman for his people and a poet of unusual ability. In *Not Without Laughter*, his first novel, his literary skill is again shown, but Mr. Hughes has not yet mastered prose as completely as verse, and the book is notable particularly as an interpretation of Negro life.

The scene throughout the greater part of the story is a small town in Kansas, the time shortly before the war. The characters are venerable Hager Williams, a laundress born in slavery days, her children and her grandson, Sandy, a likeable little boy.

In the contrast of the daughters' characters, a wide range of society is described. Tempy, the eldest of them, is a property owner and a leading figure among the Negroes; Harriett, the youngest, is a wild girl who eventually becomes a successful vaudeville performer, and Annjee is the third, Sandy's mild mother, who married for love. To these is added Jimboy Rodgers, a delightful wanderer who brightens every page on which he appears, whose philosophy is succinctly expressed in his advice to Sandy:

> Don't never let no one woman worry you . . . Treat 'em like chickens, son. Throw 'em a little corn and they'll run after you, but don't give 'em too much. If you do, they'll stop layin' and expect you to wait on 'em.

Unfortunately for the book's success, the weak parts are the opening, in which explanatory material is awkwardly introduced while the story pauses, and the conclusion, in which the scene is hurriedly changed to Chicago. Otherwise the story is well contrived, with incidents varied sufficiently to hold the attention and yet probable enough to be typical. The descriptions of a dance hall, of a carnival, or a barber shop and of a cheap hotel are vivid and full of life, and throughout the entire book Mr. Hughes has managed to impart a great deal of valuable information on how Negroes feel towards white people, and why.

Helen E. Haines
"Life 'Not Without Laughter': Langston Hughes' First Novel Contribution to a Freshly Opening Field in Negro Literature"
Pasadena Star-News,
3 January 1931, p. 36

This is the first novel of the young Negro poet whose work became known about four years ago by his volume of mingled jazz clangor and wistful cadences, *The Weary Blues.* Simple and unpretentious, it is apt to be overlooked in the continuous press of new books, more assertive or more arresting, but it deserves attention as a contribution of unusual interest and importance in a freshly opening field of Negro literature. For the Negro is taking a significant place in American art, music and literature, opening a rich vein of rhythm and emotion that so far is only just tapped and has hardly begun to yield the racial store that in time will deepen and widen our native creative art. In our fiction, especially, Negro life as yet is chiefly portrayed as seen and interpreted by white observers—often with truth and sympathy, as in Du Bose Heyward's *Porgy* and Mamba's *Daughter,* or, though with more narrowed vision, in Mrs. Peterkin's *Black April,* to my mind a finer and more valid study than her widely known *Scarlet Sister Mary.* The fiction that reflects Negro life as it is seen and known at first hand by Negro writers is less generally familiar to the reading public, but it has unquestionably more authentic value and deeper significance. Unfortunately, it often follows too closely the pattern set by many white novelists, its dominating emphasis on sensational aspects of sexual promiscuity or of vicious living; or, often too, it is distorted by a tragic violence of embitterment that is natural and inevitable but crude or repellent in effect. Yet Negro life must be portrayed by Negro writers if it is to be rendered in a living, truthful reflection in the looking-glass of American fiction. And this reflection must convey not only the excessive and the melodramatic as they are interwoven in life, but it must set before us the simplicities, the realities and achievements of everyday experience, the character, temperament and racial qualities of everyday people—patient, hardworking, warm-hearted, with ideals and standards and truly heroic virtues, as well as defects and excesses.

168

Langston Hughes gives us such a reflection in this simple chronicle of the life of a Negro family. It possesses the texture of truth; it is appealing, often poignant in its tragic implications of race discrimination, its matter-of-fact record of poverty, privation and toil; it is never violent and never artificial. The book has no sustained plot structure nor dramatic development; no sentimentality and no sensationalism. It is a quiet, restrained deeply human rendering of poor Negroes living in a small Kansas town before and during the years of the World War. Mr. Hughes knows and loves his people and he pictures them with insight and sympathy in their individual personalities and differing characters—some lazy and lovable, some hardworking and uncomplaining, some embittered, some ambitious, some talented, some vicious; but all fighting the same foes, poverty and prejudice. And it is a hard and unending fight, with odds against them, in an indifferent or hostile white world.

The tale is concerned chiefly with the life of a Negro boy from his ninth to his sixteenth year; a slim little fellow, brown-skinned but with sand-colored hair, which has given him his nickname, Sandy. His father is Jimboy, a lovable, ne'r-do-well, lazy mulatto, always with his banjo, a born wanderer following elusive jobs from place to place, perennially cheerful and gay, and adored by his serious, hard-working wife, Annjee, who is cook for an exacting family of white people. Sandy and his mother live with his grandmother, Aunt Hager, old but still strong, devoted, fervently religious, slaving always at the washtub for white people. The support of her family through three generations, called upon to nurse white and black alike, Aunt Hager is a truly heroic and beautiful figure, in spite of her dominating temper and constant conflict with the new generation that seems to her so godless and thoughtless. She herself is typical of the older generation; she had been a slave, but her memories of slavery are not bitter, for she had loved her mistress and been loved in turn. She is passionately devoted to her children, and on her little grandson she centers her ambition that he must have proper education and her hope that he shall become a helper of his race.

Annjee is patient, industrious, devoted to her Jimboy and ready to sacrifice anything for him. There is a younger sister, Sandy's Aunt Harriett, a born singer and dancer, with innate artistic capacities and an intelligence that resents the race discrimination she encounters and turns to embitterment and secret hate toward white people. Her pride and sensitiveness met constant injury in childhood and school-days—in high school particularly through isolation from companionship with others of her age. All through the book there is something very moving in the quiet chronicle of continuous incidents that stamp upon the colored children the sense of their inferiority—for example, the seating of all the Negro children in the back rows of the classroom, or the turning them away from a children's festival to which tickets to all school children had been issued, or the time that Harriett is forced to leave her high school classmates and sit in the last row of seats, the colored seats, at an educational movie. It is all personal and intimate in its sympathy, but simple and matter-of-fact, with no touch of propaganda or special pleading—and for that reason so much the more poignant.

Briefly, the story follows Sandy's life with Aunt Hager through his schooldays, his grandmother's death and his later stay with his Aunt Tempy who is well-to-do, with a prosperous husband, and holds herself above her family. It carries him after disappointments and frustrations to the opening of unexpected opportunity to finish his education and carry out his determination to fulfil Aunt Hager's hopes and make his life of service to his race. The book brings in many characters, many types; its scenes and incidents are varied, homely or ugly, harsh or mellow. It mirrors an aspect of American life that is in its essence pathetic and heroic and that is too seldom seen in the light of broad personal understanding and sympathy.

Alain Locke
"This Year of Grace"
Opportunity, 9 (February 1931), 48–51

... If this book were a trilogy, and carried its young hero, Sandy, through a typical black boy's journey from the cradle to the grave we might perhaps have the all-too-long-prayed-for Negro Novel. As it is, despite immaturity of narrative technique, this novel is one of the high-water marks of the Negro's self depiction in prose. *Not Without Laughter* owes its inspiration to a force far different from the flippant exhibitionism by which some of our younger writers aimed to out-Herod *Nigger Heaven.* Indeed it was born in Mr. Hughes' poetry, which aims to evoke the folk temperament truly and reverently; and in its best chapters, "Storm," "Guitar," and "Dance," its style palpitates with the real spiritual essences of Negro life. Should its promise be fulfilled, we shall have a Negro novelist to bracket with Julia Peterkin and Du Bose Heyward.

Frances Swan Hunter
"On the Bookshop Table"
Pike County Republican (Pittsfield, Ill.), 25 March 1931, p. 2

Modest, unassuming, but entirely convincing is Langston Hughes' story of his own colored race in *Not Without Laughter.*

Of the writer, Alfred Knopf has this to say: "Langston Hughes has written poetry in every corner of the world while working at nearly every kind of job. He has lived in Mexico, he has been to Africa where he drank palm wine on the Gold Coast, bought a monkey up the Niger and fell into the Congo. He has been a cook in a Montmartre night club. He has been a beach comber in Genoa. But when he sat down to write his first novel he chose a small town in Kansas for his scene because, he says, 'I am interested primarily in life, not in local color.'" It is the story of Hager Williams, life-long laundress; her daughter Annjee, married for love to inconsequent Jimboy Rodgers; Tempy, married for social position and economic safety to Mr. Siles, mail clerk; Harriett, seventeen, wayward, incorrigible but finally successful, and of Sandy, Annjee's little boy.

One suspects that the tale is biographical. How else could a writer give an account so intimate of the life and thought of a little colored boy? From the first sentence the reader seems to see with his eyes, think with his brain, yet he is the youngest person in the story and views the action of the rest as an interested, affectionate bystander.

Mr. Hughes' choice of the little Kansas town where the white people enter into the story only as employers whose voices are never heard, perhaps gives a slightly unreal quality—yet it as surely secures the austerity of his picture. He means only to show the lives of the colored people and that he does in a manner which enlists the sympathy of the reader.

Old Hager, washing and ironing all day long every day until she finally lies wearily down, leaving the steaming clothes in the tub, is a clear fine character. Her religion is very real and sustaining and she transmits to her children and grandchild none save admirable qualities.

Sandy, Annjee's boy, lives with Hager, whose heart's desire is to bring him up "nice" to be a help to his race. Annjee, against the mother's will, has followed her adored "Jimboy" to Detroit. Sandy has secured a job at the Drummers Hotel. Can you wonder that he was successful?

"He liked to clean things to make them beautiful, to make them shine. Aunt Hager did, too. When she wasn't washing clothes, she was always cleaning something about the house, dusting, polishing the range, or scrubbing the kitchen floor until it was white enough to eat from. To Hager a clean thing was beautiful, also to Sandy, proud every evening of his six unblemished brass spittoons. Yet each day when he came to work they were covered anew with tobacco juice, cigarette butts, wads of chewing gum, and phlegm. But to make them clean was Sandy's job—and they were beautiful when they were clean."

Sandy's was a sensitive soul. It is this which makes the reader wonder if Langston Hughes' own poetic spirit does not speak in such lines as these:

"He had discovered already, though, that so-called jokes are often not really jokes at all, but rather unpleasant realities that hurt unless you can think of something equally funny and unpleasant to say in return."

The presence of the Negro race among us today has furnished the theme for some of the best of contemporary literature. None has been written with a more sympathetic touch. Every word is interesting. It might have happened in Pittsfield.

Martha Gruening
"The Negro Renaissance"
Hound and Horn, 5
(April–June 1932),
[504]–514

. . . But if there have been few if any good novels written about the Negro Bourgeoisie there have been at least three first rate novels about Negro Proletarian life. All three were written by Negro poets. Negro poets have very generally been spare-time poets—and proletarians. They have been cooks, dishwashers, floor-scrubbers, shoe-shiners, waiters, stevedores, Pullman porters, stokers, or have worked at any of the various forms of rough and casual menial labor open to American Negroes.

Langston Hughes is one of these poets, who having spent much of his life in the world of labor has inevitably been close to the life of the masses of his race. It was out of this experience that he wrote *Not Without Laughter,* which is not only uniquely moving and lovely among Negro novels but among books written about America. It is affirmative in a sense in which no other book by an American Negro is, for it is the story of a Negro happily identified with his own group, who because of this identification tells what is essentially, despite the handicaps of poverty and prejudice, the story of a happy childhood. The poverty was never sordid; for one thing it was country poverty in a growing small town of the Middle West, and the child had a backyard to play in, in which there was an apple tree, and flowers as well as clothes lines.

. . . It was poverty, but never sodden or defeated, though the child's grandmother toiled all day at her washtub washing the white folk's clothes and his mother sweated all day in the white woman's kitchen, while his handsome, vagabond father went fishing and played the guitar; even though eventually there was no place in Stanton for his pretty, fun-loving Aunt Harriett but the sinful house in the "bottoms". . . . It was poverty enlivened by singing and laughter, by strong, if casual, family affection and occasional family quarrels; by carnivals and camp meetings, by lodge meetings and regalia after the day's work was done, for: "Evening's the only time we niggers have to ourselves— Thank God for night—'cause all day you give to the white folks." Simple and touching, yet by some miracle always avoiding sentimentality, the story is told with a happy tenderness which recalls Katherine Mansfield's dictum that in fiction the beginning of art is remembering. It has the courage of its tenderness for Negro things, a serene and robust acceptance of the common things, the sights and smells and sounds, the folkways and idiosyncrasies of the people who made up one little Colored boy's background; and through this acceptance and evocation of them it communicates the very feeling and texture of life.

The only other American novel I know which seems to me comparable with *Not Without Laughter* is Willa Cather's *My Antonia*. Both books have, in common, somewhat the same quality of radiant sanity. Both communicate, in spite of relatively small canvases, a feeling of earth and sun and air, of a strong life with deep folk roots. In both a poetic quality is due in part to the fact that the story is told reminiscently through the eyes of a child reflecting a child's curiosity and sensibility

and wonder, and that the child in each case was a potential poet. In both there is ugliness and hardship and pain, but in both these incidents are dominated by a triumphant vitality, an open-eyed resilience in the face of life. And this, too, is a quality that is characteristic of Langston Hughes and which sings through his poems whether he is writing of "Beale Street Love" or "Railroad Blues" or of

> The steam in hotel kitchens
> And the smoke in hotel lobbies
> And the slime in hotel spittoons
> Part of my life

and is implicit in his high-hearted chant, "I, Too". . . .

. . . Thus *Not Without Laughter* is not merely a chronicle of Negro family life. The story of hard working, stay-at-home Annjee's helpless love for her vagabond husband, of Harriett's rebellion against her mother's puritanism, the true and sensitive picture of Sandy's boyhood and adolescence are rich and warm and full-flavored because of certain Negro qualities that Langston Hughes knows and loves, but the book's hold on our emotions is independent of these. They merely enhance the truth of what the perceptive artist in Hughes has felt about love between a man and a woman, about the clash of the generations, and the awakening consciousness of a boy. . . .

Checklist of Additional Reviews

Warren D. Abbott, Jr., "Under the Reading Lamp," *Tulsa World*, section 5, 17 August 1930, p. 3.

"Fiction," *Among Our Books*, 35 (October 1930), 70.

"The American Scene, Past and Present," *Open Shelf,* December 1930, p. 148.

"Fiction," *Booklist,* 27 (December 1930), 160.

K.P., "Take Notice, White Folks!" *World Tomorrow,* 13 (December 1930), 520–1.

David H. Pierce, "Here and There," *Cleveland Call and Post,* 28 February 1931, [p. ?].

"Aunt Hager's Boy Sandy Finds Life Puzzling in Hughes' Picture of Family," *Indianapolis Recorder,* section 2, 28 November 1942, [p. 1].

THE DREAM KEEPER AND OTHER POEMS

"The Dream Keeper"
Boston Evening Transcript, Book Section, 30 July 1932, p. 2

One of the better known poets has brought together in this small, varied collection for young people selections which reveal a number of interests and talents. The poems are all short, and they typify some of the aspects of the natural interests of a race. There are poems of nature, poems characteristic of Negro philosophy. The brevity of many of the selections greatly enhances their effectiveness. They are simple, human, vivid, singing with sincerity.

Horace Gregory
"Sandburg of Negro Verse"
New York Evening Post, 2 August 1932, p. 9

About five years ago Countee Cullen published an anthology of Negro poetry. In this collection over thirty-five living Negro poets were represented. Here was a sudden renaissance of Negro literature and its results were often more than merely promising. So much for the movement at full tide. It was inevitable that a reaction should set in, a reaction not unlike the lull that followed the American poetry renaissance of 1912–1916. Today one hears almost nothing of the general movement, but a few names survive: Charles Weldon John-son, Claude McKay, Stirling A. Brown, Countee Cullen and Langston Hughes.

In some respects Langston Hughes is the most interesting figure in the group. When *The Weary Blues,* his first book of poems, was published, the vogue for Negro jazz was at its height. His poetry, which employed many of the dominant elements of jazz music, struck the ear with the conviction that here was something extraordinarily fresh and invigorating. Langston Hughes never disguised his purpose: first of all he was a Negro poet and in that sense a propagandist quite without the usual apologies for being so. He had overcome the initial stages of self-consciousness and could afford to speak out loud. From the very start his poetry had an air of outdoor health and vitality. His work had something of the same physical charm that we associate with the singing of Paul Robeson.

The present volume, a collection of verse made for young people from the ages of twelve to sixteen, is an admirable example of editing. The poems are selected from his two early books and are supplemented by a group of new poems so as to complete a feeling of unity. It has been a long time since any book of verse for children has been so attractively presented. Langston Hughes's charm is here with its best foot forward and each page is deftly illustrated with a design by Helen Sewell. The little poems and the drawing seem to merge into an inseparable unit which is a rare accident in modern book illustration.

Glancing through this book one might almost say that Langston Hughes is the Carl Sandburg of Negro poetry. Surely his attraction for children springs from the same source that makes Carl Sandburg one of the few contemporary poets whose verse continues to demand attention from younger people. The direct speech and the simple image evoke an instantaneous response. Take the first stanza of "Homesick Blues":

De railroad bridge's
A sad song in de air.
De railroad bridge's
A sad song in de air.
Every time de trains pass
I wants to go somewhere.

Or the poem called "The Negro," which contains these stanzas:

I've been a slave:
    Caesar told me to keep his
        doorsteps clean.
    I brushed the boots of Washington.
I've been a worker:
    Under my hand the pyramids arose.
    I made mortar for the Woolworth
        Building.

There is a kind of emotional validity in these lines that gives them genuine, unforced power and a quality of frankness that deserves respect. Miss Effie L. Power, director of work with children at the Cleveland Public Library, is responsible for suggesting that this selection be made into a book. Her choice was a wise one, and I believe that her enthusiasm for Langston Hughes as a poet for children will be shared by hundreds of young people throughout the country.

Clothes to the Jew, two previous works of Langston Hughes. The selection of those suitable for young readers has been made through the suggestion of Miss Effie L. Power, the director of work with young people in the Cleveland Public Library.

These delightful verses are divided into five groups. The first expresses in a lyrical mood the beauty of such common things (or so they seem to most of us) as rain, skies and little white houses in the snow. The second gives us glimpses of the sea as seen by the author, who in his youth visited many lands. There is an introduction to the third section carefully explaining the meaning of the "Blues" in poetry and the poetic pattern which is followed in writing this particular type of verse. This should prove helpful to other readers as well as to the students for whom it is intended. The next section is titled "Feet of Jesus" and contains fervent prayers from humble hearts. In the last group one notes the essence of hope in each of the poems and feels Mr. Hughes' great pride in his race and his desire to instil it in those entering into manhood and womanhood.

This book should be placed in the hands of as many children, black and white, as possible. To the former it is bound to be a great inspiration and to the latter afford a better view of what Negroes can do in the field of literature.

N.A.G.
"New Books"
New York Amsterdam News, 3 August 1932, p. 6

This collection of poems is for boys and girls between the ages of twelve and sixteen years. Many of the verses will be remembered from *Weary Blues* and *Fine*

Charles Hanson Towne
"Books—and a Number of Things"
Boston American, 13 August 1932, p. 5

After I had read Langston Hughes' poems, *The Dream Keeper,* just issued by Alfred

Knopf, and liked them all, I read a few aloud to my colored servant, James, who is from the South. I said to myself, "If he likes them, then they are authentic. If he responds, especially to the 'blues' verses, then I shall know for a certainty that Hughes has interpreted well the heart and soul of his race."

James responded with loud guffaws, and then, to my surprise, he said: "They remind me of Paul Laurence Dunbar's poems."

That was high praise, but it was deserved.

You half sing the poems to yourself. I wondered immediately if any of them had been set to music. Here is a mine for some composer like Gershwin or Deems Taylor.

In a note on the "blues" poems, Mr. Hughes says:

"The 'blues,' unlike the spirituals, have a strict poetic pattern; one long line, repeated, and a third line to rhyme with the first two. Sometimes the second line in repetition is slightly changed and sometimes, but very seldom, it is omitted. . . . The mood of the 'blues' is almost always despondency, but when they are sung people laugh."

I give only three stanzas of "Bound No'th Blues" to show what beauty and strength are obtained by this method of simple repetition:

Goin' down de road, Lawd,
Goin' down de road.
Down de road, Lawd,
Way, way down de road.
Got to find somebody
To help me carry dis load.

Hates to be lonely,
Lawd, I hates to be sad.
Says I hates to be lonely,
Hates to be lonely an' sad,
But ever' friend you finds seems
Like they try to do you bad.

Road, road, road, O!
Road, road . . . road . . . road, road!
Road, road, road, O!
On de No'thern road.
These Mississippi roads ain't
Fit fer a hoppin' toad.

The title page announces that this collection is especially for young people. True, those of the jingly, almost banjo-strumming kind, will appeal to youthful ears; but there are many verses here for a deeper significance than would at first appear. Take the simple "Song":

Lovely, dark, and lonely one,
Bare your bosom to the sun.
Do not be afraid of light,
You who are a child of night.

Open wide your arms to life,
Whirl in the wind of pain and strife,
Face the wall with the dark closed
    gate,
Beat with bare brown fists—
And wait.

But Mr. Hughes sees not only the pathos of the Negro. He can be equally sentimental over a Parisian beggar woman. Thus:

Once you were young,
Now, hunched in the cold
Nobody cares
That you are old.

Once you were beautiful,
Now, in the street,
No one remembers
Your lips were sweet.

Oh, withered old woman
Of rue Fontaine,
Nobody but Death
Will kiss you again.

The drawings and decorations by Helen Sewell are a perfect interpretation of the text.
    [. . .]

179

William Rose Benét
"Round about Parnassus: Chiefly on Langston Hughes"
Saturday Review, 9 (12 November 1932), 241

There is a great deal of verse now before me in various volumes, nor is it all negligible. But none of it arouses my enthusiasm. The size of the output of verse in these United States is truly extraordinary, and the level of the writing higher than one would suppose. At the same time, there is a great deal of wasted effort. This is due principally to the fact that it is fairly easy to write a set of verses eccentrically or on some trivial subject, and extremely hard to write poetry in any way unusual. Four books from among those before me promise something. First there is a book of poems for young people by the Negro poet, Langston Hughes, entitled *The Dream Keeper* (Knopf). This volume, with excellent illustrations by Helen Sewell, is presented with the usual good taste in evidence in Knopf books. It is aimed at children from twelve to sixteen. There is a word by way of introduction from Effie L. Power, Director of Work with Children at the Cleveland Public Library. Hughes wrote his first verses as a pupil in the Central High School of Cleveland. It is not till the third section of the book, "Dressed Up" (with a note on the Blues), that one encounters the best work of this poet, though several wistful fragments may delay us on the way. The last sentence of the poet's "Note" is a pregnant one: "The mood of the Blues is almost always despondency, but when they are sung people laugh." In this section Hughes's well-known "The Weary Blues" is included, one of his best things. "Song," "When Sue Wears Red," and "Song for a Banjo Dance," are meritorious. In the next section, "Feet o' Jesus" and "Judgment Day" contain the essence of the spirituals. Following this section, "Walkers with the Dawn" contains the tribute to Booker Washington, "Alabama Earth"; the fine, simple "My People"; "Dream Variations"; the praised "The Negro Speaks of Rivers"; and "I, Too," and "Youth," which are of Hughes's best. Langston Hughes is not a first-rate poet, even among those of his own race, but he is distinctly an appealing one, a melodist who touches with sensitiveness the stops of his black flute.

Doyne Elliott
"Children's Book Week Presents New Juveniles"
Los Angeles Times, part 3, 13 November 1932, p. 16

[. . .]

Many of the boys and girls and adults who were so fortunate as to hear Langston Hughes read his poems when he was in Los Angeles last year will be glad to read and own this collection of short lyrics, serious poems, songs and blues by one of the foremost Negro poets. Many of the poems in this collection were first printed in the *New Republic, Survey Graphic, Vanity Fair* and other magazines.

As an introduction to the group of blues, Mr. Hughes writes: "The Blues are songs about being in the midst of trouble, friendless, hungry, disappointed in love, right here on earth. The mood of the Blues is almost always despondency, but when they are sung people laugh." He then sets our feet tap, tapping with his "Negro Dancers" and makes us smile as we read "Dressed Up."

[. . .]

Jane B. Ford
"Literary Guidepost"
San Diego Union, World-Wide Features section, 11 December 1932, p. 4

Miss Effie L. Power, director of work with young people in the Cleveland Public Library, noticed that the poems of Langston Hughes were popular especially with boys and girls in their teens. At her suggestion this selection of poems for young readers was made. The book consists of 60 poems from *The Weary Blues* and *Fine Clothes to the Jew* together with 21 new ones.

The choice, representative as it is of the scope of Mr. Hughes' work, and the arrangement according to mood, subject and complexity are both thoroughly admirable. The contents is divided into five sections, called respectively: "The Dream Keeper," "Sea Charm," "Dressed Up," "Feet O' Jesus" and "Walkers with the Dawn."

The first two groups consist of short lyrics, simple in sentiment and imagery. Characteristic of these is the one-stanza lyric:

I loved my friend.
He went away from me.
There's nothing more to say.
The poem ends,
Soft as it began—
I loved my friend.

While most of these poems seem within the comprehension of quite young chil-

dren, say from six or seven, those under the title, "Dressed Up" are decidedly not of interest to the pre-adolescent. The emotions typical of adolescence, loneliness, haunting melancholy, love are the basic themes here. Five of these 15 poems are blues with "The Weary Blues" among them.

"The Walkers with the Dawn" are, of course, the youth, and these poems of inspiration, though most of them are addressed to young Afro-America, have an exaltation and earnestness that cannot fail to move readers of any age or race. The lines written at the grove of Booker Washington are as profoundly eloquent as Whitman's tribute to Lincoln:

Deep in Alabama earth
  His buried body lies—
But higher than the singing pines
  And taller than the skies
And out of Alabama earth
  To all the world there goes
The truth a simple heart has held
  And the strength a strong hand
    knows.

While over Alabama earth
  These words are gently spoken:
Serve—and hate will die unborn,
  Love—and chains are broken.

The book is decorated with numerous black and white designs by Helen Sewell. These drawings, in perfect harmony with the poems, do much to enhance the beauty of the text.

Mr. Hughes' poems are childlike in their spirit, but there is nothing childish about them. I venture to say that for the adult who wishes to arouse an interest in genuine poetry in some young heart, no recent book will serve the purpose so well as *The Dream Keeper.*

181

John Clements
"Paul James' Ironic Jests Palpable Hits at Folly: Poets, Struggling Bravely to Scale Parnassus, Offer Varied Verses of Great Charm"
Philadelphia Public Ledger, 31 December 1932, p. 9

[...]

The Dream Keeper is a culling from the earlier books of Langston Hughes with some new poems added intended for children of from 12 to 16 years. The many drawings of Helen Sewell, done in woodblock effect and depicting Negro figures, as well as the race-consciousness present in most of the poems, stamp the book as primarily one of Negro poetry, and the spirituals, blues and character pieces bring out the moods of the author's own people. However, it is in the short poems of one stanza limited to a single thought, such as "The Dream Keeper," "Irish Wake," "Sea Charm," that the beauty and delicacy of thoughts and his words show to the best advantage.

[...]

Alain Locke
"Black Truth and Black Beauty"
Opportunity, 11 (January 1933), 14–18

Meanwhile, as the folk-school tradition deepens, Langston Hughes, formerly its chief exponent, turns more and more in the direction of social protest and propaganda; since *Scottsboro Ltd.* represents his latest moods, although *The Dream Keeper* and *Popo and Fifina* are also recent publications. The latter is a quite flimsy sketch, a local-color story of Haitian child life, done in collaboration with Arna Bontemps, while *The Dream Keeper* is really a collection of the more lyrical of the poems in his first two volumes of verse, supplemented by a few unprinted poems,—all designed to be of special appeal to child readers. The book is a delightful lyrical echo of the older Hughes, who sang of his people as "walkers with the dawn and morning," "loud-mouthed laughers in the hands of fate." But the poet of *Scottsboro, Ltd.* is a militant and indignant proletarian reformer, proclaiming. . . .

Checklist of Additional Reviews

Anne T. Eaton, "The New Books for Children," *New York Times Book Review,* 17 July 1932, p. 13.
"Children's Books," *Booklist,* 29 (October 1932), 47.
Robert Harris, "The Afro-American Classics: An Essential Library," *Black*

Enterprise, 14 (June 1984), [33–34], 36, [38].

"Critically Speaking: Freshly Minted Words for a Happy New Year," *Reading Teacher,* 40 (January 1987), 463.

Janet Hickman, "Bookwatching: Notes on Children's Books," *Language Arts,* 64 (February 1987), 241.

Barbara T. Rollock, "The Black Experience in Children's Books," *Five Owls,* 2 (January–February 1988), 47–8.

THE WAYS OF WHITE FOLKS

Mason Roberson
"Hughes Talks on Tragedy of Race"
Spokesman, 7 June 1934, p. 6

Mr. Hughes talks of tragedy—and tragedy that goes far beyond any one human life or group of lives. It partakes of the nature of mankind: it is part of his history and part of himself in the mass. And it seems almost beyond our power to correct. Of course, Mr. Hughes deals with the matter of prejudice, but he deals with it in a restrained narrative manner that, for the Negro reader, brings the book into a class with the somber despair of *All Quiet on the Western Front, The Well of Loneliness,* and *Strange Interlude.* What he says in his stories is known to us all—but he possesses the artist's power of making it immensely vivid.

Some years ago a Miss Corra Harris in an essay about the South mentioned the fact that the Negro has an understanding of white people based on an intimate and at the same time divorced contact with their life. Someday, she said, a Negro would write of what he knows. It would, she thought, be one of the most completely revealing studies of American life ever published.

And now we have Langston Hughes' *Ways of White Folks* which attacks just that task and does it not only out of an intimate knowledge of the white man as he is seen by the Negro, but with a rarer understanding since his values have been shaped and widened by travel abroad.

The product is not academic. The collection of short stories which makes up this book is biased. It is definitely what a Negro thinks of the white folks. And necessarily bitterness warps the pictures of the white characters. Not that Mr. Hughes distorts. He is far too able an artist to do anything like that. His characters ring true, always. It is just that his choice of white folks fell among those who embodied the white man as he is known to the Negro when he thinks of the things the white man has done to his race. It is to be regretted that in the collection, although he was justified in the choice of white characters in each story, choosing as he did those best suited to point what he had to say in that particular story, the collected works make up a gallery of white folks all of whom are weak.

I have doubtless read into Mr. Hughes' book much that doesn't appear on the pages. That is the way with a work of art. The book is beautifully written in the easy deceptive simplicity that is Mr. Hughes' style. It will make you think, although what you think will not always be pleasant.

H.H.H.
"Books on Review"
Durham Herald Sun, part 1, 17 June 1934, p. 5

After two years of silence, Langston Hughes comes forth with a collection of dynamic, inter-racial stories which have appeared in the leading literary magazines, including *The American Mercury, Scribner's,* and *Esquire.* One of the stories, "A Good Job Gone," temporarily upset the works of *Esquire,* the magazine for men. But it was not Langston Hughes' aim to upset either a magazine or the reading audience. He has written in *The Ways of*

White Folks what the Negro thinks of the white man and what the white man has done to him to make him think that way. According to Milberry, in one of the stories, "the ways of white folks, some white folks, is too much for me. I reckon they must be a few good ones, but most of 'em ain't good—leastwise they don't treat me good and Lawd knows, I ain't never done nothin' to 'em, nothin' a-tall."

In "Cora Unashamed," the first story, Hughes has written of the naturalness of the Negro. Cora wouldn't think much of having an illegitimate child but her white folks' daughter who was going to have one died from an abortion. The old paternal, Christian attitude toward the Negro is characteristically and quite ironically carried out in "Slave on the Block" and "Poor Little Black Fellow." The first story concerns a conventional American couple who pseudo a bit in the Village while the latter is a story of a well-to-do family of whites who bring up a Negro boy as their own child. Arnie learns that in Europe there are no color race barriers. In Europe people are only tired of being poor. Hughes brings in his Marxism in a classic spot. Everything in America is like a camp, Arnie learns—segregated.

The most dramatic story, however, is that of Roy Williams, Negro, who returned to his small Missouri hometown, after touring Europe with an orchestra. According to a music teacher, he is the only one who can play Brahms, Beethoven and Franck. One day when she stopped to talk to him on the street, cries arose that he had attacked her. "And when the white folks left his brown body, stark naked, strung from a tree at the edge of town, it hung there all night, like a violin for the wind to play." Equally powerful is the one about the Little Dog. Quite satiric with amusing penetration are "The Blues I'm Playing," "Rejuvenation Through Joy" and "Passing." In these stories Hughes has combined the poetic instinct and feeling to the best technique of Erskine Caldwell, Anton Chekhov and Katherine Mansfield. The real Hughes is talking at last.

"Book Honors Noel Sullivan"
San Francisco News, 23 June 1934, p. 8

This is a splendid collection of 14 short stories written by the Negro poet and novelist. They are told with a power and a full understanding of the trends of the modern, realistic writers now coming to the front in the better magazines.

The stories for the greater part concern the relations between the Negroes and the whites in the north.

The tale of the faithful and outspoken family servant in "Cora Unashamed" stands out. The sardonic epic of the arty people who gush over colored folk is especially well done in "Slave on the Block."

Most pathetic in its stark tragedy is the story of the homecoming of a Negro pianist who became the innocent victim of a lynching bee in the tale called "Home."

The book is dedicated to Noel Sullivan, well known art patron of this city.

"White Folks' Ways: Relations of Races Interpreted by Negro Poet Hughes"
Pasadena Star-News,
23 June 1934, p. 6

We have had a full quota of stories of Negro life written from the point of view of the white man, but this is the first time a group of short stories has been gathered into a book, which sees and interprets Negro life from the point of view of a Negro. Mr. Hughes, one of the leading members of his race and the author of several volumes of poetry (*The Weary Blues, The Dream Keeper* and *Fine Clothes to the Jew*) and a novel of Negro life in the Middle West (*Not Without Laughter*) presents fourteen tales, some of which are high art, and all of which give the reader a new understanding of Negro psychology, the light-hearted gaiety of a people, and the tragedy which is their lot.

Mr. Hughes plays upon the heartstrings in such tales as "Home," the story of a little Negro boy who ran away from his mother's house, joined a circus, found his way into a jazz orchestra that went to Europe, took violin lessons from one of the great German music teachers, fell a victim of tuberculosis, had a premonition of death, and returned to his old home town in Southern Missouri to see his mother before he died. One will have to go to the Russians to find anything comparable to the unutterable sadness and tragic futility this story of Roy Williams bodies forth.

I wish that every man who bears senseless malice in his heart against men who are not of his race and color could read "Home" and be touched and revolted by the cruelty that was visited upon a hapless genius by a mob that became the murderers of an innocent boy. I don't know when I have been so deeply affected by short story or by novel as I was by this little masterpiece that is propaganda in spite of itself. If Langston Hughes never wrote another short story, he would have to be reckoned with for what this volume contains.

Lewis Gannett
"Books and Things"
New York Herald Tribune Books, 27 June 1934, p. 15

"White folks is white folks, honey, South or North, North or South," says Lucy Doves in one of the tales in Langston Hughes's *The Ways of White Folks;* and white folks do not stand out as very nice folks in any of these stories written along the color line. White folks here are proud and mean, even when surest they are being warm-hearted and generous to their brown-skinned brethren. And it happens that Langston Hughes can write as no other of the younger colored writers can; and these stories cut deep.

Nothing of the wise but patronizing romanticism of Julia Peterkin's stories here; nothing of the harsh assertiveness of some of the older, combative writers; no gentle haze. These are stories written by a Negro who is a master of the story-telling art and who writes as one of a Negro generation which asserts and assumes a pride in its own race. Three of these fourteen tales deal with the love of white men for brown women, four with the love of white women for brown men. Two end in the lynching of uppity colored boys who had dared to go to school. And three touch a note new in Negro literature, and bitter with a sudden, searing bitterness, resenting white patrons of Negro art and Negro artists. Some of them, appearing in *Esquire,* caused violent debate; others were published in the *Mercury, Scribner's* and other magazines. And they are good stories.

The Pembertons, of a Boston suburb, were very proud of the way they had brought up Arnie, son of their old Negro servants. In fact, the whole town was nice to Arnie, and very proud of its municipal good deed. He was the bright boy at high school, though, of course, he did not dance at the senior ball. The Pembertons took Arnie with them to Paris and were bitterly resentful when Arnie ran away from their lectures to play with the little Rumanian girl he had met at the apartment of Claudine, the brown-skinned Georgia beauty whose dancing had swept Paris. Claudine had greeted Arnie in the hotel corridor, not as a poor little black boy but as a human being, and for the first time in his life Arnie had been really happy. "Somebody had offered him something without charity, without condescension, without prayer, without distance, and without being nice."

Langston Hughes's Negro artists are no more grateful to their white patrons than the people at the New York City relief stations are, in confidential moments, to those who give them food. And to Vivi, the Rumanian girl, there were no blacks and whites in the world; there were only poor people and rich. She was astonished to hear about the color lines drawn even by nice white folks in Boston suburbs.

"Here it's only hard to be poor," said Vivi.

Arnie thought he would not mind being poor in a land where it didn't matter what color you were.

"Yes, you would mind," said Vivi. "But being poor's not easy anywhere.

But then," she added, "by and by the Revolution will come. Everywhere poor people are tired of being poor."

"What revolution?": asked Arnie, who hadn't heard of the revolution from the Pembertons' friends.

Vivi told him.

"Where we live, it's quiet," said Arnie. "My folks come from Massachusetts." But he didn't go back.

"I don't mind being white, Ma," wrote the light-skinned boy who had "passed"—over into the white world—to his mulatto mother in another of these poignant stories. There you have another new note. He did not really mind missing the warmth and color and humanity of his own racial tradition, since he could make more money by passing; but he recognized his loss. He was an American.

It isn't enough to be regarded as quaint and lovable, or accepted as artists, a race seems to be saying through these stories. All they ask—more than they ever get—is to be accepted as human beings without a thought of their complexion.

Harry Hansen
"The First Reader"
New York World-Telegram, 27 June 1934, p. 19; with variations also in *New Bedford Mercury,* 29 June; *Norfolk Pilot,* 30 June; *Pittsburgh Press,* feature section, 8 July, p. 10; *San Francisco News,* 8 July

Langston Hughes never had his head in the clouds, even when he wrote poetry. His feet were on the ground, and he knew where he was going. You sense that in his short stories, published today under the title *The Ways of White Folks.*

Maybe the spirit of his grandparents directed him. They were free Negroes, and even before the civil war they hustled slaves across the line from the South and gave them shelter in the North. His maternal grandmother was the last surviving widow of the raid on Harper's Ferry for which John Brown swung.

[. . .]

This ought to be enough to indicate that if experience is important to an author Langston Hughes ought to have something to say. Further evidence may be found in *The Ways of White Folks.*

The first story in the book, "Cora Unashamed," is also the best. It is based upon the strong contrast in two attitudes toward illegitimate children. Cora, the maid of the Studevants, was proud of her child, even though its father did not give it a name. But the Studevants could not tolerate the idea that their daughter, Jessie, should bear a child out of wedlock, and because appearances meant so much to them they indirectly brought about the death of their daughter.

But the story is not as simple as that. Here we see the life force welling up in Cora, who was happy with her little one until it died, and then transferred her affection to Jessie. Jessie could not confide in her mother when her own trouble came— only in Cora. There were too many barriers between her parents and natural living, whereas there were none at all visible to Cora Jenkins.

This affecting story is really more than a commentary on the difference in race; it shows how the veneer of society distorts values and makes human beings sacrifice their best interests to pride and vanity.

Certain themes are very close to the Negro way of life. We find a representative group of them treated by Hughes in the short story.

For instance, exploitation of the Negro by well-intentioned whites, who do not, however, understand that the Negro cannot be given half a loaf and denied the other half. In "Poor Little Black Fellow" the Pembertons, who have patronized Arnie and taken him with them to Paris, are shocked when he announces his intention of breaking with them and remaining in Paris with a French girl.

In "The Blues I'm Playing" Mrs. Ellsworth, who has tried to force Oceola's musical talent into conventional lines, meets her defeat when Oceola rises ecstatically to the rhythms of her own race.

In "Slave on the Block" the Carraways, who love to paint the swarthy beauty of Luther and have him sing for their guests, cannot understand why he should override their restrictions and deny them further chaperonage.

More subtly treated is the theme of "Little Dog," in which a white spinster feels herself drawn toward a colored janitor who nightly brings meat for her dog. Nothing happens, but the story suggests a bond among human beings that transcends color. Ironically, Hughes turns against those Negroes who deny their color by passing for whites in "Passing." This is the letter of a Negro to his mother apologizing for not recognizing her on the street because he was with his white fiancée. Ostensibly the mother suggested his "passing."

The collection of stories winds up with high explosive. "Father and Son" is two-thirds melodrama. In the first third it explains a problem—that of the young half-breed, son of the white planter and his Negro mistress, who returns from school at the age of 20 determined to meet his father as an equal. The working out of this tale is rather hectic and reminds one of situations in Stribling's "Unfinished Cathedral." It does not show Hughes at his best as an artist.

These and other stories are forthright tales. Hughes' method is direct and hard-hitting. Subtlety is not easily at his command, but his portraits ring true. The workmanship of the tales is uneven, but as a whole they make an admirable contribution to American writing that counts.

William Soskin
"Reading and Writing"
San Francisco Examiner,
27 June 1934, [p. 13]; also
New York American,
27 June, [p. 17]

Perhaps the Commissars and the Soviet Union of Artists and Writers will approve the latest work of the American Negro writer, Langston Hughes, and perhaps that's all the approval he wants. I don't think his stories, published under the title *The Ways of White Folks,* will appeal to that portion of his public which admired his poetry in *The Weary Blues* and his novel, *Not Without Laughter,* and which has not joined the Moscow literary ranks.

There's no reason to quarrel with the subject matter of these stories. Mr. Hughes writes with realism and cynically about the fate of his race at the hands of various classes of whites. He divorces the Negro race in America from all the self-help and advancement movements and from all the flirting with white culture and art that have been so seriously promoted in the past. He does not state his beliefs or his point of view in so many words, but the stories, bitter and hard-boiled, leave that implication. It is a thesis which Mr. Hughes' Russian friends will applaud in the best neo-Marxist manner.

Granting him the validity of his viewpoint, then, I still regret it for what it has done to his artistry. Langston Hughes was a good writer. These stories of his are, when you get outside the emotional eddies of his arguments, pretty shoddy affairs.

Mr. Carl Van Vechten, an old enthusiast for Langston Hughes' work, describes the stories as worthy of comparison with those of Chekhov and Katherine Mansfield. Neither Chekhov, with all his good humor, nor Katherine Mansfield, with all her kindliness, would have taken that lightly. These tales by Mr. Hughes are little allegories, little arguments. They have virtually no atmospheric qualities, no subtleties of omission, no haunting moods, nothing to qualify them for comparison with the two masters of the modern short story.

Throughout these stories Mr. Hughes stresses the stupidity of the white folks who made a cult of Harlem, "spirichels" and the Negro primitives, the poor whites who cultivated Negroes as a fashionable gesture. Yet there is an exaltation of the black folks in his book, a tendency to make a grand, simple, wholesome, sensitive and strong soul out of every Negro who figures in the stories.

Whether one writes of Negroes, Jews, Chinese, Hindus or Nordics, this is a fault. It leaves a sentimental and false note sounding throughout the book despite the intense sincerity of the author.

The first story glorifies a Negro servant girl who was not ashamed to bear her illegitimate child openly and to exult in her love affair with a pagan healthiness. But when the girl gets up at the funeral of the white daughter of the household, a victim of an operation by which the respectable family sought to conceal an extramarital affair, and denounces the hypocrisy of the white folks—then I think Mr. Hughes has descended to rather obvious and stupid melodrama.

A story called "Home" has considerable merit when it describes the reception which a world-famous jazz band leader receives in his small home town in the South. There all the sophistication and the glitter disappear and the boy is simply a Negro, subject to the insults and the violence all Negroes must meet in the South. When Mr. Hughes carries the situation to an extreme and has the sensitive musician lynched, I think he places himself as far from Chekhov and Katherine Mansfield as one can get. There are lynchings. There are false accusations of assault upon white women. There are sensitive Negroes. There is a race problem. But all that has very little to do with the question of whether or not a story such as "Home" is an effective one.

And my complaint is this: That as soon as writers—good writers such as Langston Hughes—get themselves involved in the machinery of propaganda, write for a so-cial or economic or political thesis primarily, and to tell a story and build character and situation only secondarily, they lose their real power.

There is a good deal of variety in this volume. One story deals with the difficulties of "passing" as a white, but it offers nothing original or striking on the subject. Another tale is a character study of a wealthy white philanderer who falls in love with a Negro girl from Harlem, is jilted for a man of her own race, and goes insane imagining himself a great lover. Some of the stories contrast the effete and imitative "culture" of the whites with the natural, unpretentious talents of the Negroes. Another tale contrasts the gay effervescence of people like Florence Mills and her Parisian pals with the cold, stuffy lives of Massachusetts social moguls.

The writing of the tales is often sloppy, and certainly not worthy of the Langston Hughes of pre-Moscow days.

"The Book of the Day: Short Stories Touching on and Appertaining to Certain Human Relations" New York Sun, 28 June 1934, p. 23

Needless to say, Carl Van Vechten is present, on the jacket of this volume of short stories by one of the most distinguished of American Negro writers. Mr. Van Vechten was always suspect in his role and by now is completely tedious. By mentioning Chekhov, citing several stories as "masterpieces" and referring generally to the book as "important art," he succeeds in writing just the wrong kind of introduction. Langston Hughes's work is entirely unpretentious; it is never "important art," but, with excellent consistency, it is earnest, interesting writing.

In his approach to short fiction Mr. Hughes may well have had in mind an article by James Weldon Johnson, whose comprehension of any of the issues of his race is always solid. Mr. Johnson wrote an article for the *American Mercury* some years ago, describing "The Dilemma of the Negro Author" as the inescapable fact that he must write for a double audience. He is, unavoidably, writing for a white audience; and in this connection he faces the handicap that even the intelligent and the interested have a whole set of stencils about the possible scope of Negro character with which they are satisfied. The author's Negro audience offers immense resistance also, to any comprehensive presentation on Negro character; because, since the failings of Negro character have already suffered from a vast literature of caricature, a Negro audience resents any attention to those failings paid by a Negro author.

Mr. Hughes chooses a very direct way of taking this bull of a double audience by the horns. He deliberately restricts himself in the way of fictional material to a relation between white and Negro. His determination to put the emphasis just there prevents him from calling upon certain powers that were very much in evidence in his novel of a few years ago. With a few exceptions, his stories develop no intensity; there is no vivid delineation of character, no remarkable detail of scene or speech. Mr. Hughes seems perhaps too much concerned with achieving a tolerant, earnest, unemotional presentation of his material—with the result that, at their worst, his stories are dull, and, laying aside possible sociologic considerations, insignificant. Yet, with his book, he has covered a good body of material with sane observation organized into readable approximations of good short story form. Given the peculiarity of his problems, his patience, his control of resentment, his careful avoidance of sentimentality or caricature are admirable achievements. His is eminently sensible writing, deserving respect.

It is also true that several stories deserve more than this unexcited commendation. In "Cora Unashamed" and "Little Dog," where he hit upon something more than just a case, where he has conceived the single, sharp incident that gives the short story form, he writes very well and has a story comparable to all but the best American work.

The quiet virtues of his attitude about all the material in his book are summed up in the speech of one of the characters which gives the book its title. "Besides, the ways of white folks, I mean some white folks, is too much for me. I reckon they must be a few good ones, but most of 'em ain't good— leastwise they don't treat me good. And Lawd knows, I ain't never done nothin' to 'em, nothin' a-tall."

His stories, without being masterpieces, contribute intensity to that speech.

Herschel Brickell
"Books on Our Table: Langston Hughes Produces a Remarkably Fine Book of Short Stories"
New York Post, 28 June 1934, p. 11

Ever since the appearance of his novel, *No More Laughter* [*sic*], Langston Hughes has seemed to me the most genuinely talented of the Negro writers in America, and his volume of short stories, *The Ways of White Folks,* completely confirms my opinion.

It is not that good and admirable work has not been done by others of his race, but that from the first in both his prose and poetry there has been a quality that challenged comparison with first-rate work by anybody, regardless of color.

So it is with the present book, from which at least half a dozen stories might be awarded the O. Henry Prize without disturbing the even temper of the reviewers, so sensitive in these matters. They are works of art, these tales that do not depend upon their material for their appeal, although the heart-breaking tragedy of race runs through them like a theme.

In general, as might be expected from the title, they are concerned with the relations of white and colored people from the angle of the Negro. They do not depend upon background or dialect—in other words, they are not related to the familiar type of genre story that has grown into a convention—but they are about human beings in a variety of situations and settings, ranging from our Middle West to New England and from the Deep South to Paris.

Mr. Hughes has a genuine gift for irony among other things, as may be seen from such stories as "Rejuvenation Through Joy," a most amusing and malicious satire on the goings-on of a cult based upon Negro music and dancing.

The irony of another of the best of the stories, "Poor Little Black Fellow," is of a different and more astringent quality. I am not sure this isn't my favorite of the fifteen stories, although it does not appear in the trio selected by Carl Van Vechten, author of the jacket blurb, as masterpieces. His choices are "A Good Job Gone," which I read in *Esquire* with an immediate realization of its excellence; "Cora Unashamed" and "Little Dog."

"A Good Job Gone" and "Little Dog" are technically perfect, particularly the latter. The former is, perhaps, a bit broad for the run of short-story anthologies, but if "Little Dog" doesn't find itself a permanent place in these collections it will certainly not be because of any lack of merit.

"Poor Little Black Fellow" is the story of a Negro boy who was brought up by a New England family after his father, their butler, had been killed in France. Grown up, he is taken to Paris for the sake of his education, where he meets a white girl from Rumania and introduces her to his "family." They are shocked beyond words and, after lecturing him severely, think of him as ungrateful for all their great generosity and kindness.

This is an unforgettably poignant story, from which there is no shade of pathos missing, and not a tear in sight, for there is no sentimentality in Mr. Hughes's writing. He can even write a Christmas story about a neglected little black boy and make it so sad that one is moved too deeply for wet eyes to be any relief.

There is no propaganda in the stories, but there are here an understanding of racial qualities and a proper pride therein, as may be seen in "The Blues I'm Playing," the story of a colored girl who was adopted by a rich white woman who wished to make a great pianist of her, but who decided she would rather marry her lover. It ends like this:

Mrs. Ellsworth sat very still in her chair looking at the lilies trembling delicately in the priceless Persian vases, while Oceola made the bass notes throb like tomtoms deep in the earth.

O, if I could holler

sang the blues,

Like a mountain jack,
I'd go up on de mountain

sang the blues,

And call my baby back.

"And I," said Mrs. Ellsworth rising from her chair, "would stand looking at the stars."

The Ways of White Folks is, I think, as distinguished a volume of short stories as has been published in this country within a decade, perhaps longer.

John Chamberlain
"Books of the Times"
New York Times, 28 June 1934, p. L21

"That wasn't no Santa Claus," says Arcie, the colored maid, to her son Joe in the sketch called "One Christmas Eve." ". . . He's just a old white man." The explanation, coming as it does from a "dead pan," carries with it a suppressed, almost weary, quality of bitterness, and it is a similar bitterness that one finds in most of the stories of *The Ways of White Folks*.

For short-story purposes Mr. Hughes has discarded the singing, vibrant rhythms of his poems, *The Weary Blues* and *Fine Clothes to the Jew*. His style, in *The Ways of White Folks*, is flat, unaccented, clipped. But the seemingly undistinguished and unimpassioned recitals of "Cora Unashamed" and "A Good Job Gone" have a queer effectiveness. In all of these stories of life at the edge of the colored line one gets a sense of a bitterness that lies too deep for hysteria and tears. Mr. Hughes has assayed the world, and he knows what to expect. Because he knows the conditions of Negro existence in a callous white world, he is able to discount disappointment before it hits him. The tragedies of his stories are undeniably real. But they sound, in the telling, like an old man recalling the troubles and defeats of his youth. An old man recalling tragedy does so with an air of "Well, it was fated so to happen." Mr. Hughes's stories have this air of finality about them.

The Negroes, in *The Ways of White Folks*, generally get a dirty deal. But the white folks suffer too. They suffer because they don't dare to be human in a world of false conventions. "Cora Unashamed," for example, is a story of Negro drudgery in a white folks' house, but it is more than that; it is also a story of any Main Street matron who had rather keep up appearances than treat her daughter with human dignity and decency. Life is tragic for Cora Jenkins, maid of all work at the house of the Studevants in a small Midwestern town. She has had her child, an illegitimate daughter who died. But Cora's nature needs objects of affection, and she can't go on living just for herself. When Mrs. Studevant's Jessie proves to be a dull, seemingly unimaginative girl, the butt of the Studevants' scorn, Cora becomes her friend. Jessie tells Cora her troubles. She may be a stupid girl, but she "was not too stupid to have a boy friend." When she learns that she is going to have a child she carries her confession to Cora, who breaks the news to Mrs. Studevant. But Mrs. Studevant is of the small-town conventional breed; she won't think of letting Jessie marry her lover, who happens to be the son of the Greek ice-cream maker. And so she carts Jessie off to Kansas City to a doctor. Jessie dies. And Cora, brooding about it all, breaks the conspiracy of silence at the funeral.

The story would have been a tragedy without Cora. But it would not have served Mr. Hughes's purpose. It would not have enabled him to say: "See, if you, Mrs. Studevant, had not been trapped by a vicious caste view of the world, which was illustrated by your treatment of Cora through many years, you would not have ended your daughter's life and spoiled your own. Your attitude toward so-called inferior races is not only bad for Negroes; it is bad for yourself. You, too, are poisoned by a system of relationships that will not permit of equal opportunity." Of course, Mr. Hughes, being an artist, never makes this moral explicit. But it runs through the stories of The Ways of White Folks—particularly through the ones called "Little Dog" and "Father and Son."

There is one story in this collection that makes use of something more than straight realism. "Rejuvenation Through Joy" is a bitterly hilarious satire on the sort of person that is forever seeking happiness in a new cult. It is also a satire on a white affectation that was rampant in the years before the 1929 crash. In "Rejuvenation Through Joy" Mr. Hughes kills two pretentious birds with one stone, polishing off those who used to run to Yoga and those who "went primitive," or thought they were going primitive, by making a cult of Harlem night clubs, Negro novels, jazz, and by singling out the "new Negro" for special friendship. Mr. Hughes is pretty well fed up with members of his own race who believe in the "new Negro." He doesn't want favors for a few lucky or talented individuals of his race who happen to be good jazz performers, good artists, good actors. For this sort of thing only adds class discrimination to race discrimination. Both, Mr. Hughes thinks, are vicious.

There is more latent hatred in The Ways of White Folks than one remembers in Mr. Hughes's fine novel of Negro life in a Midwestern town, Not Without Laughter. The depression has been getting its licks since Mr. Hughes wrote that story of a Negro boy growing up in a white world. The Negroes of The Ways of White Folks are, as a matter of fact, almost wholly "without laughter." Cora and Arcie and the little boy who gets a job in a home for crippled children in "Berry" have very little time to forget the troubles of the world; there is no gayety here. Mr. Hughes is somber. Those who like to think of the Negro as a naturally happy animal are advised to stick to Rudolph Fisher's stories, to Claude McKay's Home to Harlem. Even when Mr. Hughes resorts to a trick used frequently by bubbling Ring Lardner—that of revealing character through letter writing—he does so only to bring out the bitterness, and also the contemptibility, of the lot of a Negro who is "passing for white" and marrying a white girl without telling her he is a Negro.

Heaven knows that no one should be compelled to laugh. But "Rejuvenation Through Joy," precisely because it departs from the prevailing mood of this book, will be remembered longest—and hence have the greatest effect. One hopes that Mr. Hughes will not let bitterness betray his art into monotony when he can pull out all the stops if he chooses. He is master of a sullen, straight realism. But he can also caricature, ridicule, burlesque. I wish he would mix his methods more than he does.

L. A. Sloper
"And of Some Negroes"
Christian Science Monitor,
28 June 1934, p. 14

Not all white folks are meant by Mr. Langston Hughes in the title of his book of short stories. It's only some white folks. The title is taken from a remark of the chief character of the story called "Berry": "The ways of white folks, I mean *some* white folks, is too much for me."

And no wonder. Berry, "a nice black boy, big, good natured and strong," got a job as Kitchen man in a Home for Crippled Children. He was paid $8 a week; his white predecessor had received $10. He did most of the work around the place, and became a favorite of the children. A slight mishap befell one of them. Berry was discharged. His last week's pay was withheld to pay for the damage to the child's wheel chair.

But the beauty of this collection is that not all the stories have that twist. Not all the whites are painted black, nor all the blacks white. The author, who is a Negro, has the faculty of seeing the white man's side of the problem, too. Some of these stories expose the outrages that have been practiced by the whites against the Negro race in America; others reveal certain shortcomings of the Negroes themselves.

One story that has a particular significance from the viewpoint of the race problem is "Poor Little Black Fellow," because it deals with an attempt to handle that problem which failed, not because of lack of good will in the whites involved, but because of their inability to understand that the Negro boy they were trying to help wanted to be treated not as a deserving little black fellow, but as a person.

Another item revelatory of the mistakes that can be made in approaching the race problem is "Slave on the Block," which depicts the growth of insolence in Negroes who are treated with mistaken kindness by white people who regard them as "too charming and naive and lovely for words."

From the technical and aesthetic points of view, too, several of these stories are important. Such are "Home," "Passing" and "Little Dog." On the whole, a collection of exceptional quality, worthy to stand beside the play, *Porgy.*

Herschel Brickell
"Books on Our Table: Three Fine Books of the Current Week"
New York Post, 30 June 1934, p. 9

[. . .]
Mr. Hughes's short stories are extraordinarily well done and powerful; they cannot but add greatly to his reputation as a novelist and poet. I think he is easily the most talented of our Negro writers, and he is still young enough to have a great deal of good work ahead of him.

C.F.
"*The Ways of White Folks*"
Boston Evening Transcript, 30 June 1934, p. 3

All of us are well acquainted with stories of white and colored people from the white point of view. *The Ways of White Folks* represents a departure from the familiar. These are stories of the relations between white and colored people from the Negro point of view. Mr. Hughes has known white people intimately in both the capacity of servant and friend, and his knowledge of his own race is wide. He has already served a successful apprenticeship as a writer. A novel which has been generally accepted as the best novel yet to be written by an American Negro and several volumes of poetry highly praised have been published—but in these short stories is rare achievement.

Not only does he write from first-hand experiences with a keen yet tender understanding of human beings, but he writes well. There is much vigor in his style and honesty in his portraits. Sometimes his language is strong stuff, but always clear, concise and dramatic. At first glance some of his stories seem to be an excursion into the sensational and the sordid, but out of these ingredients the writer has made dominant the redeeming dignity of love of life. They are frank and unretouched photographs in which neither the subject nor the background is faked.

"Hughes' Stories Combine Pathos and Rare Humor" *Buffalo Evening News Magazine*, 30 June 1934, p. 3

Langston Hughes' tender and humorous *Not Without Laughter* is considered not only the best novel yet to be written by an American Negro, but a remarkable piece of work on its own account. The author has now turned his attention to the short story, in which his rare talent challenges comparison with the modern Russians.

These tales concern white and Negro people described from the Negro point of view. The author has the incomparable gift of the born raconteur. He knows with unerring instinct what to say and what to leave unsaid; he sacrifices whatever is incongruous; he adjusts his narratives so as to arouse expectation from the start and hold it to the finish. Each tale is complete and each is single.

"The Blues I'm Playing" is about a gifted colored girl whom a white woman sent to Paris to study music. But there was a young man studying medicine in Atlanta, with whom Oceola has grown up, and when she returned to give a concert in New York, much to Mrs. Ellsworth's grief, marriage triumphed over art. When they meet again, the girl played for her, not Beethoven or Chopin, but a flood of wild syncopation which sank into slow and singing blues. "This is mine," said Oceola, simply, "it was born of my love—the blues I'm playing."

"Little Dog," "Mother and Child," and "Poor Little Black Fellow" are inimitable.
[. . .]
The Ways of White Folks is a distinct contribution to American letters.

H.J.
"Superb Stories"
Baltimore Evening Sun,
30 June 1934, p. 6

This is a collection of fine and deeply disturbing stories by a Negro author. There are fourteen pieces in the book, and not one bears any of the earmarks of the pot boiler. Of the seven particularly outstanding stories Carl Van Vechten—quoted on the inside cover—seems on the right track in selecting three, "A Good Job Gone," "Cora Unashamed" and "Little Dog" as masterpieces. To this select list I should be inclined to add a fourth, "Father and Son," which describes a Georgia lynching from the black man's end of the rope.

Mr. Hughes writes well, holding in check a strong sense of dramatic values with the curb of sober and restrained English. In one story, called "Mother and Child," he shows what he can do with an instinct for rhythm and the sound effect of words. His tale of a white mother's black baby pieced together through scraps of conversation at the Salvation Rock Ladies' Missionary Society for the Rescue of the African Heathen develops a swing comparable to some parts of the stage version of *Porgy*.

The book does not have to base its claim to recognition upon technical excellence only. What lifts it near greatness (and makes it disturbing) is its frontal approach to the race problem. The full picture of the black man's life in this white man's country is not a soothing one. More limited aspects, like lynchings or disenfranchisement in the South, can be discussed with a fair degree of comfort, for among civilized people there can be no general disagreement on at least the theoretical side of these points.

But the real cleavage of which these are only parts lies, usually too deep to be touched by intellectual liberalism, in the Negro's will to social equality and the white man's refusal to grant it. The tension of these mutually exclusive viewpoints, too tangled to be judged by any flat verdict, is one of the most fruitful fields America offers its authors. Mr. Hughes has done it justice in presenting the Negro's side of the case. His book contains neither propaganda nor conscious malice, but it is bitterly frank. Had a white man written the stories he probably would have been labeled broadminded. Comment on the present author conceivably may bear a geographical relation to the Mason and Dixon line.

George Schuyler
"Views and Reviews"
Pittsburgh Courier, 30
June 1934, [p. 10] (This
page misprints "23 June,"
but review is in 30 June
issue.)

Ye Olde Cynic suspects that the microscopic minority of Senegambians that buys books will rend the air with deafening applause over Langston Hughes' collection of short stories, *The Ways of White Folks,* which has just reached the book stalls. They will have, not because of its intrinsic merit as literature but because he persistently echoes that unpleasant, carping, irritating race chauvinism which is, sad to say, becoming of late so widespread in Aframerica, chiefly among the black bourgeoisie, the so-called Talented Tenth. They will chortle with glee over this not-at-all-subtle nose-thumbing, this tongue-sticking-out-at, this jeering, this clumsy caricaturing of the white brethren which enables mentally twisted Negroes to "get back at" the Aryan folk in a vicarious manner.

Nordics, we gather from many of these stories, are saps, easy marks, ignoramuses and brutes, while the Charcolarians are clever, intelligent, lovable and noble. This is undoubtedly good race propaganda, but is it good literature? I recall that Mr. Hughes has always taken the Negro Art hokum seriously, always groaned under the burdens of "race," always glanced at the world through smoked spectacles. He is today, for all his Communistic flirtings, spiritually akin to the whole raft of sophomoric Aframerican "thinkers," apologists for a jim crow society, who go shouting down the alleys of time atop this ox cart of "Negro Culture." Mr. Hughes has become, in brief, a lamp-blacked Thomas Dixon.

This would not be an unforgivable sin if so many of Mr. Hughes' stories were not unpleasantly unreal and unconvincing. He has twisted his material to fit the pattern of Negro propaganda, which of course heightens its improbability. There is certainly no objection to caricature if it is inclusive, but here only white folk are grotesque. One feels that the author is consciously putting the Negro's best foot forward. This, as I say, is quite excusable if one is merely writing "race" propaganda under the guise of literature as Tom Dixon and his ilk have done, but why should Negroes follow their bad example?

Let me hasten to say that Mr. Hughes is a competent craftsman, though many of his tales begin and develop better than they end. He has a disappointing way of letting you down sometimes when you are pre-pared for something better. There are nevertheless precious passages in some of these stories of interracial relations—passages to which one can with profit, return, and Mr. Hughes reveals frequently an ability to chuckle or shake his midriff (and the reader's) with a guffaw. It is unfortunate that this natural fund of humor is so often spoiled by annoying racial back-patting. Only one story, "Little Dog," is thankfully free of it.

However, all of the racialistic "slanting" in the world cannot spoil a good story entirely, and Mr. Hughes has several in this volume. The orchids, I should say, go to "Slave on a Block," "Home," "Passing," "Rejuvenation Through Joy," "Little Dog," "Mother and Child" and "One Christmas Eve." The first is rich in humor, the second dramatic but improbable, the third is not done in the happiest form, being more a soliloquy than a letter. The fourth, although slightly marred by length and the same fault mentioned above, reveals a lively sense of humor. The fifth is away out in front and the last two are close behind it, albeit "Mother and Child" would be improved without the doggerel. I imagine these stories measure up to the better standards of the short story art.

On the debit side are "Cora Unashamed," "A Good Job Gone," "The Blues I'm Playing," "Red-Headed Baby," "Poor Little Black Fellow," "Berry" and "Father and Son." I dislike them because they are unreal, unconvincing, often illogical and generally untrue to life. It is hard to believe that the cabaret singer in the second tale can be duplicated in real life. Nor can I believe that any colored girl would act as did the pianiste in "The Blue's I'm Playing" or any New England white folks as in "Poor Little Black Fellow." There are far too many instances to the contrary. A similar fault can be found with "Father and Son." This may be good melodrama but it does not ring true to life. One sometimes suspicions that Mr. Hughes is not near as familiar with the ways of white and black folks as he would have us believe. Indeed, some of his slanting is ludicrous contrasted with facts, which are ever stranger than fiction. As a result his picture of interracial relations is a distorted one, quite as distorted as the short stories by Paul Morand. This seems the more strange since Mr. Hughes, being a devotee of the Communist Cult, is not expected to kowtow to race chauvinism, the counter-irritant of the Black Bourgeoisie.

I am getting rather tired of glib generalizations about the race problem, anyhow. One hears on every hand of what white folks will do and what black folks will do; of the differences between the two so-called races in customs, habits, thought, ability, etc. One hears it nowadays as frequently from colored folks as from their paler brethren.

About 90 per cent of it is Mexican confetti. When you've been in this world for any length of time, rubbed shoulders with all sorts of people and kept your eyes and ears open, you find that people are people, regardless of such superficialities as pigment, hair texture, head shape, heel length, etc. They are products largely of their environments, yet there are tremendous differences between the character of people living in the same block. There are tolerant and intolerant, hateful and lovable, miserly and generous, selfish and sacrificing, smart and dumb, cruel and kind people among all national, social and so-called racial groups. No one group has a monopoly on desirable assets. It is a distortion to paint whites as noble creatures descended from the gods, and an equal distortion to paint colored folks in such flattering pigments. There are a few exceptional individuals in this world; the rest are weak vessels. There is an intellectual aristocracy in human society; the rest "don't

belong." These designations cut through class, nationality and race lines. There are colored folk finer than most whites, and white folk better than most Negroes. There are white people who will do more for colored folk than most Negroes will do. There are Negroes who will do more for white people than most Aryans will attempt. Every honest person knows this. The relations between groups are unhappy enough without distorting the picture.

A very great deal is often made of the fact that white men, fathers of children by colored women, have abandoned them, but why isn't more said about the white men who have provided for their colored sweethearts and their children, sent the latter to college and helped them after graduation? Indeed, it would be a most interesting study to ascertain how many persons prominent in Aframerica today got their start in this manner.

Much is made by race chauvinists on both sides, of the difficulties of interracial adjustment, and scores of cases are always being recited to "prove" that never shall the blacks and whites meet on common ground. Yet for every "horrible example," I can point to one proving the contrary.

The ways of white folks! There are as many different ways among them as there are among any other people. Who would believe that a wealthy white Alabama planter living with a brown common-law wife, would stroll into town with his two mulatto sons and boast of them to his white friends on the main street? Who would believe that a rich Texas planter would hire an English tutor for his mulatto children and leave all of his property to them and their mother? Who would believe that a white girl, a college graduate, would insist on giving birth to a mulatto baby after its father died, and work singlehanded, braving the prejudices of groundlings to make a living, and yet giving her child the finest care? Who would believe that an elderly white woman of limited means would help a colored boy get through college (and nothing between them, either!) as much as she did her own white son? Who would believe that a retired southern white country lawyer, believing an injustice had been done a Negro accused of murdering a white man, would come out of retirement, take the Negro's case, and in face of grave danger, fight it through to a victorious conclusion?

Yet all these things I know personally to be true. And of course, there are just as many cases of love, friendship and sacrifice of colored folk for whites. There is also a great deal of hatred on both sides but to give this one side is to present a cruel caricature.

If there were not a great deal of tolerance, friendship and love between white and black Americans how would the Negroes here exist?

Most of these stories have appeared in the magazines. Not all of them are up to the Hughes standard, and none of them is "revolutionary" in the sense that Hughes is now being played up as a *revolutionary* artist. There is no class struggle in these stories, only the struggle between black and white, with deft touches here and there to emphasize the strong undercurrent that Langston Hughes knows his white folk, and knows how to laugh at their foibles along the color line.

Horace Gregory
"Genius of Langston Hughes"
New York Herald Tribune Books, 1 July 1934, p. 4

G[eorge] W. S[treator]
"The Browsing Reader"
Crisis, 41 (July 1934), 216

Langston Hughes is laughing at white people in this book. He laughs at white people on all rounds of the social ladder. He laughs with subtlety and tragic mockery in "Father and Son," when he lets Colonel Norwood abuse his black concubine and their mulatto children. He laughs at the selfish and brutal small-town crackers who lynch Norwood's sons, and declare that he died without heirs. In "Slave on the Block" Hughes laughs at two white people of uncertain talents who set out to paint and rhyme about Negroes. . . . He pauses, it seems, to laugh at a mulatto who has just met his mother on the street without being able to speak to her. He was "passing."

To those who have read Langston Hughes's early books of poems and his admirable novel *Not Without Laughter,* the effectiveness of this volume of short stories will not come as a surprise. He is one of the few young writers in America whose work has kept pace with a growing reputation and whose signs of early promise are now bearing fruit.

I find it impossible to say anything about this collection of fourteen short stories without speaking directly of the Negro problem in America; that problem lies at the center of every story in the book. It is a race-conscious, class-conscious document that often extends far beyond the familiar limitations of documentary literature and proves to me at least that the controversy raised between "art" and "propaganda" need only be considered when the writer fails to make his work convincing. Though Langston Hughes never allows his readers to forget his central purpose, he is also engaged in the art of presenting a dramatic situation in short story form. His success is by no means as easy as his skill in reciting each episode would make it appear; these were not mere "simple" situations to set down on paper; each shows the result of deliberate economy in presenting complex phenomena, of cutting below and piercing to the roots those motives that we assign to racial prejudice.

Among the best of the short stories in the book is the first, which is called "Cora Unashamed." Cora, to all outward appearances, is the usual cheerful, devoted Negro servant in a middle-class white household. She becomes attached to one child in the household, a rather dull child, a girl who happened to be of the same age as Cora's child, who died within a few weeks of its birth. "Everybody found fault with her but Cora"; she becomes Cora's special charge in an active, growing family, and through protection of her, Cora rises in revolt against the entire household. One must read the story in full to appreciate its force, to see how clearly Langston Hughes reveals that wide difference between Cora's wisdom and the short-sighted worldliness of the people who employ her.

The episode following this is a well-directed satire on those who take up Negroes as a cult, a "fad," the so-called "artistic" people who live on unearned incomes south of Fourteenth Street in New York. Any one who has lived in New York during the last ten years will recognize the Carraways, will see at once how shallow and futile their "broadmindedness" becomes when faced with the realities of two Negro servants running their establishment, sharing their social life and, with expanding freedom, occupying the center of interest in a small apartment.

A companion piece to this story is "Rejuvenation Through Joy," a burlesque on the yearnings of the rich and credulous to seek out their salvation through joining a "Colony of Joy." Lesche, a Negro who is ex-circus barker, has an attractive, imposing physique and who "passes" for a white, is the leader of the extraordinary show, whose formula for "joy" was calisthenics and dancing to the music of a Negro jazz band. Again one recognizes all the faces that appear—the neurotic, wealthy white woman and the suave Negro "leader."

The book contains two remarkable lynching stories ("Home" and "Father and Son"), and again the complex interweaving of the Negro problem with the social and economic life of America is revealed and simplified. Both stories are recited in terms of swiftly moving melodramatic action, exposing at the roots of racial antagonism widespread economic maladjustment. However familiar the devices of such melodrama may seem, Langston Hughes contributes to his material a spirited prose style and an accurate understanding of human character.

Within the range of these fourteen stories there is humor, pathos, terror and satire. I suspect that Langston Hughes is revealing here that mysterious quality in writing that we call genius. I recommend this book as one of the best books published in a season when the standard of fiction has held a higher level than any season within the last five years.

Joseph Henry Jackson "*Ways of White Folks,* Collection of Finished Work by Negro Author" *San Francisco Chronicle,* 1 July 1934, p. 4D

Langston Hughes originally came to public notice through poetry. But since 1926 when his volume *The Weary Blues* appeared, he has become known for other talents. As a novelist, for example, he received wide recognition for his *Not without Laughter,* published in 1930. More than one critic has acclaimed that book as the best novel yet written by an American Negro about his people.

Since that novel appeared Hughes has published more poetry—*The Dream Keeper* in 1932—and has been writing short stories for various magazines, *Scribner's, Esquire, The American Mercury* and others. Fourteen of those stories are now collected in this new volume. Technically excellent pieces of work, all of them, they are important chiefly for the fact that in each the author presents the Negro in his relations with white people and presents this relationship entirely from the Negro point of view. Carl Van Vechten has written of the book: "These tales are not to be regarded as fanciful embodiments of wish-fulfilments," and neither they are. Mr. Hughes, knowing his people, has been carefully objective in here putting them forward under, so to say, their own steam. If you want to know just how the ways of white folks appear in many cases to those who are not white folks, this collection of stories will show you.

The ground the author covers is wide; these are not purely Southern tales. Their settings range from Alabama to the Middle West, from Florida to New England, from New York's Harlem to Paris, where there is no color line worth mentioning. Young people and old are his characters; if you like variety in your short fiction you'll find it here.

As to selecting among the stories, that kind of thing is always a difficult task. I have, as a matter of fact, three favorites among them, which may do as well as any other choice.

One is the tale with which the volume begins, "Cora Unashamed." It is the story of a Negro woman, general servant and maid-of-all-work to a middle class family of which she loves only one member. That member is the daughter, Jessie, almost the same age as her own illegitimate child would have been had it lived. Her work leaves her little time for the exercise of emotion, but such affection as Cora has time to lavish is spent on Jessie, who has replaced her own baby in her heart.

Jessie grows up dullish and slow and her family is slightly ashamed of her, but to Cora she is everything perfect, everything grand. When she can she stands between the girl and her demanding parents; Jessie is her lone chick and she instinctively fights for her whenever fighting is necessary and sometimes when it isn't.

But eventually there comes a time when Cora must fight. Jessie—poor stupid, dull Jessie—has got herself into trouble with a boy. Here is tragedy and no one to help. Cora is ready to do battle.

Yet what can she do? As it turns out—nothing. Jessie's mother takes her on a long visit to the city. When they come back it is a different Jessie Cora sees. From her mother's viewpoint Jessie is safe now from scandal. There will be no baby. But it wasn't scandal that Jessie herself feared. She had wanted her child; it was all she could have. And she wasn't able to survive the strain.

The climax of the story, when Cora, at Jessie's funeral, forgets herself, forgets the neighbors and friends, forgets the white folks—forgets everything, in fact, but that her darling Jessie has been denied the one thing she wanted—is a really tremendous thing. Unashamed, Cora told them all what she thought, told them all what they were, impaled them with her words and showed them up for the lying, meeching hypocrites that their code made them. Mr. Hughes has written a small masterpiece in this tale; if you're interested in masterpieces you should not miss it.

My second favorite of the lot is the one called "One Christmas Eve," a brief, poignant story of how one small black boy learned, sooner than a child should have to learn, that there is no Santa Claus—at any rate, no black Santa Claus. Into this tale the author has packed the whole tragedy of his race; he has made it a thumbnail sketch of a thousand disappointments, a million refusals to those whose skin is black. Perhaps it is not as considerable a job as "Cora," but it is nevertheless a little gem in its way.

The other that I particularly liked was "The Blues I'm Playing," the story of a rich white woman who—just because of her love for art—financed the career of Oceola Jones, colored pianist. Not only a satiric picture of all Maecenas-minded people who expect to buy obedience along with credit for helping talent, the story is also a very delightful refutation of the common theory that a career is the most important thing. Written with a sure, light touch, it is certainly one of the best put together tales in the collection.

However, you are sure to have your own selections when you read the book; nothing is so much a matter of taste as choice in short stories, especially when you have a singularly high-level, evenly good group to choose from. It doesn't matter such a great deal anyway. The interesting thing

about the stories is, as I've already said, the manner in which they will show you what it seems like to be a Negro—any Negro—who is intelligent enough to wonder why the ways of white folks are as they are, and what if anything he can do about it.

Ted Robinson
"Republic of Panama Outlaws Scientist Who Discovered White Indians of Darien"
Cleveland Plain Dealer, Women's Magazine and Amusement Section, 1 July 1934, p. 15

[. . .]

Every Clevelander will, I think, want to read *The Ways of White Folks* by Langston Hughes. He was once a Clevelander, and I can assure them that they will find in this book some splendid stories written from an unusual point of view. All the stories have to do with the relations between white and colored people, but always from the viewpoint of the colored man. We shall not find in these stories very much to bolster up our pride of race intellect or understanding. The author has few illusions about the attitude of white people toward Negroes—even of such white people as made a great pride of their absolute lack of race prejudice. Some of the stories are bitter, some are humorous, but all exhibit a clear vision and surprising lack of sentimentalism. We should read these stories for the good of our souls as well as for their high literary quality. Langston Hughes has talent of the highest sort, as every succeeding book of his more amply proves.

[. . .]

Leane Zugsmith
"The Impact of Races"
New York Times Book Review, 1 July 1934, p. 6

Mr. Hughes is a talented writer; he is also a Negro; and it is difficult to decide which comes first. As an artist, it may be a limitation that he concerns himself entirely with the interrelations of the black and white peoples. It was undoubtedly his intention to include only such stories in this collection, and he is not limited in his perceptions and knowledge of either Negroes or whites.

He writes about the impact of one race upon the other with the confidence of the intelligent, self-respecting man. He is scornful of the meretricious friendliness that certain pretentious whites offer to Negroes. He deplores the slave-conditioned, scraping humility that certain Negroes possess. He can be amused as well as infuriated, malicious as well as tender. Perhaps it is because he is none of these things to excess that what he has to say is so effective.

Of the fourteen stories in this volume, "Home" is the most moving and probably represents what is nearest to the author's heart. In it a gifted young Negro violinist goes back to see his mother in a Missouri village after an absence of eight years. He is ill and a little homesick after a long period in Europe playing with a successful orchestra. In Berlin, in Vienna, in Paris, he did not have to think of the color line; but at home he is just an "uppty nigger."

Racked by his cough, humiliated by his reception, the boy plays at a church benefit at which his humble, pious mother is delighted because white folks condescend to come.

A faded music teacher is the only person who understands what he plays or how well he is playing. But she is white, and she stops him on the street one night and shakes his hand. The hometown whites, coming out of a picture show, start to mob him. The sick boy wonders feebly why she stopped him; he knows he'll never get back to his mother now. "And when the white folks left his brown body, stark naked, strung from a tree at the edge of the town, it hung there all night like a violin for the wind to play."

This theme recurs in a number of Mr. Hughes's stories; and it is important. No matter what progress the Negro makes, no matter what homage he receives in foreign lands or from small urban groups in this country, he is eventually blocked. The white folks will stop him with weapons that range from condescension to lynching. He is supposed to be something naive, charming and jungle—as in Mr. Hughes's mocking tale, "A Slave on the Block"—or a lazy good-for-nothing or a monster. White folks have defined his character and they won't let him step out of it. This is what Mr. Hughes says in his strongest stories. In his weakest, such as "The Blues I'm Playing," he seems to be guilty of the orthodox practice of upholding the primitive against the sophisticated.

Two of the best stories in the book, "Passing" and "A Good Job Gone," top others, not because of their theses but because in them the author refrains from marginal comments. His philosophy is implicit in his subject-matter; it does not need the explanations in which he occasionally indulges. Only an insecure creator wants to underline his thoughts; and Mr. Hughes is definitely not one of those. As a poet and a novelist his writing position was made sturdy. As a short-story writer he here confirms his earlier performances.

Hal Borland
"New Books: Red and Yellow"
Philadelphia Evening Public Ledger, 5 July 1934, p. 22

[. . .]

Turning from this Frenchman's vivid and brutal picture of war and lust and hatred, I find another picture of troubled people in Langston Hughes' book of short stories, *The Ways of White Folks.* Mr. Hughes has turned ironic and rather bitter about the race problem in these tales, and he concentrates his fire on miscegenation. Of the fourteen stories in the collection, seven deal with mixed love and three turn angry eyes on white patrons of Negro art and Negro artists.

There is drama here and writing of high talent. But there is a self-consciousness that robs the work of its full effectiveness. Mr. Hughes is a little too somber, a little too bitter. I should have enjoyed his stories more if there had been more of the viewpoint of the Langston Hughes who wrote *Not Without Laughter,* and even better yet if there were the admirable detachment Zora Neale Hurston showed in her novel of colored folk, *Jonah's Gourd Vine.*

Charles A. Wagner
"Books: The Negro Speaks"
New York Daily Mirror, 5 July 1934, p. 25

[. . .]

The Negro was not in the minds of the signers of the Declaration of Independence when that document was drawn, on the occasion of our celebration of yesterday. Yet the Negro belonged to that day as much as he did to Gettysburg. His independence remains unendorsed.

Langston Hughes, probably the strongest of the younger Negro voices in literature today, in his book of 14 short stories *The Ways of White Folks* still carries the torch of his race to the white fields of prejudice, misunderstanding and shrivelmindedness. He carries it high and rhythmically, and well.

There are the stories of lynchings which are inevitable in a collection by a Negro writer. But the two stories here are unlike any you have ever read on lynchings. You are lynched, with the lynched.

The tales run the gamut, rather the gauntlet of the emotions this time. Manner supersedes matter once again, and the slow magic of genius, a genius for sensing the tragic tempo of humanity's waste and frustration, lights the clean march of these pages.

"Cora Unashamed," the very first story in the book, is probably the best one in it, although there are some difficulties in grading them. Yet Cora comes nearest to universality, for she is the Negro servant in the white household and she has at last been South, North, East and West. She is Cora of the Southern drawl no longer.

Cora takes to a child in the household who is the same age as her own dead child. It is one slim spar in a sea of chiding and prejudice. Through it Cora finds ultimate escape.

Clyde Beck
"Books and Authors: The Queer Ways of the White Race"
Detroit News, 7 July 1934, p. 18

The happy-go-lucky Negro and his stage counterpart, the black-face comedian, have provided the world with much mirth; the Negro has been a natural purveyor of comedy for the white man because he contains in himself its essential elements: a marked difference in behavior and a fundamental gusto. Of late years, with the rise of a literature about Negroes and by Negroes, with the development of a pronounced Negro influence on American music, he has taken on an added interest. He has likewise emerged in many instances as an artist.

As a rule the Negro writer has applied himself to a consideration of his own race: its fortunes and misfortunes. The role of the white man has been largely incidental in his work. Often he has been a poet, and his success in that field has been marked. Some critics have declared that he has not yet arrived at distinction in prose, despite the work of Langston Hughes, Claude McKay, W. E. B. Du Bois, and others.

The day of distinction for the Negro as a prose writer has evidently arrived, however, if one can judge by Langston Hughes' new book, *The Ways of White Folks.* This is a collection of short stories that will bear comparison with the best contemporary American work in the field. That can be demonstrated either on the basis of art and technique or profound emotional appeal; better still it can be demonstrated on both grounds. In other words, when you finish one of Mr. Hughes' stories there is a sense of complete and satisfying effect.

There is a certain novelty in the book, too, inasmuch as the white man, not the Negro, provides the diverting or the tragic element, as the case may be. Sometimes, as in the story "Father and Son," both races merge in an awful irony. Again, as in "Cora Unashamed," the tragedy of the white woman as she departs from the ways of nature is contrasted with the Negro woman's all-embracing maternal instinct.

In two stories the ridiculous behavior of sophisticated white people is revealed by Hughes' keen satire. In one of them the Negro servant is appalled at the behavior of his wealthy master; he sees that it will lead to perdition, and it does. This story is "A Good Job Gone," which is a technical triumph. So is "Little Dog," which might have been written by a Frenchman.

Mr. Hughes' stories have both an artistic and a moral strength. They play on most of our human susceptibilities and interests. They do not lean heavily on one thing or another. They do not exploit sex for its own sake. They do not lug in crime for the sake of sensation. They are honest and unsentimental. Their excellence is to be found in the fact that the author is an artist, not in the fact that he is a Negro. "The ways of white folks" are simply the ways of human nature at certain levels. Mr. Hughes has held the uncommon advantage of an artist standing between two races and justly observing both.

[. . .]

H.L.M.
"About Books: Not in Uniform"
New York Amsterdam News, 7 July 1934, p. 8

Pseudo-Marxian critics who have hailed Langston Hughes as the "revolutionary voice of the Negro masses" will find scant support in *The Ways of White Folks,* a volume of intensely racial short stories; his first venture in this form of expression. There is, to be sure, a spirit of revolution articulate in "Father and Son." But it is the tragedy of the individual rebelling against white dominance rather than the class against the system which perpetuates that dominance.

If, however, you, like most Negroes, are convinced of the superior virtues of this race of ours, you will be willing to forego the class struggle and will enjoy the fun-poking at the foibles of wealthy whites in the ironical "Rejuvenation Through Joy." You will be enthralled by the story of young Bert Lewis, whose grim determination not to be a "white folks' nigger" ends in a lynching bee as set forth in "Father and Son." You will applaud the defiance of the Negro characters (yet wonder if you would have acted the same) towards the patronizing whites in "Slave on the Block," "The Blues I'm Singing" and "Poor Little Black Fellow." And you will understand the dilemma of black folk in a small Ohio town after a white married woman has given birth to a mulatto child, the son of a young Negro farmer.

Despite the unprecedented ballyhoo with which "A Good Job Gone" was publicized by *Esquire,* in which it first appeared, it turns out to be a quite com-monplace story based on the widely accepted myth of the Negro's sexual superiority and the Negro woman's known recalcitrance. Mr. Hughes writes knowingly of the white patron of art in "The Blues I'm Singing," a story of a talented Negro pianist who prefers love to the continued patronage of the wealthy white woman who schooled her. Again, in "Poor Little Black Fellow" and in "Slave on the Block," he exposes the superficial character of white people's interest in Negroes—the immense satisfaction they get out of helping somebody who needs help, and the self-righteousness with which they go about it. Nowhere, however, does the author point out the vitiating influence of the institution of philanthropy upon the Negro race.

Of the fourteen stories in this volume this reviewer likes best "Father and Son." This is a thrilling story of the dramatic conflict between a white father and his illegitimate Negro son. Technically, it is the best of the lot. It is a complete and compact story, moving swiftly, unerringly to a logical denouement, the effectiveness of which is in no sense impaired by an ironical anti-climax. Its style is consistent. The dialogue is pointed and expressed with economy of phrase and fidelity to the vernacular. The language conveys the increasing tension which the son's return to the plantation occasions. It is a good story, more emotionally satisfying than any other this reviewer has read on the conflict of black and white.

Other stories recommended are "Rejuvenation Through Joy," "Cora Unashamed," "Poor Little Black Fellow," and "The Blues I'm Singing," despite the inconclusiveness of the last two.

"Nearly Genius" *Cleveland News,* 7 July 1934, p. 8

This colored youth who distinguished himself in Central High School in Cleveland, just about puts his foot over the genius wire in this collection of short stories. With the Negro's uncanny knowledge of the white man, he exposes the cults and fads of the "Harlem runners" who have sprung up in the last ten years. He shows that their broadmindedness toward the color line is just a form of neurotic excitement and does not last when a genuine test comes. In two stories, "Home" and "Father and Son," he uncovers the color prejudice by graphic pictures of lynchings. He does not use his art as a medium for propaganda, but throughout his beautifully written work, the reader never overlooks his central purpose. This he does with satire, with burlesque on the whites who join a calisthenics class directed by an ex-barker in Harlem and with truth when whites, having turned over their domiciles to colored servants, are faced with the uncomfortable result. It seems that Langston Hughes believes that we are two races apart and all that Negroes want from the whites is a fair economic and humane treatment instead of a patronizing, insincere camaraderie.

"Negro Author Pens Stories of Race Prejudice" *Washington News,* 7 July 1934, p. 11

A brilliant Negro author, Langston Hughes, has brought one of the touchiest problems in this country to the surface in his new book of 14 short stories, *The Ways of White Folks.* The power and conviction these stories carry are the result of Hughes' own artistry in the short story form, tho the problems involved are deeply rooted in our present society.

Here is the Negro maid who devotes her life to the little white girl who is her charge; here are the servants whose employers make much of their lack of racial prejudice; here are the white folks who mingle with Negroes as an exciting fad; here is the Negro with a lynch-mad mob at his heels; here is the ex-circus barker who passes as white—a parade of persons familiar because of the conditions of our life, and the situations that necessarily follow because of conflicting official and non-official attitudes toward black-skinned citizens.

The major theme, then, of all the stories, is race prejudice. Tho it is obvious that Hughes' own views are militant, at times bitter, yet in these stories there is no artificial wrenching of realism to suit a fixed point of view.

W.N.
"Genuine Feeling"
Los Angeles Times, part 2, 8 July 1934, p. 7

These short stories and sketches by one of our best known Negro poets, who has also written a novel, *Not Without Laughter,* are decidedly uneven in quality. With Carl Van Vechten's enthusiasm for certain of the tales we cannot at all concur; but there are others, which he does not mention, that have power and a genuine feeling for the Negro. "Home," the story of a Negro musician who returns from Europe to die among his own people, only to be lynched by white folks because he talked with a white woman on the street, has peculiar meaning just now, when lynchings are becoming more frequent and brutal.

But Hughes's bitterness does not confine itself to lynchings nor to the injustice with which the Negro is treated in America, whether he is a business man or an artist or a man trying to become socially equal with white folks. Hughes lashes out almost as savagely at those white people who, for a pose or out of mistaken kindness, patronizingly take up the Negro and treat him as a "social equal." Curiously, Hughes wants us to forget that he is black, and always to remember it; and when you examine this desire, you begin to see its absolute justice.

"The Book Shelf"
Altoona Tribune, 9 July 1934, p. 6

This group of fourteen stories about the relations between white and colored people is a bit unusual because, written by a Negro, it describes these relations from the Negro point of view. We've had any number of books telling what whites think of Negroes, but very few from the other side of the fence. For this reason only it's worth your while. And Mr. Hughes can write.

It's my own opinion that the author would have done well to present his material more impersonally. A number of the stories have to do with miscegenation, and a certain amount of bitterness shows through. Nevertheless, it's distinctly worth reading.

Edwin Rolfe
"Change the World!"
Daily Worker, 10 July 1934, p. 5

Langston Hughes possesses a very rare talent—the ability to create living and altogether understandable characters and situations in every subject his pen touches. He has done this for many years and in many forms. First in his two volumes of poetry, *The Weary Blues* and *Fine Clothes to the Jew.* Then in his novel *Not Without Laughter.* Very frequently in his vigorous reportage—readers of the *Daily Worker* will recall his "Moscow and Me," published on this page more than six months ago. And now in his new book of short stories, *The Ways of White Folks.*

Unlike a host of other poets, novelists, writers of all kinds, Hughes is not afraid of sentiment or emotion. And their presence in his writings, even in his most subtle and restrained stories, his most delicate sketches, gives them the real qualities, the authenticity of life, so that the reading of his work is not merely an interesting exercise but an absorbing experience.

The fourteen stories in *The Ways of White Folks* are, as the title indicates, concerned with the feelings and doings of Negroes in relation to white people. The struggles of his own people concern Langston Hughes most in these stories, but it is the white people with whom they come in contact and among whom they live which in the majority of cases circumscribes and affects their lives. And, even though he portrays individuals for the greater part, in many of his stories these individual figures epitomize and symbolize the actions, plight, direction, of great masses of people.

Hughes very naturally writes of the Negro artists and intellectuals whom he knows so well, living in a land where the white bourgeoisie controls and directs all means of artistic and intellectual expression. And he writes of the white intellectuals as well—or of those white people of considerable wealth or weltschmerz who attempt to make up for their lack of talent and intellect by acting as sponsors and patrons and sycophants of the arts.

But he is also deeply concerned, in his stories as in his life, with the struggles of the great masses of toiling Negroes, particularly the sharecroppers and tenant farmers of the South upon whose shoulders the southern ruling class has built its backward and semi-feudal agricultural system—the entire southern economy which depends for its continued existence upon the oppression of the Negro people. Not a few of his stories are about such Negroes on large southern plantations, living side by side with the white landlords, subservient to them. And it is in the masterly depiction of the relations of these people, their struggles, aspirations, tragedies, that some of his best stories are built.

Such a story is "Father and Son," the very last in the book, which ends with the self-inflicted death of Bert Lewis, son of Colonel Norwood, a white plantation owner, and Coralee Lewis, his Negro housekeeper. Bert is Colonel Norwood's youngest and most handsome son, strongly resembling and just a shade darker of skin than his father. He is a boy who is sick of "white folks' niggers," sick of his people's oppression. Upon his return to the Norwood plantation he refuses to submit to the degradation, the slave behavior which is forced upon the Negro in the south. After the death of Colonel Norwood, he attempts to escape to the swamp but is driven back into the Norwood residence, where he shoots his white attackers and would-be lynchers with his white father's gun until but one bullet remains. His mother aids him:

"'No time to hide, Ma,' Bert panted. 'They're at the door now. They'll be coming in the back way, too. They'll be coming in everywhere. I got one bullet left, Ma. It's mine.'

"'Yes, son, it's your'n. Go upstairs in mama's room and lay down on ma bed and rest. I won't let 'em come up till you're gone. God bless you, chile.'

"Quickly they embraced. A moment his head rested on her shoulder."

Then the white men came:

"'Keep still, men,' one of the leaders said. 'He's armed. . . . Say where's that yellow bastard of yours, Cora—upstairs?'

"'Yes,' Cora said, 'Wait.'

213

"'Wait, hell!' the men cried. 'Come on, boys, let's go!'

"A shot rang out upstairs; then Cora knew it was all right.

"'Go on,' she said, stepping aside for the mob."

It is impossible to indicate in a brief discussion the consummate restraint and artistry with which Langston Hughes brings his Negroes and white folks to life. Or to give more than a suggestion of the depth and power of his stories. Of "Cora Unashamed" or of "Home," in which a young Negro violinist, returning to his southern home town after being "away seven or eight years," is lynched by white hoodlums for shaking the hand of a white woman, a friend, on the street. Or to give the full satiric flavor of "Rejuvenation Through Joy" or the quiet pathos of "Little Dog."

The last-named story, by the way, shows clearly that Langston Hughes is not trying to categorize "white folks" as a race of oppressors. He differentiates between the white worker, the white sufferer under capitalism, and the white boss and landlord, just as he distinguishes between black toilers and the black bourgeoisie. This story, permeated by a tender and understanding sympathy for this tragic, middle-aged spinster-heroine, reveals Hughes' approach as essentially a class-approach, not a racial one.

What makes all fourteen stories so intensely alive and authentic, I submit, is the author's intimate knowledge not only of the members of his own race and the white people, but of their plight in capitalist America, in which their position as an oppressed national minority has its roots in their economic position and the attempt of the white-ruling class to perpetuate this state in order to safeguard its own wealth, its own social and economic and political domination. This means terror, social subjugation, lynching for the Negro toilers, as well as similar degradation for the white workers.

The Ways of White Folks is the book of an extraordinarily gifted writer, and the working class movement in the United States may well be proud of the fact that Langston Hughes is "one of our own."

Sherwood Anderson "Paying for Old Sins" *Nation*, 139 (11 July 1934), 49–50

[...]

The Ways of White Folks is something to puzzle you. If Mr. [Carl] Carmer goes one way [in *Stars Fell on Alabama*], Mr. Langston Hughes goes another. You can't exactly blame him. Mr. Hughes is an infinitely better, more natural, story teller than Mr. Carmer. To my mind he gets the ball over the plate better, has a lot more on the ball, but there is something missed. Mr. Carmer is a member of the Northern white race gone South, rather with jaws set, determined to please and be pleased, and Mr. Hughes might be taken as a member of the Southern colored race gone North, evidently not determined about anything but with a deep-seated resentment in him. It is in his blood, so deep-seated that he seems himself unconscious of it. The Negro people in these stories of his are so alive, warm, and real and the whites are all caricatures; life, love, laughter, old wisdom all to the Negroes, and silly pretense, fakiness, pretty much all to the whites.

It seems to me a paying for old sins all around, reading these two books. We'll be paying for the World War for hundreds of years yet, and if we ever get that out of us we may still be paying interest on slavery.

214

Mr. Hughes, my hat off to you in relation to your own race but not to mine.

It is difficult. The difficulties faced by Mr. Hughes, as a story teller, are infinitely greater than those faced by Mr. Carmer. Mr. Carmer has but to take the old attitude toward the American Negro. "They are amusing. They are so primitive." If you go modern you go so far as to recognize that Negro men can be manly and Negro women beautiful. It is difficult to do even that without at least appearing to be patronizing. You begin to sound like an Englishman talking about Americans or a Virginian talking about a Texan. Even when you don't mean it you sound like that.

The truth is, I suspect, that there is, back of all this, a thing very little understood by any of us. It is an individualistic world. I may join the Socialist or the Communist Party but that doesn't let me out of my own individual struggle with myself. It may be that I can myself establish something between myself and the American Negro man or woman that is sound. Can I hold it? I am sitting in a room with such a man or woman and we are talking. Others, of my own race, come in. How can I tell what is asleep in these others? Something between the Negro man and myself gets destroyed . . . it is the thing D. H. Lawrence was always speaking of as "the flow." My neighbor, the white man, coming in to me as I sit with my Negro friend, may have qualities I value highly but he may also stink with old prejudice. "What, you have a damn nigger in here?" In the mind of the Negro: "Damn the whites. You can't trust them." That, fed constantly by pretense of understanding where there is no understanding. Myself and Mr. Carmer paying constantly for the prejudices of a whole race. Mr. Hughes paying too. Don't think he doesn't pay.

But story telling is something else, or should be. It too seldom is. There are always too many story tellers using their talents to get even with life. There is a plane to be got on—the impersonal. Mr. Hughes gets on it perfectly with his Negro men and women. He has a fine talent. I do not see how anyone can blame him for his hatreds. I think "Red-Headed Baby" is a bum story. The figure of Oceola Jones in the story, "The Blues I'm Playing," is the most finely drawn in the book. The book is a good book.

"Books of the Week" *Columbus Citizen*, 13 July 1934, p. 17

[. . .]

Langston Hughes, considered one of the foremost American Negro poets and novelists living, has turned to the short story medium. Some of the titles in *The Ways of White Folks* may be familiar to you. A few have appeared in *Esquire, Scribner's,* and the *American Mercury.*

One of the finest stories in the collection, "Little Dog," handled with disarming simplicity, stresses the problem of a bookkeeper facing middle age with no life to boast of but vague erotic feelings when confronted by her Negro janitor.

White people, as seen through the eyes of the Negro, concern Mr. Hughes for the most part. In these he appears completely at home. Stories of adoption and musical protegees, Park avenue philanthropists who prey on the Negro to make him white, the arty dowager who makes her find in Harlem, the attempts, sometimes successful, to uproot the Negro from native soil, are charged with tragic bitterness. They strike deep at the instinctive misunder-

Mark Lutz
"Stories Satirize Whites Who Make Cult of Negro"
Richmond News-Leader, 13 July 1934, p. 11

White folks who make a cult of the Negro and of Harlem are spoofed by Langston Hughes in a collection of his short stories brought out by Alfred A. Knopf. Mr. Hughes, who knows both his white folks and his Negroes, has contempt for those who think it fashionable to patronize the Negro, and has disgust for the Negroes who deliberately allow white people to exploit them under one guise or another.

His feelings about those Negroes, however, who are victims of injustice and oppression through no fault of their own, is one of sympathy and understanding. Writing with a knowledge based on observation both as a worker and a friend of white people, and as a Negro and a friend of Negroes, Mr. Hughes is so realistic in his treatment of racial problems he might be called hard-boiled, and so aware of what happens when the interests of the races conflict he might be called cynical. After all, the author has a fine scorn for the shame and pretenses which enter into the relations between the two, and he is uncompromising in his determination to show how foolish is the attitude of patron and patronized and to fight against the prejudices and ignorance with which Negroes are treated by some whites.

Two devastating shafts of satire are fired against those "arty" persons who expect their servants to dance and sing for the entertainment of guests after they have done the household chores, and against those idle and neurotic men and women who have taken up the Negro as a fad. Turning to the serious, his treatment of the plight of a Negro violinist, a musician whose training abroad had unfitted him for the antagonistic attitude of his fellow townsmen, is poignant and affecting.

One of the best tales in the book is the tragic chronicle of a humble girl whose primitive viewpoint is in sharp contrast with that of the middle-class family for whom she works. This story builds up to a highly dramatic climax which impresses the reader with the sincerity and justice of the writer's thesis.

The Ways of White Folks includes many of the problems which beset the Negro in his struggle to get along and in his treatment at the hands of the stupid and vicious. Miscegenation, the difficulties of "passing" as a white to solve economic emergencies, and contrasts in ways of thinking and living between the two races, figure in the book.

Mr. Hughes is equally at home whether he is dealing with humor, terror, pathos or satire. Besides being a most enlightening book on subjects frequently clouded over with sentiment or prejudice, *The Ways of White Folks* is of absorbing interest whether you read it for entertainment or as a social document.

Theophilus Lewis
"Harlem Sketchbook"
New York Amsterdam News, 14 July 1934, p. 8

Short stories are not my preferred form of reading. Since the passing of the O. Henry vogue and the old Mencken-Nathan Smart Set, I have read practically nothing in that field of fiction except a dozen or so of the tales of Jean Toomer and Ruth Suckow and perhaps a couple of Hergesheimer's yarns in the *Saturday Evening Post*. I would not dispute the charge that my standards have begun to date.

It is possible that my appraisal of *The Ways of White Folks*, a collection of short stories by Langston Hughes, is out of tune with the times. I leave to younger heads than mine to decide whether these tales soar above or sink below the contemporary level of the art. Measured by my ancient yardstick, *The Ways of White Folks* is a swell book. If this be praise from the rocking chair, make the most of it.

I always judge an artist—story teller, painter or sculptor of "The Old Courtesan"—by his ability to portray character under the impact of life; or, if you are of a scientific turn of mind, by his ability to reveal character adapting itself to environment. These stories show Negro character, in its various types, adapting itself to the exigencies of a society made and controlled by white people. The title, *The Ways of White Folks*, is misleading. *The Ways of Black Folks* would be more pat. For in all the tales, except one, the Negroes either conform or refuse to conform. The whites always take themselves and their point of view for granted. They have only one way—the way of the conqueror, the way of the superior, the lord of the earth.

In the eyes of the Aframerican, the Caucasian is greater than the lord of the earth. He is the earth. The black must conform to his will and whim as the tree toad seeks protective coloration. But the toad, in assuming the color of leaves, never becomes a leaf. He remains a frog. The Negro yields to the ways of white folks, but in his soul he remains a Negro.

Which is to say that American Negroes have retained their essentially racial character while adapting themselves to an alien environment. It is a debatable point. Anthropologists, stressing environment, may say no. Langston Hughes, the artist, emphasizing character, says yes. I think the artist is right.

A reviewer might compare *The Ways of White Folks* with the Wessex Tales. The comparison would be void of bathos. For the Hughes stories reek with irony. In these stories, as in Hardy's yarns, human desire perpetually palpitates ineffectually against the stone wall of natural law. In the end everything remains as it was in the beginning.

Nothing ever changes, even though the heroine of "Cora Unashamed," like a black she-Samson, attempts to pull down the temple of white prissyness. Cora passes out of the picture. White prissyness remains to assert itself in "Slave on the Block" and "Poor Little Black Fellow." "Slave on the Block" is a kind of bravura piece in which Hughes pokes fun at modern whites who are just bound to be good to Negroes because it is a fad. In "Poor Little Black Fellow" a family of old-fashioned whites, finding themselves with a colored orphan on their hands, accept the responsibility of raising the child as a Christian duty, with a great flourish of self-righteousness. Their attempt to produce a hothouse Negro is not an unqualified success, for the black fellow goes native the first time he meets people who offer him humanity "without charity, without con-

217

descension, without prayer, without distance, without being nice."

A similar attempt to cultivate Negro character under glass comes to naught in "The Blues I'm Playing," in which a wealthy white woman takes a talented black girl under her wing. The black girl simply cannot be made to believe that man was made for art. In her creed art exists to express men's joys and yearnings and no amount of polite browbeating can make her recant her faith.

In making comparisons, it hardly needs to be said, more will depend on the tastes of various types of readers than on the merit of the tales. My preference is for "One Christmas Eve" and "Little Dog" as fine specimens of the story teller's art, but "Cora Unashamed," "The Blues I'm Playing" and "Poor Little Black Fellow" are more significant as portrayals of Negro character in contrast with the ways of white folks. "Home," "Red-Headed Baby" and "Father and Son" are the least important.

Some of the stories are marred, but not seriously, by signs of narrative weakness, as Hughes takes obvious short cuts to get a tale done. But his hand never falters when he is painting a fragment of life or working in a detail of character. His aim seems to be to achieve a verisimilitude of life with all the rind and pith pared away. He succeeds. His tales throb with the urge and ache of men and women striving in the dark. More than once, as I conned them, I seemed to be reading a page from my own autobiography.

Vernon Loggins
"Jazz-Consciousness"
Saturday Review, 10
(14 July 1934), 805

Negro literature in this country has been flowing in an uninterrupted stream since it had its beginning with the much written about Phillis Wheatley just before the American Revolution. For most of its long course it has been calm, turning up little that could interest any one except the historian or the sociologist. But there have been flood periods.

One came during the twenty years preceding the Civil War; another between the years 1895 and 1905. And about 1920 a third was ushered in that is upon us still, and which has corresponded with the so-called jazz age. The Negro indeed—whether rightly or wrongly does not matter—was pointed out as the creator of jazz. Naturally he was filled with pride and the spirit of self-assertion. Jazz-consciousness was for him another Emancipation Proclamation. As an artist he was no longer obliged to speak haltingly in the idiom of the whites. They themselves were aping the idiom which he had created.

Among the Negro authors of the present no one has been more jazz-conscious than Langston Hughes. A little less than ten years ago he began publishing poems. Right from the start his aim was to put into English words the pulse and verve of jazz. Imagery and idea were of minor importance; the meaning of the poem depended upon the jazz overtones. Often—especially in his numerous specimens of the blues, which he regards as a distinct pattern, as binding in its laws as the sonnet—he has been astoundingly successful. In 1930 he published his one novel, *Not*

218

Without Laughter. The tempo is again that of jazz; but, because of the large proportions, the effect is to a great extent lost.

Now he gives us what seems to us his strongest work—*The Ways of White Folks,* a collection of fourteen stories, each an intense drama projected before the reader with the suavity and gliding grace of Cab Calloway conducting the Cotton Club orchestra. Each of the stories deals primarily with a white person—the mother who prefers her daughter's death to an illegitimate grandchild, the rich *roué* who goes insane over his thwarted love for a Harlem high-yellow, the old maid who unconsciously falls in love with her Negro janitor, the Southerner who is defied by his mulatto son, and ten other varying types. But while the force of the white person is felt, the drama of each story belongs to the Negro.

Perhaps the most satisfying tale in the volume is "The Blues I'm Playing," the chronicle of a wealthy patron of the arts who takes under her wing a black girl with extraordinary physical strength and a great talent for the piano. Mrs. Ellsworth installs the girl in a luxurious flat in Paris, engages Philippe to teach her, and makes her an interpreter of Beethoven and Brahms whom the European critics rush to praise. But to Oceola life means something else besides the glory on the concert stage. Life means Pete, the Negro boy whom she has kept in her four-room apartment back in Harlem, whom she has lain in bed with planning a formal engagement and a wedding, whom she will join again when he is through with medical school. To the starved, rich Mrs. Ellsworth art lies in looking at the stars; to Oceola it lies in sitting at the piano and letting her fingers wander from Beethoven and Brahms to the blues—laughing and crying . . . white like you and black like me . . . like a man . . . like a woman . . . warm as Pete's kiss.

The story is ideal for Mr. Hughes's jazz touch. He has given it a superb telling. His cynicism, his sarcasm, his radicalism, and his urbane humor tumble and cavort throughout the volume. And there is scarcely a line in which his sophisticated jazziness is not felt. Reading the fourteen stories one after another is like listening with eyes closed to a Paul Whiteman concert of fourteen numbers.

"The Weekly Book Shelf" *Pittsburgh Post-Gazette,* 14 July 1934, p. 10; also *Duluth News-Tribune,* Features section, 22 July, 1934, p. 3

There are 14 short stories in *The Ways of White Folks* by Langston Hughes, all of them dealing more or less directly with the relationships between white and colored people in present-day America. Three of these stories, "Home," "Cora Unashamed" and "Little Dog," are miniature masterpieces, worthy indeed of the author of that finest of all colored racial novels, *Not Without Laughter.* One or two have little to commend them except as they truthfully mirror the injustices done the colored race by their fellow Americans. All of these Langston Hughes stories, however, obvious or subtle, ironic or melodramatic, are written from the colored people's point of view, and as such should be read by all those who hope to understand the still unsettled race question, which remains a large black spot in the much vaunted American ideal of democracy.

Mr. Hughes, a novelist and poet of considerable distinction, does not concern himself very much with the type of colored man so often sentimentalized in novels even as good as *Scarlet Sister Mary*. His characters are often men and women of considerable sophistication, and their problems, not often recognized or understood by the whites, are ones that will sooner or later have to be faced and solved by intelligent persons of both races. As an introduction to these persons, as a skillful, accurate and sympathetic dramatization of these problems and the psychological forces that lie back of them, the stories in *The Ways of White Folks* are superb. In many cases, moreover, they transcend the artistic limitations of documentary literature and stand as first-rate fiction in their own right.

H. Bond Bliss
"Bitter Stories of Negro Race"
Miami Herald, 15 July 1934, p. 16

"They killed you, honey. They killed you and your child. I told 'em you loved it, but they didn't care."

That despairing cry of the negress addressed to the dead white girl at the close of "Cora Unashamed," the first story in this book, is typical of the pathetic and tragic bitterness which characterizes most of these 15 tales. Here is pictured not the joyous abandon of the black boys and girls but rather the serious aspects of their life in relation to a white world. Few of the brief plots are strictly moral, but whether the affairs should be regarded as immoral or unmoral or just the acts of nature's children may be left for readers to decide for themselves. But the modern realists, as you may note, find it difficult to refrain from dragging in the salacious and objectionable.

Langston Hughes, American Negro, turns from poetry and the novel, *Not Without Laughter*, to the simple but not easy form of the short story in this latest book. Some of the tales have previously appeared in such magazines as *Esquire, The American Mercury, Scribner's, Opportunity* and others.

These stories are dramatic, effective, interesting, even though gloomy and permeated with the futility of existence, told in short sentences with no surplus words. They are practically all action and dialogue. The Negroes usually receive the worst of the deals but the whites do not escape suffering either.

There are lynchings, some with justification, if lynching can ever be justified, and some not. "Home" tells of Roy Williams, the Negro youth who won distinction with his music in Europe and stricken with illness returned to his little Missouri home to die. Only the music teacher could appreciate his genius; the others mocked. One day Miss Reese stopped him on the street, when suddenly a ruffian hit him for talking to a white woman. There was a scream and that was the end of Roy Williams.

"Rejuvenation Through Joy" is satire, ridiculing the ways of some women, and men, in seeking relief or escape through the worship of an idiotic cult created for the sole purpose of making money. These fads were more prevalent before 1929. Here the patrons were to be rejuvenated through the merry movements of Harlem dancers. It is one of the gay moods in the volume.

The last story, "Father and Son," is the longest and possibly the most exciting. It is disagreeable and somber and tragic. Colonel Norwood, master of a Georgia plantation, had several children by his dusky servant, Cora, and he treated them well. But education in Atlanta spoiled Bert. He didn't know his place back on the plantation. He wouldn't work. He defied the master. The colonel cursed, ordered him out. Bert would leave by the front door. But no! There was a struggle. More blood, bodies swaying in the breeze.

Laurence Shropshire "Negro Writer Lends Insight into Problem" *Lexington* [Ky.] *Leader,* 15 July 1934, p. 5

Fourteen short stories by Langston Hughes, the brilliant young Negro poet whose first novel, *Not Without Laughter,* elicited high praise, make up a volume just published by Alfred A. Knopf under the title of *The Ways of White Folks.* The book is undeniably a literary treasure.

Hughes' treatment of his one general theme smacks soundly of genius in that all the stories reveal a high sense of the dramatic, moderately tempered and rated evenly to produce an impressionable and pointed climax; and because his marked economy in words and quiet approach seem to heighten the effect of his writings about tremendous social complexities. His work reveals that always he is conscious of the need to dig directly at the root of the problem, at the basic motives leading to the misunderstanding causing racial antagonism.

The problem with which all the stories are concerned is that of race-consciousness, in America particularly, since several of the tales draw contrasts between the situation here and in Europe. Hughes would show in one or two that the antagonism re-

sults not alone from recognized race differences, but in some part also from class-consciousness. He attributes, too, being very generous toward the whites, one might say, a large measure of it springing from nothing more than economic maladjustment.

Two of the stories are about lynchings which were brought on indirectly by efforts of Negroes to rise above the level of servitude in emulation of the whites. Others show Negroes' good deeds wasted in the eyes of white men purely through misunderstanding. Sill others would demonstrate a wide difference between a Negro's simple wisdom and the view of narrow-minded, short-sighted white people.

A few white writers have attempted to present the viewpoint of the Negro, and some of them possibly with a measure of success, but the fact remains that it is still one individual's opinion of another's reactions. This work by Hughes, bearing no tone of bitterness, yields more reliable testimony. The writer handles humor and satire as well as terror and pathos, and in all of it is forceful.

Dewey R. Jones "The Bookshelf" *Chicago Defender,* 21 July 1934, p. 11

Langston Hughes is still at the top of the list of young American writers, as far as I am concerned. This, in spite of the fact that George Schuyler and a few other literary observers feel that he has harped too much on the somber side of the race question in his latest book, *The Ways of White Folks.*

In this book of ten short stories, most

221

of which had been published in American magazines during the past year, Langston Hughes proves conclusively that he is a master craftsman—that he not only has things to say, but knows definitely how to say them. Indeed, there are stories in this book which, I sincerely believe should take their place as examples of the finest type of writing—and I have no doubt they will. In this class I would place "Christmas Eve," one of the most poignantly touching stories I have encountered in many years of reading.

This story is done with a feeling, yet with a restraint that gives ample testimony of the power that impels the author forward in his narration. You not only see Arcie pacing the floor as she waits for her white mistress to come home and pay her off so that she can take her little boy, Joe, to town for his Christmas shopping, but you feel with her. You sympathize with Joe as he creeps up to the edge of the crowd to get a closer glimpse of Santa Claus—a white Santa Claus—and you even understand the motive that prompts the white man to frighten the little boy.

It is this technique, of which Langston Hughes is master, that makes his stories so deeply impressive. Of hardly less depth of feeling is the story "Beery," which was printed first in *Abbott's Weekly*. Other stories which will stand out in any group of short stories are "Home," which was printed in *Esquire*; "Cora Unashamed," which I read in *The American Mercury*; "Little Dog," and "Father and Son," which I read several months ago in manuscript. The other stories were good, but, in my opinion, not up to the standard of the ones named. At the time I read "The Blues I'm Playing" in *Scribner's*, I remarked to myself that this story, while good and readable, seemed a bit far fetched.

Of "Rejuvenation Through Joy," I have little to say, except that it is quite silly, although also quite believable when one knows the silly things of which moneyed New Yorkers are capable. "A Good Job Gone" was the story that split *Esquire* into numerous camps and left its opponents and proponents gasping after it was printed. Aside from the fact that it is daring in its subject, and treatment, it offers little to the student of short story. However, even this story has its rightful place in this collection.

I have little faith in Negro critics who feel themselves called upon to take up cudgels for the white race. Everyone knows that they are of many traits and characteristics. And for that reason alone, it ought to be obvious that almost any story told about them in their relations with the black minority in this country has a good chance of being authentic. Besides, I remember, always, that the book, having been published and issued by a white firm, will stand as the best argument that all white people are not narrow-minded. Any observer of white people—and I believe Langston Hughes to be one—can find in their conduct material for hundreds of stories about their ways, and never duplicate himself. This book, judged by its merits alone, will find a permanent place in the category of the short story, and Langston Hughes, its author, will move up in the scale of American writers because of it.

John Clair Minot "Heralding the New Books" *Boston Herald*, 21 July 1934, p. 11

. . . It deserves an even larger audience than it is likely to win, for the 14 stories in the collection are superbly done, with something of prose jazz in them—if that is not a contradiction of terms—and with much of the finer feeling of a race that moves, even while it laughs, through constant tragedy.

The stories have widely varying settings and types of people, but each of them has whites, as well as colored folk, in leading roles. In fact, whites may be said to be the leading figures in most of them, but in all of them there is drama that centers in some Negro character. For example, there is the story of the southern aristocrat who has to face the vigorous enmity of his mulatto son in a crisis of his life. There is the New York spinster who falls in love with a Negro janitor in her apartment house, though she does not really know what is happening to her. There is the case of the wealthy woman who finances piano study in Paris by a Negro girl in whom she sees great talent, but the girl finds more in the love of a boy back in Harlem than in the applause of concert hall audiences abroad. And so the stories go. Langston Hughes should travel far in the world of authorship.

Bess M. Wilson
"Negro Author Turns Out
14 Short Tales: Pathos,
Humor, Satire, Terror, All
Are Present"
Minneapolis Journal,
editorial section, 22 July
1934, p. 5

Your enjoyment and appreciation of this group of stories written by a Negro, depend much upon the relation of your birthplace to the Mason and Dixon line.

Also somewhat upon the size of your bank account and the seriousness with which you take your culture. For the stories are race-conscious, class-conscious, melodramatic and ironic—and one needs poise and understanding if he is to read them well.

Fourteen of these stories there are, and ranging through them are the varied elements of pathos, satire, humor and terror. They would have been more artistic, more pleasing had they been written with less of the Negro love for startling effects, with more restraint and deeper intuitions. But even with these faults they make good reading.

The first is the best. "Cora Unashamed" was just that; a Negro woman unashamed of her illegitimate half-white child, unashamed when her white charge, a stupid girl who was all Cora had to love, was to have a child by the Greek boy at the corner grocery; unashamed to stand at the funeral of this girl following the illegal operation and tell the proud white family of its crime. Cora was wise in her ignorance, innocent in her guilt. Into her portrait has gone the best work of the young author.

Another story in which the writer is happy in his results is the story of the lonely old maid who found herself desiring the Negro janitor of her apartment house, and was brave and proud enough to leave before loneliness and desire spelled defeat for her. In this little story, quite without plot and free from episode, the writer has shown a fine restraint, good sense of values, and has written without recourse to trick or emotion.

Less pleasing because more ornate and still of interest because of racial viewpoint are the stories involving the lynching of Negroes for trivial contact with white women, the murder of a white father by his half-breed son—the tragedies of mob insanity, race prejudice and race injustice. These stories will make white readers ashamed of incidents of the past, an effect less insistent because the writer has given way to emotionalism and melodrama where he might well have kept his drama pure and high.

But the reader laughs with the author, albeit a somewhat bitter laugh on the latter's part, at the white people who go in for Negro culture, who seek to adapt superficially the qualities which make the Negro a distinctive race, or who seek that which is even worse: to remake the Negro over to fit the white man's ideas of what he should be. Here is satire, humor, art in writing, understanding of the amusing stupidities of the person with money and without brains. "Colony of Joy," the story of a Negro who, an ex-circus barker, becomes the admiration and adored of fat-minded white women, is a choice and revealing tale.

E.E.H.
"Reviews of New Books"
Albany Times-Union,
23 July 1934, p. 15

Langston Hughes, a talented writer, also a Negro, keeps his feet upon the ground. He writes about the impact of one race upon the other with the confidence of an intelligent, self-respecting man, albeit these 14 short stories constitute a race-conscious, class-conscious document that often extends far beyond the limitation of documentary literature. For instance, he scorns the pretentious friendship that some whites offer colored people, and, in the same breath, lambasts the scraping humility that certain of his race present. Yet, keeping his head, he does not indulge in this criticism to excess; therein lies the

strength of his stories and their attendant discussion.

"Cora Unashamed," first of the stories, is based upon the strong contrast in two attitudes toward illegitimate children. Cora, maid of the Studevants, was proud of her child who died, even though it was born out of wedlock. The Studevants, however, could not tolerate the idea that their daughter, Jessie, should become a mother under similar circumstances. Because appearances meant so much to them, they indirectly brought about the death of their daughter. The story tells how Cora transferred her affections to Jessie, once her own offspring died and of how Jessie could confide in Cora—there were not barriers there—but could not confide in her parents; there were too many barriers there. Here we have a depiction of how the veneer of society impels humans to sacrifice their best interests to pride and vanity.

In "Home," a decidedly moving story, a gifted young Negro violinist returns to see his mother in a Missouri village after eight years of success abroad. He is ill and humiliated by his reception in his home town where he is "just another nigger." A faded music teacher is the only person who understands how well he has played at a church benefit and stops him on the street to shake his hand. She is white, and natives, emerging from a moving picture show, mob him. The gifted artist wonders why she stopped him; he knows that he will never see his mother again. "And when the white folks left his brown body, stark naked, strung from a tree at the edge of town, it hung there all night like a violin for the wind to play."

To those who have Langston Hughes' novel, *Not Without Laughter,* and his poems, it may be said that he keeps pace with a growing reputation with these short stories. Those who have not read him will find that his work rings true and that he is

224

a master of humor, pathos, satire and terror, giving promise even of approaching genius.

Harold R. Walley
"Book Worm's Turn"
Ohio State Journal,
25 July 1934, p. 5

Langston Hughes' *The Ways of White Folks* is the latest book of a very interesting Negro writer. It is a collection of 14 sketches on a theme stated by one of the characters. "The ways of white folks, I mean some white folks, is too much for me. I reckon they must be a few good ones, but most of 'em ain't good—leastwise they don't treat me good. And Lawd knows, I ain't never done nothin' to 'em, nothin' a-tall."

The book is not so much fiction as it is a sociological study in the guise of fiction. Nor is it primarily concerned with the ways of white folks, except as they impinge upon the Negro. Against a cosmopolitan background, Langston Hughes has set himself to survey, calmly, shrewdly, and with commendable restraint and good humor the Negro problem in America. His book contains 14 case histories.

Of course, there are the usual problems of miscegenation, too much stressed, in my opinion. But Hughes is generally impressive in his dramatic realization of a variety of problems. He is peculiarly happy in his sharp differentiation of the psychology of his two races. In "The Blues I'm Playing" and "Poor Little Black Fellow" he has expressed a tremendous truth casually.

"Home" is perhaps as tragic a commentary on a blundering civilization as one can find. The brief "Passing" sums up a novel in its subacid irony. All in all, Hughes builds up an indictment which is damning in its very quietness.

But Langston Hughes is more than a sociologist, more than a Negro; he is an artist. He is sufficiently dispassionate to treat his people as human beings rather than as horrible examples. He has sufficient acquaintance with white folk to see them as they are, and he does not grow maudlin over his downtrodden people. What impresses one is the variety of his knowledge, his psychological grasp of his characters, his good humor, and his ability to depict a whole social history with a few quietly drawn strokes. Here is the whole plight of the Negro. . . .

Percy Winner
"Pity of Others Shunned by Negro Race"
New York Evening Journal, 25 July 1934, p. 24

[. . .]
So far as modern science knows there is little biological justification for the idea of essential inferiority of any one race in relation to any other. Nevertheless each race, using its own interests as a criterion, finds it psychologically and economically convenient to consider itself superior.

Negroes—the Ethiopian race, who have suffered through the ages from their subjection—do not, Langston Hughes makes clear in *The Ways of White Folks,* consider themselves inferior to the whites. They feel themselves to be different, and in many ways superior.

Hughes, one of the truly competent literary artists produced by his race in this country, writes no propaganda. He tells stories, fine, sensitive, well made stories of men and women—white and black, but he looks at life through the pages of this charming book from the viewpoint of the Negroes.

[. . .]

It may come as a surprise that Negroes don't care much for white people "who go in for Negroes"—no matter how praiseworthy their motives. "Slave on the Block" is a story which gently but firmly shows that the Negroes want to be Negroes and not what whites think they should be.

Hughes does not get bitter or violent about the cruel injustices visited upon his people. He sets them down quietly, artistically, and lets them talk for themselves; almost with compassion and sympathy for the whites who, to the Negroes, seem at times to be in the grip of incomprehensible compulsions which make them act badly while their true feelings are good.

"Recent Releases in Brief Review"
Desert News [Salt Lake City], section 3, 28 July 1934, p. vi

Mr. Knopf rang the bell again when he published this job, a superb collection of the short stories of Negro master, Langston Hughes, the writer who is unafraid of his topic, the relationships of white man and Negro.

Written with a fine and stirring blend of irony and pity, these stories do not present the white race in relation to the Negro in a pretty light. As presented in all honesty by

Mr. Hughes, it becomes very obvious that the whites most often encountered by the Negro are far from superior people. Either the whites are heavily and uncomfortably patronizing, unwilling to grant the Negro anything in the way of intelligence, or they are cultists, patronizing the Negro from a fake art-and-culture point of view.

The stories are admirably written, in a soft, uncolored and yet mellow style which makes its points firmly and surely. Here is the simple pathos of the colored woman of-all-work who wanted to be let off before 10 p.m. Christmas Eve so that she could buy her little Archie a present at the dime store. Here is the pity and terror of the story "Father and Son" in which the old southern colonel refuses to recognize his ivory-shaded son: the grim humor of "Poor Little Black Fellow," the tale of a lone Negro who was guarded from life by New England white folks until they didn't know what to do with him; and the rich flooding heartbreak of "Cora Unashamed," the Negro servant who knew enough to respect true love and honor it, when her white employers ruined the happiness of their daughter by interfering with her marriage to a Greek.

All are beautifully written—all present a side of life in this country that we must know.

Herschel Brickell
"The Literary Landscape: Good Short Stories"
North American Review, 238 (September 1934), 286

Langston Hughes's The Ways of White Folks, a volume of short stories of Negroes and whites, contains some of the best stories that have appeared in this country in years, and strengthens the Landscaper's long-held opinion that the author is far and away the most talented member of his race who has ever written in this country. They are bitter stories for the most part, often savagely ironical, but done with admirable art. . . .

E. C. Holmes
"Our Book Shelf"
Opportunity, 12
(September 1934), 283–4

Langston Hughes' development has been steady, sure and positive. His works from 1926 to 1931 are links in this evolution. Save for occasional retrogressions ("Dream Keeper," "Dear Lovely Death," "Popo and Fifina") which are allowable in the development of the sincere fellow-traveller, Hughes' career has been brilliant and straightforward. His work, it is true, has not always possessed the anti-bourgeois note so evident in his work from 1931 to 1934. Nevertheless, it was reasonable to believe that Hughes would go further in the only direction in which an artist should go, than any of his colleagues of the "New Negro Renaissance."

Langston Hughes was, in 1926, an integral part of that unhealthy "New Negro" tradition. He shared the beliefs in the new theories of bourgeois estheticism as much as Cullen, Toomer and McKay. Even so, the poems in *Weary Blues* signified the arrival of a remarkable poetic genius. And in *Not Without Laughter,* he had broken almost definitely with the "Harlem Tradition." Today, with the publication of *The Ways of White Folks,* Hughes has traveled

much further, nearer his goal of true revolutionary literature. It must be remembered that there had to be a good deal of excision, a complete denial of bourgeois traditions and parlor radicalism before he could write "Scottsboro Limited," "Columbia," "Good Morning, Revolution" and *The Ways of White Folks.*

Since it is difficult to review these fourteen stories in any but a laudatory fashion, it should not be incorrect to analyze the entire content as well as the author. First, Hughes has shown that he has mastered the objective short story form. These stories are as nearly perfect as one could desire. They are not unlike the stories of Pauteileimon Romanov, and Romanov's master, Tchekov. The resemblance extends to the superb irony, the simplicity and the splendid craftsmanship.

Every word seems to be weighted, tested, burnished and carefully inserted. There is such economy of structure, the stories are told so ably, that one experiences the feeling of having read what might have been a novel. There is in this book a sense of ease, but yet vivid writing. These stories remain indelibly on the mind. You live them. They constitute special experiences for you. These properties belong to great art.

Eight years ago, Hughes, in defending Negro Art, wrote, "If white people are pleased, we are glad. If they are not, it does not matter. We know we are beautiful. And ugly too." Now, he writes of these same white people. Now, his approach is a class approach. Now, he does not mean all white folks, but as Berry says "some white folks." Hughes, realizing the struggles in existence between two classes, conceives of those white people who in their control, circumscribe and influence the lives of the Negro masses. He writes of Negroes in relation to white people who are part of their very existence. This is so for Hughes because all men stand in relation to each other as parts of a social whole. He is interested in Negro and white class psychology, in their class differentiations. He uses working class themes, showing the intensity of the exploitation of share-croppers, bookkeeper, domestic and laborer.

When read together, these stories present a rather tightly knit pattern. Taken together, they show an indictment against the decadence of capitalistic society. When read singly, such stories as "A Good Job Gone," "Little Dog," "One Christmas Eve," etc., may evoke the remarks that they are good as stories go, but that they are not examples of bourgeois realism or of revolutionary literature. Such criticism is specious, of course, when these stories are taken together. For, one of the largest effects gained in the body of the book is in the use of irony and satire, concealed and open. Also, his ability to generalize is characteristic of his anti-bourgeois outlook. This characteristic enables him to apply his scalpel to Negroes and whites alike.

In "Father and Son," the most powerfully absorbing story in the volume, the author states his belief in the knowledge that the union of white and black workers will be the single force which will smash American Capitalism. "Crucible of the South, find the right powder and you'll never be the same again—the cotton will blaze and the cabins will burn and the chains will be broken and men, all of a sudden, will shake hands, black men and white men, like steel meeting steel!" That is why Hughes' art is social. Call it propaganda if you like. He has succeeded, nevertheless, in overcoming his former schematism and abstractness. He has succeeded in depicting social relations in a realism of the highest order.

All the stories are excellent. There are, of course, some which stand out as being more powerful, such as "Red Headed Baby," "Father and Son," "Cora Un-

ashamed," "Home," and "Rejuvenation Through Joy."

The thing which makes this volume one of the most outstanding contributions to American literature is the fact that Hughes understands the people about whom he writes. He understands their relations—exploiting and exploited—to each other. He knows what the solution of these problems of a capitalist society will be. No longer will he attempt to solve any problems, art, racial or personal, within the framework of capitalism. He knows that if he is to write in such a society, he must portray life as he sees it. He must come to terms with the life of this time. Above all, he must point the way out. In this volume, Hughes justifies his experiment and his use of the short story form finds a most felicitous outlet for his talent.

Martha Gruening "White Folks Are Silly" *New Republic*, 80 (5 September 1934), 108–9

Octavus Roy Cohen finds colored people very funny, and Julia Peterkin finds them very quaint. Langston Hughes finds white people either sordid and cruel, or silly and sentimental. Nevertheless this collection of short stories suffers a little, as a whole, from being based on such a formula. Any formula is too cheap and easy for an artist of Hughes' caliber. Oceola Jones, the Negro pianist, he tells us for instance, did not "stare mystically over the top of a grand piano like white folks and imagine that Beethoven had nothing to do with life," and when she played for her white patroness the latter looked "very cold and white" and "her grand piano seemed like the biggest and heaviest in the world." I doubt that white people—who have, of course, plenty to answer for—do any more mystical staring over the tops of pianos and imagining of silly things about Beethoven than warm, dark-skinned ones, or that their grand pianos are any bigger and heavier.

The best of these stories, however, are very good indeed. "Cora Unashamed," with its direct and shattering impact, its warmth and bitterness, is magnificent. "Home" tells with sharp eloquence of the return of a young Negro violinist from triumphs abroad to a little Missouri town where he is lynched. "Christmas Eve" is a straightforward and touching sketch of a Negro maid and her small son, reminiscent of the author's *Not Without Laughter*, though written with more bitterness. In "Little Dog" Langston Hughes has given old stuff about a frustrated old maid and her dog a new and painful reality, and in "Slave on the Block," he has written a rollicking and very funny, though merciless, satire on a certain type of white Negrophile. It is hard to understand why he should have included in this otherwise distinguished collection so heavy-handed and wearisome a satire as "Rejuvenation Through Joy," or so slick and brittle a piece as "A Good Job Gone."

R.S.M.
"About Books"
Hastings [N.Y.] *News,*
7 September 1934, p. 8

Among the interesting books in the lending library of the Bookshop is Langston Hughes' *The Ways of White Folks,* a collection of short stories about Negroes every bit as much of a document as *The Jungle.* In many ways, Hughes is just as much of a campaigner and propagandist as Upton Sinclair, but whether a state or mayhap a nation, ever crowns tireless efforts on behalf of race tolerance is doubtful, for such things take time. In the South, for instance, where the Negro Problem is greatest, to be seen reading Hughes' book would probably produce a call from the local KKK. To vow, publicly, sympathy for him would be tantamount to suicide in many sections. In 1934 down there 1864 is but yesterday.

But for those who can read stories about Negroes as they would read stories about Indians, or say Chinese—"The Good Earth" for example—and get from them the emotional kick which comes from superior artistry, then *The Ways of White Folks,* a varied collection of compelling stories, is just the book for them. Many of them first appeared in *Esquire, The American Mercury, Scribner's, Opportunity, The Brooklyn Daily Eagle, Debate* and *Abbott's Monthly.* Needless to add, Mr. Hughes is one of the outstanding writers of his race.

Mary White Ovington
"Book Chat: *The Ways of White Folks,*"
Omaha Guide, 15
September 1934, p. 6

"The ways of white folks. I mean some white folks—"

They are certainly very trying ways for a white person to read about. No single contact between the races as described in this book is satisfactory. One of the characters, Arnie, brought up by white folks, first finds happiness when he goes to a gathering among his own race. "For the first time in his life Arnie was happy. Somebody had offered him something without prayer, without distance and without being nice." According to Langston Hughes' picture, contact between the two races never makes for friendship. White folks' ways are not natural ways. Sometimes they are terrible and we have the too familiar lynching at the end, sometimes they are condescending, and the Negro escapes as soon as he can. The two worlds never meet in friendly sympathy.

The stories vary greatly. "Little Dog," to my mind the best, shows the love that a lonely white working woman gives to her Negro janitor and the complete unconsciousness of the janitor. The little dog brings the two together for a few minutes of the day. Of course, in the end, the white woman runs away. "Poor Little Black Boy" shows the good intentioned but hopelessly obtuse white Northern family bringing up a colored boy. He is kept from his own group but never receives full entrance into the white. He is always on the side lines. In a third, "Cora Unashamed," a young white girl gets into trouble and only the colored servant understands her. Here at least the two races meet in love, but the older members of the white race are antagonistic. The end of the story is poignant. Langston Hughes always writes of the overworked servant girl, upon whose back the labor of the house is placed, and who receives scant reward, with deep sympathy. That faithful mammy whom the white writer loved to depict he sees in her true light, a servile woman whose natural instincts were appropriated by her owner for her selfish uses. She was to be a mammy for her mistress's children but not for her own.

After the reconstruction period the white South took upon itself to educate Northern opinion regarding the Negro. We were flooded with books showing the black man as sullen, ungrateful. Sometimes a rapist. *The Birth of a Nation* marked the high water mark of this propaganda. Now we have the Negro's conception of the white man and woman, and it is as severe as the picture the South once drew of the black. I use the word "once" advisedly. Negro stories by white writers today are usually sympathetic, but such stories are at their best when dealing only with the black race. One sees from this most interesting and entertaining book how far the groups still are from one another, how little chance they have really to understand each other. *The Ways of White Folks* are sorry ways indeed. I especially recommend the book to the Caucasian reader.

Alain Locke
"Negro Angle"
Survey Graphic, 23
(November 1934), 565

These fourteen short stories of Negro-white contacts told from the unusual angle of the Negro point of view are challenging to all who would understand the later phases of the race question as it takes on the new complications of contemporary social turmoil and class struggle. Their sociological significance is as important as their literary value, perhaps more so, because although written with some personal reaction of disillusionment and bitter despair, they reflect the growing resentment and desperation which is on the increase in the Negro world today. Though harped upon almost to the extent of a formula, there is an important warning in what has been called "the sullen, straight, bitter realism" of this book. It has reportorial courage and presents new angles, but it offers no solutions, doctors no situations and points no morals. Its most illuminating moods are those of tragic irony as in the particularly effective concluding story, "Father and Son," the tragedy of a planter killed by his own illegitimate son who is lynched for the crime; and of caustic satire as in "Cora Unashamed." In most of the stories there is the double motif of the inconsistency of racial discriminations and the injustice of class lines, with frequent hints of the recent radical insistence that the two are below the surface closely related. This is an important book for the present time; greater artistry, deeper sympathy and less resentment would have made it a book for all times.

M.H.
"Book Reviews"
Controversy, 1 (9 November 1934), 11

Carmel has for the last year and a half numbered in its colony of artists and writers one of the outstanding American poets—the Negro, Langston Hughes. His first book of short prose, *The Ways of White Folks,* was finished in Carmel and even considering the large and important contribution from Carmel to all the arts, this book should be one of its proudest boasts. Mr. Hughes is the author of a novel, *Not Without Laughter,* but is best known for his several volumes of poetry published under the titles *The Weary Blues, Fine Clothing for the Jew* [sic], *The Dream Keeper* and other works.

The whole feeling and expression of this, his latest publication, is almost a mirror of the personality of Mr. Hughes—simple, unassuming, but with the deep and sensitive human understanding of a highly evolved yet growing artist and man. There are 14 short stories, both tragic and humorous, in this book, all of which tell of the happenings that occur every day about us in America, when black and white people mix, casually or intimately. They are put down with an expression so simple that it hardly seems an art, as we are apt to think of "art," in letters, but the natural compelling urge of a man of his race to tell of his people—these people are so inevitably a part of our lives, yet so resentfully excluded. Many of Mr. Hughes' critics have complained of his bitterness toward the whites and of his Negro propaganda. We would like to ask these critics how any Negro with an ounce of manhood, having the art to make this field his subject, could help but resent the entire situation and reflect it in his work.

After all, is not all vital art propaganda in the large sense? The glaring and historical example is the art of the Renaissance which was, almost in its entirety, propaganda for the Christian religion. We feel that Mr. Hughes has shown as very great, almost an unhuman restraint; he could very easily and with entire truth have chosen many more cruel and violent examples of the oppression of the Negroes. His art, far from suffering from this selection of subjects, we feel, is enhanced by the very natural intenseness of his natural feelings.

From the variety of these 14 tales, we choose "Red Headed Baby" as the most beautiful in expression, where the irrepressible poetic sense, obviously Mr. Hughes' natural form, flows on in a musical and creative style. "Mother and Child," the only story told in Negro dialect, is of the love between a white woman and a black man. This story exemplifies his delicate handling of a subject that is charged with dynamite, touching as it does the core of the eventual problem of the two races.

"Home" and "Father and Son," both of which end in lynchings, are tragically powerful, and in them we realize the ghost that haunts every Negro in this country—the possibility, with mis-step or accident, of lynching.

We do not feel that Mr. Hughes is so successful in his comedy pieces, such as "Slave on the Block" and "Rejuvenation Through Joy." In these we feel the writing is more mechanical and uninspired and does not seem to us to express either the deep or subtle satire of which he so often shows capacity, or the spontaneous, contagious, big-hearted laugh of his race, with which he personally has often vitalized the more self-serious and neurotic Carmel gatherings.

[. . .]

Thelma B. Miller
"Books, Old and New"
Carmel [Calif.] *Pine Cone,*
23 November 1934, p. 2

One of the best products to date of the articulate American Negro culture is Langston Hughes' *The Ways of White Folks.* This is a collection of short stories, good individually, but as powerful as a novel in the cumulative force which they attain by being grouped in one volume. In all of the stories there are both white folks and black folks; the book is therefore a study of the two alien races in enforced association.

Delicate but biting satire is directed particularly against the white people who make a vogue of Negroes. The recipients of their beneficence are not fooled for a moment. The white people are so terribly self-conscious in their graciousness. They see the objects of their patronage not as human beings but as very clever animals.

"Slave on the Block" is this sort of story, about the Carraways, who "went in" for Negroes, and are amazed by the "familiarity" with which their priceless pair of servants respond to urgent if unspoken invitation to make free of the house. Another is "Poor Little Black Fellow," about a kindly family of New Englanders who raised an orphan Negro boy as "one of themselves," without contact with his own race, and then reacted as might be expected when he picked up a white girl in Paris.

No collection of Negro stories is complete without one lynching episode; this is provided in "Father and Son," the strongest and unpleasantest story in the book. Not in so many words, but clearly, Hughes shows that instigators of southern lynchings are not the "flower of the old south," who probably could live at peace with their former slaves, but the "poor whites" who prove to their own satisfaction by mob violence, because there is no other way that they can reassure themselves and show the world, that they are "superior" to any and all blacks.

There is not much sense in blinding ourselves to the fact that racial antagonism exists and is probably inevitable. It is perhaps an insuperable obstacle to internationalism and world peace. If we whites ever settled our own family quarrels, we would probably only get together to clean up on our colored neighbors. Anthropologists tell us that Orientals find the smell of white people just as objectionable as white people find the smell of black people. Dogs and cats have the same innate antagonism. But dogs and cats can be trained to live harmoniously in the same household, and if civilization can bring enough pressure to bear, soon enough, the various races will learn to get along harmoniously on a basis of mutual respect. Mutual respect, mind you, not respect only on the side of the other fellow.

Most white people are either too gracious or too familiar when they are trying to be "nice" to Negroes or Orientals, or Indians, for that matter. The reaction is either resentment of a patronizing attitude, or response in kind to familiarity. If a "colored person" is treated with the same respectful reserve which you accord any other stranger, he will reply in kind. Not long ago I had a job which brought me in contact with a large number of Negroes and Mexicans; I was there to serve them, and not, as is the usual case, to receive service from them. Such a "demeaning" position for a white person that many people would have refused the job. I was warned that my clientele was "fresh" and disrespectful.

By treating them as individuals and not as a hostile colored mob, I was treated as respectfully as if they had been working for me and not I for them. Moreover, I received a measure of childlike gratitude that was very humbling. The strange thing was that as I got to know them, the color faded from their skins. I forgot that they were different from myself. They were individuals instead of a flock of sparrows.

Alain Locke
"The Eleventh Hour of Nordicism"
Opportunity, 13 (January 1935), 8–12

. . . only irony can make them real or effective with any considerable number of readers.

And just this mechanism has been used in the more successful of the stories of the first Negro writer whose fiction we discuss, Langston Hughes in his much discussed *The Ways of White Folks.* Here is the militant assault on the citadel of Nordicism in full fury, if not in full force. Avowedly propagandist, and motivated by radical social philosophy, we have here the beginnings of the revolutionary school of Negro fiction. But though anti-bourgeois and anti-Nordic, it is not genuinely proletarian. But it is nevertheless a significant beginning, and several stories in the volume, notably "Father and Son," rise far above the general level of rhetorical protest and propaganda reversal, achieving rare irony and real tragedy.

[. . .]

V. V. Oak
"Book Review"
Bulletin of National Association of Teachers in Colored Schools, January 1935, p. 20

Langston Hughes needs no introduction to the readers. As a poet he is well-known. As a prose writer he will be remembered by his novel *Not Without Laughter.* The book under review is a collection of stories depicting the social relations between white and colored people, relations as the Negro sees them. Some of these stories had already appeared in some "white" magazines.

Each story depicts a different type of social set-up between the two races, portraying the underlying racial hatred presenting itself in various guises. "Slave on the Block" and "Poor Little Black Fellow" bring out very vividly the utter failure of many white people (who "go in for Negroes") to understand why they generally fail to win the heart of their proteges. "Father and Son" is the story of a boy, named Bert, with a Negro mother and an aristocratic white father. The antagonistic attitude of the father who refuses to recognize his son in public though quite willing to condescend to patronize him in private leads to a growing hatred between them. Both come to a tragic end, the father being killed by his son when insulted by the epithet "nigger bastard," and the latter killing himself rather than be a prey to the ferocious mob waiting outside to lynch him. The mob, however, takes its vengeance in the southern fashion of hanging some Negro, and so poor Bert's brother was made the victim.

There are several other stories equally interesting bringing out clearly that in any social relations with the white the Negro gets the worst end. The style of the book is easy and rather poetic-prose, and captures the reader to such an extent that the book is finished at one sitting.

Checklist of Additional Reviews

Elrick B. Davis, "Cleveland Novelist Scores Success with Second Book, Made Up of Short Stories," *Cleveland Press,* 23 June 1934, p. 5.

Calvert Carroll, "Books in the News," *Baltimore News and Post,* 27 June 1934, p. 9.

"Book Chat," *Oroville* [Calif.] *Mercury,* 28 June 1934, p. 2; also in *Wilmington* [Calif.] *Journal,* 12 June 1934, *Macon News* 19 June 1934.

Clifton Fadiman, "Also Out This Week," *New Yorker,* 10 (30 June 1934), 54.

Booklist, 30 (July 1934), 351.

"Fiction," *Open Shelf,* July 1934, p. 16.

W. G. Sibley, "Along the Highway: Langston Hughes, Negro Genius," *Chicago Journal of Commerce,* 11 July 1934, p. 11; reprinted in *Gallipolis* [Ohio] *Tribune,* 26 September 1934.

Thomas W. Duncan, "Quaint Caucasians," *Des Moines Register,* magazine, 5 August 1934, p. 4.

"New Books at City Library," *Sacramento Union,* 2 September 1934, p. 13.

THE BIG SEA

Henry A. Lappin
"Langston Hughes Lives
a Literary History"
*Buffalo Evening News
Magazine,* 24 August
1940, p. 3

"A Negro Writer's Story:
Langston Hughes's Book
Called *The Big Sea*"
*Springfield Union and
Republican,* 25 August
1940, p. 7E

The title of Langston Hughes' book symbolizes its contents. Into *The Big Sea* that is literature and life in one, "I let down my nets," he writes, "and pulled. What I caught was amazing."

His record of those years of fishing is amazing, too. What catches were his in Paris and Harlem, and long before that, on freighters off East African coasts under "equatorial large few stars!" And even before that, in Mexico and in hotel work in Washington where he met and made a friend of Vachel Lindsay. Dominie Simpson had a word for it, as readers of Walter Scott—one hopes there are some left!—will remember: "Prodigious!"

Here, too, is the Negro movement in letters in the New York—and elsewhere, but mainly in New York—of the 1920's, told in a profoundly and pathetically beautiful narrative by a first-rate craftsman, done with compactness and economy.

To the best of our knowledge this is the first attempt by a Negro to write a full and manly account of the recent history of Negro literature in the United States. That literature has yielded much to his sympathetic study no less than to his occasionally scornful appraisal.

Langston Hughes has written his autobiography, and it is everything that his admirers could have wished to receive from him—intimate in its stories of his struggles, inspirations and successes; candid in its revealing references to those mean discriminations which beset the Negro who seeks to better himself and those of his race, but not vindictive; homely in its humor, broad in its philosophy and, over all, fascinating as a record of odd adventure and wide travel. He calls it *The Big Sea,* for he finds that life is a big sea, full of many fish. . . .

In a life such as this there are many critical moments and Langston Hughes was more than once rescued from what might have been, at least to one more submissive to adversities, an overpowering discouragement. His meeting with Vachel Lindsay was such a turning point. It came about indirectly because Hughes had caught a cold that winter while working in the steam of a wet wash laundry. Staying home for a week, he returned to find his job gone and soon after got a job as busboy at the Wardman Park Hotel in Washington. Lindsay was to give a reading of his poems in the little theater of the hotel and Hughes, thrilled in anticipation of his coming, prepared for the visit:

"That afternoon I wrote out three of my poems, 'Jazzonia,' 'Negro Dancers,' and 'The Weary Blues,' on some pieces of paper and put them in the pocket of my busboy's coat. In the evening when Mr. Lindsay came down to dinner, quickly I laid them beside his plate and went away, afraid to say anything to so famous a poet, except to tell him that I liked his poems and that these were some poems of mine. I looked back once and saw Mr. Lindsay reading the poems, as I picked up a tray of dirty dishes from a side table and started for the dumb-waiter. . . .

"The next morning on the way to work, as usual I bought a paper—and there read that Vachel Lindsay had discovered a Negro busboy poet! At the hotel the reporters were already waiting for me. They interviewed me. And they took my picture, holding up a tray of dirty dishes in the middle of the dining room."

Mr. Lindsay had gone, but he had left a package at the hotel desk for Hughes, a set of Amy Lowell's John Keats, with an informal and encouraging note spread over six pages of the fly leaves. A few days later Mr. Lindsay and his wife were in Washington again for a brief stay and the young poet had a short, inspiring talk with him.

This was, indeed, a rescue, for Hughes had been bewildered, his spirits lowered, by what he had found elsewhere in Washington. In Europe and Mexico he had lived with white people, worked, eaten and slept with them, and no one seemed any the worse for it. In New York he sat in the theaters with white people without untoward incident. "But in Washington I could not see a legitimate stage show, because the theaters would not sell Negroes a ticket. I could not get a cup of coffee on a cold day anywhere within sight of the Capitol." Worse, perhaps, than this, he found that his own race was divided and that the upper class colored people "were on the whole as unbearable and snobbish a group of people as I have ever come in contact with anywhere. They lived in comfortable homes, had fine cars, played bridge, drank Scotch, gave exclusive 'formal' parties, and dressed well, but seemed to me altogether lacking in real culture, kindness or good common sense."

The meeting with Lindsay revived his ambitions, but it cost him his job, because from then on, due to national publicity, he became a curiosity, required by the head waiter to go and stand before tables for the benefit of those guests who desired to see what a Negro busboy poet looked like. He continued to write poetry and won a prize offered by the magazine published by the National Urban League. He received $40, but spent it going after the award to the presentation banquet at New York. This was in the 1925–29 period, in the middle of a decade of progress for the Negro:

"The nineteen-twenties were the years of Manhattan's black Renaissance. It began with *Shuffle Along, Running Wild,* and the Charleston. Perhaps some people would say even with *The Emperor Jones,* Charles Gilpin and the tom-toms at the Provincetown. But certainly it was the musical revue, *Shuffle Along,* that gave a scintillating send-off to that Negro vogue in Manhattan which reached its peak just before the crash of 1929, the crash that sent Negroes, white folks and all rolling down the hill toward the Works Progress Administration.

"Put down the nineteen-twenties for the rise of Roland Hayes, who packed Carnegie Hall, the rise of Paul Robeson in New York and London, of Florence Mills over two continents, of Rose McClendon in Broadway parts that never measured up to her, the booming voice of Bessie Smith and the low moan of Clara on thousands of records, and the rise of that grand comedienne of song, Ethel Waters, singing 'Charle's elected now. He's in right for sure!' Put down the nineteen-twenties for Louis Armstrong and Gladys Bentley and Josephine Baker."

As for Hughes, he attended a house-rent party almost every Saturday night in Harlem, wrote lots of poems about house-rent parties, met ladies' maids and truck drivers, laundry workers and shoe shine boys, seamstresses and porters and "can still hear their laughter in my ears, hear the soft slow music, and feel the floor shaking as the dancers danced." And during the summer of 1926, with Wallace Thurman and other intellectuals, he decided to publish a Negro quarterly of the arts, to be called *Fire*. The name idea was that it would burn up some of the old, dead notions and provide an outlet for the younger Negro writers and artists. The venture, far from being economically sound, folded up when, climaxing other misfortunes, a real fire burned up the bulk of the final issue.

Hughes does not regard his own background as typical of the average Negro. His grandmother lived in Oberlin and spoke perfect English, without trace of dialect. She looked like an Indian. His mother had been a newspaper woman and stenographer, although varied fortunes led her to other occupations. His father, whom he learned to hate, was a successful, aggressive businessman in Mexico. His granduncle had been a congressman. And there were heroic memories of John Brown's raid and the underground railroad in the family record.

He didn't care much for poetry as a little boy, but he came early to a love of books. A stay with his father in Mexico gave him broadening experience, but left him miserable. He went to Africa as a sailor, after casting all his books overboard in his wish to wipe out a discouraging past. He walked as a beachcomber in Italy. He has produced several volumes of poems, a novel, *Not Without Laughter,* which did not please him, and a book of short stories, *The Ways of White Folks.* At times his work has shown that high, comforting quality of his "A House in Taos" and the consoling, spiritual note of "Brass Spittoons"; at times mournful as "The Weary Blues," and again, powerful but rebellious as his "Advertisement for the Waldorf Astoria." An ironic effort, "Red Silk Stockings," led to misunderstanding and resentment among those of his own race, while the selection of a poem titled "Fine Clothes to the Jew" as the title of the full book of verse brought wide protests.

Hughes is not prepared to accept compromises which some Negroes approve. While at Lincoln, he felt that the college, in charge of an all-white faculty and board of trustees and supported by the philanthropy of non-Negroes, was not consistent with its own aims to produce Negro leaders, since it apparently could find none among its own alumni worthy of trust. But his own survey showed that 63 per cent of his fellow students disagreed with him. Conditions have since changed and Negroes are on both faculty and board. He parted with a good patron and friend, explaining:—

"She wanted me to be primitive and know and feel the intuitions of the primitive. But, unfortunately, I did not feel the rhythms of the primitive surging through me, and so I could not live and write as though I did. I was only an American Negro—who had loved the surface of Africa and the rhythms of Africa—but I was not Africa. I was Chicago and Kansas City and Broadway and Harlem."

And this, now, is the mood of his autobiography.

Ted Robinson
"Fugitive Otto Strasser, Fate Unknown, Tells How Ex-Friend 'Missed the Bus'"
Cleveland Plain Dealer, feature section, 25 August 1940, p. 3

This unusual autobiography will be on the bookshop shelves tomorrow morning, and I trust that our dealers have supplied themselves generously to meet the special demand that will arise in Cleveland. Because Langston Hughes is a Clevelander, an old Central High boy, and his well-deserved literary reputation is a matter of pride to a great number of people in this city.

As poet, novelist and playwright, he stands well toward the top of the list of Negro writers who have a keen and articulate understanding of the significant aspects of the life of his own race in America. He feels the race's problems, but nevertheless he is able to approach them objectively. His travels, his experiences, his education, his contacts, have combined to make a cosmopolitan of him; he is less of an introvert than most other poets are. Here is no whining; no propagandizing; no mock humility on the one hand or defiant brashness on the other. The narrative of his colorful life is perfectly frank in every detail where frankness is a virtue; he knows, too, the value of reticence.

This is the story of Harlem in its heyday, of the Paris of the 1920's, of life on freight ships, in hotels, in Mexico, in college. It is the story of the "Negro Renaissance" with its remarkable flowering in music, the dance, poetry, the stage; the story of the night-club era. It is the story of contemporary literary society of every race, and its cast of characters reads like an Authors Who's Who.

I have seldom read a book so natural, so candid, and yet with such an undercurrent of humorous irony, such an effect of knowing much more than it is fitting to disclose. I think thousands of people are going to be absorbed by this book, and I cannot imagine that any of the readers will be disappointed.

Milton Rugoff
"Negro Writer's Heap of Living"
New York Herald Tribune Books, 25 August 1940, p. 5

Seaman, waiter, doorman, laundry sorter, cook's helper, truck-garden worker, busboy. . . . It is a curious thing to be a Negro writer. In fact, there are probably few ways of looking at America as curious as through the eyes of a well known Negro artist. Thus the autobiography of Langston Hughes, poet, novelist and playwright, might well have been a very disturbing confessional, filled with unpleasant truths and with bitterness. But *The Big Sea* is not like that at all. It is not like that because Hughes is not. It may be that he is naturally incapable of rancor or that he has gone beyond it to attitudes that leave little room for the note of hate. In any event, his record of this, his childhood and growing time (it goes only to 1929, his twenty-seventh year), is essentially a friendly, ramblingly anecdotal chronicle characterized by a tolerance, simplicity and unpretentiousness that borders on the naive.

But let this not mislead, for Hughes has, as they say, done a heap of living. Even his childhood was nomadic, for his wealthy father had gone off to Mexico, leaving Langston and his mother to shift for themselves. Whether he was happy-go-lucky by nature or for protection, this section of Hughes's reminiscence hardly mentions those psychological difficulties that are supposed to harass youth. It was only when his mother's troubles forced him to live with his father in Mexico that certain unpleasant truths began to make themselves felt—particularly the fact that discrimination had made his father a grasping, money-minded man whom he could not abide and that the color line was drawn more viciously inside America than in many countries outside. He was unhappy in Mexico—but this was perhaps fortunate, for when he is unhappy, he innocently admits, he writes poetry.

To get away from his father, he agreed to enter Columbia, but, once at the university, found it cold and depressing. Compared to dormitory life, Harlem seemed rich and vital, and Europe, where one could be independent, very attractive. That is why, at the end of a year, he shipped on a freighter bound for Africa. Thereafter his was the sailor's way—slavery on board, carouser on shore, sightseer in strange worlds, and then home again with nothing to show but a Congo monkey.

It was shortly after this that he succumbed to the legend of Paris. Like many another innocent, he arrived in the French capital with nothing but romantic fervor; naturally he starved. But that was the heyday of the Negro in Europe, so he landed a job as doorman in the "Grand Duc" on the Rue Pigalle and got what might be called a nightclub-eyeview of Paree. Those were the palmy twenties when Montmartre was a Mecca for American artists, eccentrics, millionaires and Negro entertainers. If Hughes didn't exactly hobnob with them he certainly rubbed their elbows. Menial though his work was he was young and exuberant, he dwelt in a Paris garret, and there was even a Russian dancer for a while. . . . So there is something of Paris-in-the-spring-tra-la in his memoirs at this point, and very few racial flies in the ointment. It was so pleasant, in fact, that he wrote hardly any poetry. When the "Grand Duc" closed he bummed through Italy and was finally reduced to beachcombing, but even that, in retrospect at least, was a lark not without laughter.

When he returned to Washington, the "Black Renaissance" had hit America, too, and the intelligentsia were hailing James Weldon Johnson, Claude McKay, Countee Cullen and a host of other Negro artists. Soon generous Vachel Lindsay discovered Hughes, the newspapers were duly surprised to find a poet working as busboy, and people even came to gape at the artist carrying dishes. Like the whites, upper-crust Negro society showed him off somewhat gingerly, for he didn't seem altogether safe—and then left him working in a laundry.

"Folks!" says Hughes. "Start out with nothing some time and see how long it takes to work up to something." Being unhappy, he wrote poetry again. Then, quite suddenly, the breaks came. Lincoln University gave him a scholarship, and being so near New York he was caught up in the Negro vogue and the Harlem craze. It lasted only until '29, but while it lasted it sizzled; it brought forth Paul Robeson, Roland Hayes, Bojangles, Ethel Waters, Josephine Baker, Jules Bledsoe, Florence Mills, the Charleston, the Cotton Club style, the Savoy dancehall, white sponsors like Carl Van Vechten, and Ethel Barrymore in blackface! It created a group of Negro literati, with cults and cliques. It brought

Hughes a white patroness, who helped him lavishly. (How gleefully amazed were his redcap friends the day she made him ride to Grand Central in her huge car with a white chauffeur!) But the decade, and prosperity, and the Negro vogue were all destined to draw swiftly to an end together. . . .

And there, quite abruptly, Hughes's chronicle stops. Abruptly, I feel, because it leaves you with a picture, genial and entertaining enough, of a footloose, adventurous young man, but with hardly a suggestion of the vigorous social attitude which was soon to mark his point of view and upon which much of his reputation depends. But perhaps *The Big Sea* is only a prelude to a less buoyant record of a darker era. Or perhaps most of the pain was poured out in those poems. Or it may be that Langston Hughes is another Negro who defends himself through the invincible amiability of his disposition.

Katherine Woods
"A Negro Intellectual Tells His Life Story"
New York Times Book Review, 25 August 1940, p. 5

It is fifteen years since Vachel Lindsay brought a new item of literary interest to the public in the discovery of a poet who was a colored bus boy in a Washington hotel. Or had he been, some asked each other, an elevator operator? As a matter of fact, he had been a great many things, in twenty-three years of a remarkably eventful history. And neither then nor in these years since, as Langston Hughes has continued to produce sensitive and thoughtful

work in prose and verse, has the full course of his extraordinary career been generally guessed. Now that it is here before us, the noteworthy quality of the poet's latest book passes well beyond its content of remarkable situation and incident. Langston Hughes's autobiography is the product and portrait of a very unusual spirit, in its narrative of crowded happenings and contrasts and the envisioning of a strange and significant time.

The Big Sea is the story of a Negro who began life as the child of a poor family in the Midwest in the first decade of this century, and who after that was a successful business man's son and also a teacher of English in Mexico, a night-club cook and waiter in Paris, a mess boy on freighters halfway around the world, a starving beachcomber in Genoa, a laundry hand in Washington, a student at Columbia and Lincoln Universities, and at once a participant in and a clear-eyed observer of Harlem's "Black Renaissance." The book can be followed through with fascination as a success story and chronicle of adventure, full of living individuals and colorful scenes. It can be remembered more thoughtfully as a personal re-creation of Negro life from pre-war days, through post-war conditions and fevers, against backgrounds of contrast both in place and time. But its profound quality and lasting worth are to be found in the fact that from first to last, through all these and other experiences and observations, it remains both sensitive and poised, candid and reticent, realistic and unembittered. "Life is a big sea full of many fish. I let down my nets and pull." It is a poet who is the fisher, and the poet's miracle of combining subjectivity with detachment is in the gathering of the nets.

[. . .]

These chapters tell the story of a sensitive youth, and tell it memorably. The episode of the child's pseudoconversion is a little masterpiece of poignant simplicity, far removed from the bitterness of the flippancy with which the same kind of story has sometimes been treated, in other memoirs. There is a passionate sincerity here which expresses itself in unstrained directness. Whether scenes and incidents are beautiful or ugly they are set down in quiet candor, without exhibitionism or apology; and only when one looks back does one realize how much reserve there is also, and how much one has read, even in this straightforwardness, by a glimpse here and there, a curtain drawn for a moment, a suggestion.

[...]

... his comprehensive picture is studded with individual portrait sketches and informed with lively thought.

... Literature, too, was a big sea where one put down one's nets and pulled: "I'm still pulling," he says.

The reference to literature strikes the right note for the autobiography's climax. Engrossing as the book is in event and illuminating as commentary, *The Big Sea* is essentially an individual evocation of life, in sentiment, response, and penetrating clarity; and it is as literature, thus, that it is to be read, in all its vivid complexity of situation and simplicity of phrase.

Harry Hansen
"The First Reader"
New York World-Telegram, 26 August 1940, p. 15

Paint chipper on a rusty tramp steamer, dishwasher in a Montmartre night club, beachcomber on the Genoa waterfront, and hero of the Harlem literati when Negro poets were the pets of sophisticated New York—these are high spots in the experiences of Langston Hughes, prizewinning poet. The story of his roving years is called *The Big Sea*. Packed with good stories, it is the amusing and ironical record of how a young man who wanted to write took menial jobs on three continents to make both ends meet.

Rarely have I been more diverted or instructed by a vagabond's confessions. For, aside from the fun, there are pertinent accounts of how an honest Negro lad gets by. Hughes does not write in bitterness here—the book does not have the stinging quality of his social poems. But the truth of his message is apparent on every page. Without moralizing he drives his point home by anecdotes.

It is not far-fetched to say that nobody ever has told the story of the American Negro in Paris night club life of the 1920s as Hughes tells it here, nor has anyone ever brought to book the ironical character of the "black renaissance," when New York made Harlem a place of pilgrimage. Hughes knows these events from personal experience and his pages are a contribution to social history.

Hughes was stranded in Paris with $7 when he ran into a Russian dancer named Sonya who "had no mon-nee nedder" and promptly found a room which she insisted on sharing with him. At first Hughes became a doorman for a small club where girls would fight each other by breaking champagne glasses on the edge of the table and attacking with the jagged stems. Then he became dishwasher at the Grand Duc.

About this time Montmartre was full of Negro jazz bands. The Grand Duc was a diminutive "boite de nuit" which had become the rage because Florence Embry was singing there. Florence's stunt was to high hat everybody and this made her highly desirable to know. Hughes found his protector in a one-eyed cook whose berserker legend is one of the high spots of the book. The story of the big fight in the Grand Duc, which resulted when Florence waded in because the owner was ejecting an obstreperous dancer who was pregnant, is a classic. Florence later deserted the Grand Duc for her own "boite" and the Duc imported Bricktop Ada Smith of Connie's Inn, who became the toast of Paris.

Hughes sees the "black renaissance" of the 1920s as a conglomeration of good and evil, of appreciative white folks helping Negro artists and snobbish hangers-on following the fashion. By 1930 "we were no longer in vogue, we Negroes. Sophisticated New Yorkers turned to Noel Coward. Colored actors began to go hungry, publishers politely rejected new manuscripts and patrons found other uses for their money. The cycle that had charlestoned into being on the dancing heels of *Shuffle Along* now ended in *Green Pastures* with De Lawd."

Hughes recalls the generosity of Joel and Amy Spingarn, "charming, quiet people," whose services to the American Negro cannot be repaid in gold; the great flair for entertaining hundreds of the late A'Lelia Walker, open-handed daughter of the woman whose invention "worked wonders on unruly Negro hair." He mourns the defection from Negro culture of Jean Toomer; recalls the gumbo suppers of James Weldon Johnson "where one met solid people," and praises the generous advice of Carl Van Vechten. He defends the latter's use of *Nigger Heaven* as the title of a book, saying that it alienated only those who did not understand it. He tells, rather sadly, how his collaboration on a play with Zora Hurston broke up a beautiful friendship.

We also learn how an artist feels when he is being supported by a rich patroness. Hughes was on Easy Street while a wealthy Park Ave. woman paid his bills, but soon the obligations became irksome. She wanted his work to be "primitive"; he felt that she hindered the free play of his spirit. He left her in distress. He has much praise for her kindness and for her position as one who has helped many. Her name is withheld.

We can laugh with Langston Hughes as he describes his plight in various difficult situations, from which he usually emerged with little more than his coat and pants. But, despite this humor, he gives by means of personal experiences, excellent sidelights on the difficulties of a young, talented, honest dark-skinned American in our paradoxical society. He could not share his father's contempt for Negroes. His father had established himself in business in Mexico and eventually married a German woman. He could not understand the snobbery of Negro society in Washington, which withdrew an invitation to his mother because she didn't have a dinner gown, and boasted of descent from Southern white families "on the colored side." Rather he took up with the "ordinary Negroes" on Seventh Ave., who sang songs and laughed out loud.

Since he was not coal-black a soda fountain clerk was willing to serve him if he declared himself a Mexican, which he wouldn't. But, ironically, the full-blood Negroes from Liberia, in Africa, denied that he was a Negro. "You white man," they asserted. He found his best welcome in Central High School of Cleveland, Ohio, where the immigrant children accepted him outright. Here everyone was eagerly interested in the Russian revolution. Hughes does not describe his turn to radicalism, nor his visit to Soviet Russia—that came after the events treated in this book. It is likely that the equal treatment given all races by the Soviet system in those days may have had considerable influence on his views. He is, however, no longer an editor of *New Masses,* and what his views are today he does not say. But what he tells, up to 1930, is not only his own but American biography.

"Life of a Black Man" *Newsweek*, 16 (26 August 1940), 44

One of the more ingratiating aspects of the fabulous 1920s has never been accorded its proper place in the history of our times. That was the slightly misnamed "Negro renaissance" (why not "Negro naissance"?). In that decade America "discovered" the Negro: Black Harlem came into furious vogue, a black-and-tan intelligentsia sprang up, wrote poems, painted pictures, sang and composed a new music, acted and danced while white America clapped hands and paid.

Langston Hughes grew up in that wonderful era and was a shining light in Harlem's literati (which Wallace Thurman, one of his cynical black friends, labeled the "niggerati"). He saw all there was to see and remembered it; in his autobiography, *The Big Sea,* published this week, he tells as much about the cultural revolution as about himself. For entertainment alone, his book is a killer.

Hughes pere was a black man who hated his race, apparently because it was poor. He early saw that the cards were stacked against an ambitious Negro businessman in the United States, so he got out, to Mexico, where he flourished and made money. He counseled Langston to do likewise.

Graduating from a Cleveland high school just after the World War, Langston spent a wretched year at Columbia University, where he was generally snubbed because of his color, then decided to go to sea. His first job had him so excited that he forgot to ask where the boat was going; he had landed a berth on the fleet of war-built tubs which rusted year in and out in the Hudson River. He wasn't going anywhere.

He got another job, on a freighter bound for Africa with a gay and mutinous crew. He drifted into Paris around 1924, working mostly in Negro nightspots (Paris was just discovering the black man, too). In Genoa, he went on the beach after his passport and money were stolen. In the end he got home safe, arriving in America at the height of the Negro cult; he worked at anything, preferring jobs in "places where you eat." And he wrote poems, especially when he felt bad, which was often.

The Big Sea is full of superb stories, about parties thrown for rent-raising purposes (the invitations ran like this: "We got yellow girls, we've got black and tan. Will you have a good time? YEAH MAN!"), and about the author's host of friends, white and black. He tells of the incredible A'Lelia Walker, Harlem's Elsa Maxwell, whose mother left her a fortune made from a "dope" to take kinks out of Negro hair. When A'Lelia died, Harlem went to town on her funeral; downtown celebrities crowded into the funeral chapel where a black vaudeville quartet swung "I'll See You Again" and Hughes' poem, "To A'Lelia," was read.

But with the depression, Hughes says in a "Postscript," came the end for the Harlem renaissance: "Sophisticated New Yorkers turned to Noel Coward. . . . The cycle that had charlestoned into being on the dancing heels of *Shuffle Along* now ended in *Green Pastures* with De Lawd." He might have added, however, that still "greener pastures" seem to lie ahead, if one lifts his eyes above Harlem and considers the strides made by the Negro—even since 1930—in America. Writers like Richard Wright and Zora Neale Hurston, singers like Marian Anderson and Dorothy Maynor, sculptors like Augusta Savage and Richmond Barthe, and actors like Rex Ingram have come up in a new renaissance of the arts.

Richard Peters
"Cleveland Poet Writes Book about His Career"
Cleveland Press, 27 August 1940, p. 13

Langston Hughes, the talented colored poet, novelist and playwright who wrote his first poems for Central High School's magazine, tells the story of his youth and young manhood in a delightful autobiography, *The Big Sea,* published today. . . .

Although his life was as varied as a professional adventurer's, with interludes in Mexico, Paris, at sea, on Park Avenue and in Harlem, his boyhood here is one of the most interesting episodes.

Mr. Hughes writes very simply. He is frank and thorough and he is completely tolerant.

"My best poems were all written when I felt the worst," he says, but there is no moodiness in this book. In fact, a lot of it sounds quite a lark.

Central High's teachers got him started—he names them with gratitude and tells what they contributed to his thoughts and ambitions. Then, at 15, he began writing for *The Belfry Owl,* the school magazine.

"Little Negro dialect poems like Paul Laurence Dunbar's and poems without rhyme like Sandburg's were the first real poems I tried to write. I wrote about love, about the steel mills where my stepfather worked, the slums where we lived and the brown girls from the South, prancing up and down Central Avenue on a spring day."

Some of the poems were terrible, but his high school days were not. He edited the year book, ran on the track team and, because of a Jewish-Gentile split among his classmates, was elected to several offices as a compromise candidate.

Then, suddenly he went to Mexico with his father, a money-mad person who was ashamed of the colored people and of himself for being colored.

Young Hughes hated his father. He left for a year at Columbia University, and then, filled with romantic notions, he sailed for Africa, and later Paris.

Returning, he was swept into the "Black Renaissance," was discovered by Vachel Lindsay while he was working as a bus boy in Washington, and taken up by society, both colored and white.

He also acquired a patroness, and his redcap friends at Grand Central were amazed one day when he appeared in her sleek town car, driven by a white chauffeur.

The story ends in 1929, when he is only 27. That was just after a temperamental episode concerning another playwright and the Gilpin Theater here.

He closes on a pleasant note: "Literature is a big sea full of many fish. I let down my nets and pulled. I'm still pulling."

[. . .]

Malcolm Johnson
"Without Bitterness"
New York Sun, 28 August 1940, p. 21

Langston Hughes, the Negro poet, says that he can't write when he is happy. He can write only when he is feeling bad, when the blues get him down. Well, he must have been feeling bad, mighty bad, when he sat down to write this book, the story of his own life, for it is a superb job, vastly entertaining, forceful and often moving.

"Life is a big sea full of many fish," the author explains. "I let down my nets and pull." Hence the title.

Mr. Hughes tells his story simply and frankly and with a delightful sense of humor. He does not permit much bitterness to creep in, not even when he is describing the difficulties of being a Negro in the United States.

Langston Hughes came of age in the turbulent twenties. He was born in Joplin, Mo., but grew up mostly in Lawrence, Kansas, reared by his grandmother until he was 12 years old. Then he lived at intervals with his mother in Topeka, Kansas City and Cleveland. He began to learn what it was to be a Negro when he was a small child. But even in school, when the white boys would call him "nigger," there was always one or more who would take up for him. "So I learned early in life not to hate all white people," Hughes says. "And ever since it has seemed to me that most people are generally good, in every race and in every country where I have been."

During his wanderings and his efforts to make a living Hughes continued to write when he felt bad. He wrote his first poetry when he was in high school in Cleveland and since then has published three volumes of verse, *Fine Clothes to the Jew, The Weary Blues, The Dream Keeper;* a volume of short stories, *The Ways of White Folks,* and a novel, *Not Without Laughter.*

Hughes has a way of remembering the interesting people he has met, whether they be celebrities or common laborers, and of making his readers remember them, too. One of the grandest passages in his book is his description of a brawl in a Paris night club, the Grand Duc, where he was working as a kitchen helper. It must have been an epic battle and Hughes describes it with a rhythm that recaptures the drunken scene. He writes of the incident under the title, "Don't Hit a Woman."

The management of the club was attempting to eject a little French dancer who was employed there to dance with the patrons and encourage them to buy champagne. Florence, the star entertainer, then one of the favorites of Paris, intervened.

"Don't touch that woman!" Florence said. "She's a woman and I'm a woman, and can't nobody hit a woman in any place where I work."

Then the battle was on, with the little French girl screaming that she was a woman and with Florence screaming that she was a woman, too, that she had a mother and nobody could hit her mother, either.

Aside from this hilarious incident, Hughes tells about other personalities of Paris: The brown-skinned Josephine Baker, the one-eyed cook in the Grand Duc who chased the owner and all the other bosses from the place with a butcher knife when they tried to fire him and of the little Harlem girl known as Bricktop, who arrived there penniless and remained to become the favored entertainer of Paris. (Bricktop is back in New York now, where she has engaged in several unsuccessful night club ventures. Times have changed!)

Hughes also tells about the renaissance during the roaring twenties when the Negro was in vogue, when Harlem was in its glory and the place for white celebrities to go.

But the depression brought an end to the renaissance and the Negro was no longer in vogue. "Sophisticated New Yorkers turned to Noel Coward," Hughes records impishly.

One finishes this book with the feeling

that it is the work of a sincere and talented Negro artist, a tolerant man, who will not let even hardships and racial barriers keep him from enjoying life and people.

Listen, everybody! This is a good book and you'd better read it!

Lewis Gannett
"Books and Things"
Boston Evening Transcript, 29 August 1940, p. 11; also as "Books and Things: Twentieth-Century America," *Washington Post,* 30 August 1940, p. 11

Langston Hughes once said to Wallace Thurman: "If I could feel as bad as you do all the time I would surely produce some wonderful books." Thurman answered that you had to know how to write as well as how to feel bad. Langston Hughes retorted that he didn't have to know how to feel bad because, every so often, the blues just naturally overtook him, like a blind beggar with an old guitar:

> You don't know,
> You don't know my mind—
> When you see me laughin',
> I'm laughin' to keep from cryin'.

Langston Hughes is colored—and an American. That is, of course, the dominant fact on every page of his autobiography, *The Big Sea.* If he had been born in Russia, or in France, or in Mexico, it would not matter so much. There he would be simply a poet and a story teller. Here he is colored.

By some grateful miracle he has not lost his native sense of humor in the process of becoming a writer. He has won fame, but never been comfortable among the consciously famous. He always—well, almost always—runs out and chuckles at them. And he chuckles at being neither black nor white but colored.

He went to Africa, the great Africa of his ancestral dreams, wild and lovely, the women dark and beautiful, the palm trees tall, the sun bright, the rivers deep. But the Africans looked at him and would not believe he was a Negro. His skin was too light. His blood is, by the crude calculation of pre-Mendelian genealogy, one-sixteenth Cherokee Indian, one-sixteenth French, five-sixteenths Southern white and seven-sixteenths Negro. One of his grand-uncles was a member of Congress from Virginia. He was born in Missouri. His mother was a stenographer in Kansas. His father was a prosperous business man in Toluca, Mexico, hating Negroes and hating being a Negro.

And when Langston Hughes asked for an ice cream soda in the St. Louis railway station, returning from a summer with his father in Toluca, the clerk looked at him and asked: "Are you a Mexican or a Negro?"

"Why?" the boy asked.

"Because if you're a Mexican I'll serve you," the clerk said. "If you're colored I won't."

"I'm colored," said Langston Hughes, and went off, probably not humming "God Bless America, My Own Sweet Land."

He was class poet at the grammar school in Lincoln, Ill.—because, he thinks, the white children in his class knew that they could not write poetry and assumed, as most white Americans do, that every Negro had a sense of rhythm. That was how Langston Hughes came to write his first poem. At the Central High School in

Cleveland he was class poet again. This time it was because the school was split between Jews and Gentiles, and the two factions compromised on a Negro. Later he wrote poetry because he could not help it or just because he felt bad. And one year in New York a white-haired Park Avenue lady supported him for the good of the arts, and he wrote almost no poetry at all. He says it was because he didn't feel bad. She said that the poetry he wrote was not properly "primitive."

Poetry is not, ordinarily, remunerative. So Langston Hughes worked as a delivery boy in Chicago (and was beaten up for wandering into a neighborhood whose gangs disapproved of colored interlopers); as a hand on a Greek truck farm on Staten Island; as a messenger boy for Thorley, the florist; as mess boy on a "mother ship" tied up at Jones Point on the Hudson River; as a seaman on most of the world's oceans—and some of the stories he tells of that life compare favorably with B. Traven's strange classic, *The Death Ship;* as doorman, second cook and waiter in Paris cabarets. He went one year to Columbia University, where he found the Chinese students friendly; later he graduated from Lincoln University, near Philadelphia, where the students were colored and the faculty, like the trustees, all white. In Washington he worked as secretary to a Negro historian, but he found the colored society of Washington stuffy; he preferred a job as bus boy in the Wardman Park Hotel. There Vachel Lindsay "discovered" him and put him in the newspapers.

He had been "discovered" before. Floyd Dell was the first editor who ever wrote him a letter along with a rejection slip. Alain Locke, colored himself and a great scholar, had read his poems in *The Crisis* and tried to visit him on his ship at Jones Point; later Dr. Locke found him in Paris and encouraged him in his writing. In the 1920's he lived through the "Negro Renaissance" that made Harlem famous; Carl Van Vechten asked him if he had not enough poems for a book and sent the manuscript to Alfred Knopf, who is still Mr. Hughes' publisher. Nothing I have ever read by or about Mr. Van Vechten does him as much honor as Langston Hughes' account of their relationship: and neither Mr. Van Vechten nor James Weldon Johnson in his *Black Manhattan* has ever pictured the Harlem of the 1920's better.

Broke in Paris, Langston Hughes ran into a Russian girl, who found him a cheap room, then explained, "I have no mon-nee nedder"; and soon he was in the midst of Paris' Negro furor. He tells of a fight on the floor of the Grand Duc cabaret, when Florence Embry, then the toast of Paris as Josephine Baker was a few years later, threw her orchids on the floor and swept across the room like a gold tigress to defend a French danseuse and men fought women as never elsewhere save in the "movie" version of *The Women.* He tells of seamen's brothels all around the world; of A'Lelia Walker's Harlem parties (and of the Park Avenue lady who, hearing a lurid version of "My Daddy Rocks Me," exclaimed, "I just love Negro spirituals," to the vast delight of the audience); of investigating voodoo with Zora Hurston; of his life as a beachcomber in Genoa and of the time he and Alain Locke were invited to lecture and to lunch at the Hill School—the faculty asked some of the boys to volunteer to sit at the same table with the distinguished but colored visitors.

Some of his favorite poems are scattered through the book. Prose or poetry, Mr. Hughes' sense of color and rhythm lights up the pages and gives them a singing lilt. You may take *The Big Sea* as a string of good stories or you may read it as a strange commentary on twentieth-century America. This, too, is the United States.

Lee Berry
"This World of Books"
Toledo Blade, 31 August 1940, p. 5

[. . .]

The theater also plays a minor part in *The Big Sea,* in which Langston Hughes chronicles his life from 1902 up through his twenty-seventh year. During that period Mr. Hughes lived for a while in Mexico, attended Columbia for one depressing year, shipped to Africa, came perilously near starvation in Paris, worked on and off as a waiter, doorman and busboy, wrote some first-class poetry and shared in the "Black Renaissance" which hit Harlem in the mid-twenties.

The lot of the Negro artist is not often a happy one, even in democratic America, and this might have been a bitter and disturbing record of poverty and frustration. But although there are momentary references to both, by and large this is an exuberant and often gleeful account of a varied and adventurous young manhood, brought to a sudden and rather arbitrary close in 1929, thereby indicating that Mr. Hughes has a sequel in mind. If it's half as entertaining as *The Big Sea,* it will be well worth reading.

Oswald Garrison Villard
"The Negro Intellectual"
Saturday Review, 22
(31 August 1940), 12

When I was more than halfway through this book I felt a strong sense of disappointment. It seemed to me that it had not justified itself. It was vulgar in spots, trivial elsewhere; neither the contents nor the style were original, noteworthy, or compelling. But when I laid it down it was with regret. It had taken hold of me, this picture of the itinerant life of a Negro intellectual, mostly at loose ends, with nothing to tie to, and no strong parental hand to direct his life during the formative years.

Primarily it is Mr. Hughes's absolute intellectual honesty and frankness which moved me. He looks at his White and Negro world with rare objectivity and paints it exactly as he sees it. He is not a propagandist, nor a too bitter critic. When he records some of the discriminations from which he has suffered and insults to which he has been subjected he does so almost like an outsider looking in. You feel also that he is not holding something back as so many colored people do when setting forth their views where they may be seen or heard by white folks. More than that, he is as severe in his criticisms of the snobbish colored intellectuals, notably in Washington, as he is of the condescending, race-proud whites.

It will be a shock to many readers to learn that a people so discriminated against as the Negroes has an intellectual uppercrust with all the arrogance, bad manners, and snobbishness of the *nouveaux riches* of Park Avenue, but here the facts are. For example, Mr. Hughes was invited to attend a formal dinner in Washington in honor of the "New Negro" writers, to represent the younger poets. He was told that he might attend although he had no dinner clothes and that his mother was included in the invitation. The afternoon of the dinner his mother was called up by one of the "ladies" of the committee and told that it would not be wise for her to come since she did not possess an evening gown! Needless to say the younger poets were not represented at that dinner by Langston Hughes. That many of these colored intellectuals boast of their illegitimate descent from Southern white families, Mr. Hughes also stresses.

As for himself he makes no claims. He does not write as if he were a genius born and admits frankly how slow he was in coming to his versifying under conditions which would have proved fatal to many a man. He has kept alive by struggling for existence as a sailor, scullion, busboy, cook, clerk, waiter, laundryman here and in France and Italy, often hungry, sometimes sleeping for weeks in a public lodging-house or leading the life of a beach-comber in a foreign city. All this was on his road to getting a college education and becoming an outstanding poet, dramatist, and writer, and winner of many prizes. There is not a trace of self-pity, nor a whine in the whole book. There is also no yielding of his manhood or his rights as an American citizen. He is one of those uncomfortable people who wish to have ethics and Christian rules of conduct applied at all times. So when at an interracial conference at Franklin and Marshall College, which bars Negro students from attending, Mr. Hughes was wicked enough to think that this, his first interracial student-conference, ought to "get at the root of the matter right there on the campus where we were in session—as to why Negro citizens could not attend that college." He proposed a resolution on the subject. As he puts it:

But I could get no action on such a resolution at all. Everybody shied away. And the white director of our conference—an adult professional Young Men's Christian Association leader—said regarding this problem in his final talk to the assembled delegates: There are some things in this world we must leave to Jesus, friends. Let us pray. So they prayed. And the conference ended.

It is not surprising that he has now discovered that "an awful lot of hooey revolves around interracial conferences in this country."

One of the most tragic episodes is Mr. Hughes's description of his being taken up by a rich resident of Park Avenue in New York, who became his patroness and most generously freed him from having to toil for his living so that he might be unhampered for creative work. She wished him to be primitive and "know and feel the intuitions of the primitive." But he was

only an American Negro. . . . I was not Africa. I was Chicago and Kansas City and Broadway and Harlem. And I was not what she wanted me to be. So, in the end, it all came back very near to the old impasse of white and Negro again, white and Negro—as do most relationships in America.

The break—it was complete—made him physically ill.

That beautiful room, that had been so full of light and help and understanding for me, suddenly became like a trap closing in, faster and faster, the room darker and darker, until the light went out with a sudden crash in the dark. . . .

Yes, this is a moving, a well worthwhile book which should have been written; a most valuable contribution to the struggle of the Negro for life and justice and freedom and intellectual liberty in America. But I warn Mr. Hughes that when our military dictator takes the saddle *The Big Sea* will burn among the first.

Roger Pippett
"Three Pilgrims File Their Stories"
PM, 1 (1 September 1940), 40

[. . .]

But the last of our trio, Langston Hughes, poet, novelist and playwright, comes through clearest of all to me. Seaman, doorman, waiter, cook, beachcomber, busboy, he has served the traditional American writer's apprenticeship, shadowed and heightened in his case by his Negro blood.

When we meet him, he is leaning over the rails of a ship, Africa-bound, throwing his library into the green water off Sandy Hook. Books had been happening too much to him, and he ached to be free of them for a while. He picked up the last one and pitched it away. "The wind caught it and ruffled its pages quickly, then let it fall into the rolling darkness. I think it was a book by H. L. Mencken."

When we leave him he is recovering from a bitter, bewildering experience with a Park Avenue patron. It made him sick for weeks, but he bears no malice. Tolerance, in fact, is his middle name. The indignities he suffered would sadden him and then he would write (he rarely wrote when he was happy)—and the sun would warm him once more.

Detached yet never aloof, Mr. Hughes stages his life-story up to the early 30s ("Ma soul's a witness for de Waldorf-Astoria!") in a series of sensitive, candid pictures which leave nothing that he desires to say unsaid. Naive? I wish other autobiographers had some of his "innocence." I clean forgot to be a detective while I was reading him.

J.S.
"Hughes' Story Unique"
Richmond Times-Dispatch, 1 September 1940, p. 8; also in *New Haven Register* and *Youngstown Vindicator*, 1 September 1940; *Durham Herald*, 8 September 1940; and, in abridged version, *Knoxville Journal*, section 5, 25 August 1940, p. 11, and *Akron Journal*, 22 September 1940

Langston Hughes is only 38 years old, and therefore young to write an autobiography. His *The Big Sea* would, if it were only an autobiography, be somewhat futile. It is more.

It is the story of a young Negro at large in the world, written in the only way it could be written, and remain effective. That is to say, it is a personal account of experience in which the experience is related to an individual and not to a concept.

There is a concept at large in the book, of course. It is the ever-present problem of the place in a world dominated by white or reasonably white people of a black, or reasonably black man. It concerns Langston Hughes as well as everyone else in the

United States. He thinks, as most Negroes think, that a Negro should enjoy the privileges of this country equally with a white man. But he is not screaming about it in print.

Because of its restraint, and its wholly delightful appearance of having "just grown," his story is unique among like projects by Negroes. It should be read and studied by young Richard Wright before it is too late. It should be read, too, by most whites, because it is true and honest and not bitter.

It tells how a Negro boy born in Joplin, Mo., and brought up mostly in Lawrence, Kansas, has made a career for himself in literature. It tells the truth about his ancestry, for a start—exactly how much white blood he has, and where it came from. It shows his father, a hard, driving man who would not endure the restrictions of this country and made much money in Mexico. And his mother, bitter about her husband, beaten down to jobs beneath her, sometimes even hungry—but still able to live life.

It shows also an amazing succession of men as a Negro sees them—George, the boy on a freighter Hughes once sailed on; Carl Van Vechten in the days of *Nigger Heaven;* a celebrated gold-digging evangelist of Harlem's prime; many of the Negro entertainers at their zenith and after. And Vachel Lindsay and Paris in the '20s, and Greenwich Village out after alcoholic art, and the parties the whites never saw in Harlem, and life as a bus boy in a Washington hotel.

Whether or not anything intelligent will ever be done about the thing which worries Hughes this writer does not know. But if something effective is done, it will be because people like Hughes tell the truth, as he has done.

Margaret Guthrie Stauffer

"Source Material of a Race"

San Francisco Chronicle This World, 1 September 1940, p. 18

"Life is a big sea," declared Langston Hughes in his autobiography, and "literature is a big sea," both "full of many fish. I let down my nets and pulled."

The haul proved by no means easy, for the odds were against him in a three-fold sense. As the child of divorced parents he never knew emotional security. As a Negro, from the moment when the "kids" in the elementary school of Topeka chased him with stones and tin cans, he found himself the victim of stupid race prejudice. He was early acquainted with poverty and the necessity of self-support. When only in the seventh grade, he found regular employment scrubbing the halls and shining the mirrors and spittoons of an old hotel for the munificent wage of 50 cents a week! The medley of jobs subsequently held included that of English tutor; truck gardener; mess boy on merchant ships; doorman, cook, and waiter in night clubs, hotels, and restaurants; and assistant in a wet wash laundry.

During this trying period he wrote poetry whenever the spirit prompted, as it usually did when he was "feeling bad." For example, out of a mood of depression en route to Mexico came "The Negro Speaks of Rivers"; out of days when he was busy dragging about bags of laundry or toting trays of dirty dishes to the dumb waiter came the blues, spirituals, shouts, and work poems of his second volume.

The years brought other compensations. There was "the quick friendship of the dispossessed"—as of Sonya, the Russian ballet dancer who shared her room and food with him when he was stranded in Paris—and the friendship of celebrities like Alain Locke, Carl Van Vechten and Vachel Lindsay, whose discovery of a bus boy who was also a poet forms one of the most dramatic episodes in the book. There was the generous woman who provided a scholarship so that he could resume his college education. And that other patron who supported him for a year in order that he might finish his novel and who might have continued to do so had not he, sensing her dissatisfaction with the quantity and quality of his output and her desire to control, preferred insecurity to shackles. Eventually there were literary prizes that meant both cash and prestige.

In a word, the book is primarily interesting as a success story and as the revelation of a personality combining courage, self-reliance, integrity, sensitivity, humor and gusto for living. But it has other angles of appeal. It is armchair travel, the scene shifting from the United States to Mexico, Africa, Holland, Paris, Italy. It is vivid characterization, as in the case of Chef One-Eye and Bricktop of the Grand Duc, Montmartre; Dr. Becton, charlatan revivalist, "mouthing inanities and whistling for God"; and A'Lelia Walker, "joy-goddess of Harlem's 1920s." As already implied, it is significant source material in the field of race relations. The author writes with controlled feeling, but with obvious intent to produce a cumulative impression of rank injustice to his people. He writes with candor, including in his composite picture of the Negro the uncultured proletarian element as well as Washington's snobbish colored society and the literati and other intellectuals of Manhattan's Black Renaissance.

The squeamish reader may be offended by rawness or rowdiness in spots. The stylist may be inclined to blue-pencil occasional awkward sentences, slang, and trivia. But he is indeed hard to suit who is not far less annoyed by the demerits than delighted by the merits of the book.

John Kinloch
"Langston Hughes' *The Big Sea* Called Best Book of the Year"
California Eagle, 5 September 1940, [p. 1B]

The Big Sea is the best Negro book of the year, which is fitting and proper, it being the autobiography of Langston Hughes.

The work is a glistening gem in the current autobiographical bevy. Within the past few years, an amazing collection of personal memoirs has clogged the literary market with everything from blushing confession to windy egomania. Never before have so many people in the midst of their lives seen fit to pen autobiographies which under all normal circumstances could only record the "first half" of their earthly wanderings. In this aspect, Hughes has outdone them all. Young as he is, the master has seen fit to reminisce only as far as the Year of Our Lord, 1932. Perhaps he is leaving room for a future self-inquisition. As it is, the reader misses Hughes' experiences in the Spanish Civil War and his part in other more recent events.

There is probably no other American Negro who could sit him down to a Corona Special and spew forth the romantic—and apparently authentic—adventures which Hughes has lavished over

254

the 335 joyous pages of *The Big Sea.* A list of locales would sound like a genuine Cook's tour: Kansas, Mexico, New York, Paris, Africa, Italy, Spain, Holland and so on into the night. And there are tales of high adventure to match the glamor of each of these places. In Ole Mehiko, a beautiful Spanish grand lady falls in love with the author; in Paris, he spends winter months in a garret romance with a Russian dancer; by Spring, he is chirping sweet nothings into the ear of a South African heiress. Beach-combing in Genoa, a Mississippi flood, parties with the Prince of Wales. All of these things flash through kaleidoscopic pages of the most cosmopolitan autobiography Afro-America has ever produced.

Just as dark rumors of Langston Hughes "losing the touch" were gaining credence in the best literary circles—witness the motion picture debacle, *Way Down South,* with which he was recently connected—the Poet Laureate of the nation's black millions has given us his finest work. From all appearances, Hughes has gained the most commanding grasp of his great powers in this simple, yet brilliant book. All literary affectation—a commodity with which the writer never had much truck—is eliminated. An amazing life stands upon its own feet—without simile or metaphor.

A striking surprise is the almost total lack of "red stuff." Vicious rumors that Hughes has lately become disaffected with the great American Democracy have made him taboo in certain quarters. If any Marxian outburst had been expected in *The Big Sea,* it certainly never appeared except through the gentlest implication. And that is good, for this book is too merry with business of living to be weighted down with sociological or political twaddle, no matter how uplifting.

Throughout Hughes displays an astonishing ability to sketch vivid pictures without apparent guile or effort. Not only are the physical dimensions of places made clear, but the literary miracle of recreating atmosphere, the very aura of reality, is everywhere evident.

I understand that there has been some discussion as to whether this book is a "masterpiece." It is contended in certain quarters that the autobiography is too "plain" to boast such a noble title. Of course, one must stay glued to the thing until it's read; of course, one gobbles every morsel of its rambling bill of fare; of course, one looks at the steadily diminishing number of pages with pained regret— but it isn't FANCY enough to be a "masterpiece." Aw, nuts!

[. . .]

David H. Appel
"Book of the Week"
Cleveland News, 7 September 1940, p. 13

Cleveland has a particular interest in Langston Hughes. He was graduated from Central High School in 1920 and some of his early literary efforts first came to light in the *Belfry Owl,* student publication at Central. Now Hughes is generally regarded as one of the most important Negro authors of our day, perhaps best known for his poetry.

In his recently-published autobiography *The Big Sea,* Hughes recounts pleasant memories of days at Central High. He praises the inspirational teaching of some of the members of its faculty, tells how he found practical democracy at work in the school. In his senior year, Hughes was class poet and yearbook editor.

After high school, Hughes lived for a

time in Mexico, attended Columbia University, traveled to Africa, worked as a cook in a Paris night club, as a worker along the docks in Genoa and eventually came back to Harlem to participate in the Negro literary renaissance of the 1920s.

Langston Hughes writes straight from the shoulder, but he has the poetic viewpoint. *The Big Sea* is at once the picture of a people and a period, a book filled with interesting personalities and places.

F. A. Breyer
"Distinguished Negro Poet"
Cincinnati Enquirer,
7 September 1940, p. 5

Langston Hughes, now a distinguished Negro poet, was born in Joplin, Mo., in 1902. Most of his childhood years were spent in Cleveland, Ohio, where Hughes wrote his first poetry in Central High School. His father and mother were separated, and Hughes went to visit his father in Mexico where the elder Hughes had acquired money and status. But father and son were not congenial and Hughes set out to make his own way.

He lived through the hectic nineteen twenties in Paris and Harlem, the two great playgrounds of the decade. Hughes knew the musicians and dancers, the queer people and the plain people, the drunks and the dope fiends. In America his poetry brought him prestige and recognition, he mingled with white and black authors, artists, and patrons of the artistic and literary world.

The Negro intellectual is engaged in pushing forward the frontiers of achievement, and Hughes is well in the van of this movement.

He is still a comparatively young man. This story of his life up to the present time is revealing and absorbing but I am sure that it leaves out much that might be told. For I have read Langston Hughes's poetry and heard him speak, and there is a fire in his speech and poetry that doesn't show up in this autobiography. On the other hand, Hughes is older now and perhaps his added years have mellowed his intensity. I hope that what has just been said (and I felt that it must be said) will not imply that *The Big Sea* is not well worth reading, for it is.

M[urray] duQ. B[onnoitt]
"Under the Covers"
State [Columbia, S.C.],
8 September 1940, p. 4B

If *The Big Sea* were considered only as the autobiography of a distinguished Negro poet it could easily be described as a fast moving and hilarious chronicle of trans-Atlantic freighters, Paris in the '20s, the Harlem Renaissance, an alcoholic Greenwich Village and a Washington hotel above and below stairs. But the book is far more than that. It carries the concept that is every Negro's concept—that the Negro should enjoy privileges equally with white citizens of these United States. What makes Hughes' book "different" and gives it a stature that towers above other books by other Negroes concerned with the same problem is that this author's thesis is presented naturally and only as it concerns matters at hand. There is no "forcing" of openings in the story for loud preachments on the racial theme, and none of the propaganda to which Richard Wright so recently abandoned himself to spoil his otherwise good work in *Native Son.* Hughes has written well and interestingly of the experiences of Langston Hughes; he has written intelligently of a problem that concerns Hughes and everyone else in the United States.

Alexander Williams "From Waiter of Montmartre to Beachcomber of Genoa" *Boston Herald,* 14 September 1940, p. 9

It is the custom nowadays to write autobiography when one is still young, and that is a tendency of which we should approve. Too often a distinguished elder takes a mellow and kindly glance at his youth when, as often as not, his emotions were far from genial and mountains were not molehills. Of course, the carping may say that it is presumptuous in anyone under 40 to write autobiography. We can honestly waive the question of right to distinction and prefer that an author, like Mr. Langston Hughes in *The Big Sea,* set forth the details of his life without pretending that they are part of a novel.

Mr. Hughes has had an exceptionally active and interesting life. He is a Negro poet whose work has attracted much attention, and he is also the author of a novel, *Not Without Laughter.* He tells us of his life with his mother in various cities and extreme poverty and by contrast of that with his father (whom he did not like)

in Mexico and comparative wealth. He has traveled extensively and originally—on a tramp steamer to Africa, again to Rotterdam, of his year as a waiter in a Montmartre night club, of a sojourn in Italy and partly as a beachcomber in Genoa, finally of his life here in America, in Harlem, in college, in the South.

All of these adventures are told modestly, with constant reflection on the social position of the Negro and the fact that the color line is most bitterly drawn in this democracy. Some of the experiences he went through are pretty shocking, some of them appear too trivial to be worth recording when they are not amusing. The section on the Harlem parties with long lists of names was certainly a boring interlude in the book.

And it is just when a book becomes boring that its faults thrust themselves upon the consciousness. Greatly as we were interested in Mr. Hughes' narrative and sympathetic to his point of view, we ended by becoming very antipathetic to his literary style. The extreme simplicity of his prose is fine for the recounting of adventure, but disastrous when the events of his life are commonplace. Almost every other clause or sentence begins with "but" or "so." For example: "Of course, I did not say so, but that was in the back of my head. So I began to gather data on the matter, quite sure that the data would not lie. It didn't." Naturally in small bits this manner of writing is not irritating, but the accumulative effect in a whole book written on that dead level is. Nevertheless, to enjoy the best parts of *The Big Sea* we can easily put up with an annoying mannerism.

P.M.
"Small Fry: Little Fish Are All That Appear in *The Big Sea*"
People's World, 18 September 1940, p. 5

I'm consistently pained with criticism harping on what this book or that play "didn't have," "failed to emphasize," and so forth. What I want to know about anything under review is what it does have, and to estimate it on that basis. But now up comes Langston Hughes with an autobiography which starts me to thinking that concerning canons of criticism I have maybe been indulging in dogmatic slumbers.

With all the good will in the world I am forced to report that this time our celebrated Negro poet, playwright and novelist has "gypped" us, for what Langston Hughes has left out of this book is remarkable.

The Big Sea is strictly not an autobiography, but really only Part I covering his first twenty-nine years and ending of all times in the year 1931. Thus we were automatically deprived of knowing anything of Langston's activity during the anvil-pounding depression years crucial in the development of American culture, the story of his adjustment to higher levels as a creative man, of his experiences, his problems during the job of sharpening and deepening his talents towards expressing (which he has done brilliantly) the wishes and dreams and strength and beauty of his people.

Instead we are served some three hundred-odd pages of charming conversational reminiscence. Maybe it's in Carmel, or Acapulco, or even Beverly Hills, and we're spending a pleasant week end, and Langston is one of the guests, and he's telling us, graciously, all about his early years, witty, poignant, romantic, his trips to sea, his big red-faced monkey, the lovely girl in Paris, Bricktop's nightclub, Van Vechten's parties, his stern bourgeois trade-follows-the-flag father, an oil man in Mexico, his bitter hard-working mother. It's all completely readable and captivating and yet, despite its disarming friendliness, curiously reticent, terpsichoreanly nimble in avoiding any use of the mind on topics apart from the poet's unique soul. All of which fails to satisfy us, for we know Langston Hughes is much more than, let us say, an earlier Saroyan.

"Life is a big sea full of many fish," says Hughes. "I let down my nets and pull." In this book he has shown us the little fishes, the ones that sparkle, the ones you throw back.

"An Adventuring Poet: Langston Hughes, Negro Author, Tells of His Wayfaring in Life and Letters"
Pasadena Star-News, 21 September 1940, [p. 8]

[. . .]

In this fine and sensitive chronicle of adventurous living, Mr. Hughes writes with serious purpose, setting down a personal record of colorful and often strange experiences. Some readers will like best the story of his childhood, while others will be more fascinated by his pictures of Negro life in Harlem. Those who have read his book of short stories, *The Ways of White Folks,* need not be reminded of the quality of his prose. Here is a book whose narrative is crowded with the life which the poet has seen across the varied years. Into it he has put the soul of the poet and the heart of the man. In it there is no spirit of bitterness and revolt but deep and sincere reflections and commentaries on the journey which he has taken through disappointments and triumphs.

Ralph Ellison
"Stormy Weather"
New Masses, 37 (24 September 1940), 20–1

Langston Hughes' autobiography, *The Big Sea,* is a story of the writer's life from his birth in 1902 up to 1930. It is a highly exciting account of a life which in itself has encompassed much of the wide variety of Negro experience (even within the Jim-Crow-flanked narrowness of American Negro life there is much variety). Before he was twenty-seven, Langston Hughes had lived in Kansas, Missouri, Ohio, New York, and Washington, D.C., on this side of the world; and on the other side he had lived in France and Italy and he had visited Africa. He had known the poverty of the underprivileged Negro family and the wealth of his successful businessman father. He had taught school in Mexico, gone to college at Columbia, shipped to Africa on a freighter, worked as a doorman in Paris, combed the beaches of Genoa, bussed dishes in a Washington hotel, and had received the encouragement of Vachel Lindsay for the poetry he was making of these experiences.

Hughes' family background is no less broad. It winds and spreads through the years from a revolutionary grandmother whose first husband had died with John Brown, to include a great-uncle who was a Reconstruction congressman from Virginia, US minister to Haiti, and the first dean of Howard Law School. Hughes' early life was marked by economic uncertainty, while his father, who left his wife and child to seek freedom in Mexico, was a rich man. Despite its revolutionary source there was even room on Hughes' family tree to include a few bourgeois Washington snobs. This wide variety of experience and background is enough in itself to make *The Big Sea* an interesting book and to recommend it as an important American document. It offers a valuable picture of the class divisions within the Negro group, shows their traditions and folkways and the effects of an expanding industrial capitalism upon several generations of a Negro family.

But *The Big Sea* is more than this. It is also a story told in evocative prose of the personal experiences of a sensitive Negro in the modern world.

In the wake of the last war there appeared that phenomenon of literary and artistic activity among Negroes known as the Negro Renaissance. This movement was marked by the "discovery" of the Negro by wealthy whites, who in attempting to fill the vacuum of their lives made the 1920's an era of fads. Negro music, Negro dancing, primitive Negro sculpture, and Negro writing became a vogue. The artificial prosperity brought by the war allowed these whites to indulge their bohemian fancies for things Negroid. Negro writers found publishing easier than ever before. And not strange to the Marxist is the fact that the same source which furnished the money of the period had also aroused the group energy of the Negro people and made for the emergence of these writers. But this in a different way.

The wave of riots and lynchings released by the war ushered in a new period in the struggle for Negro liberation. Under this pressure Negroes became more militant than ever before in attacking the shortcomings of American democracy. And in the sense that the American Negro group is a suppressed nation, this new spirit was nationalistic. But despite its national character, the group was not without its class divisions. It happened that those who gave artistic expression to this new spirit were of the Negro middle class, or, at least, were under the sway of its ideology. In a pathetic attempt to reconcile unreconcilables, these writers sought to wed the passive philosophy of the Negro middle class to the militant racial protest of the Negro masses. Thus, since the black masses had evolved no writers of their own, the energy of a whole people became perverted to the ends of a class which had grown conscious of itself through the economic alliances it had made when it supported the war. This expression was further perverted through the bohemian influence of the white faddists whom the war had destroyed spiritually, and who sought in the Negro something primitive and exotic; many writers were supported by their patronage.

Into this scene Langston Hughes made his first literary steps. Two older writers, Claude McKay and James Weldon Johnson, have treated the movement in their autobiographies. But neither has given a realistic account of the period or indicated that they knew just what had happened to them. Hughes himself avoids an analysis, but his candid and objective account of his personal experience in the movement is far more realistic than theirs. For the student of American letters it should offer valuable material.

There are many passages in *The Big Sea* in which Hughes castigates the Negro bourgeoisie, leaving no doubt as to what he thought of its value. Declining its ideological world, he gained his artistic soul: he is one of the few writers who survived the Negro Renaissance and still has the vitality to create. While his contemporaries expressed the limited strivings of this class, Hughes' vision carried him down into the black masses to seek his literary roots. The crystallized folk experience of the blues, spirituals, and folk tales became the stuff of his poetry. And when the flood of 1929 wrecked the artistic houses of his fellows, his was balanced firm upon its folk foundation. The correctness of his vision accounts for his development during that period of his life which follows the close of this book, and which we hope will be made the material of a forthcoming volume.

In his next book, however, we hope that besides the colorful incidents, the word pictures, the feel, taste, and smell of his experiences, Langston Hughes will tell us more of how he felt and thought about them. For while the style of *The Big Sea* is charming in its simplicity, it is a style which depends upon understatement for its more important effects. Many *New Masses* readers will question whether this is a style suitable for the autobiography of a Negro writer of Hughes' importance; the national and class position of the writer should guide his selection of techniques and method, should influence his style. In the style of *The Big Sea* too much attention is apt to be given to the esthetic aspects of experience at the expense of its deeper meanings. Nor—this being a world in which few assumptions may be taken for granted—can the writer who depends upon understatement to convey these meanings be certain that they do not escape the reader. To be effective the Negro writer must be explicit; thus realistic; thus dramatic.

The Big Sea has all the excitement of a picaresque novel with Hughes himself as hero. This gives the incidents presented a unity provided by a sensitive and unusual personality; but when Hughes avoids analysis and comment, and, in some instances, emotion, a deeper unity is lost. This is that unity which is formed by the mind's brooding over experience and transforming it into conscious thought. Negro writing needs this unity, through which the writer clarifies the experiences of the reader and allows him to recreate himself. Perhaps its lack of this unity explains why *The Big Sea* ends where it does.

For after 1930 Hughes was more the conscious artist. His work followed the logical development of the national-folk sources of his art. Philosophically his writings constitute a rejection of those aspects of American life which history has taught the Negro masses to reject. To this is accountable the power of such poems as "Ballad of Lenin," "Letter to the Academy," "Elderly Race Leaders," "Ballad of Ozzie Powell," and "Let America Be America Again." It is the things which he rejects in American life that make for the strength of the Negro writer. This amounts to the recognition of the new way of life postulated by the plight of the Negro and other minorities in our society. In accepting it the writer recognizes the revolutionary role he must play. Hughes' later work, his speeches before the International Congress of Writers for the Defense of Culture at Paris and his presence in Madrid during the Spanish War, shows his acceptance of that role.

Because he avoided the mistakes of most Negro writers of the twenties, Hughes' responsibility to younger writers and intellectuals is great. They should be allowed to receive the profound benefits of his experiences, and this on the plane of conscious thought. Then, besides the absorbing story of an adventurous life, we would be shown the processes by which a sensitive Negro attains a heightened consciousness of a world in which most of the

odds are against his doing so—in the South the attainment of such a consciousness is in itself a revolutionary act. It will be the spread of this consciousness, added to the passion and sensitivity of the Negro people, that will help create a new way of life in the United States.

John D. Barry
"Ways of the World: Langston Hughes' Autobiography"
San Francisco News, 26 September 1940, p. 18

Don't you agree with me that autobiography can be the most fascinating kind of writing? Oh, I know about the qualifications. It depends. But when an autobiography is sincerely and effectively done it's almost certain to have an appeal. And if it's done recklessly it has a chance of being a most significant revelation.

I don't like to say the Negro writer, Langston Hughes, has been reckless in *The Big Sea*. But he lets himself go just the same. And what he writes deserves a place among great contemporary human documents.

He has a special advantage in being a Negro. There aren't many Negroes who write autobiographies. When they do they reveal a unique outlook.

Langston Hughes has often been in San Francisco. I've met him here on several occasions. He's a quiet, modest, dignified man in the 30s. When he speaks he makes you want to listen to his pleasant voice. Quickly you realize that he has things to say. And yet he's no exhibitionist. I once heard him read from his poems, and it seemed to me that in spite of his intelligent rendering, he missed expressing dramatic effects that were in the lines. Later when I talked the interpretation over with him I suggested that intensity here and there might achieve contrast. He listened politely and shook his head, "Oh, I couldn't do that."

He had his own method and I admired him for adhering to a method that expressed his qualities.

[. . .]

A book of this kind couldn't have been published 50 years ago, it's so outspoken. Though I don't find anything shocking there, I imagine a good many people will be shocked, perhaps not unpleasantly. Langston Hughes is a product of the turbulent and audacious present. As a colored man he has been made to suffer, intensely and needlessly. Some of his misadventures he's able to laugh at. Other adventures he mentions with a bitterness altogether understandable. Throughout he reveals a sensitiveness that, at times, has rather dreadful physical manifestations.

In my opinion, he has written a really tremendous book. It can't be overlooked by any one who's concerned about present-day customs and about that strange, contradictory ideal we call democracy.

of the current national scene as well as of his own problems of race and color. *The Big Sea* is his autobiography, the story of a brief life that has been extraordinarily filled with events and experiences. For all the handicaps resulting from his color, Hughes has seen a great deal of the world. In telling of it, he reveals aspects of proletarian existence which can be pathetic but which, as in his descriptions of Harlem parties, can equally often be amusing.

In the period which this book covered Hughes never earned more than $22 a week, but he saw much of this country, Mexico and Paris, he entered the literary life of both Harlem and Park Avenue, he was cook in a Paris night club, mess boy on freight ships, laborer in a Washington laundry.

As a poet, who must study his own emotions as the source of his writing, Hughes is never quite free of self-consciousness; as a Negro, even if his family could have been "society" in Kansas had they been less poor, he naturally is never able to escape the implications of his racial handicaps; as an important member of the "Negro Renaissance" of the prosperous Twenties he narrowly escaped the precious. The frankness with which he discusses his own difficulties is one of the most engaging features of his tale.

Edward B. Schriftgiesser
"Outstanding
Biographies"
*Boston Evening
Transcript,* part 5, 28
September 1940, p. 3

Frank Mlakar
"Song in the Face of
Despair"
Common Ground, 1
(Autumn 1940), 98–9

Langston Hughes is among the finest writers the Negro race has produced. He is a sensitive poet, a short-story writer aware

Life is the big sea full of many fish into which Langston Hughes, Negro poet, novelist, and playwright, let down his nets and pulled. And the picture which the book immediately raises is that of a Negro fishing and a white man fishing. The sea is the same for both, the welter of teeming life that is America. Why should the catch be so dissimilar?

It is this circumstance which gives shape to Hughes' life. And tone to his book. It is difficult to describe this tone, which ranges from vague bewilderment to scathing if indirect criticism; but the general impression is one of personal helplessness in the face of his problem, which is also one of America's big problems and whose solution may well release rich human resources.

In Langston Hughes is also the blood of white men, reaching on his mother's side back to Francis Quarles, famous Jacobean poet who wrote *A Feast for Wormes;* on his father's side to a Jewish slave trader in Kentucky and a Scotsman said to be a relative of Henry Clay.

At 21, Hughes went to sea, Africabound. His boyhood had been unhappy, a matter of vague restlessness and encounters with poverty, but tinged with the dream life he had evoked for himself out of books. He was glad, too, to leave behind him his father, a Negro who hated Negroes, who had deserted his family and emigrated to Mexico.

Africa was an education. "When I saw the dust-green hills in the sunlight, something took hold of me inside. My Africa, Motherland of the Negro peoples! And me a Negro!" But the Africans looked at him and would not believe he was one.

Then came Paris, where the tendency was to accept Negroes on a higher level than in America. Later, Hughes was intimate also with that other playground of the 1920s: Harlem, then the magnet for those enlightened whites who had discovered in the Negro the "primitive" which was to vitalize the American scene. Only slightly attached to the real processes of the nation's life, Negro literature and art produced during the so-called "Black Renaissance" existed as in a vacuum. Now and again, when such poets as Hughes raised their voices and decried the anomalous position of the Negro in democratic America, they were shouted down by even the Negroes themselves. An exotic bloom, this Renaissance; the roots had been struck in shallow soil and the plant withered.

The book is rich in portraits of persons prominent in the Negro world: Zora Hurston, James Weldon Johnson, the Spingarns, Alain Locke. There is a warm, human picture of Carl Van Vechten, whose *Nigger Heaven* stirred attention in the late 1920s.

Indeed, Van Vechten and some of the other characters appear more clearly limned than does Hughes himself at times. What he has been doing these last years, besides "making his living from writing," is not mentioned. What problems he has resolved are not described. The spirit of *The Big Sea* comes closest to that of the "I Feel Like a Motherless Child" spiritual. It is not strange that Hughes' best writing has been in his evocative blues poetry, those childlike plaints of a trodden people, whose grasp on life is nonetheless simple and good and real, with room for joy in and acceptance of life. Hughes himself is not childlike in his acceptance, his grasp not so simple; America has touched him too deeply.

The Big Sea is perhaps most valuable as a presentation of the quandary of the Negro intellectual. Where does he fit in? If at times he sounds confused and frustrated, he is not wholly to blame. America has still to recognize him and his talents, to accept and utilize them.

The story of Langston Hughes is a song in the face of despair. That ability to sing is also a gift, and one that will accrue to the advantage of this country.

"The Check List"
American Mercury, 52
(October 1940), 245

This autobiography of a Negro poet, who has been everywhere and has met nearly everybody of the white sophisticated artistic set in New York, London, Paris and Antibes, is honest, good-natured, intelligent and entertaining. There is no book more nostalgically revivifying than Hughes' on the Drunken Decade of the 1920's, with its speakeasies and stock gambling in New York, its Surrealism and American expatriates at the Dome and Rotonde on the debased franc, its Josephine Baker and "eegh leef" in Montmartre, its vogue of primitive African woodcarving in London, its Harlem craze of New York's ermined speakeasy society. Hughes' reflections on Negro snobbery and interracial class and color discrimination dispel much cant of the communists about Negroes. Hughes is a brown Negro who has in him the blood of a Jewish slave trader, named Silas Cushenberry, of a Scotch distiller named Sam Clay and of an English paternal great-grandfather, Captain Charles Quarles of Louisa County, Virginia, who had several colored children by his colored housekeeper. African Negroes refused to accept Hughes as one of them because of his color; and the Negro literati have consistently attacked him and his work. He has found patronage and appreciation almost exclusively among the whites. An historically and socially, as well as humanly, interesting life story.

Henry Lee Moon
"New Books on Our Bookshelf: Mr. Hughes Goes Fishing"
Opportunity, 15 (October 1940), 312

Now approaching 40, Langston Hughes looks back with pardonable nostalgia upon the gay—and not all so gay—days of his twenties which came to an end as the country settled deeper into the Great Depression. Those were the glittering days of the Negro Renaissance when the youthful author, personifying the New Negro, was riding the crest of the popular vogue.

During this period he published two volumes of verse and a novel, and began work on a play. He won literary prizes and acquired a wide circle of friends, attracted as much by his personal charm as by the merit of his works. He attended college and traveled through the South. He drank gin in Harlem and champagne downtown. He had a Park Avenue angel to make life easy for him. And yet in the end, Langston Hughes was unhappy. Unhappy because he could not share his luxurious living with the hungry unemployed who sold apples on street corners and slept in subways. Unhappy because he sanely realized that only the uncertain patronage of an aged and wealthy woman stood between him and the plight of the apple vendors.

Although covering only three decades, it is a full and varied life which Mr. Hughes records in *The Big Sea.* There was poverty, and sometimes hunger, during his childhood years in Kansas and Illinois and his youth in Cleveland. There were bitter, lonely days on his father's ranch in Mexico.

There were the rigors of his seafaring expeditions which took him to the West Indies, to Africa and to Europe, where he remained long enough to master the arts of cooking, table-waiting, and beach-combing. And all the while he was observing and participating in the pageantry of life—its squalor as well as its glamor. He learned early that while wealth enhances the comfort of living, it does not always contribute to the gaiety of life; that laughter, mingled with tears, rings loudly through the black slums of Chicago, Cleveland, Washington and Harlem. Both the laughter and the tears he captured in his poems.

Even during the period when he was sitting uneasily in the lap of luxury, Mr. Hughes was being hailed by left wingers as a proletarian poet. In this review of his life he lays no claim to that role. He wrote about life as he observed it. And because he spent most of his life among working class Negroes, he wrote of them. He was a seaman, a bus boy, a laundry worker. He notes the conditions under which such employees worked and the low wages they received, but fails to mention any organized efforts to better these conditions. Possibly there were no unions at that time in the shops in which he was employed.

There is no attempt in *The Big Sea* to set down an integrated philosophy. Yet from its pages one gleans much of the author's outlook on life. At home, he experienced the perils of slum living. In mixed schools, he learned tolerance. On his jobs, he learned self-reliance. In his travels he saw European imperialism at work robbing the Africans of their labor and produce, and despoiling their women. And though for a while he was the darling of wealthy white faddists, he appears unspoiled and accords no deference to wealth and power and whiteness.

The Big Sea reveals the personality of the man—a charitable spirit, unembittered by experience, gifted with a leavening sense of humor, and sensitive alike to beauty and human suffering. His tolerance embraces all save his father, whose Yankee thrift he never appreciated or understood, and the unidentified Washington "society leaders" whose conventionalism and snobbery bewildered him. Only of these does he speak disparagingly. For all others he has a dispassionate, if not kindly, word.

Mr. Hughes' autobiography is not merely a self-portrait; it is a vivid and valuable record of a period which, though only yesteryear, seems already remote and almost legendary. He recreates Harlem's golden era when only their new-found sophistication restrained the black literati from climbing upon the pews and shouting: "Hallelujah, Freedom's come!" Things were that good to the bohemians, if not to the black masses. The author was in the midst of all this; but, he assures us, even at that time, he perceived the hard core of reality beneath the tinsel Negro vogue.

Like Claude McKay, his fellow poet and novelist, Langston Hughes has written frankly of his life; but there's a genial quality about his candor which contrasts sharply with the mordant and memorable characterizations in Mr. McKay's autobiography, *A Long Way from Home*. Nor does one find in the Hughes work the chaste restraint of *Along This Way*, James Weldon Johnson's life story.

"Literature," Mr. Hughes concludes, "is a big sea full of many fish. I let down my nets and pulled. I'm still pulling." *The Big Sea* is his latest catch. Now in the prime of his life, he may well look forward to the rich rewards of many another fishing season.

C[arter] G. Woodson
"Book Reviews"
Journal of Negro History,
25 (October 1940), 567–8

This work is a real autobiography. It conforms to the requirements of taking the reader into confidence and unbosoming to him one's inner life. This book is Langston Hughes in person as far as he can be portrayed in print. The very title shows the magnitude of his wanderlust. He believed that there were many things in the world which he could enjoy. So he set out early in his career to see the world and to give in brilliant verse his reactions to what he saw. He appropriately closed his narrative with the thought "Literature is a big sea full of many fish. I let down my nets and pulled. I am still pulling."

The narrative pictures Hughes from Kansas to the Central High School in Cleveland and then to Columbia and Lincoln for education, into Mexico with his father, up to New York City, on to Africa, back in the United States, stranded in Paris, down-and-out in Italy, and marking time in Washington. He sees the big sea with a widened horizon. The world began to mean more to the young poet when he dared to place in the hands of Vachel Lindsay three poems while Hughes was serving as a waiter in the Wardman Park Hotel in Washington. Lindsay proclaimed him to the public as a poet of worth and brought Hughes his first worthwhile publicity. He immediately received honorable mention here and there and had many to encourage his literary aspirations. He could soon bring out a book of poems entitled *Weary Blues.* Next appeared *Fine Clothes to the Jew.* Thereafter followed frequently other productions from his pen, welcomes by magazines and publishing houses. *Not Without Laughter,* a novel, was his next important production.

Langston Hughes easily excelled most of the contemporary poets of African blood. He saw in life the same forces and agencies which came under their observation. He experienced deep emotion as they did. He showed the determination to do something about these evils, and wrote poems, novels, and dramas just as they did; but, until the rise of Richard Wright, Hughes was about the only one who visioned the entire race as a mass of suffering humanity represented by the impoverished Negro who had been degraded to upholding lampposts, frequenting gambling dens, and running house parties to pay rent. Hughes's contemporaries in the field of letters have been concerned solely with the humiliation and social proscription suffered by the talented tenth of the race. Hughes, therefore, has tended to become the poet of the Negro race, while others have remained near the level of writers of interesting verse.

Yet Langston Hughes has not drifted toward clownishness as often Dunbar did. Hughes has written about the lowly without portraying them as persecuted saints or as devils incarnate. But in his writings the picture of squalor, poverty, and frustration is there, nevertheless; and it attracts more attention than the tableau left by the inept artist who does not know how to make his work tell its own story. The circulation of this book will secure for the Negro a hearing where the indignant memorialist cannot penetrate.

Booklist, 37 (1 October 1940), 34

A Negro writer describes his struggles to exist during footloose, roving years in Europe, Mexico, Africa, and the United States. Stories and anecdotes of Paris night-club life during the 1920's, of Harlem literati, of snobbish Washington Negro society, of life on a tramp steamer, and of a rich white patroness are told with irony, some criticism, and no bitterness. A few passages will offend conservative readers.

M.P.D.
"Review of *The Big Sea*," *Carmel* [Calif.] *Pine Cone*, 4 October 1940, p. 5

Langston Hughes' latest book, published by Alfred A. Knopf, is the autobiography of a Negro, told without self-consciousness and that defensive emphasis so often found in the literature of that race. It is a story of struggle and adventure, told simply and well, describing the difficulties faced by Negroes in this country in comparison to their more democratic reception in Mexico and France.

But the most impressive element in this book is not the race struggle, rather the battle with life itself—the big sea—fought by a man who could and would do many things to keep alive, but never forgot he wanted to be a writer.

Langston Hughes has led a fabulous life—early years of poverty with his mother, summers in Mexico with his father, who was a prosperous rancher and tried his best to instill in the boy a hate for his own race and a sense of property. Langston Hughes could manage neither, but did achieve a vehement dislike of the man who said: "Engineering is something that will make you some money. What do you want to do, live like a nigger all your life? Look at your mother, waiting table in a restaurant! Don't you want to get anywhere?"

The son did, but not via college in Germany where his father would have sent him. Instead he returned to the States and to the task of earning an education and a living in the gayest spots to be found in the gay twenties—Paris and Harlem. As a bus boy, sailor, cook, taking what came along and writing always, the young Negro drifted toward the recognition he now enjoys. He was often hungry—he admits to having been oppressed by fears which the very poor know so well. But he enjoyed a freedom and experience which might be envied by men who lead monotonous, protected lives.

He met the celebrities of the times, both in France and this country during that period when Harlem had been "discovered" by the great and near great of the white world. And he became a rising young poet in the center of the "Negro renaissance."

He had a patron, an elderly lady of means, who helped him to live that he might write, but who wanted him to write all the time and only what she liked. So there came a great disillusionment to the young man who found that the white lady was not interested in his life at all, only in his writings.

Langston Hughes knew James Weldon Johnson, Dr. Alain Locke, Vachel Lindsay and others. He liked *Nigger Heaven* as he liked Carl Van Vechten, and condemns his race for their objection to that fine book. The reader discovers that Langston Hughes' own books were harshly criticized by Negro reviewers, who felt on the whole that when Negroes wrote of their own people they should write only the beautiful things about them. The hero of *The Big Sea* has too true a pride to adopt such an attitude, and one feels in reading his latest book that he will continue to fish in the sea of literature and life, drawing some amazing fish into his nets.

Richard Wright "Forerunner and Ambassador" *New Republic,* 103 (28 October 1940), 600–1

The double role that Langston Hughes has played in the rise of a realistic literature among the Negro people resembles in one phase the role that Theodore Dreiser played in freeing American literary expression from the restrictions of Puritanism. Not that Negro literature was ever Puritanical, but it was timid and vaguely lyrical and folkish. Hughes's early poems, *The Weary Blues* and *Fine Clothes to the Jew,* full of irony and urban imagery, were greeted by a large section of the Negro reading public with suspicion and shock when they first appeared in the middle twenties. Since then the realistic position assumed by Hughes has become the dominant outlook of all those Negro writers who have something to say.

The other phase of Hughes's role has been, for the lack of a better term, that of a cultural ambassador. Performing his task quietly and almost casually, he has repre-sented the Negroes' case, in his poems, plays, short stories and novels, at the court of world opinion. On the other hand he has brought the experiences of other nations within the orbit of the Negro writer by his translations from the French, Russian and Spanish.

How Hughes became this forerunner and ambassador can best be understood in the cameo sequences of his own life that he gives us in his sixth and latest book, *The Big Sea.* Out of his experiences as a seaman, cook, laundry worker, farm helper, bus boy, doorman, unemployed worker, have come his writings dealing with black gals who wore red stockings and black men who sang the blues all night and slept like rocks all day.

Unlike the sons and daughters of Negro "society," Hughes was not ashamed of those of his race who had to scuffle for their bread. The jerky transitions of his own life did not admit of his remaining in one place long enough to become a slave of prevailing Negro middle-class prejudices. So beneficial does this ceaseless movement seem to Hughes that he has made it one of his life principles: six months in one place, he says, is long enough to make one's life complicated. The result has been a range of artistic interest and expression possessed by no other Negro writer of his time.

Born in Joplin, Missouri, in 1902, Hughes lived in half a dozen Midwestern towns until he entered high school in Cleveland, Ohio, where he began to write poetry. His father, succumbing to that fit of disgust which overtakes so many self-willed Negroes in the face of American restrictions, went off to Mexico to make money and proceeded to treat the Mexicans just as the whites in America had treated him. The father yearned to educate Hughes and establish him in business. His favorite phrase was "hurry up," and it irritated Hughes so much that he fled his father's home.

Later he entered Columbia University, only to find it dull. He got a job in a merchant ship, threw his books into the sea and sailed for Africa. But for all his work, he arrived home with only a monkey and a few dollars, much to his mother's bewilderment. Again he sailed, this time for Rotterdam, where he left the ship and made his way to Paris. After an interval of hunger he found a job as a doorman, then as second cook in a night club, which closed later because of bad business. He went to Italy to visit friends and had his passport stolen. Jobless in an alien land, he became a beachcomber until he found a ship on which he could work his way back to New York.

The poems he had written off and on had attracted the attention of some of his relatives in Washington and, at their invitation, he went to live with them. What Hughes has to say about Negro "society" in Washington, relatives and hunger are bitter poems in themselves. While living in Washington, he won his first poetry prize; shortly afterwards Carl Van Vechten submitted a batch of his poems to a publisher.

The rest of *The Big Sea* is literary history, most of it dealing with the Negro renaissance, that astonishing period of prolific productivity among Negro artists that coincided with America's "golden age" of prosperity. Hughes writes of it with humor, urbanity and objectivity; one has the feeling that never for a moment was his sense of solidarity with those who had known hunger shaken by it. Even when a Park Avenue patron was having him driven about the streets of New York in her town car, he "felt bad because he could not share his new-found comfort with his mother and relatives." When the bubble burst in 1929, Hughes returned to the mood that seems to fit him best. He

wrote of the opening of the Waldorf-Astoria:

> Now, won't that be charming when the last flophouse has turned you down this winter?

Hughes is tough; he bends but he never breaks, and he has carried on a manly tradition in literary expression when many of his fellow writers have gone to sleep at their posts.

Theophilus Lewis
"Adventurous Life"
Crisis, 47 (December 1940), 395–6

One contemplates an autobiography by Langston Hughes with a deal of misgiving. Hughes certainly looms large enough in Negro literature, perhaps in American literature too, to rate a biography, especially if he should be tragically removed from among the living as his career approaches midstream. Autobiography is a different matter. It is usually undertaken when an author has grown venerable in years and rich in experience, and implies that he can look backward upon his life with satisfaction. Autobiography usually indicates the waning of an author's creative powers too, a decline of his sense of objectivity and a turning inward of the spirit. There are notable exceptions, of course, and let us hope this book is one of them.

To observe that the book is interesting is hardly to praise it. Most autobiographies are interesting, for the simple reason that every man is interesting, to the limit of his capacity, when he is talking about something important; and every man thinks his own life is important. In *The Big Sea*, however, the interest is not derived solely from the subjective ardor of a man talking about himself. The narrative is crowded with experiences and incidents, and a few adventures, which make enjoyable if not exciting reading, aside from whatever influence they may have exerted upon the author's life.

After his childhood, which was no more eventful than that of most any alert, intelligent boy, Hughes began to go places and see things. He began his venture over the horizon with an arresting if not a significant gesture. All during his school days, followed by one year in Columbia University, he had been an avid reader. When he obtained a job as mess boy on a tramp steamer bound for Africa he carried a trunk full of books aboard with him. Suddenly, he decided that he had seen enough of life filtered through other men's minds and embalmed in their books. Now, he wanted to meet life at first hand, and nothing but life, with no comment or interpretation but that of his own mind. As the ship steamed past Sandy Hook, he carried his books, all of them, to the deck and threw them into the sea.

He saw quite a lot of life before he began to read again. He saw his ship mates luxuriating in the wine shops and bordellos of the Azores and the coast towns of Africa; he almost starved in the artists' quarter of Paris; he roved the waterfront of Genoa with a band of beachcombers; he was sickened by the unleashed lusts of sex-hungry sailors; he was amused by hilarious free-for-all fist fights and alcoholic orgies the like of which are seldom seen on land or sea this side of Valhalla; he experienced brief but felicitous friendships and interludes of lyrical love. He saw many of the great museums, libraries and cathedrals of Europe and rubbed hams with numerous minor celebrities. He lived precariously in the flesh but expansively in the spirit, and altogether had a grand and glorious time during his days of hunger and adventure on the far side of the Atlantic.

If he came in contact with any of the really great men and women at the time, outstanding statesmen, leading journalists or famous artists or writers, he does not mention them. His narrative refers only to the near great, the shabby and the picaresque. Hughes would probably comment that social mavericks were precisely the people he wanted to meet and observe, for it is among them that life is most lush and interesting; and he wanted to know life.

Back home in America, he circulated among the best of his own race, the second best of the white world, an order of social fauna definitely superior to his associates in the Latin Quarter of Paris. But home or abroad, in Paris or on Park avenue, he kept the common touch. If he gained anything from his travels and experiences, it was the ability to rate men according to their personal worth rather than by their station or possessions. It is probable that he has always had that talent.

Hughes refers to his literary achievements rather modestly, devoting most of his attention to his poetry. The reader gets the impression that he considers his verse more important than his prose. If that inference is correct, one might be inclined to quarrel with him. More than any other poet, Hughes caught and expressed the dominant note of his generation of Aframericans—a chord of mingled insouciance and revolt. But most of his poems reflect the spirit of the years in which they were written and have already begun to date. His prose may have a more enduring quality. *The Weary Blues,* written to the tempo of the jazz age, may be unintelligible to post–jazz age readers. *Not Without Laughter* may not be a great novel, but it is an interesting novel; and it will remain interesting as long as discriminating readers enjoy competent portrayal of the wistfulness and poignancy which are constant factors of life. Most of the tales in *The Ways of White Folks* will elude the antiquarian many a year, and two or three of them are among the finest short stories this reviewer has encountered in American fiction.

The Big Sea is a valuable addition to Hughes' growing volume of prose. He writes with enthusiasm and candor, and the latter quality gives the narrative the assurance of permanence. It will always be useful to future scholars searching for sidelights on the history of Negro literature.

Lucy F. de Angulo "Life of Adventure and Keen Observation, by Negro Author: Contribution to Study of Race Problem" *Oakland Tribune,* 29 December 1940, p. 6B

The author of *Not Without Laughter* and *The Ways of White Folks* has written an autobiography that makes excellent reading from beginning to end. One, too, that is of interest in a number of different ways.

In 1925, Carl Van Vechten in his introduction to *The Weary Blues,* spoke of Langston Hughes' experiences as being fit material for a picturesque [*sic*] romance. And from one point of view *The Big Sea* is exactly that.

For it is, on the surface, a tale of astonishingly varied adventures that lead to many parts of the world, and that are associated with an amazing variety of jobs, and ways of life filling in between jobs. It contains stories, spirited and sometimes rowdy, of adventures with sailors in seaports or on board ship when the author was messboy on the S.S. Malone; adventures as a beachcomber in Genoa; as doorman in a cafe in Montmartre; as a young writer in Harlem in the hectic 20's, when Negro art was the rage, parties the rule, and the Harlem night clubs so full of white sight-seers that local residents (those who were not entertainers or social lions) had to crowd their fun into their own apartments.

All the episodes are full of vitality, and some are irresistibly funny. Some have great beauty. Word portraits of picturesque individuals persist in one's memory, often complete in a sentence, like that of A'Lelia Walker the cosmetics heiress of Harlem, "a gorgeous dark Amazon in a silver turban," or that of the Rumanian girl in Paris (who might have stepped out of the pages of *Mademoiselle de Maupin*), "with large green paint on her eyes, who often came to the club in a white riding habit, white boots and hat, carrying a black whip."

However, *The Big Sea* is never merely amusing or picturesque. It is essentially a record of events, circumstances, relationships that have gone to make up an unusual life, and that have contributed to the development of an artist of distinction.

[. . .]

Readers who are familiar with other works of Langston Hughes will find special enjoyment in the parts of *The Big Sea* in which he tells of his awakening interest in literature, and how he himself began to write. How he was first introduced to the work of Carl Sandburg by one of his teachers, and began to write poems in the same vein; how his enjoyment of French literature commenced with the reading of de Maupassant in school, and how he then first began to want to write, and, as he says, "write stories about Negroes, so true that people in faraway lands would read them—even after I was dead." How "The Negro Speaks of Rivers" was written on a train on the way to Mexico to join his father, and (like most of his poetry) while he was "feeling very bad." And how *Not Without Laughter* was written while he was still in college, in an empty dormitory during vacation, and how people and circumstances of his childhood were translated and made more universal to build up the tale of Annjee and Jimboy, Harriett and Aunt Hager.

Mr. Hughes is not a propagandist, nor a sociologist. But he is an intelligent and deeply interested observer of social relations. He has watched and lived among groups of people of many kinds, both Negro and white. The Negro groups he writes of differ widely in type and in locale since he has known them in the South, in the mid-Western towns, and in city "black belts"; the poor, and also the well-to-do; scholars, writers, college men, and the uneducated. He is familiar with all the problems of adjustment that confront his people, both in relation to the white population and among themselves. He writes of these matters, sometimes with irony, but always with fairness, and with insight rather than bitterness. So that quite apart from literary values, this autobiography has importance as a book of source material, and should not be ignored by anyone who is interested in the sociology or psychology of racial minorities anywhere, and especially of the Negro in the United States.

The Big Sea is written throughout in a very simple style. Equally simple, whether it is a matter of how good wild strawberries can taste in Paris in the spring, or of sordid brutality in an African seaport. This simplicity of telling is arresting—at times almost appalling—in relation to the nature and the implications of what is told. To this contrast, perhaps more than to anything else, *The Big Sea* owes its odd quality

of seeming to be written in two moods— one that is explicit and another that follows through like an undercurrent.

Henrietta L. Herod
"The Big Sea"
Phylon, 2 (First Quarter 1941), 94–6

Having been acclaimed a noteworthy poet and having experimented with drama and fiction, Langston Hughes, at what may seem a too early age, has written his autobiography, *The Big Sea*. Here we find him satisfying many of the demands we make when a man writes of himself. We find him in the main recognizing the hard facts of existence and sharing them with the rest of mankind. Although we are not always able to deduce a point of view from which the whole of life appears endowed with an inner glow, he does reveal himself as serving his apprenticeship to literature—in Mexico, in Africa, in Europe, and in New York, living fully, often sensitively, and emerging the extraordinary person much of his writing has shown him to be. *The Big Sea* is, then, a forthright, objective autobiography of Langston Hughes who has made up his mind "to continue being a writer" and who, until he went to Lincoln University, "worked at other things; teaching English in Mexico, truck gardening on Staten Island, a seaman, a doorman, a cook, a waiter in Paris night clubs or hotels and restaurants, a clerk at the Association for the Study of Negro Life and History, a bus boy at Wardman Park in Washington."

In the early chapters of the book Mr. Hughes gives us an account of his ancestry. He writes of a grandfather who had followed John Brown at Harper's Ferry and of a grandmother of Negro, French, and Indian descent who "worked out her purchase." He tells of his mother who was poor, mortgage-haunted, enjoying plays and books whenever she might; of his father who was primarily interested in making money, who hated Negroes, and who had little understanding of his son who wanted to become a poet and write of himself and of the people he knew.

With the people he knew and the places in which he found them is the book chiefly concerned. Both people and places challenge his curiosity, evoke his powers of close observation, and stimulate his writing. With vivid memories from childhood, he writes best of these early years. Then follows a running account, of a diary sort, comprised of some striking adventures and unusual scenes—in Cleveland, in Toluca, in New York City, at Columbia University, or aboard an old vessel in the Hudson River as he struggled for an education and for success as a writer. Always he was avid for experience, and always there was his remarkable zest for living.

It was certainly not a true vocation which took Mr. Hughes to sea. Although there are passages which suggest that the sailor's life had trained his senses to a richness of perception as when he pictures the ocean as terrible with storm in African waters, the sea for him is not the great school of human character and conduct many writers have found it to be. One is disappointed that Mr. Hughes was no freer to respond to the imaginative appeal of the sea. Rarely in evoking elemental aspects are his sense perceptions acute. He writes of heat, "African weather was no hotter than a Chicago summer"; of the moonlight, "In the clearing, great mango trees cast purple shadows across the path, there was no wind. Only the moon."

It was after a trip from New York to Rotterdam that he found his way to Paris. Here were new and often fantastic experiences and extraordinary people ranging from Florence Palmer and Bricktop to Dr. Alain Locke. Many of the incidents he records as happening in Paris and later in Italy would better have deserved short story treatment, since in his autobiography Mr. Hughes has evaluated few of them. Paris made no rich impression on him; the wonder of the place eluded him. He does not body forth the essence of life there, and we miss the feeling of place; scene is rarely surrounded and blended with the action of which he writes.

Back again in America and after an uninspiring interlude in Washington, it was Vachel Lindsay who "discovered a Negro bus-boy poet" and confirmed Mr. Hughes' ambition to write poetry as a valid one, giving him some of the soundest advice a young writer, ambitious in the 1920's, might have followed. Mr. Hughes was later graduated from Lincoln University and returned to New York. The period of the Black Renaissance found Mr. Hughes doing much of his best writing, meeting a friendlier world, and discovering intellectual companionship. Of this period Mr. Hughes writes often with illuminating understanding and considerable force. These were the years of excessive popularity of the Negro on the stage, in art, and in literature—the years of the "whites" in Harlem—the years of the often publicized parties of Carl Van Vechten and A'Lelia Walker—the years of Mr. Hughes' acquaintance with some of the better known writers: W. E. B. Du Bois, James Weldon Johnson, Charles S. Johnson—the years of promise for a less well-known group: Wallace Thurman, Jessie Fauset, and Zora Hurston. These were also the years which saw Mr. Hughes experimenting with various forms of writing—poetry, the drama, fiction. Although some of his best known pieces such as "I've Known Rivers" came at a much earlier period, the 1920's brought *Fine Clothes to the Jew, Mulatto,* and *Not Without Laughter* as well as the Harmon award for distinguished writing. These were the years of the author's patronage from a generous lady whose identity he conceals, the years when he found he could not become "primitive"; for says he, "I did not feel the rhythms of the primitive surging through me and so I could not live and write as though I did. I was only an American Negro—who had loved the surface of Africa and the rhythms of Africa—but I was not Africa. I was Chicago and Kansas City and Broadway and Harlem."

The Big Sea is not a great book. Mr. Hughes has written amusingly sometimes, often vividly, and always, one feels, sincerely. In it he has been frank and intellectually honest, writing without reticence and yet with reserve. He seems to have understood the ephemeral nature of the vogue for the Negro in art forms and himself to have been aware always of his being an American Negro. However, it must be said that in spots the book is pedestrian and thin both as to content and style and gives greater emphasis to incident and situation than seems justifiable. Too often it is undistinguished writing. Never is it propaganda. It has not the wit or wisdom of Hans Zinsser's *As I Remember Him* or the richness and charm of J. B. Priestley's *Midnight on the Desert*. There is, however, much of the *gemuetlichkeit* of American background which one finds in James Weldon Johnson's *Autobiography of an Ex-Coloured Man;* and there is good reason for declaring that the book ought to have been written. It does help us know better Langston Hughes, poet preeminently, and writer of promise—sensitive, sincere, fully acquainted with the life about which he writes.

Alain Locke
"Of Native Sons: Real and Otherwise"
Opportunity, 19 (January 1941), 4–9

[. . .]

Our year's fiction is so factual that one turns to the biography with a positive thirst for adventure. Langston Hughes provides it—perhaps too much of it—in his biographic memoir, *The Big Sea*. Too much by way of contrast, certainly, for the broad areas of his life's wide wanderings— Europe, Africa and America from east to west coast—are not plumbed to any depth of analysis or understanding, with the possible exception of Washington society. If, as in this case, righteous anger is the mainspring of an interest in social analysis with Langston Hughes, one wishes that more of life had irked him. For time and again important things are glossed over in anecdotal fashion, entertainingly but superficially, without giving us any clear idea as to what a really important participant in the events of the last two decades thinks about the issues and trends of his generation and the Negro's relationship to them. Occasional hints of attitudes on such matters argue for an awareness of their existence, and seem to call for a more penetrating analysis even if it should sober down the irresponsible charm of the present narrative.

[. . .]

Edwin R. Embree
"A Poet's Story"
Survey Graphic, 30
(February 1941), 96

Here is a grand tale. It is no great epic of literature, and it is not intended to be. It is an adventure story—the adventures of a bubbling American boy from the plains of Kansas who sailed the seas, saw Africa, roamed happily over the face of Europe, hit Harlem at the height of its "discovery" by the literati and the thrill hunters, led a rather forlorn existence among the highbrows of Washington's colored society, and finally decided to give free rein to his talent for writing.

In many ways this autobiography is the tale of a typical Peck's "Bad Boy" of modern America. Although this is the story of a colored American, there is little searching of soul on questions of caste and class. This rambunctious youth runs up against rude bumps because the sun tanned the skin of his forefathers. But these bumps are taken with much the same bounce that other American boys would show in running into other but also painful bruises.

The peculiar flavor of this book is not that the boy was a Negro, but that he was a poet. Every few chapters the rollicking tale is lifted by sudden poetic inspiration; it is often illumined by quotations from poems written by the author in the midst of the experiences he is recounting.

This is the story of a poet, but not of a highbrow. Over and over again the young hero turns his back on respectable occupations to sail as a mess boy on a freighter, to live from hand to mouth in Paris, to go hungry in Harlem.

Young Hughes' first revolt was against the hoarding and commercial climbing of his father who was a very successful business man in Mexico. In Washington, Hughes embarrassed his highbrow fellows by throwing up a white collar job in a publishing house and turning his hand to less confining but far from dignified tasks in laundries and eating houses. Colored society wanted no traffic with a lowly washer boy, yet it longed for the reflected glory of association with one of America's leading poets. In one of the poignant incidents of the book the young poet, as a bus boy in a Washington restaurant, sees a boyhood idol, Vachel Lindsay, and shyly places some of his poems on the great man's table. But when the newspapers play up Lindsay's discovery of a bus boy poet, Hughes flees the restaurant to avoid the gaping crowds.

The story is packed with adventure, some of it gayly purple, much of it dealing with personages both Negro and white with whom the author came into odd and interesting contact. It is written in beautiful English and is a fine tale.

C.E.R.
"Book Reviews"
Liberator, 4 (May 1964), 22

The Big Sea, which is the autobiography of the Poet Laureate of Harlem, moves with the gentility of a lazy cloud floating across a clear blue sky. Yet, this gentility which perhaps is the touch of the poet, obscures the reader from any real insight into the entrails of Langston Hughes the man. Mr. Hughes tells us about himself but not of his self.

The book is written in the characteristic Hughes style, simple and lucid, but there is a certain "something" lacking. It is as if the author restrains from revealing himself. Yes, what is absent is that special quality that makes Mr. Hughes different from any other Negro writer.

What, to me, is most disturbing is that although Mr. Hughes is perhaps one of the few contemporary Negro writers who knows Harlem as if he had assisted the midwife in giving birth to this child of darkness, a man who has lived most his life on this island of forgotten people, he is not able to communicate his "negroness." It is as if he is saying to "make it" in this white man's world one has to sacrifice one's blackness.

[. . .]

I would further submit that the real Mr. Hughes, with his humor, incisive irony, peering into the "guts" of America, is the real Hughes that flows through the worldly wisdom of Jesse B. Semple and not the acculturated American who drifts through the pages of *The Big Sea*. At least, I hope not. And even good old Semple has been left behind by the present struggle.

Perhaps I may seem too critical of Mr. Hughes; if so, it is only because I sincerely feel that as a writer, Mr. Hughes is superb, and his autobiography was beautifully written, but he told us nothing of himself; thus, giving us no greater insight into the man when we closed the book.

Checklist of Additional Reviews

"A Few of the Newer Books: Interesting People," *Open Shelf*, July–August–September 1940, p. 14.

Clifton Fadiman, "Briefly Noted," *New Yorker*, 16 (31 August 1940), 46.

Ralph Thompson, "Books of the Times," *New York Times*, 3 September 1940, p. L15.

Richard Wright, "As Richard Wright Sees Autobiographies of Langston Hughes and W. E. B. Du Bois," *Chicago Daily News*, 4 December 1940, p. 40.

Philip A. Adler, "Poet Writes Story of Life: Hughes Tells How He Reached Top," *Detroit News*, sports section, 16 February 1941, p. 24.

J.P., "Books: Langston Hughes: Poet and Prophet," *People's World*, 5 October 1963, p. 7.

"Books Noted," *Negro Digest*, 13 (November 1963), 93.

Michael Sean O'Shea, "The Sardi Set: All Hail Hill and Wang," *Back Stage*, 5 (21 February 1964), 2, 11.

"Focus on: Negro History," *Bibliographic Survey: The Negro in Print*, 2 (January 1967), 7.

"Humanizing History: Books," *Booklist*, 82 (1 March 1986), 974.

Alex Raskin, "Now in Paperback," *Los Angeles Times Book Review*, 1 June 1986, p. 14.

"Paperbacks: New and Noteworthy," *New York Times Book Review*, 15 June 1986, p. 34; merely quotes Katherine Woods's 25 Aug. 1940 review.

Charles Guenther, "Black Masses Main Poetic Man," *St. Louis Post-Dispatch*, 27 July 1986, p. 4B.

"New in Paperback: Nonfiction," *Washington Post Book World*, 3 August 1986, p. 12.

Julie Parson, "Reviews: Non-fiction," *New Pages*, 11 (Fall 1986), 16.

Paula Giddings, "Books," *Essence*, 17 (October 1986), 28.

SHAKESPEARE IN HARLEM

Leonard Rowe
"Turning the Pages"
Cincinnati Times-Star,
25 February 1942, p. 14

Langston Hughes, often called the Negro poet laureate, has a new collection of poems, his first since 1932; some 60 pieces, of which one "Shakespeare in Harlem," gives the book its title. These poems are direct and forthright and intelligible; hence a great relief after my trying (in vain) to understand the surrealistic profundities and rhetorical conundrums of many so-called modern poets. Another thing I like about these Harlem poems is their frank concern with the things and people and events of urban Negro life: My most diligent searches fail to unearth a single elegy to a dead epic poet, a single ode to a nightingale or a single apostrophe to the cosmic soul. And, finally, Mr. Hughes employs the vernacular of Lenox Avenue and Twenty-fifth Street—not the putative elegant diction of Oxford and Cambridge.

The best way to get the Aframerican flavor of these poems is to open the book at random and read a stanza here and there, such as the following excerpts:

From "Cabaret Girl Dies on Welfare Island":

I hate to die this way with the quiet
Over everything like a shroud.
I'd rather die where the band's a-
    playin'
Noisy and loud.

Rather die the way I lived—
Drunk and rowdy and gay!
God! Why did you ever curse me
Makin' me die this way?

From "Down and Out"

De credit man's done took ma clothes
And rent time's most nigh here.
Credit man's done took ma clothes
Rent time's nearly here.
I'd like to buy a straightenin' comb,
And needs a dime fo' beer.

"Merry-Go-Round"

    Colored Child at Carnival.
Where is the Jim Crow section
On this merry-go-round,
Mister, 'cause I want to ride?
Down South where I come from
White and colored
Can't sit side by side.
Down South on the train
There's a Jim Crow car.
On the bus we're put in the back—
But there ain't no back
To a merry-go-round!
Where's the horse
For a kid that's black?

In one important respect the above three quotations are typical: the dominant mood of the poems is plaintive and melancholy: they are the stuff of which "blues" are made.

"Langston Hughes Puts Harlem Mood in Verse"
Springfield [Mass.] *Union and Republican,* 1 March 1942, p. 7E

A new volume of poetry by Langston Hughes is rare enough to be awaited with eager anticipation. *Shakespeare in Harlem* bears the stamp of strong personality which one expects of Mr. Hughes, and at the same time evidences growth in power and sensitivity. The book is small in the hand and each poem is brief, colloquial and hard-packed. The poet mastered his technique long ago and, being master, is free to use it as the easy medium of his mood. This ease makes the mood contagious, quick to grasp and share. It is this fluidity of expression which makes the individual's experience universal, so that others than Harlem dwellers say, "That's it. I know that, too."

Yes, this is racial poetry. Peculiarly racial in its swift transition from the bitter despair of the blues to the carefree joy of "Me and My Mule," with its undertone of defeat nagging at the reader's heart. It is racial poetry that belongs to a special group of Negroes, one suspects. It belongs to the Northern Negro without opportunity or hope of opportunity who has neither a past nor a future to fortify and stabilize the present. He loves, hates, works and plays when he can, and when he cannot he makes songs to remember what was briefly his.

The poems are no more profound than his days and nights; they are the spontaneous overflow of emotion, slight or intense. Mr. Hughes has a sympathetic ear and a voice which is faithful echo to this special section of his people. Here is the poet, speaking for Harlem in recognizable accents:—

"DECLARATION"

If I was a sea lion
Swimming in the sea
I would swim to China
And you would never see me.
No!
You never would
See me.

If I was a rich boy
I'd buy myself a car,
Fill it up with gas

And drive so far, so far.
Yes!
I would drive
So far.

Hard-hearted and unloving!
Hard-hearted and untrue!
If I was a bird I'd
Fly away from you.
Yes, way
Away
From
You.

"Negro Voices"
Newsweek, 19 (9 March 1942), 59

Blues and ballads to be "crooned, shouted, recited, and sung"—thus Langston Hughes describes *Shakespeare in Harlem*, his first book of verse since 1932. And certainly nobody would want to read silently—for instance—the ballad of Arabella Johnson who shot bold Bessie in a Harlem cabaret. Or the lament of the widow woman:

I say don't want nobody else
And don't nobody else want me—
Yet you never can tell when a
Woman like me is free!

. . . Now 40, Hughes has long been a leader of the new Negro movement and is recognized as the Negroes' most versatile writer. . . .

"The Bookworm"
San Francisco Call-Bulletin, 14 March 1942, [p. 12]; also in *Lawrence* [Mass.] *Eagle,* 21 March 1942

[. . .]

The Negro in Verse: Langston Hughes is the Negro's poet laureate. So his new book, *Shakespeare in Harlem,* is aptly described as "a book of light verse. Afro-Americana in the blues mood; poems syncopated and variegated in the colors of Harlem, Beale Street, West Dallas, and Chicago's South Side." Some are bitter, some are heartbreaking, some have the golden laughter of the Negro in them . . . Paint-chipper, dishwasher, beachcomber, Langston Hughes is an honest poet. No white man imitating the Negro spirit could approach the spirit of this book.

[. . .]

L.M.J.
"Books"
Virginia Statesman, 14 (14 March 1942), 2

There is a distinct difference in Langston Hughes' newest book, *Shakespeare in Harlem* in comparison to his last publication, *Weary Blues* back in 1932 [*sic*]. *Shakespeare in Harlem* has a sense of definiteness and maturity about it that was not present before and is easily expected since this was ten years ago, and Mr.

Hughes has probably found and grounded himself permanently in this time.

However, there is one thing present as in all of his verse—the steady beat of the Negro way of life. He brings out their emotions of love, labor, sorrow and gladness. He knows and loves his race because he has lived and worked with them so closely; and for the same reason he might be acclaimed Negro Poet Laureate by his people who know and love his works, the country over.

Shakespeare in Harlem is a book of light verse, Afro-American in mood, containing a sequence of poems on love, Harlem in New York, mammy songs and several groups of blues.

Those who have read his works before will appreciate its definiteness; those just becoming acquainted with the Hughes style will welcome a black writer akin to Sandburg.

Henry A. Lappin
"Concerning M. Proust, Van Doren Has a Doubt"
Buffalo Evening News Magazine, 14 March 1942, p. 9

Of Langston Hughes' oddly-entitled book of verse, *Shakespeare in Harlem,* there is little to say. He continues here the vein of his 1926 volume, *The Weary Blues,* and amplifies it. To one reader, however, the publisher's claim that this book is "more profound, more incisive and more mature" than the earlier volume, seems scarcely justified.

But no doubt some of the verses are touching: "Share-croppers," for example, and in the section called "Blue for Ladies," strong and astringent. We like Langston Hughes better when he writes prose.

Beatrice M. Murphy
"The Book Worm"
Baltimore Afro-American, 14 March 1942, p. 7

Mr. Hughes's first volume of poems in ten years—which was postponed many times from its announced publication date last summer—was certainly worth waiting for.

Thumbing through the pages, one is convinced anew of the poet's universal appeal. Without a doubt, Langston Hughes is the poet of his people. He caters to the tastes and intellects of high and low, literate and illiterate alike. He interprets their desires, their secret ambitions, loves and disappointments, their heart-breaks and their joys.

What intellect could not appreciate his portrait of a "Young Negro Girl," whom he describes as:

> . . . like a warm dark dusk
> In the middle of June time
> When the first violets
> Have almost forgotten their names
> And the deep red roses bloom.

And even the most humble of us could understand the child who asks "where is the jim crow section of this merry-go-round?"

His "Seven Moments of Love" are both profound and simple—as is life.

The drawings by E. McKnight Kauffer are striking, to say the least.

Mary M. Colum
"The New Books of Poetry"
New York Times Book Review, 22 March 1942, p. 9

[. . .]

Langston Hughes's *Shakespeare in Harlem* makes a text on which, if one had space, one could talk on the value of having a range in language. Langston Hughes's range is very bounded, and consequently many of his poems are monotonous. He has strong emotions; he has a form and vocabulary of his own, both familiar to us from the singers of the blues and the spirituals, but neither his imagination nor his intelligence comes anywhere near the strength of his emotions. We agree with Count Keyserling that great art is bound to come out of the Negro; some has come already, but it looks at the moment as if the richest Negro minds had not gone into literature. There is nothing, for instance, in Negro poetry that corresponds to the power and imagination of Augusta Savage's sculpture. Nevertheless, there are memorable pieces in *Shakespeare in Harlem,* and though it may be only the expression of one type of Negro, the Harlem Negro, yet it does give an insight into the African mind, and anything that gives the European stock an insight into the mind of Asiatics and Africans is bound to shake our complacence. The Europeans seem to be the only branch of the human race who ever believed much in the joy of life or went in much for the praise of life. The Negro of *Shakespeare in Harlem* is immensely sad, even hopeless. As a relief from the forlornness he rushes headlong into some activity—love, dancing, banging a musical instrument, or fighting, gambling. The most impressive poems are in the section, "Death in Harlem." This is from "Crossing":

> It was that lonely day, folks,
> When I walked all by myself.
> [. . .]
> Then I stood out on a prairie
> And, as far as I could see,
> Wasn't anybody on the prairie
> That looked like me.
> [. . .]

August Derleth
"The New Books: New Poetry"
Capital Times [Madison, Wisc.], 22 March 1942, p. 16

Long ago Carl Van Vechten hailed Hughes as "the Negro Poet Laureate," saying of his verse that it "resounds with the exultant throb of Negro pain and gladness." That description might well fit the present collection of poems, his first in ten years. Hughes writes that this is "A book of light verse. Afro-Americana in the blues mood. Poems syncopated and variegated in the colors of Harlem, Beale Street, West Dallas, and Chicago's South Side." Hughes has not overstated.

Reading these poems—they read with remarkable ease—I found, as a blues-devotee myself, that the lines seemed almost to carry their own music with them. Consider these lines, for example:

> Did you ever try livin'
> On two-bits minus two?
> I say did you ever try livin'

> On two-bits minus two?
> Why don't you try it, folks,
> And see what it would do to you?

The poems in *Shakespeare in Harlem* are only superficially light in tone, however. They are, it seems to me, as exciting and important as anything Langston Hughes has written; despite the infectious blues note so marked throughout this volume, the poems are very often profound and incisive. Moreover, Knopf have done a beautiful format for the book, colorful in the Negro sense, with drawings by E. McKnight Kauffer to illustrate it.

"Children's Page: Book of the Month"
Negro History Bulletin, 5 (April 1942), 157

Shakespeare in Harlem by Langston Hughes . . . is a volume worthy of notice. This is a book of poetry which follows the usual trend of the author, who is regarded by many as the Negro "Poet Laureate." His poems are apparently in a humorous vein, but at the same time they show the deepest thought as to the serious condition of the Negro. In this way Hughes tries to interpret the feeling of his persecuted people. The medium which the poet has chosen as the expression of this thought is the blues. To him all the world is sad and dreary everywhere he roams, and still he can laugh in the hope for a brighter day.

These poems are very simple—in words which are familiar to most children. Yet children may fail to reach the depth of the thought which these words convey. In the hands of alert teachers who desire to clarify the Negro child's understanding of his present position in this country, this work will be a valuable asset in the teaching of realistic literature. These poems tell the truth without arousing any feeling of bitterness which we sometimes find in inflammatory verse.

These poems, moreover, cover a wide range. They deal with situations in all stages of struggle where Negroes contend with the problems of life. The picture, therefore, is national although sectional. For this broad point of view and thorough grasp of things as they exist today, Langston Hughes deserves credit.

C[arter] G. Woodson
"Book Reviews"
Journal of Negro History,
27 (April 1942), 236–7

This is a slender book of poems by the distinguished Negro poet, the first collection of verse to come from his pen since 1932. These productions show more maturity than the poet's earlier creations, but it is doubtful that they have added much to his nationwide reputation for interpreting the lowly of the Negro race as reflected in the life of the unfortunately congested urban centers. The public will welcome this new thought from the author of *The Weary Blues, The Dream Keeper, The Ways of White Folks* and *The Big Sea.*

In these poems appears the same theme which runs through the other works of the author. He is decidedly in the realm of the blues. These ballads and reels are "to be read aloud, crooned, shouted, recited, and sung. Some with gestures, some not—as you like. None with a far-away voice." Here we learn of "Seven Moments of Love," "Declarations," "Blues for Men,"

"Blues for Ladies," "Death in Harlem," "Mammy Songs," and "Lenox Avenue." The book is appropriately illustrated with drawings by E. McKnight Kauffer.

On the surface this book of poems does not seem to have any historical significance; and, considered in its special sphere, the collection does not interest some ambitious Negroes and those of the other race long assisting in the elevation of Negroes. It must be conceded, moreover, that the Harlem tradition has been overemphasized. That peculiar settlement, although typical of frustrated Negroes in some other large cities of the country, is not typical of the majority of the race in the United States.

There is, however, another side which is usually ignored by those who would turn away from Harlem and vision the Negro as an essential element of our population. These poems review the history of the Negro, account for his present status, summarize his grievances and appeal for justice and equality. In verse the case of the Negro is thus brought before an audience which sociological and historical treatises would never reach. Langston Hughes, therefore, in addition to being a poet is a soldier for human rights.

Wilma Cook
"Book Review"
Carmel [Calif.] *Pine Cone,*
10 April 1942, p. 2

Carl Van Vechten has called him the poet laureate of the Negro. In the first seven poems of his new volume, *Shakespeare in Harlem,* Langston Hughes is any man's poet laureate. He tells the story of a man whose wife has left him. He tells it with simplicity, power and humor, and with a complete understanding of the average man's emotional reactions.

The group is called "Seven Moments of Love." The poems take anyman through seven emotional crises that arise when he has to face the ordinary events of his life without the woman he is accustomed to have at his side to share them. The events, and also the titles of the poems: Twilight Reverie, Supper Time, Bed Time, Daybreak, Sunday, Pay Day and Letter.

The next group of fourteen—"Declarations"—is light, some of them almost flimsy. The "Death in Harlem" group is stronger, reminiscent of our realistic playwrights, specifically Eugene O'Neill in his middle period. "Mammy Songs" group takes us down south and sings the story of race prejudice and Negro suffering. Two other collections, "Ballads" and "Blues for Ladies," bring us back to Harlem and tell of men who have loved worthless women and women who have loved worthless men, until the reader wonders if the dwellers of Harlem ever achieve a happy mating.

The poet finally pays tribute to love in the last poem of the book, the finish of the "Lenox Avenue" octet, in which he calls it a wild wonder—stars that sing—a spark dying in the dark.

Shakespeare in Harlem should succeed with a larger audience than is usually attracted to poetry. Hughes' subject is people, an eternally popular subject, and he knows his subject thoroughly. He presents it with simplicity, freshness and color warmed with an undercurrent of amusement that is the outgrowth of his understanding of the vagaries of human beings.

Pearl Strachan
"The World of Poetry"
Christian Science Monitor, weekly magazine, 11 April 1942, p. 11

A kind of savage humor, vital and important, distinguishes the best of the folk poetry of the United States. One finds it in Sandburg. One finds it to a marked degree in the work of another American poet, a Negro, Langston Hughes, whose *Shakespeare in Harlem* is just out. Here the problems are not only those such as the steel worker and prairie farmer encounter, but those of the toiler also burdened with public conceptions of race. The Afric-American blues rhythms make a perfect accompaniment for what the poet has to say. He says a good deal, too, says it with a laugh; and the thing that hurts is in the laughter. This is a work of genuine talent and skillful artistry. What is not voiced is what gives it most power, as in the poem entitled "Supper Time," which goes:

> I look in the kettle, the kettle is dry.
> Look in the bread box, nothing but a fly.
> Turn on the light and look real good!
> I would make a fire but there ain't no wood.
> Look at that water dripping in the sink.
> Listen to my heartbeats trying to think.
> Listen at my footprints walking on the floor.
> That place where your trunk was, ain't no trunk no more.
> Place where your clothes hung's empty and bare.

Stay away if you want to, and see if I
care!
If I had a fire I'd make me some tea
And set down and drink it, myself and
me.

Frank Marshall Davis
"The Browsing Reader"
Kansas City Call, 17 April 1942, p. 22; also as "Book Review," in *Chicago Bee,* 5 April 1942

After authoring volumes of short stories, a novel, an autobiography and several plays, Langston Hughes returns to his first love, poetry, in his new volume, *Shakespeare in Harlem.* And if all of this implies that Mr. Hughes is extremely versatile, that is just what is meant. Mr. Hughes is at home in any medium of expression and is one of those literary rarities: a creative writer able to live purely by his pen.

This new book is intended to be a volume of light verse. It is. What's more, this reviewer suspects it was slanted particularly for the Caucasian reader—highly desirable, if Mr. Hughes and Mr. Knopf want to sell it. . . .

The Associated Negro Press considers it an honor to have released some of the poetry prior to publication during the past year. Other compositions appeared originally in *Esquire, Poetry, The New Yorker* and other periodicals. All of it is worth reading time after time. Give ear to what Mr. Hughes suggests in the frontispiece: "Blues, ballads and reels to be read aloud, crooned, shouted, recited and sung. Some with gestures, some not—as you like. None with a far-away voice."

Section headings give a key to the content: "Seven Moments of Love," "Declarations," "Blues for Men," "Death in Harlem," "Mammy Songs," "Ballads," "Blues for Ladies," and "Lenox Avenue." As for individual poems—which range from pungent two-line epigrams to narratives of several pages—the title poem for the section, "Death in Harlem," strikes this bystander as being most impressive. It's a ballad in a Frankie and Johnnie mood, but there the resemblance ends. Hughes's creation is genuine poetry, memorable and alive. So, for that matter, is just about all of the book. It will be your loss if you fail to read *Shakespeare in Harlem.*

Alfred Kreymborg
"Seven American Poets"
Saturday Review, 25 (25 April 1942), 9

[. . .]

A new volume by Langston Hughes, with delightful drawings by E. McKnight Kauffer, is a lively event in these troubled times. He calls his *Shakespeare in Harlem* a book of light verse. . . . The intimate relation with the old music halls is a happy reminder of such mastersingers of vaudeville as Bert Williams and Eddie Leonard. For here is no highbrow verse, no heavy thinking, and nothing low-born either. The careless reader might easily fall into the error of thinking that these delicate notes and rhythms are funny or gay. It is only the skilful surface that is funny or gay; the heart of the matter is tragic. Rarely in our poetry do we find this subtle blending of tragedy and comedy. It is an exquisite art and a difficult one. The salient character behind the verse of Langston Hughes is social and sociable. And he has the perfect gift of writing quatrains with more than one meaning or overtone. "Wake" is a tiny thing with the broadest connotations.

[. . .]

Marcia Masters
"A Critique in Verse"
Chicago Sun, 25 April 1942, p. 16

Red currant lips and trombone hips,
And purple-fruited fingertips:
What lovesick verse! Oh, Mr. Hughes,
Must you still croon these Harlem
  blues?
Must you describe these skins of
  plum,
Of cider-brown and scented rum,
As if all else of joy or grief
Had vanished like the autumn leaf?
Is Juliet with dusk for hair
Your final sweet, your primal fare?
And jazz and all its bobbing song
Your glory in the Harlem throng?
Too dulcet are these words you speak
For one whose tongue rests in his
  cheek.

"Poems East and West: From Gay Harlem and Quiet Maine Farms to Greek Drama in Sierra Madre"
Pasadena Star-News, 25 April 1942, p. 18

This latest collection of Langston Hughes's poems is the first in 10 years. It is, as the author says, "a book of light verse, Afro-Americana in the blues mood, poems syncopated and variegated in the colors of Harlem, blues, ballads and reels to be read aloud, crooned, shouted, recited and sung." In none of them, he asserts, can be found "a far-away voice." It is Harlem throbbing with life, albeit life that is wistful and often sad, in which pell-mell joys and dancing are interspersed with fighting and loving and gambling.

Mr. Hughes has divided the book into eight sections, "Death in Harlem" being probably the most memorable of the eight. The title-piece of this section is a long poem celebrating the affair of Arabella Johnson and the Texas Kid who "went bustin into Dixie's bout one a.m."

The pickin's weren't bad—
His roll wasn't slim—
And Arabella Johnson had her
Hands on him.

Mr. Hughes's growth as a poet during the last decade is observable, but he is still the same reporter and interpreter of his people in their many moods of joy and sorrow, of hope and despair. He has been called "the Negro poet laureate," but we imagine that such a resounding title does not mean much to him. It is enough that he makes his people live in his verse.

[. . .]

Coleman Rosenberger
"Dark Laughter"
New Republic, 106 (27 April 1942), 577–8

Langston Hughes's poetry is an example of the vitality of the Negro contribution to American culture. . . .

The "syncopated and variegated" may be a little starched, but the commentary is more accurate than what most poets have to say about their own work. My crooning and shouting are weak, but for the past ten days I've been reading these poems aloud to anybody I can corner and have had unexpectedly happy results. People who "don't like poetry" like this, which is to say that these poems have more and not less than the poetry which goes unsuccessfully searching for an audience.

The conscious artistry is here. Hughes observes the strict poetic pattern, the formal rhyme scheme and the repetition of the blues:

> This mornin' for breakfast
> I chawed de mornin' air.
> This mornin' for breakfast
> Chawed de mornin' air.
> But this evenin' for supper,
> I got evenin' air to spare.

But, seemingly effortless, the craftsmanship does not misdirect attention to itself; it carries the attention out to the whole poem, not in to the felicitous line.

The poetry is "light verse" only within the paradox of all "blues, ballads and reels." Hughes wrote in an earlier volume: "The mood of the blues is almost always despondency, but when they are sung people laugh." The themes are grim enough: hunger, death, poverty, loneliness—and that they are themes which can be turned to laughter suggests the resilience and the strength of the Negro spirit.

The sixty-odd poems, divided somewhat arbitrarily into eight sections, play over a wide range of subjects and attitudes. From the bitterness of "Ku Klux":

> A cracker said, "Nigger,
> Look me in the face—
> And tell me you believe in
> The great white race"

the poetry moves to the recognition of common unhappiness in "Daybreak":

> I wonder if white folks ever feel bad,
> Getting up in the morning lonesome and sad?

It ranges from the urban lushness of "Harlem Sweeties" to "Mississippi Levee" and the tight-lipped "Sharecroppers." Throughout Hughes speaks richly for his race. He has been called the Negro Laureate; he is this and more; he is an authentic American poet.

"A Few of the Newer Books: Priority in Poetry" *Open Shelf,* May–June 1942, p. 12

Musical ballads, blues, and reels, done with perception and a light touch by the gifted Cleveland Negro poet.

Ruth Lechlitner "To Croon, Shout, Recite or Sing" *New York Herald Tribune Books,* 3 May 1942, p. 2

Several years ago a book of verse, *The Weary Blues,* brought considerable attention to the work of a young Negro writer, Langston Hughes. Recently a wider audience learned more about him through his exciting autobiography, *The Big Sea.* His first collection of poems since

1932, *Shakespeare in Harlem,* continues, in mood and form—but with greater variety and deeper perception—those dynamic songs on the thoughts and doings of his people as first set down in *The Weary Blues.*

Mr. Hughes himself calls these syncopated verses "blues, ballads and reels to be read aloud, crooned, shouted, recited and sung. Some with gestures, some not—as you like. None with a faraway voice." The last phrase implies both their characteristic keynote of emotional immediacy and that ever-present general conflict between the black and the "great white race." The poems built simply upon individual experience are done with so sure a touch and an insight so genuine as to make that experience universal. In first-person speech of casual idiom—not dialect—Mr. Hughes shows the combination of illogical, big-talk childlike imagination ("Just by ifing I have a good time") and the checkrein of adult reality and despair. "Seven Moments of Love" is the ordinary moods of a black boy whose wife, after a spat, has walked out on him. His are the humanly universal alternate moods of don't care, I'm free now, and aching loneliness—a universality pointed by

> I wonder if white folks ever feel bad,
> Getting up in the morning lonesome
>   and sad?

Making these verses memorable, too, is the humor that almost always surmounts near tragedy. It is never read in from the outside, but inherent in the Negro's ability to objectify his own situation, to laugh at himself. Further, the Negro's genuine feeling for poetry has its own way with an image. He doesn't say he's jobless and hungry, but

> This mornin' for breakfast
> Chawed de mornin' air,

> But this evenin' for supper
> I got evenin' air to spare.

Or he will say

> Night like a reefer man
> Slipped away.

There is an occasional luscious-colored lyric, such as "Harlem Sweeties," in the early Countee Cullen manner; in contrast the rollicking, somewhat synthetic ballad of Arabella Johnson and the Texas Kid, or the rowdy high spirits of "Hey Hey Blues." But in almost all the poems—whether the theme be love, work, or death—we sense a black world never free from the heavy intrusion of the white: the lynchers, the bossman who takes the share-cropper's money, and—no less sinister—the white woman in the ermine cape at "Dixie's" in Harlem, who

> Looked at the blacks and
> Thought of a rope,
> Looked at the blacks and
> Thought of a flame—
> And thought of something
> Without a name.

However, this collection of Hughes's poems does not have the bitterly stressed social angle one finds in the work of other Negro poets, such as Robert Hayden. But the lighter scoring is no less poignant when an old situation is given a new turn; the colored child at the carnival, for instance, looking for the "Jim Crow" section on the merry-go-round. Mostly it is a matter of economics—the underlying eternal poverty—that shapes and directs the action in Mr. Hughes's ballads: the killer boy who robs a bank to get money for his girl; the pawnbroker, asked to lend on life itself; the struggle of the poor to get enough cash together for a burial:

> I wonder what makes
> A funeral so high?

A poor man ain't got
No business to die.

The book is designed and illustrated with several striking portrait drawings, in white on black, by C. McKnight Kauffer.

Eda Lou Walton
"Nothing New under the Sun"
New Masses, 43 (16 June 1942), 23

None of these three books is really something new under the sun. Both Langston Hughes and Robinson Jeffers, in their totally different ways, are writing as they always have. Mr. Rodgers is younger and this is his first book. But not even this young poet has achieved either a new way of communicating his feeling about the world as it is now or, surely, a new vision of this world. With history moving so rapidly, poets are, of course, having difficulty in writing at all, for poetry is not mere reporting. Any poem must convey an idea made feeling, and through words and rhythms which are sufficiently emotionalized to stir the reader. Poetry, in other words, requires time for gestation.

If a poet needs a history, a culture, something implicit and of some duration to communicate, the Negro poet has this. His problem is old, his cause just. The culture out of which he writes is more or less homogeneous. The symbols of race suffering and oppression are well understood.

This new collection of Langston Hughes' "blues songs" is not unlike his earlier collections. These are the known lonely songs and rhythms of his people,

their love songs too. Back of the simple rhythms lies suffering. The poems are close to folk song. It may be said, however, that they probably had been in preparation for some time. They indicate no awareness of the changed war world; they are not even profoundly class or race-conscious. I think on the whole they are a little too easily composed. Folk poetry is always the picture of a people. But a poet like Langston Hughes should have something more to say than is said in these strummed out "blues songs" which can too easily be listened to and do not call forth enough thought.

[. . .]

Charlest R. H. Johnson
"Within These Books"
Cincinnati Union, 25 June 1942, p. 1, 3; reprinted from *Challenge,* 1 [March, May, or June] 1942, 7; remarkably like review in *Negro History Bulletin,* April 1942

This is a book of poetry, which follows the usual trend of the author, who is often regarded as "the poet laureate of the Negro today." While in a humorous vein, these poems of his reveal a depth of thought as to the serious condition of the Negro people. For blues medium, to him, "all the world is sad and dreary everywhere he roams," and still he can laugh in hope for a brighter day.

The alert teacher, who desires to clarify the Negro child's understanding of its present position in this country, will find this work a valuable asset in teaching realistic literature. These poems tell the truth without arousing that feeling of bitterness. They deal with situations in all stages of struggle where Negroes contend with problems of life. For his broad point of view and thorough grasp of things as they exist today, Langston Hughes deserves much credit. *Shakespeare in Harlem* is a book worthy of a place on your book shelf.

[. . .]

Owen Dodson "Shakespeare in Harlem" *Phylon,* 3 (Third Quarter 1942), 337–8

This Shakespeare still rolls dice in Harlem, grabs a wishbone, makes a wish for his sweet mamma, long gone, long lost; still lies in bed in the noon of the day. This Shakespeare is lazy, unpoetic, common and vulgar. In short Mr. Langston Shakespeare Hughes is still holding his mirror up to a gold-toothed, flashy nature. It is the same mirror he has held up before but somehow the glass is cracked and his deep insight and discipline has dimmed. There is no getting away from the fact that this book, superior in format, is a careless surface job and unworthy of the author Mr. Van Vechten calls the "Negro Poet Laureate," who loves his race and reports and interprets it feelingly and understandingly to itself and other races. His verse resounds with the exultant throb of Negro pain and gladness.

Once Mr. Hughes wrote

Because my mouth
Is wide with laughter

You do not hear
My inner cry;
Because my feet
Are gay with dancing
You do not know
I die.

In this volume we merely hear the laughter: loud, lewd, unwholesome and degenerate. We see and hear a cartoon doing a black-face, white-lip number, trying terribly to please the populace. None of the inner struggle is revealed, no bitter cries, no protests, no gentleness, no ladders of hope being climbed. These things are hard to say about a poet I very much admire. But they must be said.

Mr. Hughes states at the beginning of the book that this is "light verse." . . . This statement screens a thousand sins. Because verse is "light" it doesn't therefore follow that anything goes. The technique of light verse is as exacting as that of serious verse, almost more so.

If this were Mr. Hughes' first book we would say, here is some promise but in a few years he will deepen this stream, he will broaden this stream. But as this is his fourth volume of verse all I can say is that he is "backing into the future looking at the past" to say nothing of the present.

Eight sections make up the book: "Seven Moments of Love," "Declarations," "Blues for Men," "Death in Harlem," "Mammy Songs," "Ballads," "Blues for Ladies," "Lenox Avenue."

The section called "Death in Harlem" has, perhaps, some of his better work:

They done took Cordelia
Out to stony lonesome ground.
Done took Cordelia
To stony lonesome,
Laid her down.

Another poem in this section that has a haunting and poetic shine is "Crossing."

The real "nitty gritty" is a poem in the "Lenox Avenue" section called "Shakespeare in Harlem":

Hey ninny neigh!
And a hey nonny no!
Where, oh, where
Did my sweet mama go?

Hey ninny neigh!
With a tra-la-la-la!
They say your sweet mama
Went home to her ma.

But the "cup" is poems like "Hey-Hey Blues," and "Little Lyric." Whoever drinks will choke on these.

After hearing some of these poems read aloud a fellow who hadn't heard of Mr. Hughes said: "that Langston Hughes must be a cracker." Lord have mercy!

William Harrison "New Books on Our Bookshelf: A Book of Light Verse" *Opportunity,* 20 (July 1942), 219

This volume, with drawings by E. McKnight Kauffer, is characteristic of Langston Hughes as a poet. To make such an assertion is to indicate that the quality of the versification and of the poet's peculiar insights fulfills all of the reader's expectations. If not great, the poems are (in every instance) at least competent. However, at the present fateful hour when the very national independence of our country is threatened by the forces of Axis enslavement whose declared program requires the annihilation of American culture, a special task is imposed upon a Negro poet to be

more than "characteristic," to rise above and expand beyond his usual self.

Of course, Mr. Hughes is too close to the folk-experience of the Negro people to be a trifler, "the idle singer of an empty lay," but his themes are concerned over-much with the most uprooted, and hence demoralized, Negro social types with which his portrait gallery has always abounded. It is true that such types—the pimp and the prostitute—are ever with us, and it is not in the spirit of Sugar Hill scorn that I should condemn over-emphasis on their portrayal. Their interest, I submit, is comparable to that of Mr. Ol Harrington's buffoonish "Bootsie": they exist everywhere, in all Negro communities from Boston to Tampa. The question is whether they are significant in any important poetic depiction of Negro life at this time.

Another way of saying that these poems are characteristic of Mr. Hughes is to state that they add nothing to his well-merited reputation, that they evidence little growth, either in his choice of material or in his mode of expression. They are, indeed, "Afro-Americana in the blues mood."

The poet's social consciousness gleams in many poems, as in

I wish the rent
Was heaven sent.

Several poems are redolent with protest against blighting poverty and race discrimination, though the call to social action is not sounded as it once was, and the labor movement does not appear even furtively. "Sharecroppers" suffers when compared to Sterling Brown's poem of the same title, although it has a quiet dignity of its own.

Like the "people's artist" that he indubitably is, Mr. Hughes touches the depths of Negro life, but he strikes no note of hope for the future. Perhaps his abstention from revealing any attitude whatsoever toward the war, the all-encompassing event of our waking and sleeping days and nights, is what makes his volume never rise above its announced intention to be "a book of light verse." His admirers, among whom is enrolled the present reviewer, look forward eagerly to the appearance of a book of serious verse from his pen.

H. R. Hays
"To Be Sung or Shouted"
Poetry, 60 (July 1942), 223–4

This is a book of light verse and, as such, the only demands that should be made upon it are those of entertainment. It has charm and spontaneity. It expresses temporary nostalgias, passing moods of weariness or gaiety and, occasionally, irony and racial bitterness. Mr. Hughes writes easily without much caring about formal pattern. As he says himself, the poems are to be crooned, shouted or sung. Perhaps the best in the volume are those in which he captures a genuine folk feeling. In the following:

> Levee, levee,
> How high have you got to be
> To keep them cold muddy waters
> From washin' over me

he achieves what might be an actual work song. In a poem called "Ku Klux," he strikes hard at white brutality:

> They hit me in the head
> And knock me down
> And then they kicked me
> On the ground.
> A cracker said "Nigger,
> Look me in the face
> And tell me you believe in
> The great white race."

It is interesting to compare the work of Hughes with the Cuban, Nicolas Guillen or the Puerto Rican, Pales Matos, who are creating a new Negro art in Spanish. The Latin-Americans are much closer to their African origins; they employ primitive folklore and write with great sensual abandon and gusto. The American Negro poet expresses, especially in the Harlem poems, a certain feeling of rootlessness, a sense of isolation in the crowd, of not belonging. Says Hughes:

> Say! you know I believe I'll change my
>   name,
> Change my color, change my ways
> And be a white man the rest of my
>   days!
> I wonder if white folks ever feel bad
> Getting up in the morning lonesome
>   and sad.

In countries like Cuba or Puerto Rico where there is a mulatto majority, the artist feels sure of himself and his work breathes a certain optimism even though it is full of protest. But the American Negro can never rid himself of the realization that he is on a racial island surrounded by a dominant people which does not understand him. He is already urbanized and frustrated. Hence the blues mood is characteristic, a restless seeking for small pleasures and small compensations.

Much of *Shakespeare in Harlem* is in popular song style and really calls for music. Mr. Hughes would be an excellent lyricist for a singer such as Ethel Waters. Having already explored the medium, he is the logical poet to write a blues opera. One hopes he will some day try his hand at a libretto.

"Book Reviews"
Michigan Chronicle,
25 July 1942, [p. ?]

Langston Hughes' latest book, *Shake-speare in Harlem,* is a collection of light verse "Afro-Americana in the blues mood." It is the author's first book of poems to be published since 1932.

The poems are for the most part excellent and in Mr. Hughes' best style, light, witty, laughing and sometimes poignant. But there are a few like the one entitled "Little Lyric":

I wish the rent
Was Heaven sent

which are not poetry at all and not even lyrical prose.

Mr. Hughes has an unquestionable gift for this type of writing, but we would like to see him do more of the type of poem like his protest songs which are a truer portrayal of the Negro today. These few poems are called "Share-Croppers," "Merry-Go-Round," "West Texas," "Ku-Klux" and "Southern Mammy Sings." Although the other poems are also true pictures of Negroes in Harlem and elsewhere, they are superficial and picture only the most obvious and most stereotyped aspects of the Negro's life. The light touch of a Langston Hughes is as praiseworthy as the greater depth and sincerity of a Richard Wright, but Richard Wright seems more attuned to the times in which we are living.

There are a number of excellent drawings by E. McKnight Kauffer which catch the spirit of Mr. Hughes' poetry. The book is one that should be extremely popular.

"In Brief"
Nation, 155 (8 August 1942), 119

This book by the "Negro Poet Laureate" describes itself as a "book of light verse. Afro-American in the blues mood. . . ." Death, frustration, poverty, and persecution are related in tones that ask, as it were, for sympathy through laughter rather than for sympathy through understanding. From the drawings (in reverse) by E. McKnight Kauffer to the title and lavender print on the black-cloth cover, the book attempts a folklore atmosphere and succeeds in being lugubrious. In the main, the lyrics, more in the category of Americana than poetry, are sincere and very readable, a kind of tragic light verse of today.

"Shakespeare in Harlem"
Stowe [Vt.] *Sentinel,*
15 October 1942, [p. ?]

The prolific pen of Langston Hughes has again consummated a book of poems. *Shakespeare in Harlem,* as do his other three collections, concerns itself with a subject close to the soul of the young poet, the lot of the Negro Race. The pieces are as refreshing as he has ever written. Stripped of sophistication and ornateness, they are symbolic of the people they portray. They are also free from the mechanics of technical pattern which has ofttimes disturbed the intrinsic charm of otherwise good poetry. If you have aspiration to write verse, you will do well to read *Shakespeare in Harlem*.

It is a Negro book, which is about exploitations and drollery, at a time when the subject of oppression is unpopular in light of the international situation. On the brighter side it is also a book about loyalty, which is particularly fashionable. It is a book of mistreatment and human violations. You may agree with the reviewer that in its realistic portrayal of the life and character of lowly Negroes it is axiomatic. We know that in any case it is a thought-provoking discussion, written for the most part in free verse.

Checklist of Additional Reviews

Booklist, 38 (1 April 1942), 271.

L. D. Reddick, "Publishers Are Awful," *Negro Quarterly*, 1 (Summer 1942), 187–9. [reviews only the book's cover]

"Literature," *Pratt Institute Library Quarterly Booklist*, 22, Series 6 (October 1942), 17.

FIELDS OF WONDER

Mary S. Churchill
"Poetry"
Virginia Kirkus Bulletin,
15 (15 March 1947), 187

Langston Hughes' *Fields of Wonder* is a new volume of poems in which there is a slight, fragile, nostalgic charm. Hughes has worked out his own method of shortline versification; he is definitely a lyric poet, something rare in this day; but he lacks real skill or strength; the perfume of *Fields of Wonder* is faint. Those interested in the development of Negro poetry will read this as a part of the Negro contribution, but scarcely for itself.

Arna Bontemps
"The Harlem Renaissance"
Saturday Review, 30 (22 March 1947), 13, 44

New books of poems by Langston Hughes and Countee Cullen have appeared this year. Some readers, no doubt, will be reminded of the shy, disarming bows made by these new writers before literary circles back in the twenties, when neither of them had yet finished college. In the case of Cullen, who died a year ago January, there will be a tendency to summarize as well as reflect. His stature as a poet will be estimated. With Hughes, of course, only a tentative and partial measurement can be attempted. But whatever evaluations may follow, whatever ranks and positions may finally fall to them in American literature,

there isn't likely to be much question about their importance to the Harlem renaissance, so well remembered by many. They were its heralds and its brightest stars.

Except for their ages (there was a difference of about a year) and the fact that each was a Negro American, they were not much alike. An observer got the impression that while they were drawn together by the common experience of writing poetry, they actually had remarkably little in common. Their personal backgrounds, their reading, their moods, their attitudes, their tastes and preferences—everything one saw in their personalities was different. Even when they wrote poems on identical subjects, as in Cullen's "Epitaph for a Poet" and Hughes's "The Dreamkeeper," the contrast was striking. Cullen's stanza goes:

I have wrapped my dreams in a silken
  cloth.
And laid them away in a box of gold!
Where long will cling the lips of the
  moth,
I have wrapped my dreams in a silken
  cloth;

I hide no hate; I am not even wroth
Who found earth's breath so keen and
  cold.
I have wrapped my dreams in a silken
  cloth,
And laid them away in a box of gold.

Hughes puts the same idea in these words:

Bring me all of your dreams,
You dreamers,
Bring me all of your
Heart melodies
That I may wrap them
In a blue cloud-cloth
Away from the too-rough fingers
Of the world.

Cullen's verses skip; those by Hughes glide. But in life Hughes is the merry one.

Cullen was a worrier. If these traits in the two poets stood out with less emphasis in the days of cultural and artistic awakening among Negroes, twenty-odd years ago, they were nevertheless present. Equally evident, then as later, was Cullen's tendency to get his inspiration, his rhythms and patterns as well as much of his substance from books and the world's lore of scholarship; while Hughes made a ceremony of standing on the deck of a tramp steamer and tossing into the sea, one by one, all the books he had accumulated before his twenty-first birthday. He need not have done it, of course, for he had never been chained to any tradition, and there isn't the least danger that he ever will be; yet this stern renunciation was in keeping with his old habit of using living models and taking poetic forms as well as content from folk sources.

[. . .]

Notice was paid, on a more limited scale, to the adolescent writing of Langston Hughes. In his case this happened to consist of delightfully innocent little pieces like "Dressed Up," perhaps inspired by a childhood fondness for the work of Paul Laurence Dunbar. They appeared in the school publications of Central High in Cleveland, and it is unlikely that anyone used them as texts for sermons in those days. To achieve that special distinction, Hughes had to wait until a number of years later when, in a moment of puzzlement, no doubt, he composed and allowed to be published a little item called "Goodbye, Christ," which not only misrepresented himself, in the light of his total writing, but caused him to be misinterpreted, denounced, and abused from dozens of rostrums and platforms, picketed by the followers of Amy McPherson and the supporters of Gerald L. K. Smith, and derided before the nation in newspapers and magazines.

Mainly, however, the response to Hughes's early writing was neither sudden nor spontaneous. Even "The Negro Speaks of Rivers," a poem written in the weeks following his graduation from high school and which few people in any part of the world have been able to read without feeling, caught on slowly. It was hard for those readers who noticed a new Negro poet at that time to know what to make of a young man who wrote what he called a "Suicide's Note," saying:

> The calm,
> Cool face of the river
> Asked me for a kiss.

Was this a poem or not? There was another one that said only:

> I loved my friend.
> He went away from me.
> There is nothing more to say.

If these were puzzling to people whose reading experiences had been formal and conservative, the one which began:

> My old man's a white old man
> And my old mother's black,

was downright shocking. So was the free verse work in which Hughes insisted that a clean spittoon is "beautiful to the Lord." His preoccupation with low life, with the singers of blues, with rounders and cabaret girls, with the misery and exaltation of road workers and of shouting church folk bothered even those who had found something which they could admire in his "Fantasy in Purple" or his "Dream Variation." Nevertheless there were those who felt, even then, that this poet of broad human sympathies, this writer of effortless, almost casual, verses, this singer with an ear for street music and for the folk idioms of our modern urbanization was indeed an American original.

The career which began with the magazine publication of "The Negro Speaks of Rivers" in 1921 yielded *The Weary Blues,* a first book of poems, in 1926, and Langston Hughes, home from world wanderings, found his lines being used as touchstones of an awakening movement. His poems were set to music, they were painted, they were danced. They were recited, they were interpreted, they were translated—the Latin Americans are particularly fond of them. They were dramatized, they were recorded, they were imitated. To rest and perhaps recuperate from too much excitement—and perhaps to take stock—the poet went back to college and completed his interrupted schooling. The experience did him no more harm than had been done by the books he discarded at sea. On the other hand, it provided the calm security necessary to write his first novel. What he did about the curriculum is something of a mystery, but obviously he satisfied the requirements, for Lincoln University not only gave him a bachelor's degree but an honorary doctorate.

The literary and artistic movement which Cullen and Hughes highlighted was regarded sympathetically, but it was never quite certified or approved as a phase of America's cultural growth. In the twenties the Negro's gifts were still departmentalized. There were poets in the United States, and there were Negro poets. There were musicians, and there were Negro musicians. There were painters, and there were Negro painters. Cullen abhorred this attitude. Almost his only public comments about the art in which he expressed himself were pleas for an evaluation of his work strictly on its own merits, without racial considerations. He was to learn, however, that this was no small matter.

Cullen did not live to see another springtime resurgence of his own creative powers comparable with the impulse that produced his first three books of poetry, the books which give his selected poems most of their lilt and brightness. He did not live to see young poets like Gwendolyn Brooks and Robert E. Hayden coming up for the kind of evaluation he had hoped to receive. Before he was forty, a second generation of the renaissance, owing much to him and to Langston Hughes, was on the way.

A curious footnote to these events now reveals that Langston Hughes, whose work seemed to have such a definite Negro flavor in the days of the Dark Tower, has not only written the lyrics for the successful musical adaptation of *Street Scene* but has also published *Fields of Wonder*, a volume of poems which contains not a single blue note. The renaissance isn't over yet.

William Harrison
"*Fields of Wonder*"
Boston Chronicle, 29 March 1947, p. 6

Readers familiar with all the published work of a poet are prone to expect novelty and development in each successive volume. That expectation meets with disappointment in this latest book by Mr. Hughes, for his most characteristic as well as most highly individualized notes are absent. None of the poems will move anybody other than persons hitherto entirely unfamiliar with one of the talents which thrilled the thirties and burnished the shield of the so-called Negro Renaissance. Some are pleasant like a brook near a meadow in early spring; others are fanciful with delicate hints of profundity like a fairy tale in tracing single strokes of unusual imagery, reminiscent of Japanese hokkus [*sic*]. Nowhere is evident the surging oceanic turbulence with which Mr. Hughes invigorated American poetry in his youth. All communicate a mellow

301

chewing of the cud, ruminant contemplation of those elements in human life which are not the sole possession of any particular epoch in history, though a few recall the crisis of our times.

To say that this volume adds nothing to the poet's reputation is not to imply that it detracts from it. It is merely a chore, an exercise in craftsmanship by a competent worker who seems too tired to blow a herald's horn summoning the spirits of progressive mankind to greater and intenser endeavors.

Russell Jelliffe and Rowena Jelliffe
"Langston Hughes Fulfills Promise of Great Destiny in New Book"
Cleveland News Week-End Review, 30 (29 March 1947), [1], 8

Langston Hughes came from a little town in Kansas to live in Cleveland (at the age of 13) in the same year that we came to Cleveland, tucked ourselves in a little rear cottage on E. 38th St. and set about the building of Karamu House. Books and theories were now behind us and we began to learn from people. Among that first group of children from whom we learned so much, upon whose lives our Karamu program came to be based, was Langston Hughes.

The debt we owe to him and to other children of that period can scarcely be defined, much less repaid. Here we learned from a child's unfolding. He was one of a score or more whom we watched and interpreted as honestly as we knew how, searching for the thing which would meet the basic need. This searching shaped Karamu.

In Langston Hughes the outstanding thing to see was his wonder at the world. It shone through his deep hurt, his struggle to understand, his gaiety, his fine sense of humor, his sensitiveness to beauty and his deep liking for people.

There are outstanding moments to treasure. There was the moment when his wondering eyes fell upon a little brown girl in a red dress and he fell in love with her. One of his poems is written to her. There were the times when he fell asleep over books in our living room. We have the memory of his eager invitation to come to his home to see his Grandfather Leary's shawl with the bullet holes, the shawl which his grandfather had worn when he fell beside John Brown at Harper's Ferry. He became one of our first volunteers and drew and painted with a group of younger children.

In his adult years again he came very close to us at Karamu through his plays, most of which are unpublished. He has written for Karamu Theater more plays than any other one playwright. Six of his plays we premiered, though but one of these, *Mulatto,* has so far reached Broadway. None is more beloved, by both children and adults at Karamu, than he, and he returns to us just often enough to implant that same love in each generation of people.

It seems altogether fitting and logical to us that this last book of poems should be one of lyric poems, and further that it should bear the name *Fields of Wonder.* We have through it a sense of seeing his own destiny approaching its fulfillment, of a fine maturing, of the coming to fruition of the best of those things of which he gave promise a good many years ago. Surely he is one of those rare people given rare vision to see all nature and man alike very truly indeed and to crystallize that seeing into poetic form with an honesty and a simplicity that is deeply moving.

Repeatedly in this volume he sings of a sense of order, of peace, of triumph.

> Walls have been known
> To fall
> Dusk turn to dawn
> And chains to be gone.

Knowing the life and the honest searching of this man one can but respond confidently to his abstract conclusions, to his ideology, for he has not rushed madly toward these concepts through any wish to escape the storm of living, through a willful binding of his eyes to the sordid and the ugly. Rather, he has in the past written of these things sharply, concisely, sometimes bitterly, always honestly.

Sometimes Negroes have disapproved of his writing, feeling that he is not enough concerned about putting forth the best racial foot for the world at large to see. Somewhere back of this misunderstanding is his deep conviction that either foot is very good indeed and that all art should be used to reveal life, to hunt out its truths about all men, humble as well as great, rather than to conceal it with superficial drapings. For the people he is most concerned about there is a poem called "Prayer" in which he says—

> Gather up
> In the arms of your love
> Those who expect
> No love from above.

In *Fields of Wonder* he sings of many of the things about which he has sung before. He writes of life in a night club, of the southern cabin, of the wail and ache of jazz, of old sailors, of the secrets of Harlem, of the Mexican market place and the Cuban bar, of children at play, of the religious shout, of black motherhood, of the Mother, Africa, of the waste and sting of segregation, of night and sunrise, of the sea and the desert, of human destiny, of God, of immortality.

Of all these things he has written before. But it is as though the path of his life had been that of a spiral (a spiral with a very wide base indeed) and that now, when the same point is viewed, it is from a higher level, with a wider vision, through a clearer atmosphere. While there is maturing, there is no withdrawing from life and there is the unvarying basis of honesty. It is as though he had long ago made a pact with himself and his readers always to tell so truly what he sees.

When this poet was growing up his greatest pleasure came from his writing. He glowed from it. Years later he said to us, "I never quite escape the feeling of guilt about taking money for my poems. It doesn't seem decent to earn money from anything that you enjoy so much. Maybe I ought to make my living some other way."

As there was, during his adolescence, the need to reach very often within himself for pleasant experience (for his real life was not easy) he wrote abundantly. He wrote for the Central High School paper, which he loved so much, as well as his numerous "letters to God." It interests us deeply to note that in this current collection is a reference again to these "letters." He writes—

> In an envelope marked
> Personal
> God addressed me a letter
> In an envelope marked
> Personal
> I have given my answer.

But if the final achievement of his writing gave him pleasure, that prior period, when a thought was twisting through his being but had not yet gotten itself into words, was one of haunting misery. Thus he describes it under the caption, "Burden."

It is not weariness
That bears me down
But sudden nearness
To song without sound.

At the moment he is no doubt best known as the writer of the lyrics to Elmer Rice's *Street Scene*, now running on Broadway, and for which Kurt Weill wrote the music. Here are lyrics so sensitive and true to character they seem to rise at the instant of hearing spontaneously from the heart of the singer, so true are they to the character they portray. Likewise are they true to the culture and emotions of America.

If it is true, as it seems to us to be, that in this group of poems, Langston Hughes rounds out and approaches the sensitiveness which his childhood promised, it is true also that another and larger destiny is here attained. It has to do with the destiny of his race as he sensed it long before he put it into words.

Long ago he saw that in those values in which we, as the American people, are weak, the Negro was strong. The emotive, esthetic values of life, the rich enjoyment of life as the goal of living, he knew to be strong and deep within his race. That America, which this poet so deeply loves, needs this element more strongly woven into her life he also knew. Well aware of the predominant emphasis which we in this country give to economic, political, technological and practical matters and of the gap that is there in the realm of the esthetic, he knew that along the latter line the Negro will achieve his fullest giving.

That he himself has here and in this way given to us more fully than ever before is evident. That here he fulfills a racial as well as a personal destiny seems equally true.

Bertram L. Woodruff
"Of Myth and Symbol"
Phylon, 8 (Second Quarter 1947), 198–200

[. . .]

Langston Hughes' latest volume *Fields of Wonder* charms with its simplicity. A far cry from the complex significance of Cullen, the poetry of Mr. Hughes matches the symbolic canvases of Horace Pippin in the release of the evocative power of personal and traditional metaphors. Mr. Hughes apostrophizes the "fields of wonder" which give birth to the stars and the poet with his cosmic destiny.

To distinguish between the beauty of poetic matter and poetry itself is to hear a word and a tone in silence, Langston Hughes avers. He offers the beauty of poetic matter in such lines as

In times of silver rain
The butterflies
Lift silken wings
To catch a rainbow cry.

But, although pictorial and musical beauties are poetic, they do not constitute poetry itself. Explicit description of onomatopoeia must be refracted and reflected obliquely by metaphor in order to acquire intensity of poetic feeling. Mr. Hughes therefore succeeds with the personal symbols that awaken for the reader old memories and reflections:

Rocks and the firm roots of trees.
The rising shafts of mountains.
Something strong to put my hands on.

Empathy is aroused in the reader by the exquisite speculation on the little snail on a rose "drinking the dew drop's mystery," and by the loneliness of a likker bottle on a table "All by itself." The use of sexual imagery deepens from adumbrations in "Sleep" and "Desire" to the seething surge of the waves in "Moonlight Night: Carmel." To reinforce kinesthetic sensations by aural recollections, folk speech is used. Langston Hughes calls the graveyard a "no stretching place" and "that-never-get-up-no-more Place." Also, when he becomes cryptic, all the stops of mystery and suspense sound in such poems as "Night, Four Songs," "Poppy Flower," and "End."

This body of poetry is not without social implications. Mr. Hughes drops a given symbol like a pebble in the reader's consciousness to spread widening ripples of emotional agitation. The circles thus set in vibration have power to limn suggestfully the economic and political nightmares of our times. For example, "Dust Bowl" conjures up the curse on American agriculture and the baffled love for the land at the same time that it reaffirms man's harmony with nature. Like Cullen, Langston Hughes is deeply religious. In "Prayer" he asks for pity for

All the scum
Of our weary city

and he trusts that divine love will gather up those who expect no love.

In fine, these two volumes satisfy. Both Cullen and Langston Hughes reveal growth in poetic stature. Theirs is a more serious and effective art.

Ellen Barnette "Book Review" *Campus Mirror* [Spelman College], April 1947, p. 5

If Mr. Hughes should think for years to come, there is great doubt that he would pick a more appropriate title for his latest volume of poems.

On reading this collection, one is, above all, amazed to find lines woven so intricately fine that he gets a full picture of situations within a small compass. Reading the poems separately, one is sometimes at a loss as to the meaning of some of them. The titles are very helpful, but in some cases do not explain what the poem is about. It is well to be careful about giving our own interpretation to a poet's works unless we are absolutely sure of the meaning. There is, however, something which makes us listen to an exquisite melody when we know very little about music, and it is that same compulsion which makes us hear the exquisite flow of rhythm in these poems.

We do not need to know what the poet meant by every word. It is at times when we read poems like the following that we see the significance in McLeish's words that a poem should not mean, but be.

[. . .]

This is the first volume of poems by Mr. Hughes containing lyric poems only. For those of us who know his works, this new collection has, perhaps, a deeper significance. We can see some of the same ideas that we find in his verse that concerns race, and in some of them we see and feel the touches of his blues.

Whatever we find in them, it is enough to know that his genius is bright and his poems are: . . .

[. . .]

Beatrice M. Murphy
"New Books Reviewed"
Pulse, 5 (April 1947), 26

As the title implies, Mr. Hughes' latest book of poems is a far cry from *Shakespeare in Harlem*. In this new book he has almost abandoned the blues completely, and has turned out a volume of lyrical poetry concerning things like "Dream Dust," "Poppy Flower" and "Silver Rain."

Time and time again Mr. Hughes has demonstrated his versatility—he has written short stories, plays, music, and poetry, and showed himself as much at home in one field as in another.

Here he has demonstrated that even a poet from Harlem can forget the sordidness and earthiness long enough to indulge in lyrical fantasy. He does not ignore the race question but he touches upon it in such a way, the reader is left with the idea, that this too, he has taken in his stride, and moved on to other things.

"Too Many Tunes; Very Little Music"
Springfield [Mass.] *Daily News*, 2 April 1947, p. 6

Here is a prolific young writer possessed of one of the most dangerous of all gifts, a facile pen. He has written poetry, a novel, an autobiography. *Fields of Wonder* is another book of verse, if you can call it that.

The feeling you get from this particular opus is of a writer who thinks he can do anything without trying. It is a book that is lazy to the point of being shiftless. The biggest surprise contained in it is that Alfred A. Knopf, or anyone else, published it.

It is filled with ideas of poems; shows without substance. He has written his own best criticism in a verse called "Fragments."

Whispers
Of Springtime.
Death in the night.
A song
With too many
Tunes.

In *Fields of Wonder*, this writer has too many tunes and no music.

Constance Curtis
"About Books and Authors"
New York Amsterdam News, 5 April 1947, p. 11

One reading of the lyrics included in Langston Hughes' new book of lyric poems, *Fields of Wonder*, is not enough for a fair judgment of their worth. Short in length, averaging little over four lines, the poems, to the casual reader, may appear to be only slight word pictures, many without too much meaning. Such a judgment is unfair, however, for Mr. Hughes has a good many things he wishes to say—and he says them neatly, without loss of time.

The poem "Communion" is deceptively guileless—on the surface:

I was trying to figure out
What it was all about
But I could not figure out
What it was all about

So I gave up and went
To take the sacrament
And when I took it
It felt good to shout!

And if the author holds that religion is an opiate, he holds too that the little jobs of the little people do not offer fulfillment for man's needs:

Lonely people
In the lonely night
Grab a lonely dream
And hold it tight.

Lonely people
In the lonely day
Work to salt
Their dream away.

The early poems written by Langston Hughes showed the fascination rhythms held for him. Later poems, in which he allowed his awareness of social issues to overpower his poetic ear, suffered because of this fact. *Fields of Wonder* has bound together his interest in rhythm with the message which he has, without losing sight of the need for technique in the handling of both.

Not all of *Fields of Wonder* concerns itself with social themes. The author has the ability to catch the flavor of the language heard in the ten cent beer halls and at the old-time rent parties, without resorting to any dialect usage. In a poem such as "One," he takes a phrase and makes it build to such a picture. . . .

Readers of this new volume of poetry will find Mr. Hughes matured in his talents. The careful workmanship and fresh viewpoint inherent in the material contained here go well together to make a satisfying compilation of his newer poems.

Byron Herbert Reece
"Memorable"
Atlanta Journal, 6 April 1947, p. 13C

Langston Hughes explores one of the narrowest veins in contemporary poetry. The poems are even narrow on the page. That he manages to make authentic poetry out of material so tenuous and sheer is a great tribute to his disciplined technique. In a few instances he writes merely notes for poems, but the six or eight truly memorable lyrics are compensation for these lapses. This book adds little to his stature as a poet but it does not confirm the continuity of his talent, which is often as much as we can ask of a poet's work.

[. . .]

E.J.
"Book Review: Nothing Said, Little Insight in Hughes' *Fields of Wonder*"
People's World, 10 April 1947, p. 5

The illusion that poetry can subsist without content, or that a poet who has nothing to say can still be a fine poet, if he can be nostalgic, rhyme "song" with "along" and make words cut a precise dark pattern down a white page, should by now be anachronism. If it is not, Hughes should help to make it so.

Unobscured by the passion of a D. H. Lawrence, or the poignancy of a Millay, these vignettes stand out in all their nakedness as the empty lyricisms of a man who is fugitive from his origins and his sources of strength.

For Hughes in the past has been a writer to contend with—a writer with insight into the position of his people, with a keen biting satiric pen, with a love of the working man, with a sense of the strength of his tradition as a Negro. From his "The Negro Speaks of Rivers" to "Comrade Lenin of Russia" he has had a sense of belonging to the struggle, of writing from and for it, that gave his work the vitality a Countee Cullen's lacked.

But in the present collection, which apparently includes much old and some new, there is virtually nothing said, and very little of insight or originality even into that minimum lyrical content necessary to burgeon words into consciousness and thence onto paper.

Lest you think the reviewer exaggerates, I quote:

"NIGHT: FOUR SONGS"

Night of the two moons
And the seventeen stars,
Night of the day before yesterday
And the day after tomorrow,
Night of the four songs unsung:
Sorrow! Sorrow!
Sorrow! Sorrow!

And again:

"SONGS"

I sat there singing her
Songs in the dark.
She said,
I do not understand
The words.
I said,
There are
No words.

To which one should add only one line: "And there are no songs either."

There are a few poems that spark to life in the book. There is the one which is also currently printed in the new quarterly *Mainstream,* which has a certain real poetic quality:

"TRUMPET PLAYER: 52ND STREET"

The Negro
With the trumpet at his lips
Has dark moons of weariness
Beneath his eyes
Where the smoldering memory of
     slave ships
blazed to the crack of whips
About his thighs.
But softly
As the tune comes from his throat
Trouble
Mellows to a golden note.

But even this poem is marred by a quality of separation from and condescension towards subject matter.

In the section called "Words Like Freedom" there is some smoke from the flame that should make Hughes a poet. I cite such a poem as:

"TODAY"

This is earthquake
Weather!
Honor and Hunger
Walk lean
Together.

This reviewer does not mean to measure Langston Hughes against the yardstick of solid revolutionary contribution (though she is not convinced at this moment that it would be wrong to do so).

But flashing his poems upon the screen of the reader as poetry-lover and revolutionist, one finds they fail to deepen understanding or to enrich feeling about any

308

material. I am reminded of a polemic of Vishinsky's on Soviet law in which he says that the final decision rests with the socialist legal conscience of the judge. As in aesthetics the final decision rests with the socialist aesthetic conscience of the reader.

However, in the field of aesthetics the problem must be posed somewhat differently. For in this day of monopoly capital and capitalist decadence, the working class in a real sense has the monopoly on humanism, and those who do not draw their sustenance from this well-spring have little sustenance and are weak and perishable. Hughes had drunk of that spring. He can and should again.

Minnie Lomax
"Current Reading:
Without a Smile"
Los Angeles Tribune,
12 April 1947, p. 11

There can be little doubt that *Fields of Wonder,* latest collection of poems by Langston Hughes, will win him a place among American poets without the qualifying adjective, Negro. The tragic sense of life which he has caught, the unhappy awareness of the futility of existence, are expressed with a feeling, a pathos and beauty that few lyricists have excelled. In this group of poems, he has turned away from the particular racial problem to a more inclusive theme and seeks to convey the idea that it isn't worth the trouble.

The mood is predominantly blue as Mr. Hughes, with his gift for significant detail and feeling for cadence, chants of life's loneliness and man's inevitably unhappy destiny. Beginning with the idea that only

Heaven is
The place where
Happiness is
Everywhere,

he says life is short and cruel, love fickle, and, perhaps, suicide isn't bad after all, for

The sea is deep,
A knife is sharp,
And a poison acid burns—
But they all bring rest,
They all bring peace
For which the tired
Soul yearns.

The quatrain "Remembrance," speaking of wandering through this living world leaving "uncut the roses," may be a warning to gather the rosebuds while we may.

Although he may dwell upon a path of life which shows nothing but the night, he may even recommend suicide, but he does at the same time remind us that a brief recompense for the harshness of our lot lies in a glimpse of natural beauty or the solace of a song:

Songs that break
And scatter
Out of the moon:
Rockets of joy
Dimmed too soon.

His grim and impassioned apostrophe to the wind, beseeching it to blow quickly through our bodies to the terrible snarl of our souls is reminiscent of Shelley's appeal to this same aspect of nature in "Ode to the West Wind."

Relief from this morbid preoccupation with the vanity of life is found in a few poems like "Trumpet Player: 52nd Street" and "Harlem Dance Hall." Two or three treat of the race problem. A strange musical vagueness characterizes the ballad, "When the Armies Passed."

Since the publication of his earlier

works—*The Weary Blues, The Dream-keeper,* and *Shakespeare in Harlem,* Hughes has grown in depth and vision. At first he felt more than he thought. He has seen enough of the misshapen lives of his own people and of the havoc wrought in the lives of all mankind by the tragedy of two world wars to justify the brooding sense of frustration and barren spirituality apparent in his present work. We know that he is thinking of the contemporary scene when he writes of our not being really wise, for

If we were
We'd open up the kingdom
And make earth happy
As the dreamed of skies.

Oddly enough, it is in a Carolina cabin that he finds peace, laughter and love.

Technically, Hughes uses a variety of forms, including the pure verse type. He shows a preference for uneven, run-on lines, some consisting of a single word. There is little rhyme and some repetition. Simplicity of language and a certain amount of tenderness qualify his pungent observations, which are expressed in ironical reflection rather than lyrical protest. A sense of mystery and awe overcomes him in the presence of sun, moon, and stars, even of the serpent and the snail.

[. . .]

J. Saunders Redding
"Book Review"
Baltimore Afro-American,
12 April 1947, p. 4

Of all the writers who figured prominently in the renaissance of the late twenties, Langston Hughes is perhaps the most du-rable. He is certainly the most eclectic and the most versatile.

He has practiced in all the forms (sometimes, it is true, with more determination than success) and he has used a variety of methods, not fearing to create new ones when he felt that his material demanded.

He has written a novel, dozens of short stories, plays, the libretto for an opera, radio scripts and, of course, verse; and only recently he has done the lyrics for the musical version of the play *Street Scene.* But of all this, I wish to write at greater lengths later.

What I have before me at the moment is Hughes's latest book of verse, *Fields of Wonder.* This is the first book of lyrics Hughes has issued in a long while—the first, indeed, since 1940 or '41. That fact alone is enough to make the publication of the book an event.

But this is not all. *Fields of Wonder* is important because it marks, it seems to me, at least in some of its pieces, a new maturity and a new mellowness and a control in Hughes. The development is organic.

Had this latest book been merely smartly oblique and cynically inclined and sophisticated, as some of his things undeniably have been, I would have been deeply disappointed and doubtful that the poet's earlier experiments—his successes and failures in verse—had taught him anything. There are others who would have felt the same way.

But there is no need for anyone to feel that way now. *Fields of Wonder* is pure lyricism, and some of the poems ("Little Song," "Dream Dust," "Exits," and "Border Line" are examples) have the intensity and the hard definition of emotion that have always been most admirable in Hughes.

One gets the idea from these that Langston Hughes has rediscovered himself. He has come back to the importance of emotional insight and to an awareness of the power that the simple, colloquial idiom can pack.

There has always been a simplicity in Hughes, but too often it has seemed a kind of mode rather than mood. In *Fields of Wonder*, simplicity is implicit in sincerity.

As to subjects, Hughes is concerned with the same things as always—the finiteness of man's life on earth, the cruelty of love, the futility of desire, the perversity of fortune.

There is little "race" in the book, but those poems in the final section which deal with it are among the best. Of the 74 poems in the book, at least 22 rank with the finest Hughes has ever done, 26 are good second bests, and the rest are only run-of-the-mill Hughes.

Reach up your hand,
Dark boy, and take a star
Out of the little breath of oblivion
That is night,
Take just
One star.

Cecil Boykin
"Along the Bookshelf"
Detroit Tribune, 19 April 1947, p. 16

Langston Hughes, modern poet of our times, has scored again in a collection of lyric poetry that stimulates the imagination and challenges the powers of understanding.

Short, apparently simple and direct, most of the verses call for a second reading to properly appreciate them. They are filled with a quality and depth of thought that is apt to be missed in a casual reading.

Such writing comes only after an author has lived and experienced fully, and the result is a delightful philosophical bit of reading.

[. . .]

In his latest work, *Fields of Wonder,* he covers a variety of subjects, ranging from love to oppression, and description to philosophy. His poems are eloquently simple, bearing his own individual unique style.

Charles Lawrence
"Simplicity Marks New Langston Hughes Verse"
Cleveland Plain Dealer, 20 April 1947, p. 17B

The reader who puts down this volume of lyrics and exclaims, "This is real poetry!" is not necessarily indulging in a banality. He is more likely to be passing intuitive judgment on most of what is being written by the modern poets.

In a time when reading so much of the new poetry requires as great concentration as unraveling an atomic formula, the simple lyrics of Langston Hughes give one the feeling of coming suddenly into bright sunlight after long traveling in deep fog.

If, as I believe, the highest art, in any of its forms, is that which succeeds most completely in transmitting the innermost feelings of the artist to his audience, then Langston Hughes' poetry is of the highest art.

Seldom can a man succeed in telling others as much about himself as Hughes does in "Snake":

He glides so swiftly
Back into the grass—

311

Gives me the courtesy of road
To let me pass,
That I am half ashamed
To seek a stone
To kill him.

This is typical of the sincerity and the depth of the worth of this man who started writing as a pupil at Cleveland's Central High School and who has gone on to become one of America's finest poets.

S.H.
"Looks at Books: Poetry" *La Jolla Light,* 24 April 1947, p. 3B

The latest collection of poems by Langston Hughes must be reread many times for complete understanding. They are all short, lyrical and free-flowing.

"BURDEN"

It is not weariness
That bows me down
But sudden nearness
To song without sound.

At times his style is very reminiscent of Carl Sandburg in his use of native colloquialisms and his subject matter. He expresses every mood and emotion of which humans are capable, but even those expressing bitterness and irony are true poetry.

[. . .]

Hubert Creekmore
"Poems by Langston Hughes"
New York Times Book Review, 4 May 1947, p. 10

This fifth book of poems by Langston Hughes is notable for the brevity and leanness of its lyrics. Many are only four to six lines long, and others would be, if the regular lines were not broken up. For instance, the last stanza of "Snail":

Weather and rose
Is all you see,
Drinking
The dewdrop's
Mystery.

However, the physical appearance of a poem has little to do with its effect or its value. In most cases, the effect here is of a sudden, sensitive gasp of feeling. Often the poems project a sketchiness of image, a questionable logic (as in the lines quoted above), or a suspicion in the reader that the emotional climate has not been rendered fully.

Since the poems are so stripped, so direct, except in the abundance of repetition and abstract or general terms, their brevity allows for little expansion within the reader. Among the successful ones, "Snake," "Songs" and "Personal" have the hardness of Greek epigrams. But others—poems of nature, longing, love or "Dreamdust," as one is called—are frugally romantic in treatment. Little in the book is regionally or racially inspired, and much of the latter seems strained and lacking in the easy power of Mr. Hughes' earlier poems. However, after a trite beginning,

312

"Trumpet Player: 52nd Street" shows fine penetration in its last page.

For all its variety of subject matter, the collection seems monotonous in treatment. In spite of a certain individuality in Mr. Hughes' approach, there are such strong echoes of other poets that the names of Emily Dickinson, Stephen Crane, and a whisper of E. A. Robinson and Ernest Dowson (there are even two Pierrots and a Pierrette) keep coming to mind. "Montmartre" is pure Imagism:

Pigalle:
A neon rose
In a champagne bottle.
At dawn
The petals
Fall.

This matter of influences or resemblances is, of course, unavoidable and no censure of Mr. Hughes' work. His poems have their own qualities of delicate lyricism and honesty of vision, and undoubtedly many of them will appeal to the great audience now crying for verse that appeals to their emotions without being stereotypes of the Victorian models.

John Frederick Nims
"Imaginative, Tart Rhetoric by Stevens"
Chicago Tribune Magazine of Books, 4 May 1947, p. 4

[. . .]

Stevens communicates ideas thru image and melody; Langston Hughes too often makes statements without the help of either—a proper method for song lyrics.

(Mr. Hughes wrote the much admired lyrics for the new production of *Street Scene.*) But, without orchestra, these poems seem to remain pretty flat on the page. There is much force behind them: a childlike freshness, wide sympathy, quick sensibility, sincere emotion—all qualities which, in this collection, have not found adequate outlet. Merely to state mood and attitude is not enough; poetry is not that way. It seems to me that Mr. Hughes, the distinguished author of *The Weary Blues* and *Shakespeare in Harlem,* has deserted the vigor of his earlier work for a rather conventional facility.

Pearl Strachan
"Lyrics by Mr. Hughes"
Christian Science Monitor, Magazine Section, 10 May 1947, p. 11

Spare and forceful are the lyrics which fill this new volume, by an American poet who long since proved his ability. Langston Hughes packs as much into nine lines as some poets get into ninety. So short as to appear almost fragmentary are some of the lyrics in *Fields of Wonder.* Yet most of them offer the reader a stimulating experience. And the reader goes eagerly from one poem to another.

Probably one of the most useful tricks in this poet's artistry is knowing when to stop—a rarer gift than most people might suppose. This is evident in many of the new lyrics.

Some of the shorter poems are merely scraps of observation, of no marked importance, yet they are said with distinction. Deep tragedy lies at the core of some; for example, "Genius Child," with its poignant refrain: "Nobody loves a genius child." Penetrating, compassionate, mellow in his cynicism, completely mature, the poet writes of many different things in many different places. In "Montmartre" he gives a deft, quick sketch of the Rue Pigalle. The old world and the new are both represented. The section called "Stars Over Harlem" brings to mind an excellent book of poems by the same author, *Shakespeare in Harlem*. Direct and apparently simple, these Harlem poems in both books show the most skillful and practiced hand, and an unerring poetic instinct. The poem about the Negro trumpet player of 52nd Street ends with the stanza:

> But softly
> As the tune comes from his throat
> Trouble
> Mellows to a golden note.

When the band begins to play in a Harlem dance hall, flowers, trees, and air appear:

> And like a wave the floor—
> That had no dignity before!

[. . .]

Guide Post [Cincinnati Public Library], 22 (June 1947), 11

Though lacking real skill, this lyric poet shows a fragile nostalgic charm. For those interested in the development of Negro poetry.

"Theatre Arts Bookshelf: *Fields of Wonder*" *Theatre Arts,* 31 (June 1947), 74–5

[. . .]

When the musical version of Elmer Rice's *Street Scene* appeared, a good many people noted the fact that the lyrics, by Langston Hughes, had all the quality of street speech underlying their poetry. Those who were familiar with Hughes' poetry took this for granted since this matter of the simple word tied to the poet's forms and thoughts was an essential part of his poetic expression. And never was this more so than in the slim new volume which he calls *Fields of Wonder,* and which opens with four typical Hughes lines:

> Heaven is
> The place where
> Happiness is
> Everywhere

Mr. Knopf, as publisher, has been generous with his poet; each poem, many of them only eight or ten lines long, has a page to itself. But the generosity is rewarded; the lines of the poems have wings that spread across the empty spaces, like these from an eleven-line poem called "Stars." . . .

Harriet Hambarin
"Dreamdust"
New Masses, 63 (10 June 1947), 26

Ever since poetry began, the plain, the solid, the monosyllabic (Keats': "And no birds sing"), the direct and everyday (Shakespeare's: "Pray you, undo this button"), the momentous because the common (Wordsworth's: "And never lifted up a single stone") have been the stuff that poetry is made of. Langston Hughes follows this tradition.

In "Juliet," for example, the simple conventional words alone produce the starkness of the situation:

> There are wonder
> And pain
> And terror,
> And sick silly songs
> Of sorrow,
> And the marrow
> Of the bone
> Of life
> Smeared across
> Her mouth.
>
> The road
> From Verona
> To Mantova
> Is dusty
> With the drought.

In "Trumpet Player: 52nd Street," which *Mainstream* has published, the poet has employed simple words still but has added to them the fierceness of the unconventional image without distortion of language. There is no ambidextrous word play in both poems cited. Realism is present, and the greater suggestiveness inherent in simplicity projects the meaning.

The suggestiveness of the direct symbol is also used by the poet with good effect, as the use of the symbol of the Red Star in the poem "When the Armies Passed."

However, side by side with a poem of this order are poems reminiscent of the Romantic era. Too often the poet's fields of wonder are only the silver rain, the moonlight night, the snake (pretty much as D. H. Lawrence saw him), dream-dust, snails, rainbows, trees, and the "half-shy young moon/ Veiling her face like a virgin/ Waiting for a lover." Stars and sun and moon, not felt with the passion that Hughes has for the social outrages of our time, can only produce the curious self-indulgence of "A House in Taos," in which "three smitten by beauty" fear the "windlessness" of their Taos home. When Hughes leaves the Taos atmosphere and with no romantic backwash reminds us that

> Walls have been known
> To fall,
> Dusk turn to dawn
> And chains be gone!

we are reassured that the poet's deep sense of reality will lead him to more passionate fields of wonder.

"U.S. Treasury vs. Axis"
Newark Evening News,
10 June 1947, p. 12

Hughes, with his gift of simple wonder and of effortless (or seemingly effortless) melody, writes on the poet's usual themes—nature, human emotions, people, faith and the lack of it, freedom—with a special section called "Stars Over Harlem." He can look at a snail and imagine that

Weather and rose
Is all you know.

More vibrant with thought is his picture of "Trumpet-Player: 52nd Street," and understandable pessimism pervades his thought of the little southern girl who, in a Northern school, is afraid to play with the white children. His impression "Harlem Dimout" is description of the immediate and at the same time a symbol. All of these poems are brief; they reveal Hughes as still one of our most likable and most lyrical poets.

Frank Marshall Davis
"A Look at Books"
Los Angeles Sentinel,
12 June 1947, [p. 7]

Langston Hughes writes with such ease and disarming charm that many people who ordinarily would have little patience with poetry are completely captivated by his work. That, I think, is the secret of his popularity which has made him the most widely read of Negro poets for some two decades.

His fifth and latest volume, recently published, is devoted to lyric poems. Brightly polished they are, and carefully cut like small diamonds. They range from pure imagery to glimpses of reality. Best of all, they communicate directly with the emotions.

Of course Mr. Hughes is modern, having a command of both rhyme and free verse, but giving rhyme the living feeling of today instead of the stuffiness of the departed past. For instance, here is his "Little Song":

In the lonely night
Grab a lonely dream
And hold it tight.
Lonely people
In the lonely day
Work to salt
Their dream away.

In this volume Mr. Hughes is not preoccupied with what is known as "the race problem." He uses a universal approach, on behalf of all humanity, so that the reader may see the world through the eyes of a poet who happens to be a Negro instead of as an open propagandist. There are just enough verses that could have been written only by a Negro to assure the success of this indirect approach.

George Scarbrough
"'Simple' Poems"
Chattanooga Times,
22 June 1947, p. 19

To say very little things amounts to very little, even if they are said well, for the way of saying is equal only to the things said. But when the meaning of what is said hopelessly outdistances the manner of saying, then the poet has laid hold merely upon the shadow of his dilemma and is caught within the maze of his two purposes, at cross with each other: his desire to communicate a thought, an idea, or an emotion, on the one hand, and his inescapable knowledge that his style of conveyance must be suitable to the tone of his statement, yet somehow acceptable to the people who read it, on the other.

Langston Hughes, it occurs to me, has considerably confused himself in the *Fields of Wonder*. Matters of large import are tossed off with a few and frequently non-sensical lines, whose rhymes are those a child might apply to a similar theme. He is lost in simplicity, or rather was lost in his search for that somehow ordained and natural quality, and the result he obtains is simple, well enough, but could hardly be termed effectual simplicity, in the good sense of that word. A bit of the old "spiritual" ardor might have resurrected these poems; it surely would have fleshened his lines and given their meaning a commensurate expression. But there is no such ardor. These poems are neither this nor that. Some of them are the stuff of love songs, more of them are the germs of spirituals; but all of them are the frail breathings of a strong poet grown pretty and indolent. Mr. Hughes should reconsider.

> Great lonely hills.
> Great mountains.
> Mighty touchstones of song.

True, Mr. Hughes, but where are the songs?

Henry C. Tracy
"One World—of Many Creeds and Colors"
Common Ground, 7 (Summer 1947), 109–11

[. . .]

All turmoil of race and hate drops behind as we enter Langston Hughes' *Fields of Wonder,* a book of lyric poems. Pioneering in brevity of poetic expression, Hughes has caught in fewest words an elusive meaning, a surprise, a wordless wonder; held it for an instant and let it go, leaving but a slight imprint on the page. But his imprint, by some magic, makes a poet of the man who reads. This is a height few lyricists have attained.

[. . .]

Dora Hagemeyer
"Have You Read . . . ?"
Carmel [Calif.] *Pine Cone,* 4 July 1947, p. 8

The title of the new collection of poems by Langston Hughes, *Fields of Wonder,* attracts the reader before he has opened the book. And the "wonder" is to be found before many pages are turned, the clear sunny singing, the grief transmuted, the questions still unanswered but containing their own answer. "In time of silver rain . . . the wonder spreads."

Here is the true charm of poetry: the ecstasy merely hinted, never too completely; so that the reader experiences the fresh delight for himself. He is the discoverer. The poet has merely opened the gate. These little lyrics, of short lines deeply felt or merely brushed with thought, are in themselves "mighty touchstones of song." They kindle, they shatter, they awaken. Grief, race-grief, drives its dark thrust; joy enters like star-beams; mere happiness is an earth-song. These free-moving rhythms, caught before they become obvious, release rather than curb the music. It is a beauty of spirit beyond that of mind and heart. It does not stay to complete. It kindles and moves on.

Langston Hughes has kept his heart open to all human problems. His awareness is keen and sensitive. He gives himself freely to a wide range of moods and emotions but—he never loses hold of his contact with reality. He is primarily a human being, threading his way through the city, toiling in the fields, subject to peace and persecution, praise and condemnation. But above and beyond this he listens for the sudden song in the most unexpected places. Out of the chaos of modern living he retrieves "one handful of dream-dust, not for sale."

[. . .]

Although much honor has come to him, Langston Hughes has retained his humility and natural simplicity. His spirit is wreathed with the sun. He "wanders through this living world and leaves uncut the roses," and perhaps that is why we become so aware of their fragrance.

[. . .]

Ruth Lechlitner
"Stevens, Cullen, Hughes, Bynner, Greenberg: An Interesting Selection of Contemporary Poetry by Five Poets New and Not So New"
New York Herald Tribune Weekly Book Review,
31 August 1947, p. 4

[. . .]

Fields of Wonder, Langston Hughes' latest book, is a grouping of slight, softly-syncopated lyrics. In contrast to the more formal, literary manner of Countee Cullen, Hughes's work has always been simple, colloquial, with a natural, "folklore" charm. Several of the verses in *Fields of Wonder* recapture the mood and manner of his earlier poems in *The Weary*

Blues. Such are "Trumpet Player: 52nd Street," "Harlem Dance Hall," "Migration." Some of the short nature pieces remind one of Sandburg; others have the artless, childlike quality found in Vachel Lindsay:

Heaven is
The place where
Happiness is
Everywhere.

Animals
And birds sing—
As does
Everything.

To each stone,
"How-do-you-do?"
Stone answers back
"Well! And you?"

But in still others the very simplicity seems shallow, or forced and contrived. The fault may rest not so much with the individual poems, but on the fact that their range of theme is too narrow, their lyric patterns too alike, to make an effective book collection.

John Russell McCarthy
"Four Poets for Public"
Pasadena Star-News,
31 August 1947, p. 17

This reviewer believes that the four books mentioned above were well chosen and hopes that the publishers and authors make out fairly well with the reading public. (No point in hoping more than that.) All four books are addressed to the ordinary citizen—no effort here to reach only advanced teachers of English and more advanced college sophomores.

Langston Hughes, author of *Fields of*

318

Wonder, has been writing some of America's better lyrics for about a quarter of a century. The music is always there, and the feeling. When one sees his name one expects a good lyric—and what better reputation could the poet ask? Mr. Hughes does well when he sings against racial prejudices; he is clear and convincing and does not say too much. Nevertheless those of his lyrics which have to do only with being human are surer, and surer of remembrance. Consider his "Songs." . . .

[. . .]

John W. Parker
"Lyrics of Our Times"
Journal of Negro Education, 16 (Fall 1947), 562–4

When Langston Hughes sat down to complete his newly-published collection of poems, *Fields of Wonder,* he was a worried man; the atmosphere about him was tense, and the reader who is touched off by what he reads, will swallow hard before he is through. Recalling something of the pathos and occasionally the tragedy implicit in Gwendolyn Brooks' *A Street in Bronzeville,* the volume abounds in phrases that betray the inner struggle of Brown Americans who must move in an "out group" set apart for them—"vague dreams all mixed up," "earth quake weather," "we the desperate," "weariness that bows me down," and "death in the night."

Wonder is the natural consequence when, as Hughes sees it, Southern-born Negroes stream to metropolitan areas only to add to the "scum of our weary city," and even a return to the soil offers nothing more satisfying than "a broken song in October." Although the reader finds between the covers of this book momentary flashes of sunshine, the shadows predominate. Hughes is preoccupied with people and things, with hopes and frustrations, each as a segment of a larger whole—sometimes the South, sometimes American democracy, and sometimes the whole matter of life itself.

The author has chosen to group his poems, seventy-three in all, under nine headings—"Tearless," "Marital Storm," "Words like Freedom," and "Fields of Wonder," appearing among the number. The divisions are more formal, however, than organic, for in each group the reader finds modern lyrics that vary in meter, in mood, and in quality. By and large the most powerful from the point of view of penetrating analysis is the group of poems which appears under the heading "Tearless." It is in this section that the author touches upon the familiar topic of what it means to the totality of one's personality to be segregated and exploited, to move with the "have nots" in a land of plenty. A section of the poem "Vagabonds" shall speak for itself:

> We are the desperate
> We do not care,
> The hungry
> Who have no where
> To eat,
> No place to sleep.

And certainly the poem "Walls" points unmistakably to the unwholesome socioeconomic conditions which surround America's largest minority group. In it Hughes becomes a Mr. Looking Both Ways:

> Four walls can shelter
> So much sorrow
> Garnered from yesterday
> And held for tomorrow.

In the section, "Fields of Wonder," one finds poems which surpass in freshness and delicacy. There is something beautiful and almost touching, something distinctly Wordsworthian about the ditty "Snail," which runs to an even nine lines:

Little snail,
Dreaming you go,
Weather and rose
Is all you know.

Weather and rose
Is all you see
Drinking
The dewdrop's
Mystery.

Moreover, the reader will discover intensity and majesty in the "great lonely hills" that constitute the framework of the poem "Big Sur."

Least impressive of all are the poems which fall under the heading "Stars Over Harlem." Here the poet returns to his first love—a reflection on the ways of the Harlem dweller and the social milieu of which he is a part. The whole appears little more than a rehash of topics previously treated in one way or another; one finds here more of the glitter and tinsel and less of the soul of an urban Negro community struggling against the odds. A larger concern with the total American scene and a lessening of emphasis upon Harlem *per se* is perhaps one indication of Hughes' enlarged perspective.

Like the four collections of poetry which have preceded it, *Fields of Wonder* suggests the vast possibilities of the modern American lyric in natural, free-flowing patterns. As to flavor and form, the book is reminiscent of the work of Carl Sandburg. Hughes has included a variety of themes which range from the cotton field to the cabaret; almost everywhere the stream of lyricism runs deep and the entire collection is heightened by the poet's remarkable insight into human experience. The reader will find in this new volume of poems a charm and a buoyancy, an intensity and a breadth of appeal not characteristic of his earlier collections. By all standards, Langston Hughes is now a significant American poet. In *Fields of Wonder* he has discovered what it is that makes poetry "tick."

Harold C. Gardiner "Poetry, Criticism, Short Stories" *America*, 78 (15 November 1947), xviii

[. . .]
Good sampling of modern American verse can be had in *Fields of Wonder* by Langston Hughes, which is sensitive but oppressed with a sense of futility. . . .

ONE-WAY TICKET

M. B. Tolson
"Books and Authors: Let My People Go"
Southwestern Journal, 4
(Fall–Winter 1948), 41–3

In his latest book of poems, *One-Way Ticket,* which is fittingly illustrated by Jacob Lawrence, Langston Hughes reveals that he has not lost the magic touch of his initial *The Weary Blues.* Few poets in America have equaled the globe-trotting Missourian in faithfulness to a milieu and the artistic exploration of it. In the kingdom of poetry there are many mansions. Hughes selected one early and has lived in it ever since.

One-Way Ticket shows that he is still the sophisticate and humanist on Vine Street, Lenox Avenue, Rampart Street, Beale Street, South Parkway, South Street, Elm Street, Texas Avenue, and Central Avenue. Langston Hughes is the poet of the urban Negro as Paul Laurence Dunbar was the poet of the rural Negro:

Could be Hastings Street,
Or Lenox Avenue,
Could be 18th & Vine
And still be true.

Could be 5th & Mound,
Could be Rampart:
When you pawned my watch
You pawned my heart.

To evaluate Hughes, one must see him moving in and out of beauty parlors, barber shops, taverns, flats, churches, byway stations, jails, policy offices, barbecue joints—the *poietes* sucking in the sights and sounds and smells of the black proletariat in a white man's wilderness. He has turned the naive ballads of the dusky bard into the conscious art of the poet. He is the blues troubadour par excellence. In the mansion of the blues he is the wise host. He and his urban proletarian are souls in one skin clad.

His sensitive ear catches the nuances of comedy and tragedy, the subtle implications of dark laughter, as they buoy up in "Madam to You," "One-Way Ticket," "Midnight Raffle," and "Home in a Box."

I pick up my life
And take it away
On a one-way ticket—
Gone up North,
Gone out West,
Gone!

One observes how the meters fit the brevity of the decision, the tempo of modern life. The urban Negro is caught in the crush of the black metropolis. The blues forms are products of modern industrialism. They build up in short, dramatic lines, like the pains of a woman in travail; then comes the O. Henry crack at the end. Here it is in the poignant "Deceased":

Harlem
Sent him home
In a long box—
Too dead
To know why:
The licker
Was lye.

Sometimes he gives the biography of his people cryptically, ironically, yet damningly, in a few staccato words, as in "Madam's Calling Card":

There's nothing foreign
To my pedigree:
Alberta K. Johnson—
"American" that's me.

Again he reaches universality, with an effortlessness that belies his ingenuity:

The graveyard is the
Cheapest boarding house:
 Some of these days
 We'll all board there.

Despite the differences in techniques, his "Florida Road Workers" made me think of Archibald MacLeish's "Burying Ground by the Ties" in *Frescoes for Mr. Rockefeller's City*. MacLeish's road builders—Negroes, Magyars, and Polacks—are dead; so the poet has to speak for them. Hughes is the black worker, sweatingly aware—the black worker himself speaking:

I'm makin' a road
For the cars to fly by on,
Makin' a road
Through the palmetto thicket
For light and civilization
To travel on.

So anyone who reads Langston Hughes as the sophisticate and humanist, the inheritor of the magnificent heritage of blues-singers and work-song bards, will be able to appreciate his fine contribution to his people and to America.

"The Poetry of the Negro: *One-Way Ticket*" *Virginia Kirkus Bulletin*, 16 (15 November 1948), 609

One-Way Ticket is a new volume by the poet. . . . This time he seems both overwhelmed and subdued by the trials and tribulations of his race. It is all a one-way street for him, the street of discrimination and despair. The form of these poems is light, the subject matter heavy. The result is not quite a satisfactory mixture either as

pure poetry or human appeal. Stronger, finer things have been written by other Negro poets. The defiance here seems feeble, as is the poetic gift—a disappointment from Langston Hughes in a time when powerful expression is called for. The sale of the book will be largely from his admirers (who will be disappointed) and from those who are interested in any expression of this race.

Gladys P. Graham "Books on Review: A Poet Speaks Out for Black Americans" *New Jersey Herald News,* [January or February ?] 1949, [p. ?]

Versatile Langston Hughes has returned to his original forte, poetry.

His *One-Way Ticket* breaks his long hiatus from this literary realm.

Dubbed the Negro Poet Laureate by no less a personality than the noted Carl Van Vechten, Hughes attains the height of quintessence in this ebullient collection.

There is a deep and underlying racial philosophy embedded in the rhythmical distillation of Langston Hughes' poetry. The author has attempted to mirror his conception of some of the trials and tribulations of those unfortunates who are non-Caucasian.

"Madam to You," concerning the life and times of one Alberta K. Johnson, a humorous character created by the Missourian, is indicative of many of the writer's reflections on prosaic phrases of the thought and actions of the common folk.

Hughes is loath to ignore the second class citizenship accorded America's largest minority. He is therefore on home ground when he lambasts "Restrictive Covenants. . . ."

When I move
Into a Neighborhood
Folks fly
Even every foreigner
That can move, moves
Why?

The author's "Lunch Song," is the mournful dirge of that "Black Boy's Still Body."

The splendid illustrations by Jacob Lawrence, the human relations artist, enhance and make more vivid the written words from the pen of the incomparable Langston Hughes, one of the nation's most versatile young authors.

The renowned artist has performed a unique and distinctive service to his race and to the literary world.

Those who think deeply and who are stirred to action by the underlying semantics herein will find in *One-Way Ticket,* published by Knopf, a book to be reckoned with. The text is one from which the most untutored reader will gain some insight into the complex racial patterns of our time.

Rudolph Aggrey
"Hughes' New Book *One-Way Ticket* Offers Frank, Humor-Spiked Verse"
Cleveland Call and Post,
1 January 1949, p. 4B

Langston Hughes, who once said he received his first inspiration from Miss Ethel Weiman, former English teacher at Central High School, has completed his sixth book of verse.

One-Way Ticket . . . goes on sale Jan. 10. As Hughes' ninth volume it is another well-fashioned notch on the achievement stick of a distinguished writer who roamed the area around Karamu House and ran track under the banner of Central High as a youth.

Unlike *Fields of Wonder,* Hughes' 1947 volume of delicate lyric poems, *One-Way Ticket* comprises stanzas of hard-boiled verse, written without fear or favor, depicting unvarnished aspects of modern Negro life. It is poetry some Negroes will not like because it deals with situations and circumstances many hold have been over-played by writers of color.

But much that one finds between the telling illustrations of Jacob Lawrence, rising young painter, which help the reader catch the spirit of the book, is bitter truth cleverly spiked with humor.

It is this ability to sympathetically blend comedy with tragedy in arresting word patterns that has given great readability to Hughes' poetry as well as his prose. *One-Way Ticket* is divided into 10 groups of poems, each selection in a group being related either in subject or in setting. Entitled "Madam to You," the first group depicts the late Madam Alberta K. Johnson, of hairdressing preparation fame, and her response to varying situations and people.

With tongue in cheek Hughes describes the Madam's thoughts on her past history, her madam, calling cards, the rent man, a number writer, the phone bill, the charity child, the fortune teller, the wrong visitor, the minister, her "might-have-been," and the census man.

In the section "Life is Fine" the author offers several earthy poems on the "hush, hush" subject of illegitimacy. Also in this group is a sermon-type poem of the pattern made famous by the late James Weldon Johnson and typified in his "The Creation" and "Go Down Death."

There is much satire in Hughes' sermon. For example he ends "Sunday Morning Prophecy" on this note:

Come into the church this morning
Brothers and Sisters
And be saved—

And give freely
In the collection basket
That I who am thy shepherd
Might live.

Amen!

In the group "Dark Glasses" he writes of vacations at Atlantic City, a stage show at the old Philadelphia Lincoln Theatre, of Billie Holiday. Here he reveals more his keen musical sense of rhythm. In a short selection, "Still Here," he says:

I've been scarred and battered
My hopes the wind done scattered
Snow has froze me, sun has baked me
Looks like between 'em
They done tried to make me
Stop laughing; stop lovin'; stop
    livin'—
But I don't care!
I'm still here.

Lynching and flight from mobs are the subject matter of the selections entitled "Silhouettes"; immigration from the south to the north and midwest that of "One-Way Ticket"; and the battle for freedom in this country that of "Making a Road."

The last-mentioned section includes a bit of moving verse, "Democracy," which ends with the assertion:

Freedom
Is a strong seed
Planted
In a great need.
I live here too.

I want freedom
Just as you.

Songs of despair in love, of frustration comprise a group called "Too Blue." Of the same mood are six selections under the heading "Midnight Raffle." Hughes offers five different thoughts of death in the section "Home in a Box."

The last group has its setting in Chicago's South Side and describes in panorama life in that area. Selections in this group are of strong verse mirroring several aspects of the sweep and power of the Windy City.

One-Way Ticket is hardly a book of great poetry, but few volumes are. It is a collection of significant verse; highly original and unpretentious. Certainly it deserves a place on the shelf with the vagabond poet's other volumes: *The Weary Blues,* his first book of sensitive, subjective verse, *Not Without Laughter,* his candid novel which chronicles the life of a Negro boy in the middle west, *The Ways of White Folks,* a collection of short stories viewing Negro-white relations from the Negro viewpoint, *The Big Sea,* a narrative of the rich experiences of his early years, *Fine Clothes to the Jew* and *Shakespeare in Harlem,* satiric verse of the urban East, *The Dream Keeper,* poetry for young readers, and *Fields of Wonder.*

Author of nine books, a Broadway play, *Mulatto,* and the lyrics for the well-received musical *Street Scene,* Hughes at 46 has come a long way from his Central High School days. But he still insists that it was encouragement given him by a patient English teacher that started him on the way.

"Hughes' Latest Book Traces Race Pattern" *Philadelphia Tribune,* 8 January 1949, p. 4

In returning to his original forte, poetry, Langston Hughes pictures an America that is "no bed of roses for the darker brother" in his latest volume, *One-Way Ticket.*

There is a deep underlying racial philosophy embedded in the rhythmical distillation of Hughes' poems. He has attempted to mirror his conception of some of the troubles and futilities of the Negro race.

His poem "Restrictive Covenants" asks a pertinent question:

When I move
Into a Neighborhood
Folks Fly.
Even every foreigner
That can move, moves.
Why?

Some poems like "Madam to You" demonstrate the poet's humor, through the character of Alberta E. Johnson, to give his prosaic phases of thought and actions of the common folk. His "Lynch Song" is a mournful dirge.

Those who think deeply will find in *One-Way Ticket* a book that can give them invaluable insight on the cultural patterns of our time.

David Daiches "Poetry of Negro Moods" *New York Herald Tribune Weekly Book Review,* 9 January 1949, p. 4

Langston Hughes's poetry is what, in terms of the art of the motion picture, would be called documentary. His concern is to document the moods and problems of the American Negro, to set side by side in simple and lively form pictures and impressions which will add up to a presentation of the American Negro's present situation. This kind of writing is worlds apart from the subtle distillation of meaning aimed at by other serious contemporary poets. For Mr. Hughes, the idiom of poetry is valuable only to the degree that it pins down a situation and draws it to the attention of his readers. The ultimate meaning, the subtler vision of reality, the oblique insight into man's personality and man's fate are not him; he has a more urgent and immediate problem, to project the living American Negro onto the page. And he does so, on the whole, with success.

The simple jazz rhythms run through much of Mr. Hughes's verse, and they combine with a more general folk idiom—or at least the "feel" of folk poetry—to produce a strange and sad sense of inevitability:

Number runner
Come to my door.
I had swore
I wouldn't play no more.
He said, Madam,
6—0—2
Looks like a likely
Hit for you.

The function of rhyme in such poems as "Madam to You" is to emphasize the points:

> If I ever catch him,
> Lawd have pity!
> Calling me up
> From Kansas City!
>
> Just to say he loves me!
> I knowed that was so.
> Why didn't he tell me some'n
> I don't know?

Sometimes the poems are mere versified observations, significant as fact rather than as poetry. Sometimes—as in "Florida Road Workers"—the observations are so precise and are conveyed so directly and unpretentiously that the result is a perfect documentary poem. Sometimes—as in the section "Too Blue"—the blues idiom (a very special kind of folk idiom) is used to capture that characteristically Negro sense of melancholy.

Jacob Lawrence, the interesting young Negro painter, contributes some half-dozen illustrations—one might call them stylized documentaries in black and white—which provide effective comment on the poems.

R.S.
"A Negro Poet: Jazz Tradition and a Primitive Beat"
Charlotte News, 13 January 1949, p. 10A

Negro poet Langston Hughes is a poetic sophisticate who apparently prefers to be a poetic primitive, a sort of Grandma Moses à la T. S. Eliot.

He is one of America's most accomplished poets; his work always strikes a reverberating note of artistic independence; it sounds a determined tocsin of artistic now-or-never and it gives issue to a cry of artistic anguish.

His music, and actually it can't be called poetry, is solidly in the New Orleans jazz tradition. Most of his songs are flat, melancholy blues that could be set to a W. C. Handy melody without difficulty.

He writes of the man who comes around to take your regular morning bet in the numbers racket, of the pimp and the madam. And—sometimes sadly and sometimes with wry laughter—he tells you that no one can live a decent life if his fortune is dependent on the butter-and-eggs number or if his pleasure is dependent upon the other two. Or if he cannot find a philosophy of living outside the world of these three.

You'll like Hughes' music in *One-Way Ticket*—it is simple and direct and has courage and energy and drive. But you won't say he is versatile; you may get a little tired of the same old madam in the same old beat.

Charles A. Brady
"Two Poets' Work Stands Out in Sharp Contrast"
Buffalo Evening News Magazine, 15 January 1949, p. 5

Langston Hughes' best lines would sound even better crooned to boogie-woogie background music; they are compact of "voice of muted trumpet; cold brass in warm air." One can grow weary of the invariable Frankie-and-Johnny-tempi, as well as of an occasional phony primitivism. But one must applaud the poetic anthropology that can find such fine objective correlatives for its mournful themes as "soft sad black feet" dancing "drowsy as the rain" in a city gin mill; and, to counterpoint that immemorial sadness of resignation, this perfect affirmation of survival:

Since I'm still here living,
I guess I will live on.
I would've died for love—
But for livin' I was born.

A historian of jazz recently made the claim that Negro "blues" express the colored man's revolt and despair against the status white society accords him. Harlem is the ultimate expression of that status and of that revolt; Harlem, so terribly indicted by Thomas Merton as "what God thinks of Hollywood" which "is all Harlem has, in its despair, to grasp at, by way of a surrogate for heaven."

But Harlem is more than a dark steaming slum. It is also a state of mind, and, as Mr. Hughes puts it, it is "the edge of hell." Mr. Hughes' recognition of this fact is at once the justification for and the limitation of his kind of poetry.

[. . .]

Rolfe Humphries
"Verse Chronicle"
Nation, 168 (15 January 1949), 80

The virtues of Mr. Hughes' poetry are, mainly, those of forbearance. Given the single theme, he treats his data with great restraint: basic vocabulary, simple rhymes, short line; no violence, no hyperbole, no verbalizing. The rhetoric, such as there is, is that of understatement; this kind of rhetoric is easier to slide over than that of exaggeration, but it contains, no less, the contrived element, and in the long run Mr. Hughes's use of these devices induces in the reader an effect opposite, I feel sure, to that which he intends. The studied artlessness pretty soon puts the reader too off guard, makes him condescending, patronizing. "How simple the Negro is," he will be saying to himself if he doesn't watch out, and, in a few minutes, "How quaint!" I for one should like to see what Mr. Hughes could do if he would try his hand on work more elaborate, involved, complex, be less for a change the spokesman than the individual, exploit more fully than he has seemed to want to so far his own personal resources of education, travel, reading, music other than blues.

Gertrude Martin
"January Hughes' Month of Books"
Chicago Defender, 15 January 1949, [p. 7]

[. . .]

Mr. Hughes' bright, down-to-earth poems shine with greater brilliance in this new collection. He speaks out in no uncertain terms, but without malice, against the powers that be who keep the Negro in the slums. In "The Ballad of Margie Polite" he takes a jab at the—

Colored leaders
In sound trucks.
Somebody yelled,
Go home, you hucks!

Two of the divisions of his poems "One-Way Ticket" and "Making a Road" are concerned with the Negro's life in the ghetto, in Harlem, on Chicago's South Side.

> You can talk about
> Across the railroad tracks—
> To me it's here
> On this side of the tracks. . . .

In these unpretentious poems Langston Hughes expresses the gay, undefeated philosophy with a serious undertone which makes his columns and other prose writing such an interesting commentary on the Negro as he is. *One-Way Ticket* is, I think, superior to Mr. Hughes' more recent poems. Here his rhythm is sure and lilting, and his poems tell much about the Negro that their author says extremely well. The illustrations by Jacob Lawrence are an excellent accompaniment for Mr. Hughes' poetry.

J. Saunders Redding
"Book Review"
Afro-American Magazine,
15 January 1949, p. 4

One of the arresting things about Langston Hughes is that, in spite of the fact that his verse is often jejune and, in these latter years, iterative, his reputation keeps glowing as bright as a hearth fire on a dull day. That reputation, which he has well-earned, goes marching on, while a goodly portion of his poetry lags somewhere back in the not-too-critical days of the colored renaissance.

Though one recognizes this intellectually, emotionally one rejects it—partly because an old loving admiration will not die, and partly because Langston Hughes occasionally still produces a lyric, or creates an effect so fresh, or sweet, or startling that one fears not to read him would be to miss a nugget of purest gold in an amount of dross.

Last year Hughes published *Fields of Wonder,* a volume which contains some of his finest pieces. Now, at the beginning of '49, comes *One-Way Ticket,* a collection of poems which falls back upon the old forms, the old rhythms, the old moods, the old idioms.

There is nothing in it to match the minted perfection of "Man," the subtle magic of "Trumpet Player: 52nd Street," or the low, pulsing melancholy of "Jaime." *One-Way Ticket* is stale, flat and spiritless.

And I think the reason for this dull plane of lifelessness is very simple: Hughes has long since matured beyond the capacity of the idiom he uses to express himself in *One-Way Ticket.*

It is many a year since he was the naive and simple and almost elemental lyricist of *Weary Blues* and the folk story-teller of *Ways of White Folks.* Intellectually and emotionally he has traveled a far piece—and he has not traveled in circles.

That, at least in this present volume, Hughes refuses to recognize this—while it shows an admirable loyalty to his self-commitment as the poet of the colored peasant, the laborer, the slum-dweller, and "common" folk—does a disservice to his art, his fully developed talent, and his intellectual awareness.

And the fact remains that Langston Hughes is not now, nor ever really was one of the "common" folk.

Back in the '20's and '30's, his sympathy for them had a blunt emotional forthrightness that was as fresh and genuine as any youthful outpouring of emotion.

But lately that sympathy seems a bit labored, a bit strained, like a conversation between old acquaintances who have had no mutual points of reference in a dozen years.

Nor are the colored "common" folk

quite like that any more. No one should know this better than Hughes. Sue and Ruby no longer "put on their red silk stockings and go out and let the white boys look" at their legs for free.

The price is now $4.40 for a balcony seat. And Big Boy, who boxes for a living, didn't choose fighting because he was dumb. "Johnson—Madam Alberta K"— knows more than Harlem or the Southside of Chicago now.

One-Way Ticket will interest—and perhaps entrance—those who know only this one volume of the author's work, but it will disappoint those who know the brilliance of some of Hughes's other books.

August Derleth
"The New Poetry"
Capital Times [Madison, Wisc.], 16 January 1949, [p. 36]

. . . Every reader who is interested in genuine emotional poetry with strong racial roots will enjoy *One-Way Ticket*, the first collection of poems on Negro subjects since Hughes' excellent *Shakespeare in Harlem* some years ago. This new book has all the virtues of its predecessor, and in addition it has striking illustrations by Jacob Lawrence, admirably complementary to the text. There is a generous selection of verse in this new collection, ranging from a dozen poems recounting the history of Madam Alberta K. Johnson to a section of poems celebrating Chicago's South Side. There is again a fine section of blues poems which have a music all their own.

It is perfectly patent that Hughes loves his race, and that he interprets it as well as anyone in his chosen medium. His in-

tensely, passionately subjective verse is lyrical and dramatic, affirmatively musical and always deeply sensitive. *One-Way Ticket* is a distinguished volume to put beside those collections from his pen which have preceded it.

[. . .]

Margaret L. Hartley
"Negro Poetry in America"
Dallas Morning News, section 2, 16 January 1949, p. 13

Two books bearing the name of Langston Hughes on their title pages have been issued this month, within a few days of each other. With *One-Way Ticket* the Negro poet returns, after the excursion represented by the poems in his previous book, *Fields of Wonder*, to his best and truest vein. *One-Way Ticket* follows the line of poetic development which began with *Weary Blues* and was continued in *Shakespeare in Harlem*.

When Langston Hughes was first introduced to the public, in the twenties, both he and the country had been having some pretty gaudy adventures. In that decade every emotion was blown up a little oversize, paced a little too hectically. And even the most deeply felt protest of the poet in that day sounds, read after these years, just a trifle rhetorical. But now that shadow has disappeared. The new poems are uniformly honest and living.

The mood of *One-Way Ticket* is varied. There are the blues rhythms of which Hughes has such a thorough mastery, and there is the wry humor of the section entitled "Madam to You: The Life and Times of Alberta K. Johnson." There are sharply drawn pictures of Harlem and of Chicago's South Side. The poems hum and moan with a rich-throated melody. And they also speak with an eloquence which contains no bombast. If they are sometimes awkward, it is with the awkwardness of wood-carvings cut with quick deep strokes from wood so fresh that pitch still oozes from the marks of the knife.

[. . .]

Walter Spearman
"The Literary Lantern: Negro Poems"
Charlotte Observer, 16 January 1949, [p. 6D]

[. . .]

Langston Hughes, a Negro poet who was born in Missouri in 1902, has written short stories, books, plays and songs in which he has aptly and movingly expressed the joys, the sorrows and the philosophies of the Negro race in America. Such earlier books as *The Weary Blues* and *Shakespeare in Harlem* and *The Dream-Keeper* have established him as one of the most eloquent spokesmen for the Negro.

His new book of verse is *One-Way Ticket.* Most striking in both theme and execution is the poem which gives the book its title, a heart-felt presentation of why the Negro wants a "one-way ticket" out of the South. Other poems in a similar vein are "Restrictive Covenants," "Negro Servant," and "Democracy," in which he laments that "I do not need freedom when I'm dead. I cannot live on tomorrow's bread."

The rhythm of his blues songs and the gay humor of his poems about "Alberta K.

Johnson—Madam to You" are as amusing as his dirges under the title of "Home in a Box" are pathetic. "The Graveyard Is the Cheapest Boarding House" is a particularly good example of the latter.

[. . .]

"Cover to Cover"
Atlanta Journal, 23 January 1949, p. 10C

This is a refreshing new book of poems by the gifted Negro writer, who has made some refreshing contributions to the literature of our day. Predominantly, Langston Hughes is a troubadour of the "blues," the rhythm of which he utilizes with extreme effectiveness.

In this collection he portrays sometimes whimsically, sometimes bitterly, the comedy, the tragedy, the everyday experiences of the members of the Negro race. The volume opens with a collection entitled "Madame to You! The Life and Times of Alberta K. Johnson," profuse with droll humor and a delight to read. Much of the work in the volume, however, is pervaded by a deep bitterness, an anguished resentment at the lot of the Negro in America.

Irving Dilliard
"Poetry: New Volumes by and about Negro Poets"
St. Louis Post-Dispatch, 23 January 1949, [p. 4B]

These two books present Langston Hughes as Negro poet and anthologer.

One-Way Ticket, his sixth volume of verse, is in the passionate, keenly sensitive style that blended comedy and tragedy in such earlier collections as *Shakespeare in Harlem* and *The Weary Blues.*

Some of the lines have an impact that is no less strong because it happens to be quietly expressed. For example, after Roland Hayes was beaten in Georgia in 1942, Hughes wrote:

> Negroes, Sweet and docile,
> Meek, humble and kind;
> Beware the day
> They change their minds!

[. . .]

W. T. Scott
"Round Up of Books in Poetry Field: Negroes and Irish in Anthologies"
Providence Journal, section 6, 23 January 1949, p. 8

[. . .]

Langston Hughes himself has a new collection, *One-Way Ticket,* including some black-and-white illustrations by Jacob Lawrence. The poems read easy: they are further humorous, pathetic notations of misadventures in the jazz-narrative or blues-repetitive style Hughes has developed consistently over the years.

[. . .]

John Broderick
"Briefly Noted: Verse"
New Yorker, 24 (29 January 1949), 72

True folk song sounds intense and inevitable; imitation folk song tends to be just verse. The Negro in America has succeeded many times in producing folk poetry, often of an interesting, urban kind, but only in the anonymous and semi-collective way that all folk poetry is produced. Mr. Hughes is a highly sophisticated individual, and, like all imitation folk artists, he often sounds thin and artificial.

Hubert Creekmore
"Two Rewarding Volumes of Verse"
New York Times Book Review, 30 January 1949, p. 19

In his new book Langston Hughes returns to the kind of poetry that made him famous twenty years ago—songs that express the intricate, paradoxical soul of the Negro. The backgrounds, the simplicity, the humor, the passion and the song, all are here. Yet a rather intangible change in feeling and form makes these poems slightly different. The lyric, blues and folk-song forms that Mr. Hughes has used to project, often with the lightest touch, the most devastating emotions and moral commentaries on life in the United States, have now been stripped almost to bare-ness. It is as if the poet, suspecting softness in his early work, were pushing toward an even more direct and forceful method.

The disappearance of the light touch is noticeable in the harshness of a few poems of "social protest." In a sense, most of Mr. Hughes' poems are protesting, subjectively for him and for the reader, even when they concern something as universal as physical love. One has no basis for objecting to such violent speech except that it doesn't often produce very good poems. Just the same, Mr. Hughes' forthrightness works well in many instances—"Negro Servant" and "Visitors to the Black Belt," for example.

The better poems are affirmations of joy in life, and sing of fun, love and courage. Their emotional appeal is immediate. The technique, instead of obscuring this appeal, urges it on, so that the lines seem spoken by a friend. This kind of work sustains an unfortunately dying tradition— that of oral poetry, song without melody, which can delight in varying ways the laborer and the don. . . .

[. . .]

apparently simple that they are disarming. Often they seem little more than jingles, yet underneath is a social consciousness and that elemental theme of all contemporary Negro writers, the groping for equality and a place in humanity's sun.

Hughes is facetious at times, especially in the section of the book entitled "Home Is a Box." Here we find:

DECEASED

Harlem
Sent him home
In a long box—
Too dead
To know why:
The licker
Was lye.

Probably it is an injustice to quote this poem. Hughes has done many better and more serious ones. He still, fortunately, uses his blues rhythm. He still writes of his own people. The format of the book is but another testimony to the pre-eminence of Alfred A. Knopf in the field of book making.

[. . .]

Kenneth Rockwell
"Mr. MacNeice Writes More Vagro Verses: Langston Hughes"
Dallas Times-Herald, section 6, 30 January 1949, pp. 4–5

[. . .]

This is also true of the work of Langston Hughes, outstanding American Negro poet and author of One-Way Ticket. As a matter of fact, Hughes' songs are so

---

Leo Kennedy
"Negro Life in Poetry"
Chicago Sun-Times, 31 January 1949, p. 37

[. . .]

His newest book, One-Way Ticket, carries sketches of ghetto Negro life, the South Parkway jitney, the interne at Provident, the numbers writer and the rent collector, to a higher point of skill. Hughes is probably the most noteworthy Negro poet writing today because he has synthesized observation, sensibility and political conviction into a hard, drill-sharp instrument of popular art and protest.

Millard Lampell
"Hughes and Guillén"
Masses and Mainstream,
2 (February 1949), 78–81

Langston Hughes occupies a rather special place in American life. Poet, novelist, playwright—he has become half artist, half institution. Over the years he has earned many and mixed honors: awards, grants, scholarships and fellowships—and persecution by the American Legion and other reactionary groups which are conducting a campaign to force cancellation of his lectures.

Hughes' verses continue to glow with pride and respect, and a wry cutting edge. And yet, in *One-Way Ticket* (his seventh volume of verse) there is something lacking—some sweep and intensity—the exploding anger, the exultance, the moving passion which would lift his work above the middle realm where it has circled for twenty-five years. The verses glow, but they do not burn.

There is something subtly disturbing in these latest poems. There is just the slightest edge of isolation—a sense of Hughes as a solitary onlooker watching the scene from his own hill. At its worst, this leads to painting a scene that is picturesque and "quaint," reminiscent of the gaudy Twenties when Van Vechten was discovering the "New Negro" and Hughes was writing "Jazzonia":

In a Harlem cabaret
Six long-headed jazzers play.
A dancing girl whose eyes are bold
Lifts high a dress of silken gold.

Now, more than twenty years later, the speakeasy has become a juice joint, and Hughes is on the bandstand tooting the same saxophone:

There is a gin mill on the avenue
Where singing black boys dance and
    play each night. . . .

Play your guitars, grinning
night-dark boys,
And let your songs drift
through the swinging doors.

The opening section of *One-Way Ticket* comprises a dozen short poems dealing with "The Life and Times of Alberta K. Johnson," a Harlem domestic worker. These deftly trace the familiar pattern: playing the numbers, visiting the fortune teller, flashing rebellion at the white madam, mourning the long-gone man. The verses have a simple dignity and the clear rhythms of street-corner talk, of the old ballads. By themselves, they are well-made. But a whole volume in this tempo—and a *seventh* volume at that—shows little indication that Hughes is still on the high crags he reached in "Let America Be America Again" and "Song to a Negro Wash-Woman." There is something missing from the Harlem of *One-Way Ticket*—the garbage, the ominous cops prowling the darkness, the outrage, the growing power of organization uniting an oppressed people. In other words, the poetic realization of experiences out of which are distilled such lines as:

A man comes home from work:
Knowing all things
Belong to the man
Who becomes
Men.

[. . .]

G. R. Cameron
"Langston Hughes Is Over-rated as No. 1 Poet, Critic Claims"
Pittsburgh Courier, 5 February 1949, p. 21

Langston Hughes has been writing for twenty-seven years, but one would never believe it from a perusal of his latest book of so-called poetry entitled *One-Way Ticket.* It is a sad commentary on the state of American poetry that Hughes ever won recognition as a poet.

It was apparent from publication of *The Weary Blues* a generation ago that Hughes lacked about everything one expects in a poet. But he was a Negro and at that time there was around New York a group of literary dilettantes "taking up" the Negro as an avocation.

Any young man or woman who was literate, engaging and eager to symbolize "The Negro" could get a publisher, regardless of the mediocrity of his work. Hughes became one of the literary darlings of this crowd upon whose word he has been accepted as an important poet.

At its best Langston Hughes' work is planless, maundering sentimentality, revealing the gnawing self-consciousness and inferiority complex of so many American Negro "intellectuals." At its worst it is cheap doggerel that would shame the most mediocre practitioner in Tin Pan Alley.

Indeed, a number of ordinary Negro lyric writers have ground out better stuff between drinks—and are still doing so. Put anything Hughes ever wrote alongside the second best American or British poetry and the gulf between them is depressingly vast. It is equally deep between his work and that of William Stanley Braithwaite, Joseph S. Cotter, Frank Marshall Davis, Margaret Walker, Georgia Douglas Johnson, Countee Cullen, Claude McKay and Paul Laurence Dunbar.

Even so, the pieces in the latest Hughes opus rise to Olympian heights above the incredible trash he ground out during the Thirties when he inflicted his proletarian verse upon a long-suffering public in "The Negro Mother" and other tripe.

Mr. Hughes is living evidence that anything can be put over if there is enough ballyhoo behind it from important sources. This is proved by the publication of *One-Way Ticket.* Happily there is some evidence that there may be a trend away from this so-called racial literature which has been a phoney ever since the fraudulent Negro Renaissance of the Twenties.

What we need now are more novelists and poets who are competent workmen first and only incidentally Negroes; people who are not ballyhooed to prominence by prominent people eager to "do something for the Negro," but who win high place because of the intrinsic merit of their work. Several such are now on the literary stage and we would welcome more of them.

Abner W. Berry
"*One-Way Ticket,* New Book of Poems by Langston Hughes"
Worker Magazine, 13 February 1949, p. 13; also in *People's World,* 18 February 1949, as "A New Book of Poems by Langston Hughes"

Langston Hughes, 20 years ago, was the eloquent singer of "New Negro." His *Weary Blues,* a slender volume published in the late 'twenties, established Hughes as the poetic spokesman of the Negro people. Using blues rhythms, blank verse and the folk imagery and idiom of a people then moving into a political struggle for their full rights, Hughes caught in his poems the mood and aspirations of America's oppressed and neglected darker brothers.

Hughes functioned in poetry as Duke Ellington did in music and as Aaron Douglas did in the graphic arts, to mention only two of the important cultural contributors of the times. But *One-Way Ticket,* unfortunately does not build further upon the well-established foundation.

In *One-Way Ticket,* Hughes shows that he still possesses the magic of transferring the blues rhythm to literature; he has the magic of the colloquial usage blended with simple and dramatic imagery. For example in his little poem:

> I pick up my life
> And take it with me
> And put it down in
> Chicago, Scranton,

Any place that is
North and East—
And not Dixie. . . .

 I am fed up
With Jimcrow laws.
People who are cruel
And afraid. . . .
I pick up my life
And take it away
On a one-way ticket—
Gone up North
Gone out West,
Gone!

Hughes here seems to be speaking for himself. No struggle. No hope of victory. No reflection of the Negro people—the Negro workers especially—who are today utilizing the blues and the spiritual and the beautiful and sometimes terrifying imagery of the sermon as weapons in their fight for their rights—in Dixie. The Negro people have carried on since 1928. Hughes, in his own personal expressions, has shown himself to be a part of this carrying on. But his poetry here misses by a mile the mood and the temper of the people for whom he has been so virile a spokesman.

His "Madam" poems in the present volume, despite their mood, are static pictures of static people caught in an inescapable net of exploitation. Some of them border on the rejected stereotype. In other poems there is an echo of the "Bigger Thomas" school of Richard Wright in which he envisions a blind struggle: "Wind / In the cotton fields, / Gentle breeze: / Beware the hour / It uproots trees." And except in one poem the Negro is placed in isolation—black against white. The one exception is "October 16," dedicated to John Brown.

The poem to John Brown, I would say, is the only one with perspective. The rest, although worth while reading for their craft and the charm with which they are suffused, are "tame" pieces, minor recordings of minor doings in the ghetto. There is none of the social insight which Hughes' readers have known in his "White Worker, Here's My Hand," or "Let America Be America Again," or "The Freedom Train."

If Hughes were a new poet and if *One-Way Ticket* were his new work, we could say that here is a star full of promise which will rise. But with 20 years of activity behind him, we must say of Hughes that *One-Way Ticket* indicates a waning of his star. He was once the booming and beautifully defiant voice of the Negroes' spokesman in North America, matching that of Nicholas Guillen, the Afro-Cuban, in Latin America. *One-Way Ticket* is the well-turned product, though, of a charming singer of little songs. Langston Hughes is capable of better.

Edwin Tribble
"Reviewing the New Books"
Washington Star, 20 February 1949, p. C3

One-Way Ticket is Mr. Hughes' first collection of verse on Negro themes in several years. It is made up of laments and blues in a style which he has popularized. The content is, if anything, sadder than before.

There is perhaps a trace more of bitterness and a shade less of the bittersweet. The style has been pared almost to the point of obscurity. There is none of that full and convincing articulateness in song that distinguished Mr. Hughes' lyrics for Kurt Weill's brilliant opera, *Street Scene.*

On the credit side there are flashes of wit, as in this quatrain:

> When you turn the corner
> And you run into yourself,
> Then you know that you have turned
> All the corners that are left.

[. . .]

"The Poetry Bulletin"
Tiger's Eye, 1 (March 1949), 117

This is one of the gayest of Langston Hughes' volumes and has many verses in it that would show to their best advantage when recited from a platform or a stage. Underlying these pleasant verses there is a persistent note of self-pity for the Negro and the poet, a quality which has led too many critics and readers of Negro verse to patronize and to regard it as having less value than it actually has.

Van Allen Bradley
"New English Poet Dims MacNeice"
Chicago Daily News, 2 March 1949, p. 30

Slang is a standby in the honest and often deceptively simple lyrics of Langston Hughes, whose *One-Way Ticket* is his first collection of poems on Negro subjects since *Shakespeare in Harlem.* Most of these poems are delightful, but they somehow lack the fire he was displaying a decade or so ago.

William Harrison
"The Bookshelf"
Boston Chronicle,
19 March 1949, p. 6

Mr. Langston Hughes is at once the most distinguished, the most prolific, and the most influential of living American Negro poets. In terms of distinction it would be redundant to emphasize his world-wide fame; he has practiced his art abundantly and fruitfully; and he may be said to be a constant inspiration to younger practitioners, many of whom have not hesitated to imitate his free verse technique. The present volume is a collection of poems. Illustrated by Jacob Lawrence, it adds nothing to the poet's reputation, although it does not detract. Familiar is the subject-matter; Mr. Hughes describes mostly the peculiar social types in Negro life who figured in his earliest books. "Madam to You," one of the longest poems, is of the folk in that it articulates the thoughts and feelings of a Southern migrant domestic worker.

In a sense, this book is, as the title poem indicates, fundamentally a poetic chronicle of the migrations of the Negro people from the rural South to the urban North. It is never uninteresting, even if it rarely comes to grips with the labor problems engaging the interest of the migrants, such as their employment in basic industries like steel and meat-packing. This is not to say that occasional poems do not vibrate with the old militancy universally associated with Mr. Hughes' literary reputation. "Silhouette" sounds a vigorous protest against lynching. "Restrictive Covenants" responds significantly to a fundamental social problem, housing, as it affects Negroes. It conveys the spiritual confinement

of the ghetto. However, the thematic overweight is on the side of poems like "Song for Billie Holiday," which are entertaining, though void of greatness, since they lack depth.

"The Ballad of Margie Polite" is twentieth century Villon, and that is its level. "Graduation" and "Interne at Provident" mirror aspiration and achievement. The note of struggle is not sounded often, however, and the total effect of the volume is entertainment rather than either instruction or exaltation derived from the loftiest poetry. The variety of moods represented by the various poems proves what all his readers should know by now, that Mr. Hughes is one of the most versatile American poets, never academic in the boring sense, and sometimes startling in his effects.

G. Lewis Chandler
"Selfsameness and a
Promise"
Phylon, 10 (Second
Quarter 1949), 189–91

Beginning brilliantly in 1921 with his "The Negro Speaks of Rivers," Hughes has consistently entertained, stimulated, and shared experiences with his public in autobiography (*The Big Sea*), in drama (*Mulatto*), in the novel (*Not Without Laughter*), in a volume of short stories (*The Ways of White Folks*), in innumerable articles, letters, and essays, and in several volumes of poetry. Chaucerian sly humor and realism, Wordsworthian simplicity, Shakespearean blending of comedy and tragedy, Emersonian individualism and precision, Whitmanesque earthiness and cosmopolitanism—all of these flow throughout Hughes' prose and poetry, with every now and then a note struck reminding us of the dramatic monologues of Browning and Dunbar, the bohemian vagabondia of Bliss Carman and Richard Hovey, the puzzling irony of Frost and Emily Dickinson, and the spiritual exploration of Edgar Arlington Robinson.

One-Way Ticket is indeed a legitimate and normal member of Hughes' family of works. All the basic family traits (humor, irony, tragedy, folksiness, earthiness, brevity, subtlety, puckishness, hope) are in it. And, as a whole, it is neither stronger nor weaker than the rest. It is not new in look nor different in manner. The blues are here—note particularly "Bad Morning"; the spirit of "Brass Spittoons" comes to life in the section entitled "Madam to You"; racial themes ironically expressed are in such poems as "The Ballad of Margie Polite," "Roland Hayes Beaten," "Who But the Lord," and "Lynching Song." The features of the well known "I Too Sing America" and of "Mother to Son" are found in the countenance of "Man into Men" and in "Democracy."

Besides expressing typical family themes, *One-Way Ticket*, in voice and manner, also resembles the other members of Hughes' literary siblings. Prevalent in the work is that first person singular pronoun "I," which is not personal, the way Hughes employs it, but is universal and all inclusive—something like the "I" in Whitman. For this reason and for his treatment of an individual or racial experience as a universal, human one, Hughes is a synechdochist, as most good poets are. Moreover, Hughes, through the medium of informal talk (like that of Frost—only, of course, in a different rhythm and on a somewhat different linguistic level) time and time again effectively places before us solid common sense and truths—the one-way ticket to real living—under the disguise of non-sense, or frustration, or ignorance, or depravity, or protest. Read, for example, the title poem "One-Way Ticket," or "Madam and the Charity Child," or "Blue Bayou," or "Puzzled," or "Boarding House," or "Final Curve," or "Third Degree," or "Jitney," or "Honey Babe."

It seems clear that although *One-Way Ticket*—replete with Hughesian dirges, soliloquies, ballads, blues love songs, vagabondia—adds nothing new to its family, the work is certainly not an albino or a black sheep. What is really important in an artist is not so much that he adds but that he digs. In digging he might find something new, something different—and then he might not. If he does not, he is still an artist despite our protest: "Old stuff!"

[. . .]

Louie M. Miner
"Books of the Day: Art and Mediocrity in Pair of Poetry Books"
Brooklyn Daily Eagle, 14 April 1949, p. 22

[. . .]

Langston Hughes also writes of heartbeats but he wears his woe with a difference. Pick up *One-Way Ticket* of an evening when you are too weary to exert yourself; ten-to-one before you know it you will find yourself at page 136 wishing there were more. Hughes calls it "blues" poetry and he plays his instrument with practiced hand:

> Play your guitar, boy,
> Till yesterday's
> Black cat

Runs out tomorrow's
Back door
And evil old
Hard luck
Ain't no more!

"The Ballad of Margie Polite" is based on the riots in Harlem on August 1:

Margie warn't nobody
Important before—
But she ain't just nobody
Now no more.

Mark August 1st
As decreed by fate
For Margie and History
To have a date.

Mayor LaGuardia
Riding up and down.
Somebody yelled,
What about
Stuyvesant Town?

Margie Polite!
Margie Polite!
Kept the Mayor
And Walter White
And everybody
Up all night!

Humor, understanding of the human heart, and first hand knowledge of the difficulties peculiar to his race are the burden of Hughes's song. Note these titles: "The Life and Times of Alberta K. Johnson (Madam to You)"; "Daybreak in Alabama"; "South Side: Chicago"; "Juice Joint: Northern City"; "Life Is Fine." The poems are all short. They excite in the reader tenderness, mirth, indignation. Langston Hughes knows how to make the language sing. Jacob Lawrence provides apt illustrations. "Play your guitar, boy," the world is in need of song.

Thomas Hornsby Ferril "The New Poetry in Review" *San Francisco Chronicle This World*, 29 May 1949, p. 10

Through previous books of poetry, *The Weary Blues, Shakespeare in Harlem, Fields of Wonder,* together with his short stories, autobiography and writing for the theater, Langston Hughes has won recognition as one of America's outstanding Negro writers. I am not disposed to impose my notions on any writer's responsibilities, but it does seem to me that Mr. Hughes, in this book, is coasting along too easily on synthetic folklore and romanticization of the racial underdog. These poems are perceptive and lyrical, they include some nice blues, but they labor dogmas of protest to a point where race-consciousness itself becomes too hospitable to intolerance to suit me.

"Poetry" *Guide Post* [Cincinnati Public Library], 24 (July 1949), 5

[. . .]
Collection of poems on Negro subjects executed in lyrics, dirges and romantic soliloquies. Mr. Hughes' genius is stretching thin these days.
[. . .]

"Two Good Books"
Cresset, 12 (September 1949), 47–8

[. . .]

Langston Hughes' latest volume is made up of very short poems, written in short, catchy lines, with emphatic rhythms. For the most part, the ideas are saucy, with a pay-off at the end. In "Madam to You," for example, the trials of a Negro woman are presented; she recognizes the injustice of her white mistress, the irony of life, the cruelty of Fate, but she takes life as a comic experience and has pert, common-sense answers for persecutors.

Some of the poems are directed more seriously against certain abuses; in "Note on Commercial Theatre" Hughes writes:

You've taken my blues and gone—
You sing 'em on Broadway
And you sing 'em in Hollywood Bowl,
And you mixed 'em up with
     symphonies
And you fixed 'em
So they don't sound like me.
Yep, you done taken my blues and
     gone.

Some of the comparisons are remarkable:

Pain on hind legs rising,
Pain tamed and subsiding
Like a mule broke to the halter.

Alain Locke
"Wisdom de Profundis: The Literature of the Negro, 1949: Part 1: Poetry and Belles Lettres"
Phylon, 11 (First Quarter 1950), 11–12

[. . .]

. . . Whereas in *One-Way Ticket,* Langston Hughes seems merely to have turned out, on a now overworked formula, glibly synthetic, one-dimensional folk vignettes, reflecting varied shrewdly observed facets of the present scene. Facility, undisturbed by fresh vision and new insight, can dim and tarnish almost any talent of whatever potential magnitude. Especially with the field of seriously experimental young contenders, Mr. Hughes, should he persist in his facile superficiality, will have to surrender his erstwhile cloak and laurels.

[. . .]

Harvey Curtis Webster
"One-Way Poetry"
Poetry, 75 (February 1950), 300–302

Because the poetry of Langston Hughes is so uneven and so far removed—even at its very good best—from the formal traditions the dominant school of criticism respects, it has been neglected unduly. Much of Hughes' poetry, of course, deserves this neglect—more, I should say, than is usual for a writer of talent who publishes many poems. As one can see by looking at the selections he himself has made for *The Poetry of the Negro,* his range of subject matter is limited and he tends to write almost the same poems many times: long, loosely phrased and constructed poems about what the Negro needs (and I think deserves); short, over-cute verses about the lighter aspects of Negro experience. Still, as one reads such excellent poems as "Song for a Dark Girl" and "Cross" in the same anthology, he realizes that Hughes' talent must be treated with respect and that there may be pleasure of a high order in each new book he publishes.

There is great pleasure for the reader of *One-Way Ticket,* Langston Hughes' most recent volume of verse. Almost all of the poems read well the first time; about a dozen reread well: "Madam and the Wrong Visitor," "Madam and Her Might-Have Been" (the saga of Madam Johnson, Alberta K, is almost consistently pleasurable), "Juice Joint: Northern City" (which is more ambitious and most of the way more successful than the others before it relapses into carelessness), "The Ballad of Margie Polite," "Man into Men," "Roland Hayes Beaten," "Late Last Night," "Little Old Letter," "Too Blue," "Little Green Tree" (which I like better than any of Hughes' earlier blues), "Request for Requiems." As these titles indicate, Hughes writes of a variety of experiences; as the poems indicate, he writes of them in a variety of tones despite the fact that he usually uses the form he made popular in his early modifications of the blues. Compare, for example, the skillful lightness with which Hughes manipulates the blues form in "Madam and the Wrong Visitor" and the restrained seriousness with which he uses it in "Roland Hayes Beaten":

A man knocked three times
I never seen him before.

He said, Are you Madam?
I said, What's the score?

He said, I reckon
You don't know my name,
But I've come to call
On you just the same.

I stepped back
Like he had a charm.
He said, I really
Don't mean no harm.

I'm just Old Death
And I thought I might
Pay you a visit
Before night.

He said, You're Johnson—
Madame Alberta K?
I said, Yes—but Alberta
Ain't goin' with you today!

No sooner had I told him
Than I awoke.
The doctor said, Madam,
Your fever's broke—

Nurse put her on a diet,
And buy her some chicken.
I said, Better buy two—
Cause I'm still here kickin'!

Negroes,
Sweet and docile,
Meek, humble, and kind:
Beware the day
They change their minds!

Wind
In the cotton fields,
Gentle breeze:
Beware the hour
It uproots the trees!

In these two poems and in many of the others in which he skillfully varies the rhythm and rhyme of the simple blues form, Hughes is as distinguished a craftsman as, say, W. H. Auden in his manipulation of the couplet.

But the comparison brings one up short

by its suggestion of limitation. Auden is almost always careful, even when he writes badly; Auden knows and experiments with and has mastered dozens of forms; Auden writes of an infinite variety of subjects, has extensity and intensity, breadth and depth. Hughes is careless when he strays from the one form he has chosen to master. So many admirable and banal sentiments come out like this—

> Democracy will not come
> Today, this year
> Nor ever
> Through compromise and fear—

and one fears Hughes is so undisciplined that he doesn't know when he writes well or badly. And Hughes, though he is an inspired reporter of the surface of things and of those upper layers of emotions that concern an individual as a member of a group rather than as a singular human being, never moves one deeply. Perhaps this limitation in depth is as much a product of second-class citizenship as is his restriction of substance to the American Negro and what he does and faces. Without trying to exonerate myself or my society of a social blame that, at least, contributes to aesthetic demerit, I hope that Hughes, like Robert Hayden, Gwendolyn Brooks and a few others, will move in new directions and to new depths in the many volumes of his poetry I still hope to have the pleasure of reading.

Checklist of Additional Reviews

J. Saunders Redding, "Old Forms, Old Rhythms, Old Words," *Saturday Review,* 32 (22 January 1949), 24.

"Literature," *Booklist,* 45 (1 February 1949), 189.

Orvilla M. Thompson, "A Selected List of Current Books," *Wisconsin Library Bulletin,* 45 (April 1949), 64.

SIMPLE SPEAKS HIS MIND

Virginia Kirkus Bulletin, 18 (15 February 1950), 109

These stories might be called a Harlem Mr. Dooley—a comparison that will carry substantial weight with the past generation who still remember Finley Peter Dunne's classic character. Langston Hughes, a Harlemite himself, has captured the idiom, the pattern of thinking, the personality of not only his stock character, "Simple," but many of his fellows. Simple airs his views over women, taxes, unemployment, government, Jim Crowism, religion, sex, The Law, with the moot problem of race relations a constant itch. He needs his beer (and sometimes when profoundly disturbed promotes himself to whiskey)—and usually needs the money to pay for it as well. He's a lowly philosopher of no mean gifts, an observer and commentator on the ways of his fellow man, a humorist albeit usually unconsciously. His problems and interests are any man's problems and interests, and Langston Hughes, using himself as catalyst, has caught their very fundamental qualities, the essence of the almost illiterate of his race, Southern-born, city bred. There's understanding and tenderness, and skilled avoidance of any semblance of sentimentality. The stories were written originally for the *Chicago Defender,* and well merit publication in book form. Hughes' hard-earned reputation in varied literary fields will stand him in good stead in launching this volume.

G.W.K. "Simple Speaks His Mind in Tales by Langston Hughes" Milwaukee Journal, section 5, 16 April 1950, p. 4

"Simple" is the nickname for Jesse B. Semple, an ordinary man who happens to be a Negro and who happens to live his fictional life in Harlem. Simple speaks his mind to Langston Hughes, who also happens to be a Negro and a Harlemite, and in addition, a widely known poet, playwright and author. Simple first made his appearance in a series of short, pointed stories by Hughes in the *Chicago Defender,* a Negro newspaper. This book is made up of 45 of these stories.

What makes it different from other books by and about Negroes is that *Simple Speaks His Mind* was written originally for a Negro audience. The stories are almost entirely conversation between Hughes and the imaginary Simple.

Simple says what you would expect him to say. He is deeply resentful of the treatment he and his race have received at the hands of the whites, from the whippings he got when he was a boy in Virginia to the hardly more subtle slights he is given up north. Segregation in the army, Negro lynching in the south, few opportunities for good jobs, "restricted" bars, hotels and apartments—all these are rushed over time and time again.

Aside from this preoccupation, however, the book shows Simple as a man who has his sorrow and joy just as any other man, Negro or white. Simple is a great man with the women, and many of the conversations deal with his trouble in convincing Joyce, his "good" girl, that he is a sincere, honest, hard working man. The background for nearly all the tales is a Harlem bar, where Simple pours out his heart to his friend Hughes as readily as the bartender draws the beer.

There is a lot of humor in this book, but the laughter, as the author points out, almost always is just a surface on the inner sorrow and worry. These conversations are not intended as high grade literature, but the insights they give into an average Negro's thoughts make them worth the reading.

Emerson Price
"Simple Not So Simple"
Cleveland Press, 18 April 1950, p. 38

[...]

Simple is by no means so simple as he seems in *Simple Speaks His Mind....* Simple is a Negro born in Virginia and living in Harlem. He's in trouble a good part of the time; his life has been filled with toil and travail. Yet he provides readers with the sources of laughter and hilarious fun. Beneath his simple recitations concerning his experience, however, is a profound philosophy which often touches the very core of life.

[...]

Charles Poore
"Books of the Times"
New York Times, 20 April 1950, p. 27; as "Between Book Ends: A Negro Mr. Dooley," *St. Louis Post-Dispatch,* 29 April 1950, p. 4A

Not since Finley Peter Dunne wrote his immortal Mr. Dooley sketches has anyone used casual dialogues to discuss issues of the day as effectively as Langston Hughes does in *Simple Speaks His Mind.* Outwardly the book is a collection of entertaining Harlem conversations. Inwardly it is better than a dozen vast and weighty and piously pompous studies in race relations. You learn here at first hand what it really means to be a man of color in the land of the free and the home of the brave—the tragic undertones of laughter.

[...]

Maxine Baxter
"Some of the Recent Fiction"
Cincinnati Enquirer, 22 April 1950, p. 7

These stories were published originally in the *Chicago Defender* and were meant for Negro readers. As a white, I found them embarrassing, interesting and sad, for the Negro viewpoint is exposed nakedly.

Simple is a primitive Negro who tells

these tales to the author, an educated and cultured man. The two men have only their color in common, but a deep friendship and understanding exists between them.

Simple has three loves—beer, women and Jackie Robinson. He is a man of violent emotions and who gets into brawls and riots. He fights the injustice done his race with the only weapons he owns—his fists and feet. The author disapproves of violence and wants his race to advance by slow and lawful progress, and he tries to point out the sense of such a course to Simple.

Simple has too many memories of Jim Crowism and insults to agree with his friend, but they drink together and talk, and out of their talk come these stories of Simple's loves and hopes.

Most of his troubles come from women. He has a wife in Baltimore and two girl friends in Harlem, and the three of them manage to keep him broke and miserable. Most of the time he has to cadge drinks, but the author pays up willingly in order to get Simple to talk.

The characteristics of the two men are contrasted in a most interesting manner. This is a provocative book that will provide much material for sober reflection for the white reader.

Jack Conroy
"Browsing"
Chicago Globe, 22 April 1950, p. 7

Langston Hughes has created a lively and convincing character in Harlem's Jesse Semple, whose name inevitably was shortened to Simple in his youth. Simple, however, is far from being simple in the sense of being dim-witted or unduly naive. He is both shrewd and keenly humorous.

Simple fans (and they must be legion) who have been enjoying his pungent and pertinent remarks in Hughes' newspaper column will be overjoyed to have the judicious selections offered in *Simple Speaks His Mind*.

The book, by the way, is one being used in an interesting publishing experiment. The European fashion of bringing out a new book in paper binding at a cheap price has been followed. This idea is not new, of course, but in this case a hard-cover edition is being issued simultaneously. Thus, more conservative book buyers who want library editions may also be accommodated. It is hoped that by issuing a huge printing of the dollar edition on somewhat less expensive paper the plan may be made economically feasible.

Hughes' book should be an excellent trial balloon. Simple has the easy but vigorous folk speech at which the author is so adroit. There are few readers who will not enjoy the Harlem homespun philosopher's comments on race relations (an obsession with him), the iniquities of landladies, the whims of women, the disastrous consequences of careless love, and the curious workings of the social and economic systems as they affect colored citizens.

Simple Speaks His Mind is a humorous book, but it is also a thoughtful and searching one. Some of the sketches are marked by pathos or irony. A touching episode is that concerning the one-legged soldier for whom two women are contending. [. . .]

349

Gertrude Martin
"Simple Speaks His Mind Has Its Amusing and Serious Sides"
Chicago Defender,
22 April 1950, [p. 7]

Defender readers probably are all familiar with Langston Hughes' character, Simple, and will welcome an opportunity to read this book in which Simple's philosophy of life is well expressed: *Simple Speaks His Mind* by Langston Hughes.

For any one who may have missed Mr. Hughes' witty columns, Simple is an earthy character who spends most of his free time in bars. The rest of his leisure he spends with Joyce, his girl friend, whom he is ready to marry if someone will finance a divorce from his first wife.

In the course of his book, Simple holds forth on a variety of subjects: women (especially women), Harlem restaurants, intermarriage, race relations, and Negro life in all its aspects.

Readers who do not know Simple already have an amusing time ahead as they make his acquaintance. Even faithful followers of Simple will find it interesting to read these selections as a connected whole.

According to the cover blurb Simple represents "the basic Harlemite" who laughs to keep from crying, and material for the book came from actual conversations overheard in bars and on Harlem street corners. It has an authentic ring, and Simple, himself, for all his preoccupation with wine and women, has a serious side. It would be difficult to tell how accurate Mr. Hughes' picture of Simple is as an average Harlemite, but there is no doubt that he is an interesting character.

[. . .]

"Negro Voice: Harlemite's World View"
Denver Post, 23 April 1950, p. 4C

Langston Hughes, one of America's leading Negro writers, invented Jesse B. Semple, nicknamed "Simple," for a series of articles in the *Chicago Defender,* articles in which Simple, in imaginary conversation with the author, spells out the ideas of an ordinary Harlemite in humorous and pungent talk.

Simple is a racist. He hates Jim Crow. Nearly every subject on which he discourses turns at last to the race discrimination issue. But Simple is good-natured; when he speaks hate out of his bitter frustration, he quickly softens it with wry humor.

His lot is not invariably bitter. He likes beer and the teeming life of Harlem. He likes laughter and jokes. He loves Joyce and Joyce loves him, and he even gets some rewards—for instance, his wife in Baltimore persuades her new boyfriend to pay for her divorce from Simple.

But he doesn't like his landlady, nor the Negro sales people in Harlem stores who treat their kind worse than white sales people treat them, nor Dixiecrat publications, nor the white owners of Harlem businesses, nor the Uncle Toms of his race. Simple's mind is not Simple; it is fascinatingly complex. Nor does Hughes in his own words or in Simple's solve any race problems; he poses them in all their variety

350

and he develops, with humor and wisdom, all the proposed solutions, however.

Simple and the things which happen to him are rich human tragicomedy, and Hughes is a master of the light lift that keeps tragedy and pathos from becoming unbearable. *Simple Speaks His Mind* is a clever, special pleading and rich in character.

M.C.W.
"*Simple Speaks His Mind*"
Augusta [Ga.] *Chronicle* 23 April 1950, [p. 1D]

One would scarcely describe this book as a masterpiece, nor would one consider it an important book, by any stretch of the imagination.

It deals with race outlook and reactions, from the Negro standpoint, but has the merit of not seeking to be unduly emotional or controversial. It has a meditative quality and it does, in many ways, present an interesting sidelight on the Negro mind and emotional reactions of the dominant figure in the book, his name being "Simple," to express certain qualities of the author's approach to his subject.

The book is well written and might prove diverting, in the absence of other reading matter.

H[enry] G[ilfond]
"In the Books"
New York Teachers News, 10 (29 April 1950), 3

Jesse Semple, Negro, nicknamed Simple, is a troubled man. His troubles range from women to international affairs. What troubles him most, however, is Jim Crow, lynching and every other phase of anti-Negro expression and action in our American way of life.

Simple is simple only in his approach to the Negro problem. He doesn't care to deal with generalities and fine phrases. He wants to talk about people, individual people. He doesn't like the housing situation, the unemployment situation, the eating situation. He lambasts segregation and takes a good cut at the press and radio and the Law for their double-standard dealing. He is mad enough to toss a brick at a window when a Negro gets shot by a white policeman.

Jesse is the man-out-of-the-South-in-Harlem. Much of his talk, Langston Hughes writes, "is derived from actual conversations heard or overheard in bars and on the corners of Harlem." He is the Harlem "man in the street." He has been bounced around, shoved around and his hard knocks are too many to count, but he isn't beaten. He has a love for life and the good things in it, and he intends to stick around and enjoy as much of them as he can.

Hughes writes his conversations in his own syncopated blues style, warm, human, humorous, and angry. He is always the poet. A good part of the material has seen print in the *Chicago Defender*, where the stories originated, the *New Republic,* and *Phylon.*

Lucia Barber
"Valuable Book"
Hartford Courant Magazine, 30 April 1950, p. 14

For anyone interested in what Harlem is really like, for anyone who seeks greater understanding of what it means to be a Negro in America, *Simple Speaks His Mind* is a valuable book. You won't find a melodramatic story such as Ann Petry wrote in *The Street.* You won't find the cool scholarly approach of Roy Ottley's *New World A-Coming.*

What Langston Hughes has done is to gather together forty-five representative columns, some of which were printed in a Negro newspaper, *The Chicago Defender,* through which runs a very thin story thread: whether Jesse Simple can get a divorce in order to marry the girl he really loves. Their real purpose is to allow Langston Hughes, the poet and intellectual, to carry on a conversation with his alter ego, a man of his people.

The chief difficulty with this unpretentious and delightful book is that the average white reader will not recognize what he finds in it. Mr. Hughes' ear is that of a poet, and his pen has been trained to use language precisely. His writing reflects accurately a picture of a Harlem too few whites know, etched with grace and charm by a man whose youthful bitterness has been transmuted by maturity into an understanding broad enough to extend to all who read his book with an open heart.

Ted Poston
"Simon Not So Simple: Harlem Polemicist a New Dooley"
New York Post, 30 April 1950, p. M15

When Langston Hughes paused for a beer in a Harlem gin mill one hot day back in 1943 and cocked his ear to the conversation around him, it is doubtful if he knew that he was preparing to open a new facet of an already successful career as a poet, novelist, playwright, and lecturer.

For Hughes, with that high sensitivity for the spoken word which characterizes most of his work, remembered one of the conversations, attributed it to a character named Jesse B. Semple, and published the result in his weekly column in the *Chicago Defender,* a Negro weekly.

The result was so gratifying to the majority of the *Defender's* 200,000 predominantly Negro readers that, at their request, Simple (Semple) appeared again and again until finally he had used up 150 columns of newsprint to discuss everything under the sun—from jet propulsion to Jackie Robinson, from Creation to cosmic conflict.

Simon and Schuster have chosen 45 of the Hughes-Simple dialogues for *Simple Speaks His Mind,* thereby giving the rest of America an opportunity to chuckle at and then ponder the hilariously funny but bitingly cutting comments of Harlem's first man-in-the-street on race relations, world relations, and as Jesse puts it "jes' plain relating!"

Because no one has really listened to him so closely before, it is difficult to assign Simple his niche in American folklore.

He is far more than an uptown Mr. Dooley, a tart-tongued Will Rogers or a very hipped Lenox Av. Uncle Remus. He is probably the best combination of all three, but one who can never forget that "there are certainly a lot of disadvantages in being colored."

Not that his comments are all racial. Many, like his discussion of Rudolph, the veteran who "come back from occupying Japan this morning and is occupying a jail tonight," are all too universal. Rudolph found his wife had done him wrong, but even while sympathizing with him, Simple observes:

"A soldier should always let his old lady know when he plans to return to the fold . . . and a weekend is the wrong time to come home anyhow."

Simple is never an all-out extremist. Even when wishing that the Lord would smite all white folks down, he adds: "But I hope he lets Mrs. Roosevelt alone."

While damning Harlem for its segregation and discrimination—and the very low quality of service in its restaurants and stores—he can still say that "But as long as what IS is—and Georgia is Georgia—I will take Harlem as mine. At least, if trouble comes, I will have my own window to shoot from."

Simple's imagined testimony before "Chairman Georgia" of the House Un-American Committee, his envisioned command as "Mr. General Captain" over a regiment of Mississippi "cracker boys," and his dissertations on Creation and the Garden of Eden, have a quality unequaled in either poetry or prose since Sterling Brown created Slim Green in *Southern Road*.

Hughes, as interlocutor, often chides Simple for being too race conscious. "You look at everything, I regret to say, in terms of black and white," he tells him.

And Simple retorts simply: "So does the law."

There's nothing simple about Jesse B. Semple but his name.

Peggy Randolph
"Simple Was Very Far from Simple"
Tulsa Daily World, section 5, 30 April 1950, p. 9

These conversations between the author and an imaginary character called Simple have an appeal in spite of the book's obvious propaganda. The language is quietly poetic and some of the expressions are hilariously funny and some unutterably sad. [. . .]

These are wry, often shrewd, conversations that will make many laugh and sympathize with Simple. Others, no doubt, will feel very strongly that the author sometimes goes too far. [. . .]

Peter E. Hogan
Best Sellers, 10 (1 May 1950), 27–8

Langston Hughes, despite the pinkishness associated with his name, is a forceful writer, in either poetry or prose. Here in *Simple Speaks His Mind,* he uses Jesse Semple, a character of his newspaper column, to present views of Negro life in Harlem. The background plot is uninspiring. Jesse is an uneducated Negro who has left the Jim Crowism of Virginia and a wife in Baltimore for the freedom of Harlem. There is no need for him to choose between Joyce, whom he respects, and Zarita, the good time bar girl, until Zarita makes life too complicated for him. When his wife's fiancé pays for her divorce from Jesse, the way is finally paved for him to settle down in security with Joyce, but not until Langston Hughes has used him as a foil to bring out the foibles and feelings of Harlemites.

To understand *Simple Speaks His Mind* it is necessary to know something of the medium in which it was first brought forth. *Phylon* and *New Republic* get some of the credits, but the *Chicago Defender* was the main incubator. This is a Negro newspaper and as such has a psychology widely different from "white" papers. Directed to a repressed minority, it is ordinarily sensational in its presentation, racially extreme in view, and one place where a Negro can allow himself full expression in writing. The feature columns generally fall into types that may be termed "protest literature," genre pieces, and "satire to bring self-correction." Of the forty-five "chapters" in the book, twenty are of the "protest" variety. To the critical and easily frightened eye of white supremacy, they would be an extremely alarming indication of the "vicious" bent of the Negro mind, if they were not considered in their proper background, which greatly softens the overall effect. Seven of the pieces are in the "satire for self-correction" category; two of them, "Banquet in Honor" and "A Ball of String," dealing with appreciation as a racial characteristic, are particularly effective. The remaining eighteen are genre pieces which, by their simplicity and reality, lay open the humor and pathos of Harlem life in a manner that justifies the publisher's blurb—of giving "a sense of eaves-dropping." As a unit, they explicitly present a well-rounded and uninhibited view of the lower class city Negro mind, and implicitly the upper class Negro outlook and the stratification

of Negro society. The plot is secondary and merely a vehicle for unifying the various incidents.

To the mature reader capable of sympathetic understanding, *Simple Speaks His Mind* will afford warming and rewarding reading. To the less mature or sympathetic it will be disturbing. To all who read it, many things will come back to the mind long after the final page has been turned.

Abner W. Berry "Langston Hughes' 'Simple' Speaks for Harlem" *Daily Worker*, 3 May 1950, p. 11

Jesse B. Semple—his friends call him "Simple"—could just as easily have been called "Mr. Harlem." For in this character Langston Hughes has uncovered the unspoken conscience of America's largest Negro ghetto. Simple IS Harlem, fretting at the white folks' wrongs, humorously escaping the dead end of utter frustration, militantly poised for the fight out of which will be won an America which will be America to ALL—black and white alike.

Partly because of background, and partly out of choice, Simple uses the Harlem vernacular, that colorful speech form which avoids the formal grammar and vocal mannerisms of the purists.

Much of Simple's time is spent leaning on bars, carrying on his folksy philosophy with the author. . . .

But, like Harlem, which he personifies, Simple isn't frustrated, nor is he seeking to drown reality in beer. "Here's to Harlem!" Simple toasts. "They say Heaven is Paradise. If Harlem ain't Heaven, then mouse ain't mice!" Simple claims the territory from "Central Park to 179th, from river to river." This territory is "Harlem, where I can thumb my nose at the world!" He is chided by his friend for his "belligerent attitude" in the prophecy—". . . if trouble comes (to Harlem) I will have my own window to shoot from."

"It will not be my attitude," Simple answers wryly, "I will have out my window."

In one of his conversations, Simple remembers the riot of 1943. "I was in it," Simple says.

"Grabbing hams out of broken windows?" his friend asks.

"No," came the answer, "I didn't want no ham. I wanted Justice."

He and his friends argue as to what breaking up stores had to do with Justice, but Simple comes out on top with:

"That is the way the Allies got it—breaking up Germany, breaking up Hiroshima, and everything in sight. But these white folks are more scared of Negroes in the U.S.A. than they ever was of Hitler, otherwise why would they stop Jackie Robinson playing baseball to come to Washington and testify how loyal he is? I remember that night after the riots they turned on all the street lights in Harlem, although it was during the war and New York had a dim-out. . . ."

Then Simple speaks for Harlem in a one-sentence summary of the things the people were tired of. They were tired—

"Of hearing the radio talking about the Four Freedoms all day long during the war and me living in Harlem where nary one of them Freedoms worked—nor the ceiling prices neither."

In one of his barroom conversations, Simple imagines himself before the Un-American Committee. The Un-Americans came up after Simple was called down for his "race-consciousness." "I am black," said Simple, "also I will be red if things get

worse. But one thing is sure, I will not be yellow. I will fight for my rights." His set-to with the Un-Americans is too long to deal with here, but take it from this reviewer that he poses some tough questions to the witch-hunters. His final shot, after the Un-Americans' Georgia chairman says jail awaits those Negroes who don't ride the jimcrow coach, is a good sample:

"Then I will break your jail up, because I am entitled to liberty whilst pursuing happiness."

Hughes and Simple deal with almost everything of the phase and mood of Harlem life: marriage, love, vacations in the country, dogs, baseball, business and jobs in Harlem. This is one of the first books in which the so-called "off guard" conversation of Harlemites is set down with sympathy and skill. Young Negro writers have much to learn from Hughes, and his readers will gain enjoyment and understanding from his work. Hughes' naturalism sometimes simplifies many of the issues with which his character deals, a weakness which has also shown in his poetry; but this collection of sketches is one of the best of his works since his *Weary Blues,* in this reviewer's opinion.

V.P.
"'Simple' Speaks Out"
Springfield [Mass.] *Sunday Republican,* 7 May 1950, p. 8C

Langston Hughes, the gifted Negro poet, has collected his various writings about Simple in *Simple Speaks His Mind* and created another appealing character. There is a folksy simplicity in Simple's turn of thought and honesty of statement, whether it be about war plants, love, his job, relatives or just the details of his daily round. He is one of Harlem's most authentic characters.

"Simple Tells His Troubles"
Long Beach Press-Telegram, Southland Magazine Section, 7 May 1950, p. 7

This is not a novel; it does not begin anywhere and it does not end anywhere. But throughout the entire mindful speaking of Simple, the reader will find more than any conventional novel could give him. This is the Negro; neither the clown nor the dark menace—simply a man who grows more and more bewildered and tells of it so the reader may retain the illusion of eavesdropping.

What he hears is sorrowful, but not tragic. Tragedy is never completely accepted by those involved in it. But for all the sorrow, it must be dug out from beneath the humor which overlays Simple's spicy account of what has happened to him, and what will be apt to happen to him in the future.

[. . .]

But Simple will not die, nor will he go away if you don't look at him. And if you listen to him, and keep listening, you may hear this: "Gimme another beer, Tony! I can lean on this bar, but I ain't got another thing in the U.S.A. on which to lean."

Carl Van Vechten
"Dialogues—but Barbed"
New York Times Book Review, 7 May 1950, p. 10

On frequent occasions the late James Weldon Johnson, Negro author, was heard to observe: "There is no doubt in my mind that the solution of the 'race problem' depends on a sense of humor." Then he would say that persons who would permit Negroes to prepare their food, to lave their garments, to suckle their children, and then refuse to allow these same Negroes to sit next to them in street cars or buses (although they often sat next to them in their carriages and motor cars) must be a trifle cracked. "The only way to make these benighted souls see the light," he would continue, "is to convince them that their conduct is a huge joke."

Langston Hughes, the poet, may be performing that very service in a book which is perhaps not new in form (Mr. Dooley comes to mind as a similar creative effort), but which presents the Negro in a new way. Jesse Semple is wise, witty, as mad as the Madwoman of Chaillot—and invariably race conscious. He is the naive propagandist, through a series of dialogues.

Since these papers were originally written for a Negro newspaper and, consequently, an exclusively Negro audience, there is no attempt at obfuscation. The papers probably exhibit the Negro in bedroom slippers and pajamas—that is, as nearly himself as it would be possible to show him. Simple is completely frank in his opinions about white people: he dislikes them intensely. The race problem is never absent, but the flow of the book is light-hearted and easy.

This is a sane approach to real insanity, and I wouldn't be surprised if this book reaches more people and has wider influence than any volume on a similar subject since *Uncle Tom's Cabin*. *Simple Speaks His Mind* will start a lot of people thinking hard. For those who have to swallow bitter pills it provides a sugar-coating of humor. Only a Negro could have written this book, and only a Negro as wise as Langston Hughes.

Mary Scott Dean
"*Simple Speaks His Mind*"
El Paso Herald-Post, 13 May 1950, p. 4

Langston Hughes, one of the most notable writers of the Negro race, with many books and many literary honors to his credit, has done what no white author has dared do for a decade or more. He has created a funny Negro character. It may be a hopeful straw in the stormy racial wind that has swept this country for the last dozen years. It could mean that tension is lessening a little. It could indicate growth in the Negro race, since it is only the immature who cannot bear to be laughed at.

But whether a special significance attaches to this book or not, it is good to meet again that peculiar blend of dignity and absurdity, of wisdom and folly that makes up the typical non-literate American Negro, and to hear him speak an English that never was on land or sea but which somehow takes on a richness from the land, a depth and roll from the sea that the white-man's more careful syntax can never approach.

To entertain the reader was not, however, the author's sole purpose, perhaps not even his prime purpose in creating the character Simple and letting him speak his mind. He uses Simple as a mouthpiece for the problems and issues that trouble the Negro race. In his native idiom and from his man-in-a-Harlem-street vantage, Simple tells the world what is wrong with it, usually leaning on a bar as he does so, because a bar, he says, is all he has to lean on.

In the process the reader learns what is wrong with Simple, too. He has a woman problem consisting of a superfluous wife, a good girl friend, and Zarita, a nighttime friend who complicates matters in one of the most hilarious chapters in the book. He can't let beer alone, nor dice. He can't keep his money.

There is a smile or a laugh in every chapter. But there is also meat. These slight sketches, amplified many times, mean the Negro race and his problems. It is a microscopic slide taken from one of the segments of our country by a man who knows his people through to the heart.

J. Saunders Redding
"Book Review"
Baltimore Afro-American Magazine, 13 May 1950, p. 4; as "What It Means to Be Colored," *New York Herald Tribune Book Review*, 11 June 1950, p. 13

The tradition is an old one, for it goes back to the "horse-sense humorists" of the final quarter of the last century. It goes back to Charles Heber Clark and his "Cooley"; to the irrepressible Josh Billings and Artemus Ward and Finley Dunne, who created "Mr. Dooley."

The tradition demands a rich awareness, an unclouded eye, an unstopped ear. It demands the salt of sincerity. It requires a sense of humor nicely balanced between gross, playful burlesque and stinging satire.

In *Simple Speaks His Mind* Langston Hughes has completely fulfilled the tradition and gone a far step beyond. Whereas Clark's Cooley and Dunne's Mr. Dooley bespeak only the contemporary mind at work with merely contemporary issues, Hughes's Jesse B. Semple ("Simple") ranges the universe.

It is true that Simple has equipment insufficient to cope with the universal, but this merely enlarges one's sympathetic understanding of him. It is also true that he relates world-wide problems to his own and reduces everything to a personal level, but this only evidences his humanity and arouses one's smiles and tears with equal facility and point.

Simple speaks his untutored mind on every conceivable subject and, though his accents are those of Harlem, he utters a great many of the world's hopes and fears. "Lord, kindly please, take the blood off my brothers' hands, and make us shake hands clean and not be afraid. . . .

"Too many mens and womens are dead. The fault is mine and theirs, too. So teach us all to do right, Lord, *please,* and to get along together with that atom bomb on this earth. . . ."

Instances are numerous, but "Simple's" spoken mind is a revelation in another way too. What he says opens windows on a corner of life much publicized but little known. For though "Simple" is first a man, he is one qualified by the color of his skin.

As he himself states, he knows more about being colored than he knows about anything else. What he knows, he says. That he was created originally to speak only to his own people makes the revelation more complete.

Thus one is made acquainted with the complexities of our life and Harlem life—the real complexities which cannot be resolved by the moral and social equivalents of sticks of red peppermint candy.

But let me append a warning: Read *Simple Speaks His Mind* as if each piece were a weekly column—as, indeed, each is. Otherwise, Simple's thinking and his speech may grow monotonous, in spite of flashes of sheer social brilliance and wisdom and humor.

Joseph Payne Brennan "Sessions in a Harlem Bar" *New Haven Register Magazine,* 14 May 1950, p. 11

This book began as a series of separate stories written for *The Chicago Defender,* a Negro newspaper. In chapters only loosely integrated by a weak narrative thread, Simple, an average Southern-born Negro settled in Harlem, recounts his varied adventures and reveals his wry and often bitter philosophy, almost exclusively in terms of race. Most of the sessions take place in a Harlem bar with an unnamed individual (Langston Hughes) acting as foil.

Simple's endless struggles with a hostile environment, his observations and his quixotic adventures are often amusing, occasionally hilarious. Sometimes they are poignant or savagely astringent.

Simple's version of his troubles with his landlady, his girl friend Joyce, and his estranged wife are especially human and appealing. In the matter of race relationships he tends to be a harsh and dogmatic extremist, but bitterness often has ample justification.

I wish Langston Hughes had made the book more a unified narrative and less a series of disjointed dialogues. He appears to have overlooked one of the basic tenets of all good writing: It is always far more effective to show, than it is merely to tell. Simple's experiences hold our interest, but his racial-sociological assertions become tedious even though we may agree with them. Simple is too often and too obviously only a sort of mouthpiece for Hughes' more radical opinions. It seems to me that a robust, well-rounded, closely-knit narrative, omitting the somewhat stilted dialogue and focusing more on Simple's adventures per se, would have been a more effective vehicle than the present volume.

But even with its faults, *Simple Speaks His Mind* is a keen, alternately humorous and caustic commentary. General audiences, as well as those very specifically interested in race relationships, will find it well worth reading.

J.D.C.
"News and Views of Today's Books"
Columbus Citizen Magazine, 14 May 1950,
p. 25

Langston Hughes is one of the outstanding Negro writers on the American scene and his latest book is an engaging effort which the publishers claim presents an insight into the mind of a Harlemite.

Not being a Harlemite, we are in no position to judge the truth of this statement. However, there is no question that *Simple Speaks His Mind* is a gently humorous and humorously philosophical plea for racial tolerance.

Jesse B. Semple, nicknamed "Simple," is a not particularly well educated Negro factory worker who has been "cut, shot, stabbed, run over, hit by a car and tromped by a horse . . . robbed, fooled, deceived, two-timed, double-crossed, dealt seconds and mighty near black-mailed" just to mention a few of his unhappy experiences.

He has also married the wrong woman, is in love with another whom he wants to marry and keeping a third one on the string to keep him company during his drinking evenings.

The book is a series of conversations between Jesse and the author which took place in various Harlem bars for the most part. It largely concerns itself with Simple's woman troubles, money troubles and race relations but touches briefly many other phases of his life.

The publishers say Hughes wrote the pieces in it for a Negro newspaper and originally had no idea it would ever be read by whites. This should make it doubly interesting to most whites—at least that portion of them who feel the solution to the race relations problem is a little give and take by both sides.

[. . .]

W.A.I.
"Sunny Preachment"
Columbus Dispatch,
14 May 1950, p. E15

"If you want to know about my life," said Simple . . . "don't look at my face, don't look at my hands. Look at my feet and see if you can tell how long I've been standing on them."

Thus begins one of the most delightful books we've seen in many a day. If we want to know Simple we don't have to look at those feet which he says have supported "everything from a cotton bale to a hongry woman," and which have walked ten thousand miles working for white folks and another ten thousand keeping up with colored.

All we have to do is to read this book in which Simple and his friends who ask the right questions do all the talking. We will find that Simple has a mind of his own, that sparkles all the time, and a heart that is as big as the out of doors.

Those who want to get a better understanding of the way the Negro looks at the problems of race relations will find some more than adequate suggestions here.

This is not a bitter book, but it is filled with many biting things always told with a sunny, good nature that makes them sting that much harder.

Harlem is the setting, and Langston Hughes makes that center of Negro life and culture come vividly to life. He also makes very real almost every problem that the Negro faces in white America.

"Latest Books in Review: Negro Insight"
Sacramento Union,
14 May 1950, p. 22

Langston Hughes is probably best known as a poet, though he has written a novel, short stories, plays, songs, magazine articles and done motion picture work.

Simple Speaks His Mind began as a series in the *Chicago Defender.* Written for a Negro paper and for Negro readers, it is revealing far beyond the average book. Hughes says Simple started talking to him: he talked about the things Harlemites discuss in the half-humorous, half-serious way peculiar to persons of his station. Much of the material is derived from actual conversations.

Simple is naive and wise, outspoken and witty. The race problem is present at all times but with sharpness, humor with point. The reader is given pause, sensing that what afforded him a joyous chuckle had hidden depths. Bitterness, pain and frustration there may be, but Simple asks no pity and keeps it light.

Carl Van Vechten sums it up: "Only a Negro could have written this book, and only a Negro as wise as Langston Hughes. Simple will start a lot of people thinking hard." And Simple himself contributes, "When people care for you and cry for you, they can straighten out your soul. Ain't that right, boy?"

Henry Butler
"Collection of Columns Paints New Kind of Portrait"
Indianapolis Times,
20 May 1950, p. 8

Langston Hughes' *Simple Speaks His Mind* is a new kind of literary portrait of a Negro.

It's not a race problem book. It's a collection of columns Mr. Hughes wrote for the *Chicago Defender,* intended primarily for Negro readers.

Mr. Hughes, who did such a beautiful job with the simple and expressive libretto for the Elmer Rice-Kurt Weill *Street Scene,* here sets down conversation and opinions of Simple, a composite Harlem character.

The series of dialogs between Mr. Hughes' narrator and Simple, mostly over beers the narrator obligingly sets up, deal with Simple's marital troubles and heart throbs, his job difficulties in the unofficial Jim Crowism that exists even in New York, his nostalgia for the climate and food of the South along with his reminiscent hatred of Southern Jim Crowism.

Simple thinks New York has some advantages—not climate. At least, it's a town where a Negro has some chance for interesting jobs, like the motorman on the Eighth Ave. Subway—"That cat were really driving that train."

He comments with wistful admiration on celebrities like Duke Ellington and Lena Horne. He dislikes landladies, white merchants and tavern-owners who draw income from Harlem but live away from it.

He hates all policemen, Negro more than white, because he says the Negro "polices" are rougher than the white.

In a typical flight of imagination, he would like to see the government set up "a game preserve for Negroes," where nobody could shoot, lynch or Jim Crowishly molest the inhabitants.

And he has small respect for the "Summer Time" and "That's Why Darkies Were Born" school of popular-song presentation of Negro life.

The book has humor and angles which undoubtedly will mean more to Negro than to white readers. For one thing, Mr. Hughes makes his narrator a "straight man," who has all the right sentiments of the serious-minded "tolerance" advocates. Like the well-meaning persons who pass resolutions and form committees for "better understanding," the narrator uses all the clichés.

But Simple, from insight and bitter experience, has answers for the nice-sounding but shallow generalities. An honest and sensitive, as well as somewhat deliriously imaginative guy, he says he'll believe some of those things when he sees them translated into action.

I think you'll agree with Simple when you read the book. Not to editorialize at too great length. I'll begin to believe Indianapolis is the nice town it likes to think it is when it gets sensibly busy abolishing discrimination.

William Pfaff
"Books"
Commonweal, 52
(26 May 1950), 181

A series of brief, anecdotal newspaper columns (they first appeared in the *Chicago Defender,* a Negro paper), the effect of this collection is more polemical than artistic.

But it is painless polemics: a strong, sometimes near bitter defense of the Harlem Negro who is hired by a white man to make cranks. What kind of cranks? "Cranks! Just cranks!" What do they crank? "I don't know. I don't crank with them cranks. I just makes 'em. They don't tell colored folks what cranks crank."

The episodes are humorous in a sensitive, dignified way. They do not furnish any deep picture of the meaning of jim-crow living, but time after time they produce in the white reader the sensation of being hit; hit right for the part he unconsciously plays in maintaining a racist social structure.

The pieces are conversations between the educated narrator and his friend, the colored citizen Jesse Semple. The latter, in his own way, is probably as much of a caricature as Amos or Andy, but he exists tellingly to express the simple and direct responses of the uneducated man who is black and who lives in Harlem.

Read them for what they are: newspaper columns that are neither art nor truth, but which come close to both—uncomfortably close, for those of us who live near Park Avenue where the ladies walk with dogs but not with Negroes.

Myron Galewski
"Langston Hughes Speaks His Mind"
[New York] *Sunday Compass Magazine*, 28 May 1950, p. 5

The sketches by Langston Hughes collected in this book first appeared as a series of newspaper pieces in *The Chicago De-*

fender, and were intended not for intellectuals or professionals, but for the average non-literary Negro. Their origin and function are cited by the book's jacket as proofs of their unself-conscious character and authenticity. This claim seems more or less well founded, and slight and unimportant though they may be from a strictly literary or sociological point of view, they are unique.

Simple is the nickname of Jesse B. Semple, the appealing Negro character created by Mr. Hughes through a series of dialogues in which Mr. Hughes functions as a slightly didactic interlocutor. Simple is usually to be found in Paddy's bar in Harlem and, while Mr. Hughes plies him with beer, holds forth on a number of themes.

Naturally, race relations is the most ubiquitous among them, and Simple is often chided by Mr. Hughes for being a race-obsessed man. Simple is not to be blamed, however, and I think he would be poorer company if Mr. Hughes succeeded entirely in converting him into a model citizen.

Besides the cross of being black in a white man's world, Simple has other burdens to bear. He can't afford a divorce from his nagging first wife Isabel. He quarrels with his culture-hungry girl friend Joyce. His landlady is an ornery old party who overcharges him for his Third Floor Rear, and fails to give him enough heat in winter.

When he rebels against her tyranny by destroying the signs in the bathroom which read: "Guest Towels—Roomers Do Not Use," "Wash Face Only in Bowl—No Sox," "Do Not Wash Clothes in Hear," "Turn Out Lights—Costs Money," he is not only completely defeated and browbeaten into restoring the signs, but is compelled to add a new one: "Don't Nobody Tear Down These Signs—Else Move."

Simple is also pursued by a loose lady named Zarita, which results in a temporary misunderstanding with Joyce. A Negro salesgirl, for whose right to work in the dime store he has picketed in the cold, fails to treat him with the proper courtesy.

It is small wonder then that Simple demands the right to get drunk, at least in principle, and resents being told that misbehaving while in one's cups makes one a disgrace to one's race. A white man can get drunk without representing his race in the process. When Simple's deliverance, in the form of a divorce from Isabel, is granted, the reader is happy for him.

These sketches make an agreeable vaudeville on Negro themes, to an accompaniment of fetching blues music. In one of the best of them, an ancient Negro artist berates the Sugar Hill citizens, who are honoring him with a banquet, for not buying his songs, plays and books, while he still had the teeth with which to enjoy a good chicken dinner.

Mr. Hughes has a good ear for authentic Harlem talk, and if occasionally the jokes are cornier than they should be, remember this is vaudeville. Mr. Hughes' book can be recommended to all those who want to learn, while being entertained, how Negroes feel about life in America.

Lloyd L. Brown
"Not So Simple"
Masses and Mainstream, 3 (June 1950), 81–4

Langston Hughes' new book comes as something of a jolt to those of us who have insisted that the Man-on-the-Street is a myth. Since meeting his Jesse B. Semple—the nickname "Simple" was inevitable—I for one am ready to concede that the composite man really exists, at least in Harlem.

Of course there are some 400,000 Negroes living in this world center of Negro life, and among us there are all kinds of people; but when Simple speaks his mind he is truly speaking the mind of the common people of this community.

So I urge you: Don't miss reading this book. It is revealing, it is stimulating; you are sure to enjoy it. It is especially recommended for all who have been chilled by the cold war; here is a chance for them to warm their bones before the glow of Simple's humor, the humor of a people who have come through 300 *years* of cold war.

There are a number of unusual features to this work which consists of monologues in the Mr. Dooley tradition, with the author playing it straight, asking a few questions and occasionally trying, without much success, to get a word in edgewise.

Especially notable is the fact that Simple is talking to Negroes, the book being largely a compilation of columns which have appeared in the Negro press. Offered now to the general public, the special quality that results from this approach, the intimacy of uninhibited expression, is of unique value.

Of special interest too is that here Langston Hughes has tapped the bubbling wellsprings of authentic Negro humor, the wonderful quality of which is the direct opposite of that noxious sewer-flow with which Amos 'n' Andy and Octavus Roy Cohen have drenched the nation for too many years.

The humor of the Negro people, one of the most significant features of their national psychology, is not of the "gag" variety; it is subtle, compounded of double-meanings, indirection, allusions, colloquialisms. It has a bitter-sweet tone, this laughter in the shadows, that is difficult to describe and more difficult to render without distortion; that he succeeds so well in getting much of its elusive quality into print is further evidence that Langston Hughes retains his close touch with his people and his top place among Negro creative writers.

Simple speaks of many things, of almost everything: rents, prices, wages, baseball, the F.B.I., $2,000 fur coats for dogs, the un-Americans, his landlady, why lingerie is pink, the police and courts ("I definitely do not like the Law"), the South, Congress, atom bombs, Negroes, white people, the Army, the last war, the cold war, his love life, literature—everything in Harlem and the rest of the world too; in fact, Simple looks forward to the coming Rocket Age and figures out what he will do in all the far-away places to which he'll zoom.

And through it all he wrestles with his implacable enemy, Jim Crow. For Simple is a militant Negro—though he would use the expression "race-man"—and if Judge Medina overheard his forceful talk he'd probably double his daily dose of dry Martinis. If Simple were to pray what was really on his mind, "the Lord would shut his ears and not listen to me at all."

Simple would have the Lord wipe out all the white people and let *him* rule a while. But as Simple goes on to outline the beneficent program he would install as world ruler, it seems there would still be white people around.

"First place, with white folks wiped out, I would stop charging such high rents—so my landlady would charge *me* less. Second place, I would stop hoarding up all the good jobs for white folks—so I could get ahead my self. Third place, I would make the South behave. . . ."

And lest somebody wrongly accuse him of being a reactionary nationalist for even thinking of this prayer which he didn't pray, I should hasten to add that Simple is a staunch union man and that he would not deny a white man his just reward—only he'd like to see, for once, a *black* general

pinning a medal on a *white* soldier, instead of the other way around all the time.

I have heard it said that there are some people who are a little leery about the Simple language of this book; that eyebrows have been lifted because the idiom is other (I wouldn't say "less") than pure Churchillian. I've heard tell that some were even so mad about this that they forgot to be angry about the things that anger Simple—lynchings, police brutality, Redbaiting and the rest. At one place in the book his girl friend, Joyce, also accuses him of something like that, saying reproachfully, "You are acting just like a Negro." Well, he also *talks* like a Negro, or rather, like a great many Negroes talk; and as for me, I'd rather listen to his salty speech than to all the mush-mouthed sons of Marlborough in the King's own England.

Lambasting the ways of white folks, Simple does not fail to swing a few left-hooks at some of the Negro upper-crust. Joyce takes him to a banquet sponsored by Mrs. Sadie Maxwell-Reeves, who "lives so high up on Sugar Hill that people in her neighborhood don't even have roomers." He is filled with delight when the guest of honor, a venerable artist-writer whom they are feting because the *New York Times* called him a genius, turns upon the assemblage and says:

"Now to tell you the truth, I don't want no damned banquet. . . ."

There are some weak spots in the book, and I have in mind particularly the treatment of Negroes in relation to foreigners. Simple inveighs against the situation where a new immigrant has rights that his people, "old Americans," are denied. The situation is real and that's how Simple sees it, but I was hoping that author Hughes would butt in to indicate the danger of pitting Negroes against foreign-born, and I was disappointed when he didn't. With all his wisdom, the Man-on-the-Street can be wrong too; folk-wisdom is not without its fallacies.

But in spite of such weaknesses and the limitations of this literary form, Jesse B. Semple is a splendid character, full of the zest for living and the spirit for fighting; he has nothing in common with the warped, frustrated and above all *doomed* Negro that Richard Wright, Chester Himes and others of that school have given us. That is because his creator, truly knowing his people, *loves* them. Loves them as they are, for what they are, and to hell with the white chauvinists.

No, there is nothing doomed about Simple, with all his troubles which he is quick to recite. . . .

But listen to this—and here I come back to those people who have been doomed by the way things are or seem to be: after going through the list of his grievances (which I have quoted only in part), Simple concludes by saying:

"—but I am still here. Daddy-o, I'm still here!"

That's right, Simple is still here just the same; and he and his people are going to *be here* come A-bombs or H-bombs, McCarthys, Mundts and Trumans. So all of us who aim to be here too had better get acquainted with him now if we aren't already.

Hugh H. Smythe
"Hughesesque Insight"
Crisis, 57 (June 1950),
377–8

American literature has waited a long time for a folk character of color without the stereotyped cloak of uncle tomism. The pen of Langston Hughes has finally brought to life such an individual in the person of Jesse Semple, popularly known as "Simple." This urbanized, yet folksy character that travels across the pages of Mr. Hughes' latest prose work provides entertainment unmatched in literature of recent times. Here at last is a worthy rival of the famous "Mr. Dooley," only Simple has more color—in more ways than purely physical. Here is a fresh, newly created character destined to take his place in the hall of fame of American folk characters, and he will be read and enjoyed for years to come.

From the time Simple opens his mouth to describe his feet—"big, long, broad, and flat"—and you begin to travel down his road of life which is narrow and restricted because of poverty and color, you will find yourself laughing, crying, thrown into moods of anger and disgust, but through it all Simple's sense of humor will keep you sane and amused. A review cannot do justice to this book but a glance at some of the Hughesesque titles provides an insight into what goes on here. Whether Simple is discussing "Income Tax," merely "Letting off Steam," expounding on "Equality and Dogs," or just running off at the mouth "For the Sake of Argument," you are sure to find him funny and real and human. His lingo has a delightful expressive quality that picturesquely portrays exactly what he means— "I was dancing, holding Polly Joe closer than a hanger hold a suit." And Simple has opinions on practically everything, from the Un-American Committee to pampered pets, from whiskey to women; he talks incessantly. Of course, there are his girl friends; Joyce, the real lady love; Zarita, to pass the time; and his estranged wife in Baltimore, from whom he is perennially trying to obtain a divorce—if she will pay for it.

Mr. Hughes has brought to life a character that has universal appeal. Simple may be a product of Harlem but his prototype exists in the numerous black ghettoes scattered from the Atlantic to the Pacific, from Canada to the Gulf. When Simple speaks a literature of protest is created and his philosophizing on racial injustice is clear and sensible and pointed: "The government protects and takes care of buffaloes and deers—which is more than the government does for me or my kinfolks down South." Only Langston Hughes, "the people's poet," could turn his hand to prose and create a Simple. Lifted bodily from the author's columns in the *Chicago Defender*, woven together into a cleverly joined collection of conversational pieces, you'll agree with Simple that very few men can become President "but almost anybody can get drunk." And you will find this so, after imbibing this folk humor with a protest punch that carries a powerful down-to-earth truthful quality, even as it entertains. This is one of Langston Hughes' finest contributions: a combination book of humor, a sociological monograph, a piece of race relations literature, in short a *tour-de-force* in which he can take extreme pride, for he has produced a volume any and all can enjoy.

C. B. Barnard
"Langston Hughes' Common Man"
New Leader, 10 June 1950, p. 25

Jesse B. Semple, known as Simple, is a man who lives in a prison. Like those most men seem to inhabit, Simple's is made, not of breakable concrete and iron, but of bone-tough, self-knitting custom, of blood and anxiety and the protective rituals of survival and power. Unlike most men except those of his race, Simple can clearly objectify the walls about him, can give them a name, "Jim Crow," and can with absolute justification place the blame for them, and for his imprisonment, on someone else.

In one sense this clear picture and assignment of responsibility is his strength. He can at times find freedom in unconcern, a passive acceptance of a white culture's rules without any deeper commitment. But it may also be his weakness. In his obsessive certainty that the enclosure of which he is blameless is the source of discomfort, he has denied himself the will to wear it down or to make the space within more habitable than he found it.

Simple is not a complete character. He exists as the major voice in a series of dialogues with a nameless first-person narrator and questioner, published originally as a weekly column in the Chicago *Defender*, a newspaper for Negroes. It might have been better to read the dialogues this way, episode by episode, before they were gathered into a book.

Although the book has a moment of heightened suspense at the end and a denouement implying a happier future, it has no developing structure to hold it together. It is cemented primarily by the humorous, bitter, and often deeply cutting insights Simple verbalizes for his questioner. He lacks flesh and blood—he cannot be visualized, and the fact seems consistent with his origin and purpose.

Langston Hughes, his creator, describes him on the jacket as "the ordinary 'man in the street'," a popular phrase in these popular-phrase-repeating times.

Simple is a partial collection of the surface reactions common to many people caught in the situation of colored residents of Harlem. This may be why he has no discrete reality of appearance or gesture—he is many-faced, unfused by imagination. He is slick and sophisticated and funny, and at the same time touching in his strength and sensitivity. But collected in a book, his total performance may be more depressing than moving. Although he describes many intimate and troubling situations, there is no sense of the beat of a pulse or the contraction of viscera. He is not realized with sufficient concreteness to be identified with.

This is not meant to obscure the fact that Simple as he exists is shrewd and perceptive and sympathetic, nor to deny the persistent bright spots in the book. Simple loves the people of Harlem with an embracing warmth that, while it admits criticism, is not divisible. He can indulge in shiny and elaborate escapist fantasies, like one of a personal rocket ship that will carry him beyond the boundaries of race prejudice, while at the same time recognizing their unreality. He knows that a bar is something to lean on, and admits that he leans on bars often, because everything else he has leaned on fell down, "including," he says, "my people, my wife, my boss, and me."

The finest episode in the book may be that of the one-legged veteran who falls while he is hurrying along a wet, slippery street. It is a subject that has been used too often as a sympathy-arousing device, but Mr. Hughes has more to give it. The problem is the soldier's dignity. He can maintain it in spite of his physical deficiency, if he is left alone, but with the deficiency he cannot escape two pursuing women, described as "dopey." They overtake and capture him, each one angrily attempting to establish possession for the purpose of showering him with destructive sympathy. Mr. Hughes has neatly turned the knife. The metaphor is complete and brilliant. It leaves one with a haunting and unpleasant fear of sympathetic over-extension.

Although he admits to breaking windows during the Harlem riots, Simple is not violent by nature. He is verbally vio-

lent, but it is the release of bitter humor with which he drains off his frustrations. In spite of the unpleasantness of his situation, Simple holds tight to life and finds a tremendous satisfaction in the immediate act of living. This and the deflecting armor of humor are his greatest assets.

Yet Simple is essentially formless. As a person this is justified by his family background: shifted from relative to relative, he seldom felt loved or wanted. But characters in books are not people and cannot be judged by the same standards. He lacks concreteness and shape—he has no narrative structure. He is not made important as a character, and the people, some of whose facets he represents, are important and more alive than he is.

William Harrison
"The Bookshelf"
Providence Chronicle,
10 June 1950, p. 2

The genius of Langston Hughes is axiomatic; it is in the order of certainty with facts of nature like falling rain or twinkling stars, inevitable and brilliant, abundant and common like green grass. His fount of inspiration never runs dry, for streams of thought constantly pour into its various channels. I think the scientific reason for this is more than any special genetic gift or endowment, but is rather the poet's closeness to his people, which is akin to that of the great Paul Robeson. Despite achievements, which would have turned the head of a second-rater less fortified than he with the saving grace of common sense, Mr. Hughes has not become the prisoner of any fashionably desiccating coterie of literary snobs. Indeed, it would be a contradiction in terms for him to be contemptuous of the masses of the Negro people, his original source of inspiration, the inexhaustible reservoir of both his poetry and his prose.

Since Mr. Hughes is a practicing journalist who always meets his deadlines, the content of all his writing is alive with the urgencies of his time. The present volume comprises some columns which originally appeared in the *Chicago Defender*, of which Mr. Hughes is a contributing editor. Each chapter is cast in the form of a conversational dialogue about topics of the day which purports to be between the sophisticated author and one Jesse B. Semple, otherwise known as Simple, representative of the mass sentiments of the Negro people. Only a writer who has done much coming and going down the highways and bypaths of Negro life could so truthfully record the average urban Negro American's reactions to social, economic, and political problems. Mr. Hughes chronicles the small beer of numerous conversations which he must have overheard in Harlem "greasy spoon" eateries and taverns. At the end Simple becomes so familiar that he almost comes to living flesh and blood. We have all seen and heard his counterparts in every urban area where Negroes reside in large and significant numbers, in Boston's South End as well as in Chicago's South Side, for instance.

As Dryden said of Chaucer's *Canterbury Tales*, "here is God's plenty." Each reader will select favorites according to personal taste or experience. For me most memorable is Simple's tale of his signposting landlady, because Negro humor (peculiar and universal) is there retailed at its best and most characteristic. However, there are others in which Simple's domestic troubles, although presented with tragicomic seriousness, create understanding sympathy, and in which his militant aspirations for a peaceful world with jobs and security for all literally burst with compelling force.

Ben H. Bagdikian "Hughes' Wry Humor" *Providence Sunday Journal*, section 6, 11 June 1950, p. 8

Langston Hughes, Negro poet, playwright and novelist, has collected here a series of short, Runyonesque dialogues which first appeared serially in the *Chicago Defender*. The author, a literary, temperate sort of fellow, is forever restraining the fierce pronouncements of Jesse B. Semple, or Simple, who says typically, "No matter what a man does, sick or well, something is liable to happen, especially if you are colored."

Simple lives a complicated Harlem life. He has trouble with his landlady, who puts up signs like "No Co. after 10" and "Wash Face Only in Bowl—No Sox." Simple also has trouble with his girl, who refuses to pay for Simple's divorce, his boss, who sometimes forgets that Simple puts in a hard day's work for his pay, and, most of all, with Jim Crow.

"This here movie," he tells his companion, "showed great big beautiful lakes with signs up all around: 'No Fishing—State Game Preserve.' But it did not show a single place with a sign up, 'No Lynching.'"

When his companion tells him he is disgracing his race by yelling in a Harlem barroom, Simple says, "I think I should have as much right as the next one to be a disgrace—if I want to be—without anybody talking about my race."

This is wry humor, filled with that typical Hughes quality of being both gentle and cutting. It is written, Hughes says, for people who laugh with Negroes, not at them.

Theodore Stanford
"Book Review"
Philadelphia Tribune,
17 June 1950, p. 4

In the year 1943 Langston Hughes created and first introduced thru the medium of his weekly column in *The Chicago Defender,* a character familiarly known by the sobriquet of "Simple."

There is a suspicion that many of Hughes' readers met this innovation with a reaction bordering on deep mistrust. Over the years, they had grown accustomed to the conventional stylings of the writer's comment on current topics. Here, however, was something startlingly unconventional. This creature, Simple, was a novelty, a departure. He was a man with problems on his mind. He was emphatically vocal. He talked to you. Failing that, he talked at you. He insisted on being heard, clamored to be understood. Somewhere, hidden in the often devious processes of his logic, there lay a hard and imponderable core of social truth. He was, at once, distinctly disturbed and decidedly disturbing. Simple was his name; yet he was anything but simple. Over and above it all, Simple was a creature of joy. At the same time, he was a creation irresistibly to be enjoyed.

It was not long, however, before readers of the *Defender* began to develop an unaffected interest in the flowering of Simple's mythical but determinedly convincing personality. Today, there must be thousands who, like this reviewer, picked up their copies of the Chicago newspaper in eager anticipation of chuckling over the very latest of what a certain character named Simple has had to say.

Seen from the customer's side of a lower Lenox Avenue bar, Simple is merely an easy-going, ordinary, Virginia-born resident of New York City's Negro ghetto. Christened Jesse Semple, he is dark-skinned, virile, and in the prime of life. A beer-loving habitué of the cheaper taprooms, he craves companionship and will develop an argument just for the sake of its comradely interchange of conversation. Poorly educated, hard-working, but usually down to his last dime, Simple divides his limited talents for relaxation between nightly drinking bouts and complicated episodes of philandering. Gifted with a flare for narrative and an effervescent sense of humor, he takes unabashed delight in spinning hilariously exaggerated yarns about his flint-hearted landlady, his absent wife, and his assorted love interests.

Viewed from another angle, Simple is discovered to be an exceedingly sober-minded and complex personality. Bound up with his beer-guzzling sprees, his affairs with women, and the various compulsions of his nocturnal ramblings is an inescapable loneliness of spirit, a disquieting sense of social unbelonging, and a burdensome consciousness of the necessity to do daily battle with the miscellany of his personal misfortunes. The effects of hard times, hard work, and a hard fate are written all over Simple; from the palms of his leathery hands to the soles of his callused feet. And Simple never loses an acute and rebellious awareness of that fact. Proud of his color, he is race-conscious to the core. A caustic and uncompromising critic of the practices of anti-Negro discrimination and segregation, Simple wastes no love on white people. For the white world, generally, he has only a feeling of complete contempt, a sense of righteous resentment, and a brick in either fist.

In debating the merits of Simple as an authentic "type"—and quite a bit of pro and con already has been argued on that subject—it seems patently shortsighted to limit the discussion to whether Simple is or is not a "typical" Harlemite. There are many types of Negroes in Harlem. It is a fact, however, that most of Harlem's Negroes are culturally blighted, politically underprivileged, economically exploited, and socially oppressed. Scattered among them, individually, one can find all of the characteristics manifested in Jesse Semple. Simple, himself, is a composite character. For the sake of illustrative convenience, there has been combined in his fictional person that whole complex of emotions and reactions which, in real life, actually is distributed in varying combinations among a broad segment of the Harlem population.

This technique of concentrating characteristics, employed here by Hughes, does not destroy the realities of the situation but, rather, highlights them. Simple, therefore, is not merely a reasonably "typical" representative of the great majority of Harlem's low-income-bracket Negroes. The more important fact is that Simple is unquestionably symbolic of millions of Negro proletarians penned in urban ghettoes throughout vast sections of our country north of the Mason and Dixon Line. Therein lies a lesson, a warning and, in a peculiar sense, the dim foreshadowings of a certain kind of hope.

Langston Hughes should justifiably feel happy for the impulse which led him to collect his popular newspaper columns into this book. The fortunes of the professional author are so unpredictable that it is sometimes possible for a man to write his best book almost by accident. To say such is not to deprecate the genius of any author. Literary ideas—and the fictional characters which stem from them—not infrequently grow out of all size, shape, and importance to their original dimensions. *Simple Speaks His Mind* stands in eloquent testimony to this thesis. The story of Jesse B. Semple—that airy and diverting creation, once cultivated by the author as a humorous whim—has evolved into what I believe to be the most artistically satisfying, technically perfect, and socially significant product of Langston Hughes' exceptionally fertile and distinguished career.

J. Randolph Fisher "Looks at Books: Langston Hughes' Best Columns" *Pittsburgh Courier,* 22 July 1950, p. 27

Langston Hughes' *Simple Speaks His Mind* is one of the most genuinely entertaining books I have ever read. A fellow whom the author met in 1943 "evolved into the character Simple, talking about everything from war plants to love."

Simple is the ordinary man in the street, the basic Harlemite. Born in Virginia (a state named after a woman), Simple has always had trouble with women, particularly his landlady. Losing his job, failing to qualify for WPA, Simple got a good taste of hard times. Isabel, his wife, worked in a war plant and eventually insisted that Simple "take over or take off."

He took off.

Divided into four parts, which consist of forty-five chapters, the book keeps the reader laughing—and thinking—from cover to cover. Verses scattered throughout punctuate and emphasize Simple's philosophy.

Occasionally one is treated to Simple's own "poetries," which, though often without reason, now and again are pointful.

Like Lamb and Samuel Johnson, Simple is "sold" on city life; what London was to them, Harlem ("where folks is friendly") is to him. Having listened to Daddy Grace and "et" with Father Divine, moaned with Elder Lawson and prayed with Adam Powell, Simple argues that Harlem is heaven.

"It would take an atom bomb to get me out." A victim of jim-crow shock, he is allergic even to Southern accent.

Simple is a likeable fellow, the sort one is really pleased to know. Simple is one of those too-seldom-met fellows that we manage to remember not to forget. Simple is a needful race-relations tonic that enables us not only to see "the problem," but to "see it whole."

black, not always a pleasant experience though educational.

Simple is not so simple as his nickname. With his gentle barbs, more effective than sturdy righteous indignation, and his wry amusement, he's deserving of welcome to newspaper pages and to bookshelves, and we hope to see more of him.

E.B.
"Among the New Books"
San Francisco Chronicle This World, 23 July 1950, p. 21

Poet and novelist Langston Hughes has extended his talents into the daily newspaper column. Readers of the *Chicago Defender* know his Jesse B. Semple who hangs out at Paddy's Bar in Harlem and comments on life. Through a series of dialogues, half humorous, half serious, wholly interesting, he talks of the things that concern him— his landlady, his women, his relatives, his worries on and off his job, and Jim Crow.

Hughes has developed a modern Mr. Dooley without the dialect. Through Simple's humorous comments the white-skinned can see how they look to the

Philip Farish
"Haunting, if You Dare Read"
Daily Oklahoman Sunday Magazine, 30 July 1950, p. 16

This is a collection of anecdotes originally written as a series in the *Chicago Defender* that has been put together to form a novel. Written as dialogues between Jesse Semple, known generally as Simple, and his unnamed, educated friend, they form a biography of the "man in the street" in Harlem as Hughes knows him from having lived there.

Jesse's apparent problem is to get a divorce from his wife Isabel, who threw him out when he was jobless during the depression. He wants to marry another girl, but oddly enough he seems to make no move to save the money to get the divorce. However, Jesse's real problem is much bigger. It is how to be an ordinary citizen in the U.S.A. when Negroes are not permitted to be ordinary citizens.

Since these were originally published in a Negro newspaper and not intended to be collected, the actual story line is not apparent in the very beginning. But this turns out to be an advantage because it allows hundreds of digressions that establish the pressures on the Negro, even in a Negro community, that keep him a second class citizen. The other character of the dialogues, an educated man, provides a counterpoint to Jesse's impassioned and often unreasoned attitudes. Together they point up strongly the squalid and degrading kind of thinking on the part of white people which makes it impossible for a Negro to be a citizen on his terms rather than the white man's.

The writing is clear and fresh. The dialogue is particularly rich and convincing. It is a book that will haunt you if you dare to read it.

Helen Dolan
"Our Bookshelf: *Simple Speaks His Mind*"
Catholic Interracialist, 10 (August 1950), 3

Simple Speaks His Mind began as a series in the *Chicago Defender,* a weekly newspaper that has a wide circulation among the ordinary "man in the street" type of reader.

Because it was written for that group of average non-literary Negro readers, it is extraordinarily revealing in its half-humorous, half serious attitude towards the daily life and problems of the average Negro.

Simple, who is a member of the working classes, makes many penetrating remarks in the course of his dialogues with his literary friend who is observing life for literary purposes. Simple loves to talk about everything from religion to his troubles with his landlady, usually in terms of race. Many of the articles are very funny, some bitter, but all give you a feeling of

what it must feel like to be a Negro in this Land of Democracy generally, and Harlem in particular.

When his literary friend argues with him in terms of theory, Simple's retorts compounded with the wisdom of experience, and born of a constant struggle to assert his dignity and rights as an individual, leave you with the feeling that humor is the only leaven that can keep the oppressed from despair.

Since the articles originally appeared one by one in the *Defender,* there was probably no sense of monotony, but collected in one volume, and read straight through, there is a tendency to sameness, inherent in any collection of columns, so that it would be better to read a little at a time, for there is much to ponder and think about in this collection.

J.R.M.
"Negro Viewpoint Amusingly Stated"
Pasadena Star-News, 13 August 1950, p. 23

This good book began as a series of columns, or essays, in *The Chicago Defender,* a Negro paper. Author Langston Hughes was writing as a Negro for Negroes, and perhaps that is one of the reasons that the book, as finally presented, makes excellent reading for anyone.

The scene is Harlem—not the Harlem of the visitor looking for trouble, but the Harlem of a man who has lived there and understands and feels with the people. The character portrayed and quoted, Simple, is always lifelike and human in his own sometimes perverse way. A very likable fellow. Of course some of the problems which Negroes face in the United States are presented through the mind and talk of Simple. But this is not at all an angry book; rather, it is amusing.

Probably it will do more good in the way of race relations (you should hear Simple on race relations) than any half dozen angry books. Perhaps it is not a book to read straight through, but rather one to have handy on the living room table and pick up occasionally and chuckle over. Langston Hughes, a sensitive artist, has written a number of books; this one may be close to his best. He has long been one of this reviewer's favorites.

Alexander Lang
"Book Reviews"
Industrial Worker,
18 August 1950, p. 2

"One regrets, I said, that, after all, life is conflict."

"I leave them regrets to you," said Simple.

These concluding lines of the book serve well as a preface to this review. For these lines get to the heart of the casual conversations the author has with his character Simple.

Simple is one of the ordinary men on the street—and the street is in Harlem, the largest urban Negro community in the world. Sensitive, extremely perceptive, quick on the defense, ever conscious of his color, Simple candidly gives forth his thoughts and feelings on the problems of life which he daily confronts. He is full of rich humor, even though deadly serious, of the kind expressed in these lines of a blues song: When you see me laughing, I'm laughing to keep from crying.

Life in Harlem, for Simple, means pe-rennial conflict. He has bad trouble with women, in the form of his parted wife, his sweetheart, the landlady, or flirting women who cross his path. There are difficulties with boss-man, the rising costs of living, the income tax. Sickness strikes in the winter, keeping Simple in a hospital for a painful long time. At a lecture, Simple finds himself opposed to the ideas of the speaker.

Simple likes to talk; it's a form of relaxation for him. He talks freely and interestingly on subjects ranging from politics to religion, from law to sports, from his boyhood to his dreams of the future. He continues learning and yearning, for he has a robust love of life. And ever always, he keeps coming back to the theme of race relations.

Langston Hughes has done a magnificent job with this series of dialogues in getting close to the man on the street. Much of the material he derived from actual conversations heard or overheard in bars and on corners in Harlem. Though he himself has a slightly pious and pompous attitude, it in no way interferes with the frankness of Simple. He succeeds where so many writers have recently failed.

For a real picture of what life means these days to the man on the street in Harlem, this is the book. In addition, it provides an excellent education in race relations.

Alberta Eiseman
"On the Book Beat"
Seventeen, 9 (September 1950), 14

Simple isn't simple at all. He's a wise and humorous man of Harlem, who speaks his mind on the most amazing variety of subjects: landladies, Jackie Robinson, the great outdoors, concert singers who sing in foreign languages—and Jim Crow. Jim Crow is always there, behind most of his thoughts. Langston Hughes, poet, novelist and lyricist, created Simple in a series of articles he wrote for a Negro newspaper. Simple's thoughts, therefore, are set down very frankly. If you are easily hurt, some of this may bother you, but it will make you laugh, too, and think while you're laughing.

William Gardner Smith "Simple's Dialogues" *New Republic*, 123 (4 September 1950), 20

"Listen Fluently—"

Speaking is Jesse B. Semple, known as Simple to his friends—and fluently does the reader listen. For Simple is a likable guy; he has humor, sensitivity, intelligence, and something to say; he is the voice of the American Negro as few have heard him speak.

Langston Hughes knows and loves the people of Harlem, and others like them throughout the nation. He knows that though they do not speak with eloquence, theirs is the most profound understanding of what race prejudice means. Consequently he has created their symbol, a Negro Joe Doakes, to say what all of them have on their mind. Forty-four of these dialogues, which appeared originally in the Chicago *Defender*, the *New Republic* and *Phylon*, comprise the book.

Because most of these columns were written for a Negro audience, they are uninhibited, intimate, to the point. The white reader gets a rare insight into the private conversations of Negroes. Dominating the conversations, of course, is Simple, whose irresistible tongue wanders incisively over such topics as the Harlem riots, lynchings, Jackie Robinson's appearance before the House Un-American Activities Committee, The Law, why Simple can't hope to be President, the relative treatment accorded dogs and Negroes, and Simple's family life. We also come to know his friends: Hughes, who invariably comes off second-best in arguments with the hero; Joyce, his wonderful girl; his landlady; and Zarita, the *femme fatale*.

Simple makes such priceless understatements as, "White folks is the cause of a lot of inconveniences in my life." Comes World War III, he wants to reverse the usual process and "see some Negro generals pinning medals on white men." In one of his moments of cynicism, Simple wishes the Lord would smite all white folks down, with one exception: "I hope he lets Mrs. Roosevelt alone."

The best dialogues are those in which Hughes, as the supercilious straight man, disagrees with the things Simple has to say. In some of the others, we feel the cards have been stacked against us—even though we know the things discussed are true.

Unfortunately, segregation begets a degree of "segregated" humor. There are hilarious passages in this book which no white American will be able fully to appreciate. But to people who would like an idea of what the ordinary Negro thinks about the world in general, without frills and without pretension, the book will be a revelation.

Youra Qualls
"The Bookshelf: Simple—
New Observer of U.S.
Scene"
Christian Science Monitor,
12 September 1950,
[p. 14]

In the gallery of American Negro literary types is now hung the portrait of Jesse B. Semple.

A realistic, straightforward observer of the contemporary urban scene, with a racy argot in which he comments fluently upon that scene, Simple would only be puzzled by that subtle symbolist, Uncle Remus. A short-tempered man whose religious practices are informal and infrequent, Simple bears no resemblance, except in color, to saintly Uncle Tom. Too much involved in the general experience of urban life, Simple would sympathize with the single-minded Bigger Thomas, of Richard Wright, but he could not himself be a Bigger—life is too interesting. Harlem is too full of excitement, with the joys of conviviality in the company of straight man Hughes, to whom he pours out his varied observations, the excitement of trying to understand "womens"; Simple is more of a native son than Bigger; the irony and tragedy of American Negro life are in his narrative, but the psychotic element is missing.

Simple is thus a new type, greatly varied in mood, speech, and experience. He is a completely realized critic of American life, but he may be considered the stereotyped fictional Negro by people who do not believe that the Negro's lot is sternly challenging and like to see him depicted as a clown or a happy-go-lucky child. For such readers most of Simple's funny experiences might confirm the stereotype, for they seem to be characteristically "Negro," clownlike and foolish. But the alert reader finds truer humor in the experiences that are concerned with the everyday activities of an average human being, and he begins to realize that Straight Man Hughes is just as much in earnest as some of his notable ancestors—Piers Ploughman and Jonathan Swift, for instance. Mr. Hughes is for the great crowd of common men. He is as much in earnest in his solutions to the problem of protecting minorities, who do not have the protection of state laws, as Swift was in earnest about his solution to the problem of too many Irish babies in Ireland. In Simple, Mr. Hughes has created a real, contemporary man, struggling with humor, some patience, and a great deal of humaneness to adjust himself to the only country he knows. He is not "colleged"; thus some of his solutions are "simple." To curb juvenile delinquency in Harlem, he would put a juke box in the parlor to keep kids out of joints. A film about fish and game preserves gives him the thought that Congress should pass a law creating such preserves for Negroes: "The Government protects and takes care of buffaloes and deers—which is more than it does for me or my kinfolks down South. When that movie short finished, it were sunset in Virginia, and it showed a little deer and its mama laying down to sleep. Didn't nobody say 'Get up, deer, you can't sleep here,' like they would to me if I was to go to the White Sulphur Springs Hotel."

The American conscience is scourged by the somber story of a Richard Wright; it is wooed and given a healthy pricking by the gentle humor and the quiet ridicule of Jesse B. Semple's creator.

Owen Dodson
"Love and Race"
Harlem Quarterly, 1
(Fall–Winter 1950), 56–8

Langston Hughes' character, Mr. Jesse B. Semple, nicknamed Simple, in these collected conversations, *Simple Speaks His Mind,* is more than a name or a character. He has become to thousands an almost legendary figure drinking his beer at any number of bars and talking his mind on just about everything. Simple's flashlight perception reveals many acid truths and consequences concerning America's treatment of her minorities. Like Ollie Harrington's Bootsie, Simple is not all sour and negative. He could never survive in this uneven life if he didn't have considerable motherwit and hilarious humor. He cocks a cockeyed look at many messy situations and sees them straight. Simple is a common guy with shrewd ideas, few ideals and a yearning for the good life. In all these recorded conversations he speaks with simplicity and often depth. You cannot listen for long without realizing how sharply he exposes the hurt that has been troubling democracy since the first slaves were forced here. Simple at one point asks: ". . . don't you have no realization of how bad my colored condition is?"; observes during a discussion on the race question: ". . . it is not even a question, it is a hammer over our heads and at any time it may fall." The tragic implication is that the Simples of America are trapped in injustice and often rendered impotent to act by the sheer toughness of life.

The tempo of this book like that of Simple's existence tends to become samey but that is exactly the effect Mr. Hughes wishes to give. Where is the chance for va-riety in a dark cell? What is there in a rat maze but monotony and death? It is to Mr. Hughes' credit that Simple does not openly despair. There is within Simple's character a determination to live and survive and become a member. The principal themes run throughout the book: love and race. Love, Simple must have to feel himself an individual; and his acute consciousness of race serves to knife him into the living fight against his condition; at least he puts up a verbal fight.

The most successful literary accomplishment of the book is the non-contrived reporting. Two chapters are beautifully realized by Hughes: the one in which Simple's friend Joyce, whom he someday hopes to marry, happens to come to his room only to find Simple and another more casual friend, Zarita, under the bed looking for the contents of Zarita's purse that had been scattered everywhichway in an earlier moment of hilarity. Hughes handles this with wonderful comic invention; the other chapter concerns a one-legged veteran on crutches who is being followed by two women fighting for his affection. The soldier falls on ice and the scene that follows with the women yapping about who will taxi him home, the soldier's refusal of help, Simple's compassionate comments on the sidelines, all make for a memorable, heartbreaking, Charlie Chaplin balance between pathos and farce.

Set this book along with the increasing volumes of urban folklore. Although Simple's problems are immediate and their appeal wide, it is his ingratiating character and his aspiration, his humor that will outtime the problems hanging over his head and those of his fellow beer drinkers.

G. Lewis Chandler
"For Your Recreation and Reflection"
Phylon, 12 (First Quarter 1951), 94–5

Langston Hughes cannot shed his skin—no more than any author who has found his gait. This is normal and is not meant to be a criticism. For established authors have always stamped their personalities on their themes and techniques—hence adjectives like Shakespearean, Chaucerian, Wordsworthian, Emersonian, Miltonic, Byronic. Why not Hughesian? Everything Langston Hughes writes—poetry or prose; lyrics or narratives—bears his stamp: a predilection for common life and everyday situations treated with a paradoxical mixture of genial humor and uncomfortable satire. For thirty years he has done this in "thirteen books and many stories, articles, plays, poems, opera librettos, and songs." In all of them, he injects a special type of worldliness, humor, pathos, tragedy, racism, eroticism, proletarianism, optimism. Hughes cannot shed his skin. And *Simple Speaks His Mind* again illustrates this fact. It is another *Shakespeare in Harlem,* or "Madam to You" (*One-Way Ticket*), or *Freedom's Plow* done narratively in a series of prose vignettes.

Divided into four parts ("Summer Time"; "Winter Time"; "Hard Times"; "Any Time"), *Simple Speaks His Mind*—beginning as a weekly series in the *Chicago Defender*—is a book of short short-stories photographing the mind and chronicling the droll experiences of a semi-literate Harlemite, Simple, who confides in or talks back to his creator (Hughes) in much the same way as does Charlie McCarthy to Edgar Bergen. But Charlie is white and is an aristocrat. Simple is colored and is proletariat. This makes the vast difference between the two in what they see, feel, and say. Simple is completely race conscious, sex conscious, and bread conscious. Suffering from the impact of such consciousness, he makes articulate what the average Negro experiences, mentally and physically, in a segregated society struggling for integration. The capacity to feel as a Negro and to think and talk as a man makes Simple more than a marionette. He is a live character who, though not a capital debater, takes a definite stand on many issues within the areas of sex, security, and race relations. In the matter of sex, he stands firm for male supremacy; he is genuinely indifferent to his wife (Isabel), completely loves Joyce (his girl friend), thoroughly disrespects Zarita, with whom he drinks away his money and time. Again, he has not had much economic security, though he has drudged hard to earn so little. . . .

However, if Simple is anything, he is a thoroughgoing race man. He hates prejudice; he hates segregation; he hates the white man. But he loves Mrs. Roosevelt, and the Brooklyn Dodgers—because Jackie Robinson plays for them. He would have Negro officers pin medals on white soldiers. He would have Congress do less resolving and more solving. He stands squarely for F.E.P.C. and urges that Adam Powell should out filibuster Southern filibusters. Simple is indeed a character—a Hughesian character: ignorant and wise; selfish and magnanimous—a roustabout and angel; a coward and hero; an hypochondriac and idealist.

But the significance of this book does not lie wholly in the character and reflections of Simple. It lies also in Hughes' characteristic skill in treating the serious humorously, in deftly handling dialogue (he matches Hemingway here), in selecting and compressing material germane to mood, character, and action—in achieving unity out of diversity. In short, if you read *Simple Speaks His Mind* for sheer entertainment, you will not be disappointed. If you read it, however, for esthetic and civic implications, you will be challenged. This is just like Langston Hughes—in both verse and prose. He can simultaneously turn the corners of your mouth up or down. He cannot help it. That's his skin.

sembles the same writer's "Simple's Dialogues," *New Republic,* 123 (4 September 1950), 20, reprinted in this volume.]

John W. Parker
"Book Reviews"
Journal of Negro History, 36 (January 1951), 96–8

William G[ardner] Smith
"A Book Review"
Journal A.S.P. Philadelphia, January–February 1951, [p. ?]

Heretofore, there has been little of what we might call "Negro national literature"—that is, literature by Negroes to be read by Negroes. This is a serious lack. . . .

Literature by Negroes . . . has been by Negroes to be read by white Americans; Negro writers have sought to present a picture of their own people to the white American world, which exploits and oppresses it. This has led to a great deal of distortion, pamphleteering and self-consciousness.

Langston Hughes' recent book, *Simple Speaks His Mind,* is an example of "national" literature. It is a collection of columns written by Hughes, which appeared originally in the *Chicago Defender* and other Negro publications, plus several in the *New Republic.* They were written to be read by Negroes; thus, they are invariably frank, truthful and to the point.

[. . .]

[The remainder of this review re-

In his latest book, *Simple Speaks His Mind,* Langston Hughes returns to Harlem, the scene of his departure as a poet in 1922, and the spot that just a few decades back became the home of the much-discussed and not infrequently much-cussed "Negro Literary Renaissance." Although void of much of the glitter and the fanfare that it possessed during the Mid-Twenties, Harlem has remained a center of color and enchantment and has retained its firm hold on the popular imagination of the American people. *Simple Speaks His Mind* is a brilliant and shockingly accurate exposé of the social milieu of the Harlem dweller and of the accompanying frustration that results from his desperate struggle to make ends meet and from his recognition of his out-group status in a period of growing social awareness. Hughes' selection of the social and emotional situations that make up the volume attest to his familiarity with the Harlem scene and his adeptness in the artistic handling of the simple narrative as a literary medium. Everywhere the humor is that both of characterization and of situation; it is calculated for people who laugh *with* Negroes, not *at* them.

Simple Speaks His Mind began in 1942 as a series of stories written especially for readers of the *Chicago Defender,* and with the idea that none other than Negroes

378

would ever see it. Hence, its amazing intimacy and its chit chat, Harlem style, that sometimes leaves the reader almost with a sense of eavesdropping. The collection divides into four parts—Summer Time, Winter Time, Hard Times, and Any Time—but these divisions are more formal than organic. It achieves its unity through the unity of action of Simple, who, symbolic of the "ordinary man in the street," laughs to keep from crying. Himself a Harlemite, Simple talks endlessly in a half-humorous, half-serious way about the goings-on Harlem dwellers are wont to discuss.

And as it turns out, Simple has a great deal to tell (or perhaps not to tell), for his character imperfections and his social role leave much to be desired. The Virginia biracial set-up has blurred his view of life; he is separated from his wife, but cannot afford the price of a divorce; he "plays the dozens" despite his impatience with others who do so; he resorts occasionally to clandestine association with Zarita, an "uncombed woman," who calls at his room; he is resigned to the four walls of a rented room, and with too many women on his hands, clocks to punch and landladies to dodge, Simple relaxes at parties and bars, and drinks incessantly because "I'm lonesome within myself."

While the author neither justifies nor condemns Simple's irregular conduct, it is obvious, even to Simple, that the forces at play in his life lead but to his undoing. Yet a return to the soil is unthinkable; for Simple, it is Harlem today, tomorrow, next week, and then, well, forget it. He confesses that

When I am a hundred and one,
If I'm still having fun,
I'll start all over again
Just like I begun.

Implicit in Hughes' study of the world's largest urban Negro center is an obvious irony and a tragedy that are part and parcel of the Negro ghetto in an urban community above the Mason-Dixon line.

But for the character, Simple, who is typical rather than distinctive, the array of characters in the volume are but sharply-etched sketches for the reason that the stories turn upon a central theme rather than upon character. And while individually the stories for the most part make absorbing reading, collectively they piece together the inner life of Simple "the toughest Negro God's got," and constitute a definition of the situation for at least one social class in present-day Harlem. This attractively-bound book, which comes both in the one dollar and the three dollar editions, bears the characteristic Hughes trademarks—disdain for literary "Nice-Nellyism," an abiding faith in the common folk, and a clarion call for social justice for America's minority groups. All in all, the collection enhances Hughes' reputation as a story teller.

Somehow one cannot help wishing that Hughes would write a companion volume to *Simple Speaks his Mind,* that is, a book based upon Negroes who, even though they own fish-tail Cadillacs and live in ranch-style solar houses, see life steadily and as a whole. Such a study would serve to balance the present overdrawn picture of the Negro of no consequence, and to disclose the fact that sane, forward-looking Negroes do exist, even in Harlem. And it is conceivable that a few of them are worthy of literary treatment. At any rate, Langston Hughes is still fishing in the proverbial big sea of American literature, and his new book, *Simple Speaks His Mind,* represents another significant catch. It is a fresh and a thought-provoking contribution to the literature of the urban Negro community.

"Book Review: *Simple Speaks His Mind*" *U E News* [official publication of the United Electrical Radio and Machine Workers of America], 14 (9 June 1952), 11

One of the funniest books we've read in a long time is *Simple Speaks His Mind*. The humor in it didn't come out of a can of corn made on a radio-TV program assembly line; nor did any group of writers have to dig through a card file of the world's oldest jokes.

Into the talks between two ordinary men of their experiences with landladies, bosses, bartenders, women and lots of other people, author Langston Hughes has poured honest good humor which keeps bubbling page after page.

The humor is especially rewarding because these two ordinary men are Negroes whose problems in a world of discrimination are far greater than most of us have yet come to appreciate.

[. . .]

Checklist of Additional Reviews

Robert Lucas, "Jess Simple 'Speaks His Mind' in Langston Hughes' New Publication," *Chicago Defender*, 25 March 1950, p. 2.

"April 14," *Retail Bookseller*, 53 (April 1950), 68.

"Weekly Record: Hughes, Langston," *Publishers Weekly*, 157 (22 April 1950), 1853.

"'Common Man' Speaks Out," *Chicago Sun*, 23 April 1950, p. 22.

"Fiction," *Booklist*, 46 (1 May 1950), 275.

"Colorful Analysis of Racial Picture Given in Langston Hughes's Story of 'Simple,'" *Baltimore Afro-American*, 13 May 1950, p. 19.

E.C.R., "Book Review," *New Haven Journal-Courier*, 3 June 1950, p. 12.

Pat Halloran, "Simple's Barroom Chats Cover Harlem Existence," *Buffalo Evening News*, 8 July 1950, p. 7.

"Brief Browsings in Books," *Educational Forum*, 15 (November 1950), 124–6, 128.

Harry L. Jones, "Reviews," *Scandinavian Studies*, 27 (November 1955), 212–15.

Rose Marie P. Akselrad, "Simple Goes to Berlin," *Phylon*, 22 (Fourth Quarter 1961), 395.

MONTAGE OF A DREAM DEFERRED

"Montage of a Dream Deferred"
Virginia Kirkus Bulletin, 18 (1 December 1950), 721

Poems of Harlem, loosely strung together with the twilight, flickering moods of a jazz tune, with a constant drumming beat of heart sickness and bitterness at a "dream deferred." Occasionally, it is true, the demanding re-bop rhythm in some of the sections overwhelms the basic seriousness, but in general the poems speak out of the idiom, speak of husbands and wives, lovers, movies, neon signs, landlords, English themes, funerals, Joe Lewis [sic], lamp post philosophies, and a dream of a Freedom Train with no Jim Crow signs. It is his generous and fierce love of human beings and gift of expression in terms of a people's speech, which gives Mr. Hughes' work its great appeal. However, its greatest value lies in its articulation of the Negroes' demand for respect and justice in a hostile white world. And yet Mr. Hughes hints at a solution in a brief scrap of poetry called "Subway Rush Hour": "so near—no room for fear." Predictable Hughes sales.

Gladys P. Graham
"Book Review"
Philadelphia Tribune, 6 February 1951, p. 4

Montage of a Dream Deferred, Langston Hughes' most recent contribution to the sociological scene in Harlem, is a bold and exciting portrait of a community and a people in transition. Mr. Hughes has lived and worked for some 20 years close to the heart of the sepia melting pot. In his newest work he pours out in verse Harlem in transition.

The poem within a poem has for its purpose to emphasize the dynamics of a living people who in the terms of the author are a melee of individuals with bitter dreams forever deferred.

Mr. Hughes has compiled and set down from *Holiday, Tomorrow, Our World, Common Ground, The Midwest Journal, The Crisis, Phylon, Voices,* and the *Harlem Quarterly,* sections of his work which first appeared in their pages.

"In terms of current Afro-American popular music and the sources from which it has progressed—jazz, ragtime, swing, blues, boogie woogie, and be-bop—this poem of Harlem, like be-bop, is marked by conflicting changes, sudden nuances, sharp and impudent interjections, broken rhythms, and passages sometimes in the manner of the jam session in an attempt to show a community in transition."

Poet Hughes has divided his unique volume into six sections: "Boogie Segue to Bop"; "Dig and Be Dug"; "Early Bright"; "Vice-Versa to Back"; "Dream Deferred"; and "Lenox Avenue Mural."

For this writer section five, "Dream Deferred," was striking for its color and the impression of the writer in his attempt via the medium of verse to picture the various aspects of the world's largest Negro ghetto, Harlem. He begins with the church "Mystery."

The mystery
and the darkness
and the song
and me.

Mr. Hughes then picks up "Passing," telling of the darker brother who has crossed the line and lives down town and who wearily recalls his happiness in Harlem.

"Nightmare Boogie," "Argument," "Night Funeral in Harlem," "Subway Rush," and "Likewise" are all community patterns which the author has observed in goings about town. Apparently the author observes the same structure in all economically pressed and exploited peoples.

Montage of a Dream Deferred, published by Henry Holt and Company delves deep into the folklore of a people whose lives know sadness and joy—people who still dream and wait for the good times that lie ahead.

R.Y.E.
"Langston Hughes' Poems"
Opera and Concert,
16 (March 1951), 24

Although the dust cover of Langston Hughes' most recent collection of poems, published during February by Henry Holt and Co., claims the contents to be "popular poetry in the best sense of the word," the somewhat high-flown title—*Montage of a Dream Deferred*—would hardly make a great deal of sense to many of those about whom Hughes writes. The present volume is, by and large, a sincere attempt to make use of the rhythms and standard shibboleths of bop in order to give fresh emphasis to the story of Negro life in Harlem and elsewhere in this country.

If this device frequently appears to be not too successful, the fault lies not so much in any lack of its intrinsic validity but rather in the fact that Hughes writes his strongest and most compelling work

when he ties into a subject such as "The Freedom Train" or "Theme for English B" and works it over with that special brand of bitterness, not quite yet without hope, that lends the American Negro added dignity.

A number of the poems were first published in various journals, and others are almost sure to remind the reader of something he has seen before. With at least one, "Advice," Hughes could well have achieved more felicitous results by summoning in the services of Pearl Bailey.

There are several items of three or four lines which, in their form if not their choice of words, convey the succinct impact of much of the best Oriental poetry:

When I rolled three 7's
in a row
I was scared to walk out
with the dough.

The total effect of the book may not be all that Hughes intended, but we are hoping someday to come across some of the poems while thumbing through old issues of magazines in which they first appeared and take them one at a time.

Frank Marshall Davis
"Book Review"
Philadelphia Tribune,
3 March 1951, p. 4

For a quarter of a century, Langston Hughes has been in the forefront of contemporary poets. And now, with a world reputation that is almost legendary, he has authored a new book that is easily his finest among a series of fine volumes of poetry.

Montage of a Dream Deferred, published Feb. 19 by Henry Holt, is the title.

It borrows liberally from the terms and feeling of contemporary hot jazz and bop to create a movingly realistic picture of Harlem as it is, with its joys and its dreams deferred.

As was the case with *Simple Speaks His Mind,* this is primarily a book for Negroes. That, to me, is a good thing, for the tendency too often is to write about Harlem primarily for the white reader.

Like other of Hughes' books, the style is disarmingly simple—so simple that often the brilliant artistry may be overlooked. Yet this conversational simplicity makes for the charm and readability that produces a wide audience. It is only rarely that one encounters the obscurantism that too often hangs like a heavy cloud over the work of certain other highly regarded poets.

It seems to me that any poetry woven out of the daily lives of people should be written to be read by the people instead of by a small closed corps of intellectual snobs. Apparently this is also Langston Hughes' belief, for I have yet to see anything from his pen that could not be read and understood by those whose formal education ended in the lower grades.

Consider, for instance, this in "Children's Rhymes":

By what sends
the white kids
I ain't sent:
I know I can't
be President.

Hughes has his ear attuned to jive talk and uses it for sharp portraits, as in the conclusion of "Dead in There," describing the burial of a sharp cat:

Squares
Who couldn't dig him,
Plant him now—
Out where it makes
No diff no how.

The volume also contains "Freedom Train" as well as a number of other widely known poems not previously available in book form. The book is so uniformly excellent that it should bring one of the year's top literary awards to Langston Hughes— if such awards are to be made on pure merit without any other considerations.

Morse Allen
"Poems on Harlem"
Hartford Courant Magazine, 11 March 1951, p. 19

These poems on contemporary Harlem, says Langston Hughes, are composed "in terms of current Afro-American popular music.... jazz, ragtime, swing, blues, boogie-woogie, and be-bop," and the collection, as its title-word "Montage" suggests, is made up mainly of fragments. In one case, the title— "Figurine"—is longer than the poem: "De-dop!" Most of the poems give a splinter of folk wisdom, or a gulp of direct emotion, or a vivid image, as "125th Street":

Face like a chocolate bar
full of nuts and sweet.
Face like a jack-o-lantern,
Candle inside.
Face like slice of melon,
grin that wide.

This is amusingly true, but more contrived than the bare simplicity of "Wonder":

Early blue evening.
Lights ain't come on yet.
Looky yonder!
They come on now!

Recurrent through the book is the "Dream Deferred"—social equality for the Negro. Well-known is "Freedom Train" with its hope that the train has no Jim Crow car. While Langston Hughes expresses his indignation, he has an unusual sense of proportion—he knows that all mankind has its dream deferred:

You talk like
they don't kick
dreams around
Downtown. I expect they do—
But I'm telling about
Harlem to you!

Fred Holley
"Langston Hughes Pictures Harlem in Terms of Afro-American Be-Bop"
Norfolk Virginian-Pilot, part 5, 11 March 1951, p. 4

This volume seems to establish Langston Hughes as a poet of more than passing importance, although he is a long way from the "New Criticism," and as certainly the finest Negro poet this country has yet produced. In this volume he has rendered contemporary Harlem "in terms of current Afro-American popular music . . . the music of a community in transition."

He has created what is very much akin to a folk art. Using the rhythms of boogie-woogie and be-bop, alternating with riffs and other discordances, he has brought alive an entire community, a community that lives by

The boogie-woogie rumble
Of a dream deferred,

a dream that is the dream of the American Negro everywhere.

It is startling to notice how much these bebop alternations remind us of the jangling alternations of mood and tone in Eliot's "The Waste Land" and Hart Crane's "The Bridge." The chanting rhythms are admirably adapted to his colloquial diction, which succeeds in rendering dialect without elisions, apostrophes and similar distortions of spelling and punctuation.

All of Harlem is here, the Elks getting ready for a parade, immigrants from the South, Sugar Hill nabobs, numbers gamblers, war profiteers, bebop musicians, and members of the vice squad; and a host of moving and characteristic situations and personalities, all built around the theme of a "dream deferred," which results in rootlessness, poverty, impotence, and confusion:

"There's liable to be confusion when a dream gets kicked around." The poet wonders and warns: Does a dream deferred dry up, fester, stink, or sag "like a heavy load? Or does it explode?"

Humor and pathos, anger and delight, tenderness and raucous laughter, all are a part of this moving book.

The short poems in this volume, and most of them are short, are notable additions to the body of American lyric poetry. Such a long poem as "Freedom Train" is almost a folk ballad with its reminder ". . . freedom ain't freedom if a man ain't free."

Mr. Hughes, who has been called the "Negro Poet Laureate" and is a columnist for the *Chicago Defender,* was "discovered" by the late Vachel Lindsay. His poetry is reminiscent of Lindsay's own verse but draws heavily on the musical traditions and colloquial speech of his people.

Perhaps it might be said that his verse is too much devoted to a single cause. But it seems likely to last as long as man's inhumanity to man. This volume is his finest work to date.

[J.] Saunders Redding "Langston Hughes in an Old Vein with New Rhythms"
New York Herald Tribune Book Review, 11 March 1951, p. 5

In *Montage of a Dream Deferred,* Langston Hughes again proves himself the provocative folk singer who enchanted and sometimes distressed readers of *The Weary Blues, Fine Clothes to the Jew* and *Fields of Wonder.* In the interval between the publication of *One-Way Ticket* (1949) and this new book, he seems to have made a spiritually rewarding return to the heritage that was distinctly his in the days of the Negro renaissance. His images are again quick, vibrant and probing, but they no longer educate. They probe into old emotions and experiences with fine sensitiveness—

> Into the laps
> of black celebrities
> white girls fall
> like pale plums from a tree
> beyond a high tension wall
> wired for killing
> which makes it
> more thrilling—

but they reveal nothing new. He still views his function as being useful to social reform, and (though it is no fault in itself) such a view tends to date him in the same way that a poet like Byron is dated.

> The Roosevelt, Renaissance,
> Gem, Alhambra:
> Harlem laughing in all the
> wrong places

> at the crocodile tears
> of crocodile art
> that you know
> in your heart
> is crocodile:
> (Hollywood
> laughs at me,
> black—
> so I laugh
> back.)

The idiom, like the heritage to which he returns, is also distinctly Hughes'. In earlier work, however, it was adapted to the smooth and relatively simple rhythm of jazz. In *Montage of a Dream Deferred* it is fitted to the jarring dissonances and broken rhythms of be-bop. The result is a bold and frequently shocking distortion of tempo and tone, and this will fret and repel some readers. But Hughes has always required of his readers a sophisticated ear. It is the price of admission into the meanings of his experiences, and when he is at his best, it is not too high a price. In some of the pieces in *Montage,* he is at his best, in "Island," for instance, and "Freedom Train" and "Tell Me."

Yet it seems to me that Hughes does have a too great concern for perpetuating his reputation as an "experimenter." That he was this cannot be denied. Few present-day poets have been so impatient of tradition and so zealous in seeking new and more flexible forms. But experimentation is for something: it leads to or produces a result. One would think that after twenty-five years of writing (*The Weary Blues* appeared in 1926), Hughes has long since found his form, his idiom and his proper, particular tone. If he has, let him be content with the apparatus he has fashioned, and let him go on now to say the things which many readers believe he, alone of American poets, was born to say.

Gerald D. McDonald
"Poetry"
Library Journal, 76
(15 March 1951), 519

Although it is divided into sections and presented as units with separate titles, this book is really one poem, with a recurrent theme of the dream deferred. The total effect is one of improvisation, as in a jam session, where Harlem tag lines, street wisdom, impromptu banter and deeply felt emotion take the place of trumpet, piano and drums. Langston Hughes meant it to be like this, and one must measure one's reading to the rhythms of jazz, ragtime, swing, blues, boogie-woogie or be-bop (something of all of them is here) to get the full effect of what Hughes is trying to do.

Rolfe Humphries
"Verse Chronicle"
Nation, 172 (17 March 1951), 256

Montage of a Dream Deferred, by Langston Hughes, troubles and confuses me as work by this author often does. On the one hand, no white man living in Jackson Heights is fully competent to enter into the emotions of a Negro at home in Harlem; on the other, there seems to be a split—apparent in his book's title—between the sophistication of Mr. Hughes the individual and the innocence of Mr. Hughes the spokesman, so that the statement, in terms of be-bop—another matter of which I know very little—seems both oversimplified and theatrical.

John W. Parker
"Poetry of Harlem in Transition"
Phylon, 12 (Second Quarter 1951), 195–7

With the recent publication of *Montage of a Dream Deferred,* his second book on the contemporary Harlem scene to appear within a year, Langston Hughes has rejuvenated the Harlem theme of the Mid-Twenties, and re-asserted his faith in popular verse, particularly that which draws upon popular Negro folk music. Implicit throughout the volume is a seriousness of purpose and a sense of awareness of times transhifting [sic]. And, like such previous studies as *The Weary Blues* (1926), *The Street* (1946), and even *Simple Speaks His Mind* (1950), *Montage of a Dream Deferred* runs the gamut of the ups and downs that constitute the way of life for present-day Harlem; unlike them, however, it betrays the inner conflict of Harlem's Brown Americans, and a consciousness of the steady pull exerted by this urban community in transition. It is a fast-moving story of a people who, despite their own imperfections and the bitter and corroding circumstances they face from day to day, have never relinquished their dream of a tomorrow that will be better. But it is a dream born out of a heartache, a dream much like life in dark Harlem—"all mixed up."

Montage of a Dream Deferred, Mr. Hughes' first book-length poem in his twenty-odd years of writing, is divided into six parts—"Boogie Segue to Bop," "Dig and Be Dug," "Early Bright," "Vice Versa to Bach," "Dream Deferred" and "Lenox Avenue Mural." A good many of these "poems within a poem" have appeared previously in such publications as *Tomorrow, Our World, Common Ground,* and *The Harlem Quarterly.* Scattered generously throughout the volume are poems written after the style of Negro folk songs known as boogie-woogie and be-bop. Of the manner in which he has appropriated popular Negro folk music to heighten the effectiveness of poetry that is equally popular, Hughes writes in the introductory statement: "In terms of current Afro-American popular music and the sources from which it has progressed—jazz, ragtime, swing, blues, boogie-woogie, and be-bop—this poem on contemporary Harlem, like be-bop, is marked by conflicting changes, sudden nuances, sharp and impudent interjections, broken rhythms, and passages sometimes in the manner of a jam session." Thus the reader is prepared for innovations as he may find them—the occasional omission of the latter part of a line, the excessive employment of the dash for a sudden and sometimes unwarranted break in thought, the insertion of such otherwise meaningless expressions as "oop-pop-a-da," and, of course, "Figurine," a one-line poem that is limited to an even two words. By and large the measures throughout the book are cut to absolute simplicity, and the language, the imagery, and the easy flow of syllables enhance one of the collection's strong features—its popular appeal. Unlike the position taken by James Joyce a few years back, Hughes is convinced that comprehensibility in poetic expression is a virtue, not a vice.

The goings-on in Harlem as disclosed by *Montage of a Dream Deferred* leave much to be desired. The "bad nigger," who can out Herod Herod, proceeds from joint to joint; wide-eyed newcomers from the South encounter "bars at each gate"; the low and the high look, not across, but up and down at one another; pimps make the rounds at Lenox Avenue ginmills while hustlers wait in dark doorways; and in the effort to get along on a "dime and a prayer," many sicken and die. It is the same old story of "dig and be dug" and of "trying to forget to remember the taste of day."

The nine-line poem, "Jam Session," which appears in the section, "Early Bright," defines a situation that is fraught with tragedy and comedy, hope and despair, faith and disillusionment, but one that reveals the black man's struggle to salt his dreams away:

Letting midnight
out of jail
pop-a-da
having been
detained in jail
oop-pop-a-da
for sprinkling salt
on a dreamer's tail
pop-a-da.

First and last, *Montage of a Dream Deferred,* like the six books of poetry that have preceded it, suggests the manner in which Mr. Hughes has gone on loving life and writing upon those aspects of it that have stirred his emotion deeply—"Negro life, and its relations to the problems of Democracy." Convinced that the writing of poetry about Brown Americans is serious business in these times of transition, he has remained indifferent to criticism sometimes levelled at his "predominantly-Negro themes," and at the extreme popular aspect of his poetic output. Likewise, he has shied away from the recent tendency on the part of some Negro writers in the direction of a "return to form" and of international and global perspective.

But that is Langston Hughes. And it is perhaps one of the reasons that his name has become synonymous with popular Negro poetry. With its freshness of approach, its powerful rhythm, and its moving quality, *Montage of a Dream Deferred* further justifies its author's claim to the title by which he is frequently designated in literary circles, "The Negro Poet Laureate."

Arthur P. Davis
"Book Reviews"
Journal of Negro History,
36 (April 1951), 224–6

Carl Van Vechten has called Langston Hughes the "Negro Poet Laureate," but this title, it seems to me, is too ambitious. I prefer to think of Hughes as the "Poet Laureate of Harlem." He has been associated with that community since the days of the Negro Renaissance; he has written about Harlem oftener and more fully than any other writer; and in this, his latest, work, he gives a picture of that city, which in sympathy, depth and understanding has rarely been equalled.

In *Montage of a Dream Deferred,* Mr. Hughes has recaptured some of the magic of phrase and tone which characterized *Weary Blues* (1925), his first publication. Decidedly superior to *Shakespeare in Harlem* (1942), the present volume is a sensitive and fascinating work. Sometimes tender and pathetic, sometimes playful and satiric, and sometimes profoundly moving, *Montage of a Dream Deferred* is, in some respects, the most mature verse that Hughes has yet produced.

In this volume, the poet has made effective use of a technique with which he has been experimenting since 1925. Mr. Hughes explains this technique in a brief prefatory note:

"In terms of current Afro-American popular music . . . this poem on contemporary Harlem, like be-bop, is marked by conflicting changes, sudden nuances, sharp and impudent interjections, broken rhythms, and passages sometimes in the manner of the jam session, sometimes the popular song, punctuated by the riffs, runs, breaks, and disc-tortions of the music of a community in transition."

According to this scheme, we are to consider the whole book of ninety-odd pieces as really one long poem, marked by the conflicting changes, broken rhythms, and sudden interjections characteristic of a jam session. This "jam session" technique is highly effective because it not only ties together fragmentary and unrelated segments in the work, but it also allows the poet, without being monotonous, to return again and again to his over-all theme, that of Harlem's frustration. Like the deep and persistent rolling of a boogie bass—now loud and raucous, now soft and pathetic—this theme of Harlem's dream deferred marches relentlessly throughout the poem. Hughes knows that Harlem is neither a gay nor healthy but basically a tragic and frustrated city, and he beats that message home. Because of the fugue-like structure of the poem, it is impossible for the reader to miss the theme or to forget it.

Langston Hughes, as I have said above, knows and loves and understands Harlem. He can see the pathos in a Harlem night funeral or a fraternal parade. He understands the grim realism of poverty-stricken slum-dwellers who like war because it means money for them. He sympathizes with the Harlem wife who can play, via a dream book, the number suggested by her husband's dying remarks. He realizes the appeal which black celebrities have for white girls, and he knows the explosive possibilities of such alliances. He is conscious of Harlem's bitter anti-Semitism. He is aware that Harlem, white opinion to the contrary, is not one city but several; and he can, therefore, understand the bitterness of the Negro masses when they are snubbed by their Cadillac-riding professional men. But he also understands the shame of the "respectable" Harlemite when he sees the crudeness and the violence of the masses. All of these things and many more, Langston Hughes knows thoroughly, and he writes convincingly about them.

There are a few false notes in *Montage of a Dream Deferred*. Poems like "Not a Movie," "Ballad of a Landlord," and "Freedom Train," especially the last, seem alien to the mood of the work. Essentially, they are protest pieces of a type now definitely outmoded. Their tunes have been played so often and so long they have lost their power to move us. Even in a montage arrangement, they still impress me as being out of key with the mood and spirit of the rest of the work.

Each reader will pick his favorite poems from the *Montage of a Dream Deferred*, and he will have a wide and diversified field of choice. One of the loveliest poems in the book for me and one of the most delicate Hughes has ever done is "College Formal: Renaissance Casino." "Theme for English B" is also a moving presentation of the Negro's peculiar "Americanism," and "Night Funeral in Harlem" has the kind of folk pathos which is effective because it is genuine. The pieces in the work carrying the title-theme are generally well done and, as I have intimated above, serve admirably their purpose in this type of "jam session" presentation. Taken all in all, *Montage of a Dream Deferred* is a provocative and highly delightful work.

Mona Harrop "Robert Frost and Langston Hughes Publish Their Poetry" *Cincinnati Times-Star,* 4 April 1951, p. 25

Poems, some written to be-bop rhythm, some with the lilt of a jazz song, most of them with the sad beat of heart-sickness heard in Africo-American music, speak of Harlem: of husbands and wives and lovers, of neon signs and hotdog stands and funerals, of Joe Louis. And the heartsickness? That comes from too little respect shown men with dark skins in a hostile white world.

William Harrison "Book Review" *Boston Chronicle,* 14 April 1951, p. 6; also in *Providence Chronicle* as "The Bookshelf"

To quote his own fine phrase, we can always hear "way up in the treble the tingle of a tear" in the verse of Mr. Hughes, for his genius blends the pathos inseparable from the joy of Negro life in Harlem. Each pulsating line makes our hearts throb and our feet keep time to both crude and subtle rhythms. Here, in these "poems within a poem," is the massive architecture of the spirit, soaring on foundations laid in the solid earthiness of a people striving for dignity with majesty.

Some of the poems have appeared in periodicals, such as the powerful "Freedom Train," expressive of the authentic folk feeling, language and all. Its puzzled and perplexing queries are the shame of America.

With deft artistry Mr. Hughes employs varied rhythms to match the discords and the harmonies of our existence as we struggle for the freedom of full citizenship on the basis of complete equality. Resounding is "the boogie woogie rumble of a dream deferred." Even a gentle and unobtrusive note of religion, very pious, is audible to the keen ear, in "Mystery" and "Testimonial," for example. Nor is the infinite variety surprising, since versatility has distinguished the poetry of Mr. Hughes from the beginning. He is a poet with a message, in this instance the glory and grandeur of Harlem, but he is not narrow or monotonous. He understands that nature is comprehensive, because it includes peaks and valleys, and that the poet cannot stay too long on any level, but must try to sing on even ground as well as from the heights. He is a humanist to whom nothing human is alien; hence his preoccupation, like Socrates, with mankind in the city.

This volume is pictorial, and it is also musical. It quickens the imagination to behold visions of what ought to be, can be, and will be in the midst of what is. For instance, take this sermon entitled "Brothers" (p. 66):

> We're related—you and I
> You from the West Indies,
> I from Kentucky.
>
> Kinsmen—you and I
> You from Africa,
> I from U.S.A.
>
> Brothers—you and I—

This noble sentiment precedes by two poems the humorous quatrain entitled "Hope" (p. 68):

> He rose up on his dying bed
> and asked for fish.
> His wife looked it up in her
> dream book
> and played it.

To mix the sublime with the ridiculous is a bold undertaking which affrights the timorous among Negro versifiers, and that is why Mr. Hughes is peerless, though this volume adds nothing to his reputation, nor does it detract.

Robert Friedman
"Langston Hughes' New Book of Poetry"
Sunday Worker, magazine section, 22 April 1951, p. 7

There is music and there is iron in Langston Hughes' newest book of poetry, *Montage of a Dream Deferred.* The "dream deferred," of course, is the Negro people's liberation, and the montage, the picture of many-sided Harlem—Harlem the refuge from Southern lynch terror; Harlem the jimcrow ghetto; the Harlem of slums and struggle; of children's street games, musicians' jam sessions.

The burning consciousness of white ruling class oppression is in page after page of this poetry, complementing somehow—and not contradicting—the gay lilt of its lines.

> By what sends
> the white kids
> I ain't sent;

I know I can't
be President.

In the seeming simplicity of that child's
jingle, to which one can hear the rhythmic
bouncing of a rubber ball, there is the devastating puncturing of American capitalism's pretensions to 'equality.'

In his poem "Relief," Hughes registers
the Negro people's unwillingness to be
used by the white ruling class in a new imperialist war. But there is a dangerous un-
clarity here. Hughes is arguing that the
Negro people can be satisfied to stay on
the sidelines and 'let' the war happen. Of
course, such neutrality is impossible. And
what this poem leaves out is the Negro
people's stake in fighting for peace—for
world survival and as the foremost factor
in the struggle for national liberation—
along with white workers everywhere who
want peace too.

The poem:

I know what relief can be—
it took me two years to get on WPA.

if the war hadn't come along
I wouldn't be out of the barrel yet.
Now, I'm almost back in the barrel
    again.

To tell the truth,
if these white folks want to go ahead

and fight another war
or even two,
the one to stop them won't be me.

Would you?

Of those Negro reformist leaders
whose own personal advancement is
falsely identified by the government with
the status of the oppressed 14 million Negroes, Hughes writes bitterly:

How can you forget me?
But you do!
You said you was gonna take me

Up with you—
Now you got your Cadillac,
you done forget that you are black.
How can you forget me,
When I'm you?

The Freedom Train has ended its much-
publicized travels around the country,
showing the country's precious documents—the Bill of Rights, the Declaration
of Independence—which are violated every day from Negro-hating Harlem cops
up to the august justices of the Supreme
Court who turned thumbs down on life
and liberty for Willie McGee.

The hypocrisy of the Freedom Train is
still with us in the Crusade for Freedom,
and all the other gimmicks to cover up jimcrow and the Wall Street drive toward war.

The Freedom Train is gone, but
Hughes' Freedom Train rolls powerfully on:

Who's the engineer on the
Freedom Train?
Can a coal black man drive
the Freedom Train?
Or am I still a porter on the
Freedom Train?
Is there ballot boxes on the
Freedom Train?
Do colored folks vote on the
Freedom Train?
When it stops in Mississippi
will it be made plain
Everybody's got a right to
board the Freedom Train?

There is music in *Montage of a Dream
Deferred*, music with the sharp edge of a
sword. As in his *Simple Speaks His Mind*,
Hughes has written of the realities of Negro life—oppression and struggle—in poetry that is of and for the people.

Joseph P. Clancy
"Books"
America, 85 (28 April 1951), 103–4

It would be difficult to imagine two more differing styles in poetry than these, yet both represent dominant tendencies in the verse of our century. Miss Lewis' lyrics are cool, careful, controlled: it is quite natural to find a four-line epitaph to Landor. Hers is reflective, not dramatic lyric, with its obvious debts to Marvell and Yeats.

[. . .]

To turn from Miss Lewis' classical rhythms to the blues tunes of Mr. Hughes is to enter another poetic world. As is indicated by the title, this is an attempt to make a single poem from a series of widely different short poems pointing to one effect, the delineation of the community that is Harlem. Langston Hughes, who has been called "The Negro Poet Laureate," uses the dialect of his people and the rhythm of their songs; in his portrait of Harlem he captures the qualities of its talk and action, mingling poignancy, bitterness, raucousness and innocence very often to good effect.

But there is too strident a note of protest, too much sentimentality in the poem called "Freedom Train"; here, as elsewhere, a certain overconsciousness of his position as poet of his people spoils the poetry by causing a descent to polemic. Most of all, partial failure in many of the poems seems to be due to a lack of music *within* poems themselves: they seem to need musical accompaniment for full effectiveness, which gives something of the effect of reading Gilbert without Sullivan.

It is, however, difficult to capture a blues tune in verse, and Mr. Hughes has succeeded, if not in giving us a whole poem, at least in providing some striking images ("High noon teeth/ In a midnight face"), the vivid sound of talk and song in Harlem, and a sometimes bitter meditation on "The boogie-woogie rumble/ Of a dream deferred."

Alice H. Howard
"Montage of a Dream Deferred"
Common Sense Historical Reviews, 9 (May 1951), 5

When and if individuals, distinguishing themselves in a chosen field of the arts and sciences, are accepted as tradition, Langston Hughes will be first among modern poets and writers thus honored. He will for sure be an American tradition, because in every line he writes is voiced that unmistakable rejection of the American way of life. His latest book *Montage of a Dream Deferred* deletes no phase of Negro life, their blasted hopes and inhibited ambitions.

In his opening number, "Dream Boogie," he tactfully debunks the bearded idea of a black boy's heart being as feathery as his flying feet. In his "Children's Rhythm," he pin-points the fallacy of every American lad having a chance to be president and the evidence that child problems in this great country of ours are as varied as the color of their skins. Then "Necessity," assigned through the ages to be "mother of invention," has been assigned a newer role in Mr. Hughes' "Work," which follows: "I don't have to work. I don't have to do nothing but eat, drink, stay black, and die. This little old furnished-room's so small I can't whip a cat without getting fur in my mouth and my landlady's so old her features is all run together and God knows she shure can overcharge—which is why I reckon I does have to work after all." And on through his "Question," which is a 64 dollar one—to "Freedom Train," "Theme for English B," "De dop," "Buddy," "Ulti-matum," "Croon," "Night Funeral in Har-lem," to his closing, "Letter." Langston Hughes tells a convincing though poignant miniature story of his people, his Harlem, and all the Harlems throughout America where blacks must coalesce with blacks until their whole world is engulfed by the blackness of its misery and despair. Well might he say in his "Relief," "To tell the truth, if these white folks want to go ahead and fight another war, or even two, the one to stop 'em won't be me." He is convinced the powers that be will go on in the future as in the past, fighting wars in every corner of the globe to establish good will, univer-sal peace, and the brotherhood of man with cursory thought and attention to the poetic pleas of Mr. Hughes for a little more home-work. But he will go on writing, and his work will live, long after there are no Jim Crow cars, theaters and hotels, poll-tax and grand-father clauses; cur-tained dining cars, separate waiting rooms and drinking fountains: Because Langston Hughes is a nominee for tradition, an American tradition that will endure, incul-cated with the spirit and belief in the words of his "Brother"—"We're related—you and I, you from the West Indies, I from Kentucky. Kinsmen—you and I. You from Africa, I from U.S.A. Brothers—you and I."

C.M.R.
"Harlem in Poetry"
Boston Traveler, 2 May 1951[?], [p. ?]; not in Blue Streak edition

In his new book, Langston Hughes again turns to contemporary Harlem and gives us a series of episodes and portraits, "poems within a poem," of that locality whose voice he knows so well. Its terms, as he states, are those of current Afro-American music, and the sources from which it progressed—jazz, ragtime, swing, blues, boogie-woogie, and be-bop, well described as "disc-tortions of the music of a community in transition." There is heart-break in these poems, and sometimes laughter. There is much unpleasant read-ing, occasional tenderness, and often bit-ter satire, as in "Freedom Train," but always there is life pulsing with all the ex-citing irregularity of today's "be-bop."

Babette Deutsch
"Waste Land of Harlem"
New York Times Book Review, 6 May 1951, p. 23

The title of this little book of verse tells a good deal about it. The language is that of the work-a-day urban world whose plea-sures are sometimes drearier than its pains. The scene is the particular part of the Waste Land that belongs to Harlem. The singer is steeped in the bitter knowledge that fills the blues. Sometimes his verse invites approval, but again it lapses into a facile sentimentality that stifles real feeling as with cheap scent. As he bandies about the word "dream," he introduces a whiff of the nineteenth century that casts a slight mustiness on the liveliest context.

Langston Hughes can write pages that throb with the abrupt rhythms of popular music. He can draw thumbnail sketches of Harlem lives and deaths that etch themselves harshly in the memory. Yet the book as a whole leaves one less responsive to the poet's achievement than conscious of the limitations of folk art. These limitations are particularly plain in the work of a man who is a popular singer because he has elected to remain one. His verse suffers from a kind of contrived naivete, or from a will to shock the reader, who is apt to respond coldly to such obvious devices.

It is a pity that a poet of undeniable gifts has not been more rigorous in his use of them. There are several contemporaries, especially among the French, whose subject matter and whose method are not too different from his, but who, being more sensitive artists, are also more powerful. Mr. Hughes would do well to emulate them.

Betty Vaughn
"On the Book Shelf"
California Eagle, 17 May 1951, p. 4

Carl Van Vechten has called Langston Hughes the "Negro Poet Laureate." *Montage of a Dream Deferred,* his latest collection, proves this statement. It captures the heart and feeling of the Negro and in so doing reveals also that of all minority groups both racially and economically.

The poems reflect the desires, the frustrations and the life of Harlem, the largest Negro ghetto in the world. Written for all people both young and old, this collection of word pictures runs the gamut of human emotions always with the background of a wish or desire that is deferred.

There are a few that leave the reader cold, which may be due to the fact that they were strictly written for those that are truly "hep to the jive," the real be-bopper, but the great majority are moving and enjoyable.

[. . .]

"Literature: Poetry"
United States Quarterly Book Review, 7 (June 1951), 146

[. . .]

If this loosely constructed poem sequence is to be taken at the poet's own valuation, its various but always predictable moods must not only be expected but be allowed: pathos, joy-of-life, blues-ironies, moments of bleak realism, and, brought in as a recurring and deeper motif, the anger and bitterness of the sensitive Negro in America. Mr. Hughes has a very fine ear for the idiom of present-day Harlem and for the jazz-rhythms which have so deeply embedded themselves in our culture. The poem, not unexpectedly therefore, has a great deal of gusts, freedom of movement, and human warmth. It begins with a key-question that combines the basic themes with the vernacular phrasing and musical-comedy tempo of much of the book:

Good morning, daddy!
Ain't you heard

The boogie-woogie rumble
Of a dream deferred?

Montage of a Dream Deferred startles the reader with its echoings of neighborhood talk and children's street-songs; it wins and moves him with its wistful characterizations. This sort of verse is only distantly related to the kind which has won most of the critical attention in the twentieth century. In a sense, Mr. Hughes' poetry is "easy," lacking precision of diction, intensity, or intellectual concentration, but in its own, more "popular" genre, it is alive, suggestive, and very appealing.

Arna Bontemps
"Harlem's Poet Scores Again"
Nashville Tennessean,
17 June 1951, p. 10B

The writing of no contemporary poet bears a clearer or more distinctly individual signature than that of Langston Hughes. Readers may vibrate sympathetically to his notes or not, depending on their own pitch, but they cannot mistake him for anybody else, and the very first lines of his newest book proclaim it as authentic Hughes in his most spontaneous manner.

Good morning, daddy!
Ain't you heard
The boogie-woogie rumble
Of a dream deferred?

Back in the 20s, when the young Hughes was discovered by Vachel Lindsay, the poems with which he made his bow often tried to capture the jazz rhythms that seemed to fit his mood. *The Weary Blues,*

his first book, fairly rocked with the new and infectious music. It was Hughes who first called attention to the beat of sadness so unmistakable in the beat of jazz.

In the carefully worked out long poem which he calls a Montage his own rhythms, like those of the old-time blues, have evolved into the complexities of boogie-woogie. Harlem is 25 years older now. It has seen the last of such old favorites as Florence Mills and Bill Robinson. It held back tears when a flock of blackbirds was released suddenly in the street after Florence's funeral. And it has experienced a crushing depression and a bloody riot. Naturally its music has grown more complicated. A sardonic note has been added, and Langston Hughes has provided lyrics in keeping.

Representative of the new work, perhaps, is the fragment called "Sliver":

Cheap little rhymes,
A cheap little tune
Are sometimes as dangerous
As a sliver of the moon.
A cheap little tune
To cheap little rhymes
Can cut a man's
Throat sometimes.

Harlem's favorite poet is still an American original.

Madeleine O'Connor
"Books on the Table:
Harlem Be-bop"
[San Francisco] *Argonaut,*
130 (29 June 1951), 23

With a tempo frequently reminiscent of the works of Vachel Lindsay, Langston Hughes, "The Negro Poet laureate," has sketched a panorama in poetry of the life of his race in this country. Harlem, with its Lenox Avenue busses, cold-water flats, boogie, night funerals, Cadillacs and dreams deferred forever, struts and creeps and walks across the lines of his verse. A critic of contemporary society who appears more resigned than bitter, Langston Hughes joins the idiom of the billboard slogan, the popular song and everyday speech to themes which reveal the materialistic core of our civilization. The result is not a pretty picture by a long shot. That "white enamel stove" and that "television set" and those "two new suits" constitute the dreams deferred, but the pathos lies in the other, nobler dreams that "dry up like a raisin in the sun."

Don West
"Reviews: *Montage of a Dream Deferred*"
Appeal for Peace and Unity, 1 (August 1951), 5

For such an excellent little book of poems, this reviewer thinks the title was an unfortunate selection. For Langston Hughes usually speaks the people's language, articulating the hurt and anger and hope, particularly of the Negro people.

Always conscious, intensely aware, of his people's suffering, of their unfair treatment in a land boasting of its democracy, even claiming to send armed forces to fight for democracy thousands of miles from her shores—in Korea—Hughes pours out the music and yearning of his people in sharp, beautiful words.

Langston Hughes has irony not only for the whites who talk double talk about democracy, but also for those leaders

among his own race who have been placed in soft positions by a government eager to buy their support in order to use them as "representative" of the "opportunity" the 14 million Negro people have in America.

But the finest poem in Hughes' new book is still "The Freedom Train." This poem is a powerful indictment of Jim Crow and segregation, discrimination and lynchings.

These poems are definitely for the people. They are sharp like a two-edged sword. Hughes is a great American poet. He is great because his heart stays close with the people. His poems come fresh from the people's lives. This is America.

Erling W. Eng
"Three Worlds"
Antioch Review, 11 (September 1951), 379–81

The various configurations of values expressed in these three groups of poems can be arranged in order of their closeness to, or departure from, the sensuous surfaces of life and common shared experience.

Langston Hughes' evocation of feeling, scenes, and figures from Harlem life lies closest to the deceptively simple and seemingly discontinuous happenings of everyday life. As a medium suitable for the transmission in concentrated form of the kaleidoscopic imagery and contrasting moods of Harlem life, he has modelled different portions of his sequence after the forms of "jazz, ragtime, swing, blues boogie-woogie, and be-bop." In juxtaposition, these swiftly changing styles with their sudden shifts of key, pitch and tempo give rise to intermittent dramatic contrasts and intensifications of feeling resembling those elicited by music. Moreover, it is in keeping with Hughes' emphasis on the everyday and the impermanent that discontinuity is basic to the structure of the sequence; in particular, it suggests the disjointedness of much modern urban existence, Negro or otherwise. Yet this Negro world to which Hughes admits us seems a closed world, autonomous and set apart from the influences affecting those in the city life outside. There is no awareness here of what is happening in the even larger world beyond the city. Despite Hughes' insistence on the themes of care in this little world, there is something of romantic color in his images, as if an American were writing about Arab life in a North African medina. But more important than this is an awareness of inferior social and economic status, a feeling of being different and having different interests that insulates this little world from the larger one. And it is largely this awareness and feeling that gives unity to Hughes' work.

The *Double Root* by John Holmes reveals a world to us at some distance from the more simply accessible world of protest and pathos of Langston Hughes. . . . Unlike Hughes' world without a past, oriented toward the future by a "dream deferred," this world is one in which the past and the timeless predominate. . . .

With Auden's *Nones* . . . the forms and sounds of its words are related to chamber music as Langston Hughes' language patterns are related to jazz forms. . . .

[. . .]

In the compass of these three books we are given an experience of three different worlds, each with a different principal focus: socioeconomic status, family ties, and solitary gnosis.

Ruth Lerrigo Parker "Book Reviews" *International House Quarterly*, 15 (Autumn 1951), 249

As much musician as poet, Mr. Hughes speaks for his race with sincerity and intense emotion, often with lyric beauty. His ideas are heavily freighted with his emotions and further blurred, sometimes, by his use of colloquial diction so that their precise meaning is not always clear to the reader. Not so the emotions expressed, which hit home surely and unmistakably and ring with truth and experience.

Some hypothetical reader of the future, stranger to "be-bop," "boogie-woogie," and their conventions and phrases may find the poems of Mr. Hughes as cryptic as the original "Beowulf" to today's scholar. For that matter, any reader today who is unfamiliar with the raw and dizzy rhythms of the contemporary version of jazz wander, vaguely lost but intrigued, among the strange phrases of this little book. The stark economy of the author's expression intensifies that experience.

While mood and emotion predominate in almost every specific verse or poem, yet there is no danger of missing the basic idea which underlies and motivates the entire work. The surging hope, the striving, the bitter disappointment of a goal never reached but never lost from sight, the slow, heart-breaking struggle of the American Negro for his birthright of freedom in a free society are ever present. Mr. Hughes' work could be read merely for its "be-bop" rhythms, its high-pitched, hot-blooded sketches from life, but such a reading would miss the real intent of the book by about 150 per cent.

"Let that page come out of you," says a professor to a young Negro college student in Mr. Hughes' poem "Theme for English B." Mr. Hughes has learned that lesson by heart and from it this book has sprung. The musical quality of his verse seems also to come from an instinctive and very personal source. It is perhaps this intense subjectivity that makes the reader feel at times that the poet has impaled himself on the point of a phrase and is unable to free himself by explaining fully what he wants to convey. For examples, the fragments "Warning," "Warning Augmented," "Tomorrow," where the thought lurks but is not resolved.

Along with the mood of bitterness which thunders intermittently through the whole book come occasional flashes of spirit and gaiety—"125th St.," "Jam Session," "Testimonial," "Juke Box Love Song." Their presence strengthens rather than weakens the mood of the whole.

A steady progression and building toward the theme of Mr. Hughes' *Montage,* a tangled blending of moods, of dreams and disappointments, is the distinguished accomplishment of this book. The average reader will enjoy its sincerity, its warmth and the author's lyric gift. He may be vaguely let down by its unevenness, he may regret that the title theme is phrased in words unsuitably "fancy" for the subject matter it treats, but most certainly he will be moved by what he has read and he will not forget the lyric gift of this poet of today.

Carl H. Grabo
"*Montage of a Dream Deferred*"
Chicago Jewish Forum, 10 (Winter 1951–52), 152

In the rhythms of these verses, which are the rhythms of boogie-woogie, bebop, jazz, or what have you, are caught the inarticulateness, the longing, and the frustration of a people who dream of the Freedom Train which has no Jim Crow cars. The total impress is one of pathos. They arouse sympathy, like the songs of slaves set in a minor key, the pathos of a people who find in such a place as Harlem some slight alleviation of their woes. Harlem, with all its limitations, is a better place for the Negro than the South, where degradation and economic injustice prevail. But Harlem, though "better," is the place of a "dream deferred":

> The Jews:
>   Suits
>   Fruit
>   Watches
>   Diamond rings
>   The Daily News
> Jews sell me things.
> Yom Kippur, no!
> Shops all over Harlem
> Close up tight that night.
> Some folks blame high prices on the
>   Jews.
> (Some folks blame too much on Jews).
> But in Harlem they don't answer back,
> Just maybe shrug their shoulders,
> "What's the use?"
>
> Sometimes I think
> Jews must have heard
> the music of a
> dream deferred.

Alain Locke
"The High Price of Integration: A Review of the Literature of the Negro for 1951—Poetry and Belles Lettres"
Phylon, 13 (First Quarter 1952), 11–12

[. . .]

There is another volume of verse from Langston Hughes, *Montage of a Dream Deferred,* a golden title and a potential bonanza of the Negro's urban frustration moods. Here is a subject and a poet made for each other, and here and there are occasional glints of this gifted poet's golden talent—as in "Night Funeral in Harlem."

When it was all over
And the lid shut on his head
and the organ had done played
and the last prayers been said
and six pallbearers
Carried him out for dead
And off down Lenox Avenue
That long black hearse done sped.
The street light
At his corner
Shined just like a tear—
That boy that they was mournin'
Was so dear, so dear
To them folks that brought the
    flowers,
To that girl who paid the preacher-
    man—
it was all their tears that made
That poor boy's
Funeral grand.

But then one finds the flip doggerel and an unevenness of artistic conception which careful self-criticism could easily have avoided. Surely if, as the publisher's blurb says, "a poet laureate of the Negro folk," then a carelessly tipsy laureate who wears his laurel askew and sometimes with the cap-backward antics of sandlot baseball. For the skeptical reader, just let me cite two:

Daddy,
don't let your dog
curb you!

and

I don't give a damn
for Alabam'
Even if it is my home.

Checklist of Additional Reviews

"February 19," *Retail Bookseller,* 54 (February 1951), 105.

J. Saunders Redding, "Book Review," *Baltimore Afro-American Magazine,* 24 February 1951, p. 3.

"Literature," *Booklist,* 47 (1 March 1951), 233.

"The Week's Books," *Pittsburgh Courier Magazine Section,* 10 March 1951, p. 15.

D.P., "Among the New Books," *San Francisco Chronicle This World,* 11 March 1951, p. 16.

Jay Hall, "World Beyond the Tracks," *Greensboro Daily News,* Feature Section, 25 March 1951, p. 3.

LAUGHING TO KEEP FROM CRYING

"*Laughing to Keep from Crying*"
Virginia Kirkus Bulletin, 20 (1 January 1952), 9

A collection of piquant, sweeter than sugar, more sour than green apples, sketches about Negroes from Harlem to Hong Kong and back to Johannesburg. A well known Negro poet and writer, Langston Hughes is endowed with a wit that is as strong and clear as his feeling and knowledge of Negroes and the peculiar yet common situations in which they find themselves. He knows the confusion that can arise, change behavior and ideas in the twinkling of an eye when "colored" people pass for white, then recant and say they are colored, only re-recant later and say they are really white. He knows the humor of the brawl that turns into friendship between a north-of-the-Missouri colored man and a Kentucky colonel when they meet in a bar in Hong Kong. All barbed, all short, these stories go beyond tolerance, beyond the false pride of being a Negro, beyond the purposeful ignoring of color and culture traits that is so often the educated man's invisible but weighty burden. Under the skillful results of his observations, situations where Negro and white are natural with one another come sharply into focus—there being no set pattern but as in all life—a fortuitous and happy occasion brought about by being happy. Good reading.

Milton S. Byam
"Fiction"
Library Journal, 77 (15 February 1952), 361

These short prose pieces concern the Negro, and other minority groups in their relationships among themselves and among the dominant whites. Generally in a humorous vein, the emotion underneath rings with bitterness. As a whole, the work is of uneven quality though some individual pieces will pierce the toughest hide with compassion. Mr. Hughes, a famous Negro poet, has given little attention to people so that motives are always, at best, murky. For him the little stories are all-important, slightly pleasant, slightly tart to the taste with little body. Recommended with reservations.

"Briefly Noted: Fiction"
New Yorker, 28 (22 March 1952), 133

Twenty-four slight, short sketches, most of them dealing, in one way or another, with interracial relations, chiefly between whites and Negroes. Mr. Hughes writes easily and chattily, but not to very much effect, about the visit of some white Iowans to Harlem, the viewing of a Negro revival meeting by some white people, the action of a scholarship committee against a Negro schoolgirl, and other such matters and incidents.

Bucklin Moon
"Laughter, Tears and the Blues"
New York Times Book Review, 23 March 1952, p. 4

Few writers have worn so well over the years for this reviewer as has Langston Hughes. There have been more important writers, perhaps, or others who worked a broader canvas, but few have been so versatile or as workmanlike. *Laughing to Keep from Crying,* which contains pieces dating from as far back as the Twenties, is a short book, but it is a highly successful one.

In these twenty-odd stories, almost all of them concerned with minority groups, there is little special pleading, as such, and no attempt to show only the best in the people about whom Hughes is writing. What the reader senses, however, if he happens to be a human being, is that the worst of them are caught between their environment and our inhumanity to a point where it got to be more than they could handle. It is this quality, I think, which makes every story (with the possible exception of "One Friday Morning," which seems overly familiar because of similar stories which followed it) become amazingly fresh and free from the stereotype, and the self-consciousness of too much of our protest writing.

It could be said, I suppose, that these are not the best short stories that Langston Hughes ever wrote, but the best of them are very good, indeed. "Professor" is a highly successful story. It tells of the feelings of a Negro from the faculty of a small colored college in the South who is going to dinner at the home of a prominent Midwestern philanthropist where he will have to sing for his supper because of the job he needs and knows he will get only if he Uncle Toms a little.

The story concludes: "As the car sped him back toward town, Dr. Brown sat under its soft fur rug among the deep cushions and thought how with six thousand dollars a year earned by dancing properly to the tune of Jim Crow education, he could carry his whole family to South America for a summer where they wouldn't need to feel like Negroes."

Almost as effective, though the irony is directed in another direction, is "Trouble with the Angels," in which a young singer on the road with a successful Broadway Negro folk musical tries to get the rest of the cast to go on strike when they hit a theatre in Washington where Negroes are turned down at the box office—only to find "God" suddenly acting as a strikebreaker.

Some of the shorter vignettes come alive with a sudden flash of imagery, or the poet's fine ear for the spoken word and the patterns of sound. Though less than two pages long, "Rouge High," the bitterly fatalistic story of two Harlem prostitutes, seems to hang in the air long afterward, like a song you want to forget but cannot.

Other stories are less successful; they seem a little dated, almost archaic, because in the meantime our racial thinking has subtly changed. None the less, each is the work of a "writer" in the finest sense of the word; for here is underwriting and an economy of words that put to shame many a writer who has said less in an overblown novel than is often said here in less than a dozen pages. That is rare enough these days for special mention.

William E. O'Connor
"A Master Writer"
Hartford Courant Magazine, 23 March 1952, p. 19

The publisher does Langston Hughes a dis-service in describing him as "probably the outstanding Negro writer in the United States." The author of the collection, *Laughing to Keep from Crying,* will stand out in any company of short story writers, regardless of race.

True, most of Hughes' stories are about Negroes who wrestle, in one way or another, with problems of prejudice. However, like the Normans of Maupassant's tales or the Russians of Chekhov's, these Negroes struggle with external and internal conflicts that plague people everywhere.

The writer apparently sees this clearly. The victim in the most nearly bitter story in the volume is not a Negro at all, but a Chinaman born on an American Pacific island. The call to battle against discrimination is voiced in another story by a stern Irish high school principal who remembers the suffering of her own people in prejudiced America.

Equally important, the young sociology professor who "agrees" with his benefactors in spite of his convictions acts only incidentally as a Negro. The same is true of the inept braggarts who fight a comic duel in "Slice Him Down," the young scoffers who remain to pray at "The Big Meeting," and the intellectuals whose joke backfires in "Who's Passing for Who."

A master of words, Hughes creates powerful moods of religious fervor, tender love and irony and individual desperation; and vivid pictures of north, south, east and west—wherever the Negro walks and works in America. The excitement of his stories will draw the reader from one to the next almost as if they were chapters in a novel.

Gladys P. Graham
"Book Review"
Philadelphia Tribune, 25 March 1952, p. 4; with variations in *New Jersey Herald News,* 29 March 1952, [p. ?]

Laughing to Keep from Crying, published in a handsome volume by Henry Holt, is the twelfth book penned by the dynamic literary genius Langston Hughes.

Its 24 brief, interrelated stories explore the subtleties of interracial behavior, seldom revealed in fiction, that reflect the color and feel of Negro America.

Hughes has depicted for the reader in trim conversational chatter a resume of his travels across the world. The backgrounds and peoples of the stories described stem from Manhattan to Africa and numerous parts of Asia.

Notable is "Who's Passing for Who?" In this vignette the writer exposes the busy body who is always trying to solve the race question via the mode of chit-chat. Says Hughes of such an individual:

"One of the great difficulties about being a member of a minority race is that so many kindhearted, well-meaning bores gather around to help. Usually they have nothing to help with, except their company—which is often appallingly dull. You see, Caleb and his white friends too were all bores."

The book is related to the total environment in which those of minority groups find themselves in their daily living via the tears, laughter and conversational medium, in America and other parts of the globe.

The Brown Bard of Harlem, Langston Hughes has become deeply philosophical with his opus.

Laughing to Keep from Crying is a well-written book and indeed a unique contribution to the literary arts. It requires more than surface reading for it is a book that is vigorous and stimulating, despite the sensitive and personal touches Langston Hughes has given it.

Frank O'Neill
"Books in the News: Mr. Hughes in Shorts"
Cleveland News, 25 March 1952, p. 12

Bittersweet is the word for Langston Hughes' new book of short stories. These twenty-four tales speak out like that many volumes about the Negro's struggle in the world.

From the very first page they bite and sting. . . .

Life as depicted here is remorseless and brutal, but Hughes evokes a compassionate strain. In Harlem, in Hong Kong, in Africa, in Reno, in Chicago—Hughes seeks out the little people for his dramas. Everywhere their lives are much the same—grim and severely uncompromising. This is somber but skillful penwork.

Esther Boghosian
"The Library Corner"
Medford [Mass.] *Daily Mercury,* 26 March 1952, p. 7

[. . .]

A far cry from state affairs is the collection of stories entitled, *Laughing to Keep from Crying* by Langston Hughes. These interrelated stories reveal the same laughter, rhythm, and tears that characterized the popular *One-Way Ticket* and other previous works that have made Langston Hughes one of the outstanding Negro writers in the United States. Some stories explore the subtleties of interracial behavior seldom found in fiction. Reflecting the author's own travels across the world, the background of these stories varies from Manhattan to Africa, from Hong Kong to Havana, from Washington to Mexico City.

All of these stories are personal and heartwarming, like the traditional blues song from which the title was borrowed: "When you see me laughing, I'm laughing to keep from crying."

Lewis Gannett
"Books and Things"
New York Herald Tribune, 26 March 1952, p. 27

Langston Hughes has blues rhythms in his bones, and the blues that gives him the title for this book of color-line stories runs

When you see me laughing,
I'm laughing to keep from crying.

In fact, few of these twenty-four evocative stories laugh aloud, and none of them cries; some of them merely record, and the best of them sing—sing in that minor blues key that is half-way between laughter and tears. Mr. Hughes has been around; he writes in many moods, but in his best stories, he catches conflict in the modes of a single moment.

Some of these are O. Henry stories with a Negro twist. There is the almost too neat tale of the two derelicts, one white, one black, insulting each other and fighting in a Hong Kong bar; then, in the gutter, becoming allies determined together to revenge themselves upon the Limey bartender who had had the temerity to throw two Americans out.

Still another tale pictures a white Harlem tourist, Edward Peedee McGill 3d, surviving a mugging with delight: "This is the first exciting thing that's ever happened to me," he says. "This is the first time in my life I've ever had a good time in Harlem. Everything else has been fake, a show. You know, something you pay for. This was real." Whereupon one of the black muggers says to the other: "What's the matter with rich white folks? Why you reckon they ain't happy?"

Mr. Hughes has followed the color line around the world. He tells a poignant tale of a brown-skinned boy in black Nigeria, who knows that his father will return to England and his mother's people will cast him out; he paints a weird scene in a Mexican bathhouse; reports a lively knifing in a Reno dive; recounts a Filipino experience in New Orleans. But the best of his stories are pictures of emotional border lines in what we call the border states of America. (The "border" sometimes reaches far into the North.)

"Big Meeting" tells of two dark boys

contemptuously watching a revival meeting in which their mothers participate—until a white couple parks near by and echoes their own contempt. Langston Hughes subtly catches the dark eloquence of such Negro preaching—and the confusion in an "emancipated" man's reaction to its genuine emotion and piety.

"Professor" is another story of inner conflict. T. Walton Brown, professor of sociology at a Southern colored college, goes to dinner with the Ralph P. Chandlers, "liberal" philanthropists in a city somewhere on the latitude of Baltimore or St. Louis, where the local municipal college does not admit Negroes. Maybe the Chandlers will give generously to T. Walton Brown's college and provide scholarships to send boys from the Chandlers' town to the deeper South to study. Maybe, if T. Walton Brown says nothing to offend, his salary might be raised to a point where, some summer, he can take his family to South America where they won't need to feel like Negroes. So what does he say?

Then there is "One Friday Morning," a story almost too good to be true. Nancy Lee, colored, a few years out of the south, has earned the one scholarship from George Washington High to her city's only art school. Her teacher has told her so; and she has written her acceptance speech, in warm gratitude for the credo repeated each morning in the flag salute— "One nation, indivisible, with liberty and justice for all." And then a higher committee changes the rules, and Miss O'Shay has a speech to make to Nancy. Miss O'Shay handles it well. So does Nancy. The story, heartbreakingly convincing, brings a lump into your throat. Perhaps, after reading it, you may recall one of Langston Hughes' poems, called "Border Line":

I used to wonder
About living and dying—

I think the difference lies
Between tears and crying

I used to wonder
About here and there—
I think the distance
Is nowhere.

Gertrude Martin
"Book Reviews"
Chicago Defender, 29
March 1952, [p. 11]

Langston Hughes has a way of selecting apt and provocative titles for his books. His latest, *Laughing to Keep from Crying,* is no exception. It is taken from the blues song that runs: "When you see me laughing, I'm laughing to keep from crying." The book itself is a collection of short stories, most of which are concerned with Negro-white relations. They have to do chiefly with the small, everyday events of living in the Negro world; there is little or no violence, but the hurt is there. Mr. Hughes does not take himself nor his characters too seriously, but his oblique approach to prejudice and discrimination— with the exception of one story—is all the more effective.

"Trouble with the Angels" is the story in which Mr. Hughes makes a frontal attack on conditions as they are, and indulges in considerable moralizing. The result is that it has a preachy quality, which detracts from an incident which had great possibilities. The angels in this case are characters in a play which is unnamed, but is obviously *Green Pastures.* The trouble arises when the play reaches Washington, where Negroes are not to be allowed to attend. Some of the angels protest, but "the Lord" pulls them in line with a tearful appeal, and the show goes on.

Few writers have the sympathy and understanding of the little man that Langston Hughes shows in all his writing. The character in "Why, You Reckon" is as real and as human as the professor in the story by that name. There is irony and gentle wit in most of these tales and a quiet telling, which adds to their effect. There is no pretension here. Some of the stories are not as impressive in style and character portrayal as others, but all have something to say. *Laughing to Keep from Crying* is another important step in Mr. Hughes' distinguished literary career.

A.S.H., Jr.
"Little Vignettes"
Worcester [Mass.]
Telegram, 30 March
1952, p. 11D

This collection of two dozen short stories by Langston Hughes gets its title from an old traditional blues: "When you see me laughing / I'm laughing to keep from crying."

Nearly all of the stories are either little vignettes of Negro life in America, or stories concerned with interracial behavior. "Professor," for instance, tells how a professor from a Southern Negro college goes up North in the interests of his college. He swallows gentle insults in order to get money for his college's expansion.

There are stories here of white people sightseeing in Harlem or at a revival meeting, of Negroes mildly acquiescing to Jim Crow because of their own self-interest. And there are stories which take place in Hong Kong and Mexico City.

Though one can find a few poignant moments in this collection, the stories generally leave us unmoved. Hardly more than sketches, they do not really grip life, and their surface narrative is often flat and commonplace.

Though the stories are written with obvious sincerity, they lack altogether the breathless lyricism of most of Langston Hughes' poetry.

Worth Tuttle Hedden
"Laughter and Tears across the Barriers of Race"
New York Herald Tribune Book Review, 30 March 1952, p. 6

Too often, reading a collection of short stories is like eating too many hors d'oeuvres—one's palate is satiated before one's hunger is appeased. The nineteen stories and five vignettes in *Laughing to Keep from Crying,* however, satisfy hunger for mental stimulation and emotional involvement and do not impair the sense of taste; one turns the page between the end of one tale and the beginning of another with impatient curiosity. Now what human foible or quality or behavior will I find to laugh at, to pity? Will the locale be Hong Kong, Reno, Harlem or Havana? Foible or quality beneath light or dark skin, in Southern lady or water-front prostitute, in gentleman or hobo, Mr. Hughes knows how to get at it and give it to you straight. The laughter and/or the tears are your choice. He knows his way around, too. He is equally at home in the principal's office of a Mid-Western high school, the furnace room of a Harlem fast house, the home of a border-state philanthropist, a village of the Niger delta, a Hollywood faith-healer's parlor and at a revival meeting on the outskirts of a Southern town.

In the fifteen of these stories concerned with Negro life on our planet a nuance in racial or interracial behavior sometimes is obvious, more often barely discernible— as in "Slice Him Down." You laugh through the whole of this picaresque drama of the "Southern shines," Terry and Sling, then turn back to re-read three words in their context. "Reno! The Biggest little City in the World blazing its name in lights. . . . But they couldn't read the sign too well. Hunger and rain and a bad education all stood between them and the reading of that sign," and are reminded that they're riding the rails, rather than the cushions, to Reno was as much society's fault as their own. Adding up the dynamic and reflex action, the stimulated and passive reflection, in these "spooks," "spicks" and "ofays," "white chicks" and "chocolate babies," you have a graphic racial philosophy: animosity of one human being toward another because of physical variation is ridiculous. In "Who's Passing for Who," a white couple pass, or pretend to pass, for colored, thereby causing four Negroes (a painter, two writers and a social worker) to drop their "professionally self-conscious 'Negro' manners . . . and really have fun." In "Something in Common" two old bums, a Missouri Negro and a Kentucky white man fight each other at a Hong Kong bar, are thrown out by the Cockney barman and stagger back, arm in arm, "united to protect their honor against the British." In "Professor" the Negro emissary from a Negro college receives from a white chauffeur and from the white Chandlers the courtesy due a dinner guest, but with the latters' generous gift to his department of sociology he must accept a stupid patronizing—so that, on his enhanced salary, he may take his family vacationing in South America and live for awhile like a white man.

411

Sociological treatment for humanity's psychic ills may be too solemn and too slow. Perhaps a quicker way to sanity in racial relations is through relaxation and laughter. Negroes always have had a personal close-up of the seamy side of white life and their laughter at white people is bitter. White people view Negro life panoramically and their laughter is light and condescending—until they hear a Negro preacher like the Reverend Braswell in "Big Meeting" describe the Betrayal and the Crucifixion. Compare that scene with a white writer's sincere effort to portray the uneducated Negro's religious manifestations and you have a travesty as surely as you have only an Amos 'n' Andy when the white writer tries for the essence of Negro humor. Mr. Hughes' laughter, fraught with some essential tears, is provoked by what is ironically funny in human beings. And he has an advantage over all white American authors in that he is not looking down on this country from the majority grandstand but is mingling with individuals on all levels. He, like Nancy Lee working with her art teacher in "One Friday Morning," can do his own best, "not anybody else's copied best. For anybody else's best, great though it might be, even Michelangelo's, wasn't enough to please Miss Dietrich dealing with the creative impulses of young men and women living in an American city in the Middle West and being American."

Leona T. Reed
"Proud to Be an American"
Birmingham News, 30 March 1952, p. E6

The fight for security during the depression of the hungry '30s, the struggle for the survival and revival of a nation—the Negro race in particular—inspired Langston Hughes to write *Laughing to Keep from Crying*. With his cosmopolitan heritage the author has every reason to be unbiased in presenting his observation of society.

To glance at a few models, which represent the general characteristics of this anthology, one finds such an interrogatory title as, "Why, You Reckon?" This story gives a vivid account of two hungry colored boys who had suffered the horrors of the depression. They concluded robbery was a solution after charities had refused them aid.

As one trails the "Pushcart Man" through three scant pages of *Laughing to Keep from Crying*, he sees as many varied aspects of life as in any Negro cosmopolitan area.

Headlines, illicit love affairs, gruesome outcomes provided the theme for "Name in the Paper." A unique presentation of similar harsh and brutal facts of life is conveyed in "Saratoga Rain," "Heaven to Hell," and "Tragedy at the Baths."

A creative painting won for Nancy Lee Johnson the scholarship award in the Art Club contest. Because the artist was a Negro, the judges withdrew their decision; still, Nancy was proud to be an American. Her voice rang among the others in quoting "... one nation, indivisible, with liberty and justice for all." "One Friday Morning" tells why this youth realized this is a land we must make.

Laughing to Keep from Crying is packed with varied emotions. The intricately developed plots are treated from a realistic phase. Langston Hughes offers a challenge which should cause American thinkers to set the evils of our much cherished democracy aright.

T.M.W.
"Life in Harlem"
Boston Traveler, 2 April 1952[?], [p. ?]

Not precisely a major literary effort, either in individual selection or in total impact, this book of short fiction sums up to ironic grinning rather than laughter and to ill-concealed bitterness instead of tears. There is no denying the accuracy of Mr. Hughes' appraisal of the American Negro's shabby lot, but somehow his pleading is not, in the main, calculated to evoke the sympathy he seeks.

This apparently aimlessly-arranged collection of skits, sketches, scraps, and semi-stories leaves the reader diverted, perhaps, interested always, but only infrequently moved by the implicit tragedy in the kaleidoscope of life in Harlem. "Professor" states the author's thesis as obviously as any other piece in the volume, while "Pushcart Man" and "Tragedy at the Baths" suggest this writing competence.

Laughing to Keep from Crying is, after a fashion, a pretty grim affair, but fortunately such a reaction comes upon reflection—not while one is being flashed past its cheap, carnival lights.

"Book of the Week"
Jet, 1 (3 April 1952), 54

The potent pen of the acknowledged dean of U.S. Negro writers, Langston Hughes, has unfortunately lain virtually fallow in recent years despite occasional bursts of inconsequential poetry and fluffy Simple stories. Despite his tremendous ability, Hughes has been detoured from really creative writing by a variety of other activities ranging from speaking tours to sponsoring causes. Perhaps his failure to write consistently and seriously is illustrated by his newest book, a shallow out-of-date collection of stories called *Laughing to Keep from Crying.*

The title is about the best thing about the volume. The stories are often crude and callow pieces evidently extracted from a long-neglected file cabinet, dusted off and sold hastily to a publisher. Practically all have been printed in magazines, most of them out of business because of their sorry quality. Some of the pieces date back more than 20 years and do not stand the test of time.

Most certainly Hughes has and can do better than this old collection of stories. He has proved time and again that he has a feel for Negro life today as few other men, but he has failed in recent years to reflect that remarkable talent. In his *Laughing to Keep from Crying,* Hughes sometimes putters to life in stories like "Why, You Reckon?" or "Professor" but mostly the collection is far, far from the Hughes of the 20's and 30's. Certainly pieces like "Who's Passing for Who?" have an amateurish ring that is not worthy of the Hughes name on it.

Hughes deserves better, as do his readers.

Arna Bontemps
"Black and Bubbling"
Saturday Review, 35
(5 April 1952), 17

Few people have enjoyed being Negro as much as Langston Hughes. Despite the bitterness with which he has occasionally indicted those who mistreat him because of his color (and in this collection of sketches and stories he certainly does not let up), there has never been any question in this reader's mind about his basic attitude. He would not have missed the experience of being what he is for the world.

The story "Why, You Reckon?," which appeared originally in *The New Yorker,* is really a veiled expression of his own feeling. Disguised as a young Park Avenue bachelor who comes with a group of wealthy friends for a night of colorful, if not primitive, entertainment in a Harlem night club, the Langston Hughes of a couple of decades ago can be clearly detected. He too had come exploring and looking for fun in the unfamiliar territory north of 125th Street. The kidnapping and robbing of the visitor in the story is of course contrived, but the young man's reluctance to rejoin his friends or to go back to the safety of his home downtown reflects the author's own commentary. "This is the first exciting thing that's ever happened to me," he has the white victim say to the amazement of his abductors as he stands in a coal bin stripped of his overcoat and shoes, his wallet and studs. "This was real."

Over this tale, as over most of the others in *Laughing to Keep from Crying,* the depression of the Thirties hangs ominously, and it serves as more than just an indication of the dates of their writing. It provides a kind of continuity. After a while it begins to suggest the nameless dread which darkens human lives without reference to breadlines and relief agencies.

A sailor, for example, makes a fast pick-up on the West Coast in jive talk ("Well, all reet! That's down my street! Name it!" "White Horse, Send it trotting!" "Set her up, and gimme a gin. What's your name, Miss Fine Brown frame?") only to learn that the hard times and the general hopelessness of their lives frustrate pleasure even on that level.

A dark mother, in another story, consoles herself by attributing the prohibition-time ruin of her good-looking mulatto son to his Spanish blood. In another a rounder laughs at his misfortunes: "The next thing I knew I was in the hospital, shot everywhere but in my big toe. He fired on me point-blank—and barefooted. I was nothing but a target." And elsewhere a pushcart man becomes a sort of tape-recorder for grim, depression-shaded, Saturday night talk on Eighth Avenue; a blossoming girl painter is denied through prejudice a prize she had won; and in the occasionally anthologized Christmas story "On the Road" an unemployed black man, given a quick brush-off by a high-toned preacher, breaks into a church and sees a vision of Christ before the police arrest him and start breaking his knuckles with their sticks.

Langston Hughes has practised the craft of the short story no more than he has practised the forms of poetry. His is a spontaneous art which stands or falls by the sureness of his intuition, his mother wit. His stories, like his poems, are for readers who will judge them with their hearts as well as their heads. By that standard he has always measured well. He still does.

Constance Curtis
"About Books: Glimpses at the Negro"
New York Amsterdam News [New York edition], 5 April 1952, p. 7

The ever-complex and ever-simple Langston Hughes once again has brewed a little of the essence that is his personality in this newest collection of short stories. They are, as were the thoughts and experiences of the fellow who was "Just a Little Simple," glimpses into the lives and thoughts of the Negro people.

There is a unique objectivity about the author that makes it possible for him, while understanding and experiencing the madness of being a Negro in America, to still set down this life without rancor. Indeed, *Laughing to Keep from Crying* is filled with humor, a good bit of it wry, but much of it the shoulder-shaking variety heard rippling along dark Southern streets and swelling up through the open court windows in a thousand ghettos across America.

Readers will find a certain unevenness in the stories included in the volume. Three or four, however, stand out as exquisites, cutting sharply to the shrieking core of tension in our lives that is usually betrayed only by a lowered eye or the quick flush that is not seen too easily under dark skin. Such a vignette is "The Professor," which deals with the subtler forms of torture visited upon dark Americans by well-meaning "liberals."

The laugh-provoking aspect of the "problem" is exemplified in "Why, You Reckon?", revolving about the encounter between a hungry Harlemite and a young white visitor in the confines of a dark Harlem basement.

Past criticisms of Mr. Hughes have stated that much of his writing is so "special" that it can only be understood by the people about whom he writes. It has been charged that the larger audience of white readers find him confusing and incomprehensible. In *Laughing to Keep from Crying*, as in past novels and collections of short works of the author, I feel that he touches and expresses moods and emotions which are common to people everywhere, no matter what their skin tones. That some of their experiences are different does not preclude understanding of the mind of one man, reaching out in his very humanity toward another.

There is much of entertainment, of philosophy, laughter and tears to be found in the book. It is good reading!

Frank H. Jesse
"Struggle of a Racial Minority Explored with Moving Passion"
Louisville Courier-Journal, section 3, 6 April 1952, p. 7

Recognized for many years as America's most outstanding Negro poet, Langston Hughes presents in this latest volume a series of heartwarming sketches and short stories which reveal the same heartbreak, rhythm and laughter that characterized the popular *Montage of a Dream Deferred* and his memorable autobiography, *The Big Sea*. Some of these stories take the form of vignettes which explore the subtleties of interracial behavior to an extent not often found in modern fiction; others measure in brilliant fashion the rapid pulsebeat of Negro America from the bootleg era of the Roaring Twenties (when Harlem was in vogue with the midnight pleasure-seekers) to the present.

This volume is a significant contribution to the struggle of the racial minority for life and justice and intellectual freedom in America and abroad. Few writers would approach such a theme without a certain amount of bias, but not many could present it, as Langston Hughes does, with so few overtones of bitterness and rancor. Whether scenes and incidents are beautiful or ugly, they are set down in quiet candor without exhibitionism or apology, and only on reflection does the reader realize how much reserve there is also.

Hughes has lived feverishly and adventurously, and he deals with personages both Negro and white with whom he has come into odd and interesting contact. He has a genuine talent for exposing the many stupidities of racial prejudice through the use of subtle characterization and simple, poetic images. The American conscience is scourged by the many injustices prevalent in contemporary society. Although the stories are told in a sensitive, dignified manner, the white reader has the sensation of being hit; hit right for the part he plays in maintaining a racist social structure.

In Langston Hughes we can't help but praise equally his uncompromising dedication to the cause of his own people and the universality of his sympathies. Into this free-flowing prose style, he injects a moving passion, for he is determined not to let America forget the shame of lynch-law and Jim Crow. This style is original and compelling and is marked by a clarity and succinctness evidencing a steady recognition of the realities of our time. Taken all together, these stories represent a penetrating, sane approach to the study of human behavior problems; I wouldn't be surprised

if they reach more people and have wider influence than any book treating a similar subject has had for a long time.

[Author's initials illegible] "Among the New Books" *San Francisco Chronicle This World*, 13 April 1952, p. 20

The author again "speaks his mind," this time in a series of short stories, some of them no more than sketches, vividly revealing the state of the Negro today.

The writing is direct, honest and clear in purpose. Hughes presents interracial problems deftly and is not afraid to criticize both sides of an issue. Scenes of Harlem during the Twenties, or of a Southern tent meeting, flow with a simple warmth and beauty that is powerful and compelling. Again Hughes demonstrates that he is one of the outstanding Negro writers in America today.

"Books in Brief" *Nation*, 174 (26 April 1952), 408

When Mr. Hughes is good, he is very very good, and when he is bad he is either insincere or superficial. Both extremes are represented in his latest collection of stories and sketches about Negro life, ranging from Shanghai to Havana. At his best, Mr. Hughes manages the nice feat of dragging out into the open a number of unpleasant truths about racial discrimination and presenting them in a playful and extremely engaging manner.

J. Saunders Redding "Book Review" *Baltimore Afro-American Magazine,* 26 April 1952, p. 3

I am only making a definition when I say that in the best work of Langston Hughes simplicity and beauty are one. This is not as in the work of those who make simplicity the criterion, for simplicity for its own sake is an intemperance as much to be avoided as any other.

Make simplicity the test in writing, and you end up with the unilluminating literal, the untransfigured "real," and with uninspired intelligibility. Simplicity actually is a matter of emotions rather than of intellect.

It is a way of seeing things; it is a kind of reaction to experience. And when this way of seeing things combines with a sense of beauty, then you have a Langston Hughes at his best.

He is at his best in *Laughing to Keep from Crying,* a collection of vignettes, stories and sketches. Nearly all of them have a sharp poignancy which derives partly from Hughes's sense of the tragedy that is frequently just below the laughing surface of life, and partly from the fine restraint with which he creates and recreates experience.

Reading him, one feels there is something more, something deeper and darker that he could tell us if he would and that yet is as ambiguous and as impossible to pin-point as the exact causes of adolescents' sadness on a June night when the moon is full.

Not that the pieces in *Laughing to Keep from Crying* leave one unsatisfied. They do not. They are complete, whole and even those that end without roundness—that at first seem to stop rather than end—give you a feeling of completion.

"Sailor Ashore" is such a piece. Nothing happens but an unsuccessful flirtation, and the sketch breaks off at the highest emotional point; there is no resolution, but, by heaven, you finish reading it with the strangest admiration for its fullness, and with the strongest sense that Azora and her sailor are each as real and eternal as human sorrow.

"On the Way Home" is another such piece. In "Mysterious Madame Shanghai," (which appeared in this magazine, March 15) Langston Hughes comes close to being fantastic, but he nevertheless has caught and illumined for us an old and elusive and precious truth.

Some of the pieces—"Who's Passing For Who," "Slice Him Down," and "Something in Common," for instance—are amusing in their details and make amusing though oblique comments on colored-white relations.

Others—"African Morning" and "One Friday Morning"—are not amusing and, instead of making oblique comments, speak as directly to the mind as to the emotions. But none is bald, bare. Each is subtle and, as I have said, poignant.

There are few American writers who come close to Langston Hughes's range, or who begin to approach his complex sensibilities. When he is good, he's superb, and in *Laughing to Keep from Crying* he is good.

Sarah Patton Boyle
"Negro Author's Short Stories Show Subtleties of Behavior"
Richmond Times-Dispatch, 4 May 1952, p. 8A

Langston Hughes was one of the first Negro writers, way back in the roaring twenties, to be read by "white" America, not only for the novelty of partaking of a Negro's point of view, but for sheer pleasure in good writing and in poignant emotion.

The hidden theme throughout is the suffering which all Negroes endure because of the white man's failure to grasp the truth that, except in personal appearance, they are human beings exactly like ourselves.

As the cover blurb points out, Hughes "explores the subtleties of interracial behavior seldom revealed in fiction." This is certainly true. Yet to us it seems that he presents an even more striking portrayal of the subtleties of interracial misinterpretation.

The deep, concealed wounds, the disappointments, the disillusionments which result from the white man's stereotyped conceptions of Negroes are poignantly set forth. But along with this conscious revelation is an unconscious revelation of another facet in this tragedy of errors: that of the Negro's stereotyped conception of the white man. In no story in the collection does this second masked spectre fail to rear its head.

The Negroes in the volume come warmly and humanly to life, while the whites stalk about like statues, bearing placards instead of characters. The plac-

ards all say, "This person is indifferent to the Negro's welfare. He is fixed in his determination to preserve white supremacy in some form. He is aloof, self-centered and chilly within." It's worth the price of the book just to get a look at ourselves as the Negroes see us.

Also, it's worth something to have the maturing experience of learning how it feels to be generalized about. Suddenly one grasps what Negroes mean when they demand that they be regarded as individuals and not unfailingly dealt with as representatives of a group.

Perhaps the most significant story in the collection is "Professor." In it both stereotypes spring into sharp focus—the one deliberately set forth, the other obtruding itself in the pathway of the narrative.

This story tells about the visit of a distinguished Negro professor to the home of a wealthy white couple who had promised to make a substantial contribution to Negro education. As they question him concerning the Negro's educational needs, he tells them what he thinks they want to hear—in order to secure the donation.

Both character and author are convinced that because these people are white they do not wish to know the truth. So the black professor lays himself, sighing, on a griddle of lies, and finally goes home in refreshed bitterness because Negroes are inevitably misunderstood.

Stanley Cooperman
"Fiction before Problem"
New Republic, 126 (5 May 1952), 21

Langston Hughes does not really write about Negroes. Of course the people who appear in the neat, pungent sketches and stories of *Laughing to Keep from Crying* have "colored" skin; but they appear as themselves and not as additional case histories for the indictment against racism. Fiction dealing with the problem of the Negro is understandably bitter, but this very bitterness tends to abstract injustice. Such books are limited despite their power, and the intensely human, individualized prose of Langston Hughes gives a more specific insight into racism than can be achieved by even the best problem fiction. The individuals in *Laughing to Keep from Crying* are individuals first and victims second, so that racism is seen as effecting not "Colored People" but men and women who have been met on their own terms.

Hughes writes a lucid, conversational style intimate as a personal letter and casual as a feature column. However the apparently effortless, facile prose contains undercurrents of sly humor, quiet bitterness and social consciousness that echo in the mind. It is the sort of lean, compact writing that implies as much as it states; an active, rhythmical prose without excess literary fat.

Laughing to Keep from Crying ranges from an amusing piece about two American drifters in Hong Kong (one white and the other Negro) to the memorable portrait of the Jim Crow Negro college professor who "thought how with six thousand dollars a year earned by dancing to the tune of Jim Crow education, he could carry his whole family to South America for a summer where they wouldn't feel like Negroes." For the most part it is a pleasant, relaxed book that gets its message across because it doesn't always insist on it.

John Bennett Shaw
"Warmth Lies in Hughes' Stories"
Tulsa Daily World, section 5, 25 May 1952, p. 9

I have mentioned several times in my poor attempts at book reviewing that I admire good style (but I also admit that style is a difficult thing to define—Note: I do not say "I don't know anything about style but I know what I like," which is known in aesthetics as the "no savvy" approach.) This book of short stories by Langston Hughes is one book for which I will waive my stylistic requirements, as the style in most of them is but average. These stories are of a type, in content and emotion and effect, that should be read more with the heart than with the head.

Langston Hughes is a noted Negro and a famous writer. As a writer I think that he is best as a poet of the American Negro—a singer in verse of the blues. His prose is always readable and usually interesting. I particularly relished his autobiography *The Big Sea* as it is an absorbing story of the awfulness of being a Negro and of being an intellectual while being a Negro. Hughes, however, has enjoyed, perhaps sardonically, being a Negro. It is true that in these stories bitterness occasionally creeps in, but the reader can feel that the writer has lived these events himself and has lived them fully.

Laughing to Keep from Crying contains stories dating back to the Twenties. In these 24 stories, almost all of them concerned with minority groups, there is little political pleading or sociological exposing. But there is much warm humanity

419

with its components humor, pathos, love and hate. In most of the stories the events happen to Negroes—sometimes because they are Negroes but, thank goodness, the events are not contrived to show the treatment or the quaintness or the plight of the Negro.

The plots are real and seem to be actual happenings. Of course some of the stories are dated, but some are most memorable, especially the oft anthologized Christmas story "On the Road" and the revealing "Why, You Reckon?"

These stories are good for one to read not only because they are interesting yarns but because they are about the American Negro who has to be understood. Naturally most of those who do not see the necessity of this understanding or who do not want to understand cannot read anyway.

Elizabeth Yates
"Interesting Commentary on Freedom"
Christian Science Monitor,
29 May 1952, p. 15

[. . .]

Langston Hughes' book of 24 short stories, *Laughing to Keep from Crying*, shows the effects and some of the slowly maturing fruit of the freedom that has existed for the Negro for nearly a century. The range of the stories is as varied as their lengths, and the different subjects are handled well by one who has in equal proportions a writer's skill and a poet's penetration.

In the midst of violence and uncertainty, the drama of human love is poignantly played in "Saratoga Rain." In "African Morning" a little boy whose skin is golden cannot understand why he has no place in the world. He is not black like his mother nor white like his father, yet in all other respects he is like everyone else. Here is the rough and the coarse and the tender; and underlying them all is the unmistakable attitude of one world of color to another, in which emotions are hidden so there will be no betrayal of real feeling. There is subtle humor evidenced in "'Tain't So" and violence in "Powder-White Faces"; but always the sympathetic heart guides the pen, and even with the violence the reason for it is shown. It may lie deep in the mind, but it is there for the reader to ponder. There is growth and the patient task of achieving a place in the world. In no story is this more evident than in "One Friday morning" that tells of Nancy Lee.

Nancy Lee is a young high school girl who is proud of being an American and equally proud of her African heritage. Talented and gently reared, she alone of the Senior class qualifies for a prize that will help her on to Art School. But the prize is not given to her when the committee learns of her color. The school principal, wise and kind, who being Irish knew what it had been to suffer as a minority, explains to Nancy Lee that "America is only what we who believe in it, make it." The girl is able to salute the flag with her classmates at assembly with lifted head and a smile ". . . one nation indivisible, with liberty and justice for all." "That is the land we must make," Nancy Lee said in her heart, though tears were in her eyes.

In these stories, curiously assorted and not all of them pleasant, is evidence of what is happening to a people who secured freedom by proclamation and who have traveled a long road to its realization. The end of the road is not yet in sight, but the movement along it is a forward one.

August Meier
"Poignancy"
Crisis, 59 (June–July 1952), 398–9

Langston Hughes' latest book is a collection of short stories of Harlem life and the color line, marked by the author's usual folksiness, whimsy, and satire. They range in time from the days of the Harlem Renaissance to the present, and in subject matter from vignettes of Harlem life, through tragedies of love and sex, to incisive commentaries on race and caste in America.

Included are such items as the humorously told incident of a white couple passing as Negroes; the heart-rending story (apparently based on an experience recorded in Hughes' autobiography, *The Big Sea*) of an African youngster with a white father who finds himself rejected by every one; the realistic portrayal of a pushcart vender on a Harlem street; the satirical study of a jaded, wealthy white youth who found fun and excitement in being held up and stripped of his valuables while on his way to a Harlem night club; and the bitter account of a Negro actor breaking up a strike called by his fellow performers in protest against playing to audiences from which Negroes are excluded. Two of the best are "One Friday Morning," the all-too common story of a high school girl who is deprived of a well-merited award because of her color, and the one about the Professor who, "dancing to the tune of jim crow education," toadies to white philanthropists in order to obtain money for his school.

As usual with Langston Hughes these stories are told with insight into the life he records, and with the verve, spice and droll good humor which provide the laughter necessary to keep the reader from crying. They will universally be found entertaining and pungent, and Hughes' admirers will consider them first rate.

Mabel Knight
"Laughing to Keep from Crying"
Catholic Interracialist, 11 (June 1952), 7

A poet and storyteller who has kept in touch with people has given us in this book of short stories suspense, surprise twists, tears and laughter. He has deep sympathy and understanding for his variegated characters of different races in many countries. Prejudice hits some of them—the schoolgirl who is denied her prize, the college professor who has to agree to Jim Crow education in order to get a position which will enable him and his family to escape for the summer to South America where they can forget that they are Negroes. Other sins—lust, jealousy and drunkenness—injure others. Poverty joins with prejudice against other characters. Christ walks with one of these and gets invited to a hobo jungle where there are no doors, in sharp contrast to the relief shelter, parsonage and church where the homeless and hungry Negro had sought help in vain.

"Big Meeting" is the climax of the book. Those who came to be amused were swept up into the drama of the Crucifixion. The story is reverently and powerfully told, with poetic impact.

Readers who feel that they are above reading fiction will find in this book an understanding, deeper than mere facts, which will enlarge their knowledge of race relations.

William Harrison
"Book Review"
Boston Chronicle, 28 June 1952, p. 6

Of few prolific writers can it be truthfully said what is almost banal to say of Mr. Hughes: he has never written a bad book. While this collection of short stories is not his masterpiece by any means, paling in comparison with *Simple Speaks His Mind* or the earlier *The Ways of White Folks,* for instance, it would be a major work if penned by another author without genius. Simplicity is its hallmark, for Mr. Hughes profoundly understands the common people the world over—their turns of phrase and habits of thought and usual reactions to events. In itself such understanding is the distinctive feature of literary genius which separates the poet from the poetaster or the writer of serious prose from the hack who composes for a mutual admiration coterie whose vanity leads it to suppose that its esoteric nonsense is precious because few readers bother with it.

Mr. Hughes touches numerous tangents and centers of Negro-white relations in various climes, from Harlem to Hong Kong, from Havana to Africa. He reveals facets of life which most of us will never know except through the printed page, and his revelation is trustworthy. He does not allow his political insight, which is considerable, to be heavily laden with partisan bias, to underscore points which are best left implicit. Mordant as his humor can be, it is never devoid of sympathy, as in the tale entitled "Professor," which is one of the best fictional treatments of segregated institutions of higher learning in the United States. If we compare that story with O'Wendall Shaw's *Greater Need Be-* low or J. Saunders Redding's *Stranger and Alone,* we recognize how much more effective the gently satirical method of Mr. Hughes can be in its total effect. On another theme, the attitude of Africans to persons of Negro-white ancestry, which is illustrated in "African Morning," Mr. Hughes is original in the sense that his presentation is perhaps the first in the history of prose fiction.

John W. Parker
"Literature of the Negro Ghetto"
Phylon, 13 (Third Quarter 1952), 257–8

Of the constantly-expanding volume of books that Langston Hughes has turned out since the appearance of *The Weary Blues* back in the early Twenties, perhaps no one of them has landed upon the bookstands with a title that is richer in emotional content than *Laughing to Keep from Crying,* a heart-warming sequel to an earlier collection of short stories, *Simple Speaks His Mind.* The stories in both collections are in the main exploratory rather than exegetical in character, and are characterized by the same humor and repartee, the same frustration and futility as that revealed by *Montage of a Dream Deferred. Laughing to Keep from Crying,* however, is written against the background of the color and feel of Negro America and of the author's own travels across the world; and while it employs the Harlem scene as a point of departure, it sets about to explore the ebb and flow of life in the Negro ghetto in such widely separated points as Manhattan and Pasadena, Mexico City and Havana, Hong Kong and Africa. It is predicated upon the assumption that minority-majority problems are no unique American creations; they are part and parcel of a pathological social phenomenon that embraces points throughout the world where people of color are concentrated.

A total of twenty-four stories of fairly even quality makes up the collection. One of them discloses the flavor of Bohemian primitivism of the mid-twenties; another deals with a "big meeting" down South where sinners "remain to pray," but where white people came sightseeing; and yet another brings into focus the escapades of a mixblooded Harlem fop, whose total conduct left much to be desired. "One Friday Morning" is a study of the operation of color prejudice in the case of Nancy Lee Johnson, Negro prize-winning painter in a northern high school, who had to go home with a "strange emptiness" in lieu of a first prize. And in the story "Professor," the Negro intellectual loses face. Dining by invitation with a wealthy white family in the Midwest for the purpose of securing funds for his segregated university in the South, Professor Walton Brown, holder of a Ph.D., breathes hard when the etiquette of the situation warranted a watering down of his position on the question of integration in American education. The medal is reversed, however, in "Saratoga Rain." Here one finds two broken parcels of humanity resorting to illicit love as a means of escape from themselves and from the totality of their social milieu. To each other they whisper, "We will never be angels with wings."

These interrelated stories turn primarily upon theme rather than upon character; taken together, they range from the bootleg era of the Roaring Twenties to the present. The author has managed a spontaneity as well as an intensity and a charm that all but assure reader interest. That one finds in this volume what is perhaps a conscious blending of humor of characterization and of situation is a tribute to Hughes' creative genius in an area of Negro literature hitherto largely neglected. Everywhere the laughing comes as a means of comic relief; it prevents crying eternally.

Despite the fact that segments of his subject matter go back to the early Twenties, it is hard to see how in a period of growing social awareness Mr. Hughes' new book is almost totally lacking in perspective for the Negro people. A sort of a consistent vanity of vanities, it points up disillusionment and loss of faith. The roads lead nowhere; nothing amounts to anything; and almost nobody is too much concerned. The implications in some of the stories are that the Negro's conduct—passing, raising cane, saying, "Yes, Sir," and looking down dead-end streets—is not so much his own responsibility as that of the social order of which he is a part. Nor does one find sufficient evidence that the white man is either aware of or concerned about the Negro's reaction to his plight. This note of unwavering pessimism leaves one wondering when he remembers the author's firm faith in our tomorrows.

This weakness, however, in no sense negates the basic force of this significant book. To his task, Langston Hughes has brought an intimate and a sympathetic knowledge of his subject matter and of the technique and province of the short story. *Laughing to Keep from Crying*, illuminating as it does the "Negro theme" in American literature (aspects of which yet remain largely unexplored), is an eloquent plea for social awareness and social justice for minorities in America and throughout the world.

423

J.R.M.
"Recent Fiction Shelf"
Pasadena Star-News,
6 July 1952, p. 37

Langston Hughes is one of our favorite authors, and in this book of short stories he proves again that he is one of America's better writers. Mr. Hughes, with his quiet, subtle honesty, does more for his race and for all persons who do not happen to have what is called "white" skin, than any dozen of angry "white" writers. The Negro "problem" will never be solved by hysteria, and Langston Hughes is one of those who realize this fact. Hughes is a great traveler; the various backgrounds of these stories—Harlem, Hong Kong, Washington, Africa, Mexico City—prove that his talent for observation equals his delightful imagination. The only story in this book we did not like is "One Friday Morning," which is both obvious and sentimental. The other will all catch you and hold you, especially "Who's Passing for Who?" "Why, You Reckon?" "'Tain't So." This is a book which, with another recent volume by Hughes, *Simple Speaks His Mind,* will remain on our crowded shelves.

David Steinberg
"Negro Life"
Newark Sunday News,
section 3, 6 July 1952,
p. 32

This is an assorted collection of short stories, vignettes, impressionistic fragments and thinly disguised essays, all concerned with the life problems, subtle and overt, that confront a Negro in a white world. Because the collection spans a long period of publication, from the Prohibition era through World War II, the total effect is panoramic, an injured bird's eye view of the Negro void. Not all the items are set in America, but the most poignant derive from the social and other prejudices that clot our democracy.

Hughes, recognized by many as our outstanding Negro author, often exasperates the reader because of literary laziness. A little effort here and there could round a vignette into a complete story. But it is to Hughes's credit as a writer that, despite the underlying theme of all these pieces, there is little monotony of technique such as too frequently dulls anthologies of stories by individual authors.

He plucks the wings of Jim Crow to bare unappetizing truths. Here is a story ("Professor") about the educated Negro who can get funds from the whites for his college only by self-degradation. Or there's Nancy Lee ("One Friday Morning") robbed of an art scholarship because of the color of her skin rather than the colors of her painting. But Nancy finds some joy in the person of her sensitive Irish teacher who abhors the prejudice that afflicts her superiors. The recital of the Pledge of Allegiance, which ends the story, becomes a sardonic, ironic vow.

The title of the book is derived from a Blues: "When you see me laughing, I'm laughing to keep from crying." That is precisely what Hughes does in some of these stories. He resents the superiority assumed by some Negroes over most of their race and lambasts white dogooders whose "tolerance" is a transparent veneer. But he appreciates decency and humanity.

424

R.G.
"Fine Collection of Short Stories"
Montgomery Advertiser, 3 August 1952, p. 8D

Intensely interesting stories, short stories, from the pen of a brilliant Negro writer, fill this book with laughter, rhythm, tears. A splendid collection, we agree, and one of the best books of the year. Langston Hughes is a writer! His book is well worth the reading. There are 24 stories in the volume, and here is one Negro writer whose stories will interest white people.

For his characters are human and they live. It all is personal and heart-warming. The title is taken from a blues song; do you remember it? Here are stories to laugh at or feel bad about. They are human. Some are simply vignettes; most of them are stories. There is no bitterness, no uncompromising dedication to his own. Langston Hughes has intelligence and sense plus good writing.

The reader will not find such stories elsewhere. These stories explore interracial behavior; they reflect the color and feel of American Negroes. From the bootleg era (the roaring twenties) to the present, they are variable stories covering a lot of territory. The South, Harlem, and all over the world, Africa, Hong Kong, Havana, Washington, Mexico City, stories from everywhere.

There is a tender, but illicit love affair. Read the book. It is one that will be liked by all races and creeds and colors. Most of the stories came from magazines.

Leonard Feather
"Bittersweet"
New Leader, 35 (18 August 1952), 19

Perhaps because of the multiformity of the world in which he has lived, possibly because of a predominant sense of humor, Langston Hughes rarely demonstrates any consistency of approach as a "Negro writer."

An analysis of his work through the past two decades reveals as loose a pattern of ideas as can be found in the assortment of sketches and short stories embodied in his latest anthology. His book of poems last year, *Montage of a Dream Deferred,* vacillated quaintly between the trivial and the profound, the sacred and the profane. One never expects him to come up with a *Native Son,* a big problem work dedicated to the exposition of one major racial issue. To this extent at least, he is not a Negro writer in the accepted sense any more than Frank Yerby, even though, unlike Yerby's, most of his writing does concern the members of his race.

In *Laughing to Keep from Crying,* Hughes is at his most typical level of charming inconsistency. Sometimes he seems less angry at the bigots than at the do-gooders, the whites whose racial attitude takes the form either of patronizing or of mild, misunderstanding disdain. At other moments, he seems willing to poke fun at both races as he throws a sardonic light on the confused nature of their relationship. ("Who's Passing for Who?" is a delightful sample.)

There are moments when he is concerned simply with a vivid depiction of the seamier side of Negro or white life, as in "Slice Him Down" and "Rouge High," two of the pieces in this volume. Then again, there are moments when he strikes an optimistic note, as in "Something in Common," which shows us a Negro and a white at a bar in Hong Kong whose potential animosity is quieted by their common resentment of a Briton's anti-Americanism.

But Hughes's basically humorous approach sometimes gives way to a note of pathos. In "One Friday Morning," this is beautifully effective as he describes the feelings of a school-teacher and of a Negro girl in a Northern high school whose color deprives her of a prize in a competition. The book's closing episode, "Big Meeting," with its curious whites eavesdropping on a Negro revival meeting, has the same quality.

Perhaps the most significant aspect of *Laughing to Keep from Crying* is that in one of the best pieces of writing, "On the Way Home," the characters have no racial identification. This vignette, concerned with the emotions of a man who has just learned of his mother's death and finds himself drowning his sorrow at a bar, could be the story of a Negro or a white.

Hughes writes about what he sees. Because he is a Negro, much of what he sees concerns Negroes and interracial subjects. Because he has traveled, his settings wander from New York to Cuba, from Washington to Mexico. Because he seems more concerned with diverting the reader than with reforming him, some of his tales may seem insignificant, may even have an anti-Negro effect if they fall into the hands of a simple susceptible white. But whether he be laughing or crying, casual or earnest, bitter about Jim Crow or amused by the ways of white folks, the mirror Langston Hughes holds up to the world he sees invariably reveals a colorful and highly entertaining picture.

E[drie] V[an] D[ore] "Of Negro Problems" *Hartford Times*, 30 August 1952, p. 14

Most of the short sketches in this volume, reprinted from various magazines, are conventional in their treatment of Negro problems and the attitudes of white people toward them.

They have an air of already being outdated and proving only that the world makes progress.

Peter E. Hogan *Best Sellers*, 12 (1 November 1952), 177–8

In April, 1950, *Simple Speaks His Mind*, a group of essays and genre pieces tied together around a central character, was marketed by Mr. Hughes. It was a rather good compilation. In this book he has tried to repeat his former success. Unfortunately, he seems to have had to dig so deeply into the barrel for some that they are, at least, moldy and odorous. It might be that the magazines in which several originally appeared have cast their pattern over the story, e.g., *The Anvil, Esquire, Stag,* and *The New Yorker*.

Four of the twenty-four pieces are very good: "Who's Passing for Who" and "Trouble with the Angels" are satire in a high vein of his own race; "Slice Him Down" is a psychological development of the "tough guy" attitude among the lower class; "One Friday Morning," the story of a Negro girl rising above the loss of an art scholarship. "Professor," wherein the hero supports Jim Crow education for personal advantage, "'Tain't So" and "Something in Common," dealing with Southern-schooled Negro-white relations far from their original locale, are good. "On the Road" is next door to sacrilegious. Nine seem to exist only for the element of brutally frank sex contained in them. The others seem either rusty revivals from immature days or pointless "protest literature" of the early depression period.

Langston Hughes has turned out some fine stories, but the present collection could not be used to support that contention. The title of the book is used to indicate the ability of an abused minority to overcome the pathos of its existence. The reader gets little more than an extremely depressed and morbid feeling. Because of the predominance and glorification of sex it cannot be recommended to any group.

Alain Locke
"From Native Son to Invisible Man: A Review of the Literature of the Negro for 1952"
Phylon, 14 (First Quarter 1953), 34–44

[...]

Laughing to Keep from Crying is typical Langston Hughes. That means many things, among them uneven writing, flashes of genius, epigrammatic insight, tantalizing lack of follow-through, dish water—and then suddenly crystal springs. Fortunately, this is a motley of anecdotal scenes and stories, scattered from his own cosmopolitan experience—Africa, Hong Kong, Frisco, Paris and the like, but all pointing up to Harlem and its theme of color. The title story, a very good one, has the dominant key and clue: "Who's Passing for Who?" It pokes ironic fun at the color line, as for example also does "Something in Common"—the encounter of a white Kentuckian and a color-weary Negro in a Hong Kong bar, where after falling out violently over the color question and being ejected by the bartender, they stagger back together to fight for their rights, presumably including the right to fight over the color question. This is a fair sample; as thumb nail sketches both are well observed and in that sense anecdotally good; one, however, is well told, the other, just an anecdote. And so it goes, not alternately as in this case, but spotty to the end. "Saratoga Rain," a two-page cameo of incisive etching, suggests that this type of thing is Hughes' forte, and that sustained development is not, whether it be plot or character. Why complain? Simply because from the point of evoking it, Langston Hughes knows Harlem so much more surely than all the rest that his vignettes are, with all their faults, worth dozens of so-called "Harlem novels," and with just a little more art, Hughes could be Harlem's Daumier, or to change to the right figure, its Maupassant. How true what W. C. Handy says of another book of his, "Read it for yourself and have a laugh on Harlem, not at it." There's the difference—and the right approach for all writing about this province of Negro life: to see, feel and show not its difference but its different way of being human.

[...]

427

Checklist of Additional Reviews

Max Putzel, "Between Book Ends: Choked with Bitterness," *St. Louis Post-Dispatch*, 18 March 1952, p. 2B.

"Fiction," *Booklist*, 48 (1 April 1952), 247.

SIMPLE TAKES A WIFE

"Simple Takes a Wife" *Virginia Kirkus Bulletin*, 21 (1 March 1953), 156

Langston Hughes has been called the "O. Henry of Harlem" and this second volume of stories about Jesse B. Semple, familiarly known as "Simple," justifies it. Here is immediate, rollicking laughter, the tang of highly seasoned speech, the solid impact of forceful feeling that should appeal to a wide variety of both Negro and white readers. This is the story of Simple's courtship of Joyce, a respectable, hard-working, church-going girl, whose morals have not affected her good times. Unfortunately nobody can afford the three payments necessary to obtain Simple's divorce from Isabel, who also wants her freedom. Finally, Isabel pays two thirds, and Simple painfully accumulates the other third, and hangs the decree on Joyce's Christmas tree. But with months of waiting, Joyce "jumps salty" at Simple's slowness, his stopping at bars, his derelictions. It is not the plot that makes the book memorable, but Simple's digressions and philosophy. One is caught between laughter and a catch in the throat, for though Simple's grammar is laughable, his thinking is not.

Althea P. Montgomery "Crust of Bread, Jug of Wine and Thou . . ." *Birmingham News*, 17 May 1953, p. F6

At some time, all of us have been accused of taking life too seriously as we worry about money, love, social obligations and just ordinary day-to-day living. When we meet someone who is able to face these problems casually, discuss them in witty dialogue, and forget them over a glass of beer, we have to admire, respect and possibly envy him for making life so simple, uncomplicated and amusing. Such a man is Jesse B. Semple (better known as Simple), the "arm-chair philosopher" as he appears in Langston Hughes' latest novel.

Perhaps Simple's uncomplicated approach to life's problems is due to the simplicity of the man himself. Simple asks very little of life. As long as he can get a glass of beer, borrow money from his frequently tried and true friend, persuade his landlady to skip a week's rent, and marry his girl, then all's right with the world. There are times, however, when he ponders such great problems as why there are so many different colored three-cent stamps, or why darkness is synonymous with badness, or why landladies are so bossy.

At the moment, the problem of expensive divorce is for Simple a pressing one. For there is a small but seemingly monumental sum of money which stands between Simple and his real love, Joyce. He cannot marry his high society girl friend until he pays for his first wife's divorce. Upon seeing that this cannot be accomplished by his favorite "wait and see" method, Simple makes the supreme sacrifice and gives up one of his daily pleasures—drinking several glasses of beer.

Readers who met Simple in *Simple Speaks His Mind* will probably agree after this second encounter that here is a character for whom the line "a crust of bread, a jug of wine and thou" might have been made-to-order.

431

William O'Connor
"A Changed Man"
Hartford Courant Magazine, 17 May 1953, p. 18

Jesse B. Semple—the Simple in Langston Hughes' story—could have figured out in advance that a white man would get the job of reviewing his book. Like a lot of other jobs, Simple observed, book reviewing for newspapers is seldom done by Negroes.

That means, of course, that the reviewer can only say that Simple seems like an authentic person. He can go a little farther on circumstantial evidence. People all over the world read Langston Hughes, whose following includes many readers of his own race. Therefore, Negroes must accept Hughes' writings as true and fair. If they thought he misrepresented them, they'd tell him off and stop reading his books.

Simple's courtship, told over cold beers in Harlem bars, provides a backdrop for a few dozen well chosen episodes of daily Negro life. His big problem was to raise $133.33⅓, his share in a $400 divorce for his wife in Baltimore. The wife and her intended next husband paid a third each but Simple faced a set of difficulties—high cost of living, low wages and a taste for beer, the last a sore point with his fiancee—that delayed his contribution.

Simple raises the money and gets through the ceremony a self-pronounced "changed man." The pronouncement, of course, was made over a glass of beer.

Simple is the sort of companion who grows on you. As the chapters roll on, it becomes increasingly easy to drop something else in for a vicarious visit to a Harlem bar. The expense runs low too, thanks to the publisher's use of a stripped down but still attractive format.

Hughes has written the sort of book that almost suggests a light and happy movie. Almost but not quite. They don't make movies about men like Simple.

Ted Poston
"Wit and Wisdom from Harlem"
New York Post, 17 May 1953, p. 12M; in another edition as "Wit and Wisdom from a Harlem Gin Mill"

Simple is back. And high time too. He's been away too long.

Mr. Jesse B. Semple, Langston Hughes' loquacious beer-drinking pal, is back at his old stand in a Harlem gin mill, discoursing again on everything from lynching to lexicography, from intermarriage to international relations.

Mr. Semple, some 80,000 readers of *Simple Speaks His Mind* will recall, is a mythical typical Harlemite whom Hughes first created in his weekly column in *The Chicago Defender,* a Negro newspaper. And his acidulous comments on the foibles of both colored and white folks were first intended for Negro eyes alone.

And in *Simple Takes a Wife,* one fears momentarily that the prospect of impending marriage has mellowed our not so simple-minded hero, or that the knowledge that he is not talking to Hughes alone may have softened him up.

But not Simple. Who else would have

the temerity to discuss the antipathy of Negro women to the marriage of prominent Negro males and white women—"Especially pretty white womens?"

And he quotes Joyce (his intended) as being completely unmoved when Britain booted the African prince who married a white typist.

"Any black king that wants to marry a white woman ain't got no business with a throne on which to sit," Joyce said. "Let him sit on a park bench."

Not that intermarriage holds Simple long. He's too fascinated at the failings of white people. But he understands why they can't play or imitate Be-Bop music. They don't know where it comes from.

[...]

Simple suspects that the English language "and that word black" helps to hold Negroes back, and when he gets around to it, he's going to revise the language so that people will be accused of white mail, or be caught behind the white ball, or be placed on Simple's white list with "everybody who ever Jim Crowed me from Rankin to Hitler, Talmadge to Malan, South Carolina to South Africa."

Not that Simple doesn't have faith in the coming generations. As Jesse Semple Santa Claus, he sends a requested rifle to a little cracker boy, and, after advising him to "Don't be rowdy," adds:

"If you see me on Christmas Eve, you will know me by my white beard and black face. Up North, the FEPC has given a Negro the Santa Claus job this year. Dark as I am, though, I intend to treat you equal."

And there was the brownskin son of an interracial marriage, who refused to be born down in Arkansas, no matter how liberal his white grandparents-to-be were.

Joyce corners Simple in the closing moments. But one hopes she lets him go to the neighborhood gin mill occasionally. Langston Hughes and thousands of his admirers would be lost without him.

Kent Ruth
"Simple Samples the Worst of Life"
Daily Oklahoman Sunday Magazine, 17 May 1953, p. 24

Anyone who has chuckled over the delightful tales of Damon Runyan will love these continuing adventures of Jesse B. Semple. (*Simple Speaks His Mind* was Poet Hughes' first volume.) All the guys and dolls are present . . . only in black-face. From his third floor rear to Paddy's bar and back to his third floor rear, Simple plods his easy pleasure-loving way, sweating out—for 240 pages—his divorce from Isabel (final when he can scrape together the money for the final installment) so that he can marry social-climbing Joyce, speaking his mind in the meantime on the multitudinous cares that weigh him down.

There's Joyce and her steady round of up-lift teas, to which he must sell tickets. There's the constant chore of cadging beer, of raising the rent money, of walking his rheumatic landlady's feist. And then there's the temptation of the flesh, name of Zarita. And the problem of young Cousin F.D., late of the South, who moves in with him. And, of course, the minor annoyances, like heatless radiators, grocers that don't know B from bull-foot when it comes to old-fashioned greens, mothers-in-law-to-be for whose opinion Simple gives "less than a small damn," and people who "try to pass" on chitterlings by pretending they don't like them when they do.

True, Simple is fiercely race conscious. He knows that dark skin means dark days. And he complains, with justification, that "white folks can measure their race prob-

433

lem by how far they have come. But Negroes measure ours by how far we have got to go." But he plugs along, patience and an unfailing good humor his two most important assets. And finally he does get Joyce. The result is several hours of delightfully entertaining reading ... and a picture of Negro life in New York City as revealing as a whole shelf-full of sociologies.

"Briefly Noted"
New Yorker, 29 (23 May 1953), 133

Simple (Mr. Jesse Semple, a Negro) is anxious to marry for the second time, but he finds many obstacles in his way. He discusses his troubles in a series of barroom conversations, but more often than not he turns the talk into an offhanded philosophical discussion of some of the problems of humanity, and of the Negro race in particular. Simple expresses his ancient and homey truths in a loud and jocular voice, but when his laughter has died away and he has stopped waving his arms, we see that he is excited not because he is standing in a Harlem bar drinking with his friends but because he is alone on a stage with an oversized prop glass empty in his hands and a good deal of uncertainty in his heart about the reception he is going to get from beyond the footlights. He is a pathetic figure, and in indulging his showmanship he has forgotten his dignity.

Florence Anshen Zetlin
"Barbed Dialogues: Life in Harlem Sketched"
Norfolk Virginian-Pilot, part 2, 24 May 1953, p. 10

If Simple had three wishes they would be "that all white folks was black and then nobody would have to bother about white blood and black blood anymore"; "that all poor folks was rich"; and "that all sick folks was well." But Simple was born black, stayed poor, and sometimes got sick. What he thinks about himself and the life he leads is the subject of these barbed and humorous dialogues. Simple has a tradition and a vein of his own. The vein is folk humor with its ribald gusto. The tradition is that of the clown who cloaks his disturbing truths with a grin.

In this book, a sequel to *Simple Speaks His Mind,* the troubles start with wanting to get married. One reason is so Simple will not have to mess with any more landladies. The other reason is he is in love. A wife already on hand, no money for divorce, and an altogether admirable morality on the part of Joyce his girl friend who refuses to commit bigamy, are the subject of long barside conversations. Simple is completely frank in his opinions about women, jobs, beer, police, white folks. "The closest you can get to heaven is loving," Simple says, but there's a lot of the world in the way of it.

These sketches on life in Harlem appeared originally as a weekly series in *The Chicago Defender.* Hughes writes with a poet's color and rhythm. His Simple is a naive propagandist for his race whose generosity and infectious humor make his points about injustice more sharply than many a treatise on discrimination.

Gertrude Martin
"Book Reviews"
Chicago Defender,
30 May 1953, p. 7

Langston Hughes in *Simple Takes a Wife* has succeeded in the difficult task of making a sequel better than the book it follows. Even more than in *Simple Speaks His Mind* Jesse B. Semple is an original, sparkling, three-dimensional character. There is interest here for a wide range of readers and on a number of different levels. For instance, there is Simple as a humorous, witty fellow, as a race man; there is also his friend who speaks for the author and often offers a philosophy of his own. There is besides a picture of life in Harlem which is remarkably complete.

Simple's problems in *Simple Takes a Wife* are manifold: no money, a girl he loves and wants to marry, a wife who writes for money for the divorce she had promised her wealthy boy friend would furnish, cranky landladies, and overshadowing all—race. Mr. Hughes has unpretentiously given a very perceptive look at what it means to be a Negro in the United States today. Simple lives in Harlem and although the details of living might differ elsewhere the all-pervasiveness of race does not.

Simple's wit is always fresh whether he is discussing his former girl friends, his fiance's moralizing, Negro colleges, Negro women's ideas on intermarriage or any of the many other subjects on which he voices an opinion. Simple is an original, the likes of whom has not been seen in American literature for many a day. Mr. Hughes has an eye for detail and an ear for language which combined make *Simple Takes a Wife* a thoroughly entertaining book. *The Chicago Defender* can take pride in the fact that Simple came to life in Mr. Hughes' excellent *Defender* column.

Henry F. Winslow
"Book of the Week"
Pittsburgh Courier,
30 May 1953, p. 6

Simple Takes a Wife, the second collection of Harlem sketches turning upon the rooming house and barroom adventures of Langston Hughes' lovable folk-hero, Jesse Semple, is a kind of triumph in protest humor.

In this volume Simple begins to reveal an active moral conscience and moves out of his static role by marrying Joyce, his long-wooed sweetheart. And it maintains that sheer naturalness of tone and diction which vitalizes the hero and the environment in which he moves.

Here and there, it communicates a home-spun truth singing with poetic beauty: "June-time is a good month, Sugar, but it goes away and stays all winter. When it comes back in the spring, it don't always come back the same. And for some folks, June don't come back a-tall."

But when he is most himself, Simple utters easy words revealing the hard fact of his Harlem life: ". . . every dog has its day—but the trouble is there are more dogs than there are days, more people than there are houses, more roomers than there are rooms, and more babies than there are cribs."

A little man, Simple puts his case to

"Dear Dr. Butts" in a letter to Negro leaders which they may well hang on their office walls with their other imposing credentials: it has as much truth and more meaning. If Simple and Joyce find an apartment it will be Langston Hughes' greatest creation.

Helen Beals
"New Novels Being Discussed"
Boston Sunday Herald, section 3, 31 May 1953, p. 2

Once more Langston Hughes has given us the life, adventures, and philosophy of Harlem's Jesse B. Semple, (known as "Simple") and once more Simple becomes so real that probably still more fans will proceed to send him gifts.

This time Simple discourses on such topics as race prejudice, intermarriage, divorce, and even the three cent stamp.

However, Simple's philosophy is often gay and care-free. He makes wry comments on New York rooming-houses, admits that love is as near heaven as a man gets on this earth, and loves New York where everybody is free.

Hughes, the O. Henry of Harlem, has the largest reading public among his own race of any Negro. He knows how to mirror life, its sadness, its hilarity, its frustrations and aspirations. He has an understanding heart.

James E. Kelley
"It's 'Unsignificant' but Packs a Wallop"
Denver Post, 31 May 1953, p. D23

This loosely constructed novel by one of the most articulate of our contemporary Negro writers is a warm portrayal of life in the Harlem rooming-house set.

In it, Jesse B. Semple (tagged Simple by his pals) is up to his old tricks—freeloading off his friends, courting his girl Joyce, fussing with his landlady. He's one of the most engaging fictional characters around currently.

Readers first discovered Simple in Hughes' column in the *Chicago Defender;* later on, a sampling of his antics was put between covers in *Simple Speaks His Mind.*

In his latest episode—put out in an inexpensively bound edition—Simple devotes himself to the pursuit of Joyce and happiness.

Meanwhile, and almost as an aside, he comments on everything. He discusses greens and grammar, second-hand clothes and second-hand love, possum and politics, 3-cent stamps and $300 divorces.

"I don't know which I hate to remember worse," Simple remarks to a beer-buying buddy in a moment of philosophical calm, "Baltimore womens or Baltimore bugs."

This is not one of Hughes' "significant" novels.

Yet in its quiet way and with its wry, pungent comments ("If I were not of the colored race, smart as I am, I would have money") it quite possibly packs more wallop than his embittered works of social protest.

Carl Van Vechten
"In the Heart of Harlem"
*New York Times Book
Review,* 31 May 1953,
pp. 5, 13

It is not as generally known as it should be that Langston Hughes laughs with, cries with, and speaks for, the Negro (in all classes) more understandingly, perhaps, than any other writer. Harlem is his own habitat, his workshop and his playground, his forte and his dish of tea. He is so completely at home when he writes about Harlem that he can afford to be both careless and sloppy. In his Simple books he is seldom either, and *Simple Takes a Wife* is a superior achievement to the first of the series, *Simple Speaks His Mind.* The new book is more of a piece, the material is more carefully and competently presented; it is more brilliant, more skillfully written, funnier, and perhaps just a shade more tragic than its predecessor.

The genre has been employed extensively by other writers: by Finley Peter Dunne in *Mr. Dooley,* by A. Neil Lyons in *Arthurs* and by Joel Chandler Harris in *Uncle Remus;* it is not too far, indeed, from the scheme of Gorky's *The Lower Depths.* The locale, however, is original, the taste truly Harlem, the matters discussed pertinent to the inhabitants, and the effect, prevailingly evocative. The question and answer formula is used throughout the book, but frequently Simple's replies are somewhat protracted. The views expressed for the most part have a sane basis, and it is probable that at least a modicum of these are the beliefs of Mr. Hughes himself, although they find expression on Simple's tongue.

It would be easy to refer to the author as the Molière of Harlem who has just got around to writing his *School for Wives* (or is it his *School for Husbands?*). At any rate, Mr. Hughes (himself a bachelor) seems to be as cynical in his viewpoint as Colette, when he deals with the war between the sexes. Here and there he suggests that he is writing the Harlem version of Colette's *Chéri.*

There are several women in this book. The first is Mabel, "the woman like water." "'Do you want me to tell you what that woman was like? Boy, I don't know. She was like some kind of ocean, I guess, some kind of great big old sea, like the water at Coney Island on a real hot day, cool and warm all at once—and company like a big crowd of people—also like some woman you like to be alone with, if you dig my meaning. Yet and still, I wasn't in love with that woman.'" Simple passes on to other conquests and to discussions of other ideas. For instance, in chapter seven there is a long and cheerful lesson in English grammar and usage. Chapter two is an addition to the folklore of Harlem, in which Simple describes the custom under which each roomer in a house is allotted a different ring.

[. . .]

Somewhat further on, there is a learned discussion of Bebop, which Simple declares has its origin in the police habit of beating up Negroes' heads. "'Every time a cop hits a Negro with his billy club that old club says Bop! Bop! . . . BE-BOP! . . . MOP! . . . BOP!'"

In chapter sixteen, Simple and Joyce, his lady friend, warmly discuss the disturbing subject of miscegenation. There is a touch of Mr. Hughes' special kind of poetry in his description of night: "'Night, you walk easy, sit on a stoop and talk, stand on a corner, shoot the bull, lean on a bar, ring a bell and say "Baby, here I am."'" In chapter fifty-seven, Simple dilates on the unpleasant connotations of the word black. "'What I want to know,' asks Simple, 'is where white folks get off calling everything bad *black*? If it is a dark night, they say it's *black* as hell. If you are mean and evil, they say you got a BLACK heart. I would like to change all that around and say that the people who Jim Crow me have a WHITE heart. People who sell dope to children have got a WHITE mark against them. And all the gamblers who were behind the basketball fix are the WHITE sheep of the sports world.'"

This is true humor with a bite to it, spoken in the authentic language of 135th Street and set down good-naturedly in a book which tells us more about the common Negro than a dozen solemn treatises on the "race question."

Henry Seidel Canby
"Simple Takes a Wife"
Book-of-the-Month-Club News, June 1953, p. 7

The famous technique of dialogue and commentary which made Mr. Dooley famous has not for many years been used so successfully as in this book. Simple, a Harlem philosopher who escapes from bedbugs, predatory women and a job that binds him too much, is, I am sure, likely to become a figure in American literary folklore. For his role is complex. He does not merely escape; he pursues wives who can cook and keep him happy, although better husbands would make them more prosperous, if certainly less amused. Langston Hughes, one of the best poets of his race, is the interlocutor in this instance. But he very skilfully is merely the supplier of beer and pertinent questions—a push button to

which Simple always responds. Do not suppose this book is merely a contribution to Negro humor. It is deeply humorous and often superbly witty; you can and will laugh constantly. But there is more wisdom in Simple's comments on social relationships and in his estimates of human nature than in a hundred books on the perennial theme of racial contrasts. *Simple Takes a Wife* is, I believe, an informal masterpiece worthy with a little compression of a long life in American literature. It belongs to a distinguished line, whose shining examples, far different and yet offering at least an unforced comparison, are *Uncle Remus* and *Huckleberry Finn.*

"Fiction"
Booklist, 49 (1 June 1953), 322

Before Mr. Jesse B. Semple, the untutored philosopher of the Harlem rooming-house set, can divorce his wife and espouse the morally impeccable Joyce, he has to run the gauntlet of many problems. He discourses on them in Harlem bars over beers he has cadged from his sympathetic and more literate listener. Under the folklike humor of "Simple's" monologs runs a bitter undercurrent of racial consciousness. This sequel to *Simple Speaks His Mind* first appeared in the *Chicago Defender*, and should appeal to a wider Negro audience.

"Life in Harlem"
Nation, 176 (6 June 1953), 488

These popular and entertaining sketches of Negro life in Harlem form an interesting contrast with Richard Wright's *The Outsider.* Mr. Hughes is not unaware of the race problem either; it is really the central issue of his book, viewed here from the standpoint of the common man and with bitter laughter. But the animal pleasures and all too human follies of ordinary life, black or white, are also stressed—the binding cord of humanity which Wright temporarily at least has severed. One may regret only that Mr. Hughes has made these stories a little too popular and somewhat mechanical in execution.

J. Saunders Redding
"Book Review"
Baltimore Afro-American Magazine, 13 June 1953, p. 9

There are amateurs and there are pros in writing.

The amateur not only has no real respect for writing as a craft, but also he generally has no knowledge of it.

The amateur is all spirit and dash.

He waits for the "right mood" and he goes around "looking for material" and when he thinks he has found it, he waits some more until the lightning strikes, and he calls the lightning "inspiration."

He doesn't bother to learn the trade he professes to love, because he says he "hates to write," though he loves writing. But he doesn't know what writing is.

He knows how to spell words, and he has an idea of what some words mean, and he can set them down in a grammatical sequence, and now and then, even in a meaningful sequence; but he doesn't know what words can do, or what you have to do with them to get them to do the things they can do.

The pro, on the other hand, is a workman who loves every bit of his work. He has respect for it.

He has respect for it because acquiring the craft and the skill of it has caused him much labor and much time and much pain, and he knows that putting the craft and the skill to work will go on causing time, labor and pain.

If occasionally inspiration comes, he's thankful; but he doesn't wait around for it any more than a professional ball player waits for it before he snags a fly in deep center or lays into a home run pitch.

He's in there trying to maintain a good percentage, and so long as he maintains it he can go to bed at night feeling pretty swell—and thanks for inspiration when it comes, and to hell with it when it doesn't.

Langston Hughes is a pro. You might even say that he is an old pro; and he's kind of quietly proud of himself, and he has every right to be.

He's maintained a good average over a lot of years.

Some of the zing and fire may be gone now, as it eventually goes from all of us, no matter what the game, but he has confidence in his craftsmanship. He knows what he can do, and how it can be done in several ways, and what he's doing is all about.

And all he's doing is creating one of the richest folk characters since Paul Bunyan, Appleseed Johnny and Uncle Remus. That's all.

The amateurs say it's quite easy to do this.

In fact, it's Simple.

All you have to have is a superb ear, an absorptive eye and a whole heart.

That's all you have to have—except, of course, something to say and the skill to say it. And to get the skill all you have to do is spend nine years, eleven months and twenty-nine days out of every ten years working at it.

And in order to work at it, you have to love it; and loving it hurts; but eventually the hurting love goes into the writing and diffuses all over everything you write and informs all the characters you create with hurting-loving-truth. And then you have it.

You have created a Simple, a Jesse B.

Jesse B. is a guy. He's just the pure stuff of a life that's so common that almost no one, except those who live it, recognize it.

He's a guy of the sort that most people think of as belonging in burlesque of the sort that Dusty Rhoades and Huggins and Butter Beans used to do on the Harlem circuit. But Simple is no burlesque character.

He's not even a comic character, not really—though everybody I know laughs at his witticisms, and some of those I know think they're laughing at him.

But they're not: they're laughing with him.

And when you laugh with somebody, instead of at somebody, you're in the same boat.

That's the wonderful thing that Langston Hughes does to you with words—he puts you in the same boat with Simple. That doesn't mean that you'd do the things Simple does, or talk the way he does, or even—not necessarily—feel the way he does. It only means that you understand and sympathize with him.

And that's a pro's test. He's no good if he doesn't make you understand and sympathize with the level of life he's writing about; if he doesn't broaden your experience; if he doesn't enlarge your soul.

And Langston Hughes has done just that in all the ways there are of doing it—in poetry, drama, fiction, anecdote and essay.

He does it again now in *Simple Takes a Wife.*

Arna Bontemps
"That Not So Simple Sage, Mr. Simple"
New York Herald Tribune Book Review, 14 June 1953, p. 12

There is no convenient category for the Simple books. Like much of Langston Hughes' writing, they go a merry way without too serious a regard for form or fashion. *Simple Takes a Wife* is neither a novel nor a collection of stories. To call it humor is insufficient. A series of dialogues in the idiom of a transplanted Southerner, it is as outlandish as the hubbub in a Harlem bar, as noisy and startling as voices in a rooming house, but it has too much bite to be just funny. Categories aside, however, the new book bears a signature which is indeed unmistakable.

The character called Simple was first introduced in a weekly column of *The Chicago Defender,* a Negro newspaper. He began his public career, so to speak, as a bewildered observer of the war effort. Langston Hughes first employed his languid asides as a commentary on discrimination in defense plants. Once started, however, Simple would not be shushed. He became almost embarrassingly frank about his domestic problems. At the same time he revealed a certain sensitiveness to life's

440

philosophic overtones and a tendency to let his moods overpower him:

> I got the Dallas blues
> And the Fort Worth heart's disease.

More important, he made friends fast. Readers of the column addressed letters to Simple instead of his author. One impetuous admirer sent a possum from Tennessee packed in dry ice. The first book in which these pieces were brought together was *Simple Speaks His Mind*. To a considerable extent it represented a reworking of the material rather than a collection of columns from *The Defender*. The second book goes still farther in this direction and it makes even better reading.

Between the time when Simple began to hanker for a divorce from the wife he had left in Baltimore and the day when he finally achieves freedom to marry his girl Joyce, almost everything happens, and most of it Simple reports in his own words to an interlocutor in Paddy's Bar. His troubles with his landlady are peculiarly disturbing, but scarcely more so than those precipitated by another landlady when he calls on Joyce and rings seven times for the third floor rear, as the instruction on the bell directs. When Joyce fails to respond to the first seven, he must ring seven more. At the end of a third such cluster the fat landlady comes out storming.

By then, of course, the complexity of Simple's life as a whole has been underscored, but he lives it to the hilt, nevertheless. As he pauses for beer, he has his say about ladies' hats, bed bugs, afternoon teas, be-bop music, grammar, college education, moving pictures, intermarriage, and a host of equally vital matters. He befriends an aspiring young nephew, sidesteps the party girl Zarita, and indulges a heavenly feeling as he heads for the City Hall with Joyce.

Harlem hasn't a more authentic citizen.

Esther Todfeld
"A Simple Man Finds Living Isn't Easy"
Bridgeport Sunday Post, 14 June 1953, p. B4

Not too many years ago one of our favorite characters in light fiction was one Florian Slappey, an enterprising and delightfully unpredictable young Negro created by Octavus Roy Cohen. We mourned his passing from the magazine scene when some folk took objection and felt the series might appear to be light ridicule.

Comes now, after some few years, another young Negro fictional character, Jesse B. Semple, hereinafter to be known merely as Simple, and he promises to fill the void without the possibility of appearing to discredit his race. Simple and his story are brought to us by poet Langston Hughes who enjoys the justifiable distinction of having the largest reading public among his race.

We've already had *Simple Speaks His Mind*. Now, to follow *Simple Takes a Wife*, what could be more logical than a whole string of Simple stories. . . . *Simple Settles Down, Simple Starts a Family, Simple Runs a Rooming House,* etc?

Practically all of Simple's story is told in conversations at a neighborhood bar as he cons the author into satisfying his thirst for beer by spinning the tale of his premarital woes during the long courtship of his girl, Joyce. Both Simple and Joyce live in crowded rooming houses under the eagle eyes of demon landladies who give advice freely but are mighty tightfisted when it comes to sending up heat for freezing roomers. As Simple says, "Why else does a man marry if not to get away from rooming house landladies?"

441

We found Simple quite the amusing bar-room philosopher who believes that this would be a perfect world if he could find a "good fairy to grant me three wishes—That all white folks was black; that all poor folks was rich; and that all sick folks was well—then nobody would suffer."

[. . .]

and wizard-like Langston Hughes artfully conceals a profound sociological treatise. Simple, strutting up Lexington in his new suit, draped down, reet-pleated and pegged, is a facade from behind which peers Harlem of the wide smile, rapturous dance and wet pillow. Or as Simple puts it, "I did not hear her crying, but the next morning her pillow were wet."

Will Wharton "Word-Wizard Langston Hughes" *St. Louis Post-Dispatch,* 16 June 1953, p. 2C

Among their other fascinating capabilities, Aframericans have a sort of child-like genius for "putting English" on words. Thus Mr. Jesse B. Semple, the amiable and impecunious hero of these sketches, is known as "Simple" in the Harlem rooming-house set.

A sequel to *Simple Speaks His Mind,* this book continues the story of Simple's mainly hilarious but sometimes pathetic adventures with various women, with a conclusion indicated by the title.

Years ago Langston Hughes was wont to make fiery and forthright pronouncements on the plight of his race. But, mellowing with time, he has learned to get his message across more effectively with a skilled fictional mingling of humor and pathos.

Most moving is Simple's account of "when this same-floor roomer of mine died. . . . He went in the night when he were alone by hisself" and "They could not find no address for that man's people for nobody to claim the funeral."

The relaxed, witty prose of a matured

Ben H. Bagdikian "Harlem's Simple Speaks His Mind Again" *Providence Sunday Journal,* part 6, 21 June 1953, p. 8

"Sometimes I wonder what made you so race-conscious," Simple's educated drinking friend said.

"Sometimes I wonder what made me so black," Simple replied.

And so it appeared at first that things were the same with Mr. Jesse B. Semple, better known as Simple to those who have read Hughes's columns in the *Chicago Defender* and his first book about Simple, *Simple Speaks His Mind.*

But, the fact is the gay old dog is getting quieter, he's settling down, he is, while never dull, less apt to be impertinent. He makes, for example, a New Year's Resolution:

"To let the Race Problem roll off my mind like water off a duck's back—pay it no attention any more. I have been worrying as long as I have been black. Since I have to be black a long time yet, what is the sense of so much worriation? The next time I read where they have lynched or bombed a Negro, I will just shrug my

442

shoulders and say, 'It warn't me.' The next time I hear tell of a colored singer barred out of Constitution Hall in Washington, I will say, 'I ain't no singer.' Next time I hear that colored folks can't eat in the Stork Club, I will say, 'Chitterlings is better than filet mignon anyhow.'"

Simple, the barfly philosopher of Harlem, still makes Harlem come alive in the sound and flavor of his talk. His essays on Harlem doorbell rings, on the cooking of greens, on second-hand clothing stores, are enough to let you know that he is still a living part of the city. They also hint that there is more to Simple (and his author) than meets the eye. We'd hate to see Simple become respectable or cowed. It is becoming discreet to keep one's mouth shut when angry, but if this happened to Simple it would be a great loss.

Luther P. Jackson
"Lenox Avenue Is Sad"
Newark Sunday News, section 3, 21 June 1953, p. 48

Manhattan's Harlem is one of America's best known communities and one of the least understood. This, in spite of the fact that Harlem has been overrun with writers of every hue and description. But most of these invaders go into Harlem with a preconception of what they will find there. They search out the jazz, the women and the after-hour joints, then scurry back to their typewriters to dash off eyewitness reports. It is through these brief invasions that Harlem has gained the dubious reputation of being one of the "pleasure capitals" of the world.

Here are two books that puncture the myth. *Go Tell It on the Mountain* explores the store-front church. Baldwin, the 29-year-old son of a preacher, takes off where other writers end. He not only vividly describes the physical contortions of Harlem evangelists but explains how and why they got that way.

[. . .]

Baldwin's storefronts have been so seldom examined in literature that the reader has difficulty establishing a relationship with his characters. But this is no fault of the young author. He honestly and brilliantly depicts a human experience that can be real only to those who endure it.

On the other hand, Langston Hughes's Jesse B. Semple is the familiar barroom character who trades his opinion for a beer and would die before he would pick up the tab. Simple, as he is better known, unloads his troubles on Hughes—a technique employed by Finley Peter Dunne in his "Mr. Dooley" stories. Simple has an opinion on everything from "greens to grammar." But his major subjects are women folks and white folks. He admits, though, that he can't understand either of them.

Though Baldwin's storefront could very well be in the same block as Hughes's tavern, their books are miles apart in treatment and mood. The evangelists are tormented by their failures. Simple jokes about his. But one gets the impression that Simple is "laughing to keep from crying," as Hughes expressed it in the title of another book.

On the basis of evidence submitted here, sadness stalks Lenox Avenue.

Kent Ruth
"Breaking Out of the
'Cage' of Negro Writing"
Louisville Courier-Journal, section 3, 21 June
1953, p. 12

A single swallow, they say, does not make a summer. Nor does a single tornado make a spring or a single blizzard a winter. Which is to say, albeit left-handedly, that a well curved bust no more makes an historical romance than does a brutal lynching a Negro novel. History, alas, is more than a bosom. And Negro life, fortunately, is more than tragedy.

For a 29-year-old Negro publishing his first novel, James Baldwin appreciates this weakness that seems to characterize so much Negro fiction. *Go Tell It on the Mountain* is, he admits, "a fairly deliberate attempt to break out of . . . the 'cage' of Negro writing. I wanted my people to be people first, Negroes almost incidentally." He wants the reader to close the book "knowing more about himself, and therefore more about Negroes. . . ." If he has not succeeded as completely as has Old Hand Langston Hughes, he has at least recognized the problem and met it honestly.

Three recently published novels on the Negro point up what he and Hughes have accomplished. Cross Damon in Richard Wright's disturbing *The Outsider*, Asher Brown in William Fisher's *The Waiters* and William Ransom Edwards in Water B. Lowrey's excellent *Watch Night* are all well drawn characters in well written novels. And yet none of them, by virtue of what they are and do, holds up a mirror before the average reader, prompts him to understand himself and/or the Negro in a more intimate way.

Baldwin's John Grimes and Hughes' Jesse B. Semple do just that. Basically as unalike as grits and molasses, both are as easy to recognize, just about as common. Young John hungers for salvation and the security of knowing that, despite the sin all about him, he can lift himself above it and find God. Aging Simple thirsts for beer and the security of marriage with Joyce (once he scrapes together the last installment on his divorce from Isabel). Both of them finally win out. And the average reader, having struggled along with them, sympathetically and understandingly, has gained a new insight into two completely different sides of Negro big-city life.

[. . .]

Simple's background, a pleasantly aimless barroom-rooming house existence, is definitely Runyanesque. Pleasure loving and weak, Simple's life is filled with simple problems: cadging beers, providing himself with sharp clothes, meeting the rent, struggling with the flesh in the person of Zarita, trying to persuade Isabel to pay his share of their divorce, meeting Joyce's exacting standards of culture and gentlemanly deportment. Patience and unfailing good humor are his only tangible assets, but they carry him through.

James Baldwin is deeply moving. Langston Hughes is uproariously amusing. Each pinpoints a basic human longing, particularly characteristic of the Negro, yet common to all man: the search for God and the desire for material peace and comfort. Each in his own way has broken out of the "cage" of Negro writing and achieved a memorable picture of human frailty and the just-as-human urge to do something about it.

Blyden Jackson
"'Simple' Continues His Happy Way"
Nashville Tennessean, 28 June 1953, p. 19C

As a rule sequels are letdowns. They are reminders that the lightning strikes in the same place only once. But the lightning of creative genius has broken the rule for Langston Hughes and his good friend, Jesse B. Semple. *Simple Takes a Wife* is at least as good as *Simple Speaks His Mind.* In some ways—that have to do both with aesthetics and social comment—it is better.

Simple's taking of a wife is just as hilarious as Simple's speaking of his mind. It is just as acute a job of observation of Negroes and the contemporary scene. Simple's speech is still a triumph of high-fidelity recording as well as a delight to the ear and the sense of humor.

His perception of the many ironies, big and little, that complicate his Negro existence is still keen and true. And underneath the laughter there are still the thoughts that lie too deep for tears.

When is Simple at his best here? It is hard to say. But two of his finest moments rather complement each other. They involve imaginary letters: The first, from Simple as a black Santa Claus to a little white boy down in Dixie; the second from Simple, as the common Negro he is, to a Negro leader. Put together they show the comprehensiveness, for all its seeming lightness of touch and its genuine provision of good fun, with which this book does span the race problem.

The book is attractively presented in laminated board covers at a moderate price.

Harvey Curtis Webster
"Frank's Fine Novel"
New Republic, 128 (29 June 1953), 21–2

[. . .]

Already a best-seller in the sense that many of its chapters have been read by the million readers of the *Chicago Defender,* Langston Hughes' *Simple Takes a Wife* is less ambitious and less carefully sustained than Mr. [Lion] Feuchtwanger's novel, a good deal more successful than the other three I've mentioned. Simple is an ignorant Harlem Negro, full of good sense and delectable jive talk. The chronicle of Simple's ventures, opinions, and mistakes—though it is as uneven as even the best collection of newspaper columns is bound to be—has a continuity of both theme and tone. Negroes are not uniformly bright, satisfied, or dangerously subversive is the theme; light banter that means serious business is the usual tone. Not as good as the best of Mr. Hughes' short stories and poems, *Simple Takes a Wife* unpretentiously and with mild anger reveals the average Negro as he probably is in actuality rather than as the too good or too bad man he appears to be in most of the fiction written about him.

Ira O. Guy
"Simple Takes a Wife" Common Sense Historical *Reviews,* 12 (July 1953), 5

While some may speak disparagingly of a typical Harlem scene, or look on in disgust and others make apologies, Langston

Hughes at his typewriter will reveal the souls of the participants, buried under the debris of 250 years of slavery, making their way to freedom 90 years after the physical chains have been broken.

With Biblical frankness, in *Simple Takes a Wife* Mr. Hughes gives the world the naked truth, clothed immaculate for presentation in rich, beautiful English, so pure, that with the occasional digressions due to Simple's brogue, one is carried to the scene to be, as it were, unobserved listener to every word.

Many of the World's best authorities have visited and told of Harlem; possibly none made a diagnosis quite so understandable as Mr. Hughes'.

As Simple tells of his experience in Baltimore the reader remembers how Frederick Douglass told of the big house where men, women and children were quartered like animals. Others know of similar conditions since emancipation and can easily visualize sympathetically causes for many rooming house evils.

Mr. Hughes does not pamper, neither veneer, as members of other races too often do. He presents the facts and conditions for guidance of those interested to correct.

We are all members of the same human race. Though variated, all men act and develop alike under similar conditions and environments.

George Cooper
"A Fixture in U.S. Fiction"
Dayton Daily News,
section 2, 5 July 1953,
p. 6

In this sequel to *Simple Speaks His Mind* Langston Hughes again presents Simple, the oracle of the Harlem bars, who discusses and argues with vigor about love, marriage, death, ladies' hats, college education, Negro leaders, and numerous other subjects. (These philosophical comments take place during the period Simple waits for his divorce from Isabel to become final so he can marry Joyce.)

Hughes writes in entertaining, humorous dialogue form, but although parts of it are rollicking, don't be misled; underneath the humor runs an undercurrent of bitter truth and emotion that delves deep into our American pattern of living.

The down-to-earth descriptions of everyday situations and Simple's never-to-be-forgotten reactions to them leave the reader refreshed. At the same time, Hughes gives real insight into the feelings of one element of our population and also rather clearly indicates something of the background of such feelings. While the book is based on a segment of Negro life in Harlem—the author has succeeded in unearthing some of the broader feelings of a way of life in America.

This reviewer recommends it for those who are interested in a study of group feelings as well as those seeking light, hilarious reading. Simple is truly a fixture in American fiction.

R.F.H.
"Simple's Troubles Many and Varied"
Springfield [Mass.] *Republican,* 5 July 1953, p. 4C

Simple Takes a Wife by Langston Hughes, is a continuation of the adventures of Jesse B. Semple of Harlem, whose opinions on a variety of subjects were chronicled in *Simple Speaks His Mind.* How he does take a wife, in spite of a previous marriage, rooming house troubles, race problems, and financial difficulties, provides warmly amusing reading, and a look from backstage at what belonging to a minority really means.

As in the previous Simple chronicles, the book is a series of short articles, 58 in all, sometimes discussing Simple's troubles with girlfriends and landladies and sometimes allowing him to expand on his theories of life. Simple is more real than most people you meet in books, and while the present volume does not quite meet the pace of the first one, it is an excellent piece of work.

C[arter] B[rooke] J[ones]
"Simple Takes a Wife"
Washington Sunday Star, 5 July 1953, p. C11

It is not surprising that most Negro novelists have felt impelled to write seriously of their race, if not tragically. The dilemmas and perplexities of a held-down minority have not suggested easy answers. And yet there is a humorous side to Negroes, apart from the vaudeville of Amos and Andy and Florian Slappey. Just as there is humor to be drawn from the doings of all other races and nationalities, Langston Hughes, writing of Harlem, extracts wise and gentle fun from his people. And they lose nothing of dignity and decency at his hands.

This is another book about Jesse B. Semple. He is called by his friends Simple, not because he is lacking in intelligence—the contrary is true, as you'll find out—but perhaps because of a certain naivete in his outlook and also because Semple is temptingly like Simple. A novel about Harlem's rooming-house set, it is a conversation piece, with Simple doing most of the talking. He'll never bore you. While he is sipping beer and talking to his college-educated friend, Simple describes the scrapes he drifts into and his ideas about life in general. There's many a laugh in Simple's words and quite as much shrewd instruction in what it's like to belong to Harlem's never-quite-prosperous middle class.

J.R.M.
"Simple Continues Philosophic Way"
Pasadena Star-News, 5 July 1953, p. 33

"Simple," otherwise Mr. Jesse B. Semple, has a fair chance to become a permanent American character, in some ways similar to the renowned Mr. Dooley (from the pen of Finley Peter Dunne). He started on his way to boundbook fame in *Simple Speaks His Mind,* but he was "born" earlier in a column Mr. Hughes was writing in 1943 in *The Chicago Defender.* This column and Simple were intended only for Negro readers, but the forthright and amusing Jesse B. Semple gained a larger and larger audience.

Simple Takes a Wife continues our character in the same mood as that of his previous appearance in covers—at least till toward the end, when marriage may, or may not, change him somewhat. Simple is very conscious of race, he is extremely frank about his troubles with his girl friend and he does like to relax with a glass of beer.

Publishers Simon and Schuster have made an interesting step in this volume, combining the board cover with the usual jacket and thus bringing the price down to somewhere near what most persons think books should cost. The cover is attractive, does not soil and makes permanent the information usually soon lost with the dust jacket.

and the insuperable difficulties which prevent him, temporarily, from starting life anew with Joyce.

Simple's adventures with his ex-wife and his next wife are many, and laughs for his readers not a few.

Langston Hughes, well-known Negro poet, has also written *Simple Speaks His Mind,* to which this new novel is a follow-up.

A. P. Wennergren "'Simple' Back with Advice for All" *Rocky Mountain News,* 5 July 1953, p. 38

Remember "Simple"? Perhaps lesser known as Jesse B. Semple? You who met him in *Simple Speaks His Mind* will applaud his return in *Simple Takes a Wife,* and you who are strangers to "Simple" will have the good fortune to meet Harlem's "first citizen."

You see, "Simple" is indeed an informed man and that is to your advantage. Over numerous glasses of beer, he discusses thoroughly that which touches his rooming house life; Joyce, who will be his June bride if he can ever save up $133.34 for his divorce from Isabel, and the community called Harlem and politics and the race problem, ad infinitum.

The majority of books written about our Negro populace are primarily books of violence, an emotion attendant to the race problem. But humor is also an attendant emotion to the colored race, and "Simple's" got more than a fair share.

The pleasure in meeting Jesse B. Semple—it was all mine! I hope it will be all yours.

Peggy Randolph "'Simple' Is Back, and Wife-Hunting" *Tulsa Sunday World Magazine,* 5 July 1953, p. 21

In Langston Hughes' new novel, Harlem's Jesse B. Semple (better known as Simple) talks about everything from the landladies he despises to Joyce whom he loves.

In a series of conversations, he reveals the beat of the street on which his people live, and the hazards and race problems they have to surmount to exist.

Over a glass of beer with Simple, we learn in his warm-hearted, gossipy language, the intimate details of his past loves

Garfield Hinton
"Negro Writer Hits
Happy Medium in His
Dialog Series"
Buffalo Courier-Express,
19 July 1953, p. 29B

Jesse B. Semple first appeared in the columns of the *Chicago Defender,* one of the larger Negro weekly newspapers, during World War II. In 1950 Simple's wit and wisdom were published in book form as *Simple Speaks His Mind.* This second book consists of a series of dialogues between Langston Hughes and Simple, usually at a bar over glasses of beer.

Simple is a philosophical fellow, who has learned the technique of laughing at color prejudice. For people who have been reading such heavy stuff as *Native Son* and *Invisible Man, Simple Takes a Wife* is a happy balance. Simple doesn't join the Communist Party and he doesn't commit any crime. He does keep people laughing, if not at himself, then at ourselves.

Simple lives in Harlem and tries to pay his share on a divorce from his first wife, Isabel. He wants to be free so that he can marry Joyce, a church-going girl. Joyce wanted a big June wedding. In the end, however, Joyce and Simple leave their creator, Langston Hughes, behind and marry in March, three months early.

In between humorous gripes about his landlady and conditions generally, Simple sometimes strikes home. Concerning Negroes working on railroads Simple says, "Carry and clean, that is all they let Negroes do on trains and in stations, carry and clean. If I'm man enough to buy a ticket, I do not see why I'm not man enough to sell a ticket."

Simple Takes a Wife is Langston Hughes' 13th book. As a writer of life among Negro Americans, he is a master. The lack of a basic continuity in this book is offset by its interest.

Frank Marshall Davis
"Frank-ly Speaking:
Simple Takes a Wife"
Honolulu Record, 20
August 1953, pp. 7, [8]

If I were teaching a course in sociology and wanted my students to get a good understanding of the thought processes and behavior patterns of what is called the average urban Negro, I would insist that they read Langston Hughes' latest book, *Simple Takes a Wife.*

Here in some 240 pages of fiction is as penetrating and memorable a picture of how it feels to be a Negro as you will find anywhere, including the lengthy and scholarly studies from the pens of social scientists. What's more, it's easier to read and at times, downright hilarious.

This is the 13th book from the prolific pen of Hughes, not counting a number of which he was co-author. You can buy it from the publishers, Simon and Schuster, 630 Fifth Ave., Rockefeller Center, New York, for the low price of $1.95 if you cannot obtain it at your local bookstore.

Langston Hughes, incidentally, has the largest following among Negroes of any Negro writer. He is also described by leading critics as "the poet laureate of the Negro people." I might add he is the same Langston Hughes who, complains the local Commission on Subversive Activities, I have "staunchly defended."

The book is about one Jesse B. Semple, better known as Simple. This character

449

was created in Hughes' regular column in the *Chicago Defender* and became an instant hit. A couple of years ago there appeared the first book, *Simple Speaks His Mind*. The new volume is an extension of Simple's day-to-day existence. But it hits harder and digs deeper than the first.

Simple tells his story in everyday Harlemese over his beer at the neighborhood tavern. It can be uproariously funny. It is never boring. The style permits a running and pithy commentary on anything and everything. For that reason, Simple seems as alive as your best friend.

Like most Negroes, Simple can never forget his color. And he has a logical answer for any question. When he is asked: "I often wonder why so many colored people say, 'I taken,' instead of 'I took,'" he answers:

"Because they are taken, I reckon. Lord knows I have been taken in more ways than one—for a ride, for my week's salary, my good name and everything else but undertaken. Someday I will be undertaken, too, and it will cost me five hundred dollars. Funerals is high."

"Funerals ARE high."

"Neither IS nor ARE reduces expenses," said Simple.

Commenting on radio and television, he says: "You would think no Negroes lived in America except Amos and Andy. White folks have all kinds of plays on the radio about themselves, also on TV. But what have we got about us? Just now and then a song to sing. Am I right?"

Taking a poke at the attitudes of some whites, Simple speaks of his experiences where he works:

"Them white folks are always telling me: 'Isn't it wonderful the progress that's been made amongst your people? Look at Dr. Bunche!'

"All I say is 'Look at me.'

"That jars them because I don't look nothing like Dr. Bunche.

"Then they say, 'Well, take Marian Anderson.'

"I say, 'Take Zarita,' which shakes them, because when I get through describing all the furnished-room gals in Harlem that never heard of Marian Anderson they change the subject."

Consider also this trenchant bit when Simple describes a conversation with his young cousin, Carlyle:

"Carlyle said: 'I'm a man now, so I want to get paid like a man.'

"'You mean a white man,' I said.

"'I mean a GROWN man,' says Carlyle."

Still another gem is Simple's discourse on the word "black":

"What I want to know is where do white folks get off calling everything bad black? If it is a dark night, they say it's black as hell. If you are mean and evil, they say you got a black heart. I would like to change that around and say that the people who Jim Crow me have got a white heart. People who sell dope to children have got a white mark against them. And all the white gamblers who were behind the basketball fix are the WHITE sheep of the sports world."

What I have quoted has little connection with the book's title, *Simple Takes a Wife*. Fact is, that while Simple is waiting for a divorce from his first wife so he can marry again, which happens at the end of the volume, he continues to live. And, being black, he lives black. All of which means that he has a daily struggle with the race problem.

It seems that Langston Hughes, who has been world-famous as a writer for close to 30 years, gets better with the passing of time. Just as his latest volume of poetry, *Montage of a Dream Deferred,* was his finest in that field, his *Simple Takes a Wife* is his best fiction.

Since Simple is a living, breathing human who will rub up against problems as long as he lives, the supply of source material for future volumes is as rich as life itself. Already I am looking forward to the next in the series. And if you will read *Simple Takes a Wife*, you will join me in anxious waiting.

E. Merrill Root
"Black Is Beautiful"
Freeman, 3 (24 August 1953), 857–8

Mephistopheles led Faust first through "the Little World" of love and private heart, and then through "the Great World" of politics, culture, and the escape of man into the exterior which is social life. In Langston Hughes' projection of Simple, the order is fortunately reversed. In this latest of his books, we traverse not the world of politics (where Hughes made his worst mistakes, which he has admirably admitted and rejected in recent weeks), but that private world of the heart which is most fruitful for the artist and for the individual—in whom alone the world really *lives*. Here Simple takes a wife.

The result is a book that has guts and gusto. I know of no modern character more tanged and shrewd and racy and wise, more subtle in simplicity, more serious in laughter; more richly fun-splashed about the decorum of marriage, more headlong or healthy in his hilarity about, and his devotion to women. Simple knows why the weaker sex is so strong—for he knows why the stronger sex is so weak.

"I like to drop ashes on the floor sometimes," says Simple, "so I would want Joyce to be home in the daytime only to cook, because if I had a Million Dollars, I would be home all the time myself. I would not go out to work nowhere—I would just rest and get my strength back after all these years I been working. I could not rest with no woman around the house all day, not even Joyce. A woman is all the time saying, 'Do this' and 'Do that.' And 'Ain't you got the grass cut yet?'

"I would say, 'No I ain't baby. Let it go till next week.'

"Then, if she's like the rest of the women, she would say, 'You don't take no pride in anything. I have to do everything.' And she would go out and cut it just to spite me."

Langston Hughes' style is like arterial blood. He is no "intellectual"—that fog in search of a wind. He finds a word for things; he is one of God's born artists. "Walter," he has Simple say, "were a slick hustler with a Buick car and no morals."

The book has little plot, no great drama. It is, by design and victory, a contemplative savoring of the gaudy spectacle of life by a grown Huckleberry Finn, so fascinated by characters, experiences, loves, that he could live a million years; it has the zest and zip of a single sip of champagne. Here in Simple is a man and philosopher whom we would love to meet in some heavenly tavern, cheek by jowl with Montaigne and Rabelais, and pause to pass with him our happy eternity.

Here is a book to make us thank God that so many of our fellow Americans have darker skin and warmer blood. As Mr. Simple says: "The night is black, which has a moon and a million stars, and is beautiful. . . . What is wrong with black?"

Abner Berry
"Not So Simple"
Masses and Mainstream,
6 (September 1953), 55–8

Among the 66,000 furnished room dwellers who live in Harlem between the two rivers from 110th Street, on the south, to just beyond the Polo Grounds, on the north, is one Jesse B. Semple—called "Simple," for short, by his friends. We don't know Simple's exact address, but it appears from his salty comments on landladies, bars, upper class Negroes and patronizing whites that he lives in the "valley," in "Deep Harlem," east of Seventh Avenue in the 130's.

Simple and his neighbors, refugees from the sterner racism of the South, understand and denounce the jimcrow nuances of New York City with a fierce race consciousness. This rooming house set, whose addresses denote the place where they bathe, sleep and change clothes, and for whom their favorite tavern must serve as a living room, furnish the characters and the action in Langston Hughes' *Simple Takes a Wife.*

Hughes takes us with Simple as he moves among his friends, understanding their problems, discussing his own, working hard to get a divorce so that he can marry Joyce. To pay for this divorce from his estranged wife in Baltimore, Simple explains that it took "a whole lot of NOT having what you want, to get what you want most." But most of Simple's conversations range far from the purely personal. Simple doesn't think Negroes have made as much progress as some say. "I tell them," says Simple to his friend, "that white folks can measure their race problem by how far

they have come. But Negroes measure ours by how far we have got to go." He then continues, hitting at the theory of Negro progress that is limited to advancing a few big shots:

"Them white folks are always telling me, 'Isn't it wonderful the progress that's been made amongst your people. Look at Dr. Bunche!'

"All I says is 'Look at me.'"

When it is pointed out to Simple that Negroes can now stay at the Waldorf-Astoria, he answers, "Mr. Semple cannot stay there right now—because Mr. Semple ain't able." And he will not accept the explanation that his disability is due to money and not race for "if I were not of the colored race, smart as I am, I would have money." Nor is Simple satisfied with two Negroes in Congress when "there ought to be *two dozen* colored Congressmen" who aren't there because southern Negroes are not allowed to vote. Reminded of the Supreme Court's mandate against voting restrictions, Simple asks rhetorically:

"Can a Negro take time off from work to go running to the Supreme Court every time the Klan keeps him from voting? We can't enforce no laws by ourselves."

Simple has a word for the cops, too, and in saying it, he uses the Negro folk characteristic of treating a serious problem, like police brutality, with humorous derision. Be-Bop, says Simple, "makes plenty of sense," because it originated "from the police beating Negroes' heads . . . beaten right out of some Negro's head into them horns and saxophones and piano keys. . . ." Policemen, says Simple, are likely to question him any time about "what are you doing in this neighborhood?"

"Then I have to go into my whole pedigree because I am a black man in a white neighborhood. And if my answers do not satisfy them, Bop! Mop! . . . Be-Bop! . . . If they do not hit me they have already hurt my soul."

In Simple, Hughes has found the perfect protagonist for the thousands of racial battles that are fought in conversations in every ghetto throughout the United States. It is a warm and human story of distant relatives arriving unexpectedly and sharing the cubicle of a room until they can get a foot on the ladder of New York life. We share the problems of a young couple falling in love, marrying and rearing their first child in their own one-room home. But we sense the quality of laughing at heartbreak, or being able to "escape" through the humor derived from commonplace situations, of bitterness which evades frustration. For Simple, the composite of Harlem's common man, is not defeated nor dejected, even though the road ahead is not clearly marked.

One thing Simple is irrevocably determined: to be free from jim crow and to avenge the many insults the South has handed him and his people. He dreams one night he was a bird and wishes on awaking he could make the dream true for a while. Among the things he would like to do as a bird is to "just fly *over* the South, stopping only long enough to spread my tail feathers and show my contempt." And musing on the racist "blood theories," Simple twits their proponents:

"Why is Negro blood so much more powerful than any other kind of blood in the world? If a man has Irish blood in him, people will say, 'He's *part* Irish.' If he has a little Jewish blood, they'll say, 'He's *half* Jewish.' But if he has just a small bit of colored blood in him, Bam!—'He's a Negro!' . . . Now, that is what I do not understand—why one drop is so powerful. . . ."

I suspect it is the author who steers Simple away from more basic political topics, keeping the discussions on the level of "race talk." For there was a much wider topical range in Hughes' first volume about Simple—*Simple Speaks His Mind.* Whereas in the first book, Simple had some sharp observations to make on the Un-American Activities Committee, he now limits his discussion of Congress to the absence of Negroes. And it should be remembered that Hughes, since the appearance of *Simple Speaks His Mind,* has been a "guest" of Sen. Joseph McCarthy.

It is also notable that Hughes before McCarthy did not fare nearly as well as did Simple before the Un-Americans, for Simple really "told off" that "old Georgia chairman" with some biting comments on jimcrow. Simple still has bite in discussing jimcrow, but he "talks at the big gate," out of earshot of the oppressors, to his anonymous friend. However, Simple remains a healthy representative of Negro ghetto dwellers continuing in every way they know to struggle for first class American citizenship.

I hope that in future stories, Hughes will let us see and hear Simple (who is a poorly-paid worker) in his relationships with other workers and his employers. So far we have only seen him after work, relaxing over a beer, discussing his and other Negroes' problems, within the relationship of Negro to Negro. Hughes should give us more of Simple's sides, for as one colloquy in *Simple Speaks His Mind* went:

"'Life is not so simple,' cautioned his friend on one of Simple's propositions.

"'Neither am I,' said Simple."

The present volume exhibits an artistic weakness: Hughes combines the reporter's eye, the novelist's ear, but misses the third dimension of the ghetto scene as reflected in the real characters of whom Simple is a composite. One feels that Simple and those around him can do little more than complain, futilely, of the oppressive jimcrow conditions under which they live. Despite the charm and the many nuggets of wisdom in this panorama of Harlem, the reader can conclude that Simple and his friends will remain as they are indefinitely.

It would be a mistake to say that this makes *Simple Takes a Wife* poor or insubstantial reading. On the contrary, with all of his weaknesses, Hughes has given us a vivid picture of Negro life and its richness, a picture which is sharply opposed to the "arty" degeneracy of writers like Richard Wright and Ralph Ellison. For even though he is held under wraps by the author, Simple is a healthy, probing, salty young Negro, a pleasant relief from Ellison's *Invisible Man* and Wright's fascistic killer in *The Outsider*. Simple may not show us the way to the future, but he certainly gives us a seldom seen and delightful picture of today.

William Harrison
"Book Review"
Boston Chronicle, 5
September 1953, p. 6

Mr. Hughes has no rival as the foremost American Negro creative writer, for he is so many laps ahead that others can scarcely see the dust of his galloping mount. Moreover with him the race is continuous, and his pace never slackens. He is as prolific as he is original, "not in the paltry sense of being new," to use the late G. K. Chesterton's phrase. Like all folk-characters Harlem's Jesse B. Semple, otherwise known as Simple, is too real to be new. There is much of the hardy perennial about Simple, whose cartoon opposite number is Ollie Harrington's Mr. Bootsie, and whose counterparts in actuality abound in the bars and rooming-houses where the less sophisticated Negro Americans congregate. Quite literally, Simple's number is legion. He is representative and typical, being a sort of spiritual and even intellectual statistical average of our people.

In recounting Simple's reaction to the ordinary events of life as it passes in a Negro ghetto among persons who are never invited to interracial teas even during Brotherhood Week, Mr. Hughes invests his character with such authentic human dignity that the various reports hardly seem fiction, but appear to be biography. That is why letters have been addressed to Jesse B. Semple in care of the *Chicago Defender,* where Mr. Hughes published some of the pieces in this volume.

As in previous narratives Simple's terse comments on a wide variety of topics often cause convulsive laughter, and sometimes have a satiric sting when they touch barbarous racial prejudice in all its nefarious aspects. The subject of intermarriage, for example, is discussed without recourse to evasions.

Here is the humor of the pavements, audible on Lenox Ave., in the locutions of these who have not had the advantages of considerable formal instruction in the niceties of English grammar. Mr. Hughes reveals through the agency of Simple's refugee nephew from Dixie the unquenchable desire of the Negro masses for education. His revelation is a hundred times more effective than most academic treatises.

John W. Parker
"More of Simple and His Milieu"
Phylon, 14 (Fourth Quarter 1953), 441–2

But for *The First Book of Negroes* which falls in the area of Juvenile literature, Langston Hughes' new book, *Simple Takes a Wife,* adds up to his fourth consecutive study based wholly or partially upon the romance and the tragedy that characterize the Harlem scene, and his second to stem from the exploits of one Mr. Jesse B. Semple and his social milieu. Between *Simple Speaks His Mind* (1950) and the present volume, came *Montage of a Dream Deferred* (1951), a poetic portrait of a community and a people in transition, and *Laughing to Keep from Crying* (1952), a collection of short sketches that disclose the way of life in Harlem and in widely-separated Negro ghettoes throughout the world.

Taken together, this series of investigations points up Mr. Hughes' abiding interest in Harlem, the scene of his departure as poet in 1922, and his faith in the potentialities of the Negro theme, aspects of which have yet to be tapped. Likewise, they may suggest the author's abandonment, temporarily at least, of poetry in favor of prose as a means of penetrating life in Harlem, obviously "all mixed up." *Simple Takes a Wife*, like the volumes that precede it, reveals the touch of a sympathetic hand; it is the product of an author whose background and whose sense of fellow feeling lead him to laugh with the Harlem dweller, not at him.

The book divides into three groups of stories—"Honey in the Evening," "Manna from Heaven" and "Sassafras in Spring," but these divisions are almost entirely formal and have little or nothing to do with holding the collection together. And the fifty-six sketches that comprise the volume make easy and for the most part fascinating reading; a goodly number of them exist primarily for the purpose of providing a social situation in which Simple is led to "out Herod Herod" and thus to reveal the true character of his personality.

The theme is not always easy to isolate. One finds in varying degrees fear, frustration, love, hate, inconsistency, hypocrisy and much of the goodness and the evil that is concealed in the hearts and minds of men. And as to the matter of plot, the book has a beginning and an end, scarcely anything else. The reason for this narrows down to one word, one character—Simple. Almost from the beginning, with one digression after another, he gets completely out of hand and wanders all over the place. His exploits so completely dominate the scene that the reader is likely to forget all else. Even Joyce, the "uncombed woman," like Isabel and Zarita, passes merely as a sharply-etched character sketch designed for the most part to enhance the inner nature of the protagonist. Obviously, Simple's irregular movement from woman to woman and from bar to bar will work havoc with any well-designed plot novel; and that is what happens in the case of *Simple Takes a Wife*. Such unity as the volume exhibits is contingent upon the unity of action of Simple, who invariably turns out to be consistently inconsistent.

Simple's total conduct which Hughes neither justifies nor condemns leaves one wondering. Following her seventh proposal, he married Joyce because he loved her and because he wanted to escape Harlem's Rooming House Set, but he never took the trouble even to think through the forces at play in his own life that were leading inevitably to his undoing. Harlem, with "everything he wanted from A to Z," was good at least by comparison with the by-racial set-up in Virginia, so that was that. It was Harlem, then some more Harlem, and then some more. He somehow refused ever to entertain the thought that away from the "great dark city," he could be simple again—simple and clean and pure. Perhaps it is just as well that we see Simple and Joyce to a hard-earned wedding and then forget the whole thing.

If *Simple Takes a Wife* did nothing more than to lengthen the shadow of Simple it would add considerably to the stature of Mr. Hughes as a man of letters, for despite the fact that Mr. Simple was born in a typewriter, without benefit even of a midwife, he has managed to assume the proportions of a person more real than many of those one meets on the street. In the role of a real person, he invites comparison with such rich folk characters as Appleseed Johnny and Uncle Remus. The letters fans address directly to him rather than to his creator attest to the flesh and blood character of his being. But the book goes farther—much farther; it discloses Hughes' adeptness in the handling of humor both of characterization and of situation and his mastery of the simple narrative as a literary medium. Stylistic niceties abound, and from cover to cover one finds a generous sprinkling of wit and repartee. Here as elsewhere the typical Hughes spontaneity, sensitiveness, and charm are evident.

Despite his persistent good nature and the modesty of his approach in his newest volume, *Simple Takes a Wife,* it is invigorating to note that over the years, Hughes has remained true to his ideal of a social poet—a writer who probes into the problems of the here and now rather than turn

out long dissertations on sunshine and roses, sweetness and light. *Simple Takes a Wife* comes as another major portrait of present-day Harlem to crown Langston Hughes' many years of effort as a creative artist.

Stanley E. Read "Book Review: *Simple Takes a Wife*" *International House Quarterly,* 17 (Autumn 1953), 258

Most readers of *The Quarterly* will already know the name of Langston Hughes as poet, prose writer and a leading spokesman for that great minority group composed of American Negroes. Some readers, too, will have the pleasure of remembering him as a former resident of the International House at the University of Chicago.

In this, his latest work, he continues recording the somewhat tempestuous career and impulsive comments of his warmhearted and warmblooded character, Mr. Jesse B. Semple (nicknamed Simple), to whom he has already devoted an earlier volume, *Simple Speaks His Mind.*

The publishers refer to *Simple Takes a Wife* as a novel. This is an unfortunate misnomer, for there is no plot—that is unless Mr. Semple's attempts to save $133.34 to pay for one-third of his divorce constitute a plot. Personally, I don't think they do. Actually, the book is a series of dialogues between two thoroughly delightful people—the fictional Simple, a witty, uninhibited Harlem Negro of middle age, and the omnipresent author, schol-

456

arly, controlled, tolerant, philosophical. The setting for the dialogues is nearly always the same—a warm, smoke-filled bar, where men relax over their beer, unless temporarily distracted by such delightful bar-drifters as Zarita, who holds such a fascination for Simple and who makes it difficult in the extreme for him to save that much-wanted divorce money.

The importance of the book lies in the subject matter of the dialogues, and its charm in the unrestricted play of Simple's imagination and the witty warmth of his conversation. Simple is the talker; the author, except for the occasional philosophical interjection, is the listener. And Simple just overflows with talk—talk about landladies and rooming houses; wives—past and future; balls and burials; second-hand clothes; beer and whisky and gin; food— all kinds of food, but especially greens: "mustard greens, collard greens, turnip greens, dandelions, dock, beet-tops, lamb's tongue, pepper grass, sheep cress, also poke. Good old mixed greens! Spinach or chard, refined greens! Any kind of fresh greens." But most of all Simple talks about race, especially the difficulties encountered by the Negro because he is a Negro; restrictions, segregation, discrimination. And here, an uneducated, simple man, he is frequently a pathetic figure, questioning the justice of the world in which he lives, the workings of a constitution that proclaims man free and equal in a society that does not always provide real freedom and equality. Here it is, too, that the author tries to help Simple and his people, as well as those who are not of Simple's race, towards tolerance and understanding.

Some sections of the book appeared earlier in the *Chicago Defender* and in *Phylon*. Perhaps for this reason it is at times repetitious; but it is nearly always bright and amusing, and can help many of us to a somewhat better understanding of one of the continent's most serious sociological problems.

"Book Reviews"
Crisis, 60 (October 1953), 506

Simple Takes a Wife concerns the frets of Mr. Jesse B. Semple in his efforts to get a divorce so that he might marry Joyce. Of course, he marries her in the end. He is still speaking his mind as in the previous *Simple Speaks His Mind*, but this time it is mostly about women, marriage, and Harlem rooming houses. While he is beset by the usual restrictions of ghetto living, Simple takes these things in his stride and always manages to get in some pungent comment to show up the ridiculousness of race prejudice. Since he does not always have luck with his girl friends, much of his talk is about their petty squabblings, his frustrations, and the vicissitudes of Harlem rooming-house life. The atmosphere is strictly Harlem, and so is the idiom. An entertaining novel with many vivid descriptions that bring alive Harlem streets, bars, and cares, although Simple's forced punning is sometimes annoying.

Mabel C. Knight
"How Things Are with Simple"
Catholic Interracialist, 12 (November 1953), 7

This is a book of how things are, not how they ought to be, with Mr. Jesse B. Semple, popularly known as Simple, who came from Virginia and now lives in Harlem. He is not "The Negro," but he has problems which are common to many Harlem men as well as some which are common to many big-city dwellers. They are set forth in vigorous dialogues between Simple and the narrator, usually at a bar. They report conversation with Isabel, Simple's would-be divorced wife; Joyce, his more cultured fiancée; Zarita, who is always around; F.D., Simple's nephew who has benefited from the improvement in Virginia's schools since Simple's time there; landladies, hardbitten and hardbiting. These people come to life. They are "respectable" people, hardened by their struggles to keep that way.

Some of the questions they discuss are "Why is be-bop?" "Would you like F.D. to go to a Negro college?" "Why so many kinds of 3 cent stamps?" "Should heat be turned on because there are babies in rooming houses?"

A "spunky little nurse" got a "yes" to that one at least the days when she visited, although the landlady had laid down the law against babies in the house. Difficulties in leading a decent family life in slums are brought out here more clearly than in any sociology book. Simple feels the lack of housing or a living wage or a secure job or a Christian concept of sex and family life, but he never expresses it in such dull terms. Concrete and humorous stories are his way.

This is a Pagliacci type of book. On the surface it seems "The funniest book of the year" to the *Baltimore Afro-American*. And its language has been called by the London *Times* "Eccentric and splendid. Mr. Hughes exploits to the full the vigor of the Harlem idiom."

For people who go below the surface, the book will give new understanding of some of their Negro brothers in Christ. They will feel new interest in promoting

housing so that Simple and Joyce won't be separated by rooming house difficulties as he and Isabel were and so that they can have some "little old babies" too.

Philip Burnham
"Critics' Choice for Christmas"
Commonweal, 59 (4 December 1953), 236

Jesse Semple is a thoroughly aware, reasonably educated, but resolutely free Negro. He balances delicately, but one hundred per cent confidently, between hearty adjustment and hearty disadjustment to a world which neither he nor his race ever made—except, to be sure, for marvelously vivid sections of upper Manhattan Island and their extensions into the cosmopolitan countryside. Jesse Simple came to Harlem, U.S.A. from back home in Virginia, Dixie: a country he knocks with vehemence which only deep and loving nostalgia could create. Jesse knows he likes Harlem. *Simple Takes a Wife* is the second poetic and sympathetic and funny and realistic chronicle of the lives and conversations of Simple, taken from Langston Hughes' column in the *Chicago Defender*. If your neighbor hasn't yet made this friend, now is a good time.

Checklist of Additional Reviews

"Weekly Record: Hughes, Langston," *Publishers Weekly*, 163 (16 May 1953), 2044.

Rev. L. Gillespie, "Community Relations," *Cleveland Plain Dealer,* 7 June 1953, p. 13B.

"Half Dozen Novels Give Varieties of Americana," *Los Angeles Times,* part 4, 7 June 1953, p. 12.

"Three New Ones Laugh at Big City," *Miami Herald,* 5 July 1953, p. 4F.

Walter Spearman, "Literary Lantern: 'Unfair Sex,'" *Charlotte Observer,* 12 July 1953, p. 12C.

THE SWEET FLYPAPER OF LIFE

Almena Lomax
"Book Review"
Los Angeles Tribune, 11 November 1955, p. 9

This commentator has never been an admirer of Langston Hughes, except in the isolated instance, a poem here and there, and Part I of his autobiography, the title of which we have long since forgotten.

Trying to pin this disillusionment down, we think it is because he always seemed no more to us than a folklorist, a reporter and not an interpretative one, either, a photographer, maybe, a fellow who went around recording for Negroes what they said and were and did, without any more idea than his subjects of what it all meant, what it added up to, the why and wherefore.

It is ironic, therefore, that in the one book in which Langston Hughes has the forethought to arm himself with, not a camera, but better yet a marvelously articulate cameraman, in the book in which there is the least of Hughes, we should like him best, and feel that at last he has added up the why and wherefore and has emerged with something more than folklore, some of life, itself.

This is a charming little book, one which we can even imagine you, dear *Tribune* readers, whose reading proclivities we frankly think nothing of, buying, reading, picking up again and again, perhaps never wholly tiring of. Such is the advantage over words of pictures, when they are "really real" and really life. They leap at you, smack you in the face, saying something with no effort on your part, which is something words do not do; also, they say something different each time. When they are good pictures, they are almost as multi-

dimensional as live people. These, we might say, are great pictures.

This is a strictly Hughes story, really no more than a character sketch of an old woman, of the type whom we have come to know that Langston Hughes admires, above all men, somebody small, probably black, wiry, gutty, salty, gallant, philosophical . . . the "Life for me ain't been no crystal stair"-type, with a dash of Mehitable who had a "dance in the old girl, yet."

Possibly if you could read the manuscript, which is entirely a monologue, without the pictures, it might not be quite so complete a document of a woman's life.

But you can't read the words without looking at the pictures . . . leastways we didn't try . . . who would want to? . . . and you end up having the complete epic of life in Harlem . . . the why, the wherefore . . . and something which we are not too sure Hughes has ever been able to say for himself, a relatedness of that life to life, itself.

This is not, we might point out, the dilemma summed up by Mr. George Lamning, the British West Indian writer of novels which we were never able to read. *The Castle of My Skin,* for instance— lovely title, but we could never wade through the density of words, the fugues of words, introspective, lovely sombre thoughts, funnelling down into the hero until we felt as lost as Alice in Wonderland, falling through an endless tunnel in the earth.

Talking a commoner type of English to the students at Atlanta University last week than he has talked thus far in his novels, Mr. Lamning said the dilemma of the Negro writer is that he can't relate himself to the world he lives in.

This, you might say, has been the dilemma, particularly of Mr. Hughes, as a writer, and is the dilemma which has kept him the "laughing boy" of Negro literature for all the years of his writing career, dulling his talent with diffidence and self-deprecation, hinting at truths which he should have been expressing outright.

But there is nothing diffident, deprecatory, nor mute about *The Sweet Flypaper of Life*. Here is a full lecture on life as it is lived in Harlem, and the lecture says of Harlem: Life there is real, rounded, and fully packed, nothing shadowy, fragmentary, nor disoriented from the stuff of life, and none of the real living hemmed in appreciably by being black.

The story begins right on the cover with the arrival of a telegram for "Sister Mary Bradley ... at 113 W. 134th St., New York" from "The Lord," telling her to "'Come Home,'" a particular bit of ante-bellum corn, incidentally, which we wouldn't expect the new-found Hughes to rid himself of a tendency toward, all in one easy lesson.

Being a doughty old dame, Mary Bradley tells the Lord's messenger to take the Lord's wire on back because she isn't ready yet, "ain't no ways tired," and the rest of the book is sort of a decalogue on why Mary isn't ready, a recital which in spirit is so familiar that it will immediately put her "one" with all the women who know their little worlds hinge on them, and who can't take a trip, or who hope the baby won't come tonight and send them traipsing off to the hospital before they have fully prepared for all eventualities, or who, whether anybody writes a book about it or not, probably reject the summons of St. Peter with an "I'm not ready yet, Lord. There's so much here for me to do ... I'm needed around here so. . . ."

Among the things Mary Bradley has to do is "look after Ronnie Bell," a winsome lass with big eyes whom you know Mary has identified with herself and wants to keep on scrubbing floors for, so she can give her "some of the advantages" she never had. And she's got to set her mind to rest about Rodney, her easy-does-it "favorite grandson," whom everybody

but her and his girl "downs," but about whom she knows "there's something." How could she die not seeing what that "something" is?

You can see that she wants to stick around and help her youngest daughter Melinda, who has been "married four years and got five children. . . . Two is twins," and who is "getting ready to populate the colored race again." You can see that Melinda's particularly contented-looking baby who "never cries, except when it's not setting on a lap," or Jerry, a blood-thirsty demon of two who "wants a gun that shoots both ways at once," are all special concerns of Mary's, who leave her no time to die, as well as "this integration the Supreme Court has decreed," about whose workings she is curious, particularly in South Carolina, which she was planning to visit once more before she dies. And last but not least, there is the mildly attractive proposition of the man downstairs, whose wife is dead, and "who's crazy about children" and "I kinder like him myself," and "Do you reckon I'm too old to get married again?"

To make a long story short, says Mrs. Mary Bradley, standing by her "front stoop" in her "best clothes" and with the dignity of her mien in her black hat and black dress with the gold hoop earrings and thingamajig on her bosom, belying the veined, big knuckled testimony to humility and oil of her hands, "I got my feet caught in the sweet flypaper of life—and I'll be dogged if I want to get loose."

This is the story which we can sketch in for you, but the story of Mr. DeCarava's marvelous pictures defies description. Suffice to say that it is the first pictorial of the Harlems of the United States, whether found in the pages of a Negro newspaper, the motion picture, or newsreel, which made the writer glad to be alive, and not ashamed or set apart in the freakish, phony existence which people tell us is Negro life.

Here is all of the realism and the redemption of a family album.

"Our Opinions: *Sweet Flypaper of Life*" New York Age Defender, 12 November 1955, [p. 10]

It doesn't take any particular talent to put some words together, or coin a clever phrase, and just about everybody admits that "One picture is worth a thousand words." But it isn't often that words and pictures are wed together so warmly, and with such passion and inspiration as in a literary offering by photographer Roy De-Carava, a young Guggenheim Fellow, and our own poet laureate, Langston Hughes, under the title: *The Sweet Flypaper of Life.*

The Sweet Flypaper of Life describes, in words and pictures, what the authors have seen and known about the people of Harlem, their people, and you'll want to sing, to cheer and to cry as their tale unfolds. "New York is not like back down South, with nothing happening outside," they observe. "In Harlem something is happening all the time, people are going every which-a-way. No matter which way you look, up or down, somebody is always heading somewhere, something is happening."

The Harlem of DeCarava and Hughes didn't "just happen"; it is the fruit of blood, sweat and tears shed by a determined few through the dark days of its history. In a small way, the *New York Age Defender* is currently doffing its hat to those fighters and builders of the community, through a series of articles entitled: "The Harlem Story." Through a happy co-

incidence, *The Sweet Flypaper of Life* is also scheduled for national release on November 22. We believe that both literary efforts will be a welcome addition to every Harlemite's library.

Gilbert Millstein "While Sister Mary Sticks Around" New York Times Book Review, 27 November 1955, p. 5

This small, well-designed book of text by the poet Langston Hughes and pictures by the photographer Roy DeCarava is a delicate and lovely fiction-document of life in Harlem, told, with astonishing verisimilitude, in the words of an elderly Negro woman, a grandmother ten times over, and seen, with a corresponding truth, through her bright old eyes. Its tone is by turns quiet and lively, its rhythms are soft and emphatic, its insights are constant—the very musings of just such a worn, optimistic lady in a decent black dress and a hat long since out of style.

[...]

There is a tendency in a good many books of text and pictures for the one to be at wide variance with the other and for no true organic relationship to exist between the two. When this is the case, when a link has been forced, the text invariably becomes pretentious and acquires a portentousness that is almost never justified by the pictures. The photographs themselves seem then even less integrated and so arbitrarily selected as to have only a highly private meaning, if any at all. But Mr. DeCarava's photographs are peculiarly apposite, without being merely a collaborative effort. In this book, the story and the pictures are not so much dependent on each other as they are justifications of each other.

The text weaves through the photographs; the photographs reflect, with marvelous understanding, what Sister Mary Bradley is saying and thinking and the whole effect is one of fine unity. A book like *The Sweet Flypaper of Life* should be bought by a great many persons and read by a good many more. It is probably hortatory to say so, but the chances are it could accomplish a lot more about race relations than many pounds of committee reports.

Abel.
"Literati: *Sweet Flypaper of Life*"
Variety, 30 November 1955, p. 23

An unusual $1 paperback booklet by Roy DeCarava and Langston Hughes is *The Sweet Flypaper of Life* which is a graphic photo-and-prose tour of Harlem. It is done in a warm, human, understanding style, with no more accent on the sordid environs than necessary.

In fact, the objective seems to be to point up the plus values, and the authors (camera and typewriter) have more than succeeded.

M.W.
"Reviews"
Image, 4 (December 1955), 71

This charming little book is of the handful that attempt to work in the difficult medium of words fused to pictures. The picture *and* text kind of book is still so infrequently seen that readers are in need of instructions on the flyjackets as to how to read them. Visual-minded persons look at all the photographs first, word-minded ones read. But the only way to feel the import of this book is to read the text and the photographs together—otherwise it's like looking at TV with the sound turned off.

The story is a quiet one. The simple narrative is put into the mouth of a grandmother who is caught in the business of living. She enumerates the everyday trivia, the commonplace consequences, the little tragedies, the no bigger joys. Her gift is to make these ordinaries the framework of satisfaction. The writer, well known Langston Hughes, spins the yarn. It's almost anybody's story, hence general, even though told in the first person. Roy DeCarava's photographs, made largely in Harlem, give it the poignancy of individuality.

"Now you take Rodney"—the words appear beside the photograph of a man and in a trice he is economically described, outward appearance, character and all. The same economy turns the grandmother's middle daughter into a person, the youngest into a housewife, their husbands into fathers and their children are instantly real. The camera tells us in a quick glance why the grandmother worries and likes the no-account Rodney best of all.

The subtle, the almost exquisite interplay of text and photographs as they roll out the story together is best expressed between the grandmother and Rodney. She says in words, folk-philosophywise what she likes; the photographs explain why. This exchange of roles, for we normally expect the words to explain the unseen reasons, is a major reason for the delightfulness of *The Sweet Flypaper of Life*.

Best Sellers, 15 (1 December 1955), 257

A disarmingly charming plea for mutual understanding in race relations is this brief, but effective little book of photographs linked and illumined by the text of poet Langston Hughes. Sister Mary Bradley, who lives in Harlem, New York, taking care of her children and children's children, tells the Lord's messenger to get right back on his bike and take that telegram of summons back with him, "because I am not prepared to go. . . . I ain't no ways tired. . . . I done got my feet caught in the sweet flypaper of life . . . (but) . . . When I get through with my pots and pans. . . ."

Sister Bradley is worried about her grandchild Rodney, chiefly. But she feels there is some good in him; it's only those streets that seem to generate trouble. Most of her other children are doing nicely and are nice, themselves. She will reveal a great deal about Harlem and its inhabitants to all who take the trouble to read her reflections, so beautifully illustrated by Roy De-Carava's perceptive camera.

"Happiness in Harlem" *New York Amsterdam News*, 3 December 1955, p. 8

This is not a book review but we feel that a comment on a new book by Langston Hughes is in order because Mr. Hughes is the "poet of Harlem" and because his *The Sweet Flypaper of Life* relates some of the happier phases of life in our community.

All too often, outsiders get the impression that life in this area is just a series of fights and numbers playing and loud-talking and dirty ash cans. In this new book we follow the activities of a Harlem family through the eyes of a lively old grandmother and get the rare opportunity to find our friends and neighbors portrayed in fiction as the real life and blood characters we know them to be.

Harlem is more than run down tenement houses and alleys filled with garbage. All of its residents don't clutter up the sidewalks and live by out-smarting the social welfare inspectors.

There is family life and parents who love and work for their children and children who go to school and church and dream of becoming solid citizens. This new glance at genuine happiness in Harlem is a welcome relief from the overdoses of drabness and frustration which writers so often use when telling the so-called Harlem story.

James Hicks
"Big Town"
Baltimore Afro-American, 3 December 1955, p. 13

Langston Hughes has a new book out called *The Sweet Flypaper of Life.* The book is typically Langston Hughes, which is about the highest praise I can give. But while you're laughing or loving with Langston, take a look at the pictures in the book.

It contains some of the best photography I've ever seen, bar none. The work is done by Roy DeCarava, a Guggenheim photographer. Prettiest picture in the book is a study of Danlyn Lee, one of the most sexy looking gals in Harlem.

Mary Chilton Chapman
"Books in Brief: Harlem Photos Are Expressive"
Charleston [W. Va.] *Gazette's State Magazine,* 4 December 1955, p. 19M

People look out at you from every page of this remarkable little book of photographs-with-text. Some of them look accusingly, some joyously, some sullenly, some indifferently. Their eyes are hard to ignore.

The setting is Harlem. The people are Negroes. Some of them are striving for a better life—some of them are perfectly content—some of them have given up caring.

Pictured here are vibrant youth and ex-hausted age. Most of all, pictured here are children. Many of them are poor in worldly goods but almost all are rich in happiness.

The text is fictional, but the pictures are real. The words—although they seem barely needed in many cases—are chosen from the warp and woof of a daily existence which, as Hughes writes about it, is pretty much like life everywhere—sometimes good and sometimes bad.

D.L.C.
"Stuck with It, They Find Life Has Sweet Taste"
Hartford Times, 10 December 1955, p. 18

This is an experiment in makeup, and the result is a slim, arresting volume in which pictures and words complement each other.

The story of Sister Mary Bradley who was too busy with the business of living to die begins right on the cover. A pair of eloquent eyes looking out over the type stab the consciousness of the prospective reader even before he takes the book from the shelf.

This is a fine item for the bedside table or an adult's Christmas stocking—wonderful for the doctor's or dentist office, too. It makes one forget his troubles reading about people who have worse ones and still can be glad to be stuck up in the sweet flypaper of living.

T.S.
"Picture Book on Harlem Is Masterpiece"
Air Force Times Magazine, 10 December 1955, p. M6

Photographer Roy DeCarava and writer Langston Hughes have teamed up to produce a work of art, a minor masterpiece. The book is a description, in words and pictures, of life in Harlem.

By presenting the life and feelings of one woman and her family, the authors have successfully presented the lives and feelings of many people. For once, the theory that you can present the "whole" by presenting the "specific" succeeds. This is an excellent piece of work. The text jibes well with the photographs and the photographs are superb.

James N. Rhea
"Things Are Wrong, Getting Better and Must Get Better"
Providence Journal, part 6, 11 December 1955, p. 10

[...]

Mr. Hughes writes with his tongue in his cheek a good bit of the time. When Sister Bradley describes the gay excitement of a particular Harlem girl all dressed-up for a party, the accompanying picture shows the prettied one standing in the center of one of Harlem's ugly littered courts. He shows you Harlemites looking easygoing and happy frequently, but in the same scenes you won't miss the silent comment: Things are wrong, getting better, and must get better. DeCarava's pictures are works of art, no less.

Lewis Gannett
"Book Review: New Marriage of Arts"
New York Herald Tribune, 13 December 1955, p. 25

Here, finally, is an unpretentious little book, *The Sweet Flypaper of Life,* in which words are so married to pictures that you cannot rightly say that the pictures illustrate the text or the text explains the pictures. They are one whole: the meditation of Sister Mary Bradley, of W. 134th St. in Harlem, whose blues "roll like thunder in a rocky sky." She worries about her grandson Rodney, who never gets "integrated with neither white nor colored, nor with work." But she knows that "reforming some folks is like trying to boil a pig in a coffeepot—the possibilities just ain't there." She herself "done got her feet caught in the sweet flypaper of life." Langston Hughes' words and Roy DeCarava's photographs achieve a harmony which is more than poetry or photography alone, but its own kind of art.

[...]

George B. Wright
"Photography: A Yea-saying Book, a Pro-human Show"
Village Voice [New York], 14 December 1955, p. 9

Those wistful eyes above the column are now staring out from the jacket of a new book, one which is small enough to fit into your pocket and big enough to fill your heart. *The Sweet Flypaper of Life* combines photographs made by Roy DeCarava on his Guggenheim Fellowship with a fictional text by Langston Hughes.

The theme is Harlem and the problems and victories of its people. No, that's not exactly right. This is a yea-saying about all of human life.

The photographs are a mixture of the warm and the stark, the tender and the slightly terrifying—in short, very like life itself. They are strongly felt and tightly composed. In actuality, they were made of many scenes and families, related only by geographic accident. Langston Hughes has selected and pulled them together with a fictional text, as if these people were a family, its friends and neighbors.

They do become a family—our family.

This is photography, used as it should be used. If any of the above sounds as if this book had a "message," don't be misled. Of course it has, and one which some day may actually penetrate into the Confederate States. What is much more to the point, you will enjoy this and it will remain with you, warmly, for a long time. I wish I could send the book to everyone I know as a Christmas card.

Robert Hatch
"Closing Notes"
Nation, 181 (17 December 1955), 538

Despite a title that might have come off the advertising mill, this is a small work of quality. The pictures are what make it so. The story—an old Negro woman musing about her Harlem children and grandchildren, with an occasional ogle at her own youth—is perceptive and tender, but also a little cute and patronizing, as though Hughes were no longer in touch with his world. But the pictures are in touch; they are alight with affection and amusement, intimate without the clinical prying of much candid photography.

Thomas A. Webster
"The Joy of Life in Harlem"
Kansas City Star, 17 December 1955, p. 16

This paper-back, pocket-size book, portrays in prose and pictures the joy of life in Harlem, as well as some of its problems, as two artists record it with camera and words. The text is fictional, the names of characters false, but the scenes are real, interesting pages from the life of the almost half million Negroes who are crammed into Harlem.

This potpourri of Harlem life is intended to show the joy and warmth of living between the East and the Harlem rivers, from Morningside Heights to

Washington Heights, since as the author says, "we've had so many books about how bad life is" in Harlem.

There are characters like Sister Mary Bradley, who refuses to sign for the telegram sent to summon her to her heavenly home because, as she says, "I done got my feet caught in the sweet flypaper of life and I'll be dogged if I want to get loose."

Life in Harlem is a constant shuffle—something is always happening, somebody is always headed somewhere. They are climbing up and down subway steps, partying in basement apartments, listening at night to street corner preachers, getting up each morning and going to work, knowing that today will be like yesterday and tomorrow. Life is hard, but it has its rewards and satisfactions.

"I'd rather be a lamp-post in Harlem than a king in Mississippi" is no idle boast to many of the people of Harlem.

Roy DeCarava, a young Guggenheim fellow whose prints hang in several museums, provided the documentary photographs, and Langston Hughes wrote the narrative.

gro life in upper Manhattan. Hughes' statement best describes the quality of the tiny volume. "We've had so many books about how bad life [in Harlem] is," he says. "Maybe it's time to have one showing how good it is."

The meaning of the delightful provocative title will be found in the completely charming text. It is Mary Bradley, mother and grandmother of a large brood who, in telling the story of and describing the members of her family, is inspired to use the words. When she receives a wired summons from St. Peter to "come home," she refuses to obey it, for life, in spite of its hardships and problems, is still too good to leave. In speech that holds the gentle rhythms of poetry, she explores the color and variety of the persons dear to her. Closest to her heart is her favorite "grandboy," the brooding and difficult one, who came to live with her when his parents turned him out.

There are probably less than a thousand words in the lyric narrative, but with the wonderfully human portraits with which Roy DeCarava illustrates them they glowingly add up to a world of experience. Each man is a poet of his people, one with language, the other with his camera.

Rose Feld
"The Warm Human Essence of Harlem"
New York Herald Tribune Book Review, 18 December 1955, p. 3

Orville Prescott
"Books of the Times"
New York Times, 23 December 1955, p. 15

Langston Hughes has been called "the O. Henry of Harlem." With Roy DeCarava, brilliant young photographer whose work has found a place in museums, he has collaborated on a little gem of a book that captures the warm human essence of Ne-

[. . .]

Two little books that also convey some of the spirit of Christmas are Paul Horgan's *The Saintmaker's Christmas Eve* and *The Sweet Flypaper of Life*, by Roy De-Carava and Langston Hughes. The first is a Christmas story and a beautifully written one. The second is only indirectly a book for Christmas, but its deeply moving affirmation of the joy of living, of a fine woman's love for others, and of the essential humanness of some of our less fortunate fellow citizens could, if widely read, help to spread goodwill toward black men among white men.

[. . .]

The Sweet Flypaper of Life is an extraordinary fusion of Roy DeCarava's superb photographs and Langston Hughes' expert text. I cannot recall any other book in which the two elements of pictures and words were so artfully mixed. It is impossible to tell whether the great emotional impact of this little book is produced more by the pictures or by the words.

The words are those of an old Negro woman in Harlem who was sick but did not want to die. . . .

[. . .]

Sister Mary had to look after lots of others, too, children and grandchildren, good ones and bad ones. She understood, forgave and loved them all. And she loved living itself, not expecting too much of people or of life.

[. . .]

The text of *Sweet Flypaper of Life* rings with the poetry of folk speech and is written by a man who has been writing poetry for more than thirty years. The pictures are wonderful portraits and ironic commentaries on the text, for they reveal the sordid slums in which the characters live.

[J.] Saunders Redding
"Book Review"
Afro-American Magazine,
24 December 1955, p. 2

"When the bicycle of the Lord bearing His messenger with a telegram for Sister Mary Bradley saying 'Come home' arrived at 113 West 134th Street, New York City, Sister Bradley said, 'Boy, take that wire right on back to St. Peter because I am not prepared to go. I might be a little sick, but as yet I ain't no ways tired.'"

Thus begins another of those deceptively simple folk discourses that Langston Hughes, having temporarily—and I hope Temporarily—turned his back on poetry, has made (for my money) his very own.

In the ecological sense, the colored "folk" are passing out of American life. This is the destiny (a word I prefer to "fate," which has a dark and ominous meaning) of "folk," and it is a proper destiny. But in the case of colored "folk" are pass-hastened by the dynamics of society.

It is hastened, particularly in America, by a process called acculturation. This reviewer happens to think that acculturation is a good process for folk to pass through: he does not quarrel with it.

But this reviewer also thinks that "folk" contribute many things of much value to the society that mothers and harbors them. Austria would not be the Austria of smaltz and waltz and dream (Listen to the violins! Hear the Blue Danube!) but for the Gypsy "folk."

Imagine Spain without the Moors; India without the Parsees. And America without the colored people.

What these "folk" contribute to the mother society should not pass without a memorial—without being enshrined in its own idiom, set forth in its own pattern, recognized in its true identity.

Otherwise history forgets, as it has already forgotten, or nearly forgotten, Black Samson of Brandywine, Chinook of Canada, and the Obijways.

Almost thirty years ago a poet wrote:

Thy son, I have returned in time to
    thee. . . .
Though late, O soil, it is not too late
    yet
To catch thy plaintive soul, leaving,
    soon gone,
Leaving, to catch thy plaintive soul
    soon gone.

That is the tradition Hughes has resumed in these discourses. He is a son returned in time to the folk soul, that is passing; and this it is that gives his work its special value. This it is that contributes to its very special enchantment.

Contributes to, but is by no means all. For art is here—and not just peripherally. Art, indeed, is the core of it—and art so simple—as all true folk is—that one does not always recognize it for what it is, and thinks instead that it is "life."

And this, too, is good. It is the supreme measure of the artist working sincerely in the reality he loves. But creating this illusion of life and of reality is not simple. It is as complex as love, and as hard to achieve as birth.

Sister Mary Bradley now, of course—. But let her speak for herself: "I got plenty of time to come home when I get to be eighty, ninety, or a hundred and one. . . . I done got my feet caught in the sweet flypaper of life."

But Langston Hughes hasn't got "plenty of time"—no man has, even with a guarantee of Methuselah's span—to catch the plaintive soul of a folk leaving, soon gone. I hope Hughes has more time than most, and I hope he continues to make the best of it.

H. E. Clark
"Harlem Life"
Oregon Journal Northwest Living Magazine, 25 December 1955, p. 6M

The Sweet Flypaper of Life is a unique presentation of the thoughts of a single aged resident of New York's Harlem. Seen through her eyes, the reader is shown with a minimum of text and much superb photography the daily life of her friends, relatives and neighbors as they go their ways in the world's greatest city. She faces her daily problems with a philosophical calm, and gladly accepts the simple joys brought to her through living a peaceful and collected existence. Langston Hughes is well-known as a writer, and the pictures taken by Roy DeCarava are really excellent. The combination of the two has worked out a very fine little story.

"The Sweet Flypaper of Life"
Afro Arts and Theatre Spotlight, First Quarter 1956, p. 15

This enchanting little book far exceeds its size in its contribution to a better understanding of a segment of "The Family of Man." Indeed, it is worthy of the exhibition created for the Museum of Modern Art and the recent volume of the same name. (Several pictures from this volume are included.)

But *Sweet Flypaper of Life* will long be remembered as an entity in its own right because of its honest and forthright picture of a family in Harlem, U.S.A. By accentuating the positive, Roy DeCarava has pictured the essence of a family bond. He has been fortunate in having the innermost feelings of this family. If it seems whimsical for an old woman to defer a messenger of death, to allow her time to personally find out how integration is going to work out here on earth—not in heaven. Then, too, there are a few matters pertaining to her family that she just ought to be around to help out with. Not to mention the fact that she still has some more living to do.

Yes, you've seen their faces—or have you? Certainly not in the dearth of films, plays about American life that are seen in the theatre and on TV. Nevertheless, you know them. Of course, because they're just people—people who are deeply concerned about living. They're all too involved to die.

Not since the early illustrated copy of the complete works of Paul Laurence Dunbar has there appeared an adult volume so understanding of the true spirit and nature of a people. This is a book of hope and one that you can feel proud to show to anyone.

That it leaves you wanting to see and hear more about this particular family and friends is all to the good.

The collaborative creations of Langston Hughes and Roy DeCarava should be continued in the sorely needed interpretation of the lives of Afro-American people.

"Book Reviews" *Professional Photographer*, 83 (January 1956), 59

There is nothing to say about this beyond the fact that it is, with a minimum of text because the pictures speak for themselves, a picture story of life in New York City's Harlem. The illustrations are all "candid" of course and, even though the book is printed in gravure the illustrations suffer because skin color, hair and even clothing have been lost against too dark backgrounds. The publishers tell us that Mr. DeCarava "is a young Guggenheim Fellow whose remarkable photographs are in many museums." We have said before that much modern photography leaves us cold, and this is no exception. To us—and we think to most of our readers—photographs like these are little more than snapshots.

V[ictor] P. H[ass] "About Life in Harlem" *Omaha World-Herald Magazine*, 22 January 1956, p. 28G

Roy DeCarava is a young cameraman whose remarkable photographs hang in many American museums. Langston Hughes has been called "the O. Henry of Harlem."

Out of their friendship has come this superlative mating of talent to produce a loving look at life in New York City's Harlem.

This is no mere text by Mr. Hughes to accompany pictures by Mr. DeCarava (or the other way around). Text and pictures here grow out of each other. One would not be complete without the other and together they become a single, exciting work.

It began, Mr. Hughes writes, because "we've had so many books about how bad life is" and he and Mr. DeCarava thought "maybe it's time to have one showing how good it is."

So they fashioned one . . . this little, paperbound volume on an excellent quality paper running to 98 pages only 7x5 in size. Not much to look at as books go, but impressive inside, rich with the juices of life.

A grandmother tells the story. The messenger of the Lord has come with a telegram telling her to "Come home." But she isn't ready. So she wouldn't even sign the message, being "in no way tired" and having her feet still stuck "in the sweet flypaper of life."

She tells you about that life in Harlem, about her family, even about Ronnie who's always hanging around the beer cellars and might come to no good.

These are good people in these pages, gay people, sad people, people worn near to death with work, people just starting out in life, and in inspired words and inspired pictures you come to know them.

We've had hundreds upon hundreds of books with "pictures by————, commentary by————" etc., but not many books with the heart of this one.

Nat Hentoff
"Counterpoint"
Down Beat, 23 (25 January 1956), 28

There is one small picture project recently published I would like to recommend unreservedly. It's *The Sweet Flypaper of Life*. Though not concerned directly with jazz, it should appeal to anyone who digs music and being alive. A marvelously warm, tasteful, and gentle picture of some of the people of Harlem, the book contains superb photographs by Roy DeCarava, a Guggenheim Fellow. The simple honest text is by Langston Hughes.

There are these lines, for example: "Young folks nowadays, I don't understand them. They gets their hair all done up just to go and set and listen to a jukebox." "But now the kids don't lean on the piano no more unless the piano is playing off-time." And there is this blues verse:

My blues ain't pretty.
My blues don't satisfy—
But they can roll like thunder
In a rocky sky.

"New Books"
U.S. Camera, 19 (February 1956), 50

The authors of this fictional document are imaginative and creative young men. Through the perfect blending of words and pictures the authors have told a tender story about life in Harlem. "We've had so many books about how bad life is," Lang-

475

ston Hughes says. "Maybe it is time to have one showing how good it is." Roy De-Carava is a young Guggenheim Fellow whose works are hung in many museums and published in many periodicals, including *U.S. Camera*. Langston Hughes is a writer who has been called the O. Henry of Harlem. The two men have created a work which is worthy of attention and acclaim.

John W. Parker "Parcels of Humanity" *Crisis,* 63 (February 1956), 124–5; with variations also as "Hughes Book Looks into Harlem Homes," *Charlotte Observer,* 26 February 1956, p. 5B, and as "The Bright, Right Side," *Christian Century,* 73 (1 August 1956), 905

Far in excess of that of any other single spot, Harlem both as a place and as a symbol has exerted a steady pull on Langston Hughes' imaginative powers during the nearly three decades of his devotion to *belles lettres*. This has been due in part to Hughes' interest in the Great Dark City as an experiment in urban living and in the fluid character and the ever-shifting emphasis that have rendered it a topic of never-ending discussion. So many studies have concerned themselves solely with the seamy and the pathological side of human existence on the Harlem scene that a book calculated to unearth the sunshine happily blended with the shadow has long been overdue. Such a book is Mr. Hughes' little vignette, *The Sweet Flypaper of Life.*

This Simon and Schuster publication is an intimate exposé of the goings on in the Black Metropolis as seen through the eyes of a worn but a lively grandmother, Sister Mary Bradley, for whom the clock has ticked away many a year. Her simple black dress and hat of the same color, both long since out of style, belie her grip on the here and now. The story gets off in dramatic fashion when the bicycle of the Lord bearing His messenger with a telegram inviting Sister Mary to come home made its appearance at 118 West 134th Street in New York City.

But Sister Mary declined the invitation. Having read the telegram while pretending that she could not locate her glasses, she proceeded to treat the whole incident with complete indifference. "Boy, take that wire right on back to St. Peter," she admonished the messenger, "because I am not prepared to go. I might be a little sick, but I ain't no ways tired." And to herself she reasoned, "I'm so tangled up in living, I ain't got time to die."

And she was. In a musing sort of way, she recounted the problems implicit in the rearing of her sizeable crop of grandchildren. One of them was Rodney for whom she had "ridden a million subways." But Rodney would not work; he thought only of good times. And there was her son-in-law, Jerry, with whom she had gone to live. Now Jerry was a good husband and father, but he could never quite shake off the nocturnal side of his existence. In addition, there were the houses with no porches to lean on, the eternal friction between the "dicties" and the "nobodies" and, of course, the street to think through and to speculate about—people in infinite variety throwing Saturday night parties, praying, cussing, talking sweet nothing to one another. It was to the janitor, however, who came upstairs to see her when she was ill that Sister Mary confided, "I done got my feet caught in the sweet flypaper of life— and I'll be dogged if I want to get loose."

And contrary to what is sometimes the case with books of text and pictures, *The Sweet Flypaper of Life* demonstrates the fact that neither needs necessarily to be dependent upon the other, but that each may bear an equal organic relationship to the message of the book. The tone, now quiet, now lively, is consistent with the ups and downs that characterize life in Harlem.

Fortunately enough, *The Sweet Flypaper of Life* presents a somewhat balanced picture of the world's largest Negro ghetto. Harlem has never been, as some writers have been wont to picture it, a one-dimensional city of shabby tenements, reckless abandon, and broken parcels of humanity moving irregularly from bar to bar. These aspects of it do represent realism, but realism that is misleading because it is limited to one side of the story. In Mr. Hughes' new volume, nobody is running wild, the bar has been severely de-emphasized, and a genuine regard for love, family life, and children in the home assume a place of primacy in the community. The Negro woman who has taken a sound lashing in many of Hughes' books can thank Heaven for *The Sweet Flypaper of Life,* for by implication it suggests that by and large she is a clean, loyal person who has a husband and a job and who gets the children off to school every morning.

Beneath it all, one discovers a strong undercurrent of seriousness. Since the impact of the hectic, the coarse, and the sensational of the Mid-Twenties, Harlem dwellers have come a long way. They have experienced the disillusionment that runs through *Shakespeare in Harlem* (1942), the sombre, questioning mood that characterized *Fields of Wonder* (1947), and the vague, mixed-up dream one encounters in *Montage of a Dream Deferred* (1951). To-

day, like Sister Mary Bradley, they are bent upon seeing "what this integration the Supreme Court has done decreed is going to be like." While Harlem *is* sweet, it is to them no end in itself. Theirs is a higher loyalty to a democratic order that will render unnecessary the Harlem Negro ghetto and similar ones around the world.

D[onald] H[arrington] "Thumbnail Book Review" *Community News*, 10 (12 February 1956), 3

This little book of words and pictures catches the essence of life in that part of New York known as Harlem. It has both joy and sadness, hardness and softness, boredom and excitement, poverty and dirt, yet a rare and unearthly beauty, the beauty of the caring, searching, yearning, hoping human soul.

[. . .]

The story is heartwarming and touches the deep places of the soul. Life in Harlem is changing. Integration is coming. It is good to have this intimate picture of a moment in the changing life of the Negro people in New York. May they never lose their tragedy-nurtured deep feeling for and love of life.

Sarah E. Wright
"Hughes Book Artistic
and Encouraging"
Philadelphia Tribune,
3 March 1956, p. 8

One of the most immediate impressions we get from this new book by the Messrs. Hughes and DeCarava is that of movement. We are not allowed to feel one thing too long before we find ourselves caught up in an entirely different feeling. Joy, sorrow, anger and love rush together here, crowding each other, pushing for priority. It is this overwhelming sense of movement that convinces us this is life—this is real.

We are carried on an emotion-packed journey in and out of the lives touched by Sister Mary Bradley. It is a "half-a-loaf" journey that denies the old adage: "half-a-loaf is better than none." Instead it merely whets our appetite for the other precious half.

Langston Hughes' use of Sister Mary Bradley, a woman whose years have spanned three generations, was in all senses wise. She is well equipped to make the important evaluations assigned her. She is totally familiar with the "emancipation" we all share in. From the moment she receives the telegraphed invitation from St. Peter to enter the Pearly Gates and replies, "... But right now, you understand me Lord, I'm so tangled up in living, I ain't got time to die," to the moment when she announces to her prospective man-friend, the building's janitor, "I done got my feet caught up in the sweet flypaper of life—and I'll be dogged if I want to get loose," we are convinced that this woman knows what she's talking about. She speaks to us and for us.

Sister Mary Bradley's greatest joy comes from sharing her multiple gifts, wage earning being very important among them, with her family. Although the main recipient of this benevolence is her young nephew, Rodney, her humanity readily expands to include all about her: Rodney's girlfriends, his illegitimate child, the grandchildren of her youngest daughter, Melinda, and her husband, Jerry, the neighbors, the Negro people generally, and so on and on and on. Wherever life is in the making, Sister Mary finds herself necessary. Sister Mary is love.

Mr. Hughes has given us what we expect from him: the best. His unerring faithfulness to the character of his material reflects an artistic integrity that commands our greatest respect.

Mr. DeCarava's striking photographs that give page by page illustration to the narrative, hit depth immediately. He has the unusual facility of showing us the beauty we suspected we saw in life about us, and convincing us that it was there all the time. This is photography making a difference that matters.

The Sweet Flypaper of Life is a happy book, a proud book that makes no literal plea for dignity; it is dignity. It is a fine achievement—an artistic triumph that encourages us to find and create beauty out of the raw realities we are all involved in.

"The Poetry of Harlem"
Picture Week, 2 (13
March 1956), 54–[7].

"We've had so many books about how bad life is," says Langston Hughes. "Maybe it's time to have one showing how good it is." In *The Sweet Flypaper of Life,* photographer Roy DeCarava and writer Langston

Hughes have woven out of words and pictures a moving story of the people of Harlem. It contains the trivial and the tragic, the songs and the sadness, but underlying the thread of daily living is a new note: hope, a feeling of a future.

Life is good here. It is no longer, to Hughes, the Harlem he described in "Dim-out in Harlem."

Nor is it the Harlem in "Visitors to the Black Belt."

The Sweet Flypaper reflects that side of Hughes that wrote "Youth":

> We have tomorrow
> Bright before us
> Like a flame. . . .

Bryan Collier
"Books and Arts: A Pleasing Goulash of Literary Efforts"
Charleston News and Courier, 17 June 1956, p. 13C

[. . .]

The next two items in the stack have been there a long time. They are as different as night and day, and my reasons for wanting to comment are also at opposite poles.

First: a thin paperback called *The Sweet Flypaper of Life,* published by Simon & Schuster and written and illustrated by Roy DeCarava and Langston Hughes, two talented young men who know Harlem and Negroes intimately and who set out (says the cover blurb) to describe what they have personally "seen and known and felt deeply about their own people."

Theirs is a delightful small picture story about an old Negro woman in Harlem who became ill, but when the Lord sent his message saying "Come" she asked him to wait a while because she was so happily tangled in life's sweet flypaper—loving and working and seeing her children and grandchildren grow—that she wasn't prepared to go right now.

I hope these two Harlem authors won't be too dumbfounded to read that a South Carolina book editor thinks their work quite, quite fine.

And I am reasonably certain Simon & Schuster will not be shocked when I express skepticism about the publication chances of such a book had it been written by a Southerner, white or black. Yet here, sharply and cleanly reflected, is the way old-line Southerners feel about Negroes—or used to feel—and the way many of them used to write about Negroes, until such subjects became strangely taboo and Northern editorial doors were slammed in their faces. Curious world, isn't it?

[. . .]

W. Edward Farrison
"Book Reviews"
CLAJ, 11 (March 1968), 261–3

The Sweet Flypaper of Life was first published in 1955 and has been out of print for some time. The new edition listed above was reprinted from a personal copy of the first edition which Langston Hughes presented to the present publishers not long before he died. Roy DeCarava's more than a hundred photographs of Harlemites fill most of the space in the little volume, and each of these photographs tells a story, as every picture has been said to do. But Sister Mary Bradley's prose monologue which Hughes supplied as running comments pertaining to the photographs add what excellent photography alone could not have communicated. Together with the photographs, these comments afford a kaleidoscopic view of day-to-day life in Harlem as it was and doubtless still is for many, and as it has been familiar to DeCarava and Hughes, two of its most careful observers. This is not to say that the work gives a typical picture of Harlem life or even tells the story of an average Harlem family, as some critics opined in reference to the first edition. There is no reason to believe that DeCarava and Hughes intended for the work to do such things, being conscious as they must have been of the limitation of its scope—its limitation to the portrayal of some selected phases of Harlem life with their humorous as well as serious moments.

A widow and an emigré of many years from segregation-ridden South Carolina, Sister Bradley is familiar with many of the highways and byways of life as well as with the folkways of Harlem. Without knowing anything about Henry Wadsworth Longfellow, she is quite cognizant of the reality and earnestness of life, to which that poet referred in an age scarcely remembered by hers. Indeed she has been "so tangled up in living" that she refused to give up life even "when the bicycle of the Lord bearing his messenger with a telegram" summoning her to Heaven arrived at her apartment, where she was critically ill (p. 7). "I done got my feet caught in the sweet flypaper of life—and I'll be dogged if I want to get loose," she explains in natural, not mutilated, illiterate dialect (p. 92).

To those who remember the days when well patronized sheets of flypaper could be seen in many places, sometimes close to food in grocery stores, Sister Bradley's metaphor is not likely to prove a stimulant to

gulosity. Nevertheless her creator could hardly have found a more expressive and yet compressed figure with which to describe her earthbound existence. For her, life's sweetness and stickiness, its joys and troubles, its pleasures and pains, its fortunes and misfortunes are inseparable, as they are, in fact, for all who follow a straight way between blind optimism and sightless pessimism.

One of Sister Bradley's joys is the little ones among her ten grandchildren, although she admits that "sometimes, old as I is, they tries even my impatience." One of her troubles is her grandson Rodney, a young man of the midnight streets and "king-kong basements," the despair of his parents, but the hope of his grandmother, who is sure that "there's something in that boy" despite his present waywardness. Anyway, says the grandmother, the waywardness "just might not be his fault," for as she remembers, "I were myself when I were young."

Beyond her family is a panorama of Harlem life, in which Sister Bradley naturally finds intense as well as extensive human interest. "In Harlem," she observes, "something is happening all the time, people are going every which-a-way." Some are out watching parades, "some have been where they are going," some seem unable to decide which way to go, and some seem to be going nowhere at all. There being no front porches in Harlem, there are only stoops, steps, or park benches to sit on when one wants to sit outside. Here and there are "some folks selling, other folks buying, . . . picket lines picketing," speakers haranguing crowds on street corners at night, romantic and not so romantic lovers in love, and so on. Like Sister Bradley herself, some occasionally find themselves down "but with no intentions of going out." Instead they put on the best they have and go out to face life anew. As an observer of the life around her,

Sister Bradley is a distinctive addition to the folk characters portrayed in Hughes's works—a portrayal which greatly enlivens and is in turn enlivened by DeCarava's photography.

Checklist of Additional Reviews

Alice Hackett, "PW Buyers' Forecast," *Publishers Weekly,* 168 (12 November 1955), 2086.

"Weekly Record: DeCarava, Roy and Hughes, Langston," *Publishers Weekly,* 168 (26 November 1955), 2227.

Sam Ragan, "Southern Accent," *Raleigh News and Observer,* part 4, 27 November 1955, p. 5.

Robert Sylvester, "Dream Street," *New York Daily News,* 29 November 1955, p. 48.

J.D., "Pictures and Words," *New York Times,* 18 December 1955, p. 20X.

"Photographer Captures Spirit of Harlem," *Rochester Democrat and Chronicle,* 25 December 1955, p. 9C.

Lincoln University Bulletin, 59 (Winter 1955–56), 19.

Don Langer, "Available-Light Photography," *New York Herald Tribune,* section 3, 5 January 1956, p. 3.

"Life's Sweet Misery Traps a Grandmother," *Washington Post and Times-Herald,* 8 January 1956, p. E6.

Jan Olincy, "How Life Can Be Good in Harlem," *Tulsa Sunday World Magazine,* 22 January 1956, p. 25.

Hugh H. Smythe, "The Week's Books: Photo Light on Harlem," *Pittsburgh Courier Magazine,* 28 January 1956, p. 6.

"Social Sciences," *Booklist,* 52 (1 February 1956), 222.

"Nonfiction: *The Sweet Flypaper of Life,*" *Publishers Weekly,* 192 (30 October 1967), 52.

"Your Guide to Forthcoming Books," *Book Buyer's Guide,* 70 (November 1967), 76.

Edward Margolies, "Photography," *Library Journal,* 93 (1 March 1968), 983.

I WONDER AS I WANDER

"I Wonder as I Wander"
Virginia Kirkus Bulletin,
24 (15 September 1956),
728

An autobiographical travelogue from the Negro poet and writer should come as a revealing gift to those who have known his other work. It is an amusing and often deeply serious account of the interchange between himself and people and countries—personal and international adventures that have filled his life as a true man of the world. The period of which Hughes writes is in the thirties and encompasses the years from the start of the depression to the time when he was a correspondent in the Spanish Civil War. All of it illustrates character and principle inductively, by colorfully descriptive and conversational narratives. On an early trip to Cuba, Hughes looked to a lifting of the color bar. Though he found prejudice there too, he was freer by far than in his own home and leads us to enjoy with him the artists he met and the feelings of a people whom he describes through their music and the good times they have. At home in the early Thirties Mary McLeod Bethune helped him start on a reading tour through Negro colleges and these trips are sharply indicative of what segregation means. His further and very extended trips through Russia and the east on a journey that took him around the world as far more than a traveler, carry the same interest. Hughes has the knack of living in and being a part of wherever he is. His acquaintances too—Arthur Koestler, Cartier-Bresson, Covarrubias—become new people. A book concerned with the individual, with social issues, and with art as it is a part of these things, will bring its rewards as a documentary and an important diary.

W. G. R[ogers]
"Poet Had Love for All Humans Met in Travels"
Hartford Times, 10 November 1956, p. 18 (with minor variations, also as "Travels and Adventures of Poet Langston Hughes," *Davenport Democrat Times,* Entertainment Section, 11 November 1956, p. 6; as "Book Review," *Saratogan,* during November 1956; *Syracuse Post-Standard,* 11 November 1956; *Bridgeport Post,* 18 November 1956; as "Langston Hughes Finds U.S. Best," *Topeka Daily Capital,* 18 November 1956, p. 27A)

Back a quarter of a century ago before we heard of A-bombs and learned to turn pale, or livid, at the mention of Russia, when we worried only about apple-selling, bank holidays and the three-day work week or not any work week at all, Hughes set out to see the world.

He couldn't earn much staying home, couldn't spend much traveling, so he traveled—from Cleveland to the Caribbean, through the South reading his poems, out to California, on a movie assignment to Russia, on to the Pacific, to Mexico, back to California, to Spain and the civil war and home.

There were newsworthy aspects to his wandering years, as when the police ordered him out of Japan. There was and is news in the names of the people he met and spent hours or days with: Koestler in Russia, Hemingway in Spain, Saroyan in California, Rivera in Mexico. There is even news in people he didn't see, like Julia Peterkin who wrote richly about the Negro but whose house was closed to this one when he called on her in South Carolina.

But the best of this book is the unnewsworthy people and events—the trains, hotels, food, dirt, joviality, the fleshiness and earthiness of the common Russian. Natasha who liked her husband but liked Hughes more; the women in Madrid; the boys and women in Shanghai.

"I love you," says Hughes to humans around the world, and they love him. But this is a democratic rather than a proletarian view, and Hughes in the end finds it is "fun to get back to capitalism."

Fletcher Martin
"Negro Poet's Life Told in a Profound Tale"
Chicago Sun-Times, section 2, 11 November 1956, p. 6

As a Kentucky schoolboy, I received a weekly fare of Langston Hughes.

His poetry wasn't included in the regular English classes, but in our high school we had a Negro History Club. Each Wednesday we were afforded delightful dosages of Hughes, James Weldon Johnson and Claude McKay.

Such works of Hughes' as *The Weary Blues, The Dream Keeper* and *Shakespeare in Harlem* never failed to deepen the gnawing inside us to bust through walls of social and economic restraint in my town.

He made us laugh and he made us cry—but, more importantly, he said things that made us feel that we belonged. Charles Lamb, Thoreau and Emerson gave us parlor fare, but Hughes gave the kitchen talk with a deep-seated feeling we knew.

Even now, in the midst of changing conditions, I refer to his *Fields of Wonder* and *One-Way Ticket* when complacency threatens. For Negroes, Hughes is the constant reminder of the distance from which they came and the far piece they have to go.

His latest book, *I Wonder as I Wander,* is a delightful recollection of his autobiographical journey through life. But, in addition, it is the profound and compounded story of Negro life.

486

Ted Poston
"The Brighter Side"
New York Post, 11 November 1956, p. M11

This world sometimes seems to be made for certain people. And Langston Hughes, one of America's most distinguished poets, is one of them.

Langston Hughes remains himself whether he is stranded in Samarkand with Arthur Koestler, gallivanting around Moscow with a fabulous old Negro actress named Emma Harris, ducking shells with Hemingway in Spain, or warmly humoring three genteel, aging Mexican sisters who inherited all of the property of his well-to-do father.

This personal narrative of travel and adventure takes up pretty much where his first autobiography, *The Big Sea,* left off. He opens it with:

"When I was 27 the stock market crash came. When I was 28, my personal crash came. So when I was almost 30, I began to make my living from writing. This is the story of a Negro who wanted to make his living from poems and stories."

He has done just that—with 21 books of poems, fiction and autobiography already published, and a new one coming out in a week or so.

But it was not always a good living. For few people have been stranded, or near-stranded, in as many out-of-the-way places of the world as has Hughes. But somehow it doesn't appear to have thrown him.

As a matter of fact, nothing seems to awe him. He admits to certain irritations. He can discuss his impecunious mother, his penurious father, his irresponsible brother with the same petulance that made him stage a sit-down strike with Japanese secret servicemen. . . .

The bulk of the book deals with Hughes' trip in the early '30s to the Soviet Union on a hilarious trip with 22 other Negroes of whom this reviewer happened to be one.

If the Moscow which he describes is hardly the one this reviewer recalls, it is at least a little larger than life and more interesting for all that. And that is the charm of this book. The whole world of Langston Hughes is just a little larger and a little livelier than any world we lesser mortals may know.

Charles Wilder
"A Poet Retraces '30s"
Washington Post and Times Herald, 11 November 1956, p. E7

In this "autobiographical journey," poet Hughes covers significant distances both in time and in space—from the crash of 1929 to the Spanish Civil War, from the Caribbean to the Soviet Union to the Far East to Paris and Madrid. It is the 30s which are evoked here, and not without considerable nostalgia for that tense and troubled decade.

A tireless traveler who apparently takes, and keeps, copious notes, Hughes gives detailed accounts of his wanderings—whether for pleasure or as a correspondent or, in the case of his visit to the Soviet Union, as a member of a group of Harlem intellectuals who go to Moscow to make an ill-fated movie about race relations in the United States.

Always with good humor, he describes

the disordered and various world through which he moves, the way he is received, the rooms he lives in, the food he eats, the people he encounters.

Along the route, the reader gets to know such famous figures as Koestler and Hemingway, and such appealing ones as Emma Harris, a kind of public Negro hostess of Moscow, and "Grasdani," a former upper-class Russian woman living out her old age in the middle of Soviet Asia.

And there are glimpses of the modernization of Turkmenistan, a trip on the Trans-Siberian Railway, dinner with Madame Sun Yat-sen in Shanghai, police state methods in Japan, Bohemian life in Mexico City, Madrid under Franco's bombardment. As in an abundant smorgasbord, there is something for absolutely every taste.

Perhaps it is the very fullness of Hughes' coverage which finally inundates the reader, making him wish for more direction and, above all, more meaningful emphasis. Even in the poignant sections dealing with war-torn Spain, the effect is so diffuse that emotional impact is sacrificed. One has the impression that this is expert reportage where it might have been poetry. One would like to know quite a bit more about just what Langston Hughes did wonder as he wandered.

Milton S. Byam
"Too Late for Last Issue"
Library Journal, 81 (15 November 1956), 2686

When the Great Depression gripped America, it propelled Langston Hughes into a poetry-reading odyssey through the southern states of the United States to raise eating money. Before his traveling was done, Mr. Hughes had visited the West Indies, Germany, Russia, France, Japan and Spain. His most interesting and fully-reported trip was made to Russia to scriptwrite a motion picture. Perhaps he waited too long to tell us about it, for this book has none of the beauty or visual quality of his *Big Sea* in spite of his having oriental Russia to write about. It does give something of the quality of the man—a man who in rebellion against his father does not want anyone to think him white. Recommended for Negro and autobiographical collections in all libraries.

Roi Ottley
"Personal History: Politics, Poetry and Peccadillos"
Saturday Review, 39 (17 November 1956), 35

Langston Hughes is perhaps the most versatile and best-known Negro poet in the world. If some twenty-one books of poetry, fiction, juveniles, and autobiographies have not given his name circulation, certainly his thirty-odd years of travel about this planet have served to give currency to the name. For it seems that wherever he goes he is lionized, taken up by the best and most literate people, and is often the object of considerable newspaper attention. Many of his books, as well, have been given wide circulation by translation into foreign languages.

His new book, *I Wonder as I Wander*, essentially autobiographical, recalls his personal adventures and misadventures in the world of politics and poetry from Moscow Hill in San Francisco to Moscow in Russia, from Harlem to Tashkent. Along the way we meet a galaxy of characters, plus such contrasting types as Arthur Koestler and the top-hatted dignitaries of Haiti; Miguel Covarrubias and Emma, the Black Mammy of Moscow.

Hughes has written warmly and amusingly about these people, with asides which give flashes of social and racial insights. I think, though, I liked Emma, Moscow's mammy, best. Emma was an expatriate from Dixie who had been living in Moscow since Czarist days and still managed to maintain her individuality.

Before the Revolution she had arrived with a theatrical troupe and attracted the attention of a grand duke. When the duke fell along with the czar naturally Emma was left without the servants and mansion he had bestowed upon her. The Soviets cut up her mansion into a dozen apartments, but permitted her a sizable flat on the first floor. She lived quite comfortably, Hughes reports. Not alone did she have a speaking acquaintance with the black market, but she also knew where every speakeasy, Russian version, was located, and never seemingly worked.

She told Hughes, "I'm like a cat with nine lives. I always land on my feet. Been doing it all my life wherever I am. These Bolsheviks ain't gonna kill me."

Emma had little use for the Soviet system as compared to Czarist days, but was a featured speaker at all the big rallies held in Moscow on behalf of "depressed" and "exploited" Negroes in the U.S. Emma, says Hughes, could make a fiery speech in Russian, denouncing American lynch law, then come off the platform and sigh, "I wish I was back home."

I don't think I've done Langston Hughes's book an injustice in describing Emma in such detail—for indeed he has much more to say about her and her peccadillos. But Emma is typical of the sort of characters he met and he recalls their stories with obvious relish.

I Wonder as I Wander is actually Hughes's personal history intertwined with personal narratives of his travels—a sort of vagabondia, with a dash of racialism. As such it proves excellent fare as he recalls dramatic and intimate moments in a life well and vigorously spent.

James Brewer
"Poet's Travels: Wayfaring Wonderer"
Virginian Pilot and Portsmouth Star, 18 November 1956, p. 6C

These are sketches of Langston Hughes' travels about our world, in conversation with famous and unknown people. This is an autobiographical journey—not an autobiography.

Langston Hughes has the ability, in most of his writings and poetry, of giving sensitive insights into people, personalities and situations. It was hoped that in this book he would give us sensitive insights into himself. He does not. The book is interesting and factual, but the writing is shallow and slick for a person of Hughes' accomplishments.

He mentions, at the close of the book, this being just before World War II, that he had seen people walking tightropes everywhere—"the tightrope of color in Alabama, the tightrope of transition in the Soviet Union, the tightrope of repression in Japan, the tightrope of the fear of war in France . . . and myself everywhere on my tightrope of words." This might have been a better book if Langston Hughes could have forgotten his tightrope of words.

489

The book is easy reading, with many wanderings, but with little depth in the wondering.

Marjorie B. Snyder "Philosophical Autobiography" *Boston Herald,* section 3, 18 November 1956, p. 7

It just doesn't make sense, says the early part of this philosophical autobiography of the world's most famous Negro poet, that a man of culture and attainments should be denied a place to eat and a place to sleep because of the color of his skin. Hughes' story of his life begins in 1929 when he was twenty-seven and continues for only about three years. It is a long, detailed, fascinating account; poetic, frank and humorous.

When the poet was outside the United States, in Cuba and Haiti, he found the color line almost non-existent. Later, as he traveled all over the world, he was received everywhere—often with acclaim. Probably the best part of his book is of the time he spent in Russia and particularly in Soviet Central Asia. He tells of the people—he met and talked with the lowliest as well as their masters—of their trials, hardships, and occasional joys.

Still wondering about prejudice, still writing poems and short stories, still delighted with music, girls, and dancing, he crossed Siberia by railroad and shipped to Korea, China and Japan. In Tokyo, he encountered the police, not because of his color but because he had been seen talking (as usual) with everyone he could, and making many notes. The final informative section of his book tells of Spain at the time of the Spanish Civil War; it is nearly as interesting as the Russian adventure.

Throughout the world, Hughes knew many famous persons: Mary McLeod Bethune, George Washington Carver, Arthur Koestler, Madam Sun Yat Sen, William Saroyan, Ernest Hemingway, and many others. With all his wandering and wondering, he remains a talented American of whom we are proud.

Don Stanley "The Book Corner: Poet's Work Is 'Uneven'" *San Francisco Examiner,* section 3, 19 November 1956, p. 3

Put aside for a moment the fact that Langston Hughes is a poet, and probably the world's most famous Negro poet. Put aside, while you are at it, the title to his latest book, *I Wonder as I Wander,* for Hughes really seems to do precious little wondering in his wandering.

Ignore these things and this "autobiographical journey" is a peppery, if slight, amusement based on seven years in the life of a gregarious writer.

Just before Hughes left for his first Russian visit in the early 1930's, he stopped for a last chat with Lincoln Steffens in Carmel.

"It's time Negroes were getting around the world," the salty old muckraker told him. "Can you tell me why in hell they stay home so much?"

The question seems to have haunted Hughes. He didn't stop until he had circled the globe. In the process he starved a little with beginning photographer Henri

490

Cartier-Bresson in Mexico City, walked the white steps down to the sea at Odessa where Eisenstein filmed "Potemkin," and split a fifth of Scotch with Ernest Hemingway in bomb shattered Madrid.

But along the way there is a strange unevenness of writing. There are, it turns out, at least three Hugheses. First, and most painfully apparent, is a person whose memory for famous names outdoes the most retentive of Hollywood gossip disgorgers.

Then there is the voice of the militant propagandist whose judgments seem often to arise from a sense of vaguely distasteful obligation rather than from a dogmatic conviction.

The third Hughes is a poet. There should be more of him. He is not a poet of labored imagery, but a man with the eye and feeling for the essence of experience.

He bobs up here and there in the book—most often in Spain, once or twice in Russia and Asia, never in Haiti (ironically, since that Caribbean island is the symbol of Negro rebellion against white persecution).

In Spain, there's a memorable vignette of La Nina de los Peines—a great flamenco singer who refused to go over to Franco—crying her Gypsy Spanish songs of heartbreak in a barren theater of a Madrid under bombardment.

From the standpoint of local interest, Hughes' most carefree days seem to have been spent as guest of the late Noel Sullivan in the Hyde Street mansion of that Nephew of Senator Phelan. It was from this, "the best of American capitalism" that he left for "the show place of Soviet communism—from Russian Hill to Russia itself."

Hughes seems never to have committed himself too firmly or finally to any political group. He leans to his grandmother's early counsel:

"What's the matter with you, boy? You can't expect every apple to be a perfect apple. Just because it's got a speck on it, you want to throw it away. Bite that speck out and eat that apple, son. It's still a good apple."

Webster Gault
"Days of Travel"
Hartford Courant Magazine, 25 November 1956, p. 13

Langston Hughes, the globe trotting Negro poet, has turned to prose to describe his many travels in a new book aptly titled, *I Wonder as I Wander.*

Though his journeys to Russia, Japan, Spain and other spots took place in the thirties, he has recorded them in keen, deft strokes and given his work a sense of immediacy. Particularly creditable are his wonderful tales of the desolate but spicy life in Soviet Central Asia, that remote area of which too little has been written. It was there in Ashkhabad that he first met Arthur Koestler, the Communist who was later to startle the world with his attacks on Soviet "justice."

Not so successful are his descriptions, often in pompous prose, of his travels in his own country. Using his poetry as a passport, he swept through the South and across the country on a lecture tour trailed by controversy. He had every right to buck the color barrier (as he did at Chapel Hill, N.C.). But one wonders if he might serve his people better with greater humility.

There is much that is self-conscious in *I Wonder as I Wander,* as the title would certainly imply. Agreed, autobiographical journeys have a place in print, as evidenced by the award winning work *An American in Italy* by Herbert Kubly. Like Kubly, Hughes has also chosen to include his own love affairs in his book and neither can be credited with good taste for doing so.

When he concentrates on the world around him, Hughes is on much better ground. . . .

[. . .]

R.F.
"An Autobiographical Journey by Langston Hughes"
Daily Worker, 29 November 1956, p. 7

Across half the world, and a generation ago, Langston Hughes wandered. This is the story of his travellings, set down from the remembrance of a poet's eye, and dominated by a life's experience with racial inequality. In a decade which began with the crash of 1929, concluded with the Franco conquest of Spain as the orchestra of global war tuned up in the wings, Langston Hughes journeyed to distant places— Cuba, Haiti, Spain, Russia, Japan.

Although an awful lot of history has thundered by since then, and many books have been written by participants and observers, great and small, the period comes to life as in a story never told before, due largely to Hughes' zestful joy of recollection, his gift of anecdotage and his deft portrayals of people, some prominent, some not.

But whether facing the crushing and degrading code imposed by Southern white supremacists as readily upon the Negro poet as on the Negro sharecropper, watching the colored peoples of Soviet Asia emerge into socialism from the Czarist version of jimcrow, or recording the Spanish Republican's care to avoid racist reactions to Franco's use of Moorish troops, *I Wonder as I Wander* is uniquely a Negro American's experience.

An international who's who of the arts parades through the pages of this book. Some are included, one suspects, in deference to the view, widely held among publishers, that the reader interest in an autobiography is measured by the number of "big names" the author has rubbed shoulders with.

Others, notably Hughes' sketch of Arthur Koestler, with whom he toured Russia, are memorable portraiture.

In these days of great decision of the Soviet Union and the world socialist movement, it is of particular interest to read what Langston Hughes has to say about the Russian experiment; for though he is speaking of Russia, 1932, he is writing in 1956.

"I think most idealists expected too much of Russia in too short a time," he writes. "The Soviet Union was then only fifteen years old. I kept thinking of what someone once said about the freed Negroes in America, 'Don't try to measure the progress of the Negro by how far he has gone but rather by the distance from which he had to come.' Maybe my having gone to Central Asia gave me a broader viewpoint on Soviet achievements. In Turkestan the new setup was only eight years old, dating from 1924—yet there they had already come from almost complete illiteracy to schools for all the children, from ancient feudal serfdom to wages and work for all, from veils and harems and marriage marts to women treated like human beings and not cattle, and from jimcrow cars to a complete lack of segregation—all in less than a decade."

And again, "As to the purge trials, the liquidations, the arrests and censorship, deplorable as these things were, I felt about them in relation to their continued denunciation in the European and American press, much as Frederick Douglass felt before the Civil War when he read in the slave-holding papers that the abolitionists were anarchists, villains, devils and atheists. Douglass said he had the impression that 'Abolition—whatever else it might be—was not unfriendly to the slave.'"

Always, the reader is drawn back, as Langston Hughes was time after time, to the ugly facts of racism and white supremacy in America. "I am the darker brother," the poet Hughes sang, "they sent me to eat in the kitchen when company comes," but "I, too, am America."

Much has changed since Langston Hughes first read his biting, poet's challenge to jimcrow to intent Negro student audiences in the South. His book is not only a readable tale of one man's journeyings, it is a reminder both of what America has gained from great talents like his own and lost in others crushed beneath the weight of racism.

Leon Baisier
Best Sellers, 16
(1 December 1956), 311

[. . .]

A most interesting book, beautifully written, and of vital interest. There are times when the author sees the red issue with colored glasses, yet he delineates clearly the things which he saw, and the problems which he, as a member of a minority group, faces the world over. As he ends he justly states "Anybody is liable to fall off a tightrope in any land, and God help you if you fall the wrong way." With dignity, personal warmth and lucidity poet

Langston Hughes relates his experiences on three continents.

P.L.P.
"Wandering Langston Hughes Has Lived an Exciting Life"
Pittsburgh Courier, 1 December 1956, p. 7

Even if you added up all the toothaches, upset stomachs and "thin dimes" which have been the lot of Langston Hughes as he pressed his way "curiouser and curiouser" to the ends of the world, you would have to conclude that this gentle poet and sometimes weary traveler, has lived the life of Riley.

It is perhaps unpardonably crude to try to reduce Mr. Hughes' autobiographical journal to catalogue terms, but it seems necessary because, in essence, what *I Wonder as I Wander* reveals, is not so much of the writer's life as his relationship to certain important happenings and what he thought about what happened.

One passes quickly from the fact that during the Negro Renaissance in the twenties, he was maintained by an elderly white woman patron whom he ultimately lost because he was just not primitive enough. This forced him to answer the question as to how he was going to make a living. He decided he would be a writer.

Mrs. Mary McLeod Bethune gave him his first push. After some months in Haiti and Cuba, Mr. Hughes and a friend returned to the States—broke as usual. But he did organize by dint of Mrs. Bethune's persuasion, a highly successful tour of Southern schools and colleges which took him to the West Coast and a meeting with legendary Noel Sullivan.

While on the West Coast he received a bid to join a group of Negroes who had been invited to the Soviet Union to make a motion picture, *Black and White*. The picture never came off and now, for the first time, Mr. Hughes tells why. He stayed many months in Russia, particularly in Central Russia, land of the Uzbeks and other dark and exotic peoples. So far did he travel he was sure several times he was going to fall off the rim of the world.

From Russia he went to Japan, to China, back to Japan (from where he was deported), and thence to Hawaii and San Francisco and Carmel-by-the-Sea, Noel Sullivan's retreat.

There was to be a hectic period during which his play *Mulatto* was to be produced, acclaimed in many cities and banned in others. The financial returns helped to make up for what he did not receive from a well-to-do father who died in Mexico.

Most of this living hobnobbing with the most colorful personalities of the times in many lands occurred between 1929 and 1934.

In 1937, Mr. Hughes was off again, to cover the civil war in Spain for the *Afro-American*. He was under constant bombardment, but was slightly nicked by only one bullet.

There is important sociological significance in Mr. Hughes' book, but he has also woven a yarn of bright, glittering texture. As a reader turns the pages, he wonders continually what this wandering poet will wonder about next.

Martha Bacon
"A Humane Man"
Providence Sunday Journal, section 6, 2 December 1956, p. 8

A talented writer who has lived a fascinating life seems like an almost foolproof combination for a successful autobiography. Mr. Hughes' book, *I Wonder as I Wander,* largely justifies this premise. The faults of this book lie only in its style, and they are the more irritating because Mr. Hughes, when he will take the pains, writes vividly and excitingly, as has been shown many times, not only in the present instance but in other works that have come from his pen. It is as though a kind of good-natured indolence overtook him from time to time, when he can scarcely trouble himself to construct a proper sentence: he then falls back on folksy usages that mar an otherwise alluring text and which extract the verve from his phrases as though he had drenched good tobacco in molasses.

It is the more exasperating of him because he doesn't need to write this way. When a rich subject really captures his imagination, as does the sojourn of the would-be movie company in Moscow, which he joined as a writer, then the full flow of his humor, his warmth and his wry sympathy spurts into generous language that makes the most of a hundred miraculously funny situations. The movie troupe in question were all highly educated urban young Negroes faced with having to interpret folkways for the Comintern-approved Russian movie about Negro-White relations in America, never having heard a spiritual sung outside of a concert hall and being northerners, ignorant of the cabin and the cotton patch. The whole thing was a superb comedy of errors and nobody appreciated its charms and its subtleties more highly than did Mr. Hughes.

His account of Emma, "The Mammy of Moscow," is a classic of its kind and supplies one of the few truly funny stories of life under Communism. Emma, a young colored "artiste" of undoubted charm and beauty, having found favor with a grand duke, managed to keep one floor of the palace that he gave her right through the revolution and was one of the few that managed to eat heartily in fat times and in lean. Russia had its disadvantages however in spite of its lack of a color bar. "Why I used to have six servants and a boot-boy," complained Emma, under Stalin. "Now best I can do is one old baba, older'n me, part time."

These are but hints of the highlights that flicker through Mr. Hughes' book. Langston Hughes has seen the world, taken part in its conflicts and come to a number of reasonable and humane conclusions. The horrors of civil war in Spain, the idiocies of the color bar and of Communism have not destroyed his essential enjoyment of men, women and countries, and take him for all in all he is a rewarding writer and an interesting man. The quotation at the beginning of the book perhaps sums him up more clearly than any other comment: Paul's epistle to the Romans, 1:14. I am debtor both to the Greeks and to the barbarians: both to the wise and to the unwise.

Charles H. Nichols
"Laughing World of Langston Hughes"
Dayton Daily News, section 5, 2 December 1956, p. 19

The time is the years between 1931 and 1938; the place spans three continents and the islands of the sea; the characters are of every color and political persuasion. This is the "autobiographical journey" of Langston Hughes. It is not only a personal history, but an expression of faith, reminding us that a great spirit lay behind the events of those days. For although there was depression and despair, Fascism and Nazism, the Spanish Civil War and the rape of Ethiopia, the spirit of liberty was very much alive. Langston Hughes concludes his book with the words, "My world will not end." And the whole history of the world seems to be on his side, for his is an extraordinarily indestructible world. It is a world filled with lovable people, with laughter and the lust for life. Though it has its share of big names, it is essentially a world of little people on the march, stretching in an unending line from Havana to Tokyo and from Paris to Samarkand.

I Wonder as I Wander is a delightful caravan of incidents in Langston Hughes' life drawn from a time when, as a poet, he was at the height of his fabulous career. It is a simple, direct and intimate story. His accounts of Mary McLeod Bethune, Arthur Koestler, Emma, "the Black Mammy of Moscow," are memorable. But they are not more lasting than the nameless Uzbeks, Tartars and Cuban peasants who are

495

brought to life with such sympathy in these pages.

No doubt most readers will find Langston Hughes' experiences in Soviet Russia the most exciting part of the book. For here is the Soviet world 15 years after the Revolution, floundering in bureaucratic red tape and depressing in its dirt, delinquency and disorder. Hughes and 22 other Negroes were invited to Russia to make a motion picture on the exploitation of the American Negro. Though this project fell through, Hughes remained in the Soviet Union to tour Southeastern Asia—a vast, primitive land just emerging from illiteracy, wife-buying and tyranny. It was a land not yet emancipated from the shadow of Genghis Khan. Among the people Hughes encountered were those western converts to communism who came to Moscow like pilgrims to Mecca. There are some sad and some hilarious instances of their disillusionment.

Indeed, whether he is drinking tea with Uzbek camel drivers, or sharing a bed with a Tartar maiden, playing his Louis Armstrong records for a Haitian or reading his poetry for college students in Florida, Langston Hughes is the people's poet. He senses unerringly the warm human spirit clothed in any language or dress. No doubt there are more artistic and accomplished authors in America, but few have caught so clearly and with such consistent good humor the heart-warming quality of common people everywhere.

H. A. Sieber
"A Poet's Wanderings in a World of Wonder"
Winston-Salem Journal and Sentinel, 2 December 1956, p. 5C

The American poet, James Langston Hughes, was born some 54 years and 20 books ago in Joplin, Mo.

I Wonder as I Wander is an autobiographical narrative of his journey from Joplin—a journey which takes poet and reader to the four poem-bevelled corners of the world, to Harlem, Samarkand, Turkestan, North Carolina.

In these corners of Mr. Hughes' "world without end," he systematically acquired a Catholic reputation as the outstanding Negro poet. Indeed, his most prominent white contemporaries hardly enjoy the international stature as a poet which "being Negro" has given Mr. Hughes.

The clean observations with which Langston Hughes returns from his travels in the world of poetry and politics certainly deserve understanding reading. Occasionally, Mr. Hughes is tempted to quote his former, more poetic self (from his volumes of verse, *Shakespeare in Harlem, The Dream Keeper, The Weary Blues*). The incidents are pleasantly interwoven with reminders that our wandering wonderer is, above and despite all, a poet.

The chapter entitled "Color at Chapel Hill" will be especially interesting to those North Carolinians with a long memory—one which extends back to the early thirties. This was a time when the ill-fated Scottsboro boys were very much in the headlines. The anecdote which Mr. Hughes relates involves his lecture visit to the university village and the untimely noises which were uttered on his arrival by *Contempo,* the short-lived left-wing literary journal published by Buttita and Abernethy.

I am tempted to quote a provocative poem by Mr. Hughes because it reveals the theme of his "wondering" and the impetus for his "wandering."

> My old man's a white old man . . .
> My old mother's black.
> But if ever I cursed my white old man
> I take my curses back.
> If ever I cursed my black old mother
> And wished she were in hell,
> I'm sorry for that evil wish
> And now I wish her well.
> My old man died in a fine big house,
> My ma died in a shack.
> I wonder where I'm gonna die,
> Being neither white nor black.

Audrey Weaver
"Hughes' *I Wander* Is Thoughtful and Amusing"
Chicago Defender, 3 December 1956, p. 8

Ardent followers of "Simple" with his racial philosophies, get an opportunity to go on an autobiographical journey with his prolific creator in *I Wonder as I Wander.*

In his newest book Langston Hughes tells of his travels all over the world—of the people he meets and the racial incidents he encounters just as "Simple" experiences and has experienced from time to time in his "native" Virginia and his "adopted" New York City.

Appropriately titled, the writings are interesting, amusing and thought provoking.

Daily Negroes wonder about the race situation in the U.S., and become frightfully depressed.

For those who believe that the answers to all the U.S. Negroes' problems lie in a government of their own in Africa, there is much to wonder about in Hughes' revelations of picturesque Haiti . . . the sole Black Republic in the Western hemisphere.

In Haiti, there is not only a color problem, but a class one as well.

Most upsetting is the class problem on which Hughes comments:

"All of the work that kept Haiti alive, paid the interest on American loans and enriched foreign trade, was done by people without shoes—Yet shoes were of great importance . . . to be seen barefoot marked one of low-cast, a person of no standing."

While he tells of "color around the globe," Hughes says, "I have learned that there is at least one Negro everywhere." He even finds a "Mammy" in Moscow . . . Emma Harris who went there as an entertainer and stayed permanently, becoming a favorite of the Soviets.

In the wake of the South's current fight against desegregation, it is interesting to find that racial conditions were even worse during the Depression era when Hughes toured the section reading his poems to strictly Jim-Crow audiences.

Certainly of best-seller caliber, *I Wonder as I Wander* rates well with the other books and poems that Hughes has written.

Jonathan F. Beecher "Hughes' *I Wonder as I Wander*: Reveries of an Itinerant Poet" *Harvard Crimson*, 13 December 1956, p. 5

"Most of my life from childhood on has been spent moving, traveling, changing places, knowing people in one school, in one town or in one group, or on one ship a little while, but soon never seeing most of them again," Langston Hughes writes in *I Wonder as I Wander*. The book, which he calls an autobiographical journey, describes Hughes' travelings from 1930 to 1937.

"When I was twenty-seven," he begins, "the stock-market crash came. When I was twenty-eight my personal crash came. Then I guess I woke up. So, when I was almost thirty, I began to make my living from writing." Hughes had been a long time getting through college. He graduated in 1929, and had worked in a hat store, on a truck farm, in a flower shop, and as a doorman, second cook, waiter, beachcomber, bum, and seaman, on the way. In that time he was writing poems too, and a novel, *Not Without Laughter,* which earned him a $400 award, which was what he had in 1929 when he lost his patron and decided to go to Haiti for a while.

He knew pretty well by then that he wanted to be a writer, but it was not so easy for a Negro to get a living out of writing. In Haiti he started to think about making poetry pay, and during the next few years which took him from Port au Prince to Havana, through the south via New York to San Francisco, and then to Moscow, Tashkent, Tokyo, Shanghai, Carmel, California, Mexico City, Harlem, Cleveland, Madrid, and finally Paris, he got along.

With stops in Russia during the "heroic days" of the second Five Year Plan and in Spain in 1937, Langston Hughes' journey from 1930 to 1937 paralleled those of many writers and journalists born around 1900. But Hughes' story is not much like those of such men as Stephen Spender, Louis Aragon, Louis Fischer, George Orwell, and Arthur Koestler.

The difference is that the travels of the latter group often served some carefully thought out intellectual purpose, and Hughes never cared much for ideology. Orwell chose to go down and out in Paris and London, and Koestler's trips to Palestine, Russia, and Spain were motivated by prior and (he thought) complete ideological commitments to Zionism, Communism, and finally the Popular Front. These men, particularly those who joined the Communist Party, were afflicted, wherever they went by an all-embracing purpose which made it difficult for them to see anything except in relation to that purpose.

Hughes and Koestler met by chance in Ashkhabad in 1932, and it is interesting to compare their accounts of the weeks they spent together in Russian Central Asia. Koestler had come to inspect the accomplishments of the Soviet Five Year Plan in backward areas such as Ashkhabad, while Hughes was enjoying a free vacation at the expense of the Russians after the movie he had come to Russia to make had turned into a fiasco.

"As I lay on the sheetless bed," Koestler writes in *The Invisible Writing*—"enveloped by gloom and stench, counting the familiar stains on the wall which crushed bed-bugs leave behind, I heard the sound of a gramophone in the next room." It was Hughes, playing Sophie Tucker on his phonograph, not bothering to notice the dirt. While Koestler was disgusted by the filth and unsanitary living habits, and only briefly amused by a local purge trial, Hughes was enjoying lavish Turk hospitality and occasionally reading the voluminous notes Koestler took each day. What Koestler found most everywhere failed to meet his expectations, and Hughes, having none, was mostly satisfied.

When Koestler described those days in 1953, he apologized, "I found it impossible to revive the naive enthusiasm of that period." This was not Hughes' way. His enthusiasm stayed fresh because it was for people and things, not ideas, which date faster. While he protested violently against the Scottsboro decision and later against Franco's bombing Madrid, his protest was not a Party member's, but always that of an individual. As he was convinced by the discovery of a swank little restaurant in Tashkent: "The system under which the successful live—left or right, capitalist or communists—did not seem to make much difference to that group of people, in every city around the globe, who managed by hook or crook to live well."

Though it was often by crook, Hughes usually managed to live well, or fully. Unlike those who distorted themselves and what they saw to correspond with prefixed ideas, Hughes was willing to take things pretty much as he found them and, if possible, to get fun out of them. In Russia for instance a free dental filling "seemed to me a minor miracle." "Moscow dental customs, the unveiling of the harem women in Turkestan, and the disappearance of the color line throughout Soviet Asia, are the three achievements I remember best of the whole USSR."

Of course he could never forget the barriers that faced a Negro at home; and it made him more tolerant of the Russians, for all their purge trials and liquidations. He said he felt about Communism as Frederick Douglass thought of abolition, "Whatever else it might be—it was not un-friendly to the slaves." "After all," he concluded, "I suppose how anything is seen depends on whose eyes look at it."

Hughes' willingness to take things as they came sometimes reached astonishing proportions. There was the day when he arrived in Shanghai, not knowing a soul, nor a word of the language: "Hardly had I climbed into a rickshaw than I saw riding in another along the Bund a Negro who looked exactly like a Harlemite. I stood up in my rickshaw and yelled, 'Hey man!' He stood up in his rickshaw and yelled, 'What ya sayin'?' We passed each other in the crowded street, and I never saw him again."

Hughes made few prejudgments about the people that passed his way, and knew that few judgments—least of all those one makes about oneself—are final. He was not so absorbed in his own purposes as not to notice what was going on around him. And often enough it was the funny side of things that got his attention, in besieged Madrid for instance, where Franco broadcasted each day the Falangists' dinner menus to the hungry loyalists, and where he and his friends would play Jimmie Lunceford's "Organ Grinder's Swing" all night to drown out the noise of the bombing.

What he saw in Madrid could only be wondered at—a girl practicing her piano the morning after a shell had passed through her house taking with it part of the living room wall and the top corner of the piano. "The will to live and laugh in this city of over a million people under fire, each person in constant danger, was to me a source of amazement." Langston Hughes is that kind of traveler who seeks after little, and, so, discovers much to wonder at.

499

Nick Aaron Ford
"Literature of Race and Culture"
Phylon, 18 (First Quarter 1957), 88–9

In *I Wonder as I Wander* Langston Hughes has apparently attempted a four-fold task: to entertain, to present historical and cultural information about far-away places, to point out attitudes toward race and color in various parts of the world, and to reveal his philosophy of art and of life. This latest of his more than twenty books is a grand mixture of autobiography, history, gossip, legend, sociology, travel guide, compendium of names of famous contemporary writers and artists, and poetry.

It is divided into eight chapters, each chapter containing from six to eighteen sub-divisions. The most successful chapters, in this reviewer's opinion, are "South to Samarkand," which deals with life, legends, customs, and human interest experience encountered in Soviet Central Asia; "Writing for a Living," which gives intimate glimpses into the heart and soul of the author as well as a thoroughly enjoyable discussion of the trials and tribulations he endured in the process of having his play *Mulatto* produced on Broadway; and "World Without End," which effectively dramatizes first-hand experiences of the Spanish Civil War.

This book begins where *The Big Sea* (1940) ended. Using the incident of his break with his wealthy patron, which had served as the climax of the earlier volume, he proceeds to relate his most notable experiences from 1929 to 1938. In addition to tours through the states to read his poetry, his travels during those years extended through Cuba, Haiti, Russia, China, Japan, Hawaii, France, and Spain. He tells intimate anecdotes of his association with such famous writers and artists as Arthur Koestler, Ernest Hemingway, Robinson Jeffers, Lincoln Steffens, Diego Rivera, and a host of others not so well known to the American public.

Assuming that I have rightly stated Hughes' four objectives in the writing of this book, I now address myself to the question of his success in accomplishing those objectives. On the whole, his peculiar wit, his humor, the content of his legends and anecdotes, and often his style and language make entertaining reading. But at times dull hunks of historical backgrounds of events and places get in the way. Sometimes the historical and cultural information appears to be extraneous, dragged in to demonstrate the author's knowledge. For the most part, this type of information is delightfully and successfully conveyed through legend and anecdote.

Almost every sub-chapter contains one or more incidents calculated to reveal attitudes toward race and color. The author makes it clear that he thoroughly enjoys associating with members of his own race and seeks them out wherever he goes. He makes it equally clear that for him friendship and camaraderie are not limited by race or color. He is impatient at discrimination and segregation of all kinds, but seldom bitter. He points with derision and pity at those who are committed to the doctrine of racial inferiority and superiority, some of whom he finds in every country.

His philosophy of art and of life shows up at intervals throughout the volume. He states his artistic credo thus: "I did not want to write for the pulps, or turn out fake 'true' stories to sell under anonymous names as Wallace Thurman did. I did not want to bat out slick non-Negro short stories in competition with a thousand other commercial writers trying to make *The Saturday Evening Post.* I wanted to write seriously and as well as I know how about Negro people, and make that kind of writing earn for me a living."

Stretching his philosophy beyond art to life, he says, "In the last few years I had been all around the embattled world and I had seen people walking tightropes everywhere—the tightrope of color in Alabama, the tightrope of transition in the Soviet Union, the tightrope of repression in Japan, the tightrope of the fear of war in France—and of war itself in China and in Spain—and myself everywhere on my tightrope of words. Anybody is liable to fall off a tightrope, in any land, I thought, and God help you if you fall the wrong way."

Despite the many favorable aspects, there are several shortcomings that cannot be ignored. First, the book is eighteen years too late. The material is topical, documentary, polemical, treated for the most part journalistically. If it had been published in 1938 or 1939 when it was written (or should have been) while the topical events were still fairly fresh, it could have had a powerful impact. But it takes more than humor and wit and a few philosophical comments to transform yesterday's news copy into today's literature.

Secondly, the overemphasis on the amatory experiences of the author is unfavorable. The normal reader expects to find sex in literature when it serves a necessary purpose, but for Hughes to relate intimate details of his own sex life, especially with other men's wives, seems in bad taste, to say the least. It appears that he is bragging about his virility or sex appeal or both.

Thirdly, his constant references to praise of his work by others and his reproduction of news items attesting to his notoriety suggest an immaturity that is not expected of serious writers.

Fourthly, there is too much serious attention given to gossip and hearsay.

Although these faults detract, they do not prevent *I Wonder as I Wander* from affording many moments of pleasure and profit to those who take the time to read it.

Alvin R. Rolfs
"Artist on the Wing: Peripatetic Life of Negro Poet"
St. Louis Post-Dispatch, 6 January 1957, p. 4D

It might be said that Langston Hughes was born walking, was educated running, and was "discovered" flying—this last on Pegasus itself. For since childhood he has wandered in a modern odyssey, rubbing shoulders with widely—and often wildly—diverse people in all corners of Africa, Asia, Europe, and America. And in poems, novels, short stories, plays, essays (and of course autobiography) he has recorded his ample, adventurous experience.

He absorbed myriad-faced, multimannered humanity while a doorman at one Paris cabaret and second cook at another, ordinary seaman on freighters, menial in Washington's Wardman Park Hotel. Here he gave three of his poems to Vachel Lindsay. Lindsay read them to his audience in the hotel's little theater, and the next day Hughes found himself "more or less a public curiosity in the dining room—a colored busboy who wrote poetry."

Within the next few years he won substantial awards for his poetry and fiction and consolidated his position as one of the most versatile, prolific, and representative of the New Negro artists.

A good deal of this he has told well in a previous volume of autobiography, *The Big Sea* (1940). His second such, and his twenty-first book, *I Wonder as I Wander,* picks up his life story in 1931 and carries it down to the end of 1937.

We first follow him to the Caribbean ("I went to Haiti to get away from my troubles")—an area that teemed with materials which he sagaciously marshals for the enrichment of travel literature, but never without a keen awareness of social constraints and divisions to which as a poet and liberal he was rawly sensitive. Then, back in the States, he spends some months, on the suggestion of Mary McLeod Bethune, taking "poetry to the people" via the lecture platform; and he goes through the East and South and Southwest to the Golden Gate itself, "the first Negro poet in America to span the continent, coast to coast, with his poetry."

From San Francisco's Russian Hill he leaps to Russia's Moscow—from the best of American capitalism to the showplace of Soviet Communism—invited to serve as a writer of English dialogue for a Negro motion picture group being organized in Harlem to go to the U.S.S.R. to make a film.

Here the book expands into a medley of melodrama, anti-climax, propagandistic fable, folklore. Also, some of the best objective reporting yet done on the Russia of the early Thirties, especially interesting to set alongside Truman Capote's highly praised report (*The Muses Are Heard*) on the tour of the all-Negro *Porgy and Bess* company behind the Iron Curtain in 1955.

The Meschrobpom Films' hilariously improbable scenario was typical of the naivete of the whole program involving the "Negro-worker-comrades," and nothing came of it but "an international scandal and front-page headlines around the world," Hughes writes. *Black and White*

died before a foot of it was shot, and the 22 would-be moviemakers scattered to the four winds.

Hughes knocked about for more than a year as writer and journalist—from Moscow to Samarkand, Odessa to Tashkent, Turkmenistan to Uzbekistan, back to Moscow and away again—before he came home.

The value of all this? Good autobiography answers that question with the powerful pulsebeat of living men and women, with panoramas of living history. And this is good autobiography. In it, moreover, unmistakable, implicit and explicit, are those observations and convictions that have led one distinguished contemporary to call Langston Hughes the Negro artist "most divinely capable of realizing and giving expression to the dark perturbations in the soul of the Negro."

[J.] Saunders Redding "Book Review" *Baltimore Afro-American Magazine,* 12 January 1957, p. 2

Traveling is a drug to which one can quickly become addicted, especially if he happens to have all the equipment that goes into the making of a fine writer, and also especially if he begins to travel at that very early time before the possession of the equipment is realized as a responsibility.

Langston Hughes began early—out of necessity.

He has kept at it since out of habit and also probably because, like most of today's writers, he believes that traveling is good for him, for any writer.

(On this latter point though, I must say that there is room for argument.

Except for one brief trip to Belgium, Jane Austen never left her backyard; and all the traveling Anthony Trollope did was on a dinky commuter train from Barchester to his dinky job in the London Post Office; and all Leo Tolstoy did . . . etc. etc. Staying at home did not hurt them any.)

While still a schoolboy, Langston Hughes moved from one Mid-western city to another, and on to Mexico where for a time he lived with his father and was cared for by three lovely and very religious ladies.

Still in his teens, he joined up as a merchant seaman and sailed half around the world.

At twenty-one or twenty-two he had seen more of "strange peoples and their stranger ways" than ten ordinary men see in a lifetime.

And much of what he had seen and done before he reached his legal majority made delightful and significant reading in the first volume of his autobiography, *The Big Sea.*

I Wonder as I Wander is the second volume. It begins in time approximately where the first volume ends.

Mr. Hughes went to college late, and his college days are over and the depression is on when *I Wonder as I Wander* opens.

He is beginning to feel the responsibility a writer has both to himself and the world.

It is pertinent to recall that among the things he did at the beginning of his career was to visit the Scottsboro Boys in the death house at Kilby prison, where he read them poetry.

If the sense of responsibility had begun, so had the expressions of it which make Langston Hughes a particular delight.

But his visit to the Scottsboro Boys is only an incident in a long, long journey around the eastern half of the world, from Moscow to Ashkhabad, to Tashkent, Samarkand, to Hong Kong and Shanghai—and eventually to Spain.

He went to Russia to write for the Russian production of a film about American Colored people. When he got there, the film had already been written—and badly—by a famous Russian writer, but Mr. Hughes stayed on for a year in the USSR.

He went everywhere there and saw everything and had a delightful time, and his humor is such that even the misery he suffered is transmuted into pleasurable moments for the reader.

In Russia he met and traveled with Arthur Koestler, had Ivy Litvinoff for a friend, and Karl Radek for an editor. In Shanghai he met the fabulous Teddy Weatherford.

In Tokyo he brushed with the Japanese police. In Spain he drank with Ernest Hemingway. Such names naturally have a special attraction, but Langston Hughes does not give up the personalities that go with the names.

The one personality that shines through the pages of *I Wonder as I Wander* is Langston Hughes' own, and it is especially delightful, for it is a personality without pretense, or brass, or side. *I Wonder as I Wander* may not be a "significant book," but it is a fascinating one.

503

Anthony West
"Books: Briefly Noted"
New Yorker, 32 (12 January 1957), 103–4

Mr. Hughes was born in Missouri and raised in Kansas, Illinois, and Ohio, and has been mostly on the move ever since. In this autobiographical volume, a kind of complement to his *The Big Sea,* he recalls his travels, intellectual as well as physical, during the nineteen-thirties—in the Soviet Union (where he found little, beyond the absence of a color line, to admire), in China (where he dined with Mme. Sun Yat-sen), in Japan (from which he was deported for his acquaintance with Mme. Sun), in California (where he fell in with the Jim Tully set), and in Spain (where he covered the civil war for the Baltimore *Afro-American*). An immensely interesting book, written with bounce and zest, about a time that now seems very long ago.

Frank Marshall Davis
"Frank-ly Speaking: *I Wonder as I Wander"*
Honolulu Record, 31 January 1957, pp. [8], 6

It was around 1930 that Langston Hughes decided to make a living from writing. How he came to this decision, and the people, places and events which contributed to his literary activity from that period through his experiences with the Loyalists during the Spanish Civil War, form the basis for the distinguished au-

thor's newest volume, *I Wonder as I Wander,* recently published by Rinehart.

This is not an inexpensive book since it has a price tag of $6. But for those interested in literature, events of the recent past as viewed by a discerning observer, and a sensitive Negro's reactions to people and society from the Caribbean through Dixie, Russia, China, Japan and Spain, it is hard to find a better buy than this fascinating 405 page volume.

Langston currently has 21 books to his credit including poetry, fiction, juveniles and autobiography. His life has been extraordinarily full and rich. *I Wonder as I Wander* is his second autobiography—*The Big Sea* was his first—and it covers a period less than a decade. He has crammed so much into his life that he undoubtedly has enough experiences for perhaps two more autobiographical volumes although only in his early 50's.

With some $400 from his first novel, *Not Without Laughter,* and after a complete break with an elderly Park Avenue woman who had been his patron, Langston and a companion, a Cleveland art student, set out in a borrowed car for Florida and then to Cuba and Haiti. He had already won national acclaim, so when they stopped at Bethune Cookman college in Florida to visit Mary McLeod Bethune, long recognized as America's leading Negro woman, his reception was such as to germinate the idea of annual tours of Southern Negro schools which he still continues.

His experiences with the color line in Cuba and Haiti as well as life in those areas make interesting reading. As one might expect, he had many brushes with jim crow on his literary tours of the South. He also became acquainted, through a friend, with Noel Sullivan of San Francisco and both there and at Carmel he met many of the coast's leading writers, artists and actors. It was while in California that he received an offer to join a Negro motion picture troupe being formed in Harlem to make a film in Russia. Hollywood, of course, had its doors barred to Negro writers no matter how talented, so Langston jumped at this opportunity.

The Soviet Union, in which Langston lingered after the rest of the troupe went home when the film plan fell through, impressed him for its lack of discrimination. There were many inconveniences and annoyances, but what disturbed many white journalists and tourists did not bother him because he was looking through the eyes of a Negro long conditioned in his homeland by racism. He visited many sections of the vast country and witnessed the actual struggle of the new order to get rid of the patterns of the czarist regime.

Coming home by way of Siberia, he touched Korea on his way to Japan, had dinner with Madame Sun Yat Sen in Shanghai, then returned to Japan where he ran into trouble—because he had been in Moscow, had dined with Madame Sun Yat Sen, and was personally acquainted with many radical writers. After long sessions with the Tokyo police who finally decided he was not a Communist, he was ordered out of Japan. He stopped briefly in Honolulu on his way back to California.

Langston was writing at Carmel when he got word that his father had died in Mexico City. He spent some time in Mexico where he came to know such personages as Diego Rivera and Cartier-Bresson. After several months he returned to California and then Broadway where his play, "Mulatto," was being produced. While in New York, he was hired by the Baltimore Afro-American to serve as war correspondent in Spain because of the large number of Negro volunteers among the Loyalists. Despite the rigors of life under bombardment, he left Spain reluctantly. The book ends with him in Paris wondering if Hitler and Mussolini would start a world war.

The author's style is, as usual, disarmingly simple. The book is warm and human and shows Langston's love for people. You also get glimpses of world renowned personages whom he has met in his travels, as well as a completely fresh and different perspective on places and events.

I Wonder as I Wander is one of the most refreshing literary experiences of the decade.

Abner Berry
"Langston as Traveler"
Mainstream, 10 (February 1957), 61–2

Since the publication in the Mid-'Twenties of his best-seller book of poems, *The Weary Blues,* Langston Hughes has earned an enormous reputation as a Negro writer in the folk idiom. Novels, short stories, poems, sketches, plays and travel books have cascaded from his typewriter, all of them revealing an essentially earthy quality of Negro life. In *I Wonder as I Wander* Hughes sums up his experiences and impressions from the time when he wrote "mostly because, when I felt bad, writing kept me from feeling worse ... put my emotions into exterior form" to the fall of the Spanish Republic. And in doing so he has achieved a work of charm, suffused with a rare, uninhibited honesty and good will, unblemished by personal ax-grinding and the erosion of vagrant political winds.

Hughes is frankly a "Negro writer" whose work dates to the "Harlem Renaissance" of the 1920's. Barred because of his race from jobs with big publishers, from Hollywood and the offices of the slick magazines, he settled down to doing what he most wanted to do. As he puts it: "I wanted to write seriously and as well as I knew about the Negro people, and to make *that* kind of writing earn me a living."

Hughes succeeded, first through the support of patrons, and later, when rich patrons' tastes became jaded, by taking his poems to the people, touring southern Negro college campuses, and by his own prodigious literary production. He gives the reader a peek at the process of his own development in the book under review.

We go with Hughes to Cuba, Haiti, Mexico and across the southern United States. In Mexico, where his father, an attorney, had become an extensive landowner, he learned Spanish and was introduced to Spanish literature. It was his reading of Cervantes' *Don Quixote,* he informs us, that gave him the inspiration for the character Jesse B. Semple, through whose eyes Hughes later gave readers revealing insights into American Negro life.

But perhaps the most engaging of Hughes' travel sketches are those concerning his experiences in Spain and the Soviet Union. To the Soviet Union where he had gone with a Negro group to write a scenario for a film on Negro life, he brought the vision and perception of an American Negro. The film was cancelled, causing the disillusionment of many of those with whom he came, but Hughes stayed on to visit the Soviet East. In Tashkent, Samarkand, Bokhara and other towns in an area newly freed from Czarism, Hughes had some of his most hilarious—and interesting—associations. He covers such items as love making among the Tartars, Christmas with American Negroes in Uzbekistan, and reflections on the similarity of the Czarist segregation from which these Asian people had been freed and the kind he had experienced in the United States. Hughes' utter goodwill permits him to understand the sensibilities of the displaced Russian aristocrats while his sympathies

for the ascendant brown Asians under socialism remain firm.

Hughes met the young reporter, Arthur Koestler, in Soviet Asia. Koestler was continually complaining about the dirt and wondering why the revolution had to come to this land and not to nice clean Germany. Hughes' memory of the American South caused him to take a different view from Koestler's. For one thing, Hughes concluded, even if dirty, these people had power and were not jimcrowed as they had been under the Czar.

With a literary deftness, Hughes separates the red tape and bureaucracy, of which he complained goodnaturedly, from the advances made by the people he came in contact with. He could not say with Koestler: "What a hell of a place to have a revolution!" Hughes gives his readers a revealing glimpse of the Soviet Union during the early 1930's and then moves on to other adventures in Korea, Japan and China.

Writing of Spain where he served as a correspondent during the Civil War, Hughes reminds us of the continuing tragedy of that fascist-ruled country. And his memoirs contain the record of the American Negroes who fought on the loyalist side in addition to pen portraits of other Americans including Ernest Hemingway, Lillian Hellman and an anonymous lady who nearly lost her life at Madrid because she wanted to see the front.

From Harlem to Havana, Port au Prince, Mexico City, Moscow, Tashkent, Tokyo, Shanghai, San Francisco and points south, Langston Hughes traveled and remembered that he was the son of the oppressed. And no matter what city or country he visited there is no mistaking what side he was on.

And the greatness and one-ness of humanity shine through every page. To this reviewer, the book was a rewarding experience.

Luther P. Jackson, Jr.
"Globe-trotting Bard"
Crisis, 44 (February 1957), 119–20

Langston Hughes is the last practitioner among the corps of novelists whose star ascended in the 1920s. Countee Cullen, Claude McKay, Wallace Thurman and Rudolph Fisher are long gone to their great reward. Some perhaps suffered the fate of the depression's Giles Johnson, Ph.D., who—as Frank Marshall Davis tells it— "could orate in Latin or cuss in Greek and, having learned such things, he died of starvation because he wouldn't teach and he couldn't porter." Others, however, gladly sought refuge in Seats of Higher Learning.

Only Hughes stuck it out and he is now being well compensated for any privations he suffered during his long artistic career. In addition to this six-dollar autobiography, other Hughes books on current booklists include *A Pictorial History of the Negro in America, Simple Takes a Wife,* and *The Sweet Flypaper of Life.* Hughes also has written lyrics for folksongs, juvenile books, newspaper columns, jazz criticism and reams of poetry.

Whereas most writers settle for one autobiography, Hughes already has written two, *The Big Sea* and *I Wonder as I Wander.* His latest only covers the years from 1930 to 1938, so it could well be sub-titled Volume II of the life and times of one of America's most colorful (no pun intended) talents. But like most of Hughes' works, *I Wonder* is marked by a lack of reasoning of whys and wherefores of race relations. Hughes is at his wonderful best when he reports on the troubles of poor Harlem Negroes or the ways of white folks. In his "Simple" stories and in much of his poetry

Hughes captured the Negro idiom with unequaled warmth and compassion. But when it comes to telling on himself or his friends, Hughes is strangely evasive, two autobiographies to the contrary notwithstanding.

Almost half of Volume II is devoted to Hughes' wanderings in Soviet Russia. Hughes made the trip as a member of a theater group which was to have made a Russian movie which never materialized. As for Hughes' opinions of the Soviet system, suffice it to say that he seems to take a middle-of-the-road position, neatly balancing the pros and cons until they add up to zero.

Hughes also hop-scotches to Japan, China, Spain and France, but the book's best sections are the first two which deal with hungry night in the Caribbean and lecture tours of southern Negro colleges. Best of all is his account of his trip from Daytona Beach, Florida, to New York with an artist friend and the late Mrs. Mary Bethune riding the single seat of a Ford coupe. It seems that Mrs. Bethune had planned a trip to New York by train, so she rode along with the boys to save the fare. Hughes reports that whenever the trio got hungry on the road, they stopped at the home of some of Mrs. Bethune's friends. He continues:

"According to a popular saying in Florida, before Mrs. Bethune reached the wayside home of any friend anywhere, the chickens, sensing that she was coming, went flying off frantically seeking a safe hiding place. They knew some necks would surely be wrung in her honor to make a heaping platter of southern fried chicken."

It was the remarkable Mrs. Bethune who urged Hughes to go all over the South reading his poems. Hughes tells how he bargained with college officials for fees, scaling them from $100 down to a square meal. He recaptured the attention of slumbering audiences with a poem about miscegenation—"a very provocative subject in the South," he slyly adds.

These little insights into Hughes' warm personality are too few and far between. Maybe in his next volume he'll tell more about how he made poems pay at a time when Negro writers were dropping like flies.

Antoinette Scudder
"Wandering Poet"
Newark Sunday News, section 3, 17 February 1957, p. E2

The well-known Negro poet and journalist has in this very substantial volume told his own life history, from the time when the great depression and his desertion by his early patrons threw him on his own resources through his coverage of the Spanish Civil War for the *Baltimore Afro-American* and other papers.

It is a stirring and colorful chronicle, describing his jaunts about Cuba and Haiti, his troubadourlike journeyings to bring his poetry to the Negro populations of the South, his trip to Moscow to take part in the production of the famous—or infamous—Meschrobpom production of a film supposed by its Russian authors to portray race and labor conditions and struggles in the U.S.A. This last venture ended in serio-comic frustration but resulted likewise in more fantastic journeying to places known to most of us only by name—Bokhara, Tashkent, Samarkand, the Karakum Desert, then briefly back to Moscow and from there to China and Japan.

Dirt, discomfort, dreariness, danger—

make up most of the picture but not dullness—Hughes is a first-rate narrator with a hearty humor which triumphs over all difficulties and perils and the rare gift of quick and vivid portrayal whether of characters or incidents. His outlook on humanity and its problems has both breadth and keenness; his sympathy for the "under dog," whether represented by his own race or the proletariat in general, does not inhibit a tender and charming rendering of the other side—as in the fragile Russian aristocrat who fed him with chicken and blintzes when he was ill in Moscow or the gentle Mexican spinsters with their candle lit Madonnas and their tiny packets of rice, soap and sugar for the poor.

His adventures in the sex line, if drawn with a frankness which may startle some readers, are at least free of the elaborate vulgarity common in present day writing.

John W. Parker
"Poet Wanderer"
Raleigh News and Observer, part 3, 10 March 1957, p. 5

I Wonder as I Wander is an intimate narrative of travel and adventure—a humorous-serious disclosure of the personality of an American author once labeled as the "Negro poet laureate." It is a chronicle of significant and dramatic moments viewed in retrospect—moments which Langston Hughes experienced with people and places and things in far-flung regions of the globe. In point of time, it takes up approximately where the first volume of his autobiography, *The Big Sea* (1940), leaves off. And even though the newly issued publication is grounded in solid fact, it is written in lucid, buoyant prose that makes it read like a novel.

The fascination which attaches to *The Big Sea,* written nearly two decades earlier, is perhaps intensified in *I Wonder as I Wander.* The latter treatise, which covers the period of Hughes' literary maturity, points up the writer's increasing mastery of his art and portrays his implicit faith in his way of life and in the business of probing the emotional heights and depths of the Negro people in America.

"What's New at the Library"
Middleboro [Mass.] *Gazette,* 14 March 1957, p. 2

Mr. Hughes is the world's most famous Negro poet. He has looked into his life and recalled its most dramatic and intimate moments in this narrative of travel and adventure in the world of poetry and politics. *I Wonder as I Wander* is a continuously amusing and revealing picture of an American writer journeying around an exciting world he loves.

N.K.D.
"The New Books"
San Francisco Chronicle This World, 17 March 1957, p. 24

Langston Hughes, the poet, is a man for the "blues." "The mood of the 'blues,'" he

has said, "is most always despondency, but when they are sung people laugh." To illustrate the point, he once wrote a short story titled "Laughing to Keep from Crying."

Now, in putting down his "autobiographical journey," Hughes cites his debt to both Greek and barbarian, "wise" and "unwise," then proceeds on a moderately happy-go-lucky hegira—laced though it sometimes is with angry "incident"— through the Depression Decade of the 1930s.

Whether traveling through the U.S. reading his poems at Negro colleges or making his way around the world as a journalist (a trek which includes a lengthy stay in the Soviet hinterlands of Turkestan, an Oriental excursion, and Spanish Civil War coverage), Mr. Hughes strikes one as a pretty smooth cat who always lands gracefully on his feet. The blue note lurks in his life but, for the most part, the basic beat sounds real joyous.

Whenever his money runs low, a lucky assignment or a sale of work allows Mr. Hughes more happy wandering. Yet, he maintains his protest.

Frank Greenwood
"Book Review"
Los Angeles Tribune, 16 May 1958, [p. ?]

I Wonder as I Wander is a rich, big book, written by one of the richest men in America, Langston Hughes, poet, playwright and satirist. Hughes isn't a rich man monetarily speaking, but he is rich in experience, having traveled around the world several times, visiting countries and people seldom visited by other writers. He shares his riches with the world in this big book, which is very rewarding in its humor, ideas, philosophy, adventure, etc. The greatest compliment I can pay it is to say that I read it twice and plan to reread its 405 pages.

The book covers the travels of the world's most famous Negro poet from the crash in 1929 to the eve of World War II in 1938. There is a lifetime of experience and observations packed in those 9 years. Armchair travelers will vicariously visit the deep South, the USSR, Haiti, Cuba, China, Japan, Spain, etc., meeting such world famed personages as Ramon Novarro, Arthur Koestler, Madam Sun Yat Sen, Jacques Romain, Lincoln Steffens, Ernest Hemingway, and Mary McLeod Bethune. When the journey is finished the traveler is exalted and wiser from having met so many peoples of the world and experiencing their customs.

Because of the richness of the book, it is most difficult to review it. I can only cover the portions that were the most rewarding and revealing to me.

Langston Hughes begins the book when he made up his mind to make his living as a writer of poems and stories. This, in itself, is a difficult thing, but to make it really difficult, he decided he was going to write HONEST poems and stories about Negroes, and still make a living at it. How he did it is told in this book.

Mary McLeod Bethune made the most valuable suggestion during the Depression, of taking his poetry to the Negro colleges in the South. He did so and made it pay. He read poetry and lectured to college professors and sharecroppers. Many of the ideas presented are feasible today for Negro artists struggling to make a living and finding an audience. From these experiences and others similar to them, Hughes writes "I have discovered in life that there are ways of getting almost anywhere you want to go if you REALLY want to go. You might have to squeeze through a knothole, humble yourself, or drink muddy tea from consumptive bowls, or eat camel sausage, pass for Mexican, or take the LAST chance. If you want to see the world or write honest books, you do such things by taking a chance."

Jeffrey White [tenth grader]
"What the Young Readers Have to Say: A Special Report by Junior Critics"
Winston-Salem Journal and Sentinel, 29 October 1967, p. D5

This autobiographical account of the travels of a famous Negro poet deals generally with race. The method the author uses is interesting. Whenever he sees a different class of man, he tells his history and his traits. Although the setting of the book is the 1930s, the main topics—music, government, war and sex—perfectly suit the present.

Geography plays a key role, and the author's skillful use of words enables the reader to picture every detail of the people he met. If travel interests you, you should read this book. If not, its drawn-out text may prove boring.

Charles Guenther
"Heroic Black Voices, Praise at Last"
St. Louis Post-Dispatch, section D, 1 February 1987, p. 5

Though rather neglected since his death, Langston Hughes is still the main exemplar of modern black poets of social expression. His autobiography, *I Wonder as I Wander,* first published in 1956, is now reprinted with a new foreword by his longtime friend, Margaret Walker. The book takes its title from an old folk-song or spiritual, and begins about 1930, where his earlier journal, *The Big Sea,* leaves off.

In his poetry Hughes had a genius for pithy messages in vernacular language. His journals are written in a crisp, plain style any journalist might admire. And his world travels are something anyone (including business travelers) might envy. In Japan, for instance, a half century ago, Hughes writes, "At the Imperial Hotel I was given a cream and beige room with deep rugs, a wide soft bed and a big bath. It was on the first floor just off the lobby and, at the rate of exchange then, did not cost very much." (How times have changed!)

I Wonder as I Wander is filled with wondrous revelations, confessions, descriptions. Some of the most fascinating parts deal with his journeys to the Soviet Union and Central Asia. Others deal with "Writing for a Living" and the production of his play, *Mulatto,* in 1935–36 (a play banned in Philadelphia). Scores of eminent world writers, from Asia to Civil War Spain, befriended Hughes along with artists of all expressions. As Walker points out, these vignettes show Hughes' kaleidoscopic mind and experiences, and, however briefly, give us "the exhilarating pleasure of his presence."

Checklist of Additional Reviews

"150 Major Promotion Campaigns of the Fall Season: Rinehart: *I Wonder as I Wander,*" *Publishers Weekly,* 170 (17 September 1956), 1351.

Jessie Kitching, "Nonfiction Forecast," *Publishers Weekly,* 170 (8 October 1956), 1817.

"Samples for Readers," *Memphis Commercial Appeal,* section 5, 11 November 1956, p. 10.

"Weekly Record: Hughes, Langston," *Publishers Weekly,* 170 (12 November 1956), 2238.

L. M. Collins, "Negro Lives Spot Strain on Society," *Nashville Tennessean,* 18 November 1956, p. 4H.

Francis A. Klein, "Book Marks," *St. Louis Globe-Democrat,* 18 November 1956, p. 4F.

"Biography," *Booklist,* 53 (1 December 1956), 174.

John LaFarge, "Every Tenth American," *America,* 96 (15 December 1956), 331–2.

[J.] Saunders Redding, "Travels of Langston Hughes: Events as Seen in Passing," *New York Herald Tribune Book Review,* 23 December 1956, p. 6.

Roi Ottley, "Extraordinary Books on American Negroes," *Chicago Tribune Magazine of Books,* part 4, 6 January 1957, p. 9.

E.G., "Footloose Poet: Langston Hughes Recalls Roving Life of 1930s: Up from Slavery in Prose and Pictures,"

Milwaukee Journal, part 5, 13 January 1957, p. 4.

O. B. Duthie, "Wanderings of a Poet," *Richmond Times-Dispatch*, 3 February 1957, p. L5.

L.B.S., "Poet Langston Hughes Uses Travel in Autobiography," *Indianapolis Star*, section 6, 3 February 1957, p. 14.

A.S.H., "Second Volume of His Life," *Worcester Telegram*, 10 February 1957, p. D11.

Michael Sean O'Shea, "The Sardi Set: All Hail Hill and Wang," *Back Stage*, 5 (21 February 1964), 2, 11.

"Nonfiction," *Bibliographic Survey: The Negro in Print*, 3 (May 1968), 5.

"New in Paperback: Nonfiction," *Washington Post Book World*, 16 (9 November 1986), 20.

Patricia T. O'Conner, "Paperbacks: New and Noteworthy," *New York Times Book Review*, 23 November 1986, p. 42.

Alex Raskin, "Now in Paperback," *Los Angeles Times Book Review*, 23 November 1986, p. 14.

A PICTORIAL HISTORY OF THE NEGRO IN AMERICA

"A Pictorial History of the Negro in America" Virginia Kirkus Bulletin, 24 (1 October 1956), 769

Coverage of the life of the Negro in the United States from pre-revolutionary days to the present provides a straight-forward text along with some 1000 illustrations from prints, engravings, woodcuts, photographs, paintings. They take in the important events and episodes in economic and political history, cite the general lot and trend of a people's progress as well as specific legislation and action, people who have worked for the cause of equal rights and Negroes who have made exceptional contributions. Cinque, Harriet Beecher Stowe, the Fugitive Slave Act, the Montgomery bus boycott—all are here—and through this writing we see the theme of slavery versus equality stretching from the country's early days to now. Clear historical perspective on an easy-reading level. (Illustrations not seen.) Recent *Life* article may direct interest.

J. Mason Brewer "Slavery Fills Many Pages in New Book" American-Statesman [Austin], 18 November 1956, p. B9

This volume of one thousand illustrations highlights the activities and problems of the American Negro from the period of exploration to the present time.

The bulk of the pictures and narratives depicts the social system of slavery, presenting an array of historical figures, both black and white, who were active in the abolitionist and underground railroad movements and in antislavery societies, as well as major authors of the period.

The economic, social, cultural and political aspects of the Negro's American existence are commented on only in a limited manner.

As usual, the most sparsely treated section is on the reconstruction. Following the pattern of its predecessors, this book simply mentions the fact that Negroes met their white contemporaries in Congress and state legislative halls, but the manner in which they served and the significance of their serving are omitted.

In harmony with the trend in American education which stresses visual education, this book meets a long-felt need. It has ingredients that lend themselves admirably to the causes of both intercultural and intracultural education at a time when these areas are so badly in need of development.

Although the book is a noteworthy contribution to American pictorial history, it falls short of its own goal of presenting pictures of every famous and important Negro from Nat Turner, Frederick Douglass and Dred Scott to modern leaders such as Adam Clayton-Powell, William Hastie and Ralph Bunche.

Grave omissions include Negroes such as Dr. Mordecai Johnson, present incumbent, and first Negro president of Howard University; the late L. K. Williams, world renowned Baptist leader, who served as vice-president of the Baptist World Alliance, and whose church, the Olivet Baptist Church in Chicago, was purported to have had the largest Protestant membership in the world during his pastorate; Jack Johnson, first Negro heavyweight boxing champion of the world; Oscar DePriest, first Negro to serve as a member of Congress since reconstruction days; Josh White, internationally known folk-singer; and Frederick D. Patterson, founder and director of the United Negro College Fund, without which many small church-related colleges would long since have ceased.

Many basic source materials which could have added to the stature of the work were not consulted—a fact always evident when authors, as in the case here, attempt to write books in fields where they are not trained technicians.

"Langston Hughes' Best Effort"
Black Dispatch [Oklahoma City], 23 November 1956, p. 6

A relative, who teaches school in another state, recently wrote us a letter deploring her idea there is nothing historically available about Negroes in the public school libraries, and requesting information about where she could look for this material. We told the young lady about a half dozen texts she could secure, regarding the history of Negroes since the days of Herodotus, who was the father of history. You know it was Herodotus, who lived a long time before the days of so-called "White Supremacy," who spoke in superlatives about the blacks of Africa and said, "They are beautiful people."

There is no reason for any school teacher to feel there is no background to dark people. If one is familiar with Josephus, and all of the early records to be found, especially in Spanish, Portuguese

and French, he will find much that will stir and thrill him about the history of sable-hued units of humanity. Delfosse's *Negroes of America* is one of this sort of books that gives a picture of the past when black people had great civilizations and empires. Of course we cannot blame the Negro school teachers, who know nothing about these texts, because they as well as their pupils are victims of present day phobias which dodge the background of the past. Such narrations destroy the propaganda of those who direct present-day thinking.

Despite this voluminous record of the past, we know Negroes, especially those who instruct in the public school system, will be delighted to know Langston Hughes and Milton Meltzer have placed on the market during the month of August *A Pictorial History of the Negro in the United States* [sic], a volume containing more than 1,000 historical drawings and pictures regarding the dent black folk have made upon American life since the day slave ships arrived on the shores of this nation from Africa.

In the three hundred and sixteen pages the authors have sought to condense a complete panoramic view of the black man from the days when he was inspired to seek God's guidance, without letting anyone hear him pray in the wilderness of despair. Here is a fascinating story, told in extremely readable language, that should not only be in the public schools but in every forward-looking black man's home. Pictures dot this text from the days of Nat Turner, that Virginia Negro who refused to be a slave, on down to Frederick Douglass, Booker T. Washington, Du Bois and Ralph Bunche.

We really feel that this book should grace the book shelves of everyone's library. It is a compendium that includes the trail the black man has made from the slave markets in New Orleans to the gold rush in California. The invention of the cotton gin is given its proper setting, as well as the background of Indian leadership in those early days when Osceola was dominant among the Seminoles.

Early day skilled workers of color find their place as well as the place of the black soldier in the American revolution up to and including the Korean police action of the Truman administration. Most of the pictures have been reproduced from material stored away in the Library of Congress, which convinces one of their authenticity, and one should be especially impressed of the dastardliness of slavery by the photostats made of printed "raffles" when "pretty Negro girls" were sold to the lucky ticket holders. One hand bill featured "One bay horse" and "mulatto girl." Quite evidently slaves in that period were more highly educated than free citizens today, for the handbill said the Negroes for sale could speak both French and English.

The days of the African Colonization Society are retold in this intriguing book. It encloses the *Alphabet of Slavery*, published in 1856, and a handbill announcing the 5th anniversary of the "Massachusetts Anti-Slavery Society" is listed, carrying one back to 1837. Those were the days when it was foolhardy to oppose human bondage in the southern section of the United States. This book lists numberless scores of white people who fought out in the open for equality under law for all people in the United States. The book is invaluable in that it unfolds the scores of both white men and women who were willing to give their all, back in those days, that black men and women have the same and identical freedom they possessed. It should surely be a tonic for all blacks who need confidence in the good intentions of present day white liberals. Pages 100 to 109 are given over to these revealing facts and personalities.

The Underground Railroad, the antebellum system by which this writer's father escaped from slavery, is given elaborate presentation, as well as black civil war heroes, which ended in Lincoln's Emancipation Proclamation. Fort Wagner, Fort Pillow and the federal army marching through Richmond are all pictorialized. A wonderful drawing of scenes in Congress when the 13th Amendment was passed graces one of the pages, and then Langston Hughes brings us up to the days of Booker T. Washington and the Ku Klux Klan, the period when so many blacks entered state legislatures of the South, and the national congress.

We do not want you to stop with this editorial. Send and get a copy. . . .

This book does not miss a thing worthwhile in American life. It carries pictures of Rev. Martin Luther King, Thurgood Marshall, and Autherine Lucy. This will be the best Christmas present any white or black man can contribute to his home. You'll even see the picture of Gloria Lockerman spelling "chrysanthemum."

P.L.P.
"The Week's Books"
Pittsburgh Courier Magazine, 24 November 1956, p. 2

I had hardly expected to live to see the day when such a startlingly superlative book as *A Pictorial History of the Negro in the United States* [*sic*], by Langston Hughes and Milton Meltzer, should be researched, planned, written and published. Its publication in itself is an event in Negro history. Other inferior attempts have been made to tell the story of the Negro with words and pictures. This is the first time it has been done with such skill, such artistry, such insight and such genuine craftsmanship.

If this book receives the circulation it deserves, it will, by its own strength and perfection, lift concretely the status of all Negroes. It is the focal point of racial pride, sought by Woodson, Franklin, Rogers, and others, in a strikingly graphic presentation.

Here is the focal point of racial pride in 320 large pages and 1,000 illustrations, superbly reproduced from old prints, engravings, woodcuts, photographs and paintings. The significance of these illustrations boldly captures your interest and attention from each of the printed pages.

Mr. Hughes, it is easy to surmise, has given this history the benefit of his known genius by reading between the lines of the old, old stories and reproducing with his gifted pen (or typewriter) something that makes sense. He writes discerning, sensitive prose. He also writes unassailable logic.

The authors have divided their history into seven parts, somewhat chronological, although the ante-bellum first three periods, or parts, are concurrent. They begin with the Negro's origins in Africa and come up to date with the Supreme Court decision on school segregation.

Their first story covers slavery, from Jamestown to Emancipation. The second covers the same period but is concerned with the Free Negro. Then they weave the thread-like fortunes of slaves and Free Negroes into the fight for freedom or the Anti-Slavery Movement.

The last four sections of the history are aptly and happily captioned: Up From Slavery: 1863–1900. Souls of Black Folk: 1900–1920. The New Negro: 1920–1941. Toward One World: 1941.

The cause of brotherhood and democracy would be inestimably advanced if copies of this remarkable history could be placed in every public school, college and university in the United States.

And Negro children of today and tomorrow would hold up their heads in pride if Negro parents of today would make *A Pictorial History of the Negro in the United States,* a part of the family library.

William Hogan
"A Graphic Document on the Negro in America"
San Francisco Chronicle, 29 November 1956, [p. 29]

Most of the history books used in our schools slight the Negro as a factor, Langston Hughes and Milton Meltzer declare in a foreword to their extraordinarily interesting *A Pictorial History of the Negro in America.*

Hughes, who has been called the poet laureate of the Negro people, and his collaborator on this project explain: "When a story about a Negro is printed on the front pages of today's newspapers, many readers have little or no background to which to relate the news."

The authors have tried to remedy this in a skillfully edited text accompanying some 90 photographs, drawings, handbills, anti-slavery posters and similar memorabilia that is devoted solely to the Negro's relationship to America's past.

While a history of the Negro in 316 pages, with illustrations, might suggest a once-over-lightly treatment, the authors have presented a surprisingly varied, stirring, informative—and often touching—document that attempts to strip legend and myth from the truth.

What particularly struck me about the book is that the authors permitted not a shred of propaganda, ax-grinding or special pleading in their capsule history. They have done a sound job of research, no emotion involved, unless it be a tinge of sadness and embarrassment a reader might feel when coming to grips with some of the more bleak facts of our national background.

The story goes back some 350 years, to when "black gold" poured into the Western world at the rate of 10,000 a year or more. There was the time when a Charlestown advertisement (reproduced in the book) made a great point of announcing a shipment of fine, healthy Negroes from the Windward and Rice coasts. "The utmost care," the handbill read, "has already been taken to keep them free from being infected with smallpox."

We follow this history through the age of great reformers; the Underground Railroad of the Civil War era; the pathetic "back to Africa" movement under which Negro colonists sailed for Liberia in 1850; less than 15,000 left, for America was their home.

The authors bring their story down to the present, with prideful accounts of such members of the Negro community as Harry Belafonte, the ballad singer; Federal Judge William Hastie; Marguerite Cartwright, educator; Jackie Robinson and many, many others. They are not complacent in mentioning the accomplishments of these citizens.

It being a running history, the results of the Supreme Court decision on desegregation and the recent Montgomery, Ala., bus boycott are included. The "trouble I seen" of the Negro's familiar lament, the authors suggest, is by no means ended.

D. E. S[aunders]
"Book of the Week"
Jet, 11 (29 November 1956), 46

In the authors' foreword, Langston Hughes and Milton Meltzer, who have collaborated in the compiling of *A Pictorial History of the Negro in America,* explain that their aim is to convey to the reader "the sweep of history" as it relates to the American Negro. They have succeeded in portraying not only the sweep, but the majesty that is inherent in the dramatic story of an enslaved people's struggle for full citizenship.

The text is brief and well written. Contrary to many history texts which are arranged in strictly chronological fashion, the first section of this volume deals with the concurrent streams of history, slavery, free Negroes and the fights of the abolitionists. The events since the Emancipation Proclamation are handled in the order of their occurrence—ending with the period in which we now live.

Many little known but highly important events and personalities are brought into sharp focus by the painstaking research that has gone into this work and the smooth manner in which the words and pictures have been woven into one swift-moving panorama. This is one of those rare books which should be in every Negro home and readily available for information and reference for grown-ups and children alike.

Mr. Meltzer and Mr. Hughes have unearthed documents and photographs, broadsides and posters that will give even a non-reading person an insight into the past of the Negro race in the United States. The illustrations give life and motion to the text and make this book an important contribution to the rapidly filling shelves devoted to the history of the Negro.

Milton S. Byam
"Too Late for Last Issue"
Library Journal, 81 (1 December 1956), 2849

Another volume in the pleasurable Crown series of pictorial histories, this is designed to "convey the sweep of history" (preface). It succeeds in giving the best one volume picture of the Negro's niche in America—not in any depth but interestingly and pleasurably. The authors have managed to collect some excellent and apt photographs and drawings to illustrate their subject. This is popular history at its most popular with emphasis on little-known facts. The articles are briefly and lucidly written by the famous Negro poet. Recommended for even the tiniest public library and young adult collection and browsing collections.

Webster Schott
"Negro's Big Part in History and Culture"
Kansas City Star, 1 December 1956, p. 14B

A *Pictorial History of the Negro in America,* with text by the poet-dramatist Langston Hughes (born in Joplin, Mo.) and illustrations gathered by Milton Meltzer, is probably the biggest book of its kind ever put together.

Illustrated with more than a thou-sand reproductions of pictures, paintings, broadsides, drawings, woodcuts and cartoons, it presents a panorama of the Negro in America from the arrival of the African slave ships to integration in the schools.

There is a minimum of sentimentality and a maximum of historic fact in Hughes's text, and it would take an expert in this area to find anything about the Negro in America that these two men have left untouched.

The most lasting impression one gets from this book—a document filled with pertinence to our times—is how intimately the history of the Negro is bound up with the mainstream of American history itself.

The big events in the life of the Negro have also been big events in American social, economic and political history. In this there is meaning for everyone.

R.F.
"Negro History Comes Alive in Pictures"
Worker, 9 December 1956, pp. 8–9

The highlight of the Negro people's history in America—their enslavement, their joys, their sorrows, their struggles to be free, their contributions to the culture of the land of their oppression—are effectively captured in this handsome pictorial study by Langston Hughes and Milton Meltzer.

From the slave traders to the Montgomery bus boycott, there are few aspects of Negro life in America that have escaped the attention of the authors, either in their brisk, readable text, or in the prints and photographs which make up the bulk of the large-size volume.

Such pictorial presentations of history have proved highly successful and effective in the past, and it is welcome news that one should now be available on the Negro people. Because so much has had to be done in the field of original, scholarly research on Negro history to combat the outright suppression or misrepresentation of the truth, popular treatments of the subject have been almost entirely lacking.

A Pictorial History of the Negro in America helps to fill this void. It should certainly encourage its readers to go deeper into the subject and to obtain such works as those of the Negro historians Carter Woodson and Dr. W. E. B. Du Bois and Herbert Aptheker's *Documentary History of the Negro People in the U.S.*, all of which are cited in the authors' bibliography.

The authors grind the axe for no particular political dogma in their book. Nevertheless it is marked by a definite identification with liberal thought and by a vigorous confirmation of that viewpoint which holds that the Negro people have fought—and properly so—during and since slavery times for full equality.

Many of the prints and pictures used were new to the reader. Some of the most striking and chillingly effective are reproductions of slave sales and fliers advertising for fugitive slaves.

There is only a fleeting reference to American Communists in the book, and that a tribute to their campaign for the Scottsboro Boys. In the interest of completeness, the volume might have included mention or photographs of James L. Ford, first Negro ever to run for the Vice-Presidency (he ran on the Communist ticket in 1932 and 1936), or of Benjamin J. Davis, first Negro ever to win election to the New York City Council or, for that matter, to an important municipal post in any major American city.

Speaking of firsts, Mrs. Charlotta Bass,

first Negro woman ever to run for the Vice-Presidency (on the Progressive Party ticket in 1952) rated a mention.

But these, and other deficiencies of organization of the text in relation to the pictures are minor in comparison to the volume's interest and worth.

It is a book which will stimulate deeper interest in Negro history. It deserves space alongside such works as the aforementioned *Documentary History* and, in this age of comic books and television, it is a particularly attractive gift to consider for students and other young people who like their education visual.

Kinchen Exum "Pictorial History of Negro Carries 1,000 Illustrations" *Chattanooga News–Free Press*, 13 December 1956, p. 6

Langston Hughes, sometimes called the poet laureate of the Negro people, and Milton Meltzer, who has one of the best collections of material on Negroes, have joined forces in preparing this survey of the Negro's role in American history.

More than 1,000 illustrations enliven the text, and some of these pictures appear several times. The text itself is comparatively free of bias, but the approach to the Southern concept of slavery is somewhat different than Southerners will recall it.

The horrors of slave ships are pictured in diagrams, showing how bodies were crowded for the fitful passage from the Guinea Coast, but it must be remembered that the New England "traders" supplied

Southern demands. The authors are fair to point out that the needs of the North and South were vastly different: New England had small farms while the South, in part, was adjusted to a larger scale of agricultural pursuits. What "traders" from New England could not use they sold, just as they always have.

A fairly comprehensive account, the book will be valuable for a review of accompanying problems that have followed the Negro from his first arrival until the so-called "Integration Decision" of the Supreme Court. But one closes the final page with considerable wonderment as to an apparent lack of understanding of the close bond that existed between servant and master in the old South.

My great-grandfather's "body servant," who accompanied him throughout the War Between the States in the Confederate Army, could have told these writers much. When this "body servant" died I was a small boy, but I look back towards his memory with the happiest of recollections. He was indeed "free," but bonds of love tied him, and later his memory, to us in such a way that no Emancipation Proclamation could ever separate him from us.

J. A. Rogers
"History Shows"
Pittsburgh Courier, 15
December 1956, p. 8

Since 1934, the *Courier* has been carrying an illustrated feature on the history of the Negro. Now one of America's leading publishers—Crown of New York—has stepped off the beaten track of what white publishers usually get out on the race question—and has given us *A Pictorial History of the Negro in America.*

Research on the pictures was done by Milton Meltzer, white. He spent four years on it, and it's certain that the 1,000 or more pictures in the book are but a part of his collection. Some of the pictures are rare—at least I'm seeing them for the first time. Langston Hughes, I understand, was called in to write the story around the pictures. The whole is published in fine style and is a bargain at $5.95. I, for one, am grateful to Crown for the innovation.

And it's because I'm grateful, I regret I cannot speak in the unbounded praise a work on this theme ought to elicit. It simply does not fit into the inspirational needs of the Negro. Why? Because of the 312 pages, 185 are devoted to the slavery period. Now Negroes are sick of hearing about slavery. It has been rubbed into them so much as proof of their alleged inferiority that they are anxious to forget it—as anxious as the whites of Virginia, Maryland and other states to hide the fact that most of their ancestors were convicts, thieves, prostitutes. The colonies were the dumping ground for England's human refuse. They continued to arrive until 1783. That year when two shiploads of them arrived, America, now independent, turned them back. The celebrated Dr. Johnson said then of Americans, "They are a race of convicts." Abundant evidence of that may be found in such little known books as J. D. Butler's *British Convicts Shipped to America.* White people were chattel slaves, too, and even bought by Negro slavemasters, according to eyewitness accounts. But better not remind proud whites of Maryland, Virginia and Georgia of that.

And Negroes have less cause to be ashamed of their African stock. The parts of Africa from which they came had neither criminals nor prostitutes. Still it's human nature to wish to forget a slave past. Especially those who are struggling against great obstacles.

Further, as Schuyler said of this book in his radio broadcast, the emphasis is placed on what HAS BEEN DONE FOR the Negro rather than on what he HAS DONE FOR HIMSELF, which is far more important. There's little or nothing he says about Negro banks, insurance, farms and the role of the Negro Church. Very much of the most important accomplishments of the Negro as given in "Your History" over the past 22 years is lacking.

Of course, as the preface of the work rightly says, no book of this length can tell the full story. In such a case, selection and relative value of matter is of first importance. This wasn't exercised here. I shall give my reasons next week.

Garrett D. Byrnes
"Cameras over the World: Fine Photographs of '56"
Providence Sunday Journal, section 6, 16 December 1956, p. 8

One of this year's most dramatic—and important—picture books is *A Pictorial History of the Negro in America* by Langston Hughes and Milton Meltzer. Here, apparently, is a brand new field in graphic history, discovered some four or five years ago by Mr. Meltzer, a Worcester man. His collection of pictorial material is a fine one. Although there is no way of telling how the co-authors divided the work, it is likely that Mr. Hughes, the poet, contributed largely to the sensitive text.

Reminded as we are almost daily by stories out of Clinton, Tenn., and other places of violent antagonism in the South that the struggle for freedom and equality

for colored people continues to be an issue sorely trying to our democracy, this record will give the reader much that he probably never knew before. Certainly the book will put the present crises of racism in perspective as just one more action in a battle that has been going on within our gates since the Declaration.

[. . .]

[J.] Saunders Redding
"Book Review"
Afro-American Magazine,
22 December 1956, p. 2

There will be academic historians who will not like this effort by a skilled story teller and a percipient illustrator. The academic historians will say that history is a specialty—that the study of it is one of the higher disciplines, and the writing of it the task of professional scholars. Whether this is largely bunk or not, certainly this much is true: most of the academic historians who have dealt with Southern history and with history of colored people as a part of Southern history have not been very careful to exercise their vaunted discipline to tell the colored man's full story.

From Phillips to Morison, the record is not only full of holes but plainfully distorted by preconceptions—not the least of which is the notion that the colored man's place in Southern history is merely incidental.

And not only the colored man's place, but the colored man's part—his many parts.

This is where Mr. Hughes and Mr. Meltzer come in, for what they have done to happy effect is to emphasize the colored man's significance to the development of the economic, political and social life—in short, the history—of America.

If some details are slighted, it is for the reason of getting at other details which represent the truth more accurately.

After all, what is more representative—ten slaves singing for ol' massa's guests at a barbecue, or the mass suicide of more than two hundred colored people on a slave ship in Charleston harbor?

The academic historian's point of view seems to be that the latter is too dramatic to be representative, but "as a matter of cold fact, it summarizes the truth of the colored man's hatred of his slave condition."

Few people learn from history written by scholars. Drama is a better teacher.

Carlyle's *History of the French Revolution* has more truth in it than all the archivists and all the statistics of the scholars.

Langston Hughes' text has not slighted the drama, and his swift narrative style sweeps the story along from excitement to excitement.

The superb illustrations help. Indeed, never before have so many photographs, drawings, cartoons and prints illustrative of the life of the colored man been brought between the covers of a single book.

The whole story is here, beginning in 1619 and ending with yesterday.

It makes clear who and what the American colored man is and how, himself affected, he has affected American life and thought.

This is a clarification of knowledge particularly needful in these times when the world press is full of news about American race relations.

But apart from recreating the past and examining the present, Mr. Hughes takes a considered look at the future, and what he sees should give hope to all those who believe that the idealism expressed in the American creed is still an active force in the lives of the American people.

J. A. Rogers "History Shows" *Pittsburgh Courier,* 22 December 1956, p. 8; continues his 15 December review

I said last week that the *Pictorial History of the American Negro* [sic] by Langston Hughes and Milton Meltzer was overloaded with slavery. I also mentioned Schuyler's criticism, namely, that too much had been said on what had been done for the Negro and too little on what he had done to help himself.

Now, the above is the habitual white viewpoint. And it is understandable. Books got out by white publishers, even when by Negro authors, sell mostly to white people and what the whites, even many of the most unbiased, want on the Negro is generally different from what Negroes want on themselves.

The reason is that the whites, from their earliest years, are made to feel that their colored fellow-citizens are different. Negroes are set apart as an inferior breed, and this has penetrated so deeply that very, very few even of the Negro's best friends can succeed in entirely rooting it out—even when they are ashamed of it. In fact, it is so typically American that the Negro himself (typically American, too) has come to accept the dogma of his alleged inferiority to a large extent.

The white reader, with his usual superiority complex, prefers books like *Native Son* and *Intruder in the Dust,* because they show the Negro a down-trodden, underprivileged group. Such books touch his sympathy but do not offend his feeling of superiority. On the other hand the Negro, who is more and more rebelling against the doctrine of inferiority, wants literature that will inspire him to fight it still more. Right here, he comes in opposition to what the whites want because the latter, even some of the most unbiased, feel that praise given to the Negro is praise taken from themselves. Believe me, I know what I'm talking about.

The above is merely a statement, not a complaint. Why aren't Negroes getting out themselves the kind of literature they want? Other minority groups in America do. There are more American Negroes than the combined population of Sweden, yet they do not have a single firm that finances a book and pays the author a royalty. They leave this most urgent duty to white people.

I have met, over the years, Negroes who are anxious to write some book that will inspire but they haven't a chance unless they write what will please the white reader. And publishing one's book is very tough. I know what I'm talking about. Next year will make 40 years since I published my first. I might add that since 1934 I've been collecting material for "A Pictorial History of the American Negro from 1513 to the Present." If ever that comes out I'll have to do that, too.

Until Negroes are ready to get out their books, *A Pictorial History of the American Negro* [*sic*] is the best of its kind yet. I do hope it will be bought and read.

"The Story of One-Tenth" *Saturday Review,* 39 (22 December 1956), 19

The story of one-tenth of the American people is told in an intelligently conceived and ably executed text-and-picture album, *A Pictorial History of the Negro in American History* [*sic*], edited by Langston Hughes and Milton Meltzer. Through more than 1,000 illustrations and an equal amount of space devoted to text, the story of the American Negro is told from his African past to the recent Supreme Court anti-segregation rulings. There is a nice combination of scholarly scrupulousness, objectivity, and attractive presentation. Among the figures discussed are Joseph Cinque, who led the famous Amistead mutiny, and Pierre Toussaint, who worked as a hairdresser in nineteenth century New York to support his master's widow.

N.S. "The Negro in America" *Lexington Herald Leader,* 23 December 1956, p. 29

In this king size book with more than 1,000 reproductions of pictures, paintings, woodcuts, drawings, and cartoons is a panoramic story of the Negro in America from the arrival of the first African slave ship to the present day.

This is a fascinating book and other than the pictures of all important Negroes from Nat Turner to Ralph Bunche and pictorial accounts of events involving the Negro, there are numerous absorbing narratives of Negro history, which heightens the interest in this well written volume.

Publishers of this book state that years of study and research went into its preparations, and one has only to glance through it to believe that statement. It is a blend of clear narrative style and sound scholarship without any attempt to do more than to present a true picture. One thing is certain: The book provides a source from which the reader can gain a clear understanding of the background and the rich heritage of the Negro people. It is a worthy addition to the history, not only of the Negro, but of the United States.

"About Books"
Atlanta World, 25 December 1956, p. 3

The book is the first panoramic picture of the story of the Negro in America and covers every aspect of Negro life in this country from the landing of the first Africans in 1610 to the present times.

There are more than 900 illustrations gathered over many years from all over the United States and abroad, and their total impact is both extraordinary and moving; here is the Negro as a slave, as a freeman, as a leader, as someone on whom the particular circumstances of his position in society have wrought certain effects, and as someone who, because of his position and aspirations, has made his own unique contribution to the country as a whole and often served as the conscience of his countrymen.

There are concise pictorial accounts of all the important events in the Negro's dramatic struggle for freedom, and pictures of all the famous and important Negroes in American history.

Years of study and research went into the preparation of this volume, and because of Langston Hughes' happy blend of sound scholarship and clear narrative style, the reader gains from these pages a remarkable background, the rich heritage and the unquenchable spirit of the Negro people.

Every reader will find *A Pictorial His-*tory of the Negro in America amazingly interesting throughout and, of course, it is a book that belongs in every Negro home, school and church.

James Egert Allen
"Book Review: New Book on Negro in America Praised"
New York Amsterdam News, 29 December 1956, p. 16; also as *"A Pictorial History of the Negro in America,"* Atlanta World, 27 December 1956 and Waco Messenger, 28 December 1956

Persons interested in the history of the Negro, especially in our culture, can turn the pages of a remarkable new volume, profusely illustrated with pictures, facsimiles of important documents, vivid cartoons and literary reproductions all pertaining to the historic struggle of the black man in his meteoric rise toward full and first class citizenship in this nation.

The authors follow an orderly sequence and include a plethora of background material which enables the reader to understand the varied problems identified with the Negro in history. Adequate attention is given to the period of slavery without paying tribute to the iniquitous system.

The part played by free men of color is not disregarded as is often true, in many histories of the past. Each division of the volume is indicative of the rich store of factual information and real achievements so seldom found in the current historical volumes issued in the past half century.

Here are the hidden agendas of scores of meetings initiated by Negroes which led to the formation of separate organizations so as to provide opportunities for their leadership and accomplishments to come to light under the glow of creative genius.

The Negro church, business, school and social organizations evolved out of this period of national expansion.

The contents of this volume should lift the morale of our nation, breaking down artificial barriers in our culture and society and paving a way for better communications among people of varied ethnic groups.

To place this volume in every library, every school, and, in fact, every home in America would add greatly to the moral courage and physical stamina of the entire country.

With consummate skill and graphic artistry Messrs. Hughes and Meltzer have made a wonderful contribution to Americana.

Ray Past
"The Book Shelf"
El Paso Herald-Post, 29
December 1956, [p. 4]

In many ways this *Pictorial History* is a very impressive book. It is big, its pictures are often striking, it gives a quick if somewhat superficial view of a large and important subject, which is doubtless too little known, and what it has to say in both text and pictures is thought-provoking.

Of course, the biggest impression left with the reader of this book is the obvious one that the Negro people have been much sinned against.

The authors are, of course, prejudiced and their emphasis is on the long catalog of wrongs the Negro has suffered, but the thoughtful reader comes away from the volume with a feeling of pride in the way this country has handled its racial problems. Of course, many remain to be worked out, as we are all aware, but it is encouraging to take a look back at the long way we have come. It is easy for countries with homogeneous populations to point out our sins, but let them look around the globe for another country with large numbers of different races living together which has done nearly so well.

Like many authors with an ax to grind, though, these two occasionally get carried away. In their anxiety to present their subject in the most favorable light they sometimes lose sight of reality. Thus, for instance, your reviewer was surprised and interested to learn that Father Divine did and is doing a very great deal of admirable "rescue" work with New York's colored underprivileged. But he still feels that a discussion of the man with no mention of his ludicrous antics is not a real picture at all.

The book is very cheap for one of its size, which may account for the generally poor quality of its printing, particularly of its illustrations.

P. L. Prattis
"Horizon: Dead
Paragraph"
Pittsburgh Courier, 29
December 1956, p. 8

[. . .]

Among the many unusual "revelations" in Langston Hughes' and Milton

Meltzer's *A Pictorial History of the Negro in the United States* [*sic*] is a paragraph from the first draft of the Declaration of Independence as written by Thomas Jefferson. In this paragraph, Jefferson denounced King George III of England for enslaving Africans, imposing slavery on the colonies and freeing the slaves to "murder" their masters.

The South, the same South as today, rejected the paragraph which reads:

"He has waged cruel war against human nature itself, violating its most sacred right of life and liberty in the persons of a distant people who never offended him, captivating and carrying them into slavery in another hemisphere, or to incur miserable death in their transportation thither. This piratical warfare, the opprobrium of INFIDEL powers, is the warfare of the Christian king of Great Britain. Determined to keep open a market where MEN should be bought and sold, he has prostituted his negative for suppressing every legislative attempt to prohibit or to restrain this execrable commerce; and that this assemblage of horrors might want no face of distinguished die, he is now exciting those very people to rise in arms among us, and to purchase that liberty of which HE deprived them by murdering the people upon whom HE also obtruded them; thus paying off former crimes committed against the liberties of one people with crimes which he urges them to commit against the LIVES of another."

White school children, or colored, who read the Declaration of Independence, can never suspect that the author of the Declaration, Thomas Jefferson, sought to indict the institution of slavery and was thwarted by the Eastlands, Talmadges, Ellenders and other Southerners of his day.

My colleagues, Messrs. Rogers and Schuyler, have expressed some criticism of Mr. Hughes' book, largely because of what he has left out about the achieve-

ments of Negroes since slavery and the amount of space devoted to slavery and the slavery period. The criticism may be valid, although it would be impossible for any author to write a book to suit all the desires of other authors.

Mr. Rogers is gracious enough to concede that *A Pictorial History of the Negro in the United States* [*sic*] is the best of its kind yet to be published. It is not profound, but it is discerning.

E.S.
"Books and Authors"
Lewiston [Maine] *Daily Sun,* 5 January 1957, p. 4

Important among the current pictorial, outsize volumes so popular this season is this authoritative and revealing record of the Negro's place in American history and the world of today, compiled by Milton Meltzer, writer, research and public relations expert, and Langston Hughes, poet, author, playwright and columnist, often called Poet Laureate of his race.

In view of the grave problems in the Deep South due to the U.S. Supreme Court's decision of May 17, 1954, outlawing racial segregation, these authors believed—and rightly—that a better knowledge of the Negro in America, his background, his struggle first for freedom, then for equality is badly needed at this time. Years of research went into the preparation of this volume. Over a thousand pictures have been assembled including photographs of outstanding personalities and reproductions of handbills, cartoons and newspaper illustrations. The text is soundly documented and written in clear, narrative style.

The first cargo of African slaves arrived at Jamestown, Va., in 1619, just a year, ironically enough, before the Pilgrims, seeking freedom, landed at Plymouth. The early N.E. colonists who could afford to keep a few slaves of their own apparently saw no inconsistency in following the example of their Southern neighbors.

Not until the Fugitive Slave Bill became a law in 1850 did the northerners become thoroughly aroused to the evils of slavery. In 1775 Thomas Jefferson had written into the first draft of the Declaration of Independence a clause condemning slavery, but it was too profitable a business in the South and on urgent insistence of the Southern delegation the Continental Congress omitted the paragraph from the final version.

A large section of the book is devoted to the decade or so preceding the Civil War when abolitionist activities brought to the front such free Negro leaders as Frederick Douglass, Prince Saunders and others; such distinguished fair-skinned sympathizers as Lloyd Garrison, Charles Sumner, Horace Mann, Harriet Beecher Stowe. The list is an impressive one.

Statistics are given of Negro participation in the wars from the Revolution to World War II. Before the close of the latter conflict, it is asserted that more than a million colored men and women were in uniform, including 6,000 officers.

High honors and brilliant achievement have been won in recent years by Negroes in many fields—not only in the world of literature, music and drama, but in athletics, in science and education. The "American Who's Who" lists 150 famous darkskinned Americans, including of course Dr. Ralph Bunche and U.S. Senator Clayton Powell, Jr., whose swarthiness is slight indeed. Marian Anderson became the first Negro prima donna of the Metropolitan Opera Company and Janet Collins its first colored ballerina.

The closing chapters deal with the desegregation issue, the reactionary attitude of certain of the seventeen Southern and border states affected, and recent outbreaks of violence in Montgomery, Ala. and elsewhere in the Deep South. While it will assuredly be some time before desegregation problems will be resolved, coauthors Hughes and Meltzer are confident that their racial brethren will eventually attain full citizenship, concluding "With the increasing integration of education at all levels, a new generation of Negroes is now growing to adulthood with a fuller share of the privileges and a greater understanding of the basic tenets of American democracy."

Benjamin E. Mays
"My View"
Pittsburgh Courier,
26 January 1957, p. 8

Langston Hughes and Milton Meltzer have rendered a great service in their *Pictorial History of the Negro in America,* published by the Crown Publishers, Inc., of New York. The book is a picture story of the Negro in America, from the arrival of the first slave ship to the present time. It carries more than 1,000 reproductions of pictures, paintings, drawings, etc.

If anyone believes the the Negro did nothing to free himself from physical bondage he should read this book. It shows that Negro abolitionists played as conspicuous a part in the emancipation of the Negro as did white abolitionists. Their biographies of the persons chosen are short but so dramatic that one will not forget. For example, Harriet Tubman, who could neither read nor write, but who led more than 300 slaves to freedom, her aged parents among them, carrying a pistol saying to a faltering slave who wanted to go back to slavery: "You'll be free or die!"

No Negro can read the book without gaining added respect and new appreciation for the sacrifices that Negroes themselves made to free themselves from slavery. No white person can read it without increasing sympathy for the Negro in his long struggle to be free to walk the earth with dignity. The story is simply but movingly and profoundly told.

The book fits the times. Many of the characters in the book fought for physical freedom. Other characters of contemporary time are fighting to be free from segregation and discrimination based on race and color. The work of the NAACP and that of the Negroes in Montgomery is a continuation of the fight waged for freedom by Harriet Tubman, Douglass, Garrison and Stowe.

The book indirectly says two things: Negroes have achieved mightily in the United States in spite of handicaps, better perhaps to say because of handicaps. It also says that many white Americans, such as Washington and Jefferson, had an uneasy conscience about slavery and many others fought for the emancipation of the slaves. Today, thousands of white Americans have an uneasy conscience about segregation and discrimination and are united with the Negro in his efforts to be free.

The authors tell their story in love and objectivity. Once you start reading, you want more.

It is unfortunate that the publishers claim too much for the book and the authors seem to acquiesce in it. The publishers say: "There are pictures of every famous and important Negro." It is impossible to include the picture of every important and famous Negro. Nevertheless, this is an important book and commends itself to every reader.

Herbert Aptheker
"Negro Panorama"
Mainstream, 10 (February 1957), 62–3

I think the most dramatic feature in the record of our nation is the history of the American Negro people. Its exciting quality makes the idea of Langston Hughes and Milton Meltzer—to portray that history visually, with a minimum of text—particularly apt. On the whole, they have realized their vision well and produced an excellent gift-volume of permanent value.

The scope of the book encompasses the Africa of pre-Columbus days to those immediately following the Supreme Court's desegregation decision of 1954. Many of the hundreds of illustrations are exceedingly scarce; all are of great interest and the quality of reproduction throughout is very high.

The general attitude of the volume is sharply anti-racist; its political orientation is New Dealish. As one might expect from a volume of illustrations, the work is descriptive, not analytical, and its overall approach strives for simplicity, and once in a while falls into simplifications.

Factual errors are sprinkled through the text—thus, slaves from Georgia and South Carolina did fight as soldiers in the Revolution, the Negroes brought to Virginia in 1619 were not sold as slaves, etc.—but their number is not extraordinary, and generally they are not very serious. The absence of any real concern with cause produces somewhat more serious errors of omission and commission. For example, in discussing the era of the Populist movement, one reads: "Whites of all parties decided to keep the franchise lily-white and to fight their political battles among themselves," ignoring imperialism, ignoring class-divisions among the whites, which made their reactions much more complex than this sentence would suggest, etc.

No doubt the form of the work dictates this kind of superficiality, but its presence must be pointed out, nevertheless. Yet the volume does convey an overall sense of achievement in the face of extraordinary odds, some feeling of the constant struggle by the Negro people, and a general impression of noteworthy contributions in all areas by Negro men and women. In regard to the latter, there is, too, less of an atmosphere that the book is a record of "distinguished" Negroes, and more that it is one of a mass accomplishment than is generally true with works of this kind; that, of course, is all to the good.

Two-thirds of the volume is devoted to the period up to and including Reconstruction. This reviewer would have preferred a contrary arrangement, with most of the space devoted to the last seventy or eighty years, but then historical writing as a whole still suffers from this unbalance, and one must not blame Messrs. Hughes and Meltzer for a failing that marks the historical guild as a whole, up to the present.

Related to this disproportion is the volume's underplaying of the Left, and particularly the impact of socialist and communist thinking and organizations upon the history of the Negro people. The fact is that since the founding of the NAACP (in which Socialists played an outstanding part), through the struggles of the New Deal era, and to World War II, the Marxist ingredient was a major feature in American Negro life and thought and organizational activity. To ignore this, as the present book does, is to misrepresent history. Connected with this is a picture of Negro life today that is prettified. For example: "As citizens of the U.S., Negroes are Americans and their way of life is much the same as that of other Americans." At the same time, the impact upon other Americans of the policy of second-class citizenship is obscured.

But we repeat, the work is distinctly anti-racist and its message is directed towards the elimination of Jim Crow. This, plus of course, the frequently fascinating pictures makes the volume enjoyable.

Arthur L. Crookham "2 Books Tell Negroes' Story" *Oregon Journal,* 10 February 1957, p. 6C

You could ransack all the libraries in Portland and read all the pages on the history of the American Negro but likely end with less information than is contained in this highly valuable volume.

Hughes is the eminent Negro poet, playwright and musical lyricist. Meltzer is a public relations man who has spent many years collecting photographs and countless items on the Negro.

In this collaboration they have produced a volume authentic, factual and fascinating. The handsomely printed book is more picture than text. It contains more than 1000 pictures, reproductions of paintings, photographs, drawings, woodcuts and facsimiles of pamphlets and books.

Nothing is omitted to present a complete panorama of all known facts about the Negro in Africa, his forced immigration into America, slavery, the Civil War, Reconstruction and his progress up from slavery.

The beginnings of Negro history about

1000 A.D. are outlined, and then by well-delineated stages the reader continues his march through history. And it is amazing in how many theatres of action the Negro has entered into every memorable American event, from Jamestown and the Boston Massacre to World War II and the current army. The Negro leaders in music, education, philanthropy, poetry and drama all have their pages and photographs. The book is so much down to date that it contains pictures of Autherine Lucy and of Gloria Lockerman, the $64,000 spelling wizard.

If those who inspect the book expect to find its 9-by–11-inch format crammed with pro-Negro propaganda, they will be surprised to discover that it is free from bias and distortion.

It is factual and authentic, I believe, in all particulars. Libraries that "stock" this book may find they will need several copies. It is a moving history of "our United States," valuable and worthwhile.

J.B.
"Negro in America Well Researched"
Youngstown Vindicator,
17 February 1957, p. B14

Four years of searching for the right illustrations have, we are told, gone into this massive pictorial history.

Certainly the authors have spent their time well: their aim of integrating the American Negro with the mainstream of American history has been admirably fulfilled.

This history begins all the way back in Africa, dwells on the painful era of American slavery (some rare old prints are re-produced here), passes through the Armageddon of the Civil War, and brings the story down to the Supreme Court's desegregation decision of 1954. It is, on the whole, a heartening story, and one of steady progress.

The text is knowledgeable and eloquent, and, although the approach is generally objective, the reader is left with the feeling that final fulfillment for the American Negro is inevitable.

John W. Parker
"A Part, Not Thing Apart"
Raleigh News and Observer, part 3, 17
February 1957, p. 5

Langston Hughes and Milton Meltzer are "backing into the future looking at the past," but a past calculated to illuminate the present and perhaps the future American scene. The book is reminiscent of Hughes' *The Sweet Flypaper of Life* (1955), (which also appears in pictures and prose and is confined to the Harlem scene), but unlike that volume, it spans the entire history of the Negro in America from 1619 to the present.

The authors set out to tell who the Negro is, where he came from, what he has contributed to American culture, how he has affected it and, in turn, been affected by it. They underscore the activity of American Negro folk as part and parcel of the stream of American life, and not a thing apart from it.

Steering clear of the propaganda angle, the book discloses the black man's inner being—his frustrations and hopes and desires to be one with a country to which he has given his blood. The authors have, therefore, proceeded on the sound assumption that the so-called Negro problem is but one segment of the larger problem of American minorities and those in far-flung parts of the world. And despite the artificial line that separates them, humble folk of all races and all walks of life face a common lot: they march toward a common destiny.

Never intended to be a great book, *A Pictorial History of the Negro in America* is nevertheless a serious one. It sheds light upon the Negro's social milieux and perhaps more important still upon what is going on within.

Mary Dolan
"A Pictorial History of the Negro in America"
Community, 16 (March 1957), 7

Over 900 pictures—three of which are shown here—with accompanying narrative trace the history of Negroes from their arrival in America to the present day. A fascinating record, one that will be a welcome addition to every library of race relations or American history. Some have criticized the material on the slavery period for being overly ample, but it seemed to this reviewer a well-rounded, valuable book.

Joan Doyle
"Other New Books"
Catholic World, 185 (April 1957), 74–5

To the growing list of books dealing with the subject of relations between white and Negro Americans must be added these two titles. The first is a handsomely produced, folio-size narrative-in-pictures of the Negro element in our population. Beginning with the arrival of the first African slave ship and continuing through such recent events as the Emmett Till murder case, its 1,000 illustrations tell a moving and very human story of suffering, progress against odds, and the hope of ultimate triumph in the search for justice.

Mr. Meltzer, himself the owner of an outstanding collection of pictures in the field of Negro history, has culled through hundreds of thousands of illustrations for the very excellent ones used in the book. To his work has been added the considerable literary talents of Mr. Hughes. As is sometimes the case in publishing histories of minority groups, the authors have occasionally erred in relying too heavily on sources biased in their direction—in giving unquestioned credence, for example, to the writings of Theodore Weld and Hinton R. Helper; and in basing the section of the Negro during the Abolition-Civil War period largely on the memoirs of Frederick Douglass. On the whole, however, this is an outstanding piece of work—one of the best, indeed, in its field, and it well deserves a permanent place in private as well as public libraries.

Leo Glassman
"About Books"
American Examiner,
16 May 1957, p. 13

Tinsley L. Spraggins
"Book Reviews"
*Virginia Magazine of
History and Biography,* 65
(July 1957), 390–1

One thousand illustrations taken from various sources, but mostly from the private collection of Milton Meltzer, are used to trace pictorially the history of the Negroes, beginning with their origins in Africa through their slavery in America and their gradual emergence into the light of freedom and equality.

Like the Jews and other minorities, the Negroes are self-conscious about their position in the world and suffer from an over-eagerness to prove that they are as advanced, as gifted and as deserving as those who belong to the majority groups. This may account for some of the shortcomings in this excellent volume.

It seems to this reviewer, for instance, that the Negro has proven his worth sufficiently without having to include in a roster of outstanding Negroes a number of very fine and talented but nevertheless unimportant individuals. Also, the expert text falls down here and there as in the handling of the Father Divine and the Scottsboro case stories which are lumped together on one page in a casual and unconvincing way.

Finally, one gets the feeling from this book that the Negro is trying to curry the white man's favor and appealing for his mercy. The illustration of the title page shows a chained Negro kneeling and asking: "Am I Not a Man and a Brother?" I think it is time for the Negro to stand up erect and demand what is his by right.

Although this book adds nothing that is substantially new to the field of Negro history, it is an important work to the writing of Negro historiography, in that the book is an attempt to assemble in a single volume, for the first time, a collection of illustrations describing graphically the life of the Negro. The reproductions are designed primarily to show the Negro's relationship to American history from the time of the Africans' arrival at Jamestown in 1619 until the present. In pursuing this goal Messrs. Hughes and Meltzer trace in photographs, prints, engravings, cartoons and in text the story of the Negro as a slave and as a freeman, who he is, where he came from, what he has contributed, how he has been affected by American life and, finally, where he is headed. The life of the Negro is also narrated by the use of a series of editorials, letters, posters, handbills, and pamphlets which range from the early days of the slave trade until the recent desegregation decision of the United States Supreme Court.

In viewing the illustrations in the book and in reading the textual material, however, one gets the idea that the authors planned to have their *Pictorial History* depict the Negro's dramatic struggle for freedom. This is inferred by placing on the title page of the work a picture of a chained Negro who is looking to heaven and saying, "Am I not a Man and a Brother?" Another inference of this probable aim is demonstrated by the type of poems the authors selected to illustrate the life of the Negro. For example, they used a poem of a slave, George Moses Horton of North Carolina, which said:

> How long have I in bondage lain
>   And languish to be free!
> Alas! and must I still complain—
>   Deprived of liberty.

The suggestion is also brought to the reviewer's mind by the authors' use of reproductions of documents which are synonymous with freedom such as the Declaration of Independence, the *Appeal* of David Walker, the Emancipation Proclamation, and famous court decisions relative to the constitutional history of the Negro. In addition to these illustrations the authors also present pictorial accounts of Negro participation in all movements which had as their goal freedom either for the Negro people or for all Americans. In the book, for example, are illustrations showing the Negro as a participant in the abolition movement, in all of the nation's wars, including the one which was "to save the world for democracy," and in the march on Washington for legislation dealing with fair employment practices. Finally, the concluding picture summarizes very well the results of the struggle depicting a young Negro child, Allen Turner, who aspires to become a pilot when he reaches manhood. The authors comment on this aspiration by saying Turner and other similar Negroes can look forward to entering any career they choose.

Perhaps the *Pictorial History of the Negro in America* will have little appeal to the student of history because what Messrs. Hughes and Meltzer have shown in the book has already been told by Doctors John Hope Franklin, Carter G. Woodson, Herbert Aptheker, and other students of Negro history. But, the work, no doubt, would be helpful to the casual reader who wishes to get a factual and vivid pictorial history of the Negro's struggle for freedom.

Edna Burke Jackson
"Book Reviews"
Journal of Negro History, 50 (January 1965), 62–3

This history of the Negro in America told in pictures and in easily understandable story form is a significant contribution to not only a deeper comprehension of United States history but also of the long history of humiliation and degradation to which a minority group in the United States has been subjected. The carefully selected illustrations and reproductions of important documents reveal the bestial regime that slavery was, puncture for all time any romantic concepts the ignorant may have of the antebellum South, expose vividly what is omitted from the teaching of United States history on the secondary and college levels. One has but to view many of the pictures and one understands why the present "Negro revolution" is the inevitable result of the years of struggle by the Negro to become a part of the mainstream of American life!

The book begins with the origins of the Negro and chronologically spans his history from 1619 to the present. However, the first three parts of this eight-part volume are concurrent as follows: "The Peculiar Institution, 1619–1863," "Freemen of Color, 1619–1863," and "The North Star, 1619–1863." The rest of the book concerns the years from the end of the Civil War to the present. The authors highlight the achievements of the Negro and stress particularly his struggle to escape bondage and, then, to acquire acceptance into full citizenship in the United States. A text accompanies the pictures, reproductions of handbills, newspapers, pamphlets and laws. The authors have been sufficiently careful to write so that the ordinary reader may grasp this history.

The authors are frank enough to state in their Foreword that this is not a treatment in depth of their subject but that they planned simply to "convey the sweep of history." They devote considerable space to that history prior to the turn of the century. In fact, approximately two-thirds of the book spans the early history. Perhaps this is as it should be, for the Negro, if mentioned at all in the texts used in the teaching of history, is usually allotted one or two sentences referring to his bondage and then dismissed. It has been the pattern of the past to deny that the Negro had any past! However, this reviewer feels that too much of importance in more recent events has been omitted in order to conserve space and would like to see an enlargement of the present volume.

This book should be in every school and college library and in every home, for it would supplement vividly the study of United States history of which the Negro is a dynamic and neglected part. The authors have delved deeply and widely in their own studies prior to the writing of this volume, have included a reading list for the reader, and have approached their subject with scholarly scrupulousness. This presentation is further credit to Mr. Hughes and Mr. Meltzer, already renowned for their great works.

Everyone interested in Civil Rights, race relations and United States history would further mankind's cause if he would see that young people read this book, which concludes its picture sequence with a photograph of a Negro boy: "This is Allen Turner. The horizons of his world are very wide, the limits of his dreams not what they used to be" (p. 340).

Checklist of Additional Reviews

"September 21," *Retail Bookseller, 59* (September 1956), 139.

Jessie Kitching, "PW Forecast for Booksellers: Nonfiction Forecast," *Publishers Weekly,* 170 (3 September 1956), 990.

Francis A. Klein, "Book Marks," *St. Louis Globe-Democrat,* 18 November 1956, p. 4F.

"The Record," *New York Times Book Review,* 18 November 1956, p. 36.

[J.] Saunders Redding, "The American Negro's Role in History," *New York Herald Tribune Book Review,* 18 November 1956, p. 7.

W.J.M., Jr., "Vanishing Race," *Montgomery Advertiser–Alabama Journal,* 25 November 1956, p. 2F.

B.H.H., "Book Reviews: Critic Takes Look at Three New Volumes," *Anniston* [Ala.] *Star,* 26 November 1956, pp. 4, 6.

"Nonfiction," *Bookmark,* 16 (December 1956), 58.

Thomas E. Cooney, "Picture Books," *Saturday Review,* 39 (1 December 1956), 45–6.

"Picture Books of All Sorts," *Columbus Dispatch,* Tab Section, 2 December 1956, p. 12.

H.A.W., "The Negro," *Trenton Sunday Times-Advertiser,* part 4, 2 December 1956, p. 16.

Edward Wagenknecht, "The American Negro," *Boston Sunday Herald,* 2 December 1956, sec. 5, p. 15.

"Pilgrim's Progress of Negro Told," *Hartford Times,* 5 December 1956, p. 44.

George Helmer, "Handsome Pictorial Volume Tells Story of the Negro in

America," *Sacramento Bee,* 6 December 1956, p. D12.

Luther J. Carter, "Negro History in Pictures," *Virginia-Pilot and Portsmouth Star,* 9 December 1956, p. 6C.

Thomas Cole, "Pictorial Records," *Chattanooga Times,* 9 December 1956, p. 22.

John LaFarge, "Every Tenth American," *America,* 96 (15 December 1956), 331–2.

Van Allen Bradley, "The *Carol* in Facsimile," *Chicago Daily News,* 19 December 1956, p. 16; as "Dickens *Carol* Out in Facsimile Edition," *Newark Star-Ledger,* 24 December 1956, p. 4.

Scul., "Literati: *Negro in America,*" *Variety,* 19 December 1956, p. 77.

Audrey Weaver, "Book Reviews," *Chicago Defender,* 22 December 1956, p. 2.

Mary Bingham, "The American Negro's Story—In Pictures," *Louisville Courier-Journal,* sec. 4, 30 December 1956, p. 7.

"Worth a Thousand Words," *Balance Sheet,* 8 (First Quarter 1957), [p. ?].

"Social Sciences," *Booklist,* 53 (1 January 1957), 216–17.

Roi Ottley, "Extraordinary Books on American Negroes," *Chicago Tribune Magazine of Books,* 6 January 1957, part 4, p. 9.

"Completely Absorbing," *Cleveland Press,* 8 January 1957, p. 31.

Richard Bandolph, "Negro Americans," *Greensboro Daily News,* Feature Section, 13 January 1957, p. 3.

E.G., "Footloose Poet: Langston Hughes Recalls Roving Life of 1930's: Up from Slavery in Prose and Pictures," *Milwaukee Journal,* part 5, 13 January 1957, p. 4.

James W. Ivy, "Book Reviews," *Crisis,* 64 (February 1957), 123.

"Negro in Books: New Collections," *Arkansas Gazette,* February 1957, p. 6F.

"Pictorial Books," *Picturescope,* 5 (April 1957), 4.

Margaret C. Scoggin, "Outlook Tower," *Horn Book,* 33 (April 1957), 150.

Dorothy Dunbar Bromley, "The Negro Freedom-Fighters," *New Leader,* 40 (22 April 1957), 21–2.

"America Balances the Books: Interracial Problems," *America,* 97 (25 May 1957), 264.

"Historical Publications," *Missouri Historical Review,* 52 (October 1957), 85–6.

Hubert Herring, "Books: Recent U.S. Non-Fiction," *Americas,* 10 (August 1958), 38–40.

Book Buyers' Guide, 65 (November 1962), 69.

"Against the Odds," *Saturday Review,* 46 (20 April 1963), 52.

George Freedley, "*The Negro in America* Excellent," *New York Morning Telegraph,* 20 May 1963, p. 2.

George Forsythe, "Clear and Timely History of Negro," *Boston Herald,* 23 June 1963, p. 52.

Ruben F. Kugler, "New Books Appraised," *Library Journal,* 88 (July 1963), 2692.

Frances Neel Cheney, "Current Reference Books: Social Sciences," *Wilson Library Bulletin,* 43 (February 1969), 568.

Bernadette Young, "The Parish and Lending Library: Racism and the Parish Library," *Catholic Library World,* 41 (November 1969), 185–6.

Lynne Stewart, *Library Journal,* 95 (15 February 1970), 789.

James Johnson and Frances O. Churchill, "Black and Bibliographical," *Wilson Library Bulletin,* 47 (January 1973), 417.

"Books—Intermediate," *Booklist*, 69 (1 May 1973), 837.

Frances Neel Cheney, "Recent Reference Books: Blacks," *Reference Services Review*, 2 (April–June 1974), 18.

Choice, 11 (June 1974), 663.

Woodie King, Jr., "The Black Book," *Black World*, 23 (July 1974), 72.

"Reference and Subscription Books Reviews: Notes and Comments," *Booklist*, 71 (1 November 1974), 301.

Randall M. Miller, "History," *Library Journal*, 109 (1 June 1984), 1128.

"Reference Books Bulletin," *Booklist*, 81 (1 December 1984), 507.

Connie Lawson, "General Nonfiction," *Voice of Youth Advocates*, 7 (February 1985), 345.

Linda Blaha, Priscilla Drach, and Craighton Hippenhammer, "SLJ's Reference Books Roundup 1985," *School Library Journal*, 31 (May 1985), 42.

Virginia B. Moore, "Black Materials," *Voice of Youth Advocates*, 9 (February 1987), 274.

SIMPLE STAKES A CLAIM

"Simple Stakes a Claim"
Virginia Kirkus Bulletin, 25 (15 July 1957), 497

Jesse Semple, philosopher, helps Langston Hughes, writer, to view the race problem from various new angles. "Simple" is a sort of Negro Mr. Dooley, and his opinions on race, politics, the atom bomb, desegregation, the South vs the North, housing, and the inconsistencies of the whites add up to a remarkably many-faceted view of life from a corner in Harlem. These pieces are definitely not stories; the preceding three books about "Simple," while contributing their share of Simple's philosophy of life, contributed also numerous anecdotes about his way of life. These brief views of Simple's and his answers to Hughes' arguments let one in on the emotional factors involved in the race problem. There is, only implicitly, a humorous angle here, though; if one keeps one's reasoning out of sight, Simple is funny.

Mary Elisabeth Edes
"Fiction Forecast: *Simple States* [sic] *a Claim*" *Publishers Weekly*, 172 (19 August 1957), 62

A series of very well written vignettes about Mr. Hughes' familiar hero, Simple, and his neighbors in New York's Harlem. Simple's philosophy, which undoubtedly reflects the thinking of many Northern Negroes, is considerably more interesting than the stories about the adventures of Simple's wife and his cousin from the South.

Barbara Klaw
"*Simple Stakes a Claim*" *Book-of-the-Month-Club News*, September 1957, p. 11

We have already had *Simple Speaks His Mind* and *Simple Takes a Wife*. In this new book, Langston Hughes' eloquent spokesman again expresses his prejudices, airs his furies, and speculates on things that strike his fancy. As always, Simple is a delight! A funny, belligerent, uneducated but highly articulate Negro, Simple is a man with a chip on his shoulder—in fact, his head is "beat with chips" falling from above. He is full of ideas. He thinks white people should proclaim a White History Week, for instance, in which they might set about the serious business of unveiling a monument to Jim Crow, as well as make a nice gesture and cancel Joe Louis' back income taxes. Furthermore, Simple has convictions about himself. One of the things he has worked out is an auto-obituary—a eulogy he wants delivered over his body by the Reverend. In less skillful hands, Simple could easily become tedious, but Langston Hughes is above all a writer, and his wit is rich and sure. Mr. Hughes is, in fact, one of the few authors working today who can write about race relations with humor—never allowing his fury at injustice to override his taste as an artist.

Milton S. Byam
"New Books Appraised"
Library Journal, 82 (1
September 1957), 2021

Another of that series of sardonic appraisal of Negro-white relationships by
Jesse B. Semple, familiarly known as
"Simple." These essays range from discussion of whether Mississippians will share
atom shelters with Negroes to the influence of Nasser, Nehru and Chou on American race relations. If Simple were a giant,
he would say to Malan of South Africa
"apart your own hide." He does not understand why Eisenhower (sic) "goofs" in
Georgia where Negroes cannot go. This,
the best of the "Simples" so far, is a delight
to read. Essentially a spoof of racial questions plaguing America, the book reveals
that Simple is not really so simple after all.
Recommended for all adult collections.

Arthur P. Davis
"Wisdom in Laughter:
Simple's Bar Humor Is Bar
None Fun"
*Washington Post and
Times Herald*, 15
September 1957, p. E9

In this work, the third in a series, Langston
Hughes again presents Jesse B. Semple,
or Simple for short, one of the freshest and most fascinating Negro characters in American fiction. Simple is an "uncolleged" Harlem man-about-town who
speaks a delightful brand of English, and
who from a bar stool comments both
wisely and hilariously on many things but
principally on race.

Conceived in 1943, Simple has appeared in two other full-length works and
at present is enjoying a highly successful
run on Broadway in the play *Simply Heavenly*. At the rate he is going, Simple bids
fair to become as well known as Uncle
Remus.

But there is nothing of Uncle Remus in
Simple's make-up. An intelligent and observant fellow, he has all of the modern Harlem Negro's militancy and impatience and compromise. Though definitely
a comic character, he is not a mouthpiece
for corny racial humor.

In short, Simple, like the overwhelming
majority of Harlemites, is an honest, hard-
working, highly human and highly race-
conscious Southern Negro who has been
in the North long enough to realize how
much he has been short-changed in the
matter of democracy.

When accused of "always bringing up
race," Simple readily admits it. "I do," he
says, "because that is what I am always
coming face to face with—race. I look in
the mirror to shave—and what do I see?
Me, colored." Whatever else he may be,
Simple is a realist. He knows that a black
face in a color-conscious world is THE
problem, and much of the humor in the
work is based on Simple's realistic awareness of this all-important fact.

Nash K. Burger
"Books of the Times"
New York Times, 17
September 1957, p. 33

A timely volume this morning, indeed, is the new collection of ruminative conversations between Harlem's Jesse B. Semple (or Simple, as he is better known) and his creator, the poet, novelist, short-story writer, Langston Hughes. The title: *Simple Stakes a Claim.* Simple, who has already lent his name and philosophy to a pair of books, *Simple Speaks His Mind* and *Simple Takes a Wife,* not to mention this year's Broadway play, *Simply Heavenly,* seems well on his way to becoming one of those fictional characters who cease being fictional and become historical. Sitting at a bar, speaking his mind on a great variety of topics, most of them somehow related to the pleasures and tribulations available to a Negro in America, Simple enlightens as well as entertains. His comments are not without relevance to recent events in Little Rock, Birmingham, Nashville—and New York. Shrewd and amiable, Simple isn't solemn, but he deals with solemn matters. This can be a very effective *modus operandi,* as these dialogues prove.

[. . .]

So it is that Simple, discussing housing in Harlem, Supreme Court decisions, atom bombs, miscegenation, politicians, integration, job opportunities, brotherhood and its opposite, tempers his often disillusioned comments with humor, even nonsense. And he is not above directing some of his humor and criticism at himself or members of his own race.

Simple is grateful but unenthusiastic over the Supreme Court decision banning segregation in the public schools. His viewpoint is revealed by the title of a dialogue in which the decision is discussed: "Great But Late."

[. . .]

And so it goes. Simple stakes his claim, has his say on President Eisenhower, the United Nations, teen-age delinquents (just imitating the old folks, he says), Negro magazines, race-relations conferences (these he thinks could be speeded to a more profitable conclusion by replacing most of the speeches with a little dixieland jazz), Puerto Ricans, refugees, funerals, his wife Joyce and his cousin Minnie. His opinions are often errant, sometimes contradictory, but always firm and always his own.

"You are not a man with whom I can always agree," says Mr. Hughes. "I cannot always agree with myself," replies Simple. Let us leave him there.

Albert Anderson
"Langston Hughes'
'Simple' Achieves
National Status"
Philadelphia Tribune,
21 September 1957, p. 4

Langston Hughes is about to be successful in making "Simple" a national character. Simple has long ago burst his original racial boundaries and he brings a smile to the lips of all who stop and chat with and about him.

Simple in this new book is looking after the welfare of his people. He talks about housing in Harlem with many a sage remark in their description. He tells about house-rent parties in Harlem. He describes the Puerto-Ricans who moved in the adjacent blocks to Harlem and discourses on the odd ways segregation flourishes.

There is an infectiousness in Langston Hughes' humor which is almost irresistible even when he is making fun of your racial foibles because you know he is laughing at himself as well. One wonders if this humor may not be one of the ways in breaking up those barriers of differences. Everybody likes humor and everyone likes Simple. More power to him.

Maurice Dolbier
"Book Review"
New York Herald Tribune, 21 September 1957, p. 6

Jesse B. Semple ("Simple," to his friends) is not a violent man, but when another Negro claimed that Mississippi was no worse than Simple's home state of Virginia, Simple took these as fighting words. Not that Simple has an unbounded affection for Virginia, which he left as soon as he was big enough to wear long pants. "But nobody fourteen years old like Emmett Till was ever lynched in Virginia. Neither does Virginia shoot a Negro for trying to vote."

Simple wouldn't trade all the states in the South for one barstool in New York. The North needn't sprain its shoulder trying to pat itself on the back. There are social and economic injustices here, but to Simple it's a part of the Free World (he thinks that the President should confine his golfing activities to the Free World: "I'll bet you Lincoln would not have been caught dead playing golf in Georgia").

Since 1950, Langston Hughes has been meeting Simple at a respectable rendezvous somewhere near the left-hand corner of 125th St. and Lenox Ave. and reporting the conversations. Simple has always spoken his mind forcefully, and he still does, although when his wife Joyce is around he does it with more circumspection. His writer friend sometimes chides him for looking on the dark side—"I am dark," says Simple—or accuses him of having a chip on his shoulder—"I remove this one," says Simple, "white folks will put another chip up there tomorrow"—or attempts to slow down the wilder flights of his imagination—"I would like to be a giant," says Simple, "I would sneeze, and blow the Ku Klux Klan plumb out of Dixie. I would clap my hands, and mash Jim Crow like a mosquito. . . ."

Sometimes Simple has other things on his mind—the problems imposed by the arrival of his bothersome borrowsome cousin Minnie, the boring physical fact that if he gets tired of sleeping on his left side, he has nothing to turn over on but his right side, troubles with the family budget and with the attempts of his beloved Joyce to improve his manners.

But most of the time, the conversational subject is the Negro's position in America. In this latest book, Simple does more than speak his mind; he stakes his claim, in his country and in his rights: "It is not enough for white folks just to be nice and shake my hand and tell me I am equal. I know I am equal. What I want is to be treated equal." The Supreme Court decisions are fine, but Simple sees no reason for whites to be proud about them, "talking about how wonderful it is that colored children can run through brickbats to go to school with white children down South. What's so wonderful about that? They should have been going to school together all these years."

Mr. Hughes' foreword is called "Let's Laugh a Little," and suggests that "since we have not been able to moralize the Dixiecrats out of existence with indignant editorials, maybe we could laugh them to death with well aimed ridicule." I think Mr. Hughes is going to have some words from Simple about that foreword. Whether Simple is brooding over the fact that "everybody but a Negro has seen a flying saucer, and if he did, I bet the papers wouldn't report it," or considering the contrariness of white people who canceled a Brotherhood Week in the interests of brotherhood because the choirs were going to be mixed, or blazing with anger and agony over the Emmett Till case, he is as serious as a man can be.

Arthur S. Harris, Jr. "Too Serious Says Author" *Worcester Sunday Telegram,* 22 September 1957, p. D11

In the introduction to his newest book, Langston Hughes wonders why so much writing about Negroes is serious, even in the Negro press. "Colored people are always laughing at some wry Jim Crow incident or absurd nuance of the color line." Why not, then, a humor magazine, or at least a little levity?

To fill the need, Mr. Hughes has been writing a weekly column for the *Chicago Defender,* possibly the best Negro newspaper in America. His down-to-earth spokesman is Simple, a man of wisdom and humor. He is often foolish, but he is never dull as he ruminates on Harlem house-rent parties, Negro magazines, gold, the atom bomb, Negro vacations.

Mr. Hughes admits that the race problem in America is serious, but must it always be written about in cheerless novels,

weighty volumes, sad tracts? Perhaps Mr. Jesse B. Semple (better known as Simple) points the way for writers of both races who can, as Hughes puts it, "write about problems with black tongue in white cheek, or vice versa."

William Hogan "Langston Hughes Uses Humor as a Weapon" *San Francisco Chronicle,* 24 September 1957, [p. 19]

In introducing a new collection of stories, *Simple Stakes a Claim,* the poet and novelist Langston Hughes writes: "The race problem in America is a serious business, I admit; but must it always be written about seriously?" Mr. Hughes goes on: "Humor is a weapon, too, of no mean value against one's foes."

Mr. Hughes wields his humor deftly and mercilessly through his character Jesse B. Semple (or "Simple") who originally appeared in the pages of the Negro newspaper, the *Chicago Defender.*

An instant success with Negro audiences, Simple's fame grew beyond the Negro Community. A warm, wise, philosophic, often downright funny fellow, Simple might be related to the Kingfish of the old Amos and Andy radio show. He is a more dignified figure, however, than any cliché character in a comedy act, and certainly discusses harsher realities: segregation, housing, the school situation, crime, U.S. race problems in general.

Simple Stakes a Claim, third collection of "Simple" stories to be published in book form, could not be more timely.

Jesse B., who believes "None of them Jim Crow States is worth as much as the left-handed corner of 125th street and Lenox avenue," is a fresh and unique spokesman for his race. Mr. Hughes is to be congratulated on him, for Jesse B. Semple is entertainment and level-headedness of vintage blend. Here is a very human book which should be widely distributed in Little Rock, but won't.

"Be Serious All the Time?"
Miami Herald, 29 September 1957, p. 4G

Mr. Hughes, who writes a column in the *Chicago Defender,* has made Jesse B. Semple into kind of an African Mr. Dooley.

Through his monologues we hear what he thinks about the Atom Bomb, his cousin Minnie, house rent parties, white folks in Mississippi, Puerto Ricans in Harlem, sex in colored magazines and Congress sending tanks to Saudi Arabia.

This cheerful black boy from Harlem would doubtless give his view on integration in Arkansas too, except that it had not happened yet. In the character of interrogator Mr. Hughes gives some of his own views:

"There is nothing printed in the world like the American Negro press. It is unique, intriguing, exalting, low down and terrific. It is tragic and terrible, brave, pathetic, funny and full of tears.

"The race problem in America is serious business, but need it always be written about seriously? So many weighty volumes, cheerless words, sad tears."

Gilbert Millstein "Negro Everyman" New York Times Book Review, 29 September 1957, p. 41

In this third volume of what are probably best described as interlocutories between the author and his Negro Everyman, Jesse B. Semple, Langston Hughes finally makes explicit the point of view that plainly underlies *The Sweet Flypaper of Life, Not Without Laughter,* the other Simple books, and some of his poetry. These are singled out at random. "The race problem in America is serious business, I admit," writes Hughes in a foreword to *Simple Stakes a Claim.* "But must it always be written about seriously?" . . .

This is a more courageous stand for a writer, particularly if he is a Negro, to take than might ordinarily be thought. He is apt to become the target of his own people, whose sensitivity (the word is the mildest of descriptives) to slurs, few of which are imagined, has been little mitigated, despite legislation, committee meetings or low-rent housing. (More than one case has been noted, for example, of the recordings of popular Negro singers being removed from Harlem jukeboxes when the artists were felt to have "put down their own people.") He is equally open to the regretful tongue-clickings of humorless liberals. Finally, he will do no more than confirm the rabid in their intransigence.

Like its predecessors, *Simple Stakes a Claim* is funny and sharp and indignant and tolerant, even of whites; and full of veiled warnings and demonstrations of the stupidities, callousness and cruelties of both whites and Negroes (but more of

whites than of Negroes; the other would hardly have been expected, nor would it have been accurate as things are). Sometimes, it swings, like a good jazz tune. . . .
    [. . .]
    Elsewhere in the book, Hughes has Simple light into Negro gradualists, the atom bomb, Jim Crow (the description of whose funeral is a small masterpiece), his wife, Joyce, integration, the treatment accorded refugees (in dismal contrast to that accorded native Negroes), rent parties, Negro magazines, the reason why Negroes get all tired out on vacations (they don't get as much time off as whites and tend to half kill themselves having a good time); in one form or another throughout, he lightly tans the hide of segregation. Some day all of the Simple books ought to be bound together in an omnibus volume. That day ought, of course, to be deferred until the time Hughes stops writing about Simple.

John W. Parker
"The Remarkable Mr. Simple Again"
Phylon, 18 (Fourth Quarter 1957), 435–6

While Langston Hughes' recently published *Simple Stakes a Claim* is his "umpteenth" book to stem partially or wholly from the romance and the tragedy of the Harlem scene, it is likewise his third over a period of seven years to penpoint the exploits of one Jesse B. Semple (better known as Simple), a man born on a Chicago typewriter without benefit of midwife. With a way of life peculiarly his own, Simple masquerades now as a carefree onlooker, now as the tragic embodiment of the ups and downs that beset American Negroes, but

always as a Harlemite who laughs with black folk, not at them. In a word, this new Simple volume adds up to a definition of a situation in which Brown Americans in a northern ghetto, despite their own imperfections and corroding influences to which they must face up daily, move on the assumption that tomorrow will be better.

Simple Stakes a Claim is a fresh and a vital collection of short pieces, dialogues, and discussions, many of which make absorbing reading themselves, but which, taken together, constitute an intimate exposé of the problems incident to the movement of Negroes in a democracy—Harlem rent parties, Negro gradualists, the atom bomb, Negro journals, Simple's alcoholic cousin Minnie, the need for housing, and of course that ever-present, two-headed monster, jim crow. Even items that point up the seamy side of human existence in Harlem *per se* suggest by indirection that Negro ghettoes (and all others for that matter) have no place in a democratic society.

Ranging all the way from the comic to the tragic, many of the pieces abound in laughter and love, sadness and bitterness. Himself a lover of the color and the enchantment that characterize the Black Metropolis, and one who knows his way about within her gates, Mr. Hughes has been adept in the selection of his details and sympathetic in the treatment of them. Throughout he has sought "total effect" rather than organic unity. The volume therefore is held together mainly by the unity of action of Simple, and by the unity of impression which it leaves upon the reader.

So also does this new Hughes study disclose his expanding interest in humor as an approach to the problems of race, a tendency observed in such previous books as *Simple Speaks His Mind* (1950), *Simple Takes a Wife* (1953), and *The Sweet Flypaper of Life* (1955). All in all, Simple is mainly a humorous-serious character: he is many things to many people. Humor is therefore the logical consequence when an occasional thrust aimed at another boomerangs to assify him.

Perhaps typical of the rugged, penetrating humor scattered generously through the volume is that which surrounds the forthrightness with which a well-to-do widower wrote off the probability of a fifth wife:

> Wife number 1 was OK, and wife number 2 did do. Wife number 3 quit me, and wife number 4 ain't no more. And all of them cost me money's mammy. But with what dough I got left, I intends to look out for myself. No jive, as long as I am alive, there will be no number 5.

The author takes the position that certain Negro-white problems that do not respond to moralizing may well be laughed out of existence by the employment of well-directed lampoon. Mr. Hughes suggests that white authors sometimes follow a similar procedure in writing on the question of race.

But if *Simple Stakes a Claim* does nothing more than lengthen the shadow of Simple, now about as American as turkey at Thanksgiving, it will add to the stature of Mr. Hughes as a creative artist. The fact that Simple fans are wont to address mail directly to him rather than to his creator attests to Simple's flesh and blood existence. As such he invites favorable comparison with such rich folk characters as Appleseed Johnny, Uncle Remus, and with his contemporary, Mr. Dooley.

Since the impact of the hectic, the coarse and the sensational of the Mid-Twenties, the average Harlem dweller has come a long way in outlook and in seriousness of purpose. For him it is no longer Harlem today, tomorrow, forever. Not nearly everybody is running wild any

more; and in a measure, certain anti-intellectual tendencies have given way to somber thought and questioning. American Negroes, Harlemites included, concur with Simple; they insist that America will be.

Frank Greenwood
"Simple Stakes a Claim"
Los Angeles Tribune,
9 October 1957, p. 13

Langston Hughes deserves a medal! With the creation of the character Jesse B. Semple, he has shown with consummate artistry how things of great seriousness can be tellingly said with adroit humor and satire. And by Simple alone, world-renowned playwright, poet, lyricist Hughes has every right to be considered one of America's leading satirists.

As he himself so nimbly expressed it in his foreword, "Since we have not been able to moralize them out of existence with indignant editorials, etc., maybe we could laugh them to death with well-aimed ridicule." And this he does brilliantly in *Simple Stakes a Claim*. Mr. Hughes has shown how humor can serve as a weapon to devastate the Dixiecrats. And for this he deserves a medal.

Format of this "Simple" book follows closely those of the others, in that it is a series of discussions between the author and his fictional friend, Jesse B. Semple. Their chats cover the atom bomb, Puerto Ricans, Hungarian refugees, housing, rent parties, labor, segregation, Uncle Toms— a sweeping catalogue of topics, including Simple's alcoholic Cousin Minnie. The range of conversation is from the ridiculous to the sublime. Very often what

Simple contributes is foolish and inconsequential, but almost without exception he is entertaining. His down-to-earth humor makes you laugh loud and long. This reviewer literally rolled in the aisles—and for several days after putting the book aside, often to his embarrassment and to the puzzlement of friends.

Only visible weakness of the book, so far as this reviewer is concerned, is the fact that the sharpest wit and satire are postponed until the last third of the book, which creates the hazard that some readers will not persevere long enough to reap the greatest rewards the book has to offer. It is suggested in all seriousness, therefore, that those who are as yet unacquainted with Simple should read this book backwards.

Yes, Langston Hughes deserves a medal, but it's no good waiting around until he gets it. Advise you to run, not walk, to the nearest bookstall for a copy of *Simple Stakes a Claim*.

As the inimitable Louis Armstrong would put it: "Man, that cat is a natural gasser. . . . That cat fractures me!"

"Book Review"
Philadelphia Independent,
12 October 1957, p. 14

Langston Hughes' latest entry in the "Simple" series has Jesse B. Semple (plain "Simple" to his friends) not only speaking his mind, as has been his custom since he began meeting the writer back in 1950, but this time Simple stakes a claim (as the title suggests) a claim in his country and in his rights.

Looking at the school situation and the Supreme Court's decision, Simple observes that the Court's decisions are fine, but sees no reason for whites to be proud of them.

[. . .]

Although Simple wouldn't trade all the states in the South for one barstool in New York, he sees no reason for the North straining a shoulder in patting its back with its prevalent social and economic injustices.

Indulging himself in whimsy, Simple says, "I would like to be a giant. I would sneeze, and blow the Ku Klux Klan plumb out of Dixie. I would clap my hands, and mash Jim Crow like a mosquito . . ."

In the foreword, Langston Hughes suggests that "since we have not been able to moralize the Dixiecrats out of existence with indignant editorials, maybe we could laugh them to death with well aimed ridicule."

His latest book, *Simple Stakes a Claim*, aims a double-barreled volley of biting satire at America's treatment of the Negro that demands to be read.

[J.] Saunders Redding
"Book Review"
Baltimore Afro-American
Magazine, 19 October
1957, p. 2

Mama, the man's here again!

The man, of course, is Simple—Jesse B.—and he looms in and over the life of colored America with indisputable authority. He has this authority because he is more real than thought, more vital than a birth cry, and more true than knowledge. He is Experience's very self.

He is as old and wise as the gods and yet as young and pure as the primal dawn. He is man, but he is also child.

He is endowed with all that the consciousness and conscience of a folk people endow heroes with—courage and integrity, honor and virtue—but he is so common and ordinary that he walks and talks like a common man among common men.

He is a sudden sting of pain. He is perpetually a sheer delight.

Mama, that man's here again!

Actually, of course, he has never been any place but here. Here in "America USA." It is his home, his only soil, and he is more than native to it, and much more than kin to it. He knows everything about it inside out and outside in.

He has distilled wisdom from his knowledge; and from knowledge, humor; and from humor insight. He does not merely see, he sees through. He knows that sense is no good without sensibility. He is not content with discovery: he reveals.

And what does he reveal? Why nothing if not us to ourselves in all the tough, tender, bitter, sweet, tragic, gay, hopeful, hateful, loving, desperate circumstances of colored life in America.

He reveals us to ourselves and even while the sharp pain of self-recognition stabs to the brain, he makes our hearts ready for healing laughter.

". . . I would not bother nobody, unless they bothered me. Of course, better not nobody look at me cross-eyed, neither. I know my rights in a public place up North."

[. . .]

(But why try to reproduce Simple's great gift of laughter in this botched way. It simply can't be torn out of context. One has to read the book.)

Langston Hughes has endowed Simple with the gift of laughter for two serious purposes, one of which goes back in literary tradition most to written literature's beginnings.

"Humor," Hughes says, "is a weapon . . . of no mean value against one's foes."

This is one use he puts it to—as Cervantes did in *Don Quixote*, as Fielding did in *Joseph Andrews*, Dickens in *Oliver Twist*, and Thackeray in *The Yellowplush Papers*.

But there is a second and perhaps greater use for humor in *Simple Stakes a Claim*. "If colored people took all the white world's boorishness to heart and wept over it . . . we would have been dead long ago."

Mama, that man's here again!

God willing, may he never go away.

Thomas Cole "Negro Writer on Desegregation" *Chattanooga Times*, 20 October 1957, p. 18

This is the third volume to appear of these conversations with Simple, whose real name is Jesse B. Semple. By one of the most distinguished of American Negro writers the themes discussed relate generally to some phase of racial discrimination in America.

As an example, Simple remarks upon the strange phenomenon of using a foreign language. "Just say 'Si,'" he points out, "and folks will think you are a foreigner, instead of only a plain old ordinary American Negro. . . . Why does a language, be it pig Latin or Spanish, make all that difference?" It's a pretty good question to ponder.

Simple is in a good American tradition. He is a folk philosopher, who picks up themes of serious meaning but discusses them in such a way as to contain humor. One can read them for fun, but should never overlook the deeper implications. This is a good tract for the times.

Luther P. Jackson, Jr.
"Grade-A Simple"
Crisis, 64 (November 1957), 576–7

In a foreword to this book of sketches on the life and times of Harlem's Jesse B. Semple, better known as Simple, the author suggests that a humorous Negro monthly magazine would be a welcome addition to American life. Expanding this idea, Hughes lists 16 potential contributors—including cartoonists, journalists, novelists and comedians, ranging from Jackie Mabley to George S. Schuyler.

This reviewer would never sell a Hughes idea short, for his literary brain-children have enjoyed some 30 years of artistic success. But with Simple, Hughes has struck commercial gold. He has exploited the vein to the extent of three books and a Broadway theatrical production, all adapted from newspaper columns from the *Chicago Defender*.

Hughes' and Simple's successes are well deserved, for in Jesse B. the author has created a tribute to the dignity of a common man who happens to be a Negro. This is no mean trick. In hands less skilled than Hughes', portrayals of some Negroes—"colleged" as well as "uncolleged"—are apt to wind up in racial embarrassment.

Of the 16 named by Hughes for his magazine, Harlem's Nipsey Russell is one comedian who can tell a racial joke in an integrated audience without any loss of dignity. Perhaps America's best literal interpreter of life among poor, urban Negroes is the cartoonist, Ollie Harrington. His "Mr. Bootsie" is a constant delight to his fellow Negroes, but he is hardly the type they would want to introduce to a new white neighbor.

Although Hughes' awareness of racial sensitivities is clearly shown in the Broadway production of "Simply Heavenly," which he obviously tidied up for white consumption, *Simple Stakes a Claim* is pure, unadulterated Grade-A Simple. In this new book, Simple reaches new glorious heights of racial indignation and disgust. Everybody goes when Simple's wagon comes.

[. . .]

Simple comments on everything from the atomic age to chicken necks, but no matter what he starts talking about, he always winds up on the racial problem. But, alas, Simple is almost forced to admit that he doesn't know the answers. In this exchange between himself and the author: "Inscrutable are the ways of nature," says Hughes. "Screwed up and unscrewable," Simple replies.

Charles Alexander
"Book Briefs and Best Sellers: Simple Semple: He Staked His Claim as a Colored Man"
Albany Democrat Herald, 16 November 1957, p. 10

The race problem in America is serious business, Langston Hughes writes in "Let's Laugh a Little," foreword to his new *Simple Stakes a Claim*. "But must it always be written about seriously?" Even the serious colored magazines such as *Crisis* or *Phylon* don't publish humor. "Such earnestness," says the famous Negro poet and writer, "is contrary to mass Negro thinking. Colored people are always laughing at some wry Jim Crow incident or absurd nuance of the color line."

Hughes wrote his first verse as class poet in the eighth grade in a Lincoln, Ill., public school. Seven volumes of poetry have followed, seven novels, two volumes of his autobiography, six juveniles. He's one of the foremost American Negro writers. His *Simple Speaks His Mind, Simple Takes a Wife* and now, *Simple Stakes a Claim* are in that lighter vein—though Jesse B. Semple ("Simple") can be caustic.

The pieces aren't chapters of a whole, but interchanges in which the author acts as interlocutor while Simple lays down the laws of life as he sees them, the whole strung together by the daily life of Simple, his wife Joyce who yearns after culture and won't have him gnawing porkchop bones in their Harlem front window, his job, his annoying alcoholic outlaw cousin Minnie—out of law because Simple's uncle and aunt neglected to get married up.

Simple takes it out on gradualists, Negro and white, on the white man's bomb—he'd like to have just one and drop it on Mississippi—on the pretenses, fancy alibis and posturings of pretenders of both races. He's a little harder on the whites, but that's only right under the circumstances.

The annals of Jesse B. Semple are good medicine for folks on either side of the color line, or just passing over.

Phillip Bondsky
"Humor and Hope"
Mainstream, 11 (January 1958), 53–7

For once the jacket blurb isn't far wrong, and few readers will feel their arm has been twisted into agreeing that they have found, in Langston Hughes' Jesse B. Semple, a "contemporary Mr. Dooley."

If space allowed, it would be fascinating to analyze in detail the means Simple employed to sneak up on the American public, as he did, beginning so inconspicuously, even casually, as a character originated by Hughes to serve as a convenient stalking horse for his newspaper comments on topical events. These short pages were originally published in the *Chicago Defender,* and were intended as transient comments on the passing scene. Instead one of those exciting and baffling miracles of literature occurred: a human being was born—a permanent and characteristic American type, Negro in color and race, but excruciatingly American.

Excruciatingly because the reader's mind and heart are accurately and sometimes painfully scored upon time after time by Jesse Semple (Simple), whose power to do so rises from convictions deeply shared by all Americans on the human side of Little Rock.

And characteristic, too, is the implicit sanity in even the "wildest" statements which Simple, the original race man, makes to his more-than-conventional barroom friend, the "I" of these essays; for no matter how extreme Simple is, nor how serious he threatens to become, the situation is always rescued, sometimes at the last moment, with the saving grace of humor—humor that ranges from the subtle to the not-so-subtle day-dream of what one, Jesse B. Semple, American Negro, would do if he could fly over Mississippi!

Simple knows his own worth and will not concede an inch of his pride and integrity; but at the same time he is quite conscious of how ludicrous it also is to be Jesse B. Semple in Harlem, U.S.A., in the decade of hydrogen bombs and space travel. In fact, Langston devotes his introduction to a plea for greater humor in the Negro (he could have added, the whole) press, pointing out that few stuffed shirts survive a well-aimed barb, sharpened with wit.

It's interesting to note Hughes' method, which seems like simplicity itself. There are only two characters present, usually at a bar: Simple and his somewhat high-flown, conventional friend. They talk: that is, his friend supplies the thesis, there is an answer to it, and by the end of the piece there is a satisfying literary resolution. In this bare dialectics, which Plato used of course on rather similar themes, a clash of opinion—of idea—takes place, and out of that clash arises a person. Writers ought to study this in Hughes a little more closely, for they will find proven here that at the core of every character there must be an intellectual content—an idea, a thesis.

Simple reacts sharply to life. He also reacts upon life: and in that exchange we have drawn for us the lineaments of a person, and the shape of the life—the world acted upon and acting. He is always in combat; he has a definite stake in life, he believes in something, and all this supplies him with a compass by which to measure the conflicting events of our fast-developing times.

He knows what he is: a Negro in Harlem, the eternal butt of the official American joke that all here enjoy democracy; his unrhetorical life includes an acute consciousness of high rents, high prices for food, an all-surrounding Jim Crow, and daily insults and woundings on a thousand fronts.

It's amazing to see how, with this reality constantly aching in him, he can set other matters into their more-or-less accurate place. Whereas some of the most subtle minds fainted away at the Hungarian episode last year, since events there didn't coincide with their imperatives so neatly arranged in their minds, Simple sees all this a bit differently: "'I am not talking about what the USA is made of,' said Simple, 'I am talking about who runs this country. . . .'"

He does not fail to note that the Hun-garian escapees are given the red carpet treatment here, while he, a native-born American, but unfortunately black, is lucky to get into the back door of the places the Hungarians come in free!

[. . .]

Simple is staggeringly unimpressed by largesse bestowed on his race to the tune of national self-congratulatory editorials in the newspapers—like the Supreme Court decision suggesting that segregation be eliminated from the nation's schools.

To this invitation to the dance, Simple merely remarks: "It's about time."

"I love my race," he says, "But"—and he has a lot of *buts*. "I do wish my feet pointed straight instead of sideways."

The juiceless and conventional language of his interlocutor, which embodies all the hopes and illusions of a handker-chief-headed and rising educated middle-class, contrasts deliciously with Simple's tasty idioms. Jesse B. Semple appals his friend for his outspokenness; he thinks Jesse B. is too race-conscious, too bigoted even, too irreverent, insensitive to the "finer things"; but worst of all, too belligerent.

"'Take that chip off your shoulder,' I said.

"'I will not,' said Simple."

And God help us and Langston—we hope Simple never does!

Checklist of Additional Reviews

Victor R. Yanitelli, *Best Sellers*, 17 (1 October 1957), 208.

Sarah F. Cockey, "New Adult Books for Young People: Fall 1957," *Library Journal*, 82 (15 October 1957), 2674.

Robert Sylvester, "Dream Street: The

Book Shelf," *New York Daily News,* 29 October 1957, p. 51.

John W. Parker, "Simple: Symbol of a New Day," *CLAJ,* 1 (November 1957), 46–7; also as "Hughes Stories," *Greensboro Daily News,* 10 November 1957, p. D3.

"Fiction," *Booklist,* 54 (1 November 1957), 136.

Whitney Balliett, "Books: Briefly Noted," *New Yorker,* 33 (2 November 1957), 195.

"A List of 250 Outstanding Books of the Year . . . A Christmas Guide," *New York Times Book Review,* 1 December 1957, p. 68.

THE LANGSTON HUGHES READER

Gladys P. Graham
"Book Shows Pen Mightier than Sword"
Philadelphia Tribune,
5 April 1958, p. 4

The Langston Hughes Reader is among the first to come off the press in 1958 for one of America's most prolific writers. This compilation of the writings of Langston Hughes is drawn from every category of his prodigious literary production.

It combines the highlights of the novels, stories, plays, poems, songs, essays and many new writings that have never been published before in book form. . . .

Dedicated to Hughes' Uncle John, this tremendous literary undertaking is divided into ten divisions. Short stories (*The Ways of White Folks, Laughing to Keep from Crying,* and other stories), Poems, Children's Poetry, Song Lyrics, Novels and Humor (including his famed Simple Works), Plays, Autobiography, Pageant, Articles and Speeches and Bibliography of the Writings of Langston Hughes.

Langston Hughes, highly considered because of his art and wit, dignity, deep sense of humility and sincerity, has defined the place of the Negro in all of the diverse forms of American literary expression in this comprehensive anthology packed in some 501 pages of (you can't put it down) reading for all tastes from the lowly to those in the palaces.

The high point for this reviewer is in "My America" (under articles and speeches), which he considers his land. "Naturally, I love it—it is home—and I am vitally concerned about its mores, its democracy, and its well being. Yet many Americans who cannot speak English—so recent is their arrival on our shores—may travel about this country at will securing food, hotel, and rail accommodations wherever they wish to purchase them. I may not."

[. . .]

The Langston Hughes Reader has been long overdue. It is a needed and necessary addition to the works of this gifted artist who is a true believer in the fact that the pen is mightier than the sword. He has fought the battle of Jim Crow through the printed word; his appearances before audiences and his literary works are silent monuments to the fact that the Negro in America all things being equal is able to span the tide in many tangential ways.

Felton A. Gibson
"The 'New Negro': An Anthology Offers Wide Choice of Hughes' Work"
Virginian-Pilot and Portsmouth Star, 6 April 1958, p. 6G

The Langston Hughes Reader is probably one of the most refreshing collections to come out in a long time. It is an anthology of Hughes' works which includes stories, plays, poems, songs, blues, articles, speeches and a pageant.

[. . .]

One of the most humorous sections of the book hinges on the perennial fictitious Hughes character, "Simple." The Simple series features the daily activities of "Simple," his friends and associates in New York City's Harlem.

[. . .]

The Langston Hughes Reader is

packed with many hours of good reading and will offer a treasure full of humor, when times are dull and days are tense.

Margaret Parsons
"Variety in This Reader"
Worcester Sunday Telegram, 6 April 1958, p. D9

Carl Van Vechten called Langston Hughes "the Negro poet laureate," even before his first book of poems was published in 1926, and a second title was later added, after he showed himself as proficient in prose as in poetry: "the O. Henry of Harlem."

That both titles have been well earned one acknowledges with enthusiasm after reading this well-selected 500-page *Langston Hughes Reader.* It had a further more personal interest for us, as Hugh Weideman, editor of George Brazillers and one of our reviewers, brought him to call on us in New York.

Langston Hughes is a northern Negro, born and educated in the Middle West, until he took his college work at Lincoln University, Penn., and at Columbia University. He made long visits with his father, a successful business man in Mexico, where he lived for the sake of personal freedom. So Hughes sees and sizes up the situation in the South from both inside and outside points of view. His attitude of the world citizen looking upon the prejudice of a narrow-minded minority is expressed in relating a personal experience in Virginia, when his blood undoubtedly boiled but he saw the ridiculous side and added: "The strange, silly, pathetic South!"

There is variety in this Reader. We en-joyed very much the short stories, which are humorous or tragic, or sometimes both, and have the sharpened point of O. Henry, now in disfavor with some modern writers who set forth their slice of life with no particular beginning or ending or high spot of climax. The autobiographical chapters show wide and varied life, with the extra difficulties and problems which America deliberately adds for the Negro to the ups and downs one encounters in the best of circumstances.

Of course, we were taken with Simple—called Semple by the Negroes after the habit of both black and white Southerners of pronouncing "i" and "e" with a sort of middle sound, which always strikes the Northern ear as being the wrong one. So in the script of the musical show *Simply Heavenly,* given complete, his name as speaker is Simple but he is addressed as Mr. Semple. Irresistibly funny, he says much in a back-handed way for Hughes, sugar-coating the author's philosophy and satire with his original brand of humor.

The poems we have not space to discuss in detail, but here they are, a wide variety to choose from, lyrics and blues and children's verse and poems which have deep overtones of the suffering of an individual and of a race.

Ted Poston
"A Hughes Omnibus"
New York Post, 6 April 1958, p. M11

Although many readers have followed the works of this poet, novelist, playwright, lecturer and wanderer for more than a quarter century, few can have realized the scope of his prodigious output.

It is difficult, for example, to reconcile the tenderness of Hughes' photo-essay, *Sweet Flypaper of Life* (which incidentally, is not included in this collection) with the acid-tipped portrait of condescending white patrons of the Negro Renaissance as portrayed in "Slave on the Block," one of the author's most biting short stories.

And Broadwayites who laughed warmly and long at his musical play, *Simply Heavenly*, the complete libretto of which is included here, will be brought up short by the harshness of *Soul Gone Home*, a one-act play seldom performed outside the Harlem Y or some similar forum.

There will be protests from some of the early Hughes fans, of course. How, for instance, could "A Good Job Gone" be excluded from any collection of his short stories?

And although there are solid and satisfying selections from the enduring trilogy of Jesse B. Semple, one may feel a sense of personal loss in not encountering "Surprise," the story of the returning GI who didn't notify his wife. No story of a Jodie and an unfaithful World War II wife has ever been so hilariously told.

But there is so much crammed into these 500-odd pages that one may not even miss old favorites. Combined are highlights of his novels, autobiography, short stories, poems, songs, speeches, essays and other material never published before.

His publishers describe Hughes as "the unchallenged spokesman of the American Negro." In that, they play him cheap. Hughes is so much more than that. He is the unchallenged spokesman of little people everywhere, of little people who love life and live it with love.

"Work by 'O. Henry of Harlem'"
Charlotte News, 12 April 1958, p. 5A

This is a large collection of all the literary forms to which the "O. Henry of Harlem" has put a pen, from poetry to song lyrics. But within all these forms the basic theme is the problems that beset the American Negro.

Langston Hughes is not always a delicate writer. Cleverness and subtlety are surely not his most outstanding attributes. Basically he writes as ruggedly as a pamphleteer, spicing his contempt with laughter and sorrow.

But this is no matter. The great value of this collection, aside from entertainment, is the reflection of a member of a large minority on the workings of our democracy.

Hughes is a Northerner and his character "Simple" speaks his mind on everything from Jim Crow to divorce. Simple too is a Harlem resident, but his mind wanders often to Mississippi and the conversation subjects that reoccur are not always cheerful.

This is not to say that the *Hughes Reader* is merely a selection of protest literature. On the contrary, it overflows with color and humor. The autobiographies *The Big Sea* (1940) and *I Wonder as I Wander* (1956) are beautifully human.

Hughes has been writing a long time and has not been hesitant to voice his opinions as an individual and as a Negro. Anyone who is interested in facing problems and solving them will not feel it offensive.

Those who think him bold might scan the table of contents and see the title of one section that typifies all his works. It's called "Laughing to Keep from Crying."

[W. G. Rogers]
"Literary Corner:
Biographer Traces Al
Smith's Rise"
Oregon Statesman, part 3,
13 April 1958, p. 27, AP
release; variations, with or
without attribution, in *San
Jose Mercury News,* 13
April 1958; *Portland
[Maine] Telegram,* 13
April, 1958; *Manchester
[N.H.] News,* 13 April
1958; *Klamath Falls
[Ore.] Herald and News,*
20 April, 1958; *Niagara
Falls Gazette,* 27 April
1958; *Grand Rapids
Herald,* 8 June 1958

This is a fine rich dish of Hughes—500 pages from his voluminous writings, poems dated as early as 1926, short stories, some translations from French, some of the "Simple" pieces, some plays, speeches and autobiography.

There are many explanations for Hughes' popularity, such as his sure knack for telling a story, his ability to get five-syllable thoughts into one-syllable words. But best of all, I think, is the wonderful light touch; who is more serious among our writers, and who makes us enjoy it so much?

John Wilcock
"Books: *The Langston
Hughes Reader*"
Village Voice [New York],
16 April 1958, pp. 10–11

This anthology is a delight, and there is no reason to delay saying so. Since the publication of his first book of poetry, *The Weary Blues,* in 1926, Missouri-born Langston Hughes has been turning out vast quantities of poetry, prose, and plays (and sometimes these categories seem inseparable) of uniform sensitivity and humor. The *Reader* offers a representative sampling.

Despite such recent forays into the public eye as his appearances at the Village Vanguard reading poetry, Hughes is probably known to his widest audience through Jesse B. Semple, the subject of about 400 of his weekly columns for the *Chicago Defender.* The columns became books, the books became a play—*Simply Heavenly,* which closed at off-Broadway's Renata Theatre in December—and the both-sides-of-the-argument dialogues between Simple and his creator have probably generated as much good will for Negroes as the combined endeavors of Joe Louis and Jackie Robinson.

The text of *Simply Heavenly* plus several earlier Simple columns, is reprinted in the *Reader,* providing ample proof for Brooks Atkinson's assertion that "Simple begins as a mouthpiece but steadily grows in subtlety, coherence, and significance. Now he is not only entertaining but lovable and illuminating; he is humorous and also logical and believable."

The blurb declares, rather grandiosely, that Langston Hughes' "best school has been the world," but fails to tell the whole astonishing story. In his 56 years Langston has visited a score of countries. He has taught in Mexico, farmed in New York, sailed up and down the coast of Africa, worked in a Montmartre cafe, and hustled as a bus boy in a Washington, D.C., restaurant (where he got his first break by slipping some poems in front of a customer, Vachel Lindsay, who plugged his work thereafter).

During the Civil War in Spain, Hughes was there as correspondent for the *Baltimore Afro-American,* and he has been responsible for some translations of Garcia Lorca's works. From his extensive visits to Haiti he wrote, with the collaboration of composer William Grant Still, an opera, *Troubled Island,* based on the life of Haiti's liberator, Jean Jacques Dessalines. He toured Russia with Arthur Koestler. He wrote a forceful color-bar play, *Mulatto,* which lasted a year on Broadway in 1939, went on tour, and only last year was revived in Buenos Aires, Rio, and Rome. Extracts from all these works, and from his two volumes of autobiography, are included in the *Reader.*

In high school in Lincoln, Ill., young Hughes was named class poet for no other reason than that he was one of two Negroes in his class and the teacher was always stressing that poetry, like Negroes, possessed good rhythm!

Many of Hughes' shortest poems are among his best:

SUBWAY RUSH HOUR

Mingled
breath and smell
so close
mingled
black and white
so near
no room for fear.

His admirers have given him many tags—"The Negro Poet Laureate," "The Molière of Harlem"—but as much as anything he's probably proud of the late Kurt Weill's explanation that Weill and his collaborators chose him to do the lyrics of *Street Scene* in 1948 because they felt that the lyrics of the show "should lift the everyday language of the people into a simple, unsophisticated poetry."

His sense of poetry pervades everything he writes, notably the text of one of the most charming books this reviewer has ever read, *The Sweet Flypaper of Life,* a pictures-and-text story with Roy De Carava of life in Harlem which, regrettably, is not represented in the *Reader* (in paperback form it may still be available . . .).

Prefacing a chapter in the *Reader* on "Children and Poetry," for example, he explains: "Children are not nearly so resistant to poetry as are grown-ups. In fact small youngsters are not resistant at all. But in reading my poems to children from kindergarten to junior-high-school age, I sometimes think they might want to know why people write poetry. So I explain to them:

If you put
Your thoughts in rhyme
They stay in folks' heads
A longer time."

It is hardly necessary to explain that, though he has no children of his own, Hughes, a bachelor, has a shrewd understanding of other people's. A few years ago when the neighborhood kids used to stray off the Harlem streets onto his tiny but well-tended garden at 127th Street— he still lives there—he called them in and handed them little wooden stakes on which to write their names.

The stakes were solemnly planted, each beside a different bulb, and from then on the doctrine of protective coexistence took complete charge.

[J.] Saunders Redding
"Book Review"
Afro-American Magazine,
19 April 1958, p. 2

I must say that the *Langston Hughes Reader* worries me a bit.

It is not that it's not a good book. As a matter of fact, so far as anthologies go, it's a spanking good book.

It contains the complete libretto of *Simply Heavenly,* some of Hughes' best short stories, twenty-odd of the "Simple" pieces, snatches of his two autobiographical volumes, and a spate of poems. The poems are not in every instance his best.

This is a fact that, while it is perfectly understandable, emphasizes the shortcomings of all anthologies: you can't include everything.

The poetry is special, and doubtless the best of it will be saved for a definitive collection of Hughes' verse.

But as I've said, I'm not worried on the score of the quality of the Reader.

All the best qualities of Hughes are here in some measure, and though the tastes of Hughes' readers are as various as Hughes' own talents, there's something to satisfy nearly all.

I say "nearly all," for those who, like myself, thoroughly enjoyed those early experiments in "racial rhythms"—"The Cat and the Saxophone," "Saturday Night," etc.—will have to be content with what is distinctly second-best in this line—that is, pieces from *Montage of a Dream Deferred.*

You're walking down Fifth Avenue, or Madison, or Lexington, and all is pretty right with the world, and suddenly you're stopped by a big sign pasted on the shop window of one of your favorite shops.

"BARGAIN SALE," the sign says: "LEASE EXPIRING. CLOSING OUT!"

You don't like the idea of a favorite shop closing out.

You've got too many good things there, things that you've loved and lived with for years and that time, contrary to time's usual custom, has made finer and somehow better and more precious.

The sign jars you. That's the way the *Reader* jarred me.

I've got many fine things from Langston Hughes. "Mother to Son" grows more precious as it and I grow older.

"Mulatto," "The Negro Speaks of Rivers," "A Christmas Story"—dozens of well-loved things.

And I want to go on getting more from the same rich source. That's what worries me about the *Reader.*

Common sense tells me I'm probably worrying needlessly. Hughes' lease on his talents—those various, versatile talents—is not about to run out.

My time sense just will not allow that he's had the lease long enough, really, and *Simply Heavenly* (which, incidentally, opens soon in London) proves he's not begun to use it up. "Closing out," indeed!

Common sense tells me to stop worrying and go back and enjoy the good things which it wouldn't let me enjoy when I first opened the book.

"Books: Briefly Noted"
New Yorker, 34 (26 April 1958), 155

A five-hundred-page sampling of the work of Langston Hughes—poetry, autobiography, fiction, essays, and drama. Since Mr. Hughes is a Negro who writes mostly about Negroes, seeing some thirty years of his work spread out before you is like attending an unusually subtle tolerance lecture—perhaps the last thing Mr. Hughes had in mind—for what is most striking about his book is that his American Negroes are remarkably unexotic and unalien, and, in fact, more like everybody else than most Americans realize.

Milton S. Byam
"New Books Appraised"
Library Journal, 83
(15 May 1958), 1535

A selection of the short stories, poems, novels, plays, autobiographical writings and speeches of the entertainingly prolific Langston Hughes. Here are selections from the enjoyable "Simple" stories, *The Big Sea, The Weary Blues* and the still to be published *Simply Heavenly.* Never has so much Hughes ever been available at one time in one place. It is an excellent sampling and will saturate any reader in full Hughes flavor. More useful for the home library than for those desiring complete works, it is nonetheless of value to other libraries for its birds-eye view of an author and his growth to artistry.

John W. Parker
"Minority in Transition"
Greensboro Daily News, 18 May 1958, p. D3; also as "The Growth of a Poet's Mind," *Phylon,* 19 (Third Quarter 1958), 339–40

A little better than three decades separate the publication date of *The Weary Blues* (1926), Langston Hughes' initial volume, and that of his *The Langston Hughes Reader,* fresh from the press. This new book brings into sharp focus not only much that has gone on in the mind of America's foremost Negro popular poet during thirty-odd turbulent years, but likewise something of the inner life of a major American minority in transition.

Flashed against the black man's socio-economic-cultural background in Harlem, in America, and in varying degrees around the world, the collection covers the period of the Negro Literary Renaissance of the late Twenties with much of it emphasis upon reckless abandon; the disillusionment of the Forties as expressed in a piece like *Shakespeare in Harlem* (1942); the sombre questioning mood that characterizes *Fields of Wonder* (1947); the vague, mixed-up dream one encounters in *Montage of a Dream Deferred* (1951); and the stubborn insistence upon a place in the sun that underscores the thinking of the present-day American Negro.

The Langston Hughes Reader is a comprehensive anthology replete with snatches of Mr. Hughes' novels, stories, plays, poems, songs, and essays that have justified the label by which Carl Van Vechten designated him many years back—the "Negro Poet Laureate." Included also is the complete libretto of the popular musical comedy, *Simply Heavenly,* the entire text of his pageant, *The Glory of Negro History, Soul Gone Home,* a one-act play, an assortment of his Simple pieces, generous samplings from his autobiographical selections, and certain new writings that have never before been published in book form.

It may well be assumed that it is upon this compilation of data that Mr. Hughes has elected to rest his case. And one is convinced that, all in all, the book strikes a fair balance in organization as in the selection of data. If more space is devoted to poetry than to the short story, for example, one may assume that the author included the selection that best fitted into the underlying purpose of the volume.

So far as lyric quality is concerned, however, and the other literary niceties that distinguish poetry from prose, the poems, by and large, found in *Fields of Wonder* (a volume not included in the collection) are superior to those in *Montage of a Dream Deferred.* A good many of them substitute a universal emphasis for that of a limited locale. Here is probably Hughes' finest collection of poems borne up by sheer charm and buoyancy.

A signal deduction one may draw from *The Reader* is that of the manner in which it points up the growth and diversity of the author's mind. Beginning in 1926 with the poetry medium, Hughes moved on to the short story, the plays, song lyrics, novels, and pageants, and geographically from Harlem, throughout the United States, to the West Indies and in *Laughing to Keep from Crying* and *I Wonder as I Wander* around the world. *The Langston Hughes Reader* is pulled together on the assumption that the author's message, a sort of *argumentum ad populum,* warrants a wider reading public and that the book should

eventually make its way into the nation's public schools.

Perhaps one reason Langston Hughes has managed to maintain a wide reading public over the years (almost all the young Negro penmen who began with him have fallen into obscurity) is that his message has come both from *within* and *without*— he looked into his heart and wrote. His new volume, *The Langston Hughes Reader,* adds up to a penetrating definition of the situation as regards the role of the American Negro and to a subtle disclosure of the growth of a poet's mind.

Henry F. Winslow
"Poet of the Common Man"
Crisis, 65 (June–July 1958), 376–8

At 56, the poet Langston Hughes, to quote and paraphrase a clause from a sketch in his *Laughing to Keep from Crying* (1952), has succeeded in establishing a literary reputation out of "little indirections" which finally add up to one "tremendous fact": the man from Joplin is the chief advocate and preserver of a folk tradition, and it is this tremendous fact that *The Langston Hughes Reader* makes evident throughout.

Here are brought together perhaps the most representative of those selections (articles, autobiographies, blues, novels, poems, plays, etc.) which have appeared since June 1921, when encouragement from one-time *Crisis* editor Jessie Fauset, the novelist, led to the publication (in *The Crisis*) of the poem, "The Negro Speaks of Rivers." His beginnings, literary and otherwise, Mr. Hughes has dutifully recorded in

The Big Sea (1940), his autobiography, enough of which is included in *The Langston Hughes Reader* to delineate the principal influences of the poet's life and career.

He experienced early in life the insecurity occasioned by separated parents and poverty. His father, for whom making money to keep was the main business of life, broke with his mother when she left him (for the second and last time) in Mexico City. His mother and stepfather, for whom making money to spend—on gadgets and good times—was the whole meaning of living, were poor examples to a child of so sensitive a temperament. So his grandmother took him with her to Lawrence, Kansas, when he was in the second grade, whereupon the unhappiness and shame that stemmed from their poverty led him to escape to the world of books.

The question of the relative merit as between Christians and sinners was settled for him in the respective personalities of Auntie and Uncle Reed (friends of his grandmother who took him after her death), each of whom he found equally kind and considerate. Marginal status gained him student offices at Central High School in Cleveland when deadlocks between the predominantly Jewish and Catholic elements enabled him often to get elected.

Again living with a querulous mother from 14 to 17, he left her to go back to his father in Mexico, whom he came to know—and hate—for his high-pressure hustling for money. From this Langston Hughes went for a year to Columbia University, and then out into the world, alone; and from this and more he has come all the way up as man and artist without losing the naturalness on which true humanity and art rest.

Langston Hughes has not needed to be sent in search of his identity because he has never lost it; he has kept his art at home and true to its origins. In doing this, he has succeeded not so much in underscoring the problems of a group as in depicting the humanity of a people. As a poet of the twentieth century, he has neither lost himself in the language of the skies nor soiled himself with that of the streets, yet he moves freely in both areas. Clean and clear, he has grown wise rather than arty.

Among the pieces included here from his poetic treatment of Harlem, *Montage of a Dream Deferred* (1951), is one illustrating his capacity to capture in a flash of verse-light a human condition (in this case the way of living currently emerging as the prime tragedy of average, urban Negro family life):

NUMBERS

If I ever hit for a dollar
gonna salt every dime away
in the Post Office for a rainy day.

I ain't gonna
play back a cent.

(Of course I might
combinate a little
with my rent.)

Those "genuine folk-songs born out of heartache," the Blues, he hopes that Marian Anderson and Paul Robeson will one day include on their programs, "as well as the Spirituals which they now sing so effectively."

But the poet Langston Hughes will probably be best remembered for creating and filling with all his meaningful purpose the folk-hero Jesse B. Semple. Beginning as a column in the *Chicago Defender* and as of now already three published books, . . . the *Simple* series has brought him the distinction he dreamed of while reading Guy de Maupassant as a boy: "To be a writer and write stories about Negroes, so true that people in faraway lands would read them—even after I was dead." Out of this creation has come *Simply Heavenly* (1956), the musical folk comedy which opened on Broadway at the Playhouse in August, 1957. It is in this comedy, the complete libretto of which is printed in *The Reader,* that one may find the essence of Langston Hughes. Here, Mamie, the hard-talking, soft-hearted domestic, tells the world: "I like watermelon and chitterlings both, and I don't care who knows it." Or, again, she probably speaks for Hughes, who has made Harlem his home: "I didn't come here to Harlem to get away from my people. I come here because there's more of 'em. I loves my race. I loves my people." Or, Simple himself tells his friend Melon when the latter presents him books: "I wish you'd of brought me a quart of beer and some pigs feet. I ain't much on books."

Simple's friend Boyd reads to him a letter from Isabel, the wife in Baltimore who has at last found a mail clerk willing to finance her divorce from Simple: "Let me hear from you tonight as my husband-to-be has already passed the point where he could wait." But most touching of all is the account Simple gives of how in whipping him for the last time, Aunt Lucy, "dead and gone to glory," taught him right from wrong. Aunt Lucy had cried and complained that for all her whippings she had failed to set him right. And her tears succeeded where the switches had failed. Talking to his girl-friend, Joyce, Simple sets forth the credo of the humble heart: "When peoples care for you and cry for you—and love you—Joyce, they can straighten out your soul."

The selections presented in *The Langston Hughes Reader* may not in every instance be the best of Hughes—one looks in vain for that moving piece with which the Rev. Martin Luther King electrified an overflow audience in Brooklyn's Concord Baptist Church back in 1956: "Son, Life for Me Ain't Been No Crystal Stair"—but he is here for all that he means as a poet of the common man. The man from Joplin deserves a garland, and his *Reader* a place in every living room in the world, for he speaks the language of people the world over.

Rev. Joseph G. McGroarty "The Best of Hughes" *Stray Notes from the Shrine of the Little Flower,* 34 (July–August 1958), 7–9

One-author anthologies have become a growing fad for modern readers. These bulky volumes provide a convenient and relatively painless way for one to become acquainted with what someone else considers to be the best or most representative of a particular writer's extensive output. A selection has been made recently of the varied and prodigious writings of Langston Hughes, that one-time controversial figure in contemporary Negro letters. The compilation is called *The Langston Hughes Reader.* It contains all kinds of things from the rich pen of Mr. Hughes: novels, short stories, plays, songs, poems, speeches and a pageant.

Though not arranged in the chronological order of their composition, the component items are dated. This enables the reader to observe a gradual mellowing in Mr. Hughes' racial attitude. Though he never betrays an unawareness of those injustices to which he and his people in the United States have fallen heir, there is less of outspoken bitter resentment over this state of affairs in his more recent writings.

Sections from two of his autobiographical sketches, *The Big Sea* (1940) and *I Wonder as I Wander* (1956), make up most of the latter half of the *Reader*. Here Hughes writes with disturbing frankness about everything and everybody, including himself. He was born in 1902, in Joplin, Missouri, the child of a broken marriage. During most of his childhood and youth he lived with his mother. Occasional intervals spent with his father were brief and unhappy. Family circumstances caused the family to move from city to city. During these years he experienced often the indignities arising from racial discrimination and segregation. These were wounds which he would never forget, nor, seemingly, permit to heal.

Selections from the 1956 work recount his experiences in Spain during the troubled and widely misrepresented days of that poor land's Civil War. No one even remotely informed about Langston Hughes' political past needs to be told that his sympathies lay with the Loyalists. In Spain he met up with Herbert L. Matthews, the *New York Times* one-slanted correspondent of Spain's troubles. Together they have both attempted to keep alive the old leftist myth that communist Russia did not effectively and materially espouse the Spanish Loyalist cause.

Mr. Hughes is a poet of recognized talent and ability. Like his prose, most of his verse depicts the joys, longings and sufferings of his people. While the few religious poems printed in the "Reader" have a simple and tender reverence, they can not make one forget the blasphemous verses of Hughes' "Goodbye, Christ." It was in those lines that he sacrilegiously dismissed the Son of God, and voiced his preference for Marx and Lenin. In these days when Marxism is no longer so fashionable among the off-beat literati, it is no wonder that that one was not deemed suitable to be included in the compilation of his more representative poems.

Excerpts from the three enjoyable volumes of Hughes's *Simple* series find merited space in the *Reader*. It is too bad that a more generous sampling of Jesse B. Semple's cleverly imaginative view of things is not given in these pages. Worthwhile deletions of other included matter could have been made in order to give space for more of that medium in which the author excels, humorous dialogue—clear, crisp and topical. Last year he used his "Simple" stories for the book and lyrics of the Broadway musical *Simply Wonderful* [i.e., *Heavenly*]. In its entirety, the script of this new musical folk comedy is presented in *The Langston Hughes Reader*.

A great deal that Langston Hughes has written has not always been well received in the Negro press. With the aplomb of a successful writer, safely above and beyond the sting of adverse critics, he quotes defiantly their unfavorable notices. It was his poems especially which drew their hostile fire. They were shocked because he made Negro porters and prostitutes the subjects of his verses. Complacently Hughes concludes his evaluation of their opinions:

"So I didn't pay any attention to the critics who railed against the subject matter of my poems, nor did I write them protesting letters, nor in any way attempt to defend my book. Curiously enough, a short ten years later, many of those very poems in *Fine Clothes to the Jew* were being used in Negro schools and colleges."

Hughes' influence and place in American literature can not today be denied. The *Reader* is proof of his assured recognition and success.

G.E.G.
Chattanooga Times, 6 July 1958, p. 14

The author is among the most distinguished of contemporary American Negro writers. This volume contains representative selections from his novels, short stories, poetry, plays, speeches, and articles, as well as sections of his two autobiographical volumes, *The Big Sea* and *I Wonder as I Wander.* Among the more interesting portions are a number of sketches about his famous Jesse B. Semple, Harlem Negro, whose homely folk-humor is entertaining and enlightening about Negro attitudes. I was disappointed not to find more from *Not Without Laughter,* which, though out of a dimmer past, contains as much truth as Semple's reflections.

Inez Shacklett
"A Fine, Rich Dish"
Tulsa Sunday World Magazine, 6 July 1958, p. 23

By his wit and literary excellence, Langston Hughes has established himself as the unchallenged spokesman of the American Negro—called the "O. Henry of Harlem" and the "Negro Poet Laureate" (this last by Carl Van Vechten).

[. . .]

He is a restless traveler and a brilliant writer, having that rare gift of empathy with which he has observed life from many points of view.

The 500 pages of this remarkable anthology have skimmed the cream off his many literary achievements, and contain everything from children's poetry to novels and humor. (Remember *Not Without Laughter,* 1930? And the unforgettable Simple Trilogy: *Simple Takes a Wife, Simple Speaks His Mind,* and *Simple Stakes a Claim?*)

There are numerous facets to the autobiographical section from *The Big Sea* (1940) to *I Wonder as I Wander* (1956).

Among noteworthy articles and speeches are "My Most Humiliating Jim Crow Experience" and "How to Be a Bad Writer (In 10 Easy Lessons)."

In addition to plays and poetry, there are some new selections such as *Simply Heavenly,* a musical comedy; all of the text of his pageant *The Glory of Negro History;* a one-act play, *Soul Gone Home,* and other poems, stories and children's lyrics.

A reader will not soon forget "Science Says It's a Lie" or lightly dismiss "Out Loud Silent." ("If I kicked my gizzard out now, it will not bring back one glass of the beer that has gone through my gullet, nor restore nary wasted dime to pocket.")

This is a volume to restore one's faith in a little bit of everything.

Hermes Nye
"Entertaining Selections from Langston Hughes"
Dallas Times Herald, Roundup Section, 27 July 1958, p. 15

Here in one thumping 500-page volume you have the heart of Langston Hughes' works. This versatile Negro has been batting out stories, poems, novels and speeches for over a quarter of a century and has earned the respect and admiration of both races.

Hughes is a handsome cosmopolite, a sensitive soul with a twinkle in his eye and hope in his heart. I would not call him a profound man but then he is probably the last to claim that he was out to give Plato or even Jacques Maritain any serious competition. He is concerned over the race problem to the point of fanaticism, but has never achieved enough objectivity to see that the colored problem starts out with the white problem—that persecution starts not with the persecuted but with the neurotic needs of the persecutor—. Be that as it may, Hughes has struck many a blow for freedom and has given heart to many by his wit and grace.

In writing as in living he is pretty much the "natcheral man," and he is as easy and universal as water.

In story telling, as has often been said, he is "the O. Henry of Harlem," but his "Simple" stories of a seemingly footloose and vacant-minded barfly strike more deeply than any tales spun by William Sydney Porter. I doubt if our man is a great writer but he is a distinguished and what is perhaps even more important, an interesting and entertaining one, and his influence may well be felt long after his works are forgotten.

A.C.H.
"Selections from Prolific Writer"
Savannah Morning News Magazine, 28 September 1958, p. 11

Selections from the Writings of Langston Hughes drawn from his prodigious production of novels, stories, plays, poems and even the libretto of his popular new musical comedy, *Simply Heavenly,* are included in *The Langston Hughes Reader.* We have here, too, words of many spirituals, a one-act play, *Soul Gone Home,* and even some children's lyrics.

The spirituals are not given as nostalgic slave songs but as a cry of a people wanting freedom. This is a point only for the experts, but he goes to lengths as for instance presenting "Swing Low, Sweet Chariot" as Harriet Tubman singing of freedom. There are blues songs and parts of his autobiography. There is a great deal of humor and fun in the children's poetry included, as for instance, "Old Dog Queenie was such a meanie, She spent her life barking at the scenery."

Esther J. Walls
"Book Review"
NAACP Voice, November 1958, p. 2

This new volume of selected writings by the well-known and well-loved author, playwright, and poet can only be described in superlative terms. Langston Hughes is without doubt one of the most prolific and versatile of contemporary writers. Regardless of your preferences, you will find all literary forms in *The Langston Hughes Reader*—poetry, plays, novels, short stories, essays, and autobiographical works—arranged conveniently for browsing and for rediscovering the delightful output of the author.

To anyone already familiar with Hughes' work, no expansive comments are necessary. Mr. Hughes' books are marked by humor, honesty of portrayal, integrity and simplicity—in fact, he is deceptively simple. Underlying all his writing there is real insight and perception of human foibles, limitations, dreams and aspirations. His characters and situations are those familiar to anyone who has lived in a Negro community. The people are simple folk—domestics, barmaids, ordinary people who walk on Seventh Avenue, or dance at the Savoy, or sit and talk in the neighborhood bar. It is Langston Hughes' own special magical touch that makes them so alive and real that they practically leap from the page of the book.

In the autobiographical section of the book, portions of *The Big Sea* and *I Wonder as I Wander* are reprinted. Through them the reader is able to relive the glorious period of the renaissance in Negro literature during the Twenties, the former days of house-rent parties. One shares the author's exciting and stimulating life as a young boy growing up in the Middle West, as a globetrotter, correspondent during the Spanish Civil War, and the many other highlights of this writer's career.

Here is a volume that can be read aloud with the family. It is sure to provide continuing enjoyment and pleasure.

Raymond Lowery "Sometimes Bitter but More Often Humorous" *Raleigh News and Observer,* part 3, 2 November 1958, p. 5

Although Richard Wright is generally recognized as America's most important living Negro author, Langston Hughes, by virtue of his prodigious literary production, possibly should be regarded as the leading spokesman of the American Negro.

Both writers' books deal with the difficulties of a proud and passionate, uneducated Negro in a civilization dominated by the idea of white supremacy. But Hughes' literary endeavors—if terribly uneven—are less exaggerated and more convincingly presented. He is by all odds the most versatile of all Negro writers.

This 500-page compilation is drawn from every category of a huge body of work. It offers the highlights of his novels, stories, plays, poems, songs, essays and speeches. And there are some new writings that have never before been published in book form.

Like Wright's works, much of Hughes' are clearly propaganda in purpose. But their convincing presentation of characters, thoughts and actions, which leave the reader to draw his own conclusions, makes them artistically satisfying as well.

Among the new selections are the complete libretto of his humorous, fairly successful musical comedy, *Simply Heavenly;* all of the text of his stirring pageant, *The Glory of Negro History;* an interesting one-act play, *Soul Gone Home;* and several other stories, poems and children's lyrics.

Parts of his autobiographies, *The Big Sea* and *I Wonder as I Wander,* are included. One chapter relates the hullabaloo at Chapel Hill back in the 1930's when the proprietors of a slightly notorious bookshop printed one of his more controversial poems prior to a speaking engagement on the campus and attempted to entertain him as a guest in their rooming house.

And of course there are generous selections from his incomparable "Simple" trilogy. . . .

It's a comprehensive anthology, crowded with characteristic scenes and sentiments—often more humorous than bitter—that have established Hughes' position in American literature.

Of the enormous and varied output, the reviewer has always preferred Hughes' poetry, particularly that portion not concerned so obviously with "the cause." His verses sing. Like these lines from *The Weary Blues:*

". . . And far into the night he
    crooned that tune.
The stars went out and so did the
    moon.
The singer stopped playing and went
    to bed
While the weary blues echoed
    through his head.
He slept like a rock or a man that's
    dead."

Dayton Kohler
"Echo of 1920's: Hughes Rugged, Honest"
Richmond News Leader,
8 April 1959, p. 9

For readers with long memories, the name of Langston Hughes is likely to set a bell tolling for those middle years of the 1920's when, to the accompaniment of the aesthetic snobbery of *Vanity Fair,* novels like Carl Van Vechten's *Nigger Heaven,* and the drawings of Covarrubias, the Negro writer suddenly found himself in literary fashion.

Before long, however, the Negro writer came to be judged by standards which had nothing to do with race or color. Some of the poets and novelists popular thirty-odd years ago have now disappeared because they offered little except novelty and a sense of race. A few have survived because their values ran deeper.

Of this second group, Langston Hughes has proved the most durable of all. Perhaps the most surprising feature of this edition of his selected writings is the variety of his work since his beginning as a poet with *The Weary Blues* in 1926. There is a generous selection of his poems, many in the blues rhythms which he helped to popularize, but there are also short stories, plays, essays, speeches, translations, and extensive selections from his novels and autobiographies, including the three volumes of the Simple series.

All in all, the volume offers a cross section of a literary career marked by rugged honesty and deep feeling. Some of the material is presented with wryness and satire, some with zestful good humor, some with proletarian aggressiveness. The best selections are those in which the writer has been able to look through the problems of race and into the condition of man.

Checklist of Additional Reviews

"Literature," *Booklist*, 54 (15 May 1958), 526.

"Another Collection," *Atlanta Journal and Constitution*, 25 May 1958, p. 4E.

"Books in Brief," *New York Herald Tribune Book Review*, 25 May 1958, p. 13.

TAMBOURINES TO GLORY

"Tambourines to Glory"
Virginia Kirkus Bulletin,
26 (1 November 1958),
832–3

A Harlem folk tale in modern guise—so one might characterize this story of two sides of the coin in an independent, non-denominational religious racket. Two women on relief—one a lusty realist, took her sex where she could get it, used what funds she had to "buy" her man (preferably young and good looking), and came up with the idea of putting on an act on a street corner using religion in freewheeling style; the other whose chief characteristic was sheer indolence, liked to sit better than to stand, but was at heart sincere, well-meaning and honest. A tambourine to accompany the singing—and collect the sheckels; a gift of gab and high sounding phrases in the best Billy Sunday tradition, a soulful voice and a soulful appearance, these were their stock in trade. But when Laura took on a young man with ideas, she progressed from street corner to a two room Garden of Eden, then to a refurbished ex-theatre, while the crowds grew and the money flowed. Laura doled it out to her Charlie; Essie put it into good works—and to her preparations for her teen-age daughter to come North. And a few people got religion. That it ends on a note of melodrama bordering on tragedy somehow fails to touch the heartstrings. But the telling in the vernacular has its poetic overtones and its sense of authenticity.

Marsh Maslin
"The Browser: Two Negro Writers, Two Novels"
San Francisco Call-Bulletin, 12 November 1958, p. 15

Here are two books by two capable Negro writers who feel, as every sensitive man must, deeply and strongly about the position of the Negro in a white society. Richard Wright has written 11 books, of which his *Native Son* is the best known. He has lived in France for the past 10 years, and his current novel, *The Long Dream,* gives The Browser the feeling that he has been away too long from the United States. . . .

Fishbelly's flight solved nothing—and that's bad writing.

The Browser, as an individual and a reviewer, has more respect for Langston Hughes, poet and novelist who wrote *Tambourines to Glory.* Hughes feels as deeply as Wright about his people—and he, too, once lived in Paris and discovered for himself that the race consciousness of the European is also present but more deeply buried. His story, which he calls "an urban folk tale," is set within the confines of the New York Negro community. It is the story of two Harlem women who organized their own religion and did well for themselves for a while, "preying upon the gullibility of simple people." It is funny, it is touching, it is sad—and a much better book in its narrower compass than *The Long Dream.*

Marion Turner Clarke
"Selected New Books in Review: Fiction of Harlem, Ireland, Maine"
Baltimore Evening Sun,
21 November 1958, p. 28

Job 11–7 to Essie meant a text from the Bible, "Canst thou by searching find out God?" To Laura it meant numbers, and numbers meant gamblers to swell their congregations—and congregations meant money in their pockets. These two women, one the sincere evangelist and one the charlatan, are the founders of a gospel church and the main characters in *Tambourines to Glory* by Langston Hughes.

This is a short story of Harlem, rough and unvarnished but pulsing with the life of a vigorous race. Mr. Hughes sees his people as they are and presents them with their weaknesses and with their strengths, neither sentimentalized nor caricatured. There is humor in this little book and there is tragedy. It is well done and will be memorable for those readers who are not repelled by the surface crudity. Mr. Hughes calls it an "urban folk tale," intended to expose the type of "gospel racketeers" who prey on the ignorant and on the simple hearted.

[. . .]

Richard Gehman
"Free, Free Enterprise"
Saturday Review, 61 (22 November 1958), 19–20

Sometimes, especially after I have finished a new book of his, I think Langston Hughes is one of the greatest folk poets our country has produced. I am not entirely sure what a folk poet is, but whatever a folk poet is, Langston Hughes is. His new book, which is about the Gospel business in Harlem, has the clean, simple line of a gospel song by Clara Ward; it develops with a natural, effortless simplicity and an unassuming authority, as Miss Ward sings her songs, and it is full of vitality, earthiness, joy, unashamed religious feeling, and humorous perspective. It is a book that takes delight in the classic behavior of its characters, yet never condescends. Reading it, I was reminded of Joseph Mitchell's note at the beginning of *McSorley's Wonderful Saloon.* The people in his stories, Mr. Mitchell remarked, were those of the kind "that many writers have recently got in the habit of referring to as 'the little people.'" He added, "I regard this phrase as patronizing and repulsive. There are no little people in this book."

There are no little people in Hughes's book, either. They are all drawn in bold, Rouault-like strokes. *Tambourines to Glory* is about two Harlem ladies, Laura Reed and Essie Belle Johnson, who decide that they are tired of being poor. Essie wants desperately to have her daughter, who is down South, with her. Laura wants—just as desperately—men, mink coats, big cars, and booze. Essie likes to sit; she is a slow and deliberate lady. Laura's favorite posture is less upright.

"I'm a she-male minister," she says,

"and there ain't nothing in the Bible says male or female shall not make love. Fact is, Essie, the very first book is just full of be-gats, which runs from Genesis through to Tabulations."

The two ladies found a church. That is, they put a down payment of two dollars on a Bible and spend thirty-five cents for a camp chair and fifty cents for a tambou-rine and go out into the street to look for business. They both sing. Laura is fiery, Es-sie is holy. Within a short time they rent an abandoned flat, and a short time after that they are operating in an old theater. Then Laura's boyfriend, an opportunist who has connections with a white racketeer, moves in on them. He goes for Essie's daughter, up from the South. Laura stabs him and blames Essie, and—

I don't really want to tell the whole story; not that it would spoil it, for it would not; it is just that its very simplicity might drive the reader away. This is a funny book and should be read aloud; it is a book that reaffirms its writer's talent—and, more important than mere talent, his belief in the miracle of human behavior.

[. . .]

Marty Sullivan
"'Folk Tale' of Harlem Is Praised"
Fort Wayne News Sentinel, 22 November 1958, p. 4

Too many novels about Negroes, be they written by white or Negro authors, turn into sociological theses.

Tambourines to Glory is a blessed ex-ception to this rule.

Written by Langston Hughes, a leading Negro author and poet, *Tambourines* tells the story of two jobless, relief-drawing Harlem women who found a church.

The two founders are a contrast in mood, character and belief. Laura Reed is out for one thing—money. Essie Belle Johnson, in a fumbling, often blind way, wants to help people.

Together the duo create a church that grows from a street corner revival meet-ing into an extravaganza that rivals a De Mille production and attracts thousands of faith-seekers.

Around the two women gather an assortment of characters from Deacon Crow-for-Day and lady trap drummer Birdie Lee to slick, evil Big-Eyed Buddy, Harlem lover-man.

Written almost exclusively in dialogue, the book offers a fine look into the color-ful, earthy and endlessly inventive Negro speech.

Lurking on the edges of this urban folk tale is a deeper and often darker scene—a portrait that shows the workings of unor-thodox churches which have mushroomed in Harlem during the past dozen years, churches where, the author says, "unscru-pulous leaders who might be called 'Gos-pel racketeers' prey upon the gullibility of simple people."

Gilbert Millstein
"Laura and Essie Belle"
New York Times Book Review, 23 November 1958, p. 51

About the most convenient capsule de-scription of this short novel by Langston Hughes is to call it a sort of Negro "Elmer

577

Gantry," mildly sardonic where Sinclair Lewis' gaudy assault on evangelism was savage, and gently funny where the other was undeviatingly and harshly satirical. As a literary work, *Tambourines to Glory* is skillful and engaging—the consistently high quality of Hughes' production over the years is, considering its great quantity, a remarkable phenomenon and the mark of an exuberant professionalism. Yet in the end, the book is a minor effort, a side glance at a major phenomenon, with an industriously contrived climax.

[. . .]

What has happened here, in the reviewer's opinion, is that the author elected to avoid the serious implications of his thesis. He has done it gracefully, it is true, but he has avoided it. The technique of using humor to make a point in deadly earnest is as old as mankind—Hughes has done it innumerable times and with great success in his "Simple" stories. In *Tambourines to Glory*, it has fogged up the things he clearly meant to say.

Hoke Norris
"A Store-Front Church That Sang On to Glory"
Chicago Sun-Times, section 3, 23 November 1958, p. 4

The store-front church has become a familiar sight in American cities. It is non-denominational or creates its own denomination and gives it a rather fanciful name. It is often loud and boisterous and sometimes it arises from dubious motivation. It advertises itself with crudely lettered signs and sometimes with neon. And in the city's slums—on the West Madison and North Clark streets and on the South Sides and in the Harlems of the world—the store-front church, though its facade is decaying and its front windows dusty and cracked, fills a need as all institutions must if they are to endure.

This is the world of the new novel from the distinguished Negro novelist and poet, Langston Hughes. He writes of two Harlem women, Laura, who drinks her wine and longs for money, and Essie, who wants to do good. Out of this unlikely combination of motives grows the Reed Sisters' Tambourine Temple—from street curb to first-floor apartment to abandoned theater.

Laura pays off the cop on the corner, she pays the landlord under-the-table for the apartment, she pays the politicians who must be bribed before she and Essie may use the fire-trap theater. Along the way Laura acquires a lover and a taste for Scotch whisky, Essie brings her daughter up from the South, Laura kills her faithless man and tries to frame Essie, and justice triumphs and Essie sings the gospels and plans the good works.

Out of evil, then, will come good. Even at the outset evil is not unmixed with good—Essie, though tolerant and sometimes purposefully blind, deplores her partner's greed and adultery and longs for the day of salvation for her people. Yet the Tambourine Temple would never have come into being without Laura's thirst and greed and her lover and his acquaintanceship with the helpful politicians. Once established, however, the church must be purged of evil before good can be done. Purged it is, with a knife, a confession and a song. In the Tambourine Temple the people may now feed their spiritual hunger, and in its day nursery, working mothers may now leave their children.

Much of this may seem improbable indeed to many readers, and to some even a perversion of the religious instinct. And seldom does good arise from evil (though Hughes convinces us that it does in this story). But before we judge preacher and penitent in the store-front church, perhaps we should ponder the ways of some others: the popular clergy-man, for instance, with his host of press agents and his arenas and television shows, his books and his big church, his happiness-made-easy nostrums and be-good-and-make-money brand of the gospel. Essie Bell Johnson is fumbling and ignorant, but she feels the song she sings and the gospel she preaches. Langston Hughes has written with knowledge and compassion about a memorable woman and her longing for fulfillment.

D[oris] E. S[aunders]
"Book of the Week"
Jet, 15 (27 November 1958), 58

Langston Hughes not only knows well the mores and folkways of the urban Negro, but he loves his Harlem people, and through his warmth and sympathy he brings life to the characters in his latest novel, *Tambourines to Glory.* With slight, deft strokes the "Boswell of Harlem" has chronicled the saga of Essie and Laura, relief clients and fellow residents of one of Harlem's overcrowded kitchenette buildings, who decide to establish their own church with their own denomination so they "won't be beholding to nobody else."

Laura, the good-looking one, "more well-built than plump," with a weakness for strong, young men is followed as she makes the climb up the status ladder from cheap wine to Scotch, from no clothes to wear to the Baptist Church on Easter Sun-

day morning to a mink coat and many robes of varied hue that she wears while leading the congregation in singing gospel songs and praying at the reconverted theatre which she and Essie re-christen Tambourine Temple.

Essie, fat and placid, whose efforts were directed in trying to pray Laura into a better and less sinful way of life, meanwhile "trying to do some good in Harlem because there is such a need of it."

There is much in this slim volume to remind the reader of Jesse Semple, the hero of his *Simple Takes a Wife,* etc. The language and the people are the same. Simple could easily have been standing on the corner of 126th and Lenox when Essie and Laura launched their curbstone church. If he was, no doubt we will read his opinions of such goings-on in Harlem.

Albert Anderson
"Book Review"
Philadelphia Tribune,
29 November 1958, p. 4

Although the author carefully points out that his latest effort *Tambourines to Glory* is "in no sense an attack on organized religion, or on cults as such," he hits pretty close to home in his exposé of the way in which religion is misused, especially in large city communities.

Laura Reed and Essie Belle Johnson, two typical Hughes characters, hit upon the bright (and unoriginal) idea of starting a church for profit. As to be expected, things get out of hand when money (from their duped followers) starts to pour in.

Aside from interesting reading, there is a lesson here for all of us.

[. . .]

M[argaret] P[arsons]
"Hilarious with Barbs"
Worcester Sunday Telegram, 30 November 1958, p. E7

Langston Hughes is said to be one of the few colored writers whose books are full of humor, although Negroes are by nature gay and carefree.

Beneath Hughes' humor there is a strain of seriousness because of the sin and unethical standards which mark the time in which we live. And this applies to whites as well as blacks.

Two middle-aged colored women are on relief in Harlem. Essie Belle Johnson, who is not so much older than her friend as she looks, is essentially a good soul, but she is heavy with discouragement. When things that happen strike her wrong, she goes into a "pause" which may last for an hour or so.

Laura Reed, a smart-looking woman who hankers for men younger than herself, is a sinner if there ever was one. She lives on relief when she could work, she drinks, she has a succession of lovers, sometimes overlapping each other, she is utterly unscrupulous in her ways of making money, such as by filling empty bottles with Harlem water and selling them for $1 apiece as blessed water from Jordan to the ignorant people who come to her church.

For she has a church. She persuades Essie to start one with her, as it looks like an easy way to get rich (which proves right), and fat, shapeless Essie has a beautiful voice which hypnotizes the sinners. Laura reaches the heights of Cadillac, mink coat, and fine apartment. Essie puts her surplus profits back into the "church."

Now all this is hilariously funny. Despicable though Laura is, we can't help having a sneaking affection for her when she gets caught in planting a murder on her friend. The goodness that is in Essie is released at last to accomplish results.

We have had many a hearty laugh in this satire on a sham revivalist movement and we have been shown more clearly than by many a serious book the corruption, the unfair practices, the despair of Harlem.

Howard Blair
"Among New Novels: East Europe and Harlem"
San Francisco Chronicle, 4 December 1958, p. 3–3RD

An essential item in the intellectual equipment of some poets is the ability (perhaps sometimes the misfortune) to be repelled and fascinated at the same time by certain people and phenomena. Such a poet is Langston Hughes, and in his latest book, *Tambourines to Glory*, a novel, he has cast the eye of a bitter clown upon two Harlem women who decide to start a church of their own.

Essie is a good, honest woman. Too honest, according to Laura, whose motives are simply to make money and live it up. Make money they do, and Laura gets herself a steady boy friend, two Cadillacs, a chauffeur, and a mink coat. It all functions profitably and smoothly until "Big-Eyed Buddy," the boy friend (a saint now), introduces a numbers game into all the other hocus-pocussing, and gets himself a new girl.

Through it all the tambourines trill, the

drums roll, the round, full notes of the trumpets sound, the holy water (as the tap is holy) is sold for one dollar a bottle, and Langston Hughes succeeds in contriving a slight, Rabelaisian exposé of a certain type of evangelistic chicanery.

Leslie Hanscom
"Urban Folk Tale in Curbstone Piety"
New York World-Telegram and Sun, 5 December 1958, p. 27

[. . .]

. . . on a fateful Palm Sunday, the two lady evangelists "get the call." Essie, the honest one—"she's so straight, she's square"—is hesitant at first. But Laura's vision and enterprise sweep the inert Essie along. "I'm telling you," says Laura, "this religious jive is something we can collect on."

Hitherto, the only thing the two Harlem tenement women have had to collect on is city relief. But Laura has just been affronted by the lady investigator who wants to know why, healthy as she is, Laura can't keep a job. "And me," steams Laura, "I done stooped myself over, uncombed my hair, tottered and tried to look as consumptive as I could for her benefit."

Luckily, Laura's histrionic gifts are much better appreciated once she and Essie have invested in a Bible and a tambourine and have planted their feet on "the rock of 126th and Lenox."

"All you loose-limbed sons and daughters of Satan," she harangues the passing sinners, "throwing your legs every which-a-way, dancing, letting your feet lead you every-which-a-where, sinning, playing cards . . . turn, I say, turn!" The lost sheep turn, and the girls take in $11.93 the first night.

The worldly Laura, jubilant at the high wages of a "servant of the Lord," heads for the liquor store and hopes fate will send her some "king-size Hershey bar" of a man. "I'm a she-male minister," she exults, "and there ain't nothing in the Bible says male nor female shall not make love. Fact is, Essie, the very first book is just full of begats, which runs from Genesis through to Tabulations."

"Revelations," corrects Essie, who genuinely wants to help the new converts and is troubled by Laura's no-account attitude.

As Langston Hughes develops this uproarious and touching "urban folk tale," the girls go on to glory in their partnership, graduating from the curbstone to a tabernacle of their own in a condemned theater.

The untamed Laura finds herself a "chocolate boy with coconut eyes" who talks her into selling Jordan Holy Water (from the kitchen tap) at $1 a bottle and teaches her how to multiply her congregation by reading out lucky Biblical texts from the pulpit. (The numbers of chapter and verse—"Job 11-7" "Wow! 7-11"—are taken by the faithful for tips on the numbers game.) Meantime, Essie's lifelong trance turns into a genuine religious vocation.

Toward the end, the story turns serious and the climax of the plot is a violent death, but the pleasantest thing about this very ingratiating little novel is the way a distinguished Negro author revives the wonderful Amos and Andy humor that has been out of fashion ever since it supposedly became bad taste to find comedy in the manners of ethnic groups.

G. W. Adams
"Zest for Life"
Hartford Courant Magazine, 7 December 1958, p. 13

Laura Reed and Essie Belle Johnson live in an ancient Harlem apartment where, "If you didn't see all those names under the different bells, you wouldn't believe so many people lived there." Laura, fond of wine and her men friends, is as carefree and talkative as Jesse B. Semple. She convinces her religiously inclined friend Essie they can start a gospel church. "Raise your fat disgusted self up out of that relief chair and let's we go make our fortune saving souls."

They begin on street corners with enthusiastic response and are soon renting a theatre with their names in lights over the marquee. Laura, light-heartedly cynical, continues her life unchanged and quickly brings tragedy for herself. Essie's earnestness saves herself, the daughter she has brought up from the South, and apparently the "Church" they have founded. There's much here to make you smile or burst out laughing every few pages. As always, Hughes makes you feel you are listening to real people talk.

Arna Bontemps
"How the Money Rolled In!"
New York Herald Tribune Books, 7 December 1958, p. 4

About thirty years ago a completely insolvent quartet of male students from an obscure Negro school in Alabama came to Harlem featuring, among other rollicking but unpolished numbers, a somewhat irreverent spiritual in which these lines occurred:

> Crap shooter in the church—
> Now what we gonna do?
> Take his money, kick him out,
> Let the church roll on.

Whether these particular words were in the song at the time the boys headed North or added along the way is not clear, but they catch the mood of Langston Hughes' new novel as if they had been written for it.

There were these two women, it seems, Laura and Essie, living on relief in one of those fantastically over-crowded and run-down apartment buildings in Harlem, each nourishing a little dream. Essie's was the hope of someday being situated so she could send for the teen-age daughter she had left with her mother in the south. Laura's was a vision of a mink coat by Christmas. While Laura seemed energetic enough, and unscrupulous enough to attain hers, Essie just sat and pined.

She was therefore considerably indebted when Laura shook her up with an outlandish suggestion. What was to keep the two of them from going out on Lenox Avenue and starting a church? They didn't need a building. A street corner would do at first. Essie could sing real good, and Laura—well, she had enough fool-hearted nerve to do the preaching. They could bill themselves as the Reed Sisters. Both could shake tambourines, and after the singing and the carrying on they could pass these around for the collection.

While Essie balked at the little deception this required, she accepted Laura's explanations (like the one about their being "sisters in God"), and in time a wave of real religious feeling came over her. For this she thanked the hypocritical and shameless Laura.

Their street corner church, wholly independent of all denominations, prospered as Laura made regular payoffs to avoid any possible complaints or action against them for obstructing the side-walks. When the cold weather drove them indoors, they were able to acquire a reconstructed brownstone house. Success here led them to a condemned theatre building, which in their hands, assisted by assorted finaglers, became Tambourine Temple. Needless to say, the place jumped. The music was the new gospel kind with a powerful beat.

Laura kept the money rolling in, even when this meant a tie-up with the numbers racket, and she obtained an elegant apartment for the Reed Sisters by means not quite straightforward. She also admitted a darkly handsome young rascal called Big-eyed Buddy to the Temple and to the apartment, with disastrous results.

The story as told by Langston Hughes is as ribald, as effortless, and on the surface as artless as a folk ballad. It ends in violent action, but it is violence of a kind that recalls the lines,

It was not murder in the first degree,
It was not murder in the third;
That woman just got her man
Like a hunter gets a bird.

It is also told with fondness and humor. More and more the writing of Langston Hughes tends to become an affair of the heart with Harlem.

Tambourines to Glory is funny as all get out, but it's no joke.

Dud Chamberlain, Jr. "Citizen Book Reviews" *Columbus Citizen Magazine,* 7 December 1958, p. 14

"If you've got a tambourine,
  Shake it to the glory of God . . ."

That's a song they sang in the Reed Sisters' Tambourine Temple in Harlem.

And before the great gold curtain the Tambourine Chorus sang and rattled their tambourines. And among the thousand worshippers passed other helpers with tambourines, collecting the quarters, dimes and nickels.

The Reed Sisters were really a couple of middle-aged Negro women, Essie Belle Johnson and Laura Reed. Both were out of work when they decided to start their own gospel church, so they started it on a street corner.

Essie Belle was a good hearted woman, who spent a lot of her time sitting and just thinking. She really believed in the gospel she preached. Laura Reed sometimes believed and sometimes didn't. But Laura had other interests even more important to her than gospel: Money, men and liquor, in more or less that order.

Langston Hughes shows the two sides of the gospel churches of the type the Reed Sisters organized. On one side was Essie Belle, a woman who really wanted to do good and who did do good. The rewards Essie Belle got from the community were well earned and for them she paid in good works. On the other side was Laura, who used the collection money to buy a Cadillac and a mink coat, who was a cynic, and who passed out numbers tips in the church.

Hughes has written a folk story laid in the teeming city streets. His prose has the liquid rhythm of poetry and his story line is as clean and sharp as an arrow.

Louis E. Burnham
"A Story of a Store-Front Church in Harlem"
National Guardian, 11 (8 December 1958), 8

If American Negroes were to bestow upon their creative writers such titles as Poet Laureate or People's Writer, Langston Hughes would be a likely candidate for both. His literary production is prodigious. Books of poetry, anthologies of folklore, picture histories, juveniles, plays, short story collections, librettos and novels almost overtake each other as they reel off his hot typewriter. On top of all this, he has managed a busy lecture schedule, occasional poetry recordings and recent night club appearances devoted to the merger of poetry and jazz.

It is not surprising that the quality of such quantity is not uniformly excellent. *Tambourines to Glory* is certainly one of Hughes' lesser efforts. It is a minor treatment of one of the major social outcroppings of the last two decades: the unorthodox, non-denominational, evangelistic gospel church in the urban Negro community.

The plot is a rather thin contrivance spun around wine-drinking, man-loving Laura Wright Reed and trance-bound, long-suffering Essie Belle Johnson. These two kitchenette neighbors in a Harlem tenement parlay Laura's brass, Essie's voice and an $18.50 gilt-edge Bible into a small fortune and a big crime: murder.

As they abandon the relief rolls and raise their church from street corner to apartment to an abandoned movie house, they carry along with them Sister Birdie Lee, as energetic a gospel-drummer as God ever had in any of His kingdoms; Big-Eyed Buddy Lomax, Laura's young lover and the church's link with the downtown numbers' bosses, and pretty Marietta, Essie's teen-age daughter recently up from the South.

When Buddy steals $100 from Laura's purse and taunts her with his infidelities, she kills him with malice aforethought and with Essie's switchblade knife. Her efforts to pin the crime on Essie fail. Laura winds up behind bars, repentant. Essie becomes sole high priestess of the Tambourine Tabernacle and sets out really to save souls, which is what she intended in the first place.

Hughes' social commentary depends largely on his penchant for the sardonic twist, his mastery of the bitter-sweet flavor of Negro life. Here, however, he relies too heavily on language and too little on life to convey his message. And the language is not always apt.

"Let's we ascend," would fall naturally from the lips of Negro inhabitants of Charleston, the Sea Islands, the territory surrounding the Ogeechee River, or Bahamians, Jamaicans and their Florida relations. But it doesn't ring true when spoken by Virginia-born Laura Reed. And such renditions as "from Genesis through to Tabulations," and "Laura's going to have nervous prostitution if she don't watch out," belong where they probably originated—in a minstrel show.

Tambourines to Glory does not live up

to its jacket description as "a fictional exposé of 'gospel racketeers,' preying upon the gullibility of simple people." But Hughes is an able craftsman and the reading is easy. Taken for what it is—a literary divertissement—some readers may use it for a half-evening of light, after-dinner reading.

Luther Nichols
"A Poet's Novel of Harlem"
San Francisco Examiner, section 3, 11 December 1958, p. 3

It's usually a pleasure to read prose stories by poets. They have a magic with words and ideas that more than makes up for their ineptness at plotting. Dylan Thomas, Frederic Prokosch, e. e. cummings and Lawrence Durrell are a few of the poets whose prose I like to read—and to that list you can add Langston Hughes.

Hughes, now in the Bay area on a lecture tour, exhibits some of the traditional virtues and faults of poets writing prose in his latest novel, *Tambourines to Glory.*

To sweep the main fault under the rug first, the book's plot is as old fashionedly melodramatic as the lyrics to "Frankie and Johnny."

On the brighter side, *Tambourines to Glory* offers a rare sense of life through the speech of its Negro characters, sheds some revealing light on the sort of religious fakery that tries to cash in on Christ, and has some things to say about corruption in Harlem that ought not to escape the authorities. And it does all this with a light spirit and robust humor that never let its treatment of contemporary social problems grow dull.

The tale begins when two Harlem women, Essie and Laura, decide their relief money isn't enough and start their own open air church on a Lenox Ave. curbstone.

In no time, nontaxable coins are pouring in as the girls bang tambourines, preach and sing. A small jazz combo puts enough spirit in the spirituals to make the snake in the Garden of Eden wiggle, the congregation jumps and sinners repent in the general uproar.

But the money doesn't roll in fast enough to suit Laura and her mobster boyfriend, Big-Eyed Buddy, who has connections with "The Man," a white Harlem gang overlord. Buddy introduces such refinements as holy water from the Hudson River, selling it at $1 a bottle, and "Lucky Texts," that convert the sermons into a kind of numbers racket.

Laura buys a mink coat and Cadillac and supports her man in style. But Essie, a fundamentally good woman, begins to have grave moral doubts. In time she and Laura split, and Author Hughes leads the reader into a murder for jealousy and a rather odd denouement in which it is seen that sin doesn't pay—at least not as well as commercial piety.

Hughes does little moralizing. He accepts human beings as they are, and as they are in *Tambourines to Glory* their activities make for entertaining and significant reading. They might make for an even more entertaining and significant stage musical.

Theodore M. O'Leary "Sympathy for Ways of Races" Kansas City Star, 27 December 1958, p. 7

[J.] Saunders Redding "Book Review: Work of a 'Pro'" Afro-American Magazine, 27 December 1958, p. 2

The American Negro, once a stock and comic figure in our fiction, is now being shown to us in varying aspects by numerous novelists who are breaking the old stereotypes and viewing him as an individual. Certainly the Negroes in these two novels have almost nothing in common except the superficiality of color.

[. . .]

Langston Hughes calls his story of fakery, faith and jealous violence "an urban folk tale." Its setting is Harlem, its leading characters two women who start their own gospel church on a street corner. Laura Reed sees the church as a financial racket. Essie Johnson starts with a woozy desire to help her fellow men and women which turns into a solid conviction.

Like most of the Hughes novels and stories *Tambourines to Glory* is characterized by its simple but singing prose, its humor, its tolerance of human weakness. But underneath it all is an awareness of the tragic plight of his own people. Describing a service in the old theater which the two women turn into a church to accommodate their growing congregation, Hughes tells of the two grand pianos, the guitar, the rolling drums, the golden notes of the trumpet, the girls in golden slippers and mauve robes singing a song about the glory of touching God's garments. "For many there," writes Hughes, "living in the tenements of Harlem, to believe in such wonder was worth every penny the tambourines collected."

Years ago, this reviewer read a magazine article entitled "Let Us Prey."

It was, justifiably, a rather severe castigation of the charlatans who set up storefront churches in Harlem and, hiding crass venality behind a splendid show of Christian virtue, bilked the ignorant, beguiled the innocent, and preyed upon the deep religious feelings of the lost lonely and oppressed. The article examined a social phenomenon which was then—in the 1920's—of relatively recent origin.

The store-front churches, the wildly fundamentalist splinter-baptist groups, and the audacious, cynical and sometimes charming rascals who ran them were something new.

This special kind of corruption of religion seemed a likely theme for a novel, and now Langston Hughes, the "old pro," has put it to this use in *Tambourines to Glory*.

Hughes calls his story an "urban folk tale," and if one takes him at his word, there is no quarrel with what he has done.

The simplicity of characterization, the naive overlooking of psychological motivation, the clean, direct narrative line, and the use of the tangy local jargon are all in the folk tradition, and Langston Hughes is more sensitive to that tradition and follows it more closely perhaps than any present-day American writer.

Laura and Essie, the protagonists of *Tambourines to Glory,* are not analyzed; they are presented.

Laura's sins and Essie's sudden transformation from a lazy bag of fat, given to unconscionably long "pauses," into a woman of dynamic energy and purpose are not explained; they are told.

And, considering the folk tradition, this is as it should be.

Yet there is something a little pat, and a little too self-conscious and contrived about *Tambourines to Glory*.

But a tale it is—and a highly moral one, principally about the sins of Laura Reed and the virtues of Essie Johnson.

When these two decide to start a church, Laura's only thought is to make money, but Essie's is to do good.

Each accomplishes her aim, and in spite of the differences in temperament, they get along fine until a snake called Big-Eyed Buddy walks into their Garden of Eden.

He divides the women without destroying the church, for the church is a lucrative "racket."

He pumps up Laura's ambition and he feeds Laura's lust, but it costs her the price of his upkeep, many dollars spending change a week, and a red convertible for his very own.

Since Laura is old enough to be his mamma, Buddy is soon sporting a younger woman in his convertible.

The climax comes when Laura, unable to take it any more, kills her lover and tries to fix the crime on Essie.

But sin never has managed a final victory over virtue.

The truth is revealed in the end, and, with Essie returning in triumph to her church, the book closes with offending the sense of reality it has created.

Nevertheless one feels cheated. And I think this is because the book gives the impression of playing around with materials worthy of serious treatment.

Tambourines to Glory is authentic Langston Hughes, but it is not Hughes at his best.

Lois de Banzie
"Hughes' Tale of Glory! Glory!"
News [Mexico D.F., Mexico], 28 December 1958, pp. 8A, 11A

"Get holy, sanctify yourself," urges man-loving Laura Reed to her friend and neighbor. "Say, Essie, why don't you and me start a church like Mother Bradley's? We ain't doin' nothing else useful and it would beat Home Relief."

And so another gospel church is started in Harlem, with results far beyond Laura's greedy dreams. For Essie Belle Johnson, who has done nothing but "set" for years, suddenly genuinely "finds God," and just her calm, placid presence on the street corner, and her lovely persuasive singing voice make the congregation—and the collection—grow miraculously.

Laura and Essie's initial outlay of $19.35 is soon parlayed into enough to rent the first floor of an old brownstone and convert it into a chapel, complete with biblical pictures painted on the front windows to make them look like stained glass.

Sister Essie piously saves her cut of the collection to bring her sixteen-year-old daughter Marietta up from the South, while Sister Laura, still considering the saving of souls as a racket, buys herself a Cadillac, and "a tower-tall, a big-featured, a handsome lighthouse-grinning chocolate boy of a man" several years younger than herself named Buddy. The profit on the sale of bottles of Holy Water, one of Buddy's ideas, is soon large enough to move the church into an old theater, with, in great big lights on the marquee out front, the legend: The Reed Sisters' Tambourine

Temple. There, Buddy and Sister Laura set about introducing the numbers game at the nightly services, by announcing "lucky texts," and add to their already considerable fortune.

Sister Essie, good soul that she really is, is very unhappy about Sister Laura's behavior and cynical attitude towards religion, and she and Marietta move to Mount Vernon, leaving Laura to struggle with Big-Eyed Buddy, who is beginning to cast eyes at younger women. Eventually there is violence and greed, and lying, and it seems as if the peace of Tambourine Temple is threatened, until Sister Essie and another believer, Birdie Lee, manage to save it from the infidels. They are last seen planning to build a recreation hall, playground, and children's creche next door, to loud and happy shouts of "Halleloo!" and "Praise His Name!" and "Amen!" from the enthusiastic congregation.

Tambourines to Glory is by no means an anti-religious or blasphemous book. Author Langston Hughes has written a fascinating commentary on the phenomenon of the large number of colorful, independent, unorthodox churches which have sprung up all over Harlem in the last decade. Written with humor, and in a suitably colorful style, there is food for thought in the undoubted success of the oft-times unscrupulous founders of these churches. A people who love color and music and rhythm, and have a wonderfully personal relationship with God, as the Negro people do, evidently find in these slightly bizarre religious sects something they miss in their repressed everyday lives: perhaps a hope for the future, even though it will be encountered only "on the other side."

"Book Notes"
Lincoln University Bulletin, 60 (Winter 1958–9), 20–1

Tambourines to Glory is the story of two attractive Harlem tenement women, Laura Reed and Essie Belle Johnson, who start their own gospel church on a street corner. Essie honestly desires to help people, but Laura is only interested in the money she can get to take care of her boy friend. The church prospers beyond all expectations and moves from the street corner to a reconstructed brownstone house and finally to a condemned theatre. The Reed sisters are so successful that they move into a swank apartment to which Essie brings her daughter from the South and Laura her new boy friend, Big-Eyed Buddy, handsome front man for a numbers ring. When Buddy shows his true colors to Laura, she stabs him to death and blames the murder on Essie. It would be criminal to reveal the ending of Hughes' authentic novel of Negro life in Harlem.

The work is in no sense an attack on organized religion, or on cults as such, but it is a fictional exposé of certain ways in which religion is misused in many communities by various types of unscrupulous leaders who might be called "gospel racketeers," preying upon the gullibility of simple people. But after you have read the book you can decide the merits of this statement which serves as a kind of foreword: "All the characters and situations depicted in this novel are entirely imaginary. All names used as participants in this story are fictitious, and any relation to persons living or dead is purely coincidental."

John W. Parker
"Another Revealing Facet of the Harlem Scene"
Phylon, 20 (First Quarter 1959), 100–101

Since the publication of *The Weary Blues,* poetic account of the enchantment, romance, and tragedy that was Harlem's back in the Twenties, Langston Hughes has maintained a healthy nostalgia for the Harlem scene, not only because it marks the point of his departure as a man of letters, but likewise because it remains a city within a city, a widely-discussed experiment in large-scale living in the urban ghetto. The impact of the Black Metropolis both as a place and a symbol is illuminated by such Hughes publications as *Shakespeare in Harlem* (1942), *Montage of a Dream Deferred* (1951), *Simple Takes a Wife* (1953), *The Sweet Flypaper of Life* (1955), and now *Tambourines to Glory.* A casual glance at the dates of these volumes attests to the fact that by and large each follows the other in rapid succession.

Tambourines to Glory is an urban folk tale which results from the skillful fusion of some thirty-six smaller segments into a whole more meaningful by far than any of the parts. Such organization as the book displays stems from its consistency in mood and atmosphere and from the unity of action exhibited by the characters. Artistically handled, too, is the selection and arrangement of the details in such a way as to assure suspense and movement. Starting as it does *in medias res, Tambourines to Glory* has a middle, but scarcely a beginning or an end.

The volume turns mostly upon the sham and pretense of two attractive Harlem tenement women who, with their names on the relief rolls and time on their hands, set about to establish an independent, unorthodox church, the predominance of their own worldly interests notwithstanding. Only Essie's half-hidden seriousness of purpose and the power that sometimes stems from the singing of powerful hymns lighted up an otherwise drab, second-floor kitchenette in which the idea of a new church was crystallized.

These gospel racketeers, wisely enough, gauged their public utterances to the gullibility of unsuspecting people, and suppressed in their own hearts the knowledge that whiskey, loose women, the numbers game, and the Gospel of Christ make strange bedfellows. Just the same, the church prospered and before long the Reed Sisters (as they elected to designate themselves) moved the church from the corner block to a converted theater building with a thousand seats and their names in lights on the marquee.

The total situation, however, leaves much to be desired. The two-dollar downpayment on the Bible for the new church resulted from Laura's having hit the numbers. In the absence of proper credentials, Laura and Company found it necessary to produce cash periodically to keep back the law-enforcement officers. And with too many men on her hands and whiskey to buy, Laura frequently put in late appearances at the church services. Before long, however, tragedy settled down upon the enterprise. Laura finally stabbed her boy friend, Big-Eyed Buddy, landed in prison, and left it to Essie and Birdie Lee to purify the church for the first time in its brief history.

Tambourines to Glory is in no sense a satire upon organized religion, or even upon cults as such, but rather a close-up exposé of the manner in which what sometimes passes as religion turns out to be nothing more than a commercial venture in the hands of unscrupulous racketeers.

Touched upon in this new novel are several themes treated elsewhere in Hughes' published writings. One observes, for instance, that the characters fall for the most part in the category of the nothings, not the dicties; that the author shuns sweetness and light and digs into the difficulties that aggravate men here and now; that an underlying Darwinian emphasis takes its toll upon conventional morality; and that fallen women, wandering irregularly from bar to bar, abound. Mr. Hughes cites facts, but does not draw conclusions; himself a Harlemite, he continues to laugh with the people, not at them.

All in all, *Tambourines to Glory* underscores a wide knowledge of the New York ghetto (and by implication others around the world) in a period of increasing racial awareness.

J[ames] W. I[vy]
"Book Reviews"
Crisis, 66 (January 1959), 59

Tambourines to Glory is the quite touching and funny story of Laura Reed and Essie Belle Johnson, two Harlem women who start their own gospel church on a corner of Lenox Avenue. Both women are on relief and both women have dreams: in Laura's case it is a mink coat; in Essie's, to bring her young daughter up from the South. Billing themselves as the Reed Sisters, they invest in a gilt-edge Bible, a tambourine, and a folding camp stool. "Including the Bible, we have invested $2.85 in this holy deal," said Laura. Singing and shaking their tambourine, the two women collected enough money to take over a reconstructed brownstone house,

and finally a condemned theatre which became the Tambourine Temple. The Reed Sisters are so successful they get an elegant apartment and Laura a "dingdong daddy," Big-Eyed Buddy, who brings tragedy to the Temple.

The life Mr. Hughes describes is completely authentic. Much of the humor and the pathos of the book comes from Mr. Hughes's mastery of the Harlem idiom.

Milton S. Byam
"New Books Appraised"
Library Journal, 84 (1 January 1959), 119

This suggestion of a novel by Langston Hughes will be read chiefly by those attracted by the author's fame. It is a loosely framed narrative that tells a story of two ne'er-do-well Negro women who become famous and rich ministers of the gospel with little equipment other than tambourines. The book leans too heavily on the Negro malapropism for its humor, but the true ring of language is obvious throughout. Unfortunately, the characters are stereotypes and the labored plot creaks and groans but goes nowhere. As a series of sketches this comes closer to the mark but it is still unworthy of the man who gave us "Simple." A limp and pallid recommendation for those who must have Hughes because of subject or author.

Thomas A. Webster
"About Books"
Kansas City Call, 2 January 1959, p. 21

Langston Hughes, one of America's distinguished writers, has made another significant contribution in a folk tale of big city life. Hughes came out of the "Negro Renaissance" period which roughly is from 1912 to the late twenties.

These writers of the "New Negro" were realists, attempting to throw off some of the handicaps of their predecessors' era, which was marked by the apology and self-pity of the Paul L. Dunbar school and Charles W. Chesnutt's attempt to overcome the conventional stereotyping of Thomas Nelson Page and Thomas Dixon, who wrote "The Klansman."

Hughes expressed the independence of this group at that time when he said, "We younger Negro artists who create, now intend to express our individual, dark-skinned selves without fear or shame. If white people are pleased we are glad. If they are not it doesn't matter. If colored people are pleased we are glad. If they are not their displeasure doesn't matter either. We build our temples for tomorrow, strong as we know how, and we stand on the top of the mountain, free within ourselves."

With this spirit of independence, realism, consummate skill and unmatched wit, Hughes gives us an urban folk tale about independent, unorthodox churches which have sprung up all over Harlem in the last decade or so.

Tambourines for [sic] *Glory,* first written as a two-act music drama, was never produced as such. Now, written as a novel, Hughes terms it "a fictional exposé of certain ways by which religion is used in large cities by unscrupulous 'gospel racketeers' preying upon the gullibility of simple people." In no sense does the author imply or intend the book as an attack on organized religion or cults as such.

Historically, the Negro church's role in "serving the Lord (and man)" is as old as the Negro's presence in America. During slavery the Negro church often was a "station" in the "underground railroad" and the "flight to freedom" for Negro fugitives. Slave masters allowed unrestricted attendance at religious meetings with the belief that there was an advantage to having "ole Mose" work off his frustration in hymn singing and shoutin'.

Hughes's setting, far removed from the plantation, is that of deep Harlem, where on almost any block packed with humans, in run-down areas, there is an abundance of "storefront" churches.

They are noted by their striking variety and the colorful extravagance of names— "I Will Arise Baptist Church," "Tambourines for Glory Temple," etc. Many are located in churches which still bear the marks of the previous ownership—the six pointed star of David, Hebrew, Swedish, or Scientist inscriptions or names chiseled on old cornerstones or over doorpieces which do not tally with those on new bulletin boards.

"Tambourines for Glory Temple" was started as a gospel church on a street corner by two jobless women with time on their hands and with disparate purposes. Laura Reed, wine-sipper, numbers player and cradlerocker, is greedy for money, while Essie Johnson is honestly desirous of saving souls and helping folks.

These two are subsequently joined by Essie's hymn-singing daughter who is "sweet" on the young boy who plays a "nice gospel guitar" in the Temple's band. He is J.C. (the initials do not stand for a name). The others are Birdie Lee, the trap drummer, and Deacon Crow for Day, who comes to Christ after a long spell of sin and lush living.

Laura Reed, the principal character, weak for a young slick Harlem "pimp" known as "Big-Eyed Buddy," is sucked into political and racketeering connections by her young lover. He becomes promoter par excellence for the Temple and introduces the idea of selling "holy water" not from the River Jordan but from the Harlem river via the kitchen tap. He also persuades Laura to give out lucky texts and hymns which sell for $1 apiece and may mean a "hit" on the numbers' bank.

With Big-Eyed Buddy's big ideas and Fuller brush salesmanship, Laura's greed for money to spend on Buddy and Essie's sincere soul-saving obsession, the street-corner gospel church grows beyond its expectations and moves into a converted theater of 1000 seats with "The Reed Sisters' Tambourine Temple" emblazoned in lights on the marquee.

Laura wraps Buddy up in fine-living sport cars, Brooks Brothers clothes, ready cash, steaks and premium liquors, and his head eventually turns to young, tender "chicks," and ends in his untimely, sudden and violent meeting with his Maker. Laura stabs him in the back right in the cloak-room of the Temple and with Sister Essie's switchblade which she carries for protection against Harlem muggers and pocket-book snatchers.

The tale does end in the triumph of the Lord since Essie and Bird inherit Laura's mantle and take over the affairs of the Temple after Laura is jailed for Buddy's murder.

Hughes' familiarity with Negro religious folk sermons and his interpretations of the uninhibited speech and antics of the typical folk preacher are unsurpassed genre pictures of a typical Negro church life.

Read it and then take a look at *Simple* *Takes a Stand* or *The Langston Hughes Reader* as gifts for Christmas.

M.M.
"Hallelujah, This Is Fun"
New York Post, 11 January 1959, p. M11

Langston Hughes' new novel is a bitter-sweet tale of two women who set up a gospel church in Harlem. Sister Laura is what is known as a Bad Girl; Sister Essie has the tonnage and stupidity of a Good Woman.

"I wish I had me some more wine," says Sister Laura, who drinks it by the gallon.

"The wine of God is all we need," replies Essie, who's "so straight she's square."

Laura has vitality, Essie piety; between the two they make a go of their mission. At first they operate on a street corner. Thirty-five cents for a camp stool, 50c for a tambourine, $2 Laura won on a number for the down payment on a big Bible—and they're in business.

When a cop asks for their license, Laura gives him $10: "This is my license." The mission flourishes; every night there's a big collection, until Essie begins to feel guilty. "He driv the money-changers out of the temple," she reminds Laura.

"Money-changers," Laura answers. "Us is different. We are money getters."

Mr. Hughes calls this novel a folk tale and says it's based on fact—"unscrupulous leaders who might be called gospel racketeers preying upon the gullibility of simple people—colorful, independent, unorthodox churches which have sprung up all over Harlem in the last decade."

Well, unscrupulous Laura certainly is,

but it all sounds like more fun than television. As the collections get bigger, there's a chorus and a band and the girls move inside and commission a mural.

Here Laura has very definite ideas. "God must be black, or at least dark brown. As to the lambs, you know what color my Lenox Ave. lambs are. If you put the Devil in, make him white.

"Adam is to look just like Joe Louis. Champeen! I love that man!" says Laura, and she reminds stuffy old Essie of all the begats in the Book of Genesis.

This is a wonderfully funny yet touching book, a blend of comedy and fantasy in Langston Hughes' poetic style. It would make a marvellous musical.

And along with all the fun is Hughes' pity for the drab, hard-working lives which find their pleasure in this tawdry show.

people, or at least to do something that seems important. Laura wants money. They team up, beginning on a street corner, and playing up to the deeply religious feelings of their neighbors, build a new church. "What denomination we gonna be?" asks Essie. "Start our own denomination," replies Laura, "then we won't be beholden to nobody else." And so they do! The result is the extraordinary story of a phenomenon of our time which almost certainly is a passing phase. Langston Hughes does not spare these people. He shows them as they are, some simple and sincere, others wicked and conniving. The need of the human heart for religion is what makes them possible. This book should be a challenge to all churches to do their jobs better and reach the deepest needs of their people.

D[onald] H[arrington]
"Thumbnail Book
Review"
Community News, 13
(8 February 1959), 3

One cannot walk or drive in Harlem without noticing that almost every block along the main avenues contains one or more churches. There are the big, corner churches, the legitimate ones, and then there are the storefronts and the made-over houses with gaudy pictures in the windows—hundreds and hundreds of them. In this short novel, Langston Hughes tells a typical story of the rise of a storefront church. Laura and Essie Belle have time on their hands, and no money, so they decide to start a church. Essie Belle wants to help

"Book Review"
Press Facts [Detroit],
14 February 1959, p. 2

Langston Hughes takes his readers to church in his beloved Harlem in this pleasant novel and without attempting to make an exposé of the religious racketeers which have infested our independent churches he does unveil some of the sins of our cultists.

Following the philosophy of his "Simple" that it does take all kinds of people, Hughes very skillfully blends many different types of personalities into his story of the "Tambourine Sisters" who organized a church which caught on like wildfire in Harlem.

Laura Wright Reed, the well shaped, hard-drinking, glib-tongued, man-lover and the good, but lazy Essie Belle Johnson decide to start a church. Laura's idea was that it was a good way to turn a fast buck; Essie Belle thought it was a good way to serve God. Together they became the Reed sisters, and from a corner on Harlem's Lenox Avenue they started a church that became one of the biggest independent churches in the city, "The Tambourine Temple."

It was Laura who succumbed to the serpent in Eden, Bright-Eyed Buddy, front man for the numbers racket, but it took Essie Belle and her drum beating aide, old Birdie, to withstand the assaults of Satan and keep the temple firmly on the rock.

Langston Hughes, the poet, is still superior to Hughes the novelist, but his deep feelings for his simple people come through in this excellent bit of story telling. Hughes does advise against the many innocents who are being victimized by the evil influences that have invaded the Independent church, but he also illustrates that great good can come out of the void served by these churches.

William H. Robinson, Jr.
"Budget Religion"
Greensboro Daily News,
22 February 1959, p. D3

If all God's Chilluns don't have shoes, it won't be the fault of Laura Reed and Essie Belle Johnson, two of Langston Hughes' most audacious and hilarious "folks" who live "up North in Harlem" and who animate this, one of the season's better folk tales. Among the gallery of simple people whom Hughes has drawn—with wearing regularity—surely these two will be among those longest remembered. Who can forget two tenement women, both living on Home Relief—Laura admittedly in love with men and the bottle; Essie in-

tending to do good—who decide to overcome ennui and utilize their human assets, Laura's shapely body and Essie's wonderful voice, to capitalize on the gullibility of fellow humans? These two intrepid women decide to open a church of their "own denomination, then we won't be beholding to nobody else." Total investment? $19.35: one folding camp stool: 35c; one tambourine: 50c; one Holy Bible (from Bernstein's, Two Dollars Down, Two Dollars a Month): $18.50. Economical religion.

Because many people are incurably foolish all over the world and not only in Harlem, Laura and Essie succeed with fantastic ease, moving from 126th Street and Lenox Avenue, original site of their church, into an empty, three-room apartment, on up to occupancy of an entire motion picture theater, now converted into a temple, REED SISTERS TAMBOURINE CHURCH. By design, Laura thrives in her satisfactions, which include a Cadillac for her and her acquired lover, Big-Eyed Buddy, whose connections with "up-town folks" help her in no little measure. Essie, on the other hand, continues to worry about the wrong they have done, but to look forward to the day when her daughter, down in Richmond, may have a proper New York home to visit. Converts are made, money pours in, a little old lady, Birdie Lee (who plays a wicked set of trap drums and a money-getting tambourine) joins them, things look bright, so bright that hapless Laura is blinded. Gladly cooperating with Big-Eyed Buddy's scheme to intersperse a "lucky number" or two in between other shouted prayers, she gains more than the expected monetary rewards. Thriving also, Buddy proves his genius by sporting other young girls in the Cadillac paid for by Laura. Still Laura is tolerant, but when she discovers him to be a thief, stealing a hundred dollar bill from her pocketbook; and when she cajoles him into a frank and arrogant opinion of her, her phoney church, her phoney Holy Water—this becomes the celebrated straw that broke the camel's back. From this point on, the novel assumes dimensions of a full scale tragedy, but these dimensions are never developed; they serve only to end the book.

Hughes' narrative skills have not improved, but then the fabliau tolerates many narrative violations. However, other users of this genre—Chaucer, Cervantes, Rabelais—show a more powerful command of form, in which Mr. Hughes seems lacking. To interrupt a story line with expository asides and flashbacks might be acceptable in an outline or preliminary version of a novel, but hardly in the publishable version. Too, Hughes waxes poetic in the most unexpected places throughout the book. Viewed as a picaresque, *Tambourines* succeeds and, rounding out its purport of being "in no sense an attack on organized religion, but a fictional exposé of certain ways in which religion is misused in large city communities today by various types of unscrupulous leaders . . . 'gospel racketeers,'" the book is a rollicking indictment of people both simple and sophisticated. For those who wonder about this being the best of all possible worlds, *Tambourines* might provoke at least another view: The view that that world laughs best that laughs at itself.

Richard A. Long
"Book Reviews"
CLAJ, 2 (March 1959), 192–3

Langston Hughes has literally become writer-in-residence to Harlem. In *Tambou-*
rines to Glory he mines further his motherlode and produces a novel which for all its simplicity of plot and character possesses interest and charm. Essentially it is a fable. Selecting the lower-class urban Negro milieu usually exploited only for serious and tragic treatment by novelists, Hughes weaves a sepia Horatio Alger saga.

In acknowledgment of certain features of Negro life, the protagonists—there are two—are women, Essie Belle Johnson and Laura Wright Reed, and their field of endeavor, religion. Residents of the same tenement house, Essie and Laura eke out an existence on relief. Laura is devoted to men and wine; fat, easy-going Essie merely sits and thinks about her teen-age daughter, Marietta, whom she cannot afford to have in New York with her. From a joking suggestion of Laura's that they save souls to improve their finances, they begin holding street corner revivals, then set up church in a brownstone first floor, and move finally to a deserted movie house which they christen Tambourine Temple.

Essie takes her new mission seriously and is overjoyed to have the money to bring her daughter to live with her, first in an apartment she shares with Laura, then in a porch-front house in Mount Vernon. Laura forsakes sherry for Scotch, walking for a chauffeured Cadillac, and acquires in the process a mink coat and an "idea" man, Buddy Lomax, a "king-size Hershey bar." Buddy's insolent admission of cupidity and infidelity leads Laura to kill him and, after an unsuccessful attempt to place the guilt on Essie, to jail. Essie, alone at Tambourine Temple, sets up a program of good works. Virtue has triumphed.

A certain folkloric element is created in the novel by the presence of such characters as Sister Birdie Lee and Deacon Crow-For-Day, redeemed sinners, who enliven several pages with their "testimony." Hughes' mastery of the Negro speech idiom, already well-illustrated in the Jesse

Semple epos, is always present, both in the dialogue (the novel is virtually a series of conversations) and in the panoramic passages. This mastery must unfortunately be its own reward, for much of it will certainly be lost to non-Negro readers. For example, the person who had never heard "Do, Jesus" would hardly know what to make of it.

All in all, we may say of *Tambourines to Glory* that the achievement is slight, but the craftsmanship assured. The result is charming.

Order was eventually restored to the "garden" from chaos, which resulted from greed and murder. Sisters Essie and Birdie Lee, a trap drummer, were instrumental in the restoration of serenity.

A panoramic view of a segment of Harlem's population is impellingly told by "the poet laureate of the Negro people." The story is compact and lucid. The reader will want only to stop after the final chapter, of a violation of the Third Commandment, has been gleaned.

[. . .]

Hortense D. Lloyd
Negro Educational Review, 10 (April 1959), 100–101

C. Q. Mattingly
"Recommended Books"
Marriage, 41 (May 1959), 63

[. . .]

With the expression of these ideas, the inception of another of the many cults which have spawned throughout Harlem was begun in the store-front church exposé, *Tambourines to Glory,* by Langston Hughes. With Laura Reed, preaching from the Bible, purchased from money customarily spent for wine, and Essie Johnson, singing to the beat of a tambourine, the congregation and collections grew to sufficient size to warrant the housing of the church for the first time. Outgrowing their store front, the congregation moved to a vacant moving-picture theatre.

Contributing factors to the prosperity of the church were the exploitation of a naive and deeply engrained religious people by Laura and the serpent, Buddy, a handsome confederate to a policy ring, who conceived the idea of selling "holy water" (tap) at a dollar a bottle and the giving of "lucky texts" (numbers), to the audience.

Two Harlem neighbors decide to start their own church: Laura because she needs money to live high; Essie Belle because she needs an anchor. The idea goes over and becomes a comfortable racket, giving the author a chance to broadside gospel church racketeers. This is adult reading, partly satire, partly just good fun. You will like Essie Belle, whose religion is a dear and necessary counterpart to her former shiftless existence.

Mimi Clar
"Reviews: Books: Langston Hughes' *Tambourines to Glory*"
Jazz Review, 2 (June 1959), 32, 36

"Girl," says Laura Reed to Essie Belle Johnson, "with your voice, raise your fat disgusted self up out of that relief chair and let's go make our fortune saving souls." And so, one June night Essie and Laura begin to shake their tambourine and save souls on the corner of 126th and Lenox Avenue in Harlem. With the help of two converted sinners—Birdie Lee, a little old lady drummer who follows the church into its first home in an old apartment building, and Chicken Crow-For-Day (a *real sinner*) who becomes an upright deacon even though he lies about his age on the night of his conversion—Essie and Laura see their Tambourine Temple grow until it moves into a rundown theater with a thousand seats, an upstairs, and a marquee.

Big-Eyed Buddy Lomax, Harlem flunky for a white leader of the numbers game, has his eye on the church (and on Laura, too) and soon moves in to take advantage of a good thing by selling bottles of Holy Water from the Jordan at a dollar a bottle ("Just turn on the tap, that's all") and by having Laura give out numbers from the pulpit in "Lucky Texts."

Of course, the plot is but one more variation on the good versus evil theme. Essie, whose rock is Jesus and whose meaningless life has suddenly taken on purpose thanks to her church work and to her daughter's coming from the South to live with her again ("I thrills when I touches the Bible!"), stands for the "good"; Laura, whose rocks are men, liquor, and numbers and who can indulge in her vices thanks to the church funds ("I thrills when I touch that man!"), is the "bad." Good naturally triumphs as Essie, Birdie, and Crow-For-Day make plans to add a day nursery, clubhouse, and playground to their facilities, and as Essie's innocent daughter, Marietta, will marry young C.J. from the church without any interference from Buddy or Laura, who eventually outsmart themselves.

Although Hughes stresses that all characters are imaginary and that the book "is in no sense an attack on organized religion, or on cults as such, but is a fictional exposé of certain ways in which religion is misused in large city communities today by various types of unscrupulous leaders who might be called 'gospel racketeers,' preying upon the gullibility of simple people," I hope that no one will be misled into thinking of *Tambourines to Glory* as a portrait of *the* Negro, either as represented by the lust and weaknesses of pleasure-seeking Laura and Buddy or by the artlessness of Essie or the impressionability and pliability of some of the congregation. The characters have been necessarily stereotyped or caricatured to limn more realistically a small segment of the community at large.

To those who would misconstrue or condemn the goings-on as anything beyond the circumstances and plight of a people victimized by an environment, I would recommend a more careful reading of the book's "One Lost Lamb" chapter, which unobtrusively gets in a little preaching of its own.

Primarily, *Tambourines* illustrates the power and function of the church . . . as an outlet for social contacts and convivial life; the church as a source of entertainment ("They like color, glitter, something to look at along with these fine rhythms we're putting down."); the church as a front for unscrupulous persons out for personal gain; and the church as an avenue of emotional escape for those whose lives are otherwise empty and frustrated. In short, the Negro church is a unique, picturesque institution where both festive drama and spiritual communion stand side by side.

Hughes tells his tale in a vivid folk idiom. The language of his characters swings with jive talk (Is your wig gone? Dig? put down, neat-all-reet, cool, solid), proverbial lore (Wine is a mocker and strong drink is a tempter; You should be as good on Monday as you are on Sunday; Blessed is he that giveth, and blessed is he that receiveth; to burn a candle at both ends), proverbial comparisons (purple as Devil's ink, lower than a snake's belly, innocent as a lamb, naked as a kangaroo, grinning like a chesscat, temper like a tiger, float away like soap bubbles and bust, to look like a grand piano; full in front, streamlined rear), alliterations (green as gall), beliefs and superstitions ("I was borned to bad luck," says Essie . . .), poetic adjectives (tower-tall, lighthouse grin), slang terms (do-re-mi, simoleons, conk, Abe Lincolns, live high on the hog, grease your palm, let your hair down), racial terminology (brownskin, ofay, rounder, songster, musicianer), a slavery-time joke based on a folk tale ("Thank God for this ham, even if the Devil did bring it!"), and references to the heroes of the folk—those who have "made it," who have risen above their surroundings and "the problem" to achieve national recognition (Cozy Cole, Sarah Vaughan, Joe Louis, Milt Jackson, Dorothy Dandridge, Mahalia Jackson, Ward Sisters, Teddy Wilson, Eartha Kitt, Lena Horne).

Tambourines to Glory is fast, light, entertaining reading and could be adapted to other media besides literature; it lends itself to TV, radio and theater presentation as well. I kept visualizing it as a play even before I noticed on the lp accompanying the book that the author has dramatized it too.

The *Tambourines* record album (Folkways FG 3538), with songs written by Langston Hughes and Jobe Huntley and sung by the Porter Singers with Ernest Cook at Second Canaan Baptist Church in Harlem, sounds like the unrehearsed and spontaneous waves of music and rhythm that nonprofessionals perform in churches all over the country. With the garbled words, the spur-of-the-moment "Hallelujah's" and "Amen's," the tambourine player and other "musicianers" create an authentic live-service atmosphere that matches that of the Tambourine Temple in the book. It does not represent the best in Negro church music, though, and I'd recommend tuning in radio broadcasts from the churches or the gospel disc jockeys over a period of time in order to grasp more fully the various musical qualities of gospel music. Song texts are those appearing in the pages of the book.

LeRoi Jones
"Reviews: Books: Langston Hughes' *Tambourines to Glory*" *Jazz Review,* 2 (June 1959), 33–4

I suppose, by now, Langston Hughes's name is synonymous with "Negro Literature." For many, he is the only Negro in the world of books. This, of course, is unfortunate. But in quite another sense this is as it should be. Hughes is probably the last "major" Negro writer who will be allowed to write what could be called a "Negro Literature" (as differentiated from literature in general): to impose upon himself such staggering limitations.

Now, don't for a moment take this to be a plea for "assimilationist" literature (i.e. novels, etc. written by Negroes that assiduously avoid any portrayal of Negro life in much the same way that the "Black Bourgeoisie" avoid any attempt to connect them, even vicariously, with blues, jazz, "greens" or anything else even remotely "Negroid"). I am merely saying that the Negro artist, and especially the Negro writer, A.E. (After Ellison), has come too far and has experienced so much that cannot be, even vaguely, attributed to the "folk tradition." And that to confine all of his thinking, hence all his writing to that tradition (with no thought as to where that tradition has got to; what significance that tradition has, say, in relation to the macrocosm of American life in general, or for that matter, man's life on earth) is to deny that there is any body of experience outside of that tradition. A kind of ethnic solipsism. Poet Robert Creeley says (in quite another context—but with the same general implications), "A tradition becomes inept when it blocks the necessary conclusion: it says *we* have felt nothing; it implies others have felt more." This does not mean that the Negro writer, for instance, ought to stop using Negro Life In America as a theme; but certainly that theme ought only to be a *means*. For the Negro writer to confuse that means with the end (let us arbitrarily say that end is "art") is stultifying and dangerous. For these reasons, Hughes, to my mind, is a folklorist. He abdicated from the world of literature just after his second book of verse (*Fine Clothes to the Jew:* 1927); since then, he has sort of crept backwards and away from significant literature, until finally (with this book) he has gotten to a kind of meaningless ethnic name-dropping.

I am pretty well acquainted with the Negro in literature. I know of Hughes's early writing: his first novel (*Not Without Laughter*, 1930), his early poetry (some of it very beautiful, a rough mixture of spoken blues, Masters, and Imagists). I know of his affiliation with the "Harlem School" (Claude McKay, Jean Toomer, Countee Cullen, and a few others) and the importance and merit of the "School" (Toomer's novel *Cane* is among the three greatest novels ever written by a Negro in America. The others: Richard Wright's *Native Son,* Ralph Ellison's *Invisible Man*). I also know of the "School's" (or at least Hughes's) wonderful credo, "To express our individual dark-skinned selves without fear or shame. If the white people are pleased we are glad. If they are not, it doesn't matter. . . . If colored people are pleased, we are glad. If they are not, their displeasure doesn't matter either." This credo almost singularly served to notify the world that the Negro artist had got to the point where he was ready to challenge that world solely on the basis of his art. Hughes's attitude, along with the even fiercer attitude of Claude McKay, and the more intellectually sound attitudes of Jean Toomer and Countee Cullen, was a far cry from the "head patting" parochial "literature" of Chesnutt, Dixon, Dunbar and the so-called "Talented Tenth" of the 1890's. Hughes and the rest were interested in dispelling once and for all the Negro novel of apology, (For example, from an early novel by a Negro, Charles Chesnutt, he relates an incident where "A refined Afro-American is forced to share a Jim Crow car with dirty, boisterous, and drunken Negroes.") of fawning appeals for "an alliance between the better class of colored people and the quality white folks." The "School" was also reacting against the need for a Negro artist to be a pamphleteer, a social organizer, or, for that matter, anything else except an artist. This, of course, was the beginning of the Negro in literature; and the beginning of the end for a "Negro literature."

"Negro literature" is simply *folk litera-ture,* in the sense I choose to take it. It has the same relationship to literature *per se* (that is, to that writing which can be fully significant to all the world's peoples) that any folk art has to art in general. It is usu-ally too limited in its appeal, emotional nuances, intellectual intentions, etc. to be able to fit into the mainstream of world art. Of course, when a folk art does have enough breadth of intellectual, emotional, and psychological concern to make its presence important to those outside of its individual folk tradition, then it has suc-ceeded in thrusting itself up into the area of serious art. And here, by "serious," I mean *anything* containing what Tillich calls an "Ultimate Concern" (God, Death; Life after—the concerns of art) and not as some people would have it, merely any-thing taught in a university. "Negro Lit-erature" is only that; a literature of a particular folk. It is of value only to that particular folk and perhaps to a few schol-ars, and certain kinds of literary *voyeurs.* It should not make pretensions of being anything else.

Of course, utilizing the materials of a certain folk tradition to fashion a work of art (the artist, certainly, must work with what he has, and what is closest to him) can lead to wonderful results: Lorca, Vil-lon, Joyce and Dublin, Faulkner, Ellison. But merely relying on the strength and vi-tality of that tradition, without attempting (either because one lacks talent or is insin-cere) to extend the beauty or meaning of that tradition into a "universal" statement cannot result in art. Bessie Smith is cer-tainly in the folk tradition, but what she finally got to, through that tradition, is, as they say, "something else." *Nobody Knows You When You're Down and Out* could almost be sung by Oedipus leaving Thebes. As Pound said of great literature,

"language charged with meaning to the ut-most possible degree." That is art. A work that never leaves or points to some human reference outside a peculiar folk tradition is at best only folklore.

Ralph Ellison is a Negro writer. His novel *Invisible Man* won the National Book Award as the best American novel of 1952. It is among the best books written by an American in the last twenty years. The novel clearly deals with what is super-ficially a "Negro theme." Its characters are primarily Negroes, and its protagonist is a Negro. And although it is this "Negro theme" that gives the book its special twist, the theme is no more than a point of departure for Ellison. It is no more a "folk tale" than Faulkner's *The Sound and the Fury.* Ellison's horrifying portrait of a man faced with the loss of his identity through the weird swinishness of American society is probably made more incisive by its con-centration on one segment of that society. Ellison uses the folk materials: jazz, blues, church songs, the southern heritage, the whole phenomena of Harlem. But he "charges them with meaning," extending the provincial into the universal. He makes art. Ellison, by utilizing the raw materials of his environment and the peculiar cul-tural heritage of the Negro, has not written a "Negro novel" but a novel. Ellison is a Negro writing literature and great litera-ture at that.

To get back to Langston Hughes. Hughes and the "Harlem School" pro-posed (the credo was written around 1926 in *The Nation*) essentially to resist writing mere folklore. They were to become "full-fledged" artists, though bringing in the whole of the Negro's life. Jean Toomer's novel *Cane* succeeded; some of Cullen's poetry, and Langston Hughes's early verse. Toomer's is perhaps the greatest achieve-ment. His *Cane* was the most significant work by a Negro up until Richard Wright's *Native Son.* Cullen's failure to produce

600

great art is not reproachable. He just wasn't talented enough perhaps. Perhaps Langston Hughes is not talented enough, either. But there are the poems of his early books. "The Negro Speaks of Rivers" is a superb poem, and certainly there must be something else where that came from. And though he is never as good as a prose writer, *Not Without Laughter,* his first novel, with all its faults did have a certain poise and concern nowhere after so seriously approached. Some of the famous "Simple" pieces (started as a series of sketches for *The Chicago Defender*), at their best, contain a genuine humor: but most of them are crushed into mere half-cynical yelping (through a simulated laughter) at the almost mystical white oppressors. At any rate, Hughes has not lived up to his credo. Or perhaps the fault is that he has only lived up to a part of it: "To express our individual dark-skinned selves." Certainly, that is not the final stance of an artist. A writer must be concerned with more than just the color of his skin. Jesse B. Semple, colored man, has to live up to both sides of that title, the noun as well as the adjective.

Since this is a review of a particular book rather than a tract on the responsibilities of the Negro artist, as it must seem I have made it, I must mention the book, *Tambourines to Glory.* There's not much I can say about the book itself. Probably, if a book of similar literary worth were to be written by another author it would not be reviewed (probably it would have never gotten published). But the Negro writer (especially Hughes, since he is so well known as such) raises certain peculiar questions that are not in the least "literary." I have tried to answer some of them. But the book is meaningless, awkward, and never gets past its horribly inept plot. In fact, were it not for, say, the frequent introduction of new characters within the book, it would be almost impossible to distinguish the novel itself from the blurb summary on the jacket. "Laura Reed and Essie Belle Johnson, two attractive Harlem tenement women with time on their hands and no jobs, decide to start their own gospel church on a street corner. Laura wishes to make money. Essie honestly desires to help people." The characterizations don't get much past that.

Even as a folklorist Hughes leaves much to be desired. His use of Harlem slang is strained and rarely precise. When a Harlem con man, "Big-Eyed Buddy," is trying to make little Marietta (from the South), he says hiply, "men don't start asking a sharp little chick like you what school you're in." "Sharp?" Marietta replies incredulously. Buddy says, "Stacked, solid, neat-all-reet, copasetic, baby!" It reeks of the Cab Calloway–Cotton Club–zoot suit era. No self-respecting young Harlemite hipster would be caught dead using such passé, "uncool" language today. As they say, "Man, that stuff went out with pegs." At least a folk artist ought to get the tradition of the folk straight.

But there are so many other faults in the very structure and technical aspect of the novel as to make faults in the writer's own peculiar stylistic device superfluous. None of the basic "novelistic devices" are used correctly. Any advance in the plot is merely stated, never worked into the general texture of the novel. By mentioning the landmarks of Harlem and its prominent persons occasionally, and by having his characters use a "Negro" dialect to mouth continually old stock phrases of Negro dissatisfaction with white America, Hughes apparently hoped to at least create a little atmosphere and make a good folk yarn out of it. But he doesn't even succeed in doing that this time.

It's like a jazz musician who knows that if you play certain minor chords it sounds kind of bluesy, so he plays them over and over again; year in, year out. A kind of tired "instant funk." Certainly this kind of thing doesn't have anything much to do with jazz: just as Hughes's present novel doesn't really have anything to do with either literature *per se,* or, in its imperfect and shallow rendering, the folk tradition he has gotten so famous for interpreting.

Frances Ring
"Novel Is an Opera of Harlem"
Los Angeles Times, part 5, 30 August 1959, [p. 6]

Tambourines make rhythmic music and in the hands of those who pray they make God's music. The coins that jingle in them are the sinner's toll on the Glory Road.

Langston Hughes in his brief, dramatic novel tells that story of fat, placid Essie and Eve-like Laura who decide one Sunday, when the relief money is low, to start a new denomination, find a good street corner and bestir Harlem to follow the path to the Lord.

Their success is quick and remunerative. While Essie is sincere and invests in a Bible and a rostrum, Laura invests in liquor, Cadillacs and a 6-ft. male named Buddy. Buddy's got connections with white fronts and is full of petty racket ideas. He wants to turn tap water into bottled holy water and dollars, and an old movie house into a Tambourine Temple with a stage from which Laura dramatically sings out to those waiting to be saved.

But one day Buddy refuses to bite the apple and Laura lets him have a knife in his back. She pays like any sinner while Essie continues to preach with true fervor—onward to glory!

The colored people of Harlem have little enough to be grateful for and they find comfort in the Gospel church and its music, no matter who sings it. That these lambs are led to the slaughter by the unscrupulous is the blight Langston Hughes exposes here.

His dialogue and characters are vivid but one wishes he had put his talents and understanding of his people to work in a stronger book. As it stands, it reads more like the libretto of an opera than a novel and undoubtedly could be effectively adapted.

B.H.
"Realistic Writing without Bitterness"
Durham Herald, 29 May 1960, p. 5D

Langston Hughes is one of the few Negro writers who can write realistically of his own race without bitterness.

His place in contemporary American literature is thus enhanced.

His newest book is a humorous tale concerned with the colorful independent, unorthodox churches which have arisen in many places, particularly in Harlem, in recent years. Of course there is an underlying tone of seriousness, a consciousness of the social conditions which make these cults possible, and it gives his novel body.

In his story, Laura, an unattached woman given to fleshly ways, and Essie, a less colorful individual content to vegetate through her days, combine forces to found a church. Their initial motive is to raise funds to supplement their welfare checks.

In no time at all they rise from shaking tambourines on a street corner to holding magnificent services in a converted although condemned theater.

Their success means different things to the two of them. To Laura it means a mink coat, a chauffeured Cadillac and a younger man friend.

To Essie it means a richer life with the opportunity to help others and the way to bring her daughter north.

Tragedy strikes, of course, and the expected things happen, the pat ending being the only thing disappointing about the book.

In the telling, the folk ways are marvelously depicted, and the light touch is strengthened by the underlying meaning of the story.

One scene even has great power. Midway the story Laura builds up the congregation for the "conversion" of her boyfriend, and as she sings, the pathos of a struggling race is brought forth. It is a great example of Hughes' poetic gift.

Tambourines to Glory is a wonderfully readable, a strikingly contemporary book.

Checklist of Additional Reviews

"Forthcoming Books," *Booklist,* 55 (1 November 1958), 112.

"Weekly Record: Hughes, Langston," *Publishers Weekly,* 174 (17 November 1958), 64.

Malcolm Bauer, "Author Blames Greedy Whites for Indian Troubles in West," *Oregonian,* 7 December 1958, p. 47.

Ed Wellejus, "The Bookshelf: Names in Light," *Erie Times-News,* 7 December 1958, p. 15E.

[Esther R.] M[ahoney], "To Fast Money!" *Montgomery Advertiser–Alabama Journal,* 28 December 1958, p. 6F.

"Books: Briefly Noted," *New Yorker,* 34 (24 January 1959), 124–5.

Nikki Giovanni, "Books," *Essence,* 16 (May 1985), 32.

SELECTED POEMS OF LANGSTON HUGHES

"Selected Poems of Langston Hughes"
Virginia Kirkus Bulletin, 27 (15 January 1959), 80

Langston Hughes, who has been a foremost spokesman for his race for over three decades, needs no introduction to the American public. This new volume is a collection of what he considers his best poems from earlier works—along with a few additional, newly printed poems. The poetry comes from *The Weary Blues, Fine Clothes to the Jew, Shakespeare in Harlem, Fields of Wonder, One Way Ticket, Montage of a Dream Deferred,* and from the privately printed *Dear Lovely Death.* Hughes' gifts as a spontaneous poet, shaped by the pathos and humor and colorfulness of his people, are too well accepted to need comment. What he lacks in craft, is equated by sincerity; if he is not a great poet, he hardly seems to claim to be one. Yet he has flashes now and then of real insight, and he communicates a tenderness that has a wide audience appeal.

Clark Emery
"Poetry Shows a Keen Insight"
Miami News, 22 March 1959, p. 6B

A problem of the modern Negro is to achieve middle-class respectability without becoming "a good nigger" and without losing his identity as a Negro, an equal of but different from his white compatriot.

The problem is even more acute for the Negro poet. He will, naturally, be dedicated to the economic and social betterment of his race. But the end-result of such betterment is urban middle-class respectability; and respectability, being dull, is not the stuff of poetry.

For color, excitement, humor, raciness of language, earthiness, and religious intensity, he will need to go to those whom the middle class—White and Negro—consider disreputable.

This is not easy. As Mr. Hughes has Low say to High, "Now you've got your Cadillac, you done forgot that you are black." And, further, if he focuses on Low instead of on High, he tends to divert attention from the social gains made by thousands of Negroes.

And, by exploiting the poetical values of colloquial language, native humor, and the like, he will tend to perpetuate the White-reactionary myth that Negroes (always quaintly singing and laughing) are really better off as they are.

In this volume, Mr. Hughes shows his awareness of the problem. His poems deal with share-cropper and college graduate, Bach and the blues, lynchings and festive Saturday nights.

He is proud of the gains his race has made, and militant against those who would halt them. But he is not blind to the poetical potential which exists in the milieu of those who still suffer exploitation.

If he is not a poet of real stature, he is good enough to prove that there is no field of endeavor in which the Negro is not the equal of the White.

Charles Guenther
"Poet of the Blues"
St. Louis Post-Dispàtch,
22 March 1959, p. 4B

Poets today are no longer considered to be "born." They are made by the long discipline of graduate English courses. This is especially noticeable in poets under 40, whose work appears in increasing abundance in the best literary magazines. But if any poet can be said to have a mainly natural talent, that poet is Langston Hughes. The reason for this is that Hughes draws his inspiration not so much from books as from life around him and from his experience.

[. . .]

The contents of his new "selected poems" were chosen by Hughes from seven earlier books and include some work never published before. The several hundred poems are grouped under 13 sections having titles like "Afro-American Fragments," "Shadow of the Blues," "Lament Over Love" and "Montage of a Dream Deferred." Altogether the collection is handsomely designed and printed.

Hughes is most successful in his poems and ballads which have a definite rhythm or beat; the free verse, written mostly in the '20s, has not worn so well. Whether or not he is the "original jazz poet," as Arna Bontemps has acclaimed him, he remains the most active lyricist of that category of jazz still known as the "blues." He was the first poet fully to exploit and appreciate the regular poetic pattern of the blues. The best elements of Hughes's poetry are its clarity, its depth and authenticity of feeling, and its varied treatment of moods and themes. In the conventional sense his technique is not outstanding, but his verse of-ten carries a power lacking in verse by more fussy craftsmen. The poems here range from fast-moving conversational pieces to ballads on traditional topics. Hughes has a mystical strain, too; certain poems ("Cross," "Silhouette," "Genius Child") are reminiscent of Blake's "Songs of Experience."

Underlying these "selected poems," both the grim and the glad, is a voice of pain and isolation, of a deeply felt contemporary anguish. "I am the American heartbreak," the poet writes; and the song of his "Night of the four songs unsung" repeats like a cante hondo or lament: "Sorrow! Sorrow! Sorrow! Sorrow!" By whatever name it is known—"angoisse," "agonia" or the "blues"—the voice of this suffering spirit is true, timeless and universal.

James Baldwin
"Sermons and Blues"
New York Times Book Review, 29 March 1959, p. 6

Every time I read Langston Hughes I am amazed all over again by his genuine gifts—and depressed that he has done so little with them. A real discussion of his work demands more space than I have here, but this book contains a great deal which a more disciplined poet would have thrown into the waste-basket (almost all of the last section, for example).

There are the poems which almost succeed but which do not succeed, poems which take refuge, finally, in a fake simplicity in order to avoid the very difficult simplicity of the experience! And one sometimes has the impression, as in a poem like "Third Degree"—which is about the beating up of a Negro boy in a police station—that Hughes has had to hold the experience outside him in order to be able to write at all. And certainly this is understandable. Nevertheless, the poetic trick, so to speak, is to be within the experience and outside it at the same time—and the poem fails.

Mr. Hughes is at his best in brief, sardonic asides, or in lyrics like "Mother to Son," and "The Negro Speaks of Rivers." Or "Dream Variations.". . .

I do not like all of "The Weary Blues," which copies, rather than exploits, the cadence of the blues, but it comes to a remarkable end. And I am also very fond of "Island," which begins "Wave of sorrow / Do not drown me now."

Hughes, in his sermons, blues and prayers, has working for him the power and the beat of Negro speech and Negro music. Negro speech is vivid largely because it is private. It is a kind of emotional shorthand—or sleight-of-hand—by means of which Negroes express, not only their relationship to each other, but their judgment of the white world. And, as the white world takes over this vocabulary—without the faintest notion of what it really means—the vocabulary is forced to change. The same thing is true of Negro music, which has had to become more and more complex in order to continue to express any of the private or collective experience.

Hughes knows the bitter truth behind these hieroglyphics: what they are designed to protect, what they are designed to convey. But he has not forced them into the realm of art where their meaning would become clear and overwhelming. "Hey, pop! / Re-bop! / Mop!" conveys much more on Lenox Avenue than it does in this book, which is not the way it ought to be.

Hughes is an American Negro poet and has no choice but to be acutely aware of it.

He is not the first American Negro to find the war between his social and artistic responsibilities all but irreconcilable.

Fred S. Holley
"Vivid Sense of Image: Future of a Dream Deferred"
Virginian-Pilot and Portsmouth Star, 29 March 1959, p. 6F

Jamestown's great mistake was, of course, the introduction of slavery and the consequent myth of an inherent Negro inferiority into English-speaking North America. The tragic results of this mistake are the raw materials of the poetry of Langston Hughes.

Hughes' "Selected Poems" are for the most part culled from his earlier volumes, but a section of new poems is appended. The new poems are written under the pressure of integration difficulties in the South and violence at Little Rock and they suffer from it. They have become collections of democratic clichés, exhortations in the manner of Norman Corwin and even, save the mark, Walt Whitman. Even so impressive a poem as "Freedom Train" suffers from this weakness.

But Hughes at his best, and it is a very good best, captures the spirit of the northern big-city Negro and the transplanted southern Negro with feeling and truth. His music is "the boogie-woogie rumble / of a dream deferred," and he is concerned with the future of a "dream deferred." Will it explode? he wonders. "There's liable to be confusion when a dream gets kicked around."

In a sense, Hughes is a folk poet. His songs spring from the tenements of Harlem, not from the halls of academe. There are no ambiguities here, no "objective correlatives." But there is an intense sense of image that seems to me to lift him above the rank of the mere versifier and to make of him a poet in the sense of being a creator as well as a mirror. A few words say much: "Lonely / As a bottle of licker/ On a table / All by itself." With wry yet sympathetic humor, he visualizes the "Be-Bop Boys": "Imploring Mecca / to achieve / six discs / with Decca."

In "Hope," "a dying man rose up on his dying bed / and asked for fish. / His wife looked it up in her dream book / and played it." His "Madam Alberta K. Johnson" is a true characterization of the big-city Negro woman.

There is a vast enjoyment of life here, an appreciation of the teeming vitality of the Harlem pavements. There is sorrow, too, and bitterness. He writes of the South: "I, who am black, would love her / But she spits in my face."

But I think that wonderment is the major characteristic of Hughes' poetry, wonderment at the spectacle of bi-racial cultures in America and an even more profound wonderment about the future.

> So we stand here
> On the edge of hell
> In Harlem
> And look out upon the world
> And wonder
> What we're gonna do
> In the face of
> What we remember.

John W. Parker
"The Poetic Faith of a Social Poet"
Phylon, 20 (Second Quarter 1959), 196–7; excerpted in "Not of Moonlight but of People," *Raleigh News and Observer,* section 3, 14 June 1959, p. 5

Much in the same fashion as its companion collection, *The Langston Hughes Reader* (which spotlights perhaps the best of the most popular work Langston Hughes has turned out in the prose medium), his *Selected Poems of Langston Hughes* brings between the covers of a single volume what the author himself has isolated as the most effective of his poetic contribution to American letters. In at least one respect the two collections are similar; each discloses a totality of impression different from that exhibited by any single selection included in it, or by any combination of them. The oneness of impression that underscores these recent Hughes volumes is reminiscent of a similar purposiveness that runs through his complete literary output—namely, that of bringing into sharp focus the turbulent "inner life" of Brown Americans in their struggle to outdistance their present social milieux.

Between the advent in 1926 of *The Weary Blues,* Hughes' initial book of poems, and that of his *Selected Poems of Langston Hughes,* issued in 1959, have appeared such collections of poems as *The Dream Keeper, Shakespeare in Harlem, One-Way Ticket,* and *Montage of a*

Dream Deferred. Even a casual perusal of this newly-published collection of poems reasserts a feeling that enjoyed vogue when *The Weary Blues* came out—namely, that there had appeared on the literary scene a fresh voice and a clear tone and something of a new literary genre capable of penetrating the emotional heights and depths of the Negro people in Harlem and in other ghettos around the world.

Selected Poems of Langston Hughes appears not always quite clear in organization; the thirteen chapters that go into its making are more formal than organic. In lieu of the chronological order or the organization by types, the selections are sometimes grouped on the basis of the mood they create. For example, the chapter "Feet of Jesus" portrays the penitent Negro facing up to the character imperfections that have overtaken him, just as "Lament over Love" digs into the phenomenon of unrequited love and "Magnolia Flowers" in such poems as "Cross," "Ruby Brown," and "Porter" serves as a definition of a situation inconsistent with the provisions of the Declaration of Independence.

This new volume contains not only selections from his published books (including those privately published), but also poems that either have never been published before or have appeared only in periodicals. It points up the fact that in poetry as elsewhere Mr. Hughes has gone on writing interestingly and feelingly about people and things and incidents in almost infinite variety—the taking of one's troubles to the gypsy, wreckless abandon in Harlem after midnight, the impact of the unhappy mulatto stereotype, the plight of the American Negro woman, and, of course, daybreak in Alabama. Here are such well-known favorites as "The Negro Speaks of Rivers," "The Weary Blues," "Mother to Son," "Negro," and "Freedom's Plow."

Sophisticated selections that stamp their author as a lyricist of keen sensitivity and insight include poems like "Litany" and "Snail." . . .

And among the new pieces that ring true to today's social situation are "Africa," "Democracy," and "In Explanation of Our Times."

Langston Hughes stands by his conviction that poetry, like truth and right, never quite is, but is forever in the process of becoming. As a social poet, he insists that poetry fulfills its chief purpose when it serves as a criticism of life. Hence, over the years he has been concerned not nearly so much with moonlight and roses, sweetness and light, as with the problems that beset men here and now—share-croppers, the way of the ghetto, color-lines, dead-end streets, restrictive covenants, and the ultimate freedom of the human soul, race and previous condition notwithstanding.

C.G.
"The New Books"
San Francisco Chronicle
This World, 5 April 1959,
p. 20

Since a Complete Works of Langston Hughes seems unlikely (he has published 27 books since *The Weary Blues* appeared in 1927 and gives no sign of tiring), readers will have to be content with these Selected Poems. This is no compromise, however, for Hughes' selection contains the essence of his poetic work. Unlike many anthologies or collections, one is not here conscious so much of omissions as of the consistent fineness of what has been chosen for the book.

Between his opening "Afro-American

Fragment" ("So long, / So far away / Is Africa") and his closing, "Freedom's Plough," we have some of the saddest, most humorous and beautiful insights ever given into the heart of a race. Throughout this collection the poet uses his strong evocative power to awaken in us something infinitely more important than sympathy. When queried in the poem "Misery": "Can't you understand, / O, understand / A woman's cryin' / For a no-good man?" we do understand.

This volume alone would be enough to earn Hughes the recognition that many believe is his, as America's greatest Negro lyric poet.

Ethel Phipps
"New Book of Poems Is Praised"
Charlotte Observer,
5 April 1959, p. 12F

Langston Hughes is a Negro. Of course, everybody knows that already. But he is also a universal poet. His short poem "I, Too" has been translated into many languages. South Americans claim it as the apt expression of their desire for acknowledgment by the great white nation to the north.

Langston Hughes' poetry is full of meaning, as poetry should be. His poetry is full of passion, as great poetry must be. His verses yearn and plead for the fulfillment of the wordless wishes of his people.

Consider, if you will, "Georgia Dusk." . . .

American-Negro poets, from the time of Phyllis Wheatley until now, have been consumed by a strange homesickness for Africa, the dark mother of the Negro peoples.

Nowhere is this longing more poignantly expressed than in the poem called "Afro-American Fragment." . . .

H.A.W.
"Speech and Song"
Trenton Sunday Times and Advertiser, part 4,
5 April 1959, p. 14

It was in 1926 that Langston Hughes had his first volume of poems published and since that time (and what decades he has gone through) seven volumes of his highly original verses, beating out the rhythms of his race, have been sent winging out into the hinterlands and read with understanding, for his lines carry their own built-in meanings.

"Selected Poems" is a collection of some of the poems that have appeared in those previous volumes as well as poems that either have never been published before or have appeared only in periodicals. It is an important collection for it reveals in more than one way the power he possesses to put a thought, a meaning, a feeling into a few lines, something like that difficult form of the Japanese. Some of his poems are only three lines long, but that does not mean they are fragments.

He has imagery to spare. Thus he speaks of "The lazy, laughing South with blood on its mouth," or of a colored child at a carnival—"Where is the Jim-Crow section of this merry-go-round," or "The Juke Box Love Song"—"I could take the Harlem night and wrap around you."

Or he becomes rueful:

"I put my nickel
In the raffle of the night.

612

Somehow that raffle
Didn't turn out right."

Here are religious poems that include the spirituals, poems that deal with the Blues, poems on the sea and the land and a number of other categories, but all bear the Hughes stamp of intensity, unexpected twistings and turnings, and exploring regions he has been over for so many times and yet finds not altogether explored so that he must return again and again to ponder and sing.

These selected poems, making up a good-sized book, represent the poet's own decisions as to which of his poems he most wants to preserve and reprint. He has served himself well as a critic. And the fine drawings by E. McKnight Kauffer add something to the collection.

for something more permanent than propaganda even when he is writing on strictly social themes. And at their best, the poems ring with stirring conviction.

On the other hand, honesty and passion are not always enough; nor do the essentially fragmentary perceptions that sometimes disguise themselves as complete poems really add up. The jazz rhythms, the authentic use of idiom, the genuine insights are all here but all too frequently they fail to fuse together. It is a tribute to Hughes that his poems of social protest are more durable than those of many of his contemporaries; and it is a greater tribute of him as a poet that his best poems need no apology for their social content.

Samuel F. Morse
"A Real Poet"
Hartford Courant Magazine, 12 April 1959, p. 13

This very generous selection of poems by Langston Hughes begins almost at the beginning of his long publishing career, and comes down to the present. It spans, astonishingly enough, a period of more than thirty-five years. "The Negro Speaks of Rivers" was first published in 1921; the most recent poems—a number of them here published for the first time—belong to the last two or three years.

The early poems remain the most convincing ones; those from *The Weary Blues* and *Fine Clothes to the Jew* have a polish and certitude that the later, more bitter pieces lack. Hughes strives for affirmation,

Charles H. Philbrick
"The Strength and Weakness of Racial Poetry"
Providence Sunday Journal, 19 April 1959, p. W22

Here Langston Hughes has drawn from seven previous volumes of verse, and added some new material. The book contains many poems which at once and without posturing announce themselves as excellent. But there are as many more which may look at first glance the same, and then turn out to be embarrassing impostors, undetected by their sponsor. Now, what disturbs me about all this—and it may be a good thing for me to be so disturbed—is that I can here only indicate my sense of this split, when I ought really to be driven by it into detailed comparative analyses which would have to suggest, at least, my definition of a poem. This, obviously, I cannot do here.

But Hughes is trapped in a predicament which is far more serious and far more pitiful, more tragically determined, than mine. Hughes is a poet, and he is black in a society which is largely white in power and white in its poetry. He is a poet condemned to be black; and he both triumphs and falters because of this fact. His race is the theme of nearly all his song—its strength and its limitations—and his best work stands without jostling or withdrawal in the same line with his worst. Thus this book is at one and the same time an accusation of, and an adjustment to, the atmosphere in which the Negro poet tries to work as an artist and live as a person. The poetic spirit shrinks from gray; in conflict, black and white result in the red of human blood; the pulse of people, rather than the banner of politics.

Yet quite a few of these pieces quietly emerge from their sources into poetry—from gospel-shout, say, into literary art—and we are then conscious of the color of the art, so to speak, and not of the color of the artist. Examples are "Spiritual," "Shadow of the Blues," "Wake," "Song for a Dark Girl" and some of the "Madam" poems. In such as these, anger and wit, affection and idealism are poetic, rather than occasional; they are graced with rhythmic verve and the permanence of lyric form, be they sweet and melting or hard and crisp. They have the authority of not being conceivable otherwise, of being at the same time inevitable and unpredictable.

But there are other poems which seem to me marred by a number of faults which are all, perhaps, indigenous to their provenience. Some remind me of the sinkings of Robert Burns, as folksong paints itself with pretentious diction. Others seem so studiedly simple as to be childish in a way that children seldom speak, and I hesitate

to call them poems at all; they are sketches or echoes, rather than developed poems, though they may masquerade as such behind their simplicity and exclamation. That which tries too hard to be deceptively simple can sometimes become simply deceiving. Still other pieces are embarrassing because their sentiments are so obviously right, their paradoxes so clearly and unjustly true, their clichés so drearily unquestionable. Causes, of course, live on truisms, but poems tend to die of them in their triteness; and, while I sympathize with Hughes' causes, I sidle away from some of his poems of purpose.

Enough of carping catalogues. Langston Hughes is always worth listening to as a person, and also as a poet—admirably much of the time.

[J.] Saunders Redding "Book Review: The Best of Hughes" *Baltimore Afro-American Magazine,* 9 May 1959, p. 2

Langston Hughes is the most prolific and also the most versatile of colored writers in America.

He is not just a writer of prose; he is not just a poet.

He is in the tradition of the 18th-Century man of letters: poet, novelist, dramatist, popular historian and biographer, essayist and pamphleteer.

He is a writer of many moods, from the sublime to the ridiculous, from the reverent to the satirical and scornful.

He has made his living from purely literary pursuits since 1926.

Distinguished at home, he is well known abroad, where his works have been translated into French, German and (earlier) Russian.

Last year, when Mr. Hughes published an anthology of his prose, some of his readers were disturbed.

They were afraid he was closing up shop, writing "the end" to a long and fruitful career. But the fear was groundless.

Since then, Mr. Hughes has published a novel, *Tambourines to Glory,* and now comes a volume of his selected poems.

It is a good collection, and it will be especially acceptable to those who do not have the seven separate volumes of Hughes' poetical works.

Nearly all the best pieces are here, though not all the favorites—for it frequently happens that a poet's best pieces are not those most favored by his reading public.

Browning's "From Aix to Ghent," for instance, is not so good as "Pippa Passes," but it is more favored.

In this collection of Mr. Hughes' poems, the present reviewer misses especially "The Cat and the Saxophone," which he thinks to be, indisputably, the poem of the jazz age in Harlem.

This reviewer does not claim that it is one of Hughes' best poems, but he does feel that, more than any other poem, it expresses the spirit and the tempo of the age in which the poet grew to maturity.

And that it, more than any other poem, catches the sublimation of despair which is too often mistaken for the joie de vivre that is commonly supposed to characterize the colored American.

It is, indeed, a poem that might well serve as Langston Hughes' signature, and this reviewer misses it from this volume.

But, as has been said, nearly all the best poems are here, and they are of several kinds, in several idioms and a variety of

moods, including the blue, the jazzy, the religious: "The Weary Blues," "Mother to Son," "The Negro Speaks of Rivers" (not only one of the best, but a universal favorite), "Water-Front Streets," "Cross," and a score of others.

There are also some new pieces, such as "Africa," "Democracy," and "In Explanation of Our Times."

They are topical, and the interest in them may wane as the subjects of which they treat recede in time, but just now they are what might be called "hot" verse.

There are several ways in which these selections might have been organized—chronologically, by types, by subject, by mood—but Mr. Hughes seems to have chosen none of them, and though the selections themselves are certainly not haphazard, the putting of them together is.

It would have been helpful and revealing had Langston Hughes chosen the order of time.

This arrangement would have outlined his own poetic development and would have helped to indicate the changing moods, the "varied lights and weathers" of the souls of black folk in America during the last quarter of a century.

H.N.
"Hughes Shouldn't Object to Some Obsolescence" *Chicago Sunday Sun Times,* section 3, 17 May 1959, p. 4

This is Langston Hughes' third appearance in a few months. First came a collection of folk literature (in collaboration), then a novel *Tambourines to Glory,* and now this selection of old and new work by a man who is surely one of our most prolific writers.

The poet Hughes, more so than the novelist or editor Hughes, is a man of the brief, quick thrust, of the simplicity that hides a complex of art and of humanity. Typical of this artlessness that is at the core of art is the poem "Harlem" that gave a name to the play *A Raisin in the Sun*.

Such a prolific writer as Hughes will inevitably write topical poems that lose some of their force with the passage of time. "Lunch in a Jim Crow Car," for instance, belongs now to history, as do others in the Hughes canon. But Hughes himself would probably not object. Perhaps, by writing his poems, he has contributed to their own obsolescence.

Harry M. Meacham
"Race Feeling Bitter-sweet in Hughes' Poems"
Richmond News-Leader, 27 May 1959, p. 11

This handsome volume contains Langston Hughes' own selection from seven previously published books of verse dating from 1926, when his first volume, *The Weary Blues,* appeared. A Missouri Negro now living in New York, Hughes is at his best when he is echoing the simple songs of his people.

In quatrains such as "Wake" . . . one can almost hear the funeral bands on Beale Street. "Daybreak in Alabama" . . . conveys the yearning of the ignorant for means to communicate a deep feeling for beauty.

However, Hughes' slender talents cannot support the bitter racialism which per-

vades too many of the poems. One closes the volume with the conviction that if the poet had continued to use the subject matter Paul Laurence Dunbar found so rewarding, his work might have some enduring qualities.

Alvaro Cardona-Hine
"Open Handshake"
Mainstream, 12 (July 1959), 55–6

Langston Hughes, that warm, world-wide sight-seer in depth, has here, in a tall, elongated book, put together what he would want to save after a deluge, what he would grab for in case of fire. The results make for a limpid congregation of effortless rhyme and folk-like simplicity.

The whole of the black man's world is dealt with: Africa, Spirituals, blues, Jim Crow, the South, Harlem, and the dream of freedom. There are also less implicated poems, those dealing with love and the sea, for instance, which give the book a well-rounded nature of complete human experience.

There is no doubt that Hughes understands the roots of his people's faith. It is only with understanding and sympathy that a lovely, painful thing like his "Sinner" can be written:

Have mercy, Lord!

Po' an' black
An' humble an' lonesome
An' a sinner in yo' sight.

Have mercy, Lord!

Conventional morality does not mar these pages; the politics is in the poetry. Hughes moves quietly through the everyday world of good and bad, the next-door world of gossip, and the absent world of necessary dreams intent upon catching their actual flavor. . . .

He is thoroughly and maliciously on the side of life. . . .

Debiting the book are two items in my estimation. One is the use of drawings in white against a black background; the other, a few longer poems at the end of the volume. The drawings, by E. Mc-Knight Kauffer, are reproduced from one of Hughes' earlier volumes, his *Shakespeare in Harlem,* published by Knopf in 1942. With one or two exceptions, these drawings do not merit their company. The longer poems alluded to are gathered under the heading of *Words Like Freedom.* Welcome as they may be in a political way, these poems on freedom and equality fail their subject because they never depart from the abstract principles involved. Poetry cannot exist apart from concrete and Hughes, not being a rhetorical poet, does not render the length of his utterance in a solid fashion. His essential qualities are, in its best sense, flute-like. He is almost always sweet, dear and delicate—great virtues in a man and needed ones in an art as ill with violence and intellectual strutting as poetry today.

The poetry of Langston Hughes inhabits the open handshakes of his nature, and in its joy, proclaims its freedom. . . .

John Henrik Clarke "Book Reviews" *Chicago Defender,* 4 July 1959, p. 3

While emphatically disagreeing with James Baldwin's inept review of the *Selected Poems of Langston Hughes* in the *New York Times,* the writer Lloyd L. Brown gave a truer evaluation of Langston Hughes as a poet in the following excerpt from his letter to the book review editor of that paper:

"He is indeed the poet laureate of our people, and that is because in his writing he is a Negro, voicing with a rare genius the very heart of the Negro in America."

Unlike the small, though increasing group of alienated Negro writers, who spend so much of their time running from other Negroes and cursing God for making them black, Langston Hughes has never left home. The publication of his *Selected Poems,* thirty-three years after he made his debut with his first volume of poems *The Weary Blues,* was needed and welcome.

For more than a quarter of a century the steady and prolific pen of Langston Hughes has poured forth, with what seems to be untiring consistency. Being our most versatile writer, he has the largest Negro reading audience and for many years he has also been universally read and appreciated.

No writer with the tremendous output and diversity of Langston Hughes can be expected to reach the heights of literary form with every effort. Some of his poems are weak and topical, others are strong and enduring. His most enduring poems can be found in this volume.

In his poems of protest, Langston Hughes has given us a dimension and a point of view not found elsewhere—a philosophical bitterness tempered with humor. His range as a poet extends far beyond his unique method of protest. He is also a poet who celebrates the joy of living.

Nearly all of his best known poems are included in this selection. "The Negro Speaks of Rivers," "Mother to Son," "The Weary Blues," and "Cross" show the early flourishing of his talent.

In utilizing Negro speech and idioms,

he has shown us values in the thought patterns of Negro life that we had not previously considered.

I began this review by disagreeing with James Baldwin's evaluation of Langston Hughes as a poet. I am still of the same opinion. Speaking of Hughes in his *New York Times* review of March 29, 1959, Baldwin said: "He is not the first American Negro to find the war between his social and artistic responsibilities all but irreconcilable."

Quite the contrary, I think what Mr. Baldwin calls a war between the writer's social and artistic responsibilities is only a long bridge that every seriously minded writer will have to learn how to cross. For years, Langston Hughes has been crossing this bridge, in style.

C. L. Anderson
"Thirty Years with Poetry"
Dallas Times-Herald,
Roundup Section, 5 July 1959, p. 15

Langston Hughes has been publishing his verse since the mid-twenties, and has figured so long in public notice as one of our leading Negro poets that it is a pleasure to be able to look back with him over his work of more than three decades in a volume recently published by Knopf, *Selected Poems*. It is a handsomely printed book with illustrations in the right mood by E. McKnight Kauffer.

The mood is principally the blues, as it perhaps should be, for Hughes can almost make the lines shuffle as they lament in syncopated time a tale of betrayed love,

lost love, easy love. He gives glimpses of lovers' spats, which sometimes take in the poem the sound of injured and militant indifference, sometimes that of an amusingly shrill taunt.

Mixed in with love, especially the despairing kind, are hints, threats, and hope of quick death; and the mood again is the blues.

The best of the poems find the proper balance between the sounds of speech and the blues rhythms. Obviously, not all can be the best; the lesser poems fail, it seems to me, chiefly through faulty choice of a word (for example, "Listen closely" seems a little prissy in ragtime verse) or through an inadvertent breakdown here and there of the wonderful, shuffling slackness of this poetry into dullness. Fortunately, there is plenty of Hughes at his best in this volume, and all of it gives the pleasure of seeming very close to the life and song of the urban American Negro.

Henry F. Winslow
"Enduring Exuberance"
Crisis, 66 (October 1959), 512–13

It is somewhat difficult to accept the fact that Langston Hughes has for thirty-eight years been before the public as a poet, because there is throughout his works, in whatever form, an enduring exuberance of spirit such as one usually finds and expects only in the young.

Of the 186 entries included in his *Selected Poems,* a majority—and certainly the best known—originally appeared in *The Crisis;* indeed, the widely translated and often anthologized "The Negro Speaks of Rivers"—with which he set the course of his career as a poet—appeared first in *The Crisis* for June, 1921; and as recently as December, 1958, he contributed, through *The Crisis*, "Four Christian Poems." Hence Langston Hughes has warmed the house that welcomed him with a steady flow of soft, living language.

His poetry comes to us from within—it is easy to come from within, provided one ever gets there; ay, there's the rub. And because he is humble enough to live within the experience of his people, one finds more authenticity in those twenty lines of, for example, "Mother and Son," than in imposing cultural histories:

> Well, son, I'll tell you:
> Life for me ain't been no crystal stair.
> It's had tacks in it.
> And splinters,
> And boards torn up,
> And places with no carpet on the
>   floor—
> Bare. . . .

In this poetry words serve the mood and convey the feeling: they are words of wisdom rather than a wisdom with words. He has a way with words which brings the sense all the way home, as in the concluding lines of "Trumpet Player." . . . He is at his best in short sweet songs of saddest thought, as in "Suicide's Note." . . . He is at his bitterest on "The South." . . . He is in his idiom singing the blues—he *can* sing them because he has them!—as may be felt in "Late Last Night." . . . Speaking of life through people, he points to "Ruby Brown" whom Mayville offered no "fuel for the clean flame of joy / That tried to burn within her soul," so she changed occupational traps, leaving the white woman's kitchen for the sinister shuttered house where white men paid her more money.

In general, his subjects (they are never his objects) are those people with whom he lives and who like him have made the journey from rural to urban setting—from the scorching sun of corn and cotton fields to hovels in Harlem: his overall theme is how they fare with dreams deferred; his big sea is their restless hopes and hearts; his poetry the songs of their experience.

One wishes that these magnificently bound poems were dated so as to provide for some chronological approach to Hughes as a writer. One wonders how he would sound if he treated the church-centered, spiritual aspect of Negro life as faithfully as he deals with the secular problems; or the evil-natured with unsparing truth. But this perhaps asks him to be what he is not. For certainly, as they are, these poems are worthy of having and handing down to unborn generations.

Checklist of Additional Reviews

Jessie Kitching, "Nonfiction Forecast: *Selected Poems of Langston Hughes*," *Publishers Weekly*, 175 (23 February 1959), 80.

"Books in Brief: Poetry," *New York Herald Tribune Book Review*, 22 March 1959, p. 11.

Milton S. Byam, "New Books Appraised," *Library Journal*, 84 (1 April 1959), 1140.

"Literature," *Booklist*, 55 (1 April 1959), 413.

"Nonfiction," *Bookmark*, 18 (June 1959), 229.

John Henrik Clarke, "African World Book Shelf," *New York Citizen-Call*, 6 August 1960, p. 27.

Cecil Brown, "Brown's Ten," *Black Scholar*, 12 (March–April 1981), 82.

THE BEST OF SIMPLE

"Profiles: Gay Memoir Vivid"
Portland Oregonian,
15 October 1961, p. 49

These short sketches of dialogue with Jesse B. Semple, Harlem's Everyman, provide an apt introduction to Hughes' genius in portraying compassionately, but with toughness, the American Negro's burden.

[Miles A. Smith] "Book Reviews: Simple Story"
Asheville Citizen-Times, 15 October 1961, p. 3D; variations in *Bridgeport Sunday Post,* 15 October 1961; *High Point Enterprise,* 29 October 1961, p. 10C; *Tacoma News Tribune,* 12 November 1961; *Hayward Review,* 19 November 1961; *Presque Isle Star Herald,* 23 November 1961; *Lansing State Journal,* 3 December 1961; *Cleveland Plain Dealer,* 21 January 1962, p. 7H

Poet, dramatist and prose writer Hughes began creating his folk character Simple (Jesse B. Semple) years ago, and this book is a composite of three earlier works now in print, in which Hughes, as the narrator in the background, lets Simple speak his mind about blacks and whites.

The setting is Harlem, the Negro district of New York City. The slim thread of narrative that connects these vignettes is the story of Simple's love for Joyce, his long attempts to gain his freedom from his first wife, Isabel, and his many distractions, among which are beer joints and a footloose female named Zarita.

The author keeps chiding Simple for harping continually on the racial theme, but, of course, this is a low-pressure technique for insinuating the theme itself.

Simple is a dark-skinned version of the homely philosopher, who, in earthy language and striking metaphor, comments upon his state in life and slyly pokes the probing finger of ridicule at the white folks' notions of supremacy. To leaven this social comment, Hughes throws in a few examples of the Negro's own foibles about social pretensions.

If you haven't met Simple before, you probably will find him to be an interesting character in an interesting setting.

H.N.
"Book Notes"
Chicago Sun-Times, section 3, 22 October 1961, p. 5

Jesse B. Semple—Simple—in another book, this one including 15 stories that were in *Simple Stakes a Claim,* plus 55 more. Langston Hughes has staked his claim—Harlem and its people—and he works that rich vein for all it is worth. Simple is no simpleton. He, and Hughes, know the score: They're way ahead of the rest of us.

Serena Turan Scheer
"Simple Offers Poignant Humor"
Oakland Tribune, 12 November 1961, p. EL5

Langston Hughes has been writing Simple stories for a long time, and although all of them are short (many appeared originally in the *Chicago Defender*) Hughes is able to evoke the spirit of Harlem, poor, but gay; angry, but humorous.

Jesse B. Semple (nicknamed Simple) is an American Negro born in the South and now living in Harlem. Through him Hughes expresses the character of the Negro who is angry and baffled by the mean and hypocritical ways of the white world and yet never loses his sense of humor.

Simple has reason to be angry, as he says in one piece:

"I looked around me, out yonder at Orchard Beach and almost everybody on that beach besides me and Joyce were foreigners. They were speaking Italian, German, Yiddish, Spanish, Puerto Rican and everything but English. So I got to thinking how any one of them foreigners could visit my home state down South and ride anywhere they want to on the trains—except with me, and I've been here 300 years."

All the characters in these stories are drawn from the mainstream of Harlem life. . . .

John W. Parker
"Book Reviews"
CLAJ, 5 (December 1961), 155–7

In his new volume, *The Best of Simple*, Langston Hughes has returned to the sunshine and shadow that are wont to characterize the Harlem scene, and to the exploits of one of the Black Metropolis's best-known citizens, Jesse B. Semple, whom back in 1950 he brought into existence by means of a Chicago typewriter without benefit of midwife. *The Best of Simple* appears, not so much as an extension of the Simple tradition as a collection of choice pieces culled from Hughes' previous Simple volumes—*Simple Speaks His Mind, Simple Takes a Wife*, and *Simple Stakes a Claim*. A preponderance of those literary gems was taken from his middle book, *Simple Takes a Wife*. The very appearance of this new Simple treatise points up two tendencies obvious in Mr. Hughes' recent published writing—the forsaking, at least temporarily, of poetry for prose as a literary medium and the keeping of Simple, a character by which his literary reputation as a writer of belles lettres has been greatly enhanced during the past decade.

Like the previous Hughes chronicles concerned with Simple, *The Best of Simple* is written against the background of a culture that admits of so-called second-class citizens who object, audibly and otherwise, to the role they are called upon to play in American life—that of looking *up* to certain people rather than *across* at them all. In point of proof, Hughes cites the selection "Bop" which, as he affirms, makes little sense to folk who have not known suffering, but to black people, conditioned by the way of life as led in ghettoes, it is reminiscent of the sound of a police club against a black head. Likewise is social distance implied in "Simple Prays a Prayer": "Lord, take the blood off my hands," he insists, "and off my brothers' hands and make us shake hands clean and not be afraid."

Not nearly all the selections included in Hughes' new volume are serious in character: far from it. "Empty Room," for example, discloses a situation in a Harlem rooming house in which a solitary, little-known roomer died during the night, but since the rent money had to maintain a steady flow, daybreak found a sign in the window which read: ROOM FOR RENT. And humor of situation attaches to "Feet Live Their Own Lives," as in this piece Simple enumerates the spots to which his feet have carried him.

Many things to many people, Simple is no better than he should be. Character imperfections abound: he is separated from his wife, but cannot afford the cost of divorce; he plays the dozens with his friends despite his impatience with them when the situation happens in reverse; he resorts to occasional clandestine association with Zarita, an "uncombed woman," who calls at his room; and he is resigned to the four walls of a rented room. With too many women on his hands, clocks to punch and landladies to dodge, Simple relaxes at parties and wanders irregularly from woman to woman as from bar to bar. Even with the conviction that the life he is leading points inevitably to his undoing, Simple has lost the will to do anything about it. He shares the feeling of a fellow Harlemite who toasts a pretty girl sitting on a Harlem stool:

Here's to the night;
It's a delight;

With you at my right,
May it never be
Good night.

But Simple as a creation of art is another story. As such, he invites comparison with Appleseed Johnny or with Uncle Remus. The letters fans address directly to him rather than to his creator attest to his flesh and blood character. Many critics insist that Mr. Hughes could scarcely have done better in a new book than to bring Simple back to the printed page, for as a sort of Everyman for the Negro people, he is perhaps the best-known fictional character in contemporary literature, not only in America, but in Europe, Asia, Africa, and in the West Indies. As a matter of fact, the illustrations in *The Best of Simple* appeared first in the German edition of *Simple Speaks His Mind*.

The other characters in this new volume, even such prominent ones as Joyce, Zarita, and Cousin Minnie, suffer by comparison with Simple: They pass simply as sharply-etched character sketches. Their appearance is merely a segment of the preparation of the stage and of the atmosphere for the masquerade of Simple.

The Best of Simple does more than bring Simple into sharp focus. It discloses Langston Hughes' adeptness in the handling of humor both of characterization and of situation and his mastery of the simple narrative as a literary medium. Stylistic niceties are multiplied and from cover to cover one finds a generous sprinkling of wit and repartee. Likewise are spontaneity, sensitiveness and charm exhibited as hallmarks of Mr. Hughes' literary style.

John Henrik Clarke
"Book Reviews"
Freedomways, 2 (Winter 1962), 101–2

The character Jesse B. Semple, born quite by accident according to its creator, Langston Hughes, is now a permanent and very important part of Afro-American literature. Simple is an urban folk hero and philosopher whose appearance in our literature is long overdue. The author has stated that much of the material for the books on Simple is derived from actual conversations overheard in bars and on the corner of the largest urban Negro community in the world, reflecting not the Harlem of the intellectual and professional, but that of the ordinary "man in the street," the basic Harlemite who may not always know why, but who often laughs to keep from crying.

Simple is a later day Aesop whose fables are as entertaining as they are meaningful and true. He is a man, like most men, in revolt against the world around him and those circumstances that are forever blocking the paths of ambition. In his own earthy approach to the American race problems he says more in a few sentences than some Ph.D. "authorities" have said in a small mountain of thick books. In the following quote, the problem is put in capsule:

"Now, the way I understand it," said Simple one Monday evening when the bar was nearly empty and the juke box silent, "it's been written down a long time ago that men are borned equal and everybody is entitled to life and liberty while pursuing happiness. It's in the Constitution, also Declaration of Independence, so I do not see why it has to be resolved all over again."

In this brief statement, Jesse B. Semple has told us what the race and the problem of democracy in America is all about—a broken promise—a resolution that has been ignored.

All of the pieces in this collection are worth reading again. "Banquet in Honor," taken from the first book of the adventures of Simple, "Simple Speaks His Mind," is obviously about the shameful neglect of W. E. B. Du Bois by a black bourgeoisie class who only remember him when they wish to exploit his name and reputation to raise funds.

The book, through Simple, has many other things to say, and this talkative bar-hopper is now a major figure in American literature. With warmth, good humor and good sense, he has looked beyond the problems of colored folks—and just plain folks—at the problems of the world. The best thing that can be said about the character of Jesse B. Simple is that he will probably outlive the circumstances of his creation.

Luella Hawkins
"Book Reviews"
Negro Educational Review, 13 (January 1962), 51–2

Jesse B. Semple, often called Simple by his friends, is a transplanted Virginian who has lived in Harlem most of his thirty-odd years. He came seeking freedom. His cousins by blood and by accident come, too, but later. First was Franklin D. Roosevelt Brown and then Minnie. Minnie is a refugee from Jim Crow Virginia. She came to Harlem, U.S.A. because *Jet,* the *Defender,* et cetera, painted such a pretty picture of the life of the Negro in the North. Simple lends her five dollars to get started and he figures that if he never gets it back, he has made his contribution to freedom.

Relatives take up only a small portion of Simple's time. His chief concern is women—from Virginia to Joyce, from his wife Isabel to Zarita. Virginia is where he was born. Born in a state named after a woman, from that day on, women never allowed him any peace. Simple loved both women and beer, and occasionally to celebrate or help forget, he would take something a little stronger.

After reading about half of the seventy-odd incidents in the life of Jesse B. Semple, I found myself getting a little bored with his race-problems and his women. But his story is a compelling one. I couldn't put the book down for long. I wanted to know if Simple would get together his third of the divorce money so that Isabel and her boy friend—who had together paid the other two thirds—could get married and he could take unto himself as wife Joyce. Joyce is a refined girl who was so cultured she knew people who lived so well that they could keep a whole house for themselves and not have roomers. Then I wondered, too, what would become of Zarita, the playgirl, who added spice to the tales that Simple told. Tales that were narrated while he was hanging over the bar with his friend—his pal—who almost always had to pay for the beers downed.

Jesse B. Semple is a man who doesn't waste the night by going to bed early because as he says, "I sleep quick." He thinks that jazz, jive, and jam would be better for race relations than all this high-flown gab, gaff, and gas the orators put out. He also surmises that the sooner you find out what train to take to get to where you are going in this world, the better.

The best white person he can think of is Mrs. Eleanor Roosevelt. Most of the rest are always telling him how wonderful the progress is that's been made among his people. "And they say, 'Look at Dr. Bunche!' All I say is, 'Look at Me.'"

This seems to be the right season for the reissue of a book of humorous stories about Negro life. Most of us have accepted the return to the entertainment world of the Negro comic who dares take Negro-white relations as his subject. So look at Jesse B. Semple. You will find him a colorful, entertaining, home-spun philosopher, who can always find some reason to bring up that race problem.

A.A.A.
"*Best of Simple* Proves Most Entertaining"
New Bedford [Mass.] *Sunday Standard Times,* 18 February 1962, p. 30

A pleasant reading book, its setting the warm-hearted and colorful Harlem, is about Jesse B. Semple, whose nickname is "Simple." It is a collection of related stories, selected as the author's favorites from his three previous books, *Simple Speaks His Mind, Simple Takes a Wife* and *Simple Stakes a Claim.*

Simple is a talkative character of feeling and laughter who can see problems around him, problems of the white folks, the colored folks and just plain folks, like himself. Its humor here and there, which gently rocks your armchair, makes the book inviting and friendly—nice to relax with.

Ann Stull
"Book Reviews"
Community, 21 (March 1962), 15

The Best of Simple is just that—the best of the stories about Jesse B. Semple, the character created by Langston Hughes in his column in the Chicago *Defender,* later appearing in the books *Simple Speaks His Mind, Simple Takes a Wife,* and *Simple Stakes a Claim.*

If you haven't yet met Jesse B. Semple of Harlem, you have missed one of the warmest human beings in modern literature.

In this volume Simple, as he is called, talks steadily to his bar friend (the author) through more than 50 stories. We hear about his landlady, his ex-wife, his girl friends, his cousins, plus an assortment of other Harlem residents. Simple also gives his views on army segregation, life in the country, feet, income taxes, Bop, the South, and race. He is not just a barstool philosopher, however; he is very much a part of all that goes on in Harlem and the warmth of his feeling for the people in his life is one of his most endearing characteristics.

On racial issues he is irritated with the irritation of a normal human being anywhere at unfairness. Often he is just plain mad at the things Negroes have to put up with, but he has escaped the twin poisons of bitterness and unhealthy resignation. He is able to see the real core of the problem: "To be shot down," he says, "is bad for the body, but to be Jim Crowed is worse for the spirit." Simple's spirit has survived, however, whole and human.

Yet Simple is a character who has had little formal education, he does manual labor, his speech is sprinkled with errors in grammar—in a word, he combines stereotypes which most Negroes reject. Why, then, isn't the character of Simple offensive to Negroes? The fact that the *Defender,* a Negro paper, carries the column regularly is evidence he is not.

I think there are several reasons. For one thing Simple does not speak the heavy dialect which is characteristic of few Negroes today—if it ever was. On the contrary his speech mannerisms are lifted from life; they can be heard in 1962. But more important is the dignity of Simple himself and the obvious affection with which the writer created him. The author (and consequently the reader too) does not look down on Simple. Rather, the writer and the reader are in the position of friendly confidants.

In all this discussion of character, I have neglected the principal reason you will probably have for liking the book—its humor. In a way, Langston Hughes is the Negro Thurber or, to steal a line from Dick Gregory, Thurber is the white Langston Hughes. The humor is the kind which arises out of real-life situations, sometimes bittersweet, usually just hilarious. . . .

Perhaps it would have been best to fill this review with quotes, but it is difficult to give the precise flavor of the book by excerpts—or by just talking about it. I only hope you will read it, and soon; I would like to have been the means of your meeting a thoroughly likeable human being, Jesse B. Semple.

Irvin Zyskind
"Simple's Best Is Folktype Wry Humor"
Columbus Daily Enquirer, 19 March 1962, pp. 8, 16

Characters in fiction are the creations of authors' imaginations. Sometimes they are the results of careful study. Sometimes they emerge full-blown from an incident that impressed the author. The latter was the origination of Jesse B. Semple, alias Simple, an engaging young Harlem Negro.

His creation was the result of a tag line in the conversation of several people in a Harlem beer parlor. They were discussing the war work of one who made cranks, and when pressed as to what kind of cranks, he replied testily: "Aw woman, you know white folks don't tell colored folks what cranks crank." So was Simple born.

The Best of Simple by Langston Hughes is a collection of many stories involving Simple, the friend through whom the stories are told, the three women in his life, his wife, his girl friend and his cousin. And the Harlem he inhabits.

The stories are short individually, each containing an incident complete in itself, but all woven into a continuous, humorous and most enjoyable whole. This book *The Best of Simple* consists of stories taken from three previous Simple books by Langston Hughes. . . .

Langston Hughes has done a terrific job in bringing out a book with a sympathetic Negro character, thoroughly human (as are all the other Negro characters of which the book is composed), thoroughly American and thoroughly Negro, yet with no subservience nor falseness to detract from the richness and wholesomeness of character.

The Best of Simple is for people who like humor that is both wry and double-edged. It is well written and of the type of which "Folk Literature" emerges. For the best enjoyment, however, it should not be read all at one sitting, rather savored a little at a time over a long period.

Rev. Joseph G. McGroarty "Books in the Field: Uptown O'Henry [*sic*]," *Stray Notes from the Shrine of the Little Flower,* April 1962, pp. 68–9

When he created Simple, Langston Hughes must have known he had a good thing. And hasn't he made the most of it? . . .

Oh, we do like him. We cannot help but agree with the publisher's understandably partial claim, printed in the book's jacket blurb: "Of all the fictional characters of contemporary Negro literature, Simple is probably the most widely admired and beloved."

The author tells us that he met his "ace-boy" in a Harlem bar. It was during World War II, when Simple was employed in a New York defense plant. They became fast friends and saw each other regularly after that, usually over a cool, relaxing brew or two. It was on the occasions of these casual encounters that Simple chose to open his weary soul to his "best bar-buddy." They talk, that is Simple talks and Hughes does most of the listening, a real straight man for his star. What Simple talks about are his problems. He has a lot of them, and it is this heavy plethora which conveniently serves up to Hughes his handily parlayed copy.

Jesse B. Semple's biggest worry is how to stay alive until he dies. Another is to keep women and white folk from getting him down. It takes very little to get him started on either of these subjects, or on any of their infinite ramifications. He loves to talk about them, and Langston Hughes, remember, is that best of conversationalists, a good listener. Simple takes a dim view of white people's manners. He speculates on the likelihood of there having been no first fall from grace if Adam and Eve had only been colored. When his attentive beer-drinking companion chides him for his race-consciousness and his general antipathy toward whites, Simple replies with eclectic charity, "Mrs. Roosevelt is different."

Langston Hughes has hit upon an effective device in providing himself with so winsome a spokesman. Not all the satire on race relations is bitter. Much of it is seasoned with subtle good humor, not infrequently at the expense of his own people. There is the Negro shopper, for instance, who irked Simple by her insistence that the watermelon she had just purchased be completely wrapped before she would take it from the supermarket.

For Simple there is just no place on earth like good old "Harlem, U.S.A." Before coming to the Lenox Avenue area of the Big City, he lived in Baltimore with his first wife Isabel. Jim Crow and an unhappy marriage both contrived to make life in that "border city" unbearable, worse even than being in the deep South. Like so many others of his race he sought and found his refuge in Harlem's teeming ghetto, where despite the painful vicissitudes of segregated housing and discriminatory employment, he managed to take things in good stride. From him we learn about his friends, and get to know them almost as well as Simple does. Through it all, he demonstrates the enviable capacity of talking his troubles away, whether they are minor ones like his landlady's poodle, or big ones like his broken marriage.

Langston Hughes is a master at composing lively dialogue. Even when Simple soliloquizes at length, his unexpectedly profound commentaries on the passing scene are smooth and fast-paced, laced with gentle irony and subdued humor. The stories are short, rarely running beyond five or six pages. Almost every one of them carries a good climactic punch. On finishing a chapter, this reviewer found it no easy thing not to begin the next, even though it was for some of them the third time around. Other readers, no doubt, will have the same happy experience.

Harlemite Jesse B. Semple is bound to win for his creator a merited perpetuity in more than the circumscribed field of Negro folklore. For Simple in his way has done for Harlem what O. Henry once did for other sections of New York City. Hughes deserves the mileage he is getting out of his moderately drinking, talkative extrovert. That is more than can be said in favor of many of his other effusions, so often offensive and questionable.

Checklist of Additional Reviews

[J.] Saunders Redding, "Book Review: Hughes Scores Again," *Afro-American Magazine,* 28 November 1961, p. 2.

"Books in Brief: Collections," *New York Herald Tribune Books,* 3 December 1961, p. 34.

ASK YOUR MAMA: 12 MOODS FOR JAZZ

"Ask Your Mama"
Virginia Kirkus Bulletin,
29 (15 August 1961),
767

Allen Thornton
"The Loss of Beauty"
Dallas Times-Herald,
22 October 1961, p. E9

As a Negro poet of the Twenties, Langston Hughes coupled touching observations of his people with a Harlem low life idiom. In the Sixties, he's updated all their struggles, mixing them with the coffee house patter of the Beats or the more hip dialectic of the Village *boite*. The transformation, unfortunately, is not too successful. *Ask Your Mama* is a set of twelve moods for jazz, a kind of free verse newsreel, using the "hesitation Blues" as leitmotif, around which any number of improvisations can be woven. Most of the pieces are delivered in that declamatory brash and bouncy manner late of the San Francisco scene and now having such a vogue in the East. The rhythm is telegraphic, the phrasing fine for slogans and the images go flying all over the place. There is a sardonic, semi-revolutionary tone employed, covering everything from Southern injustice and "white mammies" to a virtual catalogue of big names, e.g. Faubus, Eastland, Martin Luther King, Belafonte, Ghana, the Congo, Leontyne, Nkrumah, NAACP, Lumumba et al. As a sensitive study of prejudice, this is out; as a rollicking, sometimes riotous indictment, this is quite fashionably in. It should be felicitous when recited at night clubs and will undoubtedly gather partisans, but lovers of real poetry won't be among them.

. . . Langston Hughes presents spontaneous reflections of the world's irremediable condition through the images of Negro dignitaries. Jazz musicians represent the undercurrent that Hughes constantly strives to raise to priestdom. Mention is made of everyone from whom notice has ever been given. This in no way gives cause for this book to be called poetic, as the jacket states.

The phrase "Ask Your Mama" is derogatory. Hughes can't discount this; my environment is his. Some readers will probably shake their heads after passing through this so-called book of poetry. This will be no intellectual fault. Hughes has studded this effort in colloquialism in a way which will cause writers of greater talent to ask, "What does it take to get one's manuscript published?"

Hughes is not a young man any more. Fifty-odd years should produce fruits of beauty. Hughes, as an artist, contradicts this. He is no longer the man who authored *I Wonder as I Wander* or *The Big Sea*. Hughes is now the man being harmed by his intellectually impotent adversary.

C.M.W.
"Book Briefs: Non-fiction"
Los Angeles Times Calendar, 22 October 1961, p. 19

Ask Your Mama by Langston Hughes is a collection of topical poems subtitled "12 Moods for Jazz." Hughes writes of the new Negro that is emerging in the United States, Africa and Latin America, and of the social, political and economic problems he lives with. Hughes remains the one poet who has been able to capture the rhythms, melodies and spirit of jazz. This is a *swinging* performance with moments of high comedy, anger, irony, sorrow and puzzlement.

Paul Engle
"Critic Approvingly Views Seferis, Ciardi, and Hughes"
Chicago Tribune Magazine of Books, 29 October 1961, p. 15

[. . .]

Langston Hughes has written these poems essentially for reading to music. They must be wholly alive and diverting that way. On the page, they are less so, but still have wit and shame and the thrust of life right now. They are full of topical references, some of them already out-of-date in a rapid world. The book is handsomely done in jazzy design and color.

Dudley Fitts
"A Trio of Singers in Varied Keys"
New York Times Book Review, 29 October 1961, p. 16

[. . .]

Langston Hughes' twelve jazz pieces cannot be evaluated by any canon dealing with literary right or wrong. They are non-literary—oral, vocal, compositions to be spoken, or shouted, to the accompaniment of drum and flute and bass. For that matter, they speak from the page, the verses being set in capitals throughout; and there is a running gloss of dynamic signs and indications for the proper instrument to use at the moment. (One of these signs, used repeatedly, is "TACIT," which I find as obscure as Mr. Ciardi's "dust like darks howling," unless indeed it stands for the orchestral indication *tacet*.)

In this respect, *Ask Your Mama* goes back to Vachel Lindsay and his "Congo"; and I suppose it is fair to say that this is stunt poetry; a nightclub turn. The fury of indignation and the wild comedy, however, are very far from Lindsay. The voice is comparable to that of Nicolas Guillen, the Cuban poet, or of the Puerto Rican Luis Pales Matos—comparable, not imitative; insistent and strong in what is clearly a parallel development.

Rudi Blesh
"Jazz Is a Marching Jubilee"
New York Herald Tribune Book Week, 26 November 1961, p. 4

Jazz and the blues have been with us all the years of this century; Langston Hughes not quite that long—"jazz poetry" began in 1926 with his well-remembered volume, *The Weary Blues*. Now, with *Ask Your Mama*, it begins to appear that perhaps we have as little understood the poet as the music. For, though jazz is "good time" music, within it has always been something else, something dark yet shining, harsh yet gentle, bitter yet jubilant—a Freedom Song sung in our midst unrecognized all these years. Just so, opening the covers of this gaily-designed book is to find poetry whose jazz rhythms hide the same fire and steel.

Langston Hughes is no mere observer of Africa's stormy, shuddering rise and the awakening of dark-skinned peoples all over the world. They are his people; he sings their marching Jubilees. But Langston Hughes is also an American: he sings to all of us, of the freedom that must go to all before it can be freedom for any.

"Go ask your Mama" is the retort—half-derisive, half-angry—to the smug, the stupid, the bigoted, the selfish, the cruel, and the blind among us, all those to whom these truths that America was built upon are, even today, not yet self-evident.

With this great theme, a talented poet finds a universal voice. Like Satchmo's golden trumpet and Yardbird's blues-haunted alto, the poetry of Langston Hughes sings for—and to—all of us.

[J.] Saunders Redding
"Book Review: Hughes Scores Again"
Afro-American Magazine, 28 November 1961, p. 2

When *The Langston Hughes Reader* was published in 1958, I was surprised and worried.

As a rule, it is only near the end, when they feel their talent going or gone and their passion and their power spent, that writers collect and publish what they consider to be their representative best work.

I wondered about Langston Hughes.

I thought he thought he was through, and the work he did for the next three years seemed to indicate that he was.

He made a play—the delightful and hilarious "Simply Heavenly"—out of his "Simple" stories, but it was after all a pastiche.

He did a lot of lecturing, always, of course, with that naive and appealing air that no one else can match and that he himself does not know he exudes.

He anthologized.

And he wrote a not very good novel called *Tambourines to Glory*. In short, Langston Hughes seemed to be like one who has given up and gone into semi-retirement to find what contentment he can in hobbies. He seemed to think that he was through.

Ask Your Mama proves that he was far from through.

These "twelve moods for jazz" go back to the tradition that Hughes himself created with *The Weary Blues* more than—Shall I say? for he scarcely seems that old—thirty years ago.

There is the same passion and the same power.

It is more sophisticated now and—oddly—less confined: the power, I mean—and the passion, transmuted to the present temper and expressed in the strange, daring rhythms of the current time, is more varied.

Twelve moods—and so there are, but modulations of a simple mood that one cannot describe as serene.

I do not mean to say that irony and satire, for instance, are new to Hughes or, further, that he discovered eloquence just yesterday (else he would never have been a poet in the first place).

But sarcasm, the sharp-tongued child of soft-voiced irony and satire, is new; and the range of subtle nuances is new. From (as an example)

"In the quarter of the Negroes

Answer questions answer
And answers with a question

And the Talmud is corrected
By a student in a fez . . ."

to

"Through the jungle of white danger
To the haven of white quakers
Whose haymow was a manger
   manger
Where the Christ Child once had lain
. . ."

is a thousand miles.

You do not need to read *Ask Your Mama* to the accompaniment of jazz music as the marginal notes suggest. I didn't.

The pieces make their own music. And it is not always jazz. It is hymns and marches and way-out swing.

There is the sound of melodious soft oboes, as well as of drums and trumpets and castanets.

Ask Your Mama is Hughes vintage 1961.

Clark Collin
"New Books Appraised"
Library Journal, 86 (1 December 1961), 4190–1

Mr. Hughes has written 12 short, related poems in anger at the Negro condition. His provocation is unarguable. But the product is as thin and topical as much of the beat material it resembles, a patchwork of today's headlines, lists of Negro African politicians, Freedom Riders, American jazz musicians and entertainers, and snatches of song lyrics. The best sections concern daily life in Southern shacks and Northern slums; they have a rhythmic drive and intensity well fitting them to be read aloud in front of jazz bands. Concluding notes, labeled "for the poetically unhep," are pretty useless. There are also, running down the margin, instructions for imaginary jazz accompaniment behind the poetic themes: this trick scarcely came off in Vachel Lindsay's day. For large poetry collections only.

Alma Parks
"Ask Your Mama"
Michigan Chronicle, section 2, 16 December 1961, p. 4

I have read *Ask Your Mama* by Langston Hughes. The poems have stayed with me. They've amused me and made me think. The melody in them runs through my mind.

Ask Your Mama is a book for everyone.

The intellectual, the hipster and "just folks." In 12 poems Hughes covers everything from our beginnings in Africa, to Pearlie Mae to Mammy Faubus.

Hughes covers his subject in the jazz medium. As you read you hear and feel the rhythm in the lines.

On the right side of each page he has instructions for musical accompaniment, from German lieder to flute to bongos.

Every tempo is there, and shot through the whole book is Langston Hughes' special Negritudeness: laughter.

His ability to settle you down to searching your mind for the Negro current topics of world magnitude and slyly slipping in a "haw haw haw" slant on an explosive situation, such as Little Rock, is unmatched.

This is the latest book from a man of many talents. Born in Joplin, Missouri, in 1902, he has devoted his life to writing and lecturing.

His poetry, short stories, autobiography, song lyrics, plays and books for young people have been widely read by Americans.

Arna Bontemps once called him "the original jazz poet" because so much of his verse reflects the tempo and mood of jazz and the life in which this music grew.

The jacket of the book is very attractive, and the paper, special type, and arrangement of the poems on the pages are all artistically done to further increase the reader's enjoyment.

Although *Ask Your Mama* will delight you, it has a serious theme too.

Many of the half-thoughts and elusive facts that explain who we are and our position in today's restless and changing society are rhythmically clarified in these 12 poems.

These are poems to read, silently and out loud, to share, and to which we should listen.

Roy Z. Kemp
"Poetry Volumes"
Greensboro News, 24 December 1961, p. D3

Langston Hughes, who has been termed "the original jazz poet," who arose to fame in the late 1920's, has dedicated his latest poetry volume to Louis Armstrong. The book is subtitled "12 Moods for Jazz" and the dedication is most appropriate.

Hughes began his career by reading his poetry to jazz, and he has appeared from coast to coast with some of America's best-known jazz combinations. Thus he appears to be the father of today's "poetry-to-jazz" movement. However, Vachel Lindsay got the jump on him with his famous "General Booth Enters Heaven" poem.

In this new volume, Hughes has updated all his observations of his race and their struggles for existence, mixing them with today's coffee-house patter and the jive of the Beats. He delivers his messages in a brash and bouncy manner, with a harsh rhythm and an irregular beat.

He writes about Harlem, the South, great Negroes, race prejudice, and other allied topics. As the blurb of the book states, this is a volume of the New Negro. The work consists almost in its entirety of the subject of headlines in today's newspapers: the segregation question. Nothing new, actually, is included, except, perhaps, his references to "white mammies."

As a documentary on today's racial problems, the book cannot in any sense be considered as a serious work. It is not good propaganda and is not an indictment. It is merely curiously interesting and enjoyable because of its novelty of presentation.

The lover of really literate work will

shun this volume entirely, but the less discriminating reader who enjoys a bounce to his poetry, will find this new book diverting entertainment. The blurb states that the work is written in language bursting with sound and rhythm—angry, blue, fiercely ironic, funny, even haunting. This is very true. But the poems are not ones which demand to be read. They are sardonic; some are even semi-revolutionary in tone. The book is enjoyable mostly because of its rollicking and rhythmic manner.

The format is original, but an awkward size for handling. The cover is composed of a distinctive modernistic painting, and the paper is salmon-colored, with the poems printed in both blue and brown printing. The publisher, apparently, has tried to issue an attention-getting volume to compensate for the lack of literary merit in the contents.

Rudd Fleming
"Passing of a Year Is Indeed 'A Time for Poetry'"
Washington Post, 31 December 1961, p. E6

[. . .]

The current American scene cannot be described without recognizing the importance of poems written not for private reading but for performance with or without music. Printed on pumpkin-colored paper, Langston Hughes' *Ask Your Mama,* although almost entirely for the ear, makes good reading too, especially with the marginal directions for the music, like: "Bop blues into very modern jazz burning the air eerie."

John Henrik Clarke
"Book Reviews"
Freedomways, 2 (Winter 1962), 102–3

"Playing the dozens" is a part of Afro-American folklore and folkways. It is part of the black man's private humor that is sometimes used to drive its victim to anger and rage. Like poison, it has good and bad uses, and if you do not understand the game, you should not play it. The subtitle of the book is "Twelve Moods for Jazz"— and this is what the book is really about. The format of playing the dozens is incidental to the contents of the book.

Like so many of Langston Hughes' books that are classified as humor, this is a book of social protest not so thinly disguised. No denying the humor is apparent throughout most of the book. The presence of humor accentuates the social protest, making it more effective and less offensive.

Langston Hughes has used the pattern of jazz, poetry and the dozens to bring another dimension to the Afro-Americans' long and agonizing struggle to have his art and the dignity of his personality accepted in a nation that proclaimed, so long ago, that all men were created equal. . . .

Unlike the small group of Afro-American writers who spend so much of their time running from other members of their race, and cursing God for making them black, Langston Hughes has never "left home." For more than a quarter of a century, this steady and prolific pen has poured forth, with what seems to be an untiring consistency. Being our most versatile writer, he has the largest Afro-American reading audience, and for many years he has also been universally read and appreciated. With justification he has been called "the poet-laureate of his people."

The publication of this book, thirty-four years after he made his debut with his first volume of poems, *The Weary Blues,* represents for him the reaching of a second generation of readers. If the second generation of Langston Hughes' readers want to know what the first generation of readers thought of his writing, the best answer is in the title of the present book—ASK YOUR MAMA.

Milton R. Bass
"A Gentle Poet Who Shakes Your Conscience"
Berkshire Eagle, 13 January 1962, p. 14

In the quarter of the Negroes, in the midst of New York's Harlem, lives a gentle poet whose words are fierce enough to shake your conscience. He is not the type of poet who sits in his little tower and ponders on life's imponderables, but one who gets his inspiration from people, from their blood, from their sweat and from their tears. But even more important, he also gets it from their laughter.

I have known and admired Langston Hughes for several years now, and his latest work, *Ask Your Mama,* increases the admiration twelvefold.

Mr. Hughes, who has been a familiar figure at the Music Inn jazz roundtables in Lenox and one of whose opera librettos was performed at Tanglewood last season, has published 30 books. They take in the fields of poetry, short stories, autobiography, song lyrics, plays, novels and stories for young people. He has edited as many books as he has written, and young Negro writers throughout the world have been encouraged by him to increase the stature of their national literature.

As I said, Mr. Hughes is a gentle man, but there is a fire in him that cries out against intolerance, injustice and inhumanity. There is warmth and humor in everything he does, but underneath it all is a sharp satiric slant that punctures phoniness in both people and things. And it's amazing how many "things" he sees that need puncturing.

Langston Hughes has been reading his poetry to jazz backgrounds for 20 years now, sensing the potential long before the so-called beatniks started pulling this "daring" feat a couple of seasons ago. Hughes has a basic beat that permeates all his writing, and the poetry cries out to be read aloud, your mind's ear furnishing all the instruments needed.

Ask Your Mama is about the world today, especially the Negro world that is bursting its seams for the first time in history. It's about a people who are forming nations in Africa and desegregating lunch counters in this country and fighting for their rightful places in the strata of society. There are both victories and defeats, but the battle has reached the point where the defeats are only temporary setbacks on the road to victory.

Mr. Hughes muses about the Negro sections of the South "where doors have no resistance to violence, danger always whispers harshly." The houses are either by the river or the railroad tracks, although nobody ever has the money or opportunity to go anywhere. Nevertheless, it always seems that somebody had gone away and has just come home, bringing with him a taste of the foreign and even the exotic. This adds a strange taste to the national staple—collard greens.

Mr. Hughes muses about Leontyne Price, the great Negro soprano who sings German lieder like an angel, and who was helped in her career by a white, Southern sponsoress. Despite her fame and acclaim, Leontyne still enters by the back door when she visits the woman who did so much for her. And neither thinks it strange.

Mr. Hughes muses about oppression, and he muses about escape from oppression. . . .

Mr. Hughes muses about the Negro who gets enough money to move to the suburbs. . . .

Langston Hughes, like every other poet, isn't quite sure where you go to get the answers. In Joyce's *Finnegans Wake,* the secret is contained in a chicken on a dump heap. The poet here thinks the answers were lost "because Grandma lost her apron with all the answers in her pocket (perhaps consumed by fire). . . ."

However, that's where the secrets are, and in the segment titled "Cultural Exchange" the poet comments: "And they asked me right at Christmas / If my blackness would rub off? I said 'Ask your Mama.'"

Aside from the poetry, this is one of the most beautifully produced books of the past year. Should you own a copy? Ask your mama.

Carl Bloice
"New Poetry from Langston Hughes: 'Overcome the Hesitation Blues'"
People's World [San Francisco], 17 February 1962, p. 7

The title of Langston Hughes' newest collection of poems has a family-like ring. To the uninitiated, it would probably bring to mind a nice mother-child relationship. Such would cause one to miss the whole point of what is being offered.

In the language of the street any reference to "your mama" is about the most evil, defiant comment one could make. Make no mistake; it's not like "your mother wears combat boots"; it's a lot worse.

It takes a good deal of courage or desperation to tell any one to go "Ask Your Mama" (and mean it). So when a man with a soul picks up his saxophone and blows, he can tell you how desperate he is with folks stepping all over him by blowing a long chorus of "your mama."

But on the other hand he can tell how free he is of caring what you're thinking by blowing a few "funky" bars of "your mama."

Along the margins of each of his poems Hughes has written directions for the musicians who play as the poem is being read aloud (Hughes invented poetry with jazz). But you need nothing more than imagination to read the direction and know what's happening on the musical side.

Leading up the first defiant cry the poet

says: "In the shadows of the Negroes / Nkrumah / In the shadow of the Negroes / Nasser Nasser / In the shadow of the Negroes / Zik Azikiwe / Cuba Castro Guinea Touré." While this is going on: "Delicate lieder on piano continues between verses to merge softly in the melody of the 'Hesitation Blues,' asking its haunting question, 'How long must I wait? Can I get it now—or must I hesitate?'"

[. . .]

With this exceedingly imaginative and engrossing format, Hughes has made a valuable contribution to modern American poetry. His efforts are contemporary, perhaps avant garde without being reckless. It all fits. It all makes sense. There is none of the startling, brilliantly conceived but unnecessary wordiness of some of the North Beach set.

Exactly what it is that Hughes is trying to get across is hard to say. But running through each of the twelve poems is a recurring thought. It's like a warning from one who knows that if you're Negro, you're Negro and there's no way around it. Wherever you go, whatever you do there will be people who will consider you an object of hate or a curio. They will ask at the PTA: "Is it true that Negroes . . . ?"

No matter how much money you acquire, no matter how far you move into the suburbs (". . . unobtrusive / Book of the Month in cases") you won't get away from it. They'll ask you out on your patio: "Where did you get your money?" And what's more if you get militant they'll call you a red. They'll ask you: "How about that NAACP / and the radicals in that Southern Conference? / Ain't you got no information / On Dr. Robert Weaver?"

Hughes' answer to the problem: Overcome the "Hesitation Blues": "When they ask you if you knew me, / Don't take the Fifth Amendment: Tell 'em like it is: Take your cue from Nkrumah, Nasser, Zik Azikiwe, Kenyatta, Touré: Tell 'em: 'Ask Your Mama.'"

SWING!

Thomas McGrath
"Poems Just for Jazz"
National Guardian,
19 February 1962, p. 9

. . . In the case of most of us who read with jazz, neither the poems nor the music had been written with the idea of putting the two together. The jazz was usually whatever happened to be going with a particular band. The poems were generally what we had on hand, suitable, we hoped, to tone and tempo. The results, good and bad, were pretty much accidental. It was to avoid the unwanted accident that Langston Hughes wrote the "twelve moods for jazz" in his new book, *Ask Your Mama*.

One can see jazz in part as improvisation around a theme, and it is this kind of organization which these poems suggest. They have, too, the quality of jazz *tone*, ranging from the blues to a happy defiance and cold anger, and they are by turns sad, joyous, ironic and funny. "In the quarter of the Negroes," the poems begin, and the line is repeated again and again in various contexts. The symbols and images of the work are sometimes as traditional as allusions to Harriet Tubman, sometimes as new as Castro and the Congo; and here it is possible for Damballa and Papa Legba to exist in the same poem with Calvary and the Cross.

The effect is to summon up the richness and range of an "underground" Negro culture in which past and present are united in the contemporary struggles of

the Negro people. Here the different attitudes and strategies of American Negroes
North and South are brought together;
traditional and cool jazz are harmonized;
and here too the liberation fight in the
South is related to the liberation movements around the world. In this work the
culture of Negro Americans has gone a
long step toward internationalizing itself.

This is all one could ask for, it would
seem. But there are reservations. All the
values we have noted are true of the book
as a whole; in individual sections they are
not so apparent. For the most part this
seems to result from a failure to state or
center on a theme solidly enough. Perhaps
some sense of this prompted the inclusion
of "liner notes" on each section at the
back of the book; but, for this reader at
least, the notes don't always clarify. In contemporary jazz, of course, a theme may be
implied rather than stated, and this seems
to be Hughes's method. But the result, for
me anyway, is that passages sometimes un-
ravel where they might, perhaps, have been
tighter knit.

These qualifications need a further
qualification: the poems were meant
for the ear. They are one voice of a jazz en-
semble and would undoubtedly gain drive
and structure in a performance. Hughes
has included marginal notes on the music,
but most of us won't really hear it until it
is recorded. So far as I know, it hasn't been.
What we have here are the poems without
their musical matrix, but it is a book well
worth having—the first substantial body
of verse directly made for jazz.

Nick Aaron Ford "Search for Identity" *Phylon,* 23 (Second Quarter 1962), 128–38

[...]

Ask Your Mama by Langston Hughes
is a group of twelve "poems" set in a pattern of jazz music with directions in the
margins for the musicians. The slender
volume contains ninety-two pages, eight
of which consist of prose interpretations of
the verses. The author describes these
pieces as "moods for jazz." Those who like
blues poetry will no doubt find pleasure in
another exhibition of the Hughes specialty. But those who have not yet accepted
this kind of writing as legitimate poetry
will sigh for the return of such moods as
those represented by "The Negro Speaks
of Rivers," "Let America Be America
Again," and even "Brass Spitoons."

Ulysses Lee "Book Reviews" *CLAJ,* 6 (March 1963), 225–6

Anyone who is still unconvinced that
Langston Hughes occupies a major position in the stream of American literary humorists and experimental poets should
find convincing proofs in *Ask Your Mama.*
This volume is a series of twelve connected
poems intended to be read aloud to musical accompaniment, much of it jazz variations and improvisations on the traditional
"Hesitation Blues" spiked with fragments

of "Shave and a Haircut," German lieder, spirituals, gospels, calypsos, Hebraic chants, "Dixie," and "The Battle Hymn of the Republic." These, in turn, are to be performed by a piano, a flute, bongo drums, guitar, maracas, and a full Dixieland band playing in blues, mambo, bop, and cha-cha rhythms, sometimes alone and sometimes in chorus. Appropriately, the whole is dedicated to Louis Armstrong, "the greatest horn blower of them all," and the volume contains codas to each poem presented as "Liner Notes for the Poetically Unhep." With their irreverent comments on the core of each poem, these are gems in themselves.

The typography of the book provides yet a fourth dimension, for the poems are printed in blue and brown inks on a laid paper the color of faded roses while the binding and dust jacket use a jazzy abstract design in blues, greens, reds, and black. The contrast of desiccated pink and the crisp blue and brown ink comments on the method of the poems: the juxtaposition of the unlikely to produce a syncopated view of the paradoxes of our racial times.

The twelve poems are allusive comments on the present situation, especially as it affects American Negroes. They impudently combine the leading cultural heroes of the day with images of plantation quarters and slum inequities. In some ways, the whole set of poems is an extension of the old insult word-game, the dozens, from which the title comes. As in the dozens, the satirical tone is incisive; the biting humor is always clever and funny even when it borders upon the shocking. Hughes' targets are always the right ones. . . .

But the more significant lines in the poems bring together unexpected images and lists of the currently well-known in the manner of the dadaists and expressionists of the European 1920's. In the opening poem, "Cultural Exchange," an African diplomat is sent by the State Department

> . . . Among the shacks to meet the
>   blacks:
> Leontyne Sammy Harry Poitier
> Lovely Lena Marian Louis Pearlie
>   Mae . . .
> Where the railroad and the river
> Have doors that face each way
> And the entrance to the movie's
> Up an alley up the side.

While delicate lieder on the piano continue, between verses, merging softly with the melody of "'Hesitation Blues,' asking the haunting question 'How long must I wait . . .'" the poem resumes:

> In the pot behind the
> Paper doors what's cooking?
> What's smelling, Leontyne?
> Lieder, lovely lieder
> And a leaf of collard green.
> Lovely lieder Leontyne.

Whether a poem evokes a dream world where Negroes have voted out the Dixiecrats, Martin Luther King is governor of Georgia with Rufus Clement as advisor, and Negro children have white mammies ("Mammy Faubus, Mammy Eastland, Mammy Patterson. / Dear, *dear* darling old white mammies—sometimes even buried with our family! *Dear* old Mammy Faubus!") or whether a poem alludes to the tangle in the Congo, it always conveys the frenetic disorders of our time. The blend of politics, economics, and the entertainment world spread against a jazz background must make fascinating sounds when read aloud as intended: it also makes fascinating sense in any case.

Checklist of Additional Reviews

William Hogan, "Between the Lines: Name-Dropping," *San Francisco Chronicle This World,* 12 November 1961, p. 39.

"Last Minute Gifts: New Books for Music Lovers," *Denver Post Roundup,* 10 December 1961, pp. 11, 14.

Melva G. Chernoff, "Books," *Sioux Falls* [S. Dak.] *Argus-Leader,* 31 December 1961, p. 9A.

Fred S. Holley, "Poetic Views Contrasted," *Norfolk Virginian-Pilot,* 21 October 1962, p. B6.

FIGHT FOR FREEDOM: THE STORY OF THE NAACP

Haynes Johnson
"A History of NAACP by Hughes"
Washington Star, p. E5,
26 August 1962

When Langston Hughes was a boy, the height of his ambition was to have something published in *The Crisis,* the magazine of the National Association for the Advancement of Colored People.

Now, years after achieving that ambition, and after his poems, plays and stories have earned him a high place in American letters, Mr. Hughes has written the history of the NAACP. It is a story that needs to be told, and Mr. Hughes tells it with his usual grace, power, and even humor.

Mr. Hughes calls the list on the organization's roll of honor and salutes the leaders of the past: W. E. B. Du Bois, James Weldon Johnson, Walter White, Joel Spingarn, Mary White Ovington, and others. He describes their achievements in building an organization, which, as Mr. Hughes writes, "has changed the legal and social history of the United States. . . ." Today, the NAACP still is effecting "monumental changes."

By its nature, Mr. Hughes' story is partisan—so much so that no differences of opinion or clashes of strong personalities mar the smooth, united front in the NAACP's march toward equality. This is unfortunate. For despite its great achievements of the past, the NAACP leadership today is under increasing attack from Negroes. The charge is made that the NAACP has failed to keep pace with the militant mood of the present. None of this appears in Mr. Hughes' book. Such an omission almost has the effect of stamping Mr.

Hughes' book as a campaign tract, or official history. This would not be an entirely fair judgment, for Mr. Hughes has made another valuable contribution toward understanding of the "race problem." (As he characteristically notes, "It has often been called the Negro problem. But this perhaps is a misnomer, for if Negroes are a problem to white Americans, whites are even more of a problem to Negroes.")

Some day a definitive history of the NAACP will be written. Until then Langston Hughes fills the gap nicely.

Manning Rubin
"NAACP Story Glosses Over Many Topics"
Charleston Evening Post,
31 August 1962, p. 8B

Some months ago W. W. Law, a Negro postman in Savannah, was discharged by the Postoffice Department, for several offenses, including misconduct and inefficiency.

Law was president of the Georgia NAACP, and the national organization brought pressure in Washington to have him reinstated.

Postmaster General J. Edward Day, in defending his department's action, said "I think it should be made clear that the fact that he (Law) is a leader of the NAACP does not make him immune to normal and ordinary department proceedings."

He also said: "I would not want a person with Law's record of conduct delivering mail to my family's home."

Alas, Mr. Day was called upon to eat his brave words. He bowed to pressure exerted by the NAACP upon the White House. Law, contrary to Mr. Day's assertion, proved himself immune. He was reinstated, and when President Kennedy said Mr. Day might wish to "recast" his criticism of Law, Mr. Day took the hint and did just that.

All this is a matter of record, but you won't find it in the pages of *Fight for Freedom*, a book by Langston Hughes, which purports to be a history of the NAACP. The author, who has long been active in NAACP circles, dismissed the notorious Law case as "an ignominious persecution of a Negro letter carrier."

This treatment of the Law incident gives you an idea of what to expect in reading *Fight for Freedom*.

"Freedom Not Free: The NAACP Story" *Indianapolis Times*, 2 September 1962, p. 17

"Freedom is not free."

This paradox, stated a couple of times in Langston Hughes' *Fight for Freedom*, could well be the book's subtitle.

Hughes, prolific poet, playwright, novelist and humorist, examines the past half-century of achievement by the National Association for the Advancement of Colored People, giving rather bitter emphasis to the increased monetary cost of racial justice in recent years.

He points out how the Deep South, entrenched in racism and diehard segregationist policies, is, in effect, still waging the Civil War. White citizens' organizations seek every legal and many extra-legal means to postpone integration in any context.

The white man seems determined to

make the Negro pay fantastically for each small gain.

Hence the role of the NAACP, which annually disburses nearly $1¼ million in legal fees.

Hence also the segregationist whites' hatred of the NAACP and ferocious attacks upon it as being "subversive."

Early in the book, Hughes says simply, "A slave had no rights his master was duty-bound to respect. Because some people in America still think that a Negro has no rights a white man is duty-bound to respect, there is need for the NAACP."

Thanks largely to that group's devotion (it has had from its inception vigorous and active support by fair-minded whites) some progress has been made from the ghoulish barbarities of pre-War I [*sic*] years.

Hughes cites the 1916 case of Jesse Washington, a 19-year-old Negro mental defective, lynched in Waco, Tex. The NAACP's publication, *The Crisis*, described the lynching as follows: "Washington . . . was dragged through the streets, stabbed, mutilated and finally burned to death in the presence of a crowd of 10,000. . . . After death what was left of his body was dragged through the streets and parts of it sold as souvenirs. His teeth brought $5 apiece and the chain that had bound him 25c a link."

Some other horrors are too strong for quotation here.

Perhaps in answer to some critics of the NAACP, Hughes quotes the Rev. Martin Luther King at the time of the Montgomery bus boycott: "One thing the gradualists don't seem to understand: we are not trying to make people love us when we go to court; we are trying to keep them from killing us."

Though the methods of repression are not commonly so murderously sadistic as they were 40 or 50 years ago, the techniques of economic and social strangulation have become so refined that not only justice-seeking Negroes, but also any venturesome whites who try to offer help may be ruined in business, harassed by telephoned or live threats, even bombed out of house and home.

A sullen, racist resistance by whites aided by an apparent conspiracy on the part of law-enforcement officers renders any attempt of Negroes to extend their voting rights hazardous. "That some portions of this country are still in rebellion against the laws of the United States as they affect the Negro is one of the problems with which the NAACP continues to wrestle."

The problem is at its worst in the Deep South. Hughes comments, "For sheer savagery, Mississippi is considered the worst state in the country. It has had more mob murders in recent years than any other state. It has the lowest percentage of Negro voters in the entire South—less than four per cent of its 45 per cent Negro population."

But Hughes does not overlook the outrages in northern states, particularly in cities like Chicago where "ghettos" confine the Negro and trouble awaits him if he attempts to escape them. The 1951 Cicero, Ill., case of the Harvey Clarks, whose apartment in a previously all-white district was destroyed, its furniture heaped by a white mob on a street bonfire, with evident approval of the police, is only one example.

Less spectacular but also damaging repression occurs in job discrimination where nearly all the choicer jobs are automatically given to whites. The Negro is "last to be hired, first to be fired." And Hughes cites the irony of a depression-caused shift of employment in Southern hotels whereby whites took over the previously Negro bellhop jobs.

Though Hughes doesn't stress the following point, it nevertheless emerges from his book: the work of the NAACP is not merely in behalf of the Negro. It is in behalf of American society at large.

For whatever the racists may argue, the nation, to use a ringing phrase from the past, cannot exist half slave and half free.

Fight for Freedom is a book for everyone.

James G. Leyburn
"Man and Men at Their Best and Worst"
Roanoke Times, 2 September 1962, p. C8

Hughes' book fills the reader with conflicting emotions, chiefly ones of shame and pride—shame that Americans can have compiled a record of such barbarity and injustice toward Negroes, pride that this disgraceful record is being altered by human courage.

The author begins by saying that "the most famous initials in America are NAACP." He is probably correct, as he is when he adds that the National Association for the Advancement of Colored People is "the most talked-about, written-about, and damned" organization in the country. Founded in 1909 by a handful of white and Negro leaders to fight the inhumanities and the rank discrimination practiced against the Negroes, the Association now has 388,000 members, 1494 chapters, and an annual budget well over a million dollars. The successes it has achieved are enormously heartening to anyone who believes in the statements of the Declaration of Independence and the Bill of Rights.

Respectable Americans of both races are likely to forget, and young Americans may not even realize, the abject condition of the Negro in this country a short 60 years ago. In 1901 alone, 105 Negroes were lynched; few Negroes could vote; everywhere they were segregated, discriminated against, paid minimal wages, given only menial jobs, denied justice in the courts. The majority were illiterate or barely able to read and write. Much more shocking than all this is the constant brutality of white mobs, who tortured, burned, and beat Negroes (even children and pregnant women) with a gloating sadism that is almost incredible.

It is infinitely heartening that a small group of undaunted men and women determined to right these wrongs, and that they fought against overwhelming odds to persuade America to begin to live up to its ideals. The fight is by no means over, but it makes daily progress. Hughes is perfectly correct in attributing most of this progress to the leadership of the NAACP. Its legal battles have been phenomenally successful; its lobbying and publicity work have been unflagging; the devotion and bravery of its investigators have been admirable. "Freedom is not free," as Negroes have discovered. It has to be fought for ceaselessly, and the struggle costs money, intelligence, ingenuity, endless faith and persistence.

The story as Hughes tells it is full of incident and fact, with most of the dramatic victories and defeats recounted. The reader feels a sense of personal involvement, since the struggle concerns the good name and the cherished principles of his own country, as it involves his individual confidence in justice and integrity. The author employs humor, sometimes mordant, sometimes actually gay. He makes the personalities of the principal leaders vivid, for he has the perceptiveness of a poet.

Our history books do not tell much of the story of racial relations; yet in the long run this story may prove the most significant one in American history. In a world predominantly colored, and one in which this majority is increasing its political power, it makes a great deal of difference what the world thinks of America. We may be forgiven our shameful record in race relations if we continue our progress. More important than world opinion, however, is what we think of ourselves. The reading of Hughes' book would have a salutary effect upon the conscience and character of every American.

One may note faults in the volume. Granted that his focus must remain upon the NAACP, it is regrettable that Hughes does not even refer to the part played in New Deal legislation or by Truman's courageous acts in securing Negro rights. Roosevelt is mentioned only three times, and then casually. It is implied that the NAACP took the leadership in the sit-ins and Freedom Rides, though this is debatable. The author's desire to pay tribute to those who fought the good fight is understandable, but mere listing of names can be a distraction. Some anecdotes about the running of the New York office of the NAACP seem extraneous. Nor is Hughes always careful about his writing, as when, for example, he speaks of the "height" of the depression.

Such cavils are minor, however. This story of the NAACP needed to be told, and it needs to be widely known. The reader ends the book with a confidence that man's unconquerable mind will eventually bring the triumph of justice and decency.

Fred Zimmerman
"Noble Promulgations No Longer Are Enough"
Kansas City Times, 7 September 1962, p. 32

The hero of three new books is the American Negro. The whites are villains. There is little pleasant reading in these, for these books tell of white men who have lynched thousands of Negroes; who have forbidden Negroes to attend zoos, museums, schools, parks, libraries; who have allowed Negroes to die rather than admit them to "white" hospitals, and who have banded together into hate groups such as White Citizens Councils, White Men, Inc., the Ku Klux Klan, etc.

The most important of the books is "Fight for Freedom," Langston Hughes's story of the National Association for the Advancement of Colored People. The history begins with the founding of the NAACP and tells of the organization's early struggles against military segregation, of the KKK, and of ugly prejudice in the Deep South. Much of the book concerns recent legal battles of the NAACP over school desegregation and the right to vote.

Hughes, a well-known Negro poet and short story writer who grew up in Kansas City, writes movingly of the NAACP and its crusades. Parts of the book are overburdened with biographical data about the group's leaders. But its minor failings are atoned for by the author's fairness, sanity and sincerity.

In his postscript, Hughes writes of the current generation of militant young Negroes, those who have rejected the gradualist philosophy preached by Booker T. Washington.

[. . .]

Era Bell Thompson
"'The Most Damned Group of Respectable Citizens'"
Chicago Tribune, part 4, 9 September 1962, p. 4

[. . .]

Why the NAACP is so feared—and hated—by those who do not believe in racial equality, why it is not whole-heartedly endorsed (less than 2 percent of the Negro population belongs to it) by those who do, are questions answered in this slim volume.

The story of the NAACP is packed with legal and moral victories. Yet, one is struck by a similarity in demands made half a century ago with those of today. In 1905, for instance, Dr. W. E. B. Du Bois said what Rev. Martin Luther King is saying in 1962: "We want manhood suffrage and we want it now." A 1908 New York survey revealed that a race problem existed in the north. The first case of the NAACP's legal committee concerned the 1912 bombing of the newly purchased homes of Negroes in a Kansas City white neighborhood, and two years later an interracial picket line marched in Memphis.

The NAACP began in a period rife with mob violence. Between 1889 and 1913, there were 3,224 lynchings in the United States. Thanks, in part, to the vigorous efforts of the organization, today there are none. Its first great United States Supreme

Court victory came not with public school desegregation in 1954, but 32 years ago, when the court invalidated Oklahoma's "grandfather clause," thus making the descendants of slaves eligible to vote.

Next year will mark the centennial of the Emancipation Proclamation. Any evaluation of Negro progress made during the past 100 years must be an evaluation of the NAACP; the two are inseparable. Written by a man who has received the NAACP's highest honor, the Spingarn medal, *Fight for Freedom* is well told. It is worth reading.

Bernard Averbuch
"Fifty-year History of NAACP Progress"
San Francisco News–Call Bulletin, 22 September 1962, p. 6

[. . .]

It is well, then, that as accomplished a writer as Langston Hughes, well known poet and author of many books, undertook this history. Without a doubt, no single organization has had a greater influence on the social structure of the United States. Such a story is not easy to research.

There is nothing more powerful, in writing history, than to be accurate, objective and interesting. Author Hughes is all three.

H.H.B.
"*Fight for Freedom* by Langston Hughes"
Springfield [Mass.] *Sunday Republican,* 23 September 1962, p. 4D

Fight for Freedom by Langston Hughes, the celebrated poet, playwright, biographer and novelist, is a well-written, interesting history of the National Association for the Advancement of Colored People, which in the last half century has been one of the most important forces in the United States working toward the goal of achieving full civil rights for those Americans who have for so long been unfairly relegated to second-class status simply because their ancestors happened to have been born in Africa instead of some other geographical area.

In this valuable book Mr. Hughes sketches the whole story of Negroes in America, giving an outline of the various movements which preceded the formation of the NAACP, and then proceeding to recount in detail the highly important and increasingly effective work which the NAACP has been doing, right up to the present time. This excellent book, which reflects new credit on its distinguished author, deserves to be widely read, and should be appreciated by all Americans who believe in democracy and fair play.

The story of the National Association for Advancement of Colored People as told by poet Langston Hughes is in part a grateful tribute to the organization (and its official publication, *The Crisis*) for its uplifting influence in the lagging human rights sector of American life and in overall importance a valuable handbook for such diverse insurgents as African nationalists, sit-ins and Freedom Riders, Southern historians and Muslims. It is a battleground report from one who grew up in terms of the objectives of the association, published his first mature poems in *The Crisis*, and in 1960 won the organization's Spingarn Medal (for creative literature).

Significantly and symbolically, the NAACP came into being out of meetings held during the first decade of the century at Niagara Falls and Harper's Ferry, each by strange coincidence the site of awesome beauty and troubled waters. It was the simultaneously begotten brain-child of a group of freedom-loving people of both races who translated their reactions to mob violence and related acts into concerted action. Radcliffe's Mary White Ovington and Harvard's W. E. B. Du Bois and their equally dedicated peers were integrated on a deeper level than color: in moral realism and humane responsibility. Hence Langston Hughes wrestles more easily with his own angel, and with the graceful authority of the natural insight which sent folk hero Jesse B. Simple forth

to charm the world. Here is the background of his many tributaries—the bitter rivers of blood and torture blended with the cool rivers of humor and progress.

The foreword by NAACP president Arthur B. Spingarn, capsule accounts of its key leaders (and accomplishments)—poet James Weldon Johnson, public relations expert Walter White and administrator Roy Wilkins—and a listing of the organization's national officers and Spingarn Medal winners add to this survey some useful sidelights.

Irving Dilliard
"A Poet Asks: How Long Is a While?"
Saturday Review, 45 (29 September 1962), 32–3

[. . .]

Langston Hughes, poet, novelist, and playwright, who tells the story of the NAACP, makes it plenty clear how the Sit-in Kids and the Freedom Riders react when some Washington officials tell them to wait a while. They want to know "what while?"

[. . .]

Langston Hughes knows what he is writing about. He has been through sixty years of it since his birth in Joplin, Mo., in 1902. In Lawrence, Kan., he could not go to the movies. He could not buy an ice cream soda. He could not even swim at the YMCA.

But he would be the first to say that a lot of ground has been gained and largely due to the NAACP. Few organizations have had such distinguished backing at the outset. Jane Addams opened Hull-House to the cause, and other supporters were

John Dewey, John Haynes Holmes, Stephen S. Wise, Lincoln Steffens, Mary E. Woolley, Ray Stannard Baker, Lillian D. Wald, Brand Whitlock, Oswald Garrison Villard.

[. . .]

Next year will be the 100th anniversary of the promulgation of the Emancipation Proclamation. This book, with its reports of the bitter racial persecutions in World Wars I and II; the great work of James Weldon Johnson, who once developed a four-year high school for Negroes in Jacksonville, Fla., by keeping the eighth grade class a ninth year, and then a tenth, and so on; the later contributions of Walter White and Roy Wilkins—this stirring book by Langston Hughes will help make that historic centennial far more meaningful than it otherwise would have been. Somebody ought to put it in every library in the country!

Ivan Gerould Grimshaw
"NAACP Story Well Written"
Fort Wayne News Sentinel, 6 October 1962, p. 4A

This history of the National Association for the Advancement of Colored People has appropriately been written by an outstanding Negro man of letters who throughout the years has been a staunch friend and supporter of the Association.

He has done an excellent piece of writing, but the book is not pleasant reading. Those who assume an air of superiority concerning "American democracy" when speaking to those from other countries may be surprised at the revealed "blots on the American democratic escutcheon."

When the NAACP was organized a half century ago, Negro status stood about where it did at the close of the Civil War. Now, thanks to that organization, the "fight for freedom" appears nearer victory.

Samuel Sass
"The Crusade against Jim Crow"
Berkshire Eagle, 6 October 1962, p. 16

In the fall of 1947, a Freedom Train visited over 300 cities throughout the nation. It carried 100 original historic documents basic to American democracy. Langston Hughes, the Negro writer, wrote a poem about it which he called "Freedom Train." This poem is too long to quote here in its entirety, but the following excerpts are enough to show what he had in mind.

I'm gonna check up on this
    Freedom Train.

Who's the engineer on the
    Freedom Train?
Can a coal black man drive the
    Freedom Train?
Or am I still a porter on the
    Freedom Train?
Is there ballot boxes on the
    Freedom Train?
Do colored folks vote on the
    Freedom Train?
When it stops in Mississippi
    will it be made plain
Everybody's got a right to board the
    Freedom Train?

If my children ask me, Daddy,
    please explain

Why there's Jim Crow stations
  for the Freedom Train,
What shall I tell my children?
   . . . You tell me—
'Cause freedom ain't freedom
  when a man ain't free.

Now, 15 years later, Langston Hughes
has written a book entitled *Fight for Freedom*, the theme of which is summed up in
that one wonderful line, "Freedom ain't
freedom if a man ain't free." The book is
the story of the National Association for
the Advancement of Colored People, and
it's a history of the struggle to make the
Freedom Train documents more than just
eloquent words on paper for the Negro
population of our country. Hughes has
written a chapter in American history
which is unknown to most white people.
Very few of the events about which he
writes find a place in school history books,
yet they have affected intimately the lives
of 20 million Americans of African descent, and in many ways have left their
mark on the rest of the population.

The book begins with events that occurred long before there was any NAACP
or any other organized effort to improve
the lot of the American Negro. It tells, for
example, of slave mutinies aboard slave
ships on the high seas, a few of which were
miraculously successful. It also tells of
slave revolts on American soil, revolts
which invariably cost the lives of their
leaders and many of the followers. Certainly, the deeds of these men should give
them a place among our national heroes,
but how many of us recognize the names
of Gabriel Proser or Denmark Vesey, who
preferred to die fighting rather than to be
subjected to the indignities of slavery.

[. . .]

Practically any current issue of a daily
newspaper will reveal that the aims enun-
ciated by Dr. Du Bois have yet to be attained in most sections of our country.

This is not for lack of effort on the part of
the NAACP, which grew out of the Niagara Movement and became incorporated
in 1911. It is worth emphasizing that from
the very beginning the NAACP has been
an interracial organization and among its
founders were some famous white Americans, including Jane Addams, John Dewey,
William Lloyd Garrison, Oswald Garrison
Villard, the Rev. John Haynes Holmes,
Rabbi Stephen S. Wise and Lincoln
Steffens.

The dramatic story told by Langston
Hughes of the work of the NAACP during
the past 50 years covers every aspect of
the Negro's effort to attain full citizenship rights. It covers the struggle against
lynching; against discrimination in employment, housing, and recreational facilities; against segregation in schools,
libraries, armed services, hospitals, and
transportation; against disfranchisement.

It is not pleasant reading, because there
is nothing pleasant about man's inhumanity to man. It is with a feeling of horror
that one reads of the death of Bessie Smith,
the blues singer, because the nearest hospital to the scene of an automobile accident
would not admit a colored person. With
equal horror one reads graphic descriptions of lynchings. . . .

Although Langston Hughes is too
much of a realist to be a Pollyanna about
the current status of the Negro in our society, he does recognize the fact that progress
is being made. He points to the improvement in the "moral climate" of the country
and to specific victories as a result of enlightened state laws and significant court
decisions. He emphasizes, however, that
these improvements have come about only
as the result of constant effort on the part
of individuals and organizations who believe in equal opportunity for all regardless
of race. Incidentally, although Hughes
mentions the Congress of Racial Equality
(CORE) and the National Urban League

in connection with this work, one looks in vain for mention of the American Civil Liberties Union, which has defended civil rights wherever they have been under attack and on numerous occasions has supported the NAACP in the courts.

The book ends on a hopeful note, and the author invites all "liberty-loving" Americans to join in the effort to eliminate second-class citizenship for the Negro. What does Langston Hughes think the Negro wants? Here is his answer:

"We want 'What so proudly we hailed at the twilight's last gleaming.' We want 'My country 'tis of thee, sweet land of liberty.' We want everything we ever heard in all the Fourth of July speeches ever spoken. Don't say it—because you might be declared subversive—but *we want freedom.*"

passes over the NAACP leadership's initial resistance to these direct-action movements. The NAACP preferred to stick with the old, if slower-actioned, weapon of litigation. After making allowances for this intramural partisanship, however, the book can be taken as a fair account of what is, in truth, an inspiring success story, one in which all Americans who are concerned with human rights can take pride.

William Peeples
"NAACP's Coming of Age"
Louisville Courier-Journal, section 4, 7 October 1962, p. 5

Len Holt
"In Praise of NAACP"
National Guardian, 8 October 1962, p. 9

[. . .]

From its pre-natal period in the Niagara movement in the early part of the century, the NAACP's struggles and coming of age are traced in this slim new volume by the distinguished Negro poet and novelist, Langston Hughes. It is a straightforward, but undefinitive, history.

Mr. Hughes writes out of undisguised admiration for the organization, and he gives the NAACP more credit than it is due for the "freedom rides" and the sit-in movement, and CORE (The Congress for Racial Equality) less than its due. He

At a time when charges that the National Association for the Advancement of Colored People is "middle-class" are being hurled and substantiated, and charges that it is conservative are being made and corroborated by segregationists who tell direct-action groups to show the good manners of the NAACP, there seemed (to some) to be a need for a book that sings the praises of the NAACP.

Fight for Freedom meets the need. Langston Hughes, the commissioned author, is one of the most skillful writers of this generation. He has done the NAACP a service.

The book is defensive. It attempts to justify the NAACP's present mode of existence by pointing to the past glories of a time when there was no Congress of Racial Equality (CORE), no Southern Conference Educational Fund (SCEF), no Southern Christian Leadership Conference (SCLC), and no Student Nonviolent Coordinating Committee (SNCC), the super-militant, aggressive organization of Southern students.

The book's defensive tone is set in the foreword by Arthur B. Spingarn, NAACP president: "There is much to be done, and I for one welcome the impatience of youth. But it should not be forgotten that the NAACP first lit the torch which is now being carried by its sons and daughters and will continue to be carried by us and them until the final goal is reached."

There is some dishonesty in the book, mixed with the praise. For example, NAACP credit for the entire sit-in movement of 1960 is claimed by mentioning that the four college students who sat at a Greensboro, N.C., lunch counter were NAACP members and that, after all, the sit-ins really began in Oklahoma, where they were conducted by NAACP youth chapters in 1958.

And there is the matter of the Freedom Rides. The connection between the NAACP and the Freedom Rides of 1961— tenuous link though this may be—is that James Farmer, national director of CORE and a participant in the First Freedom Ride, had previously been employed by the NAACP.

One wonders if there are not hidden meanings and double-talk in some of the things Hughes writes. Why, for example, does this recently written book give so much credit to Dr. W. E. B. Du Bois for his herculean efforts to found and mold the NAACP into a militant organization, while the executive officers disdained to invite Du Bois to the Golden Anniversary of the NAACP held in New York City a few years ago?

And there is the matter of "meeting violence with violence," the theme of Robert Williams, who was censured and suspended as Monroe, N.C., NAACP president for proclaiming the slogan. There is no mention of this in the book. Yet there are detailed descriptions of the lives of Negroes saved—including that of Walter White, the NAACP executive secretary—by the use of guns in an Atlanta, Ga., race riot.

Adding to the value of the book are thumbnail biographical sketches of such well-known persons as Du Bois, White, Thurgood Marshall, Roy Wilkins and James Weldon Johnson. There is the drama of the early lynchings and fights for survival, both by the NAACP as an organization and by some of its employees in the red-mud Southern jungles infested with man-killing, snuff-dipping, wool-hat personalities who carry out the bidding of racism. And these same folk and their descendants are now reverting to their primitive stages as they fire shotgun blasts at workers of the Student Non-violent Coordinating Committee in Georgia and Mississippi.

The book is a psalm of praise. Its greatest value may be to suggest a book that ought to be written about the NAACP. What about the trials of the organization, its errors, the crises, such as when the Little Rock Nine refused the Spingarn Medal unless Mrs. Daisy Bates was also awarded one?

Where is the analysis of why things happened to the NAACP, instead of the simple recitation of its history?

From time to time the NAACP has attempted to develop a mass base, but with minimal success. Why? How can such efforts be made more successful? Why, with the avowed purposes of the NAACP, has it been necessary for there to develop and to flourish three more militant integration organizations? Why for almost five years has the NAACP abandoned Alabama, allowing Alabama racists, in both federal and state courts, to make the NAACP run a never-ending legal rat race?

But this book is a song of praise. Praise be the name NAACP and all the books written about it—including this one.

Lawrence E. Nicholson
"Simply by Sitting"
St. Louis Post-Dispatch, 21 October 1962, p. 4C

At the present time it is fashionable for commentators upon the NAACP's *Fight for Freedom* to downgrade its long, patient assault on the separate but equal doctrine that relegated the Negro to second class citizenship. The essence of the downgrading is that the NAACP's orientation favors legal contests leading to future change, when the need is for mass movements (sit-ins and freedom rides), resulting in change here and now. It is to the task of dealing with this criticism that the distinguished author, poet and playwright, Langston Hughes, addresses this book. Since the NAACP has his deepest sympathies (he is the recipient of its highest honor), it is inevitable that the reader gets a sympathetic view of the organization, but at the same time, an honest view. His theme, relentlessly pursued in many variations, is that much of the Negro's defense against oppression is a cumulative legal structure that the Association has and continues to build, brick by brick, with sit-ins, freedom rides, stand-ins, pray-ins, swim-ins and read-ins.

Fight for Freedom is an exciting account from cover to cover—the story of an undeniable American value, the right of a minority to protest against what it perceives as the injustices of the majority. Placed in historical context, the genesis of the organization was the Progressive, muckraking, reformist climate that was to awaken the dormant American civic consciousness at the turn of the century. In these terms, it is expected that such names as Lincoln Steffens, Ray Stannard Baker, Brand Whitlock, John Spargo and Jane Addams would be among those sounding the call to action that brought the organization into being. The organization was thus founded by whites who were not infested with delusions of racial superiority and who were opposed to lynching as the means of maintaining the racial status quo.

The author points out that the organization's priority goal of a half century ago, the abolition of lynching, has now been replaced by others since lynching has about disappeared from American soil. Additional priorities identified at that time included equal education for every child, extension and protection of every citizen's right to vote, the freedom to purchase property and live in the area of one's choice, to travel without being segregated, to inform all America of the un-American difficulties its Negro citizens experienced, and to make clear that these continuing difficulties hindered the development of a large segment of the country's human potential.

The book is divided into six sections, respectively sub-titled the "First Decade," "Between Wars," "World War II," "Pinning Down the Law," "Victory Poses Problems," and "Making Democracy Work." Here in vivid sequence are accounts of Negroes persecuted in mass orgies of violence and expressions of raw hate; disrespect for a failure to protect the military uniform when worn by Negro men and women, the fight against the official position of racism in the armed forces, justified on the basis of "harmony and efficiency"; the fight to equalize wages of Negro firemen and teachers; America's worst race riots, Detroit and Harlem. Here are the nonviolent students who "by simply sitting on a stool at a lunch counter and waiting for service forced the nation to take a new look at the old race problems."

Mr. Hughes has written wisely and

well. He does not follow the well marked path of the academic historian, but relies on a loose chronology wedded to selective use of pertinent detail. The effect is one of completeness, for not only does he explore the dynamic working of the NAACP, but he also adroitly etches personality vignettes of the chief actors in the drama—Mary White Ovington, W. E. B. Du Bois, William Pickens, Thurgood Marshall, James Weldon Johnson, Walter White and Roy Wilkins. He has a nice ear for quotations and a sharp eye for the anecdote. Nor does Mr. Hughes fail to catch the wry humor of the minority under stress. He tells the delightful story of the little old Negro lady who in her best clothes went to one of Washington's plush integrated restaurants and found she could not be served first pig tails and blackeyed peas, then chitterlings and corn bread and finally ham hocks and collard greens. Said she to a solicitous waiter: "I knowed you-all wasn't ready for integration."

John B. Sullivan
"Books"
America, 107 (27 October 1962), 959–60

Langston Hughes, in *Fight for Freedom*, has written a primer on race relations in America. As you might expect, Hughes recounts the history of the fight for equality by the National Association for the Advancement of Colored People in language that at times is joyful, on other occasions tragic and sad, but always filled with hope. He describes the birth, growth and present-day maturity of this organization against the background of its heroic and progressively successful efforts to bring to fulfillment the spiritual and political ideal of America: the innate dignity of all men, and their right under law to equal opportunity in a free democratic society.

He documents the thesis that at every point in the history of the United States, from the mutinies and organized revolts of the slave-trade days to the freedom riders of the 1960's, the resources of our Anglo-Saxon system of jurisprudence have been used effectively not only to eliminate overt acts of illegal discrimination but, through the interpretation of the U.S. Constitution, to open up areas of opportunity such as jobs, education and housing which for many decades were not equally available to Negroes.

Fight for Freedom presents convincing facts to lay to rest the recurring and irresponsible charges of communism, subversion, un-Americanism and radicalism against the NAACP. Hughes reports that no less an authority than J. Edgar Hoover, in his book *Masters of Deceit*, describes NAACP's success in preventing Communist infiltration of its ranks. Moreover, he cites Americans prominent in the fields of religion, government, law, business, industry, labor and the arts and sciences, who have given support to the ideals and ideas of this organization. One gets the feeling, after reading Hughes' story of the NAACP, that their radicalism is that of a commitment to the supernatural virtue of Christian charity translated into social action efforts.

Rev. Joseph G. McGroarty "Books in the Field: Freedom Is Not Free" *Stray Notes from the Shrine of the Little Flower,* 42 (November 1962), 72–3

"For sheer savagery, Mississippi is considered the worst state in the country. It has had more mob murders in recent years than in any other state. It has the lowest percentage of Negro voters in the entire South—less than 4 percent of its 45 percent Negro population. Not one Negro child attends an integrated school in the entire state."

Recent events have confirmed before the world the truth of that indictment lodged by the Negro poet, Langston Hughes, against the Magnolia Sovereignty. He wrote those words months before James Meredith took his life into his hands by enrolling in the graduate school of the University of Mississippi. Violence, hoodlumism and bloodshed in Oxford, Mississippi, have since crowned with tragic fulfillment Hughes's prophetic observation in his *Fight for Freedom,* the story of the NAACP.

Not since Warren D. St. James's *The National Association for the Advancement of Colored People* appeared more than four years ago (*Stray Notes,* September 1958), have we come upon a book-length history of the so much maligned militant organization dedicated to the proposition of "equal justice under law." Since it would be no easy thing to rate one above the other, this reviewer can only recommend that you take up without delay either Mr. St. James's or Mr. Hughes's study of the NAACP—whichever one happens to be closer to hand, it doesn't matter. Having read one, you will have no need to go through the other, at least not for a while. Each writer, we found, has the same story to tell, and he tells it in pretty much the same way.

Though the NAACP has for its goal the achievement for Negroes of the rights guaranteed them under the United States Constitution, it is far from being a Negro organization. Few voluntary associations anywhere, as Langston Hughes repeatedly insists, are as thoroughly integrated as this one is. Apparently a great name-dropper, the author takes pains to list both the outstanding and the lesser known representatives of both races who have supported and joined the ranks of the NAACP, the five letters that stand for the most-talked-about, most-damned non-political organization in America.

It would be a blessing, of course, if there were no need for an association of this kind. Langston Hughes, whose creative writing won for him the coveted Spingarn Medal in 1960, tells us in effect that the happy day, when the NAACP can afford to close its doors permanently, lies far away in the unforeseeable future: "Because some people in America still think that a Negro has no rights a white man is duty-bound to respect, there is need for the NAACP."

Anyone who has never read a book on race conflict in the United States will be appalled by Mr. Hughes's itemization of countless authenticated instances of atrocity and degradation visited by white men upon defenseless members of the Negro race in the past fifty years in this country. It was to combat before the bar of justice the continuance of those instances of man's inhumanity to his darker brother that the NAACP came into being in 1909. Since then it has of necessity assumed the character of "the world's biggest law firm." Operating always for principle, not for profit, it has won many significant social victories for its clients in the troubled areas of employment, housing, education, transportation, and the use of the ballot. Because the legal battle for basic civil rights has been a costly one in terms of sacrifice, ingenuity and money, Langston Hughes reminds us more than once that "freedom is not free."

In defense of the NAACP's constant recourse to the courts, Hughes quotes the Reverend Martin Luther King: "One thing the gradualists don't seem to understand: we are not trying to make people love us when we go to court. We are trying to keep them from killing us." That statement of Montgomery's bus boycott leader is hardly an exaggeration, when one recalls that the association's first major target was the all too prevalent southern practice of lynching. Thanks to an enlightened campaign of Negro protest and public indoctrination, that is one evil that has ceased to be a current blot on our national honor. There are others, but, one by one, they are being eradicated through the courageous and persistent efforts of the NAACP.

The rabid opponents of the NAACP have passed up no opportunity to discredit it and its goals. Perhaps the tactic most frequently employed by its enemies in more recent years has been the baseless charge of Communist influence. Anyone even vaguely familiar with the aims and methods of the national association will immediately dismiss that allegation as spiteful and libelous. Besides being a very readable history of the NAACP, Langston Hughes's latest book is a shocking review of race relations in America over the past half-century. There is no gainsaying his avowed admiration for the organization that has done so much to bring to his own people a fairer share in the blessings of democracy. The reader of *Fight for Freedom* will

feel the same way about the NAACP as Mr. Hughes does. His is a convincing vindication that is bound to remove the more common misconceptions that cloud a lot of thinking about the Negro and about his right to fight for freedom.

Langston Hughes is best known, and best liked, for the gently probing satire of his "Simple" stories. But for its being serious and grammatically composed, there are times when one would think that Jesse B. Semple, better known simply as Simple, Hughes's ace-boy, had written *Fight for Freedom*. It reflects so well and faithfully the tenor and content of the refreshing Simple series.

[J.] Saunders Redding "Langston Hughes Brings Out Tears, Laughter in 'The NAACP Story'" *Baltimore Afro-American Magazine,* 10 November 1962, p. 4

Langston Hughes, who is first a poet and a writer of fiction, some months ago set himself a task that has long needed doing, one that probably no one else could do as well.

Certainly the story of the NAACP was no job for the formal historian or the sociologist, either of whom might easily and perhaps excusably have missed the drama of it.

A straight and unadorned historical or sociological treatise, written from the documents, of which there are thousands, would have been as dry as dust, a mere collection of names, dates and court actions over a period of more than half a century.

But the true story of the NAACP—of which "it is no exaggeration to say that no organization has had a greater influence on the structure of our society"—the true, real story, I say, is nothing if it is not human-ness and the drama that Langston Hughes has captured.

[. . .]

The struggle, as every one knows, has been going on ever since. How grim it has been is made clear in *Fight for Freedom*.

But there has been glory in the struggle, too, and now and then a laugh. Hughes brings the glory and the laughter through.

It is laughter with, not at, William Pickens and Thurgood Marshall, for instance; and glory, not so much for, but in Miss Ovington, Ida Wells, Mary Church Terrell, Dr. Du Bois, James Weldon Johnson and Walter White.

For after all, if institutions are but "the lengthened shadows" of the men and women who created them and gave their substance to them, then it follows that the history of an institution must be written in terms of biography and biographical narrative. That is what Langston Hughes has accomplished. He has done it simply and directly, with passion and dramatic power and truth.

George B. Tindall
"Books: The Unfinished Emancipation"
Progressive, 26 (December 1962), 63–4, 66

[. . .]

Those who are eager to see a definitive history of the NAACP's half-century struggle for emancipation will be disappointed in Langston Hughes' *Fight for*

Freedom: The Story of the NAACP. It is a useful supplement to Robert L. Jack's history in that it gives the bulk of its space to the period since the publication of that volume in 1943, and it is much more skillfully written. But it is a superficially researched publicist's tract for the NAACP rather than a critical history. It gives no treatment at all, for instance, to the important policy struggle of the Thirties between the integrationists and the Du Bois group that supported separate economic development as the basis for future gains. Nor does it analyze the policy crisis created by the rise of direct action movements in the bus boycotts, sit-ins, and Freedom Rides out of impatience with the NAACP's traditional evolutionary legal approach.

[. . .]

Gladys P. Graham
"Between the Covers"
New Jersey Herald News,
8 December 1962, p. 9

Langston Hughes, whose career was influenced by the National Association for the Advancement of Colored People (NAACP) which published his first poems (and their Spingarn medalist) has done a great service to the organization and the reading public in his newest volume *Fight for Freedom*.

Arthur B. Spingarn has written a brilliant foreword, lauding the work. Hughes reports that 50 years ago the status of the Negro in the United States was not too different from the far cry of the Civil War, with disenfranchisement, segregation in education, housing and public places the order of the day.

In 1962 the picture is different. Having

fought for and won the exciting struggle, Hughes tells the story which led to the movement, together with the story of the organization and the men who led the battles. A forecast of what still lies ahead is also included.

Hughes has divided his book into six pertinent chapters: The First Decade, Between Wars, World War II, Pinning Down the Law, Victory Poses Problems, and Making Democracy Work. He has included an Author's Postscript plus a copious Bibliography, Appendix and Index in this valuable 224 page volume (which is also published in paperback for all to secure) making it a document for all to read and have at their fingertips. This brilliant story of accomplishment with facts gathered and written by such an authority in spirit and letter as Langston Hughes is a must for your book collection.

This is the first definitive account of the record and accomplishments of the NAACP, and it is lucid, interesting, and informative, giving many unknown facts not available in print to the reading public who want to know.

Considerable coverage is given to Daisy Bates, and Little Rock, Clinton, Tennessee, the Sit-Downers and other incidents in the book point to the fact that "Freedom Is Not Free" and to be won must be earned and fought for. Langston Hughes has written a moving story which puts the reader directly on the scene of action and is worth every drop of ink from the printer's pen for all to read. *Fight for Freedom* is a must!

Jayme Coleman Williams "Book Reviews" *Negro Educational Review,* 14 (January 1963), 47–8

In the foreword to *Fight for Freedom* Arthur B. Spingarn, President of the NAACP, has pointed out that "before the founding of the NAACP the condition of the Negro was our country's greatest tragedy—so great that the newer generation have forgotten the extent of its tyranny and its cruelty." Langston Hughes, a prolific writer of more than three decades, has rendered a valuable service to all thoughtful Americans by recording the accomplishments of this organization over the past half century.

The author's purpose is to trace the history of the NAACP from its inception to the present, delineating the efforts utilized to achieve its progress in the battle against racial discrimination in the United States.

[. . .]

That some readers may find Hughes' style somewhat colloquial and that the book itself may be regarded as a recapitulation of a familiar struggle are apparent weaknesses. The style itself, while weak by academic standards, makes the book highly readable for the average reader. Despite the journalistic tone, some sections of the book are heartbreakingly moving: when Negro men and women die following traffic accidents on southern highways because the nearest hospital will not accept non-whites; when a Negro woman is burned alive and her unborn falls to the ground and is trampled underfoot; when nine teenagers walk bravely through jeering mobs to attend Central High School in Little Rock.

There are several reasons why this work is valuable. This somewhat detailed account of the indignities, injustices, and inhumane treatment accorded the Negro will appropriately remind the younger generation of Negroes that the fight for freedom did not begin with their protest. It will help the older generation, who may be rather smug over the progress being made in the area of civil rights, to recall the torturous path which has been traveled. In a world which is two-third colored, the book is a solemn challenge to all—regardless of race, who must be concerned over the disparity between America's democratic pronouncements and anti-democratic practices.

Mr. Hughes has drawn extensively upon primary and secondary sources to bring alive the story of an organization which has changed an established pattern and altered an entire way of life for many people. He has been objective in treating alike prejudice in the North as well as in the South. Although it provides no new revelations or interpretations, *Fight for Freedom* should be read by every individual who would like to see the American dream of equality become a reality.

Allan Morrison
"Book of the Week: *Fight for Freedom*"
Jet, 22 (24 January 1963), 25

The prolific Langston Hughes has produced an official authorized history of the 63-year-old NAACP which grew from the 60 distinguished white and Negro Americans who convened the organizing confer-

ence in 1909 to its present membership of 390,347 in 1,573 units in 49 states.

. . . Hughes used all official NAACP records and reports placed at his disposal and did extensive outside research to compile this history of the Association that is factually accurate, highly interesting and surprisingly objective both in its treatment of the story of the civil rights struggle led by the NAACP and its excellent appraisal of the results of NAACP action in various areas in which it has worked.

Hughes is now a mellowed 60, and this book reflects his wisdom, humor, balance and restraint. He writes with the candor and freedom of a playwright-novelist rather than a formal historian, and the result is both readable and, in parts, stirring. He recounts the rise and decline of lynching as a method of Negro repression, the long and effective legal fight waged by the NAACP and the accelerating attack on the whole structure of segregation throughout the land.

Hughes presents brief sketches of the great figures of the Association—W. E. B. Du Bois, James Weldon Johnson, Walter White, Thurgood Marshall, Roy Wilkins and others, and describes the roles they played simply and well.

Fight for Freedom should prove of enormous value to the NAACP cause, for it clearly shows that it crusades for equality for all Americans.

Arna Bontemps
"Marching Song"
Crisis, 70 (February 1963), 121–2

The story of the National Association for the Advancement of Colored People, together with the historical events leading to its formation, is certainly an American epic. While we cannot yet foretell the conclusion, we may be sure we have observed a sequence as arresting and possibly as significant as the bondage and freedom of Joseph and his brothers and their descendants in Egypt. Even the unlettered slave noted the parallel of the preliminaries and expressed it in song.

The need for organized efforts "to end racial discrimination and segregation in all public aspects of American life" is so evident to anyone who has felt or even witnessed primitive oppression he must find it astonishing to learn how many Americans are still dedicated to thwarting such efforts. Yet despite the openness and simplicity of its basic aims "more NAACP members have undergone arrest in recent years than have members of the Communist party." In some areas of the nation, as this book points out, "it is tantamount to a crime to belong" to the Association. In such an atmosphere, the air poisoned with radio-active misrepresentation, it is certainly high time the story, the real story of NAACP, should be frankly, clearly and completely told for all to read.

The selection of Langston Hughes to write it is singularly appropriate. No one else that I know could possibly do it with more feeling and none with qualities of style more suited to the subject. Hughes has a positive genius for simple, direct statement in a variety of literary forms, and he could not be trite if he tried. Neither can he escape, even in prose, the overtones of poetry. Such expression cannot be contrived. In the case of Langston Hughes, however, its origins can be traced.

He grew up with the NAACP and is now, like it, in his second half-century. "I learned to read with *The Crisis* on my grandmother's lap," he has recalled. Its throbbing editorials, written by W. E. B. Du Bois, along with passages from the Bible, were his introduction to fervor and beauty in language. As a high school boy in Cleveland he attended the Association's memorable 10th Annual Convention, called then "the greatest assembly ever held by Negroes in the United States." The summer after his graduation from high school, when he was eighteen, he wrote "The Negro Speaks of Rivers," which later appeared in *The Crisis*, his first published poem. He has lost count, I am sure, of the times this enduring poem has been reprinted, translated, set to music, sung and read in public or broadcast around the world. For me it promptly became, along with the Du Bois editorials and Jean Toomer's "Song of the Son," the voice of the Association itself.

It was fortunate that NAACP had such voices in those days. There was little else to inspire courage or sustain hope. Heroic efforts seemed to go for almost nothing. Lynchings and riots continued with sickening monotony, and in most cases, if not all, mere protest seemed about as effective as pleas for justice seem today in South Africa or in most of Mississippi, including the campus of Ole Miss.

Consider in this connection the obligations and opportunities of the writer. William Faulkner lived most of his life in Oxford, Mississippi. He attained great renown. But he told us plainly where he would stand in a show-down such as occurred near his home last year. He left nothing in his writings that a U.S. Marshal, for example, could profitably read to a mob made of students of his alma mater or to a meeting of that University's executive committee. He left nothing that James Meredith could have read for his encouragement or peace of mind in the surroundings where he spent the morning of the Centennial of the Emancipation Proclamation.

This part of the story of NAACP one must read between the lines of *Fight for Freedom*. I would submit, however, that it is important, if not crucial. The Negro who spoke of rivers, the son who returned singing and the editor who inspired them both are living. Of the three, only Langston Hughes continues to speak from the same rostrum, and only he is in a position to tell the story as it is recounted here.

When NAACP warmed to its task, as Hughes so effectively indicates, "lynching, disfranchisement, color-conscious courts, segregation in education, employment, housing and public places were the order of the day—and not merely in the South." Today, as all can see, the picture is considerably changed, *especially* in parts of the South. Yet "none of the progress came automatically or through the voluntary abandonment of cherished and favored privilege. It had to be fought for and won."

This is the stuff of which epics are made. *Fight for Freedom* is a stirring account of how it all happened, a sort of marching song. If all those who have participated in the events or even witnessed them live as long as W. E. B. Du Bois, I suspect they will still treasure the experience. Langston Hughes has insured that the younger generation will not be left in ignorance of this part of their heritage.

Milton S. Byam
"New Books Appraised"
Library Journal, 88 (1 February 1963), 570

Langston Hughes, poet and author of the "Simple" stories, has given a detailed and popular account of the history of the Negro struggle for equality of opportunity in the United States based on the activity of the NAACP. By liberal use of anecdote and personal narratives, he has made this history read like the adventure story it is. The reader is both shocked by what we have rescued ourselves from and awed by the progress yet to be made. Each of the struggles and grudged victories is spelled out—tinged with disappointment and heartbreak. Not the definitive history, this is nonetheless extremely valuable for popular collections of material on the Negro and the question of civil rights in the U.S., and it should be available in all public libraries for both adult and young readers.

Gilbert E. Govan
"Negroes' Effort for Recognition"
Chattanooga Times, 17 March 1963, p. 14

With much misinformation widespread about this organization which is so prominent in the news today, this book becomes a more valuable source. It is by one of the more gifted Negro writers and is naturally favorable to the NAACP, but the reputation of the author and the publishers warrants its accuracy.

[. . .]

. . . Readers of this book will find in it the historical reasons for the NAACP, its accomplishments over the years and some idea of its aims for the future.

Elliott M. Rudwick
Annals of the American Academy of Political and Social Science, 347 (May 1963), 178–9

Fight for Freedom, according to the subtitle, is "The Story of the NAACP." The author, Langston Hughes, is no academic historian or sociologist and makes no pretense at scholarship. While the volume is interesting, it is also superficial and uncritical. Seemingly, Hughes' purpose was to produce a company book that would (1) "sell" the National Association for the Advancement of Colored People to whites as well as impatient Negro youth, and (2) boost the morale of the NAACP's leaders and members. . . .

Since Hughes' interest is in discussing only the association's accomplishments—of which there are many—he ignores the past and current criticism leveled by friends of the organization. For example, a generation ago, Negro intellectuals considered that the NAACP lacked mass support, was "bourgeois," anti-union, and oblivious to "fundamental" economic problems. Then, as now, friendly critics maintained that the association was too committed to "legalism" and too little interested in promoting direct action by local people. Whatever the merits of these criticisms, Hughes should have analyzed them in a discussion of the tactics and strategy of the NAACP.

To show how forward-looking the NAACP has been, Hughes also twists facts. For example, he suggests that the association backed Du Bois' Pan-African Movement shortly after World War I and identified with "the destiny of all the colored people of the world." Actually, the "world" view came much later, and for most of its fifty-year history, the association focused almost exclusively on United States race problems. The board of directors was understandably reluctant to dissipate limited resources elsewhere—Du Bois, who received almost no help for his Pan-American [*sic*] Movement, charged that some Negro board members "had inherited a fierce repugnance toward anything African."

Fight for Freedom, however, is useful in providing the reader with brief accounts of the NAACP's historic battles against lynching, the denial of the ballot, inequalities in teachers' salaries, and segregation in the armed forces, in housing, and, of course, in the public schools. One of the most interesting sections of Hughes' book deals with the recent efforts by several southern states to put the association out of business. Arkansas, Louisiana, Florida, and Virginia conducted harassing "legislative investigations"; Texas secured a "temporary" injunction, demanding that the NAACP pay taxes as a profit-making organization; and Alabama sought a $100,000 fine because the association refused to reveal the names of its members.

While this volume does not adequately tell "The Story of the NAACP," it is recommended as an introduction for a general reader who knows little about the subject.

Theresa Hertel
"Versatile Langston
Hughes in Two Works—
Fiction and Documentary:
Prologue to Equality"
Community, 23 (April
1964), 14

Langston Hughes, recounting the birth of the National Association for the Advancement of Colored People (NAACP) and its half-century struggle for equality for Negro Americans, provides a heart-rending prologue to the civil rights drama of the 1960's.

Fortunately, it is prologue: the relatively few voices demanding justice in 1909 have grown to a nation-wide chorus; accumulated victories of the NAACP's first fifty years have conditioned Negro Americans to accept nothing less than complete equality; long years of frustrating protest and legal effort will reach fulfillment, hopefully, in a strong federal civil rights bill.

Fortunately, too, for the reader and for the United States, Hughes' chronicle of incredibly desperate conditions is balanced by the report of their alleviation through the dedicated and courageous work of the NAACP. Nevertheless, the report makes bitter reading; if protests were not placed in historical settings, one might assume they were voiced today. . . .

Today's methods, if different, are changed more in scope than in substance: direct action, legal redress, education, publication, even non-violent resistance were used throughout the years. The threatened March on Washington in 1941

precipitated President Franklin Roosevelt's executive order establishing an FEPC which, though feeble, did help provide jobs for thousands of Negro workers.

Hughes' history of the NAACP covers much that is seldom found in textbooks. Lynching was an everyday affair—literally every day: in the thirty years, 1889 to 1919, 3224 men and women were lynched—two every week! Yet the Dyer Anti-Lynching Bill was defeated in the Senate in 1922 by a northern Republican-southern Democrat coalition. Brief descriptions of the lives and contributions of those who worked for and with the NAACP (not often found in textbooks either, though invaluable studies of American democracy at work) are also included.

Written with pride for those successes achieved, yet with passion for what remains to be accomplished, Hughes' book is necessary background for those who seek to fulfill the dream long denied.

Checklist of Additional Reviews

Jessie Kitching, "Nonfiction Forecast: Fight for Freedom: The Story of the NAACP," *Publishers Weekly,* 182 (13 August 1962), 59.

"Weekly Record: Hughes, Langston," *Publishers Weekly,* 182 (27 August 1962), 307.

Edward Allen Kent, "Fight for Freedom," *Book-of-the-Month-Club News,* September 1962, p. 12.

Peter Kihss, "Justice Comes High," *New York Times Book Review,* 2 September 1962, p. 12.

Albert H. Miller, "Books," *Critic,* 21 (October–November 1962), 88–90.

Thomasina Norford, "On the Town," *New York Amsterdam News,* 6 October 1962, p. 12.

Wallace Terry, "Roads That Converged in Oxford, Miss.," *Washington Post,* 7 October 1962, p. G6.

"Social Sciences," *Booklist,* 59 (15 October 1962), 149.

"Books Noted," *Negro Digest,* 13 (November 1963), 93.

"Books for Young Adults," *Booklist,* 59 (1 November 1962), 216.

SOMETHING IN COMMON AND·OTHER STORIES

Ruben F. Kugler
"New Books Appraised"
Library Journal, 88 (1
February 1963), 574

Martha Huntley
"Paperbacks Put Up a
Good Front"
Charlotte Observer,
14 April 1963, p. 5C

This is a collection of 39 [*sic;* there are 37] stories, 9 of which have not been collected before. Mr. Hughes chose 30 stories from his *Laughing to Keep from Crying, The Ways of White Folks,* and *The Langston Hughes Reader.* Some are short stories as usually defined, and others are sketches covering a page or two. The relationship of Caucasians and Negroes provides the dominant motif of the book. Some readers might object to the similarity in theme, but Hughes shows versatility in style and approach. Rarely bitter in tone (as in "Father and Son"), the author's expression varies from humor ("Trouble with the Angels") to reproachfulness ("The Big Meeting") to pathos ("Sailor Ashore") and to admiration for Negro courage ("Gumption"). "Breakfast in Virginia" strikes a hopeful note by telling how the war against Hitlerism brought a white Virginian and Negro soldier together for breakfast. Hughes almost consistently avoids propagandizing, because he makes his characters real. Recommended for most libraries.

All 37 stories were wonderful. I particularly enjoyed one called "Who's Passing for Who," in which a group of Harlem intellectuals try to impress visiting white sociologists, from Iowa, with the numbers of Negroes who are light enough to pass for white. The woman then confidentially admits that she and her husband have been "passing" for 30 years.

"All at once we dropped our professionally self-conscious 'Negro' manners, became natural, ate fish and talked and kidded freely like colored folks do when there are no white folks around." Finally, the delightful evening ends, and as the thawed-out intellectuals put their new friends in a taxi, the woman admits that she and her husband are really white people passing for colored passing for white.

The book's point is that "we all have something in common." The theme appears in story after story, each one better than the one before. I put the book down reluctantly.

William Kirtz
"Mr. Hughes' Shadings"
Quincy [Mass.] *Patriot-Ledger,* 17 April 1963,
p. 32

The latest collection of short stories by Negro poet, novelist and playwright Langston Hughes is a disappointing grab-bag. It is a combination of questionable sociology and worse fiction.

The majority of the stories, written from 1933 to 1963, seem to be thinly disguised sermonettes. White spinsters lust after dark-skinned janitors. If a colored person is consistently polite to a Caucasian, that's a tip-off he'll have sold out before tale's end. And Hughes' heroines' favorite game? Pretending they're the same hue as their white keepers.

Hughes occasionally unwinds and produces some welcome flashes of in-group humor, of raucous racial gibes. But he's in the pulpit more often than not.

Much in the way of stereotypes and ethnic platitudes can be forgiven a writer with power and style. James Baldwin, for example, can carry a disbeliever for pages with just the force of his rhetoric. Not so Mr. Hughes. He doesn't seem to put words in his characters' mouths; he wedges them there. For the Thought We Doubt Ever Got Thought department, there's this neat musing, by a "professor" invited to dinner by a wealthy white family:

"The Chandlers are a power in the Middle West, and in the South as well. Theirs is one of the great fortunes of America. In philanthropy, nobody exceeds them in well-planned generosity on a large and highly publicized scale. They are a power in Negro education, too—as long as it remains *Negro* and does not get tangled up in integration. That is why I am visiting them tonight at their invitation."

One may be convinced by Hughes' theme, but not as it is more clumsily expounded and hastily rationalized. Some perfectly natural situations are convoluted into diatribe by slick, trick endings. In "His Last Affair," for example, an actress twice dupes a pompous businessman with a paternity hoax. What is Hughes' last line? "And he never did even suspicion that I'm colored." The surprise doesn't proceed from the events, but from the author's effort to startle.

In "Why, You Reckon?" two Negroes rob and strip a wealthy white boy. Their victim is titillated by this Harlem experience. The thieves opine that if they had the lad's money, they'd always have a good time. "No, you wouldn't," the boy responds. And that sets one of his captors to thinking: "What do you suppose is the matter with rich white folks? Why you reckon they ain't happy?"

Now Negroes, as Hughes repeatedly implies, may have a premium on innocence. But he certainly doesn't go far toward proving the assumption with such hoked-up homilies.

Relaxed and antic stories like "Spanish Blood" and "Slice Him Down" are unselfconscious and successful glimpses into racial striving, fighting, making up. And "The Gun," a crisp chiller, proves that Hughes can turn out disciplined, punchy prose. It tells of an old maid who flourishes as soon as she puts a .32 under her pillow.

The 40-story [*sic*] collection, however, generally exudes patronizing distrust. The author continually preaches the Negro's sexual attractiveness to the white. His characters are deathly scared of any Caucasian; his whites are polite only to snare and unnerve the superior race. His heroes pity their white counterparts for their innate guilt.

But these generalizations—which are nowhere particularized, just restated—are precisely those the Southern racists chant. Both Hughes and the White Citizens Councils prate of miscegenation, of inherent antagonism, of impossible coexistence.

Is this view really the way racial affairs must be? Has there been so little progress since the 30s? Until he pinpoints it, Hughes' case must be judged unproved—for lack of evidence. And his fiction must be termed enervating, laced together by more wrath than craft.

Richard A. Long
CLAJ, 7 (December 1963), 177

In this selection of short stories written over a rather wide stretch of time, Langston Hughes displays his ability to handle a variety of styles and moods. There are thirty-seven stories in all, eleven of which appear for the first time in book form. Many are very skillful, some are weak. Those stories written in the urban Negro idiom of which Hughes is the undisputed master are by far the best. We cite only "Rock, Church" and "Sorrow for a Midget" as examples of these, but there are others. In an entirely different manner, but deeply moving and poignant, is the brief "African Morning" whose theme of the lonely mulatto links it to the very different and long "Father and Son," a cornerstone in the *oeuvre* of Langston Hughes.

Some of the less successful stories rely too heavily on the surprise ending and others show a strange ineptness in dialogue and characterization.

Mr. Hughes is known for his skill in treating the theme of the Southern migrant in the Northern ghetto. Another theme, that of Uncle Tom as artist or intellectual, provides him with the basis for excellent stories. In this collection "Trouble with the Angels" and "Fine Accommodations," in spite of some stilted dialogue in the latter, are examples.

La Verne Hickey
"Versatile Langston Hughes in Two Works—Fiction and Documentary"
Community, 23 (April 1964), 14

Presented here are 37 short stories, differing widely in subject matter, and yet having in common the author's deep concern for humanity. Written in excellent literary style, Hughes' characters generate warmth and good humor throughout, although at times the cynicism of Hitchcock is evident. Some of the most concise tales (two pages and less) encompass several avenues of thought, and the author allows his tales to unfold with smoothness and clarity. It is interesting to note, however, Hughes' treatment of the Negro, in general. Characterization of the "minstrel" or "stereotype" Negro seems to prevail, and might be offensive to some Negro readers.

In relating discriminatory experiences, he manages to vent neither despair nor bitterness, nor for that matter, hopefulness, but projects a sort of conditioned acceptance of a double standard society, a "make the most of it" attitude. One story particularly reveals the author's total objectivity when relating a tale of a small stock company of Negro players who are booked into an all-white theater. The drama is all about "God" and his "angels." When the "angels" discover the theater is restricted to whites only, they plan a strike; but "God," who is more concerned with the performance for performance sake, "the need to bring religion to white men" (and the pay), refuses to cooperate in the strike, convinces others of its uselessness, and is successful in calling it off. The angry "angel" responsible for the strike plan is carried out of the theater bawling and shouting . . . and defeated. This tale, "Trouble with the Angels," is typical of the author's ability to keep a neutral position, making it difficult to evaluate wherein his sympathy lies.

All in all, Hughes treats a broad range of human experiences with the greatest of ease, and his delightful style and humor are worth the reading.

Checklist of Additional Reviews

"Something in Common and Other Stories," *Virginia Kirkus Bulletin,* 31 (1 January 1963), 36.

[J.] Saunders Redding, "Book Review: Langston Hughes Is Back Again," *Afro-American Magazine,* 28 May 1963, p. 2.

"Fiction," *Booklist,* 60 (1 September 1963), 30.

J.P., "Books: Langston Hughes: Poet and Prophet," *People's World,* 5 October 1963, p. 7.

FIVE PLAYS BY LANGSTON HUGHES

Louise Giles
"New Books Appraised"
Library Journal, 88
(15 March 1963), 1176

Mulatto, Soul Gone Home, and *Little Ham* were written in the 30's; *Simply Heavenly* and *Tambourines to Glory* are more contemporary. *Mulatto* is a social drama set on a Southern plantation; the remaining plays deal with varying aspects of Negro life in Harlem, usually in comic tones. Edited by Webster Smalley, this volume has a long introduction which will be of interest as a commentary on Hughes's work. Although these plays may seem rather *démodé* to more sophisticated Negro and white readers, they have a definite social and historical significance. Further, Hughes is one of our best-loved Negro writers, and there is always an audience for his work. This should be represented in all collections specializing in Negro literature or the theater and in at least one agency of all large public libraries.

[J.] Saunders Redding
"Book Review: Langston Hughes Is Back Again"
Afro-American Magazine, 28 May 1963, p. 2

I am glad I read Professor Webster Smalley's introduction to *Five Plays.* I started not to read it.

After all, nobody has to introduce Langston Hughes to me, or to no one knows how many thousands of others, at home and abroad, who have known him—that is, known his work—from way back when, and who still find much of it—not all, but a good bit—as fresh and cleanly perceptive and true as it was then.

I mean, the work then and the work now. I mean, much of his new work has the qualities of spontaneity and tart perception which certainly still marks, after all these years, the best of the old.

Proof of this fact lies in this collection of plays, which Professor Smalley has edited and introduced and in the collection of stories entitled *Something in Common.*

For instance, the tragic mulatto is a constantly recurring theme in Hughes' work—poetry, drama, fiction. He has treated it in at least a dozen poems and one long short story since the play *Mulatto* was written back in the 1930's. Nevertheless Hughes' old dramatization of this old theme seems almost as crisp today as when it was first performed on Broadway nearly thirty years ago.

And *Tambourines to Glory,* which is new, is equally crisp—although I think some of its freshness may derive from the kind of technical experimentation characteristic of the theatre of O'Neill, Williams, Inge.

What I think I'm trying to say is that Hughes has the rare good fortune of not going stale—of fresh vision and high spirits, of vitality and directness, of projection.

I think this is because, as Professor Smalley hints, Hughes lives close to his people and believes in their "strength and dignity."

Hughes has equal scorn for pretense and intolerance.

And it shows in both his methods and his materials. He is, as I have said, direct, which does not mean that he does not have his own kind of complexity.

[. . .]

"Literature"
Booklist, 60 (15
September 1963), 73–4

These folk plays, most of them full length, for all Negro casts include fantasy, melodrama, comedy, and musical comedy. Over the past 30 years they have been produced professionally in the U.S. and in other parts of the world. The same qualities that make them interesting as drama make them enjoyable reading: an earthiness, a basic respect for human beings, and an indigenous American idiom both precise and revealing.

Doris E. Abramson
"'It'll Be Me': The Voice
of Langston Hughes"
Massachusetts Review, 5
(Autumn 1963), 168–76

Ask anyone to name the contemporary Negro playwrights, and he will probably answer hastily and as if they were all: Lorraine Hansberry and Langston Hughes. In that order. As a playwright she is probably better known than he is, though he has been writing plays for three decades, whereas her first play is only four years old. Mr. Hughes is known first and praised highest for his poems, one of which gave Miss Hansberry the title for her play, *A Raisin in the Sun.* Both writers have been called propaganda or social protest writers. Neither seems seriously bothered by such labels, and both have had the interest-

ing experience of receiving applause from the objects of their protest.

It is scarcely surprising that Langston Hughes is not more widely known as a playwright. Until the recent publication of his *Five Plays,* there was no opportunity for the American public to read his plays. Those of us who didn't see the plays when they were produced knew them only by reputation, which has always been a better way to know the critics than the plays.

Mulatto, the first play in this collection, was a Broadway success during the 1935–36 season. It ran for a year at the Vanderbilt and Ambassador, toured for eight months across the United States (though not in the South, not even in Philadelphia), and has been produced all over the world. It has been translated into Italian, Spanish, French, Portuguese and Japanese and has been published in Milan and Buenos Aires. Now we may read this remarkable play by a too long neglected American playwright.

In his introduction, editor Webster Smalley blames the commercial nature of our theatres and publishing houses for the delay in the printing of these five plays. And he points out very sensibly that "a Negro playwright has all the woes of a white dramatist, with a number of others thrown in." Commercial theatre in America (one might just as well say Broadway) shows only occasional interest in Negro drama; little is produced and, consequently, little is published. Miss Hansberry and Mr. Hughes are among a handful (about a dozen) of Negro playwrights who have had their plays produced on Broadway since 1925. Only six of these plays have been published, two of them for the first time in this book. We are indeed indebted to the University of Indiana Press.

[. . .]

It has not been easy for Langston Hughes or for other Negro playwrights to get their plays produced. In a country where only a few years ago Negroes were barred even from attendance at many theatres, it has been exceedingly difficult for Negro writers to serve their necessary apprenticeship in the theatre and to get an audience for their plays. Langston Hughes has been braver (more foolhardy?) than most of his fellow Negro playwrights. He founded two dramatic groups during the thirties: the Suitcase Theatre in Harlem and the Negro Art Theatre in Los Angeles. In 1941 he established the Skyloft Players in Chicago. "Few playwrights have the heart or energy for such undertakings," Mr. Smalley observes.

On a radio symposium in 1961—in the company of Lorraine Hansberry, James Baldwin, Alfred Kazin and others—Langston Hughes said: "I am, of course, as everyone knows, primarily a—I guess you might even say a propaganda writer; my main material is the race problem. . . ." He also referred to his famous character Jesse B. Semple, or Simple, as a "kind of social protest mouthpiece." These statements contradict Webster Smalley's insistence that "he is an artist, not a propagandist." What a strange, unnecessary and impossible separation. Art that has at its center a social problem must be propaganda. Mr. Smalley correctly says Mr. Hughes is not a belligerent writer, but there is propaganda in his subtle use of humor and deflating irony.

In the plays of Negro authorship written since the 1935 production of *Mulatto*—which ran longer than any other play by a Negro until *A Raisin in the Sun* broke the record in 1959—the same problems within a problem appear repeatedly. It is not surprising. Certain problems persist in the lives of American Negroes: unemployment that breeds poverty and crime; racial tensions that explode in riots, mob violence, lynching; poor housing, slums, the frustrations of too many people living in one place; miscegenation and its real or imagined unhappy results; political and social evils and educational deprivations too numerous to mention—all the problems that grow out of the ghetto existence and general second-class citizenship forced upon most American Negroes. The plays reflect, with varying degrees of realism, life as lived by Negroes. This is true of plays written for the Negro Unit of the Federal Theatre Project as well as for commercial plays on and off Broadway.

Playwright Alice Childress commented at a writers' conference in 1959 on the possibility of Negro writers forsaking problems and just writing about people. She sees a difficulty because it turns out that human beings are more than just people.

> Many of us would rather be writers than Negro writers, and when I get that urge, I look about for the kind of white writer—which is what we mean when we say "just a writer"—that I would emulate. I come up with Sean O'Casey. Immediately, I am a problem writer. O'Casey writes about the people he knows best and I must—well, there you have it! (First Conference of Negro Writers, 1959)

Langston Hughes, too, writes about the people he knows best. The five plays in this book are *Mulatto, Soul Gone Home, Little Ham, Simply Heavenly,* and *Tambourines to Glory.* With the exception of *Mulatto,* a tragedy of the Deep South, they are all comic folk plays with Harlem settings. Only in *Mulatto* is a white man more than a peripheral character.

Mulatto is a play about miscegenation, a subject that both titillated and confused nineteenth century writers and continues to fascinate in our own time. The "germ idea" was contained in an earlier short story of his called "Father and Son" and even earlier and most effectively in a poem called "Cross."

My old man's a white old man
And my old mother's black.
If ever I cursed my white old man
I take my curses back.

If ever I cursed my black old mother
And wished she were in hell,
I'm sorry for that evil wish
And now I wish her well.

My old man died in a fine big house.
My ma died in a shack.
I wonder where I'm gonna die,
Being neither white nor black.

Critics of the play have called it melodramatic. (*Mulatto,* too black and white?) The stage version must have been rather sensational, with a rape scene not even in the original text (which is what has been published) and very strong performances by the whole cast. The heroine, Cora Lewis, was played by one of the great actresses America has produced, Rose McClendon. This was the last role she played before her untimely death in 1936.

To read *Mulatto* with a forgiving eye, as we have to read many plays of the thirties, is a good experience both emotionally and intellectually. The exposition is obvious, and there's repetition galore. But Cora's long speeches are frighteningly beautiful. (They must have made wonderful arias in the opera, "The Barrier," which was first produced in 1950, with music by Jan Meyerowitz.) Here she speaks to the dead Colonel Tom who has been murdered by their mulatto child who asked to be recognized by his own father:

He's your boy. His eyes is gray—like your eyes. He's tall like you's tall. He's proud like you's proud. And he's runnin'—runnin' from po' white trash that ain't worth de little finger o' nobody what's got your blood in 'em, Tom. (*Demandingly*) Why don't you get up from there and stop 'em, Colonel Tom? What's that you say? He ain't your chile? He's ma bastard chile? Ma yellow bastard chile? (*Proudly*) Yes, he's mine. . . . He's ma chile. . . . Don't you come to my bed no mo'. I calls you to help me now, and you just lays there. I calls you for to wake up, and you just lays there. Whenever you called me in de night, I woke up.

When you called for me to love, I always reached out ma arms fo' you. I borned you five chilluns and now one of 'em is out yonder in de dark runnin' from yo' people. Our youngest boy out yonder in de dark runnin'. (*Accusingly*) He's runnin' from you, too. . . . You are out yonder in de dark, runnin' our child with de hounds and de gun in yo' hand. . . . Damn you, Colonel Norwood! (*Backing slowly up the stairs, staring at the rigid body below her*) Damn you, Thomas Norwood! God damn you!

This is less than half of the speech just before the curtain at the end of the last scene but one. The dialect sometimes contributes something to a mood, but often it detracts both from meaning and mood. We learn to put up with it, as we do with dialect in plays by Eugene O'Neill.

We should be grateful to be able to read this play at all. It may not be produced in the United States as often as it is abroad, but now we can read it and ponder why. It is an interesting question. Why should people in France and Spain and Japan still care about problems involving the intermingling of the races to the extent that they produce this play? Why do we not produce it? Is it that we don't care as much as they do, or has our sophistication taken us beyond this particular statement of the problem? We couldn't even begin to ask, let alone to answer, these questions before the play was published.

Soul Gone Home is one of the strangest little plays ever published anywhere. On the book jacket it is called "a fantasy of people so repressed that they can no longer afford love." That's probably true. The editor says it "bristles with implications and reverberates with connotations." Mr. Hughes told me recently that it should be played for broad comedy in order to heighten the tragedy. It gets maudlin if it is done seriously. What is this play about? A dead son comes alive long enough to berate his prostitute mother for being "a no-good mama." A strange subject for a comedy! And strangely enough it works—or one has the feeling that it could work on the stage if the director listened to Mr. Hughes and avoided any hint of sentimentality.

It is unfortunate that *Little Ham* and *Simply Heavenly* are placed side by side in this volume, inviting a comparison in which *Little Ham* is surely the loser. Both plays are urban folk plays set in Harlem. In each the hero is a little man with big ideas and a capacity for enjoyment: Hamlet Jones and Jesse B. Semple. Hamlet is a lady's man under the spell of a fat lady named Tiny.

> HAM: A sweet little woman like you's got no business at a fight all alone by her little she-self.
> TINY: Now you know I ain't little. (*Coyly*) Don't nobody like me 'cause I'm fat.
> HAM: Well, don't nobody like me 'cause I'm so young and small.
> TINY: You a cute little man. You mean don't *nobody* like you?
> HAM: (*Woefully*) Nobody that amounts to nothin!

This kind of dialogue ripples along with what we take for authenticity, and *Little Ham* moves lightly through a Harlem of the "roaring twenties," introducing us to Madame Lucille Bell, Mattie Bea, racketeers, molls, dancers and kids and all kinds of under- and over-ground characters. The play is a pleasant experience, but it has little more depth than an old Amos 'n Andy sketch. Mr. Hughes has written better plays, one of which should have been put here in place of *Little Ham*. (My choice would have been his agitprop play, *Don't You Want To Be Free?*)

On the other hand, *Simply Heavenly* is a remarkable play about Harlem life, a comedy filled with characters who interest, instruct, transport—and please us. Only Saroyan has created a barroom to match Mr. Hughes' Paddy's Bar. It becomes as vivid a place as the Negroes who people it.

Of the hero, Jesse B. Semple, Langston Hughes has written the following:

> Simple is a Chaplinesque character, slight of build, awkwardly graceful, given to flights of fancy, and positive statements of opinion—stemming from a not so positive soul. He is dark with a likable smile, ordinarily dressed, except for rather flamboyant summer sport shirts. Simple tries hard to succeed, but the chips seldom fall just right.

Saunders Redding once spoke of "the poignant, pain-filled, pain-relieving humor of simple Jesse B." Originally a character in a play called *Simple Takes a Wife,* this little man has become a great favorite in Europe as well as in this country. He turns up in Mr. Hughes' newspaper columns ("I sit in that barber chair, thinking how God must love poor folks because he made so many of them in my image.") and in the earlier play without music as well as the current one with music. His opinions are being heard all over the world. *Simple Takes a Wife* has been done only abroad and is in the repertory at Prague, where it was originally produced in 1961. In that year, Mr. Hughes had this to say about the universality of Simple:

> ... a regional Negro character like Simple, a character intended for the people who belong to his own race, if written about warmly enough, humanly enough, can achieve universality. ("The Negro in American Culture," WBAI-FM, New York City)

The temptation for a reviewer is to quote great chunks of dialogue from *Simply Heavenly,* for this is a delightful play with a message, a play filled with the rich dialogue of Harlemites who make their lives bearable through humor and affection for one another. Kierkegaard has said somewhere that the more one suffers the more one has a sense for the comic. He speaks of people who have suffered deepest having "true authority in the use of the comic, an authority by which one work transforms as by magic the reasonable creature one calls man into a caricature." Langston Hughes has that authority, and in this good sense of the word Simple and his friends are caricatures.

Mamie, an unforgettable woman, has to answer the charge of being a stereotype when she feels the need to defend her tastes in the presence of a "passer," a pretender:

> Why, it's getting so colored folks can't do nothing no more without some other Negro calling you a stereotype. Stereotype, hah! If you like a little gin, you're a stereotype. You got to drink Scotch. If you wear a red dress, you're a stereotype. You got to wear beige or chartreuse. Lord have mercy, honey, do—don't like no blackeyed peas and rice! Then you're a down-home Negro for true—which I is—and proud of it! I didn't come here to Harlem to get away from my people. I come here because

there's more of 'em. I loves my race. I loves my people. Stereotype!

The play is bursting with comment, sometimes a bit too obviously.

> SIMPLE: This great big old white ocean—and me a colored swimmer.
> BOYD: Aw, stop feeling sorry for yourself just because you're colored. You can't use race as an excuse forever. All men have problems. And even if you're colored, you've got to swim beyond color, and get to that island that is you—the human you, the man you.

This kind of preaching will bother some readers. But even those who have an aversion to messages will chuckle at Simple's dream of leading white Mississippi troops into action in World War III. They will chuckle, they will wonder, and Mr. Hughes will have made his point.

Tambourines to Glory, the last play in this collection, is characterized by the editor as a "musical melodrama about some aspects of Harlem religion." As a play, greatly helped by the songs, it is far more effective than Mr. Hughes' novel of the same name. Perhaps the best way to sum up the author's viewpoint in the play is to quote his own description of it quoted in the Introduction to *Five Plays:*

> *Tambourines to Glory* is a fable, a folk ballad in stage form, told in broad and very simple terms—if you will, a comic strip, a cartoon—about problems which can only convincingly be reduced to a comic strip if presented very cleanly, clearly, sharply, precisely, and with humor.

There is something intriguing about a writer who knows that the form he has chosen for his work will be right if the presentation of the piece is as honest on stage as his writing was originally. Langston

Hughes, like Bertolt Brecht, writes for the theatre as a knowledgeable man of the theatre. *Tambourines to Glory* comes alive on the page; you can hear it.

In this play two women, Laura and Essie, start a church. In Harlem it is quite possible to "set up shop" in an old store, a movie theatre, any little corner where the faithful poor may gather. In 1930 James Weldon Johnson noted that there were one hundred and sixty Negro churches in Harlem and that one hundred of them were "ephemeral and nomadic, belonging to no established denomination and within no classification." (*Black Manhattan,* New York: Alfred A. Knopf, 1930, p. 163) There must be many more by now. Mr. Hughes himself has said that it is difficult to find a suitable location for a theatre in Harlem, because when the movie houses go out of business they are bought up by "churches." Laura and Essie, who start on a street corner, convert an old movie house into Tambourine Temple.

Essie is sincere. Laura is a charlatan. Good works with evil to the glory of God ultimately. The devil is in the guise, this time, of Big-Eyed Buddy Lomax, a handsome hustler in the employ of white gangsters. The plot is the least effective thing about the play and does not bear telling. What is impressive is the skillful use of songs to heighten emotional scenes and the characterizations, especially of the two leading ladies and the devil himself. Mr. Hughes shows sympathy, even pity, for all the participants in this story of hokum and holiness.

Buddy says, "This church racket's got show business beat to hell. But some churches don't have sense enough to be crooked. They really try to be holy—and holiness don't make money." It is the good Essie, however, who wins in the end—at least of this play.

Webster Smalley's introduction is as informative as it is laudatory. He gives us a good idea of how productive Langston Hughes—poet, playwright, novelist, short story writer—has been and refers to him as "America's outstanding Negro man of letters." It would seem necessary to qualify that praise since James Baldwin has appeared on the scene. Mr. Hughes, however, is an impressive writer, and this collection of plays gives us a chance to know an important side of his work for the first time. He is still, it seems to me, a better poet than playwright, another reason why *Don't You Want To Be Free?* should appear in print soon; for in that play he uses some of his verses effectively within the framework of a play.

Negro playwrights are scarce at the moment, but they are more than promising: Lorraine Hansberry, Alice Childress, Ossie Davis, Loften Mitchell, William Branch and James Baldwin, to name most of the handful. They will, no doubt, write out of their experiences as Negroes; and they will create white characters, because the time has come for them to let us see ourselves through their art.

It is not likely that Langston Hughes will write about white men—unless they wander into Harlem. Harlem is his home, and he records for us the speech and the dreams, the agonies and the compensating joys alive in that city within a city. We are grateful for his plays and for his wise, warm sense of humor. This book should be only a beginning; his other plays and those of younger Negro playwrights should be made available to us soon.

Waters Turpin
"Book Reviews"
CLAJ, 7 (December
1963), 180–1

Webster Smalley and the Indiana University Press have done American literature of the theatre an invaluable service with the publication of *Five Plays by Langston Hughes*. Here for the first time is the meaningful body of Hughes's contribution to the stage under one cover, making it possible for the reader to produce each play in the "theatre of the mind," and thereby evaluate for himself its worth.

That these plays are readable as well as stageable becomes evident as one goes from the turgid melodramatic tragedy of *Mulatto*, set in the plantation South, to the urban fantasy of *Soul Gone Home* and the Harlem folklorism of *Little Ham, Simply Heavenly,* and *Tambourines to Glory,* the latter four serving, no doubt, for the average buying reader as palliatives of primitivism after the strong stuff of the first.

The introductory essay by the Editor is also well worth the reader's time for its perceptive suggestions for understanding the playwright's intent. One is inclined to take with a "grain of salt," however, the somewhat extravagant claim on the flap of the jacket designed by Ronald Sterkel: "No writer has better portrayed and interpreted Negro life in America, especially in the urban North." It may well be too soon to make such a statement even about Hughes, although this reviewer is inclined to place the mantle of American Negro literary deanship upon the poet-novelist-playwright's shoulders, because he rightly deserves it—as no one else at this time does—by his long-time effort and acknowledged achievement.

Finally, this volume deserves the wide sale it should have, since its format and general publishing job are of high quality—it is hardback, neatly and durably so. This reviewer hopes that because of this fine edition, more and more community and collegiate and drama groups will turn to Hughes for their productions. They will find that he stages well.

Additional Review

Crisis, 70 (October 1963), 509.

SIMPLE'S UNCLE SAM

"Simple's Uncle Sam"
Virginia Kirkus Service, 33 (1 August 1965), 786

The main voice in these interludes, 43 newspaper and magazine pieces best described as story-anecdotes, is Jesse B. Semple, or Simple, whom Hughes has developed over the years as a "reflector" of the moods, spirit, whimsies and hopes of the tenants of the Negro ghetto. The subjects include the civil rights scene, national and local politics, even air raid shelters and marriage as an institution. Simple is the Average Man Militant. His fanciful disquisitions often lead to serious revelations—such as his dream in which Negroes rule the South and "Mammy" Eastland comes begging for a handout. Harlem is a place, and one gets the feeling of it through several characters; but Harlem is also an idea and Hughes makes it more comprehensible to anyone befuddled by its complexities. As for Jesse B., he proves by his commentary on the *de facto* racist institutions which most white people take for granted as unbiased that he is as simple as a Jesuit.

Jessie Kitching
"Fiction: *Simple's Uncle Sam*"
Publishers Weekly, 188 (18 October 1965), 50

Simple (Jesse B. Semple) of Harlem talks about Harlem, civil rights, the pleasures of beer-drinking, his Cousin Minnie ("no re-specter of persons"), his wife Joyce (sharp-tongued but loving), and other people and things. If you have not met him before, we will tell you that Simple is a philosopher of brilliant common sense and wry humor, a Will Rogers of his time and place. No wonder he is Langston Hughes' favorite character. . . .

Chester M. Hampton
"Books in Review: Some Observations on Being Colored"
Baltimore Evening Sun, 3 November 1965, p. 28A

[. . .]

Simple's fans (this writer has been one for a good twenty years), have followed their hero from his early bachelor days as a Harlem bar habitué and commenter on the American racial scene, to his present staider, married state. But just as Simple's accumulation of years, wife and respectability have not changed his drinking habits (he still hangs out in the same bar), they have not tempered his trenchant, witty observations on the indignity, inconvenience and downright peril of being colored in America.

[. . .]

This mingling of bitterness and absurdity points up the greater absurdities in the source of bitterness. It is characteristically Simple, and also characteristically American Negro humor. Because that's who Simple is—he is the Negro man on the street articulating his grief and outrage while at the same time reducing them to terms he can deal with through the objectivity of humor.

In this vein, one of Simple's devices is the cataloguing of his misfortunes, in which he so cleverly mixes the significant and the trivial or the hilarious that it would be a lachrymose person indeed who would be moved to tears. . . .

The cadence and internal rhyme . . . betray Mr. Hughes's considerable background as a poet.

[. . .]

Simple is a synthesis of all the persons Mr. Hughes listened to in all those places—a synthesis in which the catalysts are the sensitivity and compassion of the poet.

Julian Krawcheck
"Hughes' Jesse Semple Speaks for the Negro"
Pittsburgh Press Showtime, 12 November 1965, p. 15; also in *Cleveland Press,* 12 November 1965

It would be well-nigh impossible for any Negro to write anything today without major allusion to the omnipresent plight and plaint of the American Negro.

That Langston Hughes can do so with gentle wit and philosophy, albeit searching commentary, is a tribute to the man's capacities as a story teller and as a man.

It is Hughes' particular genius that he can make a point as well by suggestion as by detail; and in Jesse B. Semple—or Simple as he is known informally—the former Clevelander has created an effective instrument for laying bare the Negro's innermost thoughts.

This is so because Simple is a sort of a Negro Everyman endowed with a most uncommon if homely eloquence.

You know it is the whole Negro race wailing its heart out, and not just Simple, when Hughes' fictional character sounds off on the good old days. . . .

Hughes' stories happily do not always have a racial message. There are a number about Simple's doughty Cousin Minnie, who "in protecting her ladyhood (against designing males) does not always act like a lady."

And there is a word of reproach for Negro religious exploiters in Simple's story about five prosperous gospel singers in a Harlem church. He says:

"When you hear them singing, 'I Cannot Bear My Burden Alone,' what they really mean is, 'Help me get my cross to my Cadillac.'"

Hughes' respected place in American literature is maintained, if not enhanced, by this latest collection of Simple stories. A beguiling choice for an evening of light but not wasted reading.

L. M. Collins
"Writers Share a Common Goal"
Nashville Tennessean, 14 November 1965, p. 10C

"These are the times that try men's souls" was never so applicable to the American historical scene than now. When declared by Tom Paine during the American Revolution, it was a comment on the unprecedented struggle of the people of the Colonies to be free.

Striking a parallel are the works of two distinguished commentators on the continuing fight for freedom by millions of America's black citizens: Langston Hughes and James Baldwin—spokesmen for a people in transition.

These two writers have enjoyed the recognition of personal worth, the former as poet, story-teller, and playwright; the latter, as essayist, novelist, and dramatist, yet they have exerted their influence upon public opinion by stating that now is the time when America should decide what shall be the basic tenets of her social organization. This was emphasized some time ago when I reviewed Mr. Hughes' autobiographical journey *I Wonder as I Wander*.

Together, they urge that the Negro be allowed to succeed according to traditional American standards and encourage the discovery and promotion of individual qualities and merits.

They share a common goal: complete personal freedom without prejudice and bigotry. For them, man's inhumanity to man must not be allowed to stultify the creative, the natural, and the spiritual impulse, especially if brotherhood is to survive as a virtue of democracy in these trying times.

The word for Langston Hughes is laughter. With a flair for the comic touch, Mr. Hughes won and sustained for 35 years a devoted audience who read his poems, sketches, stories, and newspaper columns for social commentary because they were "not without laughter."

These readers of *Simple Speaks His Mind* smiled and chuckled at the merry antics and mock-serious episodes of Simple—Mr. Jesse B. Semple of Harlem, U.S.A., in the Simple series of past years.

For the Hughes following, here is a laughing matter: *Simple's Uncle Sam*, a collection of 46 stories and sketches—actually a framework for Simple's activities and philosophy of life, for Simple, the truly folk hero, who comments wisely, wittily,

not linguistically soundly but morally well of American life as seen through the eyes of a Harlem sage of the tenements.

[. . .]

Mr. Hughes' Simple is the tragic portrait of a man groping for total manhood—often blindly, sometimes magnificently informed in a raw way. Yet our hero, fighting the minor battles of little men, is a symbol of Everyman, without the salt of tears of defeat. For Mr. Hughes has endowed his creation with a delightful wit that sustains him in the Harlem jungle.

[. . .]

Lillian Gregson "Books 'n Stuff" *Dekalb* [Ga.] *New Era and North Dekalb Record,* 18 November 1965, p. 5A

Those habituated to the same newspapers or periodicals will, over the course of time, have developed a pattern of reading. Whether conscious of the procedure or not, the readers will automatically reach first for the favorite comic, the gladdening, or maddening columnist, the special feature, or what all.

Applying this theory, I'll wager that most of the *Chicago Defender*'s readers will turn at once to a column written by Langston Hughes, one of the finest literary talents in America.

I have never seen a copy of this Negro newspaper. But, if the rest of the material in it approximates the quality of Mr. Hughes' writing, other newspapers had better look to their laurels.

Langston Hughes is one of his race

who, despite the inhuman privations and oppressions of the Negro's lot, seems to have surmounted this background. He has shed the burdens of the past by acquiring compassion, a delightfully wry wit, and a writing technique subtle enough to appear artless.

Some years ago, Langston Hughes created a character, one Jesse B. Semple, more affectionately known as "Simple." Around Simple, he wove situations and adventures, each a tale complete in itself, but bearing a thread, sometimes of place, sometimes of person, which fit smoothly to make a continuing story.

The little narratives were printed in the newspaper and had a wide and happy reading. Book publishers envisioned profit if the best of the Hughes columns were gathered under a hard cover. The "Simple" stories have already made several books. The latest Langston Hughes is *Simple's Uncle Sam.*

Simple, having been born and bred in Virginia, left home for the wider, some would say, wilder pastures of Harlem. By now nearing middle age, he is married to strong-minded Joyce, his second wife, whom he obviously respects as well as loves. Little educated, Simple nevertheless admires intellectual attainments. "Being colleged," is how he puts it.

Each story's structure is similar.

The narrator in the tale is a friend of Simple's. They meet for beer in a neighborhood bar. There the narrator plies Simple not only with questions, but with many a glass of the malt. Poor Simple frequently finds himself financially strapped.

Simple is expansive with ideas and opinions on every possible subject. The topics of the day attract his philosophical attention. Naturally, items of special interest to him as a Negro, Civil Rights, for example, will stimulate an array of Simpleisms.

[. . .]

Ted Poston
"Simple of Lenox Avenue"
Crisis, 72 (December 1965), 670–1

Gad! any true aficionado is likely to exclaim after reading several early chapters of Langston Hughes' latest chronicle on Jesse B. Simple, America's most caustic commentator on contemporary concerns.

What goes on here? Is Simple becoming mellow? What's all this nostalgia about his childhood days down home where that mean old white man kicked him on his shins for nothing. Or the time his kinfolks whipped him for lying when he told them truthfully how a kindly old white man "patted me on the head and gave me a dime, saying 'Looks like you could stand an ice cream cone.'"

"They could not understand," Simple recalls "that there is some few people in the world who do good without being asked . . . that is why I do not hate all white folks today . . . not everybody has to be begged to do good, or subpoenaed into it."

But such nostalgia, pathos and wistful recollection don't last long in this fifth collection of Hughes' most pithy philosopher. Soon Simple is back on his Lenox Avenue bar stool, where Hughes first met him during World War II, and giving worldwide range to his opinions on everything under, or even near, the sun.

[. . .]

But Simple and his Boswell are at their best when our hero envisions the triumph of the Black Revolution with the Negroes finally on top. And there sits Simple on the wide veranda of his Virginia mansion, sipping mint juleps served him by that old family retainer, Old Mammy Faubus, and giving advice to her and another retainer of another Negro aristocrat, Old Mammy Eastland. . . .

No, Simple is still Simple. But Langston Hughes might find himself in trouble. In a recent column in *The New York Post* (which Simple helped this reviewer integrate after 25 years) Hughes wrote:

"Simple was born full-blown and already married when I met him in imagination 20 years ago in Harlem."

Imagination indeed! Any one who has visited any bar on Lenox or Central Avenues, on South Parkway or Deep Wylie knows that no one imagined Simple. They've seen him and heard him in person.

M.R.
"Books: The Current Crop: Mexico to Moscow"
People's World, 11 December 1965, pp. 6–7

Langston Hughes "Simple" columns are a staple in the Negro press as well as on bookshelves in their collected form. *Simple's Uncle Sam* is the fifth such collection to make hard cover form.

The author's Harlem beer drinking companion furnishes a splendid window on life in that vast ghetto. Simple is very much the average Harlem dweller—most of the time. He voices the opinions, the hopes, the frustrations, the complex and multiform problems besetting the average, uneducated Negro in an area notable for rats, roaches, overcrowding, unemployment, bully white policemen and a baker's dozen other headaches—enough to make a stoic weep.

Simple's barroom talks cover all this but are far from confined to Harlem. They range from comment on life on a Dixie farm to women's rights, the war in Vietnam, life in white America and gossip about Negro notables, to such homely topics as who gets what out of the family paycheck and how to do your bit during a race riot without being downed by a brick thrown by some careless rooftop bombardier.

As usual in these columns, the handling varies widely. Sometimes they're deadly serious, sometimes hilarious. Most often they take on the flavor of the relaxed, front-porch, rocking-chair talks neighbors engage in on a sunny Sunday afternoon.

Whatever form the dialogue takes, the sum of the book supplies the reader with about as fine an insight into the lives, the hearts and the thoughts of Harlem's citizens as one is likely to find.

"Literature"
Booklist, 62 (15 December 1965), 392

As usual, deep seriousness underlies the folk humor of the durable and enduring Jesse B. Semple, alias Simple, of *Simple Stakes a Claim* and other collections of Hughes's pieces from the *Chicago Defender* and elsewhere. Here Simple reduces race relations, civil rights, and protest movements to purely personal and hence meaningful, embraceable terms against a Harlem backdrop and in so doing pricks bombast, shortsightedness, tokenism, and tit-for-tat philosophy wherever they occur.

Maggie Rennert
"Taking the A-Train"
New York Herald Tribune Book Week, 26 December 1965, p. 10; also in *Book Week* in *Chicago Sun-Times, San Francisco Examiner, Washington Post*

These 46 sketches are not actually stories but little homilies, narrative editorials shining with wit and love. If Simple—Jesse B. Semple of Harlem, U.S.A.—is indeed what he says he is, an ordinary citizen, we are all in luck.

Langston Hughes, author of 30 years' worth of fine poems and short stories, here draws a rounded portrait of contemporary America as seen by a thoroughly human being—prejudiced and tolerant, persnickety and affectionate, impulsive and patient. Simple, down at the neighborhood bar for a beer, watches Harlem and the world go by and reports pungently on both.

In "American Dilemma," the amiable Simple and a young white policeman round a corner in Harlem from opposite directions and nearly collide—a situation normally calling for brief dialogue. But, both victims of their times, they can exchange greeting neither as man and man nor as citizen and policeman; Simple sees "Birmingham" and the cop "riot," and so they pass without a word. "Wigs for Freedom," an account of Simple's ebullient Cousin Minnie and her part in a Harlem riot, is a masterly example of the large and general shown in the passionate terms of

the small and specific. "Pose-Outs" offers the most ingenious suggestion for dealing with racial conflict since Harry Golden's "Stand-up integration." And in "Interview" and "Dr. Sidesaddle," Negro leaders, liberal newspapers, and Harlem success stories are surveyed by the far-from-simple Simple.

I was struck by the similarities between Simple's irony, the wry wit we label "Jewish humor," and the kind of joking I heard once among wartime amputees at an Army hospital. Like the "sick" joke, this humor is self-mocking, but it is also self-respecting. Is the common factor that it is the laughter of victims, realistically kidding themselves and their predicament? As a reviewer, I'm accustomed to noting parallels and resemblances—but that's all I'm qualified to do. With some relief, I leave the question to the ponderings of the social scientists.

Louise M. Meriwether
"Harlem Sage on U.S. Mores"
Los Angeles Times Calendar, 9 January 1966, p. 25

According to the gospel of Jesse B. Semple, better known to Langston Hughes fans as Simple, "If one of them white Southerners gets to the moon first, 'Colored Not Admitted' signs will go up all over heaven. . . . The NAACP will have to go to the Supreme Court, as usual, to get an edict for Negroes to even set foot on the moon . . . Martin Luther King will pray himself up there . . . and will probably be arrested."

In this collection of 46 stories, all appearing in book form for the first time, Simple, the Harlem sage, comments with ironic wit from his favorite Harlem bar on everything Americana from rock'n'roll (blues with a boogie beat) to the left-hand side of God (on which uncrowded side Simple will sit all alone).

Simple admits that economics plays a large part in love in Harlem. "He who would woo, must shell out, too," he says referring to his Cousin Minnie, who asks a man, "Baby, can you pay my rent?" before choosing a permanent friend. It's too bad love and money have to be so mixed up, says Simple, but a woman should have a man's dinner ready when he comes home, because it's hard for a man to love a woman on an empty stomach.

Simple's wife, Joyce, feels it is living in sin for a colored person to marry anybody related to Talmadge, Wallace, Eastland or Sheriff Clark. And it seems to Simple that if white Americans can learn how to fly past Venus, go into orbit and make Telstar, then white barbers could learn how to cut colored hair.

The first Simple stories appeared in a column many years ago in the *Chicago Defender*. In this new collection, Simple is just as unpredictable, irreverent and entertaining as he unleashes his mother's wit on the white and the black of it. To his Uncle Sam he says:

"If you really is my blood uncle, prove it. Before you draft me into any U.S. Army, prove your kinship. Are we is, or are we ain't related?"

James Ventola
"White Man's Burden"
Quincy [Mass.] *Patriot-Ledger*, 29 January 1966, p. 18

Simple's Uncle Sam is a collection of 46 short dialogues between Jesse B. Semple of Harlem and Boyd, his more sophisticated friend. In the course of the book, Simple (as Jesse is called) philosophizes on a wide range of subjects from beauty contests (he calls for an "ugly contest") to Uncle Sam himself (he wants Harry Belafonte or Sidney Poitier to pose for the Uncle Sam posters once in a while).

Simple points to basic incongruities in American life. Of haircuts for Negroes, he says, "If white Americans can learn how to fly past Venus, go into orbit and make Telstar, it looks to me like white barbers in Ohio could learn how to cut colored hair." He invites his white boss, who is sympathetic toward Negroes to "come uptown with me and reintergrate." But he can also be biting. Asked how he can be so sure that he is going to heaven, he replies, "Because I've already been in Harlem."

Simple is the conventional naif, the child-dreamer who has special insight into the workings of the world. The trick, of course, is that the apparently simple-minded hero is really very wise indeed, and Simple delights and charms us the way wise old farmers sometimes do, showing us by contrast just where we went wrong.

Like Damon Runyon, author of "Guys and Dolls," and Joel Chandler Harris, creator of the Uncle Remus Tales, Langston Hughes attempts to spark social comment from the interplay of a simple mind in a complex world; the childlike Simple sees

697

essential reality more clearly than his worldly friends do.

The danger in all this is that the author must be very careful never to drop the pose. Simple is most charming when he is dispensing folk wisdom. When he becomes the mouthpiece for the author's more complicated social philosophy, the facade drops, and we are left with an embarrassed Hughes made up as a simpleton. Since writing of this kind is structured by one fruitful but fragile gimmick, when the essential fiction fails, there is nothing left to hold the work up.

But for the most part, Hughes is very adept at keeping up the pose, and Simple emerges as a genuine folk hero. Inevitably, the creation of a folk hero means the over-simplification of complex realities, and some will object to Simple's lack of rancor as essentially unreal in the portrayal of the Negro American living in Harlem. But Simple is not "the Negro American"; he is just Simple. And if Simple's world is a dream-world, the implication that it is really a nightmare is always present, and readers can imagine the underlying horror of life in Harlem for themselves.

Those who aren't willing to do so can read *Simple's Uncle Sam* as a series of forty-six clever jokes about a modern day blackface clown. The rest of us can take Simple for what he is, the personified laughter of an oppressed people.

Robert O'Keefe
"Langston Hughes' Hymn to the Universe"
Community, 25 (February 1966), 13

It is a positive delight, after reading social surveys on housing, education, and employment, to read a book by Langston Hughes. He does what poets should do. He distills the essence of the matter and re-designs it in a funny, enjoyable, pleasant manner.

There are whole paragraphs in his *Simple's Uncle Sam* that clamor to be read aloud, to be sung—with guitar accompaniment. Like, take for instance, that page on "Swinging High," the second of these forty-six stories:

"... looks to me life is like a swing. ..."

That page has rhythm, a rise and fall that sets the reader swinging. But that's not all the Master has to offer. I like his one-liners that shake you up: "Oh, I don't know what has come over the human race—like that nice young white minister in Cleveland laying down *behind* a rolling bulldozer, *not* in front of it—where the driver could see him maybe and maybe stop in time before the man got crushed to death. He were protesting Jim Crow, but sometimes the protest is worse than the Crow."

There is a strain of sadness in the stories of Langston Hughes, but he can't leave out the humor. It's part of him, and it makes the book easy on the eyes. Mostly there's the touch of the poet, lightening the whole thing with a kind of joy in the way things are said, that you know that what is said must be true.

698

No photographs, only the pictures your imagination creates, and the new insights the author draws from them.

Barnabas "Looks at New Books" *Together: The Midmonth Magazine for Methodist Families,* 10 (March 1966), 60

Harlem, that part of New York City which was the scene of a riot in 1964, is both mecca and ghetto. To many a Negro in the South, it represents the ultimate in living; to many of the Negroes living there, it is a jungle.

What is it really like? We get different pictures from Langston Hughes and Claude Brown. Hughes' fictional Jesse B. Semple, known as Simple in *Simple's Uncle Sam,* and Brown, telling his own story of his early years in *Manchild in the Promised Land,* talk about the same things—crowded, inadequate housing, high prices for poor quality, white-owned stores, drug addicts, white people—but their attitudes are as different as if they inhabited different planets.

Simple, though fictional, is more real to the reader. His humorous observations on the world in which he finds himself have a wry wisdom that tells you he is his own man regardless of restrictions or inequality.

Brown tells his story in such a kaleidoscopic shower of episodes that you never are sure just what happened or how he changed from a frequent inmate of reform school to the educated, talented man he now is. He gives us only the seamy side, and without straining out any of the ugliness. Consequently, his is a shocking, unpleasant book.

This does not mean you should ignore Brown; books like his broaden our experience and, hopefully, our understanding. But Hughes, speaking through Simple, gives us people who can draw our admiration and to whom we can relate.

W. Edward Farrison "Book Reviews" *CLAJ,* 9 (March 1966), 296–300

Simple's Uncle Sam is Langston Hughes's fifth book about Jesse B. Semple, better known as Simple. The first three books were *Simple Speaks His Mind* (1950), *Simple Takes a Wife* (1953), and *Simple Stakes a Claim* (1957). These three works in the form of sketches of conversations between Simple and his friend Boyd in a Harlem bar established Simple as a realistic—almost real—character in American imaginative writing. In 1961 Hughes himself selected seventy of the 143 sketches in these three books and published them in a volume entitled *The Best of Simple.* The fifth volume consists of forty-six sketches now published in a book for the first time. Most of them were written or revised within the last few years, and some in the summer of 1965. Some of them were first published in newspapers, notably in the *Baltimore Afro-American* as well as in the *Chicago Defender.*

A denizen of Harlem transplanted from Virginia, Simple continues in this new volume his reviews of personal events and comments on life in Harlem, the various phases and ramifications of the American

699

race problem, life in the United States, and life in general. He still tells his tales and comments on people and things, as his creator said in the Foreword to *The Best of Simple*, "mostly in high humor, but sometimes with a pain in his soul" and sometimes with a resort to laughter "to keep from crying." More noticeably, perhaps, than in the preceding volumes, he is often too serious to laugh—or to do more than smile sardonically—and too philosophical to cry. Without referring to the law of compensation, he incidentally takes cognizance of its all too frequent misapplication. "Some folks think that everything in life has to balance up, turn out equal," he says in the sketch entitled "Empty Houses." "If you buy a man a drink, he has to buy you one back. If you get invited to a party, then you have to give a party, too, and invite whoever invited you. . . . But me, I am not that way." Having been "a passed-around child" because he had no home during his childhood, he learned very early to distinguish a mere house from a home, as he explains in the same sketch. Said he, "If they do not have a little love for whoever lives in the house with them, it is an empty house."

Realist that he is, Simple has no appetite for the religious provender offered by the "gospel singers" in the store-front and movie-front churches in Harlem, but he likes their singing well enough to contribute to their collections just as he pays admission fees to shows. His taste for music is radically different from that of Joyce, his wife, who he says "is the most opera-listening woman I know." (p. 40) Unsophisticated as he is, he neither pretends to tastes he does not have nor apologizes for those he has. He is no less objective about the playing of numbers, an especially popular activity in Harlem, than he is about the "gospel singers." With arresting logic he queries, "If a man can bet at the race track, or play bingo in church, why should

he not play the numbers in the barbershop, in his car, or, if you are a lady, in your beauty shop or laundromat?" (p. 88)

Simple's cousin Minnie, "an offshoot of the family," who was introduced in *Simple Stakes a Claim*, figures prominently in nine and incidentally in two of the sketches in *Simple's Uncle Sam*. Whether her creator intended for her to do so or not, she reflects a contrast between the Simple of the first book and the Simple of the most recent one. Like the former, who constantly had woman troubles, she constantly has boyfriend troubles, many of which Simple thinks that she makes for herself. On the contrary Simple has been happily married for some time and is too eager to remain so to do anything to endanger his marital bliss. Accordingly he says that "My eyes might roam, but I stay home." (p. 78) There is another notable contrast between Minnie and Simple. Like him she is a firm believer in civil rights and the freedom of which they are a part. But unlike him, who is sufficiently self-possessed to consider these things dispassionately as well as humorously, she is inclined to emotionalism concerning them. This fact is revealed in his retelling of her story that her participation in the Harlem riot cost her a head injury and the loss of her wig. (pp. 139–45)

One of the most ingenious sketches in the book is Simple's account of a coffee-break conversation between him and his white boss. The boss, Simple observes, "always says 'THE Negro,' as if there was not 50-11 different kinds of Negroes in the U.S.A." Assuming that Simple represented THE Negro, the boss inquired as to "just what does THE Negro want?" Simple replied that he neither was nor represented THE Negro, but that "I am *me*," and that "I represent my own self." Less convincingly than pharisaically, the boss avowed, "I am a liberal. I voted for Kennedy. And this time for Johnson. I believe in integration.

Now that you got it, though," he asked, "what more do you want?" To which inquiry Simple replied that Negroes want "reintegration. . . . That you be integrated with *me,* not me with you." Embarrassed by Simple's insistence that true integration is a two-way process, the boss explained that white people want integration "up to a point," whereupon Simple returned to the boss's original question and answered it succinctly. "That is what THE Negro wants," he said "to remove that *point.*" This sketch most skillfully exposes quasi-liberalism, which is an often concealed obstacle to improvement in race relations.

Another of the most ingenious sketches in the book is "Rude Awakening." This is Simple's account of a dream in which he found the South ruled by Negroes, and ironically enough, with its traditions, whether factual or fanciful, inverted. He found himself, "black as I can be," the occupant and owner of a white mansion in Virginia, with two white mammies at his service—"dear old Mammy Faubus what raised me" and Mammy Eastland. He just loved to hear white folks sing—but he could not understand how "some of these little blue-eyed crackerninnies" got the nerve to want to go to colored schools. Like a confirmed interpositionist, he declared that "Our great institutions like the University of Jefferson Lee belong to us, and not even with all deliberate speed do we intend to constitutionalize the institutionalization of our institutions." Indeed from such a dream world there could have been only a rude awakening into the turmoil of matters racial early in the 1960's.

The last sketch in the book is entitled "Uncle Sam," and from it the title of the work itself was derived. In this sketch there emerges again Jesse B. Semple, philosopher. Simple is curious and uncertain about his relationship to Uncle Sam, "the old man in the tight pants, the swallowtail coat, and the star-spangled hat who lives in the attic above the President at the top of the White House." Boyd explains that Uncle Sam is "a symbol of the government." For Simple, however, Boyd's explanation is hardly sufficient, for he has observed that Uncle Sam is always portrayed as white—never as an Indian, a Negro, a Chinese-American, or a nisei. Therefore Simple does not find the symbol truly symbolical. Nor is he satisfied with the token representation of people like himself in other symbolical situations. As he remembers, he has never seen a Negro except Booker T. Washington portrayed on a postage stamp. In brief Simple is inclined to consider Uncle Sam a relative "on the off-side"—as his cousin Minnie is.

To this reviewer it seems inappropriate to compare Simple with Paul Bunyan and Davy Crockett, as has been attempted. Both Bunyan and Crockett were heroes of the nineteenth-century American frontier, the former being altogether legendary and the latter partly so. Their histories abound in the kind of exaggeration which belongs only to the most extravagant romances. This is not true of Simple. He is no frontiersman nor romantic creation of any kind. He is a contemporary realistic character inured to city life, especially as it is in New York City and particularly as it is in Harlem, and imbued with its spirit. He is a product, not of mere fancy, but of his creator's experience, observations, and reflections vitalized by a healthy, well-disciplined imagination.

Comparisons which have been made between Simple and Mr. Dooley are somewhat more appropriate. Both men comment, sometimes in the same ways, on affairs of their times, but there are remarkable differences between them. Simple, a product of Virginia's segregated public schools, expresses himself, withal, in a dialect more natural and indeed more convincing than Mr. Dooley's mutilated English. Moreover the simple rhymes which fall casually, naturally, and frequently from Simple's lips give his remarks such zest and individuality as are not found in Mr. Dooley's lucubrations. No matter with whom Simple is compared, he remains representative of many who see life, especially in America, as it is, contemplate much of it as it should not be, and consider much of it as it should be; and *Simple's Uncle Sam* is an excellent continuation of his reading—his criticism—of life.

Dudley Randall
"Books Noted"
Negro Digest, 15 (April 1966), 52, 94

Langston Hughes's *Simple's Uncle Sam* reminds you of the Senegalese soldier in World War I who, when told by a German in hand-to-hand combat "You missed me!" answered "Just shake your head and you'll find out." These conversations in a bar with Jesse B. Semple have the lightness and casualness of the newspaper columns from which they were drawn, but when you think they are all froth and humor, there's the keen cutting steel, as when Simple remarks that even Martin Luther King, with all his love, doesn't go into a white barber shop in the South for a haircut, or when Simple makes some warm comments on leaders' advice to stay cool; or when he advises young men seeking adventure to go not to the Wild West but to the savage South. Simple glances at his own folks too. He describes an evil Harlem waitress who piles meanness upon meanness. And there's a Dr. Sidesaddle who earns his living in Harlem but moves to a white neighborhood where "we are

the only ones." This is a book of the people. It has the phrases, the accents, the feelings of the people. Simple is topical, but on topics which have been with us for three hundred years. Some of the chapters sharpen to vignettes, like "Lost Wife," which touchingly contrasts infidelity to love. Characters emerge—poised Lynn Clarisse from Fisk, bodacious maneating Minnie, a scared white rookie cop alone in Harlem at night. Sometimes Mr. Hughes does not use keen steel, but a club, as in the farcical "Rude Awakening," where Simple dreams Negroes have taken over the South and he is Colonel Semple sitting on his veranda being served by his old faithful white Mammy Faubus. This reversal of the stereotypes uproariously exposes their ridiculousness so that no one should be taken in by them any more. Yet we feel a thin edge of uncertainty. Mammy Faubus protests just a shade too much. We notice that she calls Simple not a quality "man" but a quality "Nigra." Mammy Eastland laughs a little too heartily at Colonel Semple's little joke about her not using more than half of his donation to her church to buy herself snuff. Is it possible that these two have been corrupted by the rebellious young whites, who clamor to eat with us and go to school with us? Could Mammy Faubus and Mammy Eastland be secret members of the NAAWP?

Marion Bohler
"Courier Book Shelf"
Pittsburgh Courier, 16 April 1966, p. 9

A great many people have been wondering what happened to Simple, and now they can find out. This is a collection of forty-six stories—all about Simple and the way he sees Harlem through his own eyes, because of his passionate concern for people and his intense desire to grasp the meaning of life. Simple is not really simple though, because he clearly tells about all the interesting experiences that happened to lead him to explore the secret depth of man's struggles and sins.

Checklist of Additional Reviews

"*Simple's Uncle Sam*," *Publishers Weekly*, 188 (30 August 1965), 305.

Francis D. Campbell, Jr., "New Books Appraised: Fiction," *Library Journal*, 90 (1 November 1965), 4806.

"Books," *Jet*, 29 (4 November 1965), 44.

Marceline Stapes, "Simple Probes World," *Norfolk Virginian-Pilot*, 7 November 1965, p. 6B.

Charles Poore, "Books of the Times: Satire Is the Eternal Vaudeville of Morality," *New York Times*, 11 November 1965, p. 45.

"Weekly Record: Hughes, Langston," *Publishers Weekly*, 188 (15 November 1965), 118.

"Book Shelf," *Ebony*, 21 (January 1966), 18.

William Langley, "Short, Pungent Dialogue Marks Hughes Book," *Portland* [Maine] *Evening Express*, 16 March 1966, p. 7.

"Book Review," *Sepia*, 15 (April 1966), 75.

Choice 3 (April 1966), 122.

"Paperbacks: Nonfiction," *Publishers Weekly*, 192 (14 August 1967), 52.

THE PANTHER AND THE LASH

"The Panther and the Lash"
Kirkus Service, 35 (1 May 1967), 588

Some of the poems in this collection first appeared in magazines . . . ; some have been reprinted from earlier books; some are new. Mr. Hughes has published thirty-six books since the 'Thirties, but his style has not markedly changed, except that he has more or less dropped Negro dialect; he still writes in an admirably lean, brief, matter-of-fact form which avoids the obvious pitfalls of anger, sentimentality or melodrama inherent in his subject matter—the plight of the American Negro ("I play it cool / And dig all jive— / That's the reason / I stay alive")—to write of bombings in Birmingham, Harlem, Negro cleaning women, or himself as a dinner guest ("I know I am / The Negro Problem / Being wined and dined . . ."). The problems and reactions are bluntly stated, but with the simplicity and sometimes the lyricism, of spirituals; a frankness that cannot be disliked or evaded; an objective, bitter truth stated from inside and without self-pity.

Bill Katz
"Poetry"
Library Journal, 92 (1 June 1967), 2163–4

. . . Drawn from his earliest to his latest writings, the present selection presents him at his best. He has been writing another version of Ginsberg's *Kaddish* for some 30 years, and deserves more atten-

tion than he receives. But, Lord, he's not about to conform to either liberal or reactionary views of Negroes. . . .

Douglas Wilson
"Poems of Negro Anguish"
Providence Journal, 13 August 1967, p. 16W

Langston Hughes' "poems of our times" were published eight weeks after the Negro poet's death and one week before Detroit. Almost unwittingly, the blurb on the jacket says: "Forty-four of these poems are new, and the remaining twenty-six, which are drawn from previous books, take on new significance in this collection."

Here is a spokesman of his race who speaks with controlled anger; a writer whose injury and frustration wrench the reader more certainly than the incantations of Stokely Carmichael and H. Rap Brown. Hughes' verse is cold sober, and the violence in it is warned about rather than preached. Beyond the violence in the title—the black symbol and the lash of white oppression—the poet sees the backlash. It is not white backlash but Negro backlash—outrage against the long, sore history of discrimination, like the part of it in "Harlem." . . .

The Negro backlash is coming, too, against subtle discrimination. Neither "Harlem" nor the circumstance in the following lines is Southern. For the American Negro, Hughes says, they are universal, and "Office Building: Evening" could be anywhere. . . .

The poet here could be mocking "Whitey's" bid for patience. He is not. This is more serious. Maybe colored folks cleaning for white folks is due to their difference of education, of background; maybe it does take time—some time—to change all that. But how long?

"Just wait" is Hughes' warning to the White man who has deferred the larger meaning of emancipation until it's gotten to the bursting point. If the message isn't pleasant, Newark shows, now, that it was pointed. Detroit shows it was pointed. They answer Hughes' loaded question:

What happens to a dream deferred?

. . .

This poem, which comes from an earlier collection, is grouped with other selections of the fire-next-time variety under the heading, "Words on Fire." But there is laughter and "cool" in a few of the poems, like "Motto." . . .

This summer, as these poems appear in the bookstores of cities like New York, Los Angeles, Detroit and Providence, those who read them will dig Hughes' last writings less for their artistic merit than for the discomfort of the truth of them.

Rosemary Daniell
"Hughes Poems: Not Works of Art but Written in Blood"
Atlanta Journal and Constitution, 3 September 1967, p. 4C

Some writers, passionately taking up a just and popular cause, find themselves called poets. For though rhetoric doesn't make poetry, it can sometimes be as moving. And that more than 36 volumes of the work of Negro writer Langston Hughes

have been published attests to the power of becoming spokesman for a vast and backed-up sea of emotion. As works of art, his poems may not stand; but as human documents, they are written in blood.

Uncorroded by the acid of a LeRoi Jones, somewhat in the style of Kenneth Rexroth (though without Rexroth's subtlety or Eastern influence), Hughes speaks directly to anyone who can read or listen. With the voice of early hip, he declares, "I play it cool / And dig all jive— / That's the reason / I stay alive. / My motto / As I live and learn / Is / Dig and be dug / In return." He might be describing himself when he says, "The speaker catches fire, Looking at listener's faces. His words jump down to stand in their places."

Taking its power primarily from the contents of the mind of the reader, imagery is bleak and limited. Consistent with this surface approach to literary production are the sparse American historical references that create the only dimension other than the newsprint present. "Ghosts of 1916," "American Heartbreak," and "Frederick Douglass: 1817–1895" express in figurative, underdeveloped strokes the pathos of the unfulfilled American dream of equal rights for all. In "Christ in Alabama," "Birmingham Sunday," "Bible Belt," "Ku Klux" and other poems, Hughes utilized existent situations to protest the injustices. . . .

Keneth Kinnamon
"The Man Who Created 'Simple'"
Nation, 205 (4 December 1967), 599–601

More than forty years ago Langston Hughes issued in these pages (June 23, 1926) a manifesto of racial affirmation entitled "The Negro Artist and the Racial Mountain." In it he spoke not only for himself but also for other young writers of the Harlem Renaissance against both the literary gentility of Negro critics like Benjamin G. Brawley and W. E. B. Du Bois and the flippantly superficial assimilationism of the journalist George S. Schuyler. Hughes rejected the self-denying "urge toward whiteness" that would cause the Negro artist to abandon his most distinctive materials and his unique perspective; instead, the Negro should utilize proudly "his racial individuality, his heritage of rhythm and warmth, and his incongruous humor that so often, as in the blues, becomes ironic laughter mixed with tears."

These words may now seem dated—and indeed some would insist that they could be construed to constitute a Jim Crow aesthetic ("heritage of rhythm and warmth"!). But they specify cogently some of the durable elements in a remarkable literary career that began in 1915 when Hughes was selected as class poet in a Lincoln, Ill., grammar school and ended last May when he died in Harlem, a death that seemed oddly premature for a writer so perennially and ebulliently youthful.

Hughes wrote more than forty books, edited or translated fourteen more, and contributed hundreds of essays, poems, columns, reviews and letters to scores of anthologies, magazines and newspapers. . . . Much of his enormous body of writing is admittedly hack work—children's books, popular history, occasional journalism—but Hughes supported himself for thirty-seven years solely by his pen and his platform appearances. No other serious Negro writer survived so long and did so much in an often unreceptive literary market place. In this respect, as in others, Hughes was a pioneer.

[. . .]

However valuable his services as an anthologist, it is as poet that Hughes is best known to white readers. In the posthumous *The Panther and the Lash,* his poetry is mostly that of racial protest, the snarl of the black panther under the lash—and backlash—of white oppression. Many of Hughes's recent poems catch the threatening mood of impending black retributive vengeance, but the earlier verse gathered here, going back to the *Scottsboro Limited* pamphlet of 1932, more often depicts the Negro as passive victim ("Christ in Alabama," "Jim Crow Car").

Unlike those younger writers, of whom LeRoi Jones is the most eloquent spokesman, Hughes was never quite willing to relinquish the dream of racial fraternity even in the Deep South. He affirms this again by choosing to conclude this volume with "Daybreak in Alabama." This hope, common in the thirties and surviving in Martin Luther King's address to the March on Washington in 1963, may be now all but dead among Negro writers, but otherwise *The Panther and the Lash* reminds us how accurate a poetic barometer of the Negro mood Hughes has been since his first volume, *The Weary Blues* (1926).

As a poet, he did not really improve. Of the twenty poems judged to be Hughes's best in James A. Emanuel's useful critical study, *Langston Hughes*—in which readers will find most of their favorites—all but six were written in the twenties. One could trace developments in Hughes's poetry—his movement from blues to bop rhythms, for example—but not artistic growth. Gertrude Stein's remark to Scott Fitzgerald: "One does not get better but different and older," could have been directed to Hughes as well.

[. . .]

W. Edward Farrison
"Book Reviews"
CLAJ, 11 (March 1968), 259–61

This collection of poems was prepared for publication by the author himself and was in press when he died. Its title was derived from two recent outgrowths of matters racial in America—the Black Panthers and the white backlash. The work is dedicated to Mrs. Rosa Parks of Montgomery, Alabama, who refused to move to the back of a bus, "thus setting off in 1955 the boycotts, the sit-ins, the Freedom Rides, the petitions, the marches, the voter registration drives, and *I Shall Not Be Moved*." Twenty-six of the seventy poems in the collection were selected from Hughes's previously published volumes of verse. The other forty-four are herein first published in one volume, seventeen of them having formerly appeared in periodicals, and twenty-seven now appearing in print for the first time. All of them are indeed poems of our times, for all of them pertain directly or indirectly to the Negro's continuing struggle to achieve first-class citizenship in America. The poems are written in short-line free verse or in occasional rhymes, by both of which Hughes's poetic work has long been distinguished.

The selections are grouped under seven headings, the first of these being "Words on Fire." In this group is "The Backlash Blues," one of the two title poems in the collection. Not only is this one of the new poems but also it has been said to have been the last poem that Hughes submitted for publication before he died. It is an emphatic expression of determined aggressiveness against the opponents of civil rights for Negroes. Also in the first group and new is "Black Panther," the other title poem. Avowedly militant, like Claude McKay's "If We Must Die," this poem has for its theme the determination of black men to give no further ground to oppressors but to stand and fight back desperately, like a panther when cornered.

More ironical than militant is the group called "American Heartbreak," in whose initial poem with the same title a Negro declares generically that "I am the American heartbreak— / The rock on which Freedom / Stumped its toe—." Still more ironical as a whole is the group called "The Bible Belt"—a group in which life principally in Alabama and Mississippi is portrayed at its non-Biblical worst. Singularly memorable as well as new is the poem in this group entitled "Birmingham Sunday," which consists of reflections on the deaths of four little Negro Sunday-school girls who were victims of the bombing of a church in Birmingham on September 15, 1963.

Especially noteworthy at present because of prevailing international affairs is the small group entitled "The Face of War." Two provocative poems in this group are "Mother in Wartime" and "Without Benefit of Declaration," both of which deal with the common failure to understand the wherefores and the futility of war. The mother, "Believing everything she read / In the daily news," was quite unaware that both sides "Might lose." Meanwhile the draftee must go "Out there

710

where / The rain is lead," but is told "Don't ask me why. / Just go ahead and die." What simple, convincing explanatory declaration is there to give him? Alas one is reminded of John Dewey's all but forgotten observations that "The more horrible a depersonalized scientific mass war becomes, the more necessary it is to find universal ideal motives to justify it"; and "The more prosaic the actual causes, the more necessary is it to find glowingly sublime motives."

The group puckishly entitled "Dinner Guest: Me" satirizes a variety of things. Its title poem, which is based on a personal experience, ridicules white quasi-liberalism. "Un-American Investigators" coarsely twits a Congressional committee for its arbitrary methods of dealing with persons summoned before it. "Cultural Exchange," the longest poem in the volume, envisions a radical change in Southern culture in the sociological sense—an inversion of the positions of Negroes and white people in the South with Negroes living "In white pillared mansions," white sharecroppers working on black plantations, and Negro children attended by "white mammies." The *bouleversement* imagined in this poem, which was published in *Ask Your Mama* in 1961, is more ingeniously recounted in "Rude Awakening" in *Simple's Uncle Sam,* which was published in 1965.

Finally there is the group called "Daybreak in Alabama"—a title in which there is a ray of hope for the optimistic, among whom Hughes belonged. As should now be evident, two of the poems in this group rang with prophetic tones when they were published in *One-Way Ticket* in 1949. Observing that first-class citizenship would never come "Through compromise and fear," "Democracy," now entitled "Freedom," left no doubt that other means of achieving it must be employed. And admonishing America to "Beware the day" when Negroes, "Meek, humble, and kind," changed their minds, "Roland Hayes Beaten," now entitled "Warning," foreshadowed at least implicitly the various freedom movements mentioned in the dedication of *The Panther and the Lash.* From the beginning of his career as an author, Hughes was articulate in the Negro's struggle for first-class citizenship. It is indeed fitting that this volume with which his career ended is a vital contribution to that struggle as well as to American poetry.

Theodore R. Hudson "Langston Hughes' Last Volume of Verse" *CLAJ,* 11 (June 1968), 345–8

The late Langston Hughes was never primarily a "protest" poet. Although he wrote almost exclusively of the condition of being a Negro in America, Hughes was no racist in the current sense of the word. Seemingly incapable of acrimony, he was, nevertheless, militant in his own way. Dipping his pen in ink, not acid, his method was to expose rather than excoriate, to reveal rather than revile. Indeed, in the rare instances when he approached irreconcilable bitterness, his art suffered.

The Panther and the Lash, a thematic collection of his social poems, most published for the first time, is no exception.

The poem that perhaps best expresses his attitude and his answer to America's race problem is "Motto." ... Hate is simply not his bag. Empathy is.

A major premise of this volume is that American Negroes are disillusioned—

their dream has been "deferred" indefinitely,

> And you don't
> Give a damn.

The palliatives will no longer do. . . .

America's evading and procrastinating and resultant failure to solve her race problem sorrows the innately patriotic Hughes. He does not want to be

> A Mau Mau
> And lift my hand
> Against my fellow man
> To live on my own land.

But he poses the crucial question

> What happens to a dream deferred?
> Does it dry up
> like a raisin in the sun?
>
> . . .
>
> *Or does it explode?*

And in answer he feels compelled to issue ominous warnings. . . .

Langston Hughes believes that the Negro will survive and that his cause will prevail. In the past, troubles tried to make him

> Stop laughin', stop lovin', stop livin'—
> But I don't care!
> I'm still here!

In other words, the black man's "dream dust" is "not for sale." In the final analysis the "little" Negro alone may have to solve the problem: If the Pied Piper, Moses, Uncle Tom, Dreyfus, Jesus, Father Divine, Robespierre, *et al.,* cannot "pipe our rats away," and "if nobody comes [to pipe them away], send for me," he cries.

Fortunately the humor—the whimsical, ironical, and gently satirical humor—so characteristically Langston Hughes' comes through in this book. For instance, in "Ku Klux," after being abducted by Klansmen and asked if he believes in the "great white race," a pragmatic Negro replies,

> "To tell you the truth,
> I'd believe in anything
> If you'd just turn me loose."

[. . .]

Technically, these poems differ from the blues (Negroes don't get the blues any more anyhow, for the blues is a passive reaction to trouble), jazz, and ballad structured verses of his early volumes. Though not nearly as artistically conceived and executed, the newer poems are more in the free-verse and "be-bop" style and mood of two of his later works, *Montage of a Dream Deferred* and *Ask Your Mama.* There are changing rhythms, oxymoron, counterpoint and counterstatement, cataloguing of names and places, and juxtaposed images. There is less of the urban folk idiom which Hughes is so adroit at using; instead, there is flat and direct statement.

Some of the best poems in this collection are those previously published, including "Merry-Go-Round," "Cultural Exchange," "Dream Deferred," "Christ in Alabama," and "Warning."

Many of Hughes' earlier poems have a spontaneous quality, a mystical effusion, a natural lilt. In *The Panther and the Lash* he seems to have tried too hard, seems to have forced his art—as if his urge to write were the result of exterior commitment rather than interior compulsion. The result is that this anthology is marred in places by the prosaic rather than the poetic, by lines that plod rather than soar. Although these poems may stimulate the reader's mind, they often do not reverberate in his heart. And, as in some of his previous protest poetry, when he is grimly earnest he occasionally loses his poetic touch and declaims rather than sings.

Overall, though, *The Panther and the Lash* is satisfying. His message is both valid and valuable. Hughes depicts with fidelity the Negro's situation and the Negro's reactions to this situation. Hughes has the discerning and accurate eye so necessary for a poet, and his poet's hand and eye are synchronized—which is another way of saying, in the jargon of the ghetto, that Langston Hughes "tells it like it is."

Laurence Liberman
"Poetry Chronicle"
Poetry, 112 (August 1968), 337–43

[. . .]

Langston Hughes's new poems, written shortly before his death last summer, catch fire from the Negro American's changing face. To a degree I would never have expected from his earlier work, his sensibility has kept pace with the times, and the intensity of his new concerns—helping him to shake loose old crippling mannerisms, the trade marks of his art—comes to fruition in many of the best poems of his career: "Northern Liberal," "Dinner Guest: Me," "Crowns and Garlands," to name a few.

Regrettably, in different poems, he is fatally prone to sympathize with starkly antithetical politics of race. A reader can appreciate his catholicity, his tolerance of all the rival—and mutually hostile—views of his outspoken compatriots, from Martin Luther King to Stokely Carmichael, but we are tempted to ask, what are Hughes's politics? And if he has none, why not? The age demands intellectual commitment from its spokesmen. A poetry whose chief claim on our attention is moral, rather than aesthetic, must take sides politically. His impartiality is supportable in "Black Panther," a central thematic poem of *The Panther and the Lash.* The panther, a sym-bol of the new Negro militancy, dramatizes the shift in politics from non-violence to Black Power, from a defensive to an offensive stance: Hughes stresses the essential underlying will to survival—against brutal odds—of either position. He is less concerned with approving or disapproving of Black Power than with demonstrating the necessity and inevitability of the shift, in today's racial crisis.

"Justice," an early poem that teaches the aesthetic value of rage, exhibits Hughes's knack for investing metaphor with a fierce potency that is as satisfying poetically as it is politically tumultuous:

> That justice is a blind goddess
> Is a thing to which we black are wise:
> Her bandage hides two festering sores
> That once perhaps were eyes.

But this skill is all but asphyxiated in many of the new poems by an ungovernable weakness for essayistic polemicizing that distracts the poet from the more serious demands of his art, and frequently undermines his poetics. Another technique that Hughes often employs successfully in the new poems is the chanting of names of key figures in the Negro Revolution. This primitive device has often been employed as a staple ingredient in good political poetry, as in Yeats's "Easter 1916." But when the poem relies too exclusively on this heroic cataloguing—whether of persons or events—for its structural mainstay, as in "Final Call," it sinks under the freight of self-conscious historicity.

[. . .]

Checklist of Additional Reviews

"PW Forecasts: Nonfiction: *The Panther and the Lash*," *Publishers Weekly*, 191 (19 June 1967), 81.

"Your Guide to Forthcoming Books," *Book Buyer's Guide*, 70 (July 1967), 42.

Alvin Beam, "A Topical Poet," *Cleveland Plain Dealer*, 16 July 1967, p. 13G.

Thorpe Menn, "Books of the Day: The Last of Hughes," *Kansas City Star*, 16 July 1967, p. 6E.

D. LaF., "Negro Poet of Protest Still Timely," [Albany] *Knickerbocker News Weekend*, 22 July 1967, p. 4B.

"Weekly Record: Hughes, Langston," *Publishers Weekly*, 192 (24 July 1967), 69.

"Langston Hughes," *Tulsa World Your World Magazine*, 17 September 1967, p. 12.

L. M. Collins, "Exam: Don't Flunk It!" *Nashville Tennessean*, 1 October 1967, p. 6B.

B.B., "Other Books," *Newsday*, 14 October 1967, p. 32W.

Alden Whitman, "End Papers," *New York Times*, 1 June 1968, p. 25.

BLACK MAGIC: A PICTORIAL HISTORY OF THE NEGRO IN
AMERICAN ENTERTAINMENT

H. W. F[uller]
Negro Digest, 17
(February 1968), 96–7

The late Langston Hughes did so much for black letters and for black self-esteem in his 60-plus years among us that it seems somehow a burden on his memory that he should bring gifts to us even after he is with us no more in the flesh. But it is fair to suppose that this substantial contribution, *Black Magic: A Pictorial History of the Negro in American Entertainment,* written in collaboration with Hughes' longtime friend, Milton Meltzer, and published by Prentice-Hall last fall, is not the last of the Hughes legacies. *Black Magic* is a big book, richly illustrated (although many of the photos, mere publicity stills, seem uninspired), and covering all the corners of what can be classified as theater and entertainment from the days of the arrival of the first slave ships through the Sixties, when black entertainers returned to Africa as cultural emissaries from America. *Black Magic,* then, also is an important adjunct of history. Many of the players on the Hughes-Meltzer stage are legendary—Blind Tom, the incredible prodigy from Georgia who made a fortune for his slave master; Thomas Dartmouth Rice, the original "Jim Crow" who traveled to London early in the nineteenth century; the famed Luca family which toured the North in the pre-Civil War years; Elizabeth Taylor Greenfield, the Mississippi songbird whose international career preceded Leontyne Price's by more than a century; and James A. Bland, the revered composer-performer ("Carry Me Back to Old Virginny"). The nineteenth century counterparts of Robert Hooks, Earle Hyman and James Earl Jones were Ira Aldridge and James Hewlett; "Black Patti" (Sisseretta Jones) and E. Azalia Hackley matched the flourishing careers of singers like Grace Bumbry and Gloria Davy, though, of course, without the respect for their artistry which the contemporary singers enjoy. With the onset of the popularity of the incomparable Bert Williams, black entertainers broke through into entertainment dominance in this country which—despite the usual restrictions, bigotry and double standards—they are unlikely to surrender in the foreseeable future. For those collectors of documents of Negro history in general, and on entertainment history in particular, *Black Magic* is a *must.* There has not been anything even remotely like it since Edith J. R. Isaacs' *The Negro in the American Theater,* first published in 1947.

W. Edward Farrison
"Book Reviews"
CLAJ, 11 (June 1968),
367–9

Twelve years ago Langston Hughes and Milton Meltzer published *A Pictorial History of the Negro in America,* a book which deserved many more readers than it probably acquired. *Black Magic,* as its subtitle indicates, surveys only one phase of that history, but it does so comprehensively, simply, and interestingly. The title has nothing to do with the historical meaning of the term *black magic;* it refers generically to the genius which Negroes have evidenced in the arts of music, dramatics, and dancing through the various media of expression, including motion pictures, radio, and television. The thirty chapters and their accompanying, well-chosen illustrations are arranged in approximately chronological order, beginning with an account of "the syncopated beat which the captive Africans brought with them" to the New World and ending with notations of present-day Negro performers at home and abroad. The texts of the several chapters consist of running comments in which many names of persons—famous and near-famous—incidental facts, and some interpretative and critical views are mentioned.

First among the Negro performers in the arts to be acclaimed, as Hughes and Meltzer observed, were the musicians. Especially notable among those of this group who flourished during the middle of the nineteenth century and afterwards were Elizabeth Taylor Greenfield ("the Black Swan"), the Luca Family, and Thomas Greene Bethune ("Blind Tom"). These and many of their fellow-performers might not have been so well remembered had they not been commemorated by James M. Trotter in his *Music and Some Highly Musical People,* which was published in Boston in 1879. Presumably, in their research Hughes and Meltzer became familiar with this volume. They also brought back to memory some nineteenth-century songwriters, like James A. Bland, who was already well-known, and some who have never been well-known, like Gussie L. Davis of Cincinnati and Richard Milburn of Philadelphia, the composers respectively of *In the Baggage Coach Ahead* and *Listen to the Mockingbird.*

Most of *Black Magic* is appropriately devoted to the history of Negroes in the theater as actors, writers of musical comedies, and playwrights. Still most famous among the actors is Ira Frederick Aldridge (1807–1867). Since so much misinformation about Aldridge has so long been prevalent, it would have been good if Hughes and Meltzer had written more extensively than they did about him, as they could have done authoritatively on the basis of

Herbert Marshall and Mildred Stock's thoroughly researched *Ira Aldridge: The Negro Tragedian* (New York, 1958). They did mention this biography, however, in passing.

As Hughes and Meltzer indicated, Negroes made their way on the American stage at the turn of the nineteenth and twentieth centuries in musical comedies of their own creation. This they did principally in New York, which has been the theatrical capital of the United States at least since the beginning of the republic. In many instances the composers of the words and music of the songs in which the musical comedies abounded were persons who had already achieved or were soon to achieve distinction as poets or musicians. Among the poets were Paul Laurence Dunbar and James Weldon Johnson, and among the musicians were Will Marion Cook and J. Rosamond Johnson. Throughout most of his career as a poet, Hughes himself wrote lyrics for shows. Some of these lyrics were set to music by Negro musicians and some by white musicians. From the beginning the performers in these shows have been Negroes. One of them who later became a show in himself was Bert Williams. Influenced by the tradition of the musical comedies, in which singing and dancing were featured, Negro musicians of one generation after another have been inspired to write the popular songs which Americans have sung from time to time generally without knowing who composed them. Likewise performers in these shows have brought into vogue one dance after another—like the cakewalk, now forgotten, the Charleston, and the lindy hop—only to replace each in turn with a new one.

As Hughes and Meltzer might have noted for the sake of historical completeness but did not, William Wells Brown pioneered among Negroes in the writing of dramas and published in 1858 his *The Es-*

cape; Or, A Leap for Freedom, an antislavery melodrama in five acts. This is still generally considered the first play published, although certainly not the first one written, by an American Negro. This play seems never to have been professionally produced, nor was any other play by a Negro author thus presented during the next sixty-odd years. Not until the 1910's, as Hughes and Meltzer discovered, were Negro actors cast in important roles in plays produced by white theatrical companies, and not until the 1920's were plays by Negro dramatists presented on Broadway. The reasons for both of these delays were, of course, racial rather than artistic. It should also be remembered that more often than otherwise Negro actors and playwrights arrived on Broadway by way of the Apollo and the Lafayette Theatres in Harlem.

It has indeed been a long way from the plantation buffoonery with which slaves were often compelled to entertain slaveholders even while their own hearts were breaking, to the Uncle Tom shows, to the minstrel shows, to the unfulfilled plan for Sissieretta Jones ("the Black Patti") to sing roles in *Aida* and *L'Africaine* in the Metropolitan Opera House in 1892, to the musical comedies, to the birth of jazz and the blues, to celebrated dance troupes, the gospel singing—one of the songs being Thomas A. Dorsey's *Precious Lord, Take My Hand,* to the success of those whom Hughes and Meltzer listed as "The Golden Dozens" of actors, musicians of various kinds, dancers, "jazz personalities," and "very versatile artists who can hardly be classed correctly in a single category." It has been almost as long a way from Brown's writing *The Escape* to the Broadway productions of Garland Anderson's *Appearances* in 1925, Hughes's *Mulatto* in 1935, Louis Peterson's *Take a Giant Step* in 1953, Hughes's *Simply Heavenly* in 1957, and Lorraine Hansberry's *A Raisin*

in the Sun in 1959. In *Black Magic* Hughes and Meltzer have retraced and illuminated these ways very well.

Gilbert Chase
"Book Reviews"
Notes: The Quarterly Journal of the Music Library Association, 25 (December 1968), 244

As the title indicates, the illustrations are the main feature of this handsome book. The text is adequate but makes no pretense of any scholarly apparatus. The "Credits for Photographs," however, do constitute a kind of location list for the many photographs and facsimiles that give both pictorial and historical value to the volume. There is an index but no bibliography.

The scope of the book is extremely comprehensive, ranging from African antecedents and "Plantation Days" through minstrelsy, blues, jazz and the Broadway theater, to the movies, radio and television. To borrow the title of one of its chapters, the volume covers "Just About Everything." Thus it will not please the proponents of an "Afro-American culture," since the American Negro's success in the world of entertainment has been largely purchased at the price of doing "just like the white folks"—and if possible doing it even better (which has happened more often in the performing arts than in formal artistic creation). There is a lot about James A. Bland but not a word about the urban blues singer Bobby Bland; there are five "Kings" in the index—but not B.B. King, the "King of the [Urban] Blues."

The aim of the book is obviously

to show that the American Negro has achieved success in terms of the white man's values. Taken on these terms, it is an impressive and comprehensive chronicle, a pictorial treasury that should be in every library. Langston Hughes died on May 22, 1967, shortly after completing his work on this book. His co-author has dedicated it "To Langston, with love."

Checklist of Additional Reviews

"Prentice-Hall: Black Magic," *Publishers Weekly,* 192 (28 August 1967), 228.

"Black Magic," *Kirkus Service,* 35 (1 September 1967), 1098–9.

"Your Guide to Forthcoming Books," *Book Buyer's Guide,* 70 (October 1967), 94.

"Black Magic," *Best Sellers,* 27 (15 November 1967), 321.

George J. Alfred, "Adult Books for Young Adults: Nonfiction," *Library Journal,* 93 (15 January 1968), 315.

Edward Mapp, "Theater," *Library Journal,* 93 (15 February 1968), 770.

S.J.A., "Books for Young Adults," *Catholic Library World,* 39 (April 1968), 602.

"The Arts," *Booklist,* 64 (15 April 1968), 964.

Alden Whitman, "End Papers," *New York Times,* 1 June 1968, p. 25.

Frances Neel Cheney, "Current Reference Books: Black Americans," *Wilson Library Bulletin,* 63 (April 1969), 792–3.

Appendix

Additional Reprints and Checklists

Poetry: Limited Editions and Pamphlets

The Negro Mother (1931)

Arnold C. DeMille, "Book Review," *News World Harlem Weekly*, 24 October 1931, [p. ?].

In a booklet containing a few dramatic recitations, Langston Hughes, author of *The Weary Blues*, poems, and *Not Without Laughter*, a novel, gives us five beautifully-composed ballads, entitled *The Colored Soldier, Broke, The Black Clown, The Big-Timer*, and *Dark Youth*.

Each of these ballads tells an interesting story of Negro life. They are exceedingly colorful in character, and quite suitable to be recited in churches, schools and clubs.

Four of the ballads—*The Negro Mother, The Black Clown, Broke*, and *The Big Timer*—are printed separately in broadside form ready for framing, and can be purchased at ten cents each.

According to the publishers, a limited number of booklets, containing hand-colored illustrations, will be obtainable at seventy-five cents the copy.

Aubrey Bowser, "Book Review: Converted at Last!" *New York Amsterdam News*, 13 January 1932, p. 8.

Can you imagine the feelings of a traveler in a desert who, after many thirsty days, sees the distant glimmer of an oasis? That is the way a man feels when he sights the things he has long been agitating for Negro literature—real Negro literature. By this phrase is meant literature that is written of the Negro, by the Negro, and, most important of all, for the Negro.

The attitude of this reviewer has been condemned repeatedly by the intelligentsia, by eminent Negro authors and other specialists in Negro literature. They argue that, as the Negro forms only one-tenth of the American population, it is foolish to address yourself only to him and ignore the other nine-tenths. Obsessed with the idea of winning white readers, they have overlooked their own people. Thus we have had a flood of books playing up to white people's conception of the Negro, and another flood trying to change that conception.

Nor have they won the expected success with the white public. The critics have noticed them, but critics don't buy books; they sell them, if anything. The great book-buying masses have passed them by. If you can name one of them that has sold 30,000 copies, you will have this reviewer's joyful apology. It is said that *Home to Harlem* sold 22,000 copies; but that is the outstanding exception, if it be true. When you sell your birthright for a mess of pottage, and then don't get the pottage, you are befooled indeed.

Langston Hughes has taken a step in the right direction. His writings used to make colored readers steam with rage; now he is a convert to common sense. It matters little how a man starts, it is what he grows into that counts, and Hughes is growing into something better and bigger. He has discovered (rather late, to be sure, but before the rest of the intelligentsia) that the average Negro knows little and cares less about the thing that has passed for Negro literature in the last ten years.

The Negro Mother is an appeal to a distinctly Negro public. It is a booklet of six poems intended for dramatic recitation, the kind you hear in church lyceums and concerts, with simple accessories.

Langston Hughes is to be heartily commended for this effort. It will not gain the praise awarded to his other efforts, the critics may toss it aside in scorn, and, indeed, in some of the verses it looks as if Hughes had made a deliberate effort to be banal. But it is a constructive move toward the development of a true Negro literature.

"The Negro Mother," "Dark Youth," and "The Colored Soldier," properly recited, will touch responsive chords in any average Negro audience.

Even if this effort does not succeed, one hopes that Hughes will keep on. The first step is to write the thing; the next is to get it into the hands of the people. The price is well within their reach, and all the booklet needs is a good "plugger" in the churches and lyceums.

[. . .]

Dear Lovely Death (1931)

No reviews located.

Scottsboro Limited: Four Poems and a Play in Verse

"Scottsboro Limited," *Boston Evening Transcript*, Book Section, 16 July 1932, [p. 1].

Recent events in Scottsboro, Ky., form the basis for the play and four poems included in this paper-covered booklet. *Scottsboro Limited* is reprinted from the *New Masses*, wherein it first appeared. The play epitomizes in verse and tragedy the industrial plight of the Negro. There are no superlatives, no heroics, no extraneous matter, just stark tragedy, presented in straightforward realism, realism that needs no symbolism to enhance its value as literature or as poetry. It is stern stuff with striking charcoal illustrations by Prentiss Taylor. "Christ in Alabama," one of the poems, is in the same vein as Countee Cullen's "Black Christ."

Alain Locke, "Black Truth and Black Beauty," *Opportunity*, 11 (January 1933), 14–18.

[. . .]

Meanwhile, as the folk-school tradition

deepens, Langston Hughes, formerly its chief exponent, turns more and more in the direction of social protest and propaganda, since *Scottsboro Ltd.* represents his latest moods. . . . But the poet of *Scottsboro Ltd.* is a militant and indignant proletarian reformer, proclaiming:

The voice of the red world
Is our voice, too.
The voice of the red world is you!
With all of the workers,
Black or white,
We'll go forward
Out of the night.

Checklist of Additional Reviews

"Book Marks for Today," *New York World-Telegram*, 11 June 1932, p. 15.

"New Books," *New York Amsterdam News*, 13 July 1932, p. 6.

A New Song (1938)

Anna Peters, "Books of the Day," *Daily Worker*, 30 April 1938, p. 11.

This book of poems by Langston Hughes is published by the International Workers Order; the cover is drawn by Joe Jones; the introduction is by Michael Gold; the price is fifteen cents. This is news. The first edition of *A New Song* numbers 10,000 copies, and should find the audience for poetry which exists in America as it does everywhere else in the world. "The International Workers Order published these poems in the desire to make available literature which would otherwise be out of reach of wage earners."

A New Song expresses the strength and pride of workers of all nationalities and races in the world they have built up and are about to take over. The ballads and lyrics have the simplicity, straightforwardness, and plain, rhythmical speech of all folk songs. The ballads sing; they might be added to or changed in the telling, or translated into other languages, without losing their special folk quality. For instance, there is "Ballads of Lenin":

Comrade Lenin of Russia
High in a marble tomb,
Move over, Comrade Lenin,
And give me room
I am Ivan the peasant
Boots all muddy with soil.
I fought with you, Comrade Lenin.
Now I have finished my toil.
Comrade Lenin of Russia,
Alive in a marble tomb,
Move over, Comrade Lenin,
And make me room.
I am Chico, the Negro,
Cutting cane in the sun.
I lived for you, Comrade Lenin.
Now my work is done.
Comrade Lenin of Russia,
Honored in a marble tomb,
Move over, Comrade Lenin,
And leave me room.
I am Chang from the foundries,
On strike in the streets of Shanghai.
For the sake of the Revolution
I fight, I starve, I die.
Comrade Lenin of Russia
Speaks from the marble tomb:
"On guard with the workers forever—
The world is our room!"

There are chants in this book which lose some of their effectiveness by being read instead of heard performed by mass choruses, but they are always direct, outspoken, fearless.

It is good to march to a song; sometimes songs have no meaning, and only the rhythm keeps us going. But this May Day song has sense and rhythm; Langston Hughes, American Negro poet, writes for all workers, sometimes, as now, in the moving accents of his own people, in "Sister Johnson Marches":

Here I am with my head held high!
What's de matter, honey?
I just want to cry:

Here I go with my banner in my hand!
What's de matter, chile?
Why, he owns de land!
It's de first of May!

Who are all them people
Marching in a mass?
Lawd! Don't you know?
That's de working class!

Joseph Pass, "A Living Poet," *Fight,* May 1938, p. 19.

It is a great intellectual, emotional, common sense treat to read the pamphlet of seventeen poems by Langston Hughes. We are confident the *New York Times* will not give it a spread because it sells for only fifteen cents (no money in it, friends) and because it is not published via the regular channels: a workers' fraternal order ventured this pioneering effort. In an expansive moment, Walt Whitman predicted that his *Leaves of Grass* would some day sell for $50.00 a copy and for five cents too. The first has come true, but the second, we are afraid, will have to wait a few more years. But the International Workers Order has made it possible for a living poet to be read by the people. And this recognized poet has had the vision to let his work go under the imprint of a non-commercial publisher. A rare combination.

The poetry here is easy to read; it almost begs itself to be sung. These are the people's songs, folk music. AE, the Irish poet, once remarked that in reading most American novels, it is difficult to realize that in the U.S.A. people have to work and struggle in order to eat. Not in these pages. Here are the songs of everyday living and suffering and tears and laughter and hope, in Chicago, in Spain, in Alabama:

The devil's a Kleagle with an evil will,
Ozie, Ozie Powell,

A white High Sheriff who shoots to kill
Black young Ozie Powell.

The Negro poet understands his people
so well that he is a thousand thousand
miles removed from the tradition of
Booker T. Washington, or rather he lives
today and recognizes that the white and
Negro races cannot stand apart if their
will is to come to life:

The past is done!
A new dream flames
Against the
Sun!

Is it in Spain that the people are struggling against the tyrants? (We recognize
them; their breed is in Alabama too.) The
poet, the worker, the farmer, the teacher,
packs his kit and goes to Spain:

Workers, make no bombs again!
Workers, mine no gold again!
Workers, lift no hand again
To build up profits for the rape of Spain!
. . . . . .
I must drive the bombers out of Spain!
I must drive the bombers out of the
world!
I must take the world for my own
again—

In the first poem of this little book
Langston Hughes gives us to understand
that a man, even the most exploited man
in America—

Say who are you that mumbles in the
dark?
And who are you that draws your veil
across the stars?

—will not lose hope in America if he can
dream and have his feet solid on the
ground in unity with his fellow men, and
struggle for that dream.

Therefore this poet has the courage,
sense of beauty and foresight to sing:

The past has been
A mint of blood and sorrow—
That must not be
True of tomorrow.

John Skelly, *Winston-Salem Journal-
Sentinel,* 1 May 1938, p. 28.

Michael Gold in his introduction to this
collection of poems by Langston Hughes,
says "This work is the fruit of a decade of
experiment, of travel, and of contact with
all the bewildering social esthetic theories
of our times. Many young writers have lost
their way in this period, mistaking some
dazzling skyrocket of esthetic theory for
a star."

Langston Hughes, Negro poet, has published three books of poems, two books of
fiction and is also the author of a highly
successful play on Broadway called *Mulatto.* His book *A New Song* is yet another
evidence that the best Negro literature is a
folk literature, close to the joys and sorrows of the people.

Jim Crow's Last Stand (1943)

Ben Burns, "Books: People's Poet," *Chicago Defender,* 4 September 1943,
p. 19.

Langston Hughes, who is probably one
of the most prolific of Negro writers today,
has two new little pamphlets of poems off
the press.

Freedom's Plow is a work that was read
recently by Paul Muni over a national radio hookup, while *Jim Crow's Last Stand*
is a collection of his most recent work,
much of it dealing with race prejudice and
the war.

While some of the pieces show the lack
of considered writing, most show that
there are few poets today who can match
Hughes for colorful, lilting, pointed quality. *The Chicago Defender* columnist
knows what he is talking about and speaks
out with biting, sharp words that ring
clear and hard.

These are all "Ballads to Americans"—

excellent poems like "The Bitter River" about the Shubuta Bridge lynching or "Good Morning Stalingrad" with its tribute to the fighting Soviet city or "To Captain Mulzac" telling of the first wartime Negro sea captain.

"Freedom's Plow" is the longest work and has some of the Carl Sandburg ring in its free verse. These two latest publications of Hughes show he is a real people's poet.

C[arter] G. Woodson, "Book Reviews," *Journal of Negro History,* 28 (October 1943), 492–4.

Langston Hughes has written another book of poems. It is a slender volume of only 29 poems. The publication comes from the press of the Negro Publication Society of America in New York City. This collection of poems is No. 2 of the "Race Culture Series" brought out by this society whose purpose is to "publish and promote the publication of literary and scientific works giving instruction in and interpreting the history and contributions of the Negro people in American life." The launching of this effort is justified by the belief that "certainly in times like these, America needs to draw on the experience of one tenth of the population whose efforts to help make the country 'one nation, indivisible, with liberty and justice for all,' are thwarted by the forces of ignorance and racial intolerance."

These poems are written in the spirit of this declaration. The first poem, "The Black Man Speaks," boldly says that if we are fighting for democracy we must get rid of "old Jim Crow." The second poem, "Democracy," expresses the impatience with the "friends" of the Negro who caution waiting to let things take their course. The poet does not want freedom when he is dead because he cannot live on tomorrow's bread. On "Freedom," the poet says further that some folks are wrong in think-

ing that they imprison freedom by burning books and imprisoning reformers and that by lynching a Negro they lynch freedom. "Freedom stands up in their face and says, 'You'll never kill me.'" On the "Red Cross" the poet says "An angel of mercy got her wings in the mud, and all because of Negro blood." "The Bitter River" is dedicated to the memory of Charlie Lang and Ernest Green, the fourteen-year-old boys who were lynched beneath the Shubuta Bridge over the Chicasawhay River in Mississippi on October 12, 1942. "October 16" deals with John Brown at Harpers Ferry. He died for a cause. What about you? In "Motherland" Africa is imprisoned in bitter sorrow. In "Brothers" appears the kinship of all Negroes whether from West or East, from the United States or the West Indies, from America or Africa: "We are brothers—you and I." In Captain Mulzac, Negro skipper of *The Booker T. Washington,* the poet sees a symbol of a captain conducting the ship "Victory" which will triumph over the enemies of freedom, brotherhood and democracy.

After dealing thus with the political questions now moving the Negro to radical action the poet looks at the shacks in the "Blackbelt" and gives us the "Ballad of the Landlord," who is attacked in trying to enforce an eviction. Next we have "Big Buddy" at hard labor, unrequited toil, and then the "Ballad of Sam Solomon" who is not afraid of the Ku Klux Klan. The poet looks next at the "Commercial Theatre" which takes our blues and spirituals to make money, and the way they are rendered "they don't sound like me" but "some day somebody'll stand up and talk about me, and write about me— ... I reckon it'll be me myself! It'll be me." "Daybreak in Alabama" prophesies that some of these days a colored composer will give a new picture in a new song of Alabama and Negroes triumphant will be in that song. "Me and My Song" is more prophecy of the day that is breaking. In "Good Morning Stalingrad" there is the herald of a new ally in the struggle for freedom. The picture closes with "Jim Crow's Last Stand." Jim Crow cannot fight for democracy, and it must go.

These poems bring additional evidence of the self-assertion of the subordinated Negro. Books of which this one is typical show how rapidly Negroes have advanced in recent years. Formerly the Negro ran from the aggressor. Now the Negro runs to him. The battle of the Negro for freedom is no longer defensive. The Negro is now on the offensive. He sees a difference between dying to secure democracy for others and dying to secure it for himself. He prefers death in the latter case. The point to be observed also is that the Negro of today is fearlessly expressing his thought and backing up with action what he says. He is not looking for trouble, but he is not running from it.

Looking back over the last seventy years, the historian cannot escape the stages in the development of the Negro. Immediately after emancipation, the freedmen were nominally free only. Their former masters actually reenslaved them through the black codes of 1865. The minds of the freedmen were still enslaved, and nothing else could have been expected. Federal troops stationed in the South undertook to secure the freedom of the Negro through a new plan of reconstruction at the point of the bayonet, but as soon as the troops were withdrawn the Negroes were reduced immediately to chattel slavery with a status like that of the free Negroes in the South before the Civil War. There the Negroes remained under an appeasement leadership until the First World War. One result of that rather short conflict was the awakening of the Negroes almost to the point of self-assertion but the capitalistic forces of the country were too strong, and when they joined with the plantation aristocracy to keep the Negro down he could do nothing about it. Today in the midst of a world upheaval when capitalism has been shaken and exploitation is yielding ground to cooperation in a world brotherhood, the Negro is fearlessly presenting his case before a new tribunal.

Additional Review

Arthur B. Spingarn, "Books by Negro Authors in 1943," *Crisis,* 51 (February 1944), 49.

Freedom's Plow (1943)

Lucia Trent, "Spanning the Books," *Span* [St. Louis], 2 (October–November 1943), 37.

Langston Hughes is one of the great poets of our country. His work will endure because he speaks for the people of our age. He uses his powerful artistry in the service of human freedom. His poems are gleaming stones in the citadel of a better tomorrow.

Freedom's Plow has that dynamic simplicity for which this brilliant Negro poet is noted. His style is clean and economical. His free verse has most of the devices that make that medium effective and potent as a literary weapon. In spots this long poem lapses into prose, but many of the lines are poetry of a high order, stirring poetry, poetry that is a valuable instrument in the arsenal of democracy.

William Rose Benét, "Two Powerful Negro Poets," *Saturday Review,* 28 (24 March 1945), 35–6.

[. . .]
. . . I have long thought that the Negro

728

has a special delight in the sound, shape, and color of words that most white people lack. In the past their caress upon language, whose meaning was only partially understood, may have been food for humor. There is a great deal more to it than that. They furbish and freshen words, the best of them, whether artlessly or, as here, with art; they polish them till the poetry glows from them. The established Negro poet, Langston Hughes, can do that too. But *Freedom's Plow,* reprinted this year, is more good rhetoric, rhetoric in a good cause. Paul Muni read this poem over the Blue Network a year ago last March. It has stirring rhythm. It must be deeply moving, to all who really care about this country, to have one of its Negro citizens stand up and say:

> The people often hold
> Great thoughts in their deepest hearts
> And sometimes only blunderingly express
>   them,
> Haltingly and stumbling say them . . .
> The people do not always understand
>   each other.
> But there is, somewhere there,
> Always the *trying* to understand
> And the *trying* to say,
> *You are a man. Together we are building
>   our land.*

Additional Review

Ben Burns, "Books," *Chicago Defender,* 4 September 1943, p. 19.

Popo and Fifina

With Arna Bontemps, *Popo and Fifina: Children of Haiti* (1932)

Roseanne Charlton, "Book Review," *Pittsburgh Courier,* 15 October 1932, [p. 9].

Anne T. Eaton, "Books for Children," *New York Times Book Review,* 23 October 1932, pp. 13, 16.

G.J.F., "The Book Shelf," *Norfolk Journal and Guide,* 29 October 1932, p. 6.

Alain Locke, "Black Truth and Black Beauty," *Opportunity,* 11 (January 1933), 14–18.

Letha Davidson, "Children's Librarians Notebook," *Library Journal,* 58 (15 December 1933), 1051.

The "First" Books
The First Book of Negroes (1952)

Virginia Kirkus Bulletin, 20 (1 October 1952), 659.

Anne Izard, "Fascinating Facts," *Library Journal,* 77 (15 October 1952), 1746.

"Hughes' Book Tells Gains Since Slavery," *Chicago Defender,* 18 October 1952, p. 2.

Ira O. Guy, "The First Book of Negroes," *Common Sense Historical Reviews,* 11 (November 1952), [9].

James J. Foree, "Book Review," *Baltimore Afro-American Magazine,* 1 November 1952, p. 2.

Gerri Major, "Gerri-Go-Round: Arts and Letters," *New York Amsterdam News,* 1 November 1952, p. 12.

Gertrude Martin, "Book Reviews," *Chicago Defender,* 1 November 1952, p. 11.

[Louise S. Bechtell], "Thinking Toward a Better World," *New York Herald Tribune Book Review,* part 2, 16 November 1952, p. 32.

C.G., "Terry's People," *New York Times Book Review,* 16 November 1952, p. 32.

Georgia D. Johnson, "Book Review," *Boston Guardian,* 22 November 1952, p. 4.

Augusta Baker, "Recommended Children's Books," *Library Journal,* 77 (1 December 1952), 2076.

"Children's Books," *Booklist,* 49 (1 December 1952), 129.

Gertrude Parthenia McBrown, "The First Book of Negroes," *Negro History Bulletin,* 16 (January 1953), 94–5.

June Shagaloff, "Book Reviews," *Crisis,* 40 (January 1953), 62–3.

M.H.M., "Negro Poet Writes of His Race's Abilities," *Daily Oklahoman Sunday Magazine,* 18 January 1953, p. 16.

Marie Bloch, "Books for Children," *Denver Post Roundup,* 25 January 1953, p. 21.

E.D.I., "Younger Readers," *Kansas City Star,* 31 January 1953, [p. 14].

J. Saunders Redding, "Book Review," *Afro-American Magazine,* 31 January 1953, p. 2.

Alice Henrietta Howard, "The First Book of Negroes," *Common Sense Historical Reviews,* [11] (February 1953), 7.

Frank Marshall Davis, "Frank-ly Speaking: Negro History Week and a Book," *Honolulu Record,* 12 February 1953, pp. [8], 7.

Polly Goodwin, "The Junior Bookshelf: Story of the Negro," *Chicago Tribune Magazine of Books,* part 4, 22 February 1953, p. 14.

Monica Durkin, "Much Negro History in Gay Book," *Catholic Interracialist,* 12 (April 1953), 7.

William Harrison, "Book Review," *Boston Chronicle,* 2 May 1953, p. 6; also *Providence Chronicle,* 9 May 1953.

Hallie Beachem Brooks, "For Young Readers," *Phylon,* 14 (Third Quarter 1953), 343–4.

John W. Parker, "A Book of Positive Faith in America," *Journal of Negro Education,* 22 (Fall 1953), 496–7.

John W. Parker, "The First Book of Negroes," *Social Forces,* 32 (May 1954), 396.

"Secondary and Below," *Bibliographic Survey: The Negro in Print,* 7 (May 1971), 8.

The First Book of Rhythms (1954)

Virginia Kirkus Bulletin, 22 (15 March 1954), 199–200.

[Louise S. Bechtel], "Poetry," *New York Herald Tribune Book Review,* 16 May 1954, p. 17.

[J.] Saunders Redding, "Book Review," *Baltimore Afro-American Magazine,* 5 June 1954, p. 2.

Bernice Frankel, "Children's Books," *San Diego Union,* 13 June 1954, p. E-2.

"Children's Books," *Booklist,* 50 (15 June 1954), 406.

A[ugusta] B[aker], "Books for Young People," *Saturday Review,* 37 (19 June 1954), 39.

Siddie Joe Johnson, "Older Boys and Girls," *Library Journal,* 79 (July 1954), 1325.

Pat Clark, "Everyday Wonders," *New York Times Book Review,* 15 August 1954, p. 20.

Helen Muir, "Frisky Bear Cubs Make Cuddly Picture Story," *Miami Herald,* 22 August 1954, p. 4-F.

V.W.S., "Langston Hughes Examines Rhythms," *Kansas City Star,* 30 October 1954, [p. 20].

Beatrice Landeck, "Children's Books in the Field of Music," *Horn Book,* 30 (December 1954), 457.

The First Book of Jazz (1955)

Cleveland Amory, "Trade Winds: Returning to Jazz," *Saturday Review,* 37 (4 September 1954), 5–6.

Virginia Kirkus Bulletin, 22 (15 October 1954), 711.

E[llen] L[ewis] B[uell], "Take a Blue

Note," *New York Times Book Review,* 30 January 1955, p. 24.

Orrin Keepnews, "Books Noted," *Record Changer,* 14 (19 February 1955), 6, 18.

L[ouise] S. Bechtel, "For Boys and Girls," *New York Herald Tribune Books,* 27 February 1955, p. 10.

Polly Goodwin, "The Junior Bookshelf," *Chicago Sunday Tribune Books,* part 4, 6 March 1955, p. 14.

Milton R. Bass, "Jazz Primer Tops McGuffey," *Berkshire Evening Eagle,* 12 March 1955, p. 14.

Gertrude Martin, "Book Reviews," *Chicago Defender,* 26 March 1955, p. 2.

Father Edmund Bliven, "Book Review: The First Book of Jazz," *Catholic Interracialist,* 14 (April 1955), 7.

"Books for Young People," *Booklist,* 51 (April 1955), 318.

Marshall Sprague, "A Study of Jazz, " *Colorado Springs Free Press Sunday Review,* 3 April 1955, p. 5.

Lawrence Forde, "Upper Elementary," *Library Journal,* 80 (15 April 1955), 1001.

Wisconsin Library Bulletin Book Notes Supplement, 51 (May 1955), 23.

A[ugusta] B[aker], "Of General Interest," *Saturday Review,* 38 (14 May 1955), 55–6.

Janie Smith, "Want to Know about Indians?" *Charleston News and Courier,* 29 May 1955, p. 10-C.

Bulletin of the Children's Book Center, 8 (June 1955), [1].

Virginia H[aviland], "Jazz," *Horn Book,* 31 (June 1955), 195.

John Ball, "Hughes on Jazz," *Midwest Journal,* 7 (Summer 1955), 195–6.

John W. Parker, "American Jazz: Composite of Many Influences," *Phylon,* 16 (Third Quarter 1955), 318–19.

"Parents' Bookshelf: American Music," *Baltimore Evening Sun,* 7 September 1955, p. 32.

Dorothy Montgomery, "For the Teenager," *Bookmark,* 15 (November 1955), 43.

Katherine T. Kinkead, "Books: Christmas for First and Second Readers: Books on Special Interests," *New Yorker,* 31 (26 November 1955), 230.

Carol S. Sperry, "Book Review," *Patient Voice* [San Diego], 5 (January 1958), 11.

Rose H. Agree, "Fare for the Eager Reader: Music," *Library Journal,* 83 (15 February 1958), 630.

Mimi Clar, "Reviews: Books," *Jazz Review,* 2 (May 1959), 37.

Diane Haas, "SLJ/The Book Review," *School Library Journal,* 23 (October 1976), 107–8.

"Children's Books," *Booklist,* 73 (15 November 1976), 474.

"Critically Speaking: Informational Books," *Reading Teacher,* 36 (October 1982), 116.

Holly Sanhuber, "SLJ/The Book Review," *School Library Journal,* 29 (October 1982), 152.

"Children's Books," *Booklist,* 79 (1 October 1982), 246.

The First Book of the West Indies (1956)

"First Books," *Virginia Kirkus Service Bulletin,* 24 (15 June 1956), 406.

"Weekly Record: Hughes, Langston," *Publishers Weekly,* 170 (17 September 1956), 1455.

"Children's Books," *Booklist,* 53 (1 November 1956), 125–6.

[Margaret Sherwood Libby], "Visiting Other Countries," *New York Herald Tribune Book Review,* part 2, 18 November 1956, p. 16.

James R. Newman, "Children's Books," *Scientific American,* 195 (December 1956), 157–8.

Julie Coste, "Upper Elementary," *Library Journal,* 81 (15 December 1956), 2995.

Helen Lorraine Hultz, "Island Chain," *New York Times Book Review,* 30 December 1956, p. 12.

Freddye Henderson, "Guided Tour of the Antilles," *Phylon,* 18 (First Quarter 1957), 92–3.

A[ugusta] B[aker], "Books for Young People," *Saturday Review,* 40 (16 March 1957), 31–2; also on 5 May 1957 in both *Youngstown Vindicator* and *Roanoke Times.*

Alice L. Robinson, "Books for Children," *Childhood Education,* 1 (September 1957), 38.

The First Book of Africa (1960)

Virginia Kirkus Bulletin, 28 (15 June 1960), 455.

"Weekly Record: Hughes, Langston," *Publishers Weekly,* 178 (25 July 1960), 74.

"Recommended Reading," *New York Citizen-Call,* 30 July 1960, p. 15.

"Booknotes from Public Library," *Attleboro* [Mass.] *Sun,* 8 August 1960, p. 12.

Augusta Baker, "Junior Books Appraised," *Library Journal,* 85 (15 September 1960), 3216.

Frank London Brown, "The Junior Bookshelf," *Chicago Tribune,* part 4, 18 September 1960, p. 10.

John W. Parker, "Another Hard Look at the African Scene," *Phylon,* 21 (Fourth Quarter 1960), 397–8.

Lincoln University Bulletin, 64 (Fall 1960), 17.

V.H., "Other Lands," *Horn Book,* 36 (October 1960), 414.

Miriam Wessel, "Children's Books," *Catholic Library World,* 32 (October 1960), 78.

"Children's Books," *Booklist,* 57 (1 October 1960), 102.

Jean A. Merrill, "For Young Readers: Background of African Nationalism," *Kansas City Star,* 1 October 1960, p. 4.

Barbara Moody, "Recommended for Children," *Baltimore Morning Sun,* 2 October 1960, p. A-7.

Claudia Lewis, "A Child's Eyes on the World," *Saturday Review,* 43 (15 October 1960), 30.

Mary Belle Long, "Other Lands and Peoples: Go 'Digging' in Ancient Egypt," *Detroit Free Press,* 30 October 1960, p. 4-E.

Anne Perkins, "Southland Authors Top Juvenile Parade," *Los Angeles Mirror,* part 3, 7 November 1960, pp. [1]–2.

"Ancient Lands, Africa Now," *New York Herald Tribune Book Review,* 13 November 1960, p. 32.

[J.] Saunders Redding, "The Human Side of Africa," *Baltimore Afro-American Magazine,* 3 December 1960, p. 2.

"New Titles for Children and Young People," *Bulletin of the Center for Children's Books,* 14 (June 1961), 160–1.

Beverley Githens, "Book Review," *Eureka Springs* [Ark.] *Times-Echo,* 1 October 1964, p. 2.

Geraldine Clark, "Brief Mention," *Library Journal,* 89 (15 November 1964), 4654.

The "Famous" Books

Famous American Negroes (1954)

N.T., "Biographies for Young People," *Phylon,* 15 (First Quarter 1954), 110.

Ira O. Guy, "Book Review," *Common Sense Historical Reviews,* [12] (February 1954), 12.

Gladys P. Graham, "History Wk.: Hail to Sons of Freedom," *Philadelphia Tribune,* 2 February 1954, p. 4.

William Harrison, "Book Review," *Boston Chronicle,* 13 February 1954, p. 14.

Gertrude Martin, "Book Reviews," *Chi-*

cago *Defender* [City Edition], 13 February 1954, [p. 11].

J. Saunders Redding, "Book Review," *Baltimore Afro-American Magazine*, 13 February 1954, p. 2.

Earl E. Thorpe, "Books That Are Worth Reading," *Huntsville* [Ala.] *Times*, 14 February 1954, p. 14.

Alice Howard, "Famous American Negroes," *Common Sense Historical Reviews*, 12 (March 1954), 11.

Ann Nelson, "Children's Books," *Library Journal*, 79 (1 March 1954), 461.

Nerissa Long Milton, "The Young Peoples Corner," *Negro History Bulletin*, 17 (April 1954), 164–5.

John W. Parker, "Book Reviews," *Journal of Negro History*, 39 (April 1954), 151–2.

Theodore Stanford, "Current Reviews," *Philadelphia Independent*, 3 April 1954, p. 12.

M.C.K., "Negroes You'd Like to Know," *Catholic Interracialist*, 14 (May 1954), 7.

E.L.B., "New Books for Younger Readers: Seventeen Leaders," *New York Times Book Review*, 2 May 1954, p. 26.

[Louise S. Bechtel], "New Titles in Some Popular Series," *New York Herald Tribune Book Review*, 16 May 1954, p. 22.

Miranda G. Shore, "Books for Growing-Ups," *Magnificat*, 93 (July 1954), 163.

Mabel M. Smythe, "Book Reviews," *Crisis*, 62 (January 1955), 58.

Rose H. Agree, "Fare for the Eager Reader: Citizenship," *Library Journal*, 83 (15 February 1958), 629.

Judith Higgins, "Paperbacks," *Grade Teacher*, 88 (October 1970), 148–9.

Famous Negro Music Makers
(1955)

Virginia Kirkus Bulletin, 23 (15 July 1955), 499.

Lester B. Granger, "Battleaxe and Bread," *California Eagle*, 29 September 1955, p. 4; also as "Manhattan and Beyond," *New York Amsterdam News*, 1 October 1955, p. 10, and elsewhere.

Edward (Sonny) Murrain, "Front and Center," *New York Age and Defender*, 1 October 1955, p. 8.

E.K.M., "Negro 'Musics,'" *Montgomery Advertiser*, 14 October 1955, p. 9-D.

"Role of Negro in Music Told," *Charlotte Observer*, 16 October 1955, p. 16-E.

Walter A. Hansen, "Negro Musicians Better Than Book," *Fort Wayne News-Sentinel*, 5 November 1955, p. 4.

L.M., "People and Places," *Saturday Review*, 38 (12 November 1955), 76–7; also as "Music Makers," *Washington Post and Times Herald*, 13 November 1955, p. K7.

"Books for Young People," *Booklist*, 52 (15 November 1955), 129.

John Patrick Little, "Blues to Beethoven," *Community*, 15 (December 1955), 7.

Nat Hentoff, "Counterpoint," *Down Beat*, 20 (14 December 1955), 14.

Carl Diton, "Poetic Feeling in Hughes' Book on Musicians Makes It 'Must' Reading," *Philadelphia Tribune*, 27 December 1955, p. 6.

Leonard R. Ballou, "For the Record: Jas, Chass, Jass, Jazz—and Concert, Too," *Tones and Overtones*, III (Winter 1956), 75–8.

Thomas A. Webster, "American Negro Musicians," *Kansas City Star*, 7 January 1956, [p. 15].

"Junior High," *Library Journal*, 81 (15 February 1956), 571–2.

"Children's Corner," *Greensboro Daily News*, Feature Section, 26 February 1956, p. 3.

Leah R. Fuller, "Between the Bookends," *Rockland* [Maine] *Courier-Gazette,* 22 March 1956, p. 14.

Jesse Dandy, "Growth Traced: From Spirituals to Jazz," *Birmingham News,* 10 June 1956, p. E-7.

Sister M. Etheldreda, "Books for School Libraries: Books on Minority Groups," *Catholic Library World,* 41 (January 1970), [319]–22.

Famous Negro Heroes of America
(1958)

Virginia Kirkus Bulletin, 26 (1 March 1958), 185.

"Juveniles," *Evansville Press,* 1 May 1958, p. 43.

Augusta Baker, "Jr. Books Appraised: Junior High," *Library Journal,* 83 (15 May 1958), 1609.

Best Sellers, 18 (15 May 1958), 90.

Rev. Joseph G. McGroarty, "Lives of Great Men," *Stray Notes from the Shrine of the Little Flower,* 34 (July–August 1958), 9, 16.

"Children's Books," *Booklist,* 54 (1 July 1958), 617.

Marsh Maslin, "The Browser: These Were Strong Men," *San Francisco Call-Bulletin,* 18 July 1958, p. 11.

Edmund Fuller, "Sixteen Lives," *New York Times Book Review,* 27 July 1958, p. 14.

Mary Louise Hector, "Books for Young Readers," *Critic,* 17 (August–September 1958), 58–9.

R.H.V., "Biography," *Horn Book,* 34 (August 1958), 281.

Margaret Parsons, "Heroes on Double Counts," *Worcester Sunday Telegram,* 3 August 1958, p. E7.

"The Book Column," *Bulletin of the National Association of Secondary School Principals,* 42 (September 1958), 220–1.

Frank Greenwood, "Should Only Be 'History with Negroes in It,'" *Los Angeles Tribune,* 14 November 1958, p. 23.

Books Edited by Hughes
Four Lincoln University Poets
(1930)

Aubrey Bowser, "Airplanes of Ethiopia," *New York Amsterdam News,* 4 June 1930, [p. 24].

With Arna Bontemps, *The Poetry of the Negro: 1746–1949* (1949)

"The Poetry of the Negro: One-Way Ticket," *Virginia Kirkus Bulletin,* 16 (15 November 1948), 609.

Gerald McDonald, "Poetry," *Library Journal,* 73 (15 December 1948), 1818.

Abraham Chapman, "Books: Negro Poetry," *Build Your Order,* 1949, pp. 9–10.

Charles Poore, "Books of the Times," *New York Times,* 8 January 1949, p. 13.

Hartford Courant Magazine, 9 January 1949, p. 12.

Constance Curtis, "News of Books and Authors," *New York Amsterdam News,* 15 January 1949, p. 9.

Eleanor Roosevelt, "Recommended Book," *Chicago Sun-Times,* 15 January 1949, p. 22.

Margaret L. Hartley, "Negro Poetry in America," *Dallas Morning News,* sec. 2, 16 January 1949, p. 13.

"Several Sorts," *New York Herald Tribune Book Review,* 16 January 1949, p. 17.

Irving Dilliard, "Poetry: New Volumes by and about Negro Poets," *St. Louis Post-Dispatch,* 23 January 1949, [p. 4B].

W. T. Scott, "Round Up of Books in Poetry Field: Negroes and Irish in Anthologies," *Providence Journal,* sec. 6, 23 January 1949, p. 8.

John Broderick, "Briefly Noted: Verse," *New Yorker*, 24 (29 January 1949), 71–2.

Hubert Creekmore, "Two Rewarding Volumes of Verse," *New York Times Book Review*, 30 January 1949, p. 19.

L.G., "Anthology of Negro Poetry Presents a Rounded Picture," *Washington Post*, 30 January 1949, p. 7B.

John Frederick Nims, "Inclusive Anthology of Negro Poetry," *Chicago Tribune Magazine of Books*, part 4, 30 January 1949, p. 4.

Leo Kennedy, "Negro Life in Poetry," *Chicago Sun-Times*, 31 January 1949, p. 37.

Gertrude Martin, "Key Work of 'Names,' 'Unknowns' Compiled," *Chicago Defender*, 5 February 1949, [p. 7].

Robert Friedman, "Anthology of Negro Poetry," *People's World*, Our Times Section, 11 February 1949, p. 6.

Jessie Burt, "Definitive Anthology of Negro Poetry," *Nashville Tennessean*, 13 February 1949, p. 10B.

V.E., "Dusky Poetry," *New Orleans Times-Picayune*, sec. 2, 13 February 1949, p. 19.

Thomas Hornsby Ferril, "The New Poetry in Brief Review," *San Francisco Chronicle This World*, 13 February 1949, p. 15.

"Literature," *Booklist*, 45 (15 February 1949), 207.

Charles Norman, "A Good Anthology of Negro Poetry," *Boston Traveler*, 16 February 1949, p. 24.

Rolfe Humphries, "Negro Verse," *Nation*, 168 (19 February 1949), 217.

J. Saunders Redding, "Book Review," *Afro-American Magazine*, 19 February 1949, [p. 3]. "The best collection of verse by colored people and about their experiences."

Edwin Tribble, "Reviewing the New Books," *Washington Star*, 20 February 1949, p. C3.

"A Few of the Newer Books: Reading for Understanding," *Open Shelf*, nos. 3–4 (March–April 1949), [5].

"The Poetry Bulletin," *Tiger's Eye*, 1 (March 1949), 125.

Jean Starr Untermeyer, "Anthology of and about a Race," *Saturday Review*, 32 (19 March 1949), 16.

Fred Stern, "The Hughes-Bontemps Work Evaluated," *Compass: The Intercollegiate Literary Review*, 3 (April 1949), 10–11.

Irene O. Hendrick, "Important Negro Books," *Southern Packet*, July 1949, p. 2.

William Harrison, "Book Review," *Boston Chronicle*, 9 July 1949, p. 6.

Virginia Rowland, "Our Bookshelf," *Catholic Interracialist*, September 1949, p. 3.

"Two Good Books," *Cresset*, 12 (September 1949), 47–8.

Alain Locke, "Wisdom de Profundis: The Literature of the Negro, 1949: Part 1: Poetry and Belles Lettres," *Phylon*, 11 (First Quarter 1950), 11–12.

Jerome Cushman, "Poetry," *Library Journal*, 95 (1 November 1970), 3786.

"Series and Editions," *Booklist*, 67 (15 December 1970), 330.

Regina Minudri, "Adult Books for Young Adults: At a Glance," *Library Journal*, 96 (15 January 1971), 293.

"Drama, Music and Poetry," *Bibliographic Survey: The Negro in Print*, 7 (September 1971), 14.

Choice, 8 (January 1972), 1452–3.

James Johnson and Frances O. Churchill, "Black and Bibliographical," *Wilson Library Bulletin*, 47 (February 1973), 530.

"Paperbacks: Nonfiction," *Washington Post Book World*, 12 August 1973, p. 13.

Gwendolyn E. Osborne, "Book Corner," *Crisis*, 81 (November 1974), 317.

With Waring Cuney and Bruce McWright, *Lincoln University Poets* (1954)

Arthur P. Davis, "Negro Poetry," *Midwest Journal,* 6 (Summer 1954), 74–7.

Gladys P. Graham, "Books on Review: About Books and Authors," *New Jersey Herald News,* 10 July 1954, [p. ?].

William Harrison, "Book Review," *Boston Chronicle,* 30 October 1954, p. 6.

With Arna Bontemps, *The Book of Negro Folklore* (1958)

Paul Flowers, "Book of Negro Folklore," *Memphis Commercial Appeal,* sec. 4, 30 November 1958, p. 10.

Bryan Collier, "Today's Books and the Arts: Emily Kimbrough's Latest Proves to Be Charming," *Charleston News and Courier,* 7 December 1958, p. 17-C.

Luther Nichols, "A Poet's Novel of Harlem," *San Francisco Examiner,* sec. 3, 11 December 1958, p. 3.

Richmond C. Beatty, "Under the Green Lamp," *Nashville Tennessean,* 21 December 1958, p. 2-F.

Ray B. Browne, "The Folklore a Nation Was Built By," *Washington Post and Times Herald,* 28 December 1958, p. E6.

Ruth Swenson, "Books for Adults: Social Science," *Wisconsin Library Bulletin,* 55 (January–February 1959), 53.

"Nonfiction," *Bookmark,* 18 (January 1959), 91.

"Social Sciences," *Booklist,* 55 (1 January 1959), 230.

Curt Gentry, "The Lore of the American Negro—and Other Books," *San Francisco Chronicle,* 4 January 1959, p. 22.

M[argaret] P[arsons], "Many Types of Writing," *Worcester Sunday Telegram,* 11 January 1959, p. E7.

[J.] Saunders Redding, "Sunshine and Shadows," *New York Times Book Review,* 18 January 1959, p. 5.

"Negro Folk Lore," *Pittsburgh Courier Magazine,* 24 January 1959, p. 7.

Gilbert E. Govan, "Books and Writers," *Chattanooga Times,* 25 January 1959, p. 14.

"New on the Book Shelf," *New Orleans Times-Picayune,* sec. 2, 25 January 1959, p. 12.

Mildred Hart Shaw, "Between Book Ends," *Grand Junction* [Colo.] *Daily Sentinel,* 25 January 1959, p. 4.

"A True Note in the Cultural Stream," *Albany* [Oreg.] *Democrat Herald,* 31 January 1959, p. 10.

Russell Ames, "Books in Review: More Than Just Folks," *Mainstream,* 12 (February 1959), 45–9.

"The Book Column," *Bulletin of the National Association of Secondary School Principals,* 43 (February 1959), 130–1.

D[aniel] A. P[oling], "The New Books," *Christian Herald,* 81 (February 1959), 67.

Maxine Tull Boatner, "America's Culture," *Hartford Courant Magazine,* 1 February 1959, p. 13.

B. A. Botkin, "The Negro Folk Tradition in America," *New York Herald Tribune Book Review,* 1 February 1959, p. 3.

William B. Guthrie, "U.S. Negroes' Folklore Is Fascinating Reading," *Richmond Times-Dispatch,* 8 February 1959, p. 8-L.

Sam Ragan, "Southern Accent," *Raleigh News and Observer,* sec. 3, 8 February 1959, p. 5.

William Raymond Smith, "To Make Us Love Our Country," *New Republic,* 140 (16 February 1959), 19–20.

John W. Parker, "Our Heritage of Negro Folklore," *Raleigh News and Observer,* sec. 3, 22 February 1959, p. 5.

Polly Hackett, "Negro Tales Collected," *Fort Wayne News Sentinel,* 28 February 1959, p. 4.

James W. Ivy, "Book Reviews," *Crisis*, 66 (March 1959), 181–2.

John W. Parker, "Negro Folklore: Segment of American Culture," *CLAJ*, 2 (March 1959), 185–6.

"The Library Shelf," *Centralia* [Wash.] *Daily Chronicle*, 28 March 1959, p. 7.

Stella Brewer Brookes, "The Negro's Colorful Heritage," *Phylon*, 20 (First Quarter 1959), 102.

"Books," *World Outlook*, 19 (May 1959), 62.

Luix Overbea, "A Rich Heritage of Negro Folklore," *Winston-Salem Journal and Sentinel*, 17 May 1959, p. 7C.

"Briefly Noted," *Greensboro Daily News*, 16 August 1959, p. D3.

John Greenway, "Negro Folklore," *Sing Out: The Folk Song Magazine*, 9 (Fall 1959), 37.

F.R., "Brief Reviews of Recent Books," *Durham Herald*, 1 May 1960, p. 5D.

"Potpourri," *Christian Century*, 77 (8 June 1960), 697.

John Henrik Clarke, "African World Book Shelf," *New York Citizen-Call*, 6 August 1960, p. 27.

"*The Book of Negro Folklore*—an Anthology," *Teacher News* [New York Teachers Union], February 1961, pp. 2, 4.

D[orothy] H. R[ochmis], "Books in Review," *West Coast Review of Books*, 10 (July–August 1984), 40.

An African Treasury: Essays, Stories, Poems by Black Africans (1960)

Book Buyer's Guide, 63 (May 1960), 52.

Virginia Kirkus Bulletin, 28 (15 May 1960), 398.

Jessie Kitching, "Nonfiction Forecast: *An African Treasury*," *Publishers Weekly*, 177 (23 May 1960), 56.

Inside Books, July 1960, p. 2.

Thomas J. Flanagan, "Writer Reviews Langston Hughes' Novel on Africa," *Atlanta Daily World*, 13 July 1960, p. 4.

"N.Y. Courier's Bookshelf," *New York Courier*, 16 July 1960, [?].

"Other Books of This Week," *Newsday*, 23 July 1960, p. 27.

Michael Grieg, "The Book Corner: Pertinent Book about Africa," *San Francisco Examiner*, sec. 3, 26 July 1960, p. 3.

"Books," *Jet*, 28 (28 July 1960), 50.

Van Allen Bradley, "What Else Is Worth Reading," *Chicago Daily News*, 30 July 1960, p. 7.

A.S.H., Jr., "Portrait of Troubled Land," *Worcester Sunday Telegram*, 31 July 1960, p. E7.

David E. Apter, "Universality, Humanism of Native African Mind," *Chicago Tribune Magazine of Books*, 31 July 1960, p. 2.

"Hughes Shift to Prose Seen," *Fayetteville Observer*, 31 July 1960, p. 5D.

John W. Parker, "Book Reviews: African Saga," *Crisis*, 67 (August–September 1960), 489–90.

John K. Hutchens, "*An African Treasury*," *New York Herald Tribune*, 1 August 1960, p. 11.

William Hogan, "A Bookman's Notebook: 'Politics of Upheaval': Other News and Notes," *San Francisco Chronicle*, 3 August 1960, p. 31.

Charles Poore, "Books of the Times," *New York Times*, 6 August 1960, p. 17.

J. Saunders Redding, "Newest Work of Langston Hughes," *Baltimore Afro-American Magazine*, 6 August 1960, p. 2.

"Books of the Week: *An African Treasury*," *Minneapolis Tribune*, 7 August 1960, p. 18W.

Gwendolyn M. Carter, "Vibrant and Varied, Black Africa's Writers Speak," *New York Herald Tribune Book Review*, sec. 6, 7 August 1960, [p. 1].

"Just Browsing: *An African Treasury*," *Los*

Angeles Mirror, part 2, 15 August 1960, p. 3.

Charles Poore, "A Bookman's Notebook: African Anthology with a Native Beat," San Francisco Chronicle, 18 August 1960, p. 31.

Ernest B. Furgurson, "Africa in Fact and Fiction," Baltimore Morning Sun, 21 August 1960, p. A-5.

Frank London Brown, "Book Reviews," Chicago Defender, 27 August 1960, [p. 8].

John K. Hutchens, "Critic on the Hearth," Oakland Tribune, 31 August 1960, p. D21; reprint New York Herald Tribune, 1 August.

Booklist, 57 (1 September 1960), 17.

D.O.N., Jr., "Africa Writes Its Own Story in Hughes Book," Hartford Times, 3 September 1960, p. 36.

"Modern Africa Speaks in . . . ," St. Louis Argus, 9 September 1960, p. 5A; also same date in Augusta [SC] Weekly Review, p. 4, the Omaha Star, and the Kansas City Call, and in the St. Louis American on 15 September.

Milton Bracker, "Literary Lights from the Dark Continent," New York Times Book Review, 18 September 1960, p. 38.

M.C.S., "Africa as Seen by Africans," New Orleans Times-Picayune, sec. 2, 18 September 1960, p. 2.

Fayetteville Observer, 25 September 1960, p. 5D.

Mike Newberry, "Books about Africa," Worker, 25 September 1960, p. 4.

John K. Hutchens, "Book Review: Black Natives Present Their Vision of Africa in Writings," Houston Post, sec. 3, 27 September 1960, p. 6.

Lincoln University Bulletin, 64 (Fall 1960), 17.

Margaret C. Scoggin, "Outlook Tower," Horn Book, 36 (October 1960), 422.

"Briefly Noted," New Yorker, 36 (5 November 1960), 227–8.

Richard Watts, Jr., "Two on the Aisle: Random Notes on This and That," New York Post, 29 November 1960, p. 59.

"Books," Air Transportation, 37 (December 1960), 36.

Frances Neel Cheney, "Current Reference Books: Authors and Writers," Wilson Library Bulletin, 35 (December 1960), 320.

Joseph C. Carpenter, "Stop Me If . . . ," St. Louis American, 15 December 1960, pp. 2, 11.

Victor C. Ferkiss, "Limited Light on a Disturbed Continent," Commonweal, 73 (16 December 1960), 319–20.

Eleanor Hoag, "Some Books about Africa in Review," Intercollegian, 78 (January–February 1961), 20.

Mabel Knight, "Book Reviews: African Writings Delight," Community, 20 (January 1961), 6.

L. M. Collins, "New Africa Mirrored in Anthology," Nashville Tennessean, 22 January 1961, p. 8-F.

George P. Murdock, "Black Africa Speaks," New Leader, 44 (30 January 1961), 25–6.

Loretta M. Winkler, "Books for Young Adults," Catholic Library World, 32 (March 1961), 373.

Virginia Simmons Nyabongo, "Book Reviews," Negro Educational Review, 12 (April 1961), 72–4.

P. O'Sheel, "The Bookshelf: A Review Sampler of Books on Africa," Foreign Service Journal, 38 (April 1961), 34–5.

Gertrude Parthenia McBrown, "An African Treasury," Negro History Bulletin, 25 (December 1961), 63–4.

B.G.D., "Langston Hughes, comp.," Books Abroad, 36 (Winter 1962), 75.

"Paperbacks: New and Noteworthy," New York Times Book Review, 11 December 1977, p. 49.

C.F.K., "Black Studies," Kliatt Young Adult Paperback Book Guide, 12 (Winter 1978), 34.

Poems from Black Africa (1963)

"*Poems from Black Africa*," *Virginia Kirkus Bulletin*, 31 (1 April 1963), 390.

"Weekly Record: Hughes, Langston," *Publishers Weekly*, 183 (13 May 1963), 72.

"Books," *New York Amsterdam News*, 25 May 1963, p. 8.

[J.] Saunders Redding, "Book Review: Langston Hughes Is Back Again," *Afro-American Magazine*, 28 May 1963, p. 2.

Ray Smith, "New Books Appraised," *Library Journal*, 88 (1 June 1963), 2257.

"Courier Book Shelf," *Pittsburgh Courier*, 8 June 1963, p. 10.

James A. Emanuel, "Talking Drums and New Cadences," *New York Times Book Review*, 14 July 1963, p. 3.

Stephen Stepanchev, "Chorus of Versemakers: A Mid-1963 Medley: Anti-Racist Racism," *New York Herald Tribune Books*, 11 August 1963, p. 6.

"Books Noted," *Negro Digest*, 12 (September 1963), 52, 97.

"Where God Is Black," *Time*, 82 (6 September 1963), 22–3.

Ezekiel Mphahlele, "The Pain of Being Unbound," *Nation*, 197 (21 September 1963), 161–3.

Marion Plunkett, "*Poems from Black Africa*," *South and West*, 2 (Fall 1963), 33–4.

Crisis, 70 (October 1963), 509.

Negro Digest, 12 (October 1963), 96; reprints the September 1963 review.

Richard A. Long, "Book Reviews," *CLAJ*, 7 (December 1963), 176.

Ellen Conroy Kennedy and Paulette-Michele Trout, "Books," *Africa Report*, 9 (January 1964), 26.

Michael Bullock, "*Poems from Black Africa*," *UNESCO Features*, No. 430 (10 January 1964), 7–8.

LeRoi Jones, "A Dark Bag," *Poetry*, 104 (March 1964), 394–401.

Harriet Zinnes, "General Area," *Books Abroad*, 38 (Summer 1964), 336.

Barbara A. Bannon, "PW Forecast of Paperbacks: Poetry: *Poems from Black Africa*," *Publishers Weekly*, 189 (7 February 1966), 95.

M[ary] A[nn] M[alkin], "Trade Reviews," *Antiquarian Bookman*, 37 (21 February 1966), 762.

"Weekly Record: Hughes, Langston," *Publishers Weekly*, 189 (7 March 1966), 141.

Robert J. Clements, "Poetry on the Campus," *Saturday Review*, 49 (11 June 1966), 68–9.

Obiajunwa Wali, "Black Africa Revisited," *Freedomways*, 6 (Fall 1966), 378–81.

New Negro Poets U.S.A. (1964)

"Tips: Previews, Promotions, Sales: *New Negro Poets: U.S.A.*," *Publishers Weekly*, 184 (9 December 1963), 32.

Virginia Kirkus Bulletin, 32 (1 March 1964), 265.

Charles Simmons, "Rhyme from Academe," *Saturday Review*, 47 (30 May 1964), 42–3.

"Book Reviews," *Crisis*, 71 (June–July 1964), 420.

"Love Withheld," *Time*, 83 (5 June 1964), 104.

"Books: Best Reading," *Time*, 83 (12 June 1964), 13.

Marc Schleifer, "Sepia Deb Ball," *Nation*, 198 (29 June 1964), 665–6.

Choice, 1 (July–August 1964), 179.

Herbert C. Burke, "New Books Appraised," *Library Journal*, 89 (July 1964), 2800.

Claude Billings, "Works of Local Poets Included in Collection," *Indianapolis Star*, sec. 8, 12 July 1964, p. 5.

Booklist and Subscription Books Bulletin, 60 (15 July 1964), 1026–7.

"Some Other New Volumes of Poetry," *National Observer*, 24 August 1964, p. 21.

"Books Noted," *Negro Digest*, 13 (September 1964), 51–2.

Kirby Congdon, "Brooks Dammed," *Literary Times*, September 1964, p. 4.

Charlemae Rollins, "More Universal," *Community*, 24 (November 1964), 12–13.

"And Books in Brief," *Horn Book*, 40 (December 1964), 635.

Miles M. Jackson, "Significant Belles Lettres By and About Negroes Published in 1964," *Phylon*, 26 (Third Quarter 1965), 223–4.

William Stafford, "Weighed and Found Wanted," *Poetry*, 106 (September 1965), 429–[32].

The Book of Negro Humor (1966)

Jessie Kitching, "Nonfiction: *The Book of Negro Humor*," *Publishers Weekly*, 188 (6 December 1965), 58; reprinted in *Gary Post Tribune*, 27 February 1966.

Adger Brown, "Book World," *State: The Record* [Columbia, S.C.], 30 January 1966, p. 12-D; also *Lewiston* [Maine] *Journal*, 12 February 1966.

"Negro Humor Book Covers Many Years," *Memphis Appeal*, sec. 5, 30 January 1966, p. 6.

Robert Cromie, "Cromie Looks at Authors and Books: *Book of Negro Humor* Has Variety," *Chicago Tribune*, sec. 2, 7 February 1966, p. 4.

Robert Boles, "Negro Writer: His Restrictions, Triumphs," *Boston Globe*, 13 February 1966, p. 28-A.

Miles M. Jackson, Jr., "New Books Appraised: Humor," *Library Journal*, 91 (15 February 1966), 947–8.

Wes Lawrence, "Humor in Black and White," *Cleveland Plain Dealer*, 22 February 1966, p. 15.

"Reports from Our Reviewers: A Kind of Laughter," *Independent Journal* [San Rafael, Calif.], 26 February 1966, p. M14.

"Book Shelf," *Ebony*, 21 (March 1966), 24.

Richard Armour, "Humor in the Negro Vein," *Los Angeles Times Calendar*, 13 March 1966, p. 33.

Thomas E. Murphy, "Helpful Humor," *Hartford Courant Magazine*, 13 March 1966, p. 13.

M[ary] A[nn] M[alkin], "Trade Reviews," *Antiquarian Bookman*, 37 (14 March 1966), 1088.

O[live] C. R[obinson], "Reviews of Recently Published Books: Negro Humor," *Lewiston* [Maine] *Daily Sun*, 26 March 1966, p. 4.

Marion Bohler, "Courier Book Shelf," *Pittsburgh Courier*, 2 April 1966, p. 9.

I.G.G., "Negro Humor Collected," *Fort Wayne News-Sentinel*, 9 April 1966, p. 4A.

"Books for Young Adults," *Library Journal*, 91 (15 April 1966), 2236.

Terry F. Brock, "New Books: Black Humor," *Community*, 25 (May 1966), 14.

Evelyn Marie Wynn, "About Books," *Dade County Teacher*, 18 (16 May 1966), 12.

Miles M. Jackson, Jr., "Folk Wit at Its Best," *Freedomways*, 6 (Summer 1966), 280–2.

W. Edward Farrison, "Book Reviews," *CLAJ*, 10 (September 1966), 72–4.

Francis Ward, "Books Noted," *Negro Digest*, 15 (September 1966), 90–1.

Frances Neel Cheney, "Current Reference Books: Americana," *Wilson Library Bulletin*, 41 (October 1966), 225, 227.

Terry Baker, "Humor Collected from a World of Pain," *Phylon*, 28 (Second Quarter 1967), 213.

"Books Received," *Black World*, 20 (February 1971), 68.

The Best Short Stories by Negro Writers: An Anthology from 1899 to the Present (1967)

Virginia Kirkus Service, 34 (15 December 1966), 1302.

Barbara A. Bannon, "Fiction," *Publishers Weekly,* 191 (16 January 1967), 75.

Louise Giles, "Fiction," *Library Journal,* 92 (1 February 1967), 595.

Robert Boles, "Stories Without Boundaries," *Boston Sunday Globe,* 12 February 1967, p. 18-A.

Wes Lawrence, "Stories by Skilled Authors," *Cleveland Plain Dealer,* 16 February 1967, p. 11.

Virginia Bussey, "Book Reviews: Best Short Stories of Negro Writers Collected," *Bakersfield Californian,* 18 February 1967, p. 19A.

"This Week," *Christian Century,* 84 (22 February 1967), 238.

Barbara Gold, "Negro Writing," *Baltimore Sun,* 26 February 1967, p. D-7.

Warner G. Rice, "The Negro Writer as Social Historian: A Closeup Mirror of Our Times," *Detroit News,* 26 February 1967, p. 3-E.

Robert Bone, "Not All Wright and Baldwin," *New York Times Book Review,* 5 March 1967, p. 5.

Riley Hughes, "Widest Possible Range in Best Short Stories," *Washington Sunday Star,* 12 March 1967, p. D-11.

Edward B. Hungerford, "All Sides of the Negro Suppression Revealed," *Chicago Tribune Books Today,* 12 March 1967, p. 8.

Jim Long, "Bookmarks," *Oregon Journal* [Portland], 25 March 1967, p. 6J.

Rhona Ryan Wilber, "Negro Stories," *Houston Post Spotlight,* 2 April 1967, p. 17.

Donald Gibson, "Necessary Anthologies," *New Leader,* 50 (10 April 1967), 20–2.

"For Young Adults," *Library Journal,* 92 (15 April 1967), 1760.

William Hudson, "Anthology of Negro Writing Gives Poignant Look at Neglected Field," *Denver Post Roundup,* 23 April 1967, p. 33.

R. Krozett Johnson, "The Bookshelf: The Best Short Stories by Negroes," *Boston Traveler,* 11 May 1967, p. 10.

L. M. Collins, "There Are No Frankensteins," *Nashville Tennessean,* 28 May 1967, p. 10-C.

W. Edward Farrison, "Book Reviews," *CLAJ,* 10 (June 1967), 358–60.

James W. Byrd, "Negro Writers in America's Mainstream," *Southwest Review,* 52 (Summer 1967), vi–vii, 303–4.

Bernard F. Dick, "New Books," *Catholic World,* 205 (August 1967), 318.

Dudley Randall, "Books Noted," *Negro Digest,* 16 (September 1967), 52, 93.

Keneth Kinnamon, "The Man Who Created 'Simple,'" *Nation,* 205 (4 December 1967), 599–601.

"Best Books of the Year: Books for Young Adults," *Library Journal,* 92 (15 December 1967), 4580.

Frances Neel Cheney, "Current Reference Books: Who Speaks for the Negro?" *Wilson Library Bulletin,* 42 (February 1968), 626.

Books Translated by Hughes

With Mercer Cook, *Masters of the Dew* [*Gouverneurs de la Rosée*] by Jacques Roumain (1947)

Robert Gorham Davis, "Dark Pastoral, in Vodoo Rhythm," *New York Times Book Review,* 15 June 1947, p. 5.

John Cournos, "The Reviews," *New York Sun,* 16 June 1947, p. 19.

Samuel Sillen, "Roumain's *Masters of the Dew* Superb Novel of Haitian People," *Daily Worker,* 23 June 1947, p. 11.

Hamilton Basso, "Briefly Noted: Fiction," *New Yorker,* 23 (28 June 1947), 79–80.

Constance Curtis, "About Books and Authors," *New York Amsterdam News,* 28 June 1947, p. 17.

Ben Field, "The Folk Images of Jacques Roumain," *Mainstream,* 1 (Summer 1947), 376–9.

Nash K. Burger, "Books of the Times," *New York Times,* 5 July 1947, p. L9.

Linton Wells, "Elemental Men in Haiti," *Saturday Review,* 30 (5 July 1947), 14.

Thomas McGrath, "In the Wild Grass," *New Masses,* 64 (8 July 1947), 18–19.

Elmore Bourbeau, "Up from Voodoo," *Milwaukee Journal,* sec. 5, 13 July 1947, p. 3.

John Frederick Nims, "Stark Events in a Haitian Background," *Chicago Tribune Magazine of Books,* 27 July 1947, p. 5.

J. Saunders Redding, "Book Review," *Baltimore Afro-American,* 2 August 1947, [p. 4].

Stanley Baitz, "There's a Jungle Throbbing Behind This Tale of Haiti," *Washington Star,* 3 August 1947, p. C3.

Bertram D. Wolfe, "Idyl from the Hillsides of Primitive Haiti," *New York Herald Tribune Weekly Book Review,* 3 August 1947, p. 3.

Marjorie McKenzie, "Pursuit of Democracy," *Pittsburgh Courier,* 9 August 1947, [p. 6].

William Harrison, "Book Review," *Boston Chronicle,* 23 August 1947, p. 6.

Lance Jeffers, "Books of the Day," *People's Voice* [N.Y.], 13 September 1947, p. 14.

With Ben Frederic Carruthers, *Cuba Libre* by Nicolás Guillén (1948)

Millard Lampell, "Hughes and Guillén," *Masses and Mainstream,* 2 (February 1949), 78–81.

A[bner] W. B[erry], "*Cuba Libre* by Nicolás Guillén, Cuba's Greatest Poet," *Worker Magazine,* 13 February 1949, p. 13.

"The Poetry Bulletin," *Tiger's Eye,* 1 (March 1949), 116.

Romancero Gitano: Gypsy Ballads, by Federico García Lorca, as *Beloit Poetry Chapbook* No. 1 (1951)

No reviews located.

Selected Poems of Gabriela Mistral by Lucila Godoy Alcayaga (1957)

Edwin Honig, "Poet of Womanhood," *Saturday Review,* 41 (22 March 1958), 22.

Roger Sale, "New Poems, Ancient and Modern," *Hudson Review,* 18 (Summer 1965), 299–308.

Selected Scripts in Production

Screenplay with Clarence Muse, *Way Down South*

"*Beau Geste* Good Boxoffice; *Way Down South* Passable; Direction, Players Hypo Shaky Script," *Hollywood Reporter,* 19 July 1939, p. 3.

"Film Previews: *Way Down South,*" *Daily Variety,* 19 July 1939, p. 3.

G.K., "Bob Breen's New Picture Wins Favor," *Los Angeles Times,* 19 July 1939, p. 12.

"Hughes-Muse Film Okayed," *New York Amsterdam News,* 29 July 1939, p. 16; a reprint of *Daily Variety* review.

C.S., "New Shows in Town," *New Orleans Times-Picayune,* 11 August 1939, p. 10.

Wanda Hale, "Bobby Breen's Picture

Sugar-Coats Old South," *New York Daily News,* 17 August 1939, p. 46.

Plays

Mulatto [producer rewrote script]

Kelcey Allen, "*Mulatto,*" *Women's Wear Daily,* sec. 1, 25 October 1935, p. 13.

Brooks Atkinson, "The Play: Race Problems in the South the Theme of *Mulatto,* a 'New Drama' by Langston Hughes," *New York Times,* 25 October 1935, p. L25.

John Anderson, "*Mulatto*: Play Tells Race Tragedy Involving Housekeeper in Georgia Mansion," *New York Journal,* 25 October 1935, p. 24.

Rowland Field, "The New Play: *Mulatto,* a Play by Langston Hughes, with Stuart Beebe and Rose McClendon in the Leading Roles, Opens at Vanderbilt," *Brooklyn Times Union,* 25 October 1935, p. 5A.

Gilbert W. Gabriel, "*Mulatto*: Langston Hughes Drama in the Vanderbilt Theatre," *New York American,* 25 October 1935, p. 11.

Robert Garland, "*Mulatto* Presented at the Vanderbilt: Langston Hughes' Play Called Unworthy of the Author of *Weary Blues,*" *New York World-Telegram,* 25 October 1935, p. 30.

Percy Hammond, "The Theaters," *New York Herald Tribune,* 25 October 1935, p. 14.

Richard Lockridge, "The New Play: Langston Hughes's *Mulatto* Is Played at the Vanderbilt Theater," *New York Sun,* 25 October 1935, p. 34.

Burns Mantle, "*Mulatto* Is a Georgia Drama: Ol' Marse Norwood Suffers When His Half Caste Progeny Take on Book Learnin'," *New York Daily News,* 25 October 1935, p. 61.

"*Mulatto* Not for B'way or Pictures," *Hollywood Reporter,* 25 October 1935, p. 6.

The Playviewer, "New Plays: *Mulatto,*" *Home News (Bronx and Manhattan),* 25 October 1935, p. 9.

Arthur Pollock, "The Theater: *Mulatto,* a Play by a Negro Poet about the Tragedy of Being Colored in the South, Comes to the Vanderbilt Theater," *Brooklyn Daily Eagle,* 25 October 1935, p. 23.

Edgar Price, "The Premiere: *Mulatto,* a Sincere and Stirring Play by Langston Hughes, Negro Poet, Comes to the Vanderbilt Theatre—Rose McClendon Cast in Her Best Role to Date," *Brooklyn Citizen,* 25 October 1935, p. 16.

Wilella Waldorf, "Forecasts and Postscripts: *Mulatto* Brings up the Race Problem Once More," *New York Post,* 25 October 1935, p. 10.

Kelcey Allen, "*Mulatto,*" *New York News Record,* 26 October 1935, p. 7; reprints previous day's *Women's Wear Daily* review.

Whitney Bolton, "The Stage Today: Out of Tragedy of Miscegenation Comes *Mulatto,* Poetic Melodrama," *New York Morning Telegraph,* 26 October 1935, p. 3.

Julius Cohen, "*Mulatto,* at Vanderbilt, Tells Vivid, Tragic Story," *New York Journal of Commerce and Commercial,* 26 October 1935, p. 18.

H.E.K., "*Mulatto,* Drama of Stark Realism, Opens at Vanderbilt," *New York Daily Mirror,* 26 October 1935, p. 18.

Stirling Bowen, "The Theatre: A Negro Drama," *Wall Street Journal,* 28 October 1935, p. 11.

Ibee., "*Mulatto,*" *Variety,* 30 October 1935, p. 66.

"*Mulatto* Is Well Received by Local Critics," *New York Amsterdam News,* 2 November 1935, p. 12.

"New Plays in Manhattan," *Time,* 26 (4 November 1935), 58, 60.

Loren Miller, "The Theater: *Porgy and Bess* and *Mulatto*," *New Masses,* 17 (5 November 1935), 29–30.

George W. Harris, "*Mulatto* Rips Apart Awful Dixie Morals with Raw Exposure," *New York News and Harlem Home Journal,* 9 November 1935, [p. ?].

Loren Miller, "World of the Theatre," *Daily Worker,* 15 November 1935, p. 5.

Edith J.R. Isaacs, "See America First: *Mulatto*," *Theatre Arts,* 19 (December 1935), 902.

Alain Locke, "Deep River, Deeper Sea," *Opportunity,* 14 (January 1936), 6–10.

Robert Garland, "*Mulatto,* in Its Eighth Month at Vanderbilt, Has a New Star," *New York World-Telegram,* 8 May 1936, p. 30.

Arthur Spaeth, "The Play," *Cleveland News,* 9 March 1939, p. 9.

Jack Warfel, "Gilpin Players Excel in Drama of South," *Cleveland Press,* 9 March 1939, p. 23.

Paul Jordan, "Copley Theatre," *Boston Guardian,* 30 March 1940, pp. 1, 5.

Robert Koehler, "*Mulatto*," *Los Angeles Times,* sec. 6, 24 October 1986, p. 10.

Little Ham

William F. McDermott, "Amusing Play Has First Showing by Gilpin Players at the Karamu Theater," *Cleveland Plain Dealer,* 25 March 1936, p. 17.

Arthur Spaeth, "Hughes' *Little Ham* Proves Hilarious Comedy as Gilpin Players Give World Premiere," *Cleveland News,* 25 March 1936, p. 16.

Charles Schneider, "*Little Ham*," *Cleveland Press,* 27 March 1936, p. 38.

J.C., "Cleveland Gets Poet's Comedy," *New York Amsterdam News,* 28 March 1936, p. 8.

The Rounder, "On What's Doing," *Cleveland Gazette,* 28 March 1936, [p. 1].

Bud Douglass, "Gilpins Score in *Little Ham*," *Cleveland Call and Post,* 2 April 1936, p. 3.

David H. Pierce, "The Passing Week," *Cleveland Call and Post,* 2 April 1936, p. 6.

Pullen, "Plays out of Town: *Little Ham*," *Variety,* 8 April 1936, p. 56.

With Arna Bontemps, *When the Jack Hollers*

Arthur Spaeth, "*When Jack Hollers* Is Comic *Tobacco Road*," *Cleveland News,* 29 April 1936, p. 18.

With composer William Grant Still, *Troubled Island*

William F. McDermott, "Haitian Play Has Premiere Performance," *Cleveland Plain Dealer,* 19 November 1936, p. 12.

Don't You Want to Be Free

Marvel Cooke, "Suitcase Theatre Group Is Brilliant in Premiere," *New York Amsterdam News,* 30 April 1938, p. 16.

S.R., "*Don't You Want to Be Free,* a Powerful Play of Negro Life," *New Order,* May–June 1938, p. 41.

Norman MacLeod, "The Poetry and Argument of Langston Hughes," *Crisis,* 45 (November 1938), 358–9.

C.C., "Stage: Harlem Suitcase Theatre Begins Second Season," *Daily Worker,* 12 November 1938, p. 7.

With Elmer Rice and composer Kurt Weill, *Street Scene*

G.J.K., "*Street Scene* Opens at the Shubert," *Philadelphia Record,* 17 December 1946, p. 25.

Jerry Gaghan, "Elmer Rice's *Street Scene* Set to Kurt Weill Music," *Philadelphia Daily News*, 17 December 1946, p. 44.

Linton Martin, "*Street Scene*, Musical, in Premiere at Shubert," *Philadelphia Inquirer*, 17 December 1946, p. 27.

R.E.P. Sensenderfer, "Living Theater," *Philadelphia Evening Bulletin*, 17 December 1946, p. 34B.

Waters, "Plays out of Town: *Street Scene*," *Variety*, 18 December 1946, p. 68.

"Out of Town Openings," *Billboard*, 28 December 1946, p. 42.

Brooks Atkinson, "The New Play," *New York Times*, 10 January 1947, p. L17.

Robert Garland, "*Street Scene* Bows at Adelphi Theatre," *New York Journal American*, 10 January 1947, p. 14.

William Hawkins, "Theater: *Street Scene* Has Opera Touch," *New York World-Telegram*, 10 January 1947, p. 25.

Richard Watts Jr., "Two on the Aisle: Elmer Rice's *Street Scene* Is Not Helped by Music," *New York Post*, 10 January 1947, pp. 37–8.

Howard Barnes, "The Theaters," *New York Herald Tribune*, 11 January 1947, p. 10.

Brooks Atkinson, "New York to Music," *New York Times*, sec. 2, 19 January 1947, [p. 1X].

George Jean Nathan, "Theatre Week: Read on—There's Good News Coming," *New York Journal American*, 20 January 1947, p. 12.

With composer Jan Meyerowitz, *The Barrier*

Robert Bagar, "Columbia Workshop Presents *The Barrier*," *New York World-Telegram and Sun*, 19 January 1950, p. 20.

Harriett Johnson, "Words and Music: Race Drama Presented at Columbia," *New York Post*, 19 January 1950, p. 38.

Howard Taubman, "*The Barrier* Given by Columbia Opera," *New York Times*, 19 January 1950, p. 34.

Virgil Thomson, "Music: Dramatically Forceful," *New York Herald Tribune*, 19 January 1950, p. 19.

Douglas Watt, "*The Barrier*, New Music Drama, Has College Premiere," *New York Daily News*, 19 January 1950, p. 65.

Albert J. Elias, "*The Barrier*, New Opera, Bows," *New York Daily Compass*, 20 January 1950, p. 19.

"Forceful Opera, *The Barrier*, Given by Columbia Workshop," *New York Amsterdam News* [N.Y.C. edition], 28 January 1950, p. 22.

Philip Hamburger, "Musical Events: A Georgia Interlude," *New Yorker*, 25 (28 January 1950), 71–3.

"Music: Operatic Miscegenation," *Newsweek*, 35 (30 January 1950), 68.

"Old Cross," *Time*, 55 (30 January 1950), 68, 70.

Harold Stern, "Reviews: *The Barrier*," *Show Business*, 6 February 1950, p. 7.

E.R.C., "Drama Season Opera Packs Powerful Emotional Punch," *Ann Arbor News*, 6 June 1950, p. 9.

J. Dorsey Callaghan, "Drama Season Opens: Cast of *The Barrier* in Ann Arbor Wins High Praise," *Detroit Free Press*, 6 June 1950, p. 19.

Lloyd Mallan, "Enthusiastic Audience Sees Tragic Opera at Ann Arbor," *Toledo Blade*, 6 June 1950, p. 15.

Russell McLauchlin, "Attack on Race Prejudice Proves Powerful on Stage," *Detroit News*, 6 June 1950, p. 30.

Irving Sablosky, "Exciting Experiment at Ann Arbor: Opera on Race Prejudice Marks Dynamic Trend in Drama World," *Chicago Daily News*, 8 June 1950, p. 19.

Jay Carmody, "Muriel Rahn's Negro Mother Heroic Figure at Gayety," *Wash-*

ington Evening Star, 27 September 1950, p. B-16.

Richard L. Coe, "Langston Hughes Play Adapted from His *The Mulatto,*" *Washington Post,* 27 September 1950, p. 10B.

Tom Donnelly, "Give Me a Show with Hit Tunes, Like *Carmen,*" *Washington Daily News,* 27 September 1950, p. 37.

Ernie Schier, "New Musical Drama Stars Baritone Tibbett," *Washington Times-Herald,* 27 September 1950, p. 22.

Milton Berliner, "*Barrier* Becomes Very Much Alive," *Washington Daily News,* 28 September 1950, p. 51.

Glenn Dillard Gunn, "Unfolding of *The Barrier*'s Tragic Story Slowed by Music," *Washington Times-Herald,* 28 September 1950, p. 9.

Lula Taylor, "*Barrier* in Pre-Broadway Premiere at the Gayety," *Washington Afro-American,* 30 September 1950, p. 19.

Louis Lautier, "*Barrier* Offensive, Acting Good—Lautier," *Washington Afro-American,* 3 October 1950, p. 8.

Lowe, "*The Barrier,*" *Variety,* 4 October 1950, p. 60.

G.M., "Muriel Rahn Excellent in *Barrier* at the Flatbush," *Brooklyn Eagle,* 19 October 1950, p. 7.

Brooks Atkinson, "At the Theatre," *New York Times,* 3 November 1950, p. 32-L.

John Chapman, "Tibbett, Rahn Fine in *The Barrier,* but the New Opera Defeats Itself," *New York Daily News,* 3 November 1950, p. 69.

Thomas R. Dash, "*The Barrier:* Broadhurst Theatre," *Women's Wear Daily,* 3 November 1950, p. 43.

Otis L. Guernsey, Jr., "The Theatres," *New York Herald Tribune,* 3 November 1950, p. 16.

John McClain, "Very Pleasant if You Like a Lot of Singing," *New York Journal American,* 3 November 1950, p. 20.

Arthur Pollock, "*Barrier* Is Honest, Forceful and Moving," *New York Daily Compass,* 3 November 1950, p. 18.

Richard Watts, Jr., "Two on the Aisle: The Race Problem Set to Music," *New York Post,* 3 November 1950, p. 66.

Robert Coleman, "*The Barrier* Offers Much Trimming, Thin Story," *New York Daily Mirror,* 4 November 1950, p. 12.

Wolcott Gibbs, "The Theatre: The Miseries, Light and Dark," *New Yorker,* 26 (11 November 1950), 79–81.

Alonzo Greene, "*The Barrier* Opens, Closes after Four Shows," *New York Age,* 11 November 1950, p. 17.

Walter Kerr, "*The Barrier,*" *Commonweal,* 53 (24 November 1950), 172.

J.S.H., "*The Barrier* Is Presented at Circle-in-the-Square," *New York Herald Tribune,* 9 March 1953, p. 11.

"Rahn Again Steals Show in *Barrier,*" *Baltimore Afro-American,* 28 March 1953, p. 7.

Alan Corelli, "Off-Broadway Reviews: *The Barrier,*" *Show Business,* 4 April 1960, p. 8.

Raymond Ericson, "Opera: *The Barrier:* Jan Meyerowitz' Work Is Revived at N.Y.U.," *New York Times,* 25 July 1961, p. 20.

Francis D. Perkins, "*The Barrier* Ends Summer Concert Series," *New York Herald Tribune,* 25 July 1961, p. 11.

Leighton Kerner, "*The Barrier* at NYU," *Village Voice,* 27 July 1961, p. 6.

Lee Pomex, "Off-Broadway Reviews," *Show Business,* 29 July 1961, p. 16.

With composer Jan Meyerowitz, *Esther*

Ruth Berges, "*Esther* for Urbana," *Opera News,* 21 (11 March 1957), 14.

Irving Sablosky, "New Operas Make Debut in Festival at U. of Illinois," *Chicago Daily News,* 18 March 1957, p. 24.

P. C. Brooks, "Music," *Boston Herald*, 8 May 1958, p. 39.

Cyrus Durgin, "Meyerowitz' *Esther*: Opera Has Local Premiere," *Boston Daily Globe*, 8 May 1958, p. 14.

Harold Rogers, "*Esther* Heard in Its Boston Premiere," *Christian Science Monitor*, 8 May 1958, p. 7.

Ruth Berges, "*Esther* in Boston," *Opera News*, 23 (10 November 1958), 17.

"Hunter Opera Workshop Gives *Esther*," *New York Herald Tribune*, 28 April 1961, p. 12.

Ross Parmenter, "Opera *Esther* Sung at Hunter," *New York Times*, 28 April 1961, p. 12.

Ruth Berges, "*Esther* as an Opera," *Reconstructionist*, 27 (2 June 1961), 21–3.

With composer Dave Martin, *Simply Heavenly*

Brooks Atkinson, "Theatre: A Family Entertainment: *Simply Heavenly* from Langston Hughes Book," *New York Times*, 22 May 1957, p. 28.

Tom Donnelly, "Simple Is Lost in a Detour," *New York World-Telegram and Sun*, 22 May 1957, p. 28.

Walter Kerr, "*Simply Heavenly* Staged at the 85th St. Playhouse," *New York Herald Tribune*, 22 May 1957, p. 16.

John McClain, "All-Negro Cast Simply Great in Fine Show," *New York Journal American*, 22 May 1957, p. 22.

Richard Watts, Jr., "Two on the Aisle: Bright Harlem Comedy with Songs," *New York Post*, 22 May 1957, p. 58.

Thomas R. Dash, "*Simply Heavenly*: 85th Street Playhouse," *Women's Wear Daily*, 23 May 1957, p. 56.

Rube Dorin, "*Simply Heavenly*, All-Negro Offering, Bows Off-B'way," *New York Morning Telegraph*, 23 May 1957, p. 2.

Roosevelt Ward, Jr., "Langston Hughes' *Simply Heavenly* a Simply Heavenly Musical Play," *Daily Worker*, 24 May 1957, pp. 6, 7.

John Beaufort, "Explorations in Harlem," *Christian Science Monitor*, 25 May 1957, p. 4.

"Hughes Triumphs: *Simply Heavenly* Is Exactly That!!" *New York Age Defender*, 25 May 1957, pp. 23, 28.

Jesse H. Walker, "*Simply Heavenly* Provokes Laughs," *New York Amsterdam News*, 25 May 1957, p. 16.

Ira J. Bilowit, "Off-B'Way Reviews," *Show Business*, 27 May 1957, p. 6.

Millicent Brower, "Theatre: *Simply Heavenly*," *Village Voice*, 29 May 1957, p. 13.

Alfred Duckett, "Langston Hughes' *Simply Heavenly* Gay, Tuneful and Comic-Crazed Hit," *Chicago Defender*, 1 June 1957, p. 9.

John Keating, "They're Ballin' in This Happy Harlem Comedy," *Cue*, 26 (1 June 1957), 10.

Brooks Atkinson, "Negro Laughter: New Plays by Loften Mitchell and Langston Hughes Are Full of Humor," *New York Times*, sec. 2, 2 June 1957, [p. 1].

Richard Watts, Jr., "Two on the Aisle: Excellent Off-Broadway Jobs," *New York Post*, 2 June 1957, p. 14.

Geor[ge Alan Smith], "Off-B'way Show: *Simply Heavenly*," *Variety*, 5 June 1957, p. 58.

"Hughes Play Could Be 1st for Broadway in 25 Years," *Baltimore Afro-American*, 8 June 1957, p. 11.

Josephine Schuyler, "Langston Hughes Play Is *Simply Heavenly*," *Pittsburgh Courier*, 8 June 1957, p. 24.

John Williams, "New York Theatre," *Los Angeles Tribune*, 19 June 1957, p. 18.

Euphemia Van Rensselaer Wyatt, "Theater," *Catholic World*, 185 (August 1957), 388–9.

Paul V. Beckley, "*Simply Heavenly* in

Move to Broadway's Playhouse," *New York Herald Tribune*, 21 August 1957, p. 10.

John Chapman, "*Simply Heavenly* an Affectionate and Humorous Harlem Vignette," *New York Daily News*, 21 August 1957, p. 52.

Robert Coleman, "*Simply Heavenly* Is Fun," *New York Mirror*, 21 August 1957, p. 31.

Rowland Field, "Pleasant Musical," *Newark Evening News*, 21 August 1957, p. 18.

Joan Hanauer, "*Simply Heavenly* Is Lovely," *Seattle Post-Intelligencer*, 21 August 1957, p. 14.

Frances Herridge, "*Simply Heavenly* Goes to Broadway," *New York Post*, 21 August 1957, p. 58.

Hobe, "Broadway Opening," *Variety*, 21 August 1957, pp. 1, 4.

Leonard Hoffman, "The New York Play," *Hollywood Reporter*, 21 August 1957, p. 3.

Jim O'Connor, "It's Far Easier to Score a Hit Off-Broadway," *New York Journal American*, 21 August 1957, p. 18.

William Peper, "Negro Musical Has Frail Plot," *New York World-Telegram and Sun*, 21 August 1957, p. 30.

Richard P. Cooke, "The Theatre: Harlem Tale," *Wall Street Journal*, 22 August 1957, p. 6.

Thomas R. Dash, "*Simply Heavenly:* Playhouse," *Women's Wear Daily*, 22 August 1957, p. 36.

Leo Mishkin, "*Heavenly* Comedy of Life in Harlem," *New York Morning Telegraph*, 22 August 1957, p. 2.

"*Simply Heavenly* Is Fun," *New York Mirror*, 22 August 1957, pp. 29–30.

Hobe, "Show on Broadway: *Simply Heavenly*," *Variety*, 28 August 1957, p. 58.

John A. Williams, "Langston Hughes Comedy Moves to Broadway," *Los Angeles Tribune*, 28 August 1957, p. 17.

Joan Hanauer, "Langston Hughes' *Simply Heavenly* Acclaimed in Its Broadway Revival," *Chicago Defender*, 31 August 1957, p. 19.

Emory Lewis, "Langston Hughes' Musical Is Love-Letter to Harlem," *Cue*, 26 (31 August 1957), 8.

Izzy Rowe, "*Simply Heavenly* Simply Wonderful," *Pittsburgh Courier*, 31 August 1957, p. 22.

John Chapman, "Amiable Negro Musical," *New York Sunday News*, 1 September 1957, p. 23C.

Henry Hewes, "Broadway Postscript: Home Cooking," *Saturday Review*, 40 (7 September 1957), 24.

Louis Martin, "Dope and Data," *Chicago Defender*, 7 September 1957, p. 10; also in the *Memphis Tri-State Defender*.

Harold Clurman, "Theatre," *Nation*, 185 (5 October 1957), 230.

With Robert Glenn, *Shakespeare in Harlem*

Rita Hassan, "Reviews of B'way Shows," *Show Business*, 7 September 1959, p. 8.

Doul, "Stock Reviews: *Shakespeare in Harlem*," *Variety*, 9 September 1959, p. 57.

Lewis Funke, "Stage: Bard of Harlem," *New York Times*, 28 October 1959, p. 40.

Frank Aston, "Negroes Stage Vivid Revue," *New York World-Telegram and Sun*, 10 February 1960, p. 34.

Brooks Atkinson, "Theatre: *Shakespeare in Harlem*," *New York Times*, 10 February 1960, p. 43.

Judith Crist, "*Shakespeare in Harlem* Opens at 41st St. Theater," *New York Herald Tribune*, 10 February 1960, p. 16.

John McClain, "*Shakespeare in Harlem* Is Good in Spots," *New York Journal American*, 10 February 1960, p. 22.

Richard Watts, Jr., "Two on the Aisle: Langston Hughes' Harlem Poetry," *New York Post,* 10 February 1960, p. 72.

Richard P. Cooke, "Shakespeare and Spirituals," *Wall Street Journal,* 11 February 1960, p. 12.

Charles McHarry, "An Idiot Undelighted, Save by Harlem Bards," *New York Daily News,* 15 February 1960, p. 42.

Burm, "Off-Broadway Reviews: *Shakespeare in Harlem,*" *Variety,* 17 February 1960, p. 61.

John Aigner, "The Bard Uptown," *New York Age,* 20 February 1960, p. 13.

Emory Lewis, "The Theatre: A Salvo for the Poets: Hughes, Johnson, Millay," *Cue,* 29 (20 February 1960), [7].

Brooks Atkinson, "Back to Greek Mythology," *New York Times,* 21 February 1960, [p. ix].

Henry Hewes, "Broadway Postscript: The Light Is Light Enough," *Saturday Review,* 43 (27 February 1960), 27.

Joseph T. Shipley, "Three Hits: Gilbert and Sullivan, Hughes in Harlem, Italian Theater," *New Leader,* 43 (14 March 1960), 21.

Theophilus Lewis, "Theatre," *America,* 102 (19 March 1960), 747.

Paul Mooney, "Karamu's *Shakespeare in Harlem* Is Full of Humor and Feeling," *Cleveland Press,* 19 April 1961, p. 20-C.

Glenn C. Pullen, "Characters Vivid in Hughes Play," *Cleveland Plain Dealer,* 19 April 1961, p. 19.

Len Watkins, "Langston Hughes' Spoof on Shakespear [*sic*] at Karamu," *Cleveland Call and Post,* 29 April 1961, p. 6-B.

Cliff Ridley, "*Tambourines* Isn't Perfect, but It Comes Mighty Close!" *Town Crier* [Westport, Conn.], 8 September 1960, pp. 1, 15.

John Chapman, "Show Business: *Tambourines to Glory* Magnificent in Song," *New York Daily News,* 4 November 1963, p. 79.

Martin Gottfried, "Theatre: *Tambourines to Glory,*" *Women's Wear Daily,* 4 November 1963, p. 45.

Walter Kerr, "*Tambourines to Glory,*" *New York Herald Tribune,* 4 November 1963, p. 14.

John McClain, "Hallelujah, It's Great!" *New York Journal American,* 4 November 1963, p. 24.

Norman Nadel, "Gospels Atone for Faults of *Tambourines to Glory,*" *New York World-Telegram and Sun,* 4 November 1963, p. 34.

Howard Taubman, "Theater: *Tambourines,*" *New York Times,* 4 November 1963, p. 47.

Richard Watts, "Two on the Aisle: Musical Play on Gospel Singers," *New York Post,* 4 November 1963, p. 74.

Whitney Bolton, "Stage Review: *Tambourines to Glory* Is Musical Feast; Libretto Sags," *New York Morning Telegraph,* 5 November 1963, p. 2.

Harriett Johnson, "Words and Music: *Tambourines to Glory* Is Hip," *New York Post,* 19 November 1963, p. 24.

Edward Hayman, "Enthusiasm's Not Enough: *Tambourines* Misses a Few Beats," *Detroit News,* 27 June 1984, [p. H1].

With composer Jobe Huntley, *Tambourines to Glory*

"Hazel Scott Makes Triumphant Return in Westport Play," *Norwalk Hour,* 8 September 1960, p. 10.

Jerico-Jim Crow

Jay Carr, "Hughes' *Jerico* Opens at Village Sanctuary," *New York Post,* 13 January 1964, p. 16.

John Molleson, "*Jerico-Jim Crow*: Bound

for Greatness," *New York Herald Tribune,* 13 January 1964, p. 15.

Norman Nadel, "The Theater: *Jerico-Jim Crow* Worth Seeing," *New York World-Telegram and Sun,* 13 January 1964, p. 12.

Richard F. Shepard, "Theater: A Rousing *Jerico-Jim Crow,*" *New York Times,* 13 January 1964, p. 25.

Jack Thompson, "Off-Broadway: Glorious Night with Singers," *New York Journal-American,* 13 January 1964, p. 12.

Whitney Bolton, "Stage Review: *Jerico-Jim Crow* Delightful Event," *New York Morning Telegraph,* 14 January 1964, p. 2.

Peter B. Young, "Theatre: *Jerico-Jim Crow,*" *Town and Village,* 16 January 1964, p. 13.

Jesse H. Walker, "Mr. Hughes' New Play: They Might Hear *Jerico* All the Way Up on 113th St.," *New York Amsterdam News,* 18 January 1964, p. 13.

Peter Share, "Theatre: *Jerico-Jim Crow,*" *Village Voice,* 23 January 1964, p. 10.

Emory Lewis, "The Theatre," *Cue,* 33 (25 January 1964), 14.

Kenn., "Off-Broadway Reviews," *Variety,* 29 January 1964, p. 70.

Henry Hewes, "Broadway Postscript: The Union from South Africa," *Saturday Review,* 47 (18 April 1964), 31.

Mark Bricklin, "Civil Rights Musical: *Jerico-Jim Crow* a Joyous Shout of Hope and Love for All Mankind," *Philadelphia Tribune,* 21 November 1964, p. 18.

Dan Sullivan, "Theater: A Soul-Oratorio," *New York Times,* 23 March 1968, p. 22.

The Prodigal Son

Martin Gottfried, "Theatre: *The Exception and the Rule,*" *Women's Wear Daily,* 21 May 1965, p. 25.

Norman Nadel, "Brecht, Hughes Joined at the Greenwich Mews," *New York World-Telegram and Sun,* 21 May 1965, p. 30.

George Oppenheimer, "On Stage: Plays by Brecht, Hughes Presented Off-Broadway," *Newsday,* 21 May 1965, p. 3C.

Louis Snyder, "Brecht, Hughes and Rejoicing Off Broadway," *New York Herald Tribune,* 21 May 1965, p. 12.

Howard Taubman, "Theatre: Brecht and Langston Hughes," *New York Times,* 21 May 1965, p. L19.

Jack Thompson, "Off-Broadway: *Prodigal Son*—Exciting Theatre," *New York Journal American,* 21 May 1965, p. 33.

Richard Watts, Jr., "Two on the Aisle: Escaping from Brecht to Hughes," *New York Post,* 21 May 1965, p. 36.

Michael Smith, "Theatre: The Exception and the Rule," *Village Voice,* 27 May 1965, p. 17.

Emory Lewis, "The Theatre: Two Plays—at the Greenwich Mews," *Cue,* 34 (29 May 1965), 9.

Index

Halloran, Pat, 380
Hambarin, Harriet, 315
Hamburger, Philip, 745
Hammond, Percy, 743
Hampton, Chester M., 691–2
Hanauer, Joan, 748
Hanscom, Leslie, 581
Hansen, Harry, 12, 191–2, 243–5, 733
Hansen, Walter A., 733
Harlem Quarterly, 21, 376
Harrington, Donald, 477, 593
Harris, Arthur S., Jr., 545
Harris, George W., 744
Harris, Robert, 182–3
Harrison, William, 15, 21, 292–3, 301–2, 339, 367–8, 391–2, 422, 454, 730, 732, 735, 736, 742
Harrop, Mona, 391
Hartford Courant Magazine, 22, 23, 25, 31, 37, 38, 352, 385–6, 407, 432, 491–2, 582, 613, 734, 736, 740
Hartford Times, 27, 31, 32, 426, 468, 485–6, 536, 738
Hartley, Margaret L., 331–2, 734
Harvard Crimson, 32, 498–9
Hass, Victor P., 474–5
Hassan, Rita, 748
Hastings News, 12, 229
Hatch, Robert, 470
Haviland, Virginia, 731
Hawkins, Luelle, 627–8
Hawkins, William, 745
Hayman, Edward, 749
Hays, H. R., 293
Hayward Review, 623–4
Hector, Mary Louis, 734
Hedden, Worth Tuttle, 411–12
Helmer, George, 536–7
Henderson, Freddye, 732
Hendrick, Irene O., 735
Hentoff, Nat, 30, 475, 733
Herod, Henrietta L., 13, 272–4
Herridge, Frances, 748
Herriford, Neal F., 155–6
Herring, Hubert, 537
Hertel, Theresa, 670
Hewes, Henry, 748, 749, 750
Heyward, Du Bose, 4, 5, 74–5, 99–100
Hickey, La Verne, 677–8
Hickman, Janet, 183
Hicks, James, 468
Higgins, Judith, 733
High Point Enterprise, 623–4
Hinton, Garfield, 449
Hippenhammer, Craighton, 538
Hoag, Eleanor, 738
Hobe, 748

Hoffman, Leonard, 748
Hogan, Peter E., 353–4, 426–7
Hogan, William, 518–19, 545–6, 646, 737
Holley, Fred S., 386, 609–10, 646
Hollywood Reporter, 742, 743, 748
Holmes, E. C., 13, 227–8
Holt, Len, 658–9
Home News (Bronx and Manhattan), 743
Honig, Edwin, 742
Honolulu Record, 29, 33, 449–51, 504–5, 730
Horgan, Paul, xii, 6, 119–20
Horn Book, 537, 730, 731, 732, 734, 738, 740
Hound and Horn, 8, 171–2
Houston Post, 738
Houston Post Spotlight, 741
Howard, Alice Henrietta, 394–5, 730, 733
Hudson, Theodore R., 45, 711–13
Hudson, William, 741
Hudson Review, 742
Hughes, Riley, 741
Hultz, Helen Lorraine, 732
Humphries, Rolfe, 19, 329, 388, 735
Hungerford, Edward B., 741
Hunter, Frances Swan, 170–1
Huntley, Martha, 675
Huntsville Times, 733
Hutchens, John K., 737, 738

I., E.D., 730
I., W.A., 360
Ibee., 743
Image, 31, 466–7
Independent, 6, 117
Independent Journal, 740
Independent Weekly Review, 4, 65
Indianapolis Recorder, 173
Indianapolis Star, 512, 739
Indianapolis Times, 22, 42, 361, 650–1
Industrial Worker, 22, 373
Inside Books, 737
Intercollegian, 738
International House Quarterly, 24, 29, 399–400, 456–7
Isaacs, Edith J. R., 744
Ivy, James W., 537, 590, 737
Izard, Anne, 729

J., E., 307–9
J., H., 138, 200
J., L.M., 281
Jackson, Blyden, 445
Jackson, Edna Burke, 535–6
Jackson, Joseph Henry, 205–6
Jackson, Luther P., 443, 507–8, 551
Jackson, Miles M., Jr., 740
Jazz Review, 36, 38, 597–602, 731